INSTRUCTOR EDITION

WELCOME

At Thomson Course Technology, our mission is to help people teach and learn about technology. This special Instructor Edition is all about helping you teach. We provide extensive tools and resources with every text. This Instructor Edition will help you sort through all of the available material, and choose the right combination of tools to help you teach effectively.

CONTENTS AT A GLANCE

Page IE 2: **CoursePort, Passwords, and Solution Security**

CoursePort is a powerful portal through which you can access Thomson Course Technology's online learning solutions with convenience and flexibility. Centralized access to online activities for all of your classes will increase your productivity and save you time. Use CoursePort to gain access to robust online resources including Instructor Resources, Online Companion, and more.

Page IE 2: **Instructor Resources**

An in-depth description of everything we offer to supplement the text, so you can choose what makes the most sense for your classroom.

Page IE 3: **What's New to *Discovering Computers 2007: A Gateway to Information***

Wondering what's new to this edition of *Discovering Computers?* This is the place to find out!

Page IE 8: **Annotated Table of Contents**

Thomson Course Technology has some incredible tools for you. We'd like to help you incorporate all of our instructor resources into your day-to-day teaching to enhance the classroom learning experience. This section not only provides a chapter-by-chapter explanation of what is available, but also highlights some of the new elements you'll find in *Discovering Computers 2007: A Gateway to Information*.

INSTRUCTOR EDITION

Unique ❏ Easy ❏ Secure

Take Control of Your Classroom with CoursePort and Course.com

The CoursePort Student Experience

Students will follow the instructions on the inside front cover of this text to create a CoursePort account and gain access to the Online Companion. Completing the registration process is easy! No keycode is required for students to access the Online Companion for this text!

Visit http://login.course.com.

Click **New User Registration**.

Enter the required, basic information on **New User Registration** screen.

You will then be brought to the **Choose Your Product** page.

Check the box next to the title of the text and upon clicking **Submit,** you're in!

From the My Account page, launch the Online Companion.

At anytime, students can view their own progress in the Universal Gradebook, accessed from the **My Account** tab.

If you choose to track your students' activities in the Universal Gradebook, they will need to **Join a Class** from the **My Account** tab.

The Instructor Experience

As an instructor, you'll also gain access to the Online Companion for this text. But your login will provide you with unique resources dedicated to make teaching with this textbook streamlined, powerful, and simple.

Use your Thomson Course Technology username and password to launch CoursePort. If you do not currently have a Thomson Course Technology username and password for www.course.com, contact us:

For Colleges and Universities in the US: Call Thomson Course Technology at **1.800.648.7450** and select option 3 for Support Services.

For Private Career Colleges in the US: Call **1.800.477.3692**

For High Schools: Call Thomson Learning-School at: **1.800.824.5179**

For Corporations, IT Training Centers, and Federal Government Agencies: Call Thomson CourseTechnology at **1.800.648.7450**

Ensuring students don't get their hands on the answers, test banks, or other resources that we provide you through our Instructor Resources, password protection is at the forefront of our minds at all times. Note that each and every time a caller requests a password, we verify the caller's affiliation with the school that he or she indicates.

My Instructor Login

Username: _____

Password: _____

Take Advantage of the Power and Flexibility of CoursePort

A single password allows you to access the Online Companion for this text, all of the Instructor Resources, and—if you choose—to manage your class with the Universal Gradebook.

Students can access the Online Companion and track their progress with the activities for this text regardless of how heavily you choose to use CoursePort.

By setting up a Class Code, you can easily link each student to your class and view results for the individuals or the class as a whole. Customized reporting reveals exactly what content is engaging your students and what is challenging them, so you can adjust your instruction or syllabus accordingly.

To obtain a Class Code, simply login, click on the Create a Class link and follow the onscreen instructions.

INSTRUCTOR EDITION

WHAT'S NEW TO *DISCOVERING COMPUTERS 2007: A GATEWAY TO INFORMATION*

■ All topics have been completely updated for currency, and have an increased emphasis on wireless communications, video technologies, and mobile computers and devices!

■ New Ethics and Issues boxes raise controversial, computer-related topics of the day, challenging readers to closely consider general concerns of computers in society!

■ High-Tech Talk articles at the end of each chapter expand on and present a more technical discussion of a topic covered in the chapter!

■ Learn How To exercises engage students and teach fundamental skills when using a computer and accompanying technology!

■ Web Research page features Journaling and Ethics in Action exercises bring abstract concepts to students' practical experience!

■ Case Studies exercises, featuring Research, Class Discussion, and Team Challenge Case Studies, engage students in critical thinking and working collaboratively!

■ Computer Forensics Special Feature following Chapter 11 introduces students to the exciting and evolving world of computer forensics!

■ Online Companion features a Discussion Forum and dynamic games providing students challenging vehicles for learning and reinforcement!

INSTRUCTOR RESOURCES

To teach your class effectively you need more than great textbooks. That is why we strive to provide you with outstanding instructor resources – developed by educators, for educators. Our goal is to make the teaching and learning experience in your classroom the best it can be. With these resources, you can spend less time preparing, and more time teaching.

INSTRUCTOR RESOURCES CD-ROM

When preparing for your next class, the Instructor Resources CD-ROM is the best place to start. The CD-ROM contains everything you need to get your course up and running. Most of the materials on the Instructor Resources CD-ROM also are available for download on course.com. Check the instructor download section at course.com before each semester for important updates to the Instructor Resources for this title! The Instructor Resources CD-ROM for *Discovering Computers 2007: A Gateway to Information* contains the following:

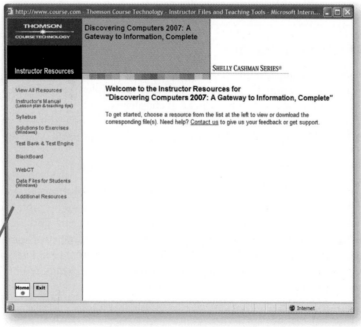

 Instructor Resources CD-ROM Menu

Instructor's Manual: Need to compile a lecture for your class that's starting in an hour? Looking for ways to challenge your students with group projects? Want to engage your students during lecture with classroom activities, or discussion topics? The electronic Instructor's Manual is a great place to look for solutions to all of these dilemmas. The Microsoft Word document for each chapter easily can be customized to include your own notes, but already comes chock-full of great ideas.

Syllabus: Need to keep your students on tract with assignments, class policies, and due dates? Our sample syllabi provide a great place to start! The syllabi come with laboratory instructions, class and school policies, sample weekly assignments, and are fully customizable by you.

Figure Files: Looking for figures in the book that are not included in the Course Presenter? Illustrations for every figure in the textbook are available in electronic form. Use this ancillary to present a slide show in lecture or to print transparencies for use in lecture with an overhead projector.

Solutions to Exercises: Need to quickly check answers to exercises? Make homework corrections a snap with all of the end-of-chapter exercises solutions right at your fingertips.

Test Bank and Test Engine: Looking for time-efficient ways to test your students effectively? ExamView features a user-friendly testing environment that allows you to not only publish traditional paper and LAN-based tests, but also Web-deliverable exams. Utilize the ultra-efficient Quick Test Wizard to create an exam in less than five minutes, take advantage of the Course Technology question banks, or even customize your own exams from scratch. Would you rather see the entire test bank in a Word document? A version of the test bank you quickly can print also is included. All of the test questions and answers found in the ExamView test bank are in one Word document per chapter.

Test Out/Final Exam: Need a way to test students out of your course? This objective-based test is the solution! It can also be used as a final examination. A master answer sheet is included.

Pretest/Posttest: Looking for ways to measure student progress effectively? Administering these carefully prepared tests at the beginning and the end of the semester enable you to do just that! A master answer sheet is included. The Pretest/Posttest makes a great addition to the ExamView Test Bank truly putting students' knowledge to the test!

Data Files for Students: Some exercises in this book require that students have access to a set of data files, to bring the lessons being learned to life in realistic settings. While these files are available for your students to download from course.com on their own, many instructors prefer to download the data files from either the Web or the Instructor Resources CD-ROM and put them on a location on their school's network for easier student access.

Putting the data files on your own network? Write the location of the titles for this book here, for easy reference:

_____

COURSE PRESENTER CD-ROM

Need to deliver engaging and visually impressive lectures? It's easy with the professionally-designed Course Presenter. Course Presenter is a one-click-per-slide presentation system on CD-ROM that provides PowerPoint slides for every subject in each chapter. Several up-to-date G4TechTV computer-related video clips are available for optional presentation. You can edit the files to fit your needs, post them to your network for students to review key concepts, or save them to the Web for your Distance Learning students.

BLACKBOARD, WEBCT, and MYCOURSE 2.1 CONTENT

Blackboard and WebCT are the leading distance learning solutions available today. In the past few years, they've also become popular class-management platforms. Course Technology has partnered with Blackboard and WebCT to bring you premium online content. MyCourse 2.1 is Course Technology's powerful online course management and content delivery system. Content for use with *Discovering Computers 2007: A Gateway to Information* is available in Blackboard Course Cartridge, WebCT e-Pack, and MyCourse 2.1 format, and includes the following:

- Topic Reviews

- Case Projects

- Review Questions

- Test Banks

- Practice Tests

- Custom Syllabus, and more!

ONLINE COMPANION

Looking to make your course more interactive? Want to integrate the World Wide Web into your course? The Online Companion (scsite.com/dc2007) offers reinforcement and the opportunity to broaden knowledge, all while having fun! On the Online Companion you'll find extensions of the features in the text, such as Career Corner, Companies, FAQs, High-Tech Talk, Looking Ahead, Technology Trailblazers, and Web Links, adding to the depth and diversity of your students' learning experience! You'll also find tools to help students review, reinforce, and solidify what they're learning with material for the Chapter Review, Checkpoint, Key Terms, Learn It Online, Learn How To, Case Studies, and Web Research. Use the CoursePort Universal Gradebook reporting to see exactly what content is engaging your students and what is challenging them. Our comprehensive Online Companion is a great tool enabling students to excel!

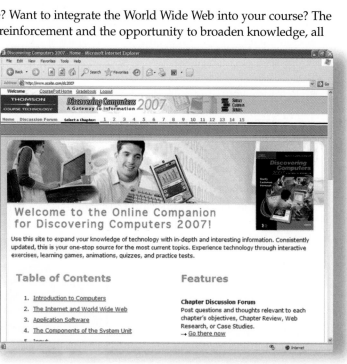

SAM COMPUTER CONCEPTS

Now you can bring the concepts and lessons presented in this text to life with **Student Edition Labs** and **SAM Computer Concepts**.

Student Edition Labs

This free, Web-based software allows your students to master hundreds of computer concepts including input and output devices, file management and desktop applications, computer privacy, virus protection, and much more. Featuring up-to-the-minute content, eye-popping graphics, and rich animation, the highly interactive Student Edition Labs help students learn through dynamic observation, step-by-step practice, and challenging review questions. Access the free Student Edition Labs from the *Discovering Computers 2007: A Gateway to Information* Online Companion at scsite.com/dc2007.

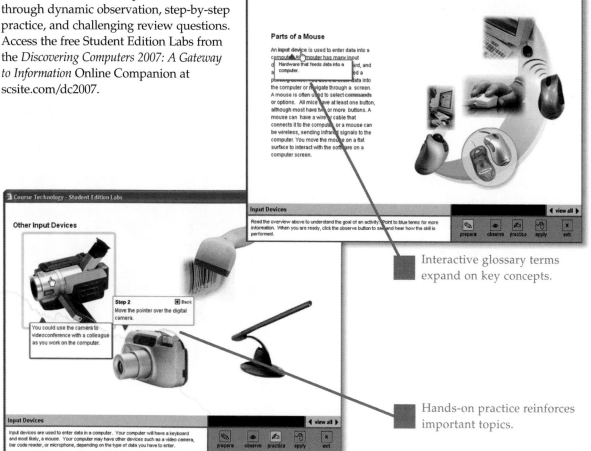

Interactive glossary terms expand on key concepts.

Hands-on practice reinforces important topics.

SAM Computer Concepts

Add more muscle and flexibility to your Student Edition Labs with SAM (Skills Assessment Manager) Computer Concepts! SAM Computer Concepts adds the power of assessment and detailed reporting to your Student Edition Labs.

By adding SAM Computer Concepts to your curriculum, you can:

- Reinforce your students' knowledge of key computer concepts with hands-on application exercises.

- Allow your students to "learn by listening," with access to rich audio in their computer concepts labs.

- Build computer concepts exams from a test bank of more than 50,000 objective-based questions or create your own test questions.

- Schedule your students' concepts training and testing assignments with powerful administrative tools.

- Track student exam grades and training progress using more than one dozen student and classroom reports.

- Teach your introductory course with the simplicity of a single system! You can now administer your entire Computer Concepts and Microsoft Office course through the SAM platform. For more information on the SAM administration system, SAM Computer Concepts and other SAM products, please visit http://samcentral.course.com.

 Choose from more than 50,000 objective-based questions to test your students' knowledge.

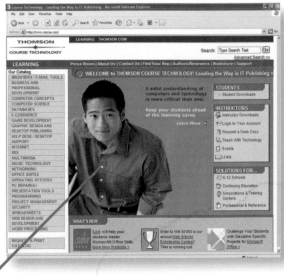

THOMSON COURSE TECHNOLOGY'S WEB SITE

Thomson Course Technology is the world's leading IT publisher. Because we focus solely on the Information Technology area, we have the unique ability to address the needs of customers like you. Find out about the latest technology trends, products, and courseware solutions on the Thomson Course Technology Web site, course.com.

Visit often to:

- Connect with your peers through our Online forums.

- Learn about the latest software releases and how they will impact you in the classroom.

- Browse our online catalog.

- Locate and contact your local sales representative.

- Register for the next Conference for Information Technology Educators and our other educational events.

- Download the files that are contained on the Instructor Resources CD-ROM.

 Course.com Home Page

ANNOTATED TABLE OF CONTENTS

Now that you have a better understanding of all the tools that come with *Discovering Computers 2007: A Gateway to Information,* how can you fit them all together? This annotated table of contents will help you begin to sort through the available tools and better define what may be appropriate where.

CHAPTER 1: INTRODUCTION TO COMPUTERS

AN OVERVIEW OF WHAT'S NEW

Chapter 1 has been completely revised to reflect the most up-to-date technologies both in the text and art features, including:

- blogs
- digital audio player
- Game Consoles
- Media Center PC
- Medical Breakthroughs with Computer Implants, Devices
- Onboard Navigation System
- podcast
- ultra personal computer (uPC)

TEACHING CHAPTER-BY-CHAPTER

Present your class using the **Course Presenter** presentation for Chapter 1. During lecture, make real the introductory computer concepts students learn in Chapter 1 with discussion topics and classroom activities in the **Instructor's Manual.** To engage students in the many questions surrounding increased computer use, introduce one of the **Discussion Topics** in the Instructor's Manual for Chapter 1. The place of computers in today's schools can be an interesting discussion topic. Advocates argue that computers add interest, reinforce skills, and even improve behavior. Critics claim that computers promote superficial thinking, lead to shortened attention spans, and even damage vision and posture. Consider having students debate the merits of computer use in schools. Students can find many works, such as Bill Gates's *The Road*

Ahead, to support the inclusion of computers (Gates is one of this chapter's Technology Trailblazers). Books such as Jane Healy's *Failure to Connect: How Computers Affect Our C hildren's Minds and What We Can Do About It* and Clifford Stoll's *High-Tech Heretic: Why Computers Don't Belong in the Classroom,* present a less optimistic view of computer use in schools. Assign one of the **Student Edition Labs** – Using Input Devices or Using Windows – in the Learn It Online exercises for Chapter 1 to assist students in learning some of the basics of computing. Encourage students to reinforce what they've learned in Chapter 1 with the new **Learn How To** video on finding out more about their computer, or with the wealth of games, activities, and exercises on the **Online Companion** (scsite.com/dc2007). Correct your students' work using the **Solutions to Exercises** files provided to instructors.

CHAPTER 2: THE INTERNET AND WORLD WIDE WEB

AN OVERVIEW OF WHAT'S NEW

Chapter 2 has been completely revised to reflect the most up-to-date technologies both in the text and art features, including:

- Atom
- blogger
- Chat Rooms
- Content Aggregator
- Google
- Internet Telephony
- Multimedia on the Web
- RSS 2.0 (Really Simple Syndication)
- Searching for Information on the Web
- Wiki
- Wireless Internet Service Provider
- Yahoo!

TEACHING CHAPTER-BY-CHAPTER

Present your class using the **Course Presenter** presentation for Chapter 2. During lecture, get students thinking practically about the Internet with the lecture notes and projects to assign in the **Instructor's Manual.** Bring some of the consequences of increased Internet accessibility and popularity to life with one of the **Projects to Assign** in the Chapter 2 IM. The Internet has had a tremendous impact on business. For some businesses, that impact has not been positive. For example, recent surveys suggest that as a growing number of

people are making their own travel plans online, travel agents are seeing a significant reduction in their customer base. What does the future hold for travel agents and other businesses that are "competing" with the Internet? Have students interview a travel agent or an individual in another business that might be impacted negatively by the Internet. What effect has the Internet had on the business? How might the Internet change the way business is done? What services does the business offer that cannot be found on the Internet? What can be done to minimize, or even take advantage of, the Internet's impact? Engage students in technology that impacts their lives with the **At the Movies** feature Instant Message From Anywhere on the Learn It Online page. Assign one of the **Student Edition Labs** – Connecting to the Internet or Getting the Most Out of the Internet – in the Learn It Online exercises for Chapter 2 to help solidify the Internet concepts presented in the chapter. Encourage students to reinforce what they've learned in Chapter 2 with the **Practice Tests,** or the wealth of games, activities, and exercises on the **Online Companion** (scsite.com/dc2007). Ensure student understanding of the chapter material by checking their Practice Test results in the **CoursePort Universal Gradebook.** Use the **ExamView Test Wizard** to create and administer an exam for Chapter 2.

CHAPTER 3: APPLICATION SOFTWARE

AN OVERVIEW OF WHAT'S NEW

Chapter 3 has been completely revised to reflect the most up-to-date technologies both in the text and art features, including:

- Adobe Systems
- backup utility
- blog software
- blogware
- Business Software
- Computer Viruses
- Copying Software – A Computer Crime!
- Distance Learning
- document management software
- file manager
- Graphics and Multimedia Software
- personal firewall
- Popular Utility Programs
- professional photo editing software
- Tax Preparation Software

TEACHING CHAPTER-BY-CHAPTER

Present your class using the **Course Presenter** presentation for Chapter 3. During lecture, get students thinking about the ways application software is used with classroom activities and discussion topics in the **Instructor's Manual.** Open class discussion on the impact of word processing software on the creative mind with one of the **Classroom Activities** in the Chapter 3 IM. Ask what effect, if any, word processors have on the creative process. Are people using word processing software more willing to adopt a "stream-of-consciousness" style, knowing that whatever they write easily can be changed? If possible, compare a formatted document to an unformatted document. Which document has more impact? Why? Engage students in a developing technology with the **At the Movies** feature Detect Spyware on Your Computer on the Learn It Online page. Assign one of the **Student Edition Labs** – Word Processing, Spreadsheets, Databases, or Presentation Software – in the Learn It Online exercises for Chapter 3 to help solidify the application software concepts presented in the chapter. Reinforce the lessons taught in Chapter 3 with the **Learn How To** videos, **Checkpoint** exercises, or the wealth of games, activities, and exercises on the **Online Companion** (scsite.com/dc2007). Schedule an end-of-chapter **SAM Assessment** exam that automatically generates a custom SAM Training lesson based on tasks performed incorrectly.

CHAPTER 4: THE COMPONENTS OF THE SYSTEM UNIT

AN OVERVIEW OF WHAT'S NEW

Chapter 4 has been completely revised to reflect the most up-to-date technologies both in the text and art features, including:

- AMD
- Athlon 64 X2 and Athlon 64 FX
- Cache
- Centrino
- Comparison of Personal Computer Processors
- Dual-Core Processors
- e-waste
- FireWire hub and ports
- Flash Memory Cards and USB Flash Drives
- Intel
- Memory Access Times
- Mobile Computers and Devices
- multicore processor
- Pentium Extreme Edition
- Pentium D
- Sound Cards
- Turion 64
- Viiv technology

TEACHING CHAPTER-BY-CHAPTER

Present your class using the **Course Presenter** presentation for Chapter 4. During lecture, make real the basic system unit information students learn in Chapter 4 with projects to assign and quick quizzes in the **Instructor's Manual.** To engage students in thinking practically about their own needs and preferences when using computers, use one of the **Projects to Assign** in the IM for Chapter 4. Some people say that, "Software drives hardware." Although this contention has several interpretations, when purchasing a computer it usually means that the system unit and peripheral devices (hardware) must be capable of running the application programs (software) in which a buyer is interested. Have students visit a store or Web site that sells computer software and make a list of application programs they would like now and those they may want to have in the future. Examine the software packages and note the capabilities required of the system unit (type of processor, amount of memory, and so on). On the basis of their findings, what are the minimum system requirements they would demand in a personal computer? What system requirements would be sufficient to provide a "cushion" so that they could be sure the system also could run other, or new, application

packages? Engage students in a developing technology with the **At the Movies** feature Chapter 4 Computing Clusters on the Learn It Online page. Broaden students' understanding of the material taught with **Web Research** exercises, or the wealth of games, activities, and exercises on the **Online Companion** (scsite.com/dc2007). Assign one of the **Student Edition Labs** – Understanding the Motherboard or Binary Numbers – in the Learn It Online exercises for Chapter 4 to help solidify the system unit components presented in the chapter. Use the **ExamView Test Wizard** to create and administer an exam for Chapter 4.

CHAPTER 5: INPUT

AN OVERVIEW OF WHAT'S NEW

Chapter 5 has been completely revised to reflect the most up-to-date technologies both in the text and art features, including:

- Audio Player Control Pad
- Bar Code Readers
- Charles Walton
- Click Wheel
- control pad
- Digital Video Camera
- gamepad
- gaming keyboard

- iPod Click Wheel
- retinal scanner
- RFID Sensors Simplify, Monitor Tasks
- Scanners
- Smart Phones
- Wearable Computers Make Performance Statement

TEACHING CHAPTER-BY-CHAPTER

Present your class using the **Course Presenter** presentation for Chapter 5. During lecture, get students thinking about input with discussion topics and classroom activities in the **Instructor's Manual.** Introduce alternative input with one of the **Discussion Topics** in the IM for Chapter 5. Consider going around the world in 80 clicks. It is possible. Take an online tour of the world at your leisure. Thousands of Web sites show live images through Web cams. These sites feature real-time (often 24-hour) views from every country in the world, and from places such as beaches, buildings, classrooms, dorm rooms, baby bassinets, fish tanks, taxicab dashboards, and even inside a refrigerator. Or, how about a camera mounted on a bike, transmitting images through a cellular telephone? Some people may question the entertainment value and the appeal of the Web cam, especially because many of the sites are rather boring. With the drop in price and the increased ease of installation and use, more people are using Web cams to share the view from their part of the world. What motivates someone to do this? Why would someone want to

see a stranger's home movies? In what type of Web cam Web site would you be interested? Why? Engage students in the world of gadgets with the **At the Movies** feature Essential Travel Gadgets on the Learn It Online page. Reinforce the lessons taught in Chapter 5 with the **Practice Tests,** or the wealth of games, activities, and exercises on the **Online Companion** (scsite.com/dc2007). Ensure student understanding of the chapter material by checking their Practice Test results in the **CoursePort Universal Gradebook.** Assign one of the **Student Edition Labs** – Working with Audio or Working with Video – in the Learn It Online exercises, or encourage students to access the **Learn How To** videos – Install and Use a PC Video Camera and Use the On-Screen Keyboard for Physically Challenged Users – for Chapter 5 to help solidify the concepts presented in the chapter. Schedule an end-of-chapter **SAM Assessment** exam that automatically generates a custom SAM Training lesson based on tasks performed incorrectly. Correct your students' work using the **Solutions to Exercises** files provided to instructors.

CHAPTER 6: OUTPUT

AN OVERVIEW OF WHAT'S NEW

Chapter 6 has been completely revised to reflect the most up-to-date technologies both in the text and art features, including:

- contrast ratio
- Digital Cinema Initiative
- earbuds, earphones, and headphones
- Flat-Panel Displays
- Force-Feedback Joysticks, Wheels, and Gamepads
- Graphics Chips and CRT Monitors
- Hewlett-Packard
- Plasma Technology
- Printing Digital Camera Images speaker systems

TEACHING CHAPTER-BY-CHAPTER

Present your class using the **Course Presenter** presentation for Chapter 6. During lecture, get students thinking about output with discussion topics and classroom activities in the **Instructor's Manual.** To introduce students to types of output with which they may not be familiar, use one of the **Discussion Topics** in the IM for Chapter 6. Imagine a library on your lap. Read your favorite Stephen King novel, delete it, and download the complete works of Hemingway. Analysts predict electronic books will revolutionize the publishing industry. An electronic book primarily is a digital storage and display unit. Some plug into a cradle that attaches to your computer, letting you download textbooks or novels from Web-based publishers. Others include a built-in modem that allows you to connect directly to the Internet. They range in size and weight from a paperback to a two-pound textbook and can hold thousands of pages or the equivalent to ten or more books. Keeping with some traits of traditional books, you can move forward or backward one page at a time, or use a stylus to write notes in the margin. What is your opinion of the electronic book? Will it replace the printed book? Why not just buy the book? Does society have a place for the electronic book? Who do you think will use electronic books and how will they use them? Assign one of the **Student Edition Labs** – Peripheral Devices or Working with Graphics – in the Learn It Online exercises for Chapter 6 to help solidify the concepts presented in the chapter. Explore the **Looking Ahead** links and view the **Learn How To** videos for Chapter 6 on the **Online Companion** (scsite.com/dc2007). Use the **ExamView Test Wizard** to create and administer an exam for Chapter 6.

CHAPTER 7: STORAGE

AN OVERVIEW OF WHAT'S NEW

Chapter 7 has been completely revised to reflect the most up-to-date technologies both in the text and art features, including:

- Disk Formatting and File Systems
- HD-DVD disc
- Heat Increases Disk Capacity
- longitudinal recording
- Maxtor
- Miniature, External, and Removable Hard Disks
- Next-Generation DVDs a Burning Question
- perpendicular recording
- SanDisk Corporation
- UMD
- USB Flash Drives

TEACHING CHAPTER-BY-CHAPTER

Present your class using the **Course Presenter** presentation for Chapter 7. During lecture, get students thinking practically about storage with the classroom activities and projects to assign in the **Instructor's Manual.** Make real the concepts of disk cache and cache controller using one of the **Classroom Activities** in the IM for Chapter 7. To reinforce the meaning of cache, ask students to use their predictive abilities and determine what they might place in "life caches" (i.e., anticipated data, instructions, or information that might be needed) to help a parent or spouse prepare dinner. A child do homework? A plumber fix a leak? Engage students with discussion of preserving CDs with the **At the Movies** feature Repair Your CD Scratches on the Learn It Online page. Expose students to the realities of maintaining a hard disk with the **Learn How To** videos, and encourage students to reinforce what they've learned in Chapter 7 with the **Practice Tests,** or the wealth of games, activities, and exercises on the **Online Companion** (scsite.com/dc2007). Ensure student understanding of the chapter material by checking their Practice Test results in the **CoursePort Universal Gradebook.** Assign one of

the **Student Edition Labs** – Maintaining a Hard Drive or Managing Files – in the Learn It Online exercises for Chapter 7 to help solidify the concepts presented in the chapter. Use the **ExamView Test Wizard** to create and administer an exam for Chapter 7.

CHAPTER 8: OPERATING SYSTEMS AND UTILITY PROGRAMS

AN OVERVIEW OF WHAT'S NEW

Chapter 8 has been completely revised to reflect the most up-to-date technologies both in the text and art features, including:

- adware
- Antivirus Programs
- Closed Source vs. Open Source Operating Systems
- Document Explorer
- File Compression Utilities
- Internet Filters
- Online Operating Systems Proposed

- Solaris
- Spyware Removers
- The Future of Linux
- Virtual Folders
- Windows Mobile
- Windows Vista
- Windows XP Professional x64 Edition

TEACHING CHAPTER-BY-CHAPTER

Present your class using the **Course Presenter** presentation for Chapter 8. During lecture, get students thinking about operating systems and utility programs with lecture notes and projects to assign in the **Instructor's Manual.** To engage students in learning about the different kinds of utility programs and their uses, introduce one of the **Projects to Assign** in the IM for Chapter 8. Many utility programs are available for users of personal computers. Have students visit a computer store, read a computer magazine, or access a vendor's Web site and choose two utility programs in which they are interested. Write a review of the two programs. What is the function of each? What are the system requirements? How easy

is the program to use? How much does the program cost? In their opinion, is the utility worth the price? Why or why not? If they could buy only one of the utility programs, which would they purchase? Why? Reinforce the lessons taught and encourage students to view the **Learn How To** videos – Installing and Maintaining a Computer, and Keeping Windows XP Up-to-Date – in Chapter 8 with the wealth of games, activities, and exercises on the **Online Companion** (scsite.com/dc2007). Assign the **Student Edition Lab** – Installing and Uninstalling Software – in the Learn It Online exercises for Chapter 8 to help solidify the concepts presented in the chapter. Correct your students' work using the **Solutions to Exercises** files provided to instructors.

CHAPTER 9: COMMUNICATIONS AND NETWORKS

AN OVERVIEW OF WHAT'S NEW

Chapter 9 has been completely revised to reflect the most up-to-date technologies both in the text and art features, including:

- 3G network
- 802.16
- 802.11 (Wi-Fi) and 802.11n
- broadband over power lines
- Cellular Radio
- Collaboration
- Dedicated Lines
- document management system
- EDGE
- Europe Develops Satellite Navigation System
- MIMO

- Networks
- Patricia Russo
- QUALCOMM
- Robert Metcalf
- video messaging
- Web Folders
- WiMAX
- Wireless Internet Access Points
- Wireless Messaging Services
- Wireless Transmission Media
- WLANs

TEACHING CHAPTER-BY-CHAPTER

Present your class using the **Course Presenter** presentation for Chapter 9. During lecture, make real the basic communications and networks concepts students learn in Chapter 9 with classroom activities and discussion topics in the **Instructor's Manual.** To broaden discussion in class, use one of the **Discussion Topics** in the IM for Chapter 9. You are on the road and need to call home. You dial your cellular telephone just as you pass a Pizza Hut. What are the first words you hear? "The Best Pizza Under One Roof." This scenario may seem a little futuristic, but today's technology makes it possible to deliver targeted advertising in all sorts of new ways. WindWire and DoubleClick, for example, both have wireless marketing and advertising networks that deliver targeted advertisements, coupons, and promotions to leading wireless Internet devices, including cellular telephones, PDAs, and two-way pagers. In one study of cellular telephone users, participants were given free text-messaging capabilities in return for the more than 100,000 targeted advertising messages. More than 60 percent of the participants liked receiving targeted advertisements, and 20 percent asked for more information after viewing the advertising

message. Will American users willingly accept wireless advertisements sent to them over cellular telephones and other mobile devices? What inducements might convince someone to accept the messages? Would you accept the advertising in return for a free service? How would you feel if the advertisements were targeted at your personal profile? Would this make a difference in your willingness to accept the advertisements? Engage students in a developing technology with the **At the Movies** feature Bluetooth in Action on the Learn It Online page. Assign one of the **Student Edition Labs** – Networking Basics or Wireless Networking – in the Learn It Online exercises or encourage students to view the **Learn How To** video – on setting up and installing a Wi-Fi home network – for Chapter 9 to help solidify the communications and networks concepts presented in the chapter. Reinforce the lessons taught in Chapter 9 with **Checkpoint** exercises, or the wealth of games, activities, and exercises on the **Online Companion** (scsite.com/dc2007). Correct your students' work using the **Solutions to Exercises** files provided to instructors. Schedule an end-of-chapter **SAM Assessment** exam that automatically generates a custom SAM training lesson based on tasks performed incorrectly.

CHAPTER 10: DATABASE MANAGEMENT

AN OVERVIEW OF WHAT'S NEW

Chapter 10 has been completely revised to reflect the most up-to-date technologies both in the text and art features, including:

- Backup and Recovery
- continuous backup
- Database Management Systems
- Oracle

- Qualities of Valuable Information
- Sybase
- Web Databases
- Windows Future Storage (WinFS)

TEACHING CHAPTER-BY-CHAPTER

Present your class using the **Course Presenter** presentation for Chapter 10. During lecture, get students thinking about database management with projects to assign and classroom activities in the **Instructor's Manual**. To help students develop research skills and practice oral and written communications skills, use one of the **Projects to Assign** in the IM for Chapter 10. The National Crime Information Center (NCIC), the FBI's index of documented criminal justice information, provides law enforcement personnel with data on wanted or missing persons and stolen property. More than a million transactions a day are processed by the NCIC database. Law officers can access the NCIC database 24 hours a day, 365 days a year when conducting their own investigations. Law enforcement agencies are extensive users of databases. Have students visit a local police department to learn about the role computerized databases play in law enforcement. What databases does the department access? What information do they contain? How are the databases used? How are they

searched? How often are they updated? In what ways does a database contribute to law enforcement? What are the advantages and disadvantages of using a computerized database? Engage students in a developing technology with the **At the Movies** feature National Identity Cards on the Learn It Online page. Assign one of the **Student Edition Labs** – Advanced Databases or Advanced Spreadsheets – in the Learn It Online exercises for Chapter 10 to help solidify the database management concepts presented in the chapter. Reinforce the lessons taught in Chapter 10 with the **Practice Tests**, or the wealth of games, activities, and exercises on the **Online Companion** (scsite.com/dc2007). Ensure student understanding of the chapter material by checking their Practice Test results in the **CoursePort Universal Gradebook**. Correct your students' work using the **Solutions to Exercises** files provided to instructors. Schedule an end-of-chapter **SAM Assessment** exam that automatically generates a custom SAM Training lesson based on tasks performed incorrectly.

AN OVERVIEW OF WHAT'S NEW

Chapter 11 has been completely revised to reflect the most up-to-date technologies both in the text and art features, including:

- Computer Viruses, Worms, and Trojan Horses
- Denial of Service Attacks
- Digital Certificates
- digital rights management (DRM)
- Encryption
- Firewalls
- Honeypots
- Intellectual Property Rights
- malicious software or malware
- McAfee

- Personal Firewall Software
- pharming
- Phishing
- Safeguards against Computer Viruses, Worms, and Trojan Horses
- Safeguards against Software Theft
- Safeguards against System Failure
- social engineering
- Spyware and Adware
- Symantec

TEACHING CHAPTER-BY-CHAPTER

Present your class using the **Course Presenter** presentation for Chapter 11. During lecture, get students thinking about computers and society, security, privacy, and ethics with classroom activities and projects to assign in the **Instructor's Manual**. Open the class with some of the more contentious issues in security and privacy using one of the **Classroom Activities** in the IM for Chapter 11. In his book, *The Cuckoo's Egg*, Clifford Stoll (one of this chapter's Technology Trailblazers) tells the fascinating story of using an audit trail to uncover computer espionage. The story is retold in a PBS *Nova* special, "The KGB, the CIA, the Computer and Me," in which Stoll plays himself. If possible, obtain a videotape of the special to show in class. Clifford Stoll is an energetic and informative speaker. Pacing, running, shouting, laughing, and cajoling, Stoll challenges his audience to consider issues they may never have thought about before. "I don't know. This is just me," Stoll observes. "Your job is to prove me wrong." Stoll believes that, "if we want good technology, we have to open it up to criticism." In one interview, Stoll said it is important for technologists (or "propeller-heads") such as himself to consider such questions as:

- Who does not benefit from computers?
- Where are computers badly applied?
- When is the Web irrelevant?
- Why are people frustrated by computers?
- How do computers change society?

Stoll listens to everyone – both computer users and non-computer users alike. In fact, Stoll decries the "cult of exclusion" or "techno-arrogance" he feels characterizes some computer users. Stoll's questions, and the issues he raises in *Silicon Snake Oil and High Tech Heretic*, could inspire an interesting end-of-term discussion. Engage students in the problems associated with spam with the **At the Movies** feature StopSpam on the Learn It Online page. Reinforce the lessons taught with **Learn How To** videos on backing up files on a offsite Internet server and using the Windows XP firewall, or with the wealth of games, activities, and exercises on the **Online Companion** (scsite.com/dc2007). Assign one of the **Student Edition Labs** – Protecting Your Privacy Online or Keeping Your Computer Virus Free – in the Learn It Online exercises for Chapter 11 to help solidify the concepts presented in the chapter. Use the **ExamView Test Wizard** to create and administer an exam for Chapter 11.

INSTRUCTOR EDITION

CHAPTER 12: INFORMATION SYSTEM DEVELOPMENT

AN OVERVIEW OF WHAT'S NEW
Chapter 12 has been completely revised to reflect the most up-to-date technologies both in the text and art features, including:

- adaptive maintenance
- Change Management
- Computer Associates
- corrective maintenance
- Object Modeling

- perfective maintenance
- Phases in the System Development Cycle
- Putting Vista to the Test
- UML
- Zebra Technologies

TEACHING CHAPTER-BY-CHAPTER
Present your class using the **Course Presenter** presentation for Chapter 12. During lecture, make real the basic information system development concepts students learn in Chapter 12 with classroom activities and projects to assign in the **Instructor's Manual**. To engage students in the class, use one of the **Classroom Activities** in the IM for Chapter 12. Software license conditions can lead to some interesting discussions. Ask students if it would be all right to share a software package in a small, family business that used just two personal computers. Should an employee be allowed to copy a software package used at the office so that he

or she could do some work on a home computer? Assign one of the **Student Edition Labs** – Project Management or Web Design Principles – in the Learn It Online exercises for Chapter 12 to help solidify the concepts presented in the chapter. Reinforce the lessons taught in Chapter 12 with **Practice Tests,** or the wealth of games, activities, and exercises on the **Online Companion** (scsite.com/dc2007). Ensure student understanding of the chapter material by checking their Practice Test results in the **CoursePort Universal Gradebook.** Correct your students' work using the **Solutions to Exercises** files provided to instructors.

CHAPTER 13: PROGRAMMING LANGUAGES AND PROGRAM DEVELOPMENT

AN OVERVIEW OF WHAT'S NEW
Chapter 13 has been completely revised to reflect the most up-to-date technologies both in the text and art features, including:

- Ajax
- C#
- Electronic Arts
- Object-Oriented Programming Languages and Program Development Tools

- RSS 2.0 or Really Simple Syndication
- Sun Microsystems
- XHTML, DHTML, XML, and WML

TEACHING CHAPTER-BY-CHAPTER
Present your class using the **Course Presenter** presentation for Chapter 13. During lecture, get students thinking about programming languages and program development with projects to assign and discussion topics in the **Instructor's Manual**. To familiarize students with some of the considerations when teaching or learning a programming language, use one of the **Discussion Topics** in the Chapter 13 IM. Many universities and community colleges require a programming logic course as a prerequisite for all programming courses. Other educational institutions integrate logic into the programming course. Proponents of programming logic as a prerequisite course point out

that programming logic is part of Step 2 within the program development cycle. They argue that a student must have the necessary background and an understanding of design before they tackle the programming language. Writing the code does not take place until Step 4. Proponents of programming logic as an integrated part of a programming course suggest that students cannot learn logic and a programming language independently. They believe that applying logic as they learn the programming language is the best approach. With which approach do you agree? Why did you choose that approach? Do you think the learning style of the individual student could determine the best approach? Should educational institutions provide both options – prerequisite and integrated approaches? Engage students in a developing technology with the **At the Movies** feature VeriChip on the Learn It Online page. Broaden student understanding of the lessons taught in Chapter 13 with the **Learn How To** video on designing and evaluating a graphical user interface, **FAQ** links, or the wealth of games, activities, and exercises on the **Online**

Companion (scsite.com/dc2007). Assign one of the **Student Edition Labs** – Visual Programming or Creating Web Pages – in the Learn It Online exercises for Chapter 13 to help solidify the concepts presented in the chapter. Schedule an end-of-chapter **SAM Assessment** exam that automatically generates a custom SAM Training lesson based on tasks performed incorrectly.

CHAPTER 14: ENTERPRISE COMPUTING

AN OVERVIEW OF WHAT'S NEW

Chapter 14 has been completely revised to reflect the most up-to-date technologies both in the text and art features, including:

- 3-D visualization
- business intelligence (BI)
- business process management (BPM)
- business process automation (BPA)
- enterprise search
- Enterprise-Wide Technologies
- Enterprise Storage Systems

- Fibre Channel
- failover
- General Purpose Information Systems
- Information Systems within Functional Units
- Mark Hurd
- SAP
- The Future of Grid Computing

TEACHING CHAPTER-BY-CHAPTER

Present your class using the **Course Presenter** presentation for Chapter 14. During lecture, make real the basic enterprise computing concepts students learn in Chapter 14 with projects to assign and classroom activities in the **Instructor's Manual**. To get students thinking practically about e-commerce as a viable business venture, use one of the **Projects to Assign** in the Chapter 14 IM. Half of all new e-commerce businesses fail within five years of their creation, and many do not last that long. What do you need to be part of the profitable 50 percent? Experts point to several factors but, at least for a successful start, two of the most important are good ideas and financial backing. Regrettably, without the first often it is difficult to get the second. Fortunately, software (such as PlanWrite Business Plan Writer Deluxe) is available to help. The software asks questions about an e-commerce idea and then provides an instant analysis with a probability for success. If a user decides to continue, the software helps to write a proposal and publish it, either by printing it or by e-mailing it to potential investors. Have students think of an idea for an e-commerce business, and then use a soft-

ware package that can help them develop their idea. According to the software, how good is the idea? Why? Do friends and relatives agree with the assessment? Why or why not? Use the software to prepare a proposal, then find a successful businessperson and ask him or her to evaluate the plan. Considering all of the evaluations they receive, do they think the idea can make them part of the successful 50 percent of e-commerce businesses? Why or why not? Engage students in developing technology with the **At the Movies** feature Confessions of a Software Pirate on the Learn It Online page. Reinforce the lessons taught in Chapter 14 with **Practice Tests**, or the wealth of games, activities, and exercises on the **Online Companion** (scsite.com/dc2007). Ensure student understanding of the chapter material by checking their Practice Test results in the **CoursePort Universal Gradebook.** Assign one of the **Student Edition Labs** – E-Commerce or Backing Up Your Computer – in the Learn It Online exercises for Chapter 14 to help solidify the enterprise computing concepts presented in the chapter. Use the **ExamView Test Wizard** to create and administer an exam for this chapter.

CHAPTER 15: COMPUTER CAREERS AND CERTIFICATION

AN OVERVIEW OF WHAT'S NEW

Chapter 15 has been completely revised to reflect the most up-to-date technologies both in the text and art features, including:

- Certification Benefits
- Certified Linux Professional (CLP)
- Certified Web Professional
- Database Certifications
- Microsoft Certified Architect (MCA)
- Microsoft Certified IT Professional (MCITP)
- Microsoft Certified Professional Developer (MCPD)
- Microsoft Certified Systems Administrator (MCSA)
- Operating System Certifications
- Professional Growth and Continuing Education
- programmer/developer
- Programmer/Developer Certifications
- Searching for Computer-Related Jobs
- Steve Ballmer
- Steve Wozniak
- Sun Certified Developer
- technical lead
- ZDNet

TEACHING CHAPTER-BY-CHAPTER

Present your class using the **Course Presenter** presentation for Chapter 15. During lecture, make real the basic computer careers and certification information students learn in Chapter 15 with classroom activities and projects to assign in the **Instructor's Manual**. To emphasize the impact location can have on business, use one of the **Projects to Assign** in the IM for Chapter 15. When people think of jobs in the computer field, they often assume the jobs are in large cities on the East or West coast – New York, Washington, San Diego, San Francisco, and so on. Many high-tech firms do call these cities home, but jobs in the computer industry also can be found elsewhere. Today, many smaller cities in the heartland of the United States have leapt on the high-tech train. Tulsa, Oklahoma, with a population of about 393,000, hosts 380 high-tech firms that employ 54,000 people, in industries ranging from the Internet

to telecommunications. Omaha, Nebraska, boasts of 4,000 high-tech companies that supply work for 50,000 of the city's 390,000 population, concentrating in telecommunications and data processing. How does a city attract high-tech corporations? Have students visit a local high-tech company and find out why the company chose its current location. Was it tax incentives? Corporate climate? Employee availability? Cost of living? Quality of life? Some other factor? Based on what they learn, what can a region, or a city, do to become a hotbed of high-tech corporations? Encourage students to learn more about careers in the various technology fields with the **Careers** information on the **Online Companion** (scsite.com/dc2007). Students can also use the **Online Companion** to reinforce the lessons taught in Chapter 15 with the wealth of games, activities, and exercises available. Use the **Test Out/Final Exam** to administer a final exam for text.

SPECIAL FEATURES

Some of the chapters in *Discovering Computers 2007: A Gateway to Information* are followed by **Special Features.** These include: Timeline 2007; Making Use of the Web; Personal Mobile Devices; Digital Imaging and Video Technology; Buyer's Guide 2007; Computer Forensics; Enterprise Order Processing:

A Case Study; and Digital Entertainment. The Special Features can be assigned as extra credit, research, or simply as part of the chapter each follows. The Special Features are another great way to diversify your students' learning experience with *Discovering Computers 2007: A Gateway to Information!*

Discovering Computers
2007

A GATEWAY TO INFORMATION

Web Enhanced — COMPLETE

Gary B. Shelly
Thomas J. Cashman
Misty E. Vermaat

Contributing Authors
Jeffrey J. Quasney
Susan L. Sebok
Jeffrey J. Webb
Gary C. Kessler

THOMSON
★
COURSE TECHNOLOGY

THOMSON COURSE TECHNOLOGY
25 THOMSON PLACE
BOSTON MA 02210

SHELLY
CASHMAN
SERIES®

Australia • Canada • Denmark • Japan • Mexico • New Zealand • Philippines • Puerto Rico • Singapore
South Africa • Spain • United Kingdom • United States

THOMSON

COURSE TECHNOLOGY

Discovering Computers 2007:
A Gateway to Information, Web Enhanced
Complete

Gary B. Shelly

Thomas J. Cashman

Misty E. Vermaat

Executive Editor:
Alexandra Arnold

Series Consulting Editor:
Jim Quasney

Product Manager:
Reed Cotter

Associate Product Manager:
Heather Hawkins

Editorial Assistant:
Klenda Martinez

Marketing Manager:
Dana Merk

Marketing Coordinator/Copywriter:
Melissa Marcoux

Print Buyer:
Justin Palmeiro

**Thomson Course Technology
Production Contact:**
Pamela Elizian

Researcher:
F. William Vermaat

Development Editor:
Lyn Markowicz

Proofreader:
Nancy Lamm

Final Reader:
Kim Kosmatka

Management Services:
Pre-Press Company, Inc.

Interior Designer:
Pre-Press Company, Inc.

Cover Image:
Pre-Press Company, Inc.

Illustrator:
Pre-Press Company, Inc.

Compositor:
Pre-Press Company, Inc.

Printer:
Banta Menasha

Contents

Special Feature

MAKING USE OF THE WEB 116

CHAPTER 3

Application Software

CHAPTER 4

The Components of the System Unit

5 CHAPTER 5

Input 232

Special Feature
PERSONAL MOBILE DEVICES 282

6 CHAPTER 6

Output 298

Special Feature

CHAPTER 9

Communications and Networks 458

Special Feature
COMPUTER FORENSICS

CHAPTER 12
Information System Development 618

CHAPTER 13
Programming Languages and Program Development 662

Special Feature

DIGITAL ENTERTAINMENT   816

Discover Computers
and make concepts real with . . .

Online Companion

Use the Online Companion at scsite.com/dc2007 to bring unparalleled currency to the learning experience. Access additional information about important topics and make use of online learning games, practice tests, and additional reinforcement. Gain access to this dynamic site through CoursePort, Thomson Course Technology's login page.

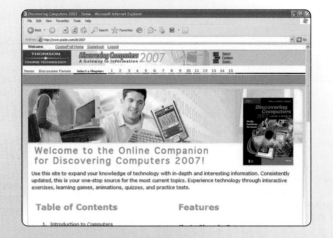

Learn How To

Apply the concepts presented in the chapter to every day life with these hands-on activities. See the Learn How To activities in action with new videos on the Online Companion.

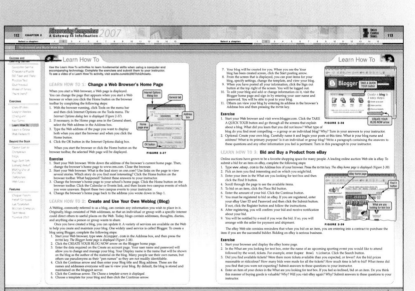

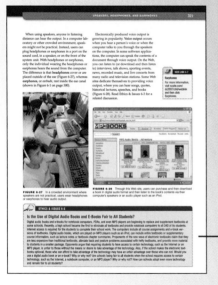

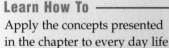

Ethics and Issues

Ethics and Issues boxes raise controversial, computer-related topics of the day, challenging readers to closely consider general concerns of computers in society.

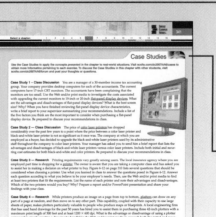

Case Studies

Exercise your mind and construct creative solutions to the thought-provoking case studies presented in each chapter. The Case Study exercises are constructed for class discussion, independent research, or examination in a team environment.

practical, hands-on elements.

High-Tech Talk

The High-Tech Talk article at the end of each chapter expands on a topic covered in the chapter and presents a more technical discussion.

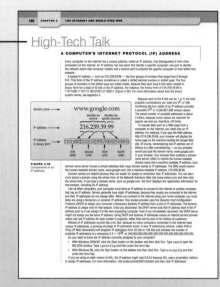

Career Corner

Each chapter ends with a Career Corner feature that introduces a computer-career opportunity relating to a topic covered in the chapter.

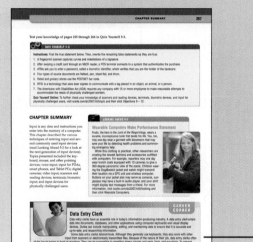

Companies on the Cutting Edge

Everyone who interacts with computers should be aware of the key computer-related companies. Each chapter profiles two of these key companies.

Technology Trailblazers

The Technology Trailblazers section in each chapter offers a glimpse into the life and times of the more famous leaders of the computer industry.

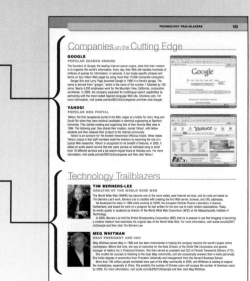

Discover Computers
and make concepts real with . . .

Web Link

Obtain current information and a different perspective about key terms and concepts by visiting the Web addresses in the Web Links found in the margins throughout the book.

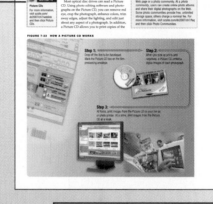

Looking Ahead

The Looking Ahead boxes offer a glimpse at the latest advances in computer technology that will be available, usually within five years.

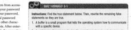

FAQ

FAQ (frequently asked questions) boxes offer common questions and answers about subjects related to the topic at hand.

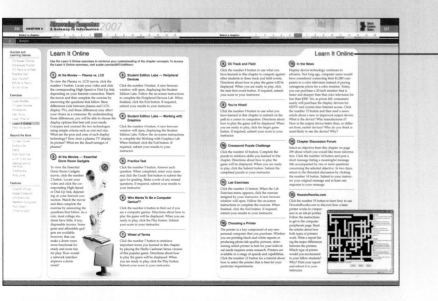

Learn It Online

The Learn It Online exercises, which include online videos, practice tests, interactive labs, learning games, and Web-based activities offer a wealth of online reinforcement.

interactive Web elements.

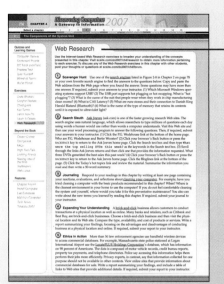

Web Research

Each Web Research exercise references an element in the book, requires follow-up research on the Web, and suggests writing a short article or presenting the findings of the research to the class.

Quiz Yourself

Three Quiz Yourself boxes per chapter help ensure retention by reinforcing sections of the chapter material, rather than waiting for the end of the chapter to test. Use the answers in Appendix B for a quick check of the answers, and take additional these quizzes on the Web for interactivity and easy use.

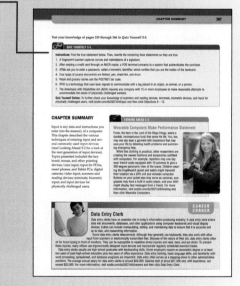

Primary and Secondary Key Terms

Before taking a test, use the Key Terms page as a checklist of terms to know. In the text, primary key terms appear in bold font and secondary key terms appear in italic font. Visit a Key Terms page on the Web and click any term for additional information.

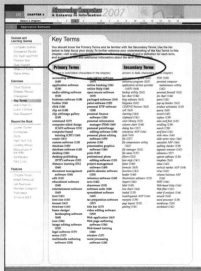

Discover Computers
and make concepts real with . . .

Picture Yourself

Picture yourself using the concepts presented in each chapter. This section at the beginning of each chapter is intended to bridge the gap between the chapter-specific material and everyday life using computers.

Chapter Objectives and Table of Contents

Before reading the chapter, carefully read through the Objectives and Contents to discover knowledge that will be gleaned from chapter.

Step Figures

Each chapter includes numerous step figures that present the more complex computer concepts using a step-by-step pedagogy.

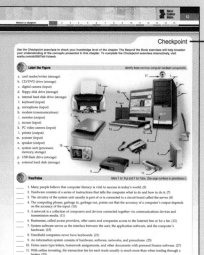

Checkpoint

Use these three pages of label-the-figure, multiple choice, true/false, matching, and short answer exercises to reinforce understanding of the topics presented in the chapter.

Initial Chapter Figure

Carefully study the first figure in each chapter because it provides an easy-to-follow overview of the major purpose of the chapter.

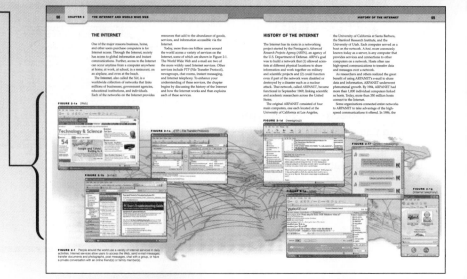

pedagogical elements.

Chapter Review

Use the two-page Chapter Review before taking an examination to ensure familiarity with the computer concepts presented. This section includes each objective, followed by a one- or two-paragraph summary. Visit a Chapter Review page on the Online Companion, and click the Audio button to listen to the Chapter Review.

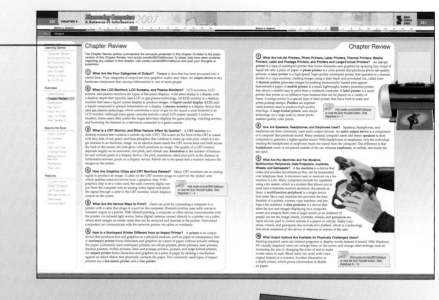

Special Features

Eight special features following Chapters 1, 2, 5, 6, 8, 11, 14, and 15 encompass topics from the history of computers, to what's hot on the Web, to a buyer's guide, to the latest in new technology.

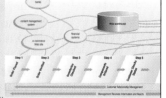

Preface

The Shelly Cashman Series® offers the finest textbooks in computer education. We are proud of the fact that the previous eleven editions of this textbook have been the most widely used in computer education. With each new edition of the book, we have implemented significant improvements based on current computer trends and comments made by instructors and students. *Discovering Computers 2007* continues with the innovation, quality, and reliability you have come to expect from the Shelly Cashman Series.

In *Discovering Computers 2007: A Gateway to Information*, you will find an educationally sound, highly visual, and easy-to-follow pedagogy that presents an in-depth treatment of introductory computer subjects. Students will finish the course with a solid understanding of computers, how to use computers, and how to access information on the World Wide Web.

OBJECTIVES OF THIS TEXTBOOK

Discovering Computers 2007: A Gateway to Information, Complete is intended for use as a stand-alone textbook or in combination with an applications, Internet, or programming textbook in a one-quarter or one-semester introductory computer course. No experience with computers is assumed. The objectives of this book are to:

- Present the most-up-to-date technology in an ever-changing discipline
- Give students an in-depth understanding of why computers are essential components in business and society
- Teach the fundamentals of computers and computer nomenclature, particularly with respect to personal computer hardware and software, the World Wide Web, and enterprise computing
- Present the material in a visually appealing and exciting manner that motivates students to learn
- Assist students in planning a career and getting certified in the computer field
- Provide exercises and lab assignments that allow students to interact with a computer and learn by actually using the computer and the World Wide Web
- Present strategies for purchasing a desktop computer, a notebook computer, a Tablet PC, and a personal mobile device
- Offer alternative learning techniques and reinforcement via the Web
- Offer distance-education providers a textbook with a meaningful and exercise-rich Online Companion

DISTINGUISHING FEATURES

To date, more than six million students have learned about computers using a *Discovering Computers* textbook. With the additional World Wide Web integration and interactivity, streaming up-to-date audio and video, extraordinary step-by-step visual drawings and photographs, unparalleled currency, and the Shelly and Cashman touch, this book will make your computer concepts course exciting and dynamic. Distinguishing features of the Shelly Cashman Series *Discovering Computers* books include:

A Proven Pedagogy
Careful explanations of complex concepts, educationally-sound elements, and reinforcement highlight this proven method of presentation.

A Visually Appealing Book that Maintains Student Interest
The latest technology, pictures, drawings, and text are combined artfully to produce a visually appealing and easy-to-understand book. Many of the figures include a step-by-step presentation

(see page 196), which simplifies the more complex computer concepts. Pictures and drawings reflect the latest trends in computer technology. This combination of pictures, step-by-step drawings, and easy-to-read text layout sets the standard for computer textbook design.

Latest Technologies and Terms

The technologies and terms your students see in this book are those they will encounter when they start using computers. Only the latest application software is shown throughout the book. New topics and terms include blog, developer, podcast, gaming desktop computer, Media Center PC, ultra personal computer (uPC), game console, digital audio player, wiki, content aggregator, RSS 2.0 (Really Simple Syndication), Atom, podcast, blogger, professional photo editing software, document management software, blog software, blogware, Centrino, multicore processor, FireWire hub, Viiv technology, gaming keyboard, control pad, Click Wheel, gamepad, retinal scanner, earphones, headphones, contrast ratio, earbuds, longitudinal recording, perpendicular recording, HD-DVD disc, UMD, adware, Document Explorer, Virtual Folders, Windows Vista, Windows XP Professional x64 Edition, 802.16, 802.11n, 3G network, MIMO, EDGE, WiMAX, wireless Internet access point,

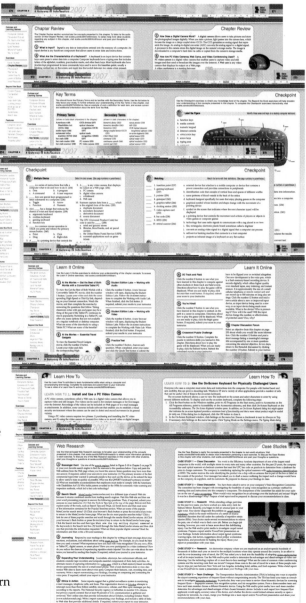

video messaging, continuous backup, social engineering, pharming, digital rights management (DRM), malicious software, malware, corrective maintenance, adaptive maintenance, perfective maintenance, Ajax, 3D visualization, enterprise search, Fibre Channel, Business intelligence (BI), Business Process Management (BPM), Business Process Automation (BPA), technical lead, Certified Linux Professional (CLP), Microsoft Certified Architect (MCA), Microsoft Certified IT Professional (MCITP), Microsoft Certified Professional Developer (MCPD), and Microsoft Certified Systems Administrator (MCSA).

World Wide Web Enhanced

This book uses the World Wide Web as a major supplement. The purpose of integrating the World Wide Web into the book is to (1) offer students additional information and currency on important topics; (2) use its interactive capabilities to offer creative reinforcement and online quizzes; (3) make available alternative learning techniques with Web-based learning games, practice tests, and interactive labs; (4) underscore the relevance of the World Wide Web as a basic information tool that can be used in all facets of society; (5) introduce students to doing research on the Web; and (6) offer instructors the opportunity to organize and administer their traditional campus-based or distance-education-based courses on the Web using WebCT, Blackboard, or MyCourse 2.1. This textbook, however, does not depend on Web access to be used successfully. The Web access adds to the already complete treatment of topics within the book.

Extensive End-of-Chapter Materials

A notable strength of the *Discovering Computers* textbooks is the extensive student activities at the end of each chapter. Well-structured student activities can make the difference between students merely participating in a class and students retaining the information they learn. The activities in the *Discovering Computers 2007* books include: Chapter Review, Key Terms, Checkpoint, Learn It Online, Learn How To, Web Research, and Case Studies.

ORGANIZATION OF THIS TEXTBOOK

Discovering Computers 2007: A Gateway to Information, Complete provides a thorough introduction to computers. The material is divided into fifteen chapters, eight special features, three appendices, and a glossary/index.

Chapter 1 – Introduction to Computers   In Chapter 1, students are introduced to basic computer concepts, such as what a computer is, how it works, and what makes it a powerful tool.

Special Feature – Timeline 2007 Milestones in Computer History   In this special feature, students learn about the major computer technology developments during the past 66 years.

Chapter 2 – The Internet and World Wide Web   In Chapter 2, students learn about the Internet, World Wide Web, browsers, e-mail, FTP, and instant messaging.

Special Feature – Making Use of the Web   In this special feature, more than 150 popular up-to-date Web sites are listed and described. Basic searching techniques also are introduced.

Chapter 3 – Application Software   In Chapter 3, students are introduced to a variety of business software, graphics and multimedia software, home/personal/educational software, and communications software.

Chapter 4 – The Components of the System Unit   In Chapter 4, students are introduced to the components of the system unit; how memory stores data, instructions, and information; and how the system unit executes an instruction.

Chapter 5 – Input   Chapter 5 describes the various techniques of input and commonly used input devices.

Special Feature – Personal Mobile Devices   In this special feature, students receive a detailed presentation of personal mobile device operating systems, built-in personal mobile device software, personal mobile device application software, and how to obtain and install personal mobile device software. Also included is a personal mobile device buyer's guide.

Chapter 6 – Output   Chapter 6 describes the various methods of output and commonly used output devices.

Special Feature – Digital Imaging and Video Technology   In this special feature, students are introduced to using a personal computer, digital camera, and video camera to manipulate photographs and video.

Chapter 7 – Storage   In Chapter 7, students learn about various storage media and storage devices.

Chapter 8 – Operating Systems and Utility Programs   In Chapter 8, students learn about a variety of stand-alone operating systems, network operating systems, and embedded operating systems.

Special Feature – Buyer's Guide 2007: How to Purchase a Personal Computer   In this special feature, students are introduced to purchasing a desktop computer, notebook computer, and Tablet PC.

Chapter 9 – Communications and Networks   Chapter 9 provides students with an overview of communications technology and applications.

Chapter 10 – Database Management   Chapter 10 presents students with the advantages of organizing data in a database and describes various types of data.

Chapter 11 – Computer Security, Ethics, and Privacy   In Chapter 11, students learn about computer and Internet risks, ethical issues surrounding information accuracy, intellectual property rights, codes of conduct, information privacy, and computer-related health issues.

Special Feature – Computer Forensics   This special feature introduces students to the scope of, process, and tools involved in computer forensics work. The feature underlines the importance of computer forensics in our increasingly digital world.

Chapter 12 – Information System Development   In Chapter 12, students are introduced to the system development cycle and guidelines for system development.

Chapter 13 – Programming Languages and Program Development   Chapter 13 presents the program development cycle, program design methods, and popular programming languages.

Chapter 14 – Enterprise Computing   In Chapter 14, students learn about the special computing requirements used in an enterprise-sized organization.

Special Feature – Enterprise Order Processing: A Case Study   This special feature introduces students to how modern-day enterprises process a customer order..

Chapter 15 – Computer Careers and Certification   Chapter 15 presents a broad overview of computer-related careers, career development, and certification.

Special Feature – Digital Entertainment   In this special feature, students are introduced to the personal computer as a digital entertainment device.

Appendix A – Coding Schemes and Number Systems   Appendix A presents the ASCII, EBCDIC, and Unicode coding schemes.

Appendix B – Quiz Yourself Answers   Appendix B provides the answers for the Quiz Yourself questions in the text.

Appendix C – Computer Acronyms   Appendix C summarizes the computer acronyms discussed in the book.

Glossary/Index   The Glossary/Index includes a definition and page references for every key term presented in the book.

SHELLY CASHMAN SERIES INSTRUCTOR RESOURCES

The Shelly Cashman Series is dedicated to providing you with all of the tools you need to make your class a success. Information on all supplementary materials is available through your Course Technology representative or by calling one of the following telephone numbers: Colleges and Universities, 1-800-648-7450; High Schools, 1-800-824-5179; Private Career Colleges, 1-800-477-3692 ; Canada, 1-800-268-2222; Corporations with IT Training Centers, 1-800-477-3692; and Government Agencies, Health-Care Organizations, and Correctional Facilities, 1-800-477-3692.

Instructor Resources CD-ROM

The Instructor Resources CD-ROM includes both teaching and testing aids. The contents of each item on the Instructor Resources CD-ROM (ISBN 1-4188-5957-5) are described below.

Instructors Manual   The Instructor's Manual is made up of Microsoft Word files, which include detailed lesson plans with page number references, lecture notes, classroom activities, discussion topics, and projects to assign.

Syllabus   Sample syllabi, which can be customized easily to a course, are included. The syllabi cover policies, class and lab assignments and exams, and procedural information.

Figure Files   Illustrations for every figure in the textbook are available in electronic form. Use this ancillary to present a slide show in lecture or to print transparencies for use in lecture with an overhead projector. If you have a personal computer and LCD device, this ancillary can be an effective tool for presenting lectures.

Solutions to Exercises   Solutions are included for all end-of-chapter exercises.

Test Bank & Test Engine   The ExamView test bank includes 220 questions for every chapter (50 multiple-choice, 100 true/false, and 70 completion) with page number references, and when appropriate, figure references. Each question also is identified by objective and type of term (primary or secondary). The test bank comes with a copy of the test engine, ExamView, the ultimate tool for your objective-based testing needs.

Printed Test Bank   A Microsoft Word version of the test bank you can print also is included.

Test Out/Final Exam   Use this objective-based test to test students out of your course, or use it as a final examination. A master answer sheet is included.

Pretest/Posttest   Use these carefully prepared tests at the beginning and the end of the semester to measure student progress. A master answer sheet is included.

Data Files for Students   All the files that are required by students to complete the exercises are included. You can distribute the files on the Instructor Resources CD-ROM to your students over a network, or you can have them follow the instructions on the inside back cover of this book to obtain a copy of the Data Disk.

Course Presenter

Course Presenter (ISBN 1-4188-5958-3) is a one-click-per-slide presentation system on CD-ROM that provides PowerPoint slides for every subject in each chapter. Use this presentation system to give interesting, well-organized, and knowledge-based lectures. Several up-to-date G4TechTV computer-related video clips are available for optional presentation. Course Presenter provides consistent coverage for multiple lecturers.

Student Edition Labs

More than thirty Web-based interactive labs will help your students master hundreds of computer concepts including input and output devices, file management and desktop applications, computer privacy, virus protection, and much more. Featuring up-to-the-minute content, eye-popping graphics, and rich animation, the highly interactive Student Edition Labs offer students an alternative way to learn through dynamic observation, step-by-step practice, and challenging review questions. Access the free Student Edition Labs from the *Discovering Computers 2007* Online Companion at scsite.com/dc2007 or see the Student Edition Lab exercises on the Learn It Online pages at the end of each chapter.

Online Content

Course Technology offers textbook-based content for Blackboard, WebCT, and MyCourse 2.1.

BlackBoard and WebCT   As the leading provider of IT content for the Blackboard and WebCT platforms, Course Technology delivers rich content that enhances your textbook to give your students a unique learning experience.

MyCoure 2.1   MyCourse 2.1 is Course Technology's powerful online course management and content delivery system. MyCourse 2.1 allows nontechnical users to create, customize, and deliver Web-based courses; post content and assignments; manage student enrollment; administer exams; track results in the online grade book; and more.

SUPPLEMENTS

Two supplements can be used in combination with this textbook.

SAM Computer Concepts

Add the power of assessment and detailed reporting to your Student Edition Lab assignments with SAM Computer Concepts.

SAM (Skills Assessment Manager) Computer Concepts helps you energize your training assignments by allowing students to learn and quiz on important computer skills in an active, hands-on environment. By adding SAM Computer Concepts to your curriculum, you can:

- Reinforce your students' knowledge of key computer concepts with hands-on application exercises.
- Allow your students to "learn by listening," with rich audio in their computer concepts labs.
- Build computer concepts exams from a test bank of more than 50,000 objective-based questions or create your own test questions.
- Schedule your students' computer concepts training and testing assignments with powerful administrative tools.
- Track student exam grades and training progress using more than one dozen student and classroom reports.

Study Guide

This highly popular *Study Guide* (ISBN 1-4188-4371-7) includes a variety of activities that help students recall, review, and master introductory computer concepts. The *Study Guide* complements the end-of-chapter material with a guided chapter outline; a self-test consisting of true/false, multiple-choice, short answer, fill-in, and matching questions; an entertaining puzzle; and other challenging exercises.

SHELLY CASHMAN SERIES – TRADITIONALLY BOUND TEXTBOOKS

The Shelly Cashman Series presents the following computer subjects in a variety of traditionally bound textbooks. For more information, see your Course Technology representative or call 1-800-648-7450. For Shelly Cashman Series information, visit Shelly Cashman Online at scseries.com

COMPUTERS	
Computers	Discovering Computers 2007: A Gateway to Information, Complete
	Discovering Computers 2007: A Gateway to Information, Introductory
	Discovering Computers 2007: A Gateway to Information, Brief
	Discovering Computers: Fundamentals, Third Edition
	Teachers Discovering Computers: Integrating Technology in the Classroom, Fourth Edition
	Essential Introduction to Computers, Sixth Edition (40-page)

WINDOWS APPLICATIONS	
Microsoft Office	Microsoft Office 2003: Essential Concepts and Techniques, Second Edition (5 projects)
	Microsoft Office 2003: Brief Concepts and Techniques, Second Edition (9 projects)
	Microsoft Office 2003: Introductory Concepts and Techniques, Second Edition (15 projects)
	Microsoft Office 2003: Introductory Concepts and Techniques, Premium Edition (15 projects)
	Microsoft Office 2003: Advanced Concepts and Techniques (12 projects)
	Microsoft Office 2003: Post Advanced Concepts and Techniques (11 projects)
	Microsoft Office XP: Essential Concepts and Techniques (5 projects)
	Microsoft Office XP: Brief Concepts and Techniques (9 projects)
	Microsoft Office XP: Introductory Concepts and Techniques, Windows XP Edition (15 projects)
	Microsoft Office XP: Introductory Concepts and Techniques, Enhanced Edition (15 projects)
	Microsoft Office XP: Advanced Concepts and Techniques (11 projects)
	Microsoft Office XP: Post Advanced Concepts and Techniques (11 projects)
Integration	Teachers Discovering and Integrating Microsoft Office: Essential Concepts and Techniques, Second Edition
	Integrating Microsoft Office XP Applications and the World Wide Web: Essential Concepts and Techniques
PIM	Microsoft Outlook 2002: Essential Concepts and Techniques • Microsoft Office Outlook 2003: Introductory Concepts and Techniques
Microsoft Works	Microsoft Works 6: Complete Concepts and Techniques[1] • Microsoft Works 2000: Complete Concepts and Techniques[1]
Microsoft Windows	Microsoft Windows XP: Comprehensive Concepts and Techniques[2] Service Pak 2 Edition
	Microsoft Windows XP: Brief Concepts and Techniques
	Microsoft Windows 2000: Comprehensive Concepts and Techniques[2]
	Microsoft Windows 2000: Brief Concepts and Techniques
	Microsoft Windows 98: Comprehensive Concepts and Techniques[2]
	Microsoft Windows 98: Essential Concepts and Techniques
	Introduction to Microsoft Windows NT Workstation 4
Notebook Organizer	Microsoft Office OneNote 2003: Introductory Concepts and Techniques
Word Processing	Microsoft Office Word 2003: Comprehensive Concepts and Techniques, CourseCard Edition[2] • Microsoft Word 2002: Comprehensive Concepts and Techniques[2]
Spreadsheets	Microsoft Office Excel 2003: Comprehensive Concepts and Techniques, CourseCard Edition[2] • Microsoft Excel 2002: Comprehensive Concepts and Techniques[2]
Database	Microsoft Office Access 2003: Comprehensive Concepts and Techniques, CourseCard Edition[2] • Microsoft Access 2002: Comprehensive Concepts and Techniques[2]
Presentation Graphics	Microsoft Office PowerPoint 2003: Comprehensive Concepts and Techniques, CourseCard Edition[2] • Microsoft PowerPoint 2002: Comprehensive Concepts and Techniques[2] • Microsoft Producer 2003: Essential Concepts and Techniques
Desktop Publishing	Microsoft Office Publisher 2003: Comprehensive Concepts and Techniques[2] • Microsoft Publisher 2002: Comprehensive Concepts and Techniques[1]

PROGRAMMING	
Programming	Microsoft Visual Basic .NET: Comprehensive Concepts and Techniques[2] • Microsoft Visual Basic 6: Complete Concepts and Techniques[1] • Java Programming: Comprehensive Concepts and Techniques, Third Edition[2] • Structured COBOL Programming, Second Edition • Understanding and Troubleshooting Your PC • Programming Fundamentals Using Microsoft Visual Basic .NET

INTERNET	
Concepts	Discovering the Internet: Brief Concepts and Techniques, Second Edition • Discovering the Internet: Complete Concepts and Techniques, Second Edition
Browser	Microsoft Internet Explorer 6: Introductory Concepts and Techniques, Windows XP Edition • Microsoft Internet Explorer 5: An Introduction • Netscape Navigator 6: An Introduction • Introduction to the World Wide Web • Mozilla Firefox: Introductory Concepts and Techniques
Web Page Creation	Web Design: Introductory Concepts and Techniques, Second Edition • HTML: Comprehensive Concepts and Techniques, Third Edition[2] • Microsoft Office FrontPage 2003: Comprehensive Concepts and Techniques, CourseCard Edition[2] • Microsoft FrontPage 2002: Comprehensive Concepts and Techniques[2] • Microsoft FrontPage 2002: Essential Concepts and Techniques • JavaScript: Complete Concepts and Techniques, Second Edition[1] • Macromedia Dreamweaver MX 2004: Comprehensive Concepts and Techniques[2]

SYSTEMS ANALYSIS	
Systems Analysis	Systems Analysis and Design, Sixth Edition

DATA COMMUNICATIONS	
Data Communications	Business Data Communications: Introductory Concepts and Techniques, Fourth Edition

[1]Also available as an Introductory Edition, which is a shortened version of the complete book, [2]Also available as an Introductory Edition and as a Complete Edition, which are shortened versions of the comprehensive book.

Discovering Computers

2007

A GATEWAY TO INFORMATION

Introduction to Computers

Picture Yourself in a Computer Class

While waiting for the instructor to begin her first lecture, you hear several classmates announce they will be meeting at the local coffeehouse to talk about homework and form study groups. Many of them sound nervous and anxious about this Introduction to Computers class. As they talk, you think about your experiences with computers. You had a beginning programming class in high school. You use the Internet regularly to chat with friends. With your digital camera, you take pictures and e-mail them to family members. No study groups for you.

During the lecture, the instructor reads several computer advertisements to the class. The ads use computer terms and acronyms you have never heard, like bus, SDRAM, USB flash drive, TFT, media player, SCSI, HT Technology, Bluetooth, Ethernet, firewall, NIC, and Wi-Fi. Now, *you* get a bit nervous and anxious. When she finishes reading, the instructor tells the class not to worry if some or most of the words in the ads are unfamiliar. "As we work through this course together," she says, "you will learn everything you need to know to buy a computer." While walking out the classroom door, you ask your friend, "What time is everyone meeting at the coffeehouse? I want to get in one of those study groups."

Read Chapter 1 to become familiar with some of the terms mentioned in the advertisement, discover practical uses of computers, and set a foundation for your further learning throughout this book.

After completing this chapter, you will be able to:

1. Recognize the importance of computer literacy
2. Define the term, computer
3. Identify the components of a computer
4. Discuss the advantages and disadvantages of using computers
5. Recognize the purpose of a network
6. Discuss the uses of the Internet and World Wide Web
7. Distinguish between system software and application software
8. Describe the categories of computers
9. Identify the elements of an information system
10. Describe the various types of computer users
11. Discuss various computer applications in society

CONTENTS

A WORLD OF COMPUTERS

Computers are everywhere: at work, at school, and at home. Many daily activities either involve the use of or depend on information from a computer. As shown in Figure 1-1, people use all types and sizes of computers for a variety of reasons and in a range of places. Some computers sit on top of a desk or on the floor; others are small enough to carry.

Computers are a primary means of communication for billions of people. People use computers to correspond with businesses, employees with other employees and customers, students with teachers, and family members with friends and other family members. In addition to corresponding via text messages, people use computers to send each other pictures, diagrams, drawings, music, and videos.

Through computers, society has instant access to information from around the globe. Local and national news, weather reports, sports scores, airline schedules, telephone directories, maps and directions, job listings, credit reports, and countless forms of educational material always are accessible. From the computer, you can meet new friends, share photographs and videos, shop, fill prescriptions, file taxes, or take a course.

At home or while on the road, people use computers to manage schedules, balance checkbooks, pay bills, track personal income and expenses, transfer funds, and buy or sell stocks. Banks place automated teller machines (ATMs) all over the world, making it easy for customers to deposit or withdraw funds at anytime. At the grocery store, a computer tracks purchases, calculates the amount of money due, and often

FIGURE 1-1   People use computers in their daily activities.

generates coupons customized to buying patterns. Vehicles include onboard navigation systems that provide directions, call for emergency services, and track the vehicle if it is stolen.

In the workplace, employees use computers to create correspondence such as e-mail messages, memos, and letters; calculate payroll; track inventory; and generate invoices. Some applications such as automotive design and weather forecasting use computers to perform complex mathematical calculations. At school, teachers use computers to assist with classroom instruction. Students complete assignments and do research on computers in lab rooms and at home.

People also spend hours of leisure time using a computer. They play games, listen to music, watch videos and movies, read books and magazines, research genealogy, compose music and videos, retouch photographs, and plan vacations.

As technology continues to advance, computers are becoming more a part of everyday life. Thus, many people believe that computer literacy is vital to success in today's world. **Computer literacy** involves having a knowledge and understanding of computers and their uses.

This book presents the knowledge you need to be computer literate. As you read this first chapter, keep in mind it is an overview. Many of the terms and concepts introduced in this chapter will be discussed in more depth later in the book.

WHAT IS A COMPUTER?

A **computer** is an electronic device, operating under the control of instructions stored in its own memory, that can accept data, process the data according to specified rules, produce results, and store the results for future use.

Data and Information

Computers process data into information. **Data** is a collection of unprocessed items, which can include text, numbers, images, audio, and video. **Information** conveys meaning and is useful to people.

As shown in Figure 1-2, for example, computers process several data items to print information in the form of a payroll check.

> **FAQ 1-1**
>
> **Is data a singular or plural word?**
>
> The word data is plural for datum. With respect to computers, however, it is accepted and common practice to use the word data in both the singular and plural context. For more information, visit scsite.com/dc2007/ch1/faq and then click Data.
>
> An **FAQ** (frequently asked question) helps you find answers to commonly asked questions. Web sites often post an FAQ section, and each chapter in this book includes FAQ boxes related to topics in the text.

Information Processing Cycle

Computers process data (input) into information (output). A computer often holds data, information, and instructions in storage for future use. *Instructions* are the steps that tell the computer how to perform a particular task. Some people refer to the series of input, process, output, and storage activities as the *information processing cycle*.

Most computers today can communicate with other computers. As a result, communications also has become an essential element of the information processing cycle.

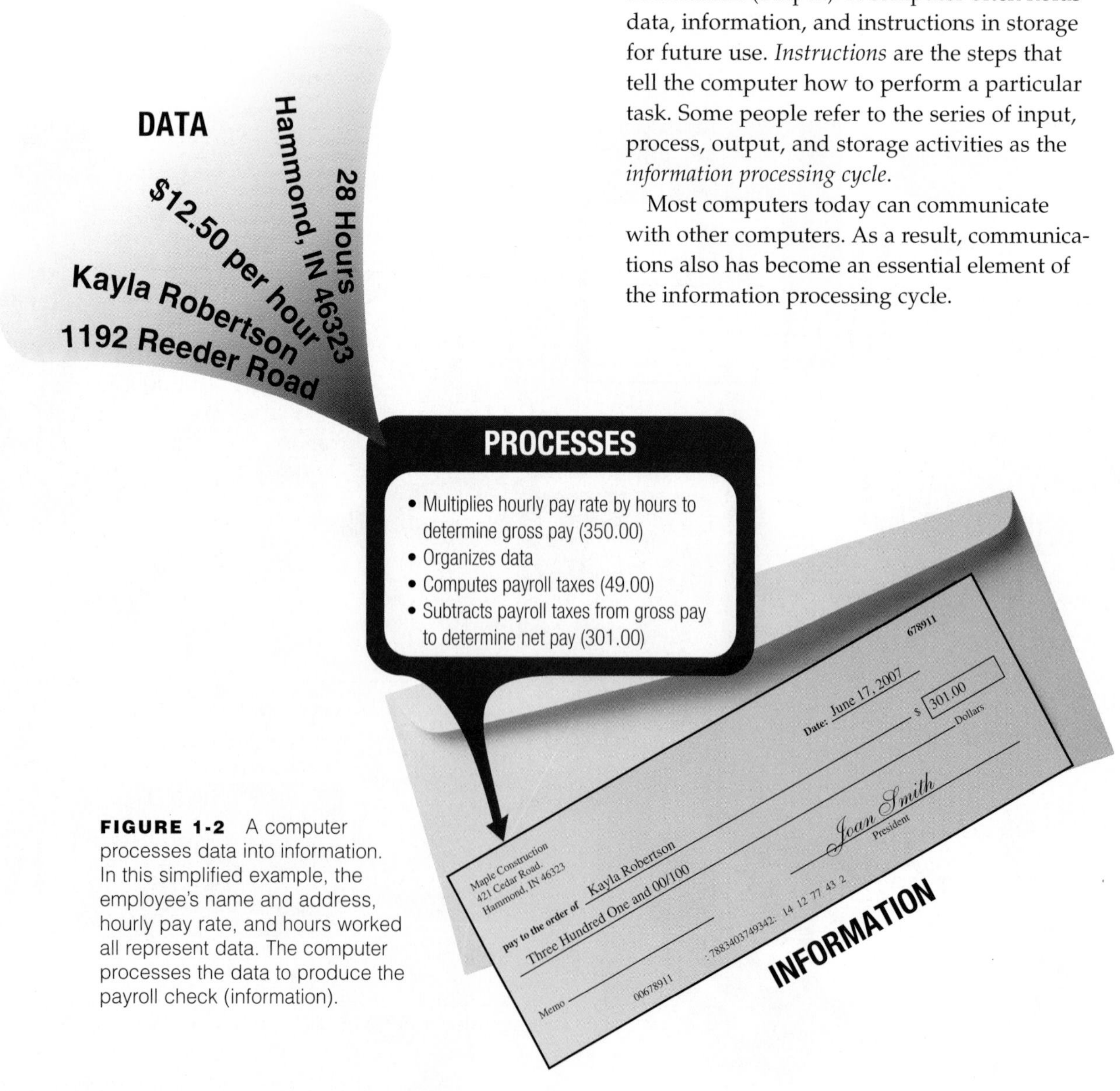
DATA
Hammond, IN 46323
28 Hours
$12.50 per hour
Kayla Robertson
1192 Reeder Road
PROCESSES
• Multiplies hourly pay rate by hours to determine gross pay (350.00)
• Organizes data
• Computes payroll taxes (49.00)
• Subtracts payroll taxes from gross pay to determine net pay (301.00)
678911
Date: June 17, 2007
$ 301.00
Dollars
Maple Construction
421 Cedar Road.
Hammond, IN 46323
pay to the order of Kayla Robertson
Three Hundred One and 00/100
Joan Smith
President
Memo
00678911
INFORMATION

FIGURE 1-2 A computer processes data into information. In this simplified example, the employee's name and address, hourly pay rate, and hours worked all represent data. The computer processes the data to produce the payroll check (information).

THE COMPONENTS OF A COMPUTER

A computer contains many electric, electronic, and mechanical components known as **hardware**. These components include input devices, output devices, a system unit, storage devices, and communications devices. Figure 1-3 shows some common computer hardware components.

Input Devices

An **input device** is any hardware component that allows you to enter data and instructions into a computer. Six widely used input devices are the keyboard, mouse, microphone, scanner, digital camera, and PC video camera (Figure 1-3).

A computer keyboard contains keys you press to enter data into the computer. A mouse is a small handheld device. With the mouse, you control movement of a small symbol on the screen, called the pointer, and you make selections from the screen.

A microphone allows a user to speak into the computer to enter data and instructions. A scanner converts printed material (such as text and pictures) into a form the computer can use.

With a digital camera, you take pictures and then transfer the photographed images to the computer or printer instead of storing the images on traditional film. A PC video camera is a digital video camera that allows users to create a movie or take still photographs electronically.

WEB LINK 1-1

Input Devices
For more information, visit scsite.com/dc2007/ch1/weblink and then click Input Devices.

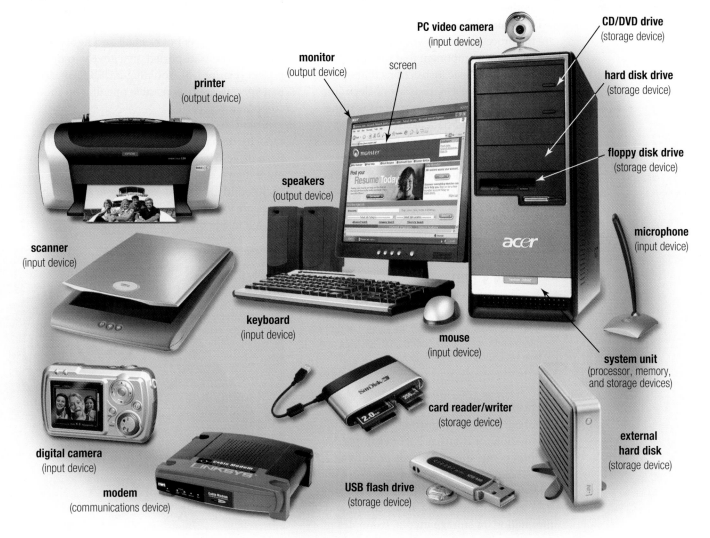

FIGURE 1-3 Common computer hardware components include a keyboard, mouse, microphone, scanner, digital camera, PC video camera, printer, monitor, speakers, system unit, internal disk drives, external hard disk, USB flash drive, card reader/writer, and modem.

Output Devices

An **output device** is any hardware component that conveys information to one or more people. Three commonly used output devices are a printer, a monitor, and speakers (Figure 1-3 on the previous page).

A printer produces text and graphics on a physical medium such as paper. A monitor displays text, graphics, and videos on a screen. Speakers allow you to hear music, voice, and other audio (sounds).

System Unit

The **system unit** is a case that contains the electronic components of the computer that are used to process data (Figure 1-3). The circuitry of the system unit usually is part of or is connected to a circuit board called the motherboard.

Two main components on the motherboard are the processor and memory. The *processor* is the electronic component that interprets and carries out the basic instructions that operate the computer. *Memory* consists of electronic components that store instructions waiting to be executed and data needed by those instructions. Although some forms of memory are permanent, most memory keeps data and instructions temporarily, which means its contents are erased when the computer is shut off.

WEB LINK 1-2

Output Devices

For more information, visit scsite.com/ dc2007/ch1/weblink and then click Output Devices.

FAQ 1-2

What is a CPU?

The processor. Most people in the computer industry use the terms *CPU* (*central processing unit*) and processor to mean the same. For more information, visit scsite.com/dc2007/ch1/faq and then click CPU.

Storage Devices

Storage holds data, instructions, and information for future use. For example, computers can store hundreds or millions of customer names and addresses. Storage holds these items permanently.

A computer keeps data, instructions, and information on **storage media**. Examples of storage media are floppy disks, Zip disks, USB flash drives, hard disks, CDs, DVDs, and memory cards. A **storage device** records (writes) and/or retrieves (reads) items to and from storage media. Drives and readers/writers, which are types of storage devices (Figure 1-3), accept a specific kind of storage media. For example, a CD drive (storage device) accepts a CD (storage media). Storage devices often function as a source of input because they transfer items from storage to memory.

A floppy disk consists of a thin, circular, flexible disk enclosed in a square-shaped plastic shell that is inserted in and removed from a floppy disk drive. A typical floppy disk stores up to about 1.4 million characters. A Zip disk looks similar to a floppy disk but has much greater storage capabilities — up to about 750 million characters. You insert Zip disks in and remove them from Zip drives.

A USB flash drive is a portable storage device that has much more storage capacity than a floppy disk but is small and lightweight enough to be transported on a keychain or in a pocket (Figure 1-3). You plug a USB flash drive in a special, easily accessible opening on the computer.

A hard disk provides much greater storage capacity than a floppy disk, Zip disk, or USB flash drive. The average hard disk can hold more than 100 billion characters. Hard disks are enclosed in an airtight, sealed case. Although some are external or removable, most are housed inside the system unit (Figure 1-4).

FIGURE 1-4 Hard disks are self-contained devices. The hard disk shown here must be installed in the system unit before it can be used.

A compact disc is a flat, round, portable metal disc with a plastic coating. One type of compact disc is a CD-ROM, which you can access using most CD and DVD drives (Figure 1-5). Another type of compact disc is a DVD-ROM, some of which have enough storage capacity to store two full-length movies. To use a DVD-ROM, you need a DVD drive.

Some portable devices, such as digital cameras, use memory cards as the storage media. You then can transfer the stored items, such as electronic photographs, from the memory card to a computer or printer using a card reader/writer (Figure 1-3 on page 7).

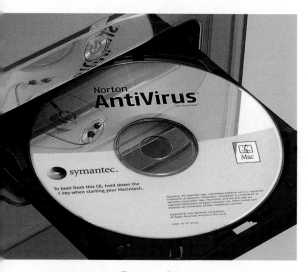

FIGURE 1-5 To use a CD or DVD, you need a CD or DVD drive.

Communications Devices

A **communications device** is a hardware component that enables a computer to send (transmit) and receive data, instructions, and information to and from one or more computers. A widely used communications device is a modem (Figure 1-3).

Communications occur over cables, telephone lines, cellular radio networks, satellites, and other transmission media. Some transmission media, such as satellites and cellular radio networks, are wireless, which means they have no physical lines or wires.

ADVANTAGES AND DISADVANTAGES OF USING COMPUTERS

Society has reaped many benefits from using computers. Both business and home users can make well-informed decisions because they have instant access to information from anywhere in the world. A **user** is anyone who communicates with a computer or utilizes the information it generates. Students, another type of user, have more tools to assist them in the learning process. Read Looking Ahead 1-1 for a look at the next generation of benefits from using computers.

LOOKING AHEAD 1-1

Medical Breakthroughs with Computer Implants, Devices

The battle to curb obesity eventually may be won with an implantable stomach device. This technology, called a gastric stimulator, would zap the stomach or 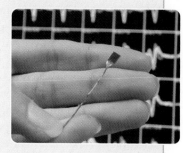 nerves with electric current, in much the same way a cardiac pacemaker stimulates the heart, to boost metabolism or regulate appetite signals.

Another possible surgery will involve implanting miniature computers or computer components in the body to help it perform basic functions. A processor, for example, could help release hormones. A brain computer interface may monitor and treat diseases, such as epilepsy and depression, that affect brain activity. A body-scanning machine will evaluate patients' pain when they cannot communicate.

In addition, robotic legs strapped to the body can assist people such as firefighters and soldiers who must bear heavy loads for extended periods of time. For more information, visit scsite.com/dc2007/ch1/looking and then click Processor Implants.

WEB LINK 1-3

Communications Devices

For more information, visit scsite.com/dc2007/ch1/weblink and then click Communications Devices.

ADVANTAGES OF USING COMPUTERS   Benefits of computers are possible because computers have the advantages of speed, reliability, consistency, storage, and communications.

- **Speed**: Computer operations occur through electronic circuits. When data, instructions, and information flow along these circuits, they travel at incredibly fast speeds. Many computers process billions or trillions of operations in a single second. Processing involves computing (adding, subtracting, multiplying, dividing), sorting (e.g., alphabetizing), organizing, formatting, checking spelling and grammar, charting, displaying pictures, recording audio clips, playing music, and showing a movie. For a more technical discussion about how computers process data, read the High-Tech Talk article on page 38.
- **Reliability**: The electronic components in modern computers are dependable and reliable because they rarely break or fail.
- **Consistency**: Given the same input and processes, a computer will produce the same results — consistently. Computers generate error-free results, provided the input is correct and the instructions work. A computing phrase — known as *garbage in, garbage out* — points out that the accuracy of a computer's output depends on the accuracy of the input. For example, if you do not use the flash on a digital camera when indoors, the resulting pictures that are displayed on the computer screen may be unusable because they are too dark.
- **Storage**: A computer can transfer data quickly from storage to memory, process it, and then store it again for future use. Many computers store enormous amounts of data and make this data available for processing anytime it is needed.
- **Communications**: Most computers today can communicate with other computers, often wirelessly. Computers with this capability can share any of the four information processing cycle operations — input, process, output, and storage — with another computer or a user.

DISADVANTAGES OF USING COMPUTERS   Some disadvantages of computers relate to the violation of privacy, the impact on the labor force, health risks, and the impact on the environment.

- **Violation of Privacy**: Nearly every life event is stored in a computer somewhere…in medical records, credit reports, tax records, etc. It is crucial that personal and confidential records be protected properly. In many instances, where these records were not properly protected, individuals have found their privacy violated and identities stolen. Read Ethics & Issues 1-1 for a related discussion.
- **Impact on Labor Force**: Although computers have improved productivity in many ways and created an entire industry with hundreds of thousands of new jobs, the skills of millions of employees have been replaced by computers. Thus, it is crucial that workers keep their education up-to-date. A separate impact on the labor force is that some companies are outsourcing jobs to foreign countries instead of keeping their homeland labor force employed.

ETHICS & ISSUES 1-1

Who Is Responsible for Identity Theft?

Using e-mail and other techniques on the Internet, scam artists are employing a technique known as phishing to try to steal your personal information, such as credit card numbers, banking information, and passwords. For example, an e-mail message may appear to be a request from your credit card company to verify your Social Security number and online banking password. Instead, the information you submit ends up in the hands of the scammer, who then uses the information to access your accounts, apply for credit in your name, or sell and trade the information with other criminals. Sadly, the result often is identity theft. Consumer advocates often blame credit card companies and credit bureaus for lax security standards. Meanwhile, the companies blame consumers for being too gullible and forthcoming with private information. Both sides blame the government for poor privacy laws and light punishments for identity thieves. But while the arguments go on, law enforcement agencies bear the brunt of the problem by spending hundreds of millions of dollars responding to complaints and finding and processing the criminals. Under current laws, who is responsible for Internet identity theft? Why? Should laws be changed to stop it or should consumers change behavior? What is an appropriate punishment for identity thieves? Given the international nature of the Internet, how can foreign identity thieves be handled?

- **Health Risks**: Prolonged or improper computer use can lead to injuries or disorders of the hands, wrists, elbows, eyes, neck, and back. Computer users can protect themselves from these health risks through proper workplace design, good posture while at the computer, and appropriately spaced work breaks.
- **Impact on Environment**: Computer manufacturing processes and computer waste are depleting natural resources and polluting the environment. The amount of resources required to manufacture a personal computer equals that of a mid-sized car. When computers are discarded in landfills, they release toxic materials and potentially dangerous levels of lead, mercury, and flame retardants. Strategies that can help protect the environment include recycling, regulating manufacturing processes, extending the life of computers, and immediately donating replaced computers.

Test your knowledge of pages 4 through 11 in Quiz Yourself 1-1.

QUIZ YOURSELF 1-1

Instructions: Find the true statement below. Then, rewrite the remaining false statements so they are true.

1. A computer is a motorized device that processes output into input.

2. A storage device records (reads) and/or retrieves (writes) items to and from storage media.

3. An output device is any hardware component that allows you to enter data and instructions into a computer.

4. Computer literacy involves having a knowledge and understanding of computers and their uses.

5. Computers have the disadvantages of fast speeds, high failure rates, producing consistent results, storing small amounts of data, and communicating with others.

6. Three commonly used input devices are a printer, a monitor, and speakers.

Quiz Yourself Online: To further check your knowledge of computer literacy, computers and their components, and the advantages and disadvantages of computers, visit scsite.com/dc2007/ch1/quiz and then click Objectives 1 – 4.

NETWORKS AND THE INTERNET

A **network** is a collection of computers and devices connected together via communications devices and transmission media. When a computer connects to a network, it is **online**.

Networks allow computers to share *resources*, such as hardware, software, data, and information. Sharing resources saves time and money. In many networks, one or more computers act as a server. The server controls access to the resources on a network. The other computers on the network, each called a client or workstation, request resources from the server (Figure 1-6). The major differences between the server and client computers are that the server ordinarily has more power, more storage space, and expanded communications capabilities.

Many homes and most businesses and schools network their computers and devices. Home networks usually are small, existing within a single structure, and often are wireless. Business and school networks can be small, such as in a room or building, or widespread, connecting computers across a city, country, or the globe. The world's largest computer network is the Internet.

FIGURE 1-6 A server manages the resources on a network, and clients access the resources on the server. This network enables three separate computers to share the same printer, one wirelessly.

The Internet

The **Internet** is a worldwide collection of networks that connects millions of businesses, government agencies, educational institutions, and individuals (Figure 1-7).

More than one billion people around the world use the Internet daily for a variety of reasons, including the following:

- Communicate with and meet other people
- Access a wealth of information, news, and research findings
- Shop for goods and services
- Bank and invest
- Take a class
- Access sources of entertainment and leisure, such as online games, music, videos, books, and magazines
- Download music
- Share information

Figure 1-8 shows examples in each of these areas.

People connect to the Internet to exchange information with others around the world. E-mail allows you to send messages to other users. With instant messaging, you can have a live conversation with another connected user.

In a chat room, you can communicate with multiple users at the same time — much like a group discussion.

Businesses, called access providers, offer users and companies access to the Internet free or for a fee. By subscribing to an access provider, you can use your computer and a communications device, such as a modem, to connect to the many services of the Internet.

The Web, short for World Wide Web, is one of the more popular services on the Internet. Think of the Web as a global library of information available to anyone connected to the Internet. The **Web** contains billions of documents called Web pages. A **Web page** can contain text, graphics, audio, and video. The eight screens shown in Figure 1-8 are examples of Web pages. Web pages often have built-in connections, or links, to other documents, graphics, other Web pages, or Web sites. A Web site is a collection of related Web pages. Some Web sites allow users to access music that can be downloaded, or transferred to storage media in a computer or digital audio player, and then listen to the music through speakers, headphones, or earphones.

WEB LINK 1-4

The Internet

For more information, visit scsite.com/dc2007/ch1/weblink and then click Internet.

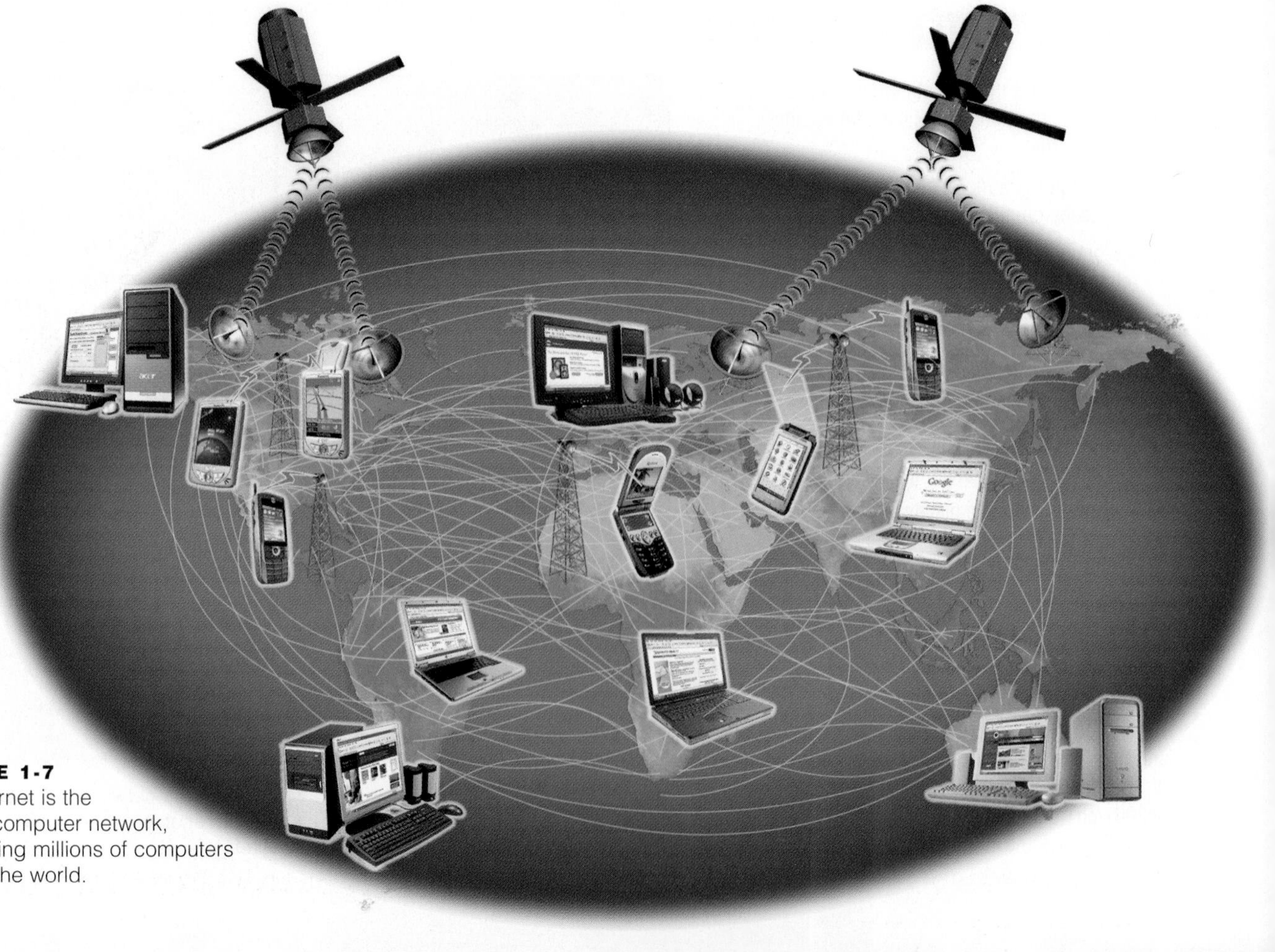

FIGURE 1-7
The Internet is the largest computer network, connecting millions of computers around the world.

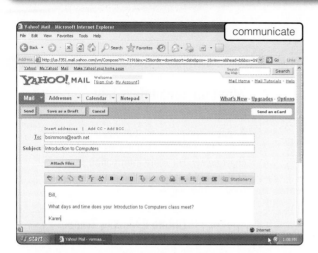

communicate

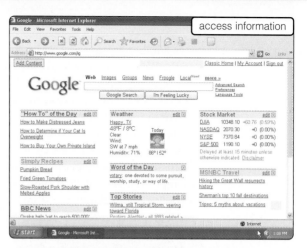

access information

shop

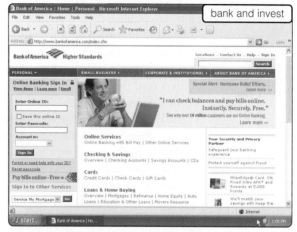

bank and invest

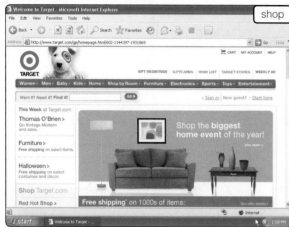

take a class

entertainment

download music

share information

FIGURE 1-8 Users access the Internet for a variety of reasons.

In addition to accessing and using information on the Web, many people use the Web as a means to share personal information, photographs, videos, or artwork with the world. Anyone can create a Web page and then make it available, or *publish* it, on the Internet for others to see (read Ethics & Issues 1-2 for a related discussion). A **photo sharing community,** for example, is a Web site that allows users to create an online photo album and store their electronic photographs (Figure 1-9). Some Web sites provide publishing services free.

Hundreds of thousands of people today use blogs to publish their thoughts on the Web. A *blog* is an informal Web site consisting of time-stamped articles in a diary or journal format, usually listed in reverse chronological order. As others read the articles in a blog, they reply with their own thoughts.

Podcasts are a popular way people verbally share information on the Web. A *podcast* is recorded audio stored on a Web site that can be downloaded to a computer or a portable digital audio player such as an iPod. At a convenient time and location, the user listens to the downloaded podcast.

FIGURE 1-9   This user posts pictures to a photo sharing community, which allows others to view, print, or download the pictures.

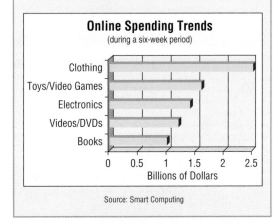

FAQ 1-3

What do consumers buy on the Internet?

A recent survey found that online consumers spend the most on clothing, as shown in the chart below. For more information, visit scsite.com/dc2007/ch1/faq and then click Internet Purchases.

Online Spending Trends
(during a six-week period)

Source: Smart Computing

ETHICS & ISSUES 1-2

Who Is Responsible for the Accuracy of Web Pages?

Since the dawn of the Web, some groups have used Web sites to try to convince people that the Holocaust in World War II did not occur. Using fake research papers and authoritative looking Web pages, these groups hope to revise history to their liking. In response, other groups have created Web sites to counter those claims and provide evidence of the truth. Many people think that anything in print is true, even what they read on the Web. Yet, authors with a wide range of expertise, authority, motives, and biases create Web pages. Web pages can be as accurate as the most scholarly journal, or no truer than the most disreputable supermarket tabloid. The Web makes it easy to obtain information, but Web page readers must make an extra effort to determine the quality of that information. In evaluating a Web page, experts suggest that you consider such factors as the purpose, scope, sponsor, timeliness, presentation, author, and permanence of the page. Ultimately, who is responsible for the accuracy of information on the Web? Why? What factors are most important in evaluating the accuracy of a Web page? Why? Should people be held accountable for what they publish on the Web? If so, by whom?

COMPUTER SOFTWARE

Software, also called a **program**, consists of a series of instructions that tells the computer what to do and how to do it.

You interact with a program through its user interface. The user interface controls how you enter data and instructions and how information is displayed on the screen. Software today often has a graphical user interface. With a **graphical user interface** (**GUI** pronounced gooey), you interact with the software using text, graphics, and visual images such as icons (Figure 1-10). An *icon* is a miniature image that represents a program, an instruction, or some other object. You can use the mouse to select icons that perform operations such as starting a program.

The two categories of software are system software and application software. The following sections describe these categories of software.

System Software

System software consists of the programs that control or maintain the operations of the computer and its devices. System software serves as the interface between the user, the application software, and the computer's hardware. Two types of system software are the operating system and utility programs.

OPERATING SYSTEM An *operating system* is a set of programs that coordinates all the activities among computer hardware devices. It provides a means for users to communicate with the computer and other software. Many of today's computers use Windows XP, which is one of Microsoft's operating systems (Figure 1-10).

When a user starts a computer, portions of the operating system load into memory from the computer's hard disk. It remains in memory while the computer is on.

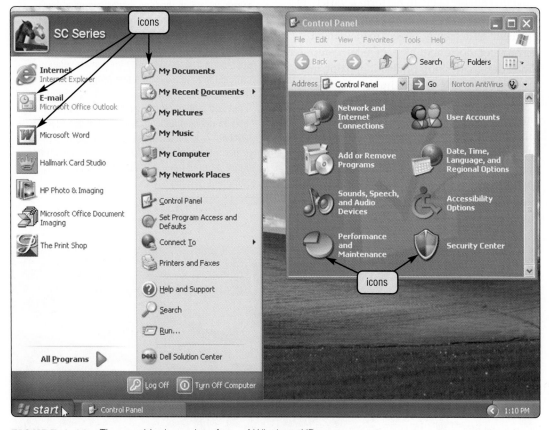

FIGURE 1-10 The graphical user interface of Windows XP.

UTILITY PROGRAM A *utility program* allows a user to perform maintenance-type tasks usually related to managing a computer, its devices, or its programs. Most operating systems include several utility programs for managing disk drives, printers, and other devices. You also can buy utility programs that allow you to perform additional computer management functions.

Application Software

Application software consists of programs designed to make users more productive and/or assist them with personal tasks. A widely used type of application software related to communications is a Web browser, which allows users with an Internet connection to access and view Web pages. Other popular application software includes word processing software, spreadsheet software, database software, and presentation graphics software.

Many other types of application software exist that enable users to perform a variety of tasks. These include personal information management, note taking, project management, accounting, document management, computer-aided design, desktop publishing, paint/image editing, audio and video editing, multimedia authoring, Web page authoring, personal finance, legal, tax preparation, home design/landscaping, education, reference, and entertainment (e.g., games or simulations, etc.). As shown in Figure 1-11, you can purchase application software from a store that sells computer products. Read Ethics & Issues 1-3 for a related discussion.

WEB LINK 1-6

Application Software

For more information, visit scsite.com/dc2007/ch1/weblink and then click Application Software.

ETHICS & ISSUES 1-3

Is Computer Gaming More Good than Bad?

Grand Theft Auto: San Andreas is one of today's most popular computer games. In the game, players advance through the mafia by conveying secret packages, following alleged snitches, and planting car bombs. Since its release, shoppers have bought millions of copies of Grand Theft Auto. Purchasers praise the game's vivid graphics, edgy characters, and wide range of allowable behaviors. Recently, the game was found to contain hidden adult content accessible by using a special code. Some parents and politicians condemn the game's explicit violence and the rewards it gives players for participating in illegal acts. They fear that games like Grand Theft Auto eventually could lead to antisocial or criminal behavior. Even worse, critics fear that the game's popularity may influence future developers of computer games aimed at younger children. Despite the fears, research has shown that playing violent games has no impact on behavior or increased crime. In fact, in the time in which gaming has become popular, violent crime has decreased by 50 percent in America. Some researchers and parents note the positive aspects of gaming, such as increased dexterity for players, use of critical thinking skills to solve problems in games, meeting goals, and following rules. What impact, if any, do violent computer games or games that include unacceptable acts have on individual behavior? On balance, is computer gaming good or bad for people? Why? What other motivations might parents have who limit their children's computer gaming?

FIGURE 1-11 Stores that sell computer products have shelves stocked with software for sale.

Installing and Running Programs

The instructions in a program are stored on storage media such as a hard disk or compact disc. When purchasing software from a computer store, you typically receive a box that includes a CD(s) or DVD(s) that contains the program. You also may receive a manual or printed instructions explaining how to install and use the software.

Installing is the process of setting up software to work with the computer, printer, and other hardware components. When you buy a computer, it usually has some software pre-installed on its hard disk. This enables you to use the computer the first time you turn it on. To begin installing additional software from a CD or DVD, insert the program disc in a CD or DVD drive. The computer then copies all or part of the program from the disc to the computer's hard disk.

Once software is installed, you can use, or **run**, it. When you instruct the computer to run an installed program, the computer *loads* it, which means the program is copied from storage to memory. Once in memory, the computer can carry out, or *execute*, the instructions in the program. Figure 1-12 illustrates the steps that occur when a user installs and runs a greeting card program.

FAQ 1-4

Which spelling is correct, disk or disc?

Both are correct, depending on usage. When referring to CD, DVD, and other *optical* (laser) storage, computer professionals typically use the term, disc. The term, disk, normally refers to floppy disks, Zip disks, hard disks, and other nonoptical storage media. For more information, visit scsite.com/dc2007/ch1/faq and then click Disk or Disc.

FIGURE 1-12 INSTALLING AND RUNNING A COMPUTER PROGRAM

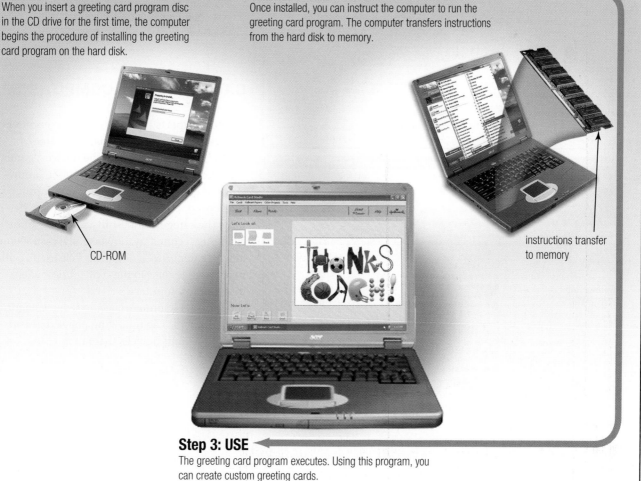

Step 1: INSTALL
When you insert a greeting card program disc in the CD drive for the first time, the computer begins the procedure of installing the greeting card program on the hard disk.

Step 2: RUN
Once installed, you can instruct the computer to run the greeting card program. The computer transfers instructions from the hard disk to memory.

CD-ROM

instructions transfer to memory

Step 3: USE
The greeting card program executes. Using this program, you can create custom greeting cards.

Software Development

A *programmer*, sometimes called a *developer*, is someone who develops software or writes the instructions that direct the computer to process data into information. When writing instructions, a programmer must be sure the program works properly so the computer generates the desired results. Complex programs can require thousands to millions of instructions.

Programmers use a programming language or program development tool to create computer programs. Popular programming languages include C++, Java, JavaScript, Visual C# 2005, and Visual Basic 2005. Figure 1-13 shows some of the instructions a programmer may write to create a Web application.

Test your knowledge of pages 11 through 18 in Quiz Yourself 1-2.

QUIZ YOURSELF 1-2

Instructions: Find the true statement below. Then, rewrite the remaining false statements so they are true.

1. A resource is a collection of computers and devices connected together via communications devices and transmission media.

2. Installing is the process of setting up software to work with the computer, printer, and other hardware components.

3. Popular system software includes Web browsers, word processing software, spreadsheet software, database software, and presentation graphics software.

4. The Internet is one of the more popular services on the Web.

5. Two types of application software are the operating system and utility programs.

Quiz Yourself Online: To further check your knowledge of networks, the Internet and Web, and system software versus application software, visit scsite.com/dc2007/ch1/quiz and then click Objectives 5 – 7.

CATEGORIES OF COMPUTERS

Industry experts typically classify computers in seven categories: personal computers, mobile computers and mobile devices, game consoles, servers, mainframes, supercomputers, and embedded computers. A computer's size, speed, processing power, and price determine the category it best fits. Due to rapidly changing technology, however, the distinction among categories is not always clear-cut. Still, many people refer to these categories when discussing computers.

Figure 1-14 summarizes the seven categories of computers. The following pages discuss computers and devices that fall in each category.

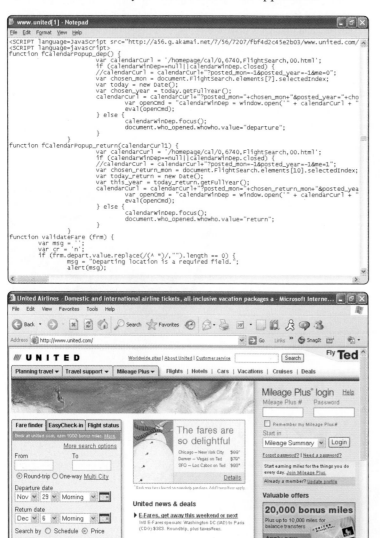

FIGURE 1-13 The top figure illustrates some of the instructions a programmer writes in JavaScript to create the Web application shown in the bottom figure.

CATEGORIES OF COMPUTERS

Category	Physical Size	Number of Simultaneously Connected Users	General Price Range
Personal computers (desktop)	Fits on a desk	Usually one (can be more if networked)	Several hundred to several thousand dollars
Mobile computers and mobile devices	Fits on your lap or in your hand	Usually one	Less than a hundred dollars to several thousand dollars
Game consoles	Small box or handheld device	One to several	Several hundred dollars or less
Servers	Small cabinet	Two to thousands	Several hundred to a million dollars
Mainframes	Partial room to a full room of equipment	Hundreds to thousands	$300,000 to several million dollars
Supercomputers	Full room of equipment	Hundreds to thousands	$500,000 to several billion dollars
Embedded computers	Miniature	Usually one	Embedded in the price of the product

FIGURE 1-14 This table summarizes some of the differences among the categories of computers. These should be considered general guidelines only because of rapid changes in technology.

PERSONAL COMPUTERS

A **personal computer** is a computer that can perform all of its input, processing, output, and storage activities by itself. A personal computer contains a processor, memory, and one or more input, output, and storage devices.

Two popular styles of personal computers are the PC (Figure 1-15) and the Apple (Figure 1-16). The term, *PC-compatible*, refers to any personal computer based on the original IBM personal computer design. Companies such as Dell, Gateway, Hewlett-Packard, and Toshiba sell PC-compatible computers. PC and PC-compatible computers have processors with different architectures than processors in Apple computers. These two types of computers also use different operating systems. PC and PC-compatible computers usually use a Windows operating system. Apple computers use a Macintosh operating system (Mac OS).

Two types of personal computers are desktop computers and notebook computers. The next section discusses desktop personal computers. Notebook computers are discussed in the mobile computers section.

WEB LINK 1-7

Personal Computers
For more information, visit scsite.com/dc2007/ch1/weblink and then click Personal Computers.

FIGURE 1-15 The PC and compatible computers usually use a Windows operating system.

FIGURE 1-16 Apple computers, such as the iMac, use a Macintosh operating system.

FAQ 1-5

How many PCs have been sold worldwide?

One billion PCs were sold during their first 25 years on the market. Experts predict that the next billion PCs will be sold between 2000 and 2008, a mere eight-year period. For more information, visit scsite.com/dc2007/ch1/faq and then click PC Sales.

Desktop Computers

A **desktop computer** is designed so the system unit, input devices, output devices, and any other devices fit entirely on or under a desk or table (Figures 1-15 and 1-16 on the previous page). In many models, the system unit is a tall and narrow *tower*, which can sit on the floor vertically — if desktop space is limited.

Some desktop computers function as a server on a network. Others, such as a gaming desktop computer and Media Center PC, target a specific audience. The *gaming desktop computer* offers high-quality audio, video, and graphics with optimal performance for sophisticated single-user and networked or Internet multi-player games. A *Media Center PC* is a home entertainment desktop computer that provides a means of accessing television programs, radio broadcasts, photographs, and videos, as well as basic computing capabilities. These high-end computers cost much more than the basic desktop computer.

Another expensive, powerful desktop computer is the workstation, which is geared for work that requires intense calculations and graphics capabilities. An architect uses a workstation to design buildings and homes. A graphic artist uses a workstation to create computer-animated special effects for full-length motion pictures and video games.

FAQ 1-6

Does the term, workstation, have two meanings?

Yes. In the computer industry, a *workstation* can be a high-powered computer or a client computer on a network. For more information, visit scsite.com/dc2007/ch1/faq and then click Workstation.

MOBILE COMPUTERS AND MOBILE DEVICES

A **mobile computer** is a personal computer you can carry from place to place. Similarly, a **mobile device** is a computing device small enough to hold in your hand.

The most popular type of mobile computer is the notebook computer. The following sections discuss the notebook computer and widely used mobile devices.

Notebook Computers

A **notebook computer**, also called a **laptop computer**, is a portable, personal computer designed to fit on your lap. Notebook computers are thin and lightweight, yet they can be as powerful as the average desktop computer. Notebook computers are more expensive than desktop computers with equal capabilities.

On a typical notebook computer, the keyboard is on top of the system unit, and the monitor attaches to the system unit with hinges (Figure 1-17). These computers weigh on average between 2.5 and 9 pounds, which allows users easily to transport the computers from place to place. Most notebook computers can operate on batteries or a power supply or both.

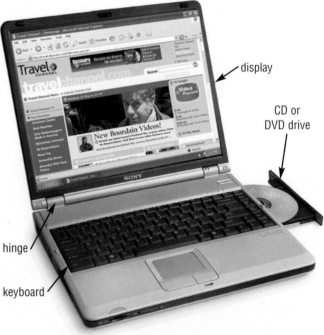

display

CD or DVD drive

hinge

keyboard

FIGURE 1-17 On a typical notebook computer, the keyboard is on top of the system unit, and the display attaches to the system unit with hinges.

TABLET PC Resembling a letter-sized slate, the **Tablet PC** is a special type of notebook computer that allows you to write or draw on the screen using a digital pen (Figure 1-18). With a *digital pen*, users write or draw by pressing the pen on the screen, and issue instructions to the Tablet PC by tapping on the screen. For users who prefer typing instead of handwriting, some Tablet PC designs have an attached keyboard; others allow you to connect a separate keyboard to the device. Tablet PCs also support voice input so users can enter text and issue instructions by speaking into the computer.

Tablet PCs are useful especially for taking notes in lectures, at meetings, conferences, and other forums where the standard notebook computer is not practical. With a cost of about $1,000 or more, some users may find Tablet PCs more appropriate for their needs than traditional notebook computers.

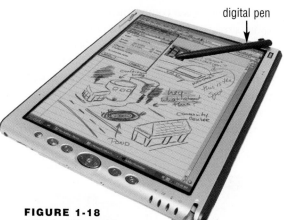

digital pen

FIGURE 1-18
A Tablet PC combines the features of a traditional notebook computer with the simplicity of pencil and paper.

Mobile Devices

Mobile devices, which are small enough to carry in a pocket, usually do not have disk drives. Instead, these devices store programs and data permanently on special memory inside the system unit or on small storage media such as memory cards. You often can connect a mobile device to a personal computer to exchange information between the computer and the mobile device.

Some mobile devices are **Internet-enabled**, meaning they can connect to the Internet wirelessly. With an Internet-enabled device, users can chat, send e-mail and instant messages, and access the Web.

Three popular types of mobile devices are handheld computers, PDAs, and smart phones. Some combination mobile devices also are available, for example, a PDA/smart phone.

HANDHELD COMPUTER A **handheld computer**, sometimes referred to as an *ultra personal computer (uPC)* or a *handtop computer*, is a computer small enough to fit in one hand (Figure 1-19). Because of their reduced size, the screens on handheld computers are small. Many handheld computers communicate wirelessly with other devices or computers and also include a digital pen or stylus for input. Similar to a digital pen, a *stylus* is a small metal or plastic device that looks like a ballpoint pen but uses pressure instead of ink to write, draw, or make selections.

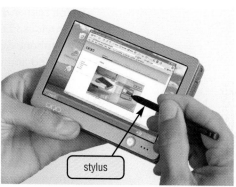

stylus

FIGURE 1-19
This OQO handheld computer is a full PC that fits in your hand and weighs less than one pound.

Some handheld computers have specialized keyboards. Many handheld computers are industry-specific and serve the needs of mobile employees, such as meter readers and parcel delivery people, whose jobs require them to move from place to place.

PDA The PDA is one of the more popular lightweight mobile devices in use today. A **PDA** (*personal digital assistant*) provides personal organizer functions such as a calendar, an appointment book, an address book, a calculator, and a notepad (Figure 1-20). Most PDAs also offer a variety of other application software such as word processing, spreadsheet, personal finance, and games.

The primary input device of a PDA is a stylus. Some PDAs do have a built-in miniature keyboard. If you prefer to type on a PDA that does not have a keyboard, you can insert the PDA in a special separate keyboard. Some PDAs also support voice input and have built-in cameras.

Many PDAs are Internet-enabled so users can check e-mail and access the Web. Some also provide telephone capabilities. Because of all the added features, increasingly more people are replacing their pocket-sized appointment books with PDAs.

stylus

FIGURE 1-20
PDAs provide personal information management functions as well as Internet access and telephone capabilities.

FAQ 1-7

Do PDAs have industry-specific applications?

Yes. Restaurant servers use PDAs to record customer orders and transmit them to the kitchen. Doctors use PDAs to access patients' records, view laboratory results, and transmit prescriptions to the pharmacy. Law enforcement officials use PDAs to run background checks and issue tickets. For more information, visit scsite.com/dc2007/ch1/faq and then click PDAs.

SMART PHONE Offering the convenience of one-handed operation, a **smart phone** is an Internet-enabled telephone that usually also provides PDA capabilities. In addition to basic telephone capabilities, a smart phone allows you to send and receive e-mail messages and access the Web. Higher-priced models have color screens, play music, and include built-in cameras so you can share photographs or videos with others as soon as you capture the image (Figure 1-21).

As smart phones and PDAs continue a trend of offering similar functions, it is becoming increasingly difficult to differentiate between the two devices. This trend, known as *convergence*, has led manufacturers to refer to PDAs and smart phones simply as *handhelds*. Some factors that affect a consumer's purchasing decision include the device's size, screen size, and capabilities of available software.

GAME CONSOLES

A **game console** is a mobile computing device designed for single-player or multiplayer video games (Figure 1-22). Standard game consoles use a handheld controller(s) as an input device(s); a television screen as an output device; and hard disks, CDs, DVDs, and/or memory cards for storage. Weighing on average between five and nine pounds, the compact size of game consoles makes them easy to use at home, in the car, in a hotel, in a camper, or any location that has an electrical outlet. Two popular models are Microsoft's Xbox 360 and Sony's PlayStation 3.

A handheld game console is small enough to fit in one hand, making it more portable than the standard game console. With the handheld game console, the controls, screen, and speakers are built into the device. Because of their reduced size, the screens are small — three to four inches. Some models use cartridges to store games; others use a miniature type of CD or DVD. Many handheld game consoles can communicate wirelessly with other similar consoles for multiplayer gaming. Two popular models are Nintendo's Game Boy Micro and Sony's PlayStation Portable (PSP).

In addition to gaming, many console models allow users to listen to music, watch movies, and connect to the Internet. Game consoles cost a few hundred dollars or less.

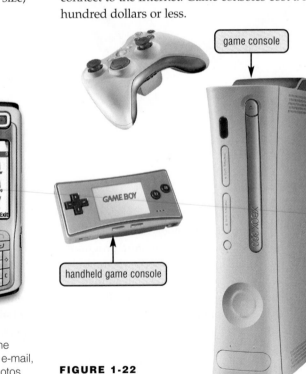

game console

handheld game console

WEB LINK 1-8

Game Consoles

For more information, visit scsite.com/ dc2007/ch1/weblink and then click Game Consoles.

FIGURE 1-21 In addition to basic telephone functionality, smart phones allow you to check e-mail, access the Web, listen to music, and share photos and videos.

FIGURE 1-22
Game consoles provide hours of video game entertainment.

SERVERS

A **server** controls access to the hardware, software, and other resources on a network and provides a centralized storage area for programs, data, and information (Figure 1-23). Servers can support from two to several thousand connected computers at the same time.

In many cases, one server accesses data, information, and programs on another server. In other cases, people use personal computers or terminals to access data, information, and programs on a server. A terminal is a device with a monitor, keyboard, and memory.

FIGURE 1-23
A server controls access to resources on a network.

MAINFRAMES

A **mainframe** is a large, expensive, powerful computer that can handle hundreds or thousands of connected users simultaneously (Figure 1-24). Mainframes store tremendous amounts of data, instructions, and information. Most major corporations use mainframes for business activities. With mainframes, large businesses are able to bill millions of customers, prepare payroll for thousands of employees, and manage thousands of items in inventory. One study reported that mainframes process more than 83 percent of transactions around the world.

Mainframes also can act as servers in a network environment. Servers and other mainframes can access data and information from a mainframe. People also can access programs on the mainframe using terminals or personal computers.

FIGURE 1-24
Mainframe computers can handle thousands of connected computers and process millions of instructions per second.

SUPERCOMPUTERS

A **supercomputer** is the fastest, most powerful computer — and the most expensive (Figure 1-25). The fastest supercomputers are capable of processing more than 100 trillion instructions in a single second. With weights that exceed 100 tons, these computers can store more than 20,000 times the data and information of an average desktop computer.

Applications requiring complex, sophisticated mathematical calculations use supercomputers. Large-scale simulations and applications in medicine, aerospace, automotive design, online banking, weather forecasting, nuclear energy research, and petroleum exploration use a supercomputer.

FIGURE 1-25 This supercomputer simulates various environmental occurrences such as global climate changes, pollution, and earthquakes.

EMBEDDED COMPUTERS

An **embedded computer** is a special-purpose computer that functions as a component in a larger product. Embedded computers are everywhere — at home, in your car, and at work. The following list identifies a variety of everyday products that contain embedded computers.

- Consumer Electronics: mobile and digital telephones, digital televisions, cameras, video recorders, DVD players and recorders, answering machines
- Home Automation Devices and Appliances: thermostats, sprinkling systems, security monitoring systems, microwave ovens, washing machines
- Automobiles: antilock brakes, engine control modules, airbag controller, cruise control

- Process Controllers and Robotics: remote monitoring systems, power monitors, machine controllers, medical devices
- Computer Devices and Office Machines: keyboards, printers, faxes, copiers

Because embedded computers are components in larger products, they usually are small and have limited hardware. These computers perform various functions, depending on the requirements of the product in which they reside. Embedded computers in printers, for example, monitor the amount of paper in the tray, check the ink or toner level, signal if a paper jam has occurred, and so on. Figure 1-26 shows some of the many embedded computers in cars.

Advanced airbag systems have crash-severity sensors that determine the appropriate level to inflate the airbag, reducing the chance of airbag injury in low-speed accidents.

Adaptive cruise control systems detect if cars in front of you are too close and, if necessary, adjust the vehicle's throttle, may apply brakes, and/or sound an alarm.

Tire pressure monitoring systems send warning signals if tire pressure is insufficient.

Cars equipped with wireless communications capabilities, called *telematics*, include such features as navigation systems and Internet access.

Drive-by-wire systems sense pressure on the gas pedal and communicate electronically to the engine how much and how fast to accelerate.

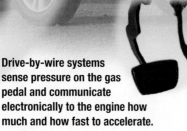

FIGURE 1-26   Some of the embedded computers designed to improve your safety, security, and performance in today's automobiles.

ELEMENTS OF AN INFORMATION SYSTEM

To be valuable, information must be accurate, organized, timely, accessible, useful, and cost-effective to produce. Generating information from a computer requires the following five elements:

- Hardware
- Software
- Data
- People
- Procedures

Together, these elements (hardware, software, data, people, and procedures) comprise an *information system*. Figure 1-27 shows how each of the elements of an information system in a large business might interact.

The hardware must be reliable and capable of handling the expected workload. The software must be developed carefully and tested thoroughly. The data entered into the computer must be accurate.

Most companies with mid-sized and large computers have an IT (information technology) department. Staff in the IT department should be skilled and up-to-date on the latest technology. IT staff also should train users so they understand how to use the computer properly. Today's users also work closely with IT staff in the development of computer applications that relate to their areas of work.

Finally, all the IT applications should have readily available documented procedures that address operating the computer and using its applications.

FIGURE 1-27   HOW THE ELEMENTS OF AN INFORMATION SYSTEM IN A LARGE BUSINESS MIGHT INTERACT

Step 1: IT staff (people) develop procedures for processing time cards (data).

Step 2: Employees (people) in the payroll department use a program (software) to enter the time cards (data) in the computer.

Step 3: The computer (hardware) performs calculations required to process the payroll and stores the results on storage media such as a hard disk (hardware).

Step 4: Paychecks (information) print on a corporate printer (hardware).

EXAMPLES OF COMPUTER USAGE

Every day, people around the world rely on different types of computers for a variety of applications. To illustrate the range of uses for computers, this section takes you on a visual and narrative tour of five categories of users:

- Home user
- Small office/home office (SOHO) user
- Mobile user
- Power user
- Large business user

The following pages discuss the types of hardware and software required by each category of user.

Home User

In an increasing number of homes, the computer no longer is a convenience. Instead, it is a basic necessity. Each family member, or **home user**, spends time on the computer for different reasons that include budgeting and personal financial management, Web access, communications, and entertainment (Figure 1-28).

FIGURE 1-28a (personal financial management)

FIGURE 1-28b (Web access)

FIGURE 1-28c (communications)

FIGURE 1-28d (entertainment)

FIGURE 1-28 The home user spends time on a computer for a variety of reasons.

On the Internet, home users access a huge amount of information, take college classes, pay bills, manage investments, shop, listen to the radio, watch movies, read books, play games, file taxes, book airline reservations, and make telephone calls. They also communicate with others around the world through e-mail, blogs, instant messaging, and chat rooms using personal computers, PDAs, and smart phones. With a digital camera, home users take photographs and then send the electronic images to others (Figure 1-29). Using a PC video camera, which costs less than $100, home users easily have live video calls with friends, family members, and others. Read Ethics & Issues 1-4 for a related discussion.

Many home users have a portable digital audio player, so they can download music or podcasts, and listen to the music and/or audio at a later time through earphones attached to the player. They also usually have one or more game consoles to play video games individually or with friends and family members.

Today's homes also typically have one or more desktop computers. Many home users network multiple desktop computers throughout the house, often wirelessly. These small networks allow family members to share an Internet connection and a printer.

To meet their needs, home users have a variety of software. They type letters, homework assignments, and other documents with word processing software. Personal finance software helps the home user with personal finances, investments, and family budgets. Other software assists with preparing taxes, keeping a household inventory, and setting up maintenance schedules.

Reference software, such as encyclopedias, medical dictionaries, or a road atlas, provides valuable information for everyone in the family. With entertainment software, the home user can play games, compose music, research genealogy, or create greeting cards. Educational software helps adults learn to speak a foreign language and youngsters to read, write, count, and spell.

FAQ 1-8

Can I listen to an audio CD on my computer?

Yes, in most cases. Simply insert the CD in the computer's CD or DVD drive. Within a few seconds, you should hear music from the computer's speakers or in your headphones or earphones. If no music plays, it is possible you need to run a program that starts the audio CD. For more information, visit csite.com/dc2007/ch1/faq and then click Audio CDs.

FIGURE 1-29 Home users take and view photographs on a digital camera.

Small Office/Home Office User

Computers assist small business and home office users in managing their resources effectively. A **small office/home office** (*SOHO*) includes any company with fewer than 50 employees, as well as the self-employed who work from home. Small offices include local law practices, accounting firms, travel agencies, and florists. SOHO users typically have a desktop computer to perform some or all of their duties. Many also have PDAs or smart phones to manage appointments and contact information.

SOHO users access the Internet — often wirelessly — to look up information such as addresses, directions (Figure 1-30a), postal codes, flights, and package shipping rates or to make telephone calls. Nearly all SOHO users communicate with others through e-mail.

Many are entering the *e-commerce* arena and conduct business on the Web. Their Web sites advertise products and services and may provide a means for taking orders. Small business Web sites sometimes use a *Web cam*, which is a video camera that displays its output on a Web page. A Web cam allows SOHO users to show the world a live view of some aspect of their business.

To save money on hardware and software, small offices often network their computers. For example, the small office connects one printer to a network for all employees to share.

SOHO users often have basic business software such as word processing and spreadsheet software to assist with document preparation and finances (Figure 1-30b). They are likely to use other industry-specific types of software. A candy shop, for example, will have software that allows for taking orders and payments, updating inventory, and paying vendors.

FIGURE 1-30a (Web access)

FIGURE 1-30b (spreadsheet program)

FIGURE 1-30   People with a home office and employees in small offices typically use a personal computer for some or all of their duties.

Mobile User

Today, businesses and schools are expanding to serve people across the country and around the world. Thus, increasingly more employees and students are **mobile users**, who work on a computer while away from a main office or school (Figure 1-31). Examples of mobile users are sales representatives, real estate agents, insurance agents, meter readers, package delivery people, journalists, consultants, and students.

Mobile users often have a notebook computer, Internet-enabled PDA, or smart phone. With these computers and devices, the mobile user connects to other computers on a network or the Internet, often wirelessly accessing services such as e-mail and the Web. Mobile users can transfer information between their mobile device and another computer, such as one at the main office or school.

The mobile user works with basic business software such as word processing and spreadsheet software. With presentation graphics software, the mobile user can create and deliver presentations to a large audience by connecting a mobile computer or device to a video projector that displays the presentation on a full screen. Many scaled-down programs are available for mobile devices such as PDAs and smart phones.

FIGURE 1-31   Mobile users have notebook computers, Tablet PCs, PDAs, and smart phones so they can work, do homework, send messages, or connect to the Internet while away from a wired connection.

Power User

Another category of user, called a **power user**, requires the capabilities of a workstation or other type of powerful computer (Figure 1-32). Examples of power users include engineers, scientists, architects, desktop publishers, and graphic artists. Power users often work with *multimedia*, combining text, graphics, audio, and video into one application. These users need computers with extremely fast processors because of the nature of their work.

The power user's workstation contains industry-specific software. For example, engineers and architects use software to draft and design floor plans, mechanical assemblies, or vehicles. A desktop publisher uses software to prepare marketing literature such as newsletters, brochures, and annual reports. A geologist uses software to study the earth's surface. This software usually is expensive because of its specialized design.

Power users exist in all types of businesses. Some work at home. Their computers typically have network connections and Internet access.

FIGURE 1-32   This scientist uses a powerful computer to study brain imaging.

Large Business User

A large business has hundreds or thousands of employees or customers that work in or do business with offices across a region, the country, or the world. Each employee or customer who uses a computer in the large business is a **large business user** (Figure 1-33).

Many large companies use the words, *enterprise computing*, to refer to the huge network of computers that meets their diverse computing needs. The network facilitates communications among employees at all locations. Users access the network of servers or mainframes through desktop computers, mobile computers, PDAs, and smart phones.

Large businesses use computers and the computer network to process high volumes of transactions in a single day. Although they may differ in size and in the products or services offered, all generally use computers for basic business activities. For example, they bill millions of customers, prepare payroll for thousands of employees, and manage thousands of items in inventory. Some large businesses use blogs to open communications among employees, customers, and/or vendors.

Large businesses typically have e-commerce Web sites, allowing customers and vendors to conduct business online. The Web site also showcases products, services, and other company information. Customers, vendors, and other interested parties can access this information on the Web. Once an order is placed, computers update inventory records to reflect goods sold and goods purchased.

The marketing department in a large business uses desktop publishing software to prepare marketing literature. The accounting department uses software for accounts receivable, accounts payable, billing, general ledger, and payroll activities.

The employees in the *information technology (IT) department* keep the computers and the network running. They also determine when and if the company requires new hardware or software.

Large business users work with word processing, spreadsheet, database, and presentation graphics software. They also may use calendar programs to post their schedules on the network. And, they might use PDAs or smart phones to maintain contact information. E-mail and Web browsers enable communications among employees, vendors, and customers.

Some large businesses place kiosks in public locations. A *kiosk* is a freestanding computer, usually with a touch screen (Figure 1-34).

Many employees of large businesses telecommute. **Telecommuting** is a work arrangement in which employees work away from a company's standard workplace and often communicate with the office through the computer. Employees who telecommute have flexible work schedules so they can combine work and personal responsibilities, such as child care.

FIGURE 1-33 A large business can have hundreds or thousands of users in offices across a region, the country, or the world.

FIGURE 1-34 Airline travelers check in using this self-service kiosk.

Putting It All Together

The previous pages discussed the hardware and software requirements for the home user, small office/home office user, mobile user, power user, and large business user. The table in Figure 1-35 summarizes these requirements.

CATEGORIES OF USERS

User	Hardware	Software
HOME 	• Desktop or notebook computer • PDA or smart phone • Game consoles	• Business (e.g., word processing) • Personal information manager • Personal finance, online banking, tax preparation • Web browser • E-mail, blogging, instant messaging, and chat rooms • Internet telephone calls • Photo editing • Reference (e.g., encyclopedias, medical dictionaries, road atlas) • Entertainment (e.g., games, music composition, greeting cards) • Educational (e.g., tutorials, children's math and reading software)
SMALL OFFICE/ HOME OFFICE 	• Desktop computer • PDA or smart phone • Shared network printer	• Business (e.g., word processing, spreadsheet, database) • Personal information manager • Company specific (e.g., accounting, legal reference) • Network management • Web browser • E-mail • Internet telephone calls
MOBILE 	• Notebook computer equipped with a wireless modem, or a Tablet PC • Video projector • PDA or smart phone	• Business (e.g., word processing, spreadsheet, note taking, presentation graphics) • Personal information manager • Web browser • E-mail
POWER 	• Workstation or other powerful computer with multimedia capabilities • PDA or smart phone	• Desktop publishing • Multimedia authoring • Computer-aided design • Photo, audio, and video editing • Personal information manager • Web browser • E-mail
LARGE BUSINESS 	• Server or mainframe • Desktop or notebook computer • Industry-specific handheld computer • PDA or smart phone • Kiosk	• Business (e.g., word processing, spreadsheet, database, presentation graphics) • Personal information manager • Accounting • Network management • Web browser • E-mail • Blogging

FIGURE 1-35 Today, computers are used by millions of people for work tasks, school assignments, and leisure activities. Different computer users require different kinds of hardware and software to meet their needs effectively.

COMPUTER APPLICATIONS IN SOCIETY

The computer has changed society today as much as the industrial revolution changed society in the eighteenth and nineteenth centuries.

People interact directly with computers in fields such as education, finance, government, health care, science, publishing, travel, and manufacturing. In addition, they can reap the benefits from breakthroughs and advances in these fields. The following pages describe how computers have made a difference in people's interactions with these disciplines. Read Looking Ahead 1-2 for a look at the next generation of computer applications in society.

LOOKING AHEAD 1-2

Robots Perform Mundane Tasks, Entertain

Playwright Karel Capek created the name, robot, for his humanoid machines that turned against their creators. Today, mobile, intelligent robots perform tasks typically reserved for humans in a $5 billion global market.

Each day, the iRobot Roomba self-propelled vacuum cleans homes, and the da Vinci Surgical System's robotic hands drill through bones and make incisions. Sony's home robot, QRIO, responds to voices and faces, displays emotions, and walks and dances fluidly.

Tomorrow's practical and versatile robots will serve a variety of personal and industrial needs. By 2010, the expected $17 billion market should include products to care for senior citizens, transport people in major cities, and perform hundreds of thousands of mobile utility jobs, such as picking up and delivering items. For more information, visit scsite.com/dc2007/ch1/looking and then click Robots.

Education

Education is the process of acquiring knowledge. In the traditional model, people learn from other people such as parents, teachers, and employers. Many forms of printed material such as books and manuals are used as learning tools. Today, educators also are turning to computers to assist with education (Figure 1-36).

Many schools and companies equip labs and classrooms with computers. Some schools require students to have a notebook computer or PDA to access the school's network or Internet wirelessly. To promote education by computer, many vendors offer substantial student discounts on software.

Sometimes, the delivery of education occurs at one place while the learning occurs at other locations. For example, students can take a class on the Web. Some classes are blended; that is, part of the learning occurs in a classroom and the other part occurs on the Web. More than 70 percent of colleges offer some type of distance learning classes. A few even offer entire degrees online.

FIGURE 1-36   In some schools, students have notebook computers on their desks during classroom lectures.

Finance

Many people and companies use computers to help manage their finances. Some use finance software to balance checkbooks, pay bills, track personal income and expenses, manage investments, and evaluate financial plans. This software usually includes a variety of online services. For example, computer users can track investments and do online banking. With **online banking**, users access account balances, pay bills, and copy monthly transactions from the bank's computer right into their personal computers.

Many financial institutions' Web sites also offer online banking (Figure 1-37). When using a Web site instead of finance software on your computer, all your account information is stored on the bank's computer. The advantage is you can access your financial records from anywhere in the world.

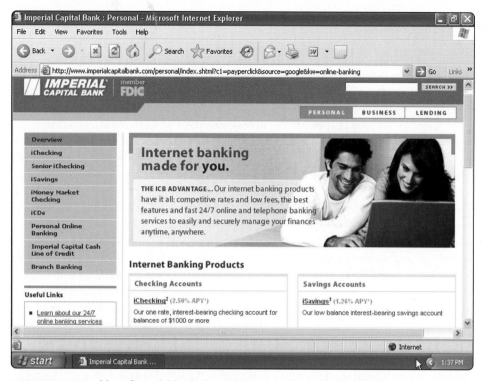

FIGURE 1-37 Many financial institutions' Web sites offer online banking.

Investors often use **online investing** to buy and sell stocks and bonds — without using a broker. With online investing, the transaction fee for each trade usually is much less than when trading through a broker.

Government

A government provides society with direction by making and administering policies. To provide citizens with up-to-date information, most government offices have Web sites. People in the United States access government Web sites to file taxes, apply for permits and licenses, pay parking tickets, buy stamps, report crimes, apply for financial aid, and renew vehicle registrations and driver's licenses.

Employees of government agencies use computers as part of their daily routine. North American 911 call centers use computers to dispatch calls for fire, police, and medical assistance. Military and other agency officials use the U.S. Department of Homeland Security's network of information about domestic security threats to help protect against terrorist attacks. Law enforcement officers have online access to the FBI's National Crime Information Center (NCIC) in police cars that have rugged notebook

computers and fingerprint scanners or through PDAs (Figure 1-38). The NCIC contains more than 52 million missing persons and criminal records, including names, fingerprints, parole/probation records, mug shots, and other information.

FIGURE 1-38 Law enforcement officials have in-vehicle computers and PDAs to access emergency, missing person, and criminal records in computer networks in local, state, and federal agencies.

Health Care

Nearly every area of health care uses computers. Whether you are visiting a family doctor for a regular checkup, having lab work or an outpatient test, or being rushed in for emergency surgery, the medical staff around you will be using computers for various purposes:

- Hospitals and doctors use computers to maintain patient records.
- Computers monitor patients' vital signs in hospital rooms and at home.
- Computers and computerized devices assist doctors, nurses, and technicians with medical tests (Figure 1-39).
- Doctors use the Web and medical software to assist with researching and diagnosing health conditions.
- Doctors use e-mail to correspond with patients.
- Pharmacists use computers to file insurance claims.
- Surgeons implant computerized devices, such as pacemakers, that allow patients to live longer.

- Surgeons use computer-controlled devices to provide them with greater precision during operations, such as for laser eye surgery and robot-assisted heart surgery.

Many Web sites provide up-to-date medical, fitness, nutrition, or exercise information. These Web sites also maintain lists of doctors and dentists to help you find the one that suits your needs. They have chat rooms, so you can talk to others diagnosed with similar conditions. Some Web sites even allow you to order prescriptions online.

An exciting development in health care is telemedicine, which is a form of long-distance health care. Through *telemedicine*, health-care professionals in separate locations conduct live conferences on the computer. For example, a doctor at one location can have a conference with a doctor at another location to discuss a bone X-ray. Live images of each doctor, along with the X-ray, are displayed on each doctor's computer.

Science

All branches of science, from biology to astronomy to meteorology, use computers to assist them with collecting, analyzing, and modeling data. Scientists also use the Internet to communicate with colleagues around the world.

Breakthroughs in surgery, medicine, and treatments often result from scientists' use of computers. Tiny computers now imitate functions of the central nervous system, retina of the eye, and cochlea of the ear. A cochlear implant allows a deaf person to listen. Electrodes implanted in the brain stop tremors associated with Parkinson's disease. Cameras small enough to swallow — sometimes called a camera pill — take pictures inside your body to detect polyps, cancer, and other abnormalities (Figure 1-40).

A *neural network* is a system that attempts to imitate the behavior of the human brain. Scientists create neural networks by connecting thousands of processors together much like the neurons in the brain are connected. The capability of a personal computer to recognize spoken words is a direct result of scientific experimentation with neural networks.

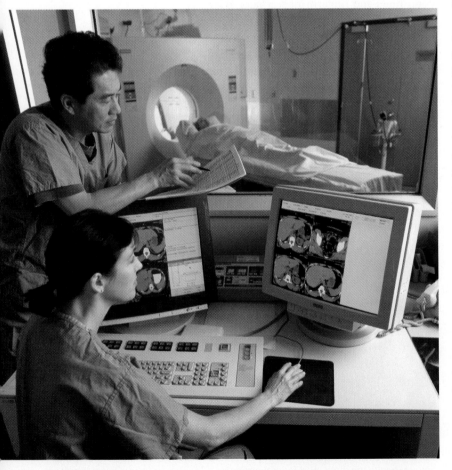

FIGURE 1-39 Doctors, nurses, technicians, and other medical staff use computers while performing tests on patients.

FIGURE 1-40 HOW A CAMERA PILL WORKS

Step 1:
A patient swallows a tiny capsule that contains a miniature disposable camera, lights, a transmitter, and batteries. The camera is positioned at the clear end of the capsule.

Step 3:
The doctor transfers the data on the recording device to a computer so it can be processed and analyzed.

Step 2:
As the capsule moves through the inside of the patient's body, the camera snaps about 50,000 pictures, which are transmitted to a recording device worn as a belt on the patient's waist.

Publishing

Publishing is the process of making works available to the public. These works include books, magazines, newspapers, music, film, and video. Special software assists graphic designers in developing pages that include text, graphics, and photographs; artists in composing and enhancing songs; filmmakers in creating and editing film; and journalists and mobile users in capturing and modifying video clips.

Many publishers make their works available online (Figure 1-41). Some Web sites allow you to copy the work, such as a book or music, to your desktop computer, handheld computer, PDA, or smart phone.

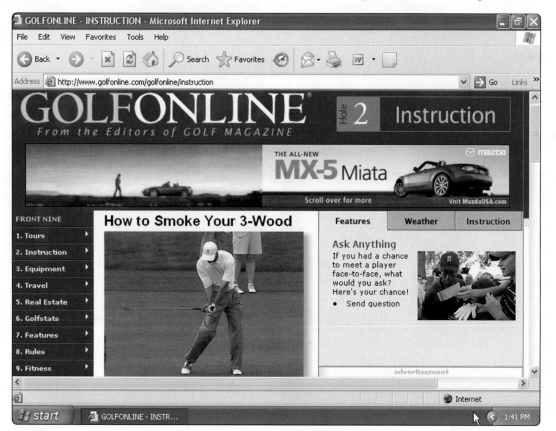

FIGURE 1-41 Many magazine and newspaper publishers make the content of their publications available online.

Travel

Whether traveling by car or airplane, your goal is to arrive safely at your destination. As you make the journey, you may interact with some of the latest technology.

Vehicles manufactured today often include some type of onboard navigation system. Many airlines now provide online access, allowing passengers to connect their mobile computer or device to the Internet (Figure 1-42). Some airlines even provide passengers with Internet-enabled devices during flights.

In preparing for a trip, you may need to reserve a car, hotel, or flight. Many Web sites offer these services to the public. For example, you can order airline tickets on the Web. If you plan to drive somewhere and are unsure of the road to take to your destination, you can print directions and a map from the Web.

WEB LINK 1-11

Onboard Navigation Systems

For more information, visit scsite.com/ dc2007/ch1/weblink and then click Onboard Navigation Systems.

FAQ 1-9

Do home users book travel on the Web?

Yes, it is estimated that nearly 22 percent ($53 billion) of the travel industry's revenues stem from leisure travel bookings. As shown in the chart, computer users of all ages visit travel agency Web sites. For more information, visit scsite.com/ dc2007/ch1/faq and then click Travel Bookings.

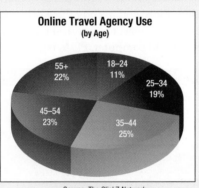

Online Travel Agency Use
(by Age)

55+ 22%
18–24 11%
25–34 19%
35–44 25%
45–54 23%

Source: The ClickZ Network

FIGURE 1-42   Airlines today offer inflight Internet connections to passengers.

Manufacturing

Computer-aided manufacturing (*CAM*) refers to the use of computers to assist with manufacturing processes such as fabrication and assembly. Industries use CAM to reduce product development costs, shorten a product's time to market, and stay ahead of the competition.

Often, robots carry out processes in a CAM environment. CAM is used by a variety of industries, including oil drilling, power generation, food production, and automobile manufacturing. Automobile plants, for example, have an entire line of industrial robots that assemble a car (Figure 1-43).

Special computers on the shop floor record actual labor, material, machine, and computer time used to manufacture a particular product. The computers process this data and automatically update inventory, production, payroll, and accounting records on the company's network.

FIGURE 1-43   Automotive factories use industrial robots to weld car bodies.

Test your knowledge of pages 18 through 36 in Quiz Yourself 1-3.

QUIZ YOURSELF 1-3

Instructions: Find the true statement below. Then, rewrite the remaining false statements so they are true.

1. A desktop computer is a portable, personal computer designed to fit on your lap.

2. A personal computer contains a processor, memory, and one or more input, output, and storage devices.

3. Each large business user spends time on the computer for different reasons that include budgeting and personal financial management, Web access, communications, and entertainment.

4. A home user requires the capabilities of a workstation or other powerful computer.

5. Mainframes are the fastest, most powerful computers — and the most expensive.

6. The elements of an information system are hardware, e-mail, data, people, and the Internet.

7. With embedded computers, users access account balances, pay bills, and copy monthly transactions from the bank's computer right into their personal computers.

Quiz Yourself Online: To further check your knowledge of categories of computers, information system elements, computer users, and computer applications in society, visit scsite.com/dc2007/ch1/quiz and then click Objectives 8 – 11.

CHAPTER SUMMARY

Chapter 1 introduced you to basic computer concepts such as what a computer is, how it works, and its advantages and disadvantages. You learned about the components of a computer. Next, the chapter discussed networks, the Internet, and computer software. The many different categories of computers, computer users, and computer applications in society also were presented.

This chapter is an overview. Many of the terms and concepts introduced will be discussed further in later chapters. For a history of hardware and software developments, read the Timeline 2007 that follows this chapter.

CAREER CORNER

Personal Computer Salesperson

When you decide to buy or upgrade a personal computer, the most important person with whom you interact probably will be a personal computer salesperson. This individual will be a valuable resource to you in providing the information and expertise you need to select a computer that meets your requirements.

Computer manufacturers and retailers that sell several types of personal computers need competent salespeople. A *personal computer salesperson* must be computer literate and have a specific knowledge of the computers he or she sells. The salesperson also must have a working knowledge of computer peripherals (printers, scanners, cameras, etc.). In addition, a successful salesperson has a friendly, outgoing personality that helps customers feel comfortable. Through open-ended questions, the salesperson can determine a customer's needs and level of experience. With this information, the salesperson can choose the best computer for the customer and explain the features of the computer in language the customer will understand. Most computer salespeople also can recommend a qualified installer for your computer or qualified service technician.

Computer salespeople typically have at least a high school diploma. Before reaching the sales floor, however, salespeople usually complete extensive company training programs. These programs often consist of self-directed, self-paced Web-training classes. Most salespeople also participate in training updates, often on a monthly basis.

Personal computer salespeople generally earn a guaranteed amount plus a commission for each sale. A computer salesperson can earn about $45,000 a year. Top salespeople can be among a company's more highly compensated employees, earning in excess of $85,000. For more information, visit scsite.com/dc2007/ch1/careers and then click Personal Computer Salesperson.

High-Tech Talk

ANALOG VERSUS DIGITAL:
MAKING THE CONVERSION

Data is processed in one of two ways: analog or digital. People generally process *analog* data — that is, continuous wave patterns. The sight and sound of a traveling subway car transmits to your eyes and ears as light and sound waves, or smooth up-and-down patterns (Figure 1-44a). A computer, by contrast, is *digital*, which means computers process data in two discrete states: positive (on, or 1) and non-positive (off, or 0) as shown in Figure 1-44b. The 1 and 0 represent the two digits used by the binary number system. While this system is at the heart of digital computing, binary digital impulses appear as long strings of 1s and 0s.

If sound and light waves are analog and a computer is digital, how does a computer record audio clips, play music, or show a movie? How can a digital computer use an analog telephone line to dial up to access the Internet?

The key lies in analog-to-digital and digital-to-analog conversions. For example, the computer's sound card allows you to record sounds and playback sounds. The sound card performs these conversions to record a digital audio clip of your analog voice. The sound card connects to the microphone, which is an analog input source. The diaphragm in the microphone converts the analog sound waves into an analog electrical signal. This signal flows to the sound card's *analog-to-digital converter (ADC)*, which converts the signal into digital data. The digital data flows to the *digital signal processor (DSP)*, compressing the data to save space. Finally, the compressed data is stored in an audio file format.

To play a recorded sound, the computer reverses the process. The processor retrieves and sends the digital data to the DSP to be decompressed. The DSP sends the decompressed digital data to the sound card's *digital-to-analog converter (DAC)*, which converts the digital data back to an analog voltage for output via a speaker or headset. In other words, a DAC takes that long binary number string of 1s and 0s and turns it into an electronic signal that the sound output devices can decode and use.

Similarly, a video card allows you to record a video or play a movie on a DVD. A camera and microphone capture and send the analog picture and sound signals to a video card. The video card's ADC converts the signals into digital data. The digital data is compressed and saved in a file format such as AVI (audio/video interleave) or MPEG (Moving Picture Experts Group). When playing a movie, the computer decompresses and separates the video and audio data. It then sends the signals to the video card's DAC. The DAC translates the digital data into analog signals and sends them to the monitor and speakers, where they are displayed as your movie.

The modem in a computer also links the analog and digital worlds. When using a dial-up modem, the computer does not transmit digital data directly across analog telephone lines. Instead, the modem converts the computer's digital signals to analog signals (called *modulation*) to be sent over telephone lines. When the analog signal reaches its destination, another modem recreates the original digital signal (*demodulation*). This allows the receiving computer to process the data. The next time you dial up using a modem, pick up the telephone. The loud, screeching noise you hear is the sound of digital data after being converted to analog sound waves. For more information, visit scsite.com/dc2007/ch1/tech and then click Analog versus Digital.

FIGURE 1-44a   (analog signal)

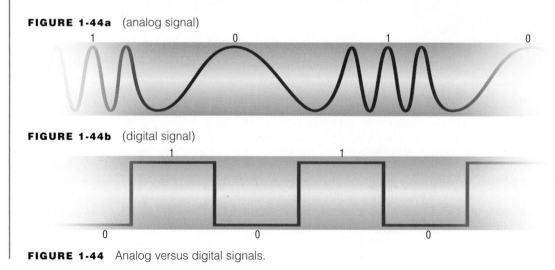

FIGURE 1-44b   (digital signal)

FIGURE 1-44   Analog versus digital signals.

Companies on the Cutting Edge

DELL
COMPUTERS YOUR WAY

As a leading manufacturer of personal computers, *Dell* prides itself on its direct approach to computer sales. Founded by Michael Dell in 1984, the company deals openly with customers, one at a time. This direct approach eliminates retailers that add cost and time to the ordering process.

Dell uses the Internet to enhance the advantages of direct marketing and hosts one of the world's largest volume e-commerce Web sites. Customers can configure and price computers, order systems, and track their orders online.

In response to the U.S. Environmental Protection Agency's estimate that 250 million computers will be discarded from 2002 to 2007, Dell began an aggressive campaign to increase the amount of computer equipment it recycles by 50 percent. For more information, visit scsite.com/dc2007/ch1/companies and then click Dell.

APPLE COMPUTER
INTRODUCING INNOVATIVE TECHNOLOGIES

Millions of computer users in more than 120 countries loyally use *Apple Computer's* hardware and software with a passion usually reserved for sports teams and musical groups.

Steven Jobs and Stephen Wozniak founded Apple in 1976 when they marketed the Apple I, a circuit board they had developed in Jobs's garage. In 1977, Apple Computer incorporated and introduced the Apple II, the first mass-marketed personal computer. Apple introduced the Macintosh product line in 1984, which featured a graphical user interface.

Under Jobs's direction as CEO, Apple introduced the iMac, the iBook, the Power Mac G5, the iPod digital audio player, and Mac OS X. Strong demand for the iPod Mini helped boost the company's earnings. Product sales jumped after Apple introduced its pay-per-download iTunes online music store in 2003. For more information, visit scsite.com/dc2007/ch1/companies and then click Apple Computer.

Technology Trailblazers

BILL GATES
MICROSOFT'S FOUNDER

Bill Gates, the founder and chief software architect of Microsoft Corporation, suggests that college students should learn how to learn by getting the best education they can. Because he is considered by many as the most powerful person in the computing industry, it might be wise to listen to him.

Gates learned to program computers when he was 13. Early in his career, he developed the BASIC programming language for the MITS Altair, one of the first microcomputers. He founded Microsoft in 1975 with Paul Allen, and five years later, they provided the first operating system, called MS-DOS, for the IBM PC. Today, Microsoft's Windows and Office products dominate the software market.

Gates consistently has been placed at the top of *Forbes'* World's Richest People list, with assets of more than $46 billion. For more information, visit scsite.com/dc2007/ch1/people and then click Bill Gates.

ANNE MULCAHY
XEROX CEO

Color printing and consulting services are the two areas where the Xerox Corporation can make a difference, according to *Anne Mulcahy*, the company's CEO and chairman of the board. She should know the nature of the business, having started her career with the Stamford, Connecticut-based corporation more than 30 years ago as a field sales representative.

One of Mulcahy's first decisions after landing the top job in 2001 was eliminating the corporation's tagline, "The Document Company." She believes the company's name, standing solo, speaks for itself in the printing, copying, and services worlds. Her decisions to revamp the company have revolved around Xerox's roots of innovation and customer care. Mulcahy believes it is essential to adapt to the world's changing technology, but the adaptations need a foundation in the basic principles that made Xerox a household word. For more information, visit scsite.com/dc2007/ch1/people and then click Anne Mulcahy.

Chapter Review

The Chapter Review section summarizes the concepts presented in this chapter. To listen to the audio version of this Chapter Review, visit scsite.com/dc2007/ch1/review. To obtain help from other students regarding any subject in this chapter, visit scsite.com/dc2007/ch1/forum and post your thoughts or questions.

① Why Is Computer Literacy Important?   **Computer literacy** involves having knowledge and understanding of computers and their uses. As computers become more a part of everyday life, many people believe that computer literacy is vital to success.

② What Is a Computer?   A **computer** is an electronic device, operating under the control of instructions stored in its own memory, that can accept data, process the data according to specified rules, produce results, and store the results for future use.

③ What Are the Components of a Computer?   The electric, electronic, and mechanical components of a computer, or **hardware**, include input devices, output devices, a system unit, storage devices, and communications devices. An **input device** allows you to enter data or instructions into a computer. An **output device** conveys information to one or more people. The **system unit** is a case that contains the electronic components of a computer that are used to process data. A **storage device** records and/or retrieves items to and from **storage media**. A **communications device** enables a computer to send and receive data, instructions, and information to and from one or more computers.

④ What Are the Advantages and Disadvantages of Using Computers?   Computers have the advantages of speed, reliability, consistency, storage, and communications. They perform operations at incredibly fast speeds, are dependable and reliable, consistently generate error-free results, can store enormous amounts of data, and can share processing with other computers. Disadvantages of computers relate to the violation of privacy, the impact on the labor force, health risks, and the impact on the environment.

connect   Visit scsite.com/dc2007/ch1/quiz or click the Quiz Yourself button. Click Objectives 1 – 4.

⑤ What Is the Purpose of a Network?   A **network** is a collection of computers and devices connected together via communications devices and transmission media. Networks allow computers to share *resources*, such as hardware, software, data, and information.

⑥ How Are the Internet and World Wide Web Used?   The **Internet** is a worldwide collection of networks that connects millions of businesses, government agencies, educational institutions, and individuals. People use the Internet to communicate with and meet other people, access news and information, shop for goods and services, bank and invest, take classes, for entertainment and leisure, download music, and share information. The **Web**, short for World Wide Web, is a global library of documents containing information that is available to anyone connected to the Internet.

⑦ How Is System Software Different from Application Software?   **Software**, also called a **program**, is a series of instructions that tells the computer what to do and how to do it. **System software** consists of the programs that control or maintain the operations of a computer and its devices. Two types of system software are the *operating system*, which coordinates activities among computer hardware devices, and *utility programs*, which perform maintenance-type tasks usually related to a computer, its devices, or its programs. **Application software** consists of programs that perform specific tasks for users. Popular application software includes Web browsers, word processing software, spreadsheet software, database software, and presentation graphics software.

connect   Visit scsite.com/dc2007/ch1/quiz or click the Quiz Yourself button. Click Objectives 5 – 7.

Chapter Review

⑧ What Are the Categories of Computers? Industry experts typically classify computers in seven categories: personal computers, mobile computers and mobile devices, game consoles, servers, mainframes, supercomputers, and embedded computers. A **personal computer** is a computer that can perform all of its input, processing, output, and storage activities by itself. A **mobile computer** is a personal computer that you can carry from place to place, and a **mobile device** is a computing device small enough to hold in your hand. A **game console** is a mobile computing device designed for single-player or multiplayer video games. A **server** controls access to the hardware, software, and other resources on a network and provides a centralized storage area for programs, data, and information. A **mainframe** is a large, expensive, powerful computer that can handle hundreds or thousands of connected users simultaneously and can store tremendous amounts of data, instructions, and information. A **supercomputer** is the fastest, most powerful, and most expensive computer and is used for applications requiring complex, sophisticated mathematical calculations. An **embedded computer** is a special-purpose computer that functions as a computer in a larger product.

⑨ What Are the Elements of an Information System? An *information system* combines hardware, software, data, people, and procedures to produce timely and useful information. People in an *information technology (IT) department* develop procedures for processing data. Following these procedures, people use hardware and software to enter the data into a computer. Software processes the data and directs the computer hardware to store changes on storage media and produce information in a desired form.

⑩ What Are the Types of Computer Users? Computer users can be separated into five categories: home users, small office/home office users, mobile users, large business users, and power users. A **home user** is a family member who uses a computer for a variety of reasons, such as budgeting and personal financial management, Web access, communications, and entertainment. A **small office/home office** (*SOHO*) user is a small company or self-employed individual who works from home. SOHO users access the Internet to look up information and use basic business software and sometimes industry-specific software. **Mobile users** are employees and students who work on a computer while away from a main office or school. A **power user** uses a workstation or other powerful computer to work with industry-specific software. Power users exist in all types of businesses. A **large business user** works in a company with many employees and uses a computer and computer network to process high volumes of transactions.

⑪ What Computer Applications Are Used in Society? People interact directly with computers in fields such as education, finance, government, health care, science, publishing, travel, and manufacturing. In education, students use computers and software to assist with learning or take distance learning classes. In finance, people use computers for **online banking** and **online investing**. Government offices have Web sites to provide citizens with up-to-date information, and government employees use computers as part of their daily routines. In health care, computers are used to maintain patient records, monitor patients, assist with medical tests and research, correspond with patients, file insurance claims, provide greater precision during operations, and as implants. All branches of science use computers to assist with collecting, analyzing, and modeling data and to communicate with colleagues around the world. Publishers use computers to assist in designing pages and make the content of their works available online. Many vehicles use some type of online navigation system to help people travel more quickly and safely. Manufacturers use **computer-aided manufacturing** (*CAM*) to assist with the manufacturing process.

connect
Visit scsite.com/dc2007/ch1/quiz or click the Quiz Yourself button. Click Objectives 8 – 11.

Key Terms

You should know the Primary Terms and be familiar with the Secondary Terms. Use the list below to help focus your study. To further enhance your understanding of the Key Terms in this chapter, visit scsite.com/dc2007/ch1/terms. See an example of and a definition for each term, and access current and additional information about the term from the Web.

Primary Terms

(shown in bold-black characters in the chapter)

application software (16)
communications device (9)
computer (6)
computer literacy (5)
computer-aided manufacturing (36)
data (6)
desktop computer (20)
embedded computer (24)
FAQ (6)
game console (22)
graphical user interface (GUI) (15)
handheld computer (21)
hardware (7)
home user (26)
information (6)
input device (7)
installing (17)
Internet (12)
Internet-enabled (21)
laptop computer (20)
large business user (30)
mainframe (23)
mobile computer (20)
mobile device (20)
mobile users (29)
network (11)
notebook computer (20)
online (11)
online banking (32)

online investing (33)
output device (8)
PDA (21)
personal computer (19)
photo sharing community (14)
power user (29)
program (15)
run (17)
server (23)
small office/home office (28)
smart phone (22)
software (15)
storage device (8)
storage media (8)
supercomputer (23)
system software (15)
system unit (8)
Tablet PC (21)
telecommuting (30)
user (9)
Web (12)
Web page (12)

Secondary Terms

(shown in italic characters in the chapter)

blog (14)
CAM (36)
convergence (22)
developer (18)
digital pen (21)
e-commerce (28)
enterprise computing (30)
execute (17)
gaming desktop computer (20)
garbage in, garbage out (10)
handhelds (22)
handtop computer (21)
icon (15)
information processing cycle (6)
information system (25)
information technology (IT) department (30)
instructions (6)
kiosk (30)
loads (17)
Media Center PC (20)
memory (8)
multimedia (29)
neural network (34)
operating system (15)
PC-compatible (19)
personal digital assistant (21)
podcast (14)
processor (8)
programmer (18)

publish (14)
resources (11)
SOHO (28)
stylus (21)
telematics (24)
telemedicine (34)
tower (20)
ultra personal computer (uPC) (21)
utility program (16)
Web cam (28)

Checkpoint

Use the Checkpoint exercises to check your knowledge level of the chapter. The Beyond the Book exercises will help broaden your understanding of the concepts presented in this chapter. To complete the Checkpoint exercises interactively, visit scsite.com/dc2007/ch1/check.

Label the Figure

Identify these common computer hardware components.

a. card reader/writer (storage)

b. CD/DVD drive (storage)

c. digital camera (input)

d. floppy disk drive (storage)

e. internal hard disk drive (storage)

f. keyboard (input)

g. microphone (input)

h. modem (communications)

i. monitor (output)

j. mouse (input)

k. PC video camera (input)

l. printer (output)

m. scanner (input)

n. speaker (output)

o. system unit (processor, memory, storage)

p. USB flash drive (storage)

q. external hard disk (storage)

True/False

Mark T for True and F for False. (See page numbers in parentheses.)

_____ 1. Many people believe that computer literacy is vital to success in today's world. (5)

_____ 2. Hardware consists of a series of instructions that tells the computer what to do and how to do it. (7)

_____ 3. The circuitry of the system unit usually is part of or is connected to a circuit board called the server. (8)

_____ 4. The computing phrase, garbage in, garbage out, points out that the accuracy of a computer's output depends on the accuracy of the input. (10)

_____ 5. A network is a collection of computers and devices connected together via communications devices and transmission media. (11)

_____ 6. Businesses, called access providers, offer users and companies access to the Internet free or for a fee. (12)

_____ 7. System software serves as the interface between the user, the application software, and the computer's hardware. (15)

_____ 8. Handheld computers never have keyboards. (21)

_____ 9. An information system consists of hardware, software, networks, and procedures. (25)

_____ 10. Home users type letters, homework assignments, and other documents with personal finance software. (27)

_____ 11. With online investing, the transaction fee for each trade usually is much more than when trading through a broker. (33)

Checkpoint

 **Multiple Choice**   Select the best answer. (See page numbers in parentheses.)

1. Computer literacy involves having a knowledge and understanding of _____. (5)
   a. computer programming
   b. computers and their uses
   c. computer repair
   d. all of the above

2. A computer can _____. (6)
   a. accept data
   b. process data according to specified rules
   c. produce and store results
   d. all of the above

3. The series of input, process, output, and storage sometimes is referred to as the _____ cycle. (6)
   a. information processing
   b. computer programming
   c. data entering
   d. Web browsing

4. Commonly used _____ devices are a keyboard, a mouse, and a microphone. (7)
   a. input
   b. storage
   c. output
   d. mobile

5. A disadvantage of computers is that _____. (10)
   a. computer operations occur at very slow speeds
   b. the components in computers are undependable
   c. prolonged computer use can lead to injuries
   d. most computers cannot communicate

6. A _____ controls access to the resources on a network. (11)
   a. server
   b. workstation
   c. client
   d. tower

7. _____ can be thought of as a library of information available to anyone connected to the Internet. (12)
   a. The Web
   b. E-mail
   c. Instant messaging
   d. A blog

8. Two types of _____ are desktop computers and notebook computers. (19)
   a. embedded computers
   b. supercomputers
   c. servers
   d. personal computers

9. A _____ is a special type of notebook computer that is useful for taking notes in lectures, at meetings, and other forums where the standard notebook computer is not practical. (21)
   a. smart phone
   b. Tablet PC
   c. game console
   d. PDA

10. A _____ is a mobile computing device designed for single-player or multiplayer video games. (22)
    a. Media Center PC
    b. gaming desktop computer
    c. game console
    d. mobile device

11. An information system should have readily available documented _____ that address(es) operating the computer and using its applications. (25)
    a. hardware
    b. procedures
    c. software
    d. data

12. Examples of the _____ category of computer users include engineers, scientists, architects, desktop publishers, and graphic artists. (29)
    a. mobile user
    b. large business user
    c. power user
    d. small office/home office user

13. When using _____, users access account balances, pay bills, and copy monthly transactions from a bank's computer right to their personal computers. (32)
    a. e-commerce
    b. personal finance software
    c. online banking
    d. accounting software

14. _____ is a system that attempts to imitate the behavior of the human brain. (34)
    a. Telemedicine
    b. A neural network
    c. E-commerce
    d. A kiosk

Checkpoint

 Matching   Match the terms with their definitions. (See page numbers in parentheses.)

_____ 1. processor (8)

_____ 2. memory (8)

_____ 3. publish (14)

_____ 4. install (17)

_____ 5. execute (17)

_____ 6. stylus (21)

_____ 7. game console (22)

_____ 8. Web cam (28)

_____ 9. multimedia (29)

_____ 10. kiosk (30)

a. stores instructions waiting to be executed and the data needed

b. carry out the instructions in a computer program

c. set up software to work with a computer and other hardware components

d. combines text, graphics, audio, and video into one application

e. video camera that displays its output on a Web page

f. collection of computers and devices connected together

g. mobile device that can connect to the Internet wirelessly

h. metal or plastic device that uses pressure to write, draw, or make selections

i. freestanding computer, usually with a touch screen

j. mobile computing device designed for single-player or multiplayer video games

k. interprets and carries out basic instructions that operate a computer

l. make a Web page available on the Internet for others to see

Short Answer   Write a brief answer to each of the following questions.

1. How is data different from information? _____ What is the information processing cycle? _____

2. How is hardware different from software? _____ What is a programmer? _____

3. Why do people use the Web? _____ What can be contained on a Web page? _____

4. What are seven categories of computers? _____ What determines how a computer is categorized? _____

5. What is telecommuting? _____ Why do people telecommute? _____

Beyond the Book   Read the following book elements, learn more about each using the Web, and then write a brief report.

1. Ethics & Issues — Who Is Responsible for Identity Theft? (10), Who Is Responsible for the Accuracy of Web Pages? (14), Is Computer Gaming More Good than Bad? (16), Does Internet Dating Really Work? (27)

2. Career Corner — Personal Computer Salesperson (37)

3. Companies on the Cutting Edge — Dell or Apple Computer (39)

4. FAQs (6, 8, 14, 17, 20, 22, 27, 36)

5. High-Tech Talk — Analog versus Digital: Making the Conversion (38)

6. Looking Ahead — Medical Breakthroughs with Computer Implants, Devices (9) or Robots Perform Mundane Tasks, Entertain (32)

7. Making Use of the Web — Fun and Entertainment (116)

8. Picture Yourself in a Computer Class (2)

9. Technology Trailblazers — Bill Gates or Anne Mulcahy (39)

10. Timeline 2007 (52)

11. Web Links (7, 8, 9, 12, 14, 16, 19, 22, 26, 36)

Learn It Online

Use the Learn It Online exercises to reinforce your understanding of the chapter concepts. To access the Learn It Online exercises, visit scsite.com/dc2007/ch1/learn.

① At the Movies — Walking the PC Pioneer Trail

To view the Walking the PC Pioneer Trail movie, click the number 1 button. Locate your video and click the corresponding High-Speed or Dial-Up link, depending on your Internet connection. Watch the movie and then complete the exercise by answering the question that follows. Many of the pioneers of the technology industry in the United States established their businesses in Silicon Valley. What explanation can you offer for why the founders of these companies all set up shop in this area?

② At the Movies — Black Viper's Windows XP Tips

To view the Black Viper's Windows XP Tips movie, click the number 2 button. Locate your video and click the corresponding High-Speed or Dial-Up link, depending on your Internet connection. Watch the movie and then complete the exercise by answering the question that follows. Windows XP is a large and powerful program that often runs many applications that you will never use. These programs require a lot of resources that can be used by other programs. Which of these programs would you turn off to make your computer run more efficiently and faster?

③ Student Edition Labs — Using Input Devices

Click the number 3 button. A new browser window will open, displaying the Student Edition Labs (screen shown in the figure below). Follow the on-screen instructions to complete the Using Input Devices Lab. When finished, click the Exit button. If required, submit your results to your instructor.

④ Student Edition Labs — Using Windows

Click the number 4 button. A new browser window will open, displaying the Student Edition Labs. Follow the on-screen instructions to complete the Using Windows Lab. When finished, click the Exit button. If required, submit your results to your instructor.

⑤ Practice Test

Click the number 5 button. Answer each question. When completed, enter your name and click the Grade Test button to submit the quiz for grading. Make a note of any missed questions. If required, submit your score to your instructor.

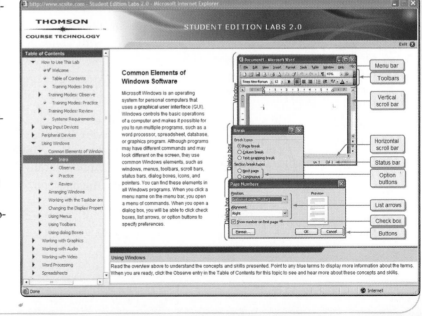

Learn It Online

⑥ Who Wants To Be a Computer Genius²?

Click the number 6 button to find out if you are a computer genius. Directions about how to play the game will be displayed. When you are ready to play, click the Play button. Submit your score to your instructor.

⑦ Wheel of Terms

Click the number 7 button to reinforce important terms you learned in this chapter by playing the Shelly Cashman Series version of this popular game. Directions about how to play the game will be displayed. When you are ready to play, click the Play button. Submit your score to your instructor.

⑧ DC Track and Field

Click the number 8 button to use what you have learned in this chapter to compete against other students in three track and field events. Directions about how to play the game will be displayed. When you are ready to play, click the start first event button. If required, submit your score to your instructor.

⑨ You're Hired!

Click the number 9 button to use what you have learned in this chapter to embark on the path to a career in computers. Directions about how to play the game will be displayed. When you are ready to play, click the begin game button. If required, submit your score to your instructor.

⑩ Crossword Puzzle Challenge

Click the number 10 button. Complete the puzzle to reinforce skills you learned in this chapter. Directions about how to play the game will be displayed. When you are ready to play, click the Play button. Submit the completed puzzle to your instructor.

⑪ Lab Exercises

Click the number 11 button. When the Lab Exercises menu appears, click the exercise assigned by your instructor. A new browser window will open. Follow the on-screen instructions to complete the exercise. When finished, click the Exit button. If required, submit your results to your instructor.

⑫ Learn the Web

No matter how much computer experience you have, navigating the Web for the first time can be intimidating. How do you get started? Click the number 12 button and click the links to discover how you can find out everything you want to know about the Internet.

⑬ Chapter Discussion Forum

Select an objective from this chapter on page 3 about which you would like more information. Click the number 13 button and post a short message listing a meaningful message title accompanied by one or more questions concerning the selected objective. In two days, return to the threaded discussion by clicking the number 13 button. Submit to your instructor your original message and at least one response to your message.

⑭ Google Maps

Click the number 14 button to learn how to locate businesses in your area, view a location's surroundings via satellite, and find directions from one location to another. Print a copy of the Google Maps page and then step through the exercise. If required, submit your results to your instructor.

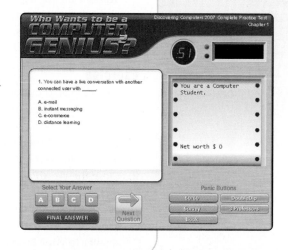

Learn How To

Use the Learn How To activities to learn fundamental skills when using a computer and accompanying technology. Complete the exercises and submit them to your instructor. To see a video of a Learn How To activity, visit scsite.com/dc2007/ch1/howto.

LEARN HOW TO 1: Start and Close an Application

An application accomplishes tasks on a computer. You can start any application by using the Start button.

Complete these steps to start the Web browser application called Internet Explorer:

1. Click the Start button ( ) at the left of the Windows taskbar on the bottom of the screen. *The Start menu is displayed.*

2. Point to All Programs on the Start menu. *The All Programs submenu appears (Figure 1-45).*

3. Click the program name, Internet Explorer, on the All Programs submenu. *The Internet Explorer browser window opens (Figure 1-46).*

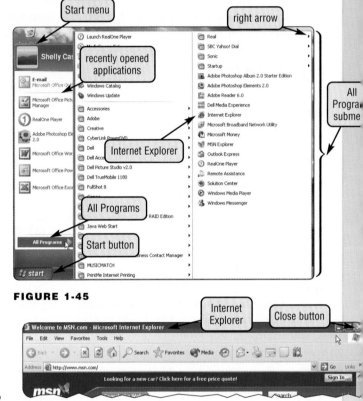

FIGURE 1-45

An item on the All Programs submenu might have a small right arrow next to it. When this occurs, point to the item and another submenu will appear. Click the application name on this submenu to start the application. Some application names might appear on the Start menu itself. If so, click any of these names to start the corresponding application.

FIGURE 1-46

Below the line on the left side of the Start menu, Windows displays the names of the applications recently opened on the computer. You can start any of these applications by clicking the name of the application.

To close an application, click the Close button (☒) in the upper-right corner of the window. If you have created but not saved a document, Windows will ask if you want to save the document. If you do not want to save it, click the No button in the displayed dialog box. If you want to save it, refer to Learn How To number 1 in Chapter 3 on page 178.

Exercise

1. Using the Start button, start the application named WordPad found on the Accessories submenu of the All Programs submenu. WordPad is a word processing application. Type the following: `To start an application, click the application name on the All Programs submenu` and then type your name. Click the Print button (🖨) on the toolbar. Submit the printout to your instructor.

2. Close the WordPad application. If you are asked if you want to save changes to the document, click the No button. Start the WordPad application again, type some new text, and then close the WordPad application. When the dialog box is displayed, click the Cancel button. What happened? Now, close the WordPad window without saving the document. Submit your answer to your instructor.

Learn How To

3. Using the Start button, start the e-mail program on the computer. What is the name of the e-mail program? In the program window, what menu names are displayed on the menu bar at the top of the window? Close the e-mail program. Submit your answers to your instructor.

LEARN HOW TO 2: Use the Discovering Computers 2007 Online Companion (scsite.com/dc2007)

The Discovering Computers 2007 Online Companion provides a variety of activities and exercises. To use the site, you first must register and establish a user name and password. Perform the following steps to register:

1. Start the Web browser.
2. Type `scsite.com/dc2007` in the Address box of the Web browser. Press the ENTER key.
3. When the registration page is displayed, click the New User Registration link.
4. Follow the on-screen instructions to complete registration.

When you first type a Web address to display a page from the dc2007 site, you must enter your user name and password to gain access to the site. When you are done using the site, close the browser so no one else can visit the site with your user name and password.

Exercise

1. Start the Web browser on your computer.
2. Type `scsite.com/dc2007/ch1/howto` in the Address box of the browser and then press the ENTER key.
3. If the registration page is displayed and you have not yet registered, complete the steps above. If you are registered, enter your user name and password, and then click the Enter button.
4. Navigate to the Chapter 1 home page.
5. Visit each of the Exercises Web pages (Case Studies, Chapter Review, Checkpoint, Key Terms, Learn How To, Learn It Online, and Web Research). Use the navigation bar on the left of the screen to display these pages.
6. Click the browser's Close button to close the application.
7. Write a report that describes the use of each of the Exercises pages you visited. Which page do you think will prove the most valuable to you when using the book and the Web site? Why? Which will be the least useful? Why? Submit your report to your instructor.

LEARN HOW TO 3: Find Out About Your Computer

By following these steps, you can find out about your computer:

1. Click the Start button on the Windows XP taskbar.
2. Point to All Programs on the Start menu, point to Accessories on the All Programs submenu, and then point to System Tools on the Accessories submenu.
3. Click System Information on the System Tools submenu. Windows displays a system summary in the right side of the window, and an index of categories in the left side of the window (Figure 1-47).

To determine more information about your computer, click any of the plus signs in the left side of the window. Then, click the item about which you want more information.

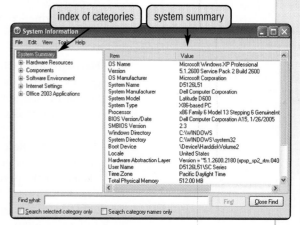

FIGURE 1-47

Exercise

1. Submit the answers to the following questions about your computer:
   a. What type of operating system (OS Name) is in use?
   b. What company manufactured the computer?
   c. How much RAM (physical memory) is on the computer?
   d. How much data can you store on the C: drive?
   e. What is the name of a CD or DVD drive found on the computer?

Web Research

Use the Internet-based Web Research exercises to broaden your understanding of the concepts presented in this chapter. Visit scsite.com/dc2007/ch1/research to obtain more information pertaining to each exercise. To discuss any of the Web Research exercises in this chapter with other students, post your thoughts or questions at scsite.com/dc2007/ch1/forum.

① Scavenger Hunt   Use one of the <u>search engines</u> listed in Figure 2-10 in Chapter 2 on page 78 or your own favorite search engine to find the answers to the questions below. Copy and paste the Web address from the Web page where you found the answer. Some questions may have more than one answer. If required, submit your answers to your instructor. (1) What are three accredited online colleges or universities that offer a bachelor's degree in computer information technology? (2) Two National Science Foundation (NSF) programs were established in 1997 to interconnect 50 university and scientific computing sites. What colleges host these two sites? What were the locations of the five original NSF-financed supercomputer centers? (3) Personal finance software helps you balance your checkbook and manage your finances. What is the name of a popular personal finance software program? (4) What is the name of the first spreadsheet program? (5) A programming language developed by the U.S. Department of Defense was named to honor a famous woman mathematician. What is the name of this programming language?

② Search Sleuth   Visit the **<u>Google Web site</u>** (google.com) and then click the About Google link at the bottom of the page. Using your word processing program, answer the following questions and then, if required, submit your answers to your instructor. (1) Below Our Company, click Corporate Info. Who are the founders of Google? (2) Click the Technology link on the left side of the page. Provide a summary on the steps Google takes to complete a query. (3) Click your browser's Back button twice or press the BACKSPACE key two times to return to the About Google page. Below Our Search, click the Google Web Search Features link. How is Google including books in its search results? What are some of Google's newest features? What weather information is available? (4) Click your browser's Back button two times to return to the Google home page. In the Google Search text box, type `computer` and click the Google Search button. Approximately how many hits resulted? Do any definitions appear? If so, list the definitions. How much time did it take to complete the search? (5) In the Google Search text box, type `personal computer` and click the Search button. Compare this to your earlier search. Are there more or fewer hits? How much time did it take to complete the second search? (6) Click one of the resulting personal computer links and review the information. Write a 50-word summary. Using the information contained within the Web site, do you think you have sufficient knowledge to purchase a computer intelligently?

③ Newsgroups   One of the more popular topics for **<u>newsgroups</u>** is the Internet. Find three newsgroups, such as those listed in CyberFiber (cyberfiber.com/internet.htm) or Google Groups, that discuss an aspect of the Internet. Read the newsgroup postings and post a reply to one message. Summarize three topics under discussion and your reply to a message.

④ Journaling   Respond to your readings in this chapter by writing at least one page about your reactions, evaluations, and reflections about computer usage in your school. For example, how many students have high-speed <u>Internet</u> access at home or in on-campus housing? Are students without this Internet access at a disadvantage for completing homework assignments and research papers? Do electronic materials in the classroom get students more engaged in learning? You also can write about the new terms you learned by reading this chapter. If required, submit your journal to your instructor.

⑤ Ethics in Action   The Internet has increased the ease with which students can plagiarize material for research paper assignments. Teachers are using online services, such as Turnitin.com, to help detect plagiarized papers and to help students understand how to cite sources correctly. Visit the **<u>Turnitin site</u>** (turnitin.com) and then write a summary of how this service is used. How prevalent is plagiarism on your campus? What action should an instructor take when a student submits a plagiarized paper? If required, submit your summary to your instructor.

Case Studies

Use the Case Studies to apply the concepts presented in the chapter to real-world situations. Visit scsite.com/dc2007/ch1/cases to obtain more information pertaining to each exercise. To discuss the Case Studies in this chapter with other students, visit scsite.com/dc2007/ch1/forum and post your thoughts or questions.

CASE STUDY 1 — Class Discussion   You are the assistant parts manager for a local car dealership. Your dealership sells cars from two different manufacturers. Your responsibilities include checking inventory, obtaining pricing and picking up parts from local auto parts stores, and performing miscellaneous tasks at the dealership. Eventually, you would like to be promoted to parts manager. The owner has just purchased a new computer for the parts department. He has told you that, in order to be promoted, you must become proficient in the use of computers and <u>computer software</u>. Review the computer courses offered at your school. Prepare a list of courses that you feel would help you acquire the computer proficiency required for you to be promoted. Draft a letter to the owner detailing your course choices and explaining why each course would be beneficial. Be prepared to discuss your findings.

CASE STUDY 2 — Class Discussion   You are a member of your local school district's board of education. Over the past year, the number of computers purchased by the district increased by 85 percent, while the supply of library books declined by almost 10 percent. School officials claim that computers extend learning opportunities and develop the <u>computer literacy</u> needed in today's technological world. Yet, some parents are complaining that computer purchases represent frivolous, status-seeking spending. Notebook computers are purchased for teachers, while textbooks and library books are too old, too worn, and too scarce. Use the Web and/or print media to learn how computers are being used in schools. As a school board member, draft a proposal recommending the percentage of the instructional materials budget that should be spent on computers versus the percentage that should be spent on library books and textbooks. Note the factors that influenced your decision. Be prepared to discuss your recommendations.

CASE STUDY 3 — Research   Computers are everywhere. Watching television, driving a car, using a charge card, even ordering fast food all involve computers, not to mention browsing the Web on your personal computer. Your car computer is an <u>embedded computer</u> that can be described as special-purpose, because it only accepts specific input and performs limited functions. Your personal computer, on the other hand, is general-purpose, meaning it accepts a wide range of input and can perform a variety of tasks. For one day, make a list of each computer you encounter (be careful not to limit your-self just to the computers you see). How is the computer used? Is the computer special-purpose or general-purpose? Why? How was the task the computer performs accomplished before computers? Write a brief report or use PowerPoint to create a presentation and share your findings.

CASE STUDY 4 — Research   You are an assistant manager at a local computer store. Your manager suspects that for cultural, financial, or societal reasons, certain groups of people are more likely to buy computers than others. To increase the impact of the store's promotions, your manager has asked you to discover if computers are purchased by individuals from a broad spectrum, or if a certain type exists that represents most <u>computer buyers</u>. Use the Web and/or print media to learn more about the demographics of computer buyers. What gender are most buyers? In what age range do they fall? What seems to be the typical educa-tional level? What is the approximate average income of a typical buyer? Do buyers tend to share any other characteristics? If you discover any trends, what reasons might be behind the results? Write a brief report or use PowerPoint to create a presentation and share your findings.

CASE STUDY 5 — Team Challenge   People use computers in a variety of fields, including education, finance, government, health care, science, publishing, travel, and manufacturing. Although the way people use computers varies, each use of a computer involves <u>computer hardware</u>, computer software, and normally some type of communications capability over networks, such as the Internet. Form a three-member team and choose a field in which you all are inter-ested. Using the Web and/or print media, assign one member of your team to investigate hardware used in the field, another member to investigate software used in the field, and the third member to investigate communications capabili-ties used in the field. After your investigation, characterize a hypothetical business or organization in the field. Based on your investigation, prepare a report that recommends specific hardware, software, and networking capabilities that would be best for the business or organization; explain your recommendations in the report.

Special Feature

Timeline 2007

MILESTONES IN COMPUTER HISTORY

Dr. John V. Atanasoff and Clifford Berry design and build the first electronic digital computer. Their machine, the Atanasoff-Berry-Computer, or ABC, provides the foundation for advances in electronic digital computers.

John von Neumann in front of the electronic computer built at the Institute for Advanced Study. This computer and its von Neumann architecture served as the prototype for subsequent stored program computers worldwide.

William Shockley, John Bardeen, and Walter Brattain invent the transfer resistance device, eventually called the transistor. The transistor would revolutionize computers, proving much more reliable than vacuum tubes.

1937 — 1943 — 1945 — 1946 — 1947 — 1951

During World War II, British scientist Alan Turing designs the Colossus, an electronic computer created for the military to break German codes. The computer's existence is kept secret until the 1970s.

Dr. John W. Mauchly and J. Presper Eckert, Jr. complete work on the first large-scale electronic, general-purpose digital computer. The ENIAC (Electronic Numerical Integrator And Computer) weighs 30 tons, contains 18,000 vacuum tubes, occupies a 30 × 50 foot space, and consumes 160 kilowatts of power. The first time it is turned on, lights dim in an entire section of Philadelphia.

The first commercially available electronic digital computer, the UNIVAC I (UNIVersal Automatic Computer), is introduced by Remington Rand. Public awareness of computers increases when the UNIVAC I, after analyzing only five percent of the popular vote, correctly predicts that Dwight D. Eisenhower will win the presidential election.

Dr. Grace Hopper considers the concept of reusable software in her paper, "The Education of a Computer." The paper describes how to program a computer with symbolic notation instead of the detailed machine language that had been used.

The IBM 305 RAMAC system is the first to use magnetic disk for external storage. The system provides storage capacity similar to magnetic tape that previously was used, but offers the advantage of semi-random access capability.

More than 200 programming languages have been created.

IBM introduces two smaller, desk-sized computers: the IBM 1401 for business and the IBM 1620 for scientists. The IBM 1620 initially is called the CADET, but IBM drops the name when campus wags claim it is an acronym for, Can't Add, Doesn't Even Try.

Fortran (FORmula TRANslation), an efficient, easy-to-use programming language, is introduced by John Backus.

1952　1953　1957　1958　1959　1960

The IBM model 650 is one of the first widely used computers. Originally planning to produce only 50 machines, the system is so successful that eventually IBM manufactures more than 1,000. With the IBM 700 series of machines, the company will dominate the mainframe market for the next decade.

Core memory, developed in the early 1950s, provides much larger storage capacity than vacuum tube memory.

Jack Kilby of Texas Instruments invents the integrated circuit, which lays the foundation for high-speed computers and large-capacity memories. Computers built with transistors mark the beginning of the second generation of computer hardware.

COBOL, a high-level business application language, is developed by a committee headed by Dr. Grace Hopper. COBOL uses English-like phrases and runs on most business computers, making it one of the more widely used programming languages.

Special Feature

scsite.com/dc2007/ch1/timeline

Dr. John Kemeny of Dartmouth leads the development of the BASIC programming language. BASIC will be widely used on personal computers.

Computer Science Corporation becomes the first software company listed on the New York Stock Exchange.

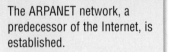

Under pressure from the industry, IBM announces that some of its software will be priced separately from the computer hardware. This unbundling allows software firms to emerge in the industry.

Digital Equipment Corporation (DEC) introduces the first minicomputer, the PDP-8. The machine is used extensively as an interface for time-sharing systems.

In a letter to the editor titled, "GO TO Statements Considered Harmful," Dr. Edsger Dijsktra introduces the concept of structured programming, developing standards for constructing computer programs.

The ARPANET network, a predecessor of the Internet, is established.

1964   1965   1968   1969   1970

The number of computers has grown to 18,000. Third-generation computers, with their controlling circuitry stored on chips, are introduced. The IBM System/360 computer is the first family of compatible machines, merging science and business lines.

Alan Shugart at IBM demonstrates the first regular use of an 8-inch floppy (magnetic storage) disk.

Fourth-generation computers, built with chips that use LSI (large-scale integration) arrive. While the chips used in 1965 contained as many as 1,000 circuits, the LSI chip contains as many as 15,000.

IBM introduces the term word processing for the first time with its Magnetic Tape/Selectric Typewriter (MT/ST). The MT/ST was the first reusable storage medium that allowed typed material to be edited without having to retype the document.

MITS, Inc. advertises one of the first microcomputers, the Altair. Named for the destination in an episode of *Star Trek*, the Altair is sold in kits for less than $400. Although initially it has no keyboard, no monitor, no permanent memory, and no software, 4,000 orders are taken within the first three months.

VisiCalc, a spreadsheet program written by Bob Frankston and Dan Bricklin, is introduced. Originally written to run on Apple II computers, VisiCalc will be seen as the most important reason for the acceptance of personal computers in the business world.

The IBM PC is introduced, signaling IBM's entrance into the personal computer marketplace. The IBM PC quickly garners the largest share of the personal computer market and becomes the personal computer of choice in business.

Ethernet, the first local area network (LAN), is developed at Xerox PARC (Palo Alto Research Center) by Robert Metcalf. The LAN allows computers to communicate and share software, data, and peripherals. Initially designed to link minicomputers, Ethernet will be extended to personal computers.

The first public online information services, CompuServe and the Source, are founded.

1971	1975	1976	1979	1980	1981

Dr. Ted Hoff of Intel Corporation develops a microprocessor, or microprogrammable computer chip, the Intel 4004.

IBM offers Microsoft Corporation cofounder, Bill Gates, the opportunity to develop the operating system for the soon-to-be announced IBM personal computer. With the development of MS-DOS, Microsoft achieves tremendous growth and success.

The first computer virus, Elk Cloner, is spread via Apple II floppy disks, which contained the operating system. A short rhyme would appear on the screen when the user pressed Reset after the 50th boot of an infected disk.

Steve Jobs and Steve Wozniak build the first Apple computer. A subsequent version, the Apple II, is an immediate success. Adopted by elementary schools, high schools, and colleges, for many students, the Apple II is their first contact with the world of computers.

Alan Shugart presents the Winchester hard drive, revolutionizing storage for personal computers.

Special Feature

3.275 Million

3,275,000 personal computers are sold, almost 3,000,000 more than in 1981.

COMPAQ

Compaq, Inc. is founded to develop and market IBM-compatible PCs.

Hayes introduces the 300 bps smart modem. The modem is an immediate success.

Apple introduces the Macintosh computer, which incorporates a unique, easy-to-learn, graphical user interface.

Hewlett-Packard announces the first LaserJet printer for personal computers.

Microsoft

Microsoft has public stock offering and raises approximately $61 million. Within 20 years, Microsoft's stock is worth nearly $350 billion or 5,735 times the amount raised in the initial public stock offering.

1982 — 1983 — 1984 — 1986 — 1988

Instead of choosing a person for its annual award, *TIME* magazine names the computer Machine of the Year for 1982, acknowledging the impact of computers on society.

Lotus Development Corporation is founded. Its spreadsheet software, Lotus 1-2-3, which combines spreadsheet, graphics, and database programs in one package, becomes the best-selling program for IBM personal computers.

Microsoft surpasses Lotus Development Corporation to become the world's top software vendor.

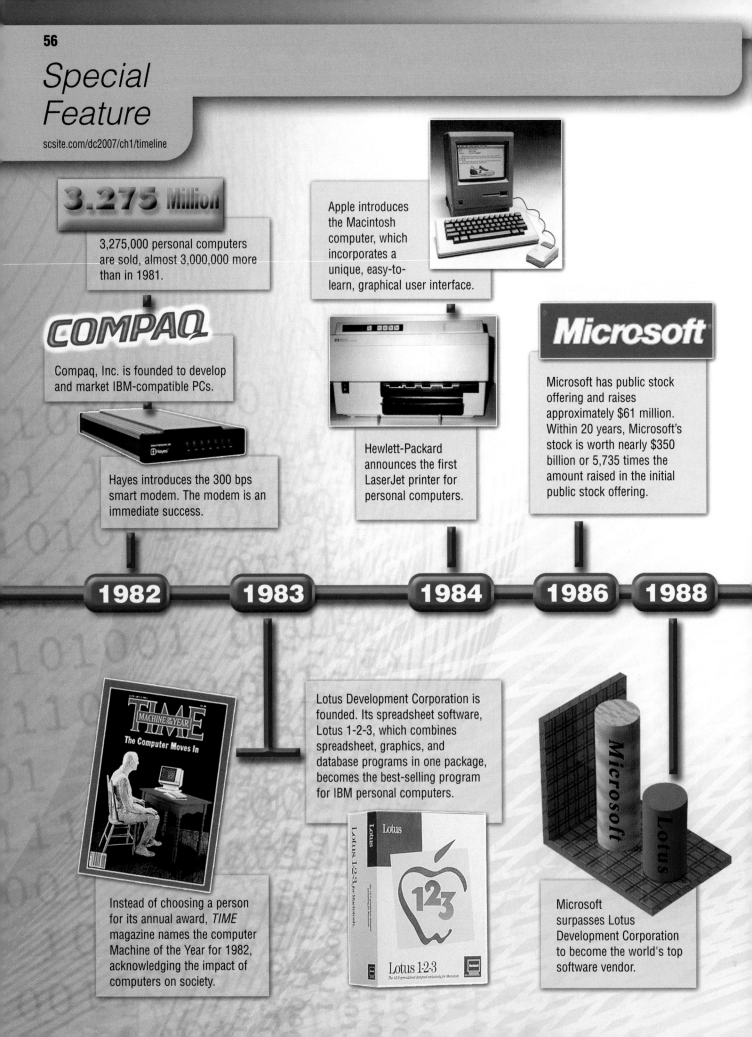

While working at CERN, Switzerland, Tim Berners-Lee invents an Internet-based hypermedia enterprise for information sharing. Berners-Lee will call this innovation the World Wide Web.

World Wide Web Consortium releases standards that describe a framework for linking documents on different computers.

Several companies introduce computers using the Pentium processor from Intel. The Pentium chip is the successor to the Intel 486 processor. It contains 3.1 million transistors and is capable of performing 112,000,000 instructions per second.

Microsoft releases Microsoft Office 3 Professional, the first version of Microsoft Office.

1989   1991   1992   1993

The Intel 486 becomes the world's first 1,000,000 transistor microprocessor. It crams 1.2 million transistors on a .4" x .6" sliver of silicon and executes 15,000,000 instructions per second — four times as fast as its predecessor, the 80386 chip.

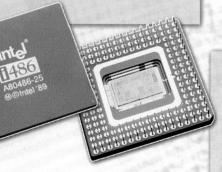

Microsoft releases Windows 3.1, the latest version of its Windows operating system. Windows 3.1 offers improvements such as TrueType fonts, multimedia capability, and object linking and embedding (OLE). In two months, 3,000,000 copies of Windows 3.1 are sold.

The White House launches its Web site, which includes an interactive citizens' handbook and White House history and tours.

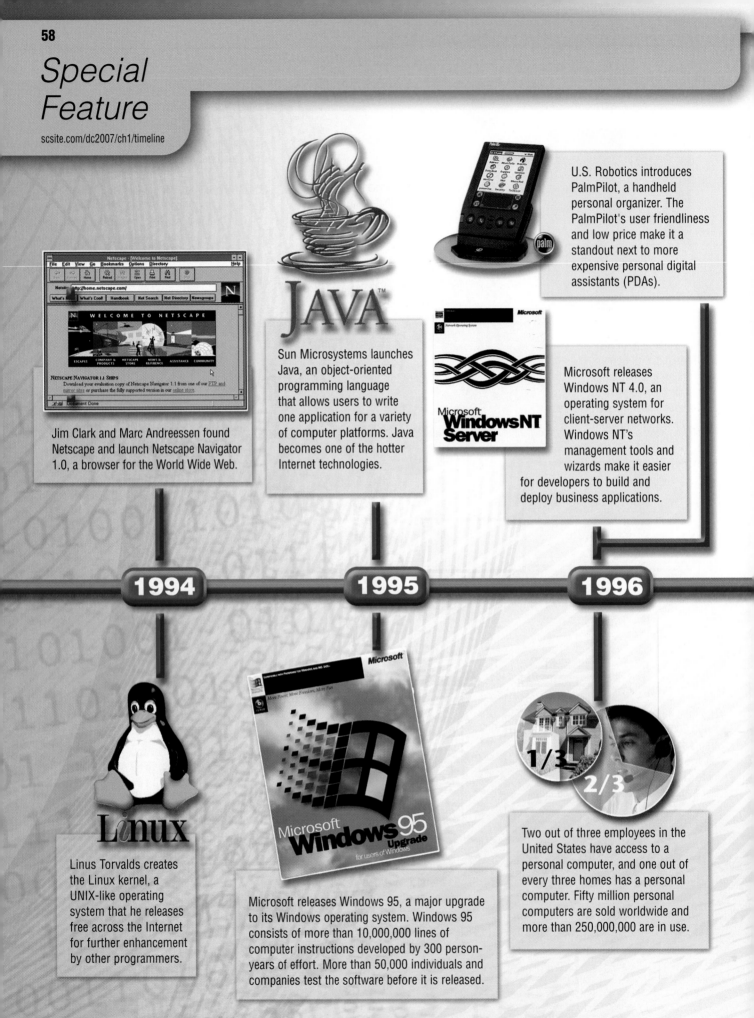

U.S. Robotics introduces PalmPilot, a handheld personal organizer. The PalmPilot's user friendliness and low price make it a standout next to more expensive personal digital assistants (PDAs).

JAVA™

Sun Microsystems launches Java, an object-oriented programming language that allows users to write one application for a variety of computer platforms. Java becomes one of the hotter Internet technologies.

Jim Clark and Marc Andreessen found Netscape and launch Netscape Navigator 1.0, a browser for the World Wide Web.

Microsoft
Windows NT Server

Microsoft releases Windows NT 4.0, an operating system for client-server networks. Windows NT's management tools and wizards make it easier for developers to build and deploy business applications.

1994   **1995**   **1996**

Linux

Linus Torvalds creates the Linux kernel, a UNIX-like operating system that he releases free across the Internet for further enhancement by other programmers.

Microsoft
Windows 95 Upgrade
for users of Windows

Microsoft releases Windows 95, a major upgrade to its Windows operating system. Windows 95 consists of more than 10,000,000 lines of computer instructions developed by 300 person-years of effort. More than 50,000 individuals and companies test the software before it is released.

1/3 2/3

Two out of three employees in the United States have access to a personal computer, and one out of every three homes has a personal computer. Fifty million personal computers are sold worldwide and more than 250,000,000 are in use.

Apple and Microsoft sign a joint technology development agreement. Microsoft buys $150,000,000 of Apple stock.

More than 10,000,000 people take up telecommuting, which is the capability of working at home and communicating with an office via computer. Increasingly more firms embrace telecommuting to help increase productivity, reduce absenteeism, and provide greater job satisfaction.

DVD, the next generation of optical disc storage technology, is introduced. DVD can store computer, audio, and video data in a single format, with the capability of producing near-studio quality. By year's end, 500,000 DVD players are shipped worldwide.

Apple Computer introduces the iMac, the next version of its popular Macintosh computer. The iMac abandons such conventional features as a floppy disk drive but wins customers with its futuristic design, see-through case, and easy setup. Consumer demand outstrips Apple's production capabilities, and some vendors are forced to begin waiting lists.

1997

1998

Intel introduces the Pentium II processor with 7.5 million transistors. The new processor, which incorporates MMX technology, processes video, audio, and graphics data more efficiently and supports applications such as movie editing, gaming, and more.

E-commerce, or electronic commerce — the marketing of goods and services over the Internet — booms. Companies such as Dell, E*TRADE, and Amazon.com spur online shopping, allowing buyers to obtain everything from hardware and software to financial and travel services, insurance, automobiles, books, and more.

Microsoft releases Internet Explorer 4.0 and seizes a key place in the Internet arena. This new Web browser is greeted with tremendous customer demand.

Microsoft ships Windows 98, an upgrade to Windows 95. Windows 98 offers improved Internet access, better system performance, and support for a new generation of hardware and software. In six months, more than 10,000,000 copies of Windows 98 are sold worldwide.

Fifty million users are connected to the Internet and World Wide Web.

Governments and businesses frantically work to make their computers Y2K (Year 2000) compliant, spending more than $500 billion worldwide. Y2K non-compliant computers cannot distinguish whether 01/01/00 refers to 1900 or 2000, and thus may operate using a wrong date. This Y2K bug can affect any application that relies on computer chips, such as ATMs, airplanes, energy companies, and the telephone system. In the end, the Y2K bug turned out not to be a problem.

Shawn Fanning, 19, and his company, Napster, turn the music industry upside down by developing software that allows computer users to swap music files with one another without going through a centralized file server. The Recording Industry of America, on behalf of five media companies, sues Napster for copyright infringement and wins.

U.S. District Judge Thomas Penfield Jackson rules in the antitrust lawsuit brought by the Department of Justice and 19 states that Microsoft used its monopoly power to stifle competition.

1999

2000

Microsoft introduces Office 2000, its premier productivity suite, offering new tools for users to create content and save it directly to a Web site without any file conversion or special steps.

E-commerce achieves mainstream acceptance. Annual e-commerce sales exceed $100 billion, and Internet advertising expenditures reach more than $5 billion.

Open Source Code software, such as the Linux operating system and the Apache Web server created by unpaid volunteers, begin to gain wide acceptance among computer users.

Dot-com companies (Internet based) go out of business at a record pace — nearly one per day — as financial investors withhold funding due to the companies' unprofitability.

Microsoft ships Windows 2000 and Windows Me. Windows 2000 offers improved behind-the-scene security and reliability. Windows Me is designed for home users and lets them edit home movies, share digital photos, index music, and create a home network.

Intel unveils its Pentium 4 chip with clock speeds starting at 1.4 GHz. The Pentium 4 includes 42 million transistors, nearly twice as many contained on its predecessor, the Pentium III.

Microsoft releases major operating system updates with Windows XP for the desktop and servers, and Pocket PC 2002 for handheld computers. Windows XP is significantly more reliable than previous versions, features a 32-bit computing architecture, and offers a new look and feel. Pocket PC 2002 offers the handheld computer user a familiar Windows interface and consistent functionality.

According to the U.S. Department of Commerce, Internet traffic is doubling every 100 days, resulting in an annual growth rate of more than 700 percent. It has taken radio and television 30 years and 15 years, respectively, to reach 60 million people. The Internet has achieved the same audience base in 3 years.

2000

2001

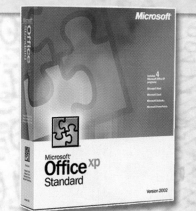

Telemedicine uses satellite technology and videoconferencing to broadcast consultations and to perform distant surgeries. Robots are used for complex and precise tasks. Computer-aided surgery uses virtual reality to assist with training and planning procedures.

Microsoft introduces Office XP, the next version of the world's leading suite of productivity software. Features include speech and handwriting recognition, smart tags, and task panes.

Avid readers enjoy e-books, which are digital texts read on compact computer screens. E-books can hold the equivalent of 10 traditional books containing text and graphics. Readers can search, highlight text, and add notes.

Special Feature

After several years of negligible sales, the Tablet PC is reintroduced as the next-generation mobile PC. The lightweight device, the size of a three-ring notebook, is ideal for people on the go.

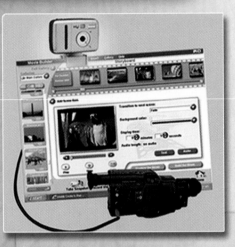

Digital video cameras, DVD writers, easy-to-use video editing software, and improvements in storage capabilities allow the average computer user to create Hollywood-like videos with introductions, conclusions, scenes rearranged, music, and voice-over.

Wireless computers and devices, such as keyboards, mouse devices, home networks, and public Internet access points become commonplace. Latest operating systems include support for both the Wi-Fi (wireless fidelity) and Bluetooth standards. Wireless capabilities are standard on many PDAs and Tablet PCs.

2002

2003

Microsoft .net

Microsoft launches its .NET strategy, which is a new environment for developing and running software applications featuring ease of development of Web-based services.

Microsoft ships Office 2003, the latest version of its flagship Office suite. More than 400 million people in 175 nations and 70 languages are using a version of Office.

DVD writers begin to replace CD writers (CD-RW). DVDs can store up to eight times as much data as CDs. Uses include storing home movies, music, photos, and backups.

Intel ships its revamped Pentium 4 chip with the 0.13 micron processor and Hyper-Threading (HT) Technology, operating at speeds of 3.06 GHz. This new development eventually will enable processors with a billion transistors to operate at 20 GHz.

In an attempt to maintain their current business model of selling songs, the Recording Industry Association of American (RIAA) files over 250 lawsuits against individual computer users who offer copyrighted music over peer-to-peer networks.

Flat-panel LCD monitors overtake bulky CRT monitors as the popular choice of computer users. Although flat-panel LCD monitors cost more, they offer several advantages including physical size, weight, true display size, better power consumption, and no radiation emission.

Companies such as RealNetworks, Microsoft, Sony, and Wal-Mart stake out turf in the online music store business started by Apple Computer. In the previous year, Apple's iTunes Music Store Web site sold nearly 20 million songs for 99 cents each.

USB flash drives, which are small enough to fit on a key chain but can store up to 4 billion characters, become a cost-effective way to transport data and information from one computer to another.

2004

Linux, the open-source operating system, makes major inroads into the server market as a viable alternative to Microsoft Windows, Sun's Solaris, and the UNIX operating systems.

Major retailers begin requiring suppliers to include radio frequency identification (RFID) tags or microchips with antennas, which can be as small as 1/3 of a millimeter across, in the goods they sell. When a transponder receives a certain radio query, it responds by transmitting its unique ID code. Besides carrying out the functions of the bar code, RFIDs may eventually eliminate long checkout lines.

Apple Computer introduces the sleek iMac G5. The new computer's display device contains the system unit.

106 million, or 53 percent, of the 200 million online population in America accesses the Internet via speedy broadband.

GERRY WEBER

Linux

Special Feature

scsite.com/dc2007/ch1/timeline

Microsoft
Windows^XP
Media Center Edition 2005

Spyware
Spam Pharming
Phishing
Spim Spit

The Mozilla Foundation, the creator of the free open source Firefox browser, claims to have captured 10 percent of the browser market, primarily at the expense of Microsoft's Internet Explorer (IE) browser.

Microsoft unveils Windows XP Media Center Edition 2005. This operating system allows users to access the routine capabilities of a Windows XP-based PC while focusing on delivering media content such as music, digital photography, movies, and television.

Spam, spyware, phishing, pharming, spim, and spit take center stage, along with viruses, as major nuisances to the 801 million computer users worldwide.

iPod the Video-Pod

Blogging
Podcasting

Blogging and podcasting become mainstream methods for distributing information via the Web.

Apple releases the latest version of its popular pocket-sized iPod audio player. First it played songs, then photos, then podcasts, and now, in addition, up to 150 hours of music videos and TV shows on a 2.5" color display.

2005

The smart phone overtakes the PDA as the personal mobile device of choice. A smart phone offers the user a cellular phone, full personal information management and e-mail functionality, a Web browser, instant message capabilities, and even the ability to listen to music, play video and games, and take pictures with its built-in camera.

Xbox360

Microsoft introduces Visual Studio 2005. The product includes Visual Basic, Visual C#, Visual J#, Visual C++, and SQL Server. Microsoft also releases a Visual Studio 2005 Express Edition for hobbyists, students, and nonprofessionals.

Microsoft releases the Xbox 360, its latest game console. Features include the capability to play music, display photos, and network with computers and other Xbox games.

Microsoft
Visual Studio 2005

IBM produces the fastest supercomputer called Blue Gene/L. It can perform approximately 28 trillion calculations in the time it takes you to blink your eye, or about one-tenth of a second. The Blue Gene/L primarily is used to explore hydrodynamics, quantum chemistry, molecular dynamics, climate modeling, and financial modeling.

Sony launches its PlayStation 3 and Nintendo launches its Revolution. Sony won the previous numbers games with worldwide sales of 90 million PlayStation 2 consoles to Microsoft's 24 million Xbox consoles and Nintendo's 21 million GameCube consoles.

Municipalities across the United States begin deploying low-cost, high-speed, broadband wireless connectivity to all points within their jurisdiction. Citizens access the Internet at broadband speeds using wireless desktop computers, notebook computers or handheld devices to connect to Wi-Fi access points. Some municipalities see the deployment of wireless networks as a way to bridge the digital divide.

Microsoft® Office

Microsoft releases the latest version of its flagship Office suite. New features include the most significant update to the user interface in more than a decade and the capability to save documents in XML and PDF formats.

2006

Windows Vista™

Microsoft ships the latest version of its widely used operating system, Windows Vista™. Windows Vista focuses on greatly improving security, deployment, manageability, and performance. Included with Windows Vista is a new version of the world's most popular Web browser, Internet Explorer 7. New features of the browser include advancements in security and enhanced browsing for end users.

Apple begins selling Macintosh computers with Intel microprocessors.

An IBM virtual supercomputer project, called the World Community Grid, links nearly 100,000 personal computers worldwide. The grid, designed to accommodate up to 10 million computers, is made up of personal computers whose owners volunteered their use when the computers otherwise would be sitting idle. The supercomputer is used to create a scientific database available to researchers around the world. The next project for this powerful grid is to maintain an up-to-date HIV/AIDS database as the virus evolves into drug-resistant forms.

CHAPTER TWO

The Internet and World Wide Web

Picture Yourself Instant Messaging

While eating popcorn and waiting for the movie to begin, you hear an alarm. Did you forget to turn off your smart phone? You look at the phone and notice that a friend is sending you an instant message from his home computer. With a few minutes until the lights dim in the theater, you open the message. At that moment, a chorus of your friends' voices singing "Happy Birthday" loudly plays through the phone while the same words appear on the phone's screen. Quickly, you turn off the phone's sound and look around — hoping no one heard. No such luck. Nearly everyone in the theater found it quite amusing.

With the phone's sound turned off, you press some buttons to reply to the instant message, thanking your musical friends for their greeting. Your friend replies that he just bought a PC video camera and wanted to try sending a video instant message over his high-speed Internet line. Everyone gathered at his house to sing and send you the message. After conversing for a few minutes, you punch in CU later on the phone and set your online status to Away — so everyone knows you will be unavailable. Then, you press another button to display the Cubs score and the weather report. Next, you decide to check e-mail messages. The movie is starting . . . time to disconnect from the Internet.

To learn how technology allows you access to your friends, sports scores, weather reports, and e-mail, read Chapter 2 and discover features of the Internet and World Wide Web.

OBJECTIVES

After completing this chapter, you will be able to:

1. Discuss the history of the Internet
2. Explain how to access and connect to the Internet
3. Analyze an IP address
4. Identify the components of a Web address
5. Explain the purpose of a Web browser
6. Search for information on the Web
7. Describe the types of Web sites
8. Recognize how Web pages use graphics, animation, audio, video, virtual reality, and plug-ins
9. Identify the steps required for Web publishing
10. Describe the types of e-commerce
11. Explain how e-mail, FTP, newsgroups and message boards, mailing lists, chat rooms, instant messaging, and Internet telephony work
12. Identify the rules of netiquette

CONTENTS

THE INTERNET

One of the major reasons business, home, and other users purchase computers is for Internet access. Through the Internet, society has access to global information and instant communications. Further, access to the Internet can occur anytime from a computer anywhere: at home, at work, at school, in a restaurant, on an airplane, and even at the beach.

The **Internet**, also called the *Net*, is a worldwide collection of networks that links millions of businesses, government agencies, educational institutions, and individuals. Each of the networks on the Internet provides resources that add to the abundance of goods, services, and information accessible via the Internet.

Today, more than one billion users around the world access a variety of services on the Internet, some of which are shown in Figure 2-1. The World Wide Web and e-mail are two of the more widely used Internet services. Other services include FTP (File Transfer Protocol), newsgroups, chat rooms, instant messaging, and Internet telephony. To enhance your understanding of these services, the chapter begins by discussing the history of the Internet and how the Internet works and then explains each of these services.

FIGURE 2-1a (Web)

FIGURE 2-1c (FTP – File Transfer Protocol)

FIGURE 2-1b (e-mail)

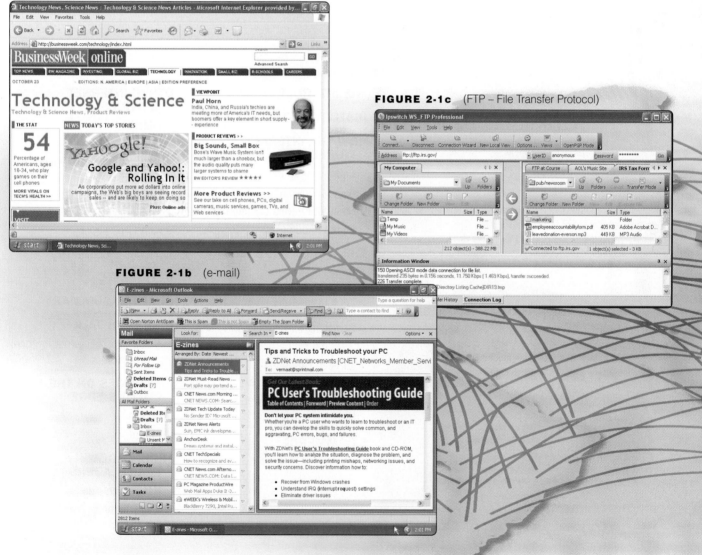

FIGURE 2-1 People around the world use a variety of Internet services in daily activities. Internet services allow users to access the Web, send e-mail messages, transfer documents and photographs, post messages, chat with a group, or have a private conversation with an online friend(s) or family member(s).

HISTORY OF THE INTERNET

The Internet has its roots in a networking project started by the Pentagon's *Advanced Research Projects Agency* (*ARPA*), an agency of the U.S. Department of Defense. ARPA's goal was to build a network that (1) allowed scientists at different physical locations to share information and work together on military and scientific projects and (2) could function even if part of the network were disabled or destroyed by a disaster such as a nuclear attack. That network, called *ARPANET*, became functional in September 1969, linking scientific and academic researchers across the United States.

The original ARPANET consisted of four main computers, one each located at the University of California at Los Angeles, the University of California at Santa Barbara, the Stanford Research Institute, and the University of Utah. Each computer served as a host on the network. A *host*, more commonly known today as a server, is any computer that provides services and connections to other computers on a network. Hosts often use high-speed communications to transfer data and messages over a network.

As researchers and others realized the great benefit of using ARPANET's e-mail to share data and information, ARPANET underwent phenomenal growth. By 1984, ARPANET had more than 1,000 individual computers linked as hosts. Today, more than 350 million hosts connect to the Internet.

Some organizations connected entire networks to ARPANET to take advantage of the high-speed communications it offered. In 1986, the

FIGURE 2-1d   (newsgroup)

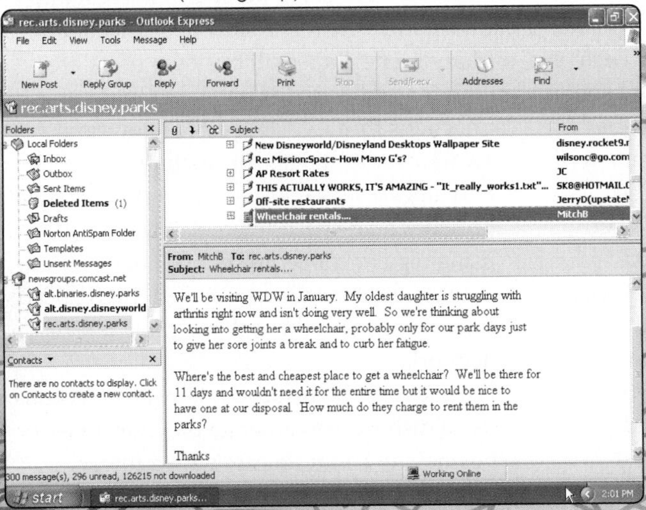

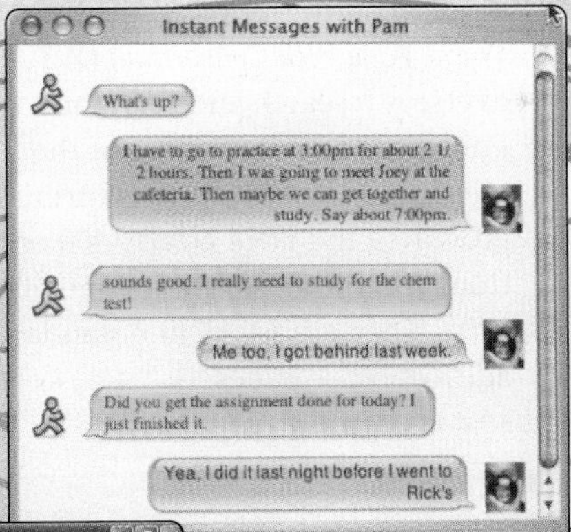

FIGURE 2-1e   (chat)

FIGURE 2-1f   (instant messaging)

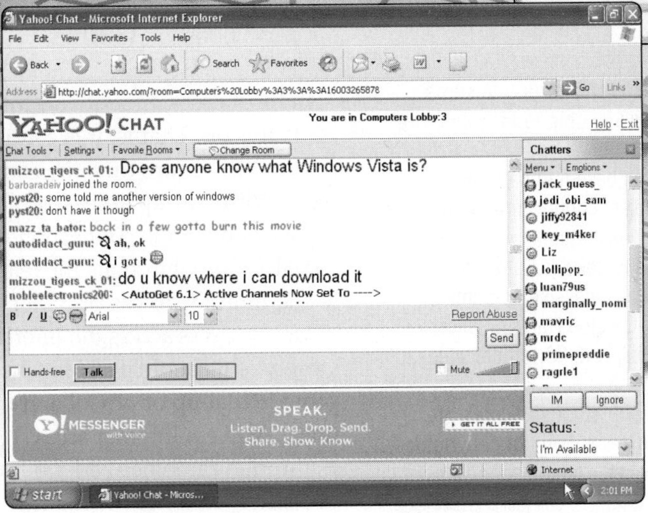

FIGURE 2-1g
(Internet telephony)

National Science Foundation (NSF) connected its huge network of five supercomputer centers, called *NSFnet*, to ARPANET. This configuration of complex networks and hosts became known as the Internet.

Until 1995, NSFnet handled the bulk of the communications activity, or **traffic**, on the Internet. In 1995, NSFnet terminated its network on the Internet and resumed its status as a research network.

Today, the Internet consists of many local, regional, national, and international networks. Numerous corporations, commercial firms, and other companies provide networks to handle the Internet traffic. Both public and private organizations own networks on the Internet. These networks, along with telephone companies, cable and satellite companies, and the government, all contribute toward the internal structure of the Internet. Read Looking Ahead 2-1 for a look at the next generation of the Internet.

Even as the Internet grows, it remains a public, cooperative, and independent network. Each organization on the Internet is responsible only for maintaining its own network. No single person, company, institution, or government agency controls or owns the Internet. The *World Wide Web Consortium (W3C)*, however, oversees research and sets standards and guidelines for many areas of the Internet. The mission of the W3C is to contribute to the growth of the Web. Nearly 400 organizations from around the world are members of the W3C. They advise, define standards, and address other issues.

LOOKING AHEAD 2-1

Internet Speeds into the Future

The Internet of the future will be much larger and faster. According to some Internet experts, in the next 20 years, Web surfers will be able to browse more than 250 million Web sites.

This increase in volume will be based, in part, on *Internet2*. This not-for-profit project connects more than 206 educational and 60 research institutions via a high-speed private network. When used solely as a research tool, Internet2 applications process massive amounts of data, such as linking observatories atop Hawaii's tallest mountains and video conferences from 20 remote sites across the world.

Recently, the recording industry charged scores of college students with copyright infringement for trading millions of copyrighted songs through Internet2 privileged access. For more information, visit scsite.com/dc2007/ch2/looking and then click Internet2.

HOW THE INTERNET WORKS

Data sent over the Internet travels via networks and communications media owned and operated by many companies. The following sections present various ways to connect to these networks on the Internet.

Connecting to the Internet

Employees and students often connect to the Internet through a business or school network. In this case, the computers usually are part of a network that connects to an Internet access provider through a high-speed connection line leased from a telephone company.

Some homes use dial-up access to connect to the Internet. **Dial-up access** takes place when the modem in your computer uses a standard telephone line to connect to the Internet. This type of access is an easy and inexpensive way for users to connect to the Internet. A dial-up connection, however, is slow-speed technology.

Many home and small business users are opting for higher-speed *broadband* Internet connections through DSL, cable television networks, radio signals, or satellite.

- **DSL** (*digital subscriber line*) is a technology that provides high-speed Internet connections using regular copper telephone lines.
- A **cable modem** allows access to high-speed Internet services through the cable television network.
- *Fixed wireless* high-speed Internet connections use a dish-shaped antenna on your house or business to communicate with a tower location via radio signals.
- A *satellite modem* communicates with a satellite dish to provide high-speed Internet connections via satellite.

In most cases, broadband Internet access is always on. That is, it is connected to the Internet the entire time the computer is running. With dial-up access, by contrast, you must establish the connection to the Internet. Usually a modem dials the telephone number to the Internet access provider.

Mobile users access the Internet using a variety of technologies. Most hotels and airports provide dial-up or broadband Internet connections. Wireless Internet access technologies, such as through radio networks, allow mobile users to connect easily to the Internet with notebook computers, Tablet PCs, PDAs, and smart phones while away from a telephone, cable, or other wired connection. Many public locations, such as airports, hotels, schools, shopping malls, and coffee shops, are *hot spots* that provide wireless Internet connections to users with mobile computers or devices.

Access Providers

An **access provider** is a business that provides individuals and companies access to the Internet free or for a fee. The most common fee arrangement for an individual Internet account is a fixed amount, usually about $10 to $25 per month for dial-up, $15 to $40 for DSL, $20 to $45 for cable, $35 to $70 for fixed wireless, and $60 to $99 for satellite. For this fee, many providers offer unlimited Internet access. Others specify

a set number of access hours per month. With the latter arrangement, the provider charges extra for each hour of connection time that exceeds an allotted number of access hours. To attract more customers, some access providers also offer Web publishing services. Web publishing is discussed later in the chapter.

Users access the Internet through regional or national ISPs, online service providers, and wireless Internet service providers (Figure 2-2).

FIGURE 2-2 Common ways to access the Internet are through a regional or national Internet service provider, an online service provider, or a wireless Internet service provider.

An **ISP** (**Internet service provider**) is a regional or national access provider. A *regional ISP* usually provides Internet access to a specific geographic area. A *national ISP* is a business that provides Internet access in cities and towns nationwide. For dial-up access, some national ISPs provide both local and toll-free telephone numbers. Due to their larger size, national ISPs usually offer more services and have a larger technical support staff than regional ISPs. Examples of national ISPs are AT&T Worldnet Service and EarthLink.

In addition to providing Internet access, an **online service provider** (**OSP**) also has many members-only features. These features include special content and services such as news, weather, legal information, financial data, hardware and software guides, games, travel guides, e-mail, photo communities, online calendars, and instant messaging. Some even have their own built-in Web browser. The fees for using an OSP sometimes are slightly higher than fees for an ISP. The two more popular OSPs are AOL (America Online) and MSN (Microsoft Network). AOL differs from many OSPs in that it provides gateway functionality to the Internet, meaning it regulates the Internet services to which members have access.

With dial-up Internet access, the telephone number you dial connects you to an access point on the Internet, called a *point of presence* (*POP*). When selecting an ISP or OSP, ensure it provides at least one local POP telephone number. Otherwise, long-distance telephone charges will apply for the time you connect to the Internet.

A **wireless Internet service provider** (*WISP*) is a company that provides wireless Internet access to computers with wireless modems or access devices or to Internet-enabled mobile computers or devices. Internet-enabled mobile devices include PDAs and smart phones. An antenna on or built into the computer or device typically sends signals through the airwaves to communicate with a wireless Internet service provider. Some examples of wireless Internet service providers include Boingo Wireless, Cingular Wireless, T-Mobile, and Verizon Wireless.

WEB LINK 2-1

Wireless Internet Service Provider

For more information, visit scsite.com/dc2007/ch2/weblink and then click Wireless Internet Service Provider.

FAQ 2-2

How many people have broadband Internet access?

According to a recent 12-month study, the number of home and small business users with high-speed Internet access grew by 34 percent, resulting in a total of more than 37 million high-speed Internet access subscribers today. The main reason users switch to broadband access is they are frustrated with the slow speeds of dial-up access. For more information, visit scsite.com/dc2007/ch2/faq and then click Broadband.

How Data Travels the Internet

Computers connected to the Internet work together to transfer data and information around the world using servers and clients. On the Internet, your computer is a client that can access data, information, and services on a variety of servers.

The inner structure of the Internet works much like a transportation system. Just as interstate highways connect major cities and carry the bulk of the automotive traffic across the country, several main transmission media carry the heaviest amount of traffic on the Internet. These major carriers of network traffic are known collectively as the *Internet backbone.*

In the United States, the transmission media that make up the Internet backbone exchange data at several different major cities across the country. That is, they transfer data from one network to another until it reaches its final destination (Figure 2-3).

FAQ 2-3

How do I find the right access provider?

The Web provides many comprehensive lists of access providers. These lists often use the terms ISP and OSP interchangeably. One of the more popular lists on the Web is called The List. For more information, visit scsite.com/dc2007/ch2/faq and then click The List.

FIGURE 2-3   HOW A HOME USER'S DATA MIGHT TRAVEL THE INTERNET USING A CABLE MODEM CONNECTION

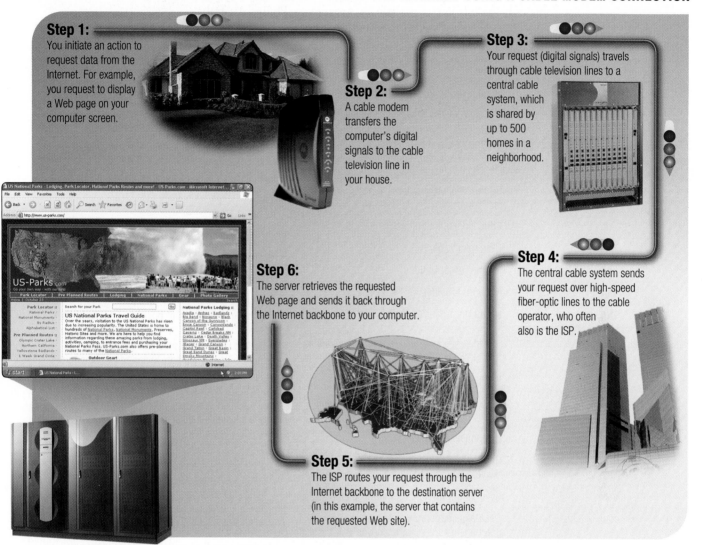

Step 1:
You initiate an action to request data from the Internet. For example, you request to display a Web page on your computer screen.

Step 2:
A cable modem transfers the computer's digital signals to the cable television line in your house.

Step 3:
Your request (digital signals) travels through cable television lines to a central cable system, which is shared by up to 500 homes in a neighborhood.

Step 4:
The central cable system sends your request over high-speed fiber-optic lines to the cable operator, who often also is the ISP.

Step 5:
The ISP routes your request through the Internet backbone to the destination server (in this example, the server that contains the requested Web site).

Step 6:
The server retrieves the requested Web page and sends it back through the Internet backbone to your computer.

Internet Addresses

The Internet relies on an addressing system much like the postal service to send data to a computer at a specific destination. An **IP address**, short for *Internet Protocol address*, is a number that uniquely identifies each computer or device connected to the Internet. The IP address usually consists of four groups of numbers, each separated by a period. The number in each group is between 0 and 255. For example, the numbers 216.239.39.99 are an IP address. In general, the first portion of each IP address identifies the network and the last portion identifies the specific computer.

These all-numeric IP addresses are difficult to remember and use. Thus, the Internet supports the use of a text name that represents one or more IP addresses. A **domain name** is the text version of an IP address. Figure 2-4 shows

an IP address and its associated domain name. As with an IP address, the components of a domain name are separated by periods.

In Figure 2-4, the com portion of the domain name is called the top-level domain. Every domain name contains a *top-level domain*, which identifies the type of organization associated with the domain. *Dot-com* is the term sometimes used to describe organizations with a top-level domain of com.

IP address ⟶ 216.239.39.99

Domain name ⟶ www.google.com

top-level domain

FIGURE 2-4   The IP address and domain name for the Google Web site.

The group that assigns and controls top-level domains is the *Internet Corporation for Assigned Names and Numbers (ICANN* pronounced EYE-can). Figure 2-5 lists some top-level domains. For international Web sites outside the United States, the top-level domain also ends with a two-letter country code, such as au for Australia or fr for France. For example, www.philips.com.au is the domain name for Philips Australia.

The *domain name system (DNS)* is the method that the Internet uses to store domain names and their corresponding IP addresses. When you specify a domain name, a **DNS server** translates the domain name to its associated IP address so data can be routed to the correct computer. A DNS server is an Internet server that usually is associated with an Internet access provider.

For a more technical discussion about Internet addresses, read the High-Tech Talk article on page 102.

EXAMPLES OF TOP-LEVEL DOMAINS

Original Top-Level Domains	Type of Domain
com	Commercial organizations, businesses, and companies
edu	Educational institutions
gov	Goverment agencies
mil	Military organizations
net	Network provider
org	Nonprofit organizations
Newer Top-Level Domains	**Type of Domain**
museum	Accredited museums
biz	Businesses of all sizes
info	Businesses, organizations, or individuals providing general information
name	Individuals or families
pro	Certified professionals such as doctors, lawyers, and accountants
aero	Aviation community members
coop	Business cooperatives such as credit unions and rural electric co-ops
Proposed Top-Level Domains	**Type of Domain**
asia	Businesses that originate in Asian countries
cat	Catalan cultural community
jobs	Employment or human resource businesses
mail	Registries to control spam (Internet junk mail)
mobi	Delivery and management of mobile Internet services
post	Postal service
tel	Internet communications
travel	Travel industry
xxx	Adult content

FIGURE 2-5 With the dramatic growth of the Internet during the last few years, the Internet Corporation for Assigned Names and Numbers (ICANN) recently adopted seven new top-level domains and is evaluating nine additional TLDs.

FAQ 2-4

How does a person or company get a domain name?

For top-level domains of biz, com, info, name, net, and org, you register for a domain name from a *registrar*, which is an organization that sells and manages domain names. In addition to determining prices and policies for domain name registration, a registrar may offer additional services such as Web site hosting. For more information, visit scsite.com/dc2007/ch2/faq and then click Registrar.

Test your knowledge of pages 68 through 74 in Quiz Yourself 2-1.

QUIZ YOURSELF 2-1

Instructions: Find the true statement below. Then, rewrite the remaining false statements so they are true.

1. An access provider is a business that provides individuals and companies access to the Internet free or for a fee.

2. A WISP is a number that uniquely identifies each computer or device connected to the Internet.

3. An IP address, such as www.google.com, is the text version of a domain name.

4. Dial-up access takes place when the modem in your computer uses the cable television network to connect to the Internet.

5. The World Wide Web Consortium (W3C) oversees research and owns the Internet.

Quiz Yourself Online: To further check your knowledge of Internet history, accessing and connecting to the Internet, and Internet addresses, visit scsite.com/dc2007/ch2/quiz and then click Objectives 1 – 3.

THE WORLD WIDE WEB

Although many people use the terms World Wide Web and Internet interchangeably, the World Wide Web actually is a service of the Internet. While the Internet was developed in the late 1960s, the World Wide Web emerged nearly three decades later — in the early 1990s. Since then, it has grown phenomenally to become one of the more widely used Internet services.

The **World Wide Web** (*WWW*), or **Web**, consists of a worldwide collection of electronic documents. Each electronic document on the Web is called a **Web page**, which can contain text, graphics, audio (sound), and video. Additionally, Web pages usually have built-in connections to other documents.

Some Web pages are static (fixed); others are dynamic (changing). Visitors to a *static Web page* all see the same content. With a *dynamic Web page*, by contrast, visitors can customize some or all of the viewed content such as desired stock quotes, weather for a region, or ticket availability for flights.

A **Web site** is a collection of related Web pages and associated items, such as documents and pictures, stored on a Web server. A **Web server** is a computer that delivers requested Web pages to your computer. The same Web server can store multiple Web sites. For example, many access providers grant their subscribers free storage space on a Web server for personal or company Web sites.

The following pages discuss how to browse the Web, use a Web address, search for information on the Web, and recognize types of Web sites. Also discussed are multimedia on the Web and Web publishing.

Browsing the Web

A **Web browser**, or **browser**, is application software that allows users to access and view Web pages. To browse the Web, you need a computer that is connected to the Internet and that has a Web browser. The more widely used Web browsers for personal computers are Internet Explorer, Netscape, Mozilla, Firefox, Opera, and Safari.

With an Internet connection established, you start a Web browser. The browser retrieves and displays a starting Web page, sometimes called the browser's home page. Figure 2-6 shows how a Web browser displays a home page. The initial home page that is displayed

Step 1:
Click the Web browser program name to start the Web browser software.

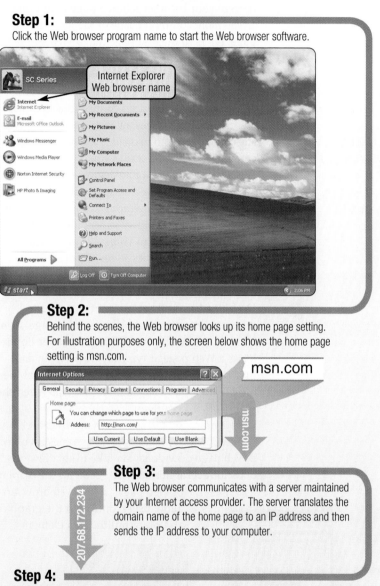

Step 2:
Behind the scenes, the Web browser looks up its home page setting. For illustration purposes only, the screen below shows the home page setting is msn.com.

Step 3:
The Web browser communicates with a server maintained by your Internet access provider. The server translates the domain name of the home page to an IP address and then sends the IP address to your computer.

Step 4:
The Web browser uses the IP address to contact the Web server associated with the home page and then requests the home page from the server. The Web server sends the home page to the Web browser, which formats the page for display on your screen.

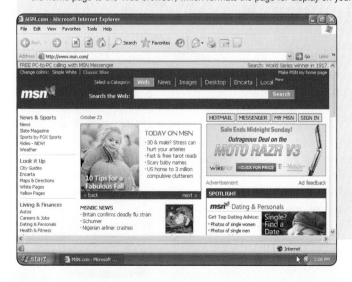

is one selected by your Web browser. You can change your browser's home page at anytime.

The more common usage of the term, **home page**, refers to the first page that a Web site displays. Similar to a book cover or a table of contents for a Web site, the home page provides information about the Web site's purpose and content. Often it provides connections to other documents, Web pages, or Web sites. Many Web sites allow you to personalize the home page so it contains areas of interest to you.

Internet-enabled mobile devices such as PDAs and smart phones use a special type of browser, called a *microbrowser*, which is designed for their small screens and limited computing power. Many Web sites design Web pages specifically for display on a microbrowser (Figure 2-7).

For a computer or mobile device to display a Web page, the page must be downloaded. **Downloading** is the process of a computer receiving information, such as a Web page, from a server on the Internet. While a browser downloads a Web page, it typically displays an animated logo or icon in the top-right corner of the browser window. The animation stops when the download is complete.

Depending on the speed of your Internet connection and the amount of graphics involved, a Web page download can take from a few seconds to several minutes. To speed up the display of Web pages, most Web browsers allow users to turn off the graphics and other multimedia elements.

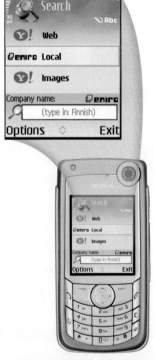

FIGURE 2-7 Sample microbrowser screens.

Web Addresses

A Web page has a unique address, called a **URL** (*Uniform Resource Locator*) or **Web address**. For example, the home page for The Weather Channel Web site has http://www.weather.com as its Web address. A Web browser retrieves a Web page using its Web address.

If you know the Web address of a Web page, you can type it in the Address box at the top of the browser window. For example, if you type the Web address http://www.weather.com/maps/activity/skinprotection/index_large.html in the Address box and then press the ENTER key, the browser downloads and displays the Web page shown in Figure 2-8.

A Web address consists of a protocol, domain name, and sometimes the path to a specific Web page or location on a Web page. Many Web page addresses begin with http://. The *http*, which stands for *Hypertext Transfer Protocol*, is a set of rules that defines how pages transfer on the Internet. The first portion of the domain name identifies the type of Internet server. For example, www indicates a Web server.

To help minimize errors, most browsers and Web sites do not require the http:// and www portions of the Web address. For example, typing weather.com/maps/activity/skinprotection/index_large.html, instead of the entire address, still accesses the Web site. If you enter an incorrect Web address, a list of similar addresses from which you can select may be displayed in the browser window. Many Web sites also allow users to eliminate the .htm or .html from the Web page name.

When you enter the Web address, http://www.weather.com/maps/activity/skinprotection/index_large.html in the Web browser, it sends a request to the Web server that contains the weather.com Web site. The server then retrieves the Web page named index_large.html in the maps/activity/skinprotection/ path and delivers it to your browser, which then displays the Web page on the screen.

When you enter a Web address in a browser, you request, or *pull*, information from a Web server. Some Web servers also can *push* content to your computer at regular intervals or whenever updates are made to the site. For example, some Web servers provide the capability of displaying current sporting event scores or weather reports on your computer screen.

For information about useful Web sites and their associated Web addresses, read the Making Use of the Web feature that follows this chapter.

protocol   domain name   path   Web page name

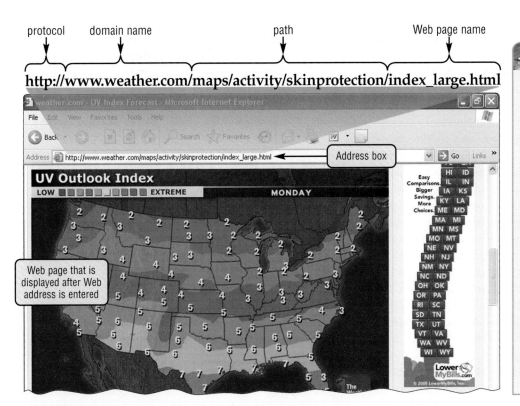

http://www.weather.com/maps/activity/skinprotection/index_large.html

FIGURE 2-8   After entering the Web address http://www.weather.com/maps/activity/skinprotection/index_large.html in the Address box, this Web page at The Weather Channel Web site is displayed.

Navigating Web Pages

Most Web pages contain links. A **link**, short for *hyperlink*, is a built-in connection to another related Web page or part of a Web page. Links allow you to obtain information in a nonlinear way. That is, instead of accessing topics in a specified order, you move directly to a topic of interest. Branching from one related topic to another in a nonlinear fashion is what makes links so powerful. Some people use the phrase, **surfing the Web**, to refer to the activity of using links to explore the Web.

On the Web, a link can be text or an image. Text links may be underlined and/or displayed in a color different from other text on the Web page. Pointing to, or positioning the pointer on, a link on the screen typically changes the shape of the pointer to a small hand with a pointing index finger. The Web page shown in Figure 2-9 contains a variety of link types, with the pointer on one of the links.

Each link on a Web page corresponds to another Web address. To activate a link, you *click* it, that is, point to the link and then press the left mouse button. Clicking a link causes the Web page associated with the link to be displayed on the screen. The linked object

might be on the same Web page, a different Web page at the same Web site, or a separate Web page at a different Web site in another city or country. To remind you visually that you have clicked a link, a text link often changes color after you click it.

FIGURE 2-9   This Web page contains various types of links: text that is underlined, text in a different color, and images.

Searching for Information on the Web

The Web is a global resource of information. One primary use of the Web is to search for specific information, including text, graphics, audio, and video. The first step in successful searching is to identify the main idea or concept in the topic about which you are seeking information. Determine any synonyms, alternate spellings, or variant word forms for the topic. Then, use a search tool to locate the information.

The two most commonly used search tools are subject directories and search engines. A **subject directory** classifies Web pages in an organized set of categories, such as sports or shopping, and related subcategories. A **search engine** is a program that finds Web sites and Web pages.

Some Web sites offer the functionality of both a subject directory and a search engine. Yahoo! and Google, for example, are widely used search engines that also provide a subject directory. To use Yahoo! or Google, you enter the Web address (yahoo.com or google.com) in the Address box in a browser window. The table in Figure 2-10 lists the

Web addresses of several popular general-purpose subject directories and search engines.

SUBJECT DIRECTORIES A subject directory provides categorized lists of links arranged by subject. Figure 2-11 shows how to use Yahoo!'s

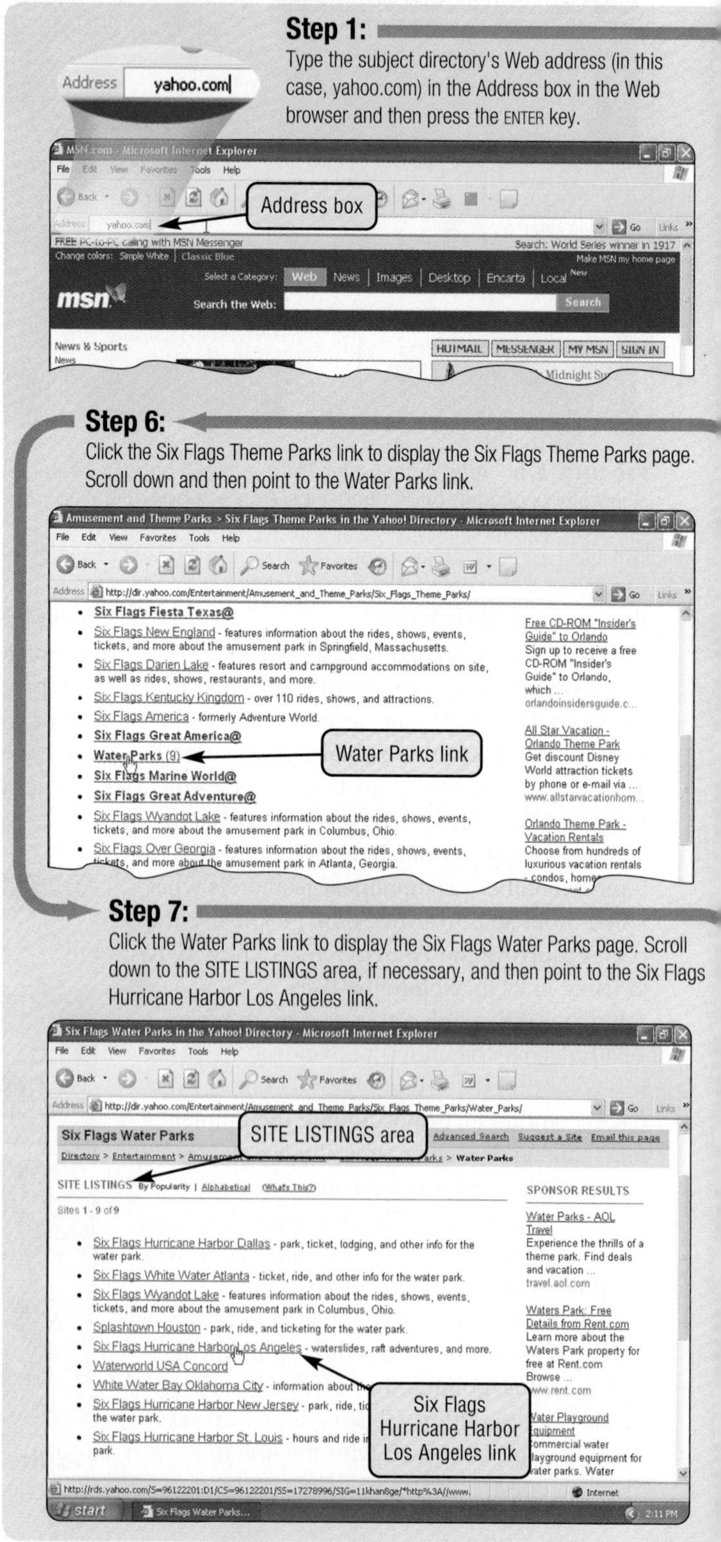

WIDELY USED SEARCH TOOLS

Search Tool	Web Address	Subject Directory	Search Engine
A9.com	a9.com		X
AlltheWeb	alltheweb.com		X
Alta Vista	altavista.com	X	X
AOL Search	search.aol.com		X
Ask Jeeves	ask.com	X	X
Dogpile	dogpile.com		X
Excite	excite.com	X	X
Gigablast	gigablast.com	X	X
Google	google.com	X	X
HotBot	hotbot.com		X
LookSmart	looksmart.com	X	X
Lycos	lycos.com	X	X
MSN Search	search.msn.com	X	X
Netscape Search	search.netscape.com	X	X
Open Directory Project	dmoz.org	X	X
Overture	overture.com		X
Teoma	teoma.com		X
WebCrawler	webcrawler.com		X
Yahoo!	yahoo.com	X	X

FIGURE 2-10 Many subject directories and search engines allow searching about any topic on the Web.

FIGURE 2-11 HOW TO USE A SUBJECT DIRECTORY

Step 1:
Type the subject directory's Web address (in this case, yahoo.com) in the Address box in the Web browser and then press the ENTER key.

Address box

Step 6:
Click the Six Flags Theme Parks link to display the Six Flags Theme Parks page. Scroll down and then point to the Water Parks link.

Water Parks link

Step 7:
Click the Water Parks link to display the Six Flags Water Parks page. Scroll down to the SITE LISTINGS area, if necessary, and then point to the Six Flags Hurricane Harbor Los Angeles link.

SITE LISTINGS area

Six Flags Hurricane Harbor Los Angeles link

subject directory to search for information about Six Flags Hurricane Harbor Los Angeles. As shown in the figure, you locate a particular topic by clicking links through different levels, moving from the general to the specific. Each time you click a category link, the subject directory displays a list of subcategory

links, from which you again choose. You continue in this fashion until the search tool displays a list of Web pages about the desired topic.

The major problem with a subject directory is deciding which categories to choose as you work through the menus of links presented.

Step 2:
When the Yahoo! home page is displayed, point to the scroll box on the right side of the screen.

Step 3:
Drag the scroll box downward to display the Yahoo! Web Directory area of the Web page. Point to the Entertainment link.

Step 5:
Click the Amusement and Theme Parks link to display the Amusement and Theme Parks page. Scroll down to the SITE LISTINGS area and then point to the Six Flags Theme Parks link.

Step 4:
Click the Entertainment link to display the Entertainment page. Scroll down to the CATEGORIES area, if necessary, and then point to the Amusement and Theme Parks link.

Step 8:
Click the Six Flags Hurricane Harbor Los Angeles link to display the Six Flags Hurricane Harbor Los Angeles Web page, which contains a variety of links to specific information about the water park. After you click one of these links, click the Home button to display this home page.

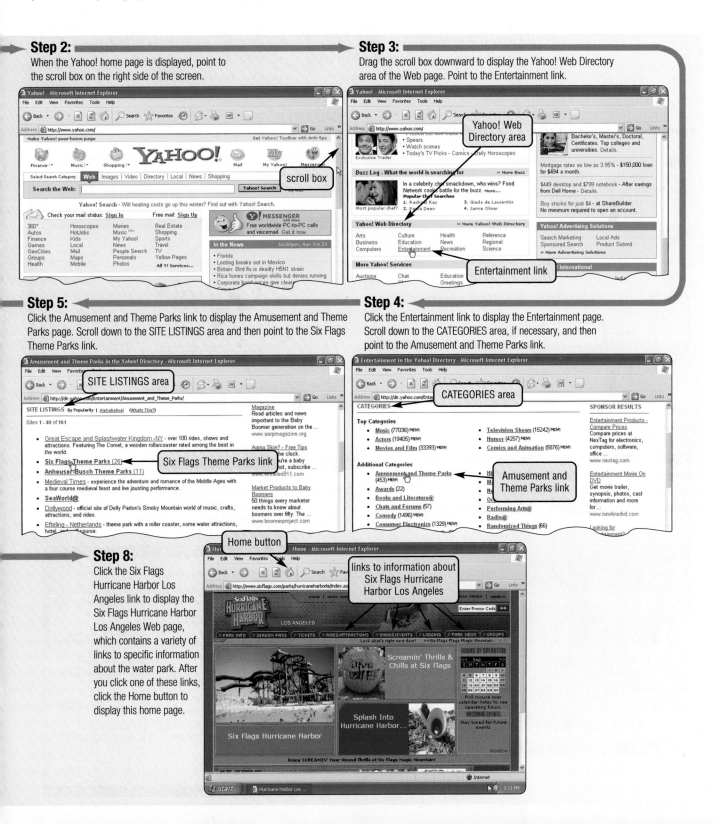

SEARCH ENGINES A search engine is particularly helpful in locating Web pages about certain topics or in locating specific Web pages for which you do not know the exact Web address. Thousands of search engines are available. Some are general and perform searches on any topic; others are restricted to certain subjects, such as finding people, job hunting, or locating real estate.

Instead of clicking through links, search engines require that you enter a word or phrase, called **search text** or *keywords*, that define the item about which you want information. Search engines often respond with results that include thousands of links to Web pages, many of which may have little or no bearing on the information you are seeking. You can eliminate the superfluous pages by carefully crafting a keyword that limits the search.

Figure 2-12 shows how to use the Google search engine to search for the phrase, Six Flags Hurricane Harbor Los Angeles coupons. The results of the search, called *hits*, shown in Step 3 include about 90,000 links to Web pages that reference Six Flags Hurricane Harbor Los Angeles coupons. Each hit in the list has a link that, when clicked, displays an associated Web site

FIGURE 2-12 HOW TO USE A SEARCH ENGINE

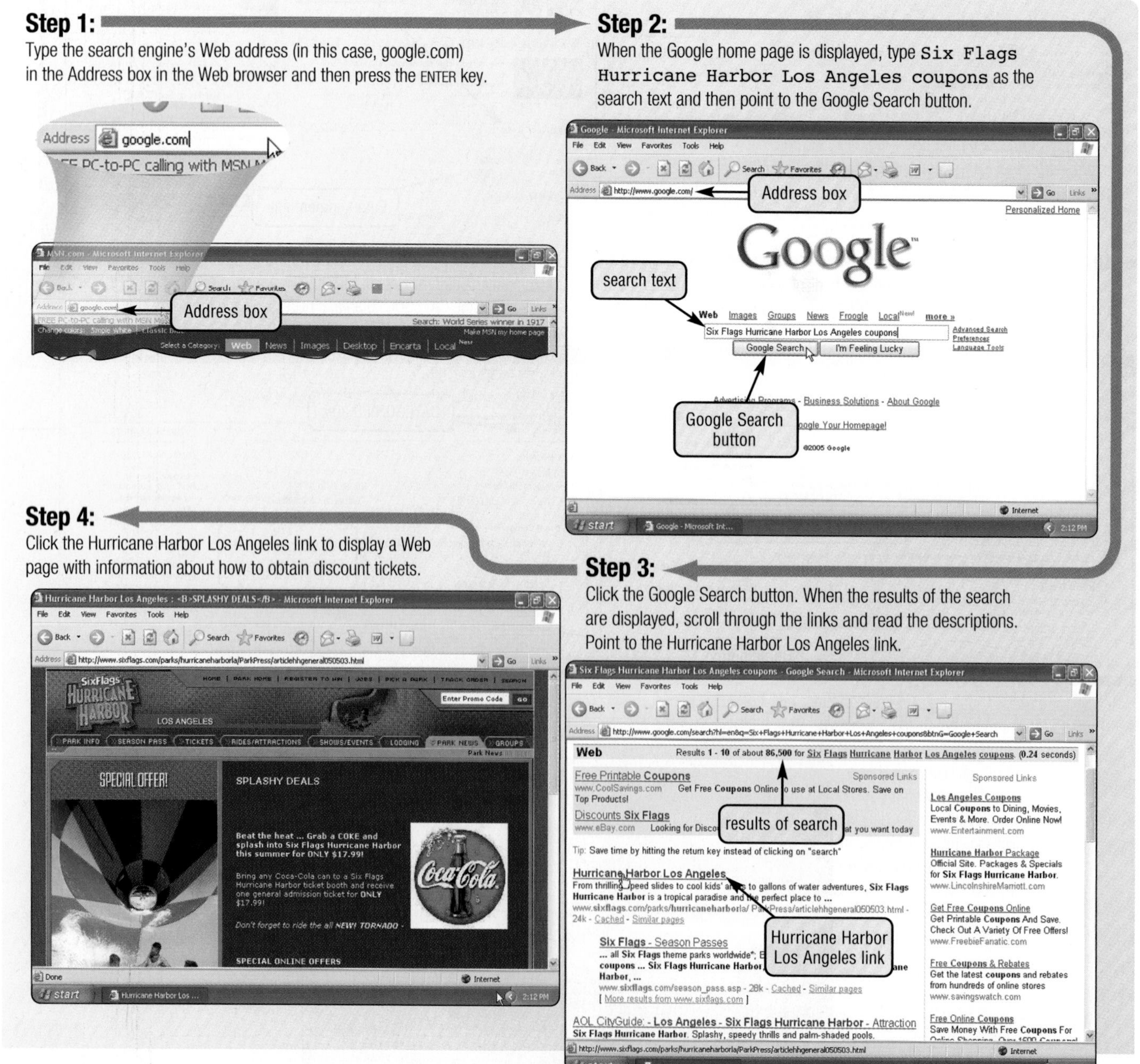

Step 1:
Type the search engine's Web address (in this case, google.com) in the Address box in the Web browser and then press the ENTER key.

Step 2:
When the Google home page is displayed, type Six Flags Hurricane Harbor Los Angeles coupons as the search text and then point to the Google Search button.

Step 4:
Click the Hurricane Harbor Los Angeles link to display a Web page with information about how to obtain discount tickets.

Step 3:
Click the Google Search button. When the results of the search are displayed, scroll through the links and read the descriptions. Point to the Hurricane Harbor Los Angeles link.

or Web page. Most search engines sequence the hits based on how close the words in the search text are to one another in the Web page titles and their descriptions. Thus, the first few links probably contain more relevant information.

If you enter a phrase with spaces between the words in the search text, most search engines display results (hits) that include all of the words, except for common words (e.g., to, the, and). The table in Figure 2-13 lists some common operators you can include in your search text to refine your search. Other techniques you can use to improve your Web searches include the following:

- Use specific nouns and put the most important terms first in the search text.
- List all possible spellings, for example, email, e-mail.
- Before using a search engine, read its Help information.

- If the search is unsuccessful with one search engine, try another.

Many search engines use a program called a *spider* to build and maintain lists of words found on Web sites. When you enter search text, the search engine scans this prebuilt list for hits. The more sophisticated the search engine combined with precise search criteria, the more rapid the response and effective the search.

In addition to searching for Web pages, many search engines allow you to search for images, news articles, and local businesses. Read Looking Ahead 2-2 for a look at the next generation of searching techniques.

FAQ 2-6

Who uses Google to search the Web?

People all around the world use Google to conduct more than 250 million searches per day. Google has been accessed in many languages including English, German, Japanese, Spanish, French, Chinese, and Dutch. For more information, visit scsite.com/dc2007/ch2/faq and then click Google Facts.

SEARCH ENGINE OPERATORS

Operator	Description	Examples	Explanation
Space or +	Use the space or plus operator (+) when you want search results to display hits that include specific words.	art + music art music	Results have both words art and music — in any order.
OR	Use the OR operator when you want search results to display hits that include only one word from a list.	dog OR puppy	Results have either the word dog or puppy.
		dog OR puppy OR canine	Results have the word dog or puppy or canine.
-	Use the minus operator (-) when you want to exclude a word from your search results.	automobile -convertible	Results include automobile but do not include convertible.
" "	Use the quotation marks operator when you want to search for an exact phrase in a certain order.	"19th century literature"	Results include only hits that have the exact phrase, 19th century literature.
*	Use the asterisk operator (*) when you want search results to substitute characters in place of the asterisk.	writer*	Results include any word that begins with writer (e.g., writer, writers, writer's).

FIGURE 2-13   Use search engine operators to help refine a search.

LOOKING AHEAD 2-2

3-D Search Engines Get the Picture

Conventional search engines, such as Google, use words to find information. But what happens when a computer user needs to locate a wing nut or camshaft based on a particular shape, not part number or model? The 3-D search engines being developed would help people who work with patterns and contours search for images. These search engines presently are being created to assist designers and engineers at large industrial companies with millions of inventoried parts, but university researchers predict image searches will be common on the Internet within 15 years.

Other search engines of the future will customize the results based on the researcher's background, include a voice interface, and use a thesaurus to keep a query in context. For more information, visit scsite.com/dc2007/ch2/looking and then click Search Engines.

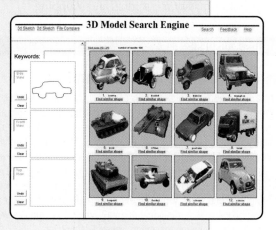

Types of Web Sites

Eleven types of Web sites are portal, news, informational, business/marketing, educational, entertainment, advocacy, blog, wiki, content aggregator, and personal (Figure 2-14). Many Web sites fall in more than one of these categories. The following pages discuss each of these types of Web sites.

PORTAL   A **portal** is a Web site that offers a variety of Internet services from a single, convenient location (Figure 2-14a). Most portals offer the following free services: search engine and/or subject directory; news; sports and weather; free Web publishing services; reference tools such as yellow pages, stock quotes, and maps; shopping malls and auctions; and e-mail and other forms of online communications. Companies often create their own portals for use by employees, vendors, and customers.

Many portals have Web communities. A **Web community** is a Web site that joins a specific group of people with similar interests or relationships. These communities may offer online photo albums, chat rooms, and other services to facilitate communications among members.

When you connect to the Internet, the first Web page that is displayed often is a portal. Popular portals include AltaVista, AOL, Excite, GO.com, HotBot, LookSmart, Lycos, MSN, NBCi, Netscape, and Yahoo!. You may notice that many of these portals are popular search engines or subject directories. Some also are Internet access providers.

A *wireless portal* is a portal designed for Internet-enabled mobile devices. Wireless portals attempt to provide all information a wireless user might require. These portals offer services geared to the mobile user such as search engines, news, stock quotes, weather, maps, e-mail, calendar, instant messaging, and shopping.

NEWS   A news Web site contains newsworthy material including stories and articles relating to current events, life, money, sports, and the weather (Figure 2-14b). Many magazines and newspapers sponsor Web sites that provide summaries of printed articles, as well as articles not included in the printed versions. Newspapers and television and radio stations are some of the media that maintain news Web sites.

INFORMATIONAL   An informational Web site contains factual information (Figure 2-14c). Many United States government agencies have informational Web sites providing information such as census data, tax codes, and the congressional budget. Other organizations provide information such as public transportation schedules and published research findings.

BUSINESS/MARKETING   A business/marketing Web site contains content that promotes or sells products or services (Figure 2-14d). Nearly every business has a business/marketing Web site. Allstate Insurance Company, Dell Inc., General Motors Corporation, Kraft Foods Inc., and Walt Disney Company all have business/marketing Web sites. Many of these companies also allow you to purchase their products or services online.

EDUCATIONAL   An educational Web site offers exciting, challenging avenues for formal and informal teaching and learning (Figure 2-14e). On the Web, you can learn how airplanes fly or how to cook a meal. For a more structured learning experience, companies provide online training to employees; and colleges offer online classes and degrees (read Ethics & Issues 2-1 for a related discussion). Instructors often use the Web to enhance classroom teaching by publishing course materials, grades, and other pertinent class information.

ETHICS & ISSUES 2-1

Is the Internet as Good as the Classroom?

College can be a rewarding experience, both personally and professionally. Some people, however, do not have the opportunity, time, or money needed to attend a traditional college. Many schools address this problem with online classes, also called Internet courses. Online classes allow students to learn whenever and wherever they can access a course's Web page, often for less cost than traditional tuitions. A student might be able to complete an entire degree program without ever physically attending a class. Many online classes present material using captivating simulations, real-life case studies, and interactive tools. And, online classes seem to work — one research report found that online students learn as well as or better than their classroom-based counterparts. Yet, even the best online classes lack some of the most important features of the bricks-and-mortar campus experience, such as casual talks with professors, informal study groups in the dorm, or enthusiastic discussions in the campus coffee shop. What are the most important advantages and disadvantages of online classes? Why? Does a degree earned online have the same value as a traditional degree? Why? Does the answer depend more on the college or on the course of study? What type of course is best, and least, suited for online classes? Why?

FIGURE 2-14b (news)

FIGURE 2-14a (portal)

FIGURE 2-14c (informational)

FIGURE 2-14e (educational)

FIGURE 2-14d (business/marketing)

FIGURE 2-14f (entertainment)

FIGURE 2-14h (blog)

FIGURE 2-14g (advocacy)

FIGURE 2-14i (wiki)

FIGURE 2-14j (content aggregator)

FIGURE 2-14k (personal)

FIGURE 2-14 Types of Web sites.

ENTERTAINMENT An entertainment Web site offers an interactive and engaging environment (Figure 2-14f on the previous page). Popular entertainment Web sites offer music, videos, sports, games, ongoing Web episodes, sweepstakes, chats, and more. Sophisticated entertainment Web sites often partner with other technologies. For example, you can cast your vote about a topic on a television show.

ADVOCACY An advocacy Web site contains content that describes a cause, opinion, or idea (Figure 2-14g). The purpose of an advocacy Web site is to convince the reader of the validity of the cause, opinion, or idea. These Web sites usually present views of a particular group or association. Sponsors of advocacy Web sites include the Democratic National Committee, the Republican National Committee, the Society for the Prevention of Cruelty to Animals, and the Society to Protect Human Rights.

BLOG A **blog**, short for *Weblog*, is an informal Web site consisting of time-stamped articles, or posts, in a diary or journal format, usually listed in reverse chronological order (Figure 2-14h). Blogs reflect the interests, opinions, and personalities of the author, called the *blogger*, and sometimes site visitors. According to a Web tracking company, more than 500,000 posts appear on blogs each day. Businesses use blogs to communicate with employees, customers, and vendors. Blogs at school provide a means for teachers to collaborate with other teachers and students. Home users also use blogs to share aspects of their personal life with family, friends, and others.

WIKI A **wiki** is a collaborative Web site that allows users to add to, modify, or delete the Web site content via their Web browser. Most wikis are open to modification by the general public. Wikis usually collect recent edits on a Web page so someone can review them for accuracy. The difference between a wiki and a blog is that users cannot modify original posts made by the blogger. A popular wiki is Wikipedia, a free Web encyclopedia (Figure 2-14i).

WEB LINK 2-3

Wiki
For more information, visit scsite.com/ dc2007/ch2/weblink and then click Wiki.

CONTENT AGGREGATOR A *content aggregator* is a business that gathers and organizes Web content and then distributes, or feeds, the content to subscribers for free or a fee. Examples of distributed content include news, music, video,

and pictures. Subscribers select content in which they are interested. Whenever this content changes, it is downloaded automatically (pushed) to the subscriber's computer or mobile device.

RSS 2.0, which stands for *Really Simple Syndication*, is a specification that content aggregators use to distribute content to subscribers (Figure 2-14j). *Atom* is another specification sometimes used by content aggregators to distribute content.

PERSONAL A private individual or family not usually associated with any organization may maintain a personal Web site or just a single Web page (Figure 2-14k). People publish personal Web pages for a variety of reasons. Some are job hunting. Others simply want to share life experiences with the world.

Evaluating a Web Site

Do not assume that information presented on the Web is correct or accurate. Any person, company, or organization can publish a Web page on the Internet. No one oversees the content of these Web pages. Figure 2-15 lists guidelines for assessing the value of a Web site or Web page before relying on its content.

GUIDELINES FOR EVALUATING THE VALUE OF A WEB SITE

Evaluation Criteria	Reliable Web Sites
Affiliation	A reputable institution should support the Web site without bias in the information.
Audience	The Web site should be written at an appropriate level.
Authority	The Web site should list the author and the appropriate credentials.
Content	The Web site should be well organized and the links should work.
Currency	The information on the Web page should be current.
Design	The pages at the Web site should download quickly and be visually pleasing and easy to navigate.
Objectivity	The Web site should contain little advertising and be free of preconceptions.

FIGURE 2-15 Criteria for evaluating a Web site's content.

Multimedia on the Web

Most Web pages include more than just formatted text and links. The more exciting Web pages use multimedia. **Multimedia** refers to any application that combines text with graphics, animation, audio, video, and/or virtual reality. Multimedia brings a Web page to life, increases the types of information available on the Web, expands the Web's potential uses, and makes the Internet a more entertaining place to explore. Multimedia Web pages often require proper hardware and software and take more time to download because they contain large graphics files and video or audio clips.

The sections that follow discuss how the Web uses graphics, animation, audio, video, and virtual reality.

FAQ 2-7

What is a file?

A *file* is a unit of storage. When you want the computer to store items (e.g., data, information, programs, graphics, audio clips, or video clips), it places them in files on storage media such as a hard disk. File sizes vary depending on items being stored. For example, graphics files usually consume more storage space than data files. For more information, visit scsite.com/dc2007/ch2/faq and then click Files.

GRAPHICS   A **graphic**, or *graphical image*, is a digital representation of nontext information such as a drawing, chart, or photograph. Today, many Web pages use colorful graphical designs and images to convey messages (Figure 2-16).

The Web contains countless images about a variety of subjects. You can download many of these images at no cost and use them for non-commercial purposes. Recall that downloading is the process of transferring an object from the Web to your computer. For example, you can insert images into greeting cards, announcements, and other documents.

Of the graphics formats that exist on the Web (Figure 2-17), the two more common are JPEG and GIF formats. *JPEG* (pronounced JAY-peg) is a format that compresses graphics to reduce their file size, which means the file takes up less storage space. Smaller file sizes result in faster downloading of Web pages because small files transmit faster than large files. The

more compressed the file, the smaller the image and the lower the quality. The goal with JPEG graphics is to reach a balance between image quality and file size.

GIF (pronounced jiff) graphics also use compression techniques to reduce file sizes. The GIF format works best for images that have only a few distinct colors. The newer *PNG* (pronounced ping) graphics format improves upon the GIF format, and thus may eventually replace the GIF format.

The BMP and TIFF formats listed in Figure 2-17 may require special viewer software, and they have larger file sizes. Thus, these formats are not used on the Web as frequently as JPEG, GIF, and PNG formats.

FIGURE 2-16   This Web page uses colorful graphical designs and images to convey its messages.

GRAPHICS FORMATS USED ON THE WEB

Abbreviation	Name
BMP	Bit Map
GIF	Graphics Interchange Format
JPEG	Joint Photographic Experts Group
PNG	Portable Network Graphics
TIFF	Tagged Image File Format

FIGURE 2-17   The Web uses graphics file formats for images.

Some Web sites use thumbnails on their pages because graphics can be time-consuming to display. A *thumbnail* is a small version of a larger graphic. You usually can click a thumbnail to display a larger image (Figure 2-18).

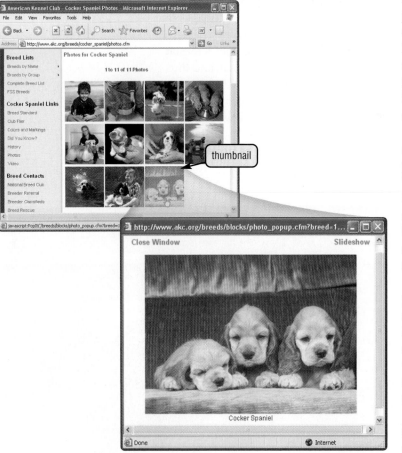

FIGURE 2-18 Clicking the thumbnail in the top screen displays a larger image in a separate window.

ANIMATION Many Web pages use **animation**, which is the appearance of motion created by displaying a series of still images in sequence. Animation can make Web pages more visually interesting or draw attention to important information or links. For example, text that animates by scrolling across the screen can serve as a ticker to display stock updates, news, sports scores, weather, or other information. Web-based games often use animation.

Web page developers add animation to Web pages using a variety of techniques. Web page authoring programs, such as Macromedia Flash, enable Web site developers to combine animation and interactivity in Web pages. Developers unfamiliar with Web page authoring programs can create an *animated GIF*, which combines several GIF images in a single GIF file.

AUDIO On the Web, you can listen to audio clips and live audio. **Audio** includes music, speech, or any other sound.

Simple applications on the Web consist of individual audio files available for downloading to a computer. Once downloaded, you can play (listen to) the contents of these files. Some common Web audio file formats are listed in Figure 2-19. Audio files are compressed to reduce their file sizes. For example, the **MP3** format reduces an audio file to about one-tenth its original size, while preserving much of the original quality of the sound.

Some music publishers have Web sites that allow users to download sample tracks free to persuade them to buy the entire CD. Other Web sites allow a user to purchase and download an entire CD of music tracks to the hard disk (Figure 2-20). Keep in mind that it is legal to download copyrighted music only if the song's copyright holder has granted permission for users to download and play the song.

To listen to an audio file on your computer, you need special software called a **player**. Most current operating systems contain a player. Popular players include iTunes, RealPlayer, and Windows Media Player. If your player will not play a particular audio format, you can download the necessary player free from the Web.

Some applications on the Web use streaming audio. **Streaming** is the process of transferring data in a continuous and even flow. Streaming allows users to access and use a file while it is transmitting. For example, *streaming audio* enables you to listen to music as it downloads to your computer. Many radio and television stations use streaming audio to broadcast music, interviews, talk shows, sporting events, music videos, news, live concerts, and other segments.

Podcasting is another popular method of distributing audio. A *podcast* is recorded audio, usually an MP3 file, stored on a Web site that can be downloaded to a computer or a portable digital audio player such as an iPod. Examples of podcasts include music, radio shows, news stories, classroom lectures, political messages, and television commentaries. Podcasters register their podcasts with content aggregators. Subscribers select podcast feeds they want to be downloaded automatically whenever they connect. Some Web sites, such as podcast.net, specialize in podcast distribution. Others, such as National Public Radio, have incorporated a podcast component in their existing Web site.

AUDIO WEB FILE FORMATS

Audio File Format	Description
AA	Audible Audio (commonly used for downloadable e-books)
AAC	Advanced Audio Coding
AIFF	Audio Interchange File Format
ASF	Advanced Streaming (or Systems) Format (part of Windows Media framework)
MP3	Moving Pictures Experts Group Audio Layer 3 (MPEG-3)
WAV	Windows waveform
WMA	Windows Media Audio (part of Windows Media framework)
RA	RealAudio sound file (supported by RealPlayer)
QT	QuickTime audio, video, or 3-D animation (included with Mac OS, also available separately)

FIGURE 2-19   Popular Web audio file formats.

FIGURE 2-20   HOW TO PURCHASE AND DOWNLOAD MUSIC

Step 1:
Display the music Web site on the screen. Search for, select, and pay for the music you want to purchase from the music Web site.

Step 2:
Download the music from the Web site's server to your computer's hard disk.

Step 3a:
Listen to the music from your computer's hard disk.

Step 3b: Download music from your computer's hard disk to a portable digital audio player. Listen to the music through headphones attached to the digital audio player.

VIDEO Video consists of full-motion images that are played back at various speeds. Most video also has accompanying audio. Instead of turning on the television, you can use the Internet to watch live and/or prerecorded coverage of your favorite programs (Figure 2-21) or enjoy a live performance of your favorite vocalist.

Simple video applications on the Web consist of individual video files, such as movie or television clips, that you must download completely before you can play them on the computer. Video files often are compressed because they are quite large in size. These clips also are quite short in length, usually less than 10 minutes, because they can take a long time to download. The *Moving Pictures Experts Group (MPEG)* defines a popular video compression standard, a widely used one called *MPEG-4*.

As with streaming audio, *streaming video* allows you to view longer or live video

images as they download to your computer. Widely used standards supported by most Web browsers for transmitting streaming video data on the Internet are AVI (Audio Video Interleaved), QuickTime, Windows Media Format, and RealVideo. Like RealAudio, RealVideo is supported by RealPlayer.

VIRTUAL REALITY Virtual reality (**VR**) is the use of computers to simulate a real or imagined environment that appears as a three-dimensional (3-D) space. On the Web, VR involves the display of 3-D images that users explore and manipulate interactively (Figure 2-22).

Using special VR software, a Web developer creates an entire 3-D Web site that contains infinite space and depth, called a *VR world*. A VR world, for example, might show a room with furniture. Users walk through such a VR room by moving an input device forward, backward, or to the side.

Games often use VR. Many practical applications of VR also exist. Science educators create VR models of molecules, organisms, and other structures for students to examine. Companies use VR to showcase products or create advertisements. Architects create VR models of buildings and rooms so clients can see how a completed construction project will look before it is built.

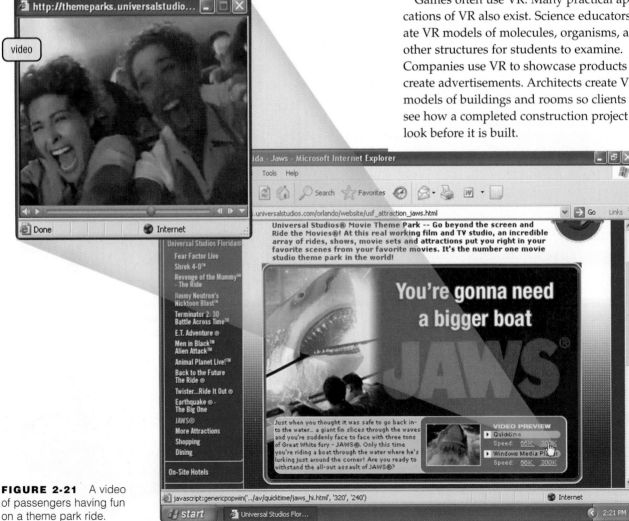

FIGURE 2-21 A video of passengers having fun on a theme park ride.

mouse pointer

FIGURE 2-22 Web site visitors use VR to see the inside of Grand Central Station in New York. As you move the mouse pointer, you see different views inside the station.

PLUG-INS Most Web browsers have the capability of displaying basic multimedia elements on a Web page. Sometimes, a browser might need an additional program, called a plug-in. A **plug-in** is a program that extends the capability of a browser. You can download many plug-ins at no cost from various Web sites (Figure 2-23). Some plug-ins run on all sizes of personal computers and mobile devices. Others have special versions for mobile devices.

Web Publishing

Before the World Wide Web, the means to share opinions and ideas with others easily and inexpensively was limited to the media, classroom, work, or social environments. Generating an advertisement or publication that could reach a massive audience required much expense. Today, businesses and individuals convey information to millions of people by creating their own Web pages. The content of the Web pages ranges from new stories to product information to blogs.

POPULAR PLUG-IN APPLICATIONS

Plug-In Application	Description	Web Address
Acrobat Reader *Get Adobe Reader*	View, navigate, and print Portable Document Format (PDF) files — documents formatted to look just as they look in print	adobe.com
Flash Player *Get macromedia FLASH PLAYER*	View dazzling graphics and animation, hear outstanding sound and music, display Web pages across an entire screen	macromedia.com
QuickTime	View animation, music, audio, video, and VR panoramas and objects directly in a Web page	apple.com
RealPlayer *realPlayer*	Listen to live and on-demand near-CD-quality audio and newscast-quality video; stream audio and video content for faster viewing; play MP3 files; create music CDs	real.com
Shockwave Player *macromedia SHOCKWAVE PLAYER*	Experience dynamic interactive multimedia, 3-D graphics, and streaming audio	macromedia.com
Windows Media Player *Windows MediaPlayer 10*	Listen to live and on-demand audio; play or edit WMA and MP3 files; burn CDs, watch DVD movies	microsoft.com

FIGURE 2-23 Most plug-ins can be downloaded free from the Web.

WEB LINK 2-4

Plug-Ins

For more information, visit scsite.com/ dc2007/ch2/weblink and then click Plug-Ins.

Web publishing is the development and maintenance of Web pages. To develop a Web page, you do not have to be a computer programmer. For the small business or home user, Web publishing is fairly easy as long as you have the proper tools. The five major steps to Web publishing are as follows: (1) plan a Web site, (2) analyze and design a Web site, (3) create a Web site, (4) deploy a Web site, and (5) maintain a Web site. Figure 2-24 illustrates these steps with respect to a personal Web site.

FIGURE 2-24 HOW TO PUBLISH YOUR RESUME ON THE WEB

Step 1:
Plan a Web site.
Think about issues that could affect the design of the Web site.

Step 2:
Analyze and design a Web site. Design the layout of the elements of the Web site.

Step 3:
Create a Web site. Use word processing software or Web page authoring software to create the Web site.

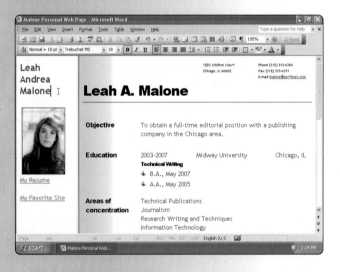

Step 4:
Deploy a Web site. Save the Web site on a Web server.

Step 5:
Maintain a Web site.
Visit your Web site regularly to be sure it is working and current.

Test your knowledge of pages 75 through 91 in Quiz Yourself 2-2.

QUIZ YOURSELF 2-2

Instructions: Find the true statement below. Then, rewrite the remaining false statements so they are true.

1. A blog is a Web site that uses a regularly updated journal format to reflect the interests, opinions, and personalities of the author and sometimes site visitors.

2. A Web browser classifies Web pages in an organized set of categories, such as sports or shopping, and related subcategories.

3. Audio and video files are downloaded to reduce their file sizes.

4. Popular portals include iTunes, RealPlayer, and Windows Media Player.

5. The more widely used search engines for personal computers are Internet Explorer, Netscape, Mozilla, Firefox, Opera, and Safari.

6. To develop a Web page, you have to be a computer programmer.

7. To improve your Web searches, use general nouns and put the least important terms first in the search text.

Quiz Yourself Online: To further check your knowledge of Web addresses, Web browsers, searching, types of Web sites, elements of a Web page, and Web publishing, visit scsite.com/dc2007/ch2/quiz and then click Objectives 4 – 9.

E-COMMERCE

E-commerce, short for *electronic commerce*, is a business transaction that occurs over an electronic network such as the Internet. Anyone with access to a computer, an Internet connection, and a means to pay for purchased goods or services can participate in e-commerce (Figure 2-25).

In the past, e-commerce transactions were conducted primarily using desktop computers. Today, many mobile computers and devices, such as PDAs and smart phones, also access the Web wirelessly. Some people use the term *m-commerce* (mobile commerce) to identify e-commerce that takes place using mobile devices.

Popular uses of e-commerce by consumers include shopping, investing, and banking. Users can purchase just about any product or service on the Web. Some examples include flowers, books, computers, prescription drugs, music, movies, cars, airline tickets, and concert tickets. Through online investing, individuals buy and sell stocks or bonds without using a broker.

Three different types of e-commerce are business-to-consumer, consumer-to-consumer, and business-to-business. *Business-to-consumer (B2C) e-commerce* consists of the sale of goods

FIGURE 2-25 E-commerce activities include shopping for goods at an online auction, such as eBay.

and services to the general public. For example, Dell has a B2C Web site. Instead of visiting a computer store to purchase a computer, customers can order one that meets their specifications directly from the Dell Web site.

A customer (consumer) visits an online business through an **electronic storefront**, which contains product descriptions, graphics, and a shopping cart. The **shopping cart** allows the customer to collect purchases. When ready to complete the sale, the customer enters personal data and the method of payment, preferably through a secure Internet connection (read Ethics & Issues 2-2 for a related discussion).

Instead of purchasing from a business, consumers can purchase from each other. For example, with an **online auction**, users bid on an item being sold by someone else. The highest bidder at the end of the bidding period purchases the item. *Consumer-to-consumer (C2C) e-commerce* occurs when one consumer sells directly to another, such as in an online auction. eBay is one of the more popular online auction Web sites.

Most e-commerce, though, actually takes place between businesses, which is called *business-to-business (B2B) e-commerce*. Businesses often provide goods and services to other businesses, such as online advertising, recruiting, credit, sales, market research, technical support, and training. For example, some MasterCard and Visa credit card companies provide corporations with Web-based purchasing, tracking, and transaction downloading capabilities.

WEB LINK 2-5

E-Commerce

For more information, visit scsite.com/dc2007/ch2/weblink and then click E-Commerce.

FAQ 2-8

How popular is online shopping?

Researchers predict that e-commerce sales will grow at a steady rate of 19 percent per year until at least 2008. At that time, online shopping will account for approximately 10 percent of all retail sales in the United States, or 63 million households. For more information, visit scsite.com/dc2007/ch2/faq and then click Online Shopping.

ETHICS & ISSUES 2-2

Should All Sales on the Internet Be Taxed?

The Supreme Court has ruled that merchants can charge state and local sales taxes only when they have a physical presence, such as a store or office building, where the purchase is made. Because Internet merchants often do not have a physical presence in a buyer's state, online purchases often are sales tax free. One study predicts that by 2011 Internet sales will cost state and local governments more than $54 billion in sales tax revenues, forcing them either to raise taxes or cut services. In response, many states have enacted "use" taxes that require residents to report, and pay sales tax on, items purchased on the Internet but used at home. Even a use tax, though, does not address other problems. The sales-tax-free status of some Internet purchases also may have a negative impact on local businesses that must charge sales tax and on lower-income families who are less likely to make purchases on the Internet. Yet, many feel any tax on e-commerce is unmanageable (forcing merchants to adjust to varying sales tax rates) and unjustified. Should sales taxes be applied to Internet purchases? Why? Is a use tax a viable alternative? Why or why not? How else can the problems of taxing, or not taxing, Internet purchases be addressed?

OTHER INTERNET SERVICES

The Web is only one of the many services on the Internet. The Web and other Internet services have changed the way we communicate. We can send e-mail messages to the president, have a discussion with experts about the stock market, chat with someone in another country about genealogy, and talk about homework assignments with classmates via instant messages. Many times, these communications take place completely in writing — without the parties ever meeting each other.

At home, work, and school, people use computers and Internet-enabled mobile devices so they always have instant access to e-mail, FTP (File Transfer Protocol), newsgroups and message boards, mailing lists, chat rooms, instant messaging, and Internet telephony. The following pages discuss each of these Internet services.

E-Mail

E-mail (short for *electronic mail*) is the transmission of messages and files via a computer network. E-mail was one of the original services on the Internet, enabling scientists and researchers working on government-sponsored projects to communicate with colleagues at other locations. Today, e-mail is a primary communications method for both personal and business use.

You use an **e-mail program** to create, send, receive, forward, store, print, and delete e-mail messages. Outlook and Outlook Express are two popular e-mail programs. The steps in Figure 2-26 illustrate how to send an e-mail message using Outlook. The message can be simple text or can include an attachment such as a word processing document, a graphic, an audio clip, or a video clip.

FIGURE 2-26 HOW TO SEND AN E-MAIL MESSAGE

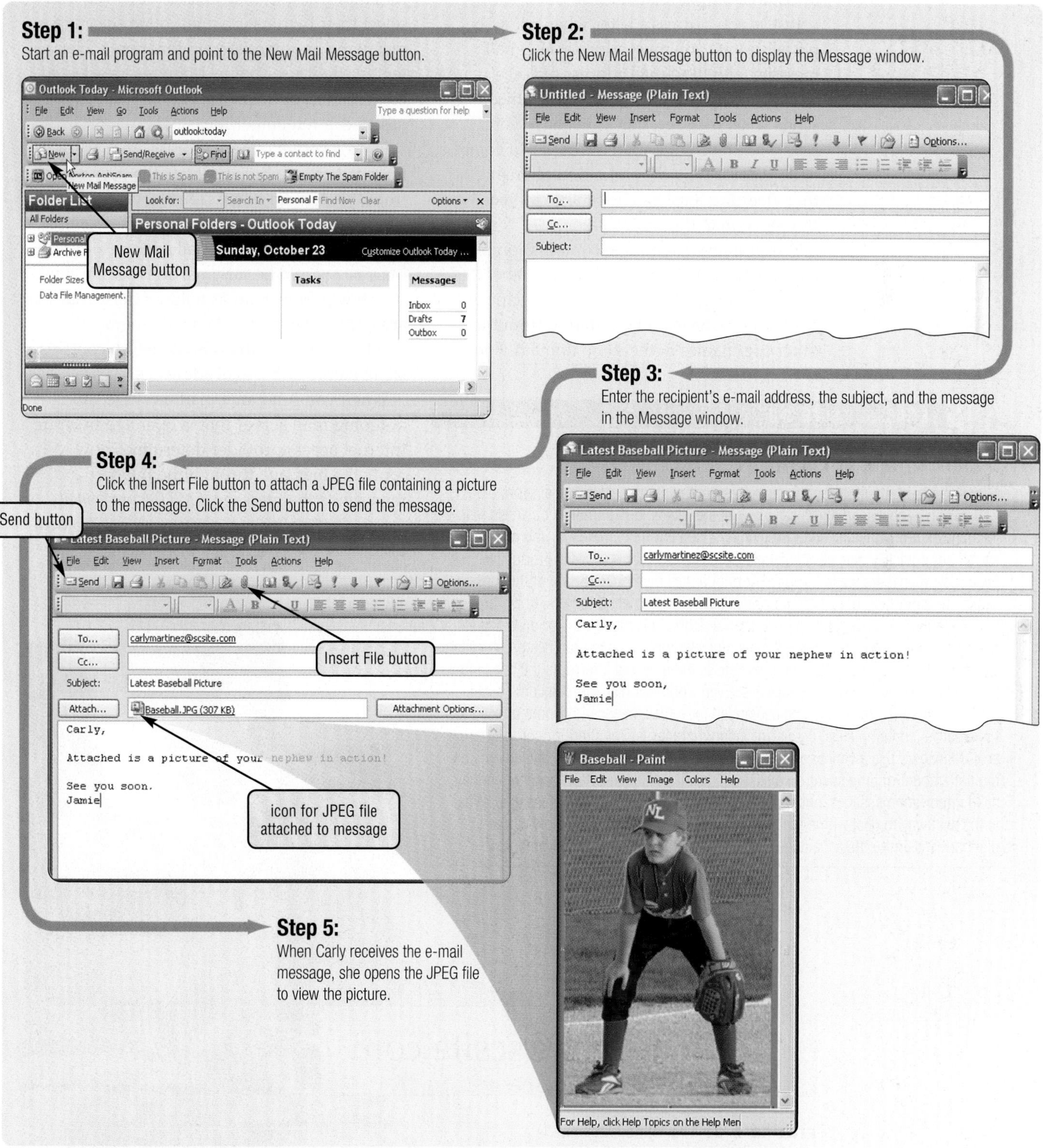
Step 1:
Start an e-mail program and point to the New Mail Message button.
Outlook Today - Microsoft Outlook
New Mail Message button
Step 2:
Click the New Mail Message button to display the Message window.
Untitled - Message (Plain Text)
Step 3:
Enter the recipient's e-mail address, the subject, and the message in the Message window.
Latest Baseball Picture - Message (Plain Text)
carlymartinez@scsite.com
Latest Baseball Picture
Carly,
Attached is a picture of your nephew in action!
See you soon,
Jamie
Step 4:
Click the Insert File button to attach a JPEG file containing a picture to the message. Click the Send button to send the message.
Send button
Insert File button
Baseball.JPG (307 KB)
icon for JPEG file attached to message
Baseball - Paint
Step 5:
When Carly receives the e-mail message, she opens the JPEG file to view the picture.

Internet access providers typically supply an e-mail program as a standard part of their Internet access services. Some Web sites, such as MSN Hotmail and Yahoo!, provide free e-mail services. To use these Web-based e-mail programs, you connect to the Web site and set up an e-mail account, which typically includes an e-mail address and a password. Read Ethics & Issues 2-3 for a related discussion.

Just as you address a letter when using the postal system, you must address an e-mail message with the e-mail address of your intended recipient. Likewise, when someone sends you a message, they must have your e-mail address. An **e-mail address** is a combination of a user name and a domain name that identifies a user so he or she can receive Internet e-mail (Figure 2-27).

A **user name** is a unique combination of characters, such as letters of the alphabet and/or numbers, that identifies a specific user. Your user name must be different from the other user names in the same domain. For

example, a user named Carly Martinez whose server has a domain name of scsite.com might want to select CMartinez as her user name. If scsite.com already has a CMartinez (for Carlos Martinez), Carly will have to select a different user name, such as carlymartinez or carly_martinez.

Sometimes, companies decide user names for employees. In many cases, however, users select their own user names, often selecting a nickname or any other combination of characters for their user name. Many users select a combination of their first and last names so others can remember it easily.

In an Internet e-mail address, an @ (pronounced at) symbol separates the user name from the domain name. Your service provider supplies the domain name. Using the example in Figure 2-27, a possible e-mail address for Carly Martinez would be carlymartinez@scsite.com, which would be read as follows: Carly Martinez at s c site dot com. Most e-mail programs allow you to create an **address book**, which contains a list of names and e-mail addresses.

When you send an e-mail message, an outgoing mail server that is operated by your Internet access provider determines how to route the message through the Internet and then sends the message. *SMTP (simple mail transfer protocol)* is a communications protocol used by some outgoing mail servers.

ETHICS & ISSUES 2-3

E-Mail: Irritant or Liberator?

E-mail is one of the more popular services on the Internet. Worldwide, more than 230 million people send and receive e-mail messages. E-mail makes business managers more productive by allowing them to share information, ideas, and opinions easily. But ironically, this easy sharing also can make managers less productive. Every day, managers wade through rivers of e-mail messages. Some of the messages are important, but many are copies of messages sent to others, notes on minor matters, or observations once shared in brief telephone calls or on walks to the water cooler. Most messages expect a quick reply, so hours can be spent dealing with e-mail. The constant flow of e-mail steals the time and interrupts the concentration needed for everyday work activities. Even worse, as managers become accustomed to the brief, rapid thinking demanded for e-mail, they can become unused to the creative, contemplative, persistent thought processes required for complex projects. Managers use a variety of measures to dam the flood of e-mail, including limiting the amount of time spent on messages, having colleagues telephone when they send important messages, and using filtering software to prioritize messages. What is the best way to deal with e-mail? Why? In terms of productivity, how can a company maximize the advantages of e-mail and minimize the disadvantages?

carlymartinez@scsite.com

FIGURE 2-27 An e-mail address is a combination of a user name and a domain name.

As you receive e-mail messages, an incoming mail server — also operated by your Internet access provider — holds the messages in your mailbox until you use your e-mail program to retrieve them. *POP3*, the latest version of POP (*Post Office Protocol*), is a communications protocol used by some incoming mail servers. Most e-mail programs have a mail notification alert that informs you via a message or sound when you receive new mail. Figure 2-28 illustrates how an e-mail message may travel from a sender to a receiver.

WEB LINK 2-6

E-Mail
For more information, visit scsite.com/dc2007/ch2/weblink and then click E-Mail.

FAQ 2-9

Can my computer get a virus through e-mail?

Yes. A *virus* is a computer program that can damage files and the operating system. One way that virus authors attempt to spread a virus is by sending virus-infected e-mail attachments. If you receive an e-mail attachment, you should use an antivirus program to verify that it is virus free.

For more information, read the High-Tech Talk article on page 168, the section about viruses and antivirus programs in Chapter 8, and visit scsite.com/dc2007/ch2/faq and then click Viruses.

FIGURE 2-28 HOW AN E-MAIL MESSAGE MAY TRAVEL FROM A SENDER TO A RECEIVER

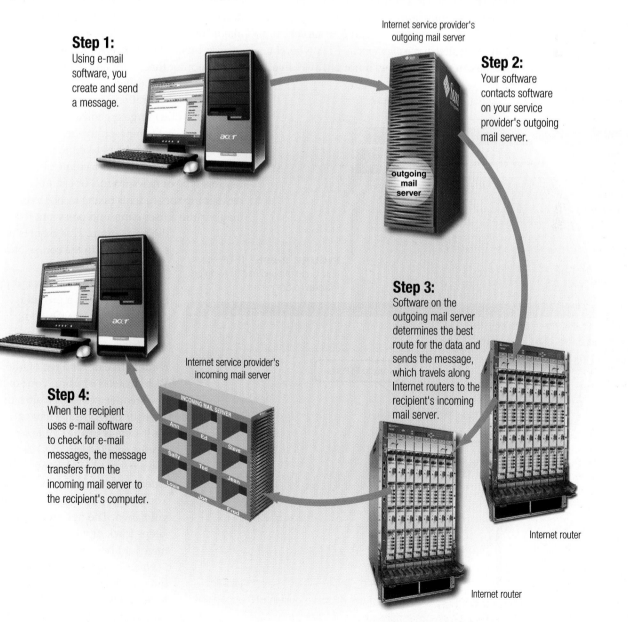

Step 1:
Using e-mail software, you create and send a message.

Internet service provider's outgoing mail server

Step 2:
Your software contacts software on your service provider's outgoing mail server.

outgoing mail server

Step 3:
Software on the outgoing mail server determines the best route for the data and sends the message, which travels along Internet routers to the recipient's incoming mail server.

Internet service provider's incoming mail server

Step 4:
When the recipient uses e-mail software to check for e-mail messages, the message transfers from the incoming mail server to the recipient's computer.

INCOMING MAIL SERVER

Ann Ed Steve Sally Ted Jean Louie Joe Fred

Internet router

Internet router

FTP

FTP (*File Transfer Protocol*) is an Internet standard that permits file uploading and downloading (transferring) with other computers on the Internet. Uploading is the opposite of downloading; that is, **uploading** is the process of transferring documents, graphics, and other objects from your computer to a server on the Internet. Web page authors, for example, often use FTP to upload their Web pages to a Web server.

Many operating systems include FTP capabilities (Figure 2-29). If yours does not, you can download FTP programs from the Web, usually for a small fee.

An *FTP server* is a computer that allows users to upload and/or download files using FTP. An FTP site is a collection of files including text, graphics, audio clips, video clips, and program files that reside on an FTP server. Many FTP sites have *anonymous FTP*, whereby anyone can transfer some, if not all, available files. Some FTP sites restrict file transfers to those who have authorized accounts (user names and passwords) on the FTP server.

Large files on FTP sites often are compressed to reduce storage space and download time. Before you can use a compressed (zipped) file, you must uncompress (unzip) it. Chapter 8 discusses utilities that zip and unzip files.

Newsgroups and Message Boards

A **newsgroup** is an online area in which users have written discussions about a particular subject (Figure 2-30). To participate in a discussion, a user sends a message to the newsgroup, and other users in the newsgroup read and reply to the message. The entire collection of Internet newsgroups is called *Usenet*, which contains tens of thousands of newsgroups about a multitude of topics. Some major topic areas include news, recreation, society, business, science, and computers.

A computer that stores and distributes newsgroup messages is called a *news server*. Many universities, corporations, Internet access providers, and other large organizations have a news server. Some newsgroups require you to enter a user name and password to participate in the discussion. Only authorized members can use this type of newsgroup. For example, a newsgroup for students taking a college course may require a user name and password to access the newsgroup. This ensures that only students in the course participate in the discussion.

To participate in a newsgroup, typically you use a program called a *newsreader*. Outlook Express includes a newsreader. You also can download newsreaders free or for a fee on the Web. Instead of using your own newsreader, some Web sites that sponsor newsgroups have a built-in newsreader. A newsreader enables you to access a newsgroup to read previously entered messages, called *articles*. You can *post*, or add, articles of your own. The newsreader also keeps track of which articles you have and have not read.

Newsgroup members frequently post articles as a reply to another article — either to

FIGURE 2-29a (FTP site being added to My Network Places folder)

FIGURE 2-29b (FTP site link is displayed in My Network Places folder)

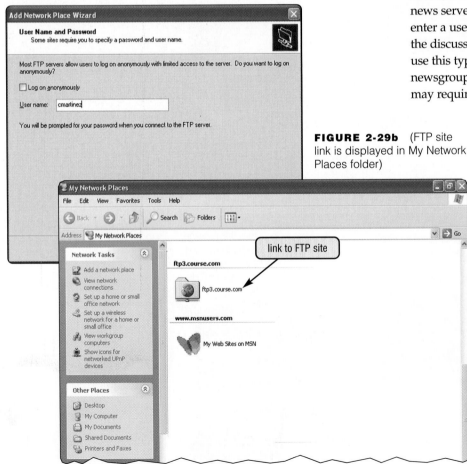

FIGURE 2-29 Many operating systems, such as Windows XP, have built-in FTP capabilities.

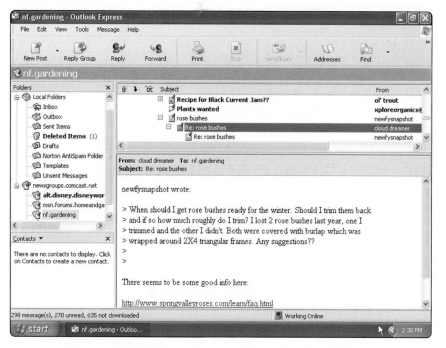

WEB LINK 2-8

Newsgroups and Message Boards

For more information, visit scsite.com/ dc2007/ch2/weblink and then click Newsgroups and Message Boards.

FIGURE 2-30 Users in a newsgroup read and reply to other users' messages.

answer a question or to comment on material in the original article. These replies may cause the author of the original article, or others, to post additional articles related to the original article. A *thread* or *threaded discussion* consists of the original article and all subsequent related replies. A thread can be short-lived or continue for some time, depending on the nature of the topic and the interest of the participants.

Using a newsreader, you can search for newsgroups discussing a particular subject such as a type of musical instrument, brand of sports equipment, or employment opportunities. If you like the discussion in a particular newsgroup, you can *subscribe* to it, which means its location is saved in your newsreader for easy future access.

In some newsgroups, posted articles are sent to a moderator instead of immediately displaying on the newsgroup. The *moderator* reviews the contents of the article and then posts it, if appropriate. With a *moderated newsgroup*, the moderator decides if the article is relevant to the discussion. The moderator may choose to edit or discard inappropriate articles. For this reason, the content of a moderated newsgroup is considered more valuable.

A popular Web-based type of discussion group that does not require a newsreader is a **message board**. Many Web sites use message boards instead of newsgroups because they are easier to use.

Mailing Lists

A **mailing list** is a group of e-mail names and addresses given a single name. When a message is sent to a mailing list, every person on the list receives a copy of the message in his or her mailbox. To add your e-mail name and address to a mailing list, you **subscribe** to it (Figure 2-31). To remove your name, you **unsubscribe** from the mailing list. Some mailing lists are called *LISTSERVs*, named after a popular mailing list program.

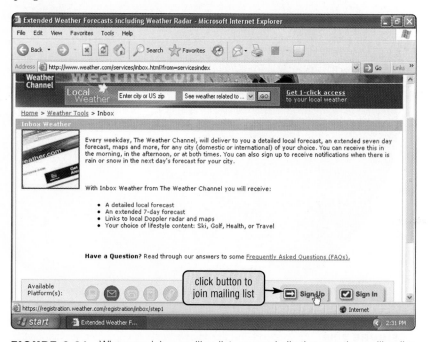

FIGURE 2-31 When you join a mailing list, you and all others on the mailing list receive e-mail messages from the Web site.

WEB LINK 2-9

Mailing Lists

For more information, visit scsite.com/ dc2007/ch2/weblink and then click Mailing Lists.

Thousands of mailing lists exist about a variety of topics in areas of entertainment, business, computers, society, culture, health, recreation, and education. To locate a mailing list dealing with a particular topic, search for the keywords, mailing list or LISTSERV, in a search engine. Many vendors use mailing lists to communicate with their customer base.

Chat Rooms

A **chat** is a real-time typed conversation that takes place on a computer. **Real time** means that you and the people with whom you are conversing are online at the same time. A **chat room** is a location on an Internet server that permits users to chat with each other. Anyone in the chat room can participate in the conversation, which usually is specific to a particular topic.

As you type on your keyboard, a line of characters and symbols is displayed on the computer screen. Others connected to the same chat room server also see what you have typed (Figure 2-32). Some chat rooms support voice chats and video chats, in which people hear or see each other as they chat.

WEB LINK 2-10

Chat Rooms

For more information, visit scsite.com/ dc2007/ch2/weblink and then click Chat Rooms.

To start a chat session, you connect to a chat server through a program called a *chat client*. Today's browsers usually include a chat client. If yours does not, you can download a chat client from the Web. Some Web sites allow users to conduct chats without a chat client.

Once you have installed a chat client, you can create or join a conversation on the chat server to which you are connected. The chat room should indicate the discussion topic. The person who creates a chat room acts as the operator and has responsibility for monitoring the conversation and disconnecting anyone who becomes disruptive. Operator status can be shared or transferred to someone else.

Instant Messaging

Instant messaging (**IM**) is a real-time Internet communications service that notifies you when one or more people are online and then allows you to exchange messages or files or join a private chat room with them. Some IM services support voice and video conversations (Figure 2-33). Many IM services also can alert you to information such as calendar appointments, stock quotes, weather, or sports scores. They also allow you to send pictures or other documents to a recipient. For IM to work, both parties must be online at the same time. Also, the receiver of a message must be willing to accept messages.

People use IM on all types of computers, including desktop computers and mobile computers and devices, such as smart phones. To use IM, you may have to install *instant messenger* software on the computer or device you plan to use. Some operating systems, such as Windows XP, include an instant messenger. No standards currently exist for IM. To ensure successful communications, all individuals on the contact list need to use the same or a compatible instant messenger.

FIGURE 2-32 As you type, the words and symbols you enter are displayed on the computer screens of other people in the same chat room.

FIGURE 2-33   AN EXAMPLE OF INSTANT MESSAGING

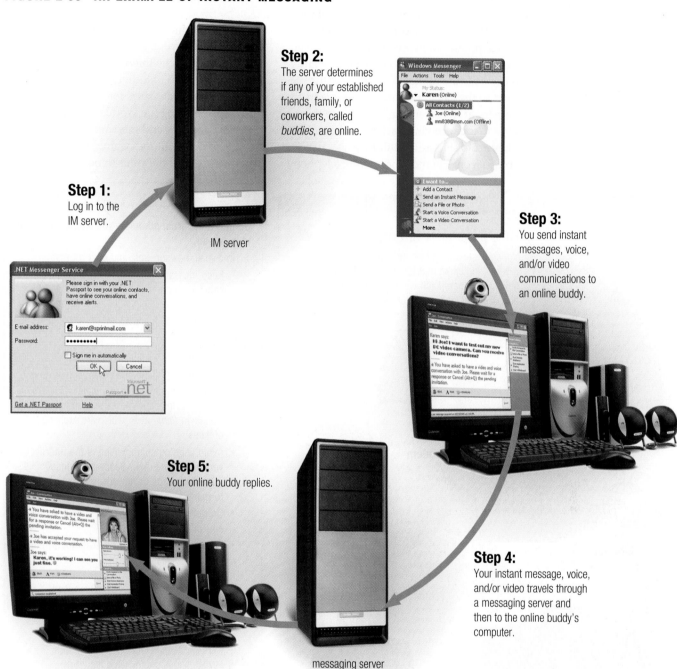

Step 1:
Log in to the
IM server.

Step 2:
The server determines
if any of your established
friends, family, or
coworkers, called
buddies, are online.

IM server

Step 3:
You send instant
messages, voice,
and/or video
communications to
an online buddy.

Step 5:
Your online buddy replies.

Step 4:
Your instant message, voice,
and/or video travels through
a messaging server and
then to the online buddy's
computer.

messaging server

Internet Telephony

Internet telephony, also called *Voice over IP* (Internet Protocol), enables users to speak to other users over the Internet using their desktop computer, mobile computer, or mobile device. That is, Internet telephony uses the Internet (instead of the public switched telephone network) to connect a calling party to one or more local or long-distance called parties.

To place an Internet telephone call, you need a high-speed Internet connection (e.g., via DSL or cable modem); Internet telephone service; a microphone or telephone, depending on the Internet telephone service; and Internet telephone software or a telephone adapter, depending on the Internet telephone service. Calls to other parties with the same Internet telephone service often are free, while calls that connect to the telephone network typically cost about $13 to $25 per month.

WEB LINK 2-11

Internet Telephony
For more information,
visit scsite.com/
dc2007/ch2/weblink
and then click
Internet Telephony.

As you speak in a microphone or telephone connected to your computer, the Internet telephone software and the computer's sound card or the telephone adapter convert your spoken words (analog signals) to digital signals and then transmit the digitized audio over the Internet to the called parties. Software and equipment at the receiving end reverse the process so the receiving parties can hear what you have said. Figure 2-34 illustrates a user's equipment configuration for Internet telephony.

> **FAQ 2-10**
>
> ### How popular is Internet telephony?
>
> Vonage, a leader in Internet telephony services, recently indicated that it is growing by 15,000 new subscribers each week. For more information, visit scsite.com/dc2007/ch2/faq and then click Internet Telephony.

cable/DSL modem

Internet

telephone adapter

personal computer

telephone

FIGURE 2-34 Equipment configuration for a user making a call via Internet telephony.

NETIQUETTE

Netiquette, which is short for Internet etiquette, is the code of acceptable behaviors users should follow while on the Internet; that is, it is the conduct expected of individuals while online. Netiquette includes rules for all aspects of the Internet, including the World Wide Web, e-mail, FTP, newsgroups and message boards, chat rooms, and instant messaging. Figure 2-35 outlines some of the rules of netiquette.

NETIQUETTE

Golden Rule: Treat others as you would like them to treat you.

1. In e-mail, newsgroups, and chat rooms:
   - Keep messages brief. Use proper grammar, spelling, and punctuation.
   - Be careful when using sarcasm and humor, as it might be misinterpreted.
   - Be polite. Avoid offensive language.
   - Read the message before you send it.
   - Use meaningful subject lines.
   - Avoid sending or posting *flames,* which are abusive or insulting messages. Do not participate in *flame wars,* which are exchanges of flames.
   - Avoid sending spam, which is the Internet's version of junk mail. *Spam* is an unsolicited e-mail message or newsgroup posting sent to many recipients or newsgroups at once.
   - Do not use all capital letters, which is the equivalent of SHOUTING!
   - Use **emoticons** to express emotion. Popular emoticons include

:)	Smile	:\	Undecided
:(	Frown	:o	Surprised
:|	Indifference		

   - Use abbreviations and acronyms for phrases:

BTW	by the way
FYI	for your information
FWIW	for what it's worth
IMHO	in my humble opinion
TTFN	ta ta for now
TYVM	thank you very much

   - Clearly identify a *spoiler,* which is a message that reveals a solution to a game or ending to a movie or program.
2. Read the *FAQ* (frequently asked questions), if one exists. Many newsgroups and Web pages have an FAQ.
3. Do not assume material is accurate or up-to-date. Be forgiving of other's mistakes.
4. Never read someone's private e-mail.

FIGURE 2-35 Some of the rules of netiquette.

Test your knowledge of pages 91 through 100 in Quiz Yourself 2-3.

QUIZ YOURSELF 2-3

Instructions: Find the true statement below. Then, rewrite the remaining false statements so they are true.

1. A chat room is a location on an Internet server that permits users to chat with each other.

2. An e-mail address is a combination of a user name and an e-mail program that identifies a user so he or she can receive Internet e-mail.

3. Business-to-consumer e-commerce occurs when one consumer sells directly to another, such as in an online auction.

4. FTP is an Internet standard that permits file reading and writing with other computers on the Internet.

5. Spam uses the Internet (instead of the public switched telephone network) to connect a calling party to one or more called parties.

6. Netiquette is the code of unacceptable behaviors while on the Internet.

7. On a newsgroup, a subscription consists of the original article and all subsequent related replies.

Quiz Yourself Online: To further check your knowledge of e-commerce, e-mail, FTP, newsgroups and message boards, mailing lists, chat rooms, instant messaging, Internet telephony, and netiquette, visit scsite.com/dc2007/ch2/quiz and then click Objectives 10 – 12.

CHAPTER SUMMARY

This chapter presented the history and structure of the Internet. It discussed the World Wide Web at length, including topics such as browsing, navigating, searching, Web publishing, and e-commerce (read Ethics & Issues 2-4 for a related discussion). It also introduced other services available on the Internet, such as e-mail, FTP, newsgroups and message boards, chat rooms, instant messaging, and Internet telephony. Finally, the chapter listed rules of netiquette.

ETHICS & ISSUES 2-4

Should Companies Be Able to Track Your Online Habits?

When you visit a Web site that includes an advertisement, someone probably is recording the fact that you visited that Web site and viewed the advertisement with your browser. Over time, companies that specialize in tracking who views which online advertisements can amass an enormous amount of information about your online Web surfing habits. This collection of information is considered to be part of your online profile. One company claims that through the use of advertisements on Web pages, it can track well over one billion Web page views per day. Through tracking the Web sites a user visits, the products they buy, and the articles they read, a company may attempt to profile the visitor's beliefs, associations, and habits. Although a user may think he or she is anonymous while navigating the Web, the company can attempt through various means to link the user's true identity with the user's online profile. The company can sell online profiles, with or without the user's true identity, to other advertisers or organizations. Should organizations be allowed to track your Web surfing habits? Why or why not? Should organizations be allowed to associate your real identity with your online identity and profit from the information? Should companies give you the option of not being tracked? What are the benefits and dangers of online tracking?

CAREER CORNER

Web Developer

If you are looking for a job working with the latest Internet technology, then Web developer could be the career for you. A *Web developer* analyzes, designs, develops, implements, and supports Web applications and functionality. Specialized programming skills required include HTML, JavaScript, Java, Perl, C++, and VBScript. Developers also may need multimedia knowledge, including Adobe Photoshop, Macromedia Flash, and Macromedia Director. Developers must be aware of emerging technologies and know how they can be used to enhance a Web presence.

A Web developer must be able to appreciate a client's needs, recognize the technologies involved to meet those needs, and explain those technologies to the client. For example, if the client is a large corporation seeking to set up an online store, a Web developer must understand e-commerce and be able to explain requirements, probable costs, and possible outcomes in a way the client can understand.

Educational requirements vary from company to company and can range from a high school education to a four-year degree. Many companies place heavy emphasis on certifications. Two of the more popular certifications are available through the International Webmasters Association (IWA) and the World Organization of Webmasters (WOW). A wide salary range exists — from $35,000 to $70,000 — depending on educational background and location. For more information, visit scsite.com/dc2007/ch2/careers and then click Web Developer.

High-Tech Talk

A COMPUTER'S INTERNET PROTOCOL (IP) ADDRESS

Every computer on the Internet has a unique address, called an IP address, that distinguishes it from other computers on the Internet. An IP address has two parts that identify a specific computer: one part to identify the network where that computer resides and a second part to pinpoint the specific computer or host within that network.

A typical IP address — such as 216.239.39.99 — has four groups of numbers that range from 0 through 255. This form of the IP address sometimes is called a *dotted decimal number* or *dotted quad*. The four groups of numbers in the dotted quad are called octets, because they each have 8 bits when viewed in binary form for a total of 32 bits in the IP address. For instance, the binary form of 216.239.39.99 is 11011000.11101111.00101001.01100011 (Figure 2-36). For more information about how the binary system works, see Appendix A.

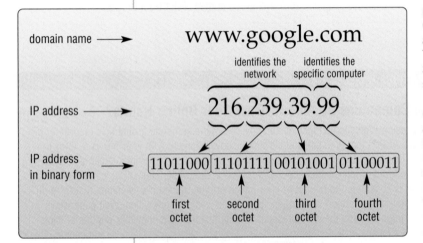

domain name → www.google.com

identifies the network   identifies the specific computer

IP address → 216.239.39.99

IP address in binary form → | 11011000 | 11101111 | 00101001 | 01100011 |

first octet   second octet   third octet   fourth octet

FIGURE 2-36
Components of an IP address.

Because each of the 8 bits can be 1 or 0, the total possible combinations per octet are 2^8, or 256. Combining the four octets of an IP address provides a possible 2^{32} or 4,294,967,296 unique values. The actual number of available addresses is about 3 billion, because some values are reserved for special use and are, therefore, off limits.

To request data such as a Web page from a computer on the Internet, you need only an IP address. For instance, if you type the Web address, http://216.239.39.99, your browser will display the home page on the machine hosting the Google Web site. Of course, remembering one IP address out of billions is a little overwhelming — so you probably would just type the domain name, www.google.com, in your browser. Your browser then contacts a domain name server (DNS) to resolve the human-readable domain name into a machine-readable IP address. Each domain name server houses a simple database that maps domain names to IP addresses. The DNS would resolve the human-readable domain name, www.google.com, into a machine-readable IP address, 216.239.39.99.

Domain names are helpful because they are easier for people to remember than IP addresses. You can learn more about a domain using the whois form at the Network Solutions Web site (www.netsol.com and then click the whois link). If you type a domain name, such as google.com, the form displays the registration information for that domain, including its IP address.

Like all other computers, your computer must have an IP address to connect to the Internet or another computer that has an IP address. Servers generally have *static IP addresses*, because they usually are connected to the Internet and their IP addresses do not change often. When you connect to the Internet using your home computer, you most likely are using a temporary or *dynamic IP address*. Your access provider uses the *Dynamic Host Configuration Protocol (DHCP)* to assign your computer a temporary dynamic IP address from a pool of IP addresses. The dynamic IP address is unique only for that session. Once you disconnect, the DHCP server puts that IP address back in the IP address pool so it can assign it to the next requesting computer. Even if you immediately reconnect, the DHCP server might not assign you the same IP address. Using DHCP and dynamic IP addresses means an Internet service provider needs only one IP address for each modem it supports, rather than one for each of its millions of customers.

Billions of IP addresses sounds like a lot. But, because so many computers connected to the Internet need unique IP addresses, a growing shortage of IP addresses exists. A new IP addressing scheme, called *IPv6* or *IPng (IP Next Generation)* will lengthen IP addresses from 32 bits to 128 bits and increase the number of available IP addresses to a whopping 3.4×10^{38}, or 340,000,000,000,000,000,000,000,000,000,000,000,000.

Do you want to know the IP address currently assigned to your computer?

- With Windows 2000/XP, click the Start button on the taskbar and then click Run. Type `cmd` to open the MS-DOS window. Type `ipconfig` and then press the ENTER key.
- With Windows 98, click the Start button on the taskbar and then click Run. Type `winipcfg` and then press the ENTER key.

If you are using an older version of AOL, the IP address might read 0.0.0.0 because AOL uses a proprietary method to assign IP addresses. For more information, visit scsite.com/dc2007/ch2/tech and then click IP Addresses.

Companies on the Cutting Edge

GOOGLE
POPULAR SEARCH ENGINE

The founders of *Google*, the leading Internet search engine, state that their mission is to organize the world's information. Every day, their Web site handles hundreds of millions of queries for information. In seconds, it can locate specific phrases and terms on four billion Web pages by using more than 10,000 connected computers.

Sergey Brin and Larry Page launched Google in 1998 in a friend's garage. The name is derived from "googol," which is the name of the number 1 followed by 100 zeros. Nearly 4,200 employees work for the Mountain View, California, corporation worldwide. In 2005, the company expanded its multilingual search capabilities by partnering with the most-visited Spanish-language Web site, Univision.com. For more information, visit scsite.com/dc2007/ch2/companies and then click Google.

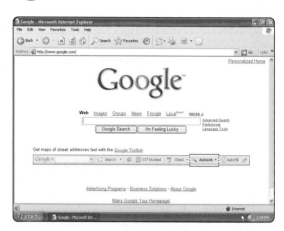

YAHOO!
POPULAR WEB PORTAL

Yahoo!, the first navigational portal to the Web, began as a hobby for Jerry Yang and David Filo when they were doctoral candidates in electrical engineering at Stanford University. They started creating and organizing lists of their favorite Web sites in 1994. The following year, they shared their creation, named Yahoo!, with fellow students and then released their product to the Internet community.

Yahoo! is an acronym for Yet Another Hierarchical Officious Oracle. What makes Yahoo! unique is that staff members build the directory by assuming the role of a typical Web researcher. Yahoo! is recognized for its breadth of features; in 2005, it added an audio search service that lets users preview an individual song or artist from 16 different services and a job search engine found at HotJobs.com. For more information, visit scsite.com/dc2007/ch2/companies and then click Yahoo!.

Technology Trailblazers

TIM BERNERS-LEE
CREATOR OF THE WORLD WIDE WEB

The World Wide Web (WWW) has become one of the more widely used Internet services, and its roots are based on *Tim Berners-Lee's* work. Berners-Lee is credited with creating the first Web server, browser, and URL addresses.

He developed his ideas in 1989 while working at CERN, the European Particle Physics Laboratory in Geneva, Switzerland, and based his work on a program he had written for his own use to track random associations. Today, he works quietly in academia as director of the World Wide Web Consortium (W3C) at the Massachusetts Institute of Technology.

In 2005, Berners-Lee told the British Broadcasting Corporation (BBC) that he is pleased to see that blogging is becoming a creative medium that resembles his original idea of the World Wide Web. For more information, visit scsite.com/dc2007/ch2/people and then click Tim Berners-Lee.

MEG WHITMAN
EBAY PRESIDENT AND CEO

Meg Whitman joined eBay in 1998 and has been instrumental in helping the company become the world's largest online marketplace. Before that time, she was an executive for the Keds Division of the Stride Rite Corporation and general manager of Hasbro Inc.'s Preschool Division. She then served as president and CEO of Florists Transworld Delivery (FTD).

She credits her success to listening to the loyal eBay community, and she occasionally answers their e-mails personally. She holds degrees in economics from Princeton University and management from the Harvard Business School.

More than 100 million people worldwide were part of the eBay community in 2005, and Whitman is looking to expand the marketplace, especially in China. She predicts the number of Chinese users will surpass the number of American users by 2009. For more information, visit scsite.com/dc2007/ch2/people and then click Meg Whitman.

Chapter Review

The Chapter Review section summarizes the concepts presented in this chapter. To listen to the audio version of this Chapter Review, visit scsite.com/dc2007/ch2/review. To obtain help from other students regarding any subject in this chapter, visit scsite.com/dc2007/ch2/forum and post your thoughts or questions.

(1) **What Is the History of the Internet?**   The **Internet** is a worldwide collection of networks that links millions of businesses, government agencies, educational institutions, and individuals. The Internet has its roots in *ARPANET*, a network started in 1969 to link researchers across the United States. In 1986, the National Science Foundation connected its huge network, called *NSFnet*, to ARPANET, creating a configuration of complex networks and hosts that became known as the Internet.

(2) **How Can You Access and Connect to the Internet?**   Employees and students often connect to the Internet through a business or school network. The networks usually use a high-speed line leased from a telephone company. Some home and small businesses connect to the Internet with **dial-up access**, which uses a modem in the computer and a standard telephone line. Many home and small business users opt for higher-speed *broadband* connections, such as DSL, cable television networks, radio signals, or satellite. **DSL** provides Internet connections using regular copper telephone lines. A **cable modem** allows access to Internet services through the cable television network. *Fixed wireless* connections use a dish-shaped antenna to communicate via radio signals. A *satellite modem* communicates with a satellite dish. An **access provider** is a business that provides access to the Internet free or for a fee. An **ISP (Internet service provider)** is a regional or national access provider. An **online service provider** (OSP) provides Internet access in addition to members-only features. A **wireless Internet service provider** (WISP) provides wireless Internet access to users with wireless modems or Internet-enabled mobile devices.

(3) **What Is an IP Address?**   An **IP address** (*Internet Protocol address*) is a number that uniquely identifies each computer or device connected to the Internet. The Internet relies on IP addresses to send data to computers at specific locations. A **domain name** is the text version of an IP address.

> *connect*
> Visit scsite.com/dc2007/ch2/quiz or click the Quiz Yourself button. Click Objectives 1 – 3.

(4) **What Are the Components of a Web Address?**   The **World Wide Web** (*WWW*), or **Web**, consists of a worldwide collection of electronic documents. Each electronic document is called a **Web page**. A **URL** (*Uniform Resource Locator*), or **Web address**, is a unique address for a Web page. A Web address consists of a protocol, a domain name, and sometimes the path to a specific Web page or location on a Web page.

(5) **What Is the Purpose of a Web Browser?**   A **Web browser**, or **browser**, is application software that allows users to access and view Web pages. When you type a Web address in the Address box of a browser window, a computer called a **Web server** delivers the requested Web page to your computer. Most Web pages contain links. A **link** is a built-in connection that, when clicked, displays a related Web page or part of a Web page.

(6) **How Can You Search for Information on the Web?**   Two commonly used search tools are subject directories and search engines. A **subject directory** classifies Web pages in an organized set of categories. By clicking links, you move through categories to display a list of Web pages about a desired topic. A **search engine** is a program that finds Web sites and Web pages. To use a search engine, you enter a word or phrase, called **search text**, that defines the item about which you want information. The search engine displays a list of *hits*. When clicked, each hit displays an associated Web site or Web page.

Chapter Review

(7) What Are the Types of Web Sites?   A **portal** is a Web site that offers a variety of Internet services from a single location. A news Web site contains newsworthy material. An informational Web site contains factual information. A business/marketing Web site promotes or sells products or services. An educational Web site offers avenues for teaching and learning. An entertainment Web site provides an interactive and engaging environment. An advocacy Web site describes a cause, opinion, or idea. A **blog** is an informal Web site consisting of time-stamped articles, or posts, in a diary or journal format, usually listed in reverse chronological order. A **wiki** is a collaborative Web site that allows users to add to, modify, or delete the Web site content via their Web browser. A *content aggregator* is a business that gathers and organizes Web content and then distributes, or feeds, the content to subscribers for free or a fee. A personal Web site is maintained by a private individual or family.

(8) How Do Web Pages Use Graphics, Animation, Audio, Video, Virtual Reality, and Plug-Ins?
Some Web pages use **multimedia**, which combines text with graphics, animation, audio, video, and/or virtual reality. A **graphic** is a digital representation of nontext information such as a drawing or photograph. **Animation** is the appearance of motion created by displaying a series of still images. **Audio** includes music, speech, or any other sound. **Video** consists of full-motion images. **Virtual reality (VR)** is the use of computers to simulate an environment that appears as three-dimensional space. A **plug-in** is a program that extends a browser's capability to display multimedia elements.

(9) What Are the Steps Required for Web Publishing?   Web publishing is the development and maintenance of Web pages. The five major steps to Web publishing are: (1) plan a Web site, (2) analyze and design a Web site, (3) create a Web site, (4) deploy a Web site, and (5) maintain a Web site.

> *connect*
> Visit scsite.com/dc2007/ch2/quiz or click the Quiz Yourself button. Click Objectives 4 – 9.

(10) What Are the Types of E-Commerce?   E-commerce, short for *electronic commerce*, is a business transaction that occurs over an electronic network such as the Internet. *Business-to-consumer (B2C) e-commerce* consists of the sale of goods and services to the general public. *Consumer-to-consumer (C2C) e-commerce* occurs when one consumer sells directly to another, such as an **online auction**. *Business-to-business (B2B) e-commerce* takes place between businesses that exchange goods and services.

(11) How Do E-Mail, FTP, Newsgroups and Message Boards, Mailing Lists, Chat Rooms, Instant Messaging, and Internet Telephony Work?   E-mail (short for *electronic mail*) is the transmission of messages and files via a computer network. **FTP** (*File Transfer Protocol*) is an Internet standard that permits file **uploading** and **downloading** with other computers. A **newsgroup** is an online area in which users have written discussions. A **message board** is a Web-based type of discussion group that is easier to use than a newsgroup. A **mailing list** is a group of e-mail names and addresses given a single name, so that everyone on the list receives a message sent to the list. A **chat room** is a location on an Internet server that permits users to conduct real-time typed conversations. **Instant messaging (IM)** is a real-time Internet communications service that notifies you when one or more people are online. **Internet telephony** enables users to speak over the Internet using a computer or mobile device.

(12) What Are the Rules of Netiquette?   **Netiquette**, which is short for Internet etiquette, is the code of acceptable behaviors users should follow while on the Internet. Netiquette rules include: keep messages short, be polite, avoid sending *flames* or *spam*, use **emoticons** and acronyms, read the *FAQ*, do not assume material is accurate or up-to-date, and never read someone's private e-mail.

> *connect*
> Visit scsite.com/dc2007/ch2/quiz or click the Quiz Yourself button. Click Objectives 10 – 12.

Key Terms

You should know the Primary Terms and be familiar with the Secondary Terms. Use the list below to help focus your study. To further enhance your understanding of the Key Terms in this chapter, visit scsite.com/dc2007/ch2/terms. See an example of and a definition for each term, and access current and additional information about the term from the Web.

Primary Terms

(shown in bold-black characters in the chapter)

access provider (71)
address book (94)
animation (86)
audio (86)
blog (84)
browser (75)
cable modem (70)
chat (98)
chat room (98)
dial-up access (70)
DNS server (74)
domain name (73)
downloading (76)
DSL (70)
e-commerce (91)
electronic storefront (92)
e-mail (92)
e-mail address (94)
e-mail program (93)
emoticons (100)
FTP (96)
graphic (85)
home page (76)
instant messaging (IM) (98)
Internet (68)
Internet telephony (99)
IP address (73)
ISP (Internet service provider) (72)
link (77)
mailing list (97)
message board (97)
MP3 (86)
multimedia (85)
netiquette (100)

newsgroup (96)
online auction (92)
online service provider (OSP) (72)
player (86)
plug-in (89)
portal (82)
real time (98)
RSS 2.0 (84)
search engine (78)
search text (80)
shopping cart (92)
streaming (86)
subject directory (78)
subscribe (97)
surfing the Web (77)
traffic (70)
unsubscribe (97)
uploading (96)
URL (76)
user name (94)
video (88)
virtual reality (VR) (88)
Web (75)
Web address (76)
Web browser (75)
Web community (82)
Web page (75)
Web publishing (90)
Web server (75)
Web site (75)
wiki (84)
wireless Internet service provider (72)
World Wide Web (75)

Secondary Terms

(shown in italic characters in the chapter)

Advanced Research Projects Agency (ARPA) (69)
animated GIF (86)
anonymous FTP (96)
ARPANET (69)
articles (96)
Atom (84)
blogger (84)
broadband (70)
business-to-business (B2B) e-commerce (92)
business-to-consumer (B2C) e-commerce (91)
chat client (98)
click (77)
consumer-to-consumer (C2C) e-commerce (92)
content aggregator (84)
digital subscriber line (70)
domain name system (DNS) (74)
dot-com (73)
dynamic Web page (75)
electronic commerce (91)
electronic mail (92)
FAQ (100)
File Transfer Protocol (96)
fixed wireless (70)
flame wars (100)
flames (100)
FTP server (96)
GIF (85)
graphical image (85)
hits (80)
host (69)
hot spots (71)
http (76)
hyperlink (77)
Hypertext Transfer Protocol (76)
instant messenger (98)
Internet backbone (72)
Internet Corporation for Assigned Names and Numbers (ICANN) (74)
Internet Protocol address (73)
JPEG (85)
keywords (80)
LISTSERVs (97)

m-commerce (91)
microbrowser (76)
moderated newsgroup (97)
moderator (97)
Moving Pictures Experts Group (MPEG) (88)
MPEG-4 (88)
national ISP (72)
Net (68)
news server (96)
newsreader (96)
NSFnet (70)
PNG (85)
podcast (86)
point of presence (POP) (72)
POP3 (95)
post (96)
Post Office Protocol (95)
pull (76)
push (76)
Really Simple Syndication (84)
regional ISP (72)
satellite modem (70)
SMTP (simple mail transfer protocol) (94)
spam (100)
spider (81)
spoiler (100)
static Web page (75)
streaming audio (86)
streaming video (88)
subscribe (97)
thread (97)
threaded discussion (97)
thumbnail (86)
top-level domain (73)
Uniform Resource Locator (76)
Usenet (96)
Voice over IP (99)
VR world (88)
Weblog (84)
wireless portal (82)
WISP (72)
World Wide Web Consortium (W3C) (70)
WWW (75)

Checkpoint

Use the Checkpoint exercises to check your knowledge level of the chapter. The Beyond the Book exercises will help broaden your understanding of the concepts presented in this chapter. To complete the Checkpoint exercises interactively, visit scsite.com/dc2007/ch2/check.

Label the Figure

Identify the types of Web sites.

a. advocacy

b. blog

c. business/marketing

d. content aggregator

e. educational

f. entertainment

g. informational

h. news

i. personal

j. portal

k. wiki

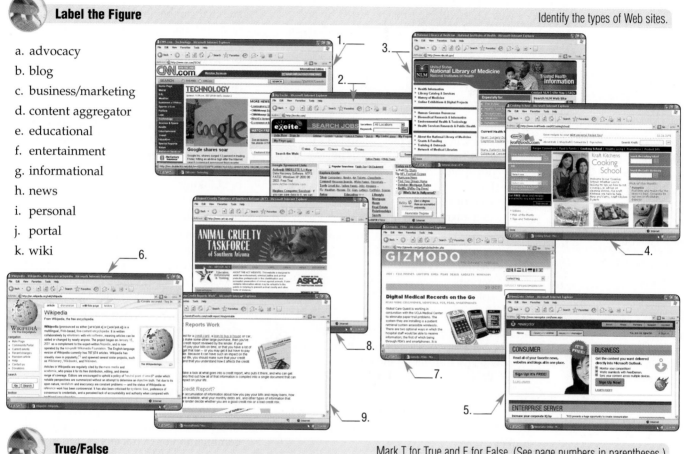

True/False

Mark T for True and F for False. (See page numbers in parentheses.)

_____ 1. A single government agency owns and controls the Internet. (70)

_____ 2. DSL is a technology that provides high-speed Internet connections over the cable television network. (70)

_____ 3. In general, the first portion of each IP address identifies the specific computer and the last portion identifies the network. (73)

_____ 4. Most current browsers and Web sites require the http:// and www portions of a Web address. (76)

_____ 5. Pointing to, or positioning the pointer on, a link on a Web page typically changes the shape of the pointer to a small hand with a pointing index finger. (77)

_____ 6. A major problem with a subject directory is deciding which categories to choose as you work through the menus of links presented. (79)

_____ 7. The purpose of an informational Web site is to convince the reader of the validity of a cause, opinion, or idea. (84)

_____ 8. A podcast is a collaborative Web site that allows users to add to, modify, or delete the Web site content via their Web browser. (86)

_____ 9. To develop a Web page, you do not have to be a computer programmer. (90)

_____ 10. An online auction is an example of business-to-consumer (B2C) e-commerce. (92)

_____ 11. A chat room is a location on an Internet server that permits users to chat with each other. (98)

_____ 12. A flame is an unsolicited e-mail message or newsgroup posting sent to many recipients or newsgroups at once. (100)

Checkpoint

Multiple Choice Select the best answer. (See page numbers in parentheses.)

1. The Internet has its roots in _____, which was a networking project started by an agency of the U.S. Department of Defense. (69)
   a. ICANN
   b. NSFnet
   c. WISP
   d. ARPANET

2. Many public locations are _____ that provide wireless Internet connections to users with mobile computers or devices. (71)
   a. hot spots
   b. ISPs
   c. Weblogs
   d. chat clients

3. As with an IP address, the components of a domain name are separated by _____. (73)
   a. commas
   b. periods
   c. colons
   d. semicolons

4. Many Web page addresses begin with _____, which stands for a set of rules that defines how pages transfer on the Internet. (76)
   a. W3C   b. http
   c. hits   d. pop

5. Some people use the phrase, _____, to refer to the activity of using links to explore the Web. (77)
   a. surfing the Web
   b. weaving the Net
   c. navigating the Net
   d. bringing in the Net

6. All of the following techniques can be used to improve Web searches except _____. (81)
   a. list all possible spellings
   b. read a search engine's Help information
   c. use general nouns and put the most important terms last
   d. if a search is unsuccessful, try another search engine

7. A(n) _____ is a business that gathers and organizes Web content and then distributes, or feeds, the content to subscribers for free or a fee. (84)
   a. WISP
   b. ISP
   c. content aggregator
   d. blogger

8. A _____ is recorded audio stored on a Web site that can be downloaded to a computer or a portable digital audio player. (86)
   a. blog
   b. wiki
   c. portal
   d. podcast

9. _____ is the process of transferring data in a continuous and even flow, allowing users to access and use a file while it is transmitting. (86)
   a. Streaming
   b. Linking
   c. Surfing
   d. Clicking

10. _____ is not a step in Web publishing. (90)
    a. Planning a Web site
    b. Deploying a Web site
    c. Creating a Web site
    d. Moderating a Web site

11. At a consumer-to-consumer (C2C) Web site, a(n) _____ allows users to purchase from other consumers. (92)
    a. news server
    b. online auction
    c. wireless portal
    d. shopping cart

12. In an e-mail address, a _____ is a unique combination of characters that identifies a specific user. (94)
    a. domain name
    b. URL
    c. user name
    d. dot com

13. The _____ standard permits uploading and downloading of files on the Internet. (96)
    a. FTP
    b. newsgroup
    c. message board
    d. LISTSERV

14. Use _____, such as :) for smile and :(for frown, to express emotions in e-mail, newsgroups, and chat rooms. (100)
    a. flames
    b. spam
    c. spoilers
    d. emoticons

Checkpoint

Matching

Match the terms with their definitions. (See page numbers in parentheses.)

_____ 1. traffic (70)

_____ 2. home page (76)

_____ 3. link (77)

_____ 4. spider (81)

_____ 5. RSS 2.0 (84)

_____ 6. MP3 (86)

_____ 7. player (86)

_____ 8. plug-in (89)

_____ 9. m-commerce (91)

_____ 10. address book (94)

a. first page that a Web site displays

b. program that extends the capability of a browser

c. specification used by content aggregators to distribute content

d. software used to listen to an audio file on a computer

e. bulk of communications activity on the Internet

f. built-in connection to a related Web page or part of a Web page

g. format that reduces an audio file to about one-tenth its original size

h. term used to identify e-commerce that takes place using mobile devices

i. contains a list of names and e-mail addresses

j. copy a program from storage to memory

k. browser designed for the small screens and limited power of PDAs and smart phones

l. program used to build and maintain lists of words found on Web sites

Short Answer

Write a brief answer to each of the following questions.

1. How is a regional ISP different from a national ISP? _____ How is an ISP different from a WISP? _____

2. How is a static Web page different from a dynamic Web page? _____ What is a Web site? _____

3. What are the differences between blogs, wikis, and podcasts? _____ When might you use each? _____

4. What three graphics formats are used frequently on the Web? _____ How are they different? _____

5. What is a threaded discussion? _____ What is a moderated newsgroup? _____

Beyond the Book

Read the following book elements, learn more about each using the Web, and then write a brief report.

1. Ethics & Issues — Is the Internet as Good as the Classroom? (82), Should All Sales on the Internet Be Taxed? (92), E-Mail: Irritant or Liberator? (94), or Should Companies Be Able to Track Your Online Habits? (101)

2. Career Corner — Web Developer (101)

3. Companies on the Cutting Edge — Google or Yahoo! (103)

4. FAQs (71, 72, 74, 77, 81, 85, 92, 95, 100)

5. High-Tech Talk — A Computer's Internet Protocol (IP) Address (102)

6. Looking Ahead — Internet Speeds into the Future (70) or 3-D Search Engines Get the Picture (81)

7. Making Use of the Web — Travel (118)

8. Picture Yourself Instant Messaging (66)

9. Technology Trailblazers — Tim Berners-Lee or Meg Whitman (103)

10. Web Links (72, 77, 84, 89, 92, 95, 96, 97, 98, 99)

Learn It Online

Use the Learn It Online exercises to reinforce your understanding of the chapter concepts. To access the Learn It Online exercises, visit scsite.com/dc2007/ch2/learn.

① At the Movies — Google Search Secrets

To view the Google Search Secrets movie, click the number 1 button. Locate your video and click the corresponding High-Speed or Dial-Up link, depending on your Internet connection. Watch the movie and then complete the exercise by answering the question that follows. Using the Internet to gather information can seem daunting. The introduction of powerful search engines has enhanced the Internet research experience. Properly utilizing a search engine can benefit almost any project. How might you go about using Google to search for information for a research paper?

② At the Movies — Instant Message from Anywhere

To view the Instant Message from Anywhere movie, click the number 2 button. Locate your video and click the corresponding High-Speed or Dial-Up link, depending on your Internet connection. Watch the movie, and then complete the exercise by answering the question that follows. Instant messaging (IM) is a fun way to stay in touch with your friends, but until now it has been limited to use on the computer. New technology developments have cut the wires, and now you can take IM on the road. What are some of the limitations of wireless instant messaging?

③ Student Edition Labs — Connecting to the Internet

Click the number 3 button. A new browser window will open, displaying the Student Edition Labs. Follow the on-screen instructions to complete the Connecting to the Internet Lab. When finished, click the Exit button. If required, submit your results to your instructor.

④ Student Edition Labs — Getting the Most out of the Internet

Click the number 4 button. A new browser window will open, displaying the Student Edition Labs. Follow the on-screen instructions to complete the Getting the Most out of the Internet Lab. When finished, click the Exit button. If required, submit your results to your instructor.

⑤ Student Edition Labs — E-mail

Click the number 5 button. A new browser window will open, displaying the Student Edition Labs. Follow the on-screen instructions to complete the E-mail Lab. When finished, click the Exit button. If required, submit your results to your instructor.

⑥ Practice Test

Click the number 6 button. Answer each question. When completed, enter your name and click the Grade Test button to submit the quiz for grading. Make a note of any missed questions. If required, submit your score to your instructor.

⑦ Who Wants To Be a Computer Genius²?

Click the number 7 button to find out if you are a computer genius. Directions about how to play the game will be displayed. When you are ready to play, click the Play button. Submit your score to your instructor.

Learn It Online

8 Wheel of Terms

Click the number 8 button to reinforce important terms you learned in this chapter by playing the Shelly Cashman Series version of this popular game. Directions about how to play the game will be displayed. When you are ready to play, click the Play button. Submit your score to your instructor.

9 DC Track and Field

Click the number 9 button to use what you have learned in this chapter to compete against other students in three track and field events. Directions about how to play the game will be displayed. When you are ready to play, click the start first event button. If required, submit your score to your instructor.

10 You're Hired!

Click the number 10 button to use what you have learned in this chapter to embark on the path to a career in computers. Directions about how to play the game will be displayed. When you are ready to play, click the begin game button. If required, submit your score to your instructor.

11 Crossword Puzzle Challenge

Click the number 11 button. Complete the puzzle to reinforce skills you learned in this chapter. Directions about how to play the game will be displayed. When you are ready to play, click the Play button. Submit the completed puzzle to your instructor.

12 Lab Exercises

Click the number 12 button. When the Lab Exercises menu appears, click the exercise assigned by your instructor. A new browser window will open. Follow the on-screen instructions to complete the exercise. When finished, click the Exit button. If required, submit your results to your instructor.

13 In the News

In her book, *Caught in the Net*, Kimberly S. Young contends that the Internet can be addictive. Young's methodology and conclusions have been questioned by several critics, but Young remains resolute. She points out that at one time, no one admitted to the existence of alcoholism. Click the number 13 button and read a news article about the impact of Internet use on human behavior. What effect did the Internet have? Why? In your opinion, is the Internet's influence positive or negative? Why?

14 Chapter Discussion Forum

Select an objective from this chapter on page 67 about which you would like more information. Click the number 14 button and post a short message listing a meaningful message title accompanied by one or more questions concerning the selected objective. In two days, return to the threaded discussion by clicking the number 14 button. Submit to your instructor your original message and at least one response to your message.

15 Google Earth

Click the number 15 button to download Google Earth. Once you have downloaded Google Earth, use it to fly to your home, school, Grand Canyon, Baghdad, Paris, and Moscow. At each location, use the buttons to change the view. Print a copy of the map showing your school, handwrite on the map the school's elevation, and submit the map to your instructor.

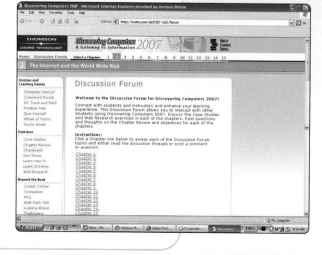

Learn How To

Use the Learn How To activities to learn fundamental skills when using a computer and accompanying technology. Complete the exercises and submit them to your instructor. To see a video of a Learn How To activity, visit scsite.com/dc2007/ch2/howto.

LEARN HOW TO 1: Change a Web Browser's Home Page

When you start a Web browser, a Web page is displayed. You can change the page that appears when you start a Web browser or when you click the Home button on the browser toolbar by completing the following steps:

1. With the browser running, click Tools on the menu bar and then click Internet Options on the Tools menu. *The Internet Options dialog box is displayed (Figure 2-37).*
2. If necessary, in the Home page area in the General sheet, select the Web address in the Address box.
3. Type the Web address of the page you want to display both when you start the browser and when you click the Home button.
4. Click the OK button in the Internet Options dialog box.

When you start the browser or click the Home button on the browser toolbar, the selected Web page will be displayed.

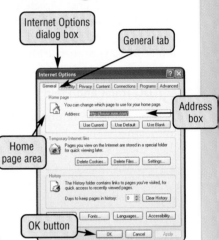

FIGURE 2-37

Exercise

1. Start your Web browser. Write down the address of the browser's current home page. Then, change the browser's home page to www.cnn.com. Close the browser.
2. Start your Web browser. What is the lead story on cnn.com? Use links on the page to view several stories. Which story do you find most interesting? Click the Home button on the browser toolbar. What happened? Submit these answers to your instructor.
3. Change the browser's home page to your school's home page. Click the Home button on the browser toolbar. Click the Calendar or Events link, and then locate two campus events of which you were unaware. Report these two campus events to your instructor.
4. Change the browser's home page back to the address you wrote down in Step 1.

LEARN HOW TO 2: Create and Use Your Own Weblog (Blog)

A Weblog, commonly referred to as a blog, can contain any information you wish to place in it. Originally, blogs consisted of Web addresses, so that an individual or group with a specific interest could direct others to useful places on the Web. Today, blogs contain addresses, thoughts, diaries, and anything else a person or group wants to share.

Once you have created a blog, you can update it. A variety of services are available on the Web to help you create and maintain your blog. One widely used service is called Blogger. To create a blog using Blogger, complete the following steps:

1. Start your Web browser, type `www.blogger.com` in the Address box, and then press the ENTER key. *The Blogger home page is displayed (Figure 2-38).*
2. Click the CREATE YOUR BLOG NOW arrow on the Blogger home page.
3. Enter the data required on the Create an account page. Your user name and password will allow you to change and manage your blog. Your Display name is the name that will be shown on the blog as the author of the material on the blog. Many people use their own names, but others use pseudonyms as their "pen names" so they are not readily identifiable.
4. Click the Continue arrow and then enter your Blog title and Blog address. These are the names and addresses everyone will use to view your blog. By default, the blog is stored and maintained on the blogspot server.
5. Click the Continue arrow. *The Choose a template screen is displayed.*
6. Choose a template for your blog and then click the Continue arrow.

Learn How To

7. Your blog will be created for you. When you see the Your blog has been created screen, click the Start posting arrow.
8. From the screen that is displayed, you can post items for your blog, specify settings, change the template, and view your blog.
9. When you have posted all your information, click the Sign out button at the top right of the screen. You will be logged out.
10. To edit your blog and add or change information on it, visit the Blogger home page and sign in by entering your user name and password. You will be able to post to your blog.
11. Others can view your blog by entering its address in the browser's Address box and then pressing the ENTER key.

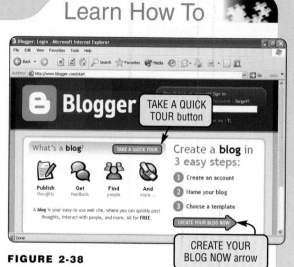

FIGURE 2-38

Exercise

1. Start your Web browser and visit www.blogger.com. Click the TAKE A QUICK TOUR button and go through all the screens that explain about a blog. What did you learn that you did not know? What type of blog do you find most compelling — a group or an individual blog? Why? Turn in your answers to your instructor.
2. Optional: Create your own blog. Carefully name it and begin your posts at this time. What is your blog name and address? What is its primary purpose? Is it an individual or group blog? Write a paragraph containing the answers to these questions and any other information you feel is pertinent. Turn in this paragraph to your instructor.

LEARN HOW TO 3: Bid and Buy a Product from eBay

Online auctions have grown to be a favorite shopping space for many people. A leading online auction Web site is eBay. To submit a bid for an item on eBay, complete the following steps:

1. Type www.ebay.com in the Address box of your browser. Press the ENTER key. *The eBay home page is displayed (Figure 2-39).*
2. Pick an item you find interesting and on which you might bid.
3. Enter your item in the What are you looking for text box and then click the Find It button.
4. Scroll through the page to see the available items.
5. To bid on an item, click the Place Bid button.
6. Enter the amount of your bid. Click the Continue button.
7. You must be registered to bid on eBay. If you are registered, enter your eBay User ID and Password and then click the Submit button. If not, click the Register button and follow the instructions.
8. After registering, you will confirm your bid and receive notification about your bid.
9. You will be notified by e-mail if you won the bid. If so, you will arrange with the seller for payment and shipment.

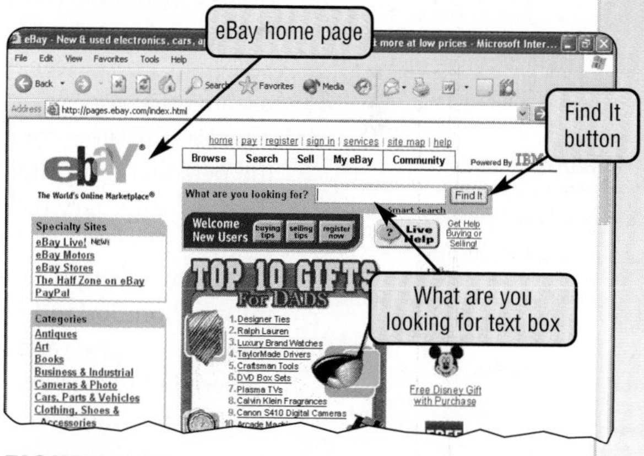

FIGURE 2-39

The eBay Web site contains reminders that when you bid on an item, you are entering into a contract to purchase the item if you are the successful bidder. Bidding on eBay is serious business.

Exercise

1. Start your browser and display the eBay home page.
2. In the What are you looking for text box, enter the name of an upcoming sporting event you would like to attend followed by the word, tickets. For example, enter Super Bowl tickets. Click the Search button.
3. Did you find available tickets? Were there more tickets available than you expected, or fewer? Are the bid prices reasonable or ridiculous? How many bids were made for all the tickets? How much time is left to bid? What items d you find that you were not expecting? Submit answers to these questions to your instructor.
4. Enter an item of your choice in the What are you looking for text box. If you feel so inclined, bid on an item. Do y this manner of buying goods is valuable? Why? Will you visit eBay again? Why? Submit answers to these que instructor.

Web Research

Use the Internet-based Web Research exercises to broaden your understanding of the concepts presented in this chapter. Visit scsite.com/dc2007/ch2/research to obtain more information pertaining to each exercise. To discuss any of the Web Research exercises in this chapter with other students, post your thoughts or questions at scsite.com/dc2007/ch2/forum.

① Scavenger Hunt Use one of the <u>search engines</u> listed in Figure 2-10 in Chapter 2 on page 78 or your own favorite search engine to find the answers to the questions below. Copy and paste the Web address from the Web page where you found the answer. Some questions may have more than one answer. If required, submit your answers to your instructor. (1) Microsoft Internet Explorer and Netscape Navigator are the two more popular Web browsers. What is the name of the first graphical Web browser? (2) What cable company was established in 1858 to carry instantaneous communications across the ocean that would eventually be used for Internet communications? (3) What American president in 1957 created both the interstate highway system and the Advanced Research Projects Agency (ARPA)? (4) Where is the location of Microsoft's headquarters? (5) How many Web pages is Google currently searching?

② Search Sleuth The Internet has provided the opportunity to access encyclopedias online. One of the more comprehensive encyclopedia research sites is **Encyclopedia.com**. Visit this Web site and then use your word processing program to answer the following questions. Then, if required, submit your answers to your instructor. (1) The site's home page lists the top five searches for the day. What are today's top five searches? Click one of these links. What magazines and newspapers contain information about this topic? (2) Type "World Wide Web" as the keyword in the Search text box. How many articles discussing the World Wide Web are found on the Encyclopedia.com Web site? (3) In the search results list, click the first link. What is the definition of the World Wide Web according to the first sentence of the article? Who is the American computer consultant who promoted the idea of linking documents via hypertext during the 1960s? What words are hyperlinks within this article? (5) Type multimedia as the keyword in the Search text box. In the search results list, click the multimedia link. What hardware typically is required to work with multimedia according to this article? What are some optional hardware devices? (6) Type "personal computer" as the keyword in the Search text box. Click one of the personal computer links, review the material, and, if required, submit to your instructor a 50-word summary of the information you read.

③ Newsgroups One of the more popular topics for <u>newsgroups</u> is netiquette. Read the information Borland Software Corporation (info.borland.com/newsgroups/netiquette.html) provides on general newsgroup conduct. Then find three newsgroups, such as those listed in CyberFiber (cyberfiber.com/internet.htm) or Google Groups, that discuss this topic. Read the information and then summarize the advice provided.

④ Journaling Respond to your readings in this chapter by writing at least one page about your reactions, evaluations, and reflections about using the <u>Internet</u>. For example, how many e-mail messages do you send and receive daily? How many Web pages do you visit each month? Have you shopped online? Have your instructors required you to access the Internet for class projects? Which search engines have you used? You also can write about the new terms you learned by reading this chapter. If required, submit your journal to your instructor.

⑤ Ethics in Action <u>Web cams</u> are video cameras that display their output on a Web page. The feasibility of installing Web cams in 47,000 locations susceptible to terrorist threats, such as nuclear and chemical plants, national airports, and gas storage facilities, is being explored. Citizens would monitor the cameras and report suspicious activity. Critics of this proposal state that the constant surveillance is an invasion of privacy. Visit the USHomeGuard Web site (ushomeguard.org) and then write a summary of the citizen corps' roles in this project. Then locate other Web sites that oppose this plan and summarize their views. If required, submit your summary to your instructor.

Case Studies

Use the Case Studies to apply the concepts presented in the chapter to real-world situations. Visit scsite.com/dc2007/ch2/cases to obtain more information pertaining to each exercise. To discuss the Case Studies in this chapter with other students, visit scsite.com/dc2007/ch2/forum and post your thoughts or questions.

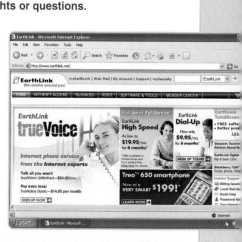

CASE STUDY 1 — Class Discussion   The owner of Deuce Investments, where you are employed part-time as a stock-research analyst, recently attended a one-day continuing education course for small businesses at the local community college. The title of the course was *Ten Reasons Why Your Company Needs the Internet to Compete in Today's Business Environment*. She now feels that the Internet might be useful as an investment-research tool, and she has asked you to investigate the costs associated with making the Internet available for use in the company during business hours. Examine the types of <u>access providers</u> available in your community, the monthly cost, and other significant factors that might influence her decision. Draft a memo to the owner summarizing your recommendations. Be prepared to discuss your recommendations in class.

CASE STUDY 2 — Class Discussion   Many retailers, such as Sports Authority, Barnes and Noble, and Toys R Us, are <u>brick-and-click businesses</u>. That is, they allow customers to conduct complete transactions at a physical location as well as online at a Web site. Choose a local brick-and-click business in which you have shopped at the physical location and visit the Web site of the business. Compare the type, availability, and cost (include tax and shipping) of products or services available. Prepare a report that summarizes the advantages and disadvantages of dealing with the physical location versus the Web site of a brick-and-click business. Would you rather shop at the physical location or at the Web site? Why? Does the answer depend on the business, the product, or some other factor? Be prepared to share your findings in class.

CASE STUDY 3 — Research   This chapter lists eleven types of Web sites: <u>portal</u>, news, informational, business/marketing, educational, entertainment, advocacy, blog, wiki, content aggregator, and personal. Use the Internet to find at least one example of each type of Web site. For each Web site, identify the Web address, the multimedia elements used, the purpose of the Web site, and the type of Web site. Explain why you classified each site as you did. Then, keeping in mind the purpose of each Web site, rank the sites in terms of their effectiveness. Write a brief report or use PowerPoint to create a presentation and share your findings with your class.

CASE STUDY 4 — Research   <u>The Internet</u> has had a tremendous impact on business. For some businesses, that influence has not been positive. For example, surveys suggest that as a growing number of people order products online, traditional brick-and-mortar businesses are seeing fewer customers. Use the Web and/or print media to learn more about businesses that have been affected negatively by the Internet. What effect has the Internet had? How can the business compete with the Internet? How has the Internet changed business in positive ways? Write a brief report or use PowerPoint to create a presentation and share your findings with your class.

CASE STUDY 5 — Team Challenge   Mr. Steve Sandberg is vice president of operations for a major luxury hotel chain. He and three of his associates want to start a new chain of discount hotels called Sleepy Hollow. They have made a plan that includes opening hotels initially in Chicago, St. Louis, Denver, and Houston. They plan to offer comfortable rooms, high-speed Internet access, and continental breakfast. Besides offering reservations over the telephone, they want to develop a Web site that will allow customers to negotiate a nightly rate as their check-in time approaches. Form a three-member team and assist Mr. Sandberg in evaluating existing major hotel Web sites by listing the advantages and disadvantages of each. Assign each member the task of evaluating three of the following hotel chains: Marriot, Hilton, Holiday Inn, Ramada, Super 8, Motel 6, Days Inn, Fairfield Inn, and Radisson. Make sure every hotel chain listed is assigned to at least one team member. Have each member print the <u>home page</u> of the hotel chain he or she is assigned. In evaluating the Web sites, each member should pay particular attention to the following areas: (1) design of Web site, (2) ease of use, (3) reservations, (4) awards programs, (5) specials, (6) online Help, (7) about the hotel, and (8) contact the hotel. Meet with your team to share each member's findings and then write a final report or create a PowerPoint presentation that summarizes the team's conclusions and ranks the sites in terms of their effectiveness.

Making Use of the Web

A wealth of information is available on the World Wide Web. The riches are yours if you know where to find this material. Locating useful Web sites may be profitable for your educational and professional careers, as the resources may help you research class assignments and make your life more fulfilling and manageable.

Because the World Wide Web does not have an organizational structure to assist you in locating reliable material, you need additional resources to guide you in searching. To help you find useful Web sites, this Special Feature describes specific information about a variety of Web pages, and it includes tables of Web addresses, so you can get started. The material is organized in several areas of interest.

AREAS OF INTEREST	
Fun and Entertainment	Learning
Travel	Science
Finance	Environment
Resources	Health
Blogs	Research
Government	Careers
Shopping and Auctions	Arts and Literature
Weather, Sports, and News	

Web Exercises at the end of each category will reinforce the material and help you discover Web sites that may add a treasure trove of knowledge to your life.

Fun and Entertainment
THAT'S ENTERTAINMENT

Rock 'n' Roll on the Web

Consumers place great significance on buying entertainment products for fun and recreation. Nearly 10 percent of the United States's economy is spent on attending concerts and buying DVDs, CDs, reading materials, sporting goods, and toys.

Many Web sites supplement our cravings for fun and entertainment. For example, you can see and hear the musicians inducted into the Rock and Roll Hall of Fame and Museum (Figure 1). If you need an update on your favorite reality-based television program or a preview of an upcoming movie, E! Online and Entertainment Tonight provide the latest features on television and movie stars. The Internet Movie Database contains credits and reviews of more than 60,000 titles.

Watch the surfers riding the waves in Hawaii and romp with pandas at the San Diego Zoo. Web cams, which are video cameras that display their output on Web pages, take armchair travelers across the world for views of natural attractions, historical monuments, colleges, and cities. Many Web sites featuring Web cams are listed in the table in Figure 2.

FUN AND ENTERTAINMENT WEB SITES

Web Cams	URL
AfriCam Virtual Game Reserve	africam.com
Discovery Channel Cams	dsc.discovery.com/cams/cams.html
EarthCam — Webcam Network	earthcam.com
Iowa State Insect Zoo Live Camera	zoocam.ent.iastate.edu
Panda Cam San Diego Zoo	sandiegozoo.org/zoo/ex_panda_station.html
The Automated Astrophysical Site-Testing Observatory (AASTO) (South Pole)	www.phys.unsw.edu.au/southpolediaries/webcam.html
CamVista.com	camvista.com
Wild Birds Unlimited Bird FeederCam	wbu.com/feedercam_home.htm
Surfrider Surf Report	surfrider.org/earth.asp
WorldLIVE	worldlive.cz/en/webcams

Entertainment	URL
AMG All Music Guide	allmusic.com
E! Online	eonline.com
ETonline	et.tv.yahoo.com
Entertainment Weekly's EW.com	ew.com/ew
MSN Entertainment	entertainment.msn.com
Old Time Radio (OTR) — Radio Days: A Soundbite History	otr.com
Rock and Roll Hall of Fame and Museum	rockhall.com
The Internet Movie Database (IMDb)	imdb.com
World Radio Network (WRN)	wrn.org

For more information about fun and entertainment Web sites, visit scsite.com/dc2007/ch2/web.

FIGURE 1 Visitors exploring the Rock and Roll Hall of Fame and Museum Web site will find history, exhibitions, programs, and the names and particulars of the latest inductees.

FIGURE 2 When you visit Web sites offering fun and entertainment resources, you can be both amused and informed.

FUN AND ENTERTAINMENT WEB EXERCISES

 1 Visit the WorldLIVE site listed in Figure 2. View two of the Web cams closest to your hometown, and describe the scenes. Then, visit the Discovery Channel Cams Web site and view two of the animal cams in the Featured Cams. What do you observe? Visit another Web site listed in Figure 2 and describe the view. What are the benefits of having Web cams at these locations throughout the world?

2 What are your favorite movies? Use The Internet Movie Database Web site listed in Figure 2 to search for information about two of these films, and write a brief description of the biographies of the major stars and director for each movie. Then, visit one of the entertainment Web sites and describe three of the featured stories. At the Rock and Roll Hall of Fame and Museum Web site, view the information about Elvis and one of your favorite musicians. Write a paragraph describing the information available about these rock stars.

Travel
GET PACKING!

Explore the World without Leaving Home

When you are ready to arrange your next travel adventure or just want to explore destination possibilities, the Internet provides ample resources to set your plans in motion.

To discover exactly where your destination is on this planet, cartography Web sites, including MapQuest (Figure 3), Maps.com, and Rand McNally, allow you to pinpoint your destination. View your exact destination using satellite imagery with Google Earth and MSN Virtual Earth.

Some good starting places are general travel Web sites such as Expedia Travel, Cheap Tickets, and Travelocity, which is owned by the electronic booking service travel agents use. These all-encompassing Web sites, including those in Figure 4, have tools to help you find the lowest prices and details on flights, car rentals, cruises, and hotels.

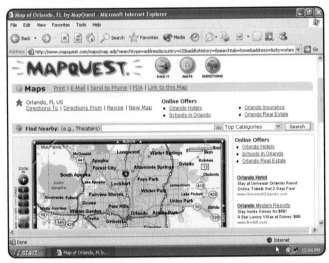

FIGURE 3 MapQuest provides directions, traffic reports, maps, and more.

TRAVEL WEB SITES

General Travel	URL
Cheap Tickets	cheaptickets.com
Expedia Travel	expedia.com
Orbitz	orbitz.com
Travelocity	travelocity.com
Cartography	**URL**
Google Maps	maps.google.com
MapQuest	mapquest.com
Maps.com	maps.com
MSN Virtual Earth	virtualearth.com
Rand McNally	randmcnally.com
Travel and City Guides	**URL**
World's Largest Cities	greatestcities.com
Frommers.com	frommers.com

For more information about travel Web sites, visit scsite.com/dc2007/ch2/web.

FIGURE 4 These travel resources Web sites offer travel information to exciting destinations throughout the world.

TRAVEL WEB EXERCISES

1 Visit one of the cartography Web sites listed in Figure 4 and obtain the directions from your campus to one of these destinations: the White House in Washington, D.C.; Elvis's home in Memphis, Tennessee; Walt Disney World in Orlando, Florida; or the Grand Old Opry in Nashville, Tennessee. How many miles is it to your destination? What is the estimated driving time? Use Google Maps or MSN Virtual Earth to view an actual satellite photograph of your destination. Then, visit one of the general travel Web sites listed in the table and plan a flight from the nearest major airport to one of the four destinations for the week after finals and a return trip one week later. What is the lowest economy coach fare for this round-trip flight? What airline, flight numbers, and departure and arrival times did you select?

2 Visit one of the travel and city guides Web sites listed in Figure 4, and choose a destination for a getaway this coming weekend. Write a one-page paper giving details about this location, such as popular hotels and lodging, expected weather, population, local colleges and universities, parks and recreation, ancient and modern history, and tours. Include a map or satellite photograph of this place. Why did you select this destination? How would you travel there and back? What is the breakdown of expected costs for this weekend, including travel expenditures, meals, lodging, and tickets to events and activities? What URLs did you use to complete this exercise?

Finance
MONEY MATTERS

Cashing In on Financial Advice

You can manage your money with advice from financial Web sites that offer online banking, tax help, personal finance, and small business and commercial services.

If you do not have a personal banker or a financial planner, consider a Web adviser to guide your investment decisions. The Motley Fool (Figure 5) provides commentary and education on investing strategies, financial news, and taxes.

If you are ready to ride the ups and downs of the NASDAQ and the Dow, an abundance of Web sites listed in Figure 6, including Reuters and Morningstar.com, can help you pick companies that fit your interests and financial needs.

Claiming to be the fastest, easiest tax publication on the planet, the Internal Revenue Service Web site contains procedures for filing tax appeals and contains IRS forms, publications, and legal regulations.

FINANCE WEB SITES

Advice and Education	URL
Bankrate.com	bankrate.com
LendingTree	lendingtree.com
Loan.com	loan.com
MSN Money	moneycentral.msn.com
The Motley Fool	fool.com
Wells Fargo	wellsfargo.com
Yahoo! Finance	finance.yahoo.com
Stock Market	**URL**
E*TRADE Financial	us.etrade.com
Financial Engines	financialengines.com
Reuters	www.investor.reuters.com
Harris*direct*	harrisdirect.com
Merrill Lynch Direct	mldirect.ml.com
Morningstar.com	morningstar.com
The Vanguard Group	vanguard.com
Taxes	**URL**
H&R Block	hrblock.com
Internal Revenue Service	irs.gov

For more information about finance Web sites, visit scsite.com/ dc2007/ch2/web.

FIGURE 5 The Motley Fool Web site contains strategies and news stories related to personal financing and investing.

FIGURE 6 Financial resources Web sites offer general information, stock market analyses, and tax advice, as well as guidance and money-saving tips.

FINANCE WEB EXERCISES

 1 Visit three advice and education Web sites listed in Figure 6 and read their top business world reports. Write a paragraph about each, summarizing these stories. Which stocks or mutual funds do these Web sites predict as being sound investments today? What are the current market indexes for the DJIA (Dow Jones Industrial Average), S&P 500, and NASDAQ, and how do these figures compare with the previous day's numbers?

2 Using two of the stock market Web sites listed in Figure 6, search for information about Microsoft, Adobe Systems, and one other software vendor. Write a paragraph about each of these stocks describing the revenues, net incomes, total assets for the previous year, current stock price per share, highest and lowest prices of each stock during the past year, and other relevant investment information.

Resources
LOOK IT UP

Web Resources Ease Computer Concerns

From dictionaries and encyclopedias to online technical support, the Web is filled with a plethora of resources to answer your computer questions.

Keep up with the latest developments by viewing online dictionaries and encyclopedias that add to their collections of computer and product terms on a regular basis. Shopping for a new computer can be a daunting experience, but many online guides, including PCWorld.com (Figure 7), can help you select the components that best fit your needs and budget.

If you are not confident in your ability to solve a problem alone, turn to online technical support. Web sites, such as those shown in Figure 8, often provide streaming how-to video lessons, tutorials, and real-time chats with experienced technicians. Hardware and software reviews, price comparisons, shareware, technical questions and answers, and breaking technology news are found on comprehensive portals.

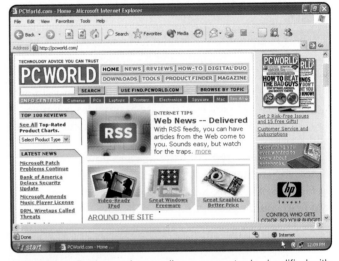

FIGURE 7 Buying and upgrading a computer is simplified with helpful Web sites such as PCWorld.com.

RESOURCES WEB SITES

Dictionaries and Encyclopedias	URL
CDT's Guide to Online Privacy	cdt.org/privacy/guide/terms
ComputerUser High-Tech Dictionary	computeruser.com/resources/dictionary
TechWeb: The Business Technology Network	www.techweb.com/encyclopedia
Webopedia: Online Computer Dictionary for Computer and Internet Terms and Definitions	webopedia.com
whatis?com	whatis.com

Computer Shopping Guides	URL
A Computer Guide: Reviews on Software and Hardware	acomputerguide.com/www/
The CPU Scorecard	cpuscorecard.com
The Online Computer Buying Guide	grohol.com/computers
TechBargains.com	techbargains.com
Tom's Hardware Guide	tomshardware.com
Viewz Desktop Computer Buying Guide	viewz.com/shoppingguide/compbuy.shtml
ZDNet Shopper	shopper-zdnet.com.com

Upgrading Guides	URL
CNET Shopper.com	shopper.cnet.com
eHow	ehow.com
Focus on Macs	macs.about.com
PCWorld.com	pcworld.com/howto
Upgrade Source	upgradesource.com

Online Technical Support	URL
Dux Computer Digest	duxcw.com
MSN Tech & Gadgets	computingcentral.msn.com
PC911	pcnineoneone.com
PC Pitstop	pcpitstop.com

Technical and Consumer Information	URL
CNET.com	cnet.com
CompInfo — The Computer Information Center	www.compinfo-center.com
NewsHub	newshub.com
PC Today	pctoday.com
Wired News	wirednews.com
ZDNet	zdnet.com

For more information about resources Web sites, visit scsite.com/dc2007/ch2/web.

FIGURE 8 A variety of Web resources can provide information about buying, repairing, and upgrading computers.

RESOURCES WEB EXERCISES

1 Visit the dictionaries and encyclopedias Web sites listed in Figure 8. Search these resources for five terms. Create a table with two columns: one for the cyberterm and one for the Web definition. Then, create a second table listing five recently added or updated words and their definitions on these Web sites. Next, visit two of the listed computer shopping guides Web sites to choose the components you would buy if you were building a customized desktop computer and notebook computer. Create a table for both computers, listing the computer manufacturer, processor model name or number and manufacturer, clock speed, RAM, cache, number of expansion slots, and number of bays.

2 Visit three upgrading guides Web sites listed in Figure 8. Write a paragraph describing available advice for buying a motherboard. Describe the strengths and weaknesses of these Web sites, focusing on such criteria as clarity of instructions, thoroughness, and ease of navigation. Would you use these Web sites as a resource to troubleshoot computer problems? Then, view two technical and consumer information Web sites listed in the table and write a paragraph about each one, describing the top two news stories of the day.

Blogs
EXPRESS YOURSELF

Blogosphere Growing Swiftly

Internet users are feeling the need to publish their views, and they are finding Weblogs, or blogs for short, the ideal vehicle. The blogosphere began as an easy way for individuals to express their opinions on the Web. Today, this communication vehicle has become a powerful tool, for individuals, groups, and corporations are using blogs to promote their ideas and advertise their products.

Bloggers generally update their Web sites frequently to reflect their views. Their posts range from a paragraph to an entire essay and often contain links to other Web sites. The more popular blogs discuss politics, lifestyles, and technology.

Corporate blogs, such as The GM FastLane Blog (Figure 9), discuss all aspects of the company's products, whereas all-encompassing blogs, such as the Metafilter Community Weblog and others in Figure 10, are designed to keep general readers entertained and informed.

Blogs are affecting the manner in which people communicate, and some experts predict they will one day become our primary method of sharing information.

BLOGS WEB SITES

BLOG	URL
A List Apart	alistapart.com
Bloglines Top Links	bloglines.com/toplinks
Boing Boing: A Directory of Wonderful Things	boingboing.net
Davenetics* Politics + Media + Musings	davenetics.com
Geek News Central	geeknewscentral.com
GM FastLane Blog	fastlane.gmblogs.com
kottke.org: home of fine hypertext products	kottke.org
Metafilter Community Weblog	metafilter.com
Scripting News	scripting.com
For more information about blogs Web sites, visit scsite.com/dc2007/ch2/web.	

FIGURE 10 These blogs offer information about technology, news, politics, and entertainment.

FIGURE 9 General Motors' executives share their insights by posting to the GM FastLane Blog.

BLOGS WEB EXERCISES

1 Visit one of the blog Web sites listed in Figure 10 that provides lists of the more popular blogs. Select three links from the lists and visit the specific blogs. Make a table listing the blog name, its purpose, the author, its audience, and advertisers, if any, who sponsor the blog.

2 Many Internet users read the technology blogs to keep abreast of the latest developments. Visit two technology blogs listed in Figure 10 and write a paragraph describing the top story in each blog. Read the posted comments, if any. Then, write another paragraph describing two other stories found on these blogs that cover material you have discussed in this course. Write a third paragraph discussing which one is more interesting to you. Would you add reading blogs to your list of Internet activities? Why or why not?

Government
STAMP OF APPROVAL

Making a Federal Case for Useful Information

When it is time to buy stamps to mail your correspondence, you no longer need to wait in long lines at your local post office. The U.S. Postal Service has authorized several corporations to sell stamps online.

You can recognize U.S. Government Web sites on the Internet by their .gov top-level domain abbreviation. For example, The Library of Congress Web site is lcweb.loc.gov, as shown in Figure 11. Government and military Web sites offer a wide range of information, and some of the more popular sites are listed in Figure 12. The Time Service Department Web site will provide you with the correct time. If you are looking for a federal document, FedWorld lists thousands of documents distributed by the government on its Web site. For access to the names of your congressional representatives, visit the extensive Hieros Gamos Web site.

FIGURE 11 The Library of Congress Web site contains more than 119 million items written in 470 languages.

GOVERNMENT RESOURCES WEB SITES

Postage	URL
Endicia	endicia.com
Pitney Bowes	pb.com
Stamps.com	stamps.com
Government	**URL**
FedWorld	www.fedworld.gov
Hieros Gamos — Law and Legal Research Center	hg.org
NARA — United States National Archives and Records Administration	archives.gov
National Agricultural Library	nal.usda.gov
The Library of Congress	lcweb.loc.gov
THOMAS Legislative Information	thomas.loc.gov
Time Service Department	tycho.usno.navy.mil
United States Department of Education	ed.gov
United States Department of the Treasury	www.treas.gov
United States Government Printing Office	www.access.gpo.gov
United States National Library of Medicine	nlm.nih.gov
United States Patent and Trademark Office	www.uspto.gov
USAJOBS	usajobs.opm.gov
White House	whitehouse.gov

For more information about government Web sites, visit scsite.com/dc2007/ch2/web.

FIGURE 12 These Web sites offer information about buying U.S.-approved postage online and researching federal agencies.

GOVERNMENT WEB EXERCISES

1 View the three postage Web sites listed in Figure 12. Compare and contrast the available services on each one. Consider postage cost, necessary equipment, shipping services, security techniques, and tracking capability. Explain why you would or would not like to use this service.

2 Visit the Hieros Gamos Web site listed in Figure 12. What are the names, addresses, and telephone numbers of your two state senators and your local congressional representative? On what committees do they serve? Who is the chief justice of the Supreme Court, and what has been this justice's opinion on two recently decided cases? Who are the members of the president's cabinet? Then, visit two other Web sites listed in Figure 12. Write a paragraph about each Web site describing its content and features.

Shopping and Auctions
BARGAINS GALORE

Let Your Mouse Do Your Shopping

From groceries to clothing to computers, you can buy just about everything you need with just a few clicks of your mouse. Electronic retailers (e-tailers) are cashing in on cybershoppers' purchases. Books, computer software and hardware, and music are the hottest commodities.

The two categories of Internet shopping Web sites are those with physical counterparts, such as Wal-Mart and Best Buy, and those with only a Web presence, such as Amazon.com. Popular Web shopping sites are listed in Figure 13.

Another method of shopping for the items you need, and maybe some you really do not need, is to visit auction Web sites, including those listed in Figure 13. Categories include antiques and collectibles, automotive, computers, electronics, music, sports, sports cards and memorabilia,

and toys. Online auction Web sites can offer unusual items, including *Star Wars* props and memorabilia and a round of golf with Tiger Woods. eBay (Figure 14) is one of thousands of Internet auction Web sites and is the world's largest personal online trading community.

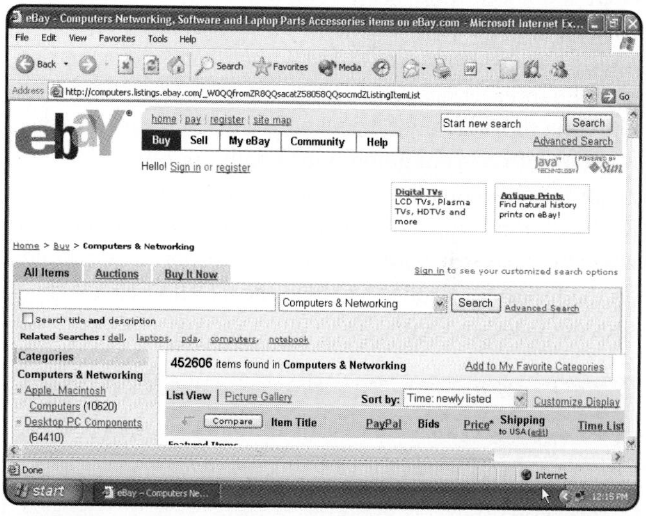

FIGURE 14 eBay is one of the world's more popular auction Web sites.

SHOPPING AND AUCTIONS WEB SITES

Auctions	URL
eBay®	ebay.com
MusicHotBid	musichotbid.com
Sothebys	sothebys.com
Yahoo! Shopping Auctions	auctions.yahoo.com
Books and Music	**URL**
Amazon.com	amazon.com
Barnes & Noble.com	bn.com
Tower Records	towerrecords.com
Computers and Electronics	**URL**
Crutchfield	crutchfield.com
BestBuy	bestbuy.com
Buy.com	buy.com
Miscellaneous	**URL**
drugstore.com	drugstore.com
Froogle	froogle.com
Sharper Image	sharperimage.com
Walmart.com	walmart.com

For more information about shopping and auctions Web sites, visit scsite.com/dc2007/ch2/web.

FIGURE 13 Making online purchases can help ease the burden of driving to and fighting the crowds in local malls.

SHOPPING AND AUCTIONS WEB EXERCISES

1 Visit two of the computers and electronics and two of the miscellaneous Web sites listed in Figure 14. Write a paragraph describing the features these Web sites offer compared with the same offerings from stores. In another paragraph, describe any disadvantages of shopping at these Web sites instead of actually visiting a store. Then, describe their policies for returning unwanted merchandise and for handling complaints.

2 Using one of the auction Web sites listed in Figure 14, search for two objects pertaining to your hobbies. For example, if you are a baseball fan, you can search for a complete set of Topps cards. If you are a car buff, search for your dream car. Describe these two items. How many people have bid on these items? Who are the sellers? What are the opening and current bids?

Weather, Sports, and News
WHAT'S NEWS?

Weather, Sports, and News Web Sites Score Big Hits

Rain or sun? Hot or cold? Weather is the leading online news item, with at least 10,000 Web sites devoted to this field. More than 20 million people view The Weather Channel Web site (Figure 15) each month.

Baseball may be the national pastime, but sports aficionados yearn for everything from auto racing to cricket. The Internet has more than one million pages of multimedia sports news, entertainment, and merchandise.

The Internet has emerged as a major source for news, with one-third of Americans going online at least once a week and 15 percent going online daily for reports of major news events. Many of these viewers are using Really Simple Syndication (RSS) technology to be notified when new stories about their favorite topics are available on the Internet. Popular weather, sports, and news Web sites are listed in Figure 16.

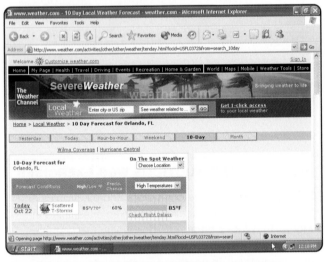

FIGURE 15 Local, national, and international weather conditions and details about breaking weather stories are available on The Weather Channel Web pages.

WEATHER, SPORTS, AND NEWS WEB SITES

Weather	URL
Infoplease Weather	infoplease.com/weather.html
Intellicast.com	intellicast.com
National Weather Service	www.crh.noaa.gov
STORMFAX	stormfax.com
The Weather Channel	weather.com
WX.com	wx.com

Sports	URL
CBS SportsLine.com	cbs.sportsline.com
ESPN.com	espn.com
NCAAsports.com	ncaasports.com
OFFICIAL WEBSITE OF THE OLYMPIC MOVEMENT	olympic.org
SIRC — A World of Sport Information	sirc.ca
Sporting News Radio	radio.sportingnews.com

News	URL
MSNBC	msnbc.com
NYPOST.COM	nypost.com
onlinenewspapers.com	onlinenewspapers.com
Privacy.org	privacy.org
SiliconValley.com	siliconvalley.com
Starting Page Best News Sites	startingpage.com/html/news.html
USATODAY.com	usatoday.com
washingtonpost.com	washingtonpost.com

For more information about weather, sports, and news Web sites, visit scsite.com/dc2007/ch2/web.

FIGURE 16 Keep informed about the latest weather, sports, and news events with these Web sites.

WEATHER, SPORTS, AND NEWS EXERCISES

1 Visit two of the sports Web sites in the table and write a paragraph describing the content these Web sites provide concerning your favorite sport. Visit Google.com and then search for stories about this sport team or athlete. Then, create a customized news page with stories about your sports interests. Include RSS feeds to get regularly updated summaries on this subject.

2 Visit the onlinenewspapers.com and Starting Page Best News Sites Web sites listed in Figure 16 and select two newspapers from each site. Write a paragraph describing the top national news story featured in each of these four Web pages. Then, write another paragraph describing the top international news story displayed at each Web site. In the third paragraph, discuss which of the four Web sites is the most interesting in terms of story selection, photographs, and Web page design.

Learning
YEARN TO LEARN

Discover New Worlds Online

While you may believe your education ends when you finally graduate from college, learning is a lifelong process. For example, enhancing your culinary skills can be a rewarding endeavor. No matter if you are a gourmet chef or a weekend cook, you will be cooking in style with the help of online resources, including those listed in Figure 17.

LEARNING WEB SITES

Cooking	URL
Betty Crocker	bettycrocker.com
recipecenter.com	recipecenter.com
Internet	**URL**
Learn the Net	learnthenet.com
Search Engine Watch	searchenginewatch.com
Wiredguide	wiredguide.com
Technology and Science	**URL**
HowStuffWorks	howstuffworks.com
ScienceMaster	sciencemaster.com
General Learning	**URL**
Bartleby.com: Great Books Online	bartleby.com
Blue Web'n	www.kn.pacbell.com/wired/bluewebn
MSN Encarta	encarta.msn.com

For more information about learning Web sites, visit scsite.com/dc2007/ch2/web.

FIGURE 17 The information gleaned from these Web sites can help you learn about many aspects of our existence.

If you would rather sit in front of the computer than stand in front of the stove, you can increase your technological knowledge by visiting several Web sites with tutorials on building your own Web sites, the latest news about the Internet, and resources for visually impaired users.

Have you ever wondered how the Global Positioning System (GPS) works? Take a look at the ScienceMaster site to find details. You might be interested in finding out about how your car's catalytic converter reduces pollution or how the Electoral College functions. Marshall Brain's HowStuffWorks Web site (Figure 18) is filled with articles and animations.

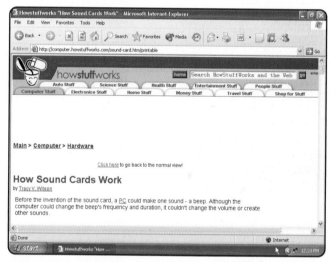

FIGURE 18 The HowStuffWorks Web site provides easy-to-understand information about technology and other facets of our lives.

LEARNING WEB EXERCISES

1. Visit one of the cooking Web sites listed in Figure 17 and find two recipes or cooking tips that you can use when preparing your next meal. Write a paragraph about each one, summarizing your discoveries. What are the advantages and disadvantages of accessing these Web sites on the new Web appliances that might someday be in your kitchen?

2. Using one of the technology and science Web sites and one of the other Web sites listed in Figure 17, search for information about communications and networks. Write a paragraph about your findings. Then, review the material in the general learning Web sites listed in Figure 18, and write a paragraph describing the content on each Web site that is pertinent to your major.

Science
$E = MC^2$

Rocket Science on the Web

For some people, space exploration is a hobby. Building and launching model rockets allow these scientists to participate in exploring the great frontier of space. For others, space exploration is their life. Numerous Web sites, including those in Figure 19, provide in-depth information about the universe.

SCIENCE WEB SITES

Periodicals	URL
Astronomy.com	astronomy.com
Archaeology Magazine	archaeology.org
NewScientist.com	newscientist.com
OceanLink	oceanlink.island.net
Science Magazine	sciencemag.org
Scientific American.com	sciam.com

Resources	URL
National Science Foundation (NSF)	nsf.gov
Science.gov: FirstGov for Science	science.gov
SOFWeb	www.sofweb.vic.edu.au

Science Community	URL
American Scientist, The Magazine of Sigma Xi, The Scientific Research Society	amsci.org
Federation of American Scientists	fas.org
NASA	www.nasa.gov
Sigma Xi, The Scientific Research Society	sigmaxi.org

For more information about science Web sites, visit scsite.com/dc2007/ch2/web.

FIGURE 19 Resources available on the Internet offer a wide range of subjects for enthusiasts who want to delve into familiar and unknown territories in the world of science.

NASA's Astronaut Flight Lounge Web site contains information about rockets, the space shuttle, the International Space Station, space transportation, and communications. Other science resources explore space-related questions about astronomy, physics, the earth sciences, microgravity, and robotics.

Rockets and space are not the only areas to explore in the world of science. Where can you find the latest pictures taken with the Hubble Space Telescope? Do you know which cities experienced an earthquake today? Have you ever wondered what a 3-D model of the amino acid glutamine looks like? You can find the answers to these questions and many others through the Librarians' Internet Index (lii.org) shown in Figure 20.

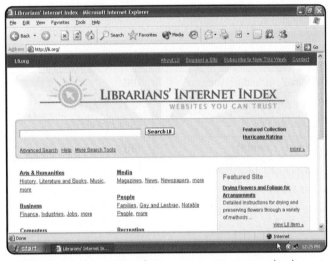

FIGURE 20 Numerous science resources are organized clearly in the Librarians' Internet Index.

SCIENCE WEB EXERCISES

1. Visit the NASA Web site listed in the table in Figure 19. View the links about spacecraft, the universe, or tracking satellites and spacecraft, and then write a summary of your findings.

2. Visit the Librarians' Internet Index shown in Figure 20. Click the Science, Computers, & Technology link and then click the Inventions topic. View the Web site for the Greatest Engineering Achievements of the Twentieth Century. Pick two achievements, read their history, and write a paragraph summarizing each of these accomplishments. Then, view two of the science Web sites listed in Figure 19 and write a paragraph about each of these Web sites describing the information each contains.

Environment
THE FATE OF THE ENVIRONMENT

Protecting the Planet's Ecosystem

From the rain forests of Africa to the marine life in the Pacific Ocean, the fragile ecosystem is under extreme stress. Many environmental groups have developed Internet sites, including those listed in Figure 21, in attempts to educate worldwide populations and to increase resource conservation.

On an international scale, the Environmental Sites on the Internet Web page developed by the Royal Institute of Technology in Stockholm, Sweden, has been rated as one of the better ecological Web sites. Its comprehensive listing of environmental concerns range from aquatic ecology to wetlands.

The U.S. federal government has a number of Web sites devoted to specific environmental concerns. For example, the U.S. Environmental Protection Agency (EPA) provides pollution data, including ozone levels and air pollutants, for specific areas. Its AirData Web site, shown in Figure 22, displays air pollution emissions and monitoring data from the entire United States and is the world's most extensive collection of air pollution data.

ENVIRONMENT WEB SITES

NAME	URL
Central African Regional Program for the Environment (CARPE)	carpe.umd.edu
Earthjustice	www.earthjustice.org
EarthTrends: The Environmental Information Portal	earthtrends.wri.org
Environmental Defense	edf.org
Environmental Sites on the Internet	www.ima.kth.se/im/envsite/envsite.htm
EPA AirData — Access to Air Pollution Data	epa.gov/air/data
Global Environmental Resources	rochesterenvironment.com/global_resources.htm
GreenNet	www.gn.apc.org
New American Dream	newdream.org
The Virtual Library of Ecology & Biodiversity	conbio.org/vl
USGS Acid rain data and reports	bqs.usgs.gov/acidrain
UWM Environmental Health, Safety & Risk Management	www.uwm.edu/Dept/EHSRM/EHSLINKS

For more information about environment Web sites, visit scsite.com/dc2007/ch2/web.

FIGURE 21 Environment Web sites provide vast resources for ecological data and action groups.

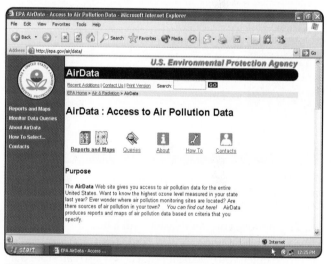

FIGURE 22 A visit to the EPA AirData Web site, with its extensive database, can assist you in checking your community's ozone and air pollutant levels.

ENVIRONMENT WEB EXERCISES

1. The New American Dream Web site encourages consumers to reduce the amount of junk mail sent to their homes. Using the table in Figure 21, visit the Web site and write a paragraph stating how many trees are leveled each year to provide paper for these mailings, how many garbage trucks are needed to haul this waste, and other statistics. Read the letters that you can use to eliminate your name from bulk mail lists. To whom would you mail these letters? How long does it take to stop these unsolicited letters?

2. Visit the EPA AirData Web site. What is the highest ozone level recorded in your state this past year? Where are the nearest air pollution monitoring Web sites, and what are their levels? Where are the nearest sources of air pollution? Read two reports about two different topics, such as acid rain and air quality, and summarize their findings. Include information about who sponsored the research, who conducted the studies, when the data was collected, and the impact of this pollution on the atmosphere, water, forests, and human health. Whom would you contact for further information regarding the data and studies?

Health
NO PAIN, ALL GAIN

Store Personal Health Records Online

More than 70 million consumers use the Internet yearly to search for health information, so using the Web to store personal medical data is a natural extension of the Internet's capabilities. Internet health services and portals are available online to store your personal health history, including prescriptions, lab test results, doctor visits, allergies, and immunizations. Web sites such as WebMD (Figure 23) are free to consumers.

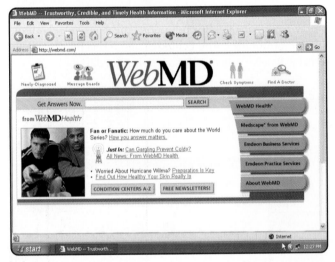

FIGURE 23 You can store health records for you and your family in the WebMD database.

In minutes, you can register with a health Web site by choosing a user name and password. Then, you create a record to enter your medical history. You also can store data for your emergency contacts, primary care physicians,

specialists, blood type, cholesterol levels, blood pressure, and insurance plan. No matter where you are in the world, you and medical personnel can obtain records via the Internet or fax machine. Some popular online health database management systems are shown in Figure 24.

HEALTH WEB SITES

Medical History	URL
Aetna InteliHealth	intelihealth.com
GlobalMedic	globalmedic.com
PersonalMD	personalmd.com
WebMD Health	my.webmd.com/ my_health_record
General Health	**URL**
Centers for Disease Control and Prevention	www.cdc.gov/
familydoctor.org	familydoctor.org
healthfinder	www.healthfinder.gov
Medical Library Association Consumer and Patient Health Information Section (CAPHIS)	caphis.mlanet.org/ consumer
MedlinePlus	medlineplus.gov
PE Central	pecentral.org/websites/ healthsites.html
www.health.gov	health.gov

For more information about health Web sites, visit scsite.com/ dc2007/ch2/web.

FIGURE 24 These health Web sites allow you to organize your medical information and store it in an online database and also obtain information about a variety of medical conditions and treatments.

HEALTH WEB EXERCISES

1. Access one of the health Web sites listed in Figure 24. Register yourself or a family member, and then enter the full health history. Create an emergency medical card if the Web site provides the card option. Submit this record and emergency card to your instructor.

2. Visit three of the health Web sites listed in Figure 24. Describe the features of each. Which of the three is the most user-friendly? Why? Describe the privacy policies of these three Web sites. Submit your analysis of these Web sites to your instructor.

Research
SEARCH AND YE SHALL FIND

Info on the Web

A 2004 Web Usability survey conducted by the Nielsen Norman Group found that 88 percent of people log onto a computer and then use a search engine as their first action. Search engines require users to type words and phrases that characterize the information being sought. Yahoo! (Figure 25), Google, and AltaVista are some of the more popular search engines. The key to effective searching on the Web is composing search queries that narrow the search results and place the most relevant Web sites at the top of the results list.

Subject directories are collections of related Web sites. Yahoo! and LookSmart have two of the more comprehensive subject directories on the Web. Their organized lists often are called trees because a few main categories, such as Entertainment, Computing, Lifestyle, and Work, branch out to more specific subtopics. Popular subject directories and search engines are listed in Figure 26.

RESEARCH WEB SITES

Search Engines	URL
A9.com	a9.com
AlltheWeb	alltheweb.com
AOL Search	search.aol.com
Gigablast	gigablast.com
HotBot	hotbot.com
Internet Archive Wayback Machine	archive.org
Overture	overture.com
WebCrawler	webcrawler.com
Subject Directories and Search Engines	**URL**
Alta Vista	altavista.com
Ask Jeeves	askjeeves.com
Excite	excite.com
Google	google.com
MSN Search	search.msn.com
Yahoo!	yahoo.com
For more information about research Web sites, visit scsite.com/ dc2007/ch2/web.	

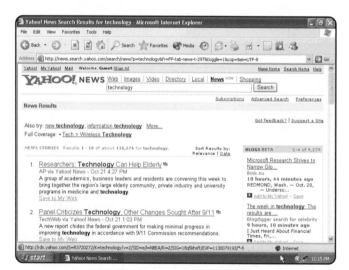

FIGURE 25 The Yahoo! News search results for the phrase, technology, lists more than 116,000 stories.

FIGURE 26 Web users can find information by using search engines and subject directories.

RESEARCH WEB EXERCISES

1 Use two of the search engines listed in Figure 26 to find three Web sites that review the latest digital cameras from Sony and Kodak. Make a table listing the search engines, Web site names, and the cameras' model numbers, suggested retail price, megapixels, memory, and features.

2 If money were no object, virtually everyone would have an exquisite car. On the other hand, drivers need a practical vehicle to drive around town daily. Use one of the subject directories listed in Figure 26 to research your dream car and another directory to research your practical car. Write a paragraph about each car describing the particular subject directory tree you used, the manufacturer's suggested retail price (MSRP) of the car, standard and optional equipment, engine size, miles per gallon, and safety features. Visit the Internet Archive Wayback Machine Web site to obtain information about previous models of this vehicle.

Careers
IN SEARCH OF THE PERFECT JOB

Web Helps Career Hunt

While your teachers give you valuable training to prepare you for a career, they rarely teach you how to begin that career. You can broaden your horizons by searching the Internet for career information and job openings.

First, examine some of the job search Web sites. These resources list thousands of openings in hundreds of fields, companies, and locations. For example, the Monster Web site, shown in Figure 27, allows you to choose a broad job area, narrow your search to specific fields within that area, and then search for specific salary ranges, locations, and job functions.

When a company contacts you for an interview, learn as much about it and the industry as possible before the interview. Many of the Web sites listed in Figure 28 include detailed company profiles and links to their corporate Web sites.

CAREER WEB SITES

Job Search	URL
BestJobsUSA.com	bestjobsusa.com
CareerBuilder	careerbuilder.com
CareerNet	careernet.com
College Grad Job Hunter	collegegrad.com
Cytiva	careerexchange.com
EmploymentGuide.com	employmentguide.com
Job.com	job.com
JobBankUSA.com	jobbankusa.com
JobWeb.com	www.jobweb.com
Monster	monster.com
Spherion	spherion.com
USAJOBS	usajobs.opm.gov
VolunteerMatch	volunteermatch.org
Yahoo!.HotJobs.com	hotjobs.com

Company/Industry Information	URL
Career ResourceCenter.com	resourcecenter.com
Forbes.com	forbes.com/careers
FORTUNE	fortune.com
Hoover's	hoovers.com
Occupational Outlook Handbook	stats.bls.gov/oco

For more information about career Web sites, visit scsite.com/dc2007/ch2/web.

FIGURE 28 Career Web sites provide a variety of job openings and information about major companies worldwide.

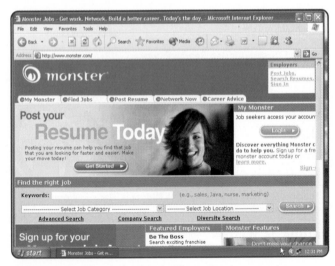

FIGURE 27 Monster's global online network connects companies with career-minded individuals.

CAREERS WEB EXERCISES

1 Use two of the job search Web sites listed in Figure 28 to find three companies with job openings in your field. Make a table listing the Web site name, position available, description, salary, location, desired education, and desired experience.

2 It is a good idea to acquire information before graduation about the industry in which you would like to work. Are you interested in the automotive manufacturing industry, the restaurant service industry, or the financial industry? Use two of the company/industry information Web sites listed in Figure 28 to research a particular career related to your major. Write a paragraph naming the Web sites and the specific information you found, such as the nature of the work, recommended training and qualifications, employment outlook, and earnings. Then, use two other Web sites to profile three companies with positions available in this field. Write a paragraph about each of these companies, describing the headquarters' location, sales and earnings for the previous year, total number of employees, working conditions, perks, and competitors.

Arts and Literature
FIND SOME CULTURE

Get Ready to Read, Paint, and Dance

Brush up your knowledge of Shakespeare, grab a canvas, and put on your dancing shoes. Visual arts and literature Web sites, including those in Figure 29, are about to sweep you off your cyberfeet.

ARTS AND LITERATURE WEB SITES

Arts	URL
Access Place Arts	accessplace.com/arts.htm
Art News — absolutearts.com	absolutearts.com
GalleryGuide.com	galleryguide.com
Louvre Museum	louvre.fr
Montreal Museum of Fine Arts	mmfa.qc.ca
The Children's Museum of Indianapolis	childrensmuseum.org
The Getty	getty.edu
The New York Times: Arts	nytimes.com/pages/arts/index.html
Virtual Library museums pages (VLmp)	vlmp.museophile.com
Literature	**URL**
Bartleby.com	bartleby.com
Bibliomania	bibliomania.com
Electronic Literature Directory	directory.wordcircuits.com
Fantastic Fiction	fantasticfiction.co.uk
Project Gutenberg	promo.net/pg
shakespeare.com	shakespeare.com
The Modern Library eBook List	randomhouse.com/modernlibrary/ebookslist.html

For more information about arts and literature Web sites, visit scsite.com/dc2007/ch2/web.

FIGURE 29 Discover culture throughout the world by visiting these arts and literature Web sites.

The full text of hundreds of books is available online from the Bibliomania and Project Gutenberg Web sites. Shakespeare.com provides in-depth reviews and news of the world's most famous playwright and his works. The Bartleby.com Web site features biographies, definitions, quotations, dictionaries, and indexes.

When you are ready to absorb more culture, you can turn to various art Web sites. Many museums have images of their collections online. Among them are the Getty Museum in Los Angeles (Figure 30), the Montreal Museum of Fine Arts, and the Louvre Museum in Paris.

Access Place Arts and The New York Times Web sites focus on the arts and humanities and provide fascinating glimpses into the worlds of dance, music, performance, cinema, and other topics pertaining to creative expression.

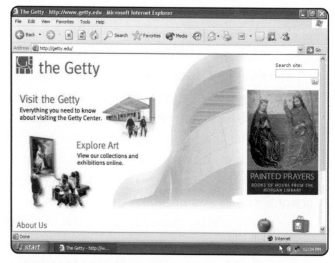

FIGURE 30 Permanent and temporary exhibitions, educational activities, and a bookstore are featured on the Getty Museum Web site.

ARTS AND LITERATURE WEB EXERCISES

1. Visit The Modern Library eBook List Web site listed in Figure 29 and view one book in the 20th CENTURY NOVELS, 19th CENTURY NOVELS, BRITISH LITERATURE, and HISTORY sections. Create a table with columns for the book name, author, cost, online store, local store, and description. Then, read the excerpt from each of the four books and write a paragraph describing which of these four books is the most interesting to you. What are the advantages and disadvantages of reading classic literature electronically?

2. Using the arts Web sites listed in Figure 29, search for three temporary exhibitions in galleries throughout the world. Describe the venues, the artists, and the works. What permanent collections are found in these museums? Some people shop for gifts in the museums' stores. View and describe three items for sale.

CHAPTER THREE

Application Software

Picture Yourself Using Software

As your biology instructor reviews for the upcoming test, you use note taking software and a digital pen to mark important points in your electronic notes. Then, you write "Professor Jenson said that this is going to be on the test." At the end of class, you start the appointment calendar software in your PDA and record the date of the test.

Later that day, when you open your e-mail program to check messages, you see a message from a friend asking what he missed in biology class. You type a reply to his message, attach a copy of your electronic lecture notes to the message, and then click the Send button.

Time to start composing your philosophy paper about Socrates. You use the research feature of your word processing program to learn about this ancient Greek philosopher and then write the paper — being sure to cite all sources. While writing the paper, your personal finance software alerts you that it is time to download transaction information from the bank's computer to your computer. With this service, your computerized checkbook balance always is up-to-date. Ready for a break, you fire up the train simulator program and experience the thrill of driving a train.

Read Chapter 3 to learn more about note taking software, PDA application software, e-mail programs, word processing software, personal finance software, and entertainment software, and discover many other types of application software.

APPLICATION SOFTWARE

With the proper software, a computer is a valuable tool. Software allows users to create letters, memos, reports, and other documents; design Web pages and diagrams; draw and alter images; record and enhance audio and video clips; prepare and file taxes; play single player or multiplayer games; compose e-mail messages and instant messages; and much more. To accomplish these and many other tasks, users work with application software. **Application software** consists of programs designed to make users more productive and/or assist them with personal tasks. Application software has a variety of uses:

1. To make business activities more efficient
2. To assist with graphics and multimedia projects
3. To support home, personal, and educational tasks
4. To facilitate communications

The table in Figure 3-1 categorizes popular types of application software by their general use. Although many types of communications software exist, the ones listed in Figure 3-1 are application software oriented. Utility programs, which are not a category of application software, are widely used to manage and protect computer resources. Successful use of application software generally requires the use of one or more of the utility programs identified in Figure 3-1.

As you become familiar with application software, it is likely you will use software from more than one of the categories in Figure 3-1. The four categories are not mutually exclusive. Software listed in one category may be used in other categories. For example, e-mail and Web browser programs, which are categorized as communications software, often are used for business or personal reasons.

Application software is available in a variety of forms: packaged, custom, open source, shareware, freeware, and public domain.

- **Packaged software** is mass-produced, copyrighted retail software that meets the needs of a wide variety of users, not just a single user or company. Word processing and spreadsheet software are examples of packaged software. Packaged software is available in retail stores or on the Web.

CATEGORIES OF APPLICATION SOFTWARE

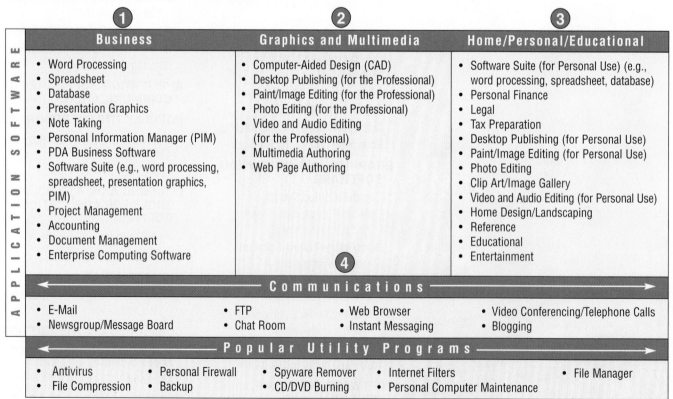

	① Business	② Graphics and Multimedia	③ Home/Personal/Educational
APPLICATION SOFTWARE	• Word Processing • Spreadsheet • Database • Presentation Graphics • Note Taking • Personal Information Manager (PIM) • PDA Business Software • Software Suite (e.g., word processing, spreadsheet, presentation graphics, PIM) • Project Management • Accounting • Document Management • Enterprise Computing Software	• Computer-Aided Design (CAD) • Desktop Publishing (for the Professional) • Paint/Image Editing (for the Professional) • Photo Editing (for the Professional) • Video and Audio Editing (for the Professional) • Multimedia Authoring • Web Page Authoring	• Software Suite (for Personal Use) (e.g., word processing, spreadsheet, database) • Personal Finance • Legal • Tax Preparation • Desktop Publishing (for Personal Use) • Paint/Image Editing (for Personal Use) • Photo Editing • Clip Art/Image Gallery • Video and Audio Editing (for Personal Use) • Home Design/Landscaping • Reference • Educational • Entertainment

④ Communications

• E-Mail • Newsgroup/Message Board	• FTP • Chat Room	• Web Browser • Instant Messaging	• Video Conferencing/Telephone Calls • Blogging

Popular Utility Programs

• Antivirus • File Compression	• Personal Firewall • Backup	• Spyware Remover • CD/DVD Burning	• Internet Filters • Personal Computer Maintenance	• File Manager

FIGURE 3-1   The four major categories of popular application software are outlined in this table. Communications software often is bundled with other application or system software. Also identified in the table are widely used utility programs.

- **Custom software** performs functions specific to a business or industry. Sometimes a company cannot find packaged software that meets its unique requirements. In this case, the company may use programmers to develop tailor-made custom software, which usually costs more than packaged software.
- **Open source software** is software provided for use, modification, and redistribution. This software has no restrictions from the copyright holder regarding modification of the software's internal instructions and redistribution of the software. Open source software usually can be downloaded from the Internet, sometimes at no cost.
- **Shareware** is copyrighted software that is distributed at no cost for a trial period. To use a shareware program beyond that period, you send payment to the program developer. Shareware developers trust users to send payment if software use extends beyond the stated trial period. In some cases, a scaled-down version of the software is distributed free, and payment entitles the user to the fully functional product.
- **Freeware** is copyrighted software provided at no cost by an individual or a company that retains all rights to the software. Thus, programmers typically cannot incorporate freeware in applications they intend to sell. The word, free, in freeware indicates the software has no charge.
- **Public-domain software** has been donated for public use and has no copyright restrictions. Anyone can copy or distribute public-domain software to others at no cost.

Thousands of shareware, freeware, and public-domain programs are available on the Internet for users to download. Examples include communications programs, graphics programs, and games. These programs usually have fewer capabilities than retail programs.

After you purchase or download software, you install it. During installation, the program may ask you to register and/or activate the software. Registering the software is optional and usually involves submitting your name and other personal information to the software manufacturer or developer. Registering the software often entitles you to product support. *Product activation* is a technique that some software manufacturers use to ensure the software is not installed on more computers than legally licensed. Usually, the software does not function or has limited functionality until you activate it via the Internet or telephone. Thus, activation is a required process for programs requesting it.

The Role of System Software

System software serves as the interface between the user, the application software, and the computer's hardware (Figure 3-2). To use application software, such as a word processing program, your computer must be running system software — specifically, an operating system. Three popular personal computer operating systems are Windows XP, Linux, and Mac OS X.

Each time you start a computer, the operating system is *loaded* (copied) from the computer's hard disk into memory. Once the operating system is loaded, it coordinates all the activities of the computer. This includes starting application software and transferring data among input and output devices and memory. While the computer is running, the operating system remains in memory.

Application Software

System Software

FIGURE 3-2 A user does not communicate directly with the computer hardware. Instead, system software is the interface between the user, the application software, and the hardware. For example, when a user instructs the application software to print, the application software sends the print instruction to the system software, which in turn sends the print instruction to the hardware.

Working with Application Software

To use application software, you must instruct the operating system to start the program. The steps in Figure 3-3 illustrate how to start and interact with the Paint program. The following paragraphs explain the steps in Figure 3-3.

Personal computer operating systems often use the concept of a desktop to make the computer easier to use. The **desktop** is an on-screen work area that has a graphical user interface (Read Looking Ahead 3-1 for a look at the next generation of user interfaces). Step 1 of Figure 3-3 shows icons, a button, and a pointer on the Windows XP desktop. An **icon** is a small image displayed on the screen that represents a program, a document, or some other object. A **button** is a graphical element that you activate to cause a specific action to take place. One way to activate a button is to click it. To **click** a button on the screen requires moving the pointer to the button and then pressing and releasing a button on the mouse (usually the left mouse button). The **pointer** is a small symbol displayed on the screen that moves as you move the mouse. Common pointer shapes are an I-beam (I), a block arrow (⇖), and a pointing hand (☝).

The Windows XP desktop contains a Start button on the lower-left corner of the taskbar.

FIGURE 3-3   HOW TO START AN APPLICATION

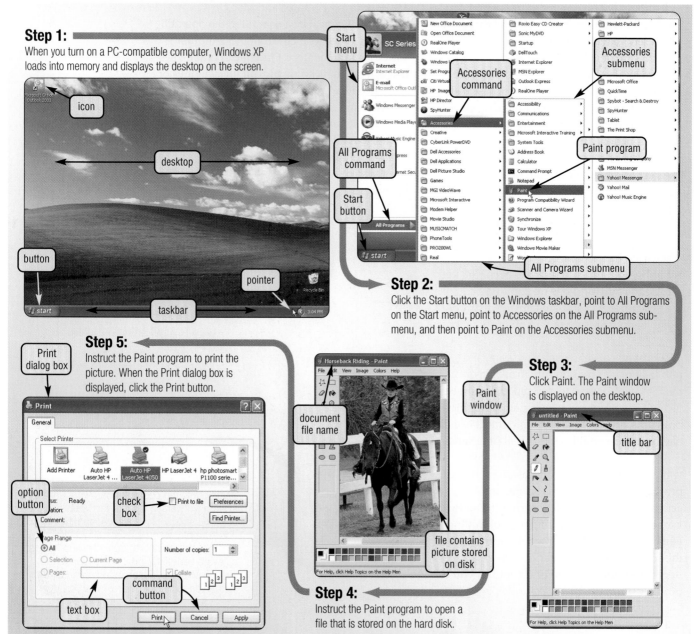

Step 1:
When you turn on a PC-compatible computer, Windows XP loads into memory and displays the desktop on the screen.

Step 2:
Click the Start button on the Windows taskbar, point to All Programs on the Start menu, point to Accessories on the All Programs submenu, and then point to Paint on the Accessories submenu.

Step 3:
Click Paint. The Paint window is displayed on the desktop.

Step 4:
Instruct the Paint program to open a file that is stored on the hard disk.

Step 5:
Instruct the Paint program to print the picture. When the Print dialog box is displayed, click the Print button.

When you click the Start button, the Start menu is displayed on the desktop. A **menu** contains a list of commands from which you make selections. A **command** is an instruction that causes a program to perform a specific action.

The arrowhead symbol at the right edge of some menu commands indicates a submenu of additional commands is available. A *submenu* is a menu that is displayed when you point to a command on a previous menu. As illustrated in Step 2 of Figure 3-3, when you click the Start button and point to the All Programs command on the Start menu, the All Programs submenu is displayed. Pointing to the Accessories command on the All Programs submenu displays the Accessories submenu.

To start a program, you can click its program name on a menu or submenu. This action instructs the operating system to start the application, which means the program's instructions load from a storage medium (such as a hard disk) into memory. For example, when you click Paint on the Accessories submenu, Windows loads the Paint program instructions from the computer's hard disk into memory.

Once loaded into memory, the program is displayed in a window on the desktop (Step 3 of Figure 3-3). A **window** is a rectangular area of the screen that displays data and information. The top of a window has a **title bar**, which is a horizontal space that contains the window's name.

With the program loaded, you can create a new file or open an existing one. A *file* is a named collection of stored data, instructions, or information. A file can contain text, images, audio, and video. To distinguish among various files, each file has a file name. A *file name* is a unique combination of letters of the alphabet, numbers, and

other characters that identifies a file. The title bar of the document window usually displays a document's file name. Step 4 of Figure 3-3 shows the contents of the file, Horseback Riding, displaying in the Paint window. The file contains an image photographed with a digital camera.

In some cases, when you instruct a program to perform an activity such as printing, the program displays a dialog box. A *dialog box* is a window that provides information, presents available options, or requests a response. Dialog boxes, such as the one shown in Step 5 of Figure 3-3, often contain option buttons, text boxes, check boxes, and command buttons. Clicking the Print button in the dialog box instructs the computer to print the picture.

FAQ 3-1

Will a document print like it looks on a screen?

Yes, because most application software is *WYSIWYG* (*what you see is what you get*). The software embeds invisible codes around the text and graphics, which instructs the computer how to present the information. For more information, visit scsite.com/dc2007/ch3/faq and then click WYSIWYG.

Test your knowledge of pages 134 through 137 in Quiz Yourself 3-1.

QUIZ YOURSELF 3-1

Instructions: Find the true statement below. Then, rewrite the remaining false statements so they are true.

1. Application software is used to make business activities more efficient; assist with graphics and multimedia projects; support home, personal, and educational tasks; and facilitate communications.
2. Public-domain software is mass-produced, copyrighted retail software that meets the needs of a wide variety of users, not just a single user or company.
3. To use system software, your computer must be running application software.
4. When an application is started, the program's instructions load from memory into a storage medium.

Quiz Yourself Online: To further check your knowledge of application software categories, ways software is distributed, and working with application software, visit scsite.com/dc2007/ch3/quiz and then click Objectives 1 – 3.

LOOKING AHEAD 3-1

User Interfaces of the Future

Most computers today use a graphical user interface. Next-generation user interfaces will be more natural and human-centric, meaning they will enable people to interact with a computer using human-like communication methods. Developments in this area include gesture recognition, 3-D interfaces, and neural interfaces.

With gesture recognition, the computer will detect human motions. Computers with this type of user interface will have the capability of recognizing sign language, reading lips, tracking facial movements, and following eye gazes.

Imagine rotating a window or object to read its flipside, switching from a desktop view to a panoramic view, or tacking sticky notes right on a Web screen. All these scenarios will be possible with the upcoming 3-D user interfaces.

Neural interfaces may help quadriplegic people gain independence with everyday activities, such as maneuvering wheelchairs and typing. These systems use a tiny chip with sensors implanted on the brain and external computers that convert brainwaves into output signals the person can control. For more information, visit scsite.com/dc2007/ch3/looking and then click User Interfaces.

BUSINESS SOFTWARE

Business software is application software that assists people in becoming more effective and efficient while performing their daily business activities. Business software includes programs such as word processing, spreadsheet, database, presentation graphics, note taking, personal information manager software, PDA business software, software suites, project management, accounting, document management, and enterprise computing software. Figure 3-4 lists popular programs for each of these categories.

The following sections discuss the features and functions of business software. Word processing and spreadsheet software have a heavier emphasis because of their predominant use.

Word Processing Software

Word processing software is one of the more widely used types of application software. **Word processing software**, sometimes called a *word processor*, allows users to create and manipulate documents containing mostly text and sometimes graphics (Figure 3-5). Millions of people use word processing software every day to develop documents such as letters, memos, reports, fax cover sheets, mailing labels, newsletters, and Web pages.

Word processing software has many features to make documents look professional and visually appealing. Some of these features include the capability of changing the shape and size of characters, changing the color of characters, and organizing text in newspaper-style columns. When using colors for characters, however, they will print as black or gray unless you have a color printer.

Most word processing software allows users to incorporate many types of graphical images in documents. One popular type of graphical image is clip art. **Clip art** is a collection of

POPULAR BUSINESS PROGRAMS

Application Software	Manufacturer	Program Name
Word Processing	Microsoft	Word
	Sun	StarOffice Writer
	Corel	WordPerfect
Spreadsheet	Microsoft	Excel
	Sun	StarOffice Calc
	Corel	Quattro Pro
Database	Microsoft	Access
	Sun	StarOffice Base
	Corel	Paradox
	Microsoft	Visual FoxPro
	Oracle	Oracle Database
	MySQL AB	MySQL
Presentation Graphics	Microsoft	PowerPoint
	Sun	StarOffice Impress
	Corel	Presentations
Note Taking	Microsoft	OneNote
	Agilix	GoBinder
	Corel	Grafigo
Personal Information Manager (PIM)	Microsoft	Outlook
	IBM	Lotus Organizer
	Palm	Desktop
PDA Business Software	CNetX	Pocket SlideShow
	Microsoft	Pocket Word Pocket Excel Pocket Outlook
	PalmOne	VersaMail
	Ultrasoft	Money

Application Software	Manufacturer	Program Name
Software Suite (for the Professional)	Microsoft	Office Office for Mac
	Sun	StarOffice Office Suite
	Corel	WordPerfect Office
	IBM	Lotus SmartSuite
Project Management	Microsoft	Project
	Primavera	SureTrak Project Manager
Accounting	Intuit	QuickBooks
	Sage Software	Peachtree Accounting
Document Management	Adobe	Acrobat
	Enfocus	PitStop
	ScanSoft	PDF Converter PaperPort
Enterprise Computing Software	Oracle	PeopleSoft Enterprise Human Resources
	Best Software	Sage MAS 500
	MSC Software	MSC.SimManager
	Oracle	Oracle Manufacturing
	SAP	mySAP Customer Relationship Management
	NetSuite	NetERP
	Apropos Technology	Apropos Enterprise Edition

FIGURE 3-4   Popular business software.

drawings, diagrams, maps, and photographs that you can insert in documents. In Figure 3-5, a user inserted a clip art image of an alarm clock in the document. Word processing software usually includes public-domain clip art. You can find additional public-domain and proprietary images on the Web or purchase them on CD or DVD.

All word processing software provides at least some basic capabilities to help users create and modify documents. Defining the size of the paper on which to print and specifying the *margins* — that is, the portion of the page outside the main body of text, including the top, the bottom, and both sides of the paper — are examples of some of these capabilities. If you type text that extends beyond the right page margin, the word processing software automatically positions text at the beginning of the next line. This feature, called *wordwrap*, allows users to type words in a paragraph continually without pressing the ENTER key at the end of each line. When you modify paper size or margins, the word processing software automatically rewraps text so it fits in the adjusted paper size and margins.

As you type more lines of text than can be displayed on the screen, the top portion of the document moves upward, or scrolls, off the screen. *Scrolling* is the process of moving different portions of the document on the screen into view.

A major advantage of using word processing software is that users easily can change what

they have written. For example, a user can insert, delete, or rearrange words, sentences, paragraphs, or entire sections. The find, or *search*, feature allows you to locate all occurrences of a certain character, word, or phrase. This feature, in combination with the *replace* feature, allows you to substitute existing characters or words with new ones.

Word processing software includes a *spelling checker*, which reviews the spelling of individual words, sections of a document, or the entire document. The spelling checker compares the words in the document with an electronic dictionary that is part of the word processing software. You can customize the

Learn how to manage time so you can balance **schoolwork and extracurricular** activities. Class also shows how to set up *and* maintain schedules using a variety of digital technologies.

Program runs for six weeks starting Tuesday, September 25. Class meets in Room 23 for one hour each week beginning promptly at 3:30 p.m.

Call 555-2858 to sign up.

document is displayed in window

printed document

clip art

FIGURE 3-5 Word processing software enables users to create professional and visually appealing documents.

electronic dictionary by adding words such as companies, streets, cities, and personal names, so the software can check the spelling of those words too.

Another benefit of word processing software is the capability to insert headers and footers in a document. A *header* is text that appears at the top of each page, and a *footer* is text that appears at the bottom of each page. Page numbers, company names, report titles, and dates are examples of items often included in headers and footers.

In addition to these basic capabilities, most current word processing programs provide numerous additional features, which are listed in the table in Figure 3-6.

ADDITIONAL WORD PROCESSING FEATURES

AutoCorrect	As you type words, the AutoCorrect feature corrects common spelling errors. AutoCorrect also corrects capitalization mistakes.
AutoFormat	As you type, the AutoFormat feature automatically applies formatting to the text. For example, it automatically numbers a list or converts a Web address to a hyperlink.
Collaboration	Collaboration includes discussions and online meetings. Discussions allow multiple users to enter comments in a document and read and reply to each other's comments. Through an online meeting, users share documents with others in real time and view changes as they are being made.
Columns	Most word processing software can arrange text in two or more columns to look like a newspaper or magazine. The text from the bottom of one column automatically flows to the top of the next column.
Grammar Checker	The grammar checker proofreads documents for grammar, writing style, sentence structure errors, and reading statistics.
Ink Input	Supports input from a digital pen. Word processing software that supports ink input incorporates user's handwritten text and drawings in a word processing document. Ink input is popular on Tablet PCs.
Macros	A *macro* is a sequence of keystrokes and instructions that a user records and saves. When you want to execute the same series of instructions, execute the macro instead.
Mail Merge	Creates form letters, mailing labels, and envelopes.
Reading Layout	For those users who prefer reading on the screen, reading layout increases the readability and legibility of an on-screen document by hiding unnecessary toolbars, increasing the size of displayed characters, and providing navigation tools.
Research	Some word processing software allows you to search through various forms of online and Internet reference information — based on selected text in a document. Research services available include a thesaurus, English and bilingual dictionaries, encyclopedias, and Web sites that provide information such as stock quotes, news articles, and company profiles.
Smart Tags	*Smart tags* automatically appear on the screen when you perform a certain action. For example, typing an address causes a smart tag to appear. Clicking this smart tag provides options to display a map of the address or driving directions to or from the address.
Tables	Tables organize information into rows and columns. In addition to evenly spaced rows and columns, some word processing programs allow you to draw tables of any size or shape.
Templates	A *template* is a document that contains the formatting necessary for a specific document type. Templates usually exist for memos, fax cover sheets, and letters. In addition to templates provided with the software, users have access to many online templates through the manufacturer's Web site.
Thesaurus	With a thesaurus, a user looks up a synonym (word with the same meaning) for a word in a document.
Tracking Changes	If multiple users work with a document, the word processing software highlights or color-codes changes made by various users.
Voice Recognition	With some word processing programs, users can speak into the computer's microphone and watch the spoken words appear on the screen as they talk. With these programs, users edit and format the document by speaking or spelling an instruction.
Web Page Development	Most word processing software allows users to create, edit, format, and convert documents to be displayed on the World Wide Web.

FIGURE 3-6   Many additional features are included with word processing software.

Developing a Document

With application software, such as word processing, users create, edit, format, save, and print documents. During the process of developing a document, users likely will switch back and forth among all of these activities.

When you **create** a document, you enter text or numbers, insert graphical images, and perform other tasks using an input device such as a keyboard, mouse, microphone, or digital pen. If you are using Microsoft Word to design an announcement, for example, you are creating a document.

To **edit** a document means to make changes to its existing content. Common editing tasks include inserting, deleting, cutting, copying, and pasting. Inserting text involves adding text to a document. Deleting text means that you are removing text or other content. Cutting is the process of removing a portion of the document and storing it in a temporary storage location, sometimes called a *clipboard*. A clipboard also contains items that you copy (duplicate) in a document. *Pasting* is the process of transferring an item from a clipboard to a specific location in a document. Read Ethics & Issues 3-1 for a related discussion.

When users **format** a document, they change its appearance. Formatting is important because the overall look of a document significantly can affect its ability to communicate clearly. Examples of formatting tasks are changing the font, font size, or font style of text.

A **font** is a name assigned to a specific design of characters. Two basic types of fonts are serif and sans serif. A *serif font* has short decorative lines at the upper and lower ends of the characters. Sans means without. Thus, a *sans serif font* does not have the short decorative lines at the upper and lower ends of the characters. Times New Roman is an example of a serif font. Arial is an example of a sans serif font.

Font size indicates the size of the characters in a particular font. Font size is gauged by a measurement system called points. A single *point* is about 1/72 of an inch in height. The text you are reading in this book is about 10 point. Thus, each character is about 5/36 (10/72) of an inch in height. A *font style* adds emphasis to a font. Bold, italic, and underline are examples of font styles. Figure 3-7 illustrates fonts, font sizes, and font styles.

FIGURE 3-7 The Times New Roman and Arial fonts are shown in two font sizes and a variety of font styles.

During the process of creating, editing, and formatting a document, the computer holds it in memory. To keep the document for future use requires that you save it. When you **save** a document, the computer transfers the document from memory to a storage medium such as a USB flash drive, hard disk, or CD. Once saved, a document is stored permanently as a file on the storage medium.

When you **print** a document, the computer places the contents of the document on paper or some other medium. One of the benefits of word processing software is the ability to print the same document many times, with each copy looking just like the first. Instead of printing a document and physically distributing it, some users e-mail the document to others on a network such as the Internet.

Spreadsheet Software

Spreadsheet software is another widely used type of application software. **Spreadsheet software** allows users to organize data in rows and columns and perform calculations on the data. These rows and columns collectively are called a *worksheet*. For years, people used paper to organize data and perform calculations by hand. In an electronic worksheet, you organize data in the same manner, and the computer performs the calculations more quickly and accurately (Figure 3-8). Because of spreadsheet software's logical approach to organizing data, many people use this software to organize and present nonfinancial data, as well as financial data.

As with word processing software, most spreadsheet software has basic features to help users create, edit, and format worksheets. Spreadsheet software also incorporates many of the features found in word processing software such as macros, checking spelling, changing fonts and font sizes, adding colors, tracking changes, recognizing voice input, inserting audio and video clips, providing research capabilities, recognizing handwritten text and drawings, and creating Web pages from existing spreadsheet documents.

The following sections describe the features of most spreadsheet programs.

FAQ 3-2

How often should I save a document?

Saving at regular intervals ensures that the majority of your work will not be lost in the event of a power loss or system failure. Many programs have an AutoSave feature that automatically saves open documents at specified time intervals, such as every 10 minutes. For more information, visit scsite.com/dc2007/ch3/faq and then click Saving Documents.

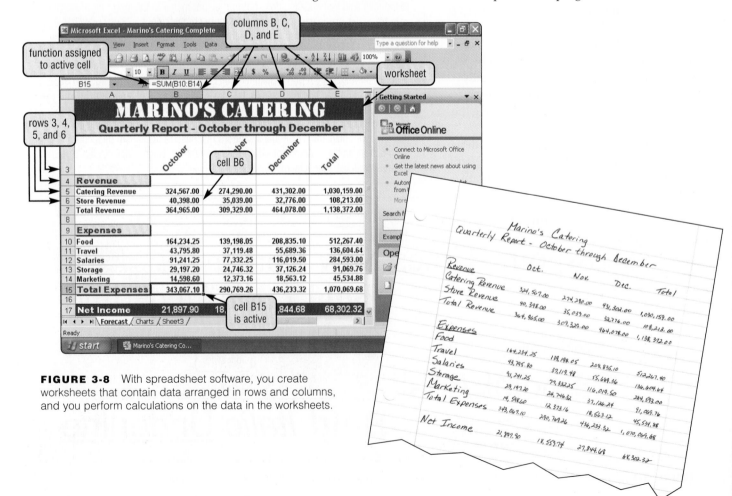

FIGURE 3-8   With spreadsheet software, you create worksheets that contain data arranged in rows and columns, and you perform calculations on the data in the worksheets.

SPREADSHEET ORGANIZATION A spreadsheet file is similar to a notebook with up to 255 related individual worksheets. Data is organized vertically in columns and horizontally in rows on each worksheet (Figure 3-8). Each worksheet typically has 256 columns and 65,536 rows. One or more letters identify each column, and a number identifies each row. The column letters begin with A and end with IV. The row numbers begin with 1 and end with 65,536. Only a small fraction of these columns and rows are displayed on the screen at one time. Scrolling through the worksheet displays different parts of it on the screen.

A *cell* is the intersection of a column and row. Each worksheet has more than 16 million (256 × 65,536) cells in which you can enter data. The spreadsheet software identifies cells by the column and row in which they are located. For example, the intersection of column B and row 6 is referred to as cell B6. As shown in Figure 3-8, cell B6 contains the number, 40,398.00, which represents the store revenue for October.

Cells may contain three types of data: labels, values, and formulas. The text, or *label*, entered in a cell identifies the worksheet data and helps organize the worksheet. Using descriptive labels, such as Total Revenue and Total Expenses, helps make a worksheet more meaningful.

CALCULATIONS Many of the worksheet cells shown in Figure 3-8 contain a number, called a *value*, that can be used in a calculation. Other cells, however, contain formulas that generate values. A *formula* performs calculations on the data in the worksheet and displays the resulting value in a cell, usually the cell containing the formula. When creating a worksheet, you can enter your own formulas.

In many spreadsheet programs, you begin a formula with an equal sign, a plus sign, or a minus sign. Next, you enter the formula, separating cell references (e.g., B10) with operators. Common operators are + for addition, − for subtraction, * for multiplication, and / for division. In Figure 3-8, for example, cell B15 could contain the formula =B10+B11+B12+B13+B14, which would add together (sum) the contents of cells B10, B11, B12, B13, and B14. That is, this formula calculates the total expenses for October. A more efficient way to sum the contents of cells, however, is to use a special type of formula, called a function.

A *function* is a predefined formula that performs common calculations such as adding the values in a group of cells or generating a value such as the time or date. For example, instead of using the formula =B10+B11+B12+B13+B14 to calculate the total expenses for October, you could use the SUM function. This function requires you to identify the starting cell and the ending cell in a group to be summed, separating these two cell references with a colon. For example, the function =SUM(B10:B14) instructs the spreadsheet program to add all of the numbers in cells B10 through B14. Figure 3-9 lists functions commonly included in spreadsheet programs.

SPREADSHEET FUNCTIONS

Financial	
FV (rate, number of periods, payment)	Calculates the future value of an investment
NPV (rate, range)	Calculates the net present value of an investment
PMT (rate, number of periods, present value)	Calculates the periodic payment for an annuity
PV (rate, number of periods, payment)	Calculates the present value of an investment
RATE (number of periods, payment, present value)	Calculates the periodic interest rate of an annuity
Date and Time	
DATE	Returns the current date
NOW	Returns the current date and time
TIME	Returns the current time
Mathematical	
ABS (number)	Returns the absolute value of a number
INT (number)	Rounds a number down to the nearest integer
LN (number)	Calculates the natural logarithm of a number
LOG (number, base)	Calculates the logarithm of a number to a specified base
ROUND (number, number of digits)	Rounds a number to a specified number of digits
SQRT (number)	Calculates the square root of a number
SUM (range)	Calculates the total of a range of numbers
Statistical	
AVERAGE (range)	Calculates the average value of a range of numbers
COUNT (range)	Counts how many cells in the range have numeric entries
MAX (range)	Returns the maximum value in a range
MIN (range)	Returns the minimum value in a range
STDEV (range)	Calculates the standard deviation of a range of numbers
Logical	
IF (logical test, value if true, value if false)	Performs a test and returns one value if the result of the test is true and another value if the result is false

FIGURE 3-9 Functions typically found in spreadsheet software.

RECALCULATION   One of the more powerful features of spreadsheet software is its capability of recalculating the rest of the worksheet when data in a worksheet changes. When you enter a new value to change data in a cell, any value affected by the change is updated automatically and instantaneously. In Figure 3-8 on page 142, for example, if you change the store revenue for October from 40,398.00 to 45,398.00, the total revenue in cell B7 automatically changes from 364,965.00 to 369,965.00.

Spreadsheet software's capability of recalculating data also makes it a valuable budgeting, forecasting, and decision making tool. Most spreadsheet software includes a *what-if analysis* feature, where you change certain values in a spreadsheet to reveal the effects of those changes.

CHARTING   Another standard feature of spreadsheet software is *charting*, which depicts the data in graphical form. A visual representation of data through charts often makes it easier for users to see at a glance the relationship among the numbers.

Three popular chart types are line charts, column charts, and pie charts. Figure 3-10 shows examples of these charts that were plotted from the data in Figure 3-8. A *line chart* shows a trend during a period of time, as indicated by a rising or falling line. For example, a line chart could show the total expenses for the three months. A *column chart*, also called a *bar chart*, displays bars of various lengths to show the relationship of data. The bars can be horizontal, vertical, or stacked on top of one another. For example, a column chart might show the total monthly expenses, with each bar representing a different category of expense. A *pie chart*, which has the shape of a round pie cut into slices, shows the relationship of parts to a whole. For example, you might use a pie chart to show the percentage each expense category contributed to the total expenses.

Charts, as well as any other part of a workbook, can be linked to or embedded in a word processing document.

WEB LINK 3-2

Spreadsheet Software

For more information, visit scsite.com/dc2007/ch3/weblink and then click Spreadsheet Software.

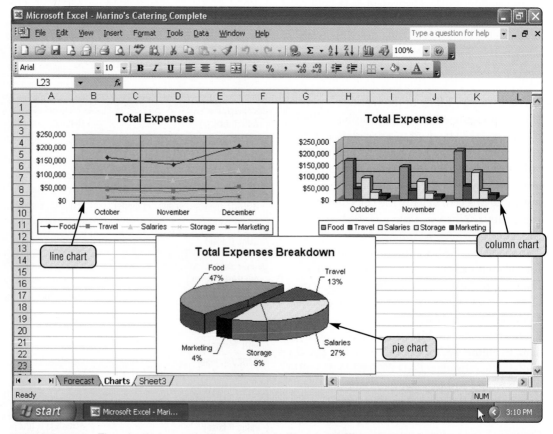

FIGURE 3-10   Three basic types of charts provided with spreadsheet software are line charts, column charts, and pie charts. The charts shown here were created from the data in the worksheet in Figure 3-8.

Database Software

A **database** is a collection of data organized in a manner that allows access, retrieval, and use of that data. In a manual database, you might record data on paper and store it in a filing cabinet. With a computerized database, such as the one shown in Figure 3-11, the computer stores the data in an electronic format on a storage medium such as a hard disk.

Database software is application software that allows users to create, access, and manage a database. Using database software, you can add, change, and delete data in a database; sort and retrieve data from the database; and create forms and reports using the data in the database.

With most popular personal computer database programs, a database consists of a collection of tables, organized in rows and columns. Each row, called a *record*, contains data about a given person, product, object, or event. Each column, called a *field*, contains a specific category of data within a record.

The Store database shown in Figure 3-11 consists of two tables: an Item table and a Supplier table. The Item table contains ten records (rows), each storing data about one item. The item data is grouped into six fields (columns): Item Code, Description, On Hand, Cost, Selling Price, and Supplier Code. The On Hand field, for instance, contains the quantity on hand in inventory. The Item and Supplier tables relate to one another through a common field, Supplier Code.

Users run queries to retrieve data. A *query* is a request for specific data from the database. For example, a query might request products that are low on hand. Database software can take the results of a query and present it in a window on the screen or send it to the printer.

FAQ 3-3

How big is the largest database?

According to a recent survey, the world's largest database holds 29 trillion characters. In the next few years, the size of the largest database is expected to exceed 5 quadrillion characters. For more information, visit scsite.com/dc2007/ch3/faq and then click Enterprise Databases.

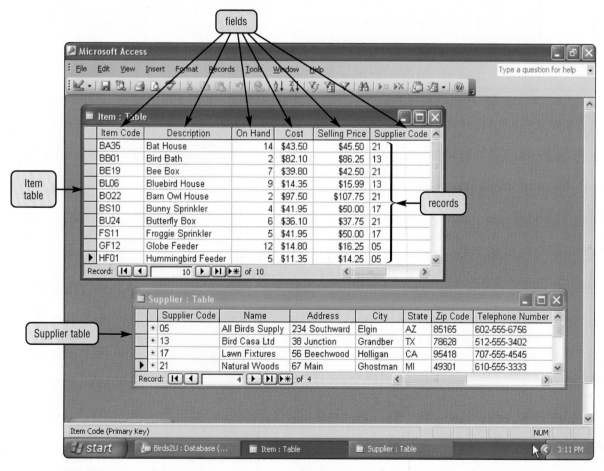

FIGURE 3-11 This database contains two tables: one for the items and one for the suppliers. The Item table has 10 records and 6 fields; the Supplier table has 4 records and 7 fields.

Presentation Graphics Software

Presentation graphics software is application software that allows users to create visual aids for presentations to communicate ideas, messages, and other information to a group. The presentations can be viewed as slides, sometimes called a *slide show*, that are displayed on a large monitor or on a projection screen (Figure 3-12).

Presentation graphics software typically provides a variety of predefined presentation formats that define complementary colors for backgrounds, text, and graphical accents on the slides. This software also provides a variety of layouts for each individual slide such as a title slide, a two-column slide, and a slide with clip art, a picture (Figure 3-13), a chart, a table, or animation. In addition, you can enhance any text, charts, and graphical images on a slide with 3-D and other special effects such as shading, shadows, and textures.

When building a presentation, users can set the slide timing so the presentation automatically displays the next slide after a preset delay. Presentation graphics software allows you to apply special effects to the transition between slides. One slide, for example, might fade away as the next slide is displayed.

To help organize the presentation, you can view thumbnail versions of all the slides in slide sorter view. *Slide sorter view* presents a screen view similar to how 35mm slides look on a photographer's light table. The slide sorter allows users to arrange the slides in any order.

Presentation graphics software typically includes a clip gallery that provides images, pictures, video clips, and audio clips to enhance multimedia presentations. Users with an artistic ability can create their own graphics using paint/image editing software (discussed later in the chapter) and then *import* (bring in) the graphics into the slide. Some audio and video editing programs, such as Producer, work with presentation graphics software, providing users with an easy means to record and insert video, music, and audio commentary in a presentation.

Presentation graphics software incorporates some of the features found in word processing software such as checking spelling, formatting, recognizing voice input, providing research capabilities, recognizing handwritten text and drawings, and creating Web pages from existing slide shows.

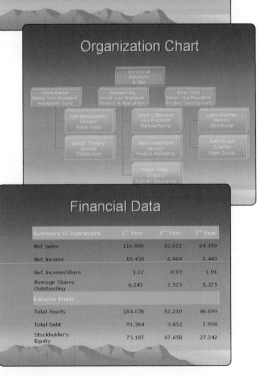
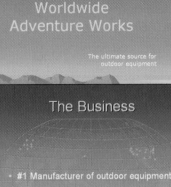

FIGURE 3-12   This presentation created with presentation graphics software consists of five slides.

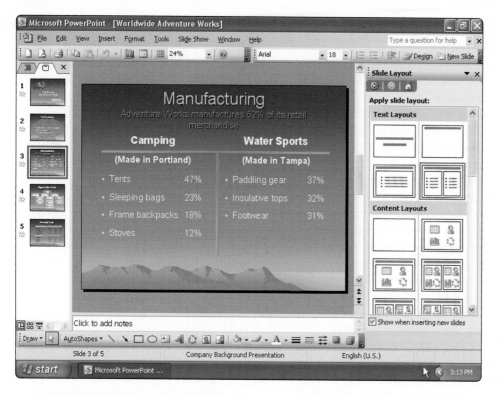

FIGURE 3-13 In presentation graphics software, users can change the design and layout of any slide in a presentation.

Note Taking Software

Note taking software is application software that enables users to enter typed text, handwritten comments, drawings, or sketches anywhere on a page and then save the page as part of a notebook (Figure 3-14). The software can convert handwritten comments to typed text or store the notes in handwritten form. Users also can include audio recordings as part of their notes.

Once the notes are captured (entered and saved), users easily can organize them, reuse them, and share them. This software allows users to search through saved notes for specific text. It even can search through an entire notebook. Users also can flag important notes with color, highlights, and shapes.

On a desktop or notebook computer, users enter notes primarily via the keyboard or microphone. On a Tablet PC, however, the primary input device is a digital pen. Users find note taking software convenient during meetings, class lectures, conferences, in libraries, and other settings that previously required a pencil and tablet of paper for recording thoughts and discussions.

Note taking software incorporates many of the features found in word processing software such as checking spelling, changing fonts and font sizes, adding colors, recognizing voice input, inserting audio and video clips, and providing research capabilities.

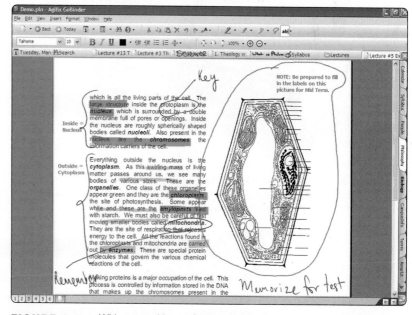

FIGURE 3-14 With note taking software, students and other mobile users can handwrite notes, draw sketches, and type text.

Personal Information Manager Software

A **personal information manager** (**PIM**) is application software that includes an appointment calendar, address book, notepad, and other features to help users organize personal information. With a PIM, you can take information previously tracked in a weekly or daily calendar, and organize and store it on your computer. The appointment calendar allows you to schedule activities for a particular day and time. With the address book, you can enter and maintain names, addresses, telephone numbers, and e-mail addresses of customers, coworkers, family members, and friends. You can use the notepad to record ideas, reminders, and other important information.

Most PDAs and many smart phones today include, among many other features, PIM functionality. Using a PDA or smart phone, you can synchronize, or coordinate, information so that both the PDA or smart phone and the computer have the latest version of the information.

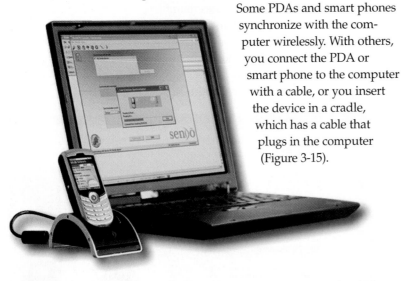

Some PDAs and smart phones synchronize with the computer wirelessly. With others, you connect the PDA or smart phone to the computer with a cable, or you insert the device in a cradle, which has a cable that plugs in the computer (Figure 3-15).

PDA Business Software

In addition to PIM software, a huge variety of business software is available for PDAs. Although some PDAs have software built in, most have the capability of accessing software on miniature storage media such as memory cards. Business software for PDAs allows users to create documents and worksheets, manage databases and lists, create slide shows, take notes, manage budgets and finances, view and edit photographs, read electronic books, plan travel routes, compose and read e-mail messages, send instant messages, and browse the Web. For additional information about software for PDAs, read the Personal Mobile Devices feature that follows Chapter 5.

Software Suite

A **software suite** is a collection of individual programs sold as a single package. Business software suites typically include, at a minimum, the following programs: word processing, spreadsheet, e-mail, and presentation graphics. Two of the more widely used software suites are Microsoft Office and Sun StarOffice.

Software suites offer two major advantages: lower cost and ease of use. Buying a collection of programs in a software suite usually costs significantly less than purchasing them individually. Software suites provide ease of use because the programs in a software suite normally use a similar interface and share features such as clip art and spelling checker. For example, once you learn how to print using the software suite's word processing program, you can apply the same skill to the spreadsheet and presentation graphics programs in the software suite.

FIGURE 3-15   With most PDAs and smart phones, you can synchronize or transfer information from the device to a desktop computer, so the updated important information always is available.

FAQ 3-4

What is the difference between Microsoft Office and Microsoft Office System?

Microsoft Office is a suite of core desktop business programs. Office is available in a variety of editions, each of which includes at least Word, Excel, and Outlook. *Microsoft Office System* is a portfolio of programs and services that are tightly integrated yet available for purchase as separate entities. In addition to Microsoft Office, other products in the Microsoft Office System include OneNote, InfoPath, Visio, FrontPage, and Project. For more information, visit scsite.com/dc2007/ch3/faq and then click Microsoft Office System.

Project Management Software

Project management software allows a user to plan, schedule, track, and analyze the events, resources, and costs of a project (Figure 3-16). Project management software helps users manage project variables, allowing them to complete a project on time and within budget. An engineer, for example, might use project management software to manage new product development to schedule product screening, market evaluation, technical product evaluation, and manufacturing processes.

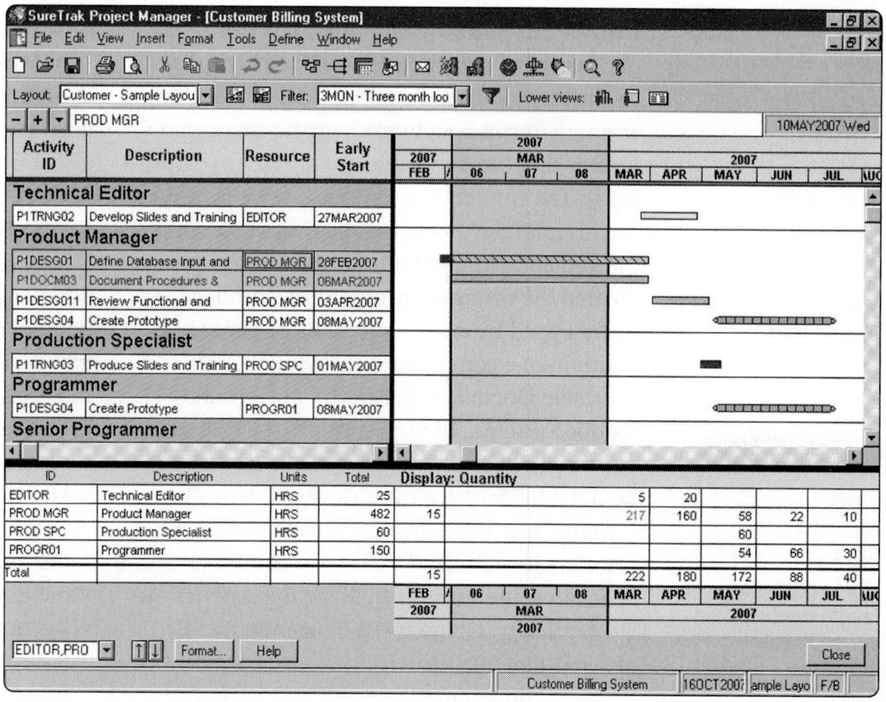

FIGURE 3-16 Project management software allows you to track, control, and manage the events, resources, and costs of a project.

Accounting Software

Accounting software helps companies record and report their financial transactions (Figure 3-17). With accounting software, business users perform accounting activities related to the general ledger, accounts receivable, accounts payable, purchasing, invoicing, and payroll functions. Accounting software also enables users to write and print checks, track checking account activity, and update and reconcile balances on demand.

Newer accounting software supports online credit checks, billing, direct deposit, and payroll services. Some accounting software offers more complex features such as job costing and estimating, time tracking, multiple company reporting, foreign currency reporting, and forecasting the amount of raw materials needed for products. The cost of accounting software for small businesses ranges from less than one hundred to several thousand dollars. Accounting software for large businesses can cost several hundred thousand dollars.

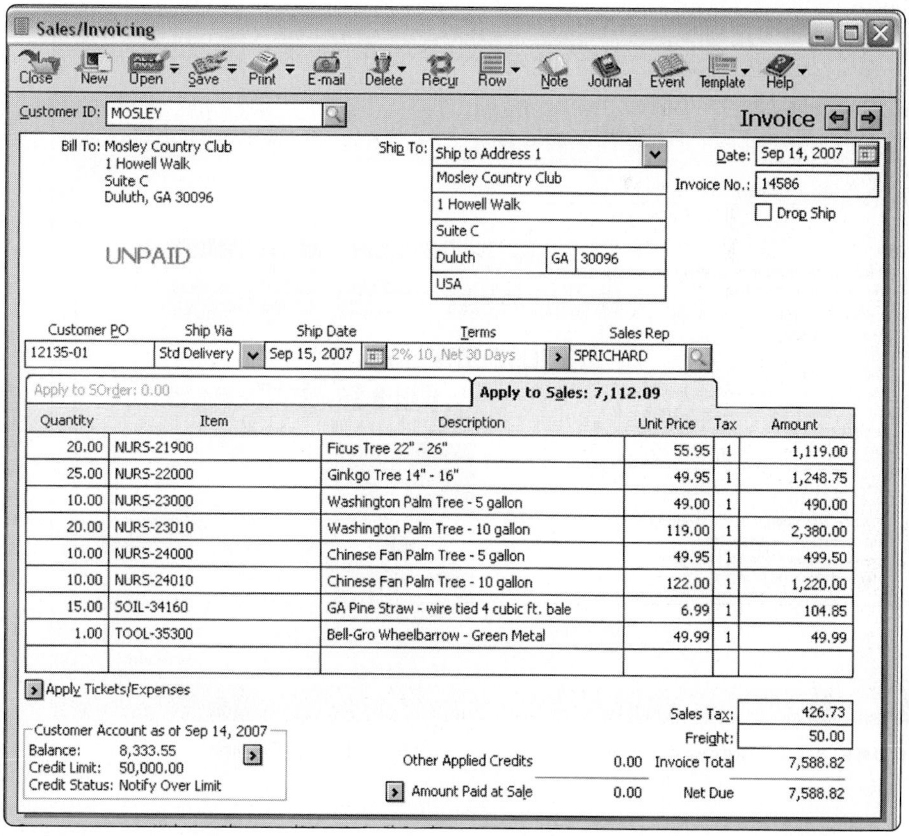

FIGURE 3-17 Accounting software helps companies record and report their financial transactions.

Document Management Software

Document management software provides a means for sharing, distributing, and searching through documents by converting them into a format that can be viewed by any user (Figure 3-18). The converted document, which mirrors the original document's appearance, can be viewed and printed without the software that created the original document. A popular file format used by document management software to save converted documents is *PDF* (Portable Document Format), developed by Adobe Systems. To view and print a PDF file, you need Acrobat Reader software, which can be downloaded free from Adobe's Web site.

Many businesses use document management software to share and distribute company brochures, literature, and other documents electronically. Home users distribute fliers, announcements, and graphics electronically. Some document management software allows users to edit and add comments to the converted document.

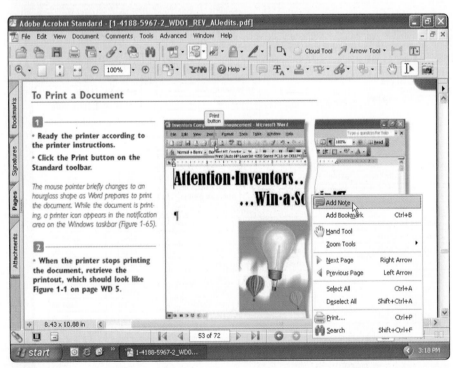

FIGURE 3-18   Adobe Acrobat allows users to create and edit PDF files.

Enterprise Computing Software

A large organization, commonly referred to as an enterprise, requires special computing solutions because of its size and large geographic distribution. A typical enterprise consists of a wide variety of departments, centers, and divisions — collectively known as functional units. Nearly every enterprise has the following functional units: human resources, accounting and finance, engineering or product development, manufacturing, marketing, sales, distribution, customer service, and information technology. Each of these functional units has specialized software requirements, as outlined below.

- Human resources software manages employee information such as benefits, personal information, performance evaluations, training, and vacation time.
- Accounting software manages everyday transactions, such as sales and payments to suppliers. Financial software helps managers budget, forecast, and analyze.
- Engineering or product development software allows engineers to develop plans for new products and test their product designs.
- Manufacturing software assists in the assembly process, as well as in scheduling and managing the inventory of parts and products.
- Marketing software allows marketing personnel to create marketing campaigns and track their effectiveness.
- Sales software enables the sales force to manage contacts, schedule meetings, log customer interactions, manage product information, and take customer orders.
- Distribution software analyzes and tracks inventory and manages product shipping status.
- Customer service software manages the day-to-day interactions with customers, such as telephone calls, e-mail messages, Web interactions, and instant messaging sessions.
- Information technology staff use a variety of software to maintain and secure the hardware and software in an enterprise.

GRAPHICS AND MULTIMEDIA SOFTWARE

In addition to business software, many people work with software designed specifically for their field of work. Power users such as engineers, architects, desktop publishers, and graphic artists often use sophisticated software that allows them to work with graphics and multimedia. This software includes computer-aided design, desktop publishing, paint/image editing, photo editing, video and audio editing, multimedia authoring, and Web page authoring. Figure 3-19 lists some popular programs in each of these categories, specifically designed for professional or more technically astute users. These programs often cost several hundred dollars or more. Many of these programs incorporate user-friendly interfaces and/or have scaled-down versions, making it possible for the home and small business users to create documents using these programs. The following sections discuss the features and functions of graphics and multimedia software.

POPULAR GRAPHICS AND MULTIMEDIA SOFTWARE

Application Software	Manufacturer	Program Name
Computer-Aided Design (CAD)	Autodesk	AutoCAD
	Quality Plans	Chief Architect
	Microsoft	Visio
Desktop Publishing (for the Professional)	Adobe	InDesign
	Corel	Ventura
	Quark	QuarkXPress
Paint/Image Editing (for the Professional)	Adobe	Illustrator
	Corel	Painter
	Macromedia	FreeHand
Photo Editing (for the Professional)	Adobe	Photoshop
	Extensis	Photo Imaging Suite
Video and Audio Editing (for the Professional)	Adobe	Audition
		Encore DVD
		Premiere Pro
	Cakewalk	SONAR
	Sony	ACID Pro
	Ulead	MediaStudio Pro
		DVD Workshop
Multimedia Authoring	SumTotal Systems	ToolBook Instructor
	Macromedia	Authorware
		Director
Web Page Authoring	Adobe	GoLive
	Lotus	FastSite
	Macromedia	Dreamweaver
		Fireworks
		Flash
	Microsoft	FrontPage

FIGURE 3-19 Popular graphics and multimedia programs — for the professional.

Computer-Aided Design

Computer-aided design (CAD) software is a sophisticated type of application software that assists a professional user in creating engineering, architectural, and scientific designs. For example, engineers create design plans for airplanes and security systems. Architects design building structures and floor plans (Figure 3-20). Scientists design drawings of molecular structures.

CAD software eliminates the laborious manual drafting that design processes can require. Three-dimensional CAD programs allow designers to rotate designs of 3-D objects to view them from any angle. Some CAD software even can generate material lists for building designs.

FIGURE 3-20 Architects use CAD software to create building designs.

Desktop Publishing Software (for the Professional)

Desktop publishing (DTP) software enables professional designers to create sophisticated documents that contain text, graphics, and many colors. Professional DTP software is ideal for the production of high-quality color documents such as textbooks, corporate newsletters, marketing literature (Figure 3-21), product catalogs, and annual reports. Today's DTP software allows designers to convert a color document into a format for use on the World Wide Web.

Although many word processing programs have some of the capabilities of DTP software, professional designers and graphic artists use DTP software because it supports page layout. *Page layout* is the process of arranging text and graphics in a document on a page-by-page basis. DTP software includes color libraries to assist in color selections for text and graphics. A *color library* is a standard set of colors used by designers and printers to ensure that colors will print exactly as specified. Designers and graphic artists can print finished publications on a color printer, take them to a professional printer, or post them on the Web.

Paint/Image Editing Software (for the Professional)

Graphic artists, multimedia professionals, technical illustrators, and desktop publishers use paint software and image editing software to create and modify graphical images such as those used in DTP documents and Web pages. **Paint software**, also called *illustration software*, allows users to draw pictures, shapes, and other graphical images with various on-screen tools such as a pen, brush, eyedropper, and paint bucket (Figure 3-22). **Image editing software** provides the capabilities of paint software and also includes the capability to enhance and modify existing images and pictures. Modifications can include adjusting or enhancing image colors, and adding special effects such as shadows and glows.

© Cher Threinen-Pendarvis

FIGURE 3-22 With paint software, artists can create and modify any type of graphical image.

Photo Editing Software (for the Professional)

Professional photo editing software is a type of image editing software that allows photographers, videographers, engineers, scientists, and other high-volume digital photo users to edit and customize digital photographs (Figure 3-23). Professional photo editing software allows users to save images in a wide variety of file formats. With professional photo editing software, users can retouch photos, crop images, remove red-eye, change image shapes, color-correct images, straighten images, remove or rearrange objects in a photo, and apply filters. Read Ethics & Issues 3-2 for a related discussion.

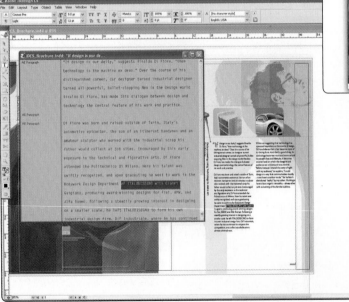

FIGURE 3-21 Professional designers and graphic artists use DTP software to produce sophisticated publications such as marketing literature.

FIGURE 3-23   With professional photo editing software, users can edit and customize digital photographs.

ETHICS & ISSUES 3-2

Altering Digital Photographs — Art or Fraud?

A *Los Angeles Times* photographer combined two digital photographs of the Iraq war, taken minutes apart, to create a single picture that appeared on the newspaper's front page. The photographer merged the photos to improve the composition, but when the source of the picture became known, the newspaper fired the photographer, citing a policy that forbids altering the content of news photos. Many commercial artists, photojournalists, and creators of cartoons, book covers, and billboards use photo editing software to alter photographs. With this software, an artist can convert photographs to a digital form that can be colorized, stretched, squeezed, texturized, or otherwise altered. The National Press Photographers Association, however, has expressed reservations about digital altering and endorses the following: "As [photo] journalists we believe the guiding principle of our profession is accuracy; therefore, we believe it is wrong to alter the content of a photograph in any way … that deceives the public." Yet, some insist that the extent to which a photo "deceives the public" is in the eye of the beholder. Is it ethical to alter digital photographs? Why or why not? Does the answer depend on the reason for the alteration, the extent of the alteration, or some other factor? If some alteration is accepted, can photographic integrity still be guaranteed? Why or why not?

Video and Audio Editing Software (for the Professional)

Video editing software (Figure 3-24) allows professionals to modify a segment of a video, called a clip. For example, users can reduce the length of a video clip, reorder a series of clips, or add special effects such as words that move horizontally across the screen.

Video editing software typically includes audio editing capabilities. **Audio editing software** lets users modify audio clips and produce studio-quality soundtracks. Audio editing software usually includes *filters*, which are designed to enhance audio quality. For example, a filter might remove a distracting background noise from the audio clip.

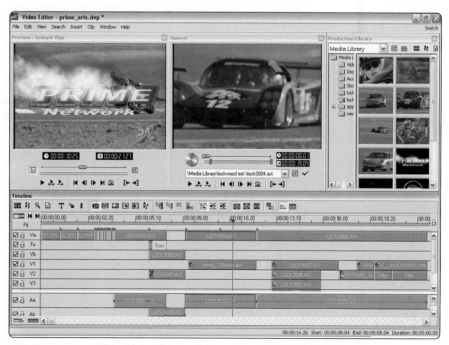

FIGURE 3-24   With video editing software, users modify video images.

Multimedia Authoring Software

Multimedia authoring software allows users to combine text, graphics, audio, video, and animation in an interactive application (Figure 3-25). With this software, users control the placement of text and images and the duration of sounds, video, and animation. Once created, multimedia presentations often take the form of interactive computer-based presentations or Web-based presentations designed to facilitate learning, demonstrate product functionality, and elicit direct-user participation. Training centers, educational institutions, and online magazine publishers all use multimedia authoring software to develop interactive applications. These applications may be available on a CD or DVD, over a local area network, or via the Internet.

FAQ 3-5

How do I know which program to buy?

Many companies offer downloadable *trial versions* of their software that allow you to use the software free for a limited time. Try a few. Read computer magazines and Web sites for reviews of various products. For more information, visit scsite.com/dc2007/ch3/faq and then click Trial Versions.

Web Page Authoring Software

Web page authoring software helps users of all skill levels create Web pages that include graphical images, video, audio, animation, and other special effects with interactive content (Figure 3-26). In addition, many Web page authoring programs allow users to organize, manage, and maintain Web sites.

Application software, such as Word and Excel, often includes Web page authoring features. This allows home users to create basic Web pages using application software they already own. For more sophisticated Web pages, users work with Web page authoring software. Many Web page developers also use multimedia authoring software along with, or instead of, Web page authoring software for Web page development.

FIGURE 3-25 Multimedia authoring software allows you to create dynamic presentations that include text, graphics, video, sound, and animation.

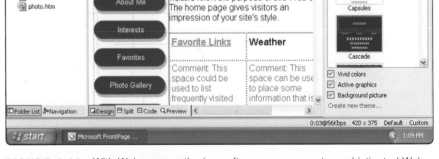

FIGURE 3-26 With Web page authoring software, users create sophisticated Web pages.

Test your knowledge of pages 138 through 154 in Quiz Yourself 3-2.

QUIZ YOURSELF 3-2

Instructions: Find the true statement below. Then, rewrite the remaining false statements so they are true.

1. Audio editing software typically includes video editing capabilities.
2. Enterprise computing software provides the capabilities of paint software and also includes the capability to modify existing images.
3. Millions of people use spreadsheet software every day to develop documents such as letters, memos, reports, fax cover sheets, mailing labels, newsletters, and Web pages.
4. Professional accounting software is ideal for the production of high-quality color documents such as textbooks, corporate newsletters, marketing literature, product catalogs, and annual reports.
5. Spreadsheet software is application software that allows users to create visual aids for presentations to communicate ideas, messages, and other information to a group.
6. Two of the more widely used CAD programs are Microsoft Office and Sun StarOffice.
7. Web page authoring software helps users of all skill levels create Web pages.

Quiz Yourself Online: To further check your knowledge of types and features of business programs and graphics/multimedia programs, visit scsite.com/dc2007/ch3/quiz and then click Objectives 4 – 5.

SOFTWARE FOR HOME, PERSONAL, AND EDUCATIONAL USE

A large amount of application software is designed specifically for home, personal, and educational use. Most of the programs in this category are relatively inexpensive, often priced less than $100 and sometimes free. Figure 3-27 lists popular programs for many of these categories. The following sections discuss the features and functions of this application software.

POPULAR SOFTWARE PROGRAMS FOR HOME/PERSONAL/EDUCATIONAL USE

Application Software	Manufacturer	Program Name
Software Suite (for Personal Use)	Microsoft	Works
	Sun	OpenOffice.org
Personal Finance	Intuit	Quicken
	Microsoft	Money
Legal	Broderbund	Family Lawyer
	Cosmi	Perfect Attorney
	H&R Block	Kiplinger's Home & Business Attorney
		Kiplinger's WILLPower
	Nolo	Quicken Legal Business
		Quicken WillMaker
Tax Preparation	2nd Story Software	TaxACT
	H&R Block	TaxCut
	Intuit	TurboTax
Desktop Publishing (for Personal Use)	Broderbund	The Print Shop
		PrintMaster
	Microsoft	Publisher
Paint/Image Editing (for Personal Use)	Corel	CorelDRAW
		Paint Shop Pro
	Sun	StarOffice Draw
	The GIMP Team	The Gimp

Application Software	Manufacturer	Program Name
Photo Editing (for Personal Use)	Adobe	Photoshop Elements
	Corel	Paint Shop Photo Album
	Dell	Picture Studio
	Microsoft	Digital Image
		Photo Story
	Roxio	PhotoSuite
	Ulead	PhotoImpact
		Photo Express
Clip Art/Image Gallery	Broderbund	ClickArt
	Nova Development	Art Explosion
Video and Audio Editing (for Personal Use)	Microsoft	Movie Maker
		Producer for PowerPoint
	Pinnacle Systems	Studio MovieBox
	Roxio	VideoWave
	Ulead	VideoStudio
Home Design/ Landscaping	Broderbund	3D Home Architect
	Quality Plans	Home Designer
	ValuSoft	LandDesigner
Reference	Learning Company	American Heritage Talking Dictionary
	Microsoft	Encarta
		Streets & Trips
	Rand McNally	StreetFinder
		TripMaker

FIGURE 3-27 Many popular software programs are available for home, personal, and educational use.

Software Suite (for Personal Use)

A software suite (for personal use) combines application software such as word processing, spreadsheet, database, and other programs in a single, easy-to-use package. Many computer vendors install a software suite for personal use, such as Microsoft Works, on new computers sold to home users.

As mentioned earlier, the programs in a software suite use a similar interface and share some common features. The programs in software suites for personal use typically are available only through the software suite; that is, you cannot purchase them individually. These programs may not have all the capabilities of business application software. For many home users, however, the capabilities of software suites for personal use more than meet their needs.

Personal Finance Software

Personal finance software is a simplified accounting program that helps home users and small office/home office users balance their checkbooks, pay bills, track personal income and expenses (Figure 3-28), set up budgets, manage home inventory, track investments, and evaluate financial plans. Personal finance software helps determine where, and for what purpose, you are spending money so you can manage your finances. Reports can summarize transactions by category (such as dining), by payee (such as the electric company), or by time (such as the last two months). Financial planning features include analyzing home and personal loans, preparing income taxes, and managing retirement savings.

Most of these personal finance programs also offer a variety of online services, which require access to the Internet. For example, users can track investments online, compare insurance rates from leading insurance companies, and bank online. **Online banking** offers access to account balances, provides bill paying services, and allows you to download monthly transactions and statements from the Web directly to your computer.

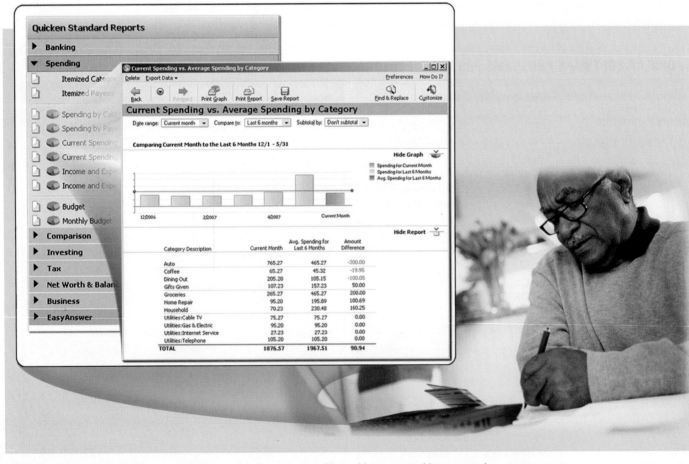

FIGURE 3-28 Personal finance software assists home users with tracking personal income and expenses.

FAQ 3-6

How many people bank online?

Currently, about 40 million people bank online. By 2010, this number is expected to grow to 50 million. The chart below depicts popular online banking activities. For more information, visit scsite.com/dc2007/ch3/faq and then click Online Banking.

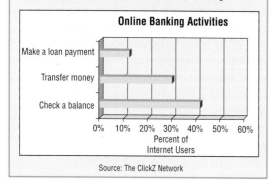

Online Banking Activities

- Make a loan payment
- Transfer money
- Check a balance

0%   10%   20%   30%   40%   50%   60%
Percent of Internet Users

Source: The ClickZ Network

Legal Software

Legal software assists in the preparation of legal documents and provides legal information to individuals, families, and small businesses (Figure 3-29). Legal software provides standard contracts and documents associated with buying, selling, and renting property; estate planning; marriage and divorce; and preparing a will or living trust. By answering a series of questions or completing a form, the legal software tailors the legal document to specific needs.

Once the legal document is created, you can file the paperwork with the appropriate agency, court, or office; or take the document to your attorney for his or her review and signature. Before using one of these software programs to create a document, you may want to check with your local bar association for its legality.

Tax Preparation Software

Tax preparation software is used to guide individuals, families, or small businesses through the process of filing federal taxes (Figure 3-30). These programs forecast tax liability and offer money-saving tax tips, designed to lower your tax bill. After you answer a series of questions and complete basic forms, the software creates and analyzes your tax forms to search for potential errors and deduction opportunities. Once the forms are complete, you can print any necessary paperwork, and then they are ready for filing.

WEB LINK 3-5

Tax Preparation Software

For more information, visit scsite.com/dc2007/ch3/weblink and then click Tax Preparation Software.

FAQ 3-7

Can I file my taxes online?

Yes, many taxpayers *e-file*, or use tax software and/or tax preparation Web sites to file federal and state returns electronically. With tax professionals available to answer questions in a chat room or via e-mail, many taxpayers find this service easy-to-use and relatively inexpensive. The IRS hopes that 80 percent of taxpayers will e-file their taxes by 2007. For more information, visit scsite.com/dc2007/ch3/faq and then click E-Filing Taxes.

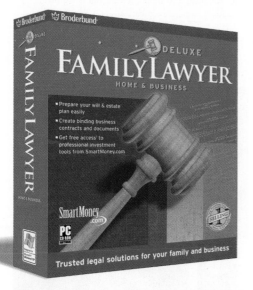

FIGURE 3-29 Legal software provides legal information to individuals, families, and small businesses and assists in record keeping and the preparation of legal documents.

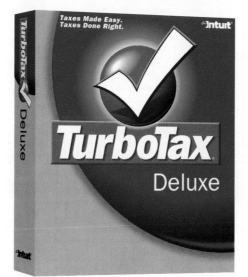

FIGURE 3-30 Tax preparation software guides individuals, families, or small businesses through the process of filing federal taxes.

Desktop Publishing Software (for Personal Use)

Instead of using professional DTP software (as discussed earlier in this chapter), many home and small business users work with simpler, easy-to-understand DTP software designed for smaller-scale desktop publishing projects (Figure 3-31). **Personal DTP software** helps home and small business users create newsletters, brochures, advertisements, post-cards, greeting cards, letterhead, business cards, banners, calendars, logos, and Web pages.

Personal DTP programs provide hundreds of thousands of graphical images. You also can import (bring in) your own digital photographs into the documents. These programs typically guide you through the development of a document by asking a series of questions, offering numerous predefined layouts, and providing standard text you can add to documents. Then, you can print a finished publication on a color printer or post it on the Web.

Many personal DTP programs also include paint/image editing software and photo editing software.

Paint/Image Editing Software (for Personal Use)

Personal paint/image editing software provides an easy-to-use interface, usually with more simplified capabilities than its professional counterpart, including functions tailored to meet the needs of the home and small business user.

As with the professional versions, personal paint software includes various simplified tools that allow you to draw pictures, shapes, and other images (Figure 3-32). Personal image editing software provides the capabilities of paint software and the ability to modify existing graphics and photos. These products also include many templates to assist you in adding an image to documents such as greeting cards, banners, calendars, signs, labels, business cards, and letterhead.

FAQ 3-8

How do pictures get in the computer from a digital camera?

Most digital cameras save pictures on miniature storage media, such as a memory card. By inserting the memory card in a card reader/writer in or attached to the computer, users can access images the same way they access files on a disk drive. With some cameras, pictures also can transfer along a cable that connects the camera to the computer. For more information, visit scsite.com/dc2007/ch3/faq and then click Digital Imaging.

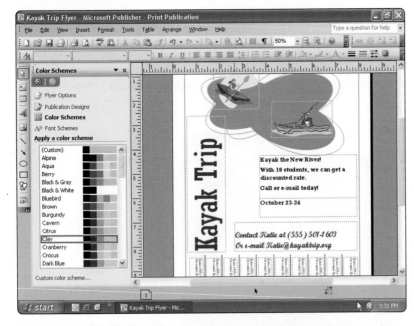

FIGURE 3-31　With Publisher, home and small business users can create professional-looking publications such as this flyer with tear-offs.

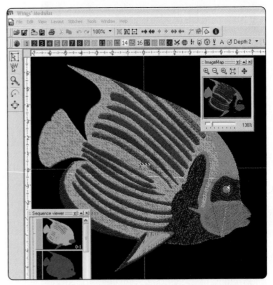

FIGURE 3-32　Home users can purchase affordable paint/image editing programs that enable them to draw images.

Photo Editing Software

Instead of professional photo editing software, many home and small business users work with easier-to-use personal photo editing software. **Personal photo editing software** allows users to edit digital photographs by removing red-eye, erasing blemishes, restoring aged photos, adding special effects (Figure 3-33), or creating electronic photo albums. When you purchase a digital camera, it usually includes photo editing software. You can print edited photographs on labels, calendars, business cards, and banners; or post them on a Web page. Some photo editing software allows users to send digital photographs to an online print service, which will deliver high-resolution printed images through the postal service. Many online print services have a photo community where users can post photographs on the Web for others to view.

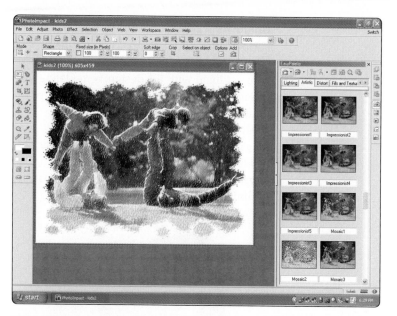

FIGURE 3-33   Personal photo editing software enables home users to edit digital photographs.

Clip Art/Image Gallery

Application software often includes a **clip art/image gallery**, which is a collection of clip art and photographs. Some applications have links to additional clips available on the Web. You also can purchase clip art/image gallery software that contains hundreds of thousands of images (Figure 3-34).

In addition to clip art, many clip art/image galleries provide fonts, animations, sounds, video clips, and audio clips. You can use the images, fonts, and other items from the clip art/image gallery in all types of documents, including word processing, desktop publishing, spreadsheet, and presentation graphics.

FIGURE 3-34   Clip art/image gallery software contains hundreds of thousands of images.

WEB LINK 3-7

Microsoft Office Clip Art

For more information, visit scsite.com/ dc2007/ch3/weblink and then click Microsoft Office Clip Art.

Video and Audio Editing Software (for Personal Use)

Many home users work with easy-to-use video and audio editing software, which is much simpler to use than its professional counterpart, for small-scale movie making projects (Figure 3-35). With these programs, home users can edit home movies, add music or other sounds to the video, and share their movies on the Web. Some operating systems include video editing and audio editing software.

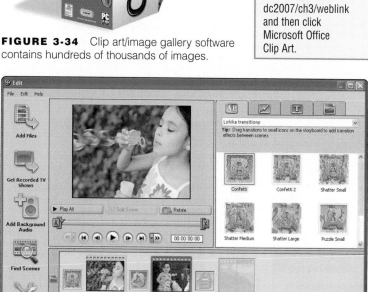

FIGURE 3-35   With personal video and audio editing software, home users can edit their home movies.

Home Design/Landscaping Software

Homeowners or potential homeowners can use **home design/landscaping software** to assist them with the design, remodeling, or improvement of a home, deck, or landscape (Figure 3-36). Home design/landscaping software includes hundreds of predrawn plans that you can customize to meet your needs. Once designed, many home design/landscaping programs print a materials list outlining costs and quantities for the entire project.

FIGURE 3-36 Home design/landscaping software can help you design or remodel a home, deck, or landscape.

Reference and Educational Software

Reference software provides valuable and thorough information for all individuals (Figure 3-37). Popular reference software includes encyclopedias, dictionaries, health/medical guides, and travel directories.

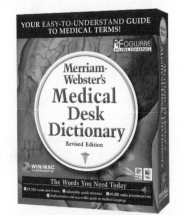

FIGURE 3-37 This reference dictionary gives text definitions and audio pronunciations of medical terms.

Educational software is software that teaches a particular skill. Educational software exists for just about any subject, from learning how to type to learning how to cook. Preschool to high-school learners use educational software to assist them with subjects such as reading and math or to prepare them for class or college entry exams. Educational software often includes games and other content to make the learning experience more fun.

Many educational programs use a computer-based training approach. **Computer-based training** (CBT), also called computer-aided instruction (CAI), is a type of education in which students learn by using and completing exercises with instructional software. CBT typically consists of self-directed, self-paced instruction about a topic. Beginning athletes, for example, use CBT programs to learn the intricacies of baseball, football, soccer, tennis, and golf. The military and airlines use CBT simulations to train pilots to fly in various conditions and environments. Schools use CBT to teach students math, language, and software skills.

Entertainment Software

Entertainment software for personal computers includes interactive games, videos, and other programs designed to support a hobby or provide amusement and enjoyment. For example, you might use entertainment software to play games (Figure 3-38), make a family tree, listen to music, or fly an aircraft.

FIGURE 3-38 Entertainment software can provide hours of recreation.

APPLICATION SOFTWARE FOR COMMUNICATIONS

One of the main reasons people use computers is to communicate and share information with others. Some communications software is considered system software because it works with hardware and transmission media.

Other communications software makes users more productive and/or assists them with personal tasks, and thus, is considered application software. Chapter 2 presented a variety of application software for communications, which is summarized in the table in Figure 3-39. Read Ethics & Issues 3-3 for a related discussion.

APPLICATION SOFTWARE FOR COMMUNICATIONS

E-Mail
- Messages and files sent via a network such as the Internet
- Requires an e-mail program
  - Integrated in many software suites and operating systems
  - Available free at portals on the Web
  - Included with paid Internet access service
  - Can be purchased separately from retailers

FTP
- Method of uploading and downloading files with other computers on the Internet
- Download may require an FTP program; upload usually requires an FTP program
  - Integrated in some operating systems
  - Available for download on the Web for a small fee
  - Can be purchased separately from retailers

Web Browser
- Allows users to access and view Web pages on the Internet
- Requires a Web browser program
  - Integrated in some operating systems
  - Available for download on the Web free or for a fee

Video Conferencing/Telephone Calls
- Meeting/conversation between geographically separated people who use a network such as the Internet to transmit video/audio
- Requires a microphone, speakers, and sometimes a video camera attached to your computer
- Requires video conferencing software

Newsgroup/Message Board
- Online area where users have written discussions
- Newsgroup may require a newsreader program
  - Integrated in some operating systems, e-mail programs, and Web browsers; built into some Web sites
  - Available for download on the Web, usually at no cost
  - Included with some paid Internet access services

Chat Room
- Real-time, online typed conversation
- Requires chat client software
  - Integrated in some operating systems, e-mail programs, and Web browsers
  - Available for download on the Web, usually at no cost
  - Included with some paid Internet access services
  - Built into some Web sites

Instant Messaging
- Real-time exchange of messages, files, audio, and/or video with another online user
- Requires instant messenger software
  - Integrated in some operating systems
  - Available for download on the Web, usually at no cost
  - Included with some paid Internet access services

Blogging
- Time-stamped articles, or posts, in a diary or journal format, usually listed in reverse chronological order
- Blogger needs *blog software*, or *blogware*, to create/maintain blog
  - Some Web sites do not require installation of blog software

FIGURE 3-39 A summary of application software for home and business communications.

ETHICS & ISSUES 3-3

Should Companies Monitor Employees' E-Mail?

According to one survey, more than 42 percent of all companies monitor (after transmission) or intercept (during transmission) employees' e-mail. Employers can use software to find automatically personal or offensive e-mail messages that have been sent or received, and intercept and filter messages while they are being sent or received. Companies monitor e-mail to improve productivity, increase security, reduce misconduct, and control liability risks. Few laws regulate employee monitoring, and courts have given employers a great deal of leeway in watching work on company-owned computers. In one case, an employee's termination for using her office e-mail system to complain about her boss was upheld, even though the company allowed e-mail use for personal communications. The court decreed that the employee's messages were inappropriate for workplace communications. Executives have not escaped scrutiny, either. Prominent leaders, such as Bill Gates, have had e-mail messages they sent used against them in court. Many employees believe that monitoring software violates their privacy rights. State laws usually favor the privacy of the employee, while federal laws tend to favor the employer's right to read employees' e-mail messages. To reduce employee anxiety about monitoring e-mail and to follow some state laws, legal experts suggest that companies publish written policies and accept employee feedback, provide clear descriptions of acceptable and unacceptable behavior, respect employee needs and time, and establish a balance between security and privacy. Should companies monitor or intercept employees' e-mail? Why or why not? How can a company balance workplace security and productivity with employee privacy? If a company monitors e-mail use, what guidelines should be followed to maintain worker morale? Why? Is intercepting and filtering e-mail more offensive than monitoring e-mail? Why?

POPULAR UTILITY PROGRAMS

Utility programs are considered system software because they assist a user with controlling or maintaining the operation of a computer, its devices, or its software. Some utility programs are included with the operating system, and others are available as stand-alone programs.

Utility programs typically offer features that provide an environment conducive to successful use of application software. One of the more important utility programs protects a computer against viruses. A computer *virus* is a potentially damaging computer program that affects, or infects, a computer negatively by altering the way the computer works without the user's knowledge or permission. For a technical discussion about viruses, read the High-Tech Talk article on page 168.

Other features of utility programs include protecting a computer against unauthorized intrusions; removing spyware from a computer; filtering e-mail messages, Web content, and advertisements; managing files and disks; compressing files; backing up; burning (recording on) a CD or DVD; and maintaining a personal computer. The table in Figure 3-40 briefly describes several utility programs. Chapter 8 discusses them in more depth.

FAQ 3-9

How much does a computer virus attack cost a company?

A recent survey found that it typically costs an enterprise about $10,000 to recover from a computer virus attack. When the virus attacks multiple servers, however, the costs can exceed $100,000. For more information, visit scsite.com/dc2007/ch3/faq and then click Computer Virus Attacks.

WEB LINK 3-9

Antivirus Programs

For more information, visit scsite.com/dc2007/ch3/weblink and then click Antivirus Programs.

WIDELY USED UTILITY PROGRAMS

Utility Program	Description
Antivirus Program	An *antivirus program* protects a computer against viruses by identifying and removing any computer viruses found in memory, on storage media, or in incoming files.
Personal Firewall	A *personal firewall* detects and protects a personal computer from unauthorized intrusions.
Spyware Remover	A *spyware remover* detects and deletes spyware on your computer.
Internet Filters	
• Anti-Spam Program	An *anti-spam program* attempts to remove spam (Internet junk mail) before it reaches your e-mail inbox.
• Web Filter	A *Web filter* restricts access to specified Web sites.
• Pop-Up Blocker	A *pop-up blocker* stops advertisements from displaying on Web pages and disables pop-up windows.
File Manager	A *file manager* provides functions related to file and disk management.
File Compression	A *file compression utility* shrinks the size of a file(s), so the file takes up less storage space than the original file.
Backup	A *backup utility* allows users to copy selected files or an entire hard disk to another storage medium.
CD/DVD Burning	A *CD/DVD burner* writes text, graphics, audio, and video files on a recordable or rewritable CD or DVD.
Personal Computer Maintenance	A *personal computer maintenance utility* identifies and fixes operating system problems, detects and repairs disk problems, and includes the capability of improving a computer's performance.

FIGURE 3-40　A summary of widely used utility programs.

APPLICATION SOFTWARE ON THE WEB

As discussed earlier in this chapter, users can purchase application software from a software vendor, retail store, or Web-based business. Users typically install purchased application software on a computer before they run it. Installed software has two disadvantages: (1) it requires disk space on your computer, and (2) it can be costly to upgrade as vendors release new versions. As an alternative, some users opt to access Web applications.

A **Web application** is application software that exists on a Web site. Users access Web applications anywhere from any computer or device, as long as it has an Internet connection (read Looking Ahead 3-2 for a look at the next generation of Web access). Web applications usually store users' data and information on their servers. For this reason, users concerned with data security may shy away from this option.

Some Web sites provide free access to the application. For example, one site creates a map and driving directions when a user enters a starting and destination point (Figure 3-41). Other Web sites allow you to use the program

free and pay a fee when a certain action occurs. For example, you can prepare your tax return free using TurboTax for the Web, but if you elect to print it or file it electronically, you pay a minimal fee.

LOOKING AHEAD 3-2

Driving Down the Web Highway

Analysts predict you will access the Internet from practically everywhere: home, office, airport, grocery store, and the local coffee shop. Why not from your car?

As it sits in your garage, your car's computer could connect to your home computer and then relay information about fluid levels and the amount of gas in the tank. It could notify you when the oil needs to be changed and when the tires should be rotated. You even could start the car remotely on chilly days by pressing a button on your notebook computer as you eat your breakfast cereal at the kitchen table.

Automobile manufacturers are touting their cyber cars of the future equipped with Internet access. They are planning in-dash screens with continuous information about traffic, weather forecasts, and restaurant guides. Their plans also call for having the Internet access disconnect when the vehicle is in motion so that drivers do not attempt to drive and surf the Web simultaneously. For more information, visit scsite.com/dc2007/ch3/looking and then click Cyber Cars.

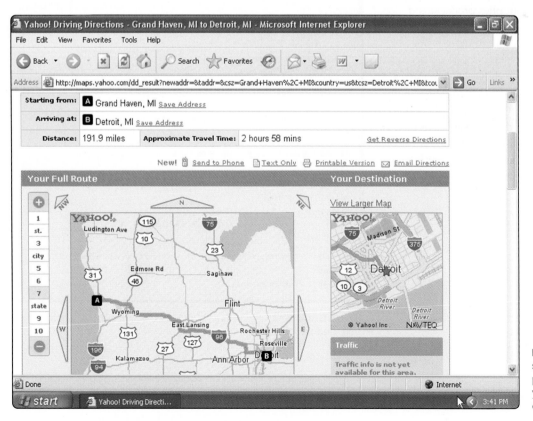

FIGURE 3-41 This Web site creates a map and provides directions when you enter a starting and destination point.

Application Service Providers

Storing and maintaining programs can be a costly investment for businesses. Thus, some have elected to outsource one or more facets of their information technology (IT) needs to an application service provider. An *application service provider* (*ASP*) is a third-party organization that manages and distributes software and services on the Web. That is, instead of installing the software on your computer, you run the programs from the Internet.

The five categories of ASPs are:

1. *Enterprise ASP*: customizes and delivers high-end business applications, such as finance and database
2. *Local/Regional ASP*: offers a variety of software applications to a specific geographic region
3. *Specialist ASP*: delivers applications to meet a specific business need, such as human resources or project management
4. *Vertical Market ASP*: provides applications for a particular industry, such as construction, health care, or retail
5. *Volume Business ASP*: supplies prepackaged applications, such as accounting, to businesses

A variety of payment schemes are available. Some rent use of the application on a monthly basis or charge based on the number of user accesses. Others charge a one-time fee.

LEARNING AIDS AND SUPPORT TOOLS FOR APPLICATION SOFTWARE

Learning how to use application software effectively involves time and practice. To assist in the learning process, many programs provide online Help, Web-based Help, wizards, and templates.

Online Help is the electronic equivalent of a user manual (Figure 3-42a). It usually is integrated in a program. In most programs, a function key or a button on the screen starts the Help feature. When using a program, you can use the Help feature to ask a question or access the Help topics in subject or alphabetical order.

Most online Help also links to Web sites that offer *Web-based Help*, which provides updates and more comprehensive resources to respond to technical issues about software (Figure 3-42b). Some Web sites contain chat rooms, in which a user can talk directly with a technical support

FIGURE 3-42a (online Help)

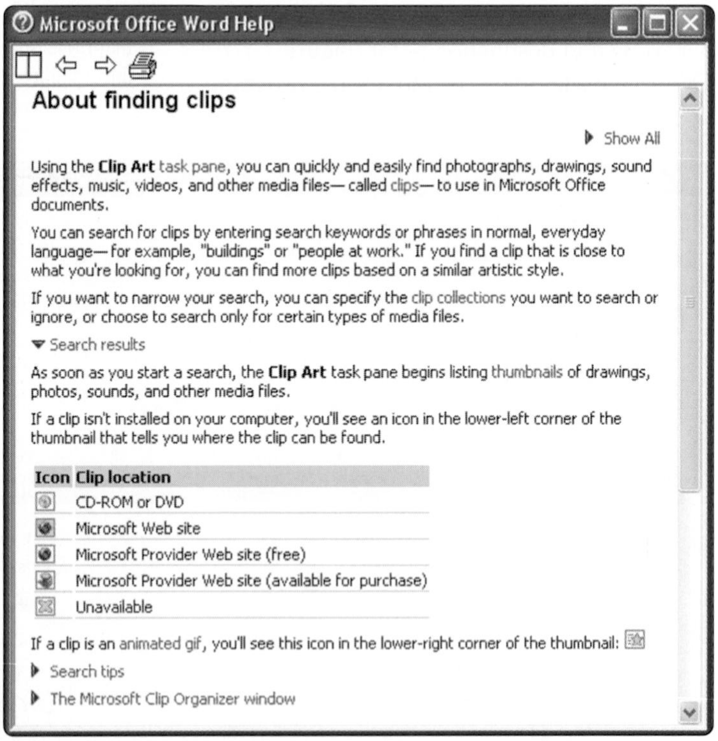

FIGURE 3-42 Many programs include online Help, Web-based Help, and templates. *(continued)*

FIGURE 3-42b (Web-based Help)

FIGURE 3-42c (template)

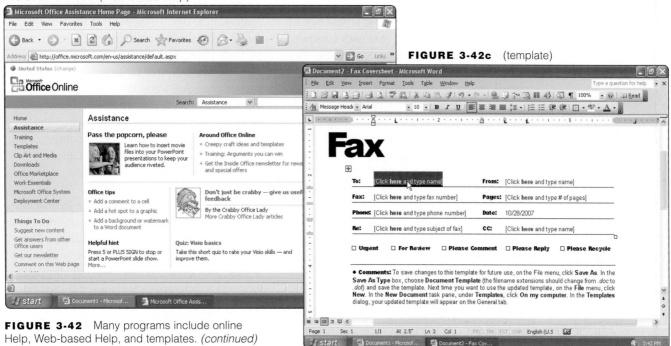

FIGURE 3-42 Many programs include online Help, Web-based Help, and templates. *(continued)*

person or join a conversation with other users who may be able to answer questions or solve problems.

A *wizard* is an automated assistant that helps a user complete a task by asking questions and then automatically performing actions based on the responses. A *template* is a document that contains the formatting necessary for a specific document type (Figure 3-42c). Many software applications include wizards and templates. For example, word processing software uses wizards for creating charts and documents and contains templates for memorandums, meeting agendas, fax cover sheets, flyers, letters, and resumes. Spreadsheet software includes wizards for creating charts and building functions and templates for invoices and purchase orders.

If you want to learn more about a particular program from a printed manual, many books are available to help you learn to use the features of personal computer programs. These books typically are available in bookstores and software stores (Figure 3-43).

Many colleges and schools provide training on several of the applications discussed in this chapter. For more information, contact your local school for a list of class offerings.

FIGURE 3-43
Bookstores often sell trade books to help you learn to use the features of personal computer application software.

Web-Based Training

Web-based training (*WBT*) is a type of CBT (computer-based training) that uses Internet technology and consists of application software on the Web. Similar to CBT, WBT typically consists of self-directed, self-paced instruction about a topic. WBT is popular in business, industry, and schools for teaching new skills or enhancing existing skills of employees, teachers, or students. When using a WBT product, students actively become involved in the learning process instead of remaining passive recipients of information.

Many Web sites offer WBT to the general public (Figure 3-44). Such training covers a wide range of topics, from how to change a flat tire to creating documents in Word. Many of these Web sites are free. Others require registration and payment to take the complete Web-based course.

WBT often is combined with other materials for distance learning courses.

Distance learning (**DL**) is the delivery of education at one location while the learning takes place at other locations. DL courses provide time, distance, and place advantages for students who live far from a college campus or work full time. These courses enable students to attend class from anywhere in the world and at times that fit their schedules. Many national and international companies offer DL training. These training courses eliminate the costs of airfare, hotels, and meals for centralized training sessions.

WBT companies often specialize in providing instructors with the tools for preparation, distribution, and management of DL courses. These tools enable instructors to create rich, educational Web-based training sites and allow the students to interact with a powerful Web learning environment. Through the training site, students can check their progress, take practice tests, search for topics, send e-mail messages, and participate in discussions and chats.

WEB LINK 3-10

Distance Learning

For more information, visit scsite.com/ dc2007/ch3/weblink and then click Distance Learning.

FIGURE 3-44   At the HowStuffWorks Web-based training site, you can learn how computers, autos, electronics, and many other products work.

Test your knowledge of pages 155 through 166 in Quiz Yourself 3-3.

QUIZ YOURSELF 3-3

Instructions: Find the true statement below. Then, rewrite the remaining false statements so they are true.

1. An anti-spam program protects a computer against viruses by identifying and removing any computer viruses found in memory, on storage media, or in incoming files.

2. Computer-based training is a type of Web-based training that uses Internet technology and consists of application software on the Web.

3. E-mail and Web browsers are examples of communications software that are considered application software.

4. Legal software is a simplified accounting program that helps home users and small office/home office users balance their checkbooks, pay bills, track investments, and evaluate financial plans.

5. Personal DTP software is a popular type of image editing software that allows users to edit digital photographs.

Quiz Yourself Online: To further check your knowledge of types and features of home, personal, educational, and communications programs, utility programs, Web applications, and software learning aids, visit scsite.com/dc2007/ch3/quiz and then click Objectives 6 – 10.

CHAPTER SUMMARY

This chapter illustrated how to start and use application software. It then presented an overview of a variety of business software, graphics and multimedia software, home/personal/educational software, and communications software (read Ethics & Issues 3-4 for a related discussion).

The chapter also described widely used utility programs and identified various Web applications. Finally, learning aids and support tools for application software were presented.

ETHICS & ISSUES 3-4

Copying Software — A Computer Crime!

Usually, when you buy software, you legally can make one copy of the software for backup purposes. Despite the law, many people make multiple copies, either to share or to sell. In a recent survey, more than 50 percent of students and 25 percent of instructors admitted that they had illegally copied, or would illegally copy, software. Microsoft, a leading software manufacturer, estimates that almost 25 percent of software in the United States has been copied illegally. Among small businesses, the rate may be even higher. The Business Software Alliance, an industry trade association, believes that 40 percent of small U.S. businesses use illegally copied software. Illegally copied software costs the software industry more than $13 billion a year in lost revenues, and the law allows fines up to $150,000 for each illegal copy of software. People and companies copy software illegally for a variety of reasons, insisting that software prices are too high, software often is copied for educational or other altruistic purposes, copied software makes people more productive, no restrictions should be placed on the use of software after it is purchased, and everyone copies software. What should be the penalty for copying software? Why? Can you counter the reasons people give for copying software illegally? How? Would you copy software illegally? Why or why not?

CAREER CORNER

Help Desk Specialist

A Help Desk specialist position is an entryway into the information technology (IT) field. A *Help Desk specialist* deals with problems in hardware, software, or communications systems. Job requirements may include the following: solve procedural and software questions both in person and over the telephone, develop and maintain Help Desk operations manuals, and assist in training new Help Desk personnel.

Usually, a Help Desk specialist must be knowledgeable about the major programs in use. Entry-level positions primarily involve answering calls from people with questions. Other positions provide additional assistance and assume further responsibilities, often demanding greater knowledge and problem-solving skills that can lead to more advanced IT positions. This job is ideal for people who must work irregular hours, because many companies need support people to work evenings, weekends, or part-time.

Educational requirements are less stringent than they are for other jobs in the computer field. In some cases, a high school diploma is sufficient. Advancement requires a minimum of a two-year degree, while management generally requires a bachelor's degree in IT or a related field. Certification is another way Help Desk specialists can increase their attractiveness in the marketplace. Entry-level salaries range from $37,000 to $60,000 per year. Managers range from $49,500 to $90,000. For more information, visit scsite.com/dc2007/ch3/careers and then click Help Desk Specialist.

High-Tech Talk

COMPUTER VIRUSES:
DELIVERY, INFECTION, AND AVOIDANCE

Bagle. Spudrag. Netsky. Qweasy. Like the common cold, virtually countless variations of computer viruses exist. Unlike the biological viruses that cause the common cold, people create computer viruses. To create a virus, an unscrupulous programmer must code and then test the virus code to ensure the virus can replicate itself, conceal itself, monitor for certain events, and then deliver its *payload* — the destructive event or prank the virus was created to deliver. Despite the many variations of viruses, most have two phases to their execution: infection and delivery.

To start the infection phase, the virus must be activated. Today, the most common way viruses spread is by people running infected programs disguised as e-mail attachments. During the infection phase, viruses typically perform three actions:

1. First, a virus replicates by attaching itself to program files. A *macro virus* hides in the macro language of an application, such as Word. A *boot sector virus* targets the master boot record and executes when the computer boots up. A *file virus* attaches itself to program files. The file virus, Win32.Hatred, for example, replicates by first infecting Windows executable files for the Calculator, Notepad, Help, and other programs on the hard disk. The virus then scans the computer to locate .exe files on other drives and stores this information in the system registry. The next time an infected file is run, the virus reads the registry and continues infecting another drive.

2. Viruses also conceal themselves to avoid detection. A *stealth virus* disguises itself by hiding in fake code sections, which it inserts within working code in a file. A *polymorphic virus* actually changes its code as it infects computers. Win32.Hatred uses both concealment techniques. The virus writes itself to the last file section, while modifying the file header to hide the increased file size. It also scrambles and encrypts the virus code as it infects files.

3. Finally, viruses watch for a certain condition or event and activate when that condition or event occurs. The event might be booting up the computer or hitting a date on the system clock. A *logic bomb* activates when it detects a specific condition (say, a name deleted from the employee list). A *time bomb* is a logic bomb that activates on a particular date or time. Win32.Hatred, for instance, unleashes its destruction when the computer clock hits the seventh day of any month. If the triggering condition does not exist, the virus simply replicates.

During the delivery phase, the virus unleashes its payload, which might be a harmless prank that displays a silly message — or it might be destructive, corrupting or deleting data and files. When Win32.Hatred triggers, it displays the author's message and then covers the screen with black dots. The virus also deletes several antivirus files as it infects the system. The most dangerous viruses do not have an obvious payload, instead they quietly modify files. A virus, for example, could randomly change numbers in an inventory program or introduce delays to slow a computer.

STEPS TO VIRUS PROTECTION

1. Install the latest Windows updates.
2. Purchase a good antivirus program.
3. After installing an antivirus program, scan your entire computer to be sure your system is clean.
4. Update your antivirus definitions regularly.
5. Be suspicious of any and all unsolicited e-mail attachments.
6. Stay informed about viruses and virus hoaxes.
7. Install a personal firewall program.
8. Download software only if you are sure the Web site is legitimate.
9. Avoid as best you can visiting unscrupulous Web sites.

FIGURE 3-45 Guidelines to keep your computer virus free.

Other kinds of electronic annoyances exist in addition to viruses. While often called viruses, worms and Trojan horse applications actually are part of a broader category called *malicious-logic programs*.

- A *worm*, such as the CodeRed or Sircam worm, resides in active memory and replicates itself over a network to infect machines, using up the system resources and possibly shutting the system down.
- A *Trojan horse* is a destructive program disguised as a real application, such as a screen saver. When a user runs a seemingly innocent program, a Trojan horse hiding inside can capture information, such as user names and passwords, from your system or open up a backdoor that allows a hacker remotely to control your computer. Unlike viruses, Trojan horses do not replicate themselves.

As with the common cold, every computer user is susceptible to a computer virus. In 1995, the chance that a virus would infect your computer was 1 in 1,000; by 2004, the odds were only 1 in 7. Even with better antivirus software, viruses are tough to avoid, as deceitful programmers craft new electronic maladies to infect your computer. Figure 3-45 lists steps you can follow to protect your computer from a virus infection. For more information, visit scsite.com/dc2007/ch3/tech and then click Computer Viruses.

Companies on the Cutting Edge

ADOBE SYSTEMS
DIGITAL IMAGING LEADER

Practically every image seen on a computer and in print has been shaped by software developed by *Adobe Systems, Inc.* The company, based in San Jose, California, is one of the world's largest application software corporations and is committed to helping people communicate effectively.

Adobe Photoshop and Photoshop Album have set the industry standard for digital imaging and digital video software, while Creative Suite is used for design and publishing. The company's Portable Document Format (PDF) and Adobe Reader are used to share documents among users electronically. More than 600 million copies of the free Adobe Reader have been downloaded in 26 languages.

In 2005, Adobe entered into an agreement to acquire Macromedia, which develops such Web page authoring software as Flash MX and Dreamweaver MX. For more information, visit scsite.com/dc2007/ch3/companies and then click Adobe.

MICROSOFT
REALIZING POTENTIAL WITH BUSINESS SOFTWARE

Microsoft's mission is "to enable people and businesses throughout the world to realize their potential." As the largest software company in the world, *Microsoft* has indeed helped computer users in every field reach their goals.

When Microsoft was incorporated in 1975, the company had three programmers, one product, and revenues of $16,000. Thirty years later, the company employs more than 57,000 people, produces scores of software titles with Office and Windows leading the industry, and has annual revenue of more than $36 billion.

The company's recent efforts have focused on security issues, with up to 35 percent of the research and development budget being spent preventing malicious software from getting onto computers, and promoting its Media Center, an entertainment hub designed for the living room. For more information, visit scsite.com/dc2007/ch3/companies and then click Microsoft.

Technology Trailblazers

DAN BRICKLIN
VISICALC DEVELOPER

When *Dan Bricklin* was enrolled at the Harvard Business School in the 1970s, he often used his calculator to determine the effect of changing one value on a balance sheet. He recognized the need to develop a program that would perform a series of calculations automatically when the first number was entered.

He named his creation VisiCalc, short for Visible Calculator. He and a friend formed a company called Software Arts and programmed the VisiCalc prototype using Apple Basic on an Apple II computer. The small program was the first piece of application software that provided a reason for businesses to buy Apple computers. It laid the foundation for the development of other spreadsheets and included many of the features found in today's spreadsheet software.

He currently is president of Software Garden, Inc., a company he founded in 1985, where he does software product development and consulting. For more information, visit scsite.com/dc2007/ch3/people and then click Dan Bricklin.

MASAYOSHI SON
SOFTBANK PRESIDENT AND CEO

Many students carry photographs of family and friends in their wallets and book bags. As a 16-year-old student in the 1970s, *Masayoshi Son* carried a picture of a microchip. He predicted that the microchip was going to change people's lives, and he wanted to be part of that trend.

While majoring in economics at the University of California, Berkeley, he earned his first million dollars by importing arcade games from Japan to the campus, developing new computer games, and selling a patent for a multilingual pocket translator to Sharp Corporation.

At age 23 he founded Softbank, which is Japan's second-largest broadband Internet service and telephone provider. He also is chairman of Yahoo! Japan. Today, he is one of the world's wealthiest entrepreneurs. For more information, visit scsite.com/dc2007/ch3/people and then click Masayoshi Son.

Chapter Review

The Chapter Review section summarizes the concepts presented in this chapter. To listen to the audio version of this Chapter Review, visit scsite.com/dc2007/ch3/review. To obtain help from other students regarding any subject in this chapter, visit scsite.com/dc2007/ch3/forum and post your thoughts or questions.

(1) **What Are the Categories of Application Software?** **Application software** consists of programs designed to make users more productive and/or assist them with personal tasks. The major categories of application software are business software; graphics and multimedia software; home, personal, and educational software; and communications software.

(2) **How Is Software Distributed?** Application software is available in a variety of forms. **Packaged software** is mass-produced, copyrighted retail software that meets the needs of a variety of users. **Custom software** performs functions specific to a business or industry. **Open source software** is provided for use, modification, and redistribution. **Shareware** is copyrighted software that is distributed free for a trial period. **Freeware** is copyrighted software provided at no cost by an individual or a company that retains all rights to the software. **Public-domain software** is free software donated for public use and has no copyright restrictions.

(3) **How Do You Work with Application Software?** Personal computer operating systems often use the concept of a **desktop**, which is an on-screen work area that has a graphical user interface. To start an application in Windows XP, move the **pointer** to the Start **button** in the corner of the desktop and **click** the Start button by pressing and releasing a button on the mouse. Then, click the program name on the Start **menu** or on the *submenu* that displays when you point to a **command**. Once loaded into memory, the program is displayed in a **window** on the desktop.

Visit scsite.com/dc2007/ch3/quiz or click the Quiz Yourself button. Click Objectives 1 – 3.

(4) **What Are the Key Features of Widely Used Business Programs?** **Business software** assists people in becoming more effective and efficient while performing daily business activities. Business software includes the following programs. **Word processing software** allows users to **create** a document by entering text and inserting graphical images, **edit** the document by making changes, and **format** the document by altering its appearance. **Spreadsheet software** allows users to organize data in rows and columns, perform calculations, recalculate when data changes, and chart the data. **Database software** allows users to create a **database**, which is a collection of data organized to allow access, retrieval, and use of that data. **Presentation graphics software** allows users to create a *slide show* that is displayed on a monitor or projection screen. **Note taking software** enables users to enter typed text, handwritten comments, drawings, or sketches on a page and then save the page as part of a notebook. A **personal information manager (PIM)** is software that includes features to help users organize personal information. A **software suite** is a collection of individual programs sold as a single package. **Project management software** allows users to plan, schedule, track, and analyze a project. **Accounting software** helps companies record and report their financial transactions. **Document management software** provides a means for sharing, distributing, and searching through documents by converting them into a format that can be viewed by any user.

(5) **What Are the Key Features of Widely Used Graphics and Multimedia Programs?** Graphics and multimedia software includes the following programs. **Computer-aided design (CAD) software** assists in creating engineering, architectural, and scientific designs. **Desktop publishing (DTP) software** enables professional designers to create sophisticated documents that contain text, graphics, and colors. **Paint software** lets users draw graphical images with various on-screen tools. **Image editing software** provides the capabilities of paint software and includes the capability to modify existing images. **Professional photo editing software** is a type of image editing software that allows

Visit scsite.com/dc2007/ch3/quiz or click the Quiz Yourself button. Click Objectives 4 – 5.

Chapter Review

photographers, videographers, engineers, scientists, and other high-volume digital photo users to edit and customize digital photographs. **Video editing software** allows professionals to modify segments of a video. **Audio editing software** lets users modify audio clips and produce studio-quality sound-tracks. **Multimedia authoring software** allows users to combine text, graphics, audio, video, and animation into an interactive application. **Web page authoring software** helps users create Web pages that include graphical images, video, audio, animation, and other special effects.

(6) What Are the Key Features of Widely Used Home, Personal, and Educational Programs?
Software for home, personal, and educational use includes the following applications. A software suite (for personal use) combines application software such as word processing, spreadsheet, and database into a single package. **Personal finance software** is an accounting program that helps users balance their checkbooks, pay bills, track income and expenses, track investments, and evaluate financial plans. **Legal software** assists in the preparation of legal documents. **Tax preparation software** guides users through filing federal taxes. **Personal DTP software** helps users create newsletters, brochures, advertisements, greeting and business cards, logos, and Web pages. **Personal paint/image editing software** provides an easy-to-use interface with functions tailored to meet the needs of home and small business users. **Personal photo editing software** is a type of image editing software used to edit digital photographs. Application software often includes a **clip art/image gallery**, which is a collection of clip art and photographs. **Home design/landscaping software** assists with the design, remodeling, or improvement of a home or landscape. **Educational software** teaches a particular skill. **Reference software** provides valuable and thorough information for all individuals. **Entertainment software** includes interactive games, videos, and other programs to support hobbies or provide amusement.

(7) What Are the Types of Application Software Used in Communications? Application software for communications includes e-mail programs to transmit messages via a network; FTP programs to upload and download files on the Internet; Web browsers to access and view Web pages; video conferencing/telephone call software for meetings or conversations on a network; newsreader/message board programs that allow online written discussions; chat room software to have real-time, online typed conversations; instant messaging software for real-time exchange of messages or files; and *blog software*, or *blogware*, to create and maintain a blog.

(8) What Are the Functions of Utility Programs? Utility programs support the successful use of application software. An *antivirus program* protects a computer against a computer *virus*, which is a potentially damaging computer program. A *personal firewall* detects and protects a personal computer from unauthorized intrusions. A *spyware remover* detects and deletes spyware. An *anti-spam program* removes spam (Internet junk mail). A *Web filter* restricts access to specified Web sites. A *pop-up blocker* disables pop-up windows. A *file manager* provides functions related to file and disk management. A *file compression utility* shrinks the size of a file. A *backup utility* allows users to copy selected files or an entire hard disk to another storage medium. A *personal computer maintenance utility* fixes operating system and disk problems.

(9) What Are the Advantages of Using Application Software on the Web? A Web **application** is application software that exists on a Web site. Web applications require less disk space on a computer than installed software and are less costly to upgrade. An *application service provider (ASP)* is a third-party organization that manages and distributes software and services on the Web.

(10) What Learning Aids Are Available for Application Software? To assist in the learning process, many programs offer Help features. **Online Help** is the electronic equivalent of a user manual. Most online Help links to *Web-based help*, which provides updates and more comprehensive resources. A *wizard* is an automated assistant that helps users complete a task by asking questions and then performing actions based on the responses. A *template* is a document that contains the formatting necessary for a specific document type.

Visit scsite.com/dc2007/ch3/quiz or click the Quiz Yourself button. Click Objectives 6 – 10.

Key Terms

You should know the Primary Terms and be familiar with the Secondary Terms. Use the list below to help focus your study. To further enhance your understanding of the Key Terms in this chapter, visit scsite.com/dc2007/ch3/terms. See an example of and a definition for each term, and access current and additional information about the term from the Web.

Primary Terms

(shown in bold-black characters in the chapter)

accounting software (149)
application software (134)
audio editing software (153)
business software (138)
button (136)
click (136)
clip art (138)
clip art/image gallery (159)
command (137)
computer-aided design (CAD) software (151)
computer-based training (CBT) (160)
create (141)
custom software (135)
database (145)
database software (145)
desktop (136)
desktop publishing (DTP) software (152)
distance learning (DL) (166)
document management software (150)
edit (141)
educational software (160)
entertainment software (160)
font (141)
font size (141)
format (141)
freeware (135)
home design/landscaping software (160)
icon (136)
image editing software (152)
legal software (157)
menu (137)
multimedia authoring software (154)

note taking software (147)
online banking (156)
online Help (164)
open source software (135)
packaged software (134)
paint software (152)
personal DTP software (158)
personal finance software (156)
personal information manager (PIM) (148)
personal paint/image editing software (158)
personal photo editing software (159)
pointer (136)
presentation graphics software (146)
print (142)
professional photo editing software (152)
project management software (149)
public-domain software (135)
reference software (160)
save (142)
shareware (135)
software suite (148)
spreadsheet software (142)
tax preparation software (157)
title bar (137)
video editing software (153)
Web application (163)
Web page authoring software (154)
Web-based training (166)
window (137)
word processing software (138)

Secondary Terms

(shown in italic characters in the chapter)

anti-spam program (162)
antivirus program (162)
application service provider (ASP) (164)
backup utility (162)
bar chart (144)
blog software (161)
blogware (161)
CD/DVD burner (162)
cell (143)
charting (144)
clipboard (141)
color library (152)
column chart (144)
dialog box (137)
enterprise ASP (164)
field (145)
file (137)
file compression utility (162)
file manager (162)
file name (137)
filters (153)
font style (141)
footer (140)
formula (143)
function (143)
header (140)
illustration software (152)
import (146)
label (143)
line chart (144)
loaded (135)
local/regional ASP (164)
margins (139)
page layout (152)
pasting (141)

PDF (150)
personal computer maintenance utility (162)
personal firewall (162)
pie chart (144)
point (141)
pop-up blocker (162)
product activation (135)
query (145)
record (145)
replace (139)
sans serif font (141)
scrolling (139)
search (139)
serif font (141)
slide show (146)
slide sorter view (146)
specialist ASP (164)
spelling checker (139)
spyware remover (162)
submenu (137)
system software (135)
template (165)
value (143)
vertical market ASP (164)
virus (162)
volume business ASP (164)
WBT (166)
Web-based Help (164)
Web filter (162)
what-if analysis (144)
wizard (165)
word processor (138)
wordwrap (139)
worksheet (142)

Checkpoint

Use the Checkpoint exercises to check your knowledge level of the chapter. The Beyond the Book exercises will help broaden your understanding of the concepts presented in this chapter. To complete the Checkpoint exercises interactively, visit scsite.com/dc2007/ch3/check.

Label the Figure

Identify these elements in the Windows XP graphical user interface.

a. Accessories command
b. Accessories submenu
c. All Programs command
d. All Programs submenu
e. Start button
f. Start menu
g. Paint command

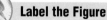

True/False

Mark T for True and F for False. (See page numbers in parentheses.)

_____ 1. The four categories of application software are mutually exclusive. (134)

_____ 2. Programmers cannot incorporate freeware in applications they intend to sell. (135)

_____ 3. To click a button on the screen requires moving the pointer away from the button and then pressing and holding down a button on the mouse (usually the right mouse button). (136)

_____ 4. A menu is an instruction that causes a program to perform a specific action. (137)

_____ 5. A font is a name assigned to a specific design of characters. (141)

_____ 6. Many graphics and multimedia programs have user-friendly interfaces and scaled-down versions, making it possible for the home and small business user to create documents using these programs. (151)

_____ 7. Professional photo editing software is a type of image editing software that allows photographers, videographers, engineers, scientists, and other high-volume digital photo users to edit and customize digital photographs. (153)

_____ 8. Legal software assists in the preparation of legal documents and provides legal information to individuals, families, and small businesses. (157)

_____ 9. Personal DTP programs never include paint/image editing software or photo editing software. (158)

_____ 10. Some communications software is considered system software because it works with hardware and transmission media. (161)

_____ 11. Utility programs are considered application software because they make users more productive or assist with personal tasks. (162)

_____ 12. Web applications store users' data and information on their servers, so users concerned with data security may shy away from this option. (163)

Checkpoint

 **Multiple Choice**   Select the best answer. (See page numbers in parentheses.)

1. _____ has no restrictions from the copyright holder regarding modification of the software's internal instructions and redistribution of the software. (135)
   a. Packaged software
   b. Custom software
   c. Open source software
   d. Shareware

2. In a document window, the _____ usually displays a document's file name. (137)
   a. status bar   b. title bar
   c. menu   d. dialog box

3. In word processing, pasting is the process of _____. (141)
   a. moving different portions of the document on the screen into view
   b. transferring an item from the clipboard to a specific location in a document
   c. locating all occurrences of a certain character, word, or phrase
   d. removing a portion of a document and storing it in a temporary storage location

4. Most spreadsheet software includes a what-if analysis feature, where you _____. (144)
   a. depict the data in a spreadsheet in graphical form
   b. enter labels to identify worksheet data and organize the worksheet
   c. review the spelling of individual words and sections of a worksheet
   d. change values in a spreadsheet to identify the effects of those changes

5. With database software, users can run a _____, which is a request for specific data from the database. (145)
   a. record   b. function
   c. query   d. field

6. Users find _____ software convenient during meetings, class lectures, and other settings that previously required a pencil and paper for recording thoughts and discussions. (147)
   a. word processing   b. database
   c. note taking   d. accounting

7. _____ software provides a means for sharing, distributing, and searching through documents by converting them into a format that can be viewed by any user. (150)
   a. Database
   b. Document management
   c. Portable Document Format
   d. Word processing

8. DTP software supports page layout, which is the process of _____. (152)
   a. creating engineering, architectural, and scientific designs
   b. arranging text and graphics in a document on a page-by-page basis
   c. enhancing and modifying existing images and pictures
   d. standardizing the colors on a page used by designers and printers

9. _____ helps home users determine where, and for what purpose, they are spending money. (156)
   a. Legal software
   b. Personal DTP software
   c. Personal finance software
   d. Tax preparation software

10. _____ is a collection of clip art and photographs. (159)
    a. Professional photo editing software
    b. Personal photo editing software
    c. Clip art/image gallery
    d. Entertainment software

11. A(n) _____, which can be used to upload and download files with other computers and on the Internet, is integrated in some operating systems. (161)
    a. FTP program   b. Web browser
    c. e-mail program   d. chat client

12. A(n) _____ restricts access to specified Web sites. (162)
    a. anti-spam program b. Web filter
    c. spyware remover   d. antivirus program

13. An enterprise ASP _____. (164)
    a. supplies packaged applications
    b. provides applications for a particular industry
    c. customizes and delivers high-end business applications
    d. offers a variety of software applications to specific regions

14. _____ is the electronic equivalent of a user manual. (164)
    a. Online Help (OH)
    b. Software wizards (SW)
    c. Online banking (OB)
    d. Distance learning (DL)

Checkpoint

Matching

Match the terms with their definitions. (See page numbers in parentheses.)

_____ 1. icon (136)

_____ 2. button (136)

_____ 3. window (137)

_____ 4. clip art (138)

_____ 5. cell (143)

_____ 6. slide sorter view (146)

_____ 7. document management software (150)

_____ 8. PDF (150)

_____ 9. volume business ASP (164)

_____ 10. wizard (165)

a. text that appears at the bottom of every page

b. provides prepackaged applications, such as accounting, to businesses

c. intersection of a row and column in a spreadsheet

d. automated assistant that helps users complete a task

e. provides a means for sharing, distributing, and searching through documents

f. collection of drawings, diagrams, maps, and photographs that can be inserted

g. popular file format used by document management software to save converted documents

h. graphical image activated to cause a specific action to take place

i. rectangular area of the screen that displays data and information

j. screen view similar to how 35mm slides look on a light table

k. small symbol on the screen that moves as you move the mouse

l. small image that represents a program, document, or some other object

Short Answer

Write a brief answer to each of the following questions.

1. When using spreadsheet software, what is charting? _____ How are line charts, column charts, and pie charts different? _____

2. What are the features of personal information manager software? _____ Where might you find personal information manager software? _____

3. What are the benefits of document management software? _____ Why do businesses use document management software? _____

4. What are disadvantages of installed software? _____ How can you access a Web application? _____

5. In most programs, how do you start the online Help feature? _____ How is a wizard different from a template? _____

Beyond the Book

Read the following book elements, learn more about each using the Web, and then write a brief report.

1. Ethics & Issues — How Should Schools Deal with Internet Plagiarism? (141), Altering Digital Photographs — Art or Fraud? (153), Should Companies Monitor Employees' E-Mail? (161), or Copying Software — A Computer Crime! (167)

2. Career Corner — Help Desk Specialist (167)

3. Companies on the Cutting Edge — Adobe Systems or Microsoft (169)

4. FAQs (137, 142, 145, 148, 154, 157, 158, 162)

5. High-Tech Talk — Computer Viruses: Delivery, Infection, and Avoidance (168)

6. Looking Ahead — User Interfaces of the Future (137) or Driving Down the Web Highway (163)

7. Making Use of the Web — Finance (155)

8. Picture Yourself Using Software (132)

9. Technology Trailblazers — Dan Bricklin or Masayoshi Son (169)

10. Web Links (140, 144, 146, 150, 157, 158, 159, 160, 162, 166)

Learn It Online

Use the Learn It Online exercises to reinforce your understanding of the chapter concepts. To access the Learn It Online exercises, visit scsite.com/dc2007/ch3/learn.

① At the Movies — Detect Spyware on Your Computer

To view the Detect Spyware on Your Computer movie, click the number 1 button. Locate your video and click the corresponding High-Speed or Dial-Up link, depending on your Internet connection. Watch the movie and then complete the exercise by answering the question that follows. Many of the programs installed on your computer also installed spyware along with the program you loaded. Several different types of spyware exist, two of which are keystroke recorders and advertising spyware. Spyware either collects information and sends it over the Internet to whoever installed it or stores it for later retrieval. Why might you want to detect and delete a keystroke recorder from your computer?

② At the Movies — History of Adobe

To view the History of Adobe movie, click the number 2 button. Locate your video and click the corresponding High-Speed or Dial-Up link, depending on your Internet connection. Watch the movie and then complete the exercise by answering the question that follows. At the dawn of the computer age, computers were used mostly by scientists, and printers were large, cumbersome machines. The advent of desktop publishing gave average people access to the power of computing. Users finally were able to publish documents and images easily, and the computer became a tool for creative expression for everyone. Compare how you complete your homework assignments now to how homework was

done in the 1950s. How has desktop publishing changed the way students research and write reports?

③ Student Edition Labs — Word Processing

Click the number 3 button. A new browser window will open, displaying the Student Edition Labs. Follow the on-screen instructions, and complete the Word Processing Lab. When finished, click the Exit button. If required, submit your results to your instructor.

④ Student Edition Labs — Spreadsheets

Click the number 4 button. A new browser window will open, displaying the Student Edition Labs. Follow the on-screen instructions, and complete the Spreadsheets Lab. When finished, click the Exit button. If required, submit your results to your instructor.

⑤ Student Edition Labs — Databases

Click the number 5 button. A new browser window will open, displaying the Student Edition Labs. Follow the on-screen instructions, and complete the Databases Lab. When finished, click the Exit button. If required, submit your results to your instructor.

⑥ Student Edition Labs — Presentation Software

Click the number 6 button. A new browser window will open, displaying the Student Edition Labs. Follow the on-screen instructions, and complete the Presentation Software Lab. When finished, click the Exit button. If required, submit your results to your instructor.

⑦ Practice Test

Click the number 7 button. Answer each question. When completed, enter your name and click the Grade Test button to submit the

Learn It Online

quiz for grading. Make a note of any missed questions. If required, submit your score to your instructor.

8 Who Wants To Be a Computer Genius²?

Click the number 8 button to find out if you are a computer genius. Directions about how to play the game will be displayed. When you are ready to play, click the Play button. Submit your score to your instructor.

9 Wheel of Terms

Click the number 9 button to reinforce important terms you learned in this chapter by playing the Shelly Cashman Series version of this popular game. Directions about how to play the game will be displayed. When you are ready to play, click the Play button. Submit your score to your instructor.

10 DC Track and Field

Click the number 10 button to use what you have learned in this chapter to compete against other students in three track and field events. Directions about how to play the game will be displayed. When you are ready to play, click the start first event button. If required, submit your score to your instructor.

11 You're Hired!

Click the number 11 button to use what you have learned in this chapter to embark on the path to a career in computers. Directions about how to play the game will be displayed. When you are ready to play, click the begin game button. If required, submit your score to your instructor.

12 Crossword Puzzle Challenge

Click the number 12 button. Complete the puzzle to reinforce skills you learned in this chapter. Directions about how to play the game will be displayed. When you are ready to play, click the Play button. Submit the completed puzzle to your instructor.

13 Lab Exercises

Click the number 13 button. When the Lab Exercises menu appears, click the exercise assigned by your instructor. A new browser window will open. Follow the on-screen instructions to complete the exercise. When finished, click the Exit button. If required, submit your results to your instructor.

14 In the News

It is a computer user's worst fear — he or she opens an unfamiliar e-mail message or uses a disk of unknown origin and a computer virus is released that damages and/or deletes files. Fortunately, specialized software prevents such things from happening to your computer. Click the number 14 button and read a news article about antivirus programs. Which program does the article recommend? What does it do? Who will benefit from using this software? Why? Where can the software be obtained? Would you be interested in this software? Why or why not?

15 Chapter Discussion Forum

Select an objective from this chapter on page 133 about which you would like more information. Click the number 15 button and post a short message listing a meaningful message title accompanied by one or more questions concerning the selected objective. In two days, return to the threaded discussion by clicking the number 15 button. Submit to your instructor your original message and at least one response to your message.

16 Google Home Page

Click the number 16 button to learn how to make the Google home page your default home page. Explore the different sections of the Google home page (Images, Groups, News, Froogle, Local, and more). On the News page, use the Customize this page feature to rearrange the page and to add other sections. Print the Google News page and then step through the exercise. If required, submit your results to your instructor.

Learn How To

Use the Learn How To activities to learn fundamental skills when using a computer and accompanying technology. Complete the exercises and submit them to your instructor. To see a video of a Learn How To activity, visit scsite.com/dc2007/ch3/howto.

LEARN HOW TO 1: Save a File in Application Software

When you use application software, usually you either will create a new file or modify an existing file. If you turn off your computer or lose electrical power while working on the file, the file will not be retained. In order to retain the file, you must save it.

To save a new file, you must complete several tasks:
1. Initiate an action indicating you want to save the file, such as clicking the Save button.
2. Designate where the file should be stored. This includes identifying both the device (such as drive C) and the folder (such as My Documents).
3. Specify the name of the file.
4. Click the Save button to save the file.

Tasks 2 through 4 normally can be completed using a dialog box such as shown in Figure 3-46.

If you close a program prior to saving a new or modified file, the program will display a dialog box asking if you want to save the file. If you click the Yes button, a modified file will be saved using the same file name in the same location. Saving a new file requires that you complete tasks 2 through 4.

Exercise
1. Start the WordPad program from the Accessories submenu on the All Programs submenu.
2. Type `Saving a file is the best insurance against losing work.`
3. Click the Save button on the WordPad toolbar. What dialog box is displayed? Where will the file be saved? What is the default file name? If you wanted to save the file on the desktop, what would you do? Click the Cancel button in the dialog box. Submit your answers to your instructor.
4. Click the Close button in the WordPad window. What happened? Click the Yes button in the WordPad dialog box. What happened? Place either a floppy disk in drive A or a USB drive in a USB port. Select either the floppy disk or the USB drive as the location for saving the file. Name the file, Chapter 3 How To 1. Save the file. What happened? Submit your answers to your instructor.

FIGURE 3-46

LEARN HOW TO 2: Install and Uninstall Application Software

When you purchase application software, you must install the software on the computer where you want to run it. The exact installation process varies with each program, but generally you must complete the following steps:
1. Insert the CD-ROM containing the application software into a drive.
2. The opening window will appear. If the CD-ROM contains more than one program, choose the program you want to install. Click the Continue or Next button.
3. Some file extractions will occur and then an Install Wizard will begin. You normally must accomplish the following steps by completing the directions within the wizard:
   a. Accept the terms of the license agreement.
   b. Identify where on your computer the software will be stored. The software usually selects a default location on drive C, and you normally will accept the default location.

Learn How To

c. Select any default options for the software.
d. Click a button to install the software.
4. A Welcome/Help screen often will be displayed. Click a button to finish the installation process.

At some point, you may want to remove software. Most software includes uninstall programming that will remove the program and all its software components. To uninstall a program, complete the following steps:
1. Click the Start button on the Windows taskbar.
2. Click Control Panel on the Start menu.
3. Click or double-click Add or Remove Programs. *The Add or Remove Programs window will open (Figure 3-47).*
4. Select the program you wish to remove. *In Figure 3-47, Macromedia Dreamweaver MX is selected as the program to remove.*
5. Click the Change/Remove button.
6. A dialog box will be displayed informing you that the software is being prepared for uninstall. You then will be informed that the process you are following will remove the program. You will be asked if you want to continue. To uninstall the program, click the Yes button.

The program will be removed from the computer.

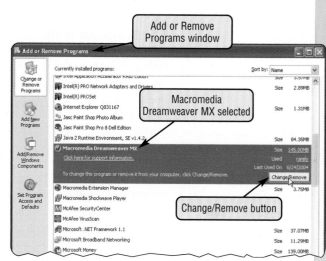

FIGURE 3-47

Exercise

1. Optional: Insert the CD-ROM containing the software you want to install into a drive and follow the instructions for installing the software. **Warning: If you are using a computer other than your own, particularly in a school laboratory, do not perform this exercise unless you have specific permission from your instructor.**
2. Optional: Follow the steps above to uninstall software you want to remove. Be aware that if you uninstall software, the software will not be available for use until you reinstall it. **Warning: If you are using a computer other than your own, particularly in a school laboratory, do not perform this exercise unless you have specific permission from your instructor.**

LEARN HOW TO 3: Check Application Software Version

Most application software will be modified from time to time by its developer. Each time the software is changed, it acquires a new version number and sometimes an entirely new name. To determine what version of software you have, perform the following steps:
1. Start the application program.
2. Click Help on the menu bar and then click About on the Help menu (the program name often follows the word, About). *The program displays the About window (Figure 3-48).*
3. To close the About window, click the OK button.

Depending on the software, in the About window you also might be able to determine further information.

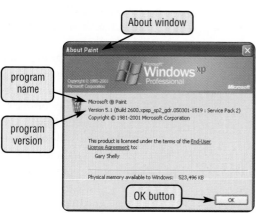

FIGURE 3-48

Exercise

1. Start your Web browser and display the About window for the browser. What is the name of the browser? What version of the browser are you using? What is the product ID? What does the copyright notice say? Submit your answers to your instructor.
2. Start any other application software. Display the About window. What is the name of the program? What is the version number? What information do you find that you did not see in Exercise 1? Which window do you find more useful? Why? Submit your answers to your instructor.

Web Research

Use the Internet-based Web Research exercises to broaden your understanding of the concepts presented in this chapter. Visit scsite.com/dc2007/ch3/research to obtain more information pertaining to each exercise. To discuss any of the Web Research exercises in this chapter with other students, post your thoughts or questions at scsite.com/dc2007/ch3/forum.

① Scavenger Hunt Use one of the <u>search engines</u> listed in Figure 2-10 in Chapter 2 on page 78 or your own favorite search engine to find the answers to the questions below. Copy and paste the Web address from the Web page where you found the answer. Some questions may have more than one answer. If required, submit your answers to your instructor. (1) What is the name of the latest Boeing flight deck added to Microsoft's Flight Simulator? (2) What video game did Atari begin selling at Sears under the Telegames label in 1975? (3) What inventor designed one of the first mechanical calculating devices, called the Codex? (4) What Web site features software that creates a game requiring a player to put numbers in nine rows of nine boxes?

② Search Sleuth A <u>virus</u> is a potentially damaging computer program that can harm files and the operating system. The National Institute of Standards and Technology Computer Security Resource Center (csrc.nist.gov/virus/) is one of the more comprehensive Web sites discussing viruses. Visit this Web site and then use your word processing program to answer the following questions. Then, if required, submit your answers to your instructor. (1) The Virus Information page provides general information about viruses and links to various resources that provide more specific details. What two steps does the National Institute recommend to detect and prevent viruses from spreading? (2) Click the Symantec link in the Virus Resources & Other Areas of Interest section. What viruses are the latest threats, and when were they discovered? (3) Click Search at the top of the page and then type "Sasser worm" as the keyword in the Search text box. How many articles discuss the Sasser worm on the Symantec Web site? What three functions does the Sasser Removal Tool perform? (4) Click one of the Latest News links and review the material. Review the information you read and then write a 50-word summary.

③ Journaling Respond to your readings in this chapter by writing at least one page about your reactions, evaluations, and reflections about the first time you used <u>home, personal, and educational software</u>. For example, have you prepared your income taxes using tax preparation programs? Have you enhanced or modified digital photos with paint/image editing software? What video games have you played on a home computer? You also can write about the new terms you learned by reading this chapter. If required, submit your journal to your instructor.

④ Expanding Your Understanding Microsoft seeks to help customers use its products by maintaining the <u>Microsoft Help and Support</u> Web site (support.microsoft.com). This Web site has a link to the Knowledge Base, which contains more than 250,000 articles written by Microsoft employees who support the company's products. Also included are software downloads and updates, public newsgroups, methods of getting online or telephone assistance, and the Security Support Center. View this site and then search the Knowledge Base for information on Microsoft Word. Also view the common issues, updates, security issues, and visitors' top links listed on the Web site. Write a report summarizing your findings. If required, submit your report to your instructor.

⑤ Ethics in Action A hacker is someone who tries to access a computer or network illegally. Although the activity sometimes is a harmless prank, it sometimes causes extensive damage. Some hackers say their activities give them a sense of excitement and test their skills. Others say their activities are a form of civil disobedience that allows them to challenge authority and force companies to make their products more secure. View online sites such as <u>Hackers: Outlaws & Angels</u> (tlc.discovery.com/convergence/hackers/hackers.html) that provide information about whether hackers provide some benefit to the Internet society. Write a report summarizing your findings and include a table of links to Web sites that provide additional details. If required, submit your report to your instructor.

Case Studies

Use the Case Studies to apply the concepts presented in the chapter to real-world situations. Visit scsite.com/dc2007/ch3/cases to obtain more information pertaining to each exercise. To discuss the Case Studies in this chapter with other students, visit scsite.com/dc2007/ch3/forum and post your thoughts or questions.

CASE STUDY 1 – Class Discussion   The owner of Mel's Hair Salon for Men and Women has decided to obtain a personal desktop computer for use in his business. In addition to using the computer for writing letters, developing advertising pieces, performing basic accounting, and maintaining lists of customers, the owner would like his employees to use a <u>digital camera</u> to take pictures of customers after they have had their hair done and create a file of printed full-color pictures of customers for marketing purposes. The owner has asked you to recommend the type of camera, software, and computer he should buy. Prepare a brief report detailing your findings and recommendations. Be prepared to discuss your recommendations in class.

CASE STUDY 2 – Class Discussion   Your manager at Dave's Office Supply Outlet intends to choose a spreadsheet program that the entire company will use. He prefers to learn about software using trade books — written texts that explain the features of a program and how to use it — rather than using online Help or tutorials. He has asked you to evaluate the <u>spreadsheet</u> trade books available in bookstores on the Web. Visit a bookstore Web site and other Web sites that sell books to survey the spreadsheet trade books available for Microsoft Excel, Lotus, Quattro Pro, and StarOffice Calc. Which spreadsheet program has the most books available? How difficult would it be to learn each program using the trade books at hand? Which trade book do you think is the best? Why? If you were going to purchase software solely on the basis of the related trade books, which program would you buy? Why? Be prepared to discuss your recommendations in class.

CASE STUDY 3 – Research   After attending a seminar on Web applications, the chief financial officer of Eastern Steel, Inc. has asked you to investigate the feasibility of using the Web to collect data from company offices and customers throughout the world. Recall that a <u>Web application</u> is application software that exists on a Web site. Users access the Web application through their browser. Use the Web and/or print media to create a brief report describing at least two Web applications and how Eastern Steel could use similar applications effectively. Include in your report a description of each application, a short overview of any online Help, and the Web address for each application. Write a brief report and share your findings with your class.

CASE STUDY 4 – Research   Frank's Custom Design frequently enhances its work with scanned photographs or graphics obtained with <u>illustration software</u>. The owner recently read that the Internet is providing a new resource for desktop publishers. Companies such as Corbis, Picture Network International, Muse, and Liaison International are offering archives of artwork and photographs. You have been asked to investigate the feasibility of using this new resource. Information about all four companies can be found on the World Wide Web. Pick two companies that provide digital images and find out more about their product. Prepare a brief report that answers the following questions. What kinds of illustrations are available? How are pictures on a specific subject located? How are the illustrations provided? What fees are involved? Would the cost be different for a high school student creating one paper than for an organization newsletter with a statewide distribution? Which company do you prefer? Why?

CASE STUDY 5 – Team Challenge   The new superintendent of Lisle Elementary School District 205 has recommended that <u>educational software</u> play a major role in the learning process at every grade level. In her presentation to the school board, she claimed that educational software is available for a wide variety of skills and subjects. She also indicated that educational software lets students learn at their own pace, shows infinite patience, and usually offers an entertaining approach. The president of the school board is not so sure. Unlike human instructors, educational software often does not recognize unique problems, fails to address individual goals, and provides limited feedback. Form a three-member team and investigate the use of educational software. Have each member of your team visit a software vendor's Web site, or an educational cooperative's Web site and list the advantages and disadvantages of using educational software. Select a program on the Web or from your school's education department library and use it. Note the subject being taught, the audience to which the software is directed, the approach used, and any special features. Then, meet with your team, discuss your findings, prepare a team report or PowerPoint presentation, and share it with your class.

CHAPTER FOUR

The Components of the System Unit

Picture Yourself Buying a Computer

Your neighbor, who is a computer guru and always has the latest computers and devices, just called to see if you want to buy one of his *old* computers. What he considers old actually still is state of the art. He says it would include the system unit, monitor, speakers, keyboard, and mouse.

He starts rattling off all the features while you frantically make quick notes. The system unit has a 3.2 GHz Pentium D processor with dual-core technology and 1 MB of L2 cache. It has 512 MB of dual channel SDRAM expandable to 4 GB, a 533 MHz bus, and integrated modem and networking capabilities. The back of the system unit has ports for a keyboard, a mouse, a monitor, speakers, a network, and a modem. It also has a serial port, a parallel port, seven USB ports (two in front and five in back), and a FireWire port. It is not Bluetooth-enabled, but you can buy a wireless port adapter if you need that capability. He says he will set up the computer for you, clean it for you once a year, and be available for personal support anytime. "Five hundred bucks," he says, "and it's yours." Sold!

After hanging up the telephone, you glance at all your notes. You know he gave you a great deal, but you have no idea what all these terms and numbers mean. To find out, you plan to read Chapter 4 to learn about processor chips, RAM, cache, adapter cards, and ports, and discover the many other components of the system unit.

OBJECTIVES

After completing this chapter, you will be able to:

1. Differentiate among various styles of system units

2. Identify chips, adapter cards, and other components of a motherboard

3. Describe the components of a processor and how they complete a machine cycle

4. Identify characteristics of various personal computer processors on the market today

5. Define a bit and describe how a series of bits represents data

6. Explain how programs transfer in and out of memory

7. Differentiate among the various types of memory

8. Describe the types of expansion slots and adapter cards

9. Explain the differences among a serial port, a parallel port, a USB port, a FireWire port, and other ports

10. Describe how buses contribute to a computer's processing speed

11. Identify components in mobile computers and mobile devices

12. Understand how to clean a system unit

CONTENTS

THE SYSTEM UNIT

Whether you are a home user or a business user, you most likely will make the decision to purchase a new computer or upgrade an existing computer within the next several years. Thus, you should understand the purpose of each component in a computer. As Chapter 1 discussed, a computer includes devices used for input, processing, output, storage, and communications. Many of these components are part of the system unit.

The **system unit** is a case that contains electronic components of the computer used to process data. System units are available in a variety of shapes and sizes. The case of the system unit, sometimes called the *chassis*, is made of metal or plastic and protects the internal electronic components from damage. All computers have a system unit (Figure 4-1).

On desktop personal computers, the electronic components and most storage devices are part of the system unit. Other devices, such as the keyboard, mouse, microphone, monitor, printer, scanner, PC video camera, and speakers, normally occupy space outside the system unit. The trend is toward a smaller form factor, or size and shape, of the desktop personal computer system unit.

FIGURE 4-1 All sizes of computers have a system unit.

On notebook computers, the keyboard and pointing device often occupy the area on the top of the system unit, and the display attaches to the system unit by hinges. The location of the system unit on a Tablet PC varies, depending on the design of the Tablet PC. Some models build the system unit behind the display (as shown in Figure 4-1), while others position the system unit below the keyboard (shown later in the chapter). The system unit on a PDA and smart phone usually consumes the entire device. On these mobile devices, the display often is built into the system unit.

With game consoles, the input and output devices, such as controllers and a television, reside outside the system unit. On handheld game consoles and digital audio players, by contrast, the packaging around the system unit houses the input devices and display.

At some point, you might have to open the system unit on a desktop personal computer to replace or install a new electronic component. For this reason, you should be familiar with the electronic components of a system unit. Figure 4-2 identifies some of these components, which include the processor, memory, adapter cards, ports, drive bays, and the power supply.

The processor interprets and carries out the basic instructions that operate a computer. Memory typically holds data waiting to be processed and instructions waiting to be executed. The electronic components and circuitry of the system unit, such as the processor and memory, usually are part of or are connected to a circuit board called the motherboard. Many current motherboards also integrate modem and networking capabilities.

FIGURE 4-2   The system unit on a typical personal computer consists of numerous electronic components, some of which are shown in this figure. The sound card and video card are two types of adapter cards.

Adapter cards are circuit boards that provide connections and functions not built into the motherboard. Two adapter cards found in some desktop personal computers today are a sound card and a video card. Devices outside the system unit often attach to ports on the system unit by a connector on a cable. These devices may include a keyboard, mouse, microphone, monitor, printer, scanner, card reader/writer, digital camera, PC video camera, and speakers. A drive bay holds one or more disk drives. The power supply converts electricity from a power cord plugged in a wall outlet into a form that can be used by the computer.

The Motherboard

The **motherboard**, sometimes called a *system board*, is the main circuit board of the system unit. Many electronic components attach to the motherboard; others are built into it. Figure 4-3 shows a photograph of a current desktop personal computer motherboard and identifies components that attach to it, including adapter cards, a processor chip, and a memory module. Memory chips are installed on memory cards (modules) that fit in a slot on the motherboard.

A computer **chip** is a small piece of semiconducting material, usually silicon, on which integrated circuits are etched. An *integrated circuit* contains many microscopic pathways capable of carrying electrical current. Each integrated circuit can contain millions of elements such as resistors, capacitors, and transistors. A *transistor*, for example, can act as an electronic switch that opens or closes the circuit for electrical charges. Most chips are no bigger than one-half-inch square. Manufacturers package chips so the chips can be attached to a circuit board, such as a motherboard or an adapter card.

WEB LINK 4-1

Motherboards
For more information, visit scsite.com/dc2007/ch4/weblink and then click Motherboards.

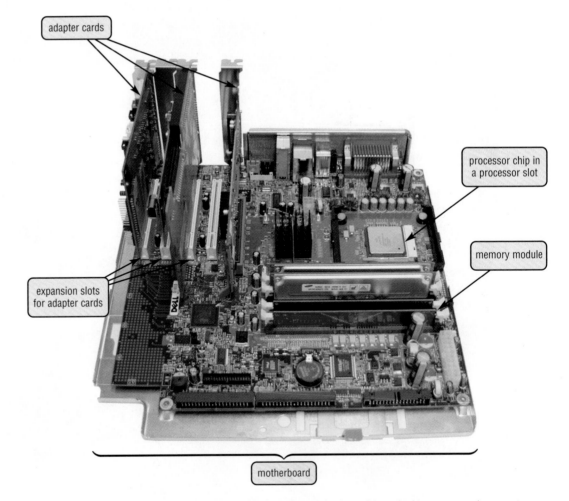

adapter cards

processor chip in a processor slot

memory module

expansion slots for adapter cards

motherboard

FIGURE 4-3   Many electronic components attach to the motherboard in a desktop personal computer, including a processor chip, memory module, and adapter cards.

PROCESSOR

The **processor**, also called the **central processing unit** (**CPU**), interprets and carries out the basic instructions that operate a computer. The processor significantly impacts overall computing power and manages most of a computer's operations. On larger computers, such as mainframes and supercomputers, the various functions performed by the processor extend over many separate chips and often multiple circuit boards. On a personal computer, all functions of the processor usually are on a single chip. Some computer and chip manufacturers use the term *microprocessor* to refer to a personal computer processor chip.

Processors contain a control unit and an arithmetic logic unit (ALU). These two components work together to perform processing operations. Figure 4-4 illustrates how other devices connected to the computer communicate with the processor to carry out a task.

The Control Unit

The **control unit** is the component of the processor that directs and coordinates most of the operations in the computer. The control unit has a role much like a traffic cop: it interprets each instruction issued by a program and then initiates the appropriate action to carry out the instruction. Read Ethics & Issues 4-1 for a related discussion.

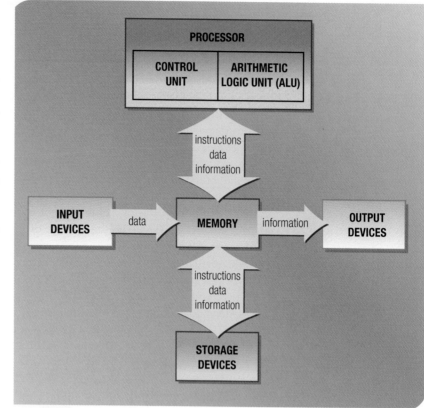

FIGURE 4-4 Most devices connected to the computer communicate with the processor to carry out a task. When a user starts a program, for example, its instructions transfer from a storage device to memory. Data needed by programs enters memory from either an input device or a storage device. The control unit interprets and executes instructions in memory, and the ALU performs calculations on the data in memory. Resulting information is stored in memory, from which it can be sent to an output device or a storage device for future access, as needed.

ETHICS & ISSUES 4-1

Can Computers Think?

Ever since a computer defeated world chess champion Gary Kasparov in a chess match, people have wondered, can computers think? As computer processors and software become more powerful, the question is more hotly debated. People who believe computers can think argue that, if a person had a conversation with a computer and was convinced the computer was really human, then the computer is intelligent. This criteria is known as the Turing Test, named after British mathematician Alan Turing who proposed the test in 1950. If a computer can pass a modern version of the Turing Test, it is considered to be intelligent, and it may win the prestigious $100,000 Loebner Prize. Opponents counter this argument by saying that, if a question written in a foreign language was submitted to a person who can read and write the language and a person who cannot read or write the language but has a list of questions and appropriate answers, it might be impossible to tell the response of one person from the other. But, the person who cannot read or write the language really does not understand it, any more than a computer really can think. Besides, computers lack an essential component of human thinking — common sense. Computers can consider millions of chess moves a second, but humans have the common sense to recognize that some moves are not worthy of consideration. Can computers think? Why or why not? If computers cannot think now, might they be able to think in the future? Why?

The Arithmetic Logic Unit

The **arithmetic logic unit** (*ALU*), another component of the processor, performs arithmetic, comparison, and other operations.

Arithmetic operations include basic calculations such as addition, subtraction, multiplication, and division. *Comparison operations* involve comparing one data item with another to determine whether the first item is greater than, equal to, or less than the other item. Depending on the result of the comparison, different actions may occur. For example, to determine if an employee should receive overtime pay, software instructs the ALU to compare the number of hours an employee worked during the week with the regular time hours allowed (e.g., 40 hours). If the hours worked are greater than 40, software instructs the ALU to perform calculations that compute the overtime wage.

Machine Cycle

For every instruction, a processor repeats a set of four basic operations, which comprise a *machine cycle* (Figure 4-5): (1) fetching, (2) decoding, (3) executing, and, if necessary, (4) storing. *Fetching* is the process of obtaining a program instruction or data item from memory. The term *decoding* refers to the process of translating the instruction into signals the computer can execute. *Executing* is the process of carrying out the commands. *Storing*, in this context, means writing the result to memory (not to a storage medium).

In some computers, the processor fetches, decodes, executes, and stores only one instruction at a time. In these computers, the processor waits until an instruction completes all four stages of the machine cycle (fetch, decode, execute, and store) before beginning work on the next instruction.

FIGURE 4-5   THE STEPS IN A MACHINE CYCLE

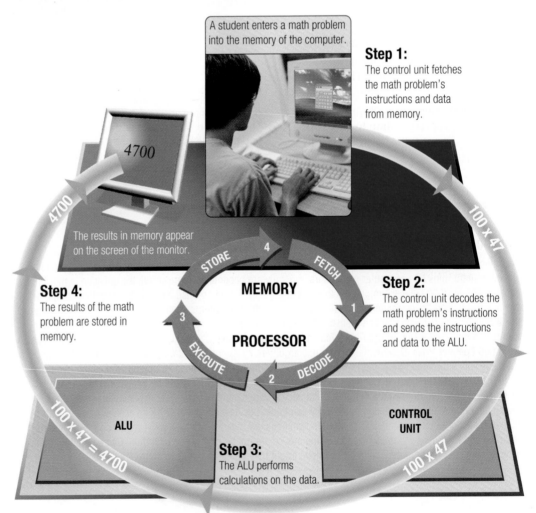

A student enters a math problem into the memory of the computer.

Step 1:
The control unit fetches the math problem's instructions and data from memory.

The results in memory appear on the screen of the monitor.

Step 4:
The results of the math problem are stored in memory.

Step 2:
The control unit decodes the math problem's instructions and sends the instructions and data to the ALU.

Step 3:
The ALU performs calculations on the data.

MEMORY
PROCESSOR
ALU
CONTROL UNIT
STORE   FETCH   EXECUTE   DECODE
4700   100 x 47   100 x 47 = 4700   100 x 47

Most of today's personal computers support a concept called pipelining. With *pipelining*, the processor begins fetching a second instruction before it completes the machine cycle for the first instruction. Processors that use pipelining are faster because they do not have to wait for one instruction to complete the machine cycle before fetching the next. Think of a pipeline as an assembly line. By the time the first instruction is in the last stage of the machine cycle, three other instructions could have been fetched and started through the machine cycle (Figure 4-6).

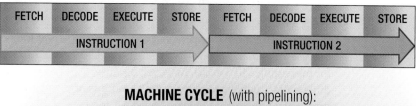

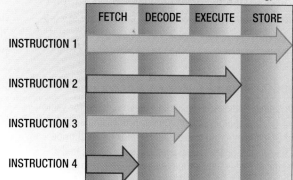

FIGURE 4-6 Most modern personal computers support pipelining. With pipelining, the processor fetches a second instruction before the first instruction is completed. The result is faster processing.

Registers

A processor contains small, high-speed storage locations, called *registers*, that temporarily hold data and instructions. Registers are part of the processor, not part of memory or a permanent storage device. Processors have many different types of registers, each with a specific storage function. Register functions include storing the location from where an instruction was fetched, storing an instruction while the control unit decodes it, storing data while the ALU computes it, and storing the results of a calculation.

The System Clock

The processor relies on a small quartz crystal circuit called the **system clock** to control the timing of all computer operations. Just as your heart beats at a regular rate to keep your body functioning, the system clock generates regular electronic pulses, or ticks, that set the operating pace of components of the system unit.

Each tick equates to a *clock cycle*. In the past, processors used one or more clock cycles to execute each instruction. Processors today often are *superscalar*, which means they can execute more than one instruction per clock cycle.

The pace of the system clock, called the **clock speed**, is measured by the number of ticks per second. Current personal computer processors have clock speeds in the gigahertz range. Giga is a prefix that stands for billion, and a *hertz* is one cycle per second. Thus, one **gigahertz (GHz)** equals one billion ticks of the system clock per second. A computer that operates at 3.8 GHz has 3.8 billion (giga) clock cycles in one second (hertz).

The faster the clock speed, the more instructions the processor can execute per second. The speed of the system clock has no effect on devices such as a printer or disk drive. The speed of the system clock is just one factor that influences a computer's performance. Other factors, such as the type of processor chip, amount of cache, memory access time, bus width, and bus clock speed, are discussed later in this chapter.

FAQ 4-1

Does the system clock also keep track of the current date and time?

No, a separate battery-backed chip, called the *real-time clock*, keeps track of the date and time in a computer. The battery continues to run the real-time clock even when the computer is off. For more information, visit scsite.com/dc2007/ch4/faq and then click Computer Clock.

Some computer professionals measure a processor's speed according to the number of *MIPS (millions of instructions per second)* it can process. Current desktop personal computers can process more than 7,000 MIPS. No real standard for measuring MIPS exists, however, because different instructions require varying amounts of processing time. Read Looking Ahead 4-1 for a look at the next generation of processing speeds.

LOOKING AHEAD 4-1

Countries Seek Computing Speed Supremacy

The United States and Japan have been battling for years over the top spot in supercomputer processing speed, and China is entering this global race for national pride.

The world's fastest computers currently are located in the United States. IBM's Blue Gene/L, built for the U.S. Department of Energy's National Nuclear Security Agency, runs at more than 138 teraflops, or trillion, calculations per second, according to the Top500 Project, a group that monitors supercomputers throughout the world.

The Japanese government has set a goal of developing a supercomputer by 2011 that can perform more than a quadrillion calculations per second.

These fast computers are used in medical research, advanced climate forecasting, and other areas. They cost more than $1 billion to develop. For more information, visit scsite.com/dc2007/ch4/looking and then click Fastest Computer.

Comparison of Personal Computer Processors

The leading processor chip manufacturers for personal computers are Intel, AMD (Advanced Micro Devices), Transmeta, IBM, and Motorola. These manufacturers often identify their processor chips by a model name or model number. Figure 4-7 categorizes the historical development of the personal computer processor and documents the increases in clock speed and number of transistors in chips since 1982. The greater the number of transistors, the more complex and powerful the chip.

With its earlier processors, Intel used a model number to identify the various chips. After learning that processor model numbers could not be trademarked and protected from use by competitors, Intel began identifying its processors with names — thus emerged the series of processors known as the Pentium. Most high-performance desktop PCs use some type of **Pentium** processor. Many notebook computers and Tablet PCs use a **Pentium M** processor. Less expensive, basic PCs use a brand of Intel processor called the **Celeron**. The **Xeon** and **Itanium** processors, are ideal for workstations and low-end servers.

Today, AMD is the leading manufacturer of *Intel-compatible processors*, which have an internal design similar to Intel processors, perform the same functions, and can be as powerful, but often are less expensive. Transmeta, also a manufacturer of Intel-compatible processors, specializes in processors for mobile computers and devices. Intel and Intel-compatible processors are used in PCs.

Until recently, Apple computers used only an *IBM processor* or a *Motorola processor*, which had a design different from the Intel-style processor. Today's Apple computers, however, use Intel processors.

In the past, chip manufacturers listed a processor's clock speed in marketing literature and advertisements. As previously mentioned, though, clock speed is only one factor that impacts processing speed in today's computers. To help consumers evaluate various processors, manufacturers such as Intel and AMD now use a numbering scheme that more accurately reflects the processing speed of their chips.

Processor chips include technologies to improve processing performance. Some of Intel's processor chips contain *Hyper-Threading (HT) Technology*, which improves processing power and time by allowing the processor chip to mimic the power of two processors. For even higher levels of performance with lower levels of power consumption and heat emitted in the system unit, several processor chip manufacturers now offer dual-core and multicore processors. A *dual-core processor* is a chip that has two separate processors. Similarly, a *multicore processor* is a chip with two or more separate processors. Most processors have built-in instructions to improve the performance of multimedia and 3-D graphics. Processors for notebook computers include technology to integrate wireless capabilities and optimize and extend battery life. For example, Intel's *Centrino* mobile technology integrates wireless capabilities in notebook computers and Tablet PCs. PDAs and other smaller mobile devices often use a processor, such as AMD's Alchemy processor, that consumes less power yet offers high performance.

Another type of processor, called *system on a chip*, integrates the functions of a processor, memory, and a video card on a single chip. Lower-priced personal computers, Tablet PCs, networking devices, and consumer electronics such as audio players and game consoles sometimes have a system-on-a-chip processor. The goal of system-on-a-chip manufacturers is to create processors that have faster clock speeds, consume less power, are small, and are cost effective.

COMPARISON OF PERSONAL COMPUTER PROCESSORS

	NAME	DATE INTRODUCED/ UPDATED	MANUFACTURER	CLOCK SPEED*	NUMBER OF TRANSISTORS
SERVER PROCESSORS	Xeon MP	2002/2005	Intel	1.4–3.66 GHz	108–169 million
	Itanium 2	2003/2004	Intel	1.3–1.6 GHz	220–410 million
	Xeon	2001/2003	Intel	1.4–3.6 GHz	42–108 million
	Itanium	2001	Intel	733–800 MHz	25.4–60 million
	Pentium III Xeon	1999/2000	Intel	500–900 MHz	9.5–28 million
	Pentium II Xeon	1998/1999	Intel	400–450 MHz	7.5–27 million
	Opteron	2003	AMD	1.4–2.4 GHz	100 million
	Athlon MP	2002	AMD	1.53–2.25 GHz	54.3 million
DESKTOP PERSONAL COMPUTER PROCESSORS	Pentium Extreme Edition (dual-core)	2005	Intel	3.2 GHz	178 million
	Pentium D (dual-core)	2005	Intel	2.8–3.2 GHz	230 million
	Pentium 4 with HT Technology	2002/2005	Intel	2.4–3.8 GHz	55–178 million
	Pentium 4	2000/2005	Intel	1.3–3.8 GHz	42–125 million
	Pentium III	1999/2003	Intel	450 MHz–1.4 GHz	9.5–44 million
	Celeron D	2004/2005	Intel	2.4–3.2 GHz	26.2–125 million
	Celeron	1998/2003	Intel	266 MHz–2.8 GHz	7.5–55 million
	Pentium II	1997/1998	Intel	233–450 MHz	7.5 million
	Pentium Pro	1995/1999	Intel	150–200 MHz	5.5 million
	Pentium	1993/1997	Intel	75–233 MHz	3.3–4.5 million
	80486DX	1989/1994	Intel	25–100 MHz	1.6 million
	80386	1985/1990	Intel	16–33 MHz	275,000
	80286	1982	Intel	6–12 MHz	134,000
	Athlon 64 X2 (dual-core)	2005	AMD	2.0–2.8 GHz	233 million
	Athlon 64 FX	2005	AMD	2.6–2.8 GHz	114 million
	Sempron	2004	AMD	1.5–2 GHz	68.5 million
	Athlon 64	2003/2004	AMD	2–2.4 GHz	105.9–114 million
	Athlon	1999/2002	AMD	500 MHz–1.4 GHz	22–38 million
	Duron	1999/2001	AMD	600 MHz–1.3 GHz	25 million
	AMD–K6	1997/1999	AMD	300–450 MHz	8.8–21.3 million
	PowerPC (G1 to G5)	1994/2005	Motorola/IBM	60 MHz–2.7 GHz	2.8–58 million
	68040	1989	Motorola	25–40 MHz	1.2 million
	68030	1987	Motorola	16–50 MHz	270,000
	68020	1984	Motorola	16–33 MHz	190,000
MOBILE PROCESSORS	Celeron M	2004	Intel	900 MHz–1.6 GHz	55 million
	Pentium M	2003/2004	Intel	1–2.26 GHz	77–140 million
	Mobile Celeron	1999/2003	Intel	266 MHz–2.8 GHz	18.9 million
	Mobile Pentium	1997/2002	Intel	200 MHz–3.46 GHz	55 million
	Turion 64	2005	AMD	1.6–2.4 GHz	114 million
	Mobile Sempron	2004	AMD	1.6–1.8 GHz	37.5 million
	Mobile Athlon	2001/2002	AMD	1.4–2.2 GHz	37.5–105.9 million
	Mobile Duron	2000/2001	AMD	1.3 GHz	25 million
	Efficeon	2003	Transmeta	1–1.7 GHz	79 million
	Crusoe	2000	Transmeta	500 MHz–1 GHz	6.7 million

* Clock speed is not the only factor that determines processor performance.

FIGURE 4-7 A comparison of some processors.

Buying a Personal Computer

If you are ready to buy a new computer, the processor you select should depend on how you plan to use the computer. If you purchase an IBM-compatible PC or Apple computer, you will choose an Intel processor or an Intel-compatible processor (Figure 4-8).

Most users will realize greater processing performance with a dual-core/multicore processor. Each processor on a dual-core/multicore chip generally runs at a slower clock speed than a single-core processor, but dual-core/multicore chips typically reduce the power consumption and heat output, while increasing overall performance. For example, a dual-core processor can deliver one and one-half times more processing speed than a single-core processor.

If you plan to purchase an entertainment desktop computer, you will want it to use Intel's *Viiv technology*, which is designed to enhance digital entertainment through a home computer.

Instead of buying an entirely new computer, you might be able to upgrade your processor to increase the computer's performance. Be certain the processor you buy is compatible with your computer's motherboard; otherwise, you will have to replace the motherboard, too. Replacing a processor is a fairly simple process, whereas replacing a motherboard is much more complicated.

For detailed computer purchasing guidelines, read the Buyer's Guide 2007 feature that follows Chapter 8. Read Ethics & Issues 4-2 for a related discussion.

WEB LINK 4-2

Dual-Core Processors

For more information, visit scsite.com/ dc2007/ch4/weblink and then click Dual-Core Processors.

GUIDELINES FOR SELECTING AN INTEL OR INTEL-COMPATIBLE PROCESSOR

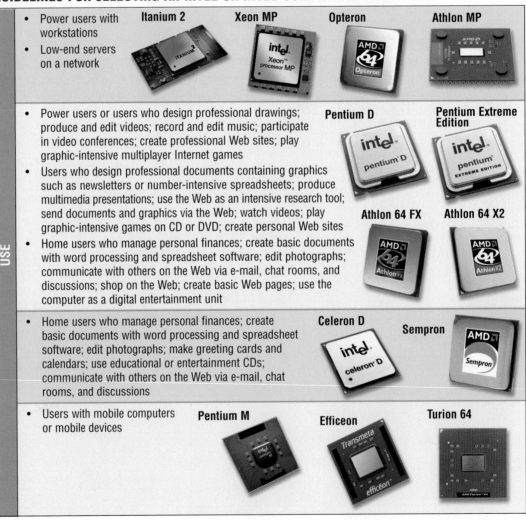

FIGURE 4-8 Determining which processor to obtain when you purchase a computer depends on computer usage.

FAQ 4-2

What is Moore's Law?

Moore's Law is a prediction made by one of the founders of Intel, Gordon Moore, that the number of transistors and resistors placed on computer chips would double every year, with a proportional increase in computing power and decrease in cost. The chart below shows the growth of Intel processors. For more information, read the Technology Trailblazer article on page 219 and visit scsite.com/dc2007/ch4/faq and then click Moore's Law.

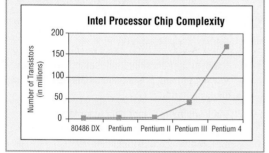

Intel Processor Chip Complexity

ETHICS & ISSUES 4-2

Discarded Computer Parts: Whose Problem Is It?

Experts estimate that about 1 billion computers will be discarded by 2010. The discarded items often are known as *e-waste*. As technology advances and prices fall, many people think of computers as disposable items. Computers contain several toxic elements, including lead, mercury, and barium. Computers thrown into landfills or burned in incinerators can pollute the ground and the air. A vast amount of e-waste ends up polluting third world countries. One solution is to recycle old computers. Some lawmakers prefer a more aggressive approach, such as setting up a recycling program that would be paid for by adding a $10 fee to a computer's purchase price, or forcing computer makers to be responsible for collecting and recycling their products. Manufacturers already have taken steps, but some claim that consumers should bear the responsibility of disposing of their old computer parts. Several have reduced the amount of toxic material in their products, and manufacturers have set up their own recycling programs, for which users pay a fee. One manufacturer admits, however, that only seven percent of the computers it has sold have been recycled. What can be done to ensure that computers are disposed of safely? Should government, manufacturers, or users be responsible for safe disposal? Why? How can computer users be motivated to recycle obsolete equipment?

Heat Sinks, Heat Pipes, and Liquid Cooling

Processor chips generate quite a bit of heat, which could cause the chip to burn up. Although the computer's main fan generates airflow, today's processors require additional cooling. A *heat sink* is a small ceramic or metal component with fins on its surface that absorbs and disperses heat produced by electrical components such as a processor (Figure 4-9). Some heat sinks are packaged as part of a processor chip. Others are installed on the top or the side of the chip. Because a heat sink consumes extra space, a smaller device called a *heat pipe* cools processors in notebook computers.

Some computers use liquid cooling technology to reduce the temperature of a processor. *Liquid cooling technology* uses a continuous flow of fluid(s), such as water and glycol, in a process that transfers the heated fluid away from the processor to a radiator-type grill, which cools the liquid, and then returns the cooled fluid to the processor.

heat sink fan

heat sink

FIGURE 4-9 A heat sink, which is attached to the top of a processor, prevents the chip from overheating. The heat sink fan, which attaches to the top of the heat sink, helps distribute air dissipated by the heat sink.

Parallel Processing

Parallel processing is a method that uses multiple processors simultaneously to execute a single program or task (Figure 4-10). Parallel processing divides a single problem into portions so that multiple processors work on their assigned portion of the problem at the same time. Parallel processing requires special software that recognizes how to divide the problem and then bring the results back together again.

Some personal computers implement parallel processing with dual-core processors or multi-core processors. Others have two or more separate processor chips, respectively called dual processor or multiprocessor computers.

Supercomputers use parallel processing for applications such as weather forecasting. Some applications draw on the idle time of home users' personal computers to achieve parallel processing.

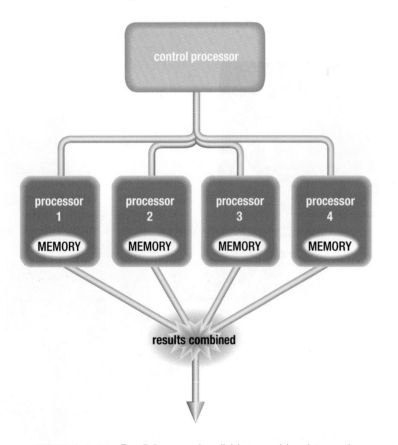

FIGURE 4-10 Parallel processing divides a problem into portions so that multiple processors work on their assigned portion of a problem at the same time. In this illustration, one processor, called the control processor, is managing the operations of four other processors.

Test your knowledge of pages 184 through 194 in Quiz Yourself 4-1.

QUIZ YOURSELF 4-1

Instructions: Find the true statement below. Then, rewrite the remaining false statements so they are true.

1. A computer chip is a small piece of semiconducting material, usually silicon, on which integrated circuits are etched.

2. Four basic operations in a machine cycle are: (1) comparing, (2) decoding, (3) executing, and, if necessary, (4) pipelining.

3. Processors contain a motherboard and an arithmetic logic unit (ALU).

4. The central processing unit, sometimes called a system board, is the main circuit board of the system unit.

5. The leading processor chip manufacturers for personal computers are Microsoft, AMD, IBM, Motorola, and Transmeta.

6. The pace of the system clock, called the clock speed, is measured by the number of ticks per minute.

7. The system unit is a case that contains mechanical components of the computer used to process data.

Quiz Yourself Online: To further check your knowledge of system unit styles, motherboards, processor components and machine cycles, and characteristics of personal computer processors, visit scsite.com/dc2007/ch4/quiz and then click Objectives 1 – 4.

DATA REPRESENTATION

To understand fully the way a computer processes data, you should know how a computer represents data. People communicate through speech by combining words into sentences. Human speech is **analog** because it uses continuous (wave form) signals that vary in strength and quality. Most computers are **digital**. They recognize only two discrete states: on and off. This is because computers are electronic devices powered by electricity, which also has only two states: on and off.

The two digits, 0 and 1, easily can represent these two states (Figure 4-11). The digit 0 represents the electronic state of off (absence of an electronic charge). The digit 1 represents the electronic state of on (presence of an electronic charge).

When people count, they use the digits in the decimal system (0 through 9). The computer, by contrast, uses a binary system because it recognizes only two states. The **binary system** is a number system that has just two unique digits, 0 and 1, called bits. A **bit** (short for *binary digit*) is the smallest unit of data the computer can process. By itself, a bit is not very informative.

When 8 bits are grouped together as a unit, they form a **byte**. A byte provides enough different combinations of 0s and 1s to represent 256 individual characters. These characters include numbers, uppercase and lowercase letters of the alphabet, punctuation marks, and others, such as the letters of the Greek alphabet.

The combinations of 0s and 1s that represent characters are defined by patterns called a coding scheme. In one coding scheme, the number 4 is represented as 00110100, the number 6 as 00110110, and the capital letter E as 01000101 (Figure 4-12). Two popular coding schemes are ASCII and EBCDIC (Figure 4-13). The *American Standard Code for Information Interchange* (*ASCII* pronounced ASK-ee) scheme is the most widely used coding system to represent data. Most personal computers and servers use the ASCII coding scheme. The *Extended Binary Coded Decimal Interchange Code* (*EBCDIC* pronounced EB-see-dik) scheme is used primarily on mainframe computers and high-end servers.

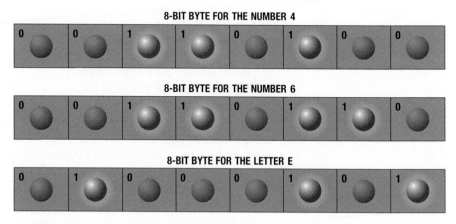

FIGURE 4-12 Eight bits grouped together as a unit are called a byte. A byte represents a single character in the computer.

The ASCII and EBCDIC coding schemes are sufficient for English and Western European languages but are not large enough for Asian and other languages that use different alphabets. *Unicode* is a 16-bit coding scheme that has the capacity of representing more than 65,000 characters and symbols. The Unicode coding scheme is capable of representing almost all the world's current written languages, as well as classic and historical languages. To allow for expansion, Unicode reserves 30,000 codes for future use and 6,000 codes for private use. Unicode is implemented in several operating systems, including Windows XP, Mac OS X, and Linux.

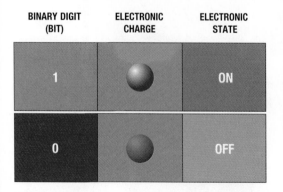

FIGURE 4-11 A computer circuit represents the 0 or the 1 electronically by the presence or absence of an electronic charge.

ASCII	SYMBOL	EBCDIC
00110000	0	11110000
00110001	1	11110001
00110010	2	11110010
00110011	3	11110011
00110100	4	11110100
00110101	5	11110101
00110110	6	11110110
00110111	7	11110111
00111000	8	11111000
00111001	9	11111001
01000001	A	11000001
01000010	B	11000010
01000011	C	11000011
01000100	D	11000100
01000101	E	11000101
01000110	F	11000110
01000111	G	11000111
01001000	H	11001000
01001001	I	11001001
01001010	J	11010001
01001011	K	11010010
01001100	L	11010011
01001101	M	11010100

ASCII	SYMBOL	EBCDIC
01001110	N	11010101
01001111	O	11010110
01010000	P	11010111
01010001	Q	11011000
01010010	R	11011001
01010011	S	11100010
01010100	T	11100011
01010101	U	11100100
01010110	V	11100101
01010111	W	11100110
01011000	X	11100111
01011001	Y	11101000
01011010	Z	11101001
00100001	!	01011010
00100010	"	01111111
00100011	#	01111011
00100100	$	01011011
00100101	%	01101100
00100110	&	01010000
00101000	(	01001101
00101001	)	01011101
00101010	*	01011100
00101011	+	01001110

FIGURE 4-13 Two popular coding schemes are ASCII and EBCDIC.

Unicode-enabled programming languages and software products include Java, XML, Microsoft Office, and Oracle.

Appendix A at the back of this book discusses the ASCII, EBCDIC, and Unicode schemes in more depth, along with the parity bit and number systems.

Coding schemes such as ASCII make it possible for humans to interact with a digital computer that processes only bits. When you press a key on a keyboard, a chip in the keyboard converts the key's electronic signal into a special code that is sent to the system unit. Then, the system unit converts the code into a binary form the computer can process and stores it in memory. Every character is converted to its corresponding byte. The computer then processes the data as bytes, which actually is a series of on/off electrical states. When processing is finished, software converts the byte into a human-recognizable number, letter of the alphabet, or special character that is displayed on a screen or is printed (Figure 4-14). All of these conversions take place so quickly that you do not realize they are occurring.

Standards, such as those defined by ASCII, EBCDIC, and Unicode, also make it possible for components in computers to communicate with each other successfully. By following these and other standards, manufacturers can produce a component and be assured that it will operate correctly in a computer.

FIGURE 4-14 HOW A LETTER IS CONVERTED TO BINARY FORM AND BACK

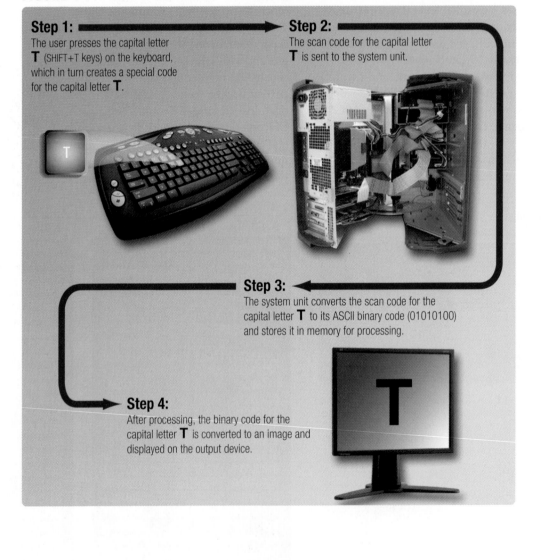

Step 1:
The user presses the capital letter **T** (SHIFT+T keys) on the keyboard, which in turn creates a special code for the capital letter **T**.

Step 2:
The scan code for the capital letter **T** is sent to the system unit.

Step 3:
The system unit converts the scan code for the capital letter **T** to its ASCII binary code (01010100) and stores it in memory for processing.

Step 4:
After processing, the binary code for the capital letter **T** is converted to an image and displayed on the output device.

MEMORY

Memory consists of electronic components that store instructions waiting to be executed by the processor, data needed by those instructions, and the results of processed data (information). Memory usually consists of one or more chips on the motherboard or some other circuit board in the computer.

Memory stores three basic categories of items: (1) the operating system and other system software that control or maintain the computer and its devices; (2) application programs that carry out a specific task such as word processing; and (3) the data being processed by the application programs and resulting information. This role of memory to store both data and programs is known as the *stored program concept*.

Bytes and Addressable Memory

A byte (character) is the basic storage unit in memory. When application program instructions and data are transferred to memory from storage devices, the instructions and data exist as bytes. Each byte resides temporarily in a location in memory that has an *address*. An address simply is a unique number that identifies the location of a byte in memory. The illustration in Figure 4-15 shows how seats in a concert hall are similar to addresses in memory: (1) a seat, which is identified by a unique seat number, holds one person at a time, and a

location in memory, which is identified by a unique address, holds a single byte; and (2) both a seat, identified by a seat number, and a byte, identified by an address, can be empty. To access data or instructions in memory, the computer references the addresses that contain bytes of data.

Memory Sizes

Manufacturers state the size of memory chips and storage devices in terms of the number of bytes the chip or device has available for storage (Figure 4-16). Recall that storage devices hold data, instructions, and information for future use, while most memory holds these items temporarily. A **kilobyte** (**KB** or **K**) is equal to exactly 1,024 bytes. To simplify memory and storage definitions, computer users often round a kilobyte down to 1,000 bytes. For example, if a memory chip can store 100 KB, it can hold approximately 100,000 bytes (characters). A **megabyte** (**MB**) is equal to approximately 1 million bytes. A **gigabyte** (**GB**) equals approximately 1 billion bytes. A **terabyte** (**TB**) is equal to approximately 1 trillion bytes.

MEMORY AND STORAGE SIZES

Term	Abbreviation	Approximate Number of Bytes	Exact Amount of Bytes	Approximate Number of Pages of Text
Kilobyte	KB or K	1 thousand	1,024	1/2
Megabyte	MB	1 million	1,048,576	500
Gigabyte	GB	1 billion	1,073,741,824	500,000
Terabyte	TB	1 trillion	1,099,511,627,776	500,000,000

FIGURE 4-16 Terms commonly used to define memory and storage sizes.

Types of Memory

The system unit contains two types of memory: volatile and nonvolatile. When the computer's power is turned off, *volatile memory* loses its contents. *Nonvolatile memory*, by contrast, does not lose its contents when power is removed from the computer. Thus, volatile memory is temporary and nonvolatile memory is permanent. RAM is the most common type of volatile memory. Examples of nonvolatile memory include ROM, flash memory, and CMOS. The following pages discuss these types of memory.

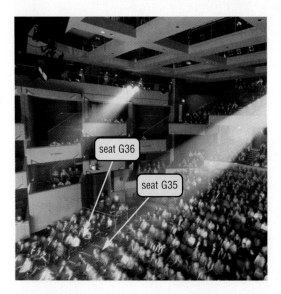

seat G36

seat G35

FIGURE 4-15 Seats in a concert hall are similar to addresses in memory: a seat holds one person at a time, and a location in memory holds a single byte; and both a seat and a byte can be empty.

RAM

Users typically are referring to RAM when discussing computer memory. **RAM** (*random access memory*), also called *main memory*, consists of memory chips that can be read from and written to by the processor and other devices. When you turn on power to a computer, certain operating system files (such as the files that determine how the Windows XP desktop appears) load into RAM from a storage device such as a hard disk. These files remain in RAM as long as the computer has continuous power. As additional programs and data are requested, they also load into RAM from storage.

The processor interprets and executes a program's instructions while the program is in RAM. During this time, the contents of RAM may change (Figure 4-17). RAM can accommodate multiple programs simultaneously.

Most RAM is volatile, which means it loses its contents when the power is removed from the computer. For this reason, you must save any data, instructions, and information you

FIGURE 4-17   HOW PROGRAM INSTRUCTIONS TRANSFER IN AND OUT OF RAM

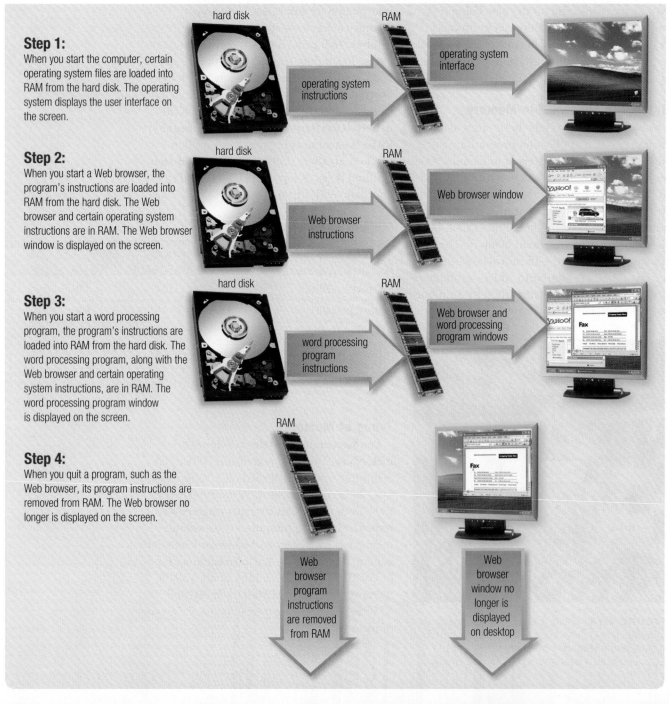

Step 1:
When you start the computer, certain operating system files are loaded into RAM from the hard disk. The operating system displays the user interface on the screen.

Step 2:
When you start a Web browser, the program's instructions are loaded into RAM from the hard disk. The Web browser and certain operating system instructions are in RAM. The Web browser window is displayed on the screen.

Step 3:
When you start a word processing program, the program's instructions are loaded into RAM from the hard disk. The word processing program, along with the Web browser and certain operating system instructions, are in RAM. The word processing program window is displayed on the screen.

Step 4:
When you quit a program, such as the Web browser, its program instructions are removed from RAM. The Web browser no longer is displayed on the screen.

may need in the future. Saving is the process of copying data, instructions, and information from RAM to a storage device such as a hard disk.

Three basic types of RAM chips exist: dynamic RAM, static RAM, and magnetoresistive RAM.

• *Dynamic RAM* (*DRAM* pronounced DEE-ram) chips must be re-energized constantly or they lose their contents. Many variations of DRAM chips exist, most of which are faster than the basic DRAM. *Synchronous DRAM* (*SDRAM*) chips are much faster than DRAM chips because they are synchronized to the system clock. *Double Data Rate SDRAM* (*DDR SDRAM*) chips are even faster than SDRAM chips because they transfer data twice for each clock cycle, instead of just once, and DDR 2 is even faster than DDR. Dual channel SDRAM is faster than single channel SDRAM because it delivers twice the amount of data to the processor. *Rambus DRAM* (*RDRAM*) is yet another type of DRAM that is much faster than SDRAM because it uses pipelining techniques. Most personal computers today use some form of SDRAM chips or RDRAM chips.

• *Static RAM* (*SRAM* pronounced ESS-ram) chips are faster and more reliable than any variation of DRAM chips. These chips do not have to be re-energized as often as DRAM chips, thus, the term static. SRAM chips, however, are much more expensive than DRAM chips. Special applications such as cache use SRAM chips. A later section in this chapter discusses cache.

• A newer type of RAM, called *magnetoresistive RAM* (*MRAM* pronounced EM-ram), stores data using magnetic charges instead of electrical charges. Manufacturers claim that MRAM has greater storage capacity, consumes less power, and has faster access times than electronic RAM. Also, MRAM retains its contents after power is removed from the computer, which could prevent loss of data for users. As the cost of MRAM declines, experts predict MRAM could replace both DRAM and SRAM.

RAM chips usually reside on a **memory module**, which is a small circuit board. **Memory slots** on the motherboard hold memory modules (Figure 4-18). Three types of memory modules are SIMMs, DIMMs, and RIMMs. A *SIMM* (*single inline memory module*) has pins on opposite sides of the circuit board that connect together to form a single set of contacts. With a *DIMM* (*dual inline memory module*), by contrast, the pins on opposite sides of the circuit board do not connect and thus form two sets of contacts. SIMMs and DIMMs typically hold SDRAM chips. A *RIMM* (*Rambus inline memory module*) houses RDRAM chips. For a more technical discussion about RAM, read the High-Tech Talk article on page 218 at the end of this chapter.

WEB LINK 4-3

RAM

For more information, visit scsite.com/ dc2007/ch4/weblink and then click RAM.

dual inline memory module

memory chip

memory slot

FIGURE 4-18 This photo shows a memory module being inserted in a motherboard.

RAM CONFIGURATIONS The amount of RAM necessary in a computer often depends on the types of software you plan to use. A computer executes programs that are in RAM. Think of RAM as the workspace on the top of your desk. Just as the top of your desk needs a certain amount of space to hold papers, a computer needs a certain amount of memory to store programs, data, and information. The more RAM a computer has, the faster the computer will respond.

A software package typically indicates the minimum amount of RAM it requires. If you want the application to perform optimally, usually you need more than the minimum specifications on the software package. Some programs, such as operating systems, also have specified maximums.

Generally, home users running Windows XP and using basic application software such as word processing should have at least 256 MB of RAM. Most business users who work with accounting, financial, or spreadsheet programs, voice recognition, and programs requiring multimedia capabilities should have a minimum of 512 MB of RAM. Users creating professional Web sites or using graphics-intensive applications will want at least 2 GB of RAM.

Figure 4-19a lists guidelines for the amount of RAM for various types of users. Figure 4-19b shows advertisements that match to each user requirement. Advertisements normally list the type of processor, the clock speed of the processor, and the amount of RAM in the computer. The amount of RAM in computers purchased today ranges from 256 MB to 16 GB. In an advertisement, manufacturers specify the maximum amount of RAM a computer can hold, for example, 512 GB expandable to 2 GB. Read Ethics & Issues 4-3 for a related discussion.

FAQ 4-3

Can I add more RAM to my computer?

Check your computer documentation to see how much RAM you can add. RAM modules are relatively inexpensive and usually include easy-to-follow installation instructions. Be sure to purchase RAM compatible with your brand and model of computer. For more information, visit scsite.com/dc2007/ch4/faq and then click Upgrading RAM.

ETHICS & ISSUES 4-3

How Much Should You Pay for a Computer?

Today, you can buy a personal computer for less than $500 that can do more than one sold at nearly twice its cost three years ago. Some manufacturers even are offering basic computers for less than $300. Part of the plunge in prices is lower-cost components, but another factor is a growing demand for cheaper machines. Many of the new buyers are from families earning less than $40,000, far below the $50,000 average that once characterized typical computer buyers. These consumers are looking for inexpensive computers that are adequate for the most popular tasks. Spending more money on a computer means faster processors, more memory, 3-D graphics cards, higher-quality sound cards, more hard disk space, and other extras that some consider to be unnecessary, frivolous expenses. As one industry analyst asks, "Why buy a Porsche when you are going to drive only 55 miles per hour?" But others point out that perhaps you should spend more money and buy for the future in anticipation of more robust software and peripherals that can take advantage of more computing power. How might a greater availability of lower costing personal computers change the way people, schools, and businesses buy and use them? With respect to computers, does a higher price always mean greater usefulness? Why or why not? Who might be satisfied with less than the latest and greatest computer technology? Why?

FIGURE 4-19a (RAM guidelines)

RAM	256 MB to 1 GB	512 MB to 2 GB	2 GB and up
Use	Home and business users managing personal finances; using standard application software such as word processing; using educational or entertainment CD-ROMs; communicating with others on the Web	Users requiring more advanced multimedia capabilities; running number-intensive accounting, financial, or spreadsheet programs; using voice recognition; working with videos, music, and digital imaging; creating Web sites; participating in video conferences; playing Internet games	Power users creating professional Web sites; running sophisticated CAD, 3-D design, or other graphics-intensive software

FIGURE 4-19b (computers for sale)

Model	A200	P320	A280	P320	X225	A240
Processor	2.00 GHz Sempron processor	3.20 GHz Celeron D processor	2.80 GHz Athlon 64 X2 processor	3.2 GHz Pentium D processor	2.25 GHz Athlon MP processor	2.40 GHz Opteron processor
Memory	256 MB SDRAM	512 MB SDRAM	512 MB SDRAM	1 GB SDRAM	2 GB RDRAM	4 GB SDRAM

FIGURE 4-19   Determining how much RAM you need depends on the applications you intend to run on your computer. Advertisements for computers normally list the type of processor, the speed of the processor, and the amount of RAM installed.

Cache

Most of today's computers improve processing times with **cache** (pronounced cash). Two types of cache are memory cache and disk cache. This chapter discusses memory cache. Chapter 7 discusses disk cache.

Memory cache helps speed the processes of the computer because it stores frequently used instructions and data. Most personal computers today have two types of memory cache: L1 cache and L2 cache. Some also have L3 cache.

- *L1 cache* is built directly in the processor chip. L1 cache usually has a very small capacity, ranging from 8 KB to 128 KB. The more common sizes for personal computers are 32 KB or 64 KB.
- *L2 cache* is slightly slower than L1 cache but has a much larger capacity, ranging from 64 KB to 16 MB. When discussing cache, most users are referring to L2 cache. Current processors include *advanced transfer cache* (*ATC*), a type of L2 cache built directly on the processor chip. Processors that use ATC perform at much faster rates than those that do not use it.

Personal computers today typically have from 512 KB to 2 MB of advanced transfer cache. Servers and workstations have from 2 MB to 6 MB of advanced transfer cache.

- *L3 cache* is a cache on the motherboard that is separate from the processor chip. L3 cache exists only on computers that use L2 advanced transfer cache. Personal computers often have up to 2 MB of L3 cache; servers and workstations have from 2 MB to 9 MB of L3 cache.

Cache speeds up processing time because it stores frequently used instructions and data. When the processor needs an instruction or data, it searches memory in this order: L1 cache, then L2 cache, then L3 cache (if it exists), then RAM — with a greater delay in processing for each level of memory it must search (Figure 4-20). If the instruction or data is not found in memory, then it must search a slower speed storage medium such as a hard disk, CD, or DVD.

ROM

Read-only memory (**ROM** pronounced rahm) refers to memory chips storing permanent data and instructions. The data on most ROM chips cannot be modified — hence, the name read-only. ROM is nonvolatile, which means its contents are not lost when power is removed from the computer. In addition to computers, many devices contain ROM chips. For example, ROM chips in printers contain data for fonts.

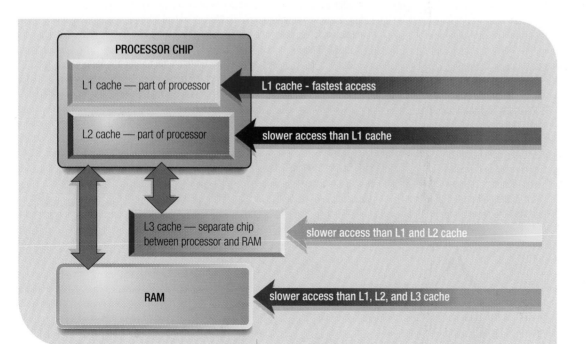

FIGURE 4-20 Cache helps speed processing times when the processor requests data, instructions, or information.

Manufacturers of ROM chips often record data, instructions, or information on the chips when they manufacture the chips. These ROM chips, called **firmware**, contain permanently written data, instructions, or information.

A *PROM* (*programmable read-only memory*) *chip* is a blank ROM chip on which a programmer can write permanently. Programmers use *microcode* instructions to program a PROM chip. Once a programmer writes the microcode on the PROM chip, it functions like a regular ROM chip and cannot be erased or changed.

A variation of the PROM chip, called an *EEPROM* (*electrically erasable programmable read-only memory*) *chip*, allows a programmer to erase the microcode with an electric signal.

Flash Memory

Flash memory is a type of nonvolatile memory that can be erased electronically and rewritten, similar to EEPROM. Most computers use flash memory to hold their startup instructions because it allows the computer easily to update its contents. For example, when the computer changes from standard time to daylight savings time, the contents of a flash memory chip (and the real-time clock chip) change to reflect the new time.

Flash memory chips also store data and programs on many mobile computers and devices, such as PDAs, smart phones, printers, digital cameras, automotive devices, audio players, digital voice recorders, and pagers. When you enter names and addresses in a PDA or smart phone, a flash memory chip stores the data. Some MP3 players store music on flash memory chips (Figure 4-21); others store music on tiny hard disks or flash memory cards. A later section in this chapter discusses flash memory cards, which contain flash memory on a removable device instead of a chip.

FAQ 4-4

How much music can I store on an MP3 player?

MP3 players that store music on flash memory chips can hold up to 700 songs. MP3 players with tiny hard disks have a much greater storage capacity — from 1,000 to 15,000 songs. For more information, visit scsite.com/dc2007/ch4/faq and then click MP3 Players.

FIGURE 4-21   HOW AN MP3 MUSIC PLAYER MIGHT STORE MUSIC IN FLASH MEMORY

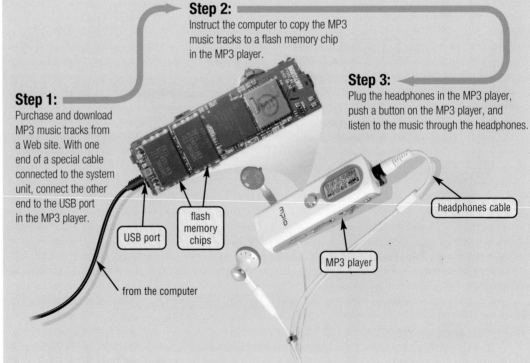

Step 1:
Purchase and download MP3 music tracks from a Web site. With one end of a special cable connected to the system unit, connect the other end to the USB port in the MP3 player.

Step 2:
Instruct the computer to copy the MP3 music tracks to a flash memory chip in the MP3 player.

Step 3:
Plug the headphones in the MP3 player, push a button on the MP3 player, and listen to the music through the headphones.

USB port

flash memory chips

from the computer

headphones cable

MP3 player

CMOS

Some RAM chips, flash memory chips, and other types of memory chips use **complementary metal-oxide semiconductor** (**CMOS** pronounced SEE-moss) technology because it provides high speeds and consumes little power. CMOS technology uses battery power to retain information even when the power to the computer is off. Battery-backed CMOS memory chips, for example, can keep the calendar, date, and time current even when the computer is off. The flash memory chips that store a computer's startup information often use CMOS technology.

FAQ 4-5

What should I do if my computer's date and time are wrong?

First, try resetting the date and time. To do this in Windows XP, double-click the time at the right edge of the taskbar. If the computer continues to lose time or display an incorrect date, you may need to replace the CMOS battery on the motherboard that powers the system clock. For more information, visit scsite.com/dc2007/ch4/faq and then click CMOS Battery.

Memory Access Times

Access time is the amount of time it takes the processor to read data, instructions, and information from memory. A computer's access time directly affects how fast the computer processes data. Accessing data in memory can be more than 200,000 times faster than accessing data on a hard disk because of the mechanical motion of the hard disk.

Today's manufacturers use a variety of terminology to state access times (Figure 4-22). Some use fractions of a second, which for memory occurs in nanoseconds. A **nanosecond** (abbreviated *ns*) is one billionth of a second. A nanosecond is extremely fast (Figure 4-23). In fact, electricity travels about one foot in a nanosecond.

Other manufacturers state access times in MHz; for example, 533 MHz DDR SDRAM. If a manufacturer states access time in megahertz, you can convert it to nanoseconds by dividing 1 billion ns by the megahertz number. For example, 533 MHz equals approximately 1.9 ns (1,000,000,000/533,000,000).

The access time (speed) of memory contributes to the overall performance of the computer. Standard SDRAM chips can have access times up to 133 MHz (about 7.5 ns), and access times of the DDR SDRAM chips reach 677 MHz (about 1.5 ns). The higher the megahertz, the faster the access time; conversely, the lower the nanoseconds, the faster the access time. The faster RDRAM chips can have access times up to 1600 MHz (about 0.625 ns). ROM access times range from 25 to 250 ns.

While access times of memory greatly affect overall computer performance, manufacturers and retailers usually list a computer's memory in terms of its size, not its access time. Thus, an advertisement might describe a computer as having 512 MB of SDRAM upgradeable to 4 GB.

ACCESS TIME TERMINOLOGY

Term	Abbreviation	Speed
Millisecond	ms	One-thousandth of a second
Microsecond	µs	One-millionth of a second
Nanosecond	ns	One-billionth of a second
Picosecond	ps	One-trillionth of a second

FIGURE 4-22 Access times are measured in fractions of a second. This table lists the terms used to define access times.

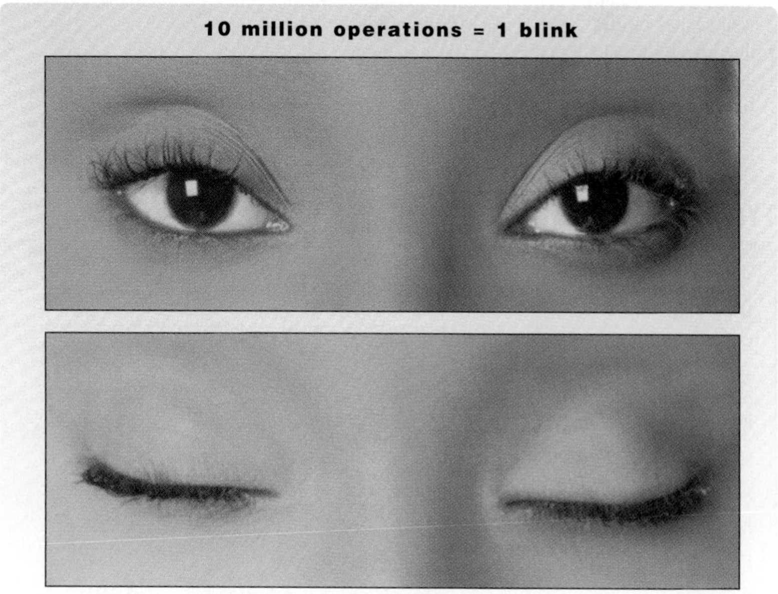

10 million operations = 1 blink

FIGURE 4-23 It takes about one-tenth of a second to blink your eye, which is the equivalent of 100 million nanoseconds. In the time it takes to blink your eye, a computer can perform some operations 10 million times.

Test your knowledge of pages 194 through 203 in Quiz Yourself 4-2.

QUIZ YOURSELF 4-2

Instructions: Find the true statement below. Then, rewrite the remaining false statements so they are true.

1. A computer's memory access time directly affects how fast the computer processes data.
2. A gigabyte (GB) equals approximately 1 trillion bytes.
3. Memory cache helps speed the processes of the computer because it stores seldom used instructions and data.
4. Most computers are analog, which means they recognize only two discrete states: on and off.
5. Most RAM retains its contents when the power is removed from the computer.
6. Read-only memory (ROM) refers to memory chips storing temporary data and instructions.

Quiz Yourself Online: To further check your knowledge of bits, bytes, data representation, and types of memory, visit scsite.com/dc2007/ch4/quiz and then click Objectives 5 – 7.

EXPANSION SLOTS AND ADAPTER CARDS

An **expansion slot** is a socket on the motherboard that can hold an adapter card. An **adapter card**, sometimes called an *expansion card*, is a circuit board that enhances functions of a component of the system unit and/or provides connections to peripherals. A **peripheral** is a device that connects to the system unit and is controlled by the processor in the computer. Examples of peripherals are modems, disk drives, printers, scanners, and keyboards.

Figure 4-24 lists currently used types of adapter cards. Sometimes, all functionality is built in the adapter card. With others, a cable connects the adapter card to a device, such as a digital video camera, outside the system unit. Figure 4-25 shows an adapter card being inserted in an expansion slot on a personal computer motherboard.

Some motherboards include all necessary capabilities and do not require adapter cards. Other motherboards may require adapter cards to provide capabilities such as sound and video. A **sound card** enhances the sound-generating capabilities of a personal computer by allowing sound to be input through a microphone and output through external speakers or headphones. A **video card**, also called a *graphics card*, converts computer output into a video signal that travels through a cable to the monitor, which displays an image on the screen.

TYPES OF ADAPTER CARDS

Adapter Card	Purpose
Disk controller	Connects disk drives
FireWire	Connects to FireWire devices
Graphics accelerator	Increases the speed at which graphics are displayed
MIDI	Connects musical instruments
Modem	Connects other computers through telephone or cable television lines
Network	Connects other computers and peripherals
PC-to-TV converter	Connects a television
Sound	Connects speakers or a microphone
TV tuner	Allows viewing of television channels on the monitor
USB 2.0	Connects to USB 2.0 devices
Video	Connects a monitor
Video capture	Connects a camcorder

FIGURE 4-24 Currently used adapter cards and their functions.

FIGURE 4-25 An adapter card being inserted in an expansion slot on the motherboard of a personal computer.

In the past, installing a card was not easy and required you to set switches and other elements on the motherboard. Many of today's computers support **Plug and Play**, which means the computer automatically can configure adapter cards and other peripherals as you install them. Having Plug and Play support means you can plug in a device, turn on the computer, and then immediately begin using the device.

PC Cards, Flash Memory Cards, and USB Flash Drives

Notebook and other mobile computers have at least one **PC Card slot**, which is a special type of expansion slot that holds a PC Card. A **PC Card** is a thin, credit card-sized device that adds memory, storage, sound, fax/modem, network, and other capabilities to mobile computers (Figure 4-26). Because of their small size and versatility, some consumer electronics products such as digital cameras use PC Cards.

All PC Cards conform to standards developed by the *Personal Computer Memory Card International Association* (these cards originally were called *PCMCIA cards*). These standards help to ensure the interchangeability of PC Cards among mobile computers. Although some PC cards contain tiny hard disks, many PC Cards are a type of flash memory card.

A **flash memory card** is a removable flash memory device that allows users to transfer data and information conveniently from mobile devices to their desktop computers (Figure 4-27). Many mobile and consumer devices, such as PDAs, smart phones, digital cameras, and digital audio players, use these memory cards. Some printers and computers have built-in card readers/writers or slots that read flash memory cards. In addition, you can purchase an external card reader/writer that attaches to any computer. Flash memory cards are available in a variety of shapes and sizes. The type of flash memory card you have will determine the type of card reader/writer you need. Storage capacities of flash memory cards range from 64 MB to 5 GB.

Another widely used type of removable flash memory is the USB flash drive (Figure 4-27). A *USB flash drive* is a flash memory storage

device that plugs in a USB port on a computer or portable device. (The next section discusses USB ports.) Storage capacities of USB flash drives range from 64 MB to 5 GB.

Unlike adapter cards that require you to open the system unit and install the card on the motherboard, you can change a removable flash memory device without having to open the system unit or restart the computer. This feature, called *hot plugging*, allows you to insert and remove the removable flash memory and other devices while the computer is running.

WEB LINK 4-7

Removable Flash Memory Devices

For more information, visit scsite.com/dc2007/ch4/weblink and then click Removable Flash Memory Devices.

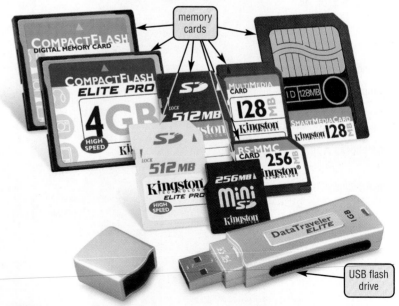

FIGURE 4-26   A PC card slides in a PC Card slot on a notebook computer.

FIGURE 4-27   Removable flash memory devices are available in a range of sizes.

PORTS AND CONNECTORS

A **port** is the point at which a peripheral attaches to or communicates with a system unit so the peripheral can send data to or receive information from the computer. An external device, such as a keyboard, monitor, printer, mouse, and microphone, often attaches by a cable to a port on the system unit. Instead of port, the term **jack** sometimes is used to identify audio and video ports. The back of the system unit contains many ports; newer personal computers also have ports on the front of the system unit (Figure 4-28).

Ports have different types of connectors. A **connector** joins a cable to a peripheral. One end of a cable attaches to the connector on the system unit, and the other end of the cable attaches to a connector on the peripheral. Most connectors are available in one of two genders: male or female. *Male connectors* have one or more exposed pins, like the end of an electrical cord you plug in the wall. *Female connectors* have matching holes to accept the pins on a male connector, like an electrical wall outlet.

Sometimes, attaching a new peripheral to the computer is not possible because the connector on the system unit is the same gender as the connector on the cable. In this case, purchasing a gender changer solves this problem. A *gender changer* is a device that enables you to join two connectors that are both female or both male.

Manufacturers often identify the cables by their connector types to assist you with purchasing a cable to connect a computer to a peripheral. Figure 4-29 shows the different types of connectors on a system unit. Some system units include these connectors when you buy the computer. You add other connectors by inserting adapter cards on the motherboard. Certain adapter cards have ports that allow you to attach a peripheral to the adapter card.

Desktop personal computers may have a serial port, a parallel port, several USB ports, and a FireWire port. The next section discusses these and other ports.

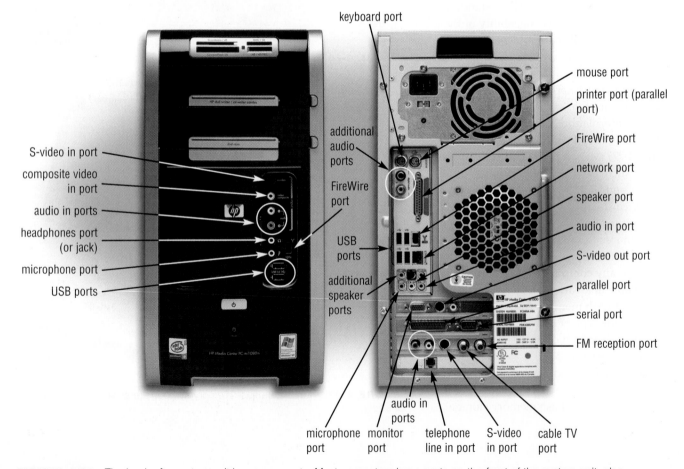

FIGURE 4-28　The back of a system unit has many ports. Most computers have ports on the front of the system unit, also.

CONNECTOR TYPES

Connector Type	Picture	Connector Type	Picture
Audio in		Mouse	
Cable TV		Network	
Composite video in		Printer	
FireWire		Serial	
FM reception		Speaker	
Headphones		S-video in	
Keyboard		S-video out	
Microphone		Telephone line in	
Monitor		USB	

FIGURE 4-29 Examples of different types of connectors on a system unit.

Serial Ports

A **serial port** is a type of interface that connects a device to the system unit by transmitting data one bit at a time (Figure 4-30). Serial ports usually connect devices that do not require fast data transmission rates, such as a mouse, keyboard, or modem. The *COM port* (short for communications port) on the system unit is one type of serial port.

Some modems that connect the system unit to a telephone line use a serial port because the telephone line expects the data in a specific frequency. Serial ports conform to either the RS-232 or RS-422 standard, which specifies the number of pins used on the port's connector.

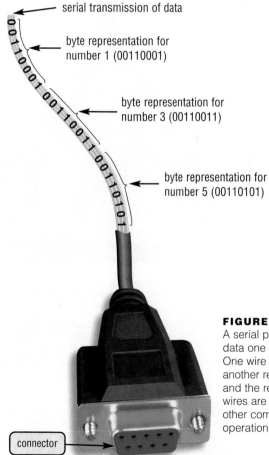

serial transmission of data

byte representation for number 1 (00110001)

byte representation for number 3 (00110011)

byte representation for number 5 (00110101)

connector

port

FIGURE 4-30
A serial port transmits data one bit at a time. One wire sends data, another receives data, and the remaining wires are used for other communications operations.

Parallel Ports

Unlike a serial port, a **parallel port** is an interface that connects devices by transferring more than one bit at a time (Figure 4-31). Originally, parallel ports were developed as an alternative to the slower speed serial ports.

Some printers can connect to the system unit using a parallel port. This parallel port can transfer eight bits of data (one byte) simultaneously through eight separate lines in a single cable.

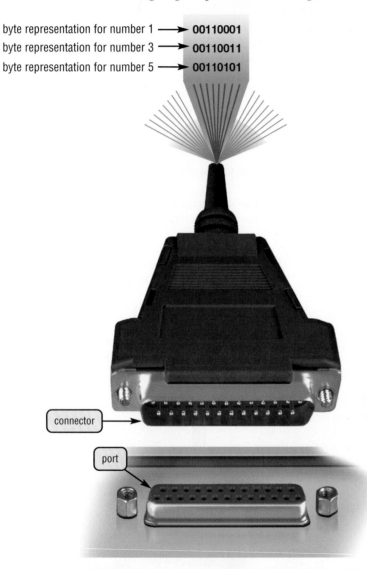

byte representation for number 1 ——▶ 00110001
byte representation for number 3 ——▶ 00110011
byte representation for number 5 ——▶ 00110101

connector

port

FIGURE 4-31 A parallel port is capable of transmitting more than one bit at a time. The port shown in this figure has eight wires that transmit data; the remaining wires are used for other communications operations.

USB Ports

A **USB port**, short for *universal serial bus port*, can connect up to 127 different peripherals together with a single connector. Devices that connect to a USB port include the following: mouse, printer, digital camera, scanner, speakers, MP3 music player, CD, DVD, and removable hard disk. Personal computers typically have six to eight USB ports either on the front or back of the system unit (Figure 4-28 on page 206). The latest version of USB, called *USB 2.0*, is a more advanced and faster USB, with speeds 40 times higher than that of its predecessor.

To attach multiple peripherals using a single USB port, you can daisy chain the devices together outside the system unit. *Daisy chain* means the first USB device connects to the USB port on the computer, the second USB device connects to the first USB device, the third USB device connects to the second USB device, and so on. An alternative to daisy chaining is to use a USB hub. A **USB hub** is a device that plugs in a USB port on the system unit and contains multiple USB ports in which you plug cables from USB devices.

USB also supports hot plugging and Plug and Play, which means you can attach peripherals while the computer is running. With serial and parallel port connections, by contrast, you often must restart the computer after attaching the peripheral.

Some newer peripherals may attach only to a USB port. Others attach to either a serial or parallel port, as well as a USB port.

FAQ 4-6

Can older USB devices plug in a USB 2.0 port?

Yes. USB 2.0 is *backward compatible*, which means that it supports older USB devices as well as new USB 2.0 devices. Keep in mind, though, that older USB devices do not run any faster in a USB 2.0 port. For more information, visit scsite.com/dc2007/ch4/faq and then click USB 2.0.

FireWire Ports

Previously called an *IEEE 1394 port*, a **FireWire port** is similar to a USB port in that it can connect multiple types of devices that require faster data transmission speeds, such as digital video cameras, digital VCRs, color printers, scanners, digital cameras, and DVD drives, to a single connector. A FireWire port allows you to connect up to 63 devices together. You can use a FireWire hub to attach multiple devices to a single FireWire port. A **FireWire hub** is a device that plugs in a FireWire port on the system unit and contains multiple FireWire ports in which you plug cables from FireWire devices. The FireWire port supports Plug and Play.

Some newer peripherals may attach only to a FireWire port. Having standard ports and connectors, such as FireWire and USB, greatly simplify the process of attaching devices to a personal computer. For newer computers that do not have a serial or parallel port, users plug the device in a USB or FireWire port — as specified by the device's manufacturer. In general, FireWire has replaced audio, parallel, and SCSI ports, which are discussed in the next section. USB ports have replaced mouse, keyboard, serial, audio, parallel, and SCSI ports. Figure 4-32 shows how FireWire and USB ports are replacing other ports completely.

Special-Purpose Ports

Four special-purpose ports are MIDI, SCSI, IrDA, and Bluetooth. These ports are not included in typical computers. For a computer to have these ports, you must customize the computer purchase order. The following sections discuss MIDI, SCSI, IrDA, and Bluetooth ports.

MIDI PORT A special type of serial port that connects the system unit to a musical instrument, such as an electronic keyboard, is called a **MIDI port**. Short for *Musical Instrument Digital Interface*, MIDI (pronounced MID-dee) is the electronic music industry's standard that defines how devices, such as sound cards and synthesizers, represent sounds electronically. A *synthesizer*, which can be a peripheral or a chip, creates sound from digital instructions.

A system unit with a MIDI port has the capability of recording sounds that have been created by a synthesizer and then processing the sounds (the data) to create new sounds. Nearly every sound card supports the MIDI standard, so you can play and manipulate on one computer sounds that originally were created on another computer.

TRADITIONAL PORTS

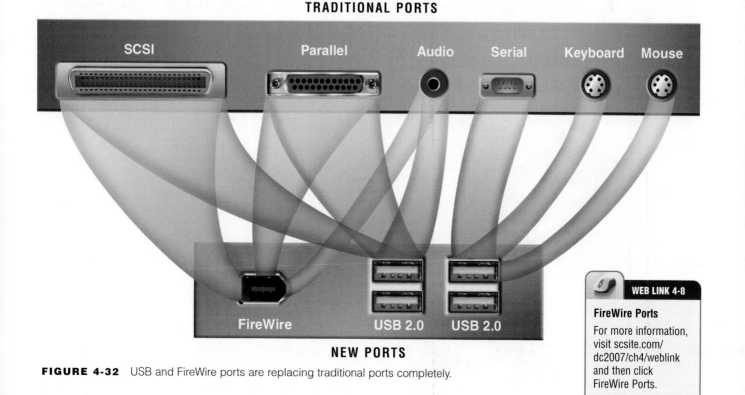

NEW PORTS

FIGURE 4-32 USB and FireWire ports are replacing traditional ports completely.

WEB LINK 4-8

FireWire Ports

For more information, visit scsite.com/ dc2007/ch4/weblink and then click FireWire Ports.

SCSI PORT   A special high-speed parallel port, called a **SCSI port**, allows you to attach SCSI (pronounced skuzzy) peripherals such as disk drives and printers. Depending on the type of *SCSI*, which stands for *small computer system interface*, you can daisy chain up to either 7 or 15 devices together. Some computers include a SCSI port. Others have a slot that supports a SCSI card.

IrDA PORT   Some devices can transmit data via infrared light waves. For these wireless devices to transmit signals to a computer, both the computer and the device must have an **IrDA port** (Figure 4-33). These ports conform to standards developed by the *IrDA* (*Infrared Data Association*).

To ensure nothing obstructs the path of the infrared light wave, you must align the IrDA port on the device with the IrDA port on the computer, similarly to the way you operate a television remote control. Devices that use IrDA ports include a PDA, smart phone, keyboard, mouse, printer, and pager. Several of these devices use a high-speed IrDA port, sometimes called a *fast infrared port*.

BLUETOOTH PORT   An alternative to IrDA, **Bluetooth** technology uses radio waves to transmit data between two devices (Figure 4-34). Unlike IrDA, the Bluetooth devices do not have to be aligned with each other. Many computers, peripherals, PDAs, smart phones, cars, and other consumer electronics are Bluetooth-enabled, which means they contain a small chip that allows them to communicate with other Bluetooth-enabled computers and devices. The latest version of Bluetooth, called Bluetooth 2.0, supports higher connection speeds and is backward compatible with its predecessors.

If you have a computer that is not Bluetooth enabled, you can purchase a Bluetooth wireless port adapter that will convert an existing USB port or serial port into a Bluetooth port. Also available are Bluetooth PC Cards for notebook computers and Bluetooth cards for PDAs and smart phones.

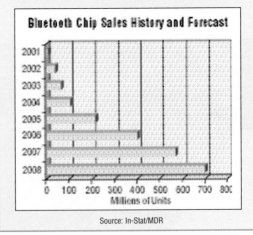

FAQ 4-7

How popular is Bluetooth?

Experts predict Bluetooth chip sales will grow to 720 million units by 2008 with revenues of $1.7 billion, as shown in the chart below. For more information, visit scsite.com/dc2007/ch4/faq and then click Bluetooth Growth.

Bluetooth Chip Sales History and Forecast

Source: In-Stat/MDR

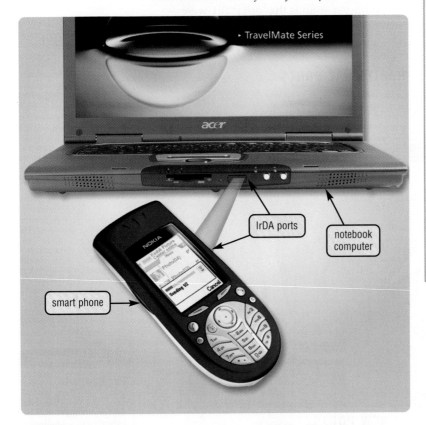

smart phone

IrDA ports

notebook computer

FIGURE 4-33   Many devices communicate wirelessly with desktop or notebook computers through IrDA ports.

FIGURE 4-34 This smart phone wirelessly communicates with a Bluetooth-enabled notebook computer.

BUSES

As explained earlier in this chapter, a computer processes and stores data as a series of electronic bits. These bits transfer internally within the circuitry of the computer along electrical channels. Each channel, called a **bus**, allows the various devices both inside and attached to the system unit to communicate with each other. Just as vehicles travel on a highway to move from one destination to another, bits travel on a bus (Figure 4-35).

Buses transfer bits from input devices to memory, from memory to the processor, from the processor to memory, and from memory to output or storage devices. Buses consist of two parts: a data bus and an address bus. The *data bus* transfers actual data and the *address bus* transfers information about where the data should reside in memory.

The size of a bus, called the *bus width*, determines the number of bits that the computer can transmit at one time. For example, a 32-bit bus can transmit 32 bits (4 bytes) at a time. On a 64-bit bus, bits transmit from one location to another 64 bits (8 bytes) at a time. The larger the number of bits handled by the bus, the faster the computer transfers data. Using the highway analogy again, assume that one lane

on a highway can carry one bit. A 32-bit bus is like a 32-lane highway. A 64-bit bus is like a 64-lane highway.

If a number in memory occupies 8 bytes, or 64 bits, the computer must transmit it in two separate steps when using a 32-bit bus: once for the first 32 bits and once for the second 32 bits. Using a 64-bit bus, the computer can transmit the number in a single step, transferring all 64 bits at once. The wider the bus, the fewer number of transfer steps required and the faster the transfer of data. Most personal computers today use a 64-bit bus.

In conjunction with the bus width, many computer professionals refer to a computer's word size. **Word size** is the number of bits the processor can interpret and execute at a given time. That is, a 64-bit processor can manipulate 64 bits at a time. Computers with a larger word size can process more data in the same amount of time than computers with a smaller word size. In most computers, the word size is the same as the bus width.

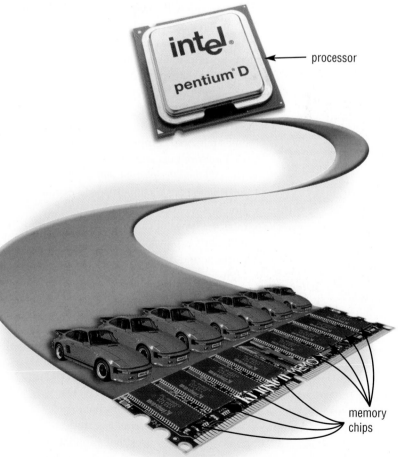

FIGURE 4-35 Just as vehicles travel on a highway, bits travel on a bus. Buses transfer bits from input devices to memory, from memory to the processor, from the processor to memory, and from memory to output or storage devices.

Every bus also has a clock speed. Just like the processor, manufacturers state the clock speed for a bus in hertz. Recall that one megahertz (MHz) is equal to one million ticks per second. Most of today's processors have a bus clock speed of 400, 533, or 800 MHz. The higher the bus clock speed, the faster the transmission of data, which results in applications running faster.

A computer has two basic types of buses: a system bus and an expansion bus. A *system bus* is part of the motherboard and connects the processor to main memory. An *expansion bus* allows the processor to communicate with peripherals. When computer professionals use the term bus by itself, they usually are referring to the system bus.

Expansion Bus

Some peripherals outside the system unit connect to a port on an adapter card, which is inserted in an expansion slot on the motherboard. This expansion slot connects to the expansion bus, which allows the processor to communicate with the peripheral attached to the adapter card. Data transmitted to memory or the processor travels from the expansion slot via the expansion bus and the system bus.

The types of expansion buses on a motherboard determine the types of cards you can add to the computer. Thus, you should understand these expansion buses commonly found in today's personal computers: PCI bus, AGP bus, USB, FireWire bus, and PC Card bus.

- The *PCI bus* (*Peripheral Component Interconnect bus*) is a high-speed expansion bus that connects higher speed devices. Types of cards you can insert in a PCI bus expansion slot include video cards, sound cards, SCSI cards, and high-speed network cards.
- The *Accelerated Graphics Port* (*AGP*) is a bus designed by Intel to improve the speed with which 3-D graphics and video transmit. With an AGP video card in an AGP bus slot, the AGP bus provides a faster, dedicated interface between the video card and memory. Newer processors support AGP technology.
- The USB (*universal serial bus*) and *FireWire bus* are buses that eliminate the need to install cards in expansion slots. In a computer with a USB, for example, USB devices connect to each other

outside the system unit, and then a single cable attaches to the USB port. The USB port then connects to the USB, which connects to the PCI bus on the motherboard. The FireWire bus works in a similar fashion. With these buses, expansion slots are available for devices not compatible with USB or FireWire.

- The expansion bus for a PC Card is the *PC Card bus*. With a PC Card inserted in a PC Card slot, data travels on the PC Card bus to the PCI bus.

BAYS

After you purchase a computer, you may want to install an additional storage device, such as a disk drive, in the system unit. A **bay** is an opening inside the system unit in which you can install additional equipment. A bay is different from a slot, which is used for the installation of adapter cards. Rectangular openings, called **drive bays**, typically hold disk drives.

Two types of drive bays exist: external and internal. An *external drive bay* allows a user to access the drive from outside the system unit (Figure 4-36). CD drives, DVD drives, Zip drives, floppy disk drives, and tape drives are examples of devices installed in external drive bays. An *internal drive bay* is concealed entirely within the system unit. Hard disk drives are installed in internal bays.

CD drive

DVD drive

floppy disk drive

FIGURE 4-36 External drive bays usually are located beside or on top of one another.

POWER SUPPLY

Many personal computers plug in standard wall outlets, which supply an alternating current (AC) of 115 to 120 volts. This type of power is unsuitable for use with a computer, which requires a direct current (DC) ranging from 5 to 12 volts. The **power supply** is the component of the system unit that converts the wall outlet AC power into DC power. Different motherboards and computers require different wattages on the power supply. If a power supply is not providing the necessary power, the computer will not function properly.

Built into the power supply is a fan that keeps the power supply and other components of the system unit cool. This fan dissipates heat generated by the processor and other components of the system unit. Many newer computers have additional fans near certain components in the system unit such as the processor, hard disk, and ports.

Some external peripherals such as an external modem, speakers, or a tape drive have an **AC adapter**, which is an external power supply. One end of the AC adapter plugs in the wall outlet and the other end attaches to the peripheral. The AC adapter converts the AC power into DC power that the peripheral requires.

FAQ 4-8

How many fans are in a system unit?

Most system units have at least three fans: one in the power supply, one on the case, and one on the processor heat sink. Some computers allow you to turn off noisy fans until they are needed. You also can purchase utility programs that slow or stop the fan until the temperature reaches a certain level. For more information, visit scsite.com/dc2007/ch4/faq and then click Computer Fan.

MOBILE COMPUTERS AND DEVICES

As businesses and schools expand to serve people across the country and around the world, increasingly more people need to use a computer while traveling to and from a main office or school to conduct business, communicate, or do homework. As Chapter 1 discussed, users with such mobile computing needs — known as mobile users — often have a mobile computer, such as a notebook computer or Tablet PC, or a mobile device such as a smart phone or PDA (Figure 4-37).

FIGURE 4-37 Users with mobile computing needs often have a notebook computer, PDA, and/or smart phone.

Weighing on average between 2.5 and 9 pounds, notebook computers can run either using batteries or using a standard power supply. Smaller PDAs and smart phones run strictly on batteries. Like their desktop counterparts, mobile computers and devices have a motherboard that contains electronic components that process data. Read Ethics & Issues 4-4 for a related discussion.

A notebook computer usually is more expensive than a desktop computer with the same capabilities because it is more costly to miniaturize the components. Notebook computers may have video, serial, parallel, modem, network, FireWire, USB, headphones, and microphone ports (Figure 4-38).

Two basic designs of Tablet PC are available: slate and convertible. With the slate Tablet PC (shown in Figure 4-1 on page 184), all the hardware is behind the display — much like a PDA. Users can attach a removable keyboard to the slate Tablet PC. The display on the convertible Tablet PC, which is attached to a keyboard, can be rotated 180 degrees and folded down over the keyboard. Thus, the convertible Tablet PC can be repositioned to look like either a notebook computer or a slate Tablet PC. Tablet PCs usually include several slots and ports (Figure 4-39).

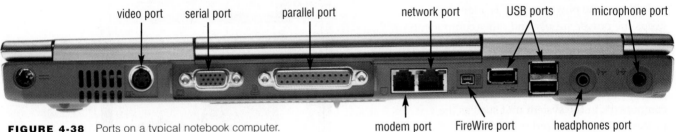

video port   serial port   parallel port   network port   USB ports   microphone port

FIGURE 4-38   Ports on a typical notebook computer.

modem port   FireWire port   headphones port

ETHICS & ISSUES 4-4

Should Smart Shoes Be Banned from Competitive Events?

Titanium golf clubs. Graphite tennis rackets. Aluminum baseball bats. Advances in technology have impacted many sports. Now, Adidas is changing the sport of running with the introduction of a computerized running shoe. The lightweight, battery-powered shoe, sometimes called a "smart shoe," contains a sensor and a microprocessor. Every second, the sensors send a thousand readings to the tiny mobile computer, which uses a motorized screw and cable system to adjust the heel cushion based on the conditions and the runner's style. The goal is to ensure ideal cushioning for the runner and the situation. The smart shoe is innovative, but is it fair? To maintain competitive balance, the governing bodies of golf and tennis place restrictions on the composition of equipment. Some racers would like similar limitations placed on running shoes. At a cost of about $250, the smart shoe could provide an unfair advantage to wealthier runners. The advantage would be evident at high school, college, and amateur races, where not all competitors could afford the shoe. Should smart shoes be banned from all races? Why or why not? Baseball banned aluminum bats at the professional level; should smart shoes be banned at the high school, college, and amateur levels, where they would be most apt to upset competitive balance? Why?

USB ports

video port

modem and network ports behind cover

FireWire port

headphones port

microphone port

smart card slot

IrDA port

PC Card slot

FIGURE 4-39   Ports and slots on a Tablet PC.

PDAs and smart phones are quite affordable, usually priced at a few hundred dollars or less. These mobile devices often have an IrDA port or are Bluetooth enabled so users can communicate wirelessly with other computers or devices such as a printer. Read Looking Ahead 4-2 for a look at the next generation of mobile computer.

LOOKING AHEAD 4-2

DNA Computer Works to Fight Cancer

One of the newest computers is so tiny that one trillion of them can fit inside a drop of water. The hardware of this biolog-ical invention is com-posed of enzymes that manipulate DNA, and the software is com-posed of actual DNA.

The concept for this computer had been proposed in 1936, but the actual computer was developed at the Weizmann Institute in Israel in 2001. Today, researchers at the Weizmann Institute are develop-ing applications that process biological information. Their most current success is being able to pro-gram the computer to diagnose and treat cancer.

The researchers are hopeful they will be able to have the medical computer function inside a human cell. For more information, visit scsite.com/dc2007/ch4/looking and then click DNA Computer.

PUTTING IT ALL TOGETHER

When you purchase a computer, it is important to understand how the components of the sys-tem unit work. Many components of the sys-tem unit influence the speed and power of a computer. These include the type of processor, the clock speed of the processor, the amount of RAM, bus width, and the clock speed of the bus. The configuration you require depends on your intended use.

The table in Figure 4-40 lists the suggested minimum processor and RAM requirements based on the needs of various types of computer users.

SUGGESTED MINIMUM CONFIGURATIONS BY USER

User	Processor and RAM
HOME	Intel Celeron D or AMD Sempron or Intel Pentium 4 or AMD Athlon 64 Minimum RAM: 256 MB
SMALL OFFICE/ HOME OFFICE	Intel Pentium D or AMD Athlon 64 FX Minimum RAM: 512 MB
MOBILE	Intel Celeron M or Intel Pentium M or AMD Turion 64 Minimum RAM: 512 MB
POWER	Intel Itanium 2 or AMD Opteron or Intel Pentium Extreme Edition or Intel Xeon MP or AMD Athlon MP or AMD Athlon 64 X2 Minimum RAM: 2 GB
LARGE BUSINESS	Intel Pentium D or AMD Athlon 64 FX Minimum RAM: 1 GB

FIGURE 4-40 Suggested processor and RAM configurations by user.

KEEPING YOUR COMPUTER CLEAN

Over time, the system unit collects dust — even in a clean environment. Built up dust can block airflow in the computer, which can cause it to overheat, corrode, or even stop working. By cleaning your computer once or twice a year, you can help extend its life. This preventive maintenance task requires a few basic products (Figure 4-41):

- can of compressed air — removes dust and lint from difficult-to-reach areas
- lint-free antistatic wipes and swabs
- bottle of rubbing alcohol
- small computer vacuum (or small attachments on your house vacuum)
- antistatic wristband — to avoid damaging internal components with static electricity
- small screwdriver (may be required to open the case or remove adapter cards)

Before cleaning the computer, turn it off, unplug it from the electrical outlet, and unplug all cables from the ports. Blow away any dust from all openings on the computer case, such as drives, slots, and ports. Vacuum the power supply fan on the back of the computer case to remove any dust that has accumulated on it. Next, release short blasts of compressed air on the power supply fan. Then, use an antistatic wipe to clean the exterior of the case.

If you need assistance opening the computer case, refer to the instructions that came with the computer. Once the case is open, put the antistatic wristband on your wrist and attach its clip to the case of the computer. Use the antistatic wipes to clean dust and grime inside the walls of the computer case. Vacuum as much dust as possible from the interior of the case, including the wires, chips, adapter cards, and fan blades. Next, release short blasts of compressed air in areas the vacuum cannot reach. If the motherboard and adapter cards still look dirty, gently clean them with lint-free wipes or swabs lightly dampened with alcohol.

When finished, be sure all adapter cards are tightly in their expansion slots. Then close the case, plug in all cables, and attach the power cord. Write down the date you cleaned the computer so you have a record for your next cleaning.

If you do not feel comfortable cleaning the system unit yourself, have a local computer company clean it for you.

FIGURE 4-41   With a few products, this computer user keeps his computer clean.

FAQ 4-9

How do I clean components in the system unit?

Never pour or spray any form of liquid on the motherboard — or on any hardware. Always apply the liquid to a cloth or swab, and then use the cloth or swab to clean the hardware. If you can squeeze liquid out of the cloth or swab, then it is too moist. For more information, visit scsite.com/dc2007/ch4/faq and then click PC Hygiene.

Test your knowledge of pages 204 through 216 in Quiz Yourself 4-3.

QUIZ YOURSELF 4-3

Instructions: Find the true statement below. Then, rewrite the remaining false statements so they are true.

1. A bus is the point at which a peripheral attaches to or communicates with a system unit so the peripheral can send data to or receive information from the computer.

2. An AC adapter is a socket on the motherboard that can hold an adapter card.

3. Built into the power supply is a heater that keeps components of the system unit warm.

4. Serial ports can connect up to 127 different peripherals together with a single connector.

5. The higher the bus clock speed, the slower the transmission of data.

6. When cleaning the inside of the system unit, wear an antistatic wristband to avoid damaging internal components with static electricity.

Quiz Yourself Online: To further check your knowledge of expansion slots, adapter cards, ports, buses, components of mobile computers and devices, and cleaning a computer, visit scsite.com/dc2007/ch4/quiz and then click Objectives 8 – 12.

CHAPTER SUMMARY

Chapter 4 presented the components of the system unit; described how memory stores data, instructions, and information; and discussed the sequence of operations that occur when a computer executes an instruction. The chapter included a comparison of various personal computer processors on the market today. It also discussed how to clean a system unit.

CAREER CORNER

Computer Engineer

A *computer engineer* designs and develops the electronic components found in computers and peripheral devices. They also can work as researchers, theorists, and inventors. Companies may hire computer engineers for permanent positions or as consultants, with jobs that extend from a few months to a few years, depending on the project. Engineers in research and development often work on projects that will not be released to the general public for two years.

Responsibilities vary from company to company. All computer engineering work, however, demands problem-solving skills and the ability to create and use new technologies. The ability to handle multiple tasks and concentrate on detail is a key component. Assignments often are taken on as part of a team. Therefore, computer engineers must be able to communicate clearly with both computer personnel and computer users, who may have little technical knowledge.

Before taking in-depth computer engineering design and development classes, students usually take mathematics, physics, and basic engineering. Computer engineering degrees include B.S., M.S., and Ph.D. Because computer engineers employed in private industry often advance into managerial positions, many computer engineering graduates obtain a master's degree in business administration (M.B.A.). Most computer engineers earn between $63,500 and $106,500 annually, depending on their experience and employer, but salaries can exceed $125,000. For more information, visit scsite.com/dc2007/ch4/careers and then click Computer Engineer.

High-Tech Talk

RANDOM ACCESS MEMORY (RAM): THE GENIUS OF MEMORY

Inside your computer, RAM takes the form of separate microchip modules that plug in slots on the computer's motherboard. These slots connect through a line (bus) or set of electrical paths to the computer's processor. Before you turn on a computer, its RAM is a blank slate. As you start and use your computer, the operating system files, applications, and any data currently being used by the processor are written to and stored in RAM so the processor can access them quickly.

How is this data written to and stored in RAM? In the most common form of RAM, dynamic random access memory (DRAM), *transistors* (in this case, acting as switches) and a *capacitor* (as a data storage element) create a *memory cell*, which represents a single bit of data.

Memory cells are etched onto a silicon wafer in a series of columns (bitlines) and rows (wordlines), known as an *array*. The intersection of a column and row constitutes the *address* of the memory cell (Figure 4-42). Each memory cell has a unique address that can be found by counting across columns and then counting down by row. The address of a character consists of a series of memory cell addresses put together.

To write data to RAM, the processor sends the memory controller the address of a memory cell in which to store data. The *memory controller* organizes the request and sends the column and row address in an electrical charge along the appropriate address lines, which are very thin electrical lines etched into the RAM chip. This causes the transistors along those address lines to close.

These transistors act as a switch to control the flow of electrical current in an either closed or open circuit. While the transistors are closed, the software sends bursts of electricity along selected data lines. When the electrical charge traveling down the data line reaches an address line where a transistor is closed, the charge flows through the closed transistor and charges the capacitor.

A capacitor works as electronic storage that holds an electrical charge. Each charged capacitor along the address line represents a 1 bit. An uncharged capacitor represents a 0 bit. The combination of 1s and 0s from eight data lines forms a single byte of data.

The capacitors used in dynamic RAM, however, lose their electrical charge. The processor or memory controller continuously has to recharge all of the capacitors holding a charge (a 1 bit) before the capacitor discharges. During this *refresh operation*, which happens automatically thousands of times per second, the memory controller reads memory and then immediately rewrites it. This refresh operation is what gives dynamic RAM its name. Dynamic RAM has to be refreshed continually, or it loses the charges that represent bits of data. A specialized circuit called a counter tracks the refresh sequence to ensure that all of the rows are refreshed.

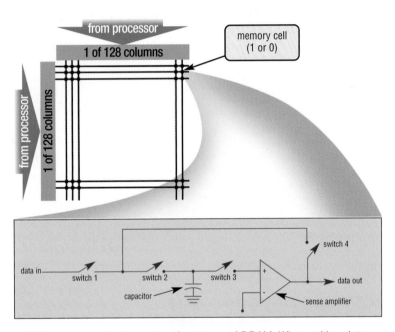

FIGURE 4-42 An illustration of one type of DRAM. When writing data, switches 1 and 2 in the circuit are closed and switches 3 and 4 are open. When reading data, switches 2, 3, and 4 in the circuit are closed and switch 1 is open. Most DRAM chips actually have arrays of memory cells (upper-left corner of figure) that are 16 rows deep.

The process of reading data from RAM uses a similar, but reverse, series of steps. When the processor gets the next instruction it is to perform, the instruction may contain the address of a memory cell from which to read data. This address is sent to the memory controller. To locate the memory cell, the memory controller sends the column and row address in an electrical charge down the appropriate address lines.

This electrical charge causes the transistors along the address line to close. At every point along the address line where a capacitor is holding a charge, the capacitor discharges through the circuit created by the closed transistors, sending electrical charges along the data lines.

A specialized circuit called a *sense amplifier* determines and amplifies the level of charge in the capacitor. A capacitor charge over a certain voltage level represents the binary value 1; a capacitor charge below that level represents a 0. The sensed and amplified value is sent back down the address line to the processor.

As long as a computer is running, data continuously is being written to and read from RAM. As soon as you shut down a computer, RAM loses its data. The next time you turn on a computer, operating system files and other data are again loaded into RAM and the read/write process starts all over. For more information, visit scsite.com/dc2007/ch4/tech and then click Memory.

Companies on the Cutting Edge

AMD
PC PROCESSOR SUPPLIER

Customer needs influence the integrated circuits *Advanced Micro Devices* (*AMD*) develops for the computing, communications, and consumer electronics industries. AMD calls this philosophy "customer-centric innovation."

As a global supplier of PC processors, AMD engineers its technologies at its Submicron Development Center (SDC) in Sunnyvale, California. The technologies are put into production at manufacturing facilities in the United States, Europe, Asia, and Japan.

Among the company's more successful line of processors is the AMD 64 family, which is composed of the AMD Athlon 64 processor for desktop and personal computers, the AMD Opteron processor for servers and workstations, and the AMD Turion mobile technology for notebook computers. The company is partnering with portable multimedia manufacturers, including TiVo, to use its Alchemy processor in providing high-performance video entertainment products. For more information, visit scsite.com/dc2007/ch4/companies and then click AMD.

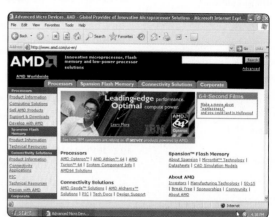

INTEL
CHIP MAKER DOMINATES THE COMPUTER MARKET

When Gordon Moore and Robert Noyce started *Intel* in 1968, their goal was to replace magnetic core memory with semiconductor memory. Noyce and Moore, together with Andy Grove, refined the process of placing thousands of tiny electronic devices on a silicon chip. In 1971, the company introduced the Intel 4004, the first single-chip microprocessor.

When IBM chose the Intel 8008 chip for its new personal computer in 1980, Intel chips became standard for all IBM-compatible personal computers. Today, Intel's microprocessors are the building blocks in countless personal computers, servers, networks, and communications devices. In 2006, Intel introduced its Viiv technology, which is designed to enhance the entertainment experience in the digital home. For more information, visit scsite.com/dc2007/ch4/companies and then click Intel.

Technology Trailblazers

JACK KILBY
INTEGRATED CIRCUIT INVENTOR

Jack Kilby was awarded more than 60 patents during his lifetime, but one has changed the world. His integrated circuit, or microchip, invention made microprocessors possible.

Kilby started his work with miniature electrical components at Centralab, where he developed transistors for hearing aids. He then took a research position with Texas Instruments and developed a working model of the first integrated circuit, which was patented in 1959. Kilby applied this invention to various industrial, military, and commercial applications, including the first pocket calculator, called the Pocketronic.

Kilby is considered one of the more influential people in the world who has had the greatest impact on business computing in the past 50 years. He was awarded the Nobel Prize in physics in 2000 for his part in the invention of the integrated circuit, a product he believed will continue to change the world. For more information, visit scsite.com/dc2007/ch4/people and then click Jack Kilby.

GORDON MOORE
INTEL COFOUNDER

More than 40 years ago, *Gordon Moore* predicted that the number of transistors and resistors placed on computer chips would double every year, with a proportional increase in computing power and decrease in cost. This bold forecast, now known as Moore's Law, proved amazingly accurate for 10 years. Then, Moore revised the estimate to doubling every two years.

Convinced of the future of silicon chips, Moore cofounded Intel in 1968. Moore's lifelong interest in technology was kindled at an early age when he experimented with a neighbor's chemistry set. Even then, he displayed the passion for practical outcomes that has typified his work as a scientist and engineer.

Moore says that the semiconductor industry's progress will far surpass that of nearly all other industries. For more information, visit scsite.com/dc2007/ch4/people and then click Gordon Moore.

Chapter Review

The Chapter Review section summarizes the concepts presented in this chapter. To listen to the audio version of this Chapter Review, visit scsite.com/dc2007/ch4/review. To obtain help from other students regarding any subject in this chapter, visit scsite.com/dc2007/ch4/forum and post your thoughts or questions.

① How Are Various Styles of System Units Different?   The **system unit** is a case that contains electronic components of the computer used to process data. On desktop personal computers, most storage devices also are part of the system unit. On notebook computers, the keyboard and pointing device often occupy the area on top of the system unit, and the display attaches to the system unit by hinges. On mobile devices, the display often is built into the system unit. With game consoles, the input and output devices, such as controllers and a television, reside outside the system unit. On handheld game consoles and digital music players, by contrast, the packaging around the system unit also houses the input devices and display.

② What Are Chips, Adapter Cards, and Other Components of the Motherboard?   The **motherboard** is the main circuit board of the system unit. The motherboard contains many electronic components including a processor chip, memory chips, expansion slots, and adapter cards. A **chip** is a small piece of semiconducting material, usually silicon, on which integrated circuits are etched. Expansion slots hold adapter cards that provide connections and functions not built into the motherboard.

③ What Are the Components of a Processor, and How Do They Complete a Machine Cycle?   The **processor** interprets and carries out the basic instructions that operate a computer. Processors contain a **control unit** that directs and coordinates most of the operations in the computer and an **arithmetic logic unit** (*ALU*) that performs arithmetic, comparison, and other operations. The *machine cycle* is a set of four basic operations — *fetching, decoding, executing,* and *storing* — that the processor repeats for every instruction. The control unit fetches program instructions and data from memory and decodes the instructions into commands the computer can execute.

④ What Are the Characteristics of Various Personal Computer Processors?   Intel produces the **Pentium** processor for high-performance PCs, the **Celeron** processor for basic PCs, and the **Xeon** and **Itanium** processors for workstations and low-end servers. AMD manufactures *Intel-compatible processors,* which have an internal design similar to Intel processors. A *dual-core processor* is a chip that has two separate processors. A *multicore processor* is a chip with two or more separate processors. Some devices have a *system on a chip* processor that integrates the functions of a processor, memory, and a video card on a single chip.

connect
Visit scsite.com/dc2007/ch4/quiz or click the Quiz Yourself button. Click Objectives 1 – 4.

⑤ What Is a Bit, and How Does a Series of Bits Represent Data?   Most computers are **digital** and recognize only two discrete states: off and on. To represent these states, computers use the **binary system**, which is a number system that has just two unique digits — 0 (for off) and 1 (for on) — called bits. A **bit** is the smallest unit of data a computer can process. Grouped together as a unit, 8 bits form a **byte**, which provides enough different combinations of 0s and 1s to represent 256 individual characters. The combinations are defined by patterns, called coding schemes, such as *ASCII, EBCDIC,* and *Unicode.*

⑥ How Do Programs Transfer In and Out of Memory?   When an application program starts, the program's instructions load into memory from the hard disk. The program and operating system instructions are in memory, and the program's window is displayed on the screen. When you quit the program, the program instructions are removed from memory, and the program no longer is displayed on the screen.

Chapter Review

(7) What Are the Various Types of Memory? The system unit contains volatile and nonvolatile memory. *Volatile memory* loses its contents when the computer's power is turned off. *Nonvolatile memory* does not lose its contents when the computer's power is turned off. RAM is the most common type of volatile memory. ROM, flash memory, and CMOS are examples of nonvolatile memory. **RAM** consists of memory chips that can be read from and written to by the processor and other devices. **ROM** refers to memory chips storing permanent data and instructions that usually cannot be modified. **Flash memory** can be erased electronically and rewritten. **CMOS** technology uses battery power to retain information even when the power to the computer is turned off.

 Visit scsite.com/dc2007/ch4/quiz or click the Quiz Yourself button. Click Objectives 5 – 7.

(8) What Are the Types of Expansion Slots and Adapter Cards? An **expansion slot** is a socket on the motherboard that can hold an adapter card. An **adapter card** is a circuit board that enhances functions of a component of the system unit and/or provides a connection to a **peripheral** such as a modem, disk drive, printer, scanner, or keyboard. Several types of adapter cards exist. A **sound card** enhances the sound-generating capabilities of a personal computer. A **video card** converts computer output into a video signal that displays an image on the screen. Many computers today support **Plug and Play**, which enables the computer to configure adapter cards and peripherals automatically.

(9) How Are a Serial Port, a Parallel Port, a USB Port, a FireWire port, and Other Ports Different? A **port** is the point at which a peripheral attaches to or communicates with a system unit so it can send data to or receive information from the computer. A **serial port**, which transmits data one bit at a time, usually connects devices that do not require fast data transmission, such as a mouse, keyboard, or modem. A **parallel port**, which transfers more than one bit at a time, sometimes connects a printer to the system unit. A **USB port** can connect up to 127 different peripherals together with a single connector. A **FireWire port** can connect multiple types of devices that require faster data transmission speeds. Four special-purpose ports are MIDI, SCSI, IrDA, and Bluetooth. A **MIDI port** connects the system unit to a musical instrument. A **SCSI port** attaches the system unit to SCSI peripherals, such as disk drives. An **IrDA port** and **Bluetooth** technology allow wireless devices to transmit signals to a computer via infrared light waves or radio waves.

(10) How Do Buses Contribute to a Computer's Processing Speed? A **bus** is an electrical channel along which bits transfer within the circuitry of a computer, allowing devices both inside and attached to the system unit to communicate. The size of a bus, called the *bus width*, determines the number of bits that the computer can transmit at one time. The larger the bus width, the faster the computer transfers data.

(11) What Are the Components in Mobile Computers and Mobile Devices? In addition to the motherboard, processor, memory, sound card, PC Card slot, and **drive bay**, a mobile computer's system unit also houses devices such as the keyboard, pointing device, speakers, and display. The system unit for a typical notebook computer often has video, serial, parallel, modem, network, FireWire, USB, headphone, and microphone ports. Tablet PCs usually include several slots and ports. PDAs often have an IrDA port or are Bluetooth enabled so users can communicate wirelessly.

(12) How Do You Clean a System Unit? Before cleaning a system unit, turn off the computer and unplug it from the wall. Use a small vacuum and a can of compressed air to remove external dust. After opening the case, wear an antistatic wristband and vacuum the interior. Wipe away dust and grime using lint-free antistatic wipes and rubbing alcohol.

Visit scsite.com/dc2007/ch4/quiz or click the Quiz Yourself button. Click Objectives 8 – 12.

Key Terms

You should know the Primary Terms and be familiar with the Secondary Terms. Use the list below to help focus your study. To further enhance your understanding of the Key Terms in this chapter, visit scsite.com/dc2007/ch4/terms. See an example of and a definition for each term, and access current and additional information about the term from the Web.

Primary Terms

(shown in bold-black characters in the chapter)

AC adapter (213)
access time (203)
adapter card (204)
analog (194)
arithmetic logic unit (188)
bay (212)
binary system (195)
bit (195)
Bluetooth (210)
bus (211)
byte (195)
cache (201)
Celeron (190)
central processing unit (CPU) (187)
chip (186)
clock speed (189)
complementary metal-oxide semiconductor (CMOS) (203)
connector (206)
control unit (187)
digital (194)
drive bays (212)
expansion slot (204)
FireWire hub (209)
FireWire port (209)
firmware (202)
flash memory (202)
flash memory card (205)
gigabyte (GB) (197)
gigahertz (GHz) (189)
IrDA port (210)
Itanium (190)

jack (206)
kilobyte (KB or K) (197)
megabyte (MB) (197)
memory (197)
memory cache (201)
memory module (199)
memory slots (199)
MIDI port (209)
motherboard (186)
nanosecond (203)
parallel port (208)
PC Card (205)
PC Card slot (205)
Pentium (190)
Pentium M (190)
peripheral (204)
Plug and Play (205)
port (206)
power supply (213)
processor (187)
RAM (198)
read-only memory (ROM) (201)
SCSI port (210)
serial port (207)
sound card (204)
system clock (189)
system unit (184)
terabyte (TB) (197)
USB hub (208)
USB port (208)
video card (204)
word size (211)
Xeon (190)

Secondary Terms

(shown in italic characters in the chapter)

Accelerated Graphics Port (AGP) (212)
address (197)
address bus (211)
advanced transfer cache (ATC) (201)
ALU (188)
American Standard Code for Information Interchange (ASCII) (195)
arithmetic operations (188)
binary digit (195)
bus width (211)
Centrino (190)
chassis (184)
clock cycle (189)
COM port (207)
comparison operations (188)
daisy chain (208)
data bus (211)
decoding (188)
DIMM (dual inline memory module) (199)
Double Data Rate SDRAM (DDR SDRAM) (199)
dual-core processor (190)
dynamic RAM (DRAM) (199)
EEPROM (electrically erasable programmable read-only memory) chip (202)
executing (188)
expansion bus (212)
expansion card (204)
Extended Binary Coded Decimal Interchange Code (EBCDIC) (195)
external drive bay (212)
fast infrared port (210)
female connectors (206)
fetching (188)
FireWire bus (212)
gender changer (206)
graphics card (204)
heat pipe (193)
heat sink (193)
hertz (189)
hot plugging (205)
Hyper-Threading (HT) Technology (190)
IBM processor (190)
IEEE 1394 port (209)
integrated circuit (186)
Intel-compatible processors (190)
internal drive bay (212)
IrDA (Infrared Data Association) (210)

L1 cache (201)
L2 cache (201)
L3 cache (201)
liquid cooling technology (193)
machine cycle (188)
magnetoresistive RAM (MRAM) (199)
main memory (198)
male connectors (206)
microcode (202)
microprocessor (187)
MIPS (millions of instructions per second) (190)
Motorola processor (190)
multicore processor (190)
Musical Instrument Digital Interface (209)
nonvolatile memory (197)
ns (203)
parallel processing (194)
PC Card bus (212)
PCI bus (Peripheral Component Interconnect bus) (212)
Personal Computer Memory Card International Association (PCMCIA) cards (205)
pipelining (189)
PROM (programmable read-only memory) chip (202)
Rambus DRAM (RDRAM) (199)
random access memory (198)
registers (189)
RIMM (Rambus inline memory module) (199)
SCSI (small computer system interface) (210)
SIMM (single inline memory module) (199)
static RAM (SRAM) (199)
stored program concept (197)
storing (188)
superscalar (189)
synchronous DRAM (SDRAM) (199)
synthesizer (209)
system board (186)
system bus (212)
system on a chip (190)
transistor (186)
Unicode (195)
universal serial bus port (208)
USB 2.0 (208)
USB flash drive (205)
Viiv technology (192)
volatile memory (197)

Checkpoint

Use the Checkpoint exercises to check your knowledge level of the chapter. The Beyond the Book exercises will help broaden your understanding of the concepts presented in this chapter. To complete the Checkpoint exercises interactively, visit scsite.com/dc2007/ch4/check.

 Label the Figure   Identify these components.

a. memory module
b. motherboard
c. adapter cards
d. expansion slots
e. processor chip in a
   processor slot

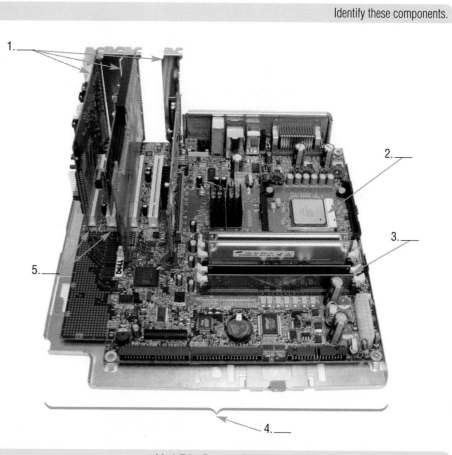

 True/False   Mark T for True and F for False. (See page numbers in parentheses.)

_____ 1. With game consoles, the input and output devices, such as controllers and a television, reside outside the system unit. (185)

_____ 2. The processor interprets and carries out the basic instructions that operate a computer. (187)

_____ 3. The speed of the system clock is the only factor that influences a computer's performance. (189)

_____ 4. A Pentium M processor typically is used for workstations and low-end servers. (192)

_____ 5. Replacing a motherboard is a fairly simple process, whereas replacing a processor is much more complicated. (192)

_____ 6. A heat sink is a small ceramic or metal component with fins on its surface that absorbs and disperses heat produced by electrical components. (193)

_____ 7. A byte is the smallest unit of data the computer can process. (195)

_____ 8. Coding schemes make it possible for humans to interact with a digital computer that processes only bits. (195)

_____ 9. Two types of cache are memory cache and disk cache. (201)

_____ 10. Read-only memory refers to memory chips storing permanent data and instructions. (201)

_____ 11. Serial ports usually connect devices that require fast data transmission rates. (207)

_____ 12. A USB port can connect up to eight different peripherals together with a single connector. (208)

Quizzes and
Learning Games

Computer Genius
Crossword Puzzle
DC Track and Field
Practice Test
Quiz Yourself
Wheel of Terms
You're Hired!

Exercises

Case Studies
Chapter Review
▶ Checkpoint
Key Terms
Learn How To
Learn It Online
Web Research

Beyond the Book

Career Corner
Companies
FAQs
High-Tech Talk
Looking Ahead
Making Use of
the Web
Trailblazers
Web Links

Features

Chapter Forum
Install Computer
Lab Exercises
Maintain Computer
Tech News
Timeline 2007

Checkpoint

Multiple Choice   Select the best answer. (See page numbers in parentheses.)

1. On _____, the display often is built into the system unit. (185)
   a. mobile devices
   b. notebook computers
   c. desktop personal computers
   d. all of the above

2. The processor also is called the _____. (187)
   a. central processing unit (CPU)
   b. adapter card
   c. motherboard
   d. chip

3. The _____ is the component of the processor that directs and coordinates most of the operations in the computer. (187)
   a. control unit
   b. arithmetic logic unit
   c. register
   d. machine cycle

4. _____ is the process of obtaining a program instruction or data item from memory. (188)
   a. Storing   b. Decoding
   c. Executing   d. Fetching

5. A processor contains small, high-speed storage locations, called _____, that temporarily hold data and instructions. (189)
   a. flash drives   b. registers
   c. jacks   d. heat sinks

6. Processors that can execute more than one instruction per clock cycle are said to be _____. (189)
   a. superscalar
   b. dual-core processors
   c. system on a chip
   d. flash drives

7. Dual-core/multicore processors _____. (192)
   a. reduce the power consumption
   b. reduce heat output
   c. increase overall performance
   d. all of the above

8. _____ is a 16-bit coding scheme that is capable of representing more than 65,000 characters and symbols, enough for almost all the world's current written languages. (195)
   a. ASCII   b. Unicode
   c. Microcode   d. EBCDIC

9. A(n) _____ is a unique number that identifies the location of a byte in memory. (197)
   a. register
   b. kilobyte
   c. address
   d. bit

10. A _____ is a type of memory module with pins on opposite sides of the circuit board that do not connect, and thus form two sets of contacts. (199)
    a. RIMM (Rambus inline memory module)
    b. DIMM (dual inline memory module)
    c. ROMM (Rambus online memory module)
    d. SIMM (single inline memory module)

11. Many of today's computers support _____, which means the computer automatically can configure adapter cards and other peripherals as you install them. (205)
    a. Pack and Go
    b. Plug and Play
    c. Pick and Choose
    d. Park and Ride

12. A _____ port is an interface that connects devices by transferring more than one bit at a time. (208)
    a. serial
    b. parallel
    c. USB
    d. mouse

13. Word size is the _____. (211)
    a. pace of the system clock
    b. size of the bus
    c. amount of time it takes the processor to read instructions from memory
    d. number of bits the processor can interpret and execute at a given time.

14. _____ usually are installed in internal bays. (212)
    a. Floppy disk drives
    b. Hard disk drives
    c. Zip drives
    d. CD drives

Checkpoint

Matching Match the terms with their definitions. (See page numbers in parentheses.)

_____ 1. motherboard (186)

_____ 2. processor (187)

_____ 3. ALU (188)

_____ 4. register (189)

_____ 5. memory (197)

_____ 6. firmware (202)

_____ 7. flash memory (202)

_____ 8. expansion slot (204)

_____ 9. PC Card (205)

_____ 10. Bluetooth (210)

a. socket on the motherboard that can hold an adapter card

b. small, high-speed storage locations that temporarily hold data and instructions

c. electronic components that store instructions, data, and results of processed data

d. performs arithmetic, comparison, and other operations

e. ROM chips that contain permanently written data, instructions, or information

f. amount of time it takes the processor to read data, instructions, and information from memory

g. thin, credit card-sized device that adds memory, storage, sound, fax/modem, network, and other capabilities to mobile computers

h. nonvolatile memory that can be erased electronically and rewritten

i. technology that uses radio waves to transmit data between two devices

j. number of bits the processor can interpret and execute at a given time

k. main circuit board of the system unit

l. interprets and carries out the basic instructions that operate a computer

Short Answer Write a brief answer to each of the following questions.

1. What is the motherboard? _____ What is a computer chip? _____

2. What are the four basic operations in a machine cycle? _____ What is pipelining, and how does it affect processing speed? _____

3. What is the system clock? _____ How does clock speed affect a computer's speed? _____

4. What is a system on a chip? _____ What types of devices typically have them? _____

5. What is a bus? _____ How does bus width affect a computer's data transfer speed? _____

Beyond the Book Read the following book elements, learn more about each using the Web, and then write a brief report.

1. Ethics & Issues — Can Computers Think? (187), Discarded Computer Parts: Whose Problem Is It? (193), How Much Should You Pay for a Computer? (200), or Should Smart Shoes Be Banned from Competitive Events? (214)

2. Career Corner — Computer Engineer (217)

3. Companies on the Cutting Edge — AMD or Intel (219)

4. FAQs (189, 193, 200, 202, 203, 208, 210, 213, 216)

5. High-Tech Talk — Random Access Memory (RAM): The Genius of Memory (218)

6. Looking Ahead — Countries Seek Computing Speed Supremacy (190) or DNA Computer Works to Fight Cancer (215)

7. Making Use of the Web — Resources (120)

8. Picture Yourself Buying a Computer (182)

9. Technology Trailblazers — Jack Kilby or Gordon Moore (219)

10. Web Links (186, 192, 199, 201, 202, 204, 205, 209, 212)

Learn It Online

Use the Learn It Online exercises to reinforce your understanding of the chapter concepts. To access the Learn It Online exercises, visit scsite.com/dc2007/ch4/learn.

① At the Movies — Computing Clusters

To view the Computing Clusters movie, click the number 1 button. Locate your video and click the corresponding High-Speed or Dial-Up link, depending on your Internet connection. Watch the movie and then complete the exercise by answering the questions below. Many graphics and animation programs have heavy data loads. When using a processing cluster, these difficult, memory-intensive tasks can be divided over several different computers linked through a network. Using multiple computers to perform a big job means it gets done faster. What types of tasks are best accomplished by a cluster? How would you handle a large, time-consuming project?

② At the Movies — USB Basics

To view the USB Basics movie, click the number 2 button. Locate your video and click the corresponding High-Speed or Dial-Up link, depending on your Internet connection. Watch the movie and then complete the exercise by answering the questions below. A universal serial bus (USB) is a peripheral bus standard developed by Intel which allows you to connect external equipment such as digital cameras and MP3 players to your computer. The USB enables the external equipment to communicate with your computer and share information and power. How can you tell if your USB port is working? What are some ways you can troubleshoot your USB ports?

③ Student Edition Labs — Understanding the Motherboard

Click the number 3 button. A new browser window will open, displaying the Student Edition Labs. Follow the on-screen instructions, and complete the Understanding the Motherboard Lab. When finished, click the Exit button. If required, submit your results to your instructor.

④ Student Edition Labs — Binary Numbers

Click the number 4 button. A new browser window will open, displaying the Student Edition Labs. Follow the on-screen instructions, and complete the Binary Numbers Lab. When finished, click the Exit button. If required, submit your results to your instructor.

⑤ Practice Test

Click the number 5 button. Answer each question. When completed, enter your name and click the Grade Test button to submit the quiz for grading. Make a note of any missed questions. If required, submit your score to your instructor.

⑥ Who Wants To Be a Computer Genius[2]?

Click the number 6 button to find out if you are a computer genius. Directions about how to play the game will be displayed. When you are ready to play, click the Play button. Submit your score to your instructor.

⑦ Wheel of Terms

Click the number 7 button to reinforce important terms you learned in this chapter by playing the Shelly Cashman Series version of this popular game. Directions about how to play the game will be displayed. When you are ready to play, click the Play button. Submit your score to your instructor.

Learn It Online

8 DC Track and Field

Click the number 8 button to use what you have learned in this chapter to compete against other students in three track and field events. Directions about how to play the game will be displayed. When you are ready to play, click the start first event button. If required, submit your score to your instructor.

9 You're Hired!

Click the number 9 button to use what you have learned in this chapter to embark on the path to a career in computers. Directions about how to play the game will be displayed. When you are ready to play, click the begin game button. If required, submit your score to your instructor.

10 Crossword Puzzle Challenge

Click the number 10 button. Complete the puzzle to reinforce skills you learned in this chapter. Directions about how to play the game will be displayed. When you are ready to play, click the Play button. Submit the completed puzzle to your instructor.

11 Lab Exercises

Click the number 11 button. When the Lab Exercises menu appears, click the exercise assigned by your instructor. A new browser window will open. Follow the on-screen instructions to complete the exercise. When finished, click the Exit button. If required, submit your results to your instructor.

12 In the News

In February 2006, the forerunner of the modern computer had its 60th anniversary. By today's standards for electronic computers, the ENIAC (Electronic Numerical Integrator And Computer) was a grotesque monster. With 30 separate units, plus a power supply and forced-air cooling, it weighed more than 30 tons. Its 19,000 vacuum tubes, 1,500 relays, and hundreds of thousands of resistors, capacitors, and inductors consumed almost 200 kilowatts of electrical power. The ENIAC performed fewer than 1,000 calculations per minute;

today, personal computers can process more than 300 million instructions per second. The rapid development of computing power and capabilities is astonishing, and the rate of that development is accelerating. Click the number 12 button and read a news article about the introduction of a new or improved computer component. What is the component? Who is introducing it? Will the component change the way people use computers? If so, how?

13 Chapter Discussion Forum

Select an objective from this chapter on page 183 about which you would like more information. Click the number 13 button, and post a short message listing a meaningful message title accompanied by one or more questions concerning the selected objective. In two days, return to the threaded discussion by clicking the number 13 button. Submit to your instructor your original message and at least one response to your message.

14 Configuring and Pricing Computers

Click the number 14 button to learn how to configure and price a custom computer. Research at least two manufacturers' Web sites, and get a quote from each site you visit. Make sure you include any software you may require. Also, add any upgrade items that you would like to have on your system including peripheral items (printer, scanner, etc.). Print the quotes from each site and submit the results to your instructor.

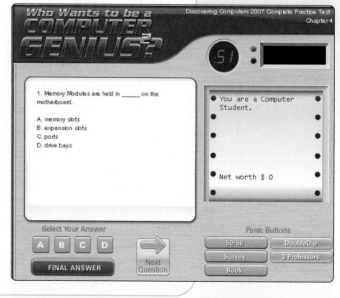

Learn How To

Use the Learn How To activities to learn fundamental skills when using a computer and accompanying technology. Complete the exercises and submit them to your instructor. Visit scsite.com/dc2007/ch4/howto to obtain more information pertaining to each activity.

LEARN HOW TO 1: Purchase and Install Memory in a Computer

One of the less expensive and more effective ways to speed up a computer, make it capable of processing more programs at the same time, and enable it to handle graphics, gaming, and other high-level programs is to increase the amount of memory. The process of increasing memory is accomplished in two phases — purchasing the memory and installing the memory. To purchase memory for a computer, complete the following steps:

1. Determine the amount of memory currently in the computer. For a method to do this, see Learn How To number 3 in Chapter 1.
2. Determine the maximum amount of memory your computer can contain. This value can change for different computers, based primarily on the number of slots on the motherboard available for memory and the size of the memory modules you can place in each slot. On most computers, different size memory modules can be inserted in slots. A computer, therefore, might allow a 128 MB, 256 MB, or 512 MB memory module to be inserted in each slot. To determine the maximum memory for a computer, in many cases you can multiply the number of memory slots on the computer by the maximum size memory module that can be inserted in each slot.

   For example, if a computer contains four memory slots and is able to accept memory modules of 128 MB, 256 MB, or 512 MB in each of its memory slots, the maximum amount of memory the computer can contain is 2 GB (4 x 512 MB).

   You can find the number of slots and the allowable sizes of each memory module by contacting the computer manufacturer, looking in the computer's documentation, or contacting sellers of memory such as Kingston (www.kingston.com) or Crucial (www.crucial.com) on the Web. These sellers have documentation for most computers, and even programs you can download to run on your computer that will specify how much memory your computer currently has and how much you can add.
3. Determine how much memory you want to add, which will be somewhere between the current memory and the maximum memory allowed on the computer.
4. Determine the current configuration of memory on the computer. For example, if a computer with four memory slots contains 512 MB of memory, it could be using one memory module of 512 MB in a single slot and the other three slots would be empty; two memory modules of 256 MB each in two slots with two slots empty; one memory module of 256 MB and two memory modules of 128 MB each in three slots with one slot empty; or four memory modules of 128 MB each in four slots with no slots empty. You may be required to look inside the system unit to make this determination. The current memory configuration on a computer will determine what new memory modules you should buy to increase the memory to the amount determined in Step 3.

   You also should be aware that a few computers require memory to be installed in matching pairs. This means a computer with four slots could obtain 512 MB of memory with two memory modules of 256 MB in two slots, or four memory modules of 128 MB in four slots.
5. Determine the number of available memory slots on your computer and the number and size memory modules you must buy to fulfill your requirement. Several scenarios can occur (in the following examples, assume you can install memory one module at a time).
   a. Scenario 1: The computer has one or more open slots. In this case, you might be able to purchase a memory module that matches the amount of memory increase you desire. For example, if you want to increase memory by 256 MB, you should purchase a 256 MB memory module for insertion in the open slot. Generally, you should buy the maximum size module you can for an open slot. So, if you find two empty slots and wish to increase memory by 256 MB, it is smarter to buy one 256 MB module and leave one empty slot rather than buy two 128 MB memory modules and use both slots. This allows you to increase memory again without removing currently used modules.

Learn How To

b. Scenario 2: The computer has no open slots. For example, a computer containing 512 MB of memory could have four slots each containing 128 MB memory modules. If you want to increase the memory on the computer to 1 GB, you will have to remove some of the 128 MB memory modules and replace them with the new memory modules you purchase. In this example, you want to increase the memory by 512 MB. You would have several options: (1) You could replace all four 128 MB memory modules with 256 MB memory modules; (2) You could replace all four 128 MB memory modules with two 512 MB memory modules; (3) You could replace one 128 MB memory module with a 512 MB memory module, and replace a second 128 MB module with a 256 MB memory module. Each of these options results in a total memory of 1 GB. The best option will depend on the price of memory and whether you anticipate increasing the memory size at a later time. The least expensive option probably would be number 3.

c. Scenario 3: Many combinations can occur. You may have to perform calculations to decide the combination of modules that will work for the number of slots on the computer and the desired additional memory.

6. Determine the type of memory to buy for the computer. Computer memory has many types and configurations, and it is critical that you buy the kind of memory for which the computer was designed. It is preferable to buy the same type of memory that currently is found in the computer. That is, if the memory is DDR SDRAM with a certain clock speed, then that is the type of additional memory you should place in the computer. The documentation for the computer should specify the memory type. In addition, the Web sites cited on the previous page, and others as well, will present a list of memory modules that will work with your computer. Enough emphasis cannot be placed on the fact that the memory you buy must be compatible with the type of memory usable on your computer. Because there are so many types and configurations, you must be especially diligent to ensure you purchase the proper memory for your computer.

7. Once you have determined the type and size of memory to purchase, buy it from a reputable dealer. Buying poor or mismatched memory is a major reason for a computer's erratic performance and is a difficult problem to troubleshoot.

After purchasing the memory, you must install it on your computer. Complete the following steps to install memory:

1. Unplug the computer, and remove all electrical cords and device cables from the ports on the computer. Open the case of the system unit. You may want to consult the computer's documentation to determine the exact procedure.

2. Ground yourself so you do not generate static electricity that can cause memory or other components within the system unit to be damaged. To do this, wear an antistatic wristband you can purchase inexpensively in a computer or electronics store; or, before you touch any component within the system unit, touch an unpainted metal surface. If you are not wearing an antistatic wristband, periodically touch an unpainted metal surface to dissipate any static electricity.

3. Within the system unit, find the memory slots on the motherboard. The easiest way to do this is look for memory modules that are similar to those you purchased. The memory slots often are located near the processor. If you cannot find the slots, consult the documentation. A diagram often is available to help you spot the memory slots.

4. Insert the memory module in the next empty slot. Orient the memory module in the slot to match the modules currently installed. A notch or notches on the memory module will ensure you do not install the module backwards. If your memory module is a DIMM, insert the module straight down into grooves on the clips and then apply gentle pressure. If your memory is SIMM, insert the module at a 45 degree angle and then rotate it to a vertical position until the module snaps into place.

5. If you must remove one or more memory modules before inserting the new memory, carefully release the clips before lifting the memory module out of the memory slot.

6. Plug in the machine and replace all the device cables without replacing the cover.

7. Start the computer. In most cases, the new memory will be recognized and the computer will run normally. If an error message appears, determine the cause of the error.

8. Replace the computer cover.

Exercise

1. Assume you have a computer that contains 256 MB of memory. It contains four memory slots. Each slot can contain 128 MB or 256 MB memory modules. Two of the slots contain 128 MB memory modules. What memory chip(s) would you buy to increase the memory on the computer to 512 MB? What is the maximum memory on the computer? Submit your answers to your instructor.

2. Assume you have a computer that contains 1 GB of memory. It contains four memory slots. Each slot can contain 128 MB, 256 MB, 512 MB, or 1 GB memory modules. Currently, each slot contains a 256 MB memory module. What combinations of memory modules will satisfy your memory upgrade to 2 GB? Visit a Web site to determine which of these combinations is the least expensive. Submit your answers and recommendations to your instructor.

Web Research

Use the Internet-based Web Research exercises to broaden your understanding of the concepts presented in this chapter. Visit scsite.com/dc2007/ch4/research to obtain more information pertaining to each exercise. To discuss any of the Web Research exercises in this chapter with other students, post your thoughts or questions at scsite.com/dc2007/ch4/forum.

① Scavenger Hunt   Use one of the **search engines** listed in Figure 2-8 in Chapter 2 on page 78 or your own favorite search engine to find the answers to the questions below. Copy and paste the Web address from the Web page where you found the answer. Some questions may have more than one answer. If required, submit your answers to your instructor. (1) Which Microsoft Windows operating systems support USB? (2) The USB port supports hot plugging or hot swapping. What is "hot plugging"? (3) What is the name of the suit that people wear when they work in chip manufacturing clean rooms? (4) What is CAS Latency? (5) What are rune stones and their connection to Danish King Harald Blatand (Bluetooth)? (6) What is the name of the type of memory that retains its contents until it is exposed to ultraviolet light?

② Search Sleuth   **Ask Jeeves** (ask.com) is one of the faster growing research Web sites. The search engine uses natural language, which allows researchers to type millions of questions each day using words a human would use rather than words a computer understands. Visit this Web site and then use your word processing program to answer the following questions. Then, if required, submit your answers to your instructor. (1) Click the P.G. Wodehouse link at the bottom of the home page. Who are P.G. Wodehouse and Bertie Wooster? (2) Click your browser's Back button or press the BACKSPACE key to return to the Ask Jeeves home page. Click the Search text box and then type What were the top selling DVDs this week? as the keywords in the Search text box. (3) Scroll through the links Ask Jeeves returns and then click one that provides the information requested. What three DVDs generated the best sales this past week? (4) Click your browser's Back button or press the BACKSPACE key to return to the Ask Jeeves home page. Click the Bloglines link at the bottom of the page. (5) Click the Today's hot topics link and review the material. Summarize the information you read and then write a 50-word summary.

③ Journaling   Respond to your readings in this chapter by writing at least one page containing your reactions, evaluations, and reflections about **cleaning your computer**. For example, have you tried cleaning a computer with the basic products recommended in this chapter? When? Where is the cleanest environment in your home to use the computer? If you do not feel comfortable cleaning the system unit yourself, where would you take it for this preventive maintenance? You also can write about the new terms you learned by reading this chapter. If required, submit your journal to your instructor.

④ Expanding Your Understanding   A **brick-and-click** business allows customers to conduct transactions at a physical location as well as online. Many banks and retailers, such as Citibank and Best Buy, are brick-and-click businesses. Choose a brick-and-click business and then visit the physical location and its Web site. Compare the type, availability, and cost of products or services. Write a report summarizing your findings, focusing on the advantages and disadvantages of conducting business at a physical location and online. If required, submit your report to your instructor.

⑤ Ethics in Action   More than 50 law enforcement agencies use handheld wireless devices to access commercial databases. For example, Massachusetts state police stationed at Logan International Airport use the **LocatePLUS Holdings Corporation**'s database, which has information on 98 percent of Americans. The data is composed of motor vehicle records, credit bureau reports, property tax payments, and telephone directories. Police say accessing this information helps them perform their jobs more efficiently. Privacy experts, in contrast, say that information collected for one purpose should not be available in other contexts. View online sites that provide information about commercial databases for sale. Write a report summarizing your findings, and include a table of links to Web sites that provide additional details. If required, submit your report to your instructor.

Case Studies

Use the Case Studies to apply the concepts presented in the chapter to real-world situations. Visit scsite.com/dc2007/ch4/cases to obtain more information pertaining to each exercise. To discuss the Case Studies in this chapter with other students, visit scsite.com/dc2007/ch4/forum and post your thoughts or questions.

CASE STUDY 1 — Class Discussion   You are the purchasing manager at TechnoInk, a company that specializes in designing and producing logos for local high school and college sports teams. The company has 35 nonnetworked computers that are used throughout the company for common business applications. The computers are four years old, and you would like to replace them. The director of information technology agrees, but he has reservations. He has asked you to complete a study on the cost of new computers, comparing the major features found on <u>system units</u> at three different price levels: less than $1,000; $1,000 to $1,750; and greater than $1,750. Prepare a brief summary report on the major features of system units at the various price levels. Include recommendations on which system units would meet the company's needs most economically. Be prepared to discuss your recommendations in class.

CASE STUDY 2 — Class Discussion   Universal Computing, Inc. has decided to upgrade several hundred PCs used in their offices nationwide. The Information Technology Department has recommended that the company again purchase PCs for approximately $1,500 each. The system units would include Pentium 4 processors with speeds of 3.80 GHz with 1 GB of RAM. From her days in college, the CFO has preferred Apple computers and currently uses an <u>Apple iMac</u> at home. She has hired you as a consultant to determine if the company would be better off purchasing iMacs in the same price range and with similar capabilities. Use the Web and/or print media to select a comparable iMac. Which one starts faster? Which one opens files faster? Which one loads Web pages faster? Is the iMac in the same price range as the PC? List any other advantages and disadvantages of each. Prepare a brief summary report and be prepared to discuss your findings in class.

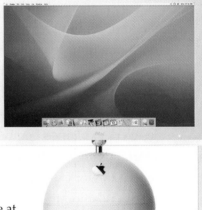

CASE STUDY 3 — Research   Your family has decided to purchase a computer for use at home. Because you are enrolled in a computer course, you have been asked to make recommendations. Your instructor has pushed the premise "software drives hardware." List the application programs you and your family members plan to use. Visit the Web sites of the manufacturers of each application program, and note the capabilities required of the system unit (type of processor, amount of <u>RAM</u>, and so on). On the basis of your findings, what are the minimum system requirements you and your family would require in a personal computer? What system requirements would be sufficient to provide a "cushion" so that you could be sure the system also could run other, or new, application packages? Write a brief report and share your findings with your class.

CASE STUDY 4 — Research   Many system unit manufacturers provide a toll-free telephone number that customers can call with technical problems or questions. If the <u>service technician</u> determines a difficulty is a hardware problem that the customer can fix, the technician might ask the customer to open the system unit and make some adjustments. For this reason, every computer user can benefit by being familiar with the inside of the system unit. If you own a personal computer or have access to a personal computer, unplug the power supply and take the cover off the system unit. Be careful not to touch any of the system unit components. Make a sketch of the system unit and try to identify each part. By referring to the computer's *User Guide*, list some of the computer's specifications (clock speed, memory size, and so on). Compare your sketch and list with a classmate who has done this exercise with a different computer. How are the computers similar? How are they different?

CASE STUDY 5 — Team Challenge   The chief financial officer of SkateJam, Inc. has asked her Information Technology Department to look into replacing the company's desktop computers with <u>notebook computers</u>. The director of information technology has hired your team as consultants to examine the advantages and disadvantages of notebook computers. Form a three-member team and assign each team member one of the following companies — Dell, HP, and Apple. Have each member of your team use the Web and/or print media to find a notebook computer and a desktop computer with comparable middle-of-the-road system units sold by the company assigned to them. What is the price of each computer? How are the processors and RAM similar? How are they different? Meet with the members of your team to discuss results of your investigations. Is the notebook computer the better buy? If so, why? Write a summary report or use PowerPoint to create a group presentation and share your findings with the class.

Input

Picture Yourself Going Digital

Your daughter claims you have been stuck in the last decade — still connected by cords, still writing appointments in a daily planner, still using the house telephone as your main method of communication, and still visiting photo labs to process 35 mm film. To get up to speed with digital technology, you have been using gift cards that you have received for birthdays and other occasions to purchase new devices for your computer.

First, you bought a wireless keyboard and mouse, which the sales clerk explained communicates via radio waves. More importantly to you, these two devices give you the freedom to work without the clutter of cords. You now can position the keyboard and mouse anywhere on your desk and not worry about whether the cord is long enough.

You then bought a smart phone that has PDA capabilities. First, you learned how to enter contact information and appointments and how to use the digital pen. Next, you learned how to send picture messages and post them to a Web site. You plan to send or post regular photo updates to keep friends and family up-to-date of all your activities.

Most recently, you purchased a digital camera. You have become quite adept at transferring the digital images to your computer, editing them with your photo editing software, printing the images in a variety of sizes, and, of course, e-mailing the pictures.

To learn more about keyboards, mouse devices, input for PDAs and smart phones, and digital cameras, read Chapter 5 and discover features of many other types of input devices.

CONTENTS

WHAT IS INPUT?

Input is any data and instructions entered into the memory of a computer. As shown in Figure 5-1, people have a variety of options for entering data or instructions into a computer.

As discussed in Chapter 1, *data* is a collection of unprocessed text, numbers, images, audio, and video. Once data is in memory, the computer interprets and executes instructions to process the data into information. Instructions entered into the computer can be in the form of programs, commands, and user responses.

• A *program* is a series of instructions that tells a computer what to do and how to do it. When a programmer writes a program, he or she enters the program into the computer by using a keyboard, mouse, or other input device. The programmer then stores the program in a file that a user can execute (run). When a user runs a program, the computer loads the program from a storage

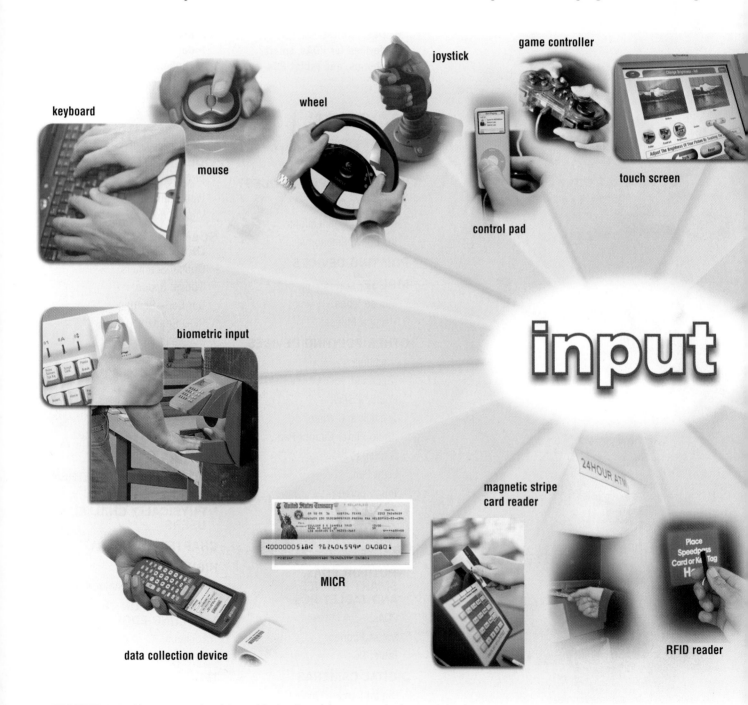

keyboard

mouse

wheel

joystick

game controller

control pad

touch screen

biometric input

input

data collection device

MICR

magnetic stripe card reader

RFID reader

FIGURE 5-1   Users can enter data and instructions into a computer in a variety of ways.

medium into memory. Thus, a program is entered into a computer's memory.

- Programs respond to commands that a user issues. A *command* is an instruction that causes a program to perform a specific action. Users issue commands by typing or pressing keys on the keyboard, clicking a mouse button, speaking into a microphone, or touching an area on a screen.

- A *user response* is an instruction a user issues by replying to a question displayed by a program. A response to the question instructs the program to perform certain actions. Assume the program asks the question, Is the time card correct? If you answer Yes, the program processes the time card. If you answer No, the program gives you the opportunity to modify the time card entries.

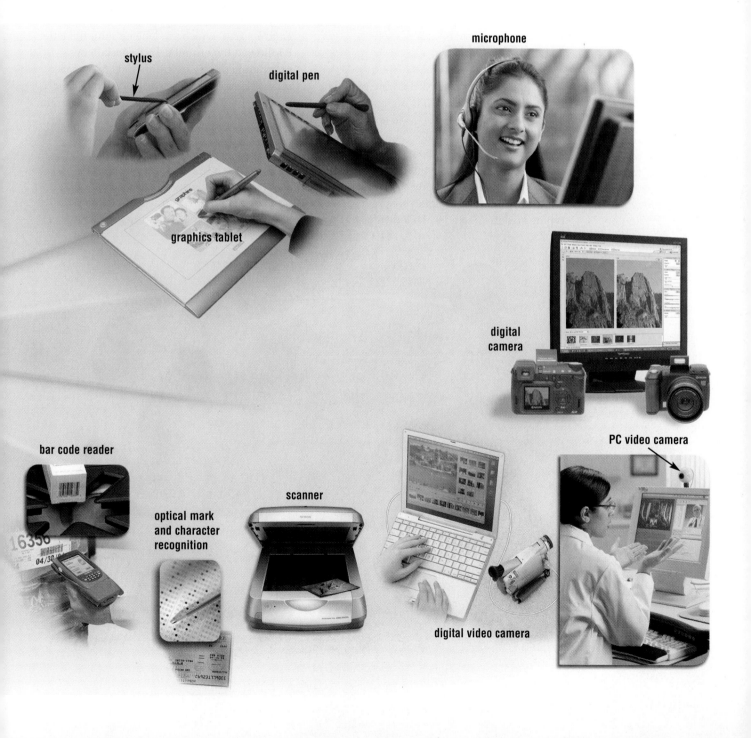

stylus

digital pen

microphone

graphics tablet

digital camera

PC video camera

bar code reader

optical mark and character recognition

scanner

digital video camera

WHAT ARE INPUT DEVICES?

An **input device** is any hardware component that allows users to enter data and instructions (programs, commands, and user responses) into a computer. Depending on the application and your particular requirements, the input device selected may vary. The following pages discuss a variety of input devices.

Storage devices, such as disk drives, serve as both input and output devices. Chapter 7 discusses storage devices.

THE KEYBOARD

Many people use a keyboard as one of their input devices. A **keyboard** is an input device that contains keys users press to enter data and instructions into a computer (Figure 5-2).

Desktop computer keyboards typically have from 101 to 105 keys. Keyboards for smaller computers such as notebook computers contain fewer keys. All computer keyboards have a typing area that includes the letters of the alphabet, numbers, punctuation marks, and other basic keys. Many desktop computer keyboards also have a numeric keypad on the right side of the keyboard. A keyboard also contains other keys that allow users to enter data and instructions into the computer. Read Ethics & Issues 5-1 for a related discussion.

Most of today's desktop computer keyboards are enhanced keyboards. An *enhanced keyboard* has twelve function keys along the top; it also has two CTRL keys, two ALT keys, and a set of arrow and additional keys between the typing area and the numeric keypad (Figure 5-2). *Function keys*, which are labeled with the letter F followed by a number, are special keys programmed to issue commands to a computer. The command associated with a function key may vary, depending on the program with which you are interacting. For example, the F3 key may issue one command to an operating system and an entirely different command to a word processing program. To issue commands, users often can press a function key in combination with other special keys (SHIFT, CTRL, ALT, and others).

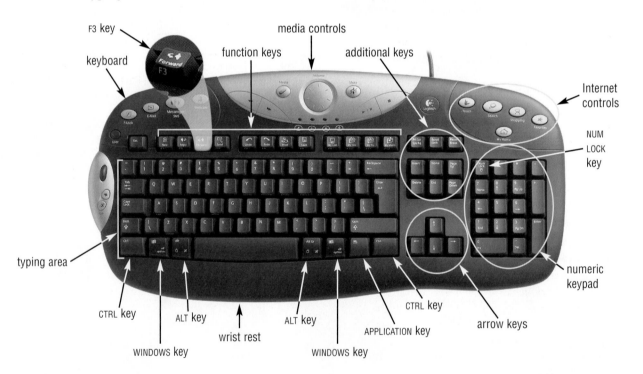

FIGURE 5-2   On a desktop computer keyboard, you type using keys in the typing area and on the numeric keypad.

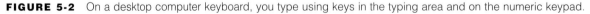

ETHICS & ISSUES 5-1

Keyboard Monitoring — Privacy Risk?

Are you curious about your spouse's long e-mail messages to a mutual friend? Are you concerned about your teenager's conversations in Internet chat rooms? Keyboard monitoring software can dispel your doubts. When installed on a computer, *keyboard monitoring software* records every keystroke in a hidden file, which later can be accessed by supplying the correct password. With keyboard monitoring software, you can see everything that was typed on the computer keyboard, including documents, e-mail, and other messages. Some programs also store a record of software used, Web sites visited, user logons, and periodic screen shots. The software can run completely undetected. With keyboard monitoring software, you can discover that your spouse is e-mailing gardening tips or recognize that your teenager has made a potentially dangerous contact in a chat room. Recently, courts ruled that law-enforcement agencies secretly can install keyboard monitoring software on suspects' computers if a proper search warrant is obtained. Many maintain, however, that keyboard monitoring software is an invasion of privacy, and some states have outlawed the secret installation of such software. Should keyboard monitoring software ever be used? If so, when? Some marketers of keyboard monitoring software recommend computer users be informed that the software is installed. Is this a good idea? Why or why not?

Nearly all keyboards have toggle keys. A *toggle key* is a key that switches between two states each time a user presses the key. When you press the NUM LOCK key, for example, it locks the numeric keypad so you can use the keypad to type numbers. When you press the NUM LOCK key again, the numeric keypad unlocks so the same keys can serve to move the insertion point. Many keyboards have status lights that light up when you activate a toggle key.

Keyboards also often have a WINDOWS key(s) and an APPLICATION key. When pressed, the WINDOWS key displays the Start menu, and the APPLICATION key displays an item's shortcut menu.

Keyboards also contain keys that allow you to position the insertion point, also known as a *cursor* in some programs. The **insertion point** is a symbol on the screen, usually a blinking vertical bar, that indicates where the next character you type will be displayed (Figure 5-3). Users can move the insertion point left, right, up, or down by pressing the arrow keys and other keys on the keyboard.

Newer keyboards include media control buttons that allow you to access the computer's CD/DVD drive and adjust speaker volume, and Internet control buttons that allow you to open an e-mail program, start a Web browser, and search the Internet. Some keyboards also have USB ports so a user can plug a USB device directly in the keyboard instead of in the system unit. Some keyboards include a fingerprint scanner, which is discussed later in this chapter.

A *gaming keyboard* is a keyboard designed specifically for users that enjoy playing games on the computer. Gaming keyboards typically include programmable keys so gamers can customize the keyboard to the game being played.

The keys on gaming keyboards light up so they are visible in all lighting conditions. Some even have small displays that show important game statistics, such as time or targets remaining.

FAQ 5-1

What is the rationale for the arrangement of keys in the typing area?

The keys originally were arranged to reduce the frequency of key jams on old mechanical typewriters. Called a *QWERTY keyboard*, the first letters on the top alphabetic line spell QWERTY. A *Dvorak keyboard*, by contrast, places frequently typed letters in the middle of the typing area. Despite the Dvorak keyboard's logical design, most people and computers use a QWERTY keyboard. For more information, visit scsite.com/dc2007/ch5/faq and then click Keyboards.

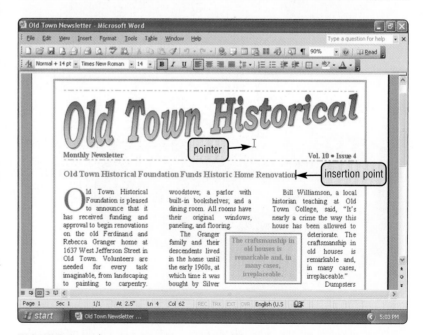

FIGURE 5-3   In most programs, such as Word, the insertion point is a blinking vertical bar. You use the keyboard or other input device to move the insertion point. The pointer, another symbol that is displayed on the screen, is controlled using a pointing device such as a mouse.

Keyboard Connections

Desktop computer keyboards often attach via a cable to a serial port, a keyboard port, or a USB port on the system unit. Some keyboards, however, do not use wires at all. A *wireless keyboard*, or *cordless keyboard*, is a battery-powered device that transmits data using wireless technology, such as radio waves or infrared light waves. Wireless keyboards often communicate with a receiver attached to a port on the system unit. The port type varies depending on the type of wireless technology. For example, a Bluetooth-enabled keyboard communicates via radio waves with a Bluetooth receiver that typically plugs in a USB port (Figure 5-4).

On notebook computers and some handheld computers, PDAs, and smart phones, the keyboard is built in the top of the system unit. To fit in these mobile computers and devices, the keyboards usually are smaller and have fewer keys. A typical notebook computer keyboard usually has only about 85 keys. To provide all of the functionality of a desktop computer keyboard, manufacturers design many of the keys to serve two or three purposes.

Keyboard Ergonomics

Regardless of size, many keyboards have a rectangular shape with the keys aligned in straight, horizontal rows. Users who spend a lot of time typing on these keyboards sometimes experience repetitive strain injuries (RSI) of their wrists and hands. For this reason, some manufacturers offer ergonomic keyboards. An *ergonomic keyboard* has a design that reduces the chance of wrist and hand injuries. Even keyboards that are not ergonomically designed attempt to offer a user more comfort by including a wrist rest or palm rest (Figure 5-2 on page 236).

The goal of **ergonomics** is to incorporate comfort, efficiency, and safety in the design of the workplace. Employees can be injured or develop disorders of the muscles, nerves, tendons, ligaments, and joints from working in an area that is not ergonomically designed.

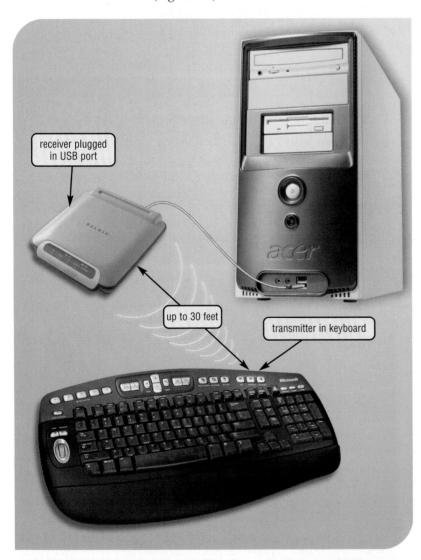

receiver plugged in USB port

up to 30 feet

transmitter in keyboard

FAQ 5-2

What can I do to reduce chances of experiencing repetitive strain injuries?

Do not rest your wrist on the edge of a desk; use a wrist rest. Keep your forearm and wrist level so your wrist does not bend. Do hand exercises every 15 minutes. Keep your shoulders, arms, hands, and wrists relaxed while you work. Maintain good posture. Keep feet flat on the floor, with one foot slightly in front of the other. For more information, visit scsite.com/dc2007/ch5/faq and then click Repetitive Strain Injuries.

FIGURE 5-4 Some personal computers have built-in Bluetooth technology. On computers that are not Bluetooth-enabled, you plug a Bluetooth receiver in a USB port on the system unit. A transmitter inside the keyboard communicates with the receiver, which should be within 30 feet from each other.

POINTING DEVICES

A **pointing device** is an input device that allows a user to control a pointer on the screen. In a graphical user interface, a **pointer** is a small symbol on the screen (Figure 5-3 on page 237) whose location and shape change as a user moves a pointing device. A pointing device can be used to move the insertion point; select text, graphics, and other objects; and click buttons, icons, links, and menu commands. The following sections discuss the mouse and other pointing devices.

MOUSE

A **mouse** is a pointing device that fits under the palm of your hand comfortably. The mouse is the most widely used pointing device on desktop computers.

With a mouse, users control the movement of the pointer, often called a *mouse pointer* in this case. As you move a mouse, the pointer on the screen also moves. Generally, you use the mouse to move the pointer on the screen to an object such as a button, a menu, an icon, a link, or text. Then, you press a mouse button to perform a certain action associated with that object. The top and sides of a mouse have one to four buttons; some also have a small wheel. The bottom of a mouse is flat and contains a mechanism that detects movement of the mouse.

Mouse Types

A *mechanical mouse* has a rubber or metal ball on its underside (Figure 5-5). When the ball rolls in a certain direction, electronic circuits in the mouse translate the movement of the mouse into signals the computer can process. You should place a mechanical mouse on a mouse pad. A **mouse pad** is a rectangular rubber or foam pad that provides better traction than the top of a desk. The mouse pad also protects the ball in the mouse from a build-up of dust and dirt, which could cause it to malfunction.

An optical mouse, by contrast, has no moving mechanical parts inside. Instead, an *optical mouse* uses devices that emit and sense light to detect the mouse's movement. Some use optical sensors, others use a laser (Figure 5-6). You can place an optical mouse on nearly all types of surfaces, eliminating the need for a mouse pad.

An optical mouse is more precise than a mechanical mouse and does not require cleaning as does a mechanical mouse, but it also is more expensive.

A mouse connects to a computer in several ways. Many types connect with a cable that attaches to a serial port, mouse port, or USB port on the system unit. A *wireless mouse*, or *cordless mouse*, is a battery-powered device that transmits data using wireless technology, such as radio waves or infrared light waves. The technology used for a wireless mouse is similar to that of a wireless keyboard discussed earlier. Some users prefer a wireless mouse because it frees up desk space and eliminates the clutter of a cord.

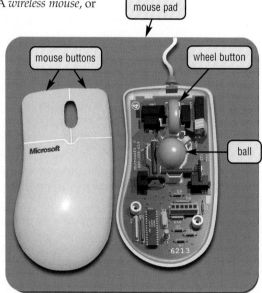

FIGURE 5-5 A mechanical mouse contains a small ball.

FIGURE 5-6a (optical mouse that uses optical sensor)

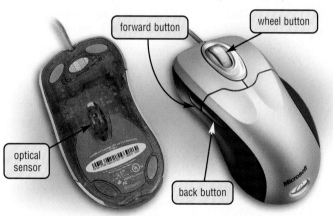

FIGURE 5-6b (optical mouse that uses laser)

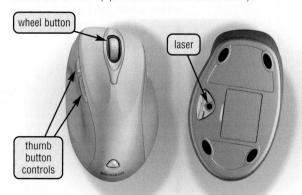

FIGURE 5-6
An optical mouse uses an optical sensor or a laser. Many also include buttons you push with your thumb that enable forward and backward navigation through Web pages.

Using a Mouse

Windows users work with a mouse that has at least two buttons. For a right-handed user, the left button usually is the primary mouse button, and the right mouse button is the secondary mouse button. Left-handed people, however, can reverse the function of these buttons.

Operations you can perform with the mouse include point, click, right-click, double-click, triple-click, drag, right-drag, rotate wheel, press wheel button, and tilt wheel. The table in Figure 5-7 explains how to perform these mouse operations. Some programs also use keys in combination with the mouse to perform certain actions. The function of the mouse buttons and the wheel varies depending on the program. Read Ethics & Issues 5-2 for a related discussion.

Some programs support *mouse gestures*, where the user performs certain operations by holding a mouse button while moving the mouse in a particular pattern. For example, moving the mouse down and to the left may close all open windows. Mouse gestures minimize the amount of time users spend navigating through menus or toolbars because users can perform these tasks by simply moving (gesturing) the mouse.

WEB LINK 5-1

Mouse

For more information, visit scsite.com/dc2007/ch5/weblink and then click Mouse.

FAQ 5-3

How do I use a wheel on a mouse?

Roll it forward or backward to scroll up or down. Tilt it to the right or left to scroll horizontally. Hold down the CTRL key while rolling the wheel to make the text on the screen bigger or smaller. These scrolling and zooming functions work with most software and also on the Web. For more information, visit scsite.com/dc2007/ch5/faq and then click Using a Mouse.

MOUSE OPERATIONS

Operation	Mouse Action	Example
Point	Move the mouse across a flat surface until the pointer on the desktop is positioned on the item of choice.	Position the pointer on the screen.
Click	Press and release the primary mouse button, which usually is the left mouse button.	Select or deselect items on the screen or start a program or program feature.
Right-click	Press and release the secondary mouse button, which usually is the right mouse button.	Display a shortcut menu.
Double-click	Quickly press and release the left mouse button twice without moving the mouse.	Start a program or program feature.
Triple-click	Quickly press and release the left mouse button three times without moving the mouse.	Select a paragraph.
Drag	Point to an item, hold down the left mouse button, move the item to the desired location on the screen, and then release the left mouse button.	Move an object from one location to another or draw pictures.
Right-drag	Point to an item, hold down the right mouse button, move the item to the desired location on the screen, and then release the right mouse button.	Display a shortcut menu after moving an object from one location to another.
Rotate wheel	Roll the wheel forward or backward.	Scroll vertically.
Press wheel button	Press the wheel button while moving the mouse on the desktop.	Scroll continuously.
Tilt wheel	Press the wheel toward the right or left.	Scroll horizontally.

FIGURE 5-7 The more common mouse operations.

Should the Government Set Computer Use Standards?

When you consider the causes of workplace injuries, you might not put clicking a mouse in the same category with lifting a bag of concrete, but perhaps you should. According to the chairman of a National Academy of Sciences panel that investigated workplace injuries, every year one million Americans lose workdays because of repetitive strain injuries. Repetitive strain injuries are caused when muscle groups perform the same actions over and over again. Once, repetitive strain injuries were common among factory workers who performed the same tasks on an assembly line for hours a day. Today, these injuries, which often result from prolonged use of a computer mouse and keyboard, are the largest job-related injury and illness problem in the United States. OSHA proposed standards whereby employers would have to establish programs to prevent workplace injuries with respect to computer use. Yet, congress rejected the standards, accepting the argument that the cost to employers would be prohibitive and unfair, because no proof exists that the injuries are caused exclusively by office work. Should the government establish laws regarding computer use? Why or why not? Who is responsible for this type of workplace injury? Why?

OTHER POINTING DEVICES

The mouse is the most widely used pointing device today. Some users, however, work with other pointing devices. These include the trackball, touchpad, pointing stick, joystick, wheel, audio player control pad, gamepad, light pen, touch screen, stylus, and pens. The following sections discuss each of these pointing devices.

Trackball

Similar to a mechanical mouse that has a ball on the bottom, a **trackball** is a stationary pointing device with a ball on its top or side (Figure 5-8). The ball in most trackballs is about the size of a Ping-Pong ball.

To move the pointer using a trackball, you rotate the ball with your thumb, fingers, or the palm of your hand. In addition to the ball, a trackball usually has one or more buttons that work just like mouse buttons.

A trackball requires frequent cleaning because it picks up oils from fingers and dust from the environment. For users who have limited desk space, however, a trackball is a good alternative to a mouse because the device is stationary.

Touchpad

A **touchpad** is a small, flat, rectangular pointing device that is sensitive to pressure and motion (Figure 5-9). To move the pointer using a touchpad, slide your fingertip across the surface of the pad. Some touchpads have one or more buttons around the edge of the pad that work like mouse buttons. On most touchpads, you also can tap the pad's surface to imitate mouse operations such as clicking. Touchpads are found most often on notebook computers.

WEB LINK 5-2

Touchpad
For more information, visit scsite.com/ dc2007/ch5/weblink and then click Touchpad.

FIGURE 5-8 A trackball is like an upside-down mouse.

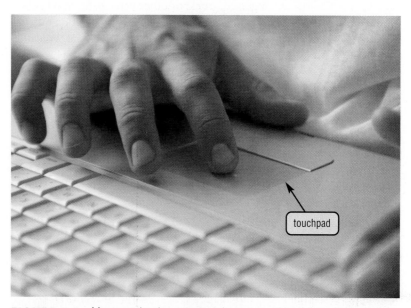

touchpad

FIGURE 5-9 Most notebook computers have a touchpad that allows users to control the movement of the pointer.

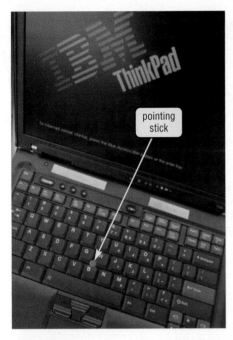

FIGURE 5-10
Some notebook computers include a pointing stick to allow a user to control the movement of the pointer.

Pointing Stick

A **pointing stick** is a pressure-sensitive pointing device shaped like a pencil eraser that is positioned between keys on a keyboard (Figure 5-10). To move the pointer using a pointing stick, you push the pointing stick with a finger. The pointer on the screen moves in the direction you push the pointing stick. By pressing buttons below the keyboard, users can click and perform other mouse-type operations with a pointing stick.

A pointing stick does not require any additional desk space. IBM developed the pointing stick for its notebook computers.

Joystick and Wheel

Users running game software or flight and driving simulation software often use a joystick or wheel as a pointing device (Figure 5-11). A **joystick** is a vertical lever mounted on a base. You move the lever in different directions to control the actions of the simulated vehicle or player. The lever usually includes buttons called triggers that you press to activate certain events. Some joysticks also have additional buttons you set to perform other actions.

A **wheel** is a steering-wheel-type input device. Users turn the wheel to simulate driving a car, truck, or other vehicle. Most wheels also include foot pedals for acceleration and braking actions. A joystick and wheel typically attach via a cable to a USB port.

Audio Player Control Pad

The *control pad* on an audio player is a pointing device that enables users to scroll through and play music, adjust volume, and customize settings. Control pads typically contain buttons or wheels that are operated with a thumb or finger. For example, users rotate the iPod's *Click Wheel* to browse through its song lists and press the Click Wheel's buttons to play or pause a song, display a menu, and other actions (Figure 5-12).

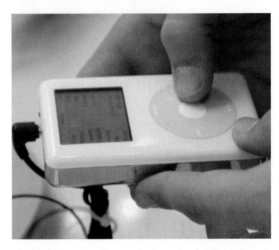

FIGURE 5-12   You rotate the wheel or press buttons on the iPod's Click Wheel to select and play songs.

Gamepad

A **gamepad**, sometimes called a game controller, is a pointing device that controls the movement and actions of players or objects in video games or computer games. On the gamepad, users press buttons or move sticks in various directions to activate events. Gamepads communicate with a game console or a personal computer via wired or wireless technology.

Light Pen

A **light pen** is a handheld input device that can detect the presence of light. To select objects on the screen, a user presses the light pen against the surface of the screen or points the light pen at the screen and then presses a button on the pen. Light pens also are ideal for areas where employees' hands might contain food, dirt, grease, or other chemicals that could damage the computer.

FIGURE 5-11   Joysticks and wheels help a user control the actions of players and vehicles in game and simulation software.

Touch Screen

A **touch screen** is a touch-sensitive display device. Users can interact with these devices by touching areas of the screen. Because touch screens require a lot of arm movements, you do not enter large amounts of data using a touch screen. Instead, you touch words, pictures, numbers, letters, or locations identified on the screen.

Kiosks, which are freestanding computers, often have touch screens (Figure 5-13). Travelers use kiosks in airports to print tickets ordered online and in hotels for easy check in and check out. To allow easy access of your bank account from a car, many ATM machines have touch screens. Many handheld game consoles also have touch screens.

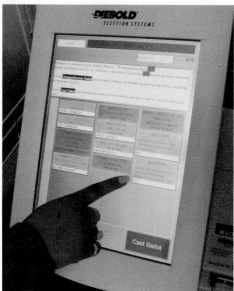

FIGURE 5-13 A voter uses a kiosk touch screen to cast ballots in an election.

Pen Input

Mobile users often enter data and instructions with a pen-type device. With **pen input**, users write, draw, and tap on a flat surface to enter input. The surface may be a monitor, a screen, a special type of paper, or a graphics tablet. Two devices used for pen input are the stylus and digital pen. A **stylus** is a small metal or plastic device that looks like a tiny ink pen but uses pressure instead of

ink (Figure 5-14). A **digital pen**, which is slightly larger than a stylus, is available in two forms: some are pressure-sensitive; others have built-in digital cameras.

Some mobile computers and nearly all mobile devices have touch screens. Instead of using a finger to enter data and instructions, most of these devices include a pressure-sensitive digital pen or stylus. You write, draw, or make selections on the computer screen by touching the screen with the pen or stylus. For example, Tablet PCs use a pressure-sensitive digital pen (Figure 5-15) and PDAs use a stylus. Pressure-sensitive digital pens, often simply called pens, typically provide more functionality than a stylus, featuring electronic erasers and programmable buttons.

Computers and mobile devices often use *handwriting recognition software* that translates the handwritten letters and symbols into characters that the computer or device can process.

FIGURE 5-14 PDAs and smart phones use a stylus.

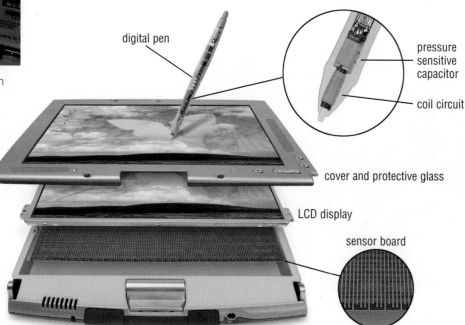

FIGURE 5-15 Tablet PCs use a pressure-sensitive digital pen.

If you want to use pen input on a computer that does not have a touch screen, you can attach a graphics tablet to the computer. A **graphics tablet** is a flat, rectangular, electronic, plastic board. Architects, mapmakers, designers, artists, and home users create drawings and sketches by using a pressure-sensitive pen or a cursor on a graphics tablet (Figure 5-16). A *cursor* looks similar to a mouse, except it has a window with cross hairs, so the user can see through to the tablet. Each location on the graphics tablet corresponds to a specific location on the screen. When drawing on the tablet with a pen or cursor, the tablet detects and converts the movements into digital signals that are sent in the computer. Large-scale applications sometimes refer to the graphics tablet as a *digitizer*.

Digital pens that have built-in digital cameras work differently from pressure-sensitive digital pens. These pens look much like a ballpoint pen and typically do not contain any additional buttons. In addition to the tiny digital camera, these pens contain a processor, memory, and an ink cartridge. As you write or draw on special digital paper with the pen, it captures every handwritten mark by taking more than 100 pictures per second and then stores the images in the pen's memory. You transfer the images from the pen to a computer (Figure 5-17) or mobile device, such as a smart phone. Some pens have a cradle for transferring images; others communicate wirelessly using Bluetooth.

WEB LINK 5-5

Pen Input

For more information, visit scsite.com/dc2007/ch5/weblink and then click Pen Input.

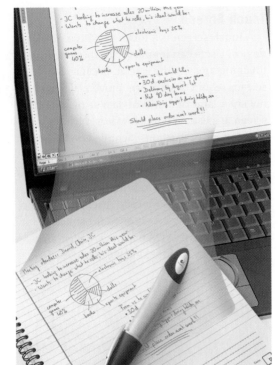

FIGURE 5-17   Some digital pens have built-in digital cameras that store handwritten marks and allow you to transfer your handwriting to a computer.

Test your knowledge of pages 234 through 244 in Quiz Yourself 5-1.

QUIZ YOURSELF 5-1

Instructions: Find the true statement below. Then, rewrite the remaining false statements so they are true.

1. A keyboard is an output device that contains keys users press to enter data in a computer.

2. A light pen is a flat, rectangular, electronic, plastic board.

3. A trackball is a small, flat, rectangular pointing device commonly found on notebook computers.

4. Input is any data or instructions entered into the memory of a computer.

5. Operations you can perform with a wheel include point, click, right-click, double-click, triple-click, drag, right-drag, rotate wheel, press wheel button, and tilt wheel.

6. PDAs use a pressure-sensitive digital pen, and Tablet PCs use a stylus.

Quiz Yourself Online: To further check your knowledge of input techniques, the keyboard, the mouse, and other pointing devices, visit scsite.com/dc2007/ch5/quiz and then click Objectives 1 – 4.

FIGURE 5-16a   (artist using a pen)

FIGURE 5-16b
(civil engineer using a cursor)

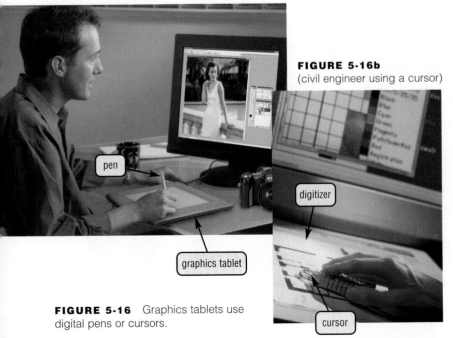

pen

graphics tablet

digitizer

cursor

FIGURE 5-16   Graphics tablets use digital pens or cursors.

VOICE INPUT

As an alternative to using a keyboard to enter data and instructions, some users talk to their computers and watch the spoken words appear on the screen as they talk. **Voice input** is the process of entering input by speaking into a microphone. The microphone may be a stand-alone peripheral that sits on top of a desk, or built in the computer or device, or in headphones or earphones. Some external microphones have a cable that attaches to a port on the sound card on the computer. Others communicate using wireless technology such as Bluetooth.

Voice recognition, also called *speech recognition*, is the computer's capability of distinguishing spoken words. Popular voice recognition programs include IBM ViaVoice and Dragon NaturallySpeaking. Many programs, such as Microsoft Office, support voice recognition. Figure 5-18 illustrates how Word recognizes dictated words and voice commands.

FIGURE 5-18 HOW TO DICTATE WORDS AND COMMANDS

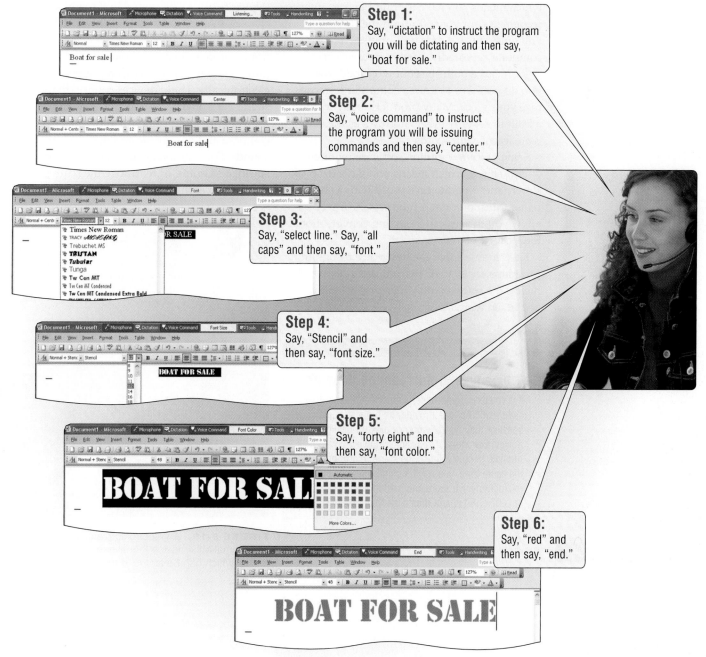

Step 1:
Say, "dictation" to instruct the program you will be dictating and then say, "boat for sale."

Step 2:
Say, "voice command" to instruct the program you will be issuing commands and then say, "center."

Step 3:
Say, "select line." Say, "all caps" and then say, "font."

Step 4:
Say, "Stencil" and then say, "font size."

Step 5:
Say, "forty eight" and then say, "font color."

Step 6:
Say, "red" and then say, "end."

Voice recognition programs recognize a vocabulary of preprogrammed words. The vocabulary of voice recognition programs can range from two words to millions of words. The automated telephone system at your bank may ask you to answer questions by speaking the words Yes or No into the telephone. A voice recognition program on your computer, by contrast, may recognize up to two million words.

Most voice recognition programs are a combination of speaker dependent and speaker independent. With *speaker-dependent software*, the computer makes a profile of your voice, which means you have to train the computer to recognize your voice. To train the computer, you must speak words and phrases into the computer repeatedly. *Speaker-independent software* has a built-in set of word patterns so you do not have to train a computer to recognize your voice. Many products today include a built-in set of words that grows as the software learns your words.

Some voice recognition software requires *discrete speech*, which means you have to speak slowly and separate each word with a short pause. Most of today's products, however, allow you to speak in a flowing conversational tone, called *continuous speech*.

Keep in mind that the best voice recognition programs are 90 to 95 percent accurate, which means the software may interpret as many as one in ten words incorrectly.

FAQ 5-4

Which type of microphone is best?

For voice recognition software, headphones that have a microphone provide the highest quality because they typically do not pick up background noises. For group discussions, however, where multiple people will use the same microphone at the same time, you need a stand-alone or built-in microphone. For more information, visit scsite.com/dc2007/ch5/faq and then click Microphones.

WEB LINK 5-6

Voice Input

For more information, visit scsite.com/dc2007/ch5/weblink and then click Voice Input.

Audio Input

Voice input is part of a larger category of input called audio input. **Audio input** is the process of entering any sound into the computer such as speech, music, and sound effects. To enter high-quality sound into a personal computer, the computer must have a sound card. Users enter sound into a computer via devices such as microphones, tape players, CD/DVD players, or radios, each of which plugs in a port on the sound card.

Some users also enter music and other sound effects into a computer using external MIDI devices such as an electronic piano keyboard (Figure 5-19). As discussed in the previous chapter, in addition to being a port, *MIDI (musical instrument digital interface)* is the electronic music industry's standard that defines how digital musical devices represent sounds electronically. These devices connect to the sound card on a computer. Software that conforms to the MIDI standard allows users to compose and edit music and many other sounds. For example, you can change the speed, add notes, or rearrange the score to produce an entirely new sound.

FIGURE 5-19 An electronic piano keyboard is an external MIDI device that allows users to record music, which can be stored in the computer.

INPUT FOR PDAs, SMART PHONES, AND TABLET PCs

Mobile devices, such as the PDA and smart phone, and mobile computers, such as the Tablet PC, offer convenience for the mobile user. A variety of alternatives for entering data and instructions is available for these devices and computers.

PDAs

A user enters data and instructions into a PDA in many ways (Figure 5-20). PDAs ship with a basic stylus, which is the primary input device. Users often purchase a more elaborate stylus that has a ballpoint pen at one end and a stylus at the other. With the stylus, you enter data in two ways: using an on-screen keyboard or using handwriting recognition software that

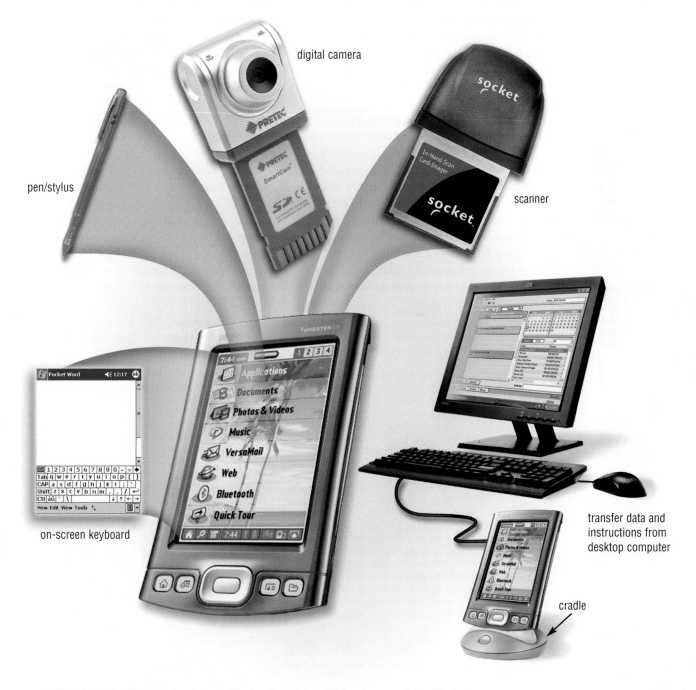

pen/stylus

digital camera

scanner

on-screen keyboard

transfer data and instructions from desktop computer

cradle

FIGURE 5-20   Users enter data and instructions into a PDA using a variety of techniques.

is built in the PDA. For example, drawing a straight vertical line in a downward motion displays the number 1 on the PDA.

For users who prefer typing to handwriting, some PDAs have a built-in mini keyboard. Other users type on a desktop computer or notebook computer keyboard and transfer the data to the PDA. Some users prefer to enter data into a PDA using a portable keyboard. A *portable keyboard* is a full-sized keyboard you conveniently use with a PDA or other mobile device. Some portable keyboards physically attach to and remove from a PDA; others are wireless. Figure 5-21 shows a pocket-sized portable wireless keyboard that unfolds into a full-sized keyboard.

As an alternative to typing, some PDAs allow users to speak data and instructions into the device. Some PDAs also have cameras built in so you can take photographs and view them on a PDA. On other models, you simply attach a digital camera directly to the PDA. You also can use a PDA to scan small documents, such as business cards and product labels, by attaching a scanner to the PDA. For more information about PDAs, read the Personal Mobile Devices feature that follows this chapter.

Smart Phones

Voice is one method of input for smart phones. Instead of voice, many people use text messaging, instant messaging, and picture messaging to communicate with others.

TEXT MESSAGING Instead of calling someone's smart phone or cellular telephone, users can enter and send typed messages using *text messaging*. To send a text message, you type a short message, typically less than 160 characters, to another smart phone by pressing buttons on the telephone's keypad. As with chat rooms and instant messaging, text messaging uses abbreviations and emoticons to minimize the amount of typing required. For example, instead of typing the text, I am surprised, a user can type the emoticon, :-O.

INSTANT MESSAGING Recall that instant messaging (IM) is a real-time communications service that allows you to exchange messages with other online users. Some wireless Internet service providers (WISPs) partner with IM services so you can use your smart phone to communicate with computer users of the same IM service. For example, with Cingular Wireless service, users can send and receive instant messages with AOL Instant Messenger and Yahoo! Messenger.

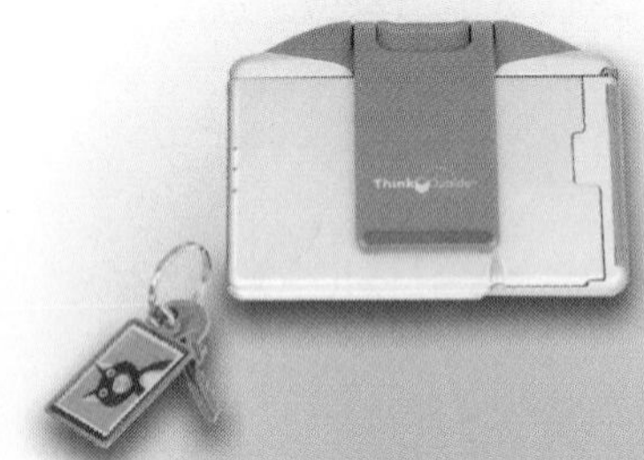

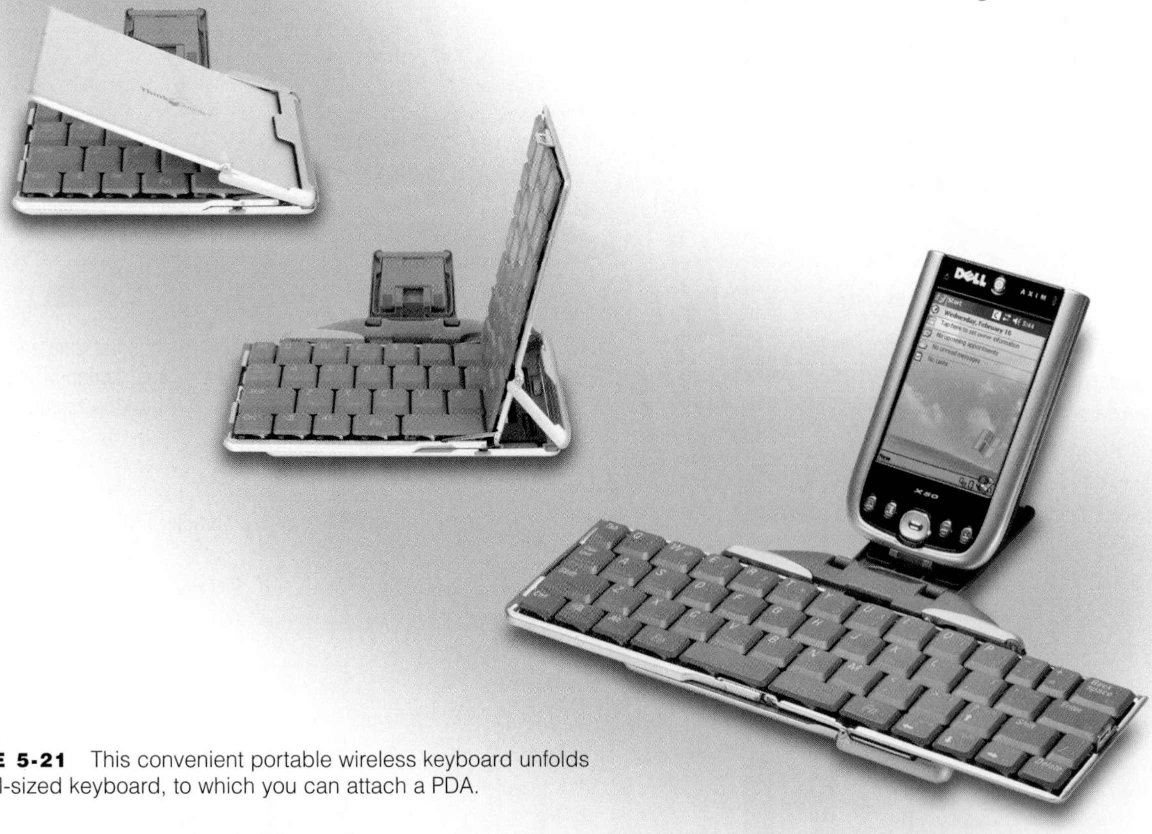

FIGURE 5-21 This convenient portable wireless keyboard unfolds into a full-sized keyboard, to which you can attach a PDA.

PICTURE MESSAGING

With *picture messaging,* users can send graphics, pictures, video clips, and sound files, as well as short text messages to another smart phone with a compatible picture messaging service. Many smart phones today have a built-in camera so users easily can take pictures and videos and even incorporate short voice recordings in their picture messages (Figure 5-22). After taking the pictures, users can send them to another smart phone, e-mail them to any e-mail address, or post them on a Web site.

FIGURE 5-22 Many smart phones include a digital camera so users can send pictures and videos to others.

As an alternative to text messaging, some users write a message with a digital pen, transfer the message from the pen to the smart phone, and then use picture messaging to send the handwritten message. Read Ethics & Issues 5-3 for a related discussion.

Most smart phones include PDA capabilities. Thus, input devices used with PDAs typically also are available for smart phones.

Tablet PCs

The primary input device for a Tablet PC is a pressure-sensitive digital pen, which allows users to write on the device's screen. A Tablet PC's handwriting recognition software works similarly to that of a PDA. The computer converts the handwriting into characters it can process.

Both the slate and convertible designs of a Tablet PC provide a means for keyboard input for those users who prefer typing to handwriting. You can attach a removable keyboard to the slate Tablet PC. The convertible Tablet PC has an attached keyboard that can be rotated 180 degrees so the computer resembles a notebook computer.

To access peripherals at their home or office, users can slide their Tablet PC in a docking

ETHICS & ISSUES 5-3

Should Talking on a Cellular Phone While Driving Be Illegal?

Cellular phone sales are soaring. In addition to talking on the phone, many drivers are using their phones to send and receive text messages, instant messages, picture messages, and e-mail, and to access and view Web pages. For drivers, however, cellular phones may be a liability. Estimates vary widely, but studies link between 800 and 8,000 fatalities on U.S. highways to phone use. Because of their additional capabilities, some experts believe cellular phones pose an even greater risk. Many countries have placed bans or restrictions on the use of phones while driving. In the United States, several states have considered or enacted similar legislation. New York, for example, permits vehicle operators to use only hands-free phones. Yet, some studies report that just talking on a phone can cause enough driver inattention to trigger an accident. Supporters of a cellular phone ban cite a British study that found drivers talking on phones had reaction times 50 percent slower than when not talking on a phone, and 30 percent slower than drivers who were intoxicated. Opponents of a ban note, however, that other driver activities, like tuning a radio or having a conversation, can be equally distracting and that phones are a factor in fewer than 1 percent of crashes. Furthermore, drivers may have good reasons to use phones while driving, and laws may not take this into account. Should the use of phones be banned while driving? Why? What other measures, if any, could be taken to prevent drivers from endangering themselves and others while using phones?

station. A *docking station*, which is an external device that attaches to a mobile computer or device, contains a power connection and provides connections to peripherals. In the docking station, Tablet PC users can work with a full-sized keyboard, mouse, CD/DVD drives, and other desktop peripherals (Figure 5-23). The design of docking stations varies, depending on the type of mobile computer or the device to which they are attached.

FAQ 5-5

Can a mobile computer or device get a virus?

Yes. Mobile computers and devices can get a virus from a downloaded Web page. A virus can transfer from a desktop computer to a mobile device when users connect the two to synchronize data. Viruses also can transmit via wireless data transfer when two wireless devices communicate with one another, such as when receiving a text or picture message. For more information, visit scsite.com/dc2007/ch5/faq and then click Viruses and Mobile Devices.

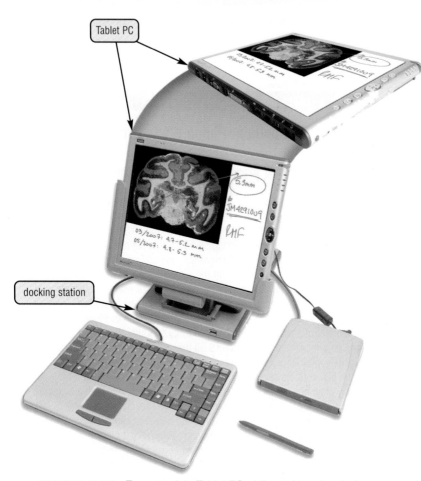

Tablet PC

docking station

FIGURE 5-23 To use a slate Tablet PC while working at a desk, insert the Tablet PC in a docking station. Devices such as a keyboard and CD drive can be plugged in the docking station.

DIGITAL CAMERAS

A **digital camera** allows users to take pictures and store the photographed images digitally, instead of on traditional film (Figure 5-24). While many digital cameras look like a traditional camera, some models attach to PDAs or are built in PDAs and smart phones. Mobile users such as real estate agents, insurance agents, general contractors, and photojournalists use digital cameras so they immediately can view photographed images on the camera. Home and business users have digital cameras to save the expense of film developing, duplication, and postage.

Some digital cameras use internal flash memory to store images. Others store images on mobile storage media, such as a flash memory card, memory stick, and mini-disc. Chapter 7 discusses these and other storage media in depth. Generally, higher-capacity storage devices can hold more pictures.

Digital cameras typically allow users to review, and sometimes edit, images while they are in the camera. Some digital cameras can connect to or communicate wirelessly with a printer or television, allowing users to print or view images directly from the camera.

FIGURE 5-24 With a digital camera, users can view photographed images immediately through a small screen on the camera to see if the picture is worth keeping.

Often users prefer to *download*, or transfer a copy of, the images from the digital camera to the computer's hard disk. With some digital cameras, images download through a cable that connects between the digital camera (or the camera's docking station) and a USB port or a FireWire port on the system unit. For cameras that store images on miniature mobile storage media, simply insert the media in a reading/writing device that communicates wirelessly or attaches to a port on the system unit. Copying images from the miniature media to the computer's hard disk is just like copying files from any other disk drive. Some cameras store images on a mini CD/DVD. In this case, insert the disc in the computer's disc drive and then copy the pictures to the computer's hard disk (or you can view the contents of the disc by inserting it in a CD or DVD player).

When you copy images to the hard disk in a computer, the images are available for editing with photo editing software, printing, faxing, sending via e-mail, including in another document, or posting to a Web site or photo community for everyone to see. Many users add pictures to greeting cards, a computerized photo album, a family newsletter, certificates, and awards.

The three basic types of digital cameras are studio cameras, field cameras, and point-and-shoot cameras. The most expensive and highest quality of the three is a *studio camera*, which is a stationary camera used for professional studio work. Often used by photojournalists, a *field camera* is a portable camera that has many lenses and other attachments. As with the studio camera, a field camera can be quite expensive. A *point-and-shoot camera* is much more affordable and lightweight and provides acceptable quality photographic images for the home or small business user. Figure 5-25 illustrates how one make of point-and-shoot digital camera works.

A point-and-shoot camera often features flash, zoom, automatic focus, and special effects. Some allow users to record short audio narrations for photographed images. Others even record short video clips in addition to still images. Point-and-shoot digital cameras often have a built-in TV out port, allowing users to

FIGURE 5-25   HOW A DIGITAL CAMERA MIGHT WORK

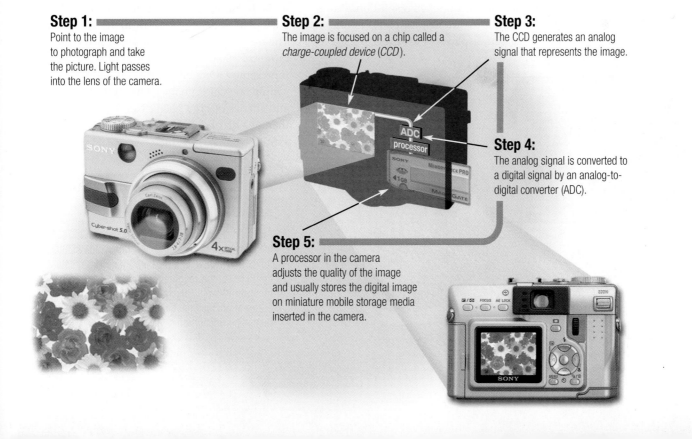

Step 1: Point to the image to photograph and take the picture. Light passes into the lens of the camera.

Step 2: The image is focused on a chip called a *charge-coupled device* (*CCD*).

Step 3: The CCD generates an analog signal that represents the image.

Step 4: The analog signal is converted to a digital signal by an analog-to-digital converter (ADC).

Step 5: A processor in the camera adjusts the quality of the image and usually stores the digital image on miniature mobile storage media inserted in the camera.

display photographed images or play recorded video clips directly on a television.

For additional information about digital cameras, read the Digital Imaging and Video Technology feature that follows Chapter 6.

Digital Camera Quality

One factor that affects the quality of a digital camera is its resolution. **Resolution** is the number of horizontal and vertical pixels in a display device. A *pixel* (short for picture element) is the smallest element in an electronic image (Figure 5-26). The greater the number of pixels the camera uses to capture an image, the better the quality of the image. Thus, the higher the resolution, the better the image quality, but the more expensive the camera.

Digital camera resolutions range from approximately 1 million to more than 8 million pixels (*MP*). A camera with a 5.1-megapixel (5,100,000 pixels) resolution will provide a better quality than one with a 3.2-megapixel resolution. As a general rule, a 1-megapixel camera is fine for pictures sent via e-mail or posted on the Web. For good quality printed photographs, users should have a 2-megapixel camera for 4 × 6 inch photographs, a 3-megapixel camera for 8 × 10 photographs, and 5-megapixel or greater camera for larger size prints.

Manufacturers often use pixels per inch to represent a digital camera's resolution. *Pixels per inch* (*ppi*) is the number of pixels in one inch of screen display. For example, a 2304 ×

1728 (pronounced 2304 by 1728) ppi camera has 2,304 pixels per vertical inch and 1,728 pixels per horizontal inch. Multiplying these two numbers together gives an approximate total number of megapixels. For example, 2304 times 1728 equals approximately 4 million, or 4 megapixels. If just one number is stated, such as 1600 ppi, then both the vertical and horizontal numbers are the same.

Many digital cameras provide a means to adjust the ppi to the desired resolution. With a lower ppi, you can capture and store more images in the camera. For example, a camera set at 800 × 600 ppi might capture and store 61 images, if it has sufficient storage capacity. The number of images may reduce to 24 on the same camera set at 1600 × 1200 ppi, because each image consumes more storage space.

The actual photographed resolution is known as the *optical resolution*. Some manufacturers state *enhanced resolution*, instead of, or in addition to, optical resolution. Optical resolution is different from enhanced resolution. The enhanced resolution usually is higher because it uses a special formula to add pixels between those generated by the optical resolution. Be aware that some manufacturers compute a digital camera's megapixels from the enhanced resolution, instead of optical resolution.

Another measure of a digital camera's quality is the number of bits it stores in a pixel. Each pixel consists of one or more bits of data. The more bits used to represent a pixel, the more colors and shades of gray that can be represented. One bit per pixel is enough for simple one-color images. For multiple colors and shades of gray, each pixel requires more than one bit of data. A point-and-shoot camera should be at least 24 bit.

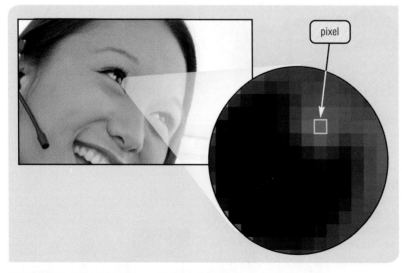

FAQ 5-7

What is dpi?

Some advertisements incorrectly use dpi to mean the same as ppi. The acronym *dpi*, which stands for *dots per inch*, is a measure of a print resolution. For screen resolution, the proper measurement term is ppi (pixels per inch). For more information, visit scsite.com/dc2007/ch5/faq and then click Resolution.

FIGURE 5-26 A pixel is a single point in an electronic image.

VIDEO INPUT

Video input is the process of capturing full-motion images and storing them on a computer's storage medium such as a hard disk or DVD.

Some video devices record video using analog signals. Computers, by contrast, use digital signals. To enter video from an analog device into a personal computer, the analog signal must be converted to a digital signal. To do this, plug a video camera, VCR, or other analog video device in a video capture port on the system unit. One type of adapter card that has a video capture port is a *video capture card*, which converts an analog video signal into a digital signal that a computer can process. Most new computers are not equipped with a video capture card because not all users have the need for this type of adapter card.

A **digital video (DV) camera**, by contrast, records video as digital signals instead of analog signals. Many DV cameras can capture still frames, as well as motion. To transfer recorded images to a hard disk or CD or DVD, users connect DV cameras directly to a USB port or a FireWire port on the system unit. Thus, the computer does not need a video capture card. Simply connect the video device to the computer and begin transferring images. After saving the video on a storage medium, such as a hard disk or DVD, you can play it or edit it using video editing software on a computer (Figure 5-27).

PC Video Cameras

A **PC video camera**, or **PC camera**, is a type of digital video camera that enables a home or small business user to capture video and still images, send e-mail messages with video attachments, add live images to instant messages, broadcast live images over the Internet, and make video telephone calls. During a *video telephone call*, both parties see each other as they communicate over the Internet (Figure 5-28). The cost of PC video cameras usually is less than $100.

Attached to the computer's USB port or FireWire port, a PC video camera usually sits on top of the monitor. For more flexibility, some PC video cameras are portable. That is, you can detach them from the base and use them as a stand-alone digital camera.

FIGURE 5-28 Using a PC video camera, home users can see each other as they communicate over the Internet.

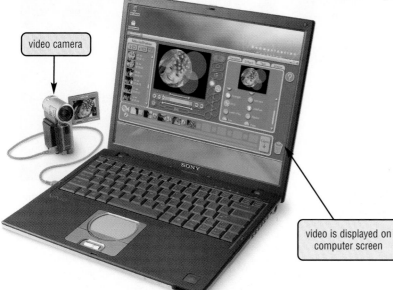

video camera

video is displayed on computer screen

FIGURE 5-27 Home users can transfer videos to their computers and then use video editing software to edit the video.

WEB LINK 5-7

Digital Video Cameras

For more information, visit scsite.com/ dc2007/ch5/weblink and then click Digital Video Cameras.

Web Cams

A **Web cam** is any video camera that displays its output on a Web page. A Web cam attracts Web site visitors by showing images that change regularly. Home or small business users might use Web cams to show a work in progress, weather and traffic information, employees at work, photographs of a vacation, and countless other images. Read Ethics & Issues 5-4 for a related discussion.

Some Web sites have live Web cams that display still pictures and update the displayed image at a specified time or time intervals, such as 15 seconds. Another type of Web cam, called a *streaming cam*, has the illusion of moving images because it sends a continual stream of still images.

ETHICS & ISSUES 5-4

Should Cameras Be Able to Monitor Your Every Move?

In the world of George Orwell's classic novel *1984*, "Telescreens" constantly monitor each citizen's every word and movement. Since its publication more than 50 years ago, most people have viewed the novel as a warning against a future that should be avoided. Today, however, you can find cameras in every corner of public life. Whether it is on a busy street corner, on a casino floor, in a subway station, in the neighborhood grocery store, in an elevator, or even in the workplace, the watchful eye continues to become more and more ubiquitous. In Chicago, cameras monitor high-crime areas and even listen for gunshots. Businesses and governments claim that advances in the technology and the low cost as compared to other options allow them to provide greater security and safety. Privacy advocates say that the cameras violate the Constitution's guarantee against unreasonable searches. Many cases of abuse of video monitoring have been noted, such as stores secretly listening in on spouses discussing a potential purchase. What are the differences between George Orwell's Telescreens and the current state of video monitoring? What are the similarities? Would you feel more secure or more paranoid living in a continuously monitored society? Why? What are the benefits of video monitoring? Should you have nothing to fear from security cameras if you have done nothing wrong?

Video Conferencing

A **video conference** is a meeting between two or more geographically separated people who use a network or the Internet to transmit audio and video data (Figure 5-29). To participate in a video conference, you need video conferencing software along with a microphone, speakers, and a video camera attached to a computer.

As you speak, members of the meeting hear your voice on their speakers. Any image in front of the video camera, such as a person's face, appears in a window on each participant's screen. A *whiteboard* is another window on the screen that displays notes and drawings simultaneously on all participants' screens. This window provides multiple users with an area on which they can write or draw.

As the costs of video conferencing hardware and software decrease, increasingly more business meetings, corporate training, and educational classes will be conducted as video conferences.

FAQ 5-8

How popular is video conferencing?

A recent survey found that 40 percent of computer users participate in video conferences with desktop equipment. Annual expenditures exceed $7.7 billion on voice and video conferencing equipment. For more information, visit scsite.com/dc2007/ch5/faq and then click Video Conferencing.

FIGURE 5-29 To save on travel expenses, many large businesses are turning to video conferencing.

Test your knowledge of pages 245 through 254 in Quiz Yourself 5-2.

QUIZ YOURSELF 5-2

Instructions: Find the true statement below. Then, rewrite the remaining false statements so they are true.

1. A digital camera allows users to take pictures and store the photographed images digitally, instead of on traditional film.
2. DV cameras record video as analog signals.
3. Instant messaging is the computer's capability of distinguishing spoken words.
4. Many smart phones today have a built-in camera so users easily can send text messages.
5. The lower the resolution of a digital camera, the better the image quality, but the more expensive the camera.

Quiz Yourself Online: To further check your knowledge of voice input; input for PDAs, smart phones, and Tablet PCs; digital cameras; and video input, visit scsite.com/dc2007/ch5/quiz and then click Objectives 5 – 8.

SCANNERS AND READING DEVICES

Some input devices save users time by eliminating manual data entry. With these devices, users do not type, speak, or write into the computer. Instead, these devices capture data from a *source document*, which is the original form of the data. Examples of source documents include time cards, order forms, invoices, paychecks, advertisements, brochures, photographs, inventory tags, or any other document that contains data to be processed.

Devices that can capture data directly from a source document include optical scanners, optical readers, bar code readers, RFID readers, magnetic stripe card readers, and magnetic-ink character recognition readers. The following pages discuss each of these devices.

Optical Scanners

An *optical scanner*, usually called a **scanner**, is a light-sensing input device that reads printed text and graphics and then translates the results into a form the computer can process. Four types of scanners are flatbed, pen, sheet-fed, and drum (Figure 5-30).

TYPES OF SCANNERS

Scanner	Method of Scanning and Use	Scannable Items
Flatbed 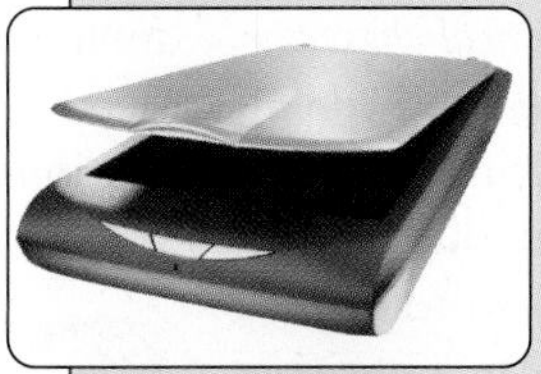	• Similar to a copy machine • Scanning mechanism passes under the item to be scanned, which is placed on a glass surface	• Single-sheet documents • Bound material • Photographs • Some models include trays for slides, transparencies, and negatives
Pen or Handheld 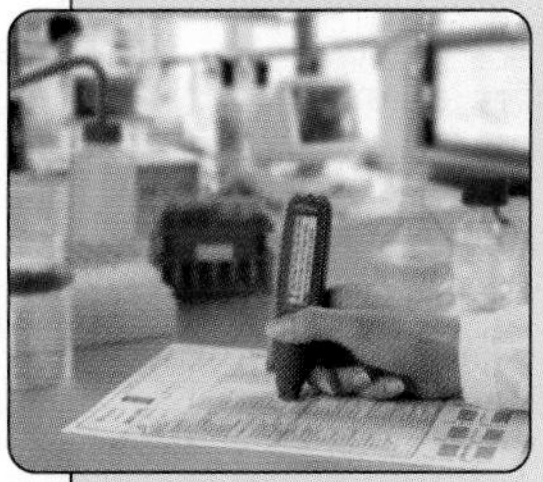	• Move pen over text to be scanned, then transfer data to computer • Ideal for mobile users, students, and researchers • Some connect to a PDA or smart phone	• Any printed text
Sheet-fed 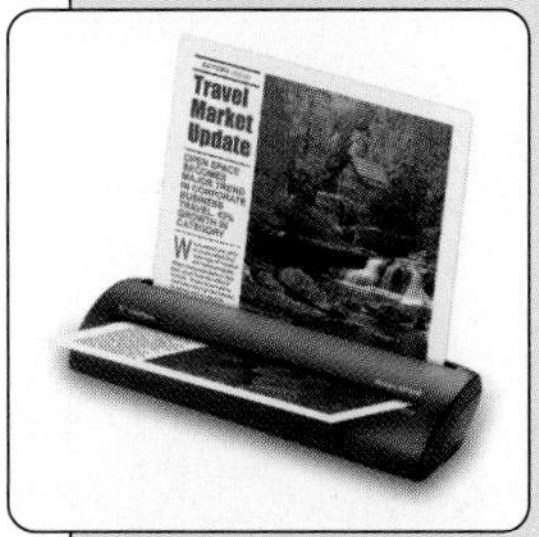	• Item to be scanned is pulled into a stationary scanning mechanism • Smaller than a flatbed scanner • A model designed specifically for photographs is called a *photo scanner*	• Single-sheet documents • Photographs • Slides (with an adapter) • Negatives
Drum 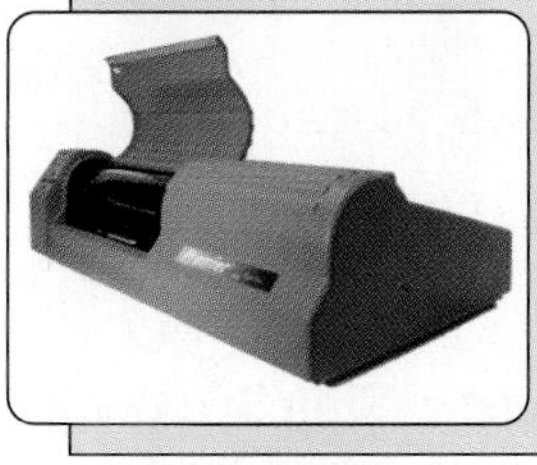	• Item to be scanned rotates around stationary scanning mechanism • Very expensive • Used in large businesses	• Single-sheet documents • Photographs • Slides • Negatives

FIGURE 5-30 This table describes the various types of scanners.

A **flatbed scanner** works in a manner similar to a copy machine except it creates a file of the document in memory instead of a paper copy (Figure 5-31). Once you scan a document or picture, you can display the scanned object on the screen, store it on a storage medium, print it, fax it, attach it to an e-mail message, include it in another document, or post it to a Web site or photo community for everyone to see.

As with a digital camera, the quality of a scanner is measured by the number of bits it stores in a pixel and the number of pixels per inch, or resolution. The higher each number, the better the quality, but the more expensive the scanner. Most of today's affordable color desktop scanners for the home or small business range from 30 to 48 bits and have an optical resolution ranging from 600 to 9600 ppi. Commercial scanners designed for power users range from 9600 to 14,000 ppi.

Many scanners include *OCR (optical character recognition) software*, which can read and convert text documents into electronic files. OCR software is useful if you need to modify a document but do not have the original word processing file. For example, if you scan a business report with a flatbed scanner and do not use OCR software, you cannot edit the report because the scanner saves the report as an image. This is because the scanner does not differentiate between text and graphics. OCR software, however, would convert the scanned image into a text file that you could edit, for example, with a word processing program. Current OCR software has a high success rate and usually can identify more than 99 percent of scanned material.

Businesses often use scanners for *image processing*, which consists of capturing, storing, analyzing, displaying, printing, and manipulating images. Image processing allows users to convert paper documents such as reports, memos, and procedure manuals into electronic images. Users distribute and publish these electronic documents on networks and the Internet.

Business users typically store and index electronic documents with an image processing system. An *image processing system* is similar to an electronic filing cabinet that provides access to exact reproductions of the original documents. Local governments, for example, use image processing systems to store property deeds and titles to provide the public and professionals, such as lawyers and loan officers, quick access to electronic documents.

FAQ 5-9

How can I improve the quality of scanned documents?

Place a blank sheet of paper behind translucent papers, newspapers, and other see-through types of paper. If the original image is crooked, draw a line on the back at the bottom of the image. Use that mark to align the original on the scanner. Use photo editing software to fix imperfections in images. For more information, visit scsite.com/dc2007/ch5/faq and then click Scanning.

FIGURE 5-31   HOW A FLATBED SCANNER WORKS

Step 1: Place the document to be scanned face down on the glass window. Using buttons on the scanner or the scanner program, start the scanning process.

Step 2: The scanner converts the document content to digital information, which is transmitted through the cable to the memory of the computer.

Step 3: Once in the memory of the computer, users can display the image, print it, e-mail it, include it in a document, or place it on a Web page.

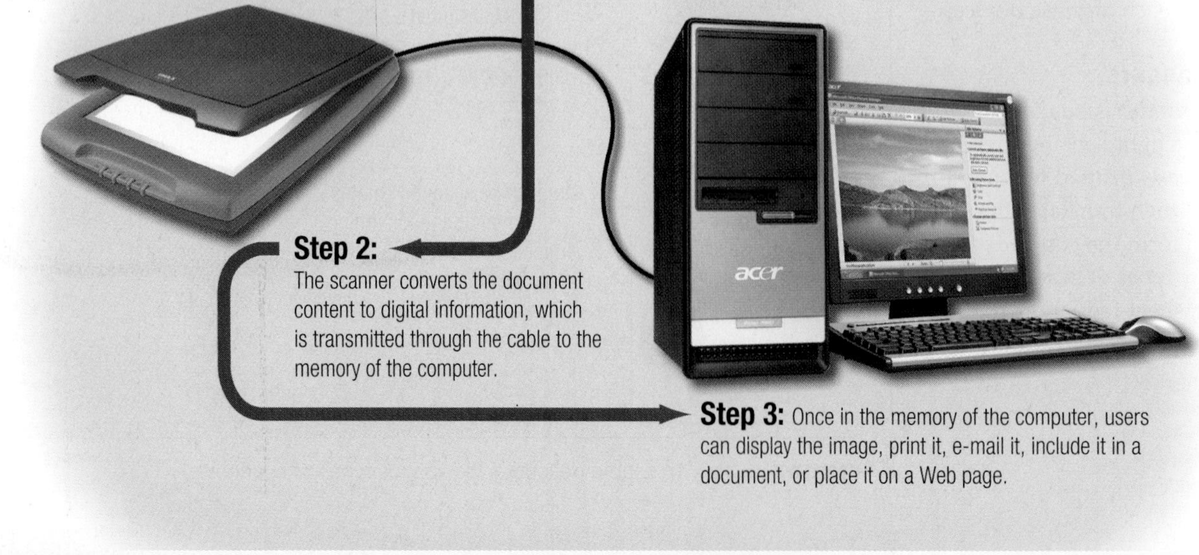

Optical Readers

An *optical reader* is a device that uses a light source to read characters, marks, and codes and then converts them into digital data that a computer can process. Two technologies used by optical readers are optical character recognition and optical mark recognition.

OPTICAL CHARACTER RECOGNITION Optical **character recognition (OCR)** is a technology that involves reading typewritten, computer-printed, or hand-printed characters from ordinary documents and translating the images into a form that the computer can process. Most **OCR devices** include a small optical scanner for reading characters and sophisticated software to analyze what is read.

OCR devices range from large machines that can read thousands of documents per minute to handheld wands that read one document at a time. OCR devices read printed characters in an OCR font. A widely used OCR font is called OCR-A (Figure 5-32). During the scan of a document, an OCR device determines the shapes of characters by detecting patterns of light and dark. OCR software then compares these shapes with predefined shapes stored in memory and converts the shapes into characters the computer can process.

```
ABCDEFGHIJKLM
NOPQRSTUVWXYZ
1234567890
-=■;',./
```

FIGURE 5-32 A portion of the characters in the OCR-A font. Notice how characters such as the number 0 and the letter O are shaped differently so the reading device easily can distinguish between them.

Many companies use OCR characters on turnaround documents. A **turnaround document** is a document that you return (turn around) to the company that creates and sends it. For example, when consumers receive a bill, they often tear off a portion of the bill and send it back to the company with their payment (Figure 5-33). The portion of the bill they return usually has their payment amount, account number, and other information printed in OCR characters.

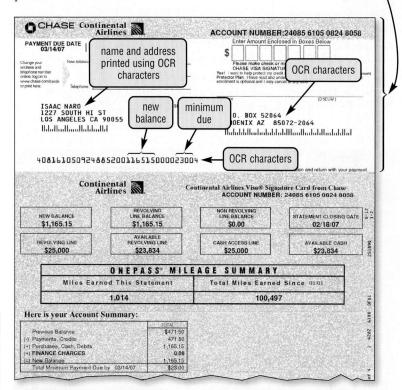

FIGURE 5-33 OCR characters frequently are used with turnaround documents. With this bill, you tear off the top portion and return it with a payment.

OPTICAL MARK RECOGNITION Optical mark **recognition (OMR)** is a technology that reads hand-drawn marks such as small circles or rectangles. A person places these marks on a form, such as a test, survey, or questionnaire answer sheet. With a test, the OMR device first scans the answer key sheet to record correct answers based on patterns of light. The OMR device then scans the remaining documents and matches their patterns of light against the answer key sheet.

Bar Code Readers

A **bar code reader**, also called a **bar code scanner**, is an optical reader that uses laser beams to read bar codes by using light patterns that pass through the bar code lines (Figure 5-34). A **bar code** is an identification code that consists of a set of vertical lines and spaces of different widths. The bar code represents data that identifies the manufacturer and the item.

Manufacturers print a bar code either on a product's package or on a label that is affixed to a product. A variety of products such as groceries, books, clothing, vehicles, mail, and packages have bar codes. Each industry uses its own type of bar code. The United States Postal Service (USPS) uses a POSTNET bar code. Retail and grocery stores use the *UPC* (*Universal Product Code*) bar code (Figure 5-35). Read Ethics & Issues 5-5 for a related discussion.

FIGURE 5-34 A bar code reader uses laser beams to read bar codes on products such as groceries and books.

ETHICS & ISSUES 5-5

Scanner Errors at the Checkout Counter?

Have you ever taken an item to a store's checkout and discovered that the price displayed when the item's bar code was scanned was different from the price shown on a shelf tag, sign, or advertisement? If you have, you are not alone. A government survey found that eight percent of the time, an item's scanned price is different from the price presented elsewhere. When an item is scanned at a store's checkout counter, a computer finds the item's price in the store's database. Store owners claim that discrepancies between the scanned price and a listed price are the result of human error — either failure to update the store's price database or incorrect shelf tags, signs, or advertisements. Yet, some consumer advocates claim that the discrepancy sometimes is intentional. They accuse stores of *scanner fraud*, insisting that some stores advertise one price and then charge another, hoping buyers will not recognize the difference. Most states have laws that protect consumers against scanner fraud. Some laws even require stores to pay consumers an immediate reward, sometimes $5 or more, if the consumer finds a scanner error. Who do you think is responsible for differences between scanned prices and posted costs? Why? Should stores be responsible for pricing errors? Why or why not?

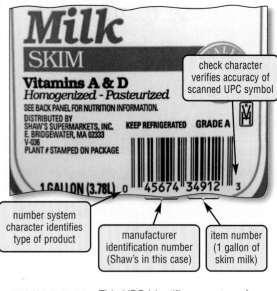

FIGURE 5-35 This UPC identifies a carton of skim milk.

RFID Readers

RFID (*radio frequency identification*) is a technology that uses radio signals to communicate with a tag placed in or attached to an object, an animal, or a person. RFID tags, which contain a memory chip and an antenna, are available in many shapes and sizes and sometimes are embedded in glass, labels, or cards. Some RFID tags are as small as a grain of sand; others are the size of a luggage tag. An **RFID reader** reads information on the tag via radio waves. RFID readers can be handheld devices or mounted in a stationary object such as a doorway.

Many retailers see RFID as an alternative to bar code identification because it does not require direct contact or line-of-site transmission. Each product in a store would contain a tag that identifies the product (Figure 5-36). As consumers remove products from the store shelves and walk through a checkout area, an RFID reader reads the tag(s) and communicates with a computer that calculates the amount due, eliminating the need for checking out each item.

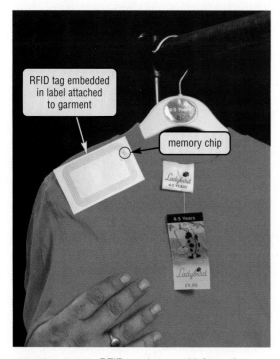

RFID tag embedded in label attached to garment

memory chip

FIGURE 5-36 RFID readers read information stored on an RFID tag and then communicate this information to computers, which instantaneously compute payments and update inventory records. In this example, the RFID tag is embedded in a label attached to the garment.

Other uses of RFID include tracking times of runners in a marathon; tracking location of soldiers, employee wardrobes, and airline baggage; checking lift tickets of skiers; gauging pressure and temperature of tires on a vehicle; checking out library books; and tracking payment as vehicles pass through booths on tollway systems. Read Ethics & Issues 5-6 for a related discussion. Read Looking Ahead 5-1 for a look at the next generation of RFID.

ETHICS & ISSUES 5-6

Ready for RFID?

Move over bar codes, make way for RFID. RFID (radio frequency identification) uses a tiny computer chip that can be mounted on a tag attached to a product or sewn into an article of clothing. For merchants, RFID can help to locate items in a warehouse and identify items that need to be replenished. For consumers, RFID can supply detailed product information, reduce costs associated with inventory management, and someday let buyers bypass check-out lines and take purchases directly from the store, with the item's cost charged to their card. Even casinos are beginning to use RFID in betting chips to stop counterfeiting and track patrons' habits. Privacy advocates worry, however, that RFID could obliterate a buyer's anonymity. They fear that with an RFID reader, any individual or organization could track a purchaser's movements and make that information available to marketers or government agencies. To protect privacy, privacy advocates insist that merchants should be forced to disable RFID transmitters as soon as buyers leave a store. Would you be comfortable purchasing a product that includes RFID? Why or why not? Should buyers be allowed to request that RFID transmitters be disabled after they make a purchase, or should merchants be required to render transmitters inoperative when the product leaves the store? Why?

LOOKING AHEAD 5-1

RFID Sensors Simplify, Monitor Tasks

Burnt microwave meals may become a thing of the past with the development of RFID technology. Just wave the packaging in front of a food-enabled scanner and let the microwave determine how long to cook the food at a particular temperature.

Many uses for RFID sensors are planned. They could determine when a soccer ball crosses a goal line or a marathon runner crosses the finish line, signal when a child passes a doorway in his pajamas or an inmate enters restricted areas, and track packages by sensing and transmitting product locations. On the battlefield, they could sense vehicle and missile movement. In hospitals, patient wristbands could monitor when a particular drug and dosage is administered. For more information, visit scsite.com/dc2007/ch5/looking and then click RFID Uses.

Magnetic Stripe Card Readers

A **magnetic stripe card reader**, often called a *magstripe reader*, reads the magnetic stripe on the back of credit cards, entertainment cards, bank cards, and other similar cards. The stripe, which is divided in three horizontal tracks, contains information identifying you and the card issuer (Figure 5-37). Some information stored in the stripe includes your name, account number, the card's expiration date, and a country code.

When a consumer swipes a credit card through the magstripe reader, it reads the information stored on the magnetic stripe on the card. If the magstripe reader rejects your card, it is possible that the magnetic stripe on the card is scratched, dirty, or erased. Exposure to a magnet or magnetic field can erase the contents of a card's magnetic stripe.

In many cases, a magstripe reader is part of a point-of-sale terminal. The function of point-of-sale terminals is discussed later in this chapter.

MICR Readers

MICR (*magnetic-ink character recognition*) devices read text printed with magnetized ink. An **MICR reader** converts MICR characters into a form the computer can process. The banking industry almost exclusively uses MICR for check processing. Each check in your checkbook has precoded MICR characters beginning at the lower-left edge (Figure 5-38). The MICR characters represent the bank number, the customer account number, and the check number. These numbers may appear in a different order than the ones shown in the sample in Figure 5-38.

When a bank receives a check for payment, it uses an MICR inscriber to print the amount of the check in MICR characters in the lower-right corner. The check then is sorted or routed to the customer's bank, along with thousands of others. Each check is inserted in an MICR reader, which sends the check information — including the amount of the check — to a computer for processing. When you balance your checkbook, verify that the amount printed in the lower-right corner is the same as the amount written on the check; otherwise, your statement will not balance.

The banking industry has established an international standard not only for bank numbers, but also for the font of the MICR characters. This standardization makes it possible for people to write checks in other countries.

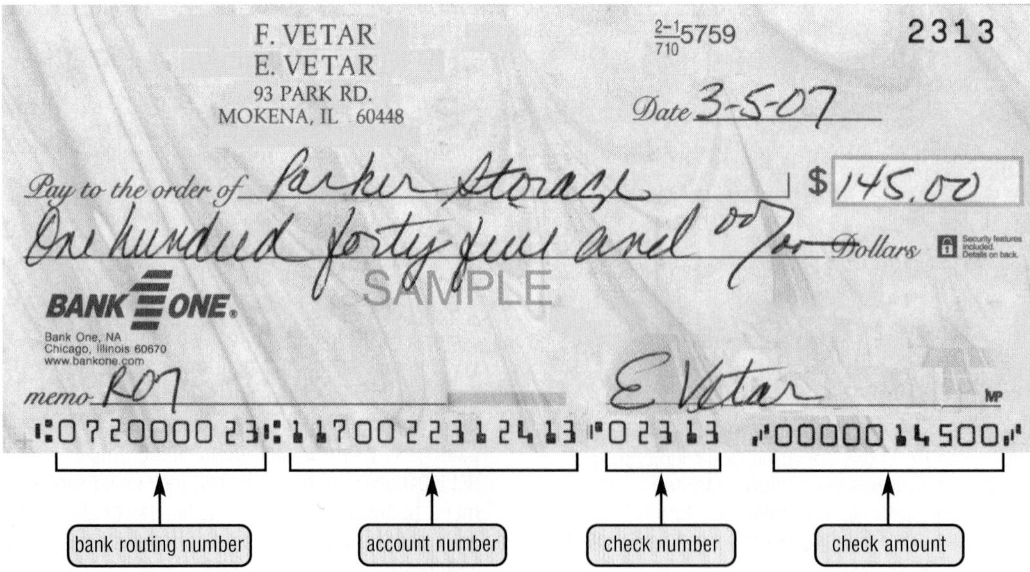

FIGURE 5-37 A magnetic stripe card reader reads information encoded on the stripe on the back of your credit card.

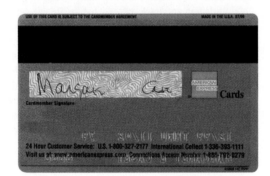

FIGURE 5-38 The MICR characters preprinted on the check represent the bank routing number, the customer account number, and the check number. The amount of the check in the lower-right corner is added after the check is cashed.

Data Collection Devices

Instead of reading or scanning data from a source document, a *data collection device* obtains data directly at the location where the transaction or event takes place. For example, employees use bar code readers, PDAs, handheld computers, or other mobile devices to collect data wirelessly (Figure 5-39). These types of data collection devices are used in restaurants, factories, warehouses, the outdoors, or other locations where heat, humidity, and cleanliness are not easy to control.

Data collection devices and many mobile computers and devices have the capability of wirelessly transmitting data over a network or the Internet. Increasingly more users today send data wirelessly to central office computers using these devices.

FIGURE 5-39 A warehouse employee uses this rugged handheld computer, which includes a bar code reader, that wirelessly transmits information about the scanned item to the company's inventory system.

TERMINALS

A *terminal* consists of a keyboard, a monitor, a video card, and memory. Often, these components are housed in a single unit.

Terminals fall into three basic categories: dumb terminals, smart terminals, and special-purpose terminals. A *dumb terminal* has no processing power; thus, it cannot function as an independent device. Users enter data and instructions in a dumb terminal and then transmit the data to a host computer over a network. The host computer processes the input and then, if necessary, sends information (output) back to the dumb terminal. The host computer usually is a server or mainframe. A *smart terminal* has a processor, giving it the capability of performing some functions independent of the host computer. In recent years, personal computers have replaced most smart terminals.

Special-purpose terminals perform specific tasks and contain features uniquely designed for use in a particular industry. Two widely used special-purpose terminals are point-of-sale (POS) terminals and automated teller machines.

Point-of-Sale Terminals

The location in a retail or grocery store where a consumer pays for goods or services is the *point of sale* (*POS*). Most retail stores use a **POS terminal** to record purchases, process credit or debit cards, and update inventory.

In a grocery store, the POS terminal is a combination of an electronic cash register, bar code reader, and printer. When the checkout clerk scans the bar code on the food product, the computer uses the manufacturer and item numbers to look up the price of the item and the complete product name in a database. Then, the price of the item in the database shows on the display device, the name of the item and its price print on a receipt, and the item being sold is recorded so the inventory can be updated. Thus, the output from a POS terminal serves as input to other computers to maintain sales records, update inventory, verify credit, and perform other activities associated with the sales transactions that are critical to running the business. Some POS terminals are Web-enabled, which allows updates to inventory at geographically separate locations.

Many POS terminals handle credit card or debit card payments and thus also include a magstripe reader. After swiping your card through the reader, the POS terminal connects to a system that authenticates the purchase. Once the transaction is approved, the terminal prints a receipt for the customer.

A self-service POS terminal allows consumers to perform all checkout-related activities (Figure 5-40). That is, they scan the items, bag the items, and pay for the items themselves. Consumers with small orders find the self-service POS terminals convenient because these terminals often eliminate the hassle of waiting in long lines.

which verifies that you are the holder of the bankcard. When your transaction is complete, the ATM prints a receipt for your records.

magstripe reader

FIGURE 5-41 An ATM is a self-service banking terminal that allows customers to access their bank accounts.

touch screen with graphical user interface

magstripe reader scans credit or debit card

bar code reader reads UPC labels

FIGURE 5-40 Many grocery stores offer self-serve checkouts, where the consumers themselves use the POS terminals to scan purchases, scan their store saver card and coupons, and then pay for the goods.

Automated Teller Machines

An **automated teller machine** (**ATM**) is a self-service banking machine that connects to a host computer through a network (Figure 5-41). Banks place ATMs in convenient locations, including grocery stores, convenience stores, retail outlets, shopping malls, and gas stations, so customers conveniently can access their bank accounts.

Using an ATM, people withdraw cash, deposit money, transfer funds, or inquire about an account balance. Some ATMs have a touch screen; others have special buttons or keypads for entering input. To access a bank account, you insert a plastic bankcard in the ATM's magstripe reader. The ATM asks you to enter a password, called a *personal identification number* (*PIN*),

BIOMETRIC INPUT

Biometrics is the technology of authenticating a person's identity by verifying a personal characteristic. Biometric devices grant users access to programs, systems, or rooms by analyzing some biometric identifier. A *biometric identifier* is a physiological (related to physical or chemical activities in the body) or behavioral characteristic. Examples include fingerprints, hand geometry, facial features, voice, signatures, and eye patterns.

A *biometric device* translates a personal characteristic (the input) into a digital code that is compared with a digital code stored in the computer. If the digital code in the computer does not match the personal characteristic's code, the computer denies access to the individual.

The most widely used biometric device today is a fingerprint scanner. A **fingerprint scanner** captures curves and indentations of a fingerprint. With the cost of fingerprint scanners less than $100, home and small business users install fingerprint scanners to authenticate users before they can access a personal computer. External fingerprint scanners usually plug into a parallel or USB port. To save on desk space, some newer keyboards and notebook computers have a fingerprint scanner built into them, which allows users to log on to Web sites via their fingerprint instead of entering a user name and password (Figure 5-42). For a technical discussion about fingerprint scanners, read the High-Tech Talk article on page 268.

A *face recognition system* captures a live face image and compares it with a stored image to determine if the person is a legitimate user. Some buildings use face recognition systems to secure access to rooms. Law enforcement, surveillance systems, and airports use face recognition to protect the public. Some notebook computers use this security technique to safeguard a computer. The computer will not start unless the user is legitimate. These programs are becoming more sophisticated and can recognize people with or without glasses, makeup, or jewelry, and with new hairstyles.

Biometric devices measure the shape and size of a person's hand using a *hand geometry system* (Figure 5-43). Because their cost is more than $1,000, larger companies use these systems as time and attendance devices or as security devices. Colleges use hand geometry systems to verify students' identities. Day-care centers and hospital nurseries use them to verify parents who pick up their children.

A *voice verification system* compares a person's live speech with their stored voice pattern. Larger organizations sometimes use voice verification systems as time and attendance devices. Many companies also use this technology for access to sensitive files and networks. Some financial services use voice verification systems to secure telephone banking transactions. These systems use speaker-dependent voice recognition software. That is, users train the computer to recognize their inflection patterns.

A *signature verification system* recognizes the shape of your handwritten signature, as well as measures the pressure exerted and the motion used to write the signature. Signature verification systems use a specialized pen and tablet.

FIGURE 5-42 Keyboard with built-in fingerprint scanner.

FIGURE 5-43 A hand geometry system verifies this student's identity before he is allowed access to the school recreation center.

High security areas use iris recognition systems. The camera in an *iris recognition system* uses iris recognition technology to read patterns in the iris of the eye (Figure 5-44). These patterns are as unique as a fingerprint. Iris recognition systems are quite expensive and are used by government security organizations, the military, and financial institutions that deal with highly sensitive data. Some organizations use *retinal scanners*, which work similarly but instead scan patterns of blood vessels in the back of the retina.

Sometimes, fingerprint, iris, retina, and other biometric data are stored on a smart card. A **smart card**, which is comparable in size to a credit card or ATM card, stores the personal data on a thin microprocessor embedded in the card (Figure 5-45). Smart cards add an extra layer of protection. For example, when a user places a smart card through a smart card reader, the computer compares a fingerprint stored on the card with the one read by the fingerprint scanner. Some credit cards are smart cards; that is, the microprocessor contains the card holder's information instead of a magnetic stripe.

WEB LINK 5-9

Biometric Input

For more information, visit scsite.com/ dc2007/ch5/weblink and then click Biometric Input.

FAQ 5-10

How popular is biometric technology?

One study estimates that revenues from biometric solutions has and will continue to grow by about 35 percent annually for the next several years, as shown in the chart below. For more information, visit scsite.com/dc2007/ch5/faq and then click Biometrics.

Revenues from Biometric Solutions

Year	
2008	
2007	
2006	
2005	
2004	

$0 $1,000 $2,000 $3,000 $4,000 $5,000
(in millions of dollars)

Source: International Biometric Group

FIGURE 5-44 An iris recognition system.

smart card reader

microprocessor on smart card

FIGURE 5-45 A smart card reader reads data stored on a smart card's microprocessor.

PUTTING IT ALL TOGETHER

When you purchase a computer, you should have an understanding of the input devices included with the computer, as well as those you may need that are not included. Many factors influence the type of input devices you may use: the type of input desired, the hardware and software in use, and the desired cost. The type of input devices you require depends on your intended use. Figure 5-46 outlines several suggested input devices for specific computer users.

SUGGESTED INPUT DEVICES BY USER

User	Input Device
HOME 	• Enhanced keyboard or ergonomic keyboard • Mouse • Stylus for PDA or smart phone • Joystick or wheel • 30-bit 600 x 1200 ppi color scanner • 3-megapixel digital camera • Headphones that include a microphone • PC video camera
SMALL OFFICE/ HOME OFFICE 	• Enhanced keyboard or ergonomic keyboard • Mouse • Stylus and portable keyboard for PDA or smart phone, or digital pen for Tablet PC • 36-bit 600 x 1200 ppi color scanner • 3-megapixel digital camera • Headphones that include a microphone • PC video camera
MOBILE 	• Wireless mouse for notebook computer • Touchpad or pointing stick on notebook computer • Stylus and portable keyboard for PDA or smart phone, or digital pen for Tablet PC • 3- or 4-megapixel digital camera • Headphones that include a microphone • Fingerprint scanner for notebook computer
POWER 	• Enhanced keyboard or ergonomic keyboard • Mouse • Stylus and portable keyboard for PDA or smart phone • Pen for graphics tablet • 48-bit 1200 x 1200 ppi color scanner • 6- to 8-megapixel digital camera • Headphones that include a microphone • PC video camera
LARGE BUSINESS 	• Enhanced keyboard or ergonomic keyboard • Mouse • Stylus and portable keyboard for PDA or smart phone, or digital pen for Tablet PC • Touch screen • Light pen • 42-bit 1200 x 1200 ppi color scanner • OCR/OMR readers, bar code readers, MICR reader, or data collection devices • Microphone • Video camera for video conferences • Fingerprint scanner or other biometric device

FIGURE 5-46 This table recommends suggested input devices.

INPUT DEVICES FOR PHYSICALLY CHALLENGED USERS

The ever-increasing presence of computers in everyone's lives has generated an awareness of the need to address computing requirements for those who have or may develop physical limitations. The **Americans with Disabilities Act** (**ADA**) requires any company with 15 or more employees to make reasonable attempts to accommodate the needs of physically challenged workers.

Besides voice recognition, which is ideal for blind or visually impaired users, several other input devices are available. A *keyguard* is a metal or plastic plate placed over the keyboard that allows users to rest their hands on the keyboard without accidentally pressing any keys (Figure 5-47). A keyguard also guides a finger or pointing device so a user presses only one key at a time.

Keyboards with larger keys also are available. Still another option is the *on-screen keyboard*, in which a graphic of a standard keyboard is displayed on the user's screen (Figure 5-48).

FIGURE 5-47 A keyguard.

Various pointing devices are available for users with motor disabilities. Small trackballs that the user controls with a thumb or one finger can be attached to a table, mounted to a wheelchair, or held in the user's hand. Another option for people with limited hand movement is a *head-mounted pointer* to control the pointer or insertion point (Figure 5-49). To simulate the functions of a mouse button, a user works with switches that control the pointer. The switch might be a hand pad, a foot pedal, a receptor that detects facial motions, or a pneumatic instrument controlled by puffs of air.

Two exciting developments in this area are gesture recognition and computerized implant devices. Both in the prototype stage, they attempt to provide users with a natural computer interface.

With *gesture recognition*, the computer will detect human motions. Computers with gesture recognition capability have the potential to recognize sign language, read lips, track facial movements, or follow eye gazes. For paralyzed or speech impaired individuals, a doctor will implant a computerized device into the brain. This device will contain a transmitter. As the user thinks thoughts, the transmitter will send signals to the computer.

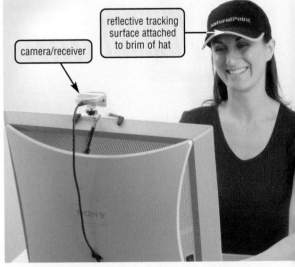

reflective tracking surface attached to brim of hat

camera/receiver

FIGURE 5-49 A camera/receiver mounted on the monitor tracks the position of the head-mounted pointer, which is reflective material that this user is wearing on the brim of her hat. As the user moves her head, the pointer on the screen also moves.

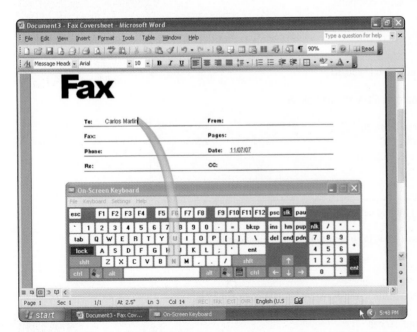

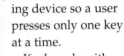

FIGURE 5-48 As you click letters on the on-screen keyboard, they appear in the document at the location of the insertion point.

Test your knowledge of pages 255 through 266 in Quiz Yourself 5-3.

QUIZ YOURSELF 5-3

Instructions: Find the true statement below. Then, rewrite the remaining false statements so they are true.

1. A fingerprint scanner captures curves and indentations of a signature.
2. After swiping a credit card through an MICR reader, a POS terminal connects to a system that authenticates the purchase.
3. ATMs ask you to enter a password, called a biometric identifier, which verifies that you are the holder of the bankcard.
4. Four types of source documents are flatbed, pen, sheet-fed, and drum.
5. Retail and grocery stores use the POSTNET bar code.
6. RFID is a technology that uses laser signals to communicate with a tag placed in an object, an animal, or a person.
7. The Americans with Disabilities Act (ADA) requires any company with 15 or more employees to make reasonable attempts to accommodate the needs of physically challenged workers.

Quiz Yourself Online: To further check your knowledge of scanners and reading devices, terminals, biometric devices, and input for physically challenged users, visit scsite.com/dc2007/ch5/quiz and then click Objectives 9 – 12.

CHAPTER SUMMARY

Input is any data and instructions you enter into the memory of a computer. This chapter described the various techniques of entering input and several commonly used input devices (read Looking Ahead 5-2 for a look at the next generation of input devices). Topics presented included the keyboard, mouse, and other pointing devices; voice input; input for PDAs, smart phones, and Tablet PCs; digital cameras; video input; scanners and reading devices; terminals; biometric input; and input devices for physically challenged users.

LOOKING AHEAD 5-2

Wearable Computers Make Performance Statement

Frodo, the hero in the *Lord of the Rings* trilogy, wears a durable, inconspicuous tunic that saves his life. You, too, may one day wear a garment with biosensors that may save your life by detecting health problems and summoning emergency help.

While this clothing is practical, other researchers are creating the newest fashions and accessories outfitted with computers. For example, reporters may one day wear trench coats equipped with 10 cameras to give a 360-degree panoramic view of the scene. Children wearing the Dog@watch jacket and watch might transmit their location via a GPS unit and wireless computer. Buttons on your jacket also may serve as cameras, sunglasses may have a built-in audio player, and your shirt might display text messages from a friend. For more information, visit scsite.com/dc2007/ch5/looking and then click Wearable Computers.

CAREER CORNER

Data Entry Clerk

Data entry clerks have an essential role in today's information-producing industry. A *data entry clerk* enters data into documents, databases, and other applications using computer keyboards and visual display devices. Duties can include manipulating, editing, and maintaining data to ensure that it is accurate and up-to-date, and researching information.

Some data entry clerks telecommute. Although they generally use keyboards, they also work with other input from scanners or electronically transmitted files. Because of the nature of their job, data entry clerks often sit for hours typing in front of monitors. They can be susceptible to repetitive stress injuries and neck, back, and eye strain. To prevent these injuries, many offices use ergonomically designed input devices and incorporate regularly scheduled exercise breaks.

Data entry clerks usually are high school graduates with keyboarding skills. Some employers require an associate's degree or at least two years of post-high-school education plus two years of office experience. Data entry training, basic language skills, and familiarity with word processing, spreadsheet, and database programs are important. Data entry often serves as a stepping-stone to other administrative positions. The average annual salary for data entry clerks is around $24,000. Salaries start at about $21,500 and, with experience, can exceed $33,000. For more information, visit scsite.com/dc2007/ch5/careers and then click Data Entry Clerk.

High-Tech Talk

BIOMETRICS: PERSONALIZED SECURITY

Biometric authentication is based on the measurement of an individual's unique physiological and behavioral characteristics. The most common measurements, described earlier in this chapter, such as fingerprints, hand geometry, facial features, and eye patterns are physiological biometrics. Some of the more novel measurements, such as body odor, brain wave patterns, DNA, ear shape, sweat pores, and vein patterns also fall into the category of physiological biometrics. Voice scan and signature scan are examples of behavioral biometrics.

Any biometric technology process involves two basic steps — enrollment and matching. To illustrate these steps, this High-Tech Talk uses the most common biometric technology, finger-scan technology.

ENROLLMENT   Enrollment is the process in which a user presents the fingerprint data to be stored in a template for future use, as shown in the top of Figure 5-50. This initial template is called the *enrollment template*. Creating the enrollment template involves four basic steps: (1) acquire fingerprint, (2) extract fingerprint feature, (3) create enrollment template, and (4) store enrollment template. The enrollment template usually is created only after the user has submitted several samples of the same fingerprint. Most fingerprint images will have false details, usually caused by cuts, scars, or even dirt, which must be filtered out.

The first step, acquire fingerprint, presents a major challenge to finger-scan technology. The quality of a fingerprint may vary substantially from person to person and even finger to finger. The two main methods of acquiring images are optical and silicon. With optical technology, a camera is used to register the fingerprint image against a plastic or glass platen (scanner). Silicon technology uses a silicon chip as a platen, which usually produces a higher quality fingerprint image than optical devices.

The second step, extract fingerprint feature, involves thinning the ridges of the raw image to a minuscule size and then converting the characteristics to binary format. Fingerprints are comprised of ridges and valleys that have unique patterns, such as arches, loops, and swirls. Irregularities and discontinuities in these ridges and valleys are known as *minutiae*. Minutiae are the distinctive characteristics upon which most finger-scan technology is based. The fingerprint-feature extraction process used is highly sophisticated, patented, and a closely-held vendor secret.

In the third step, the binary format is used to create the enrollment template. The fourth and final step involves storing the template on a storage device, such as a hard disk or smart card for future use when the same person attempts to be authenticated.

MATCHING   Matching is the process of comparing a match template to an enrollment template. A *match template* is created when the user attempts to gain access through a fingerprint scanner. Most computer and network systems are set up so that the person also must claim an identity, such as a user name, along with the fingerprint. In this case, the match template is compared directly to the enrollment template for that user name. Other systems, such as those used for criminal investigations, will search the entire enrollment template database for a match.

The match template is created in the same fashion as the enrollment template described earlier. Rather than storing the match template on disk, however, it is compared to the user's stored enrollment template, as shown in the bottom of Figure 5-50. The result of the matching process is a score. The score is compared against a threshold. The threshold is a predefined number that can be adjusted depending on the desired level of security.

The scoring process leads to the decision process. The decision process will produce one of three actions: (1) the threshold has been exceeded, thereby resulting in a match; (2) the threshold has not been met, thereby resulting in a nonmatch; or (3) the data may have been insufficient, resulting in the system requesting a new sample from the user to begin a new comparison.

Finger-scan technology is likely to continue to grow as the centerpiece of the biometric industry. For more information, visit scsite.com/dc2007/ch5/tech and then click Biometrics.

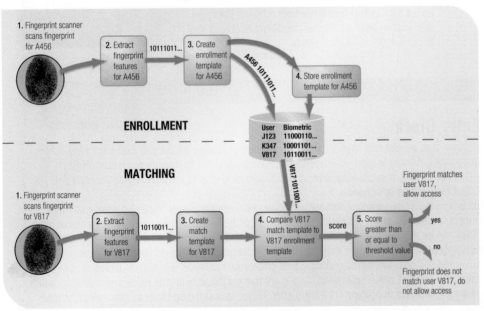

FIGURE 5-50 The two steps in biometric technology.

Companies on the Cutting Edge

LOGITECH
PERSONAL INTERFACE PRODUCTS LEADER

The average Internet user has more than 40 inches of cords on his desktop, according to a *Logitech* survey. This company is working to reduce desktop clutter with a variety of cordless peripherals, including mouse devices, keyboards, mobile headphones and earphones, and game controllers.

A market leader, Logitech has sold more than 50 million wireless devices. It also designs, manufactures, and markets corded devices. The company's retail sales account for more than 85 percent of its revenue.

Two engineering students from Stanford University, Italian-born Pierluigi Zappacosta and Swiss-born Daniel Borel, launched Logitech in 1981. Today, the corporation is the world's largest manufacturer of the mouse, having sold more than 500 million since the company's founding. For more information, visit scsite.com/dc2007/ch5/companies and then click Logitech.

Palm
HANDHELD COMPUTING DEVICES MANUFACTURER

The PalmPilot holds the distinction of being the most rapidly adopted new computing product ever manufactured. More than two million units of this PDA were sold since Palm Computing introduced the product in 1996.

Palm Computing was founded in 1992 and became a subsidiary of 3Com Corp. in 1997. In 2000, the Palm subsidiary became an independent, publicly traded company. In 2003, shareholders voted to spin off PalmSource, Inc., maker of the Palm operating system, as an independent company called palmOne, Inc., and acquire Handspring, Inc. In 2005, the company changed its name to *Palm*, Inc., after it acquired full rights to the brand name, Palm.

The Palm product family includes the Zire and Tungsten handheld devices, LifeDrive storage devices, and the Treo smart phones. For more information, visit scsite.com/dc2007/ch5/companies and then click Palm.

Technology Trailblazers

CHARLES WALTON
RFID DEVELOPER

The next time you use a key card to unlock a door, you can thank *Charles Walton* for simplifying your life. He holds the first patent in RFID technology, issued in 1973, which he called "an automatic identification system."

He believed his invention would interest General Motors executives, but they thought his automatic door lock reader was too futuristic. He then went to lock manufacturer Schlage, where management licensed his technology. Walton also created an automatic toll collection system more than 20 years ago. He has been awarded more than 50 patents, 10 of which are for his RFID-related products.

Today, Walton continues to invent RFID and other technologies in his Los Gatos, California laboratory. For more information, visit scsite.com/dc2007/ch5/people and then click Charles Walton.

DOUGLAS ENGELBART
CREATOR OF THE MOUSE

The phrase "point and click" might not be part of every computer user's vocabulary if *Douglas Engelbart* had not pursued his engineering dreams. In 1964, he developed the first prototype computer mouse with the goal of making it easier to move a cursor around a computer screen.

Ten years later, engineers at Xerox refined Engelbart's prototype and showed the redesigned product to Apple's Steve Jobs, who applied the concept to his graphical Macintosh computer. The mouse was mass produced in the mid-1980s, and today it is the most widely used pointing device.

Engelbart currently serves as director of the Bootstrap Institute, a company he founded with his daughter to form strategic alliances and consequently improve corporations' performances. For more information, visit scsite.com/dc2007/ch5/people and then click Douglas Engelbart.

270 **CHAPTER 5**

Discovering Computers 2007
A Gateway to Information

Select a chapter:
1 2 3 4 5 6 7 8 9 10 11 12 13 14 15

5 | Input

Chapter Review

The Chapter Review section summarizes the concepts presented in this chapter. To listen to the audio version of this Chapter Review, visit scsite.com/dc2007/ch5/review. To obtain help from other students regarding any subject in this chapter, visit scsite.com/dc2007/ch5/forum and post your thoughts or questions.

① What Is Input? Input is any *data* or instructions entered into the memory of a computer. An **input device** is any hardware component that allows users to enter data and instructions.

② What Are the Characteristics of a Keyboard? A **keyboard** is an input device that contains keys users press to enter data into a computer. Computer keyboards have a typing area that includes letters of the alphabet, numbers, punctuation marks, and other basic keys. Most keyboards also have *function keys* programmed to issue commands; keys used to move the **insertion point**, usually a blinking vertical bar, on the screen; and *toggle keys* that switch between two states when pressed. A *gaming keyboard* is a keyboard designed specifically for users that enjoy playing games on the computer.

③ What Are Different Mouse Types, and How Do They Work? A **pointing device** is an input device that allows users to control a small graphical symbol, called a **pointer**, on the computer screen. A **mouse** is a pointing device that fits under the palm of your hand. As you move a mouse, the pointer on the screen also moves. A *mechanical mouse* translates the movement of a ball on its underside into signals the computer can process. An *optical mouse* uses devices that emit and sense light to detect the mouse's movement. A *cordless mouse* transmits data using wireless technology.

④ How Do Pointing Devices Work? A **trackball** is a stationary pointing device with a ball that you rotate to move the pointer. A **touchpad** is a flat, pressure-sensitive device that you slide your finger across to move the pointer. A **pointing stick** is a device positioned on the keyboard that you push to move the pointer. A **joystick** is a vertical lever that you move to control a simulated vehicle or player. A **wheel** is a steering-wheel-type device that you turn to simulate driving a vehicle. The *control pad* on an audio player is a pointing device that enables users to scroll through and play music, adjust volume, and customize settings. A **gamepad**, sometimes called a game controller, is a pointing device that controls the movement and actions of players or objects in video games or computer games. A **light pen** is a light-sensitive device that you press against or point at the screen to select objects. A **touch screen** is a touch-sensitive display device that you interact with by touching areas of the screen. A **stylus** and a **digital pen** use pressure to write or draw.

> Visit scsite.com/dc2007/ch5/quiz or click the Quiz Yourself button. Click Objectives 1 – 4.

⑤ How Does Voice Recognition Work? **Voice recognition** is the computer's capability of distinguishing spoken words. Voice recognition programs recognize a vocabulary of preprogrammed words. Most voice recognition programs are a combination of *speaker-dependent software*, which makes a profile of your voice, and *speaker-independent software*, which has a built-in set of word patterns.

⑥ What Are Input Devices for PDAs, Smart Phones, and Tablet PCs? A primary input device for a PDA is a basic stylus. Some PDAs have a built-in keyboard or support voice input. You can attach a full-sized *portable keyboard* to a PDA. Voice is one input method for smart phones. Users can send typed messages using *text messaging*. Some smart phones can use IM to communicate over the Internet, and many have a camera so that users can use *picture messaging*. The primary input device for a Tablet PC is a digital pen, with which users can write on the device's screen. If you slide a Tablet PC into a *docking station*, you can use a full-sized keyboard, mouse, and other peripherals.

Chapter Review

⑦ How Does a Digital Camera Work? A **digital camera** allows users to take pictures and store the photographed images digitally. When you take a picture, light passes into the camera lens, which focuses the image on a *charge-coupled device (CCD)*. The CCD generates an analog signal that represents the image. An analog-to-digital converter (ADC) converts the analog signal to a digital signal. A processor in the camera stores the digital image on the camera's storage media. The image is downloaded to a computer's hard disk via cable or copied from the camera's storage media.

⑧ How Are PC Video Cameras, Web Cams, and Video Conferencing Used? A **PC video camera** is a digital video camera that enables users to capture video and still images and then send or broadcast the images over the Internet. A **Web cam** is any video camera that displays its output on a Web page. A **video conference** is a meeting between geographically separated people who use a network or the Internet to transmit audio and video data.

> Visit scsite.com/dc2007/ch5/quiz or click the Quiz Yourself button. Click Objectives 5 – 8.

⑨ What Are Various Types of Scanners and Reading Devices, and How Do They Work? A **scanner** is a light-sensing input device that reads printed text and graphics and translates the results into a form the computer can process. A **flatbed scanner** works in a manner similar to a copy machine except it creates a file of the document. An *optical reader* uses a light source to read characters, marks, and codes and converts them into digital data. **Optical character recognition (OCR)** reads characters from ordinary documents. **Optical mark recognition (OMR)** reads hand-drawn marks such as small circles. A **bar code reader** is an optical reader that uses laser beams to read a **bar code**, or identification code. **RFID** (*radio frequency identification*) uses radio signals to communicate with an embedded tag. **MICR** (*magnetic-ink character recognition*) reads text printed with magnetized ink.

⑩ What Are Types of Terminals? A *terminal* consists of a keyboard, a monitor, a video card, and memory. A *dumb terminal* has no processing power and relies on a host computer for processing. A *smart terminal* has a processor and can perform some functions independent of the host computer. POS terminals and ATMs are special-purpose terminals. A **POS (point-of-sale) terminal** records purchases, processes credit or debit cards, and updates inventory. An **automated teller machine (ATM)** is a self-service banking machine that connects to a host computer. To access a bank account, you insert a bankcard into the ATM's card reader and enter a *personal identification number (PIN)*.

⑪ What Are Various Biometric Devices? A *biometric device* translates a personal characteristic into digital code that is compared with a digital code stored in the computer to identify an individual. A **fingerprint scanner** captures curves and indentations of a fingerprint. A *face recognition system* captures a live face image. A *hand geometry system* measures the shape and size of a hand. A *voice verification system* compares live speech with a stored voice pattern. A *signature verification system* recognizes the shape of a signature. An *iris recognition system* reads patterns in the iris of the eye. *Retinal scanners* scan patterns of blood vessels in the back of the retina.

⑫ What Are Alternative Input Devices for Physically Challenged Users? Voice recognition is ideal for visually impaired users. A *keyguard* is a plate placed over the keyboard that allows users with limited hand mobility to rest their hands and press only one key at a time. Keyboards with larger keys or an *on-screen keyboard* displayed on a user's screen also are available. A small trackball or a *head-mounted pointer* helps users with limited hand movement to control the pointer. Two developments in the prototype stage are *gesture recognition* and computerized implant devices.

> Visit scsite.com/dc2007/ch5/quiz or click the Quiz Yourself button. Click Objectives 9 – 12.

Key Terms

You should know the Primary Terms and be familiar with the Secondary Terms. Use the list below to help focus your study. To further enhance your understanding of the Key Terms in this chapter, visit scsite.com/dc2007/ch5/terms. See an example of and a definition for each term, and access current and additional information about the term from the Web.

Primary Terms

(shown in bold-black characters in the chapter)

Americans with Disabilities Act (ADA) (266)
audio input (246)
automated teller machine (ATM) (262)
bar code (258)
bar code reader (258)
bar code scanner (258)
digital camera (250)
digital pen (243)
digital video (DV) camera (253)
ergonomics (238)
fingerprint scanner (262)
flatbed scanner (256)
gamepad (242)
graphics tablet (244)
input (234)
input device (236)
insertion point (237)
joystick (242)
keyboard (236)
light pen (242)
magnetic stripe card reader (260)
MICR (260)
MICR reader (260)
mouse (239)
mouse pad (239)

OCR devices (257)
optical character recognition (OCR) (257)
optical mark recognition (OMR) (257)
PC camera (253)
PC video camera (253)
pen input (243)
pointer (239)
pointing device (239)
pointing stick (242)
POS terminal (261)
resolution (252)
RFID (259)
RFID reader (259)
scanner (255)
smart card (264)
stylus (243)
touch screen (243)
touchpad (241)
trackball (241)
turnaround document (257)
video conference (254)
video input (253)
voice input (245)
voice recognition (245)
Web cam (254)
wheel (242)

Secondary Terms

(shown in italic characters in the chapter)

biometric device (262)
biometric identifier (262)
biometrics (262)
charge-coupled device (CCD) (251)
Click Wheel (242)
command (235)
continuous speech (246)
control pad (242)
cordless keyboard (238)
cordless mouse (239)
cursor (application program) (237)
cursor (graphics tablet) (244)
data (234)
data collection device (261)
digitizer (244)
discrete speech (246)
docking station (250)
download (251)
dumb terminal (261)
enhanced keyboard (236)
enhanced resolution (252)
ergonomic keyboard (238)
face recognition system (263)
field camera (251)
function keys (236)
gaming keyboard (237)
gesture recognition (266)
hand geometry system (263)
handwriting recognition software (243)
head-mounted pointer (266)
image processing (256)
image processing system (256)
iris recognition system (264)
keyguard (266)
magnetic-ink character recognition (260)
magstripe reader (260)
mechanical mouse (239)
MIDI (musical instrument digital interface) (246)
mouse gestures (240)

mouse pointer (239)
MP (252)
OCR (optical character recognition) software (256)
on-screen keyboard (266)
optical mouse (239)
optical reader (257)
optical resolution (252)
optical scanner (255)
personal identification number (PIN) (262)
picture messaging (249)
pixel (252)
pixels per inch (ppi) (252)
point-and-shoot camera (251)
point of sale (POS) (261)
portable keyboard (248)
program (234)
radio frequency identification (259)
retinal scanners (264)
signature verification system (263)
smart terminal (261)
source document (255)
speaker-dependent software (246)
speaker-independent software (246)
speech recognition (245)
streaming cam (254)
studio camera (251)
terminal (261)
text messaging (248)
toggle key (237)
UPC (Universal Product Code) (258)
user response (235)
video capture card (253)
video telephone call (253)
voice verification system (263)
whiteboard (254)
wireless keyboard (238)
wireless mouse (239)

Checkpoint

Use the Checkpoint exercises to check your knowledge level of the chapter. The Beyond the Book exercises will help broaden your understanding of the concepts presented in this chapter. To complete the Checkpoint exercises interactively, visit scsite.com/dc2007/ch5/check.

Label the Figure

Identify these areas and keys on a desktop computer keyboard.

a. function keys
b. media controls
c. numeric keypad
d. Internet controls
e. APPLICATION key
f. arrow keys
g. typing area
h. wrist rest

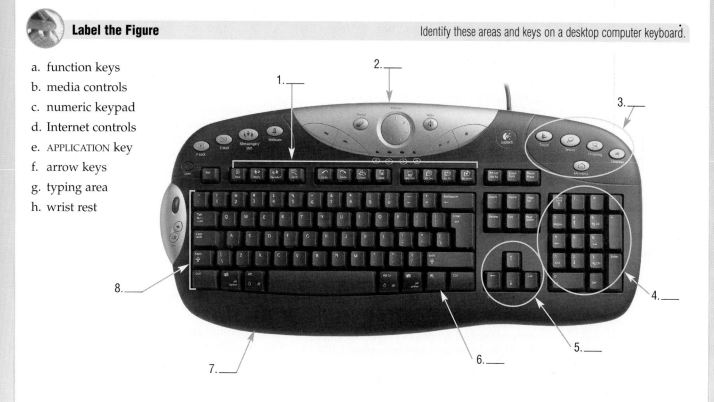

True/False

Mark T for True and F for False. (See page numbers in parentheses.)

_____ 1. Once data is in memory, the computer interprets and executes instructions to process the data into information. (234)

_____ 2. An input device is any hardware component that allows users to enter data and instructions into a computer. (236)

_____ 3. The command associated with a function key will remain the same from program to program. (236)

_____ 4. An optical mouse has a rubber or metal ball on its underside. (239)

_____ 5. A touchpad is a small, flat, rectangular pointing device that is sensitive to pressure and motion. (241)

_____ 6. A light pen is a handheld input device that can detect the presence of light. (242)

_____ 7. Pressure-sensitive digital pens typically provide less functionality than a stylus. (243)

_____ 8. A stylus is the primary input device for a PDA. (247)

_____ 9. The primary input device for a Tablet PC is a mouse. (249)

_____ 10. A point-and-shoot camera often features flash, zoom, automatic focus, and special effects. (251)

_____ 11. A scanner is a light-sensing input device that reads printed text and graphics and then translates the results into a form the computer can process. (255)

_____ 12. Many scanners include OCR (optical character recognition) software, which can read and convert text documents into electronic files. (256)

Checkpoint

Multiple Choice   Select the best answer. (See page numbers in parentheses.)

1. _____ is a series of instructions that tells a computer what to do and how to do it. (234)
   a. Data
   b. A program
   c. A command
   d. A user response

2. _____ keys are special keys programmed to issue commands to a computer. (236)
   a. Toggle
   b. Arrow
   c. Function
   d. Numeric

3. A(n) _____ has a design that reduces the chance of wrist and hand injuries. (238)
   a. ergonomic keyboard
   b. cordless keyboard
   c. gaming keyboard
   d. function key

4. _____ is a common mouse operation in which you press and release the primary mouse button. (240)
   a. Point
   b. Click
   c. Drag
   d. Right-click

5. A _____ is a pointing device that controls the movement and actions of players or objects in video games or computer games. (242)
   a. control pad
   b. gamepad
   c. gaming keyboard
   d. touchpad

6. Architects, mapmakers, designers, artists, and home users create drawings and sketches on a _____. (244)
   a. graphics tablet
   b. touch screen
   c. trackball
   d. touchpad

7. _____ is the process of entering any sound into the computer such as speech, music, and sound effects. (246)
   a. MIDI
   b. Audio input
   c. Voice recognition
   d. Voice input

8. The most expensive and highest quality digital camera is a _____, which is a stationary camera used for professional work. (251)
   a. PC camera
   b. point-and-shoot camera
   c. studio camera
   d. field camera

9. A _____ is any video camera that displays its output on a Web page. (254)
   a. PC camera
   b. digital video camera
   c. whiteboard
   d. Web cam

10. Scanners capture data from a _____, which is the original form of the data. (255)
    a. duplicate document
    b. secondary document
    c. derivative document
    d. source document

11. The UPC (Universal Product Code) bar code is used by _____. (258)
    a. retail and grocery stores
    b. libraries, blood banks, and air parcel carriers
    c. the United States Postal Service (USPS)
    d. nonretail applications such as game tickets

12. Point-of-sale terminals and automated teller machines are types of _____ that perform specific tasks and contain features uniquely designed for use in a particular industry. (261)
    a. smart terminals
    b. dumb terminals
    c. special-purpose terminals
    d. general-purpose terminals

13. The most widely used biometric device is the _____. (262)
    a. retinal scanner
    b. iris recognition system
    c. fingerprint scanner
    d. face recognition system

14. With _____, the computer will detect human motion. (266)
    a. an on-screen keyboard
    b. a head-mounted pointer
    c. gesture recognition
    d. a computerized implant

Checkpoint

Matching

Match the terms with their definitions. (See page numbers in parentheses.)

_____ 1. insertion point (237)

_____ 2. gaming keyboard (237)

_____ 3. pointer (239)

_____ 4. gamepad (242)

_____ 5. graphics tablet (244)

_____ 6. docking station (250)

_____ 7. video capture card (253)

_____ 8. bar code (258)

_____ 9. RFID (259)

_____ 10. retinal scanner (264)

a. external device that attaches to a mobile computer or device that contains a power connection and provides connections to peripherals

b. identification code that consists of vertical lines and spaces of different widths

c. scans patterns of blood vessels in the back of the retina

d. keyboard designed specifically for users that enjoy playing games on the computer

e. graphical symbol whose location and shape change with the movement of a pointing device

f. symbol on the screen that indicates where the next character typed will be displayed

g. a pointing device that controls the movement and actions of players or objects in video games or computer games

h. technology that uses radio signals to communicate with a tag placed in an item

i. flat, rectangular, electronic plastic board sometimes called a digitizer

j. converts an analog video signal to a digital signal that a computer can process

k. self-service banking machine that connects to a host computer

l. projects an infrared image of a keyboard on any flat surface

Short Answer

Write a brief answer to each of the following questions.

1. What are three different types of mouse devices? _____ What makes them different from each other? _____

2. What is a video capture card? _____ Why is a video capture card not needed with a digital video (DV) camera? _____

3. What is OCR (optical character recognition)? _____ What is OMR (optical mark recognition)? _____

4. What is a bar code reader? _____ Define RFID, and list some of its uses. _____

5. What is the Americans with Disabilities Act (ADA)? _____ How might gesture recognition and computerized implant devices help physically challenged users in the future? _____

Beyond the Book

Read the following book elements, learn more about each using the Web, and then write a brief report.

1. Ethics & Issues — Keyboard Monitoring — Privacy Risk? (237), Should the Government Set Computer Use Standards? (241), Should Talking on a Cellular Phone While Driving Be Illegal? (249), Should Cameras Be Able to Monitor Your Every Move? (254), Scanner Errors at the Checkout Counter? (258), or Ready for RFID? (259)

2. Career Corner — Data Entry Clerk (267)

3. Companies on the Cutting Edge — Logitech or Palm (269)

4. FAQs (237, 238, 240, 246, 250, 251, 252, 254, 256, 264)

5. High-Tech Talk — Biometrics: Personalized Security (268)

6. Looking Ahead — RFID Sensors Simplify, Monitor Tasks (259) or Wearable Computers Make Performance Statement (267)

7. Making Use of the Web — Blogs (121)

8. Picture Yourself Going Digital (232)

9. Technology Trailblazers — Charles Walton and Douglas Engelbart (269)

10. Web Links (240, 241, 242, 243, 244, 246, 253, 258, 264)

Learn It Online

Use the Learn It Online exercises to reinforce your understanding of the chapter concepts. To access the Learn It Online exercises, visit scsite.com/dc2007/ch5/learn.

① At the Movies — Get the Best of Both Worlds with a Convertible Tablet PC

To view the Get the Best of Both Worlds with a Convertible Tablet PC movie, click the number 1 button. Locate your video and click the corresponding High-Speed or Dial-Up link, depending on your Internet connection. Watch the movie, and then complete the exercise by answering the questions that follow. Taking classroom notes with pen and paper may be a thing of the past if the Tablet PC continues its rise in popularity. Switching to a Tablet PC can offer you some options that are not available on a regular notebook or desktop computer. What are some of the drawbacks to using a Tablet PC? What are some of the benefits?

② At the Movies — Essential Travel Gadgets

To view the Essential Travel Gadgets movie, click the number 2 button. Locate your video and click the corresponding High-Speed or Dial-Up link, depending on your Internet connection. Watch the movie and then complete the exercise by answering the questions that follow. Why would someone traveling with electronic equipment purchased for use in the United States need to carry an electric plug adapter when visiting most countries overseas? Explain how a pocket translator works. What is one drawback to this device? What are the benefits of traveling with a portable wireless device?

③ Student Edition Labs — Working with Audio

Click the number 3 button. A new browser window will open, displaying the Student Edition Labs. Follow the on-screen instructions to complete the Working with Audio Lab. When finished, click the Exit button. If required, submit your results to your instructor.

④ Student Edition Labs — Working with Video

Click the number 4 button. A new browser window will open, displaying the Student Edition Labs. Follow the on-screen instructions to complete the Working with Video Lab. When finished, click the Exit button. If required, submit your results to your instructor.

⑤ Practice Test

Click the number 5 button. Answer each question. When completed, enter your name and click the Grade Test button to submit the quiz for grading. Make a note of any missed questions. If required, submit your results to your instructor.

⑥ Who Wants To Be a Computer Genius²?

Click the number 6 button to find out if you are a computer genius. Directions about how to play the game will be displayed. When you are ready to play, click the Play button. Submit your score to your instructor.

⑦ Wheel of Terms

Click the number 7 button to reinforce important terms you learned in this chapter by playing the Shelly Cashman Series version of this popular game. Directions about how to play the game will be displayed. When you are ready to play, click the Play button. Submit your score to your instructor.

Learn It Online

⑧ DC Track and Field

Click the number 8 button to use what you have learned in this chapter to compete against other students in three track and field events. Directions about how to play the game will be displayed. When you are ready to play, click the start first event button. If required, submit your score to your instructor.

⑨ You're Hired!

Click the number 9 button to use what you have learned in this chapter to embark on the path to a career in computers. Directions about how to play the game will be displayed. When you are ready to play, click the begin game button. If required, submit your score to your instructor.

⑩ Crossword Puzzle Challenge

Click the number 10 button. Complete the puzzle to reinforce skills you learned in this chapter. Directions about how to play the game will be displayed. When you are ready to play, click the Submit button. Submit the completed puzzle to your instructor.

⑪ Lab Exercises

Click the number 11 button. When the Lab Exercises menu appears, click the exercise assigned by your instructor. A new browser window will open. Follow the on-screen instructions to complete the exercise. When finished, click the Exit button. If required, submit your results to your instructor.

⑫ In the News

Many people spend a great deal of time jotting notes on scratch pads, napkins, or self-stick notes. This may be fine for the occasional thought; however, in a situation where you would rather concentrate on the substance of the ideas being expressed, you may need a more sophisticated method for taking notes. Tape recorders have long been the mainstay for recording lectures, interviews, or one's thoughts, but they are restricted by the fact that the tapes last only so long before they have to be flipped over or switched altogether. One new development is the voice pen, which is a flash-memory-based recording device. It records digitally, which offers higher quality over standard tapes, easy indexing, and instant erasure. It is approximately the size of a small cellular telephone or remote control unit and can record up to 500 minutes on long play settings. Click the number 12 button and read a news article about a new or improved input device, an input device being used in a new way, or an input device being made more available. What is the device? Who is promoting it? How will it be used? Will the input device change the number, or effectiveness, of potential users? If so, why?

⑬ Chapter Discussion Forum

Select an objective from this chapter on page 233 about which you would like more information. Click the number 13 button and post a short message listing a meaningful message title accompanied by one or more questions concerning the selected objective. In two days, return to the threaded discussion by clicking the number 13 button. Submit to your instructor your original message and at least one response to your message.

⑭ eHow.com

Click the number 14 button to learn how to use eHow.com to locate information on a project you want to learn how to complete. Read other users contributions' and then perform the project. Write a brief report about your experience and then post your report to the topic you chose so that others can learn from your experience. Print your report and submit to your instructor.

Learn How To

Use the Learn How To activities to learn fundamental skills when using a computer and accompanying technology. Complete the exercises and submit them to your instructor. To see a video of a Learn How To activity, visit scsite.com/dc2007/ch5/howto.

LEARN HOW TO 1: Install and Use a PC Video Camera

A PC video camera, sometimes called a Web cam, is a digital video camera that allows you to capture video and still images. The videos can be used in live instant messages or for live images over the Internet. Recordings of the videos can be included on Web pages or in e-mail messages as attachments. In addition, some cameras include software that enables you to establish a visual security environment where the camera can be used to detect and record movement in its general vicinity.

Using a PC video camera requires two phases: 1) purchasing and installing the PC video camera, and 2) using the video camera to transmit live video or to record video or digital images.

To purchase and install a PC video camera, complete the following steps:

1. Determine how you want to use the video camera in order to decide the quality of camera you require and the camera software you need. PC video cameras range in price from about $25 to more than $125, and vary in picture quality, features, and accompanying software. If you are not sure of all features and prices, search the Web to determine the best camera for your use.
2. After making your purchase, you will find that most cameras are accompanied by a CD-ROM containing the software that enables the camera to communicate and work with the computer. Often, the instructions with the device will specify that you should place the CD-ROM in a CD or DVD drive and follow the on-screen instructions to install the software on the computer.
3. After the software is installed, you likely will be told to connect the camera to the computer. You do so by connecting the USB cable first to the camera and then to a USB port on your computer. When the camera is connected, you will be able to start the camera software from either the All Programs submenu or the Windows taskbar.

Once you have started the camera software, you will be able to use the camera for any of the tasks you require. Each camera and its accompanying software will allow you to create a video, use instant messaging to send live video to your IM contacts, and other uses as well. In addition, you often will be able to control the quality of your video output by modifying brightness, contrast, and clarity. With many cameras, you will be able to zoom in and out, and, from your keyboard, enter commands to move the camera lens left, right, up, and down.

On some cameras, you even can use a feature called face tracking, where the camera will remain focused on your face even when you move. This feature allows you to be more natural and not be concerned with always making sure you are placed exactly right for the camera.

As you can see, once you have purchased and installed a PC video camera, you will open an entirely new world of communication right from your computer.

Exercise

1. Assume you have decided to purchase a PC video camera to use for instant messaging. Search the Web to find the highest rated cameras available for purchase that can be used for your purposes. What is the most expensive camera you found? The least expensive? What features distinguish the two? Based on your use of the camera for instant messaging, what camera would you choose to buy? Why? Submit your answers to your instructor.
2. Optional: Purchase a PC video camera or borrow one from a friend. Install the camera software on a computer. Warning: If you are using a computer that is not your own, complete this exercise only with the owner's permission. Connect the camera to the computer. Practice with the camera and the accompanying software. What features does the software provide? Which feature do you find the most compelling? What features could you do without? Record a video of yourself answering these questions. Submit the video to your instructor.

Learn How To

LEARN HOW TO 2: Use the On-Screen Keyboard for Physically Challenged Users

Everyone who uses a computer must enter data and instructions into the computer. For people with limited hand and arm mobility, this can prove a daunting task. Windows XP and a variety of other applications provide a number of aids that can be useful. One of these is the on-screen keyboard.

The on-screen keyboard allows a user to view the keyboard on the screen and select characters to enter by using several different methods. To display and use the on-screen keyboard, complete the following steps:

1. Click the Start button on the Windows taskbar, point to All Programs on the Start menu, point to Accessories on the All Programs submenu, point to Accessibility on the Accessories submenu, and then click On-Screen Keyboard on the Accessibility submenu. *The On-Screen Keyboard window opens. In addition, an On-Screen Keyboard dialog box might appear that indicates the on-screen keyboard provides a minimum level of functionality and that a more robust product might be needed for daily use.* If this dialog box is displayed, click the OK button to close it.
2. In the On-Screen Keyboard window, click Settings on the menu bar. Ensure a checkmark is next to Always on Top.
3. If necessary, click Settings on the menu bar again. Click Typing Mode on the Settings menu. *The Typing Mode dialog box is displayed (Figure 5-51).*
4. Ensure the Click to select button is selected and then click the OK button in the Typing Mode dialog box.
5. Start your Web browser and click the Address bar.
6. Using the on-screen keyboard, enter the characters www.cnn.com and then click the ent key.
7. When the cnn.com Web page appears, click the Enter Symbol box in the Business at CNNMoney section of the page. Using the on-screen keyboard, enter ibm and then click the ent key.
8. After finding the stock price for IBM, close the browser window.
9. Start the WordPad program (see Learn How To number 1 on page 48).
10. In the On-Screen Keyboard window, click Settings on the menu bar and then click Typing Mode on the Settings menu.
11. Ensure the Hover to select button is selected in the Typing Mode dialog box. Click the Minimum time to hover box arrow and select 1.00 seconds in the list. Click the OK button.
12. Click in the WordPad window to position the insertion point.
13. You can cause a character to be entered in the WordPad window by placing the mouse pointer over the desired key (hovering) for one second. Type the following using the on-screen keyboard: Accessibility tools are vital for computer users.
14. Close the WordPad window and then close the On-Screen Keyboard window.

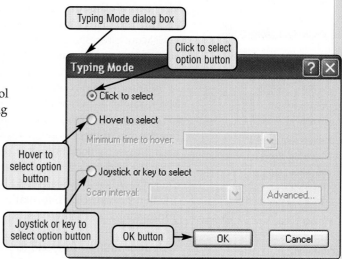

FIGURE 5-51

You have seen how one of the Accessibility tools within Windows XP functions. You are encouraged to explore all of the tools and discover how these tools can be useful to those people for whom they were designed.

Exercise

1. Start WordPad and then display the on-screen keyboard. In the On-Screen Keyboard window, click Settings on the menu bar and then click Typing Mode. In the Typing Mode dialog box, select Joystick or key to select. Click the Advanced button. Ensure the Keyboard key box contains a checkmark and then click Space in the list. Click the OK buttons to close the dialog boxes. Then, on the Keyboard menu, select Block Layout. Click in the WordPad window and then press the SPACEBAR. What happened? Keep pressing the SPACEBAR until you cause a character to be entered in the WordPad window. Use the bksp key on the on-screen keyboard to backspace and erase the character, and then use the on-screen keyboard to type On-Screen Keyboard usage in the WordPad window. When you are done, close the WordPad window and the On-Screen Keyboard window. Which means of using the on-screen keyboard (click a key, hover, or the SPACEBAR) did you find easiest to use? Why? Why would a physically challenged person prefer one method over another? Prepare your answers using the on-screen keyboard and then submit your answers to your instructor.

Web Research

Use the Internet-based Web Research exercises to broaden your understanding of the concepts presented in this chapter. Visit scsite.com/dc2007/ch5/research to obtain more information pertaining to each exercise. To discuss any of the Web Research exercises in this chapter with other students, post your thoughts or questions at scsite.com/dc2007/ch5/forum.

① Scavenger Hunt   Use one of the <u>search engines</u> listed in Figure 2-10 in Chapter 2 on page 78 or your own favorite search engine to find the answers to the questions below. Copy and paste the Web address from the Web page where you found the answer. Some questions may have more than one answer. If required, submit your answers to your instructor. (1) The primary inventor of the first commercial typewriter wanted to persuade people to buy and use the device, so he ordered the keys to allow users to type as quickly as possible. Who was the QWERTY keyboard's primary inventor? (2) What are reasonable accommodations that employers must make to comply with the Americans with Disabilities Act? (3) Who holds patents awarded in the 1950s for automatic video scanning and inspection methods, which led to bar code technology?

② Search Sleuth   <u>MetaCrawler</u> (metacrawler.com) is a different type of search Web site because it returns combined results from leading search engines. Visit this Web site and then use your word processing program to answer the following questions. Then, if required, submit your answers to your instructor. (1) Click the Tools & Tips link at the top of the page. Browse and then explore some of the tools, such as Search Tips and FAQs. (2) Scroll down and then read some of the information contained in the Popular Searches section. What are some of the popular MetaCrawler search terms? (3) Click your browser's Back button or press the BACKSPACE key twice to return to the MetaCrawler home page. What are the six most popular searches today? Click a link for one of these popular searches and scroll through the results MetaCrawler returns. (4) Click your browser's Back button or press the BACKSPACE key to return to the MetaCrawler home page. Click the Search text box and then type What are the top selling digital cameras? as the keywords in the Search text box. (5) Scroll through the links MetaCrawler returns and then click one that provides the information requested. What are three popular digital cameras? Read the information and then write a 50-word summary.

③ Journaling   Respond to your readings in this chapter by writing at least one page about your reactions, evaluations, and reflections about using <u>input devices</u>. For example, do you recall the first time you used a mouse? What experiences have you had with voice recognition? Do you own a PDA or Tablet PC, digital camera, or smart phone? Have you ever participated in a video conference? How do you reduce the chances of experiencing repetitive strain injuries? You also can write about the new terms you learned by reading this chapter. If required, submit your journal to your instructor.

④ Expanding Your Understanding   Journalists, attorneys, law enforcement officials, and students consider tape recorders and notepads essential components of their daily activities. An alternate means of capturing information is a <u>voice pen</u>, which is a flash-memory-based recording device approximately the size of a small smart phone. Visit a local electronics store or view electronics Web sites to learn more about voice pens. Compare their features, cost, recording time, and warranty. Write a report summarizing your findings, focusing on comparing and contrasting the voice pens. If required, submit your report to your instructor.

⑤ Ethics in Action   Some reports suggest that a global surveillance system is monitoring e-mail messages, telephone calls, and faxes. This organization known as <u>Echelon</u> attempts to intercept more than three billion satellite, microwave, cellular, and fiber-optic messages per day, according to the reports. The National Security Agency is forbidden to monitor U.S. citizens, but privacy experts contend that at least 90 percent of U.S. communication is gathered and reviewed. View online sites that provide information about Echelon, including Echelon Watch (www.echelonwatch.org). Write a report summarizing your findings, and include a table of links to Web sites that provide additional details. If required, submit your report to your instructor.

Case Studies

Use the Case Studies to apply the concepts presented in the chapter to real-world situations. Visit scsite.com/dc2007/ch5/cases to obtain more information pertaining to each exercise. To discuss the Case Studies in this chapter with other students, visit scsite.com/dc2007/ch5/forum and post your thoughts or questions.

CASE STUDY 1 — Class Discussion   You work in the Efficiency Analysis department of one of the largest retail companies in the world, with multiple stores in every state and many other countries. For the past 25 years, the company has used optical scanners at checkout counters that read the UPC bar code on products to determine from a database the price to charge customers. The company is considering replacing the optical scanners with **radio frequency identification**, or RFID. The reader receives the code identifying the product via a chip with an antenna that is part of the box or label on the outside of the product. Your manager has asked you to draft a memo outlining the impact such a change would have on the company, its suppliers, and its customers. Be prepared to discuss your findings in class.

CASE STUDY 2 — Class Discussion   You have been asked to serve on your company's Voice Recognition Committee. The committee has been charged with investigating the feasibility of using voice recognition as a primary method for entering data and instructions into the company's computers. The chairperson of the committee has asked for your opinion on the use of **voice recognition**. When would voice recognition be an advantage over the keyboard and mouse? Might it ever be a disadvantage? Why? Prepare a brief report and be prepared to discuss your recommendations in class.

CASE STUDY 3 — Research   While attending college part-time for the past two years, you have worked as a data entry clerk for Salmon Mirror. Recently, you began to feel an unusual pain in your right wrist. Your doctor diagnosed the problem as **carpal tunnel syndrome**, which is the most well-known of a series of musculoskeletal disorders that fall under the umbrella of repetitive strain injuries (RSIs). Your doctor made several recommendations to relieve the pain, one of which was to find a new job. Before you begin job hunting, however, you want to learn more about this debilitating injury. Use the Web and/or print media to investigate carpal tunnel syndrome. Prepare a report and/or PowerPoint presentation on your findings. Include information about carpal tunnel syndrome warning signs, risk factors, suggestions about proper workstation ergonomics, and procedures for healing the injury. Share your report or presentation with your class.

CASE STUDY 4 — Research   An electronics company where you are employed as an analyst spends hundreds of thousands of dollars each year on travel to the multiple locations where they operate around the country. In an effort to curb the ever-increasing costs of travel, the CFO has asked you to look into the feasibility of adopting **video conferencing** at all of its major locations. Use the Web and/or print media to determine the advantages and disadvantages of video conferencing. Can the technology replace all or most face-to-face meetings? What are the costs of common video conferencing systems and the recurring costs their use incurs? Compare those costs to the cost of travel for a team of three people making six trips per year between New York and Los Angeles, including hotel, airline, and food expenses. Write a brief report or use PowerPoint to create a presentation and share your findings with your class.

CASE STUDY 5 — Team Challenge   The Transportation Security Administration (TSA) is looking into ways to expedite the airport screening experience of frequent flyers without compromising security. The TSA has hired your team as consultants to investigate **biometric technology**. In particular, they want your team to review three biometric devices for screening frequent flyers — fingerprint scanner, face recognition system, and iris recognition system. Form a three-member team and have each team member choose a different biometric device. Using the Web and/or print media, have each team member determine the advantages and disadvantages of their chosen biometric device. Include in each report how frequent flyer applicants would apply, accuracy rates of the device, and whether the device would indeed enhance security or open a loophole for terrorists. As a team, merge your findings into a team report and/or PowerPoint presentation and share your recommendations with your class.

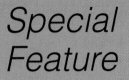

Special Feature

Personal Mobile Devices

Mobile devices that usually can fit in your pocket, such as PDAs, smart phones, and smart pagers, are referred to as personal mobile devices (Figure 1). Page 22 in Chapter 1 discusses PDAs and smart phones. A **PDA** provides personal organizer functions, such as calendar, appointment book, address book, calculator, and notepad. A **smart phone** is an Internet-enabled telephone that usually provides PDA functionality. A **smart pager** is a wireless mobile device that provides data services, such as e-mail alerts, news alerts, and Internet access. Smart pagers usually provide PDA functionality, such as an address book and calendar. Additionally, some smart pagers include telephone capabilities.

Because the various types of personal mobile devices often offer similar capabilities, they typically are categorized by their form factor. A device's **form factor** refers to its size, shape, and configuration. For example, Figure 1 shows a smart phone that has a PDA form factor and a smart phone that has a phone form factor. While the device with the phone form factor may include PDA functionality, its main purpose is to be used as a phone. Its smaller size may make using it as a PDA more cumbersome than the smart phone with a PDA form factor. The PDA form factor, while larger, provides a better interface for accessing the PDA functionality.

Most personal mobile devices allow you to enhance their functionality through the use of accessories — such as headsets, cameras, and memory cards — and software. Not long ago, PDA (personal digital assistant) software consisted of a few programs, such as a to-do list and an address book. PDAs previously contained embedded software, meaning that a user could not change the software or add programs to the PDA. Today's PDAs, smart phones, and smart pagers allow for as much choice and versatility in their software as a typical personal computer. Most personal mobile devices come equipped with a rich set of programs. In some cases, a user may want to use enhanced versions of the included software, such as an enhanced calculator program, or install additional software, such as a game. Many personal mobile devices allow the user to play music, such as MP3 files.

This special feature provides an overview of accessories and software available for personal mobile devices. The final section of the feature lists the criteria you should consider when deciding which personal mobile device is right for you.

smart pager

PDA

smart phone with
phone form factor

smart phone with
PDA form factor

FIGURE 1 Your choice of a personal mobile device depends on the features you require, the desired form factor, the available accessories, and the available software for the device.

PERSONAL MOBILE DEVICE OPERATING SYSTEMS

As with personal computers, personal mobile devices run an operating system. A personal mobile device runs software made only for the operating system of the device. Personal mobile devices can be categorized by the operating system that each runs. Figure 2 lists the common personal mobile device operating systems, the manufacturer, and a brief description of the operating system.

PERSONAL MOBILE DEVICE OPERATING SYSTEMS

Operating System	Manufacturer	Device Types	Description
Palm OS (versions 5 and later)	PalmSource	PDA Smart phone	The latest version of the operating system for Palm OS-based PDAs supports faster processors, multimedia, and more memory.
Palm OS (earlier versions)	PalmSource	PDA Smart phone	Several PDA manufacturers continue to use earlier versions of the Palm OS operating system because of the simplicity and lower power requirements, resulting in longer usage between recharges.
Windows Mobile for Pocket PC	Microsoft	PDA	The Windows Mobile operating system tightly integrates with Microsoft's Windows operating systems and includes scaled-down versions of many of Microsoft's popular programs, including Word, Outlook, Excel, and MSN Messenger.
Windows Mobile for Pocket PC Phone Edition	Microsoft	Smart phone with PDA form factor	The Pocket PC Phone Edition includes enhancements for the Windows Mobile operating system geared for phone use, such as enhancing the contact manager with the ability to dial a telephone number. This edition includes all of the Windows Mobile PDA functionality.
Windows Mobile for Smartphone	Microsoft	Smart phone with phone form factor	The Smartphone edition of the Windows Mobile operating system is designed for smaller screens and devices with less functionality than a typical PDA.
Blackberry	Research in Motion (RIM)	Smart pager Smart phone with PDA form factor	The Blackberry operating system runs on devices supplied by RIM. The devices include enhanced messaging and e-mail features when compared to smart phones.
Symbian OS	Symbian	Smart phone	Symbian OS is a popular PDA operating system commonly used on cellular telephones. Symbian OS is more popular in Europe and with business users.
Embedded Linux	Open source	PDA Smart phone	Some PDAs use a scaled-down version of the free Linux operating system.

FIGURE 2 Personal mobile device capabilities depend on the operating system that they run.

Special Feature

ACCESSORIES FOR PERSONAL MOBILE DEVICE SOFTWARE

Most personal mobile devices have the capability to take advantage of add-on accessories. For example, using an external keyboard with a device greatly enhances the ability to enter data or notes quickly. Figure 3 lists the more common accessories available for a personal mobile device.

ACCESSORIES FOR PERSONAL MOBILE DEVICES

Accessory	Description
Keyboard	External keyboards provide much faster input when taking notes as opposed to using a small, built-in keyboard on a device. Keyboards may be wireless or attached to the device using a special cable.
Memory card	Memory cards provide additional storage space for a device. Some memory cards may include hardware enhancements such as wireless capability, a camera, or Bluetooth capability. Some cards come with preinstalled software or a vast amount of data, such as a dictionary, on them.
Car kit	Car kits allow you to integrate a device with your car by providing mounting and/or hands-free operation of a device.
Chargers	Special chargers allow you to recharge a device's battery almost anywhere, such as an airplane, hotel, or foreign country. Some chargers provide emergency battery backup in case the device's batteries start running low when no electrical outlet is nearby.
Camera	Add-on cameras provide picture and video taking capability to devices with no such built-in functionality.
Case	Most mobile devices can be placed in a case or holster for protection while the device is not in use. Some devices include built-in flip screens to protect the device. You may want a case that fits comfortably in your pocket, or one that includes a belt clip. A good case protects the device when it is dropped from a height of 3 or 4 feet.
Headset/earphones	Headsets allow you to wear a combined earpiece and microphone while keeping the device in your hand, pocket, or next to you. Some headsets use Bluetooth to communicate wirelessly with the device. Earphones are used when you want to listen to sound on your device, such as when listening to music or an e-book, or when watching a video.
GPS receiver	A GPS receiver contains an antenna, radio receiver, and processor and receives signals from GPS satellites to determine a location and/or speed. GPS receivers turn a personal mobile device into a complete GPS unit. The receivers typically include software that you must install on the device.

FIGURE 3 Some accessories for personal mobile devices are common to most devices, while others are specialized.

BUILT-IN PERSONAL MOBILE DEVICE SOFTWARE

Most personal mobile devices include several programs that provide basic functionality, such as an **address book** and **date book**. Figure 4 lists the types of software that usually are preinstalled on a personal mobile device.

BUILT-IN PERSONAL MOBILE DEVICE SOFTWARE

Application	Description
Address book and contacts	Maintains a list of acquaintances, including names, addresses, telephone numbers, e-mail addresses, and notes.
To-do list	Maintains a list of tasks. Tasks can be categorized and assigned a priority.
Calculator	Offers functionality of standard desktop calculators.
Datebook and calendar	Maintains appointments and important dates, such as birthdays and holidays. A user also sets audio or visual alarms to trigger when an appointment time arrives.
Memos and notepad	Keeps track of notes.
Launcher	The interface that allows a user to execute, or launch, programs, shown on the PDA screen in the figure below.
Dialer	Smart phones typically include dialer software that assists you in using the telephone capabilities of a device. Some dialer software is integrated into the operating system so that you use dialing capabilities in other applications. For example, you can select a telephone number in the word processing program and request that the number be dialed.

FIGURE 4   Personal mobile devices typically contain this preinstalled software.

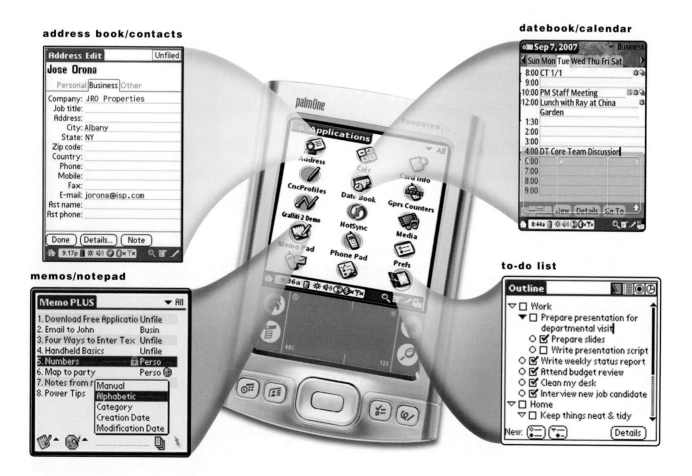

SYNCHRONIZATION SOFTWARE

Most personal mobile devices allow a user to share data and information between his or her personal computer and the device. The software that enables the sharing is called **synchronization software**. A personal mobile device may synchronize, or sync (pronounced sink), with a personal computer or a server on a network. Corporations often standardize their synchronization software so that employees share data across the corporate network, and so the data is backed up properly on a server. Figure 5 lists popular synchronization software for personal mobile devices.

SYNCHRONIZATION SOFTWARE FOR PERSONAL MOBILE DEVICES

Application	Description	Samples
Built-in	Most devices include software that the user loads on a personal computer that allows the computer to communicate with the device and share data and information.	• The Palm OS includes HotSync software • Pocket PC PDAs include ActiveSync software • Blackberry devices use the Blackberry Desktop Software
Synching many sources	Some device users have data and information stored in many places. For example, users may want to have their address books on the Web, on their personal computers, on their cellular phones, and on their PDAs. Special synchronization software allows users to keep all of the address books up-to-date.	• Intellisync Handheld Edition • PocketMirror • XTNDConnect Server
SyncML	**SyncML** is a standard that is being adopted by many companies that create personal mobile devices. SyncML allows for common information stored on a device to be shared among many devices, such as cellular telephones, other personal mobile devices, and personal computers.	• IBM WebSphere Everyplace Access • Intellisync Handheld Edition • fusionOne MightyPhone • Symbian based devices use SyncML
iSync	Apple's iSync software allows a user to keep a calendar and contact information synchronized up to the minute between a smart phone, an Apple iPod, a Palm OS device, or multiple Macs.	• Apple iSync

FIGURE 5 Personal mobile devices use synchronization software to share data and information with a personal computer or server.

BUSINESS SOFTWARE

Most programs used on a personal mobile device have some counterpart program on a desktop computer. For example, both a personal computer and a PDA or smart phone may include a word processing program. Many business programs have counterparts on personal mobile devices. The personal mobile device versions of these programs generally have fewer features and options. For example, a word processing program on a PDA may not have a spelling checker, and a spreadsheet program may not include all of the built-in calculations of its desktop computer counterpart. A smart phone with a phone form factor may allow you only to view documents, rather than edit documents. Figure 6 lists business software for personal mobile devices.

BUSINESS SOFTWARE FOR PERSONAL MOBILE DEVICES

Application	Description	Samples
Word processing	Allows for simple creation, editing, and viewing of documents.	• Documents To Go • WordSmith • PocketWord
Spreadsheet	Allows a user to create, edit, and view worksheets on a personal mobile device.	• PocketExcel • TinySheet • Quickoffice • SmartSheet
Readers	Allows read-only (view only) access to word processing documents, spreadsheets, or databases that a user downloads to a personal mobile device from a personal computer. Readers are useful for taking large documents on the road to read them without the ability to modify them. Some readers allow the user to view all of these types of documents, while others are targeted to specific desktop program counterparts, such as presentation viewers or word processing document viewers.	• Pocket SlideShow • TealDoc • iSilo • Microsoft Reader for Pocket PC
Database and list management	Allows creation, editing, and viewing of databases or lists. List management is a popular use of personal mobile devices. Some examples of lists that are handy to store on a device include shopping lists, to-do lists, exercise logs, and automobile maintenance logs.	• HanDBase • thinkDB • SmartList To Go • JFile • ListPro • Mobile Data Viewer
Financial	Financial software includes programs to manage a bank account, track expenses during a trip, manage a budget, or track an investment portfolio. Many personal computer financial programs include personal mobile device companion software that keeps the information on a device synchronized with the financial information on a personal computer or the Web.	• Microsoft Money for Windows Mobile-based Pocket PC • Pocket Quicken • BankBook • Ultrasoft Money • Handy Expense

FIGURE 6 Business software provides scaled-down versions of common desktop programs.

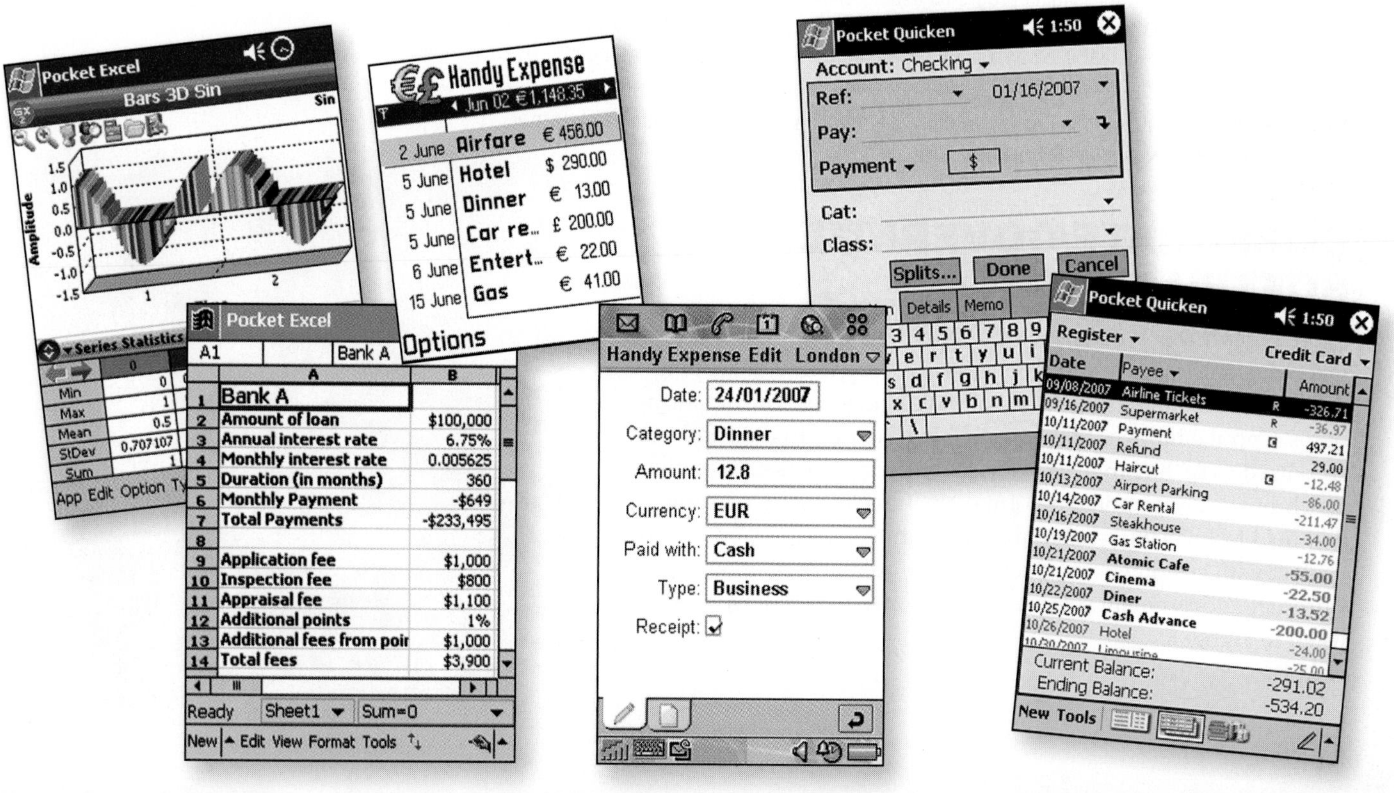

SOFTWARE FOR WIRELESS DEVICES

Most of the software used to interact with the Internet using a personal computer has a counterpart on wireless mobile devices. Some devices come equipped with e-mail software or a Web browser. Often, special servers allow the device to communicate securely with corporate databases or Web sites. For personal mobile devices that do not include wireless Internet connectivity, a special modem connects the device to the Internet. Often, a device without built-in wireless capability can be connected to a mobile phone that can connect the device to the Internet. Web content and e-mail also synchronize to the device from a personal computer, and the information may be browsed offline while using the device. Figure 7 provides a list of popular communications software for personal mobile devices.

COMMUNICATIONS SOFTWARE FOR PERSONAL MOBILE DEVICES

Application	Description	Samples
E-mail	Used for composing and reading e-mail. Many personal mobile devices include a pre-installed e-mail program.	• Pocket Outlook • riteMail • Mail+ • SnapperMail
Web browsers	Allows Web browsing. Some browsers use an **intermediate server** to make the pages smaller by stripping out images or making images smaller. Others attempt to display the full Web page on the personal mobile device. Many personal mobile devices include a preinstalled Web browser.	• Pocket Internet Explorer • ThunderHawk • AvantGo • Opera browser
Clipping	**Web clippings** are programs that gather and display only the critical elements, or clips, of a Web page.	• Travelocity.com • The Weather Channel • Moviefone.com
Instant messaging	Instant messaging programs usually allow the user to use the same instant messaging ID as that used on a personal computer.	• MSN Messenger • AIM for Palm OS • Agile Messenger

FIGURE 7 Communications software allows a mobile device to access the Internet and other data sources while the user is away from the classroom or office.

CORPORATE/GOVERNMENT SOFTWARE

Large organizations, such as corporations and government agencies, take advantage of personal mobile devices' capability of keeping current information in the hands of their personnel. The organization's central employee telephone book is kept up-to-date and synchronized to each employee's device on a regular basis. Executives synchronize key corporate information. Traveling sales personnel and field technicians synchronize appointments, e-mail, notes about contact with customers, product lists, and sales information. Corporate/government software for personal mobile devices is listed in Figure 8.

CORPORATE/GOVERNMENT SOFTWARE FOR PERSONAL MOBILE DEVICES

Application	Description	Samples
Executive	Executives keep up-to-date corporate information on their personal mobile devices. Executives may keep current sales information, financial information, and inventory information available to make informed decisions.	• mySAP.com • Siebel 7 Mobile Solutions
Sales	Sales people working out of the office are perhaps the largest group of personal mobile device users. The devices are useful for keeping product information handy, keeping scheduled appointments, and maintaining customer information.	• Siebel 7 Mobile Sales • Salesforce.com • ActionNames
Field technicians and mobile workers	Field technicians visit customer locations to troubleshoot problems. Personal mobile devices help technicians keep track of customer information, maintain up-to-date information on replacement parts, and log troubleshooting information.	• UPS and FedEx use specialized devices and software for their drivers to track package pickups and drop offs.
Military and law enforcement	The military and law enforcement agencies deploy personal mobile devices to manage the special needs of the military and law enforcement.	• Most software of this nature is custom made for the needs of particular agencies. Such programs help track cases or serve as legal references.
Connecting and synchronizing with corporate data sources	Several solutions exist for synchronizing corporate data with personal mobile devices. Special software keeps track of user permissions and makes certain that the right people get the data they require on a day-to-day basis.	• Intellisync Data Sync • MessageWireless
Large organization management issues	In organizations with thousands of personal mobile device users, the support of those devices becomes tedious, especially when users install unsupported software on the devices that may interfere with the corporate software and data for which the device was intended. Server software may detect these conflicts when the user synchronizes with the corporate server and deletes or reports the offending software.	• Much of the software of this nature is custom built for each enterprise, as needs and infrastructure of each organization are different.

FIGURE 8 Large organizations utilize special software to keep their employees synchronized.

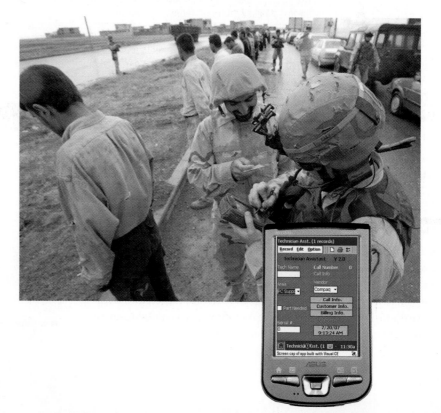

MEDICAL SOFTWARE

One of the largest communities to adopt personal mobile device software in significant numbers is the medical community. Physicians and other medical workers routinely use specialized software to track patient charts, check information on drugs, and browse electronic versions of large reference books. The end result is a savings in time and money, and an increase in the level of care for the patient. Figure 9 lists some popular medical software for personal mobile devices.

MEDICAL SOFTWARE FOR PERSONAL MOBILE DEVICES

Application	Description	Samples
Patient and case management	Patient and case management programs allow medical workers to enter information as they interact with the patient. This eliminates transcription errors or the need for the worker to find a workstation to do his or her work.	• MedLogs • PatientKeeper Personal • Handy Patients • MD Coder PocketPC Edition
Drug information and drug interactions	Allows for fast access to critical drug information, such as dosages and drug interactions.	• Epocrates Rx • eDrugsDatabase • Dr Drugs
Reference books	Medical workers often rely on a large collection of references to do their jobs. Electronic versions of many popular references, such as the *Physicians' Desk Reference*, are available in electronic format and are kept up-to-date easily through regular downloads.	• PDRDrugs • eDrugs Database • DiagnosisPro for Pocket PC • MedRules
Prescriptions	With electronic prescribing, physicians write prescriptions electronically. Physicians print legible prescriptions and hand the prescriptions to the patient. If the personal mobile device is connected to the Internet or hospital network, the physician checks the patient's medication or medical history.	• iScribe • PocketRx • Medicalis
Medical calculations	Medical workers often make quick calculations for medication dosages or patient status. Programs assist many of these calculations and target the worker's specialty.	• MedMath • MedCalc • Medical MathPad

FIGURE 9 The medical community quickly has become one of the larger users of specialized PDA software.

SCIENTIFIC SOFTWARE

The mobility of personal mobile devices makes them valuable tools for scientific use. Researchers use these devices to gather and record data in the field and later download the data to a personal computer or server. Scientists also use specialized software targeted to their specific field, such as astronomy or meteorology, as a replacement for bulky reference manuals or observation notes (Figure 10).

SCIENTIFIC SOFTWARE FOR PERSONAL MOBILE DEVICES

Application	Description	Samples
Data gathering	Scientists can enter observations quickly into a personal mobile device. These programs often are used in the field for gathering research statistics.	• iCollect
Calculations and conversions	Users can perform specialized calculations or data conversions. Many fields of science, such as astronomy, require special calculations that are useful to have available on a personal mobile device.	• ME Tools • CoolCalc for the Pocket PC • Convert It! • APCalc Converter
Reference	Scientists can look up information quickly, rather than using cumbersome manuals or textbooks.	• ChemRef Basic • Packed Periodic Table • Gene • ABC's of Science
Astronomy	Observers can follow the stars. With the large number of amateur astronomers in the world, programs specific to astronomy are some of the more popular scientific titles.	• Pocket Universe • Planetarium • Astronomist • Pocket Stars
Weather	Meteorologists' specific needs are addressed because these programs allow quick calculations or data gathering in a changing environment. Some programs are linked to add-on hardware that measure temperature, humidity, and other meteorological data.	• Weather Manager • WorldMate • Weather Calculator for Palm OS • Weather.com

FIGURE 10 Scientific programs help scientists manage complex information.

TRAVEL SOFTWARE

The portable nature of personal mobile devices makes them ideal for the business or leisure traveler. Even a night on the town can be enhanced by a list of popular hot spots. The user keeps his or her itinerary handy along with maps and directions while traveling to new places. A GPS-enabled mobile device tracks a user's route and keeps the user on course. Wireless connectivity allows the user to book flights and hotels from the back of a taxi cab. Figure 11 lists travel software for personal mobile devices.

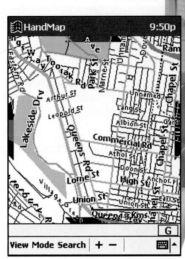

TRAVEL SOFTWARE FOR PERSONAL MOBILE DEVICES

Application	Description	Samples
Itinerary consolidation	Manages travel itineraries, including flights, hotels, and car rentals. The software may keep track of travel preferences and make suggestions about travel and accommodations when planning a new trip.	• Traveler (Pocket PC edition) • Time Traveler • WorldMate
Mapping	Mapping software may download maps from the Web or a personal computer. Or, the software may include maps. The software may suggest travel routes from point to point, or simply serve as a reference.	• Vindigo for Palm OS or Pocket PC • Pocket Streets • HandMap
City guides	City guides are one of the more popular personal mobile device programs. The user installs city guides for specific cities or an entire country. Guides include restaurant listings and ratings, hotels, directions, popular attractions, and local customs.	• Intelliguide Professional • Vindigo for Palm OS or Pocket PC • WorldMate • Frommer's Port@ble Guide • iFodor's
Hotel and flight	Users can view current hotel and flight information while planning a trip. Some of these programs require the device to connect to the Internet. Others occasionally allow downloading the information to a device from a personal computer. Some programs link to booking systems on the Internet, so the user makes reservations directly from a personal mobile device.	• OAG Club • SkyGuide
GPS	Usually requires additional GPS hardware connected to the device. Some software includes mapping data or only displays and saves GPS information, such as location and speed.	• GPS Port@ble Navigator — Travelers Edition • GPS Wireless Navigation System • GPS Atlas

FIGURE 11 Travel software acts as a personal concierge for the business or leisure traveler.

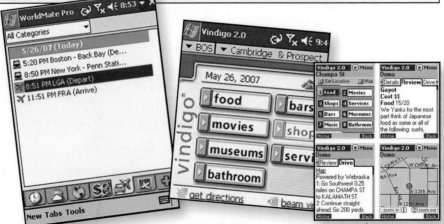

EDUCATIONAL SOFTWARE

With so much to organize, students and instructors greatly benefit from mobile software geared for educational uses (Figure 12). Students load textbook chapters or entire textbooks onto expansion cards and use special software to read the books and highlight key material. Instructors distribute electronic versions of the class syllabus, automatically updating each student's calendar on the students' devices. Some schools even acquire PDAs for the entire student body and require their use in the classroom.

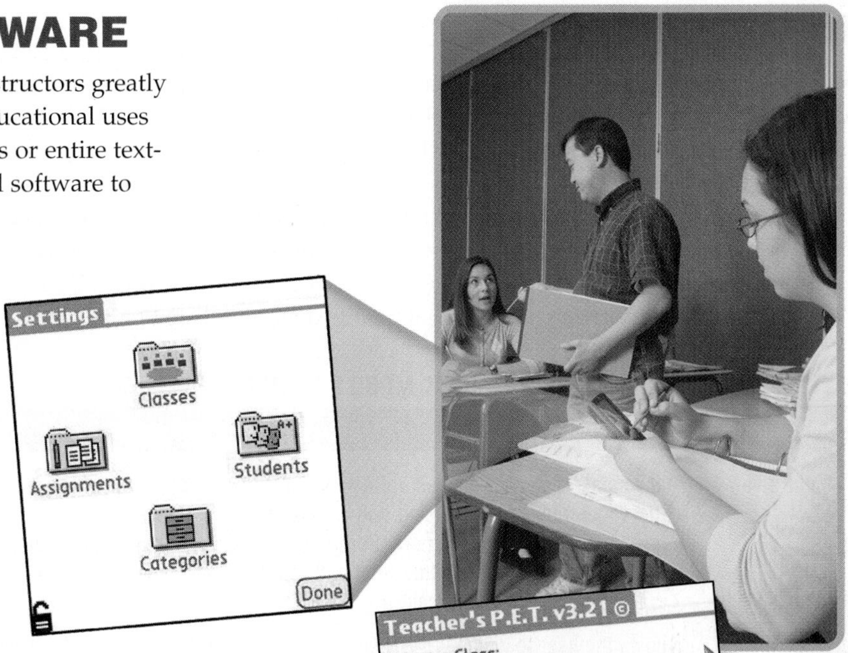

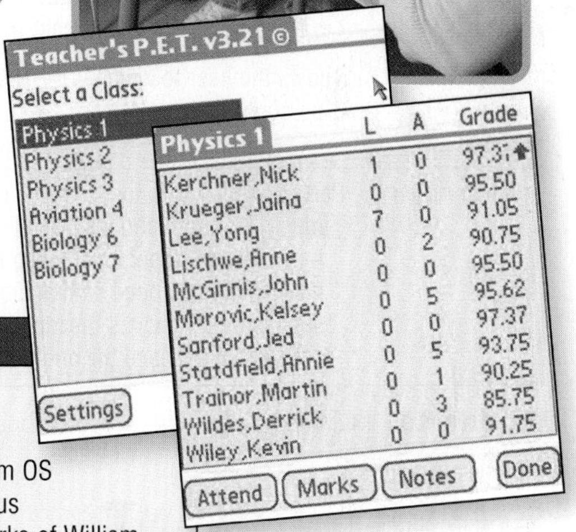

EDUCATIONAL SOFTWARE FOR PERSONAL MOBILE DEVICES

Application	Description	Samples
E-books and references	E-books are electronic versions of books. E-books are specially formatted files that may be viewed using Reader software, as noted in Figure 6 on page 287. Many e-books are available at no cost, and many authors and publishing companies make e-books available to those who have purchased a hard copy of a particular book.	• TomeRaider • PocketLingo Pro • Formulas for Palm OS • Speed Reader Plus • The collected works of William Shakespeare for Microsoft Reader • eWord for Blackberry • Mobipocket Reader Pro for Symbian OS
Class schedules and course management	Helps instructors and students manage their respective schedules. The information may include syllabus details distributed in electronic format by an instructor. The software also may link to a central data repository of a school. The software helps track grading, assignments, to-do lists, instructor office hours, and notes.	• 4.0Student by Handmark course management • Pocket ClassPro for Pocket PC • MyClasses
Roster	Manages grading, rosters, attendance, and contact information for students.	• Teachers PET • Head Start • Teach File
Review	Includes programs for quizzing students and reviewing coursework. Students often train the application to help them review troublesome material.	• Herbert's Math Time • Mental Arithmetic • Quizzler

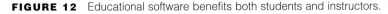

FIGURE 12 Educational software benefits both students and instructors.

MULTIMEDIA SOFTWARE

Most personal mobile devices include the capability of viewing images, and some are powerful enough to view short video clips. Some devices also double as audio players, allowing the user to take his or her favorite music anywhere. Devices that are more recent contain, or allow the user to attach, a camera or recording device to capture video or audio and then download the captured media to a personal computer. Some image viewers allow the user to use a personal mobile device as an electronic picture frame while the device rests in its cradle on the user's desk. Popular multimedia software for personal mobile devices is listed in Figure 13.

MULTIMEDIA SOFTWARE FOR PERSONAL MOBILE DEVICES

Application	Description	Samples
Picture viewer	Allows a user to view images uploaded to a personal mobile device using software on a personal computer or camera. Some viewers have a slide show mode that rotates through a list of images automatically.	• SplashPhoto • PocketPhoto • Palbum Picture Viewer • Resco Photo Viewer for Smartphone • Pictures
Video player	Allows the user to watch video clips on a personal mobile device.	• Windows Media Player Mobile • PocketTV for Pocket PC • ActiveSky Media Player
Audio player	Permits a user to listen to his or her favorite music or record and playback voice recordings for meetings or personal audio notes. Some devices are equipped with additional hardware such as microphones, headphones, or audio controls to enhance the audio experience.	• AudioPlus • Windows Media Player Mobile • Today Player

FIGURE 13 Multimedia software gives personal mobile device users the ability to view images, watch video, and listen to audio.

ENTERTAINMENT SOFTWARE

While on the train ride to work or waiting at the airport, a personal mobile device user can enjoy his or her favorite games. The infrared port or wireless connectivity of a device allows a user to play some games against other players. Most devices include buttons to control games. Figure 14 lists popular entertainment software for personal mobile devices.

ENTERTAINMENT SOFTWARE FOR PERSONAL MOBILE DEVICES

Application	Description	Samples
Strategy	Includes classic board games such as chess, backgammon, and Monopoly.	• PocketChess • ChessGenius • Handmark Monopoly • SimCity
Card	Includes casino games, solitaire games, and other card games.	• AcidSolitaire • BlackJack++ • Pocket Cribbage
Action	Games that require quick reflexes, including many arcade-style games.	• Tomb Raider • Bejeweled • Breakfast • Vexed for Symbian
Puzzle	Thought-provoking puzzles to pass time and sharpen the mind, such as crossword puzzles, mazes, and word games.	• Handmark SCRABBLE • Crossword • ChessPuzzles
Sports	Games that mimic real-life sports.	• Pocket Mini Golf • Smart Tennis • Bowling Master

FIGURE 14 Entertainment software allows a user to relax with a personal mobile device and enjoy his or her favorite games.

OBTAINING AND INSTALLING PERSONAL MOBILE DEVICE SOFTWARE

Software often is available at computer or electronics stores. A significant number of programs are available as shareware, freeware, or trial editions at various Web sites. Most of the software listed in the previous figures is accessible on the Web sites listed in Figure 15. Because software for personal mobile devices usually is smaller than the personal computer counterparts, downloading the software from the Web to your personal computer and then uploading it to your device often is the best alternative when you want to try something new. Software downloaded from the Web to a personal computer requires that the software be installed using the device's synchronization software. Additionally, some personal computer application software includes accompanying mobile device software that corresponds with the personal computer software. Wireless devices, such as smart phones and smart pagers, may allow you to download new software over the wireless connection.

Software for personal mobile devices sold in a retail location often is supplied on a CD-ROM. The CD-ROM first installs the software on a personal computer. The device's synchronization software then is used to load the software onto the device while the device is connected to the personal computer. Depending on the type of software installed, this process may be automatic. Some software is packaged as an add-on card that the user inserts into the device's expansion slot. Some Web sites allow the user to browse a software catalog from a wireless device's Web browser and download the software directly to the device. When synchronizing a personal mobile device on a corporate network, some companies automatically install software to the employees' devices with no interaction required from the employee.

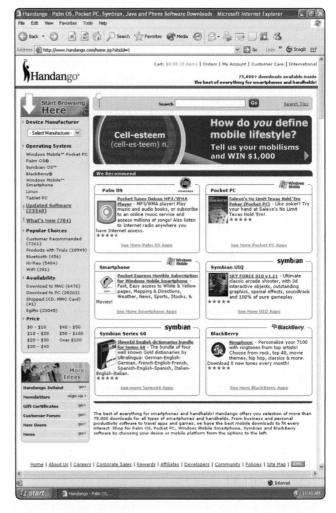

WHERE TO OBTAIN PERSONAL MOBILE DEVICE SOFTWARE

Application	Description	Samples
Web sites	Software publishers make their products available at their Web sites. Several Web sites also exist specifically to distribute mobile device software. Tens of thousands of titles are available, and most can be downloaded on a trial basis.	palmgear.com handandgo.com pdamd.com tucows.com
Retail	Many popular software titles can be purchased at electronic and computer stores. The most popular titles at these locations include productivity and entertainment software.	bestbuy.com compusa.com
Develop in-house	Many corporations develop their own personal mobile device software to use internally to meet specific needs. These programs usually tap into existing corporate databases of product and customer information. The companies that produce mobile device operating systems often make the development tools for such software available at no cost or a minimal cost.	palmsource.com microsoft.com/windows/mobile/ developers blackberry.net/developers symbian.com/developer

For an updated list of where to obtain PDA software, visit scsite.com/dc2007/ch5/pda.

FIGURE 15   Personal mobile device software is available from a number of sources.

HOW TO PURCHASE A PERSONAL MOBILE DEVICE

Whether you choose a PDA, smart phone, or smart pager depends on where, when, and how you will use the device. If you need to stay organized when you are on the go, then a PDA may be the right choice. PDAs typically are categorized by the operating system they run (Figure 2 on page 283). If you need to stay organized and in touch when on the go, then a smart phone or smart pager may be the right choice. Like PDAs, smart phones and smart pagers are categorized by the operating system they run. The six primary operating systems for these devices are the Palm OS, Windows Mobile for Pocket PC, Windows Mobile for Smartphone, Symbian OS, Blackberry, and Embedded Linux.

This section lists guidelines you should consider when purchasing a PDA, smart phone, or smart pager. You also should visit the Web sites listed in Figure 16 to gather more information about the type of personal mobile device that best suits your computing needs.

 DETERMINE THE PROGRAMS YOU PLAN TO RUN ON YOUR DEVICE.

All PDAs and most smart phones and smart pagers can handle basic organizer-type software such as a calendar, address book, and notepad. The availability of other software depends on the operating system you choose. The depth and breadth of software for the Palm OS is significant, with more than 20,000 basic programs and over 600 wireless programs. Devices that run Windows-based operating systems, such as Windows Mobile or Windows Smartphone, may have fewer programs available, but the operating system and application software are similar to those with which you are familiar, such as Word and Excel. Some Symbian-based smart phones also include the capability to read and/or edit Microsoft Office documents. Consider if you want extras on the device, such as the capability of playing MP3 music files.

2 CONSIDER HOW MUCH YOU WANT TO PAY.

The price of a personal mobile device can range from $100 to $800, depending on its capabilities. Some Palm OS devices are at the lower end of the cost spectrum, and Windows-based devices often are at the higher end. A PDA will be less expensive than a smart phone with a similar configuration. For the latest prices, capabilities, and accessories, visit the Web sites listed in Figure 16.

3 DETERMINE WHETHER YOU NEED WIRELESS ACCESS TO THE INTERNET AND E-MAIL OR MOBILE TELEPHONE CAPABILITIES WITH YOUR DEVICE.

Smart pagers give you access to e-mail and other data and Internet services. Smart phones typically include these features, but also include the capability to make and receive phone calls on cellular networks. Some PDAs and smart phones include wireless networking capability to allow you to connect to the Internet wirelessly. These wireless features and services allow personal mobile device users to access real-time information from anywhere to help make decisions while on the go.

 FOR WIRELESS DEVICES, DETERMINE HOW AND WHERE YOU WILL USE THE SERVICE.

When purchasing a wireless device, you must subscribe to a wireless service. Determine if the wireless network (carrier) you choose has service in the area where you plan to use the device. Some networks have high-speed data networks only in certain areas, such as large cities or business districts. Also, a few carriers allow you to use your device in other countries.

When purchasing a smart phone, determine if you plan to use the device more as a phone, PDA, or wireless data device. Some smart phones, such as those based on the Pocket PC Phone edition or the Palm OS, are geared more for use as a PDA and have a PDA form factor. Other smart phones, such as those based on Microsoft Smartphone or Symbian operating systems, mainly are phone devices that include robust PDA functionality. Research in Motion Blackberry-based smart phones include robust data features that are oriented to accessing e-mail and wireless data services.

 MAKE SURE YOUR DEVICE HAS ENOUGH MEMORY.

Memory (RAM) is not a major issue with low-end devices with monochrome displays and basic organizer functions. Memory is a major issue, however, for high-end devices that have color displays and wireless features. Without enough memory, the performance level of your device will drop dramatically. If you plan to purchase a high-end device running the Palm OS operating system, the device should have at least 32 MB of RAM. If you plan to purchase a high-end device running the Windows Mobile operating system, the PDA should have at least 64 MB of RAM.

6 **PRACTICE WITH THE TOUCH SCREEN, HANDWRITING RECOGNITION, AND BUILT-IN KEYBOARD BEFORE DECIDING ON A MODEL.**

To enter data into a PDA or smart phone, you use a pen-like stylus to handwrite on the screen or a keyboard. The keyboard either slides out or is mounted on the front of the device. With handwriting recognition, the device translates the handwriting into a computerized font. You also can use the stylus as a pointing device to select items on the screen and enter data by tapping on an on-screen keyboard. By practicing data entry before buying a device, you can learn if one device may be easier for you to use than another. You also can buy third-party software to improve a device's handwriting recognition.

7 **DECIDE WHETHER YOU WANT A COLOR DISPLAY.**

Pocket PC devices usually come with a color display that supports as many as 65,536 colors. Palm OS devices also have a color display, but the less expensive models display in 4 to 16 shades of gray. Smart phones and smart pagers also have the option for color displays. Having a color display does result in greater on-screen detail, but it also requires more memory and uses more power. Resolution also influences the quality of the display.

8 **COMPARE BATTERY LIFE.**

Any mobile device is good only if it has the power required to run. For example, Palm OS devices with monochrome screens typically have a much longer battery life than Pocket PC devices with color screens. The use of wireless networking will shorten battery time considerably. To help alleviate this problem, most devices have incorporated rechargeable batteries that can be recharged by placing the device in a cradle or connecting it to a charger.

9 **SERIOUSLY CONSIDER THE IMPORTANCE OF ERGONOMICS.**

Will you put the device in your pocket, a carrying case, or wear it on your belt? How does it feel in your hand? Will you use it indoors or outdoors? Many screens are unreadable outdoors. Do you need extra ruggedness, such as would be required in construction, in a plant, or in a warehouse? A smart phone with a PDA form factor may be larger than a typical PDA. A smart phone with a phone form factor may be smaller, but have fewer capabilities.

10 **CHECK OUT THE ACCESSORIES.**

Determine which accessories you want for your personal mobile device. Accessories include carrying cases, portable mini- and full-sized keyboards, removable storage, modems, synchronization cradles and cables, car chargers, wireless communications, global positioning system modules, digital camera modules, expansion cards, dashboard mounts, replacement styli, hands-free headsets, and more.

11 **DECIDE WHETHER YOU WANT ADDITIONAL FUNCTIONALITY.**

In general, off-the-shelf Microsoft operating system-based devices have broader functionality than devices with other operating systems. For example, voice-recording capability, e-book players, MP3 players, and video players are standard on most Pocket PC devices. If you are leaning towards a Palm OS device and want these additional functions, you may need to purchase additional software or expansion modules to add them later. Determine whether your employer permits devices with cameras on the premises, and if not, do not consider devices with cameras.

12 **DETERMINE WHETHER SYNCHRONIZATION OF DATA WITH OTHER DEVICES OR PERSONAL COMPUTERS IS IMPORTANT.**

Most devices come with a cradle that connects to the USB or serial port on your computer so you can synchronize data on your device with your desktop or notebook computer. Increasingly more devices are Bluetooth and/or wireless networking enabled, which gives them the capability of synchronizing wirelessly. Many devices today also have an infrared port that allows you to synchronize data with any device that has a similar infrared port, including desktop and notebook computers or other personal mobile devices.

Web Site	Web Address
Hewlett-Packard	hp.com
CNET Shopper	shopper.cnet.com
Palm	palm.com
Microsoft	windowsmobile.com pocketpc.com microsoft.com/smartphone
PDA Buyers Guide	pdabuyersguide.com
Research in Motion	rim.com
Danger	danger.com
Symbian	symbian.com
Wireless Developer Network	wirelessdevnet.com
Sharp	www.myzaurus.com

For an updated list of reviews and information about personal mobile devices and their Web addresses, visit scsite.com/dc2007/ch5/pda.

FIGURE 16 Web site reviews and information about personal mobile devices.

CHAPTER SIX

Output

Picture Yourself Saving Money Using a Computer

While eating lunch with some friends, your conversation centers around rising prices and the cost of hotels, postage stamps, greeting cards, gasoline, and services such as banking and film developing. After the discussion, each of you decides to take measures to reduce some of these costs by using your computers.

Instead of paying for personal checks and postage, you decide to use online banking to pay your bills and balance your statements while viewing them on a computer monitor. For those items that still must be mailed through the postal service, you will print the postage stamps on your printer. You also will print addresses directly on the envelopes or print mailing labels. You soon discover that not only do you save on costs but also the amount of time it takes to complete these activities. No more time spent driving to the post office!

With greeting card software, you will design your own greeting cards on the computer screen, personalizing them with pictures and special notes, and then print them in color on card paper. You also will make personalized T-shirts as gifts by printing pictures on T-shirt transfer paper and then ironing the transfer on a plain T-shirt.

The next time photo paper is on sale, you plan to stock up. With the photo paper in the printer, you will print copies of your digital pictures in a variety of sizes — wallet, 4 × 6, 5 × 7, and 8 × 10.

Read Chapter 6 to learn about various types of monitors, printers, and paper and to discover many other forms of output.

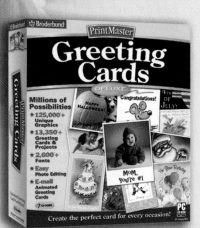

WHAT IS OUTPUT?

Output is data that has been processed into a useful form. That is, computers process data (input) into information (output). A computer generates several types of output, depending on the hardware and software being used and the requirements of the user.

Users view output on a screen, print it, or hear it through speakers, headphones, or earphones. Monitors, notebook computers, Tablet PCs, PDAs, and smart phones have screens that allow users to view documents, Web sites, e-mail messages, and other types of output. Some printers produce black-and-white documents, and others produce brilliant colors, enabling users to print color documents, photographs, and transparencies. Through the computer's speakers, headphones, or earphones, users listen to sounds, music, and voice messages.

While working with a computer, a user encounters four basic categories of output: text, graphics, audio, and video (Figure 6-1). Very often, a single form of output, such as a Web page, includes more than one of these categories.

• Text — Examples of text-based output are memos, letters, announcements, press releases, reports, advertisements, newsletters, envelopes, mailing labels, and e-mail messages. On the Web, users view and print many other types of text-based output. These include newspapers, magazines, books, play or television show transcripts, stock quotes, famous speeches, and historical lectures.

• Graphics — Output often includes graphics to enhance its visual appeal and convey information. Business letters have logos. Reports include charts. Newsletters use drawings, clip art, and photographs. Users print high-quality photographs taken with a

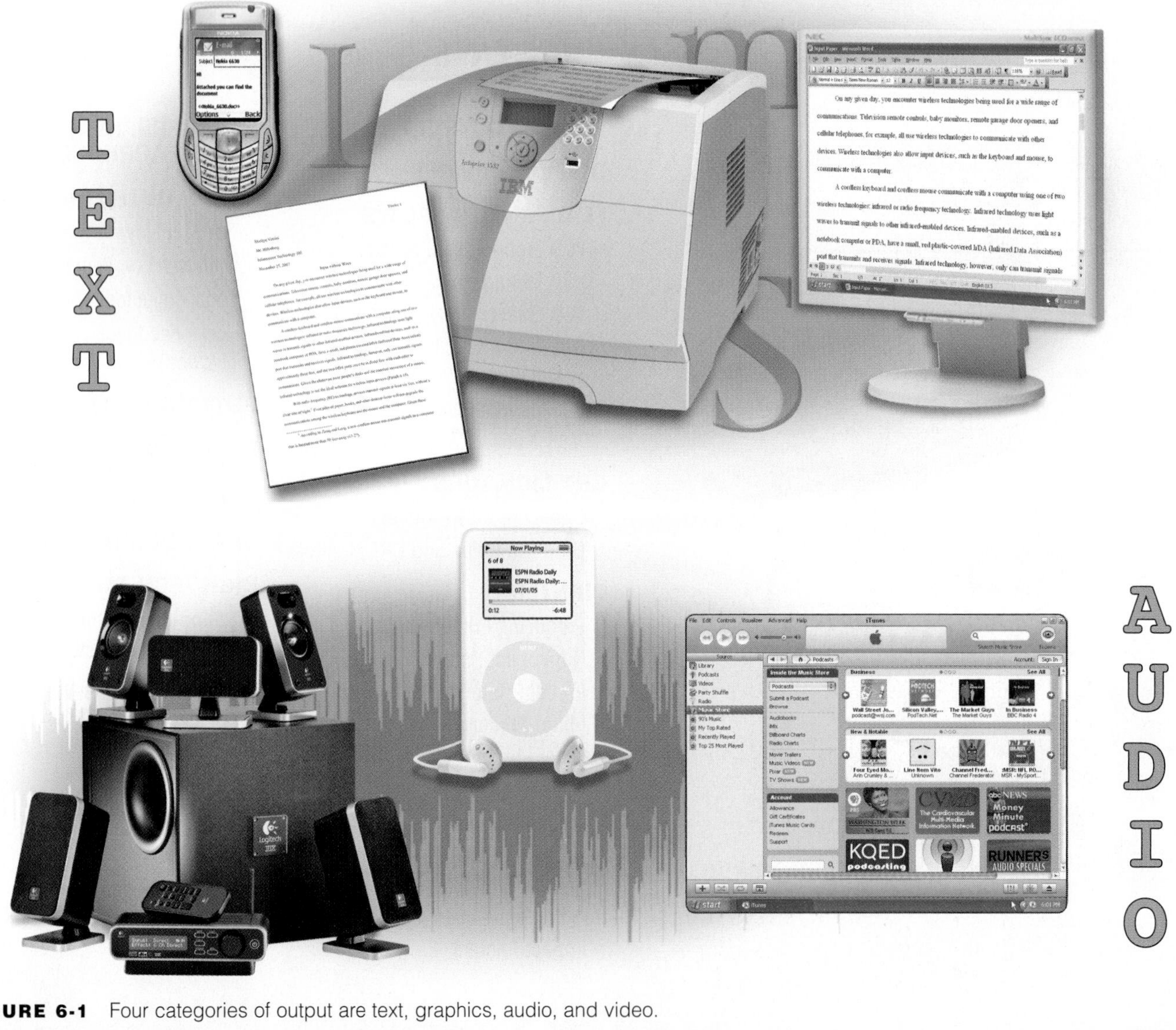

FIGURE 6-1   Four categories of output are text, graphics, audio, and video.

digital camera, eliminating the need for film or film developers. Many Web sites use animated graphics, such as blinking icons, scrolling messages, or simulations.

• Audio — Users insert their favorite music CD in a CD or DVD drive and listen to the music while working on the computer. Software such as games, encyclopedias, and simulations often have musical accompaniments for entertainment and audio clips, such as narrations and speeches, to enhance understanding. On the Web, users tune into radio and television stations and listen to audio clips or live broadcasts of interviews, talk shows, sporting events, news, music, and concerts. They also use the Internet to conduct real-time conversations with friends, coworkers, or family members, just as if they were speaking on the telephone.

• Video — As with audio, software and Web sites often include video clips to enhance

understanding. Users watch a live or prerecorded news report, view a movie, see a doctor perform a life-saving surgery, observe a hurricane in action, or enjoy a live performance of their favorite musician or musical group on the computer.

Attaching a video camera to the computer allows users to watch home movies on the computer. They also can attach a television's antenna or cable to the computer and watch a television program on the computer screen.

An **output device** is any type of hardware component that conveys information to one or more people. Commonly used output devices include display devices; printers; speakers, headphones, and earphones; fax machines and fax modems; multifunction peripherals; data projectors; and force-feedback joysticks, wheels, and gamepads. This chapter discusses each of these output devices.

DISPLAY DEVICES

A **display device**, or simply *display*, is an output device that visually conveys text, graphics, and video information. Information on a display device, sometimes called *soft copy*, exists electronically and appears for a temporary period.

Display devices consist of a screen and the components that produce the information on the screen. Desktop computers typically use a monitor as their display device. A **monitor** is a display device that is packaged as a separate peripheral. Most monitors have a tilt-and-swivel base that allows users to adjust the angle of the screen to minimize neck strain and reduce glare from overhead lighting. Monitor controls permit users to adjust the brightness, contrast, positioning, height, and width of images.

Most mobile computers and devices integrate the display and other components into the same physical case. For example, the display on a notebook computer attaches with hinges. Some PDA and smart phone displays also attach with a hinge to the device; with others, the display is built into the PDA or smart phone case.

Most display devices show text, graphics, and video information in color. Some, however, are monochrome. *Monochrome* means the information appears in one color (such as white, amber, green, black, blue, or gray) on a different color background (such as black or grayish-white). Some PDAs and other mobile devices use monochrome displays because they require less battery power.

Two types of display devices are flat-panel displays and CRT monitors. The following sections discuss each of these display devices.

FAQ 6-1

What can I do to ease eyestrain while using my computer?

Blink your eyes every five seconds. Adjust the room lighting. Use larger fonts or zoom a display. Take an eye break every 30 minutes: look into the distance and focus on an object for 20 to 30 seconds, roll your eyes in a complete circle, and then close your eyes for at least 30 seconds. If you wear glasses, ask your doctor about computer glasses. For more information, visit scsite.com/dc2007/ch6/faq and then click Eye Strain.

FLAT-PANEL DISPLAYS

A *flat-panel display* is a lightweight display device with a shallow depth and flat screen that typically uses LCD (liquid crystal display) or gas plasma technology. Types of flat-panel displays include LCD monitors, LCD screens, and plasma monitors.

LCD Monitors and Screens

An **LCD monitor**, also called a *flat panel monitor*, is a desktop monitor that uses a liquid crystal display to produce images (Figure 6-2). These monitors produce sharp, flicker-free images.

LCD monitors have a small *footprint*; that is, they do not take up much desk space. For additional space savings, some LCD monitors are wall mountable. LCD monitors are available in a variety of sizes, with the more common being 15, 17, 18, 19, 20, 21, and 23 inches — some are 30 or 40 inches. You measure a monitor the same way you measure a television, that is, diagonally from one corner to the other.

Determining what size monitor to purchase depends on your intended use. A large monitor allows you to view more information on the screen at once, but usually is more expensive. You may want to invest in a 19-inch monitor if you use multiple applications at one time or do a lot of research on the Web. Users working with intense graphics applications, such as desktop publishing and engineering, typically have larger monitors.

FIGURE 6-2 An LCD monitor is thin and lightweight.

For an even wider screen area, some users position two or more monitors side by side or stacked (Figure 6-3). For example, one monitor can show the left side of a document, game, graphic design, or other item, with the other monitor showing the right side. This arrangement also is convenient if you want to run multiple applications simultaneously. Users of side-by-side or stacked monitors include music editors, video editors, network administrators, gamers, researchers, Web developers, graphic designers, and engineers.

Mobile computers, such as notebook computers and Tablet PCs, and mobile devices, such as PDAs and smart phones, often have built-in LCD screens (Figure 6-4). Notebook computer screens are available in a variety of sizes, with the more common being 14.1, 15.4, and 17 inches. Tablet PC screens range from 8.4 inches to 14.1 inches. PDA screens average 3.5 inches. On smart phones, screen sizes range from 2.5 to 3.5 inches.

FIGURE 6-3   Users sometimes have multiple monitors stacked or side by side to increase their viewing area.

FAQ 6-2

Can I read a book on a PDA or smart phone screen?

Yes, you can download an electronic book, called an *e-book*, to a mobile device or computer. To read an e-book, your mobile device or computer requires a reader program such as *Microsoft Reader* or *Adobe Reader*. Both of these programs can be downloaded free on the Web. For more information, visit scsite.com/dc2007/ch6/faq and then click E-Books.

notebook computer

Tablet PC

PDA

smart phone

FIGURE 6-4   Notebook computers and Tablet PCs have color LCD screens. Many PDAs and smart phones also have color displays.

LCD Technology

A **liquid crystal display** (**LCD**) uses a liquid compound to present information on a display device. Computer LCDs typically contain fluorescent tubes that emit light waves toward the liquid-crystal cells, which are sandwiched between two sheets of material. When an electrical charge passes through the cells, the cells twist. This twisting causes some light waves to be blocked and allows others to pass through, creating images on the display.

LCD monitors and LCD screens produce color using either passive-matrix or active-matrix technology. An *active-matrix display*, also known as a *TFT* (*thin-film transistor*) *display*, uses a separate transistor to apply charges to each liquid crystal cell and thus displays high-quality color that is viewable from all angles. A newer type of TFT technology, called *organic LED* (*OLED*), uses organic molecules that produce an even brighter, easier-to-read display than standard TFT displays. OLEDs are less expensive to produce, consume less power, and can be fabricated on flexible surfaces. Read Looking Ahead 6-1 for a look at the next generation of OLEDs.

A *passive-matrix display* uses fewer transistors, requires less power, and is less expensive than an active-matrix display. The color on a passive-matrix display often is not as bright as an active-matrix display. Users view images on a passive-matrix display best when working directly in front of it.

LOOKING AHEAD 6-1

Rollable Displays Lock and Roll

Your newspaper arrives each morning at your front door rolled up and secured with a rubber band or in a plastic bag. Your computer monitor soon may arrive rolled up so you can transport it easily in your book bag or luggage.

Flexible screens are being developed to curve against your car's dashboard and bend around corners. In 2005, Philips Polymer Vision introduced the Readius prototype, a pocket-sized electronic document reader that unrolls a 5-inch-long display. The paper-like mobile reader can display text, graphics, and maps. When users are finished viewing the screen, they simply retract the display back into the device, which measures less than 4 inches high.

Rollable screens should prove useful as electronics shrink in size, for they will permit large displays in small, pocket-size mobile devices. For more information, visit scsite.com/dc2007/ch6/looking and then click Rollable Displays.

LCD Quality

The quality of an LCD monitor or LCD screen depends primarily on its resolution, response time, brightness, pixel pitch, and contrast ratio.

- **Resolution** is the number of horizontal and vertical pixels in a display device. For example, a monitor that has a 1600 × 1200 resolution displays up to 1600 pixels per horizontal row and 1200 pixels per vertical row, for a total of 1,920,000 pixels to create a screen image. Recall that a *pixel* (short for picture element) is a single point in an electronic image. A higher resolution uses a greater number of pixels and thus provides a smoother, sharper, and clearer image. As you increase the resolution, however, some items on the screen appear smaller, such as menu bars, toolbars, and rulers (Figure 6-5).

  With LCD monitors and screens, resolution generally is proportional to the size of the device. For example, a 17-inch LCD monitor typically has a resolution of 1280 × 1024, while a 20-inch LCD monitor has a resolution of 1600 × 1200. LCDs are geared for a specific resolution, called the *native resolution*. When set at other resolutions, the quality may not be as good as the native resolution.

- *Response time* of an LCD monitor or screen is the time in milliseconds (ms) that it takes to turn a pixel on or off. LCD monitors' and screens' response times range from 8 to 25 ms. The lower the number, the faster the response time.

- Brightness of an LCD monitor or LCD screen is measured in nits. A *nit* is a unit of visible light intensity equal to one candela (formerly called candlepower) per square meter. The *candela* is the standard unit of luminous intensity. LCD monitors and screens today range from 200 to 350 nits. The higher the nits, the brighter the images.

- *Pixel pitch*, sometimes called *dot pitch*, is the distance in millimeters between pixels on a display device. Text created with a smaller dot pitch is easier to read. Advertisements normally specify a monitor's pixel pitch or dot pitch. Average pixel pitch on LCD monitors and screens should be .28 mm or lower. The lower the number, the sharper the image.

- *Contrast ratio* describes the difference in light intensity between the brightest white and darkest black that can be displayed on an LCD monitor. Contrast ratios today range from 400:1 to 800:1. Higher contrast ratios represent colors better.

FIGURE 6-5a (screen resolution at 800 × 600)

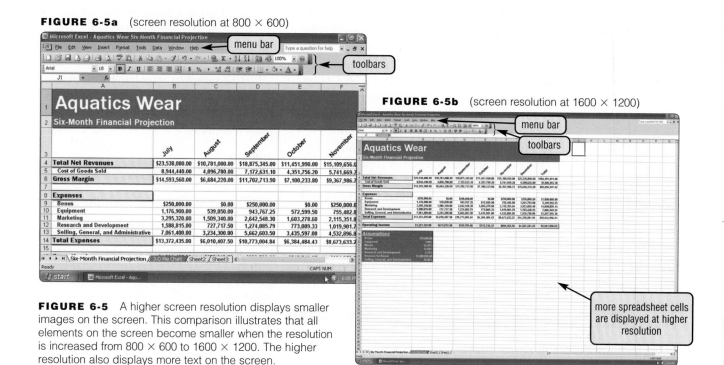

FIGURE 6-5b (screen resolution at 1600 × 1200)

FIGURE 6-5 A higher screen resolution displays smaller images on the screen. This comparison illustrates that all elements on the screen become smaller when the resolution is increased from 800 × 600 to 1600 × 1200. The higher resolution also displays more text on the screen.

Graphics Chips, Ports, and LCD Monitors

A cable on a monitor plugs in a port on the system unit, which enables communications from a graphics chip. This chip, called the *graphics processing unit*, controls the manipulation and display of graphics on a display device. The graphics processing unit either is integrated on the motherboard or resides on a video card in a slot in the motherboard. Video cards usually contain a fan or heat sink to keep this and other chips from overheating.

LCD monitors use a digital signal to produce a picture. To display the highest quality images, an LCD monitor should plug in a *DVI (Digital Video Interface) port*, which enables digital signals to transmit directly to the LCD monitor. Current models of system units either have an integrated DVI chip or contain a video card that has a DVI port. They usually also have a standard monitor port and an *S-video port*, allowing users to connect external devices such as a television, DVD player, or video recorder, to the computer (Figure 6-6).

Over the years, several video standards have been developed to define the resolution, number of colors, and other display properties.

Current video standards include *SVGA* (Super Video Graphics Array), which has a resolution of 800 × 600; *XGA* (eXtended Graphics Array), a resolution of 1024 × 768; *SXGA* (Super XGA), a resolution of 1280 × 1024; and *UGA* (Ultra XGA), a resolution of 1600 × 1200. Many display devices have resolutions beyond UGA, such as 2048 × 1536. Some display devices support all of these standards; others support only a subset of them. For a display device to show images as defined by a video standard, both the display device and graphics processing unit must support the same video standard.

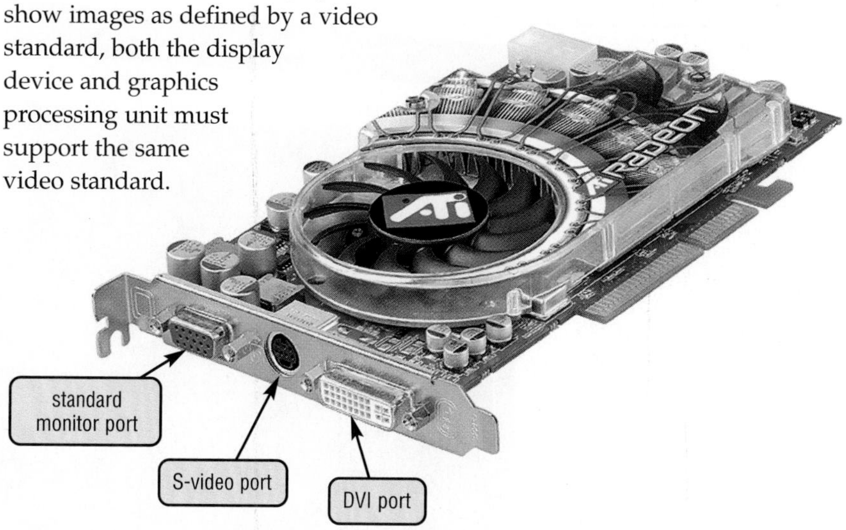

standard monitor port

S-video port

DVI port

FIGURE 6-6 Ports on current video cards.

The number of colors a graphics processing unit displays is determined by bit depth. The *bit depth*, also called *color depth*, is the number of bits used to store information about each pixel. For example, a video card with a 24-bit depth uses 24 bits to store information about each pixel. Thus, this video card can display 2^{24} or 16.7 million colors. The greater the number of bits, the better the resulting image. Today's video cards typically have a 24-bit depth or a 32-bit depth.

A video card or motherboard, in the case of integrated video, must have enough video memory to generate the resolution and number of colors you want to display. This memory, which often is 128 MB or 256 MB on current video cards, stores information about each pixel.

When voltage is applied, the gas releases ultraviolet (UV) light. This UV light causes the pixels on the screen to glow and form an image.

Plasma monitors offer larger screen sizes and higher display quality than LCD monitors but are more expensive. These monitors also can hang directly on a wall.

FAQ 6-4

What is the largest monitor to date?

The Sydney Olympics had a monitor wall that contained more than 400 screens, measuring about 150 feet wide and 7½ feet tall. For more information, visit scsite.com/dc2007/ch6/faq and then click Monitor Wall.

FAQ 6-3

How much do video cards cost?

Although video cards for the home user cost less than $100, professional artists and designers use video cards that can cost up to $1,500. These cards have more than 384 MB of memory and support resolutions of 2048 × 1536. For more information, visit scsite.com/dc2007/ch6/faq and then click Video Cards.

WEB LINK 6-2

Plasma Technology

For more information, visit scsite.com/dc2007/ch6/weblink and then click Plasma Technology.

Plasma Monitors

Large business or power users sometimes have plasma monitors, which often measure more than 60 inches wide (Figure 6-7). A **plasma monitor** is a display device that uses gas plasma technology, which sandwiches a layer of gas between two glass plates.

Televisions

Home users sometimes use their television as a display device. Connecting a computer to an analog television requires a converter that translates the digital signal from the computer into an analog signal that the television can display. The best analog televisions have a resolution of only 520 × 400 pixels. Thus, users are turning to *digital television* (DTV) for crisper, higher-quality output on their LCD or plasma televisions.

Digital television signals provide two major advantages over analog signals. First, digital signals produce a higher-quality picture. Second, many programs can be broadcast on a single digital channel, whereas only one program can be broadcast on an analog channel. Today, all broadcast stations must transmit digital signals, as mandated by the FCC.

HDTV (*high-definition television*) is the most advanced form of digital television, working with digital broadcast signals, transmitting digital sound, supporting wide screens, and providing resolutions up to 1920 × 1080 pixels. With HDTV, the broadcast signals are digitized when they are sent via over-the-air (OTA) broadcasts from

FIGURE 6-7 Large plasma monitors can measure more than 60 inches wide.

local television networks, satellite, or cable. To receive the HDTV signals via OTA broadcasts, you need a VHF/UHF antenna; via satellite, you need an HDTV-compatible satellite receiver/tuner; and via cable, you need an HDTV-compatible cable box.

With game consoles, such as Microsoft's Xbox 360 and Sony's PlayStation 3, the output device often is a television (Figure 6-8). Users plug one end of a cable in the game console and the other end in the video port on the television. Although some game consoles include a small LCD screen (usually 5 inches or smaller), home users often prefer the larger television displays for game playing, watching movies, and browsing the Internet on a television connected to a game console.

FAQ 6-5

Who plays video games?

Studies have shown that people between 18 and 34 years of age spend the most time playing video games. This age group spends more money on video games than in movie theaters. For more information, visit scsite.com/dc2007/ch6/faq and then click Video Gaming.

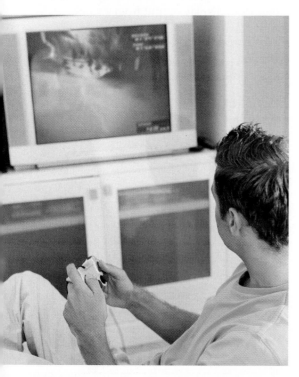

FIGURE 6-8 Video game players often use a television as their game console's output device.

CRT MONITORS

A **CRT monitor** is a desktop monitor that contains a cathode-ray tube (Figure 6-9). A *cathode-ray tube* (*CRT*) is a large, sealed glass tube. The front of the tube is the screen. Tiny dots of phosphor material coat the screen on a CRT. Each dot consists of a red, a green, and a blue phosphor. The three dots combine to make up each pixel. Inside the CRT, an electron beam moves back and forth across the back of the screen. This causes the dots on the front of the screen to glow, which produces an image on the screen.

CRT monitors have a much larger footprint than do LCD monitors; that is, they take up more desk space. CRT monitors for desktop computers are available in various sizes, with the more common being 15, 17, 19, 21, and 22 inches. In addition to monitor size, advertisements also list a CRT monitor's viewable size. The *viewable size* is the diagonal measurement of the actual viewing area provided by the screen in the CRT monitor. A 21-inch monitor, for example, may have a viewable size of 20 inches.

In the past, CRT monitor screens were curved slightly. Today's models have flat screens. A flat screen reduces glare, reflection, and distortion of images. With a flat screen, users do not notice as much eyestrain and fatigue.

A CRT monitor costs less than an LCD monitor, but it also generates more heat and uses more power than an LCD monitor. To help reduce the amount of electricity used by monitors and other computer components, the United States Department of Energy (DOE) and the United States Environmental Protection Agency (EPA) developed the **ENERGY STAR program**. This program encourages manufacturers to create energy-efficient devices that require little power when they are not in use. Monitors and devices that meet ENERGY STAR guidelines display an ENERGY STAR label.

FIGURE 6-9 The core of a CRT monitor is a cathode-ray tube.

CRT monitors produce a small amount of electromagnetic radiation. *Electromagnetic radiation (EMR)* is a magnetic field that travels at the speed of light. Excessive amounts of EMR can pose a health risk. To be safe, all high-quality CRT monitors comply with MPR II standards. *MPR II* is a set of standards that defines acceptable levels of EMR for a monitor. To protect yourself even further, sit at arm's length from the CRT monitor because EMR travels only a short distance. In addition, EMR is greatest on the sides and back of the CRT monitor.

FAQ 6-6

Is a flat display the same as a flat-panel display?

No. A *flat display* refers to a CRT monitor that has a flat screen. A flat-panel display, by contrast, has a shallow depth and uses LCD, gas plasma, or some technology other than CRT. For more information, visit scsite.com/dc2007/ch6/faq and then click Flat-Panel Displays.

Quality of a CRT Monitor

The quality of a CRT monitor depends largely on its resolution, dot pitch, and refresh rate.
- Most CRT monitors support a variety of screen resolutions. Standard CRT monitors today usually display up to a maximum of 1800 × 1440 pixels, with 1280 × 1024 often the norm. High-end CRT monitors (for the power user) can display 2048 × 1536 pixels or more. The display resolution you choose is a matter of preference. Larger monitors typically look best at a higher resolution, and smaller monitors look best at a lower resolution.
- As with LCD monitors, text created with a smaller dot pitch, or pixel pitch, is easier to read. To minimize eye fatigue, use a CRT monitor with a dot pitch of .27 millimeters or lower.
- Electron beams inside a CRT monitor "draw" an image on the entire screen many times per second so the phosphor dots, and therefore the image, do not fade. The number of times the image is drawn per second is called the *refresh rate*, or *scan rate*. A CRT monitor's refresh rate, which is expressed in hertz (Hz), should be fast enough to maintain a constant, flicker-free image. A slower refresh rate causes

the image to fade and then flicker as it is redrawn. This flicker can lead to eye fatigue and cause headaches for some users.

A high-quality CRT monitor will provide a vertical refresh rate of at least 68 Hz. This means the image on the screen redraws itself vertically 68 times in a second.

Graphics Chips and CRT Monitors

Many CRT monitors use an analog signal to produce an image. As with an LCD monitor, a cable on the CRT monitor plugs in a port on the system unit, which enables communications from a graphics chip. If the graphics chip resides on a video card, for example, the video card converts digital output from the computer into an analog video signal and sends the signal through the cable to the monitor, which displays output on the screen (Figure 6-10).

As with LCD monitors, the greater the video card's bit depth, the better the resulting image. Both the video card and the monitor must support the video standard to generate the desired resolution and number of colors, and the video card must have enough memory to generate the resolution and number of colors you want to display. Some users place additional video cards in their system unit, allowing multiple monitors to display output from a single computer simultaneously.

FAQ 6-7

What type of video content do users view on display devices?

Music videos and newscasts are the most widely viewed video content on display devices, as shown in the chart below. For more information, visit scsite.com/dc2007/ch6/faq and then click Video Output Content.

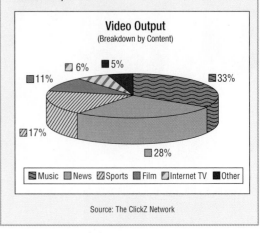

Video Output
(Breakdown by Content)

6% 5%
11% 33%
17%
28%

Music   News   Sports   Film   Internet TV   Other

Source: The ClickZ Network

FIGURE 6-10 HOW VIDEO TRAVELS FROM THE PROCESSOR TO A CRT MONITOR VIA A VIDEO CARD

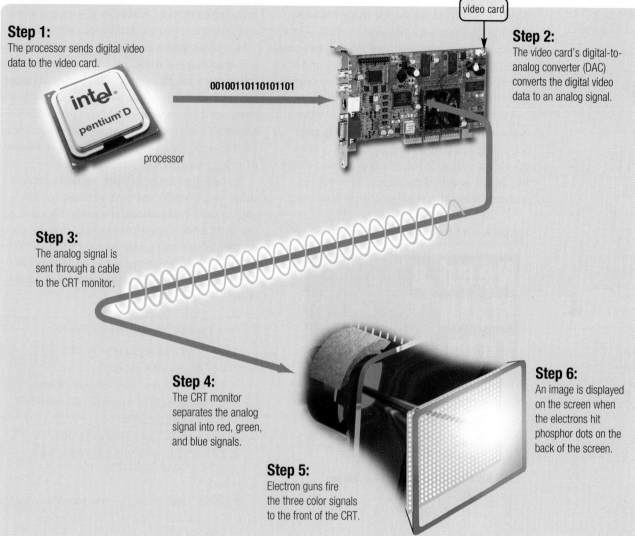

Step 1:
The processor sends digital video data to the video card.

00100110110101101

processor

video card

Step 2:
The video card's digital-to-analog converter (DAC) converts the digital video data to an analog signal.

Step 3:
The analog signal is sent through a cable to the CRT monitor.

Step 4:
The CRT monitor separates the analog signal into red, green, and blue signals.

Step 6:
An image is displayed on the screen when the electrons hit phosphor dots on the back of the screen.

Step 5:
Electron guns fire the three color signals to the front of the CRT.

Test your knowledge of pages 300 through 309 in Quiz Yourself 6-1.

QUIZ YOURSELF 6-1

Instructions: Find the true statement below. Then, rewrite the remaining false statements so they are true.

1. A lower resolution uses a greater number of pixels and thus provides a smoother image.

2. An output device is any type of software component that conveys information to one or more people.

3. Documents often include text to enhance their visual appeal and convey information.

4. LCD monitors have a larger footprint than CRT monitors.

5. Types of CRTs include LCD monitors, LCD screens, and plasma monitors.

6. You measure a monitor diagonally from one corner to the other.

Quiz Yourself Online: To further check your knowledge of output, flat-panel displays, and CRT monitors, visit scsite.com/dc2007/ch6/quiz and then click Objectives 1 – 4.

PRINTERS

A **printer** is an output device that produces text and graphics on a physical medium such as paper or transparency film. Printed information, called *hard copy*, exists physically and is a more permanent form of output than that presented on a display device (soft copy).

A hard copy, also called a *printout*, is either in portrait or landscape orientation (Figure 6-11). A printout in *portrait orientation* is taller than it is wide, with information printed across the shorter width of the paper. A printout in *landscape orientation* is wider than it is tall, with information printed across the widest part of the paper. Letters, reports, and books typically use portrait orientation. Spreadsheets, slide shows, and graphics often use landscape orientation.

Home computer users might print less than a hundred pages a week. Small business computer users might print several hundred pages a day. Users of mainframe computers, such as large utility companies that send printed statements to hundreds of thousands of customers each month, require printers that are capable of printing thousands of pages per hour.

To meet this range of printing needs, many different printers exist with varying speeds, capabilities, and printing methods. Figure 6-12 presents a list of questions to help you decide on the printer best suited to your needs.

The following pages discuss various ways of producing printed output, as well as many different types of printers.

FIGURE 6-11a (portrait orientation)

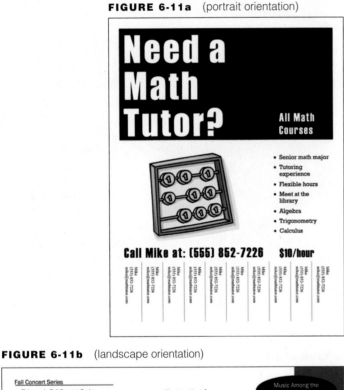

FIGURE 6-11b (landscape orientation)

FIGURE 6-11 Portrait orientation is taller than it is wide. Landscape orientation is wider than it is tall.

1. What is my budget?
2. How fast must my printer print?
3. Do I need a color printer?
4. What is the cost per page for printing?
5. Do I need multiple copies of documents?
6. Will I print graphics?
7. Do I want to print photographs?
8. Do I want to print directly from a memory card or other type of miniature storage media?
9. What types of paper does the printer use?
10. What sizes of paper does the printer accept?
11. Do I want to print on both sides of the paper?
12. How much paper can the printer tray hold?
13. Will the printer work with my computer and software?
14. How much do supplies such as ink and paper cost?
15. Can the printer print on envelopes and transparencies?
16. How many envelopes can the printer print at a time?
17. How much do I print now, and how much will I be printing in a year or two?
18. Will the printer be connected to a network?
19. Do I want wireless printing capability?

FIGURE 6-12 Questions to ask when purchasing a printer.

Producing Printed Output

Until a few years ago, printing a document required connecting a computer to a printer with a cable via the USB or parallel port on the computer. Although many users today continue to print using this method, a variety of printing options are available, as shown in Figure 6-13.

Today, wireless printing technology makes the task of printing from a notebook computer, Tablet PC, PDA, smart phone, or digital camera much easier. As discussed in Chapter 4, two wireless technologies for printing are Bluetooth and infrared. With *Bluetooth printing*, a computer or other device transmits output to a printer via radio waves. The computer or other device and the printer do not have to be aligned with each

other; rather, they need to be within an approximate 30-foot range. With *infrared printing*, a printer communicates with a computer or other device using infrared light waves. To print from a smart phone, for example, a user lines up the IrDA port on the smart phone with the IrDA port on the printer.

Users can print images taken with a digital camera without downloading the images to the computer using a variety of techniques. Some cameras connect directly to a printer via a cable. Others store images on media cards that can be removed and inserted in the printer. Some printers have a docking station, into which the user inserts the camera to print pictures stored in the camera.

WEB LINK 6-3

Printing Digital Camera Images

For more information, visit scsite.com/dc2007/ch6/weblink and then click Printing Digital Camera Images.

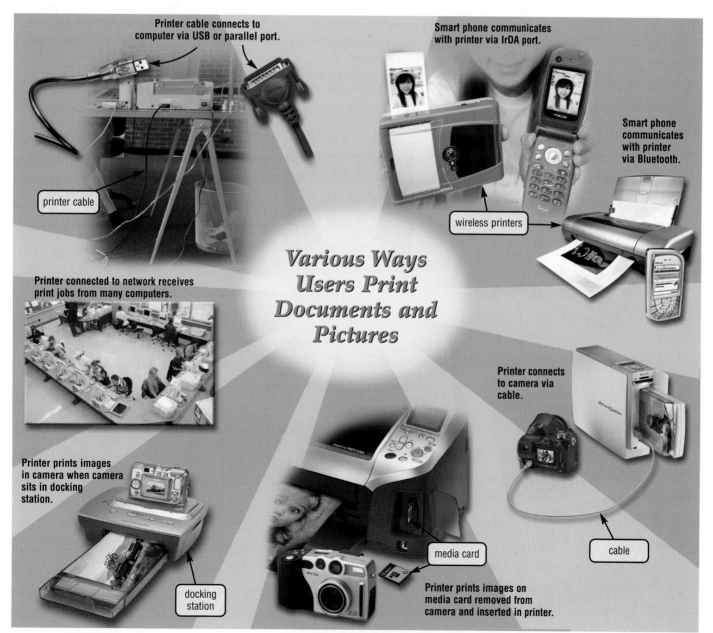

FIGURE 6-13 Users print documents and pictures using a variety of printing methods.

Finally, many home and business users print to a central printer on a network. Their computer may communicate with the network printer via cables or wirelessly.

FAQ 6-8

Where did the name Bluetooth originate?

Harald Blatand was king of Denmark circa 950. This king, whose last name they say roughly translates to blue tooth, was able to unite Denmark and Norway despite their differences. When Ericsson, Intel, IBM, Nokia, and Toshiba collectively were able to develop this wireless communications standard, they named it Bluetooth — after the Danish leader. For more information, visit scsite.com/dc2007/ch6/faq and then click Bluetooth.

Nonimpact Printers

A **nonimpact printer** forms characters and graphics on a piece of paper without actually striking the paper. Some spray ink, while others use heat or pressure to create images.

Commonly used nonimpact printers are ink-jet printers, photo printers, laser printers, thermal printers, mobile printers, label and postage printers, plotters, and large-format printers.

Ink-Jet Printers

An **ink-jet printer** is a type of nonimpact printer that forms characters and graphics by spraying tiny drops of liquid ink onto a piece of paper. Ink-jet printers have become a popular type of color printer for use in the home. A reasonable quality ink-jet printer costs less than $100.

Ink-jet printers produce text and graphics in both black-and-white and color on a variety of paper types (Figure 6-14). These printers normally use individual sheets of paper stored in one or two removable or stationary trays. Ink-jet printers accept papers in many sizes, ranging from 3×5 inches to $8^1/_2 \times 14$ inches. Available paper types include plain paper, ink-jet paper, photo paper, glossy paper, and banner paper. Most ink-jet

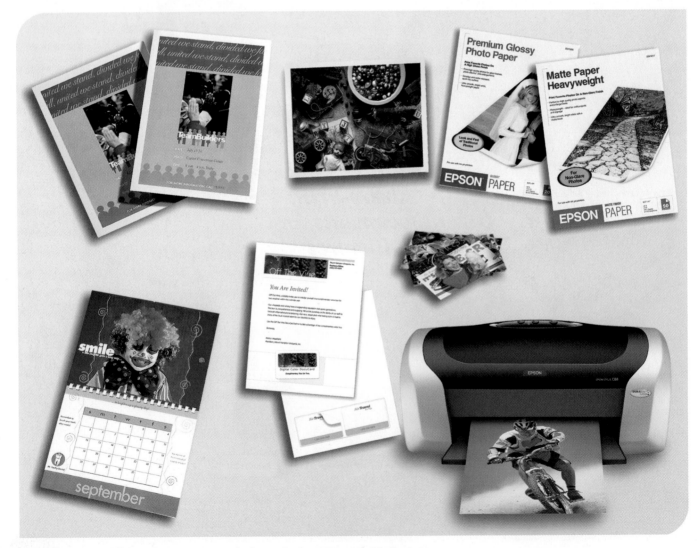

FIGURE 6-14   Ink-jet printers are a popular type of color printer used in the home.

printers can print photographic-quality images on any of these types of paper.

Ink-jet printers also print on other materials such as envelopes, labels, index cards, greeting card paper (card stock), transparencies, and iron-on T-shirt transfers. Many ink-jet printers include software for creating greeting cards, banners, business cards, letterheads, and transparencies.

As with many other input and output devices, one factor that determines the quality of an ink-jet printer is its resolution. Printer resolution is measured by the number of *dots per inch* (*dpi*) a printer can print. With an ink-jet printer, a dot is a drop of ink. A higher dpi means the drops of ink are smaller. Most ink-jet printers can print from 600 to 4800 dpi.

As shown in Figure 6-15, the higher the dpi, the better the print quality. The difference in quality becomes noticeable when the size of the printed image increases. That is, a wallet-sized image printed at 600 dpi may look similar in quality to one printed at 1200 dpi. When you increase the size of the image, to 8 × 10 for example, the printout of the 600 dpi resolution

may look grainier than the one printed using a 1200 dpi resolution.

The speed of an ink-jet printer is measured by the number of pages per minute (ppm) it can print. Most ink-jet printers print from 3 to 26 ppm. Graphics and colors print at a slower rate. For example, an ink-jet printer may print 20 ppm for black text and only 15 ppm for color and/or graphics.

The print head mechanism in an ink-jet printer contains ink-filled print cartridges. Each cartridge has fifty to several hundred small ink holes, or nozzles. The steps in Figure 6-16 illustrate how a drop of ink appears on a page. The ink propels through any combination of the nozzles to form a character or image on the paper.

FIGURE 6-15 You will notice a higher quality output with printers that can print at a higher dpi.

FIGURE 6-16 HOW AN INK-JET PRINTER WORKS

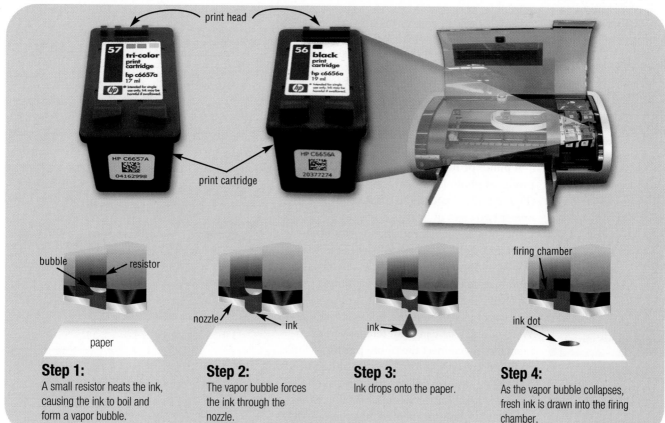

Step 1:
A small resistor heats the ink, causing the ink to boil and form a vapor bubble.

Step 2:
The vapor bubble forces the ink through the nozzle.

Step 3:
Ink drops onto the paper.

Step 4:
As the vapor bubble collapses, fresh ink is drawn into the firing chamber.

When the print cartridge runs out of ink, you simply replace the cartridge. Most ink-jet printers have at least two print cartridges: one containing black ink and the other(s) containing colors. Cartridges with black ink cost $15 to $30 each. Color ink cartridge prices range from $20 to $35 each. The number of pages a single cartridge can print varies by manufacturer and the type of documents you print. For example, black ink cartridges typically print from 200 to 800 pages, and color ink cartridges from 125 to 450 pages. Read Ethics & Issues 6-1 for a related discussion.

WEB LINK 6-4

Ink-Jet Printers

For more information, visit scsite.com/dc2007/ch6/weblink and then click Ink-Jet Printers.

ETHICS & ISSUES 6-1

Is It Ethical to Refill an Ink-Jet Cartridge?

In 1903, King Camp Gillette introduced an innovative product — a safety razor with disposable blades. Gillette accompanied his product with an even more innovative idea — sell the razor, which was purchased once, at or below cost, and rely on sales of the razor blades, which were purchased repeatedly, for profit. The idea made Gillette a millionaire. Manufacturers of ink-jet printers use a similar approach. The printers are inexpensive, often less than $100. The ink cartridges the printers use, however, can cost from $30 to $50 each time they are replaced. To avoid the high cost of cartridges, some people get cartridges refilled cheaply by a third party vendor. At least one printer company legally prohibits the practice, and violators may be breaking patent and contract law if they refill a cartridge. Additionally, some printer manufacturers have inserted special chips that keep a cartridge from being refilled and, some claim, shut down a cartridge before it really is out of ink. Opponents of these practices say that the printer companies are gouging customers and that no legitimate reason exists why someone should not be able to refill an ink-jet cartridge in the same way a soap dispenser can be refilled. Should manufacturers be allowed to prevent people from refilling ink cartridges? Why? Would you use an ink refill kit? Why or why not?

Photo Printers

A **photo printer** is a color printer that produces photo-lab-quality pictures (Figure 6-17). Some photo printers print just one or two sizes of images, for example, 3 × 5 inches and 4 × 6 inches. Others print up to letter size, legal size, or even larger. Some even print panoramic photographs. Generally, the more sizes the printer prints, the more expensive the printer.

Many photo printers use ink-jet technology. With models that can print letter-sized documents, users connect the photo printer to their computer and use it for all their printing needs. For a few hundred dollars, this type of photo printer is ideal for the home or small business user. Other photo printer technologies are discussed later in the chapter. Read Ethics & Issues 6-2 for a related discussion.

WEB LINK 6-5

Photo Printers

For more information, visit scsite.com/dc2007/ch6/weblink and then click Photo Printers.

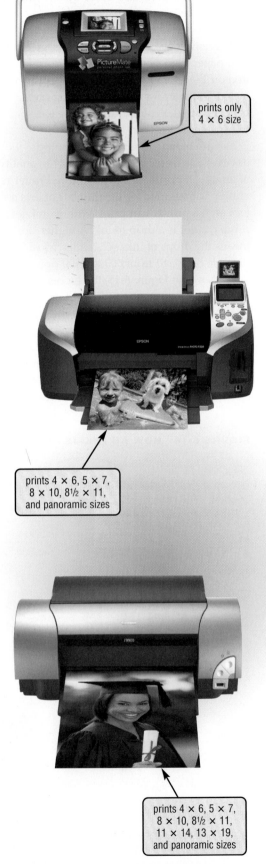

prints only 4 × 6 size

prints 4 × 6, 5 × 7, 8 × 10, 8½ × 11, and panoramic sizes

prints 4 × 6, 5 × 7, 8 × 10, 8½ × 11, 11 × 14, 13 × 19, and panoramic sizes

FIGURE 6-17 Photo printers print in a range of sizes.

Many photo printers have a built-in card slot so the printer can print digital photographs directly from a media card. Simply remove the media card from the digital camera and insert it in the printer's card slot. Then, push buttons on the printer to select the desired photo, specify the number of copies, and indicate the size of the printed image. Some photo printers have built-in LCD color screens, allowing users to view and enhance the pictures before printing them.

Laser Printers

A **laser printer** is a high-speed, high-quality nonimpact printer (Figure 6-18). Laser printers are available in both black-and-white and color models. A laser printer for personal computers ordinarily uses individual 8½ × 11-inch sheets of paper stored in one or more removable trays that slide in the printer case. Some laser printers have built-in trays that accommodate different sizes of paper, while others require separate trays for letter- and legal-sized paper. Most laser printers have a manual feed slot where you can insert individual sheets and envelopes. You also can print transparencies on a laser printer.

Laser printers print text and graphics in high-quality resolutions, usually 1200 dpi for black-and-white printers and up to 2400 dpi for color printers. While laser printers usually cost more than ink-jet printers, they also are much faster. A laser printer for the home and small office user typically prints black-and-white text at speeds of 15 to 50 ppm. Color laser printers print 4 to 27 ppm. Laser printers for large business users print more than 150 ppm.

FAQ 6-9

What type of paper is available for a photo printer?

Many photo papers are available in various surface finishes, brightness, and weights. Surface finishes include high gloss, soft gloss, satin, or matte. The higher the brightness rating, the more brilliant the whiteness. The greater the paper weight, which is measured in pounds, the thicker the paper. In the United States, the weight of paper is stated in pounds per 500 sheets of 17 × 22-inch paper, each sheet of which equals four letter-sized sheets. For more information, visit scsite.com/dc2007/ch6/faq and then click Photo Paper.

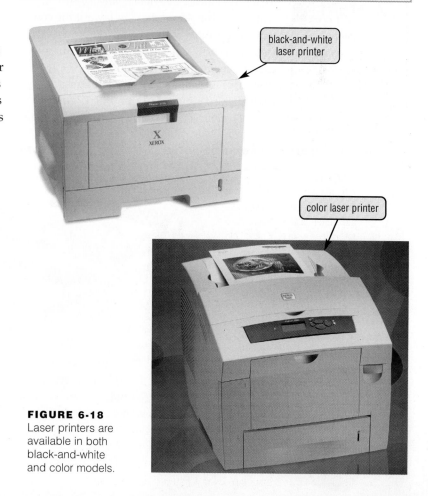

black-and-white laser printer

color laser printer

FIGURE 6-18
Laser printers are available in both black-and-white and color models.

Depending on the quality, speed, and type of laser printer, the cost ranges from a few hundred to a few thousand dollars for the home and small office user, and several hundred thousand dollars for the large business user. Color laser printers are slightly higher priced than otherwise equivalent black-and-white laser printers.

When printing a document, laser printers process and store the entire page before they actually print it. For this reason, laser printers sometimes are called page printers. Storing a page before printing requires that the laser printer has a certain amount of memory in the device.

Depending on the amount of graphics you intend to print, a laser printer for the home or small business user can have up to 544 MB of memory and a 20 GB hard disk. To print a full-page 1200-dpi picture, for instance, you might need 32 MB of memory in the printer. If the printer does not have enough memory to print the picture, either it will print as much of the picture as its memory will allow, or it will display an error message and not print any of the picture.

Laser printers use software that enables them to interpret a *page description language* (*PDL*), which tells the printer how to lay out the contents of a printed page. When you purchase a laser printer, it comes with at least one of two common page description languages: PCL or PostScript. Developed by Hewlett-Packard, a leading printer manufacturer, *PCL* (*Printer Control Language*) is a standard printer language

that supports the fonts and layout used in standard office documents. Professionals in the desktop publishing and graphic art fields commonly use *PostScript* because it is designed for complex documents with intense graphics and colors.

Operating in a manner similar to a copy machine, a laser printer creates images using a laser beam and powdered ink, called *toner*. The laser beam produces an image on a special drum inside the printer. The light of the laser alters the electrical charge on the drum wherever it hits. When this occurs, the toner sticks to the drum and then transfers to the paper through a combination of pressure and heat (Figure 6-19).

When the toner runs out, you replace the toner cartridge. Toner cartridge prices range from $50 to $100 for about 5,000 printed pages.

WEB LINK 6-6

Laser Printers

For more information, visit scsite.com/ dc2007/ch6/weblink and then click Laser Printers.

FAQ 6-10

How do I dispose of toner cartridges?

Do not throw them in the garbage. The housing contains iron, metal, and aluminum that is not biodegradable. The ink toner inside the cartridges contains toxic chemicals that pollute water and soil if discarded in dumps. Instead, recycle empty toner cartridges. Contact your printer manufacturer to see if it has a recycling program. For more information, visit scsite.com/dc2007/ch6/faq and then click Recycling Toner Cartridges.

FIGURE 6-19 HOW A BLACK-AND-WHITE LASER PRINTER WORKS

Step 1:
After the user sends an instruction to print a document, the drum rotates as gears and rollers feed a sheet of paper into the printer.

Step 2:
A rotating mirror deflects a low-powered laser beam across the surface of a drum.

Step 3:
The laser beam creates a charge that causes toner to stick to the drum.

Step 4:
As the drum continues to rotate and press against the paper, the toner transfers from the drum to the paper.

Step 5:
A set of rollers uses heat and pressure to fuse the toner permanently to the paper.

Thermal Printers

A **thermal printer** generates images by pushing electrically heated pins against heat-sensitive paper. Basic thermal printers are inexpensive, but the print quality is low and the images tend to fade over time. Self-service gas pumps often print gas receipts using a built-in lower-quality thermal printer.

Two special types of thermal printers have high print quality. A *thermal wax-transfer printer* generates rich, nonsmearing images by using heat to melt colored wax onto heat-sensitive paper. Thermal wax-transfer printers are more expensive than ink-jet printers, but less expensive than many color laser printers.

A *dye-sublimation printer*, sometimes called a *digital photo printer*, uses heat to transfer colored dye to specially coated paper. Most dye-sublimation printers create images that are of photographic quality (Figure 6-20). Professional applications requiring high image quality, such as photography studios, medical labs, and security identification systems, use dye-sublimation printers. These high-end printers cost thousands of dollars and print images in a wide range of sizes. Most dye-sublimation printers for the home or small business user, by contrast, typically print images in only one or two sizes and are much slower than their professional counterparts. These lower-end dye-sublimation printers are comparable in cost to a photo printer based on ink-jet technology. Some are small enough for the mobile user to carry the printer in a briefcase.

Mobile Printers

A **mobile printer** is a small, lightweight, battery-powered printer that allows a mobile user to print from a notebook computer, Tablet PC, PDA, or smart phone while traveling (Figure 6-21). Barely wider than the paper on which they print, mobile printers fit easily in a briefcase alongside a notebook computer.

Mobile printers mainly use ink-jet, thermal, thermal wax-transfer, or dye-sublimation technology. Many of these printers connect to a parallel port or USB port. Others have a built-in wireless port through which they communicate with the computer wirelessly.

FIGURE 6-20a (dye-sublimation printer for the professional)

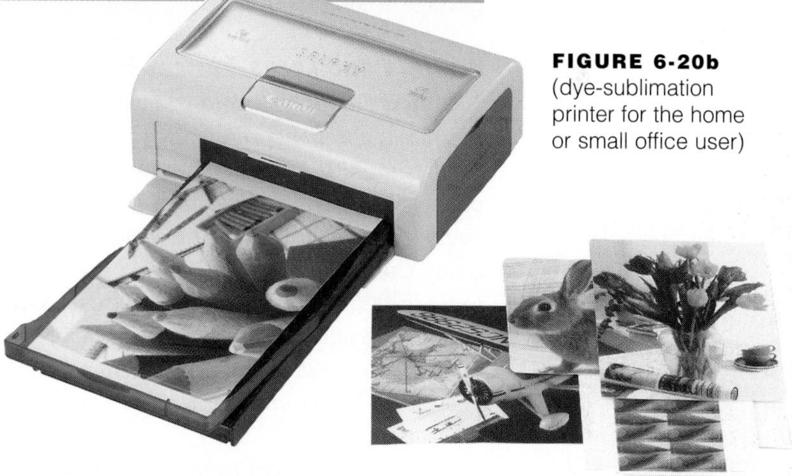

FIGURE 6-20b (dye-sublimation printer for the home or small office user)

FIGURE 6-20 The printers shown in this figure use dye-sublimation technology to create photographic-quality output.

FIGURE 6-21 A mobile printer is a compact printer that allows the mobile user to print from a notebook computer or mobile device.

Label and Postage Printers

A **label printer** is a small printer that prints on an adhesive-type material (Figure 6-22) that can be placed on a variety of items such as envelopes, packages, CDs, DVDs, audio-cassettes, photographs, file folders, and toys. Most label printers also print bar codes. Label printers typically use thermal technology.

A *postage printer* is a special type of label printer that has a built-in digital scale and prints postage stamps. Postage printers allow users to buy and print digital postage, called *Internet postage*, right from their computer. That is, you purchase an amount of postage from an authorized postal service Web site. As you need a stamp, you print it on the postage printer. Each time a postage stamp prints, your postage account is updated.

FIGURE 6-22
A label printer.

Plotters and Large-Format Printers

Plotters are sophisticated printers used to produce high-quality drawings such as blueprints, maps, and circuit diagrams. These printers are used in specialized fields such as engineering and drafting and usually are very costly. Current plotters use a row of charged wires (called styli) to draw an electrostatic pattern on specially coated paper and then fuse toner to the pattern. The printed image consists of a series of very small dots, which provides high-quality output.

Using ink-jet printer technology, but on a much larger scale, a **large-format printer** creates photo-realistic-quality color prints. Graphic artists use these high-cost, high-performance printers for signs, posters, and other professional quality displays (Figure 6-23).

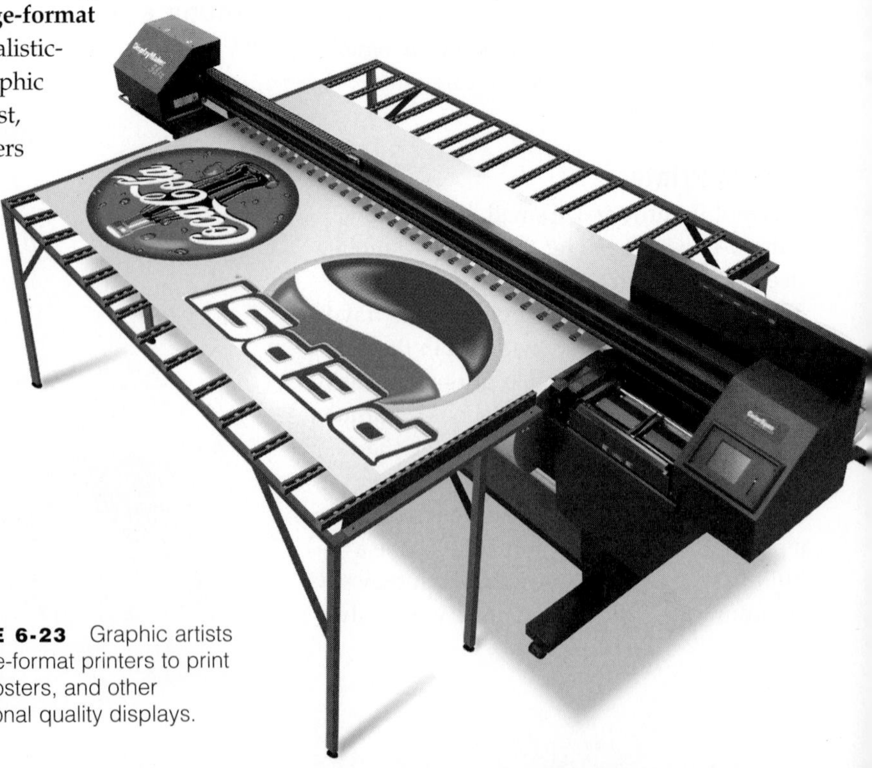

Plotters and large-format printers can accommodate paper with widths up to 60 inches because blueprints, maps, signs, posters and other such drawings and displays can be quite large. Some plotters and large-format printers use individual sheets of paper, while others take large rolls.

Impact Printers

An **impact printer** forms characters and graphics on a piece of paper by striking a mechanism against an inked ribbon that physically contacts the paper. Impact printers characteristically are noisy because of this striking activity. These printers commonly produce *near letter quality* (*NLQ*) output, which is print quality slightly less clear than what is acceptable for business letters. Companies may use impact printers for routine jobs such as printing mailing labels, envelopes, and invoices. Impact printers also are ideal for printing multipart forms because they easily print through many layers of paper. Factories and retail counters use impact printers because these printers withstand dusty environments, vibrations, and extreme temperatures.

Two commonly used types of impact printers are dot-matrix printers and line printers.

FIGURE 6-23 Graphic artists use large-format printers to print signs, posters, and other professional quality displays.

DOT-MATRIX PRINTERS A **dot-matrix printer** is an impact printer that produces printed images when tiny wire pins on a print head mechanism strike an inked ribbon (Figure 6-24). When the ribbon presses against the paper, it creates dots that form characters and graphics.

Most dot-matrix printers use *continuous-form paper*, in which thousands of sheets of paper are connected together end to end. The pages have holes along the sides to help feed the paper through the printer.

The print head mechanism on a dot-matrix printer contains 9 to 24 pins, depending on the manufacturer and the printer model. A higher number of pins means the printer prints more dots per character, which results in higher print quality.

The speed of a dot-matrix printer is measured by the number of characters per second (cps) it can print. The speed of most dot-matrix printers ranges from 300 to 1100 characters per second (cps), depending on the desired print quality.

LINE PRINTERS A **line printer** is a high-speed impact printer that prints an entire line at a time (Figure 6-25). The speed of a line printer is measured by the number of lines per minute (lpm) it can print. Some line printers print as many as 3,000 lpm. Mainframes, servers, or networked applications, such as manufacturing, distribution, or shipping, often use line printers. These printers typically use 11 x 17-inch continuous-form paper.

Two popular types of line printers used for high-volume output are band and shuttle-matrix. A *band printer* prints fully formed characters when hammers strike a horizontal, rotating band that contains shapes of numbers, letters of the alphabet, and other characters. A *shuttle-matrix printer* functions more like a dot-matrix printer. The difference is the shuttle-matrix printer moves a series of print hammers back and forth horizontally at incredibly high speeds, as compared with standard line printers. Unlike a band printer, a shuttle-matrix printer prints characters in various fonts and font sizes.

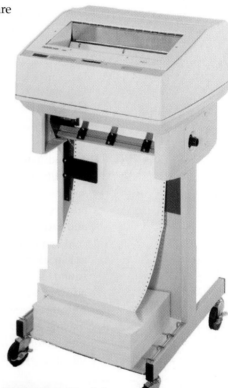

FIGURE 6-25 A line printer is a high-speed printer often connected to a mainframe, server, or network.

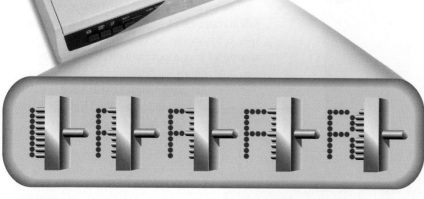

continuous-form paper

FIGURE 6-24 A dot-matrix printer produces printed images when tiny pins strike an inked ribbon.

Test your knowledge of pages 310 through 319 in Quiz Yourself 6-2.

SPEAKERS, HEADPHONES, AND EARPHONES

An **audio output device** is a component of a computer that produces music, speech, or other sounds, such as beeps. Three commonly used audio output devices are speakers, headphones, and earphones.

Most personal computers have a small internal speaker that usually emits only low-quality sound. Thus, many personal computer users add surround sound **speakers** to their computers to generate a higher-quality sound for playing games, interacting with multimedia presentations, listening to music CDs, and viewing DVDs (Figure 6-26).

Most surround sound computer speaker systems include one or two center speakers and two or more *satellite speakers* that are positioned so sound emits from all directions. Speakers typically have tone and volume controls, allowing users to adjust settings. To boost the low bass sounds, surround sound speaker systems also include a *subwoofer*.

Surround sound systems are available in a variety of configurations. For example, a 2.1 speaker system contains two speakers and a subwoofer. A 5.1 speaker system has four satellite speakers, a center speaker, and a subwoofer. A 6.1 speaker system has four satellite speakers, a front center speaker, a rear center speaker, and a subwoofer.

In many cases, users connect the speakers and subwoofer to ports on the sound card. With wireless speakers, however, a transmitter connects to the sound card, which wirelessly communicates with the speakers. To take full advantage of high-end surround sound speaker systems, be sure the sound card in the computer is compatible with the speaker system. For a more technical discussion about how sound cards produce sound, read the High-Tech Talk article on page 328.

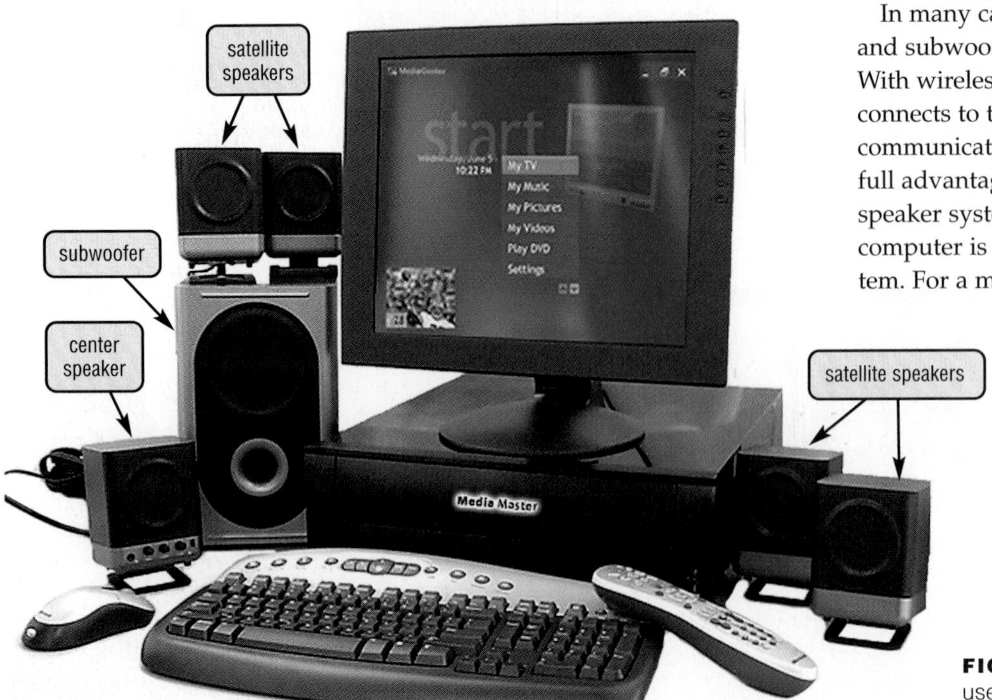

satellite speakers

subwoofer

center speaker

satellite speakers

FIGURE 6-26   Most personal computer users add high-quality surround sound speaker systems to their computers.

When using speakers, anyone in listening distance can hear the output. In a computer laboratory or other crowded environment, speakers might not be practical. Instead, users can plug headphones or earphones in a port on the sound card, in a speaker, or on the front of the system unit. With headphones or earphones, only the individual wearing the headphones or earphones hears the sound from the computer. The difference is that **headphones** cover or are placed outside of the ear (Figure 6-27), whereas **earphones**, or *earbuds*, rest inside the ear canal (shown in Figure 6-1 on page 300).

Electronically produced voice output is growing in popularity. **Voice output** occurs when you hear a person's voice or when the computer talks to you through the speakers on the computer. In some software applications, the computer can speak the contents of a document through voice output. On the Web, you can listen to (or download and then listen to) interviews, talk shows, sporting events, news, recorded music, and live concerts from many radio and television stations. Some Web sites dedicate themselves to providing voice output, where you can hear songs, quotes, historical lectures, speeches, and books (Figure 6-28). Read Ethics & Issues 6-3 for a related discussion.

WEB LINK 6-7

Earphones

For more information, visit scsite.com/dc2007/ch6/weblink and then click Earphones.

FIGURE 6-27 In a crowded environment where speakers are not practical, users wear headphones or earphones to hear audio output.

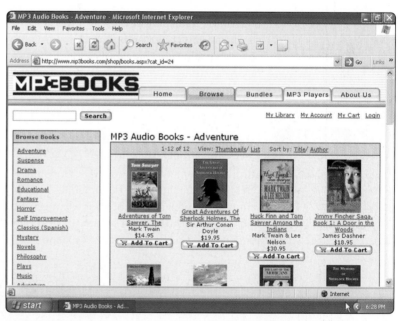

FIGURE 6-28 Through this Web site, users can purchase and then download a book in digital audio format and then listen to the book's contents via their computer's speakers or an audio player such as an iPod.

ETHICS & ISSUES 6-3

Is the Use of Digital Audio Books and E-Books Fair to All Students?

Digital audio books and e-books for notebook computers, PDAs, and even MP3 players are beginning to replace and supplement textbooks at some schools. Recently, a high school became the first to eliminate all textbooks and provide notebook computers to all 340 of its students. Internet access is required for the students to complete their school work. The computers include all course assignments and e-book versions of textbooks. Digital audio books, which are played on MP3 players such as an iPod, can include entire textbooks or supplementary course information, such as lecture notes or textbook chapter summaries. Proponents of the new wave of electronic textbooks claim that they are less expensive than traditional textbooks, alleviate back and posture problems associated with hefty textbooks, and provide more material to students in a smaller package. Opponents argue that requiring students to have access to certain technology, such as the Internet or an MP3 player, is unfair to those without the means or desire to take advantage of the technology. Also, if the school makes the electronic textbooks optional, those who can afford to take advantage of the technology may have an unfair advantage over those who can not. Would you use a digital audio book or an e-book? Why or why not? Are schools being fair to all students when the school requires access to certain technology, such as the Internet, a notebook computer, or an MP3 player? Why or why not? How can schools adopt even more technology and remain fair to all students?

Very often, voice output works with voice input. For example, when you call an airline to check the status of gates, terminals, and arrival times, your voice interacts with a computer-generated voice output. Another example is *Internet telephony*, which allows users to speak to other users over the Internet using their desktop computer, mobile computer, or mobile device.

Sophisticated programs enable the computer to converse with you. Talk into the microphone and say, "I'd like today's weather report." The computer replies, "For which city?" You reply, "Chicago." The computer says, "Sunny and 80 degrees."

OTHER OUTPUT DEVICES

In addition to display devices, printers, and speakers, many other output devices are available for specific uses and applications. These devices include fax machines and fax modems, multifunction peripherals, data projectors, and force-feedback joysticks, wheels, and gamepads.

Fax Machines and Fax Modems

A **fax machine** is a device that codes and encodes documents so they can be transmitted over telephone lines. The documents can contain text, drawings, or photographs, or can be handwritten. The term *fax* refers to a document that you send or receive via a fax machine.

A stand-alone fax machine scans an original document, converts the image into digitized data, and transmits the digitized image (Figure 6-29). A fax machine at the receiving end reads the incoming data, converts the digitized data back into an image, and prints or stores a copy of the original image.

Many computers include fax capability by using a fax modem. A *fax modem* is a modem that also allows you to send (and sometimes receive) electronic documents as faxes (Figure 6-30). A fax modem transmits computer-prepared documents, such as a word processing letter, or documents that have been digitized with a scanner or digital camera. A fax modem transmits these faxes to a fax machine or to another fax modem.

FIGURE 6-29   A stand-alone fax machine.

WEB LINK 6-8

Fax Modems

For more information, visit scsite.com/dc2007/ch6/weblink and then click Fax Modems.

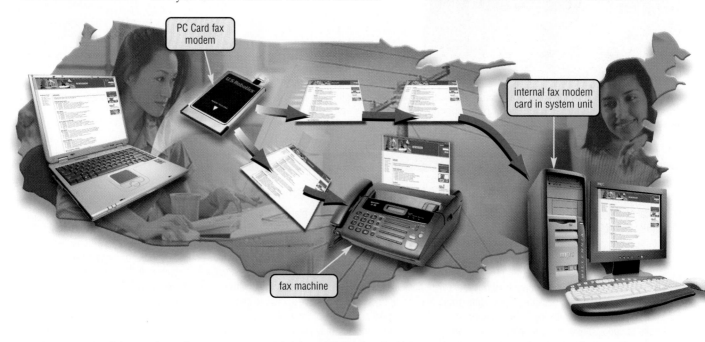

FIGURE 6-30   A fax modem allows users to send (and sometimes receive) electronic documents as faxes to a fax machine or another computer.

When a computer (instead of a fax machine) receives a fax, users can view the fax on the screen, saving the time and expense of printing it. If necessary, you also can print the fax. The quality of a viewed or printed fax is less than that of a word processing document because the fax actually is an image. Optical character recognition (OCR) software, which was discussed in Chapter 5, enables you to convert the image to text and then edit it.

A fax modem can be an external device that plugs in a port on the system unit, an internal adapter card inserted in an expansion slot on the motherboard, a chip integrated on the motherboard, or a PC Card that inserts in a PC Card slot.

Multifunction Peripherals

A **multifunction peripheral** is a single device that looks like a copy machine but provides the functionality of a printer, scanner, copy machine, and perhaps a fax machine (Figure 6-31). The features of these devices, which sometimes are called *all-in-one devices*, vary. For example, some use color ink-jet printer technology, while others include a black-and-white laser printer.

Small offices and home office (SOHO) users have multifunction peripherals because these devices require less space than having a separate printer, scanner, copy machine, and fax machine. Another advantage of these devices is they are significantly less expensive than if you purchase each device separately. If the device breaks down, however, you lose all four functions, which is the primary disadvantage.

Data Projectors

A **data projector** is a device that takes the text and images displaying on a computer screen and projects them on a larger screen so an audience can see the image clearly (Figure 6-32). For example, many classrooms use data projectors so all students easily can see an instructor's presentation on the screen.

Some data projectors are large devices that attach to a ceiling or wall in an auditorium. Others are small portable devices. Two types of smaller, lower-cost units are LCD projectors and DLP projectors.

FIGURE 6-31 This multifunction peripheral is a color printer, scanner, copy machine, and fax machine all-in-one device.

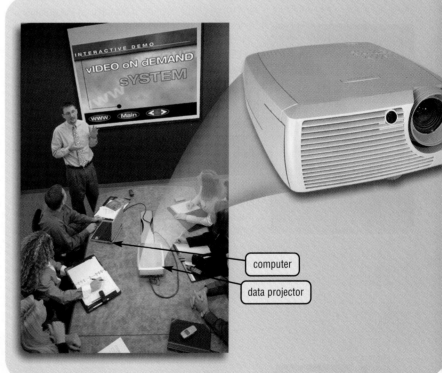

FIGURE 6-32 A data projector projects an image from a computer screen on a larger screen so an audience easily can see the image.

An *LCD projector*, which uses liquid crystal display technology, attaches directly to a computer, and uses its own light source to display the information shown on the computer screen. Because LCD projectors tend to produce lower-quality images, users often prefer DLP projectors for their sharper, brighter images.

A *digital light processing (DLP) projector* uses tiny mirrors to reflect light, which produces crisp, bright, colorful images that remain in focus and can be seen clearly even in a well-lit room. Some newer televisions use DLP instead of LCD or plasma technology. Read Looking Ahead 6-2 for a look at the next generation of digital cinema projectors.

Force-Feedback Joysticks, Wheels, and Gamepads

As discussed in Chapter 5, joysticks, wheels, and gamepads are input devices used to control movement and actions of a player or object in computer games, simulations, and video games. Today's joysticks, wheels, and gamepads also include *force feedback*, which is a technology that sends resistance to the device in response to actions of the user (Figure 6-33). For example, as you use the simulation software to drive from a smooth road onto a gravel alley, the steering wheel trembles or vibrates, making the driving experience as realistic as possible. In addition to games, these devices are used in practical training applications such as in the military and aviation.

LOOKING AHEAD 6-2

Digital Cinema Just the Right Picture

Computers have influenced the motion picture business by modifying how movies are produced, distributed, and exhibited. Major movie studios are part of the *Digital Cinema Initiative* (DCI), and they plan to release all of their theatrical feature films worldwide in digital format. The new technology's superior sound and visual clarity have been heralded as the greatest innovations since talkies replaced silent movies 80 years ago.

The seven larger Hollywood movie studios have developed final system requirements and specifications that enable manufacturers to develop standardized digital theater equipment. These uniform standards were created along with a compression scheme, which allows the studios to distribute the movies without having to make thousands of prints, thus saving millions of dollars annually.

With the equipment and compression standards in place, manufacturers now can intensify their efforts to develop digital cinema projectors. For more information, visit scsite.com/dc2007/ch6/looking and then click Digital Cinema.

FIGURE 6-33 Gaming devices often provide force feedback, giving the user a realistic experience.

PUTTING IT ALL TOGETHER

Many factors influence the type of output devices you should use: the type of output desired, the hardware and software in use, and the anticipated cost. Figure 6-34 outlines several suggested monitors, printers, and other output devices for various types of computer users.

SUGGESTED OUTPUT DEVICES BY USER

User	Monitor	Printer	Other
HOME 	• 17- or 19-inch LCD monitor	• Ink-jet color printer; or • Photo printer	• Speakers • Headphones or earphones • Force-feedback joystick, wheel, and/or gamepad
SMALL OFFICE/ HOME OFFICE 	• 19- or 21-inch LCD monitor • Color LCD screen on Tablet PC, PDA, or smart phone	• Multifunction peripheral; or • Ink-jet color printer; or • Laser printer (black-and-white or color) • Label printer • Postage printer	• Fax machine • Speakers
MOBILE 	• 15.7-inch LCD screen on notebook computer • Color LCD screen on Tablet PC, PDA, or smart phone	• Mobile color printer • Ink-jet color printer; or • Laser printer for in-office use (black-and-white or color) • Photo printer	• Fax modem • Headphones or earphones • DLP data projector
POWER 	• 23-inch LCD monitor	• Laser printer (black-and-white or color) • Plotter or large-format printer; or • Photo printer; or • Dye-sublimation printer	• Fax machine or fax modem • Speakers • Headphones or earphones
LARGE BUSINESS 	• 19- or 21-inch LCD monitor • Color LCD screen on Tablet PC, PDA, or smart phone	• High-speed laser printer • Laser printer, color • Line printer (for large reports from a mainframe) • Label printer	• Fax machine or fax modem • Speakers • Headphones or earphones • DLP data projector

FIGURE 6-34 This table recommends suggested output devices for various types of users.

OUTPUT DEVICES FOR PHYSICALLY CHALLENGED USERS

As Chapter 5 discussed, the growing presence of computers has generated an awareness of the need to address computing requirements for those with physical limitations. Read Ethics & Issues 6-4 for a related discussion.

For users with mobility, hearing, or vision disabilities, many different types of output devices are available. Hearing-impaired users, for example, can instruct programs to display words instead of sounds. With the Windows XP operating system, users also can set options to make programs easier to use. The Magnifier command, for example, enlarges text and other items in a window on the screen (Figure 6-35).

Visually impaired users can change Windows XP settings, such as increasing the size or changing the color of the text to make the words easier to read. Instead of using a monitor, blind users can work with voice output. That is, the computer reads the information that is displayed on the screen. Another alternative is a *Braille printer*, which prints information on paper in Braille (Figure 6-36).

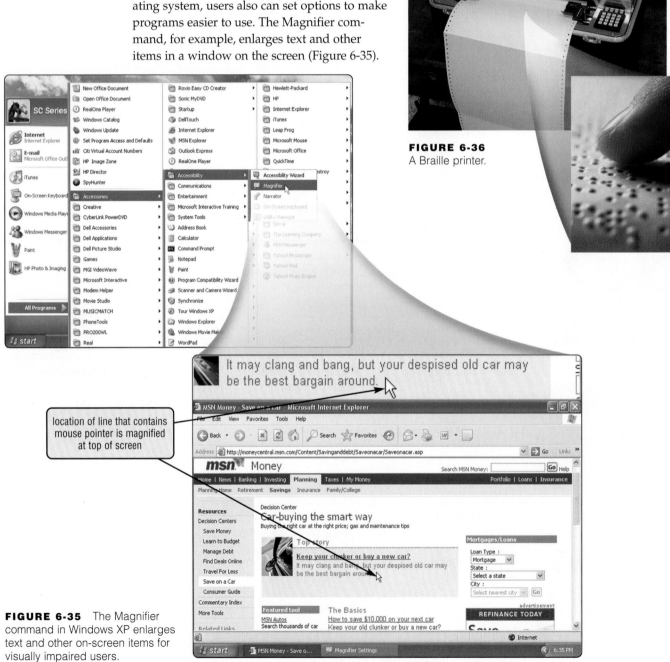

FIGURE 6-36
A Braille printer.

location of line that contains mouse pointer is magnified at top of screen

FIGURE 6-35 The Magnifier command in Windows XP enlarges text and other on-screen items for visually impaired users.

ETHICS & ISSUES 6-4

Should Web Sites Be Held Accountable for Accessibility Levels for Physically Challenged People?

The World Wide Web Consortium (W3C) has published accessibility guidelines for Web sites. The guidelines specify measures that Web site designers can take to increase accessibility for physically challenged users. Among its guidelines, the W3C urges Web site designers to provide equivalent text for audio or visual content, include features that allow elements to be activated and understood using a variety of input and output devices, and make the user interface follow principles of accessible design. A recent report found that most Web sites do not meet all of the W3C guidelines. This failure is disappointing, because many physically challenged users could benefit from the Web's capability to bring products and services into the home. Ironically, a survey discovered that more than 50 percent of the Web sites run by disability organizations also fail to meet the W3C guidelines. Critics contend that these Web sites neglect the needs of their users and fail to lead by example. Web site apologists contend, however, that many sponsoring organizations lack the funding necessary to comply with the guidelines. Should the government require that all Web sites meet the W3C accessibility guidelines? Why or why not? Do Web sites run by disability organizations have a moral obligation to meet the guidelines? Why? What can be done to encourage people and organizations to make their Web sites more accessible?

Test your knowledge of pages 320 through 327 in Quiz Yourself 6-3.

QUIZ YOURSELF 6-3

Instructions: Find the true statement below. Then, rewrite the remaining false statements so they are true.

1. A digital light processing (DLP) projector uses tiny lightbulbs to reflect light.
2. A stand-alone fax machine scans an original document, converts the image into digitized data, and transmits the digitized image.
3. Many personal computer users add surround sound printer systems to their computers to generate a higher-quality sound.
4. Multifunction peripherals require more space than having a separate printer, scanner, copy machine, and fax machine.
5. Some joysticks, wheels, and gamepads include real-time action, which is a technology that sends resistance to the device in response to actions of the user.

Quiz Yourself Online: To further check your knowledge of speakers, headphones, and earphones; other output devices; and output for physically challenged users, visit scsite.com/dc2007/ch6/quiz and then click Objectives 8 – 10.

CHAPTER SUMMARY

Computers process and organize data (input) into information (output). This chapter described the various methods of output and several commonly used output devices. Output devices presented were flat-panel displays; CRT monitors; printers; speakers, headphones, and earphones; fax machines and fax modems; multifunction peripherals; data projectors; and force-feedback joysticks, wheels, and gamepads.

CAREER CORNER

Graphic Designer/Illustrator

Graphic designers and *graphic illustrators* are artists, but many do not create original works. Instead, they portray visually the ideas of their clients. Illustrators create pictures for books and other publications and sometimes for commercial products, such as greeting cards. They work in fields such as fashion, technology, medicine, animation, or even cartoons. Illustrators often prepare their images on a computer. Designers combine practical skills with artistic talent to convert abstract concepts into designs for products and advertisements. Many use computer-aided design (CAD) tools to create, visualize, and modify designs. Designer careers usually are specialized in particular areas, such as:

- Graphic designers — book covers, stationery, and CD covers
- Commercial and industrial designers — products and equipment
- Costume and theater designers — costumes and settings for theater and television
- Interior designers — layout, decor, and furnishings of homes and buildings
- Merchandise displayers — commercial displays
- Fashion designers — clothing, shoes, and other fashion accessories

Certificate, two-year, four-year, and masters-level educational programs are available within design areas. About 30 percent of graphic illustrators/designers choose to freelance, while others work with advertising agencies, publishing companies, design studios, or specialized departments within large companies. Salaries range from $30,000 to $80,000-plus, based on experience and educational background. For more information, visit scsite.com/dc2007/ch6/careers and then click Graphic Designer/Illustrator.

High-Tech Talk

SOUND CARDS: BRINGING YOUR COMPUTER TO LIFE

Speakers, headphones, earphones, and other audio output devices rely on sound cards or integrated sound card functionality to produce sounds such as music, voice, beeps, and chimes. Sound cards contain the chips and circuitry to record and play back a wide range of sounds using analog-to-digital conversion and digital-to-analog conversion, as described in the Chapter 1 High-Tech Talk on page 38.

To record a sound, the sound card must be connected to an input device, such as a microphone or audio CD player. The input device sends the sound to the sound card as an analog signal. The analog signal flows to the sound card's analog-to-digital-converter (ADC). The ADC converts the signal into digital (binary) data of 1s and 0s by sampling the signal at set intervals.

The analog sound is a continuous waveform, with a range of frequencies and volumes. To represent the waveform in a recording, the computer would have to store the waveform's value at every instant in time. Because this is not possible, the sound is recorded using a sampling process. *Sampling* involves breaking up the waveform into set intervals and representing all values during that interval with a single value.

Several factors in the sampling process — sampling rate, audio resolution, and mono or stereo recording — affect the quality of the recorded sound during playback.

- *Sampling rate*, also called sampling frequency, refers to the number of times per second the sound is recorded. The more frequently a sound is recorded, the smaller the intervals and the better the quality. The sampling frequency used for audio CDs, for example, is 44,100 times per second, which is expressed in hertz (Hz) as 44,100 Hz. Cassette-tape-quality multimedia files use a sampling rate of 22,050 Hz; and basic Windows sounds use a sampling rate of 11,025 Hz.

- *Audio resolution* — defined as a bit rate such as 8-bit, 16-bit, or 24-bit — refers to the number of bytes used to represent the sound at any one interval. A sound card using 8-bit resolution, for example, represents a sound with any 1 of 256 values (2^8). A 16-bit sound card uses any 1 of 65,536 values (2^{16}) for each interval. Using a higher resolution provides a finer measurement scale, which results in a more accurate representation of the value of each sample and better sound quality. With 8-bit resolution, the sound quality is like that of an AM radio; 16-bit resolution gives CD-quality sound, and a 24-bit resolution is used for high-quality digital audio editing.

- Mono or stereo recording refers to the number of channels used during recording. *Mono* means that the same sound emits from both the left and right speaker during playback; *stereo* means that two separate channels exist in the recording: one each for the left and right speakers. Most sound cards support stereo recording for better playback.

After the ADC converts the analog sound through sampling, the digital data flows to the digital signal processor (DSP) on the sound card. The DSP then requests instructions from the sound card's memory chip on how to process the digital data. Typically, the DSP then compresses the digital data to save space. Finally, the DSP sends the compressed data to the computer's main processor, which stores the data in .WAV, .MP3, or other audio file format.

To play a recorded sound, such as a WAV, an MP3, or a CD track, the main processor retrieves the sound file from a hard disk, CD, or other storage device (Figure 6-37). The processor then sends the digital data to the DSP, which decompresses the data and looks to the memory chip to determine how to recreate the sound.

The DSP then sends the digital signals to the sound card's digital-to-analog converter (DAC), which converts the sound in digital format back to an analog electrical voltage. An output device, such as a speaker, uses an amplifier to strengthen the electrical voltage. This causes the speaker's cone to vibrate, recreating the sound.

All of this happens in an instant. The next time your computer beeps or chirps, consider the complex process required to make that simple sound. Then, insert your favorite CD and hear your computer come to life with the sweet music provided courtesy of the sound card. For more information, visit scsite.com/dc2007/ch6/tech and then click Sound Cards.

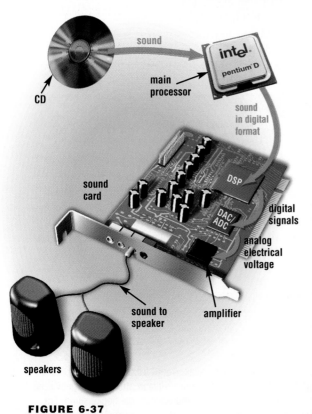

FIGURE 6-37
The path of sound from media to speakers.

Companies on the Cutting Edge

HEWLETT-PACKARD
TECHNOLOGY FOR BUSINESS AND LIFE

If you have printed a document recently, chances are the printer manufacturer was *Hewlett-Packard (HP)*. Market analysts estimate that 60 percent of printers sold today bear the HP logo, and HP says it ships one million printers each week.

HP is noted for a range of high-quality printers, disk storage systems, UNIX and Windows servers, and notebook, desktop, and handheld computers. In 2005, HP acquired Snapfish, an online photo service, and also unveiled the world's fastest home photo printing devices.

William Hewlett and David Packard started the company in a one-car garage in 1939 with the goal of manufacturing test and measurement equipment. HP has been developing personal information devices, including calculators and computers, for more than 30 years. For more information, visit scsite.com/dc2007/ch6/companies and then click Hewlett-Packard.

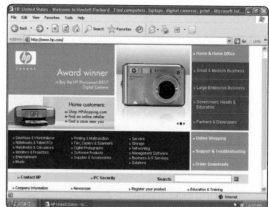

VIEWSONIC
VISUAL TECHNOLOGY LEADER

We live in a "display-centric world" according to industry leaders at *ViewSonic*. Our computer displays, whether viewed on a PDA, a desktop monitor, or a flat-panel screen, influence how we access and control the informative and entertaining output.

ViewSonic's products focus on visual technology, including CRT and LCD monitors, data projectors, plasma screens, and high-definition television. The company also designs mobile products, such as Tablet PCs and wireless monitors.

President and CEO James Chu founded ViewSonic in 1987 with the goal of increasing workers' productivity while creating an ergonomically comfortable workspace. He developed the company's logo consisting of three colorful Gouldian finches to represent outstanding quality and value, radiant color, and crisp resolution. For more information, visit scsite.com/dc2007/ch6/companies and then click ViewSonic.

Technology Trailblazers

STEVE JOBS
APPLE COMPUTER AND PIXAR COFOUNDER

Steve Jobs has an uncompromising drive for perfection. He helped build the first desktop personal computer, cofounded Apple Computer Corporation, marketed a revolutionary operating system, and became a millionaire all before his 35th birthday.

Under his direction, Apple took advantage of advances in both memory and battery technology to develop the iPod, the world's most popular digital audio player. He also is known as being a brilliant motivator and having the ability to bring out the best performance from his employees.

Under Jobs's supervision, Pixar's award-winning animation studios have created some of the most beloved animated films, such as *Toy Story*, *Toy Story 2*, *A Bug's Life*, *Monsters, Inc.*, and *Finding Nemo*. For more information, visit scsite.com/dc2007/ch6/people and then click Steve Jobs.

DONNA DUBINSKY
Palm Cofounder

PDAs are ubiquitous, partly due to the efforts of *Donna Dubinsky*. In the mid-1990s, she sensed that people wanted to own an electronic version of their paper appointment books. She and Jeff Hawkins introduced the original Palm Pilot prototype made of mahogany and cardboard at Palm Computing in 1996. Sales of more than two million units made the Palm Pilot the most rapidly adopted new computing product ever manufactured.

Dubinsky and Hawkins left Palm in 1998 to cofound Handspring, where they introduced several successful products, including the Treo smart phone. In 2003, Handspring merged with the Palm hardware group to create palmOne, now called Palm.

Dubinsky currently serves as CEO and chairman of Numenta, Inc., which develops computer memory. For more information, visit scsite.com/dc2007/ch6/people and then click Donna Dubinsky.

Chapter Review

The Chapter Review section summarizes the concepts presented in this chapter. To listen to the audio version of this Chapter Review, visit scsite.com/dc2007/ch6/review. To obtain help from other students regarding any subject in this chapter, visit scsite.com/dc2007/ch6/forum and post your thoughts or questions.

(1) What Are the Four Categories of Output? Output is data that has been processed into a useful form. Four categories of output are text, graphics, audio, and video. An **output device** is any hardware component that conveys information to one or more people.

(2) What Are LCD Monitors, LCD Screens, and Plasma Monitors? LCD monitors, LCD screens, and plasma monitors are types of flat-panel displays. A *flat-panel display* is a display with a shallow depth that typically uses LCD or gas plasma technology. An **LCD** monitor is a desktop monitor that uses a liquid crystal display to produce images. A **liquid crystal display** (LCD) uses a liquid compound to present information on a display. A **plasma monitor** is a display device that uses gas plasma technology, which substitutes a layer of gas for the liquid crystal material in an LCD monitor. Although some game consoles include a small LCD screen (usually 5 inches or smaller), home users often prefer the larger television displays for game playing, watching movies, and browsing the Internet on a television connected to a game console.

(3) What Is a CRT Monitor, and What Factors Affect Its Quality? A **CRT monitor** is a desktop monitor that contains a *cathode-ray tube (CRT)*. The screen on the front of the CRT is coated with tiny dots of red, green, and blue phosphor that combine to make up each *pixel*, which is a single element in an electronic image. As an electron beam inside the CRT moves back and forth across the back of the screen, the dots glow, which produces an image. The quality of a CRT monitor depends largely on its resolution, dot pitch, and refresh rate. **Resolution** is the number of horizontal and vertical pixels in a display device. *Dot pitch*, sometimes called *pixel pitch*, is the distance in millimeters between pixels on a display device. *Refresh rate* is the speed that a monitor redraws the images on the screen.

(4) How Are Graphics Chips and CRT Monitors Related? Many CRT monitors use an analog signal to produce an image. A cable on the CRT monitor plugs in a port on the system unit, which enables communications from a graphics chip. If the graphics chip is on a video card, the card converts digital output from the computer into an analog video signal and sends the signal through a cable to the CRT monitor, which displays output on the screen.

connect Visit scsite.com/dc2007/ch6/quiz or click the Quiz Yourself button. Click Objectives 1 – 4.

(5) What Are the Various Ways to Print? Users can print by connecting a computer to a printer with a cable that plugs in a port on the computer. *Bluetooth printing* uses radio waves to transmit output to a printer. With *infrared* printing, a computer or other device communicates with the printer via infrared light waves. Some digital cameras connect directly to a printer via a cable; others store images on media cards that can be removed and inserted in the printer. Networked computers can communicate with the network printer via cables or wirelessly.

(6) How Is a Nonimpact Printer Different from an Impact Printer? A **printer** is an output device that produces text and graphics on a physical medium, such as paper or transparency film. A **nonimpact printer** forms characters and graphics on a piece of paper without actually striking the paper. Commonly used nonimpact printers are ink-jet printers, photo printers, laser printers, thermal printers, mobile printers, label and postage printers, plotters, and large-format printers. An **impact printer** forms characters and graphics on a piece of paper by striking a mechanism against an inked ribbon that physically contacts the paper. Two commonly used types of impact printers are a **dot-matrix printer** and a **line printer**.

Chapter Review

(7) What Are Ink-Jet Printers, Photo Printers, Laser Printers, Thermal Printers, Mobile Printers, Label and Postage Printers, and Plotters and Large-Format Printers? An **ink-jet printer** is a type of nonimpact printer that forms characters and graphics by spraying tiny drops of liquid ink onto a piece of paper. A **photo printer** is a color printer that produces photo-lab-quality pictures. A **laser printer** is a high-speed, high-quality nonimpact printer that operates in a manner similar to a copy machine, creating images using a laser beam and powdered ink, called *toner*. A **thermal printer** generates images by pushing electronically heated pins against heat-sensitive paper. A **mobile printer** is a small, lightweight, battery-powered printer that allows a mobile user to print from a notebook computer. A **label printer** is a small printer that prints on an adhesive-type material that can be placed on a variety of items. A *postage printer* is a special type of label printer that has a built-in scale and prints postage stamps. **Plotters** are sophisticated printers used to produce high-quality drawings. A **large-format printer** uses ink-jet technology on a large scale to create photo-realistic-quality color prints.

> *connect* Visit scsite.com/dc2007/ch6/quiz or click the Quiz Yourself button. Click Objectives 5 – 7.

(8) How Are Speakers, Headphones, and Earphones Used? Speakers, headphones, and earphones are three commonly used audio output devices. An **audio output device** is a component of a computer that produces sound. Many personal computer users add stereo **speakers** to their computers to generate a higher-quality sound. With headphones or earphones, only the individual wearing the headphones or earphones hears the sound from the computer. The difference is that **headphones** cover or are placed outside of the ear, whereas **earphones**, or *earbuds*, rest inside the ear canal.

(9) What Are Fax Machines and Fax Modems, Multifunction Peripherals, Data Projectors, Joysticks, Wheels, and Gamepads? A **fax machine** is a device that codes and encodes documents so they can be transmitted over telephone lines. A document sent or received via a fax machine is a *fax*. Many computers include fax capability using a *fax modem*, which is a modem that allows you to send (and sometimes receive) electronic documents as faxes. A **multifunction peripheral** is a single device that looks like a copy machine but provides the functionality of a printer, scanner, copy machine, and perhaps a fax machine. A **data projector** is a device that takes the text and images displaying on a computer screen and projects them onto a larger screen so an audience of people can see the image clearly. Joysticks, wheels, and gamepads are input devices used to control actions of a player or vehicle. Today's joysticks, wheels, and gamepads also include *force feedback*, which is a technology that sends resistance to the device in response to actions of the user.

(10) What Output Options Are Available for Physically Challenged Users? Hearing-impaired users can instruct programs to display words instead of sound. With Windows XP, visually impaired users can enlarge items on the screen and change other settings, such as increasing the size or changing the color of text to make words easier to read. Blind users can work with voice output instead of a monitor. Another alternative is a *Braille printer*, which prints information in Braille on paper.

> *connect* Visit scsite.com/dc2007/ch6/quiz or click the Quiz Yourself button. Click Objectives 8 – 10.

Key Terms

You should know the Primary Terms and be familiar with the Secondary Terms. Use the list below to help focus your study. To further enhance your understanding of the Key Terms in this chapter, visit scsite.com/dc2007/ch6/terms. See an example of and a definition for each term, and access current and additional information about the term from the Web.

Primary Terms

(shown in bold-black characters in the chapter)

audio output device (320)
CRT monitor (307)
data projector (323)
display device (302)
dot-matrix printer (319)
earphones (321)
ENERGY STAR program (307)
fax machine (322)
HDTV (306)
headphones (321)
impact printer (318)
ink-jet printer (312)
label printer (318)
large-format printer (318)
laser printer (315)
LCD monitor (302)
line printer (319)
liquid crystal display (LCD) (304)
mobile printer (317)
monitor (302)
multifunction peripheral (323)
nonimpact printer (312)
output (300)
output device (301)
photo printer (314)
plasma monitor (306)
plotters (318)
printer (310)
resolution (304)
speakers (320)
thermal printer (317)
voice output (321)

Secondary Terms

(shown in italic characters in the chapter)

active-matrix display (304)
all-in-one devices (323)
band printer (319)
bit depth (306)
Bluetooth printing (311)
Braille printer (326)
candela (304)
cathode-ray tube (CRT) (307)
color depth (306)
continuous-form paper (319)
contrast ratio (304)
digital light processing (DLP) projector (324)
digital photo printer (317)
digital television (DTV) (306)
display (302)
dot pitch (304)
dots per inch (dpi) (313)
DVI (Digital Video Interface) port (305)
dye-sublimation printer (317)
earbuds (321)
electromagnetic radiation (EMR) (308)
fax (322)
fax modem (322)
flat-panel monitor (302)
flat-panel display (302)
footprint (302)
force feedback (324)
graphics processing unit (305)
hard copy (310)
high-definition television (306)
infrared printing (311)
Internet postage (318)

Internet telephony (322)
landscape orientation (310)
LCD projector (324)
monochrome (302)
MPR II (308)
native resolution (304)
near letter quality (NLQ) (318)
nit (304)
organic LED (OLED) (304)
page description language (PDL) (316)
passive-matrix display (304)
PCL (Printer Control Language) (316)
pixel (304)
pixel pitch (304)
portrait orientation (310)
postage printer (318)
PostScript (316)
printout (310)
refresh rate (308)
response time (304)
satellite speakers (320)
scan rate (308)
shuttle-matrix printer (319)
soft copy (302)
subwoofer (320)
S-video port (305)
SVGA (305)
SXGA (305)
TFT (thin-film transistor) display (304)
thermal wax-transfer printer (317)
toner (316)
UGA (305)
viewable size (307)
XGA (305)

Checkpoint

Use the Checkpoint exercises to check your knowledge level of the chapter. The Beyond the Book exercises will help broaden your understanding of the concepts presented in this chapter. To complete the Checkpoint exercises interactively, visit scsite.com/dc2007/ch6/check.

Label the Figure

Identify the ports on this video card.

a. S-video port

b. DVI port

c. standard monitor port

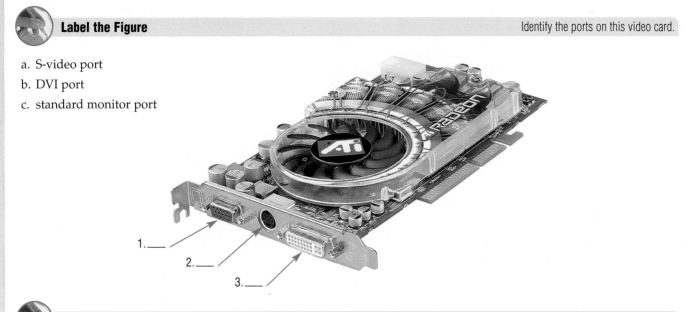

1. _____
2. _____
3. _____

True/False

Mark T for True and F for False. (See page numbers in parentheses.)

_____ 1. A computer generates several types of output, depending on the hardware and software being used and the requirements of the user. (300)

_____ 2. Information on a display device sometimes is called soft copy. (302)

_____ 3. Most mobile computers and devices do not integrate the display and other components into the same physical case. (302)

_____ 4. Some PDAs and other mobile devices use monochrome displays because they require less battery power. (302)

_____ 5. A pixel is a unit of visible light intensity equal to one candela per square meter. (304)

_____ 6. LCD monitors use an analog signal to produce a picture. (305)

_____ 7. With game consoles, the output device often is a television. (307)

_____ 8. A printout in portrait orientation is taller than it is wide. (310)

_____ 9. With Bluetooth printing, a computer or other device transmits output to a printer via infrared light waves. (311)

_____ 10. Many photo printers use ink-jet technology. (314)

_____ 11. A laser printer is a high-speed, low-quality nonimpact printer. (315)

_____ 12. A multifunction peripheral is a single device that looks like a copy machine but provides the functionality of a printer, scanner, copy machine, and perhaps a fax machine. (323)

Discovering Computers 2007
A Gateway to Information

6   Output

Checkpoint

Multiple Choice Select the best answer. (See page numbers in parentheses.)

1. Examples of text-based documents are
   _____. (300)
   a. drawings, clip art, and photographs
   b. home movies and live performances
   c. music, narrations, and speeches
   d. letters, reports, and mailing labels

2. A passive-matrix display _____ an active-matrix display. (304)
   a. uses more transistors than
   b. requires more power than
   c. often is not as bright as
   d. is more expensive than

3. _____ uses organic molecules that produce an even brighter, easier-to-read display than standard TFT displays. (304)
   a. HDTV   b. OLED
   c. LCD   d. LED

4. _____ describes the difference in light intensity between the brightest white and darkest black that can be displayed on an LCD monitor. (304)
   a. Contrast ratio
   b. Brightness
   c. Dot pitch
   d. Bit depth

5. For a display device to show images as defined by a video standard, both the display device and the graphics processing unit must _____. (305)
   a. be the same size
   b. contain a heat sink or fan
   c. use an analog signal
   d. support the same video standard

6. Plasma monitors offer larger screens _____. (306)
   a. but lower display quality than LCD monitors and are less expensive
   b. but lower display quality than LCD monitors and are more expensive
   c. and higher display quality than LCD monitors but are less expensive
   d. and higher display quality than LCD monitors but are more expensive

7. The viewable size of a monitor is the _____ measurement of the actual viewing area provided by the screen in the monitor. (307)
   a. horizontal
   b. vertical
   c. three-dimensional
   d. diagonal

8. Printer resolution is measured by the number of _____ a printer can print. (313)
   a. pages per minute (ppm)
   b. dots per inch (dpi)
   c. lines per minute (lpm)
   d. pixels per inch (ppi)

9. Laser printers usually cost _____. (315)
   a. more than ink-jet printers and are faster
   b. less than ink-jet printers and are faster
   c. more than ink-jet printers and are slower
   d. less than ink-jet printers and are slower

10. The speed of a(n) _____ is measured by the number of characters per second (cps) it can print. (319)
    a. dot-matrix printer
    b. laser printer
    c. ink-jet printer
    d. thermal printer

11. _____ occurs when you hear a person's voice or when the computer talks to you through the speakers on the computer. (321)
    a. Voice input
    b. Force feedback
    c. Voice output
    d. Internet telephony

12. A(n) _____ is a device that takes the text and images displaying on a computer screen and projects them on a larger screen so an audience can see the image clearly. (323)
    a. DLP projector
    b. LCD projector
    c. data projector
    d. all of the above

13. The disadvantage of multifunction peripherals is that _____. (323)
    a. they require more space than having separate devices
    b. if the multifunction peripheral breaks down, all functions are lost
    c. they are significantly more expensive than purchasing each device separately
    d. all of the above

14. The _____ command in Windows XP enlarges text and other on-screen items for visually impaired users. (326)
    a. Magnifier
    b. On-Screen Keyboard
    c. Narrator
    d. Utility Manager

Checkpoint

Matching

Match the terms with their definitions. (See page numbers in parentheses.)

_____ 1. soft copy (302)
_____ 2. LCD monitor (302)
_____ 3. pixel pitch (304)
_____ 4. nit (304)
_____ 5. bit depth (306)
_____ 6. electromagnetic radiation (EMR) (308)
_____ 7. hard copy (310)
_____ 8. nonimpact printer (312)
_____ 9. LCD projector (324)
_____ 10. DLP projector (324)

a. information on a display device that exists electronically and appears for a temporary period

b. printed information that exists physically and is a more permanent form of output

c. distance in millimeters between pixels on a display device

d. unit of visible light intensity equal to one candela per square meter

e. changes the brightness and contrast of pixels surrounding each letter

f. the number of bits used to store information about each pixel

g. attaches directly to a computer and uses its own light source to display information

h. a desktop monitor that uses a liquid crystal display to produce images

i. magnetic field that travels at the speed of light

j. forms characters and graphics on a piece of paper without actually striking the paper

k. uses many shades of gray from white to black to enhance the quality of graphics

l. uses tiny mirrors to reflect light, which produces crisp, bright, colorful images

Short Answer

Write a brief answer to each of the following questions.

1. What determines the quality of an LCD monitor or LCD screen? _____ What are the differences between active-matrix and passive-matrix displays? _____

2. What factors determine a CRT monitor's quality? _____ What is the ENERGY STAR program? _____

3. How is portrait orientation different from landscape orientation? _____ What is continuous-form paper? _____

4. What are two types of wireless printing technology? _____ How do they differ in how they communicate with a computer or other device? _____

5. What are two common types of impact printers? _____ What are the differences between the two types? _____

Beyond the Book

Read the following book elements, learn more about each using the Web, and then write a brief report.

1. Ethics & Issues — Is It Ethical to Refill an Ink-Jet Cartridge? (314), Who Is Responsible for Stopping Counterfeiting? (315), Is the Use of Digital Audio Books and E-Books Fair to All Students? (321), or Should Web Sites Be Held Accountable for Accessibility Levels for Physically Challenged People? (327)

2. Career Corner — Graphic Designer/Illustrator (327)

3. Companies on the Cutting Edge — Hewlett-Packard (329) or ViewSonic (329)

4. FAQs (302, 303, 306, 307, 308, 312, 315, 316)

5. High-Tech Talk — Sound Cards: Bringing Your Computer to Life (328)

6. Looking Ahead — Rollable Displays Lock and Roll (304), or Digital Cinema Just the Right Picture (324)

7. Making Use of the Web — Government (122)

8. Picture Yourself Saving Money Using a Computer (298)

9. Technology Trailblazers — Steve Jobs and Donna Dubinsky (329)

10. Web Links (304, 306, 311, 314, 316, 321, 322, 323, 324)

Learn It Online

Use the Learn It Online exercises to reinforce your understanding of the chapter concepts. To access the Learn It Online exercises, visit scsite.com/dc2007/ch6/learn.

1 At the Movies — Plasma vs. LCD

To view the Plasma vs. LCD movie, click the number 1 button. Locate your video and click the corresponding High-Speed or Dial-Up link, depending on your Internet connection. Watch the movie and then complete the exercise by answering the questions that follow. Basic differences exist between plasma and LCD-display TVs, and those differences may affect your choice as a consumer. By understanding those differences, you will be able to choose the display options that best suit your needs. Compare and contrast the two technologies using simple criteria such as cost and size. What are the pros and cons of each display technology? How does a plasma TV display its picture? What are the disadvantages of plasma?

2 At the Movies — Essential Dorm Room Gadgets

To view the Essential Dorm Room Gadgets movie, click the number 2 button. Locate your video and click the corresponding High-Speed or Dial-Up link, depending on your Internet connection. Watch the movie and then complete the exercise by answering the questions that follow. As a rule, most college students have little, if any, disposable income. Some great and affordable gadgets are available, however, that can make a dorm room more functional for study and more fun for play. How would a network interface improve a dorm room?

3 Student Edition Labs — Peripheral Devices

Click the number 3 button. A new browser window will open, displaying the Student Edition Labs. Follow the on-screen instructions to complete the Peripheral Devices Lab. When finished, click the Exit button. If required, submit your results to your instructor.

4 Student Edition Labs — Working with Graphics

Click the number 4 button. A new browser window will open, displaying the Student Edition Labs. Follow the on-screen instructions to complete the Working with Graphics Lab. When finished, click the Exit button. If required, submit your results to your instructor.

5 Practice Test

Click the number 5 button. Answer each question. When completed, enter your name and click the Grade Test button to submit the quiz for grading. Make a note of any missed questions. If required, submit your results to your instructor.

6 Who Wants To Be a Computer Genius²?

Click the number 6 button to find out if you are a computer genius. Directions about how to play the game will be displayed. When you are ready to play, click the Play button. Submit your score to your instructor.

7 Wheel of Terms

Click the number 7 button to reinforce important terms you learned in this chapter by playing the Shelly Cashman Series version of this popular game. Directions about how to play the game will be displayed. When you are ready to play, click the Play button. Submit your score to your instructor.

Learn It Online

8 DC Track and Field

Click the number 8 button to use what you have learned in this chapter to compete against other students in three track and field events. Directions about how to play the game will be displayed. When you are ready to play, click the start first event button. If required, submit your score to your instructor.

9 You're Hired!

Click the number 9 button to use what you have learned in this chapter to embark on the path to a career in computers. Directions about how to play the game will be displayed. When you are ready to play, click the begin game button. If required, submit your score to your instructor.

10 Crossword Puzzle Challenge

Click the number 10 button. Complete the puzzle to reinforce skills you learned in this chapter. Directions about how to play the game will be displayed. When you are ready to play, click the Submit button. Submit the completed puzzle to your instructor.

11 Lab Exercises

Click the number 11 button. When the Lab Exercises menu appears, click the exercise assigned by your instructor. A new browser window will open. Follow the on-screen instructions to complete the exercise. When finished, click the Exit button. If required, submit your results to your instructor.

12 Choosing a Printer

The printer is a key component of any new personal computer that you purchase. Whether you are printing black-and-white reports or producing photo-lab-quality pictures, determining which printer is best for your individual needs requires some research. Printers are available in a range of speeds and capabilities. Click the number 12 button for a tutorial about how to select the printer that is best for your particular requirements.

13 In the News

Display device technology continues to advance. Not long ago, computer users would have considered connecting their $1,000 computers to a color television instead of paying outrageous prices for a color monitor. Today, you can purchase a 20-inch monitor that is faster and sharper than that color television for less than $300. Yet, as prices fall, consumers surely will purchase the display devices for HDTV and crystal-clear Internet access. Click the number 13 button and then read a news article about a new or improved output device. What is the device? Who manufactures it? How is the output device better than, or different from, earlier devices? Who do you think is most likely to use the device? Why?

14 Chapter Discussion Forum

Select an objective from this chapter on page 299 about which you would like more information. Click the number 14 button and post a short message listing a meaningful message title accompanied by one or more questions concerning the selected objective. In two days, return to the threaded discussion by clicking the number 14 button. Submit to your instructor your original message and at least one response to your message.

15 Howstuffworks.com

Click the number 15 button to learn how to use Howstuffworks.com to discover how a laser printer works in comparison to an ink-jet printer. Follow the instructions to get to the computer peripherals page. Read the articles about how both types of printers work. Write a report listing the major differences between the printers. Which type of printer would you recommend to your fellow students? Why? Print your report and submit it to your instructor.

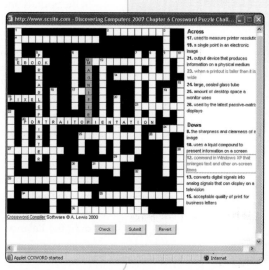

Learn How To

Use the Learn How To activities to learn fundamental skills when using a computer and accompanying technology. Complete the exercises and submit them to your instructor. To see a video of a Learn How To activity, visit scsite.com/dc2007/ch6/howto.

LEARN HOW TO 1: Adjust the Sound on a Computer

Every computer today contains a sound card and associated hardware and software that allow you to play and record sound. You can adjust the sound by completing the following steps:

1. Click the Start button on the Windows taskbar and then click Control Panel on the Start menu.
2. When the Control Panel window opens, click Sounds, Speech, and Audio Devices and then click Adjust the system volume; or double-click Sounds and Audio Devices. *The Sounds and Audio Devices Properties dialog box is displayed (Figure 6-38).*
3. To adjust the volume for all devices connected to the sound card, drag the Device volume slider left or right to decrease or increase the volume.
4. If you want to mute the sound on the computer, click the Mute check box so it contains a checkmark, and then click the OK button or the Apply button.
5. If you want to place the volume icon on the Windows taskbar, click the Place volume icon in the taskbar check box so it contains a checkmark, and then click the OK button or the Apply button. You can click the icon on the taskbar to set the volume level or mute the sound.
6. To make sound and other adjustments for each device on the computer, click the Advanced button in the Device volume area. *The Play Control or Recording Control window opens, depending on prior choices for this window (Figure 6-39).*
7. If the Recording Control window is opened, click Options on the window menu bar, click Properties on the Options menu, click the Playback option button, and then click the OK button.
8. In the Play Control window, Play Control volume is the same as the volume adjusted in the Sounds and Audio Devices Properties dialog box. The other columns in the Play Control window refer to devices found on the computer. To select the columns that are displayed, click Options on the menu bar and then click Properties. With Playback selected, place checkmarks in the check boxes for those devices you want to be displayed in the Control window.
9. To adjust volumes, drag the Volume sliders up or down for each device. To adjust the speaker balance, drag the Balance sliders.

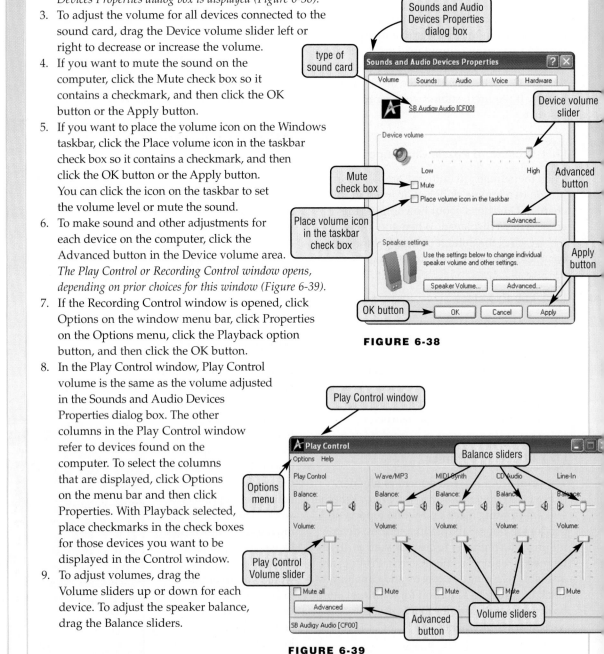

FIGURE 6-38

FIGURE 6-39

Learn How To

10. If the Advanced button is not displayed in the Play Control window, click Options on the menu bar and then click Advanced Controls on the Options menu. Click the Advanced button. You can control the Bass and Treble settings by using the sliders in the Tone Controls area of the Advanced Controls for Play Control dialog box.

Exercise

1. Open the Control Panel window and then display the Sounds and Audio Devices Properties dialog box. What kind of sound card is on the computer? Click the Place volume icon in the taskbar check box and then click the Apply button. What change did you notice on the Windows taskbar? Do the same thing again. What change occurred on the Windows taskbar? Click the Advanced button in the Device volume area. Ensure the Play Control window is open. What devices are chosen for control in the Play Control window? How would you change what devices are chosen? Submit your answers to your instructor.

LEARN HOW TO 2: Control Printing on Your Computer

When you print using a computer, you control printing at two different points: first, before the printing actually begins, and second, after the document has been sent to the printer and either is physically printing or is waiting to be printed. To set the parameters for printing and then print the document, complete the following steps:

1. Click File on the menu bar of the program that will be used for printing and then click Print on the File menu. *The Print dialog box is displayed (Figure 6-40). The Print dialog box will vary somewhat depending on the program used.*

2. In the Print dialog box, make the selections for what printer will be used, what pages will be printed, the number of copies to be printed, and any other choices available. For further options, click the Properties button (or, sometimes, the Preferences button) or click the Options button.

3. Click the OK button or the Print button. The document being printed is sent to a print queue, which is an area on disk storage from which documents actually are printed.

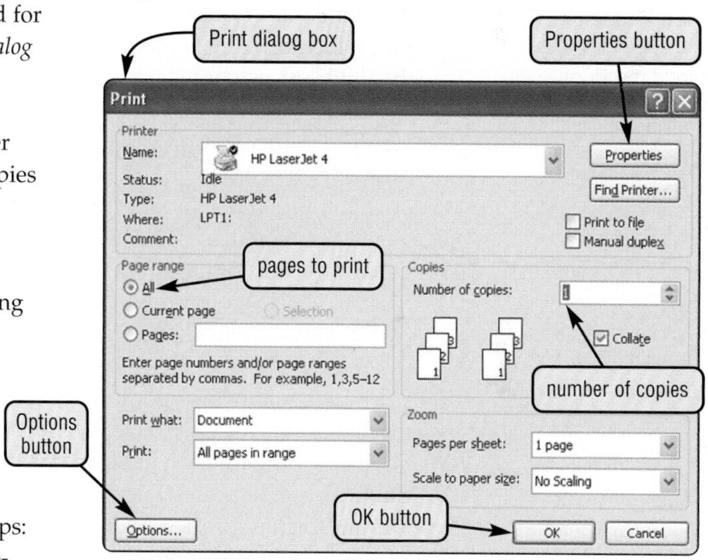

When you click the Print button to send the document to the print queue, a printer icon [] may appear on the Windows taskbar. To see the print queue and control the actual printing of documents on the printer, complete the following steps:

1. If the printer icon appears on the Windows taskbar, double-click it; otherwise, click the Start button on the Windows taskbar, click Printers and Faxes on the Start menu, and then double-click the printer icon with the checkmark. The checkmark indicates the default printer. *A window opens with the name of the printer on the title bar. All the documents either printing or waiting to be printed are listed in the window. The Status column indicates whether the document is printing or waiting. In addition, the owner of the file, number of pages, size, date and time submitted, and printer port are listed.*

FIGURE 6-40

2. If you click Printer on the menu bar in the printer window, you can set printing preferences from the Printer menu. In addition, you can pause all printing and cancel all printing jobs from the Printer menu.

3. If you select a document in the document list and then click Document on the menu bar, you can cancel the selected document for printing, or you can pause the printing for the selected document. To continue printing for the selected document, click Document on the menu bar and then click Resume on the Document menu.

Exercise

1. Start WordPad from the Accessories submenu. Type `The Print dialog box is displayed by clicking Print on the File menu.`

2. Display the Print dialog box and then click the Preferences button. What choices do you have in the Layout sheet? Close the Printing Preferences dialog box. How do you select the number of copies you want to print? How would you print pages 25–35 of a document? Submit your answers to your instructor.

Web Research

Use the Internet-based Web Research exercises to broaden your understanding of the concepts presented in this chapter. Visit scsite.com/dc2007/ch6/research to obtain more information pertaining to each exercise. To discuss any of the Web Research exercises in this chapter with other students, post your thoughts or questions at scsite.com/dc2007/ch6/forum.

① Scavenger Hunt Use one of the <u>search engines</u> listed in Figure 2-10 in Chapter 2 on page 78 or your own favorite search engine to find the answers to the questions below. Copy and paste the Web address from the Web page where you found the answer. Some questions may have more than one answer. If required, submit your answers to your instructor. (1) What company introduced the first laser printer? When? (2) What was the selling price of the first DeskJet ink-jet printer Hewlett-Packard released in 1988? (3) Who developed the liquid crystal display? (4) What is the model number of the IBM printer that could play musical notes? (5) What is an ambient light sensor on a monitor?

② Search Sleuth Some search engines use computers to index the World Wide Web automatically, so they generally find more Web sites that human indexers can catalog. One of the most aggressive automatic, or robot, search engines is <u>AltaVista</u> (altavista.com), which attempts to catalog the entire World Wide Web. AltaVista and many other search engines have a wildcard matching feature. Assume that you want to search for all information pertaining to flat-panel displays, including LCD monitors and screens, and plasma monitors. In this instance, you could use the wildcard symbol (*) to indicate missing letters. Your search query would be *flat-panel display, where the * substitutes for any variation of the words, flat-panel display. Visit this Web site and then use your word processing program to answer the following questions. Then, if required, submit your answers to your instructor. (1) Click the Help link and then click the Search link. Scroll down and then read about the different types of searches AltaVista emphasizes in its Basic Help page. What are these searches? (2) Click your browser's Back button or press the BACKSPACE key twice to return to the AltaVista home page. (3) Use the wildcard option and type *flat-panel display. (4) Scroll through the results until you reach the AltaVista News section. Read at least two of the news stories and then write a 50-word summary.

③ Journaling Respond to your readings in this chapter by writing at least one page about your reactions, evaluations, and reflections about using <u>output devices</u>. For example, have you printed photos taken with a digital camera? What type of photo paper did you use? Do you purchase recyclable printer supplies, such as toner or ink-jet cartridges? Where would you dispose of old monitors and printers and used toner? How do you attempt to reduce eyestrain while using a computer? You also can write about the new terms you learned by reading this chapter. If required, submit your journal to your instructor.

④ Expanding Your Understanding If you are using a Tablet PC and your coworker is using a PDA, it is cumbersome to transfer files from one device to the other. Engineers are developing <u>digital pens</u> that might ease the file exchange process. Using this special pen, one user can select a file on his computer and then place the pen on the other user's computer to transfer the file. Other digital pens allow users to write or draw and then retrieve all the handwritten information on a computer. Visit a local electronics store or Web site to learn more about digital pens. Compare their features, cost, file transfer process, and warranty. Write a report summarizing your findings, focusing on comparing and contrasting the digital pens. If required, submit your report to your instructor.

⑤ Ethics in Action <u>Internet addiction disorder</u> (IAD) may be affecting some Internet users. People claim to be addicted when they spend up to 10 hours a day online, they occasionally binge for extended Internet sessions, and they suffer withdrawal symptoms when they have not been online for some time. "Netomania" is not a recognized disorder, however, and some researchers believe the Internet problem is just a symptom of other psychiatric disorders, such as manic-depression. View online sites that provide information about IAD, including the Center for Online and Internet Addiction (netaddiction.com). Write a report summarizing your findings and include a table of links to Web sites that provide additional details. If required, submit your report to your instructor.

Case Studies

Use the Case Studies to apply the concepts presented in the chapter to real-world situations. Visit scsite.com/dc2007/ch6/cases to obtain more information pertaining to each exercise. To discuss the Case Studies in this chapter with other students, visit scsite.com/dc2007/ch6/forum and post your thoughts or questions.

Case Study 1 – Class Discussion   You are a manager of a 30-member income tax accounting group. Your company provides desktop computers for each of the accountants. The current computers have 17-inch CRT monitors. The accountants have been complaining that the monitors are too small. Use the Web and/or print media to investigate the costs associated with upgrading the current monitors to 19-inch or 20-inch <u>flat-panel display devices</u>. What are the advantages and disadvantages of flat-panel display devices? What is the best screen size? Why? When you have finished reviewing flat-panel display device characteristics, write a brief report to your supervisor summarizing your recommendations. Include a list of the five factors you think are the most important to consider when purchasing a flat-panel display device. Be prepared to discuss your recommendations in class.

Case Study 2 — Class Discussion   The price of <u>color laser printers</u> has dropped considerably over the past few years to a point where the price between a color laser printer and black-and-white laser printer is not as significant as it once was. The company at which you are employed as a buyer, has decided to upgrade the black-and-white laser printers used by its administrative staff throughout the company to color laser printers. Your manager has asked you to send him a brief report that lists the advantages and disadvantages of black-and-white laser printers versus color laser printers. Include both initial and recurring cost estimates for both black-and-white and color printers. Be prepared to discuss your recommendations in class.

Case Study 3 — Research   Printing requirements vary greatly among users. The local insurance agency where you are employed part time is shopping for a <u>printer</u>. The owner is aware that you are taking a computer class and has asked you to assist her in making a decision on what printer to buy. Figure 6-12 on page 310 lists several questions that should be considered when choosing a printer. Use what you learned in class to answer the questions posed in Figure 6-12. Answer each question according to what you believe to be your employer's needs. Then, use the Web and/or print media to find at least two printers that fit the requirements. List the name of each printer and note their advantages and disadvantages. Which of the two printers would you buy? Why? Prepare a report and/or PowerPoint presentation and share your findings with your class.

Case Study 4 — Research   While printers produce an image on a page from top to bottom, <u>plotters</u> can draw on any part of a page at random, and then move on to any other part. This capability, coupled with their capacity to use large sheets of paper, makes plotters particularly valuable to people who produce maps or blueprints. A local engineering firm that has used hand drawings for the past 50 years has hired you to assist them in purchasing three 42-inch plotters with a maximum print length of 300 feet and at least 1200 × 600 dpi. What is the advantage or disadvantage of using a plotter compared to simply creating a drawing by hand? Use the Web and/or print media to research both the initial and recurring costs of plotters that meet the stated requirements from three different manufacturers. Include in your research how long each plotter takes to produce an image and other noteworthy information. Prepare a report and/or PowerPoint presentation summarizing your findings.

Case Study 5 — Team Challenge   Three accountants at the company you work for want to go off on their own and set up a small accounting office with approximately 20 to 25 employees. They have hired your group as consultants to help with the setup. The goal is to determine the type of output devices you think they will need within the office. Consider the types and number of printers, types and number of display devices, <u>audio devices</u>, microphones, LCD projectors, considerations for the physically challenged, and whether fax machines, fax modems, and/or multifunction peripherals are needed. Form a three-member team and assign each team member one or more categories of output devices. Have the team members use the Web and/or print media to research their assignments. Combine your findings in a table listing the advantages and disadvantages of the various devices, your team's recommendations, and a short explanation of why the team selected each device. Share your findings with your class.

Special Feature

Digital Imaging and Video Technology

Everywhere you look, people are capturing moments they want to remember. They take pictures or make movies of their vacations, birthday parties, activities, accomplishments, sporting events, weddings, and more. Because of the popularity of digital cameras and digital video cameras, increasingly more people desire to capture their memories digitally, instead of on film. With digital technology, photographers have the ability to modify and share the digital images and videos they create. When you use special hardware and/or software, you can copy, manipulate, print, and distribute digital images and videos using your personal computer and the Internet. Amateurs can create professional quality results by using more sophisticated hardware and software.

digital camera (inp

digital video camera (input)

FireWire or USB 2.0

television (output)

FIGURE 1   The top portion of the figure shows a typical home digital imaging setup, and the lower portion of the figure shows a typical home setup for editing personal video.

Digital photography and recordings deliver significant benefits over film-based photography and movie making. With digital cameras, no developing is needed. Instead, the images reside on storage media such as a hard disk, DVD, or flash memory card. Unlike film, storage media can be reused, which reduces costs, saves time, and provides immediate results. Digital technology allows greater control over the creative process, both while taking pictures and video and in the editing process. You can check results immediately after capturing a picture or video to determine whether it meets your expectations. If you are dissatisfied with a picture or video, you can erase it and recapture it, again and again.

As shown in the top portion of Figure 1, a digital camera functions as an input device when it transmits pictures through a cable to a personal computer via a USB port or FireWire port. Using a digital camera in this way allows you to edit the pictures, save them on storage media, and print them on a photographic-quality printer via a parallel port or USB port.

The lower portion of Figure 1 illustrates how you might use a digital video camera with a personal computer. The process typically is the same for most digital video cameras. You capture the images or video with the video camera. Next, you connect the video camera to your personal computer using a FireWire or USB 2.0 port, or you place the storage media used on the camera in the computer. The video then is copied or downloaded to the computer's hard disk. Then, you can edit the video using video editing software. If desired, you can preview the video during the editing process on a television. Finally, you save the finished result to the desired media, such as a VHS tape or DVD+RW or, perhaps, e-mail the edited video. In this example, a VCR and a DVD player also can be used to input video from a VHS tape or a DVD.

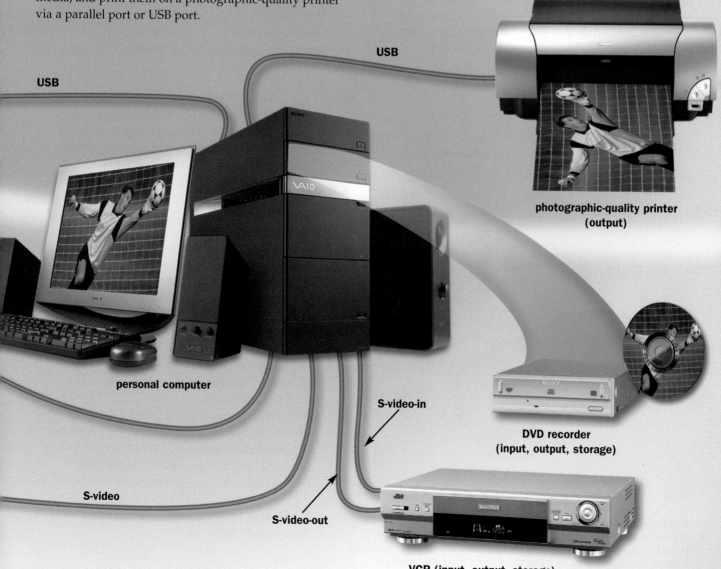

USB

USB

photographic-quality printer (output)

personal computer

S-video-in

DVD recorder (input, output, storage)

S-video

S-video-out

VCR (input, output, storage)

DIGITAL IMAGING TECHNOLOGY

Digital imaging technology involves capturing and manipulating still photographic images in an electronic format. The following sections outline the steps involved in the process of using digital imaging technology.

1 Select a Digital Camera

A **digital camera** is a type of camera that stores photographed images electronically instead of on traditional film. Digital cameras are divided into three categories (Figure 2) based mainly on image resolution, features, and of course, price. The image resolution is measured in pixels (short for picture element). The image quality increases with the number of pixels. The image resolution usually is measured in **megapixels** (million of pixels), often abbreviated as **MP**. Features of digital cameras include red-eye reduction, zoom, autofocus, flash, self-timer, and manual mode for fine-tuning settings. Figure 3 summarizes the three categories of digital cameras.

TYPES OF DIGITAL CAMERAS

Type	Resolution Range	Features	Price
Point-and-shoot	Less than 5 MP	Fully automatic; fits in your pocket; easy to use; ideal for average consumer usage.	Less than $500
Field cameras	Greater than 6 MP	Used by photojournalists; portable but flexible; provides ability to change lenses and use other attachments; great deal of control over exposure and other photo settings.	$600 to $2,000
Studio cameras	Greater than 6 MP	Stationary camera used for professional studio work; flexible; widest range of lenses and settings.	$1,500 and up

FIGURE 3 Digital cameras often are categorized by image resolution, features, and price.

2 Take Pictures

Digital cameras provide you with several options that are set before a picture is taken. Three of the more important options are the resolution, compression, and image file format in which the camera should save the picture. While a camera may allow for a very high resolution for a large print, you may choose to take a picture at a lower resolution if the image does not require great detail or must be a small size. For example, you may want to use the image on a Web page where smaller image file sizes are beneficial.

Compression results in smaller image file sizes. Figure 4 illustrates the image file sizes for varying resolutions and compressions under standard photographic conditions using a 4-megapixel digital camera. Figure 4 also shows the average picture size for a given resolution. The camera may take more time to save an image at lower compression, resulting in a longer delay before the camera is ready to take another picture. A higher compression, however, may result in some loss of image quality. If a camera has a 16 MB flash memory card, you can determine the number of pictures the card can hold by dividing 16 MB by the file size. Flash memory cards are available in sizes from 16 MB to 8 GB.

(a) point-and-shoot

(b) field

(c) studio

FIGURE 2 The point-and-shoot digital camera (a) requires no adjustments before shooting. The field digital camera (b) offers improved quality and features that allow you to make manual adjustments before shooting and use a variety of lenses. The studio digital camera (c) offers better color and resolution and greater control over exposure and lenses.

Most digital cameras also allow you to choose an image file format. Two popular file formats are TIFF and JPEG. The **TIFF** file format saves the image uncompressed. All of the image detail is captured and stored, but the file sizes can be large. The **JPEG** file format is compressed. The resolution of the image may be the same as a TIFF file, but some detail may be lost in the image.

Finally, before you take the photograph, you should choose the type of media on which to store the resulting image file. Some cameras allow for a choice of media to which you can store the image, such as a CompactFlash card or Memory Stick, while others allow for only one type of storage media. One major advantage of a digital camera is that you easily can erase pictures from its media, freeing up space for new pictures.

IMAGE FILE SIZE WITH A FOUR MEGAPIXEL DIGITAL CAMERA

Resolution in Pixels	COMPRESSION			Picture Size in Inches
	Low	Medium	High	
	Resulting Image File Size			
2272 × 1704	2 MB	1.1 MB	556 KB	11 x 17
1600 × 1200	1 MB	558 KB	278 KB	8 x 10
1024 × 768	570 KB	320 KB	170 KB	4 x 6
640 × 480	249 KB	150 KB	84 KB	3 x 5

FIGURE 4 Image file sizes for varying resolutions and compressions under standard photographic conditions using a 4-megapixel digital camera.

③ Transfer and Manage Image Files

The method of transferring images from the camera to the personal computer differs greatly depending on the capabilities of both. Digital cameras use a variety of storage media (Figure 5). If your camera uses a flash memory card such as CompactFlash, Memory Stick, SmartMedia, or Secure Digital (SD), you can remove the media from the camera and place it in a slot on the personal computer or in a device, such as a card reader, connected to the personal computer. Your camera or card reader also may connect to the personal computer using a USB, USB 2.0, or FireWire (Figure 6) port. When you insert the memory card or connect the camera, software on the personal computer guides you through the process of transferring the images to the hard disk. Some operating systems and software recognize a memory card or camera as though it is another hard disk on the computer. This feature allows you to access the files, navigate them, and then copy, delete, or rename the files while the media still is in the camera.

After you transfer the files to the hard disk on your personal computer, you should organize the files by sorting them or renaming them so that information, such as the subject, date, time, and purpose, is saved along with the image. Finally, before altering the images digitally or using the images for other purposes, you should back up the images to another location, such as a CD or DVD, so the original image is recoverable.

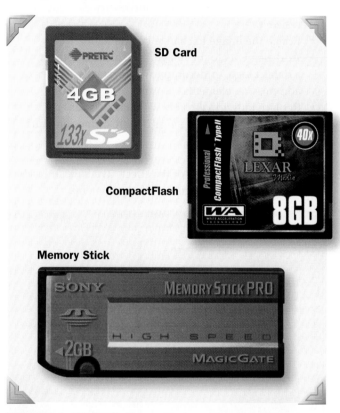

FIGURE 5 SD Cards, CompactFlash, and Memory Sticks are popular storage devices for digital cameras.

FIGURE 6 Using a USB or FireWire connection, you can add a card reader to your personal computer.

④ Edit Images

Image editing software allows you to edit digital images. The following list summarizes the more common image enhancements or alterations:

- Adjust the contrast and brightness; correct lighting problems; or help give the photograph a particular feeling, such as warm or stark.
- Remove red-eye.
- Crop an image to remove unnecessary elements and resize it.
- Rotate the image to change its orientation.
- Add elements to the image, such as descriptive text, a date, a logo, or decorative items; create collages or add missing elements.
- Replace individual colors with a new color.
- Add special effects, such as texture or motion blurring to enhance the image.

Figure 7 shows some of the effects available in Jasc's Paint Shop Pro on the Artistic Effects submenu.

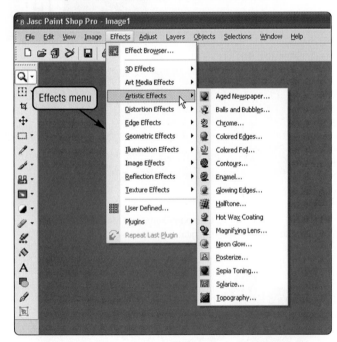

FIGURE 7 The capability of applying effects separates digital photography from film photography.

⑤ Print Images

Once an image is digitally altered, it is ready to be printed. You can print images on a personal color printer or send them to a professional service that specializes in digital photo printing.

When printing the images yourself, make sure that the resolution used to create the image was high enough for the size of the print you want to create. For example, if the camera used a resolution of 640 × 480 pixels, then the ideal print size is a wallet size. If you print such an image at a size of 8 x 10 inches, then the image will appear **pixilated**, or blurry. Use high-quality photo paper for the best results. A photo printer gives the best results when printing digital photography.

Many services print digital images, either over the Internet or through traditional photo developing locations and kiosks (Figure 8), such as those found in drug stores or shopping marts. Some services allow you to e-mail or upload the files to the service, specify the size, quality, and quantity of print; and then receive the finished prints via the postal service. Other services allow you to drop off flash memory cards, CD-ROMs, or floppy disks at a photo shop and later pick up the prints, just as you do with traditional photo developing shops.

FIGURE 8
A Pixel Magic Imaging Photo Ditto kiosk allows you to print digital images in high resolution on photo paper.

6 Distribute Images Electronically

Rather than printing images, you often need to use the images electronically. Depending on the electronic use of the image, the image may require additional processing. If you use the images on a Web site or want to e-mail a photo, you probably want to send a lower-resolution image. Image editing software allows you to lower the resolution of the image, resulting in a smaller file size. You also should use standard file formats when distributing an electronic photo. The JPEG format is viewable using most personal computers or Web browsers. Some online services allow you to upload and share your photos free of charge and will automatically change your photos to a lower resolution and JPEG format.

You can store very high resolution photos on a DVD or a CD. **DVD and CD mastering software** (Figure 9) allows you to create slide show presentations on a recordable DVD or CD that can play in many home DVD players or personal computer DVD drives.

Finally, you should back up and store images that you distribute electronically with the same care as you store your traditional film negatives.

FIGURE 9 Nero PhotoShow Elite and similar software applications allow you to create your own photo slide show on DVD or CD.

DIGITAL VIDEO TECHNOLOGY

Digital video technology allows you to input, edit, manage, publish, and share your videos using a personal computer. With digital video technology, you can transform home videos into Hollywood-style movies by enhancing the videos with scrolling titles and transitions, cutting out or adding scenes, and adding background music and voice-over narration. The following sections outline the steps involved in the process of using digital video technology.

1 Select a Video Camera

Video cameras record in either analog or digital format. **Analog formats** include 8mm, Hi8, VHS, VHS-C, and Super VHS-C. The last three formats use the types of tapes similar to those used in a standard VCR. **Digital formats** include Mini-DV, MICROMV, Digital8, and DVD. Digital video cameras fall into three general categories: high-end consumer, consumer, and webcasting and monitoring (Figure 10). Consumer digital video cameras are by far the most popular type among consumers. Digital video cameras provide more features than analog video cameras, such as a higher level of zoom, better sound, or greater control over color and lighting.

(a) high-end consumer

(b) consumer

(c) webcasting and monitoring

FIGURE 10 The high-end consumer digital video camera (a) can produce professional-grade results. The consumer digital video camera (b) produces amateur-grade results. The webcasting and monitoring digital video camera (c) is appropriate for webcasting and security monitoring.

2 Record a Video

Most video cameras provide you with a choice of recording programs, which sometimes are called automatic settings. Each recording program includes a different combination of camera settings, so you can adjust the exposure and other functions to match the recording environment. Usually, several different programs are available, such as point-and-shoot, point-and-shoot with manual adjustment, sports, portrait, spotlit scenes, and low light. You also have the ability to select special digital effects, such as fade, wipe, and black and white. If you are shooting outside on a windy day, then you can enable the wind screen to prevent wind noise. If you are shooting home videos, then the point-and-shoot recording program is sufficient.

3 Transfer and Manage Videos

After recording the video, the next step is to transfer the video to your personal computer. Most video cameras connect directly to a USB 2.0 or FireWire port on your personal computer (Figure 11). Transferring video with a digital camera is easy, because the video already is in a digital format that the computer can understand.

An analog camcorder or VCR requires additional hardware to convert the analog signals to a digital format before the video can be manipulated on a personal computer. The additional hardware includes a special video capture card using a standard RCA video cable or an S-video cable (Figure 12). *S-video* cables provide sharper

images and greater overall quality. When you use video capture hardware with an analog video, be sure to close all open programs on your computer because capturing video requires a great deal of processing power.

FIGURE 11 A digital video camera is connected to the personal computer via a FireWire or USB 2.0 port. No additional hardware is needed.

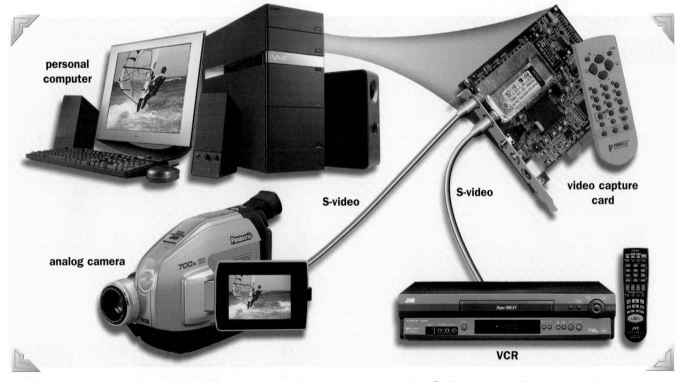

FIGURE 12 An analog camcorder or VCR is connected to the personal computer via an S-video port on a video capture card.

When transferring video, plan to use approximately 15 to 30 gigabytes of hard disk storage space per hour of digital video. A typical video project requires about four times the amount of raw footage as the final product. Therefore, at the high end, a video that lasts an hour may require up to 120 gigabytes of storage for the raw footage, editing process, and final video. This storage requirement can vary depending on the software you use to copy the video from the video camera to the hard disk and the format you select to save the video. For example, Microsoft claims that the latest version of its Windows Movie Maker can save 15 hours of video in 10 gigabytes when creating video for playback on a computer, but saves only 1 hour of video in 10 gigabytes when creating video for playback on a DVD or VCR.

The video transfer requires application software on the personal computer (Figure 13). Windows XP includes the Windows Movie Maker software that allows you to transfer the video from your video camera. Depending on the length of video and the type of connection used, the video may take a long time to download. Make certain that no other programs are running on your personal computer while transferring the video.

When transferring video, the software may allow you to choose a file format and a codec to store the video. A video **file format** holds the video information in a manner specified by a vendor, such as Apple or Microsoft. Three of the more popular file formats are listed in Figure 14.

File formats support codecs to encode the audio and video into the file formats. A particular file format may be able to store audio and video in a number of different codecs. A **codec** specifies how the audio and video is compressed and stored within the file. Figure 15 shows some options available for specifying a file format and codec in a video capture application. The dialog box in Figure 15 allows the user to determine whether the video is smoother in playback or if the video is more crisp, meaning that it includes more detail. The file format and codec you choose often is based on what you plan to do with the movie. For example, if you plan to stream video over the Web using Real's Helix software, the best choice for the file format is the RealMedia format, which uses the RealVideo codec.

After transferring the video to a personal computer, and before manipulating the video, you should store the video files in appropriate folders, named correctly, and backed up. Most video transfer application software helps manage these tasks.

POPULAR VIDEO FILE FORMATS

File Format	File Extensions
Apple QuickTime	.MOV or .QT
Microsoft Windows Media Video	.WMV or .ASF
Real RealMedia	.RM or .RAM

FIGURE 14 Apple, Microsoft, and Real offer the more popular video file formats.

FIGURE 13 Some video editing software allows you to transfer your video from any video source to a hard disk. This dialog box allows the user to set various video parameters for capturing video from a camera or other device.

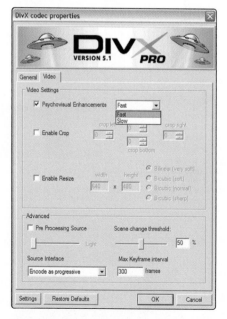

FIGURE 15 Video editing software applications allow you to specify a combination of file format and codec when saving a video.

Edit a Video

(4) Once the video is stored on your hard disk, the next step is to edit, or manipulate, the video. If you used a video capture card to transfer analog video to your computer (Figure 12 on page 348), the files may require extra initial processing. When you use a video capture card, some of the video frames may be lost in the transfer process. Some video editing programs allow you to fix this problem with **frame rate correction** tools.

The first step in the editing process is to split the video into smaller pieces, or *scenes*, that you can manipulate more easily. This process is called *splitting*. Most video software automatically splits the video into scenes, thus sparing you the task. After splitting, you should cut out unwanted scenes or portions of scenes. This process is called *pruning*.

After you create the scenes you want to use in your final production, you edit each individual scene. You can *crop*, or change the size of, scenes. That is, you may want to cut out the top or a side of a scene that is irrelevant. You also can resize the scene. For example, you may be creating a video that will be displayed in a Web browser.

Making a smaller video, such as 320 × 200 pixels instead of 640 × 480 pixels, results in a smaller file that transmits faster over the Internet.

If video has been recorded over a long period, using different cameras or under different lighting conditions, the video may need color correction. *Color correction tools* (Figure 16) analyze your video and match brightness, colors, and other attributes of video clips to ensure a smooth look to the video.

You can add logos, special effects, or titles to scenes. You can place a company logo or personal logo in a video to identify yourself or the company producing the video. Logos often are added on the lower-right corner of a video and remain for the duration of the video. Special effects include warping, changing from color to black and white, morphing, or zoom motion. *Morphing* is a special effect in which one video image is transformed into another image over the course of several frames of video, creating the illusion of metamorphosis. You usually add titles at the beginning and end of a video to give the video context. A training video may have titles throughout the video to label a particular scene, or each scene may begin with a title.

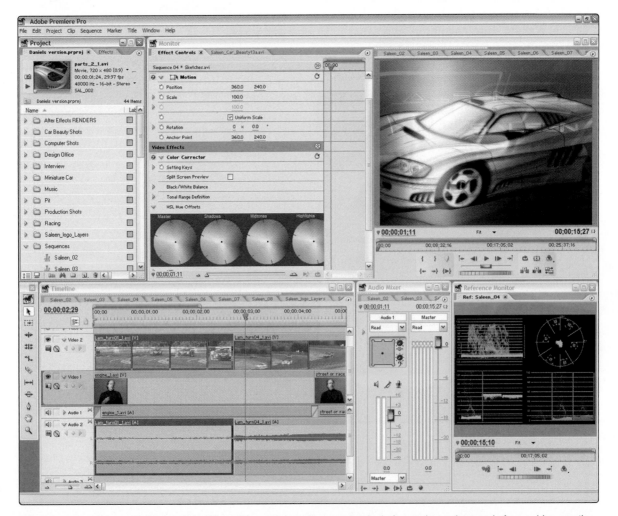

FIGURE 16   Color correction tools in video editing software allow a great deal of control over the mood of your video creation.

The next step in editing a video is to add audio effects, including voice-over narration and background music. Many video editing programs allow you to add additional tracks, or *layers*, of sound to a video in addition to the sound that was recorded on the video camera. You also can add special audio effects.

The final step in editing a video is to combine the scenes into a complete video (Figure 17). This process involves ordering scenes and adding transition effects between scenes (Figure 18). Video editing software allows you to combine scenes and separate each scene with a transition. *Transitions* include fading, wiping, blurry, bursts, ruptures, erosions, and more.

FIGURE 17 In Windows Movie Maker 2, scenes, shown on the top, are combined into a sequence on the bottom of the screen.

FIGURE 18 Smooth and dynamic transitions eliminate the hard cuts between scenes typically found in raw footage.

⑤ Distribute the Video

After editing the video, the final step is to distribute it or save it on an appropriate medium. You can save video in a variety of formats. Using special hardware, you can save the video on standard video tape. *A digital-to-analog converter* is necessary to allow your personal computer to transmit video to a VCR. A digital-to-analog converter may be an external device that connects to both the computer and input device, or may be a video capture card inside the computer.

Video also can be stored in digital formats in any of several DVD formats, on CD-R, or on video CD (VCD). *DVD* or *CD creation software*, which often is packaged with video editing software, allows you to create, or *master*, DVDs and CDs. You can add interactivity to your DVDs. For example, you can allow viewers to jump to certain scenes using a menu (Figure 19). A *video CD (VCD)* is a CD format that stores video on a CD-R that can be played in many DVD players.

You also can save your video creation in electronic format for distribution over the Web or via e-mail. Your video editing software must support the file format and codec you want to use. For example, RealNetworks's Helix media delivery system allows you to save media files in the RealVideo file formats.

Professionals use hardware and software that allow them to create a film version of digital video that can be played in movie theaters. This technology is becoming increasingly popular and has been used in such movies as the recent *Lord of the Rings* movies. Some Hollywood directors believe that eventually, all movies will be recorded and edited digitally.

After creating your final video for distribution or your personal video collection, you should backup the final video file. You can save your scenes for inclusion in other video creations or create new masters using different effects, transitions, and ordering of scenes.

FIGURE 19 DVD mastering software allows you to create interactive menus on your DVD.

CHAPTER SEVEN

Storage

Picture Yourself Working with Mobile Storage Media

At the end of the job interview, the supervisor asks, "When can you start?" You are thrilled to get this job with the local newspaper. The flexible hours are a perfect arrangement with your school schedule. As an added bonus, the job will give you experience toward your major — computer technology.

You will be working with the photojournalists in the office — more precisely, with their mobile media. The photojournalists take many pictures while on various assignments. All of them use digital cameras. Your job is to print pictures taken by the photojournalists. Because the photo-journalists each use different makes and models of cameras, the digital pictures are stored on a variety of mobile media. Some of the cameras use flash memory cards such as CompactFlash cards, xD Picture cards, and Memory Sticks. One photojournalist transfers his pictures to a USB flash drive, from which you print the images. Some copy their pictures on a CD, and another gives you a Zip disk containing all her pictures.

After you receive the media, you insert it in the appropriate card reader, card slot, drive, or port. You then begin the process of storing the images on a hard disk and finally printing the images. The office has a very liberal personal use policy that allows you to print your own digital pictures during off-the-clock time — as long as you supply the paper. When you are away from the office, however, you print personal pictures using an in-store kiosk.

To learn about these various types of mobile media, read Chapter 7 and discover many other types of storage devices.

STORAGE

Storage holds data, instructions, and information for future use. Every computer uses storage to hold system software and application software. To start up, a computer locates an operating system (system software) in storage and loads it into memory. When a user issues a command to start application software, such as a word processing program or a Web browser, the operating system locates the program in storage and loads it into memory.

In addition to programs, users store a variety of data and information on mainframe computers, servers, desktop computers, notebook computers, Tablet PCs, handheld computers,

PDAs, and smart phones. For example, all types of users store digital photographs; appointments, schedules, and contact/address information; and correspondence, such as letters and e-mail messages. Other items stored by specific types of users include the following:

• The home user might also store budgets, bank statements, a household inventory, records of stock purchases, tax data, homework assignments, recipes, music, and videos.
• The small office/home office user also often stores faxes, business reports, financial records, tax data, travel records, customer orders, payroll records, inventory records, and Web pages.

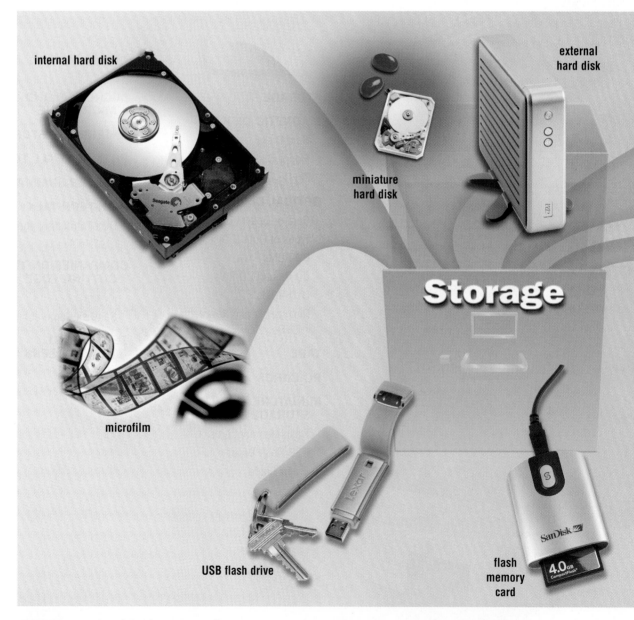

internal hard disk

external hard disk

miniature hard disk

Storage

microfilm

USB flash drive

flash memory card

FIGURE 7-1 A variety of storage media.

- The mobile user usually also stores faxes, presentations, travel records, homework assignments, and quotations.
- The power user also stores diagrams, drawings, blueprints, designs, marketing literature, corporate newsletters, product catalogs, videos, audio recordings, multimedia presentations, and Web pages.
- The large business user also accesses many stored items such as tax data, inventory records, presentations, contracts, marketing literature, and Web pages. The large business user accesses hundreds or thousands of employee, customer, and vendor records, including data and information about orders, invoices, payments, and payroll.

Storage requirements among these users vary greatly. Home users, small office/home office users, and mobile users typically have much smaller storage requirements than the large business user or power user. For example, a home user may need 160 billion bytes of storage, while large businesses may require 50 trillion bytes of storage.

A **storage medium** (media is the plural), also called *secondary storage*, is the physical material on which a computer keeps data, instructions, and information. Examples of storage media are hard disks, floppy disks, Zip disks, CDs and DVDs, tape, PC Cards, flash memory cards, USB flash drives, and microfilm (Figure 7-1). Memory, by contrast, typically consists of one or more chips on the motherboard or some other circuit board in the computer.

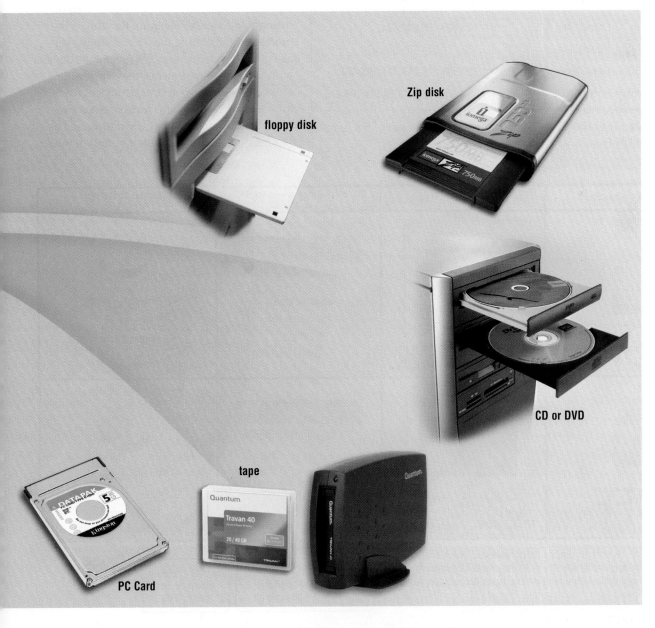

floppy disk

Zip disk

CD or DVD

tape

PC Card

Capacity is the number of bytes (characters) a storage medium can hold. Figure 7-2 identifies the terms manufacturers use to define the capacity of storage media. For example, a reasonably priced USB flash drive can store up to 256 MB of data (approximately 256 million bytes) and a typical hard disk has 160 GB (approximately 160 billion bytes) of storage capacity.

STORAGE TERMS

Storage Term	Approximate Number of Bytes	Exact Number of Bytes
Kilobyte (KB)	1 thousand	2^{10} or 1,024
Megabyte (MB)	1 million	2^{20} or 1,048,576
Gigabyte (GB)	1 billion	2^{30} or 1,073,741,824
Terabyte (TB)	1 trillion	2^{40} or 1,099,511,627,776
Petabyte (PB)	1 quadrillion	2^{50} or 1,125,899,906,842,624
Exabyte (EB)	1 quintillion	2^{60} or 1,152,921,504,606,846,976
Zettabyte (ZB)	1 sextillion	2^{70} or 1,180,591,620,717,411,303,424
Yottabyte (YB)	1 septillion	2^{80} or 1,208,925,819,614,629,174,706,176

FIGURE 7-2 The capacity of a storage medium is measured by the number of bytes it can hold.

Items on a storage medium remain intact even when power is removed from the computer. Thus, a storage medium is nonvolatile. Most memory, by contrast, holds data and instructions temporarily and thus is volatile. Figure 7-3 illustrates the concept of volatility. For an analogy, think of a filing cabinet that holds file folders as a storage medium, and the top of your desk as memory. When you want to work with a file, you remove it from the filing cabinet (storage medium) and place it on your desk (memory). When you are finished with the file, you remove it from your desk (memory) and return it to the filing cabinet (storage medium).

A **storage device** is the computer hardware that records and/or retrieves items to and from storage media. **Writing** is the process of transferring data, instructions, and information from memory to a storage medium. **Reading** is the process of transferring these items from a storage medium into memory. When storage devices write data on storage media, they are creating output. Similarly, when storage devices read from storage media, they function as a source of input. Nevertheless, they are categorized as storage devices, not as input or output devices.

AN ILLUSTRATION OF VOLATILITY

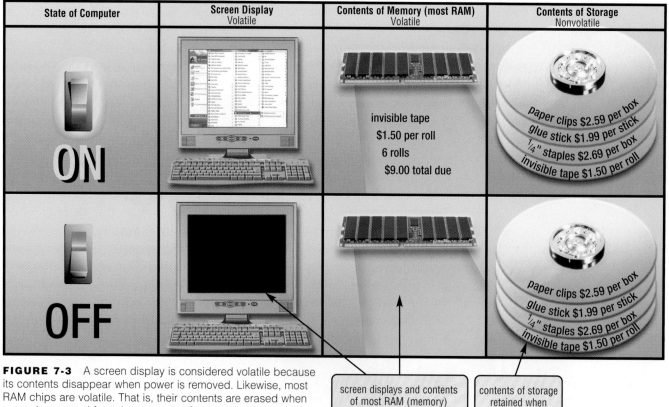

FIGURE 7-3 A screen display is considered volatile because its contents disappear when power is removed. Likewise, most RAM chips are volatile. That is, their contents are erased when power is removed from the computer. Storage, by contrast, is nonvolatile. Its contents remain when power is off.

screen displays and contents of most RAM (memory) erased when power is off

contents of storage retained when power is off

The speed of storage devices and memory is defined by access time. **Access time** measures (1) the amount of time it takes a storage device to locate an item on a storage medium or (2) the time required to deliver an item from memory to the processor. The access time of storage devices is slow, compared with the access time of memory. Memory (chips) accesses items in billionths of a second (nanoseconds). Storage devices, by contrast, access items in thousandths of a second (milliseconds).

Instead of, or in addition to access time, some manufacturers state a storage device's transfer rate because it affects access time. *Transfer rate* is the speed with which data, instructions, and information transfer to and from a device. Transfer rates for disks are stated in *KBps* (kilobytes per second) and *MBps* (megabytes per second).

Numerous types of storage media and storage devices exist to meet a variety of users' needs. Figure 7-4 shows how different types of storage media and memory compare in terms of transfer rates and uses. This chapter discusses these and other storage media.

MAGNETIC DISKS

Magnetic disks use magnetic particles to store items such as data, instructions, and information on a disk's surface. Depending on how the magnetic particles are aligned, they represent either a 0 bit or a 1 bit. Recall from Chapter 4 that a bit (binary digit) is the smallest unit of data a computer can process. Thus, the alignment of the magnetic particles represents the data.

Before any data can be read from or written on a magnetic disk, the disk must be formatted. **Formatting** is the process of dividing the disk into tracks and sectors (Figure 7-5), so the operating system can store and locate data and information on the disk. A *track* is a narrow recording band that forms a full circle on the surface of the disk. The disk's storage locations consist of pie-shaped sections, which break the tracks into small arcs called *sectors*. On a magnetic disk, a sector typically stores up to 512 bytes of data.

For reading and writing purposes, sectors are grouped into clusters. A *cluster* is the smallest unit of disk space that stores data and information. Each cluster, also called an *allocation unit*, consists of two to eight sectors (the number varies depending on the operating system). Even if a file consists of only a few bytes, it uses an entire cluster. Each cluster holds data from only one file. One file, however, can span many clusters.

Figure 7-4

	Stores...
Memory — Memory (most RAM)	Items waiting to be interpreted and executed by the processor
Storage — Hard Disk	Operating system, application software, user data and information, including pictures, music, and videos
Flash Memory Cards and USB Flash Drives	Digital pictures or files to be transported
CDs and DVDs	Software, backups, movies, music
Tape	Backups
Floppy Disk	Small files to be transported

faster transfer rates

slower transfer rates

FIGURE 7-4 A comparison of different types of storage media and memory in terms of relative speed and uses. Memory is faster than storage but is expensive and not practical for all storage requirements. Storage is less expensive but is slower than memory.

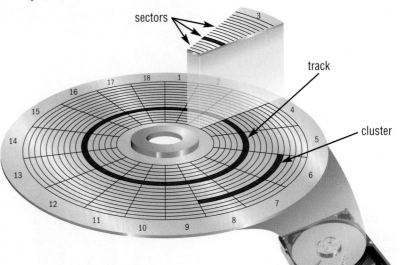

FIGURE 7-5 Tracks form circles on the surface of a magnetic disk. The disk's storage locations are divided into pie-shaped sections, which break the tracks into small arcs called sectors.

Sometimes, a sector has a flaw and cannot store data. When you format a disk, the operating system marks these bad sectors as unusable. For a technical discussion about formatting, read the High-Tech Talk article on page 382.

Three types of magnetic disks are hard disks, floppy disks, and Zip disks. Some of these disks are portable; others are not. With respect to a storage medium, the term *portable* means you can remove the medium from one computer and carry it to another computer.

Hard Disks

A **hard disk**, also called a *hard disk drive*, is a storage device that contains one or more inflexible, circular platters that magnetically store data, instructions, and information. Home users store documents, spreadsheets, presentations, databases, e-mail messages, Web pages, digital photographs, music, videos, and software on hard disks. Businesses use hard disks to store correspondence, reports, financial records, e-mail messages, customer orders and invoices, payroll records, inventory records, presentations, contracts, marketing literature, schedules, and Web sites.

The system unit on most desktop and notebook computers contains at least one hard disk.

The entire device is enclosed in an airtight, sealed case to protect it from contamination. A hard disk that is mounted inside the system unit sometimes is called a *fixed disk* because it is not portable (Figure 7-6). Portable hard disks are discussed later in this chapter.

Current personal computer hard disks have storage capacities from 80 to 500 GB and more. Traditionally, hard disks stored data using *longitudinal recording*, which aligned the magnetic particles horizontally around the surface of the disk. With *perpendicular recording*, by contrast, hard disks align the magnetic particles vertically, or perpendicular to the disk's surface, making much greater storage capacities possible. Experts estimate that hard disks using perpendicular recording will provide storage capacities about 10 times greater than disks that use longitudinal recording. Read Looking Ahead 7-1 for a look at the next generation of hard disk storage capacities. Hard disks are read/write storage media. That is, you can read from and write on a hard disk any number of times. If the computer contains only one hard disk, the operating system designates it as drive C. Additional hard disks are assigned the next available drive letter.

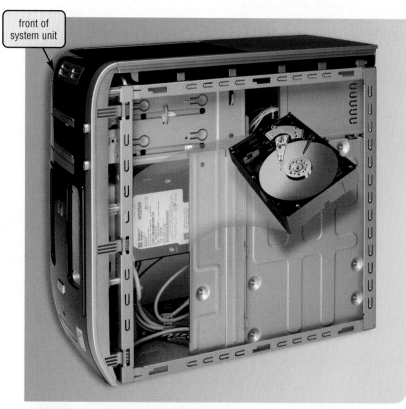

front of system unit

FIGURE 7-6   The hard disk in a desktop personal computer is enclosed inside an airtight, sealed case inside the system unit.

FAQ 7-1

Have personal computer hard disk capacities grown much since their inception?

Yes, hard disk capacities have grown phenomenally over the past several years, as shown in the chart to the right. This trend is expected to continue at a rate of 60 percent annually. For more information, visit scsite.com/dc2007/ch7/faq and then click Hard Disk Capacities.

Personal Computer Hard Disk Growth
(Historical and Projected)

LOOKING AHEAD 7-1

Heat Increases Disk Capacity

Things are heating up in the data storage industry. Engineers at IBM Research are testing the use of heat to record data inexpensively on magnetic media, such as hard disks.

Within the next ten years, the researchers predict that this new technique will allow storage of more than one terabit per square inch, which is the equivalent of 25 DVDs on an area the size of a postage stamp. With this capacity, a hard disk that can store seven terabits will be commonplace.

IBM calls this new storage system *Millipede*. It uses heated tips mounted on the ends of cantilevers, in a fashion similar to the way the stylus on an old phonograph sat on the grooves of vinyl records. For more information, visit scsite.com/dc2007/ch7/looking and then click Heated Storage.

CHARACTERISTICS OF A HARD DISK Characteristics of a hard disk include its capacity, platters, read/write heads, cylinders, sectors and tracks, revolutions per minute, transfer rate, and access time. Figure 7-7 shows characteristics of a sample 120 GB hard disk. The following paragraphs discuss each of these characteristics.

The capacity of a hard disk is determined from the number of platters it contains, together with composition of the magnetic coating on the platters. A *platter* is made of aluminum, glass, or ceramic and is coated with an alloy material that allows items to be recorded magnetically on its surface. The coating usually is three millionths of an inch thick.

SAMPLE HARD DISK CHARACTERISTICS

Advertised capacity	120 GB
Platters	3
Read/write heads	6
Cylinders	16,383
Bytes per sector	512
Sectors per track	63
Sectors per drive	234,441,648
Revolutions per minute	7,200
Transfer rate	133 MB per second
Access time	8.9 ms

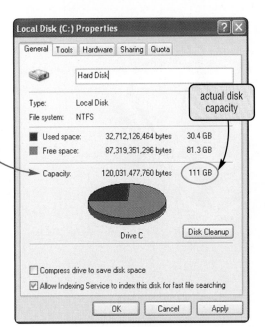

FIGURE 7-7 Characteristics of a sample 120 GB hard disk. The actual disk's capacity sometimes is different from the advertised capacity because of bad sectors on the disk.

On desktop computers, platters most often have a *form factor*, or size, of approximately 3.5 inches in diameter; on notebook computers and mobile devices, the form factor is 2.5 inches or less. A typical hard disk has multiple platters stacked on top of one another. Each platter has two read/write heads, one for each side. The hard disk has arms that move the read/write heads to the proper location on the platter (Figure 7-8). A *read/write head* is the mechanism that reads items and writes items in the drive as it barely touches the disk's recording surface.

The location of the read/write heads often is referred to by its cylinder. A *cylinder* is the vertical section of a track that passes through all platters (Figure 7-9). A single movement of the read/write head arms accesses all the platters in a cylinder. If a hard disk has two platters

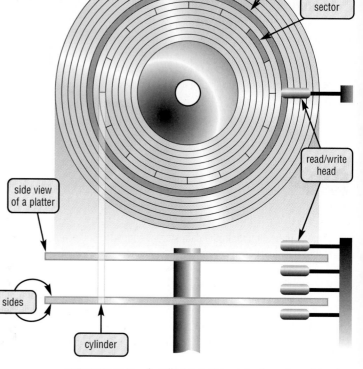

top view of a platter

track

sector

side view of a platter

read/write head

sides

cylinder

FIGURE 7-9 A cylinder is the vertical section of track through all platters on a hard disk.

FIGURE 7-8 HOW A HARD DISK WORKS

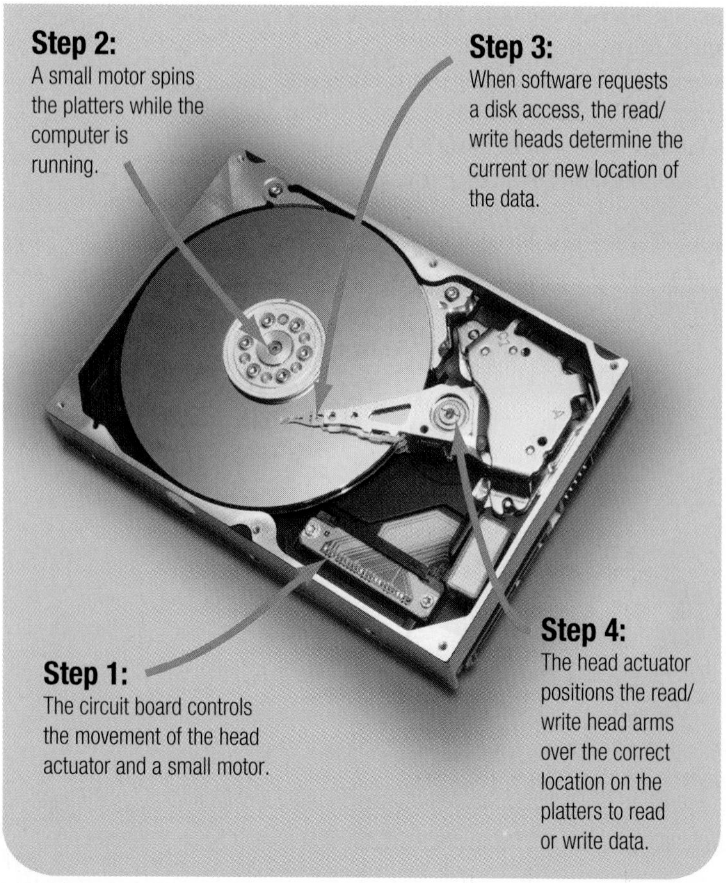

Step 2:
A small motor spins the platters while the computer is running.

Step 3:
When software requests a disk access, the read/write heads determine the current or new location of the data.

Step 1:
The circuit board controls the movement of the head actuator and a small motor.

Step 4:
The head actuator positions the read/write head arms over the correct location on the platters to read or write data.

(four sides), each with 1,000 tracks, then it will have 1,000 cylinders with each cylinder consisting of 4 tracks (2 tracks for each platter).

While the computer is running, the platters in the hard disk rotate at a high rate of speed. This spinning, which usually is 5,400 to 15,000 *revolutions per minute* (*rpm*), allows nearly instant access to all tracks and sectors on the platters. The platters typically continue to spin until power is removed from the computer. (On many computers, the hard disk stops spinning after a specified time to save power.) The spinning motion creates a cushion of air between the platter and its read/write head. This cushion ensures that the read/write head floats above the platter instead of making direct contact with the platter surface. The distance between the read/write head and the platter is about two millionths of one inch.

As shown in Figure 7-10, this close clearance leaves no room for any type of contamination. Dirt, hair, dust, smoke, and other particles could cause the hard disk to have a head crash. A *head crash* occurs when a read/write head touches the surface of a platter, usually resulting in a loss of

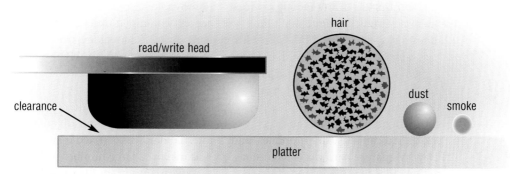

read/write head

hair

clearance

dust

smoke

platter

FIGURE 7-10   The clearance between a disk read/write head and the platter is about two millionths of an inch. A smoke particle, dust particle, human hair, or other contaminant could render the drive unusable.

data or sometimes loss of the entire drive. Although current internal hard disks are built to withstand shocks and are sealed tightly to keep out contaminants, head crashes do occasionally still occur. Thus, it is crucial that you back up your hard disk regularly. A **backup** is a duplicate of a file, program, or disk that you can use in case the original is lost, damaged, or destroyed. Chapter 8 discusses backup techniques.

Depending on the type of hard disk, transfer rates range from 15 MBps to 320 MBps. Access time for today's hard disks ranges from approximately 3 to 12 ms (milliseconds).

Hard disks improve their access time by using disk caching. *Disk cache* (pronounced cash), sometimes called a buffer, consists of a memory chip(s) on a hard disk that stores frequently accessed items such as data, instructions, and information (Figure 7-11). Disk cache and memory cache work in a similar fashion. When a processor requests data, instructions, or information from the hard disk, the hard disk first checks its disk cache — before moving any mechanical parts to access the platters. If the requested item is in disk cache, the hard disk sends it to the processor. If the hard disk does not find the requested item in the disk cache, then the processor must wait for the hard

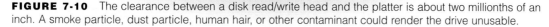

processor

Step 3: The controller transfers the requested item to the processor.

Step 2b: If the controller does not find the requested item in disk cache, it locates the requested item on the hard disk's platters.

Step 1: A special-purpose chip on the hard disk, called a controller, receives a request for data, instructions, or information from the processor.

disk cache

controller

Step 2a: The controller first checks disk cache for the requested item.

FIGURE 7-11   HOW DISK CACHE WORKS

disk to locate and transfer the item from the disk to the processor. Hard disks today contain between 2 MB and 16 MB of disk cache. The greater the disk cache, the faster the hard disk.

FAQ 7-2

How do manufacturers specify hard disk reliability?

Hardware manufacturers often specify a device's service life (expected useful life) and *MTBF* (mean time between failures), which is the total number of hours all devices were observed operating divided by the total number of failures that occurred. Although MTBF can be as high as 1.4 million hours for hard disks, many people rely on the service life estimate instead. For more information, visit scsite.com/dc2007/ch7/faq and then click MTBF.

FIGURE 7-12 This hard disk has a form factor of 0.85 inch and storage capacities up to 8 GB.

MINIATURE HARD DISKS Many mobile devices and consumer electronics include miniature hard disks, which provide users with greater storage capacities than flash memory. These tiny hard disks, some of which have form factors of less than one inch (Figure 7-12), are found in devices such as audio players, digital cameras, smart phones, and PDAs. Miniature hard disks have storage capacities that range from 2 GB to 120 GB. Miniature hard disks with greater storage capacities typically use perpendicular recording.

PORTABLE HARD DISKS Portable hard disks either are external or removable and have storage capacities up to 500 GB or higher.

An **external hard disk**, shown in the left picture in Figure 7-13, is a separate free-standing hard disk that connects with a cable to a USB port or FireWire port on the system unit. As with the internal hard disk, the entire hard disk is enclosed in an airtight, sealed case.

A **removable hard disk** is a hard disk that you insert and remove from either a dock or a drive. Sometimes the dock or drive is built in the system unit. Others are external devices that connect with a cable to a USB port or FireWire port on the system unit.

Removable hard disks that insert in a dock are self-contained units, similar to external hard disks. Removable hard disks that insert in a drive, shown in the right picture in Figure 7-13, read from and write on the removable hard disk.

External hard disks and removable hard disks offer the following advantages over internal hard disks (fixed disks):

- Transport a large number of files
- Back up important files or an entire internal hard disk (several external hard disk models allow you to back up simply by pushing a button on the disk)
- Easily store large audio and video files
- Secure your data; for example, at the end of a work session, remove the hard disk and lock it up, leaving no data in the computer
- Add storage space to a notebook computer or Tablet PC
- Add storage space to a desktop computer without having to open the system unit
- Share a drive with multiple computers

As the prices of portable hard disks drop, increasingly more users will purchase one to supplement a home or office internal hard disk. Keep in mind, though, that external or removable hard disks transfer data at slower rates than internal hard disks.

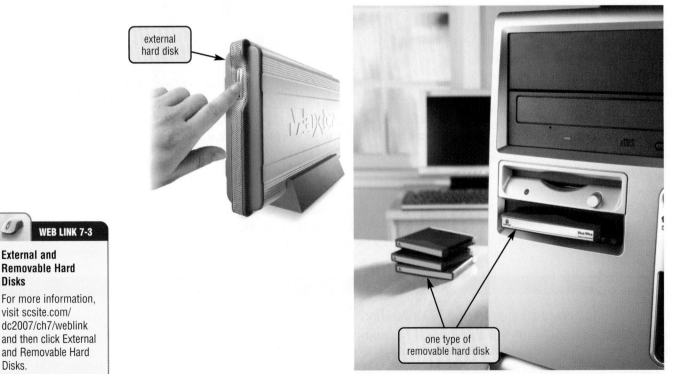

external hard disk

one type of removable hard disk

FIGURE 7-13 Examples of portable hard disks.

HARD DISK CONTROLLERS A *disk controller* consists of a special-purpose chip and electronic circuits that control the transfer of data, instructions, and information from a disk to and from the system bus and other components in the computer. That is, it controls the interface between the hard disk and the system bus. A disk controller for a hard disk, called the hard disk controller, may be part of a hard disk or the motherboard, or it may be a separate adapter card inside the system unit.

In their personal computer advertisements, vendors usually state the type of hard disk interface supported by the hard disk controller. Thus, you should understand the types of available hard disk interfaces. In addition to USB and FireWire (external hard disk interfaces), three other types of hard disk interfaces for internal use in personal computers are SATA, EIDE, and SCSI.

- *SATA* (*Serial Advanced Technology Attachment*), the newest type of hard disk interface, uses serial signals to transfer data, instructions, and information. The primary advantage of SATA interfaces is their cables are thinner, longer, more flexible, and less susceptible to interference than cables used by hard disks that use parallel signals. SATA interfaces have data transfer rates of up to 300 MBps. In addition to hard disks, SATA interfaces support connections to CD and DVD drives.
- *EIDE* (*Enhanced Integrated Drive Electronics*) is a hard disk interface that uses parallel signals to transfer data, instructions, and information. EIDE interfaces can support up to four hard disks at 137 GB per disk. These interfaces have data transfer rates up to 100 MBps. EIDE interfaces also provide connections for CD and DVD drives and tape drives. Some manufacturers market their EIDE interfaces as Fast ATA or Ultra ATA.
- *SCSI* interfaces, which also use parallel signals, can support up to eight or fifteen peripheral devices. Supported devices include hard disks, CD and DVD drives, tape drives, printers, scanners, network cards, and much more. Recall from Chapter 4 that SCSI is an acronym for Small Computer System Interface. Some computers have a built-in SCSI interface, while others use an adapter card to add a SCSI interface. SCSI interfaces provide up to 320 MBps data transfer rates.

MAINTAINING DATA STORED ON A HARD DISK Most manufacturers guarantee their hard disks to last approximately three to five years. Many last much longer with proper care. To prevent the loss of items stored on a hard disk, you regularly should perform preventive maintenance such as defragmenting or scanning the disk for errors. Chapter 8 discusses these and other utilities in depth.

ONLINE STORAGE Some users choose online storage instead of storing data locally on a hard disk. **Online storage** is a service on the Web that provides hard disk storage to computer users, usually for a minimal monthly fee (Figure 7-14). Fee arrangements for use of these Internet hard disks vary. For example, one online storage service charges $10 per month for 5 GB of storage. Many offer free trial periods.

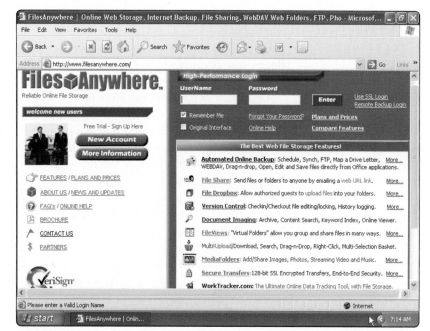

FIGURE 7-14 An example of one Web site advertising its online storage service.

Users subscribe to an online storage service for a variety of reasons:

- To access files on the Internet hard disk from any computer or device that has Internet access
- To store large audio, video, and graphics files on an Internet hard disk instantaneously, instead of spending time downloading to a local hard disk
- To allow others to access files on their Internet hard disk so others can listen to an audio file, watch a video clip, or view a picture — instead of e-mailing the file to them
- To view time-critical data and images immediately while away from the main office or location; for example, doctors can view x-ray images from another hospital, home, or office, or while on vacation
- To store offsite backups of data (Chapter 8 presents this and other backup strategies)

Once users subscribe to the online storage service, they can save on the Internet hard disk in the same manner they save on their local hard disk or any other drive.

Floppy Disks

A **floppy disk**, also called a *diskette*, is a portable, inexpensive storage medium that consists of a thin, circular, flexible plastic Mylar film with a magnetic coating enclosed in a square-shaped plastic shell. Although the exterior of current floppy disks is not bendable, users refer to this storage medium as a floppy disk because of the flexible film inside the rigid plastic 3.5-inch outer cover.

A standard floppy disk can store up to 500 double-spaced pages of text, several digital photographs, or a small audio file. Floppy disks are not as widely used as they were 15 years ago because of their low storage capacity. They are used, however, for specific applications. For example, some users work with floppy disks to transport small files to and from nonnetworked personal computers, such as from school or work to home.

A **floppy disk drive** is a device that reads from and writes on a floppy disk. A user

inserts a floppy disk in and removes it from a floppy disk drive. In the past, desktop personal computers and notebook computers had a floppy disk drive installed inside the system unit (Figure 7-15a). Most computers today do not include a floppy disk drive as standard equipment. On these computers, you can use an *external floppy disk drive*, in which the drive is a separate device with a cable that plugs in a port on the system unit (Figure 7-15b). These external drives are attached to the computer

FIGURE 7-15a (floppy disk drive installed inside a desktop computer)

FIGURE 7-15b (external floppy disk drive attached to computer with a cable)

FIGURE 7-15 Two types of floppy disk drives.

only when the user needs to access items on a floppy disk.

If a personal computer has one floppy disk drive, it is named drive A. To read from or write on a floppy disk, a floppy disk drive must support that floppy disk's density. *Density* is the number of bits in an area on a storage medium. A disk with a higher density has more bits in an area and thus has a larger storage capacity. Most standard floppy disks today are high density (*HD*).

The average time it takes a current floppy disk drive to locate an item on a disk (access time) is 84 milliseconds, or approximately 1/12 of a second. The transfer rates range from 250 to 500 KBps.

You can read from and write on a floppy disk any number of times. To protect a floppy disk from accidentally being erased, the plastic outer shell on the disk contains a write-protect notch in its corner. A **write-protect notch** is a small opening that has a tab you slide to cover or expose the notch. If the write-protect notch is open, the drive cannot write on the floppy disk. If the write-protect notch is covered, or closed, the drive can write on the floppy disk. A floppy disk drive can read from a floppy disk whether the write-protect notch is open or closed. On the opposite corner, some floppy disks have a second opening without a small tab. This opening identifies the disk as a high-density floppy disk.

A floppy disk is a type of magnetic media that stores data in tracks and sectors. A typical floppy disk stores data on both sides of the disk, has 80 tracks on each side of the recording surface, and has 18 sectors per track. To compute a disk's storage capacity, you multiply the number of sides on the disk, the number of tracks on the disk, the number of sectors per track, and the number of bytes in a sector. For example, the following is the formula for a high-density 3.5-inch floppy disk: 2 (sides) × 80 (tracks) × 18 (sectors per track) × 512 (bytes per sector) = 1,474,560 bytes. Disks often store system files in some tracks, which means the available capacity on a disk may be less than the total possible capacity.

Zip Disks

A **Zip disk** is a type of portable magnetic media that can store from 100 MB to 750 MB of data. The larger capacities make it easy to transport many files or large items such as graphics, audio, or video files. Another use of Zip disks is to back up important data and information.

Zip disks are slightly larger than and about twice as thick as a 3.5-inch floppy disk. A **Zip drive** is a high-capacity disk drive developed by Iomega Corporation that reads from and writes on a Zip disk (Figure 7-16). These drives cannot read standard 3.5-inch floppy disks.

Many users prefer to purchase an external Zip drive, which connects to a USB port or FireWire port on the system unit. The external Zip drive is convenient for users with multiple computers, because it allows them to move the drive from computer to computer as needed. As an alternative, some users prefer to order a computer with a built-in Zip drive.

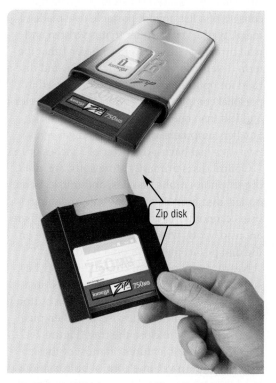

FIGURE 7-16 An external Zip drive and Zip disk.

Test your knowledge of pages 354 through 365 in Quiz Yourself 7-1.

QUIZ YOURSELF 7-1

Instructions: Find the true statement below. Then, rewrite the remaining false statements so they are true.

1. Miniature hard disks are a type of optical disc.

2. Hard disks contain one or more inflexible, circular platters that magnetically store data, instructions, and information.

3. SATA is a hard disk interface that uses parallel signals to transfer data, instructions, and information.

4. Storage media is the computer hardware that records and/or retrieves items to and from a storage device.

5. Three types of manual disks are hard disks, floppy disks, and Zip disks.

6. Users can move an internal Zip drive from computer to computer as needed by connecting the drive to a USB port or FireWire port on the system unit.

Quiz Yourself Online: To further check your knowledge of storage devices and storage media, hard disks, floppy disks, and Zip disks, visit scsite.com/dc2007/ch7/quiz and then click Objectives 1 – 4.

OPTICAL DISCS

An *optical disc* is a type of storage media that consists of a flat, round, portable disc made of metal, plastic, and lacquer that is written and read by a laser. (Recall from Chapter 1 that the term disk is used for magnetic media, and disc is used for optical media.) Optical discs used in personal computers are 4.75 inches in diameter and less than one-twentieth of an inch thick. Smaller computers and devices, however, use *mini discs* that have a diameter of 3 inches or less.

Optical discs primarily store software, data, digital photographs, movies, and music. Some optical disc formats are read only, meaning users cannot write (save) on the media. Others are read/write, which allows users to save on the disc just as they save on a hard disk.

Nearly every personal computer today has some type of optical disc drive installed in a drive bay. On these drives, you push a button to slide out a tray, insert the disc, and then push the same button to close the tray (Figure 7-17). Other convenient features on most of these drives include a volume control button and a headphone port (or jack) so you can use headphones to listen to audio without disturbing others nearby.

With some discs, you can read and/or write on one side only. Manufacturers usually place a silk-screened label on the top layer of these single-sided discs. You insert a single-sided disc in the drive with the label side up. Other discs are double-sided. Simply remove the disc from the drive, flip it over, and reinsert it in the drive

Push the button to slide out the tray.

Insert the disc, label side up.

Push the same button to close the tray.

FIGURE 7-17 On optical disc drives, you push a button to slide out a tray, insert the disc, and then push the same button to close the tray.

to use the other side of the disc. Double-sided discs often have no label; instead each side of the disc is identified with small writing around the center of the disc.

The drive designation of an optical disc drive usually follows alphabetically after that of all the hard disks and portable disks. For example, if the computer has one internal hard disk (drive C) and an external hard disk (drive D), then the first optical disc drive is drive E. A second optical disc drive would be drive F.

Optical discs store items by using microscopic pits (indentations) and lands (flat areas) that are in the middle layer of the disc (Figure 7-18). A high-powered laser light creates the pits. A lower-powered laser light reads items from the disc by reflecting light through the bottom of the disc, which usually is either solid gold or silver in color. The reflected light is converted into a series of bits the computer can process. A land causes light to reflect, which is read as binary digit 1. Pits absorb the light; this absence of light is read as binary digit 0.

Optical discs commonly store items in a single track that spirals from the center of the disc to the edge of the disc. As with a hard disk, this single track is divided into evenly sized sectors on which items are stored (Figure 7-19).

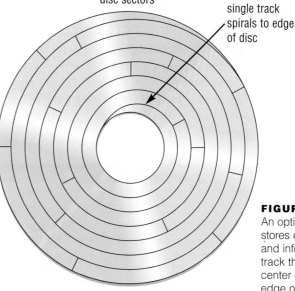

disc sectors

single track spirals to edge of disc

FIGURE 7-19
An optical disc typically stores data, instructions, and information in a single track that spirals from the center of the disc to the edge of a disc.

FIGURE 7-18 HOW A LASER READS DATA ON AN OPTICAL DISC

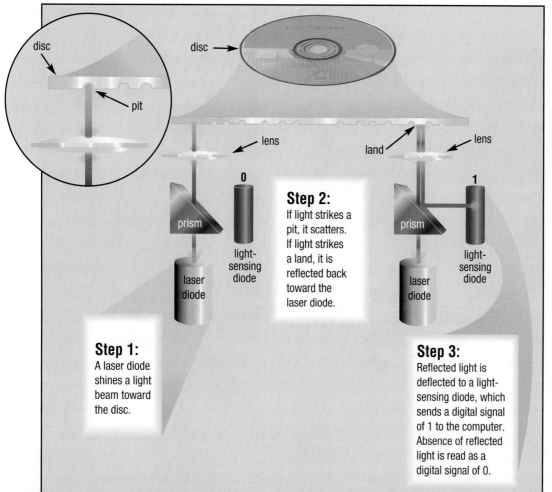

disc

disc

pit

lens

lens

land

0

1

Step 2:
If light strikes a pit, it scatters. If light strikes a land, it is reflected back toward the laser diode.

prism

prism

light-sensing diode

light-sensing diode

laser diode

laser diode

Step 1:
A laser diode shines a light beam toward the disc.

Step 3:
Reflected light is deflected to a light-sensing diode, which sends a digital signal of 1 to the computer. Absence of reflected light is read as a digital signal of 0.

Care of Optical Discs

Manufacturers claim that a properly cared for high-quality optical disc will last 5 years but could last up to 100 years. Figure 7-20 offers some guidelines for the proper care of optical discs. Never bend a disc; it may break. Do not expose discs to extreme temperatures or humidity. The ideal temperature range for disc storage is 50 to 70 degrees Fahrenheit. Stacking discs, touching the underside of discs, or exposing them to any type of contaminant may scratch a disc. Place an optical disc in its protective case, called a *jewel box*, when you are finished using it and store in an upright (vertical) position.

FAQ 7-4

Can I clean a disc?

Yes, you can remove dust, dirt, smudges, and fingerprints from the surface of an optical disc. Moisten a soft cloth with warm water or rubbing alcohol and then wipe the disc in straight lines from the center outward. You also can repair scratches on the surface with a specialized disc repair kit. For more information, visit scsite.com/dc2007/ch7/faq and then click Cleaning and Repairing Discs.

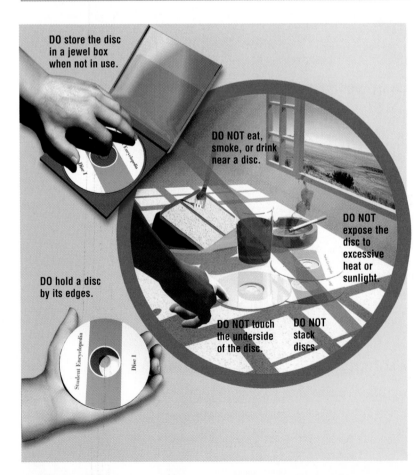

FIGURE 7-20   Some guidelines for the proper care of optical discs.

Types of Optical Discs

Many different formats of optical discs exist today. Two general categories are CDs and DVDs, with DVDs having a much greater storage capacity than CDs. Specific formats include CD-ROM, CD-R, CD-RW, DVD-ROM, DVD-R, DVD+R, DVD-RW, DVD+RW, and DVD+RAM. Figure 7-21 identifies each of these optical disc formats and specifies whether a user can read from the disc, write to the disc, and/or erase the disc. The following sections describe characteristics unique to each of these disc formats.

OPTICAL DISC FORMATS

Optical Disc	Read	Write	Erase
CD-ROM	Y	N	N
CD-R	Y	Y	N
CD-RW	Y	Y	Y
DVD-ROM	Y	N	N
DVD-R DVD+R	Y	Y	N
DVD-RW DVD+RW DVD+RAM	Y	Y	Y

FIGURE 7-21   Manufacturers sell CD-ROM and DVD-ROM media prerecorded (written) with audio, video, and software. Users cannot change the contents of these discs. Users, however, can purchase the other formats of CDs and DVDs as blank media and record (write) their own data, instructions, and information on these discs.

CD-ROMs

A **CD-ROM** (pronounced SEE-DEE-rom), or *compact disc read-only memory*, is a type of optical disc that users can read but not write (record) or erase — hence, the name read-only. Manufacturers write the contents of standard CD-ROMs. A standard CD-ROM is called a *single-session disc* because manufacturers write all items on the disc at one time. Software manufacturers often distribute their programs using CD-ROMs (Figure 7-22).

A typical CD-ROM holds from 650 MB to 1 GB of data, instructions, and information. To read a CD-ROM, insert the disc in a **CD-ROM drive** or a CD-ROM player. Because audio CDs and CD-ROMs use the same laser technology, you may be able to use a CD-ROM drive to listen to an audio CD while working on the computer. Some music companies, however, configure their CDs so the music will not play on a computer. They do this to protect themselves from customers illegally copying and sharing the music. Read Ethics & Issues 7-1 for a related discussion.

The speed of a CD-ROM drive determines how fast it installs programs and accesses the disc. Original CD-ROM drives were single-speed drives with transfer rates of 150 KBps (kilobytes per second). Manufacturers measure all optical disc drives relative to this original CD-ROM drive. They use an X to denote the original transfer rate of 150 KBps. For example, a 48X CD-ROM drive has a data transfer rate of 7,200 (48 × 150) KBps, or 7.2 MBps.

Current CD-ROM drives have transfer rates, or speeds, ranging from 48X to 75X or faster. The higher the number, the faster the CD-ROM drive. Faster CD-ROM drives are more expensive than slower drives.

WEB LINK 7-5

CD-ROMs

For more information, visit scsite.com/ dc2007/ch7/weblink and then click CD-ROMs.

ETHICS & ISSUES 7-1

Does Music Sharing Harm CD Sales?

With over a billion songs illegally available on file sharing networks, such as eDonkey, the music industry claims that sharing music is harming CD sales, which results in less money in the artists' pockets. A recent study by researchers at Harvard University and the University of North Carolina showed that the availability and sharing of recent CD releases did not have an effect on the sales of the CDs. The researchers found that those who obtained the music from the Internet were often the least likely to purchase the CDs in the first place. While music publishing companies have seen a modest decline in sales since the advent of music sharing, they have released significantly fewer titles, and some claim that the quality of music has declined. Also, CD sales may have been exceptionally high in the 1990s as people replaced older media, such as cassette tapes and vinyl albums, with the newer CD format. While clearly in violation of the music publishers' copyright, does music sharing harm CD sales? Why? Is it possible that music sharing actually results in higher sales for record companies in some cases? Why or why not? Are the music industry's complaints justified or are they being greedy? Why?

FIGURE 7-22 Encyclopedias, games, simulations, and many other programs are distributed on CD-ROM.

PICTURE CDs   A Kodak **Picture CD** is a single-session CD-ROM that stores digital versions of a single roll of film using a jpg file format. Many film developers offer Picture CD service for consumers when they drop off film to be developed. That is, in addition to printed photographs and negatives, you also receive a Picture CD containing the film's pictures. The resolution of images stored on a Picture CD usually is 1024 × 1536 pixels. The additional cost for a Picture CD is about $10 per roll of film.

Most optical disc drives can read a Picture CD. Using photo editing software and photographs on the Picture CD, you can remove red eye, crop the photograph, enhance colors, trim away edges, adjust the lighting, and edit just about any aspect of a photograph. In addition, a Picture CD allows you to print copies of the photographs on glossy paper with an ink-jet printer. If you do not have a printer to print the images, many stores have kiosks at which you can print pictures from a Picture CD or other media (Figure 7-23).

FAQ 7-5

How do I share my digital pictures with others?

You can send them as e-mail attachments, copy them to online storage, or post them to a personal Web page or a photo community. At a *photo community*, users can create online photo albums and share their digital photographs on the Web. Some photo communities provide free, unlimited storage space; others charge a nominal fee. For more information, visit scsite.com/dc2007/ch7/faq and then click Photo Communities.

FIGURE 7-23   HOW A PICTURE CD WORKS

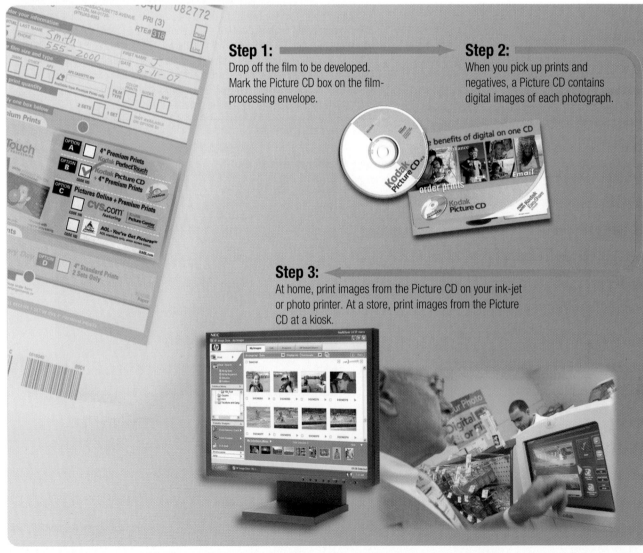

Step 1:
Drop off the film to be developed. Mark the Picture CD box on the film-processing envelope.

Step 2:
When you pick up prints and negatives, a Picture CD contains digital images of each photograph.

Step 3:
At home, print images from the Picture CD on your ink-jet or photo printer. At a store, print images from the Picture CD at a kiosk.

CD-Rs and CD-RWs

A **CD-R** (*compact disc-recordable*) is a multisession optical disc on which users can write, but not erase, their own items such as text, graphics, and audio. *Multisession* means you can write on part of the disc at one time and another part at a later time. Each part of a CD-R, however, can be written on only one time, and the disc's contents cannot be erased.

Writing on the CD-R requires a *CD recorder* or a **CD-R drive**. A CD-R drive usually can read both audio CDs and standard CD-ROMs. These drives read at speeds of 48X or more and write at speeds of 40X or more. Manufacturers often list the write speed first, for example, as 40/48.

A **CD-RW** (*compact disc-rewritable*) is an erasable multisession disc you can write on multiple times. CD-RW overcomes the major disadvantage of CD-R because it allows users to write and rewrite data, instructions, and information on the CD-RW disc multiple times — instead of just once. Reliability of the disc tends to drop, however, with each successive rewrite.

To write on a CD-RW disc, you must have CD-RW software and a **CD-RW drive**. These drives have write speeds of 52X or more, rewrite speeds of 24X or more, and read speeds of 52X or more. Manufacturers state the speeds in this order; that is, write speed, rewrite speed, and read speed is stated as 52/24/52. Most CD-RW drives can read audio CDs, CD-ROMs, CD-Rs, and CD-RWs.

Many personal computers today include a CD-RW drive as a standard feature so users can burn their own discs. The process of writing on an optical disc is called *burning*. Some operating systems, such as Windows XP, include the capability of burning discs.

Using a CD-RW disc, users easily back up large files from a hard disk. Another popular use of CD-RW and CD-R discs is to create audio CDs. For example, users can record their own music and save it on a CD, purchase and download MP3 songs from the Web, or rearrange tracks on a purchased music CD. The process of copying audio and/or video data from a purchased disc and saving it on digital media is called *ripping*. Read Ethics & Issues 7-2 for a related discussion.

WEB LINK 7-7

CD-Rs and CD-RWs
For more information, visit scsite.com/ dc2007/ch7/weblink and then click CD-Rs and CD-RWs.

 FAQ 7-6

Is it legal to copy songs or movies to a disc or other media?

It is legal to copy songs or movies from a disc that you obtained legally, if you use the copied music or movie for your own personal use. If you share the copy with a friend, however, you are violating copyright law. It is legal to download copyrighted material if the copyright holder has granted permission to do so. In most cases, you pay a fee. For more information, visit scsite.com/dc2007/ ch7/faq and then click Copying Songs and Movies.

ETHICS & ISSUES 7-2

Is It Ethical to Use Pirated CDs or DVDs?

Recently, several highly anticipated, big-budget movies were being watched in homes around the world — before the movies even were released to theaters. CD-R and DVD-R technology makes copying music and movies easy and affordable. People use CD-R and DVD-R technology to copy CDs and DVDs they have purchased, borrowed, or downloaded from the Internet. At some campuses, students use college servers to create music Web sites, download copyrighted music, and then record and distribute unauthorized copies. The recording industry claims this practice is unfair to the industry and, in essence, steals from the recording artists. Others, however, insist that bootlegged music actually is a marketing vehicle, influencing listeners who pay to attend concerts eventually to purchase the CD. The music industry has gone as far as placing technology on CDs that makes them impossible or very difficult to copy. Opponents to this practice say that these measures infringe on the CD owner's right to fair use, such as making personal backup copies, which courts have upheld as exceptions to copyright laws. Is it ethical to download and copy portions of a music CD, or an entire music CD, from the Internet? Why? If you purchase a CD, is it ethical to make copies for yourself? For a friend? Why? Should recording or movie companies be able to use formatting techniques to keep people from copying CDs or DVDs? What practices should be allowed within the doctrine of fair use?

DVD-ROMs

A **DVD-ROM** (*digital versatile disc-read-only memory* or *digital video disc-read-only memory*) is an extremely high-capacity optical disc on which users can read but not write or erase. Manufacturers write the contents of DVD-ROMs and distribute them to consumers. DVD-ROMs store movies, music, music videos, huge databases, and complex software (Figure 7-24).

The storage capacity of a DVD-ROM is more than enough to hold a telephone book containing every resident in the United States. Not only is the storage capacity of a DVD-ROM greater than that of a CD, a DVD-ROM's quality also far surpasses that of CDs because images are stored at higher resolution.

To read a DVD-ROM, you must have a **DVD-ROM drive** or DVD player. Most DVD-ROM drives also can read audio CDs, CD-ROMs, CD-Rs, and CD-RWs. DVD-ROM drives can read DVDs at speeds of 16X or more and CDs at speeds of 52X or more.

Although the size and shape of a CD-ROM and DVD-ROM are similar, a DVD-ROM stores data, instructions, and information in a slightly different manner and thus achieves a higher storage capacity. Widely used DVD-ROMs are capable of storing 4.7 GB to 17 GB, depending on the storage techniques used (Figure 7-25). The first storage technique involves making the disc denser by packing the pits closer together. The second involves using two layers of pits. For this technique to work, the lower layer of pits is semi-transparent so the laser can read through it to the upper layer. This technique doubles the capacity of the disc. Finally, some DVD-ROMs are double-sided. Two newer, quite expensive competing DVD formats are Blu-ray and HD-DVD. A *Blu-ray disc* currently has storage capacities of 27 GB, with expectations of exceeding 100 GB in the future. The *HD-DVD disc*, which stands for high-density-DVD, has storage capacities up to 45 GB. Read Looking Ahead 7-2 for a look at the competing HD-DVD and Blu-ray technologies.

A mini-DVD that has grown in popularity is the UMD, which works specifically with the PlayStation Portable handheld game console. The *UMD* (Universal Media Disc), which has a diameter of about 2.4 inches, can store up to 1.8 GB of games, movies, or music (Figure 7-26).

FAQ 7-7

What is a DVD/CD-RW drive?

It is a combination drive that reads DVD and CD media; it also writes to CD-RW media. This drive allows you to watch a DVD or burn a CD. For more information, visit scsite.com/dc2007/ch7/faq and then click DVD/CD-RW Drives.

DVD-ROM STORAGE CAPACITIES

Sides	Layers	Storage Capacity
1	1	4.7 GB
1	2	8.5 GB
2	1	9.4 GB
2	2	17 GB

FIGURE 7-25 Storage capacities of DVD-ROMs.

FIGURE 7-26 This UMD contains the movie, *Spider-Man 2*.

DVD

DVD drive

FIGURE 7-24 A DVD-ROM is an extremely high-capacity optical disc.

LOOKING AHEAD 7-2

Next-Generation DVDs a Burning Question

Two incompatible recording formats are battling for supremacy in the next generation of high-definition video discs. Traditional DVD backers, including Time-Warner, Toshiba, Intel, Microsoft, and NEC, are supporting the HD-DVD format, while several consumer electronics and high-tech companies, such as Sony, Philips, and Matsushita, are favoring Blu-ray. The major movie studios have split their support between the two technologies.

Both formats offer superior picture quality, a feature that will become increasingly important as consumers purchase more high-definition television products. Compared to the HD-DVD discs, Blu-ray discs will cost more to manufacture, but they will hold more data. The format rivalry is affecting the multibillion dollar market for DVD players, personal computer drivers, and optical discs. For more information, visit scsite.com/dc2007/ch7/looking and then click DVD Formats.

Recordable and Rewritable DVDs

Many types of recordable and rewritable DVD formats are available. *DVD-R* and *DVD+R* are competing DVD-recordable formats, each with up to 4.7 GB storage capacity. Both allow users to write on the disc once and read (play) it many times. In concept, DVD-R and DVD+R are similar to CD-R.

Instead of recordable DVDs, however, most users work with rewritable DVDs because these discs can be written on multiple times and also erased. Three competing rewritable DVD formats exist, each with storage capacities up to 4.7 GB per side: **DVD-RW**, **DVD+RW**, and **DVD+RAM**. These rewritable DVDs are similar in concept to CD-RW. With DVD-RW and DVD+RW discs, a user can erase and write (record) more than 1,000 times. To write on these discs, you must have a DVD-RW drive, a DVD+RW drive, or a DVD recorder. DVD-RW and DVD+RW drives have rewrite speeds of 12X or more, and read speeds of 40X or more. The drives usually can read DVD-ROM, DVD-R, DVD+R, and all CD media, and they can write on DVD-RW or DVD+RW, DVD-R, CD-R, and CD-RW media.

DVD+RAM (DVD+random access memory) allows users to erase and record on a DVD+RAM disc more than 100,000 times. These discs can be read by DVD+RAM drives and some DVD-ROM drives and players.

As the cost of DVD technologies becomes more reasonable, many industry professionals expect that DVD eventually will replace all CD media.

FAQ 7-8

Do any digital video cameras record movies on DVD?

Yes. Video cameras that store at least 120 minutes of recording on mini-DVD-RW/CD-RW media are available. Once recorded, users can view the DVD media in a standard computer DVD drive or a DVD player. Many video cameras include the capability of editing the video right in the camera. For more information, visit scsite.com/dc2007/ch7/faq and then click DVD Video Recorders.

WEB LINK 7-8

DVDs

For more information, visit scsite.com/dc2007/ch7/weblink and then click DVDs.

Test your knowledge of pages 366 through 373 in Quiz Yourself 7-2.

QUIZ YOURSELF 7-2

Instructions: Find the true statement below. Then, rewrite the remaining false statements so they are true.

1. A CD-RW is a type of optical disc on which users can read but not write (record) or erase.

2. A DVD-RAM is a single-session disc that stores digital versions of a single roll of film using a jpg file format.

3. DVDs have the same storage capacities as CDs.

4. Optical discs are written and read by mirrors.

5. Single session means you can write on part of the disc at one time and another part at a later time.

6. Three competing rewritable DVD formats are DVD-RW, DVD+RW, and DVD+RAM.

Quiz Yourself Online: To further check your knowledge of optical discs and various optical disc formats, visit scsite.com/dc2007/ch7/quiz and then click Objectives 5 – 6.

TAPE

One of the first storage media used with mainframe computers was tape. **Tape** is a magnetically coated ribbon of plastic capable of storing large amounts of data and information at a low cost. Tape no longer is used as a primary method of storage. Instead, business and home users utilize tape most often for long-term storage and backup.

Comparable to a tape recorder, a **tape drive** reads and writes data and information on a tape. Although older computers used reel-to-reel tape drives, today's tape drives use tape cartridges. A *tape cartridge* is a small, rectangular, plastic housing for tape (Figure 7-27). Tape cartridges that contain quarter-inch-wide tape are slightly larger than audiocassette tapes. Business and home users sometimes back up personal computer hard disks to tape. Transfer rates of tape drives range from 1.25 MBps to 6 MBps.

Some personal computers have external tape units. Others have the tape drive built into the system unit. On larger computers, tape cartridges are mounted in a separate cabinet called a *tape library*.

Tape storage requires *sequential access*, which refers to reading or writing data consecutively. As with a music tape, you must forward or rewind the tape to a specific point to access a specific piece of data. For example, to access item W requires passing through points A through V sequentially.

Hard disks, CDs, and DVDs all use direct access. *Direct access*, also called *random access*, means that the device can locate a particular data item or file immediately, without having to move consecutively through items stored in front of the desired data item or file. When writing or reading specific data, direct access is much faster than sequential access.

PC CARDS

As discussed in Chapter 4, a **PC Card** is a thin, credit-card-sized device that fits into a PC Card slot. Different types and sizes of PC Cards add storage, additional memory, fax/modem, networking, sound, and other capabilities to a desktop or notebook computer. PC Cards commonly are used in notebook computers (Figure 7-28).

Originally, PC Cards were called PCMCIA cards. Three kinds of PC Cards are available: Type I, Type II, and Type III (Figure 7-29). The only difference in size among the three types is their thickness. Some digital cameras use a Type II or Type III PC Card to store photographs. PC Cards that house a hard disk have storage capacities up to 5 GB. The advantage of a PC Card for storage is portability. You easily can transport large amounts of data, instructions, and information from one computer to another using a Type II or Type III PC Card.

FIGURE 7-28 A PC Card in a notebook computer.

PC CARDS

Category	Thickness	Use
Type I	3.3 mm	RAM, SRAM, flash memory
Type II	5.0 mm	Modem, LAN, SCSI, sound, TV tuner, hard disk, or other storage
Type III	10.5 mm	Rotating storage such as a hard disk

FIGURE 7-29 Various uses of PC Cards.

FIGURE 7-27 A tape drive and a tape cartridge.

MINIATURE MOBILE STORAGE MEDIA

Miniature mobile storage media allow mobile users easily to transport digital images, music, or documents to and from computers and other devices (Figure 7-30). Many desktop computers, notebook computers, Tablet PCs, PDAs, smart phones, digital cameras, and audio players have built-in slots or ports to read from and write on miniature mobile storage media. For computers or devices without built-in slots, users insert the media in separate peripherals such as a card reader/writer, which typically plugs in a USB port, or a device such as a *digital photo viewer*, which connects to a television port for on-screen picture viewing. The following sections discuss the widely used miniature storage media: flash memory cards, USB flash drives, and smart cards.

FIGURE 7-30 Many types of computers and devices use miniature mobile storage media.

Flash Memory Cards

Previously, this chapter discussed miniature hard disks (magnetic media) and mini discs such as the UMD (optical media). Flash memory cards, by contrast, are a type of *solid-state media*, which means they consist entirely of electronic components and contain no moving parts. Common types of flash memory cards include *CompactFlash (CF)*, *SmartMedia*, *Secure Digital (SD)*, *xD Picture Card*, and *Memory Stick*. The table in Figure 7-31 compares storage capacities and uses of these media.

Depending on the device, manufacturers claim miniature mobile storage media can last from 10 to 100 years. Transfer rates range from about 1 MBps to 10 MBps or more, depending on the device. Flash memory cards are quite expensive compared to other storage media.

For example, the cost of a 4 GB CompactFlash card is the same as a 120 GB hard disk.

To view, edit, or print images and information stored on miniature mobile storage media, you transfer the contents to your desktop computer or other device such as a digital photo viewer. Some printers have slots to read PC Cards and flash memory cards. If your computer or printer does not have a built-in slot, you can purchase a *card reader/writer*, which is a device that reads and writes data, instructions, and information stored on PC Cards or flash memory cards. Card reader/writers usually connect to the USB port, FireWire port, or parallel port on the system unit. The type of card you have will determine the type of card reader/writer needed. Figure 7-32 shows how one type of flash memory card works with a card reader/writer.

VARIOUS FLASH MEMORY CARDS

Media Name	Storage Capacity	Use
CompactFlash 	64 MB to 8 GB	Digital cameras, PDAs, smart phones, photo printers, audio players, notebook computers, desktop computers
SmartMedia 	32 MB to 128 MB	Digital cameras, photo printers, audio players
Secure Digital 	64 MB to 1 GB	Digital cameras, digital video cameras, PDAs, smart phones, photo printers, audio players
xD Picture Card 	64 MB to 1 GB	Digital cameras, photo printers
Memory Stick 	256 MB to 4 GB	Digital cameras, digital video cameras, PDAs, photo printers, smart phones, handheld game consoles, notebook computers

FIGURE 7-31 A variety of flash memory cards.

FIGURE 7-32   HOW ONE TYPE OF FLASH MEMORY CARD WORKS

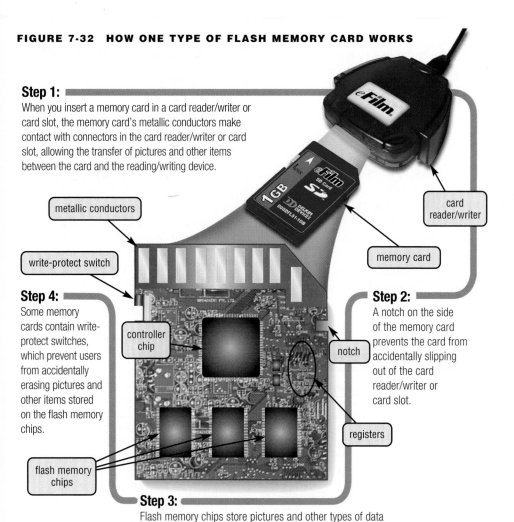

Step 1:
When you insert a memory card in a card reader/writer or card slot, the memory card's metallic conductors make contact with connectors in the card reader/writer or card slot, allowing the transfer of pictures and other items between the card and the reading/writing device.

metallic conductors

write-protect switch

Step 4:
Some memory cards contain write-protect switches, which prevent users from accidentally erasing pictures and other items stored on the flash memory chips.

controller chip

flash memory chips

card reader/writer

memory card

notch

Step 2:
A notch on the side of the memory card prevents the card from accidentally slipping out of the card reader/writer or card slot.

registers

Step 3:
Flash memory chips store pictures and other types of data and information. When requested, the controller transfers items stored on the flash memory chips to the metallic conductors, using registers for temporary storage, as needed.

USB Flash Drives

A **USB flash drive**, sometimes called a *pen drive*, is a flash memory storage device that plugs in a USB port on a computer or mobile device (Figure 7-33). USB flash drives are convenient for mobile users because they are small and lightweight enough to be transported on a keychain or in a pocket. With a USB flash drive, users easily transfer documents, pictures, music, and videos from one computer to another. Current USB flash drives have data transfer rates of about 12 MBps and storage capacities up to 4 GB.

USB flash drives have become the mobile user's primary portable storage device, making the floppy disk nearly obsolete because they have much greater storage capacities and are much more convenient to carry.

FIGURE 7-33   A USB flash drive.

Smart Cards

A **smart card**, which is similar in size to a credit card or ATM card, stores data on a thin microprocessor embedded in the card. Smart cards contain a processor and have input, process, output, and storage capabilities. When you insert the smart card in a specialized card reader, the information on the smart card is read and, if necessary, updated (Figure 7-34).

Uses of smart cards include storing medical records, vaccination data, and other health-care and identification information; tracking information such as customer purchases or employee attendance; storing a prepaid amount of money; and authenticating users such as for Internet purchases. Read Ethics & Issues 7-3 for a related discussion.

FAQ 7-9

Are some credit cards smart cards?

Yes. More than 60 million people around the world have a smart Visa card, which contains a microchip filled with their personal information. Credit card smart cards offer the consumer the convenience of using the card to make purchases in stores and online. For more information, visit scsite.com/dc2007/ch7/faq and then click Credit Card Smart Cards.

ETHICS & ISSUES 7-3

Should the World Become a Cashless Society?

Do you toss your loose change in a jar with the hopes of making a special purchase with the savings someday? Futurists predict that this practice may one day go the way of making purchases with silver and gold. Some forecasters say that the world is moving toward a cashless society. One form of payment that could end the need for cash is the smart card, which can store a dollar amount on a thin microprocessor and update the amount whenever a transaction is made. Advocates claim that smart cards would eliminate muggings and robberies, make it difficult to purchase illegal goods, and reduce taxes by identifying tax cheats. Smart cards already are common in Europe, but many Americans cite privacy concerns as reasons to avoid them. Several high-profile security breaches at credit reporting and credit card companies have heightened these concerns. In a recent survey, most Americans said that they would not use a smart card even if privacy was guaranteed. A cash purchase usually is anonymous. Yet, a smart card purchase preserves a record of the transaction that could become available to other merchants, advertisers, government agencies, or hackers. Considering the advantages and disadvantages, should the world become a cashless society? Why or why not? Would you be comfortable using a smart card instead of cash for all transactions? Why?

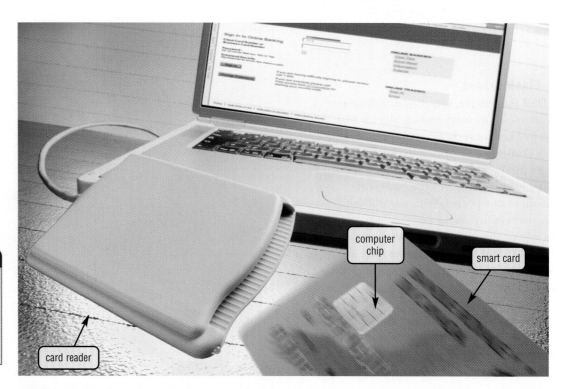

computer chip

smart card

card reader

FIGURE 7-34 A smart card and smart card reader.

MICROFILM AND MICROFICHE

Microfilm and microfiche store microscopic images of documents on roll or sheet film. **Microfilm** is a 100- to 215-foot roll of film. **Microfiche** is a small sheet of film, usually about 4 × 6 inches. A *computer output microfilm recorder* is the device that records the images on the film. The stored images are so small that you can read them only with a microfilm or microfiche reader (Figure 7-35).

Applications of microfilm and microfiche are widespread. Libraries use these media to store back issues of newspapers, magazines, and genealogy records. Some large organizations use microfilm and microfiche to archive inactive files. Some banks use them to store transactions and canceled checks. The U.S. Army uses them to store personnel records.

The use of microfilm and microfiche provides a number of advantages. They greatly reduce the amount of paper firms must handle. They are inexpensive and have the longest life of any storage media (Figure 7-36).

ENTERPRISE STORAGE

A large business, commonly referred to as an enterprise, has hundreds or thousands of employees in offices across the country or around the world. Enterprises use computers and computer networks to manage and store huge volumes of data and information about customers, suppliers, and employees (Figure 7-37).

To meet their large-scale needs, enterprises use special hardware geared for heavy use, maximum availability, and maximum efficiency. One or more servers on the network have the sole purpose of providing storage to connected users. For high-speed storage access, entire networks are dedicated exclusively to connecting devices that provide storage to other servers. In an enterprise, some storage systems can provide more than 185 terabytes (trillion bytes) of storage capacity. CD-ROM servers and DVD-ROM servers hold hundreds of CD-ROMs or DVD-ROMs.

An enterprise's storage needs usually grow daily. Thus, the storage solutions an enterprise chooses must be able to store its data and information requirements today and tomorrow.

FIGURE 7-35 Images on microfilm can be read only with a microfilm reader.

MEDIA LIFE EXPECTANCIES* (when using high-quality media)

Media Type	Guaranteed Life Expectancy	Potential Life Expectancy
Magnetic disks	3 to 5 years	20 to 30 years
Optical discs	5 to 10 years	50 to 100 years
Microfilm	100 years	500 years

* according to manufacturers of the media

FIGURE 7-36 Microfilm is the medium with the longest life.

FIGURE 7-37 An enterprise uses computers and high-capacity storage devices.

PUTTING IT ALL TOGETHER

Many factors influence the type of storage devices you should use: the amount of data, instructions, and information to be stored; the hardware and software in use; and the desired cost. The table in Figure 7-38 outlines several suggested storage devices for various types of computer users.

CATEGORIES OF USERS

User	Typical Storage Devices
HOME 	• 160 GB hard disk • Online storage • CD or DVD drive • Card reader/writer • USB flash drive
SMALL OFFICE/ HOME OFFICE 	• 250 GB hard disk • Online storage • CD or DVD drive • External hard disk for backup • USB flash drive
MOBILE 	• 100 GB hard disk • Online storage • CD or DVD drive • Card reader/writer • Portable hard disk for backup • USB flash drive and/or 5 GB PC Card hard disk
POWER 	• CD or DVD drive • 500 GB hard disk • Online storage • Portable hard disk for backup • USB flash drive
LARGE BUSINESS 	• Desktop Computer - 250 GB hard disk - CD or DVD drive - Smart card reader - Tape drive - USB flash drive • Server or Mainframe - Network storage server - 40 TB hard disk system - CD-ROM or DVD-ROM server - Microfilm or microfiche

FIGURE 7-38 Recommended storage devices for various users.

Test your knowledge of pages 374 through 380 in Quiz Yourself 7-3.

QUIZ YOURSELF 7-3

Instructions: Find the true statement below. Then, rewrite the remaining false statements so they are true.

1. A smart card stores data on a thin magnetic stripe embedded in the card.

2. A USB flash drive is a flash memory storage device that plugs in a parallel port on a computer or mobile device.

3. Flash memory cards are a type of magnetic media, which means they consist entirely of electronic components and contain no moving parts.

4. Microfilm and microfiche have the shortest life of any storage media.

5. Tape storage requires direct access, which refers to reading or writing data consecutively.

6. The only difference in size among Type I, Type II, and Type III PC Cards is their thickness.

Quiz Yourself Online: To further check your knowledge of tape, PC Cards, miniature mobile storage media, and microfilm and microfiche, visit scsite.com/dc2007/ch7/quiz and then click Objectives 7 – 9.

CHAPTER SUMMARY

Storage holds data, instructions, and information, which includes pictures, music, and videos, for future use. Users depend on storage devices to provide access to their storage media for years and decades to come. Read Ethics & Issues 7-4 for a discussion about the future of storage.

This chapter identified and discussed various storage media and storage devices. Storage media covered included internal hard disks, portable hard disks, floppy disks, Zip disks, CD-ROMs, recordable CDs, rewritable CDs, DVD-ROMs, recordable DVDs, rewritable DVDs, tape, PC Cards, flash memory cards, USB flash drives, smart cards, and microfilm and microfiche.

ETHICS & ISSUES 7-4

Who Should Be Looking at Your Medical Records?

A medical transcriber based in Pakistan and hired by a U.S. medical center threatened to post private medical records to the Internet if she was not paid more. With the widespread use of computers and an explosion in data storage capacity around the world, private information, such as medical records, requires increased diligence by companies, governments, and individuals to maintain this privacy. The government would like most Americans' health care records available in electronic format by 2014. Updates to the Health Insurance Portability and Accountability Act (HIPAA) effective in 2003 set rigorous standards for medical record privacy. The law, however, still leaves much of your medical information at risk. The law does not cover financial records, education records, or employment records — each of which may contain medical information about you. Your medical information also may be examined by insurance companies, government agencies, the Medical Information Bureau (MIB), employers, and the courts. You also inadvertently may pass on medical information to direct marketers when you participate in informal health screenings or surveys. Some people have found that discussing medical conditions via Internet chat rooms or newsgroups has resulted in unwanted attention, and they later regret the disclosures. Proponents of greater electronic access to medical records claim that more access means that physicians can be better prepared when they see patients, physicians will make fewer errors, and insurance companies can better root out fraud. Should more limits be placed on what other people can do with your medical information? Why or why not? What are the advantages of increased access to medical records? What are the disadvantages?

CAREER CORNER

Computer Technician

The demand for computer technicians is growing in every organization and industry. For many, this is the entry point for a career in the computer/information technology field. The responsibilities of a *computer technician*, also called a computer service technician, include a variety of duties. Most companies that employ someone with this title expect the technician to have basic across-the-board knowledge of concepts in the computer electronics field. Some of the tasks are hardware repair and installation; software installation, upgrade, and configuration; and troubleshooting client and/or server problems. Because the computer field is changing rapidly, technicians must work to remain abreast of current technology and become aware of future developments. Computer technicians generally work with a variety of users, which requires expert people skills, especially the ability to work with groups of nontechnical users.

Most entry-level computer technicians possess the *A+ certification*. This certification attests that a computer technician has demonstrated knowledge of core hardware and operating system technology including installation, configuration, diagnosing, preventive maintenance and basic networking that meets industry standards and has at least six months of experience in the field. The Electronics Technicians Association also provides a Computer Service Technician (CST) certification program.

Because this is an entry-level position, the pay scale is not as high as other more demanding and skilled positions. Individuals can expect an average annual starting salary of around $34,000 to $44,000. Companies pay more for computer technicians with experience and certification. For more information, visit scsite.com/dc2007/ch7/careers and then click Computer Technician.

High-Tech Talk

DISK FORMATTING AND FILE SYSTEMS

Formatting a disk can be compared to starting a library. Before any books can be put in place, you must install the bookshelves and a catalog system. Similarly, a disk must have a file system set up to make it ready to receive data. This is true of many different storage media — including floppy disks, hard disks, removable hard disks, and CDs and DVDs — all of which must be formatted, to allow a way to organize and find files saved on the disk.

This discussion focuses on the formatting process required to take a hard disk from its newly manufactured state to a fully functional storage medium. Three main steps are involved in the process of formatting a hard disk: (1) low-level (physical) formatting, (2) partitioning, and (3) high-level (logical) formatting.

A hard disk must be formatted physically before it can be formatted logically. The hard disk manufacturer usually performs a hard disk's physical formatting, or *low-level formatting*. A hard drive physically formats a hard disk by writing a pattern of 1s and 0s on the surface of the disk. The 1s and 0s act as small electronic markers, which divide the hard disk platter into its basic physical elements: tracks, sectors, and cylinders.

These elements define the way data is written on and read from the disk physically. As the read/write head moves over the spinning disks, it reads the electronic markers that define the tracks, sectors, and cylinders to determine where it is in relation to the data on the disk's surface.

Once a hard disk has been formatted physically, it can be partitioned. *Partitioning* is the process of dividing the hard disk into regions called partitions. Each partition occupies a group of adjacent cylinders. Partitioning allows you to organize a hard disk into segments and lets you run multiple operating systems on a single computer. You also can keep the entire hard disk as one partition. After a disk partition has been formatted, it is referred to as a *volume*.

After a hard disk has been formatted physically and partitioned, it must be formatted logically. Logical formatting, known as *high-level formatting*, places a file system on the disk. A *file system* allows an operating system to use the space available on a hard disk to store and retrieve files. The operating system uses the file system to store information about the disk's directory, or folder, structure.

The file system also defines the size of the clusters used to store data on the hard disk. A cluster, or *block*, is made up of two or more sectors on a single track on a hard disk. Even if a file has a size of 1 byte, a cluster as large as 64 KB might be used to store the file on large drives. The number of sectors and tracks and, therefore, the number of clusters that a drive can create on a disk's surface determine the capacity of the disk.

While creating the file system during logical formatting, the drive creates a special table in the disk's first sector, sector 0. This table stores entries that the operating system uses to locate files on a disk. Each entry in the table takes up a certain number of bits, which is why file systems often are referred to as 12-bit, 16-bit, or 32-bit. The content of each entry consists of a whole number, which identifies one or more clusters where the file is stored.

Depending on the operating system used to format the disk, the file system can be one of several types, as shown in the table in Figure 7-39. Whatever file system is used, the file system is the interface between the operating system and drives. For more information, visit scsite.com/dc2007/ch7/tech and then click Disk Formatting.

File System	Description	Key Features
FAT (also called FAT12 and FAT16)	The standard file system for DOS and Windows. Because of its widespread use, FAT also is accessible by most other operating systems.	• FAT12 is used for floppy disk drives and very small hard disks (up to 16 MB) • FAT16 is used for small to moderate-sized hard disk volumes (up to 2 GB)
VFAT (Virtual FAT)	A newer protected-mode version of the FAT file system, introduced with Windows 95.	• Supports long file names up to 255 characters • Faster than FAT because the computer can read files at least 32 bits at a time
FAT32	A 32-bit version of FAT, introduced with Windows 95.	• Same key features as VFAT • Used for medium-sized to very large hard disk volumes (up to 2 terabytes)
NTFS (NT File System)	The 32-bit file system currently used for Windows NT, Windows 2000, and Windows XP.	• 32- or 64-bit entries in file system table • Fully recoverable file system, designed to restore consistency after a system crash • Used for medium-sized to very large hard disk volumes (up to 16 billion GB)
WinFS (Windows Future Storage)	The file storage subsystem that can be used with Windows XP and Windows Vista.	• Uses database technology; allows users to query for data items • Instead of representing a file with a single name, will represent individual domain objects such as e-mail messages or address book entries

FIGURE 7-39 Comparison of various file systems.

Companies on the Cutting Edge

MAXTOR
INFORMATION STORAGE SUPPLIER

Consumers understand the need to back up their data, but fewer than 25 percent of computer users back up their data on a weekly basis. Hard-disk manufacturer *Maxtor* has been persuading people to save copies of their important documents so they will suffer less data loss in the event of a fire or natural disaster.

Maxtor is a leading manufacturer of hard disks and storage solutions for desktop computers, high-performance servers, and consumer electronics, including digital video recorders and game consoles. Its wholly owned subsidiary, MMC Technology, manufactures nearly 50 million disks each year.

Maxtor launched its Backup Awareness campaign in 2005 to educate consumers about the critical need to protect their data. For more information, visit scsite.com/dc2007/ch7/companies and then click Maxtor.

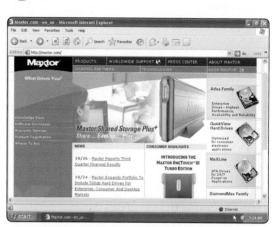

SANDISK CORPORATION
WORLD'S LARGEST FLASH MEMORY CARD SUPPLIER

The next time you buy milk at the grocery store or shampoo at the drug store, you might want to purchase a flash memory card for your digital camera, too. *SanDisk Corporation* products can be found in more than 100,000 retail stores across the United States, including Rite Aid and Kmart.

With retail sales of flash memory cards soaring, SanDisk executives believe consumers buy multiple flash memory cards to store their digital photographs in much the same manner as they formerly stored film negatives in shoe boxes. They also prefer to take a separate flash memory card to digital photo processing centers, which produce high-quality prints.

SanDisk is the only company with the rights to manufacture and sell every flash card format. For more information, visit scsite.com/dc2007/ch7/companies and then click SanDisk.

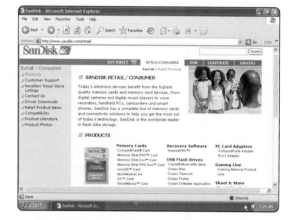

Technology Trailblazers

AL SHUGART
STORAGE EXPERT

Al Shugart enjoys fixing broken items and developing new technology. The day after receiving his bachelor's degree in 1951, he went to work at IBM to repair broken machines. IBM then promoted him to supervisor of the product development team that developed the first removable rigid read/write disk drive.

He left IBM in 1969 and went to work as vice president of product development for Memorex. In 1973, he started Shugart Associates, a pioneer in the manufacture of floppy disks. Six years later, he and some associates founded Seagate Technology, Inc., which is a leader in designing and manufacturing storage products.

Today he serves as president and CEO of Al Shugart International, a venture capital firm in California. For more information, visit scsite.com/dc2007/ch7/people and then click Al Shugart.

MARK DEAN
IBM INVENTOR

The next generation of IBM's hardware and software might be the work of *Mark Dean*. As vice president of IBM's Almaden Research Center lab in California, Dean is responsible for developing innovative products.

His designs are used in more than 40 million personal computers manufactured each year. He has more than 40 patents or patents pending, including four of the original seven for the architecture of the original personal computer.

Dean joined IBM in 1979 after graduating at the top of his class at the University of Tennessee. Dean earned his Ph.D. degree at Stanford, and he headed a team at IBM that invented the first CMOS microprocessor to operate at 1 gigahertz (1,000 MHz). For more information, visit scsite.com/dc2007/ch7/people and then click Mark Dean.

Chapter Review

The Chapter Review section summarizes the concepts presented in this chapter. To listen to the audio version of this Chapter Review, visit scsite.com/dc2007/ch7/review. To obtain help from other students regarding any subject in this chapter, visit scsite.com/dc2007/ch7/forum and post your thoughts or questions.

(1) **How Are Storage Devices Different from Storage Media?** A **storage medium** (media is the plural) is the physical material on which a computer keeps data, instructions, and information, which includes pictures, music, and videos. The number of bytes (characters) a storage medium can hold is its **capacity**. A **storage device** is the computer hardware that records and/or retrieves items to and from storage media. **Writing** is the process of transferring items from memory to a storage medium, and **reading** is the process of transferring these items from a storage medium into memory.

(2) **What Are the Characteristics of Magnetic Disks?** *Magnetic disks* use magnetic particles to store data, instructions, and information on a disk's surface. Before any data can be read from or written on a magnetic disk, the disk must be formatted. **Formatting** is the process of dividing the disk into *tracks* and *sectors*. Three types of magnetic disks are floppy disks, Zip disks, and hard disks.

(3) **What Are the Characteristics of a Hard Disk?** A **hard disk**, also called a *hard disk drive*, is a storage device that contains one or more inflexible, circular platters that store data, instructions, and information. A *platter* is made of aluminum, glass, or ceramic and is coated with a material that allows items to be recorded magnetically on its surface. Each platter has two read/write heads, one for each side. The location of a *read/write head* often is referred to by its *cylinder*, which is the vertical section of a track that passes through all platters. While the computer is running, the platters rotate at 5,400 to 15,000 *revolutions per minute* (*rpm*), which allows nearly instant access to all tracks and sectors on the platters. The spinning creates a cushion of air between the platters and the read/write heads. A *head crash* occurs when a read/write head touches the surface of a platter, usually resulting in a loss of data. A **backup** is a duplicate of a file, program, or disk that you can use in case the original is lost, damaged, or destroyed.

(4) **What Are the Differences between Floppy Disks and Zip Disks?** A **floppy disk** is a portable, inexpensive storage medium that consists of a thin, circular, flexible plastic Mylar film with a magnetic coating enclosed in a square-shaped plastic shell. A standard floppy disk can store up to 500 double-spaced pages of text, several digital photographs, or a small audio file. A **floppy disk drive** is a device that reads from and writes on a floppy disk. A **Zip disk** is a type of portable magnetic media that can store from 100 MB to 750 MB of data. The larger capacities make it easy to transport many files or large items. Another popular use of Zip disks is to back up important data and information.

Visit scsite.com/dc2007/ch7/quiz or click the Quiz Yourself button. Click Objectives 1 – 4.

(5) **What Are the Characteristics of Optical Discs?** An *optical disc* is a type of storage media that consists of a flat, round, portable disc made of metal, plastic, and lacquer that is written and read by a laser. Optical discs, which primarily store software, data, digital photographs, movies, and music, contain microscopic pits (indentations) and lands (flat areas) in their middle layer. Optical discs commonly store items in a single track that spirals from the center of the disc to its edge. Like a hard disk, the single track is divided into evenly sized sectors.

Chapter Review

Common optical discs used today are CD-ROM, CD-R, CD-RW, DVD-ROM, Blu-ray disc, HD-DVD disc, UMD, DVD-R, DVD+R, DVD-RW, DVD+RW, and DVD+RAM.

6 **How Are CD-ROMs, Recordable CDs, Rewritable CDs, DVD-ROMs, Recordable DVDs, and Rewritable DVDs Different?**   A **CD-ROM**, or *compact disc read-only memory*, is a type of optical disc that uses laser technology to store items. A typical CD-ROM holds from 650 MB to 1 GB of data, instructions, and information. Users can read the contents of standard CD-ROMs but cannot erase or modify their contents. A **CD-R** (*compact disc-recordable*) is a *multisession* disc on which users can record their own items. Each part of a CD-R can be written on only one time, and the disc's contents cannot be erased. A **CD-RW** (*compact disc-rewritable*) is an erasable disc that can be written on multiple times. A **DVD-ROM** (*digital versatile disc-ROM* or *digital video disc-ROM*) is an extremely high capacity optical disk capable of storing from 4.7 GB to 17 GB. Not only is the storage capacity of a DVD-ROM greater than that of a CD-ROM, a DVD-ROM's quality also far surpasses that of a CD-ROM. **DVD-RW** and **DVD+RW** discs are a recordable version of DVD that allows users to erase and record more than 1,000 times. **DVD+RAM** allows users to erase and record on a DVD+RAM more than 100,000 times.

> *connect*
> Visit scsite.com/dc2007/ch7/quiz or click the Quiz Yourself button. Click Objectives 5 – 6.

7 **How Is Tape Used?**   **Tape** is a magnetically coated ribbon of plastic capable of storing large amounts of data and information at a low cost. A **tape drive** reads and writes data and information on tape. Businesses and home users sometimes back up personal computer hard disks on tape.

8 **What Are PC Cards and Other Types of Miniature Mobile Storage Media?**   A **PC Card** is a thin, credit-card-sized device that fits into a PC Card slot to add storage or other capabilities to a desktop or notebook computer. Many desktop and notebook computers, Tablet PCs, PDAs, smart phones, digital cameras, and music players have built-in slots or ports for miniature mobile storage media. Common types of miniature mobile storage media include flash memory cards, USB flash drives, and smart cards. A **USB flash drive** is a flash memory storage device that plugs in a port on a computer or mobile device. Common flash memory cards include *CompactFlash* (*CF*), *SmartMedia*, *Secure Digital* (*SD*), *xD Picture Card*, and *Memory Stick*. A **smart card**, which is similar in size to a credit or ATM card, stores data on a thin microprocessor embedded in the card.

9 **How Are Microfilm and Microfiche Used?**   **Microfilm** is a 100- to 215-foot roll of film. **Microfiche** is a small sheet of film, usually about 4 × 6 inches. Libraries use microfilm and microfiche to store back issues of newspapers, magazines, and records; some large organizations use them to archive inactive files; some banks use them to store transactions and canceled checks; and the U.S. Army uses them to store personnel records.

> *connect*
> Visit scsite.com/dc2007/ch7/quiz or click the Quiz Yourself button. Click Objectives 7 – 9.

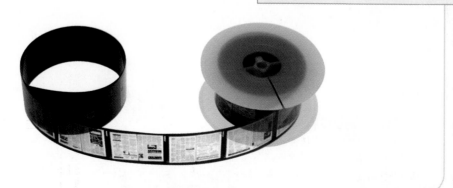

Key Terms

You should know the Primary Terms and be familiar with the Secondary Terms. Use the list below to help focus your study. To further enhance your understanding of the Key Terms in this chapter, visit scsite.com/dc2007/ch7/terms. See an example of and a definition for each term, and access current and additional information about the term from the Web.

Primary Terms

(shown in bold-black characters in the chapter)

access time (357)
backup (361)
capacity (356)
CD-R (371)
CD-R drive (371)
CD-ROM (369)
CD-ROM drive (369)
CD-RW (371)
CD-RW drive (371)
DVD+RAM (373)
DVD+RW (373)
DVD-ROM (372)
DVD-ROM drive (372)
DVD-RW (373)
external hard disk (362)
floppy disk (364)
floppy disk drive (364)
formatting (357)
hard disk (358)
microfiche (379)
microfilm (379)
online storage (363)
PC Card (374)
Picture CD (370)
reading (356)

removable hard disk (362)
smart card (378)
storage device (356)
storage medium (355)
tape (374)
tape drive (374)
USB flash drive (377)
write-protect notch (365)
writing (356)
Zip disk (365)
Zip drive (365)

Secondary Terms

(shown in italic characters in the chapter)

allocation unit (357)
Blu-ray disc (372)
burning (371)
card reader/writer (376)
CD recorder (371)
cluster (357)
compact disc read-only memory (369)
compact disc-recordable (371)
compact disc-rewritable (371)
CompactFlash (CF) (376)
computer output microfilm recorder (379)
cylinder (360)
density (365)
digital photo viewer (375)
digital versatile disc-read-only memory (372)
digital video disc-read-only memory (372)
direct access (374)
disk cache (361)
disk controller (363)
diskette (364)
DVD+R (373)
DVD-R (373)
EIDE (Enhanced Integrated Drive Electronics) (363)
external floppy disk drive (364)

fixed disk (358)
form factor (360)
hard disk drive (358)
head crash (360)
HD (365)
HD-DVD disc (372)
jewel box (368)
KBps (357)
longitudinal recording (358)
magnetic disks (357)
MBps (357)
Memory Stick (376)
mini discs (366)
multisession (371)
optical disc (366)
pen drive (377)
perpendicular recording (358)
platter (359)
portable (358)
random access (374)
read/write head (360)
revolutions per minute (rpm) (360)
ripping (371)
SATA (Serial Advanced Technology Attachment) (363)
SCSI (363)
secondary storage (355)
sectors (357)
Secure Digital (SD) (376)
sequential access (374)
single-session disc (369)
SmartMedia (376)
solid-state media (376)
storage (354)
tape cartridge (374)
tape library (374)
track (357)
transfer rate (357)
UMD (372)
xD Picture Card (376)

Checkpoint

Use the Checkpoint exercises to check your knowledge level of the chapter. The Beyond the Book exercises will help broaden your understanding of the concepts presented in this chapter. To complete the Checkpoint exercises interactively, visit scsite.com/dc2007/ch7/check.

Label the Figure

Identify the storage media.

a. CD or DVD
b. USB flash drive
c. tape
d. miniature hard disk
e. external hard disk
f. flash memory card
g. Zip disk
h. internal hard disk

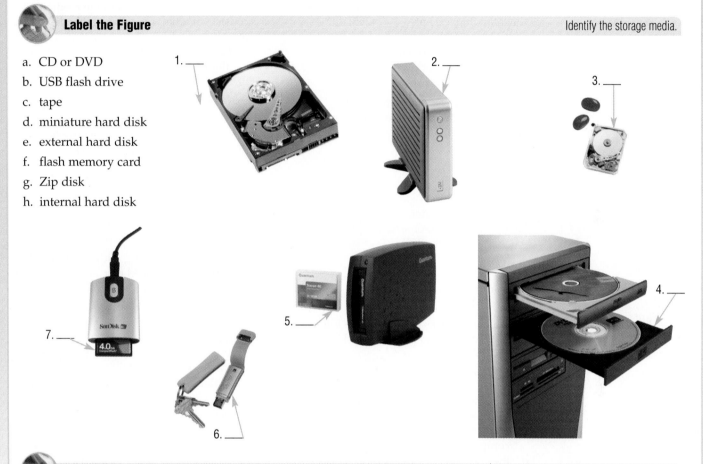

True/False

Mark T for True and F for False. (See page numbers in parentheses.)

_____ 1. Every computer uses storage to hold software, specifically, system software and application software. (354)

_____ 2. A storage medium is the physical material on which a computer keeps data, instructions, and information. (355)

_____ 3. Reading is the process of transferring data, instructions, and information from memory to a storage medium. (356)

_____ 4. Formatting is the process of dividing the disk into tracks and sectors. (357)

_____ 5. A cluster can hold data from many files. (357)

_____ 6. A typical hard disk contains multiple platters. (360)

_____ 7. A removable hard disk is a separate, free-standing hard disk that connects with a cable to a port on the system unit. (362)

_____ 8. SCSI interfaces can support up to eight or fifteen peripheral devices. (363)

_____ 9. All optical discs are double-sided. (366)

_____ 10. A UMD can store up to 2.8 GB of games, movies, or music. (372)

_____ 11. When writing or reading specific data, direct access is much slower than sequential access. (374)

_____ 12. Smart cards contain a processor and have input, process, output, and storage capabilities. (378)

Checkpoint

Multiple Choice   Select the best answer. (See page numbers in parentheses.)

1. Examples of storage media include all of the following, except _____. (355)
   a. CDs and DVDs
   b. floppy disks and hard disks
   c. monitors and printers
   d. tape and PC Cards

2. _____ is the speed with which data, instructions, and information transfer to and from a device. (357)
   a. Formatting
   b. Access time
   c. Transfer rate
   d. Reading

3. On desktop computers, platters most often have a form factor, or size, of approximately _____ in diameter. (360)
   a. 3.5 inches
   b. 2.5 inches
   c. 88 mm
   d. 1.6 inches

4. Portable hard disks offer all of the following advantages over internal hard disks, except _____. (362)
   a. they can transport a large number of files
   b. they can add storage space to a notebook computer
   c. they can be shared with multiple computers
   d. they can transfer data at much faster rates

5. Users store data and information on online storage to _____. (364)
   a. save time by storing large files instantaneously
   b. allow others to access files
   c. store offsite backups of data
   d. all of the above

6. _____ is the number of bits in an area on a storage medium. (365)
   a. Capacity
   b. Density
   c. KBps
   d. Allocation unit

7. A Zip disk can store from _____ of data. (365)
   a. 10 MB to 75 MB
   b. 100 MB to 750 MB
   c. 10 GB to 75 GB
   d. 100 GB to 750 GB

8. A(n) _____ is a type of storage media that consists of a flat, round, portable disc made of metal, plastic, and lacquer that is written and read by a laser. (366)
   a. floppy disk
   b. hard disk
   c. optical disc
   d. pen drive

9. All of the following are guidelines for the proper care of optical discs except _____. (368)
   a. do not expose the disc to extreme temperatures
   b. do not stack discs
   c. do not hold a disc by its edges
   d. do not eat, smoke, or drink near a disc

10. The process of copying audio and/or video data from a purchased disc and saving it on digital media is called _____. (371)
    a. formatting   b. ripping
    c. burning   d. reading

11. A storage technique that a DVD-ROM uses to achieve a higher storage capacity than a CD-ROM is _____. (372)
    a. making the disc denser by packing the pits closer together
    b. using two layers of pits
    c. using both sides of the disc
    d. all of the above

12. _____ storage requires sequential access. (374)
    a. Hard disk
    b. UMD
    c. Tape
    d. CD

13. Which of the following is not true of flash memory cards? (376)
    a. they are a type of solid-state media
    b. they are quite expensive compared to other storage media
    c. they can last 10 to 100 years
    d. they contain moving parts

14. Microfilm and microfiche _____. (379)
    a. greatly increase the amount of paper firms must handle
    b. are expensive
    c. have the longest life of any storage media
    d. all of the above

Checkpoint

Matching

Match the terms with their definitions. (See page numbers in parentheses.)

_____ 1. capacity (356)

_____ 2. cluster (357)

_____ 3. form factor (360)

_____ 4. cylinder (360)

_____ 5. disk cache (361)

_____ 6. disk controller (363)

_____ 7. Zip disk (365)

_____ 8. HD-DVD disc (372)

_____ 9. tape drive (374)

_____ 10. pen drive (377)

a. vertical section of a track that passes through all platters

b. the number of bytes (characters) a storage medium can hold

c. piece of metal on a floppy disk that slides to expose the surface of the disk

d. flash memory storage device that plugs in a USB port

e. smallest unit of disk space that stores data and information

f. memory chips that the processor uses to store frequently accessed items

g. reads and writes data and information on a tape

h. newer, expensive type of DVD with storage capacities up to 45 GB

i. size of hard disk platters on desktop computers

j. type of portable magnetic media that can store from 100 MB to 750 MB of data

k. special-purpose chip and electronic circuits that control the transfer of items to and from the system bus

Short Answer

Write a brief answer to each of the following questions.

1. What is access time? _____ What is the difference between a sector and a track? _____

2. Why is a hard disk inside the system unit sometimes called a fixed disk? _____ What are the different types of portable hard disks? _____

3. What is longitudinal recording? _____ What is the benefit of perpendicular recording over longitudinal recording? _____

4. How is a single-session disc different from a multisession disc? _____ How is a CD-R different from a CD-RW? _____

5. What are the common types of flash memory cards? _____ What is a card reader/writer and how might it attach to your computer? _____

Beyond the Book

Read the following book elements, learn more about each using the Web, and then write a brief report.

1. Ethics & Issues — Does Music Sharing Harm CD Sales? (369), Is It Ethical to Use Pirated CDs or DVDs? (371), Should the World Become a Cashless Society? (378), or Who Should Be Looking at Your Medical Records? (381)

2. Career Corner — Computer Technician (381)

3. Companies on the Cutting Edge — Maxtor or SanDisk Corporation (383)

4. FAQs (359, 361, 363, 368, 370, 371, 372, 373, 378)

5. High-Tech Talk — Disk Formatting and File Systems (382)

6. Looking Ahead — Heat Increases Disk Capacity (359) or Next-Generation DVDs a Burning Question (373)

7. Making Use of the Web — Shopping and Auctions (123)

8. Picture Yourself Working with Mobile Storage Media (352)

9. Technology Trailblazers — Al Shugart or Mark Dean (383)

10. Web Links (358, 362, 363, 369, 370, 371, 373, 377, 378)

Learn It Online

Use the Learn It Online exercises to reinforce your understanding of the chapter concepts. To access the Learn It Online exercises, visit scsite.com/dc2007/ch7/learn.

(1) At the Movies — Repair Your CD Scratches

To view the Repair Your CD Scratches movie, click the number 1 button. Locate your video and click the corresponding High-Speed or Dial-Up link, depending on your Internet connection. Watch the movie and then complete the exercise by answering the questions that follow. Just because your favorite CD has a few scratches is no reason to discard it. A few options are available to help you keep those scratched CDs playing smoothly longer. How does resurfacing work to restore your scratched CDs? What common household product can be used to repair a CD?

(2) At the Movies — Online Data Storage Options

To view the Online Data Storage Options movie, click the number 2 button. Locate your video and click the corresponding High-Speed or Dial-Up link, depending on your Internet connection. Watch the movie and then complete the exercise by answering the question that follows. Online data storage broadens your options for file sharing and frees up space on your personal computer. If you store files online, anyone who knows the password can access them from anywhere in the world. Several free storage systems offer a moderate amount of space; however, if you need more you can sign up and pay for additional storage for as little as $15 a month. What are some of the most important reasons for backing up your files online?

(3) Student Edition Labs — Maintaining a Hard Drive

Click the number 3 button. A new browser window will open, displaying the Student Edition Labs. Follow the on-screen instructions to complete the Maintaining a Hard Drive Lab. When finished, click the Exit button. If required, submit your results to your instructor.

(4) Student Edition Labs — Managing Files and Folders

Click the number 4 button. A new browser window will open, displaying the Student Edition Labs. Follow the on-screen instructions to complete the Managing Files and Folders Lab. When finished, click the Exit button. If required, submit your results to your instructor.

(5) Practice Test

Click the number 5 button. Answer each question. When completed, enter your name and click the Grade Test button to submit the quiz for grading. Make a note of any missed questions. If required, submit your results to your instructor.

(6) Who Wants To Be a Computer Genius²?

Click the number 6 button to find out if you are a computer genius. Directions about how to play the game will be displayed. When you are ready to play, click the Play button. Submit your score to your instructor.

(7) Wheel of Terms

Click the number 7 button to reinforce important terms you learned in this chapter by playing the Shelly Cashman Series version of this popular game. Directions about how to play the game will be displayed. When you are ready to play, click the Play button. Submit your score to your instructor.

Learn It Online

⑧ DC Track and Field

Click the number 8 button to use what you have learned in this chapter to compete against other students in three track and field events. Directions about how to play the game will be displayed. When you are ready to play, click the start first event button. If required, submit your score to your instructor.

⑨ You're Hired!

Click the number 9 button to use what you have learned in this chapter to embark on the path to a career in computers. Directions about how to play the game will be displayed. When you are ready to play, click the begin game button. If required, submit your score to your instructor.

⑩ Crossword Puzzle Challenge

Click the number 10 button. Complete the puzzle to reinforce skills you learned in this chapter. Directions about how to play the game will be displayed. When you are ready to play, click the Submit button. Submit the completed puzzle to your instructor.

⑪ Lab Exercises

Click the number 11 button. When the Lab Exercises menu appears, click the exercise assigned by your instructor. A new browser window will open. Follow the on-screen instructions to complete the exercise. When finished, click the Exit button. If required, submit your results to your instructor.

⑫ In the News

Hitachi sells a small disk drive, about the size of a quarter, which is capable of storing up to 4 GB of information, as much as 50 CDs. The drive is used in devices such as PDAs or digital cameras. What other storage devices are on the horizon? Click the number 12 button and read a news article about a new or improved storage device. What is the device? Who manufactures it? How is the storage device better than, or different from, earlier devices? How will the device be used? Why?

⑬ Chapter Discussion Forum

Select an objective from this chapter on page 353 about which you would like more information. Click the number 13 button and post a short message listing a meaningful message title accompanied by one or more questions concerning the selected objective. In two days, return to the threaded discussion by clicking the number 13 button. Submit to your instructor your original message and at least one response to your message.

⑭ Blogs

Click the number 14 button to learn how to use blogs to find information about a topic. Follow the instructions to use MSNBC.com's Blogs Etc. to find a blog about a popular topic, such as the hottest national news story or another topic of national interest. Write a report comparing opinions of two different people about the selected topic. Print your report and submit to your instructor.

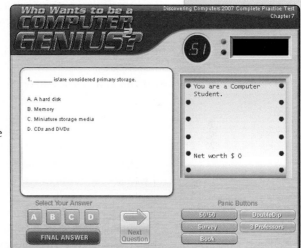

Learn How To

Use the Learn How To activities to learn fundamental skills when using a computer and accompanying technology. Complete the exercises and submit them to your instructor. To see a video of a Learn How To activity, visit scsite.com/dc2007/ch7/howto.

LEARN HOW TO 1: Maintain a Hard Disk

A computer's hard disk is used for the majority of storage requirements. It is important, therefore, to ensure that each hard disk on a computer is operating at peak efficiency.

Three tasks that maximize disk operations are detecting and repairing disk errors by using the Check Disk utility program; removing unused or unnecessary files and folders by using the Disk Cleanup utility program; and, consolidating files and folders into contiguous storage areas using the Disk Defragmenter utility program.

A. Check Disk

To detect and repair disk errors using the Check Disk utility program, complete the following steps:
1. Click the Start button on the Windows taskbar and then click My Computer on the Start menu.
2. When the My Computer window opens, right-click the hard disk icon for drive C (or any other hard disk you want to select), and then click Properties on the shortcut menu.
3. In the Properties dialog box, if necessary click the Tools tab. *The Tools sheet contains buttons to start the Check Disk program, the Defragment program, and the Backup program (Figure 7-40).*
4. Click the Check Now button. *The Check Disk dialog box is displayed.*
5. To do a complete scan of the disk and correct any errors that are found, place a checkmark in the Scan for and attempt recovery for bad sectors check box, and then click the Start button. Four phases of checking the disk will occur. While the checking is in progress, the disk being checked cannot be used for any purpose whatsoever; furthermore, once it has started, the process cannot be stopped.
6. When the four phases are complete (this may take more than one-half hour, depending on the size of the hard disk and how many corrections must occur), a dialog box is displayed with the message, Disk Check Complete. Click the OK button in the dialog box.

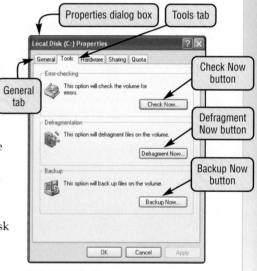

FIGURE 7-40

B. Cleanup Disk

After checking the disk, your next step can be to clean up the disk by removing any programs and data that are not required for the computer. To do so, complete the following steps:
1. Click the General tab (Figure 7-40) in the disk drive Properties dialog box to display the General sheet.
2. Click the Disk Cleanup button in the General sheet.
3. The Disk Cleanup dialog box is displayed and contains a message that indicates the amount of space that can be freed up is being calculated.
4. After the calculation is complete, the Disk Cleanup dialog box specifies the amount of space that can be freed up and the files to delete, some of which are checked automatically (Figure 7-41). Select those items from which you wish to delete files.
5. Click the OK button in the Disk Cleanup dialog box.
6. A dialog box asks if you are sure you want to perform these actions. Click the Yes button. The Disk Cleanup dialog box illustrates the progress of the cleanup. When the cleanup is complete, the dialog box closes.

Learn How To

C. Defragment Disk

The next step in disk maintenance is to defragment all the files on the disk. When a file is stored on disk, the data in the file sometimes is stored contiguously, and other times is stored in a noncontiguous manner. When a file is stored in a noncontiguous manner, it can take significantly longer to find and retrieve data from the file. Therefore, one of the more useful utilities to speed up disk operations is the defragmentation program, which combines all files so that no files are stored in a noncontiguous manner. To use the defragmentation program, complete the following steps:

1. If necessary, click the Tools tab in the Properties dialog box for the hard disk to be defragmented.
2. Click the Defragment Now button in the Tools sheet. *The Disk Defragmenter window opens (Figure 7-42). This window displays the hard disks on the computer and shows the size and amount of free space for each disk. During defragmentation, the Estimated disk usage before defragmentation area and the Estimated disk usage after defragmentation area display the layout of the data on the disk. If you click the Analyze button, the disk will be analyzed for its data layout but defragmentation will not occur.*
3. Click the Defragment button. The defragmentation process begins. The amount of processing completed is shown on the status bar at the bottom of the window. The defragmentation process can consume more than one hour in some cases. You can pause or stop the operation at any time by clicking the Pause or Stop button in the Disk Defragmenter window.
4. When the process is complete, the Disk Defragmenter dialog box displays the message, Defragmentation is complete for (C:). Click the View Report button to see a complete report about the hard disk.
5. Click the Close button to close the Disk Defragmenter dialog box.

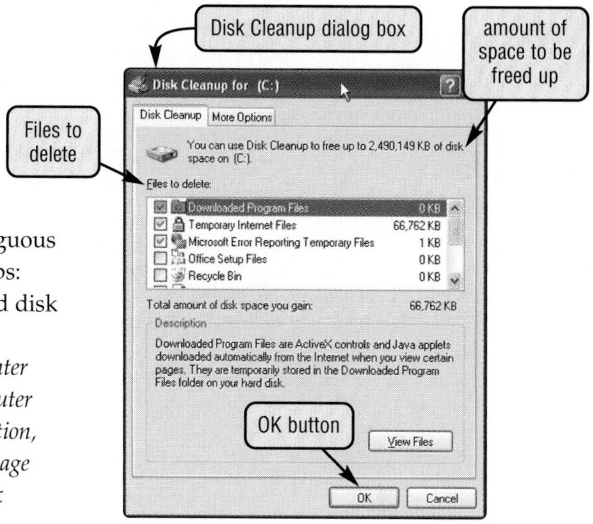

FIGURE 7-41

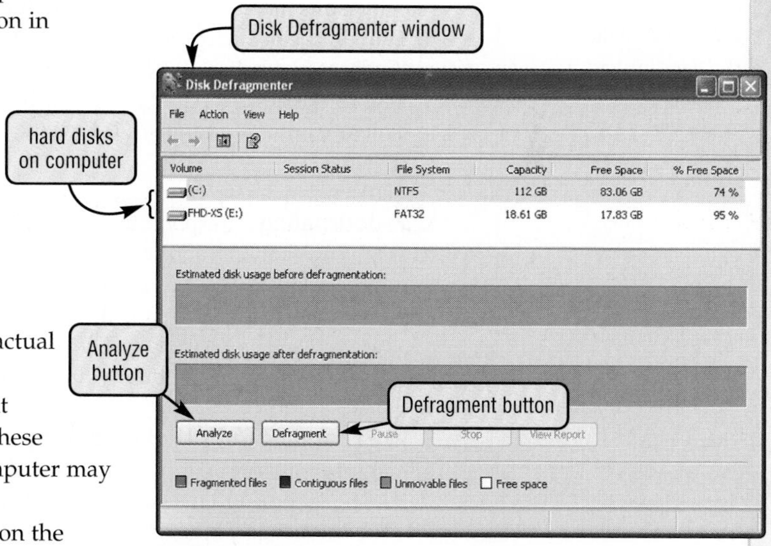

FIGURE 7-42

Exercise

Caution: The exercises for this chapter that require the actual disk maintenance are optional. If you are performing these exercises on a computer that is not your own, obtain explicit permission to complete these exercises. Keep in mind that these exercises can require significant computer time and the computer may be unusable during this time.

1. Display the Properties dialog box for a hard disk found on the computer. Display the Tools sheet. Click the Check Now button and then place a checkmark in the Scan for and attempt recovery for bad sectors check box. Click the Start button. How long did it take to complete the check of the hard disk? Were any errors discovered and corrected? Submit your answers to your instructor.
2. Display the Properties dialog box for a hard disk found on the computer. Display the General sheet. What is the capacity of the hard disk? How much space is used? How much free space is available? Click the Disk Cleanup button. How much space can be freed up if you use the Disk Cleanup program? Click the OK button to clean up the disk. How long did it take to perform the disk cleanup? Submit your answers to your instructor.
3. Display the Properties dialog box for a hard disk found on the computer. Display the Tools sheet. Click the Defragment Now button. In the Disk Defragmenter window, click the Analyze button. Does the hard disk need to be defragmented? Click the View Report button. How many files are stored on the disk? What is the average size of the files stored on the disk? If necessary, click the Defragment button in the Analysis Report window. How long did defragmentation require? Submit your answers to your instructor.

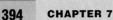
Web Research

Use the Internet-based Web Research exercises to broaden your understanding of the concepts presented in this chapter. Visit scsite.com/dc2007/ch7/research to obtain more information pertaining to each exercise. To discuss any of the Web Research exercises in this chapter with other students, post your thoughts or questions at scsite.com/dc2007/ch7/forum.

1 **Scavenger Hunt**   Use one of the <u>search engines</u> listed in Figure 2-10 in Chapter 2 on page 78 or your own favorite search engine to find the answers to the questions that follow. Copy and paste the Web address from the Web page where you found the answer. Some questions may have more than one answer. If required, submit your answers to your instructor. (1) What are the three different laser powers used in a CD-rewritable recorder? How do two of the powers affect the recording layer? During writing, to what temperature does the laser beam selectively heat areas of the recording material? (2) What was the diameter of the first floppy disk? (3) What is the Red Book standard? (4) What is the function of a hard disk's actuator? (5) What is areal density? What unit of measurement is used to describe this density? (6) What is IBM's Millipede project?

2 **Search Sleuth**   Many computer users search the World Wide Web by typing words in the search text box, and often they are overwhelmed when the search engine returns thousands of possible Web sites. You can narrow your search by typing quotation marks around phrases and by adding words that give details about the phrase. <u>Go.com</u> is a Web portal developed by the Walt Disney Internet Group. It features a search engine, the latest ABC news and ESPN sports stories, stock market quotes, weather forecasts, maps, and games. Visit this Web site and then use your word processing program to answer the following questions. Then, if required, submit your answers to your instructor. (1) What are five of the listings in the Top Ten Searches area? Click one of these search topics. What are the first three search results listed? (2) Click the Search for text box at the top of the page. Type "USB flash drive" in the box. How many pages of search results are returned that are not Sponsored links? What are Sponsored results? (3) Click the Search for text box after the words, "USB flash drive." Add +"2 GB" and +"data reliability" as the search terms. How many pages of search results are returned that are not Sponsored links? (4) Review your search results and then write a 50-word summary of your findings.

3 **Journaling**   Respond to your readings in this chapter by writing at least one page about your reactions, evaluations, and reflections about using <u>storage devices</u>. For example, have you used USB flash drives, smart cards, or Zip disks? How do you care for your mobile storage media? Do you own a credit card smart card? What is the storage capacity of your school, office, or home computer's hard disk? Have you copied a CD or DVD? You also can write about the new terms you learned by reading this chapter. If required, submit your journal to your instructor.

4 **Expanding Your Understanding**   Bill Gates, Microsoft's chief software architect, considers <u>holographic storage</u> an impressive new storage system. The holographic process can store more than 100 movie, photo, and music files on one disc holding one terabyte of data. View Web sites to learn more about holographic storage. What factors are driving the rush to develop this system? How are images stored? What companies are researching and developing this technology? Write a report summarizing your findings, focusing on the possible uses of this storage medium and current engineering efforts to commercialize the technology. If required, submit your report to your instructor.

5 **Ethics in Action**   The United States Federal Bureau of Investigation used a controversial program until January 2005 to monitor and store the e-mail and Internet activity of suspected criminals. Originally called Carnivore, the surveillance program was renamed <u>DCS1000</u>. The program was designed to track the activities of potential terrorists, spies, drug traffickers, and organized crime ring members. FBI agents needed to obtain a court order to monitor an individual, but privacy advocates claim the software tracked people not covered under the court order. View online sites that provide information about DCS1000 or Carnivore, including HowStuffWorks (computer.howstuffworks.com/carnivore.htm). Write a report summarizing your findings, and include a table of links to Web sites that provide additional details. If required, submit your report to your instructor.

Case Studies

Use the Case Studies to apply the concepts presented in the chapter to real-world situations. Visit scsite.com/dc2007/ch7/cases to obtain more information pertaining to each exercise. To discuss the Case Studies in this chapter with other students, visit scsite.com/dc2007/ch7/forum and post your thoughts or questions.

CASE STUDY 1 — Class Discussion   The owner of the motorcycle repair shop where you are employed as a part-time office manager is tired of continually upgrading the company's computer system. After attending a seminar on how small businesses can make use of the Internet, she asked you to look into the feasibility of using <u>online storage</u> (also called an Internet hard disk), rather than purchasing additional storage for the company's computer. Write a brief report outlining the advantages and disadvantages of using online storage. Compare Yahoo! Briefcase and Google's Gmail online storage offerings. Which company offers the best arrangement? Why? Be prepared to discuss your recommendations in class.

CASE STUDY 2 — Class Discussion   Paul's Trucking Company has hired you as an IT consultant. The company plans to purchase 15 computers for use in the accounting department. The first task assigned to you by the president of the company is to recommend the number and types of <u>CD and DVD drives</u> to include with the computers they plan to purchase. They want to use CDs and/or DVDs to share data and information between employees and to back up critical files. Create a brief memo that includes a table summarizing the advantages and disadvantages of using CD-ROM, recordable CD, rewritable CD, DVD-ROM, recordable DVD, and rewritable DVD. Include in the table both the approximate cost of the drive and the media. Be prepared to discuss your findings in class.

CASE STUDY 3 — Research   An old aphorism claims, "You never can have too much money." Many computer users support a similar maxim, "You never can have too much storage." Your manager at MJ National Bank where you are employed as an analyst, however, is tired of buying more hardware to meet the bank's storage needs. She wants you to investigate alternative ways to improve <u>storage capacity</u>. Use the Web and/or print media to find out more about hard disk partitions and data compression as a means of increasing storage capacity. How do partitions increase the capacity of hard disks? What kind of data compression is most suitable for communications devices? What are the most well known data compression algorithms? How can compression ratios of different algorithms be compared? What are some formats for data compression archives? Prepare a report and/or PowerPoint presentation and share your findings with your class.

CASE STUDY 4 — Research   A major national retail chain, where you are employed as a technology buyer, has grown enormously over the past few years. The growth has required the company to triple its storage capacity each year to keep pace with its expanding business. Your manager, who is up for promotion, wants to impress his boss by expanding the storage capacity by tenfold this year while staying under the budget earmarked for storage improvements. He has asked you to look into the latest cutting-edge <u>storage technologies</u>, such as holographic and heat-assisted storage. Use the Web and/or print media to develop a features/benefits breakdown that compares the latest storage technologies to the more traditional hard disk technology. What do the different technologies entail? Are they available today? If not, when? What are their costs? Prepare a report and/or PowerPoint presentation summarizing your findings.

CASE STUDY 5 — Team Challenge   Your team has been assigned to do IT research for a new local magazine-subscription telemarketing company that is about to open for business. The company's business plan calls for 150 telemarketers to make a minimum of 100 calls a day. If a telemarketer does not meet the minimum number of calls, then he or she is required to finish the calls from home. The company plans to buy used computers for each telemarketer to use at home. The company also has to decide on the type of <u>storage device</u> to provide the telemarketers so that when they have to make calls from home, they have a way to take the necessary data home with them. Senior management has narrowed down their choice to three storage devices — rewritable CDs, rewritable DVDs, or USB flash drives. Form a three-member team and have each team member choose a different storage device. Using the Web and/or print media, have each team member determine the advantages and disadvantages of their chosen device. Include such features as capacity, access time, durability of media, and cost. As a team, merge your findings into a team report and/or PowerPoint presentation and share your recommendations with your class.

CHAPTER EIGHT

Operating Systems and Utility Programs

Picture Yourself Getting a Virus through E-Mail

With a break between classes, you and some classmates sit outside and enjoy the nice weather. Everyone decides to exchange e-mail addresses and phone numbers, so you can communicate while away from school.

Later that night at home, you notice a classmate has sent you a picture via e-mail. As soon as you open the picture, your computer freezes. You click the mouse button. Nothing happens. You press a key on the keyboard. The computer beeps. You click the mouse again. Still no response. You restart the computer. The Windows XP desktop never appears.

At that moment, your smart phone rings. A panicked friend says his computer stopped working as soon as he opened that picture. Realizing the picture file probably had a virus, you call a technical support hotline. After explaining the situation, the support technician asks you several questions, and you answer: Did you have antivirus software installed on the computer? "No." Were the operating system's firewall settings enabled? "I don't know." Do you have a backup of the computer's hard disk? "No, I haven't learned how to burn CDs to make backups." Can you find the computer's recovery disc? "Yes, it's right here." The bad news is you lost *everything* on your computer and had to reinstall Windows XP — the good news is your computer is functional again. Now, you need to protect your computer from future infections.

Read Chapter 8 to learn about antivirus software, firewall settings, backups, and recovery discs, and discover features of most operating systems and utility programs.

SYSTEM SOFTWARE

When you purchase a personal computer, it usually has system software installed on its hard disk. **System software** consists of the programs that control or maintain the operations of the computer and its devices. System software serves as the interface between the user, the application software, and the computer's hardware.

Two types of system software are operating systems and utility programs. Several types of utility programs are provided with an operating system. Other utility programs are available stand-alone, that is, as programs separate from the operating system. This chapter discusses the operating system and its functions, as well as several types of utility programs for personal computers.

OPERATING SYSTEMS

An **operating system** (**OS**) is a set of programs containing instructions that coordinate all the activities among computer hardware resources. Most operating systems perform similar functions that include starting a computer, providing a user interface, managing programs, managing memory, scheduling jobs, configuring devices, establishing an Internet connection,

FIGURE 8-1 Most operating systems perform the functions illustrated in this figure.

monitoring performance, and providing file management utilities. Some operating systems also allow users to control a network and administer security (Figure 8-1).

In most cases, the operating system is installed and resides on the computer's hard disk. On handheld computers and many mobile devices such as PDAs and smart phones, however, the operating system may reside on a ROM chip.

Different sizes of computers typically use different operating systems. For example, a mainframe computer does not use the same operating system as a personal computer. Even the same types of computers, such as desktop

computers, may not use the same operating system. Furthermore, the application software designed for a specific operating system may not run when using another operating system. For example, PCs often use Windows XP, and iMacs use Mac OS X. When purchasing application software, you must ensure that it works with the operating system installed on your computer.

The operating system that a computer uses sometimes is called the *platform*. On purchased application software, the package identifies the required platform (operating system). A *cross-platform* program is one that runs the same on multiple operating systems.

provide a user interface

manage programs

manage memory

monitor performance

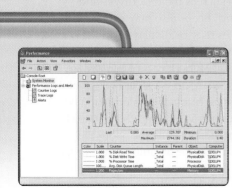

establish an Internet connection

schedule jobs and configure devices

OPERATING SYSTEM FUNCTIONS

Many different operating systems exist, designed for all types of computers. Regardless of the size of the computer, however, most operating systems provide similar functions. The following sections discuss functions common to most operating systems. The operating system handles many of these functions automatically, without requiring any instructions from a user.

Starting a Computer

The process of starting or restarting a computer is called **booting**. When turning on a computer that has been powered off completely, you are performing a **cold boot**. A **warm boot**, by contrast, is the process of using the operating system to restart a computer. A warm boot properly closes any open processes and programs. With Windows XP, you can perform a warm boot by clicking the Start button on the taskbar, clicking Turn Off Computer on the Start menu, and then clicking the Restart button in the Turn off computer dialog box (Figure 8-2). Some computers have a reset button that when pressed restarts a computer as if it had been powered off. A reset button does not properly close open processes.

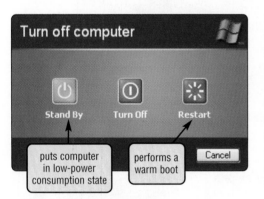

FIGURE 8-2   To reboot a running computer, click the Restart button in the Turn off computer dialog box.

When you install new software, often an on-screen prompt instructs you to restart the computer. In this case, a warm boot is appropriate. If your computer stops responding, try to restart it with a warm boot first. If it does not respond to the warm boot, then try pushing the reset button on the computer, if the computer has a reset button. As a last resort, restart the computer with a cold boot; that is, push the power button.

Each time you boot a computer, the kernel and other frequently used operating system instructions are loaded, or copied, from the hard disk (storage) into the computer's memory (RAM). The *kernel* is the core of an operating system that manages memory and devices, maintains the computer's clock, starts applications, and assigns the computer's resources, such as devices, programs, data, and information. The kernel is *memory resident*, which means it remains in memory while the computer is running. Other parts of the operating system are *nonresident*, that is, these instructions remain on the hard disk until they are needed.

When you boot a computer, a series of messages may be displayed on the screen. The actual information displayed varies depending on the make and type of the computer and the equipment installed. The boot process, however, is similar for large and small computers.

The steps in the following paragraphs explain what occurs during a cold boot on a personal computer using the Windows XP operating system. The steps in Figure 8-3 illustrate and correspond to the steps discussed in the following paragraphs.

Step 1: When you turn on the computer, the power supply sends an electrical signal to the components in the system unit.

Step 2: The charge of electricity causes the processor chip to reset itself and find the ROM chip(s) that contains the BIOS. The **BIOS** (pronounced BYE-ose), which stands for *basic input/output system*, is firmware that contains the computer's startup instructions.

Step 3: The BIOS executes a series of tests to make sure the computer hardware is connected properly and operating correctly. The tests, collectively called the *power-on self test* (*POST*), check the various system components including the buses, system clock, adapter cards, RAM chips, mouse, keyboard, and drives. As the POST executes, LEDs (tiny lights) flicker on devices such as the disk drives and keyboard. Beeps also may sound, and messages may be displayed on the screen.

Step 4: The POST results are compared with data in a CMOS chip. As discussed in Chapter 4, CMOS is a technology that uses battery power to retain information when the computer is off. The CMOS chip stores configuration information about the computer, such as the amount of memory; type of disk drives, keyboard, and monitor; the current date and time; and other startup information. It also detects any new devices connected to the computer. If any problems are identified, the computer may beep, display error messages, or cease operating — depending on the severity of the problem.

Step 5: If the POST completes successfully, the BIOS searches for specific operating system files called *system files*. The BIOS may look first to see if a USB flash drive plugged in a USB port, or a disc in a CD or DVD drive, or a disk in a floppy disk drive contains the system files. If these ports or drives do not contain media or if the system files are not

on media in the port or drive, the BIOS looks in drive C (the designation usually given to the first hard disk) for the system files.

Step 6: Once located, the system files load into memory (RAM) from storage (usually the hard disk) and execute. Next, the kernel of the operating system loads into memory. Then, the operating system in memory takes control of the computer.

Step 7: The operating system loads system configuration information. In Windows XP, the *registry* consists of several files

WEB LINK 8-1

BIOS

For more information, visit scsite.com/dc2007/ch8/weblink and then click BIOS.

FIGURE 8-3   HOW A PC BOOTS UP

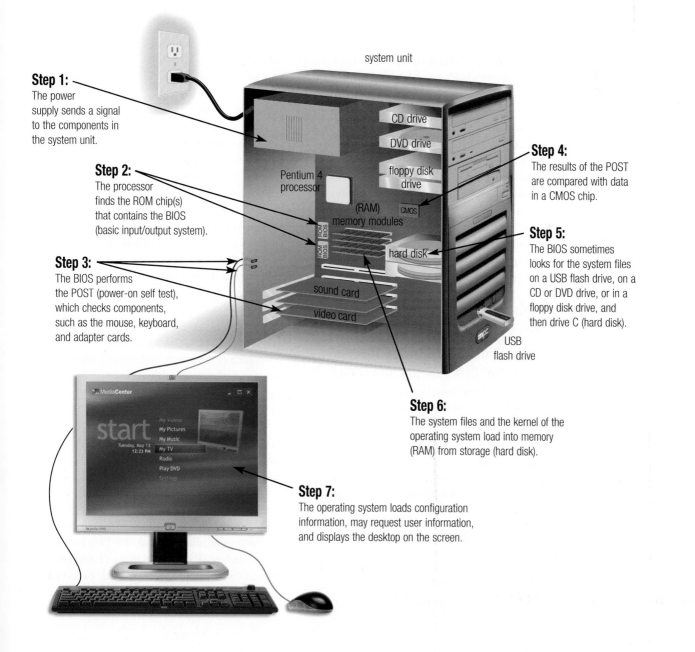

Step 1:
The power supply sends a signal to the components in the system unit.

Step 2:
The processor finds the ROM chip(s) that contains the BIOS (basic input/output system).

Step 3:
The BIOS performs the POST (power-on self test), which checks components, such as the mouse, keyboard, and adapter cards.

system unit

CD drive
DVD drive
floppy disk drive

Pentium 4 processor

(RAM) memory modules

CMOS

ROM BIOS

hard disk

sound card
video card

USB flash drive

Step 4:
The results of the POST are compared with data in a CMOS chip.

Step 5:
The BIOS sometimes looks for the system files on a USB flash drive, on a CD or DVD drive, or in a floppy disk drive, and then drive C (hard disk).

Step 6:
The system files and the kernel of the operating system load into memory (RAM) from storage (hard disk).

Step 7:
The operating system loads configuration information, may request user information, and displays the desktop on the screen.

that contain the system configuration information. Windows XP constantly accesses the registry during the computer's operation for information such as installed hardware and software devices and individual user preferences for mouse speed, passwords, and other information.

Necessary operating system files are loaded into memory. On some computers, the operating system verifies that the person attempting to use the computer is a legitimate user. Finally, the Windows XP desktop and icons are displayed on the screen. The operating system executes programs in the *Startup folder*, which contains a list of programs that open automatically when you boot the computer.

RECOVERY DISK A **boot drive** is the drive from which your personal computer boots (starts). In most cases, drive C (the hard disk) is the boot drive. Sometimes a hard disk becomes damaged and the computer cannot boot from the hard disk. In this case, you can boot from a special disk, called a **recovery disk** or a **boot disk**, that contains a few system files that will start the computer. When you purchase a computer, it usually includes a recovery disk in the form of a CD. If you do not have a recovery disk, the operating system usually provides a means to create one. Many users today create a recovery disk on a USB flash drive.

FAQ 8-1

When I am finished using the computer, can I simply turn it off?

No! You must use the operating system's shut-down procedure so various processes are closed in sequence and items in memory released properly. Depending on the computer, several shut-down options exist. The Turn Off command removes power from the computer. Restart does a warm boot. *Hibernate* saves all documents in memory and then turns off the computer. *Stand By* places the entire computer in a low-power state but does not turn it off. With Hibernate and Stand By, the next time you resume work on the computer, the desktop is restored exactly to how you left it. For more information, visit scsite.com/dc2007/ch8/faq and then click Shut-Down Options.

Providing a User Interface

You interact with software through its user interface. That is, a **user interface** controls how you enter data and instructions and how information is displayed on the screen. Three types of user interfaces are command-line, menu-driven, and graphical. Operating systems often use a combination of these interfaces to define how a user interacts with a computer.

COMMAND-LINE INTERFACE To configure devices, manage system resources, and troubleshoot network connections, network administrators and other advanced users work with a command-line interface. In a *command-line interface*, a user types commands or presses special keys on the keyboard (such as function keys or key combinations) to enter data and instructions (Figure 8-4a). Command-line interfaces often are difficult to use because they require exact spelling, grammar, and punctuation. Minor errors, such as a missing period, generate an error message. Command-line interfaces, however, give a user more control to manage detailed settings. For a technical discussion about a command-line interface, read the High-Tech Talk article on page 430.

When working with a command-line interface, the set of commands entered into the computer is called the *command language*. Programs that contain command language instructions are called *scripts*. Network administrators and Web page programmers often use scripts.

MENU-DRIVEN INTERFACE A *menu-driven interface* provides menus as a means of entering commands (Figure 8-4b). Menu-driven interfaces are easier to learn than command-line interfaces because users do not have to learn the rules of entering commands.

GRAPHICAL USER INTERFACE Most users today work with a graphical user interface. With a *graphical user interface* (*GUI*), you interact with menus and visual images such as buttons and other graphical objects to issue commands. Many current GUI operating systems incorporate features similar to those of a Web browser. The Windows XP screen shown in Figure 8-4c, for example, contains links and navigation buttons such as the Back button and the Forward button.

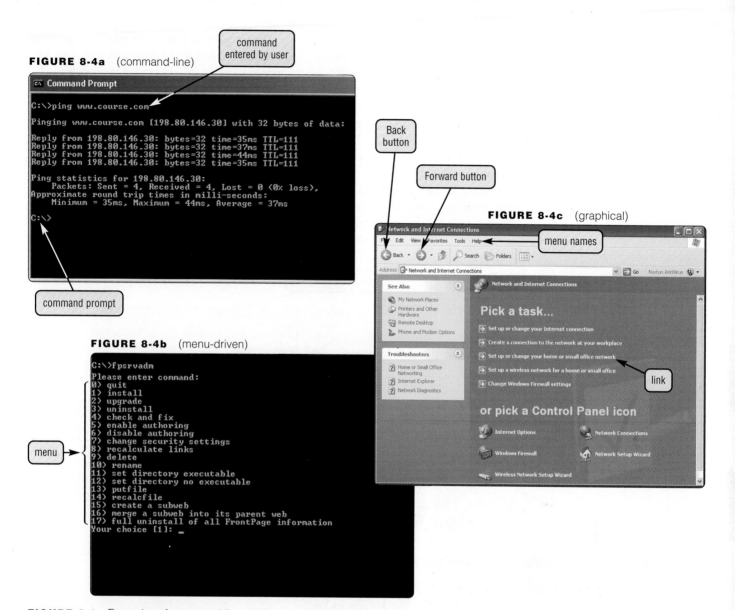

FIGURE 8-4a (command-line)

command entered by user

command prompt

FIGURE 8-4b (menu-driven)

menu

FIGURE 8-4c (graphical)

Back button

Forward button

menu names

link

FIGURE 8-4 Examples of command-line, menu-driven, and graphical user interfaces.

Managing Programs

Some operating systems support a single user and only one running program at a time. Others support thousands of users running multiple programs. How an operating system handles programs directly affects your productivity.

A *single user/single tasking* operating system allows only one user to run one program at a time. For example, if you are working in a graphics program and want to check e-mail messages, you must quit the graphics program before you can run the e-mail program. Early systems were single user/single tasking. Most of today's operating systems are multitasking. PDAs, smart phones, and other small computing devices, however, often use a single user/single tasking operating system.

A *single user/multitasking* operating system allows a single user to work on two or more programs that reside in memory at the same time. Using the example just cited, if you are working with a single user/multitasking operating system, you do not have to quit the graphics program to run the e-mail program. Both programs can run concurrently. Users today typically run multiple programs concurrently. It is common to have an e-mail program and Web browser open at all times, while working with application programs such as word processing or graphics.

When a computer is running multiple programs concurrently, one program is in the foreground and the others are in the background. The one in the *foreground* is the active program, that is, the one you currently are using. The other programs running but not in use are in the *background*. In Figure 8-5, the PowerPoint program, which is showing a slide show, is in the foreground, and three other programs are running in the background (HP Image Zone, Hallmark Card Studio, and iTunes). For example, iTunes can be playing music while you are modifying the slide show.

The foreground program typically displays on the desktop, and the background programs are partially or completely hidden behind the foreground program. You easily can switch between foreground and background programs. To make a program active (in the foreground) in Windows XP, click its program button on the taskbar. This causes the operating system to place all other programs in the background.

In addition to application programs, an operating system manages other processes. These processes include utilities or routines that provide support to other programs or

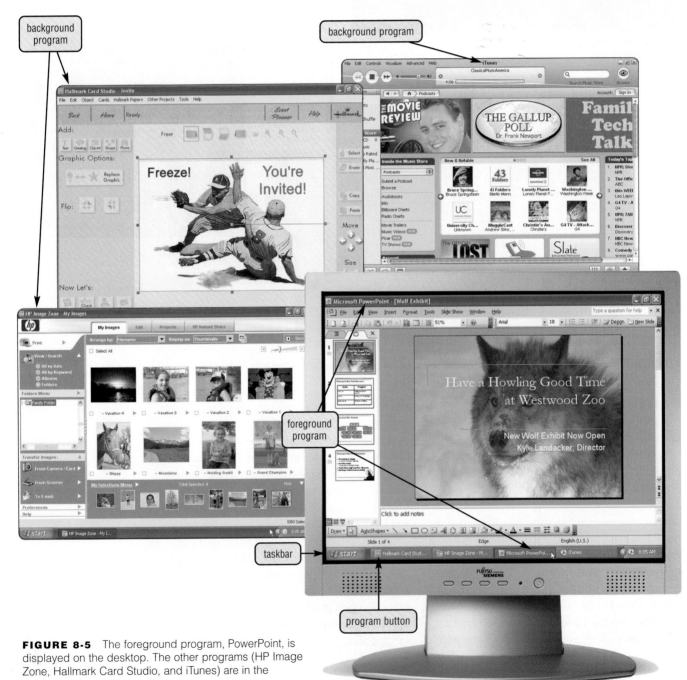

FIGURE 8-5 The foreground program, PowerPoint, is displayed on the desktop. The other programs (HP Image Zone, Hallmark Card Studio, and iTunes) are in the background.

hardware. Some are memory resident. Others run as they are required. Figure 8-6 shows a list of all processes running on a Windows XP computer. The list contains the applications programs running, as well as other programs and processes.

Some operating systems use preemptive multitasking to prevent any one process from monopolizing the computer's resources. With *preemptive multitasking*, the operating system interrupts a program that is executing and passes control to another program waiting to be executed. An advantage of preemptive multitasking is the operating system regains control if one program stops operating properly.

A *multiuser* operating system enables two or more users to run programs simultaneously. Networks, servers, mainframes, and super-computers allow hundreds to thousands of users to connect at the same time, and thus are multiuser.

A *multiprocessing* operating system supports two or more processors running programs at the same time. Multiprocessing involves the coordinated processing of programs by more than one processor. Multiprocessing increases a computer's processing speed.

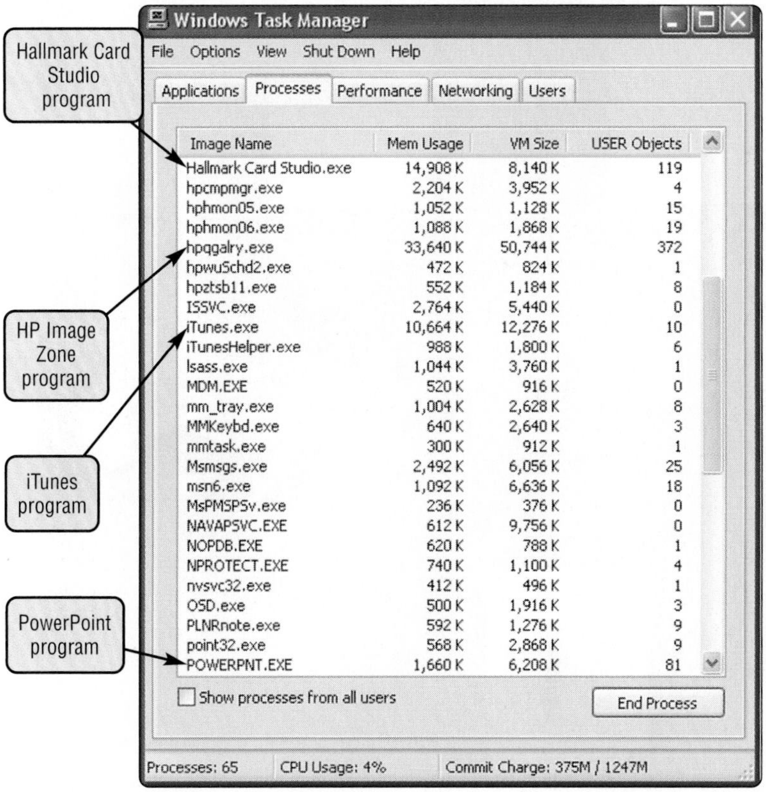

A computer with separate processors also can serve as a fault-tolerant computer. A *fault-tolerant computer* continues to operate when one of its components fails, ensuring that no data is lost. Fault-tolerant computers have duplicate components such as processors, memory, and disk drives. If any one of these components fails, the computer switches to the duplicate component and continues to operate. Airline reservation systems, communications networks, automated teller machines, and other systems that must be operational at all times use fault-tolerant computers.

Managing Memory

The purpose of **memory management** is to optimize the use of random access memory (RAM). As discussed in Chapter 4, RAM consists of one or more chips on the motherboard that hold items such as data and instructions while the processor interprets and executes them. The operating system allocates, or assigns, data and instructions to an area of memory while they are being processed. Then, it carefully monitors the contents of memory. Finally, the operating system releases these items from being monitored in memory when the processor no longer requires them.

If you have multiple programs running simultaneously, it is possible to run out of RAM. For example, assume an operating system requires 128 MB of RAM, an antivirus program — 128 MB of RAM, a Web browser — 32 MB of RAM, a business software suite — 64 MB of RAM, and a photo editing program — 128 MB of RAM. With all these programs running simultaneously, the total RAM required would be 480 MB of RAM (128 + 128 + 32 + 64 + 128). If the computer has only 256 MB of RAM, the operating system may have to use virtual memory to solve the problem.

FIGURE 8-6 An operating system manages multiple programs and processes while you use the computer.

With **virtual memory**, the operating system allocates a portion of a storage medium, usually the hard disk, to function as additional RAM (Figure 8-7). As you interact with a program, part of it may be in physical RAM, while the rest of the program is on the hard disk as virtual memory. Because virtual memory is slower than RAM, users may notice the computer slowing down while it uses virtual memory.

The area of the hard disk used for virtual memory is called a *swap file* because it swaps (exchanges) data, information, and instructions between memory and storage. A *page* is the amount of data and program instructions that can swap at a given time. The technique of swapping items between memory and storage, called *paging*, is a time-consuming process for the computer.

When an operating system spends much of its time paging, instead of executing application software, it is said to be *thrashing*. If application software, such as a Web browser, has stopped responding and the hard disk's LED blinks repeatedly, the operating system probably is thrashing.

FAQ 8-2

How can I stop a computer from thrashing?

Try to quit the program that stopped responding. If the computer does not respond and continues to thrash, do a warm boot. When the computer reboots, check whether the available hard disk space is less than 200 MB. If it is, remove unnecessary files from the hard disk and if possible uninstall seldom used programs. Defragment the hard disk (discussed later in this chapter). If thrashing continues to occur, you may need to install more RAM in the computer. For more information, visit scsite.com/dc2007/ch8/faq and then click Optimizing Memory.

Scheduling Jobs

The operating system determines the order in which jobs are processed. A **job** is an operation the processor manages. Jobs include receiving data from an input device, processing instructions, sending information to an output device, and transferring items from storage to memory and from memory to storage.

FIGURE 8-7 HOW A COMPUTER MIGHT USE VIRTUAL MEMORY

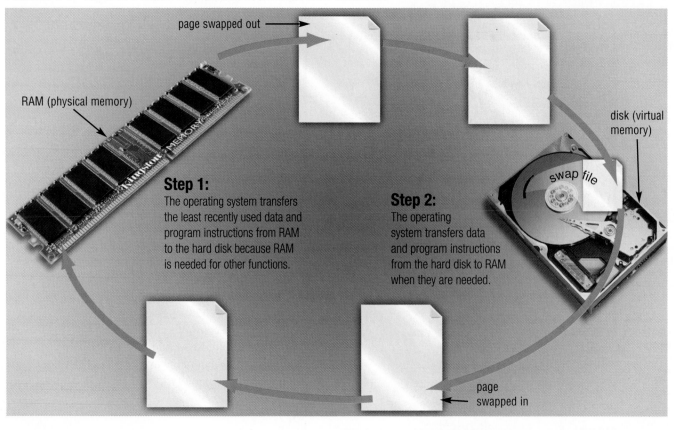

page swapped out

RAM (physical memory)

disk (virtual memory)

swap file

Step 1:
The operating system transfers the least recently used data and program instructions from RAM to the hard disk because RAM is needed for other functions.

Step 2:
The operating system transfers data and program instructions from the hard disk to RAM when they are needed.

page swapped in

A mulituser operating system does not always process jobs on a first-come, first-served basis. Sometimes, one user may have a higher priority than other users. In this case, the operating system adjusts the schedule of jobs.

Sometimes, a device already may be busy processing one job when it receives a second job. This occurs because the processor operates at a much faster rate of speed than peripheral devices. For example, if the processor sends five print jobs to a printer, the printer can print only one document at a time.

While waiting for devices to become idle, the operating system places items in buffers. A **buffer** is a segment of memory or storage in which items are placed while waiting to be transferred from an input device or to an output device.

The operating system commonly uses buffers with print jobs. This process, called **spooling**, sends print jobs to a buffer instead of sending them immediately to the printer. The buffer holds the information waiting to print while the printer prints from the buffer at its own rate of speed. By spooling print jobs to a buffer, the processor can continue interpreting and executing instructions while the printer prints. This allows users to work on the computer for other tasks while a printer is printing. Multiple print jobs line up in a **queue** (pronounced Q)

in the buffer. A program, called a *print spooler*, intercepts print jobs from the operating system and places them in the queue (Figure 8-8).

Configuring Devices

A **driver**, short for *device driver*, is a small program that tells the operating system how to communicate with a specific device. Each device on a computer, such as the mouse, keyboard, monitor, printer, card reader/writer, and scanner, has its own specialized set of commands and thus requires its own specific driver. When you boot a computer, the operating system loads each device's driver. These devices will not function without their correct drivers.

If you attach a new device to a computer, such as a printer or scanner, its driver must be installed before you can use the device. Today, many devices and operating systems support Plug and Play. As discussed in Chapter 4, **Plug and Play** means the operating system automatically configures new devices as you install them. Specifically, it assists you in the device's installation by loading the necessary drivers automatically and checking for conflicts with other devices. With Plug and Play, a user plugs in a device, turns on the computer, and then uses the device without having to configure the system manually.

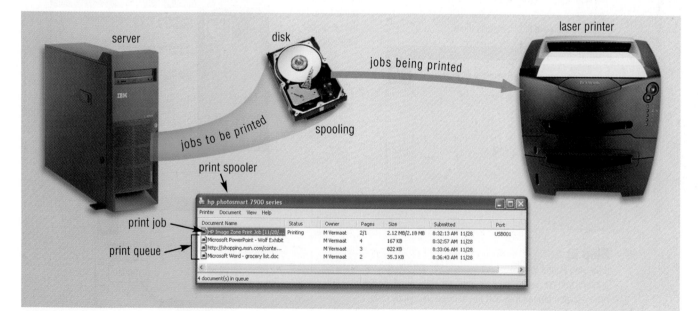

FIGURE 8-8 Spooling increases both processor and printer efficiency by placing print jobs in a buffer on disk before they are printed. This figure illustrates three jobs in the queue with one job printing.

For devices that are not Plug and Play, Windows XP provides a wizard to guide users through the installation steps. Figure 8-9 shows how to install a driver for a printer. You follow the same general steps to install drivers for any type of hardware. For many devices, the computer's operating system may include the necessary drivers. If it does not, you can install the drivers from the CD provided with the purchased device.

When you attach a Plug and Play device to a computer, the operating system determines an

FIGURE 8-9   HOW TO INSTALL DRIVERS FOR NEW HARDWARE IN WINDOWS XP

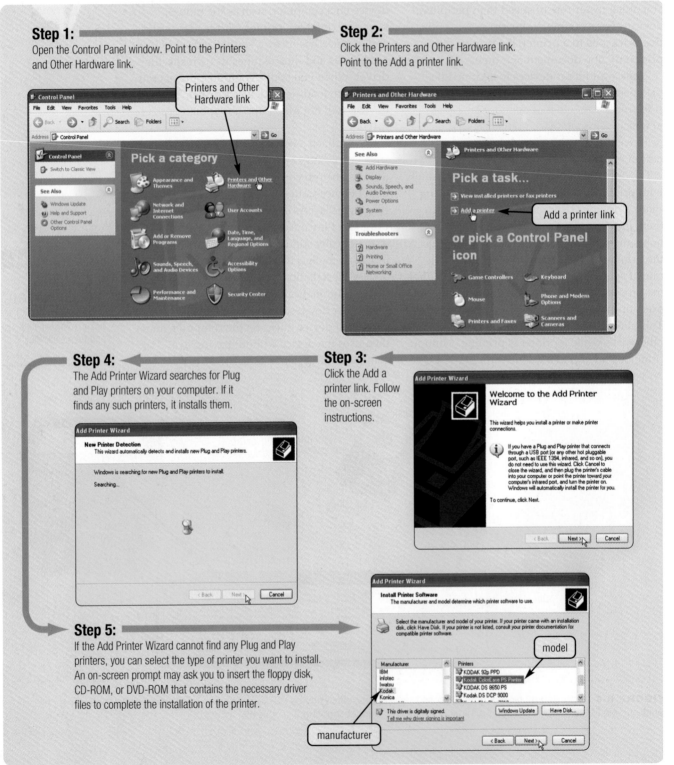

Step 1:
Open the Control Panel window. Point to the Printers and Other Hardware link.

Step 2:
Click the Printers and Other Hardware link. Point to the Add a printer link.

Step 4:
The Add Printer Wizard searches for Plug and Play printers on your computer. If it finds any such printers, it installs them.

Step 3:
Click the Add a printer link. Follow the on-screen instructions.

Step 5:
If the Add Printer Wizard cannot find any Plug and Play printers, you can select the type of printer you want to install. An on-screen prompt may ask you to insert the floppy disk, CD-ROM, or DVD-ROM that contains the necessary driver files to complete the installation of the printer.

appropriate IRQ to use. An *IRQ* (*interrupt request line*) is a communications line between a device and the processor.

FAQ 8-3

What if I do not have the driver for a device?

When reinstalling an operating system, you may have to supply a device's driver. If you do not have the original driver disc, visit the manufacturer's Web site. Most post drivers for download at no cost, or they may suggest a similar driver that will work. If you do not have Internet access, call the manufacturer and request a new disc via the postal service. For more information, visit scsite.com/dc2007/ch8/faq and then click Drivers.

Establishing an Internet Connection

Operating systems typically provide a means to establish Internet connections. For example, Windows XP includes a New Connection Wizard that guides users through the process of setting up a connection between a computer and an Internet service provider (Figure 8-10).

Some operating systems also include a Web browser and an e-mail program, enabling you to begin using the Web and communicate with others as soon as you set up the Internet connection. Some also include a built-in firewall to protect computers from unauthorized intrusions. Read Ethics & Issues 8-1 for a related discussion.

Monitoring Performance

Operating systems typically contain a performance monitor. A **performance monitor** is a program that assesses and reports information about various computer resources and devices (Figure 8-11). For example, users can monitor the processor, disks, memory, and network usage. A performance monitor also can check the number of reads and writes to a disk.

The information in performance reports helps users and administrators identify a problem with resources so they can try to resolve any problems. If a computer is running extremely slow, for example, the performance monitor may determine that the computer's memory is being used to its maximum. Thus, you might consider installing additional memory in the computer.

ETHICS & ISSUES 8-1

What Should Be in an Operating System?

Microsoft includes a Web browser, movie making software, a word processing program, plug-ins, a personal firewall, anti-spyware, and other programs, utilities, and features with its Windows operating system. Apple bundles QuickTime, CD burning software, and other programs, utilities, and features into Mac OS X. Manufacturers say that combining additional features and programs with their operating systems is a convenience for consumers and sometimes integral to the operating systems' performance. Microsoft's bundling of its Web browser with its Windows operating system was the proximate cause of an antitrust action against the software giant. Recently, the European Union ordered Microsoft to remove its media player from the Windows XP operating system as a result of antitrust action. Critics also insist that bundling applications with an operating system forces consumers to pay for programs that may be inferior to those available elsewhere. Is bundling applications with an operating system fair, or is it a monopolistic practice? Why? Who should decide what an operating system should include? Why? Should computer manufacturers be allowed to choose which bundled applications are installed on computers that they ship to customers? Why or why not?

FIGURE 8-10   To display the New Connection Wizard in Windows XP, click the Start button, point to All Programs, point to Accessories, point to Communications, and then click New Connection Wizard on the Communications submenu.

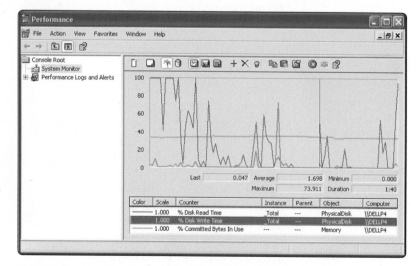

FIGURE 8-11   The System Monitor above is tracking disk read time, disk write time, and the amount of bytes in use.

Providing File Management and Other Utilities

Operating systems often provide users with the capability of managing files, viewing images, securing a computer from unauthorized access, uninstalling programs, scanning disks, defragmenting disks, diagnosing problems, backing up files and disks, and setting up screen savers. A later section in the chapter discusses these utilities in depth. Read Ethics & Issues 8-2 for a related discussion.

Controlling a Network

Some operating systems are network operating systems. A **network operating system**, or *network OS*, is an operating system that organizes and coordinates how multiple users access and share resources on a network. Resources include hardware, software, data, and information. For example, a network OS allows multiple users to share a printer, Internet access, files, and programs.

Some operating systems have network features built into them. In other cases, the network OS is a set of programs separate from the operating system on the client computers that access the network. When not connected to the network, the client computers use their own operating system. When connected to the network, the network OS may assume some of the operating system functions.

The *network administrator*, the person overseeing network operations, uses the network OS to add and remove users, computers, and other devices to and from the network. The network administrator also uses the network operating system to install software and administer network security.

Administering Security

The network administrator uses the network OS to establish permissions to resources. These permissions define who can access certain resources and when they can access those resources.

For each user, the network administrator establishes a user account, which enables a user to access, or **log on** to, a computer or a network. Each user account typically consists of a user name and password (Figure 8-12). A **user name**, or **user ID**, is a unique combination of characters, such as letters of the alphabet or numbers, that identifies one specific user. Many users select a combination of their first and last names as their user name. A user named Henry Baker might choose H Baker as his user name.

A **password** is a private combination of characters associated with the user name that allows access to certain computer resources. Some operating systems allow the network administrator to assign passwords to files

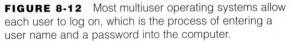

FIGURE 8-12 Most multiuser operating systems allow each user to log on, which is the process of entering a user name and a password into the computer.

and commands, restricting access to only authorized users.

To prevent unauthorized users from accessing computer resources, keep your password confidential. While entering your password, most computers hide the actual password characters by displaying some other characters, such as asterisks (*) or dots. After entering a user name and password, the operating system compares the user's entry with a list of authorized user names and passwords. If the entry matches the user name and password kept on file, the operating system grants the user access. If the entry does not match, the operating system denies access to the user.

The operating system records successful and unsuccessful logon attempts in a file. This allows the network administrator to review who is using or attempting to use the computer. Network administrators also use these files to monitor computer usage.

To protect sensitive data and information further as it travels over the network, a network operating system may encrypt it. *Encryption* is the process of encoding data and information into an unreadable form. Network administrators can set up a network to encrypt data as it travels over the network to prevent unauthorized users from reading the data. When an authorized user attempts to read the data, it automatically is decrypted, or converted back into a readable form.

FAQ 8-4

What are the guidelines for selecting a good password?

Choose a password that no one could guess. Do not use any part of your first or last name, your spouse's or child's name, telephone number, street address, license plate number, Social Security number, and so on. Be sure your password is at least six characters long, mixed with letters and numbers. For more information, visit scsite.com/dc2007/ch8/faq and then click Passwords.

Test your knowledge of pages 398 through 411 in Quiz Yourself 8-1.

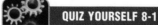

QUIZ YOURSELF 8-1

Instructions: Find the true statement below. Then, rewrite the remaining false statements so they are true.

1. A buffer is a small program that tells the operating system how to communicate with a specific device.
2. A cold boot is the process of using the operating system to restart a computer.
3. A password is a public combination of characters associated with the user name that allows access to certain computer resources.
4. Firmware that contains the computer's startup instructions is called the kernel.
5. The program you currently are using is in the background, and the other programs running but not in use are in the foreground.
6. Two types of system software are operating systems and application programs.
7. With virtual memory, the operating system allocates a portion of a storage medium, usually the hard disk, to function as additional RAM.

Quiz Yourself Online: To further check your knowledge of system software and features common to most operating systems, visit scsite.com/dc2007/ch8/quiz and then click Objectives 1 – 4.

OPERATING SYSTEM UTILITY PROGRAMS

A **utility program**, also called a **utility**, is a type of system software that allows a user to perform maintenance-type tasks, usually related to managing a computer, its devices, or its programs. Most operating systems include several built-in utility programs (Figure 8-13). Users often buy stand-alone utilities, however, because they offer improvements over those included with the operating system.

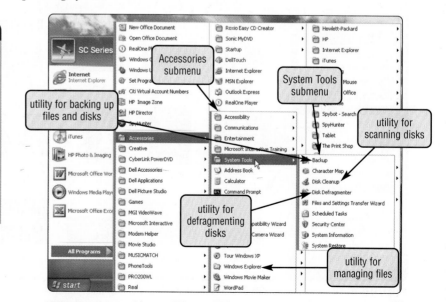

FIGURE 8-13 Many utilities available in Windows XP are accessible through the Accessories and System Tools submenus.

Utility programs included with most operating systems provide the following functions: managing files, viewing images, securing a computer from unauthorized access, uninstalling programs, scanning disks, defragmenting disks, diagnosing problems, backing up files and disks, and setting up screen savers. The following sections briefly discuss each of these utilities.

File Manager

A **file manager** is a utility that performs functions related to file and disk management. Windows XP includes a file manager called *Windows Explorer*. Some of the file and disk management functions that a file manager performs are formatting and copying disks; displaying a list of files on a storage medium (Figure 8-14); checking the amount of used or free space on a storage medium; organizing, copying, renaming, deleting, moving, and sorting files; and creating shortcuts. A **shortcut** is an icon on the desktop that provides a user with immediate access to a program or file.

Formatting is the process of preparing a disk for reading and writing. Most hard disk manufacturers preformat their disks. If you must format media, you can do so using the file manager. For a technical discussion about formatting, read the High-Tech Talk article on page 382 in Chapter 7.

Image Viewer

An **image viewer** is a utility that allows users to display, copy, and print the contents of a graphics file. With an image viewer, users can see images without having to open them in a paint or image editing program. Windows XP includes an image viewer called *Windows Picture and Fax Viewer* (Figure 8-15). To display a file in this image viewer, simply double-click the thumbnail of the image in the file manager. For example, double-clicking a thumbnail in Windows Explorer (Figure 8-14) displays the image in a Windows Picture and Fax Viewer window.

FIGURE 8-15 Windows Picture and Fax Viewer allows users to see the contents of a graphics file.

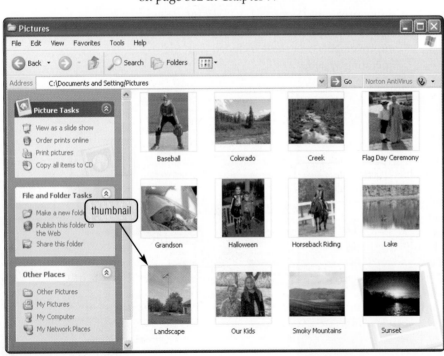

FIGURE 8-14 With Windows Explorer, which is the file manager included with Windows XP, users can display a list of graphics files on a disk. In this case, thumbnails of the files are displayed.

Personal Firewall

A **personal firewall** is a utility that detects and protects a personal computer from unauthorized intrusions. Personal firewalls constantly monitor all transmissions to and from a computer.

When connected to the Internet, your computer is vulnerable to attacks from a hacker. A *hacker* is someone who tries to access a computer or network illegally. Users with broadband Internet connections, such as through DSL and Internet cable television service, are even more susceptible than those with dial-up access because the Internet connection is always on.

The latest update to Windows XP automatically enables the built-in personal firewall upon installation. This firewall, called Windows Firewall, is easy to access and configure (Figure 8-16). If your operating system does not include a personal firewall or you want additional protection, you can purchase a stand-alone personal firewall utility or a hardware firewall, which is a device such as a router that has a built-in firewall.

Uninstaller

An **uninstaller** is a utility that removes a program, as well as any associated entries in the system files. In Windows XP, the uninstaller is available through the Add/Remove Programs command in the Control Panel.

When you install a program, the operating system records the information it uses to run the software in the system files. The uninstaller deletes files and folders from the hard disk, as well as removes program entries from the system files.

FAQ 8-5

Should I use the file manager to delete a program?

No! If you remove software from a computer by deleting the files and folders associated with the program without running the uninstaller, the system file entries are not updated. This may cause the operating system to display error messages when you start the computer. If the program has an uninstaller, always use it to remove software. For more information, visit scsite.com/ dc2007/ch8/faq and then click Uninstalling Programs.

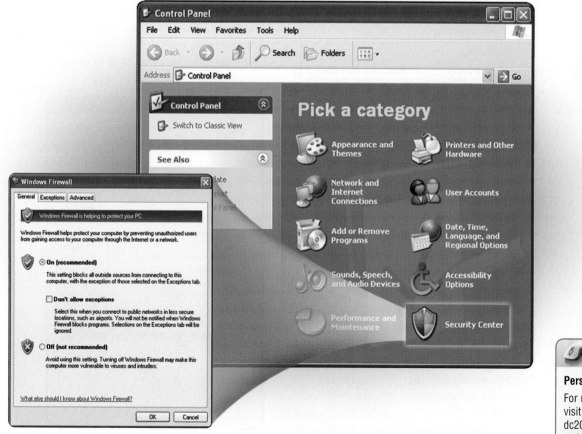

FIGURE 8-16 Through the Security Center in the Control Panel of Windows XP, users can configure Windows Firewall, which is a personal firewall utility built into the latest upgrade of Windows XP.

WEB LINK 8-3

Personal Firewalls

For more information, visit scsite.com/ dc2007/ch8/weblink and then click Personal Firewalls.

Disk Scanner

A **disk scanner** is a utility that (1) detects and corrects both physical and logical problems on a hard disk and (2) searches for and removes unnecessary files. A physical disk problem is a problem with the media such as a scratch on the surface of the disk. A logical disk problem is a problem with the data, such as a corrupt file. Windows XP includes two disk scanner utilities. One detects problems and the other searches for and removes unnecessary files such as temporary files (Figure 8-17).

FIGURE 8-17 Disk Cleanup searches for and removes unnecessary files.

Disk Defragmenter

A **disk defragmenter** is a utility that reorganizes the files and unused space on a computer's hard disk so the operating system accesses data more quickly and programs run faster. When an operating system stores data on a disk, it places the data in the first available sector on the disk. It attempts to place data in sectors that are contiguous (next to each other), but this is not always possible. When the contents of a file are scattered across two or more noncontiguous sectors, the file is *fragmented*.

Fragmentation slows down disk access and thus the performance of the entire computer. **Defragmenting** the disk, or reorganizing it so the files are stored in contiguous sectors, solves this problem (Figure 8-18). Windows XP includes a disk defragmenter available on the System Tools submenu.

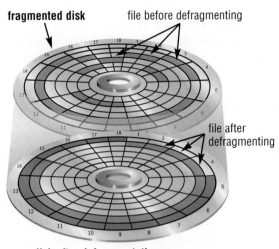

FIGURE 8-18 A fragmented disk has many files stored in noncontiguous sectors. Defragmenting reorganizes the files so they are located in contiguous sectors, which speeds access time.

Diagnostic Utility

A **diagnostic utility** compiles technical information about your computer's hardware and certain system software programs and then prepares a report outlining any identified problems. For example, Windows XP includes the diagnostic utility, *Dr. Watson*, which diagnoses problems as well as suggests courses of action (Figure 8-19). Information in the report assists technical support staff in remedying any problems.

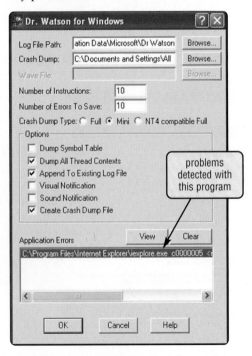

FIGURE 8-19 Dr. Watson is a diagnostic utility included with Windows.

Backup Utility

A **backup utility** allows users to copy, or *back up*, selected files or an entire hard disk to another storage medium such as CD, DVD, external hard disk, tape, or USB flash drive. During the backup process, the backup utility monitors progress and alerts you if it needs additional discs or tapes. Many backup programs *compress*, or shrink the size of, files during the backup process. By compressing the files, the backup program requires less storage space for the backup files than for the original files.

Because they are compressed, you usually cannot use backup files in their backed up form. In the event you need to use a backup file, a **restore program** reverses the process and returns backed up files to their original form. Backup utilities include restore programs.

You should back up files and disks regularly in the event your originals are lost, damaged, or destroyed. Windows XP includes a backup utility (Figure 8-20). Instead of backing up to a local disk storage device, some users opt to use online storage to back up their files. As described in Chapter 7, online storage is a service on the Web that provides hard disk storage to computer users, usually for a minimal monthly fee.

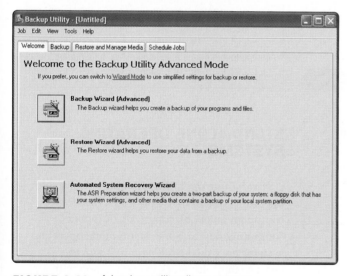

FIGURE 8-20 A backup utility allows users to copy files or an entire hard disk to another storage medium.

Screen Saver

A **screen saver** is a utility that causes a display device's screen to show a moving image or blank screen if no keyboard or mouse activity occurs for a specified time (Figure 8-21). When you press a key on the keyboard or move the mouse, the screen saver disappears and the screen returns to the previous state.

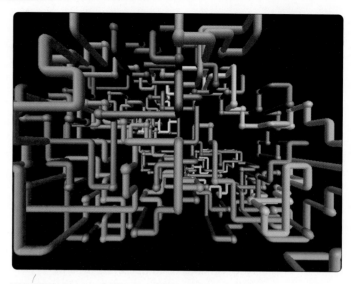

FIGURE 8-21 A Windows XP screen saver.

Screen savers originally were developed to prevent a problem called *ghosting*, in which images could be permanently etched on a monitor's screen. Although ghosting is not as severe of a problem with today's displays, manufacturers continue to recommend that users install screen savers for this reason. Screen savers also are popular for security, business, and entertainment purposes. To secure a computer, users configure their screen saver to require a password to deactivate. In addition to those included with the operating system, many screen savers are available in stores and on the Web for free or a minimal fee.

TYPES OF OPERATING SYSTEMS

Many of the first operating systems were device dependent and proprietary. A *device-dependent* program is one that runs only on a specific type or make of computer. *Proprietary software* is privately owned and limited to a specific vendor or computer model. Some operating systems still are device dependent. The trend today, however, is toward *device-independent* operating systems that run on computers provided by a variety of manufacturers. The advantage of device-independent operating systems is you can retain existing application software and data files even if you change computer models or vendors.

When you purchase a new computer, it typically has an operating system preinstalled. As new versions of the operating system are released, users upgrade their existing computers to incorporate features of the new version. An upgrade usually costs less than purchasing the entire operating system.

Some software manufacturers, such as Microsoft and IBM, release free downloadable updates to their software, often called a *service pack*. Users also can order service packs on CD for a minimal shipping fee. Service packs provide enhancements to the original software and fix bugs (errors) in the software. Read Ethics & Issues 8-3 for a related discussion.

New versions of an operating system usually are downward compatible. That is, they recognize and work with application software written for an earlier version of the operating system (or platform). The application software, by contrast, is said to be upward compatible, meaning it will run on new versions of the operating system.

The three basic categories of operating systems that exist today are stand-alone, network, and embedded. The table in Figure 8-22 lists specific names of operating systems in each category. The following pages discuss the operating systems listed in the table.

CATEGORIES OF OPERATING SYSTEMS

Category	Operating System Name
Stand-alone	• DOS • Early Windows versions (Windows 3.x, Windows 95, Windows NT Workstation, Windows 98, Windows 2000 Professional, Windows Millennium Edition) • Windows XP • Windows Vista • Mac OS X • UNIX • Linux
Network	• NetWare • Early Windows Server versions (Windows NT Server, Windows 2000 Server) • Windows Server 2003 • UNIX • Linux • Solaris
Embedded	• Windows CE • Windows Mobile • Palm OS • Embedded Linux • Symbian OS

FIGURE 8-22 Examples of stand-alone, network, and embedded operating systems. Some stand-alone operating systems include the capability of configuring small home or office networks.

ETHICS & ISSUES 8-3

Should Software Manufacturers Be Liable for Defective Software?

Several years ago in Panama, 28 patients receiving radiation treatment were given massive overdoses of radiation due to a software bug. Over the next several years, at least 12 of these patients died due to radiation poisoning and others were considered to be at risk of developing further complications. In another mishap, bugs in a sports car's braking system caused a warning light to not illuminate when problems were detected with the brakes. It is estimated that defective software costs U.S. businesses more than $60 billion annually. In a software license, software manufacturers usually include a disclaimer that limits the manufacturer's liability in the event that software malfunctions. Due to the increase in viruses, worms, and well-publicized software failures, such as the one that caused the power blackout in much of the northeastern U.S. a few years ago, many people are calling for the government to force software manufacturers to assume more liability. Software manufacturers claim that more liability — and consequently more cost — will result in less software and fewer features. They further claim that hardware manufacturers instead should be held responsible. Should the government enact more rules regarding software quality and liability? Why or why not? Who should be held accountable, if anyone, when faulty software causes injury or financial loss? Why? Will the free market or costly lawsuits eventually force makers of bug-ridden software to go out of business?

STAND-ALONE OPERATING SYSTEMS

A **stand-alone operating system** is a complete operating system that works on a desktop computer, notebook computer, or mobile computing device. Some stand-alone operating systems are called *client operating systems* because they also work in conjunction with a network operating system. Client operating systems can operate with or without a network. Other stand-alone operating systems include networking capabilities, allowing the home and small business user to set up a small network.

Examples of stand-alone operating systems are DOS, Windows XP, Windows Vista, Mac OS X, UNIX, and Linux. The following paragraphs briefly discuss these operating systems.

DOS

The term **DOS** (*Disk Operating System*) refers to several single user operating systems developed in the early 1980s by Microsoft for personal computers. The two more widely used versions of DOS were PC-DOS and MS-DOS. The functionality of these two operating systems was essentially the same.

DOS used a command-line interface when Microsoft first developed it. Later versions included both command-line and menu-driven user interfaces. At its peak, DOS was a widely used operating system, with an estimated 70 million computers running it. DOS hardly is used today because it does not offer a graphical user interface and it cannot take full advantage of modern 32-bit personal computer processors.

Windows XP

In the mid-1980s, Microsoft developed its first version of Windows, which provided a graphical user interface (GUI). Since then, Microsoft continually has updated its Windows operating system, incorporating innovative features and functions with each subsequent version (Figure 8-23). **Windows XP** is a fast, reliable Windows operating system, providing quicker startup, better performance, increased security, and a simpler visual look than previous Windows versions. Using Windows XP, home and small office users easily can set up a network and secure it from hackers with Windows Firewall. Windows Messenger, included with Windows XP, enables users to send instant messages. Windows XP also includes Windows Media Player, which allows users to listen to Internet radio stations, play

HIGHLIGHTS OF STAND-ALONE WINDOWS VERSIONS

Windows Version	Year Released	Highlights
Windows 3.x	1990	• Provided a GUI • An operating environment only — worked in combination with DOS
Windows NT 3.1	1993	• Client OS that connected to a Windows NT Advanced Server • Interface similar to Windows 3.x
Windows 95	1995	• True multitasking operating system • Improved GUI • Included support for networking, Plug and Play technology, longer file names, and e-mail
Windows NT Workstation 4.0	1996	• Client OS that connected to a Windows NT Server • Interface similar to Windows 95 • Network integration
Windows 98	1998	• Upgrade to Windows 95 • More integrated with the Internet; included *Internet Explorer* (a Web browser) • Faster system startup and shutdown, better file management, support for multimedia technologies (e.g., DVDs), and USB connectivity
Windows Millennium Edition	2000	• Upgrade to Windows 98 • Designed for the home user who wanted music playing, video editing, and networking capabilities
Windows 2000 Professional	2000	• Upgrade to Windows NT Workstation 4.0 • Complete multitasking client OS designed for business personal computers • Certified device drivers, faster performance, adaptive Start menu, image viewer, enhanced for mobile users
Windows XP	2001	• Upgrade to Windows Millennium Edition called Windows XP Home Edition • Upgrade to Windows 2000 Professional called Windows XP Professional • Windows XP Tablet PC Edition designed for Tablet PC users • Windows XP Media Center Edition designed for PCs used for home entertainment • Windows XP Professional x64 Edition designed for workstations that use 64-bit processors • Improved interface and increased performance in all editions
Windows XP SP2 (Service Pack 2)	2004	• Enhancement to Windows XP that offers more built-in security technologies • Improved firewall utility • Automatic blocking of Internet pop-up advertisements
Windows Vista	2006	• Upgrade to Windows XP • Easier to navigate user interface • Enhanced administration of user accounts • Improved firewall • Simplified customization techniques • New Document Explorer and Virtual Folders improve searching and organizing capabilities • Improved performance and reliability

FIGURE 8-23 Microsoft has released many versions of Windows.

MP3 and other music formats, copy music and data to CDs, and watch DVD movies.

Windows XP is available in five editions: Home Edition, Professional (Figure 8-24), Media Center Edition, Tablet PC Edition, and Professional x64 Edition.

- With *Windows XP Home Edition*, users easily can organize and share digital pictures, download and listen to music, create and edit videos, network home computers, send and receive instant messages, and recover from problems with easy-to-use tools.
- *Windows XP Professional* includes all the capabilities of Windows XP Home Edition and also offers greater data security, remote access to a computer, simpler administration of groups of users, multiple language user interface, and support for a wireless network.

- *Windows XP Media Center Edition* includes all features of Windows XP Professional and is designed for Media Center PCs. A *Media Center PC* is a home entertainment personal computer that includes a mid- to high-end processor, large-capacity hard disk, CD and DVD drives, a remote control, and advanced graphics and audio capabilities. These computers often use a television as their display device. Users access digital entertainment such as television programs, movies, music, radio, and photographs via a remote control device (Figure 8-25).
- *Windows XP Tablet PC Edition* includes all features of Windows XP Professional and provides additional features designed to make users more productive while working on their Tablet PC. With Windows Tablet PC Edition, users can write on the screen or issue instructions to the Tablet PC using a digital pen.
- *Windows XP Professional x64 Edition* is designed for power users with workstations that use 64-bit processors. It manages multicore processors and can support up to 128 GB of RAM and 16 TB of virtual memory.

FAQ 8-6

How many people use Windows?

According to Microsoft, the number of Windows PCs will grow to more than one billion by 2010. Studies by industry analysts estimate that 96 percent of desktop computers worldwide currently use Windows. For more information, visit scsite.com/dc2007/ch8/faq and then click Windows Users.

FIGURE 8-24 Windows XP, with its simplified look, is a fast, reliable Windows operating system.

FIGURE 8-25 With Windows XP Media Center Edition, users access recorded videos, pictures, music, television programs, radio stations, or movies via a remote control device.

Windows Vista

Windows Vista, the successor to Windows XP, is Microsoft's fastest, most reliable and efficient operating system to date, offering quicker application start up, built-in diagnostics, automatic recovery, improved security, and enhanced searching and organizing capabilities (Figure 8-26). The table in Figure 8-27 highlights features of Windows Vista.

Windows Vista is available in several editions, which are grouped in two general categories: Home and Business. The Windows Vista Home category includes several editions, each designed for a different level of user. All home editions include a firewall, parental controls, search capability, a photo library, and movie maker. For more advanced home users, other editions also include features such as media center functionality, DVD authoring, HDTV support, wireless networking automatic

configuration, and Tablet PC support. The Windows Vista Business category also includes several editions, designed for small businesses to large enterprises. To take advantage of all features and capabilities of Windows Vista, your computer should have 512 MB of RAM.

FIGURE 8-26 Windows Vista has a new interface, easier navigation and searching techniques, and improved security.

WEB LINK 8-5

Windows Vista
For more information, visit scsite.com/dc2007/ch8/weblink and then click Windows Vista.

WINDOWS VISTA FEATURES

Reliability and Performance	• New Sleep state combines resume speed of Windows XP Standby mode and low power consumption of Hibernate mode • Automatically detects and fine tunes performance problems • Built-in hardware diagnostics detect and repair problems automatically • Automatically recovers from failures, including restoring an unbootable computer to a usable state
Security	• User Account Protection allows administrators to restrict permissions • Improved firewall • Protects users from dangerous Web sites
Information Management	• *Document Explorer* (replaces My Documents in Windows XP) helps users locate documents by showing thumbnails that preview documents' content and allowing users to adjust thumbnail size to view a document without opening it • *Virtual Folders* store search criteria as part of the folder that instantly runs each time the folder opens, enabling users easily to locate documents stored anywhere on the computer • Use Quick Search to locate files based on file name or any other property saved with the file • Easily share files with other users
Appearance and Navigation	• Easy-to-navigate interface with translucent windows to minimize distraction • Flip through thumbnails of open windows using the mouse or keyboard • Windows Sidebar connects to personalized mini-applications, called gadgets, such as weather, photos, or headline news • Improved wizards • Common dialog boxes shared by all applications
Communications and the Internet	• Enhanced Internet Explorer • Improved e-mail program with built-in spam filter • Consistent and secure wireless network connections

FIGURE 8-27 Some features of Windows Vista.

Mac OS X

Since it was released in 1984 with Macintosh computers, Apple's **Macintosh operating system** has set the standard for operating system ease of use and has been the model for most of the new GUIs developed for non-Macintosh systems. The latest version, **Mac OS X**, is a multitasking operating system available only for computers manufactured by Apple (Figure 8-28).

Mac OS X includes features from previous versions of the Macintosh operating system such as large photo-quality icons, built-in networking support, e-mail, online shopping, enhanced speech recognition, CD burning, and enhanced multimedia capabilities. In addition, Mac OS X includes these features:

- New desktop search technology
- Dashboard, a desktop area for mini-applications
- Built-in, fast Web browser
- Parental controls
- Accessibility interface reads e-mail messages
- 3-D personal video and audio conferencing
- Filter to eliminate junk e-mail messages
- Contact lists synchronized with PDA or Bluetooth-enabled smart phone
- Latest version of QuickTime to listen to music and view videos on the Internet
- Easy networking of computers and devices
- Windows network connection and shared Windows documents

UNIX

UNIX (pronounced YOU-nix) is a multitasking operating system developed in the early 1970s by scientists at Bell Laboratories. Bell Labs (a subsidiary of AT&T) was prohibited from actively promoting UNIX in the commercial marketplace because of federal regulations. Bell Labs instead licensed UNIX for a low fee to numerous colleges and universities, where UNIX obtained a wide following. UNIX was implemented on many different types of computers. After deregulation of the telephone companies in the 1980s, UNIX was licensed to many hardware and software companies.

Several versions of this operating system exist, each slightly different. When programmers move application software from one UNIX version to another, they sometimes have to rewrite some of the programs. Although some versions of UNIX have a command-line interface, most versions of UNIX offer a graphical user interface (Figure 8-29).

Today, a version of UNIX is available for most computers of all sizes. Power users often work with UNIX because of its flexibility and power. Manufacturers such as Sun and IBM sell personal computers and workstations with a UNIX operating system.

FIGURE 8-28 Mac OS X is the operating system used with Apple Macintosh computers.

FIGURE 8-29 Some versions of UNIX have a graphical user interface.

Linux

Linux is one of the faster growing operating systems. **Linux** (pronounced LINN-uks) is a popular, multitasking UNIX-type operating system. In addition to the basic operating system, Linux also includes many free programming languages and utility programs.

Linux is not proprietary software like the operating systems discussed thus far. Instead, Linux is *open source software*, which means its code is provided for use, modification, and redistribution. It has no restrictions from the copyright holder regarding modification of the software's internal instructions and redistribution of the software. Many programmers have donated time to modify and redistribute Linux to make it the best possible version of UNIX. Promoters of open source software state two main advantages: users who modify the software share their improvements with others, and customers can personalize the software to meet their needs. Read Ethics & Issues 8-4 for a related discussion.

Some versions of Linux are command-line. Others are GUI. The two most popular GUIs available for Linux are GNOME and KDE. Some companies such as Red Hat market software applications that run on their own version of Linux (Figure 8-30). Many application programs, utilities, and plug-ins have Linux versions, including OpenOffice.org, StarOffice, Mozilla, Netscape, Yahoo! Messenger, RealPlayer, QuickTime, and Acrobat Reader.

Users obtain Linux in a variety of ways. Some download it free from the Web. Others purchase it from vendors such as Red Hat or IBM, who bundle their own software with the operating system. Linux CD-ROMs are included in many Linux books and also are available for purchase from vendors. Some retailers such as Dell will preinstall Linux on a new computer's hard disk on request. Read Looking Ahead 8-1 for a look at the next generation of Linux.

ETHICS & ISSUES 8-4

Closed Source vs. Open Source Operating Systems

Linux is a fast-growing, innovative operating system. One of the features that make it different from other operating systems is that Linux is open source and its source code, along with any changes, remains public. Since its introduction in 1991, Linux has been altered, adapted, and improved by thousands of programmers. Unlike Linux, most operating systems are proprietary, and their program code often is a zealously guarded secret. At one large software developer, an employee reported that application programmers had little opportunity to contribute to operating system programs because they had no access to the operating system program source code. Supporters of open source maintain that source code should be open to the public so that it can be scrutinized, corrected, and enhanced. In light of concerns about security and fears of possible virus problems, however, some people are not sure open source software is a good idea. Besides, they argue, companies and programmers should be able to control, and profit from, the operating systems they create. On the other hand, open source software can be scrutinized for errors by a much larger group of people and changes can be made immediately. Are open source operating systems a good idea? Why or why not? How can the concerns about open source operating systems be addressed? What are the advantages and disadvantages of open versus closed source operating systems? Does the open source model lead to better software?

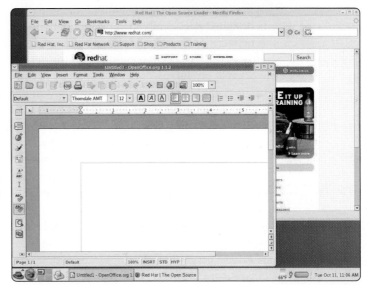

FIGURE 8-30   Red Hat provides a version of Linux called Red Hat Enterprise Linux.

LOOKING AHEAD 8-1

The Future of Linux

The Linux operating system has been altered and enhanced since Linus Torvalds wrote the initial source code in 1991. With hundreds of programmers donating their time to make Linux the best possible version of UNIX, the software literally has changed on a daily basis.

As these developers work to improve Linux, their efforts are helping to shape the software's future. Open source experts predict this operating system will command six percent of the computer market in a few years. They also believe the key to Linux's success is an initiative to get the product into schools as a viable alternative to Microsoft Windows. Expect to see Linux applications in the manufacturing, medicine, biometrics, and entertainment environments. For more information, visit scsite.com/dc2007/ch8/looking and then click Linux Future.

Test your knowledge of pages 411 through 421 in Quiz Yourself 8-2.

QUIZ YOURSELF 8-2

Instructions: Find the true statement below. Then, rewrite the remaining false statements so they are true.

1. A file manager is a utility that detects and protects a personal computer from unauthorized intrusions.

2. Fragmenting a disk is the process of reorganizing it so the files are stored in contiguous sectors.

3. Linux is available in five editions: Home Edition, Professional, Media Center Edition, Tablet PC Edition, and Professional x64 Edition.

4. Mac OS X is a multitasking operating system available only for computers manufactured by Apple.

5. Windows XP is a UNIX-type operating system that is open source software.

6. You should uninstall files and disks regularly in the event your originals are lost, damaged, or destroyed.

Quiz Yourself Online: To further check your knowledge of utilities included with most operating systems and stand-alone operating systems, visit scsite.com/dc2007/ch8/quiz and then click Objectives 5 – 6.

NETWORK OPERATING SYSTEMS

As discussed earlier in this chapter, a network operating system is an operating system that is designed specifically to support a network. A network operating system typically resides on a server. The client computers on the network rely on the server(s) for resources. Many of the client operating systems discussed in the previous section work in conjunction with a network operating system.

Some of the stand-alone operating systems discussed in the previous section include networking capability; however, network operating systems are designed specifically to support all sizes of networks, including medium to large-sized businesses and Web servers. Examples of network operating systems include NetWare, Windows Server 2003, UNIX, Linux, and Solaris.

NetWare

Novell's *NetWare* is a network operating system designed for client/server networks. NetWare has a server portion that resides on the network server and a client portion that resides on each client computer connected to the network. NetWare supports open source software and runs on all types of computers from mainframes to personal computers.

The server portion of NetWare allows users to share hardware devices attached to the server (such as a printer), as well as e-mail, databases, or any other files and software

stored on the server. The client portion of NetWare communicates with the server. Client computers also can have their own stand-alone operating system such as Windows XP, Mac OS X, or a Linux-based client.

Windows Server 2003

Windows Server 2003 is an upgrade to Windows 2000 Server, which was an upgrade to Windows NT Server. Windows Server 2003, which includes features of previous server versions, offers the following capabilities:

- Web site management and hosting
- Delivery and management of multimedia across intranets and the Internet
- Document storage in Web folders
- Central information repository about network users and resources with *Active Directory*
- Client support using Windows XP and earlier versions of Windows, Mac OS X, UNIX, and Linux

To meet the needs of all sizes of businesses, the **Windows Server 2003 family** includes five products:

- *Windows Small Business Server 2003* designed for businesses with fewer than 75 users and limited networking expertise
- *Windows Server 2003, Standard Edition* for the typical small- to medium-sized business network
- *Windows Server 2003, Enterprise Edition* for medium- to large-sized businesses, including those with e-commerce operations; available in 64-bit version

- *Windows Server 2003, Datacenter Edition* for businesses with huge volumes of transactions and large-scale databases; available in 64-bit version
- *Windows Server 2003, Web Edition* for Web server and Web hosting businesses

Windows Server 2003 is part of Windows Server System. In addition to Windows Server 2003, *Windows Server System* provides developers with dynamic development tools that allow businesses and customers to connect and communicate easily via the Internet. Through Windows Server System, programmers have the ability to use *Web services*, which are Web applications created with any programming language or any operating system to communicate and share data seamlessly.

UNIX

In addition to being a stand-alone operating system, UNIX also is a network operating system. That is, UNIX is capable of handling a high volume of transactions in a multiuser environment and working with multiple processors using multiprocessing. For this reason, some computer professionals call UNIX a *multipurpose operating system* because it is both a stand-alone and network operating system. Many Web servers use UNIX as their operating system.

Linux

Some network servers use Linux as their operating system. Thus, Linux also is a multipurpose operating system. With Linux, a network administrator can configure the network, administer security, run a Web server, and process e-mail. Clients on the network can run Linux, UNIX, or Windows. Versions of Linux include both the Netscape and Mozilla Web browsers.

Solaris

Solaris, a version of UNIX developed by Sun Microsystems, is a network operating system designed specifically for e-commerce applications. Solaris manages high-traffic accounts and incorporates security necessary for Web transactions. Client computers often use a desktop program, such as GNOME desktop, that communicates with the Solaris operating system.

WEB LINK 8-8

Solaris
For more information, visit scsite.com/ dc2007/ch8/weblink and then click Solaris.

EMBEDDED OPERATING SYSTEMS

The operating system on most PDAs and small devices, called an **embedded operating system**, resides on a ROM chip. Popular embedded operating systems today include Windows CE, Windows Mobile, Palm OS, Embedded Linux, and Symbian OS. The following sections discuss these operating systems.

Windows CE

Windows CE is a scaled-down Windows operating system designed for use on communications, entertainment, and computing devices with limited functionality. Examples of devices that use Windows CE include Voice over IP devices, industrial control devices, point-of-sale terminals, security robots, navigation systems, media players, ticket machines, and computerized sewing machines (Figure 8-31).

FAQ 8-7

How widespread is Linux usage?

Forecasters predict that Linux will command one-third of the server market by 2008. Desktop personal computers, however, have a much lower Linux usage — only six percent worldwide. For more information, visit scsite.com/ dc2007/ch8/faq and then click Linux Users.

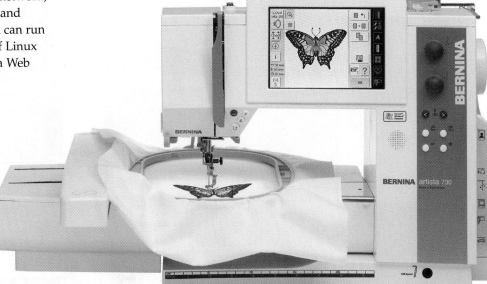

FIGURE 8-31 This sewing machine uses Windows CE to assist with stitching quilts, garments, crafts, decorations, and embroidery.

Windows CE is a GUI that supports color, sound, multitasking, multimedia, e-mail, Internet access, and Web browsing. A built-in file viewer allows users to view files created in popular applications such as Word, Excel, and PowerPoint.

Devices equipped with Windows CE can communicate wirelessly with computers and other devices using Bluetooth or other wireless technologies, as long as the device is equipped with the necessary communications hardware.

Windows Mobile

Windows Mobile, an operating system based on Windows CE, includes functionality, applications, and a user interface designed for specific types of devices. Windows Mobile-based devices include PDAs, called the **Pocket PC**, and smart phones (Figure 8-32). With the Windows Mobile operating system and a Pocket PC or smart phone, users have access to all the basic PIM (personal information manager) functions such as contact lists, schedules, tasks, calendars, and notes. Information on the PDA or smart phone easily synchronizes with a personal computer or prints on a printer using a cable or a wireless technology.

Windows Mobile, which has a Windows XP look, also provides numerous additional features that allow users to check e-mail, browse the Web, listen to music, take pictures or record video, watch a video, send and receive instant messages, record a voice message, manage finances, or read an e-book. Many applications such as Word, Excel, Outlook, and Internet

Explorer, have scaled-down versions that run with Windows Mobile. Some devices with Windows Mobile also support handwriting and voice input. With the Pocket PC Phone Edition devices, users can make telephone calls and send text messages using the PDA.

Palm OS

A competing operating system to Windows Mobile is *Palm OS*, which runs on PDAs and smart phones (Figure 8-33). With Palm OS devices, users manage schedules and contacts, telephone messages, project notes, reminders, task and address lists, and important dates and appointments. Information on the PDA or smart phone easily synchronizes with a personal computer or prints on a printer using a cable or a wireless technology. Palm users also can exchange information with other Palm users wirelessly through IrDA technology.

Palm OS includes handwriting recognition software, called Graffiti. Many Palm OS devices allow users to connect wirelessly to the Internet, browse the Web, send and receive e-mail messages and instant messages, listen to music, record voice messages, and view digital photos. The latest version of Palm OS includes improved security for data transmission, allows for biometric identification, and supports the use of smart cards.

WEB LINK 8-9

Windows Mobile

For more information, visit scsite.com/dc2007/ch8/weblink and then click Windows Mobile.

WEB LINK 8-10

Palm OS

For more information, visit scsite.com/dc2007/ch8/weblink and then click Palm OS.

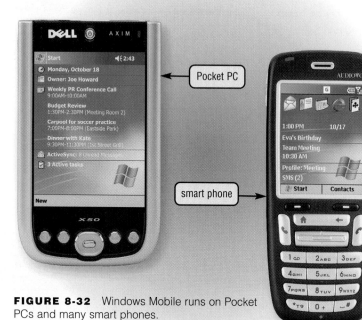

FIGURE 8-32 Windows Mobile runs on Pocket PCs and many smart phones.

FIGURE 8-33 Palm OS runs on PDAs and smart phones.

Embedded Linux

Embedded Linux is a scaled-down Linux operating system designed for PDAs, smart phones, smart watches, set-top boxes, Internet telephones, and many other types of devices and computers requiring an embedded operating system (Figure 8-34). PDAs and smart phones with embedded Linux offer calendar and address book and other PIM functions, touch screens, and handwriting recognition. Many also allow you to connect to the Internet, take pictures, play videos, listen to music, and send e-mail and instant messages. Devices that use embedded Linux synchronize with desktop computers using a variety of technologies including Bluetooth.

FIGURE 8-34
A PDA that uses embedded Linux.

Symbian OS

Symbian OS is an open source multitasking operating system designed for smart phones (Figure 8-35). In addition to making telephone calls, users of Symbian OS can maintain contact lists; save appointments; browse the Web; and send and receive text and picture messages, e-mail messages, and faxes using a smart phone. Users enter data by pressing keys on the keypad or keyboard, touching the screen, writing on the screen with a stylus, or speaking into the smart phone. Symbian OS allows users to communicate wirelessly using a variety of technologies including Bluetooth and IrDA.

FIGURE 8-35 This smart phone uses the Symbian OS.

STAND-ALONE UTILITY PROGRAMS

Although operating systems typically include some built-in utilities, many stand-alone utility programs are available for purchase. For example, you can purchase personal firewall, backup utilities, and screen savers. These stand-alone utilities typically offer improvements over those features built into the operating system or provide features not included in an operating system.

Other functions provided by stand-alone utilities include protecting against viruses, removing spyware and adware, filtering Internet content, converting files, compressing files, burning CDs and DVDs, and maintaining a personal computer. The following sections discuss each of these utilities.

Antivirus Programs

The term, computer **virus**, describes a potentially damaging computer program that affects, or infects, a computer negatively by altering the way the computer works without the user's knowledge or permission. More specifically, a computer virus is a segment of program code from some outside source that implants itself in a computer. Once the virus is in a computer, it can spread throughout and may damage your files and operating system.

Currently, more than 81,000 known virus programs exist with an estimated 6 new virus programs discovered each day. Computer viruses do not generate by chance. The programmer of a virus, known as a *virus author*, intentionally writes a virus program. Some virus authors find writing viruses a challenge. Others write virus programs to cause destruction. Writing a virus program usually requires significant programming skills.

Some viruses are harmless pranks that simply freeze a computer temporarily or display sounds or messages. The Music Bug virus, for example, instructs the computer to play a few chords of music. Other viruses destroy or corrupt data stored on the hard disk of the infected computer. If you notice any unusual changes in your computer's performance, it may be infected with a virus. Figure 8-36 outlines some common symptoms of virus infection.

SIGNS OF VIRUS INFECTION

- An unusual message or image is displayed on the computer screen
- An unusual sound or music plays randomly
- The available memory is less than what should be available
- A program or file suddenly is missing
- An unknown program or file mysteriously appears
- The size of a file changes without explanation
- A file becomes corrupted
- A program or file does not work properly
- System properties change

FIGURE 8-36 Viruses attack computers in a variety of ways. This list indicates some of the more common signs of virus infection.

Viruses are just one type of malicious software. *Malware* (short for malicious software) is software that acts without a user's knowledge and deliberately alters the computer's operations. In addition to viruses, worms and Trojan horses are malware.

A **worm**, such as Sasser or Zotob, copies itself repeatedly, for example, in memory or over a network, using up system resources and possibly shutting the system down. A **Trojan horse** (named after the Greek myth) hides within or looks like a legitimate program such as a screen saver. A certain condition or action usually triggers the Trojan horse. Unlike a virus or worm, a Trojan horse does not replicate itself to other computers. For a more technical discussion about computer viruses, read the High-Tech Talk article in Chapter 3 on page 168.

To protect a computer from virus attacks, users should install an antivirus program and update it frequently. An **antivirus program** protects a computer against viruses by identifying and removing any computer viruses found in memory, on storage media, or on incoming files (Figure 8-37). Most antivirus programs also protect against worms and Trojan horses. When you purchase a new computer, it often includes antivirus software.

The two more popular antivirus programs are McAfee VirusScan and Norton AntiVirus. As an alternative to purchasing these products on CD, both McAfee and Norton offer Web-based antivirus programs. That is, during your paid subscription period, the program continuously protects the computer against viruses.

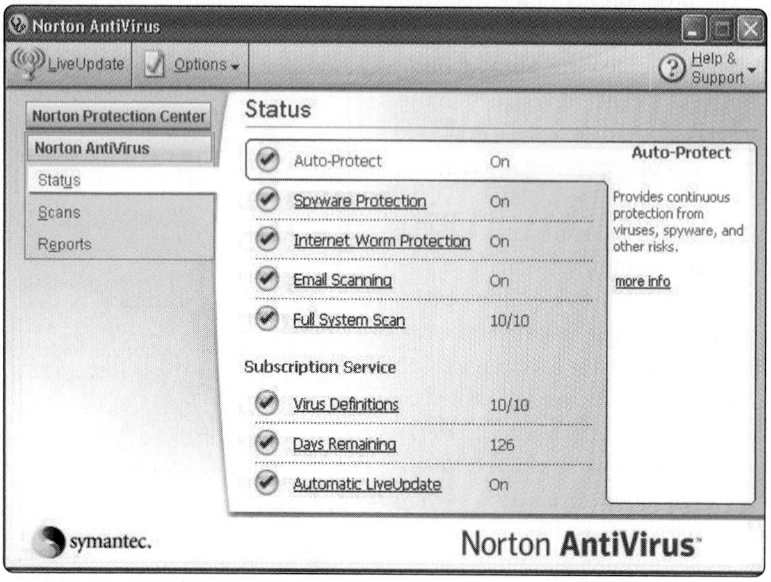

FIGURE 8-37 An antivirus program scans memory, disks, and incoming e-mail messages and attachments for viruses and attempts to remove any viruses it finds.

FAQ 8-8

What steps should I take to prevent virus infections on my computer?

Set up the antivirus software to scan on a regular basis. Update your virus definitions regularly. Never open an e-mail attachment unless you are expecting the attachment and it is from a trusted source. If you use Windows, install the latest updates. Set macro security in programs such as word processing and spreadsheet so you can enable or disable macros. Back up files regularly. For more information, visit scsite.com/dc2007/ch8/faq and then click Preventing Virus Infections.

Spyware Removers

Spyware is a program placed on a computer without the user's knowledge that secretly collects information about the user, often related to Web browsing habits. Spyware often enters a computer as a result of a user installing a new program. The spyware program communicates information it collects to some outside source while you are online.

Adware is a program that displays an online advertisement in a banner or pop-up window on Web pages, e-mail, or other Internet services. Sometimes, spyware is hidden in adware. A **spyware remover** is a program that detects and deletes spyware, adware, and other similar programs. Most spyware removers cost less than $50; some are available on the Web at no cost. Some operating systems include adware blockers.

Internet Filters

Filters are programs that remove or block certain items from being displayed. Three widely used Internet filters are anti-spam programs, Web filters, and pop-up blockers.

ANTI-SPAM PROGRAMS *Spam* is an unsolicited e-mail message or newsgroup posting sent to many recipients or newsgroups at once. Spam is Internet junk mail. The content of spam ranges from selling a product or service, to promoting a business opportunity, to advertising offensive material. An **anti-spam program** is a filtering program that attempts to remove spam before it reaches your inbox. If your e-mail program does not include an anti-spam program, many anti-spam programs are available at no cost on the Web. Internet access providers often filter spam as a service for their subscribers.

Should anti-spam programs be installed on home computers?

Yes. With more than 65 percent of all e-mail categorized as spam, home and business users could lose valuable time sifting through messages related to the variety of subjects shown in the chart below. For more information, visit scsite.com/dc2007/ch8/faq and then click Anti-Spam Programs.

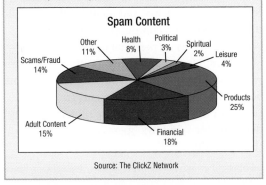

Source: The ClickZ Network

WEB FILTERS   **Web filtering software** is a program that restricts access to certain material on the Web. Some restrict access to specific Web sites; others filter sites that use certain words or phrases. Many businesses use Web filtering software to limit employee's Web access. Some schools, libraries, and parents use this software to restrict access to minors.

POP-UP BLOCKERS   A *pop-up ad* is an Internet advertisement that appears in a new window in the foreground of a Web page displayed in your browser. A **pop-up blocker** is a filtering program that stops pop-up ads from displaying on Web pages. If your operating system does not block pop-up ads, many pop-up blockers can be downloaded from the Web at no cost.

File Conversion

A *file conversion utility* transforms the contents of a file or data from one format to another. When a business develops a new information system, often the data in the current system is not in the correct format for the new system. Thus, part of the system development process is to convert data — instead of having users reenter all the existing data in the new system. On a smaller scale, when home users purchase new software, they may need to convert files so the files will be displayed properly in the new software.

File Compression

A **file compression utility** shrinks the size of a file(s). A compressed file takes up less storage space than the original file. Compressing files frees up room on the storage media and improves system performance. Attaching a compressed file to an e-mail message, for example, reduces the time needed for file transmission. Uploading and downloading compressed files to and from the Internet reduces the file transmission time.

Compressed files, sometimes called **zipped files**, usually have a .zip extension. When you receive or download a compressed file, you must uncompress it. To **uncompress**, or *unzip*, a file, you restore it to its original form. Some operating systems such as Windows XP include uncompress capabilities. To compress a file, however, you need a stand-alone file compression utility. Two popular stand-alone file compression utilities are PKZIP and WinZip (Figure 8-38).

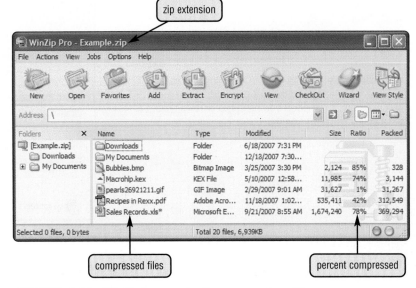

FIGURE 8-38   WinZip is a popular file compression utility.

WEB LINK 8-11

File Compression Utilities

For more information, visit scsite.com/dc2007/ch8/weblink and then click File Compression Utilities.

CD/DVD Burning

CD/DVD burning software writes text, graphics, audio, and video files on a recordable or rewritable CD or DVD. This software enables the home user easily to back up contents of their hard disk on a CD/DVD and make duplicates of uncopyrighted music or movies. CD/DVD burning software usually also includes photo editing, audio editing, and video editing capabilities (Figure 8-39).

When you buy a recordable or rewritable CD or DVD, it typically includes CD/DVD burning software. You also can buy CD/DVD burning software for a cost of less than $100.

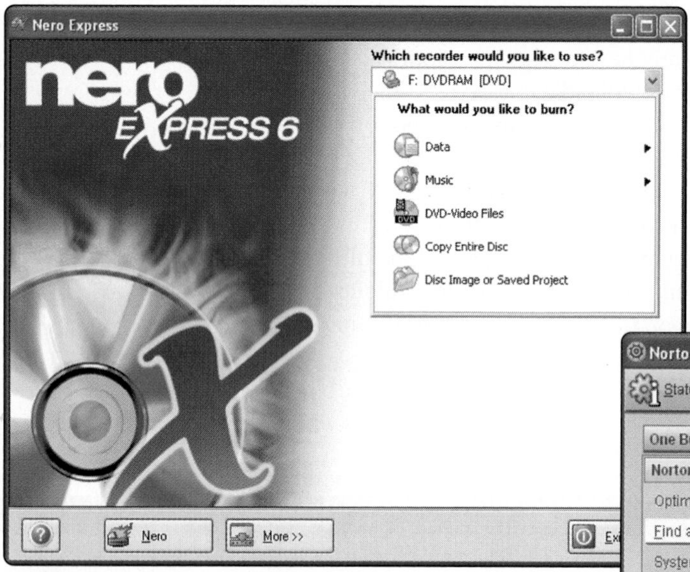

Personal Computer Maintenance

Operating systems typically include a diagnostic utility that diagnoses computer problems but does not repair them. A **personal computer maintenance utility** identifies and fixes operating system problems, detects and repairs disk problems, and includes the capability of improving a computer's performance. Additionally, some personal computer maintenance utilities continuously monitor a computer while you use it to identify and repair problems before they occur. Norton SystemWorks is a popular personal computer maintenance utility designed for Windows operating systems (Figure 8-40).

FIGURE 8-39 Using CD/DVD burning software, you can copy text, graphics, audio, and video files on CD or DVD, provided you have the correct type of CD/DVD drive and media.

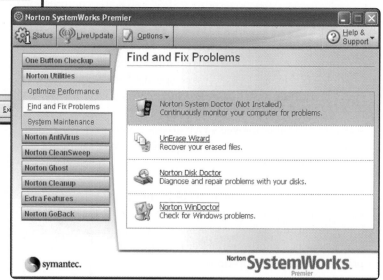

FIGURE 8-40 A popular maintenance program for Windows users.

Test your knowledge of pages 422 through 428 in Quiz Yourself 8-3.

QUIZ YOURSELF 8-3

Instructions: Find the true statement below. Then, rewrite the remaining false statements so they are true.

1. A pop-up blocker shrinks the size of a file(s).

2. An anti-spam program protects a computer against viruses by identifying and removing any computer viruses found in memory, on storage media, or on incoming files.

3. Examples of network operating systems include NetWare, Windows Server 2003, UNIX, Linux, and Solaris.

4. Pocket PCs use Palm OS as their operating system.

5. Web filtering software writes text, graphics, audio, and video files to a recordable or rewritable CD or DVD.

Quiz Yourself Online: To further check your knowledge of network operating systems, embedded operating systems, and stand-alone utility programs, visit scsite.com/dc2007/ch8/quiz and then click Objectives 7 – 9.

CHAPTER SUMMARY

This chapter defined an operating system and then discussed the functions common to most operating systems. Next, it introduced several utility programs commonly found in operating systems. The chapter discussed a variety of stand-alone operating systems, network operating systems, and embedded operating systems (read Looking Ahead 8-2 for a look at the next generation of operating systems). Finally, the chapter described several stand-alone utility programs.

LOOKING AHEAD 8-2

Online Operating Systems Proposed

Microsoft Windows' dominance in the operating system world is being challenged by proposed Web operating systems. Experts predict that within a few years computer users will see Google, Yahoo!, and Mozilla release Internet-enabled products.

If these operating systems come to fruition, computer users will access content and manage data using a Web browser. They will be unaware of when their computer is retrieving information from the Web or from their local computer. Applications will be written for this Web browser and will not be dependent upon a specific machine or cellular phone.

Proposed applications include reading e-mail, blogs, and news offline, backing up files to an online service, and managing audio and video files. For more information, visit scsite.com/dc2007/ch8/looking and then click Operating Systems.

CAREER CORNER

Systems Programmer

System software is a key component in any computer. A *systems programmer* evaluates, installs, and maintains system software and provides technical support to the programming staff.

Systems programmers work with the programs that control computers, such as operating systems, network operating systems, and database systems. They identify current and future processing needs and then recommend the software and hardware necessary to meet those needs. In addition to selecting and installing system software, systems programmers must be able to adapt system software to the requirements of an organization, provide regular maintenance, measure system performance, determine the impact of new or updated software on the system, design and implement special software, and provide documentation. Because they are familiar with the entire system, systems programmers often help application programmers to diagnose technical problems.

Systems programmers must be acquainted thoroughly with a variety of operating systems. They must be able to think logically, pay attention to detail, work with abstract concepts, and devise solutions to complex problems. Systems programmers often work in teams and interact with programmers and nontechnical users, so communications skills are important.

Most systems programmers have a four-year B.S. degree in Computer Science or Information Technology. Depending on responsibilities and experience, salaries range from $55,000 to more than $110,000. For more information, visit scsite.com/dc2007/ch8/careers and then click Systems Programmer.

High-Tech Talk

WINDOWS XP: A USEFUL WAY TO COMPLETE A WIDE RANGE OF TASKS

When Microsoft developed the Windows XP operating system, it gave it a fresh, new graphical user interface. You still, however, can complete many important tasks using the command-line interface. Microsoft's first operating system, MS-DOS, was based entirely on a command-line interface. Today, Windows XP supports many of the original MS-DOS commands — and many new commands that help you complete tasks.

With Windows XP, you enter commands via a command shell. A *command shell* is a program with a nongraphical, command-line interface that provides an environment to run text-based application software and utility programs. The Windows XP command shell is called *Command Prompt*; the file name for the Command Prompt application is cmd.exe.

To open the Command Prompt window, click the Start button and point to All Programs, point to Accessories on the All Programs submenu, and then click Command Prompt on the Accessories submenu. Clicking Run on the Start menu and then typing cmd in the Run dialog box also opens the Command Prompt window. To execute a command, type one command per line and then press the ENTER key. Many commands allow you to enter one or more *options*, or *arguments*, which are additions to a command that change or refine the command in a specified manner. To close the Command Prompt window, type exit and then press the ENTER key or click the Close button in the Command Prompt window.

The Command Prompt window allows you to complete a wide range of tasks, including troubleshooting network connections. The *ping command*, for example, allows you to test TCP/IP connectivity for network and Internet connections (Figure 8-4a on page 403). When you enter the ping command with an IP address, your computer sends a special packet called ICMP Echo to that address. If everything is working, a reply comes back; if not, the ping times out. You also can use *TRACERT* (*traceroute*), a command-line utility that traces a data packet's path to its destination. When you enter tracert scsite.com, for example, the tracert utility traces the path from your computer to the Shelly Cashman Web server (Figure 8-41). The tracert command sends information to each device (called a hop) three times. The traceroute program sends the information three times to give you some idea of the variance in transit times. The time it takes for the device to respond each time is displayed. When you access a Web site, your request usually will pass through several routers before you connect to the destination server. For example, the tracert command for scsite.com passed through 15 other routers before connecting to the destination server (www.scsite.com).

You also can use the Windows XP Command Prompt to help manage your computer. When you enter the *systeminfo command*, Command Prompt queries your computer for basic system information, including operating system configuration and hardware properties, such as RAM and disk space. If you enter the *tasklist command*, the Command Prompt window returns a list of processes running on a computer, with each process identified by a process ID (PID). You can terminate any process by entering the *taskkill command* and the PID as the argument. Network administrators can use this command to fix problems on networked computers by closing applications.

The Windows XP Command Prompt also supports commands used to manage the files and file system on your hard disk. The *chkdsk command* checks for and corrects errors on the disk. You also can defragment your hard disk by entering the *defrag command*, with an argument specifying the drive to defragment (for example, defrag c:). When you are done working, you can use the *shutdown command* to shut down or restart your local or a remote computer.

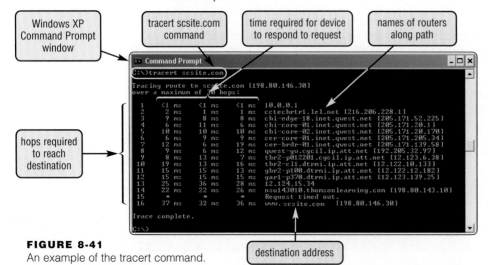

Windows XP Command Prompt window

tracert scsite.com command

time required for device to respond to request

names of routers along path

hops required to reach destination

destination address

FIGURE 8-41
An example of the tracert command.

In most cases, the command-line tools perform functions similar to the GUI application. The Disk Defragmenter utility and the defrag command, for example, provide similar functionality. In others, the command-line tools provide additional functionality. For instance, the *diskpart command* starts the command-line version of the DiskPart utility and gives you access to advanced features not available in the GUI version.

The commands discussed here are just some of the wide range of commands supported by Windows XP. For more information, visit scsite.com/dc2007/ch8/tech and then click Windows XP Command Prompt.

Companies on the Cutting Edge

RED HAT
OPEN SOURCE SOFTWARE DISTRIBUTOR

When you were young, you were taught to share. University professors share their research with colleagues throughout the world; and *Red Hat* shares software code, or instructions, with computer users.

Red Hat is the largest supplier of open source software, which allows buyers to view, modify, and perhaps improve, the software. The company delivers the software improvements to customers through the Red Hat Network, the company's Internet service.

Bob Young and Marc Ewing founded Red Hat in 1994 and started distributing a version of the Red Hat Linux operating system complete with documentation and support. Today, Linux is Red Hat's most well-known product. Subscriptions to the company's premium Linux software have helped boost the company to profitability. The subscriptions include tested updates, security fixes, and technical information updated daily. For more information, visit scsite.com/dc2007/ch8/companies and then click Red Hat.

SYMBIAN
HANDHELD COMPUTING DEVICES MANUFACTURER

The next time you send a text message using your smart phone, you may be using an operating system developed by *Symbian*. This British company's operating system is the global industry standard and is licensed to 11 leading cellular telephone manufacturers, including Ericsson, Matsushita (Panasonic), Motorola, Nokia, and Psion, which account for more than 39 million cellular phones worldwide.

In 1994, former CEO Colly Myers began experimenting with his programming expertise with the goal of developing a full operating system for a handset rivaling that found on a mainframe computer. Four years later, he convinced Ericsson, Motorola, and Nokia to invest in his product.

The Symbian open standards allow manufacturers to customize services and user interfaces, including graphics, e-mail, and touch screens. For more information, visit scsite.com/dc2007/ch8/companies and then click Symbian.

Technology Trailblazers

ALAN KAY
COMPUTER PIONEER

Chances are that every time you use your computer you use one of *Alan Kay*'s ideas. More than 35 years ago — long before the personal computer became ubiquitous — he was developing a notebook computer complete with a flat screen, wireless network, and storage. More than 20 years ago, he engineered a graphical user interface, object-oriented languages, and personal computer networks.

Kay did much of his early work at the U.S. Defense Department's Advance Research Project Agency (DARPA) and Xerox's Palo Alto Research Center (PARC). Today he is a computer science professor at UCLA and president of the Viewpoints Research Institute, a nonprofit organization dedicated to helping children develop fluency in critical thinking, math, and science. For more information, visit scsite.com/dc2007/ch8/people and then click Alan Kay.

LINUS TORVALDS
LINUX CREATOR

When *Linus Torvalds* developed a new operating system in 1991, he announced his project in an Internet newsgroup, made the source code available, and asked for suggestions. Computer users responded by reviewing the system and offering enhancements. Three years later, Torvalds released a much-enhanced version of an open source operating system he called Linux.

Torvalds developed the innovative operating system when he was a 21-year-old computer science student in Finland. Today, Linux is estimated to be running on at least 10 percent of computers and is Microsoft's main competitor. Torvalds leads the development of Linux as a fellow at OSDL (Open Source Development Labs), a not-for-profit consortium of companies dedicated to developing and promoting the operating system. In 2005, Torvalds predicted Linux will be a prominent part of the desktop market within the next 10 years. For more information, visit scsite.com/dc2007/ch8/people and then click Linus Torvalds.

Chapter Review

The Chapter Review section summarizes the concepts presented in this chapter. To listen to the audio version of this Chapter Review, visit scsite.com/dc2007/ch8/review. To obtain help from other students regarding any subject in this chapter, visit scsite.com/dc2007/ch8/forum and post your thoughts or questions.

① What Are the Types of System Software?   **System software** consists of the programs that control or maintain the operations of a computer and its devices. Two types of system software are operating systems and utility programs. An **operating system** (**OS**) contains instructions that coordinate all the activities among computer hardware resources. A **utility program** performs maintenance-type tasks, usually related to managing a computer, its devices, or its programs.

② What Is the Startup Process on a Personal Computer?   **Booting** is the process of starting or restarting a computer. When a user turns on a computer, the power supply sends a signal to the system unit. The processor chip finds the ROM chip(s) that contains the **BIOS**, which is firmware with the computer's startup instructions. The BIOS performs the *power-on self test* (*POST*) to check system components and compares the results with data in a CMOS chip. If the POST completes successfully, the BIOS searches for the *system files* and the *kernel* of the operating system, which manages memory and devices, and loads them into memory from storage. Finally, the operating system loads configuration information, requests any necessary user information, and displays the desktop on the screen.

③ What Are the Functions of an Operating System?   The operating system provides a user interface, manages programs, manages memory, schedules jobs, configures devices, establishes an Internet connection, and monitors performance. The **user interface** controls how data and instructions are entered and how information is displayed. Three types of user interfaces are a *command-line interface,* a *menu-driven interface,* and a *graphical user interface* (*GUI*). Managing programs refers to how many users, and how many programs, an operating system can support at one time. An operating system can be *single user/single tasking, single user/multitasking, multiuser,* or *multiprocessing*. **Memory management** optimizes the use of random access memory (RAM). If memory is insufficient, the operating system may use **virtual memory**, which allocates a portion of a storage medium to function as additional RAM. Scheduling jobs determines the order in which jobs are processed. A **job** is an operation the processor manages. Configuring devices involves loading each device's driver when a user boots the computer. A **driver** is a program that tells the operating system how to communicate with a specific device. Establishing an Internet connection sets up a connection between a computer and an Internet service provider. A **performance monitor** is an operating system program that assesses and reports information about computer resources and devices.

④ How Can Operating Systems Help Administrators Control a Network and Manage Security?   A **network operating system**, or *network OS*, is an operating system that organizes and coordinates how multiple users access and share network resources. A *network administrator* uses the network OS to add and remove users, computers, and other devices to and from the network. A network administrator also uses the network OS to administer network security. For each user, the network administrator establishes a user account that enables the user to **log on**, or access, the network by supplying the correct **user name** and **password**.

Visit scsite.com/dc2007/ch8/quiz or click the Quiz Yourself button. Click Objectives 1 – 4.

⑤ What Is the Purpose of the Utilities Included with Most Operating Systems?   Most operating systems include several built-in utility programs. A **file manager** performs functions related to file and disk management. An **image viewer** displays, copies, and prints the contents of a graphics file. A **personal firewall** detects and protects a computer from unauthorized intrusions. An **uninstaller** removes a program and any associated entries in the system files. A **disk scanner** detects and corrects problems on a disk and searches for and removes unnecessary files. A **disk defragmenter** reorganizes the files and unused space on a computer's hard disk. A

Chapter Review

diagnostic utility compiles and reports technical information about a computer's hardware and certain system software programs. A **backup utility** is used to copy, or *back up*, selected files or an entire hard disk. A **screen saver** displays a moving image or blank screen if no keyboard or mouse activity occurs for a specified time.

(6) **What Are Features of Several Stand-Alone Operating Systems?** A stand-alone **operating system** is a complete operating system that works on a desktop computer, notebook computer, or mobile computing device. Stand-alone operating systems include DOS, Windows XP, Windows Vista, Mac OS X, UNIX, and Linux. **DOS** (*Disk Operating System*) refers to several single user, command-line operating systems developed for personal computers. **Windows XP** is a fast, reliable Windows operating system, providing better performance, increased security, and a simpler look. **Windows Vista**, successor to Windows XP, is Microsoft's fastest, most reliable and efficient operating system to date, offering quicker application start up, built-in diagnostics, automatic recovery, improved security, and enhanced searching and organizing capabilities. **Mac OS X** is a multitasking operating system available only for Apple computers. **UNIX** is a multitasking operating system developed at Bell Laboratories. **Linux** is a popular, multitasking UNIX-type operating system that is *open source software*, which means its code is available to the public.

connect
Visit scsite.com/dc2007/ch8/quiz or click the Quiz Yourself button. Click Objectives 5 – 6.

(7) **What Are Various Network Operating Systems?** Network operating systems include NetWare, Windows Server 2003, UNIX, Linux, and Solaris. Novell's *NetWare* is a network OS designed for client/server networks. **Windows Server 2003** is an upgrade to Windows 2000 Server and includes features of previous server versions. Linux, like UNIX, is a *multipurpose operating system* because it is both a stand-alone and network operating system. *Solaris*, a version of UNIX developed by Sun Microsystems, is a network OS designed for e-commerce applications.

(8) **What Devices Use Embedded Operating Systems?** Most PDAs and small devices have an **embedded operating system** that resides on a ROM chip. Popular embedded operating systems include Windows CE, Windows Mobile, Palm OS, embedded Linux, and Symbian OS. **Windows CE** is a scaled-down Windows operating system designed for use on communications, entertainment, and computing devices with limited functionality. **Windows Mobile**, an operating system based on Windows CE, provides a user interface designed for a specific type of devices, such as PDAs, called the **Pocket PC**. *Palm OS* is an operating system used on PDAs and smart phones.

(9) **What Is the Purpose of Several Stand-Alone Utility Programs?** Stand-alone utility programs offer improvements over features built into the operating system or provide features not included in the operating system. An **antivirus program** protects computers against a **virus**, or potentially damaging computer program, by identifying and removing any computer viruses. A

spyware remover detects and deletes *spyware*, *adware*, and other similar programs. Internet filter programs can include an **anti-spam** program, **Web filtering software**, and a **pop-up blocker**. A **file compression utility** shrinks the size of a file so that it takes up less storage space. A *file conversion utility* transforms the contents of a file from one format to another. **CD/DVD burning software** writes to a recordable or rewritable CD or DVD. A **personal computer maintenance utility** identifies and repairs operating system problems or disk problems, and improves a computer's performance.

connect
Visit scsite.com/dc2007/ch8/quiz or click the Quiz Yourself button. Click Objectives 7 – 9.

Key Terms

You should know the Primary Terms and be familiar with the Secondary Terms. Use the list below to help focus your study. To further enhance your understanding of the Key Terms in this chapter, visit scite.com/dc2007/ch8/terms. See an example of and a definition for each term, and access current and additional information about the term from the Web.

Primary Terms

(shown in bold-black characters in the chapter)

anti-spam program (426)
antivirus program (426)
backup utility (415)
BIOS (400)
boot disk (402)
boot drive (402)
booting (400)
buffer (407)
CD/DVD burning software (428)
cold boot (400)
defragmenting (414)
diagnostic utility (414)
disk defragmenter (414)
disk scanner (414)
DOS (417)
driver (407)
embedded operating system (423)
file compression utility (427)
file manager (412)
formatting (412)
image viewer (412)
job (406)
Linux (421)
log on (410)
Mac OS X (420)
Macintosh operating system (420)
memory management (405)
network operating system (410)
operating system (OS) (398)
password (410)
performance monitor (409)

personal computer maintenance utility (428)
personal firewall (413)
Plug and Play (407)
Pocket PC (424)
pop-up blocker (427)
queue (407)
recovery disk (402)
restore program (415)
screen saver (415)
shortcut (412)
spooling (407)
spyware remover (426)
stand-alone operating system (416)
system software (398)
Trojan horse (426)
uncompress (427)
uninstaller (413)
UNIX (420)
user ID (410)
user interface (402)
user name (410)
utility (411)
utility program (411)
virtual memory (406)
virus (425)
warm boot (400)
Web filtering software (427)
Windows CE (423)
Windows Mobile (424)
Windows Server 2003 (422)
Windows Server 2003 family (422)
Windows Vista (419)
Windows XP (417)
worm (426)
zipped files (427)

Secondary Terms

(shown in italic characters in the chapter)

Active Directory (422)
adware (426)
back up (415)
background (404)
basic input/output system (400)
client operating systems (416)
command language (402)
command-line interface (402)
compress (415)
cross-platform (399)
device driver (407)
device-dependent (415)
device-independent (415)
Disk Operating System (417)
Document Explorer (419)
Dr. Watson (414)
embedded Linux (425)
encryption (411)
fault-tolerant computer (405)
file conversion utility (427)
foreground (404)
fragmented (414)
ghosting (415)
graphical user interface (GUI) (402)
hacker (413)
IRQ (interrupt request line) (409)
kernel (400)
malware (426)
Media Center PC (418)
memory resident (400)
menu-driven interface (402)
multiprocessing (405)
multipurpose operating system (423)
multiuser (405)
NetWare (422)
network administrator (410)
network OS (410)
nonresident (400)
open source software (421)
page (406)
paging (406)
Palm OS (424)
platform (399)
pop-up ad (427)
power-on self test (POST) (400)

preemptive multitasking (405)
print spooler (407)
proprietary software (415)
registry (401)
scripts (402)
service pack (416)
single user/multitasking (403)
single user/single tasking (403)
Solaris (423)
spam (426)
spyware (426)
Startup folder (402)
swap file (406)
Symbian OS (425)
system files (401)
thrashing (406)
unzip (427)
Virtual Folders (419)
virus author (425)
Web services (423)
Windows Explorer (412)
Windows Picture and Fax Viewer (412)
Windows Server 2003, Datacenter Edition (423)
Windows Server 2003, Enterprise Edition (422)
Windows Server 2003, Standard Edition (422)
Windows Server 2003, Web Edition (423)
Windows Server System (423)
Windows Small Business Server 2003 (422)
Windows XP Home Edition (418)
Windows XP Media Center Edition (418)
Windows XP Professional (418)
Windows XP Professional x64 Edition (418)
Windows XP Tablet PC Edition (418)

Checkpoint

Use the Checkpoint exercises to check your knowledge level of the chapter. The Beyond the Book exercises will help broaden your understanding of the concepts presented in this chapter. To complete the Checkpoint exercises interactively, visit scsite.com/dc2007/ch8/check.

Label the Figure

Identify the various elements of virtual memory.

a. Forward button

b. link

c. command prompt

d. command entered by user

e. background program

f. menu names

g. menu

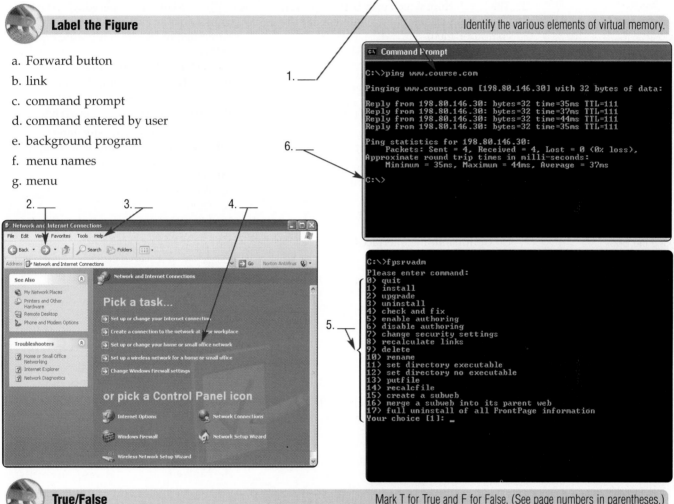

True/False

Mark T for True and F for False. (See page numbers in parentheses.)

_____ 1. All sizes of computers typically use the same operating system. (399)

_____ 2. Booting is the process of starting or restarting a computer. (400)

_____ 3. A user interface controls how you enter data and instructions and how information is displayed on the screen. (402)

_____ 4. When a computer is running multiple programs concurrently, one program is in the background and the others are in the foreground. (404)

_____ 5. Encryption is the process of encoding data and information into an unreadable form. (411)

_____ 6. A disk scanner is a utility that reorganizes the files and unused space on a computer's hard disk so the operating system accesses data more quickly and programs run faster. (414)

_____ 7. Some stand-alone operating systems are called client operating systems because they also work in conjunction with a network operating system. (416)

_____ 8. Linux is open source software, which means its code cannot be modified or redistributed. (421)

_____ 9. Most antivirus programs do not protect against worms or Trojan horses. (426)

_____ 10. A pop-up blocker is a filtering program that stops pop-up ads from displaying on Web pages. (427)

Checkpoint

Multiple Choice   Select the best answer. (See page numbers in parentheses.)

1. The _____ chip, which uses battery power, stores configuration information about the computer. (400)
   a. CMOS
   b. POST
   c. BIOS
   d. RAM

2. In Windows XP, the _____ consists of several files that contain the system configuration information. (401)
   a. shortcut
   b. page
   c. registry
   d. swap file

3. _____ often are difficult to use because they require exact spelling, grammar, and punctuation. (402)
   a. Graphical user interfaces
   b. Menu-driven interfaces
   c. Command-line interfaces
   d. All of the above

4. When an operating system spends much of its time paging, instead of executing application software, it is said to be _____. (406)
   a. booting
   b. thrashing
   c. spooling
   d. formatting

5. A _____ is a small program that tells the operating system how to communicate with a specific device. (407)
   a. buffer
   b. device
   c. performance monitor
   d. driver

6. Defragmenting reorganizes the files on a disk so they are located in _____ access time. (414)
   a. noncontiguous sectors, which slows
   b. noncontiguous sectors, which speeds
   c. contiguous sectors, which speeds
   d. contiguous sectors, which slows

7. Windows XP includes the _____, Dr. Watson, which detects problems as well as suggests courses of action. (414)
   a. file manager
   b. backup utility
   c. image viewer
   d. diagnostic utility

8. _____ is a complete operating system that works on a desktop computer, notebook computer, or mobile computing device. (416)
   a. A stand-alone operating system
   b. A network operating system
   c. A stand-alone utility program
   d. An embedded operating system

9. _____ used a command-line interface when Microsoft first developed it, although later versions included menu-driven user interfaces. (417)
   a. Windows XP
   b. DOS
   c. Mac OS X
   d. UNIX

10. _____ store(s) search criteria as part of the folder that instantly runs each time the folder opens, enabling users easily to locate documents stored anywhere on the computer. (419)
    a. Virtual Folders   b. Document Explorer
    c. A buffer   d. A screen saver

11. _____, developed by Sun Microsystems, manages high-traffic accounts and incorporates security necessary for Web transactions. (423)
    a. Solaris
    b. Linux
    c. Windows Server 2003
    d. Netware

12. _____ is an open source multitasking operating system designed for smart phones. (425)
    a. Solaris
    b. Linux
    c. Palm OS
    d. Symbian OS

13. A _____ is malware that does not replicate itself to other computers. (426)
    a. virus   b. Trojan horse
    c. worm   d. all of the above

14. _____ is a program that displays an online advertisement in a banner or pop-up window on Web pages, e-mail, or other Internet services. (426)
    a. Spyware
    b. A Trojan horse
    c. Adware
    d. A pop-up ad

Checkpoint

Matching

Match the terms with their definitions. (See page numbers in parentheses.)

_____ 1. recovery disk (402)

_____ 2. fault-tolerant computer (405)

_____ 3. page (406)

_____ 4. spooling (407)

_____ 5. IRQ (409)

_____ 6. user name (410)

_____ 7. image viewer (412)

_____ 8. restore program (415)

_____ 9. proprietary software (415)

_____ 10. virus (425)

a. communications line between a device and the processor

b. hides within or looks like a legitimate program such as a screen saver

c. continues to operate when one of its components fails

d. with virtual memory, the amount of data and program instructions that can be swapped at a given time

e. reverses the backup process and restores backed up files

f. unique combination of characters that identifies one specific user

g. potentially damaging computer program that affects, or infects, a computer negatively by altering the way the computer works without the user's knowledge or permission

h. disk that contains a few system files that will start the computer

i. privately owned and limited to a specific vendor or computer model

j. a utility that allows users to display, copy, and print the contents of a graphics file

k. process that sends print jobs to a buffer instead of sending them immediately to the printer

l. program that tells the operating system how to communicate with a device

Short Answer

Write a brief answer to each of the following questions.

1. How is a cold boot different from a warm boot? _____ How is a memory-resident part of an operating system different from a nonresident part of an operating system? _____

2. What is a user interface? _____ How are a command-line interface, a menu-driven interface, and a graphical user interface different? _____

3. What is the purpose of memory management? _____ What is the purpose of virtual memory, and where is virtual memory stored? _____

4. What is the difference between device-dependent and device-independent software? _____ What is proprietary software? _____

5. What is the difference between spyware and adware? _____ What are three widely used Internet filters? _____

Beyond the Book

Read the following book elements, learn more about each using the Web, and then write a brief report.

1. Ethics & Issues — What Should Be in an Operating System? (409), Who Is Responsible for Operating System Security? (410), Should Software Manufacturers Be Liable for Defective Software? (416), or Closed Source vs. Open Source Operating Systems (421)

2. Career Corner — Systems Programmer (429)

3. Companies on the Cutting Edge – Red Hat or Symbian (431)

4. FAQs (402, 406, 409, 411, 413, 418, 423, 426, 427)

5. High-Tech Talk — Windows XP: A Useful Way to Complete a Wide Range of Tasks (430)

6. Looking Ahead — The Future of Linux (421) or Online Operating Systems Proposed (429)

7. Making Use of the Web — Weather, Sports, and News (124)

8. Picture Yourself Getting a Virus through E-Mail (396)

9. Technology Trailblazers — Alan Kay or Linus Torvalds (431)

10. Web Links (401, 407, 413, 415, 419, 420, 423, 424, 427)

Learn It Online

Use the Learn It Online exercises to reinforce your understanding of the chapter concepts.
To access the Learn It Online exercises, visit scsite.com/dc2007/ch8/learn.

① At the Movies — Windows XP Media Center Edition

To view the Windows XP Media Center Edition movie, click the number 1 button. Locate your video and click the corresponding High-Speed or Dial-Up link, depending on your Internet connection. Watch the movie and then complete the exercise by answering the questions that follow. Windows XP Media Center Edition 2004 is software that easily can enable advanced multimedia interactivity on your computer. With one touch of the remote control, you can activate your music, photographs, videos, radio shows, or television programs. Why is the Windows XP Media Center prone to viruses? How can you make sure your computer is protected from viruses?

② At the Movies — Beam DVDs From Room to Room

To view the Beam DVDs From Room to Room movie, click the number 2 button. Locate your video and click the corresponding High-Speed or Dial-Up link, depending on your Internet connection. Watch the movie and then complete the exercise by answering the question that follows. With a moderately priced audio/video sender and receiver system you easily could hook up a small camera and monitor in any room in the house. What are the pros and cons of using video monitoring in your home?

③ Student Edition Labs — Installing and Uninstalling Software

Click the number 3 button. A new browser window will open, displaying the Student Edition Labs. Follow the on-screen instructions to complete the Installing and Uninstalling Software Lab. When finished, click the Exit button. If required, submit your results to your instructor.

④ Practice Test

Click the number 4 button. Answer each question. When completed, enter your name and click the Grade Test button to submit the quiz for grading. Make a note of any missed questions. If required, submit your results to your instructor.

⑤ Who Wants To Be a Computer Genius²?

Click the number 5 button to find out if you are a computer genius. Directions about how to play the game will be displayed. When you are ready to play, click the Play button. Submit your score to your instructor.

⑥ Wheel of Terms

Click the number 6 button to reinforce important terms you learned in this chapter by playing the Shelly Cashman Series version of this popular game. Directions about how to play the game will be displayed. When you are ready to play, click the Play button. Submit your score to your instructor.

⑦ DC Track and Field

Click the number 7 button to use what you have learned in this chapter to compete against other students in three track and field events. Directions about how to play the game will be displayed. When you are ready to play, click the start first event button. If required, submit your score to your instructor.

Learn It Online

(8) You're Hired!

Click the number 8 button to use what you have learned in this chapter to embark on the path to a career in computers. Directions about how to play the game will be displayed. When you are ready to play, click the begin game button. If required, submit your score to your instructor.

(9) Crossword Puzzle Challenge

Click the number 9 button. Complete the puzzle to reinforce skills you learned in this chapter. Directions about how to play the game will be displayed. When you are ready to play, click the Submit button. Submit the completed puzzle to your instructor.

(10) Lab Exercises

Click the number 10 button. When the Lab Exercises menu appears, click the exercise assigned by your instructor. A new browser window will open. Follow the on-screen instructions to complete the exercise. When finished, click the Exit button. If required, submit your results to your instructor.

(11) In the News

When Windows XP was introduced in October 2001, hundreds queued up at computer outlets. It is unclear, however, whether the anticipation was caused by the new operating system or by the promotions many dealers offered. Click the number 11 button and read a news article about the impact, quality, or promotion of an operating system. What operating system was it? What was done to sell the operating system? Is the operating system recommended? Why or why not?

(12) Chapter Discussion Forum

Select an objective from this chapter on page 397 about which you would like more information. Click the number 12 button and post a short message listing a meaningful message title accompanied by one or more questions concerning the selected objective. In two days, return to the threaded discussion by clicking the number 12 button. Submit to your instructor your original message and at least one response to your message.

(13) Airline Schedules

Click the number 13 button to learn how to use the Internet to price, reserve, and track airline flights. Follow the instructions to use Southwest Airlines' Web site to price a flight from Chicago to Las Vegas. Using the Schedules link, check for available flights for the dates you select. Once you have selected a flight, use the Reservations link to price the flight. Print a copy of the pricing for your selected flight. Check the status of a current flight comparable to the flight you priced. Write a report comparing the different fares available and summarizing what information is available when you check the status of a flight. Include in your report what the circumstances would have to be for you to choose a more expensive flight. Print your report and submit it to your instructor.

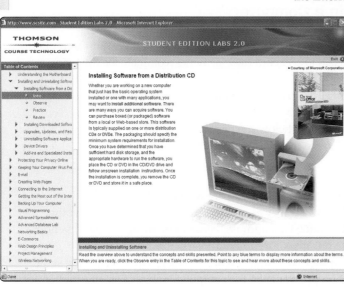

Learn How To

Use the Learn How To activities to learn fundamental skills when using a computer and accompanying technology. Complete the exercises and submit them to your instructor. Visit scsite.com/dc2007/ch8/howto to obtain more information pertaining to each activity.

LEARN HOW TO 1: Install a Computer

Once you have purchased a computer, you must install it for use. Based on years of experience, a set of guidelines for installing and using your computer has been developed. To examine these guidelines, complete the following steps:

1. Start the browser on your computer.
2. Type the Web address scsite.com/dc2007 in the Address box and then press the ENTER key.
3. Click the Chapter 8 link in the top navigation bar.
4. Click Install Computer in the left sidebar below the heading, Beyond the Book.
5. Read the material presented about how to install a computer.

Exercise

1. Using your Web search skills, research the latest recommendations with respect to proper ergonomics for using a computer. What information did you find that you did not know before? What changes would you make to your current computer setup that might make you more productive? Submit your answers to your instructor.
2. Many people report illnesses or injuries from using computers. Perform research in a library or on the Web to discover the five most common ailments associated with using a computer. Determine the actions people can take to minimize or eliminate these ailments. Submit a report to your instructor describing your findings.
3. Your computer lab at school contains multiple computers for student use. Using the knowledge you have obtained from this Learn How To activity, evaluate the computer installation in your school lab. In a report to your instructor, specify those items you think can be improved in the lab.

LEARN HOW TO 2: Maintain a Computer

While computers are amazingly resilient and reliable, you still should perform certain activities to ensure they maintain peak performance. To learn about these activities, complete the following steps:

1. Start the browser on your computer.
2. Type the Web address scsite.com/dc2007 in the Address box and then press the ENTER key.
3. Click the Chapter 8 link in the top navigation bar.
4. Click Maintain Computer in the left sidebar below the heading, Beyond the Book.
5. Read the material presented about how to maintain a computer.

Exercise

1. On either your computer or the computer on which you are working, perform a hardware and software inventory of at least five hardware devices and five application programs on the computer. List the vendor, product, vendor Web address, vendor e-mail address, and vendor support telephone number. Submit your inventory to your instructor.
2. Record the serial number of the computer on which you are working. Then, record the serial number for seven different application programs on the computer. Submit this information to your instructor.

Learn How To

LEARN HOW TO 3: Keep Windows XP Up-to-Date

Keeping Windows XP up-to-date is a critical part of keeping your computer in good working order. The updates made available by Microsoft for no charge over the Internet will keep errors from occurring on your computer and will ensure that all security safeguards are in place. To update Windows, complete the following steps:

1. Click the Start button on the Windows taskbar, point to All Programs, and then click Windows Update on the All Programs submenu (Figure 8-42). *A browser window will open and display the Windows Update page.*
2. Click the Express Install (Recommended) link. Your computer will be examined and then a list of recommended updates for your computer will be shown.
3. If necessary, select those updates you wish to install and then click the Install button. Be aware that some updates might take 20 minutes or more to download and install, based primarily on your Internet access speed.
4. Often, after installation of updates, you must restart your computer to allow those updates to take effect. Be sure to save any open files before restarting your computer.

You also can schedule automatic updates for your computer. To do so, complete the following steps:

1. Click the Start button on the Windows taskbar and then click Control Panel on the Start menu.
2. In the Control Panel window, ensure that Category view is displayed, and then click Performance and Maintenance.
3. In the Performance and Maintenance window, click System.
4. In the System Properties dialog box, click the Automatic Updates tab. *The Automatic Updates sheet is displayed in the System Properties dialog box (Figure 8-43).*
5. Select the option you want to use for Windows updates. Microsoft, together with all security and operating system experts, strongly recommends you select Automatic so updates will be installed on your computer automatically. Notice that if you select Automatic, you also should select a time when your computer will be on and be connected to the Internet. A secondary choice is to download the suggested updates and then choose when you want to install them.
6. When you have made your selection, click the OK button in the System Properties dialog box.

Updating Windows on your computer is vital to maintain security and operational integrity.

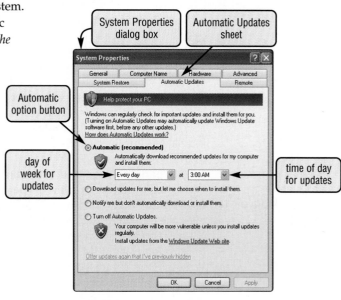

FIGURE 8-42

FIGURE 8-43

Exercise

1. Open the Windows Update window in your browser. Make a list of the recommended updates to Windows XP on the computer you are using. Add to the list the Custom Install updates that are available. If you are using your own computer, install the updates of your choice on your computer. Submit the list of updates to your instructor.
2. Optional: If you are not using your own computer, do not complete this exercise. Display the Automatic Updates sheet in the System Properties dialog box. Select the level of automatic updates you want to use. Write a report justifying your choice of automatic updates and then submit the report to your instructor.

Web Research

Use the Internet-based Web Research exercises to broaden your understanding of the concepts presented in this chapter. Visit scsite.com/dc2007/ch8/research to obtain more information pertaining to each exercise. To discuss any of the Web Research exercises in this chapter with other students, post your thoughts or questions at scsite.com/dc2007/ch8/forum.

① Scavenger Hunt　Use one of the search engines listed in Figure 2-10 in Chapter 2 on page 78 or your own favorite search engine to find the answers to the questions that follow. Copy and paste the Web address from the Web page where you found the answer. Some questions may have more than one answer. If required, submit your answers to your instructor. (1) What is the UNIX billennium? (2) The term, spool, is an acronym for what words? What company invented the term? (3) What did Gary Kildall develop in 1974 while working for Intel? (4) What is the basis of the lawsuit Caldera Inc. filed against Microsoft in 1996? (5) What is Larry the cow's relationship to Linux?

② Search Sleuth　A search engine using a concept-based search system seeks Web sites containing a search term along with related concepts. For example, if you search for "operating systems," this type of search engine also returns links to books, professional organizations, and other operating system-related topics. Many researchers consider Excite (excite.com) the best concept-based search engine. Visit this Web site and then use your word processing program to answer the following questions. Then, if required, submit your answers to your instructor. (1) Click the Help link at the bottom of the page. What are some Search Tools & Tips listed in the Searches and Classified area? (2) Click the Back button, click the Search the Web text box, and then type Linux in the box. How many search results are returned that are not sponsored links? (3) Click the View Results by Search Engine option button near the top of the page. What are three search engines Excite used to return results? Which search engine returned the most links? (4) Click two of the links that discuss Linux news and information. Review these articles and then write a 50-word summary of your findings.

③ Journaling　Respond to your readings in this chapter by writing at least one page about your reactions, evaluations, and reflections about using stand-alone utility programs. For example, does your computer have an antivirus program? If so, how often do you check for new virus definition updates? Has a virus ever infected one of your files or your computer? Do you have a backup of your hard disk? Do you have a recovery disk? Do you have a personal firewall? You also can write about the new terms you learned by reading this chapter. If required, submit your journal to your instructor.

④ Expanding Your Understanding　Instant messaging (IM) is moving into the workplace. According to America Online, 59 percent of Internet users use IM, and 27 percent of these people use IM at work. Computer industry analysts predict this method of electronic communication will overtake e-mail during the next few years. With IM's popularity comes spim, a junk message. Yahoo! reports that 2 percent of the instant messages sent over its network are spim. View Web sites to learn more about IM's popularity and spim. What programs allow you to filter instant messages? Write a report summarizing your findings, focusing on the possible uses of this method of communication in the workplace. If required, submit your report to your instructor.

⑤ Ethics in Action　Several automobile insurers, including Progressive Casualty Insurance Company, are promising drivers insurance premium discounts if they install a data recorder in their cars to track their driving and then exercise good driving behavior. Progressive customers voluntarily taking part in this TripSense program upload the data from their monitors monthly and hope to decrease their insurance bills by a maximum of 25 percent. Privacy experts predict more insurance companies will offer this monitoring system and that it eventually will become mandatory. These critics fear that negative data will be used against poor drivers and possibly be subpoenaed in litigation. View online sites that provide information about vehicle monitoring devices. Write a report summarizing your findings and include a table of links to Web sites that provide additional details. If required, submit your report to your instructor.

Case Studies

Use the Case Studies to apply the concepts presented in the chapter to real-world situations. Visit scsite.com/dc2007/ch8/cases to obtain more information pertaining to each exercise. To discuss the Case Studies in this chapter with other students, visit scsite.com/dc2007/ch8/forum and post your thoughts or questions.

CASE STUDY 1 — Class Discussion   Many students at the local college have been using the college's computers to download music from the Internet. You have been asked to serve on a student committee to draft a policy addressing this questionable use of the college's computers. Is it the college's responsibility to block music downloads? Why or why not? How would the college prevent students from **downloading music**? What is the difference between taping a song heard on the radio and downloading music from the Internet? Should violators be expelled, fined, required to attend a seminar on the ethical use of computers, or given a verbal warning? What recommendations would you give to the committee regarding the downloading of music? Draft a memo addressed to all students regarding this matter. Be prepared to discuss your recommendations in class.

CASE STUDY 2 — Class Discussion   It is legal to **copy songs from a CD**, provided it was purchased legally. A principal at a local high school, however, has learned that students have been copying popular tracks from purchased music CDs to other CDs using the school's computer and then selling the CDs for $1.00 each. As the dean of students, what action would you take against the students copying the CDs? What action would you take against students buying the illegal copies? Write a brief report, and be prepared to discuss your recommendations in class.

CASE STUDY 3 — Research   Your uncle is buying a new computer both for personal use and to operate his consulting business, which he runs out of his home. He is undecided on the Windows operating system to purchase with his new computer. **Windows XP** Professional is intended for business and power users. Windows XP Home Edition is designed for home computing. He has asked you to help him decide if he should buy one or the other. Use the Web and/or print media to develop a report that lists the differences. Which Windows XP Professional features are not available in Windows XP Home Edition? Submit your report or use PowerPoint to create a presentation and share your findings with your class.

CASE STUDY 4 — Research   Many programs are available for users of personal computers. The owner of the party supply store, Crazy Pete's Party Palace, where you work part time is interested in purchasing an **antivirus program**. Because you are taking a computer class, he has asked you to help him choose the best program. Choose at least two competing manufacturers of antivirus programs. Use the Web and/or print media and compare the programs. For each program, answer the following questions: What is the program's function? What are the system requirements? How easy is the program to use? Does it include a firewall? Does it protect against spam, spyware, and adware? How do you obtain updates to the program? How much does the program cost? In your opinion, is the program worth the price? Why or why not? Which one would you buy? Why? Write a brief report or use PowerPoint to create a presentation and share your findings with your class.

CASE STUDY 5 — Team Challenge   Your team members are employed as analysts at Soap-n-Suds, an international manufacturer of laundry soaps. The company currently uses an early version of the Windows operating system on its 5,000 desktop computers. Next year, the company plans to upgrade the operating system and, if necessary, its desktop computers. The vice-president of information technology has asked your team to compare the latest desktop versions of the Windows operating system, the **Mac operating system**, and the Linux operating system. Assign each member of your team an operating system. Have each member use the Web and/or print media to develop a feature/benefit report. What is the initial cost of the operating system per computer? What are the memory and storage requirements? Will the operating system require the company to purchase new computers? Are training costs involved? Which one is best at avoiding viruses, spam, and spyware? Which operating system is easier to use? Why? Can Microsoft Office run under the operating system? As a team, merge your findings into a team report and/or PowerPoint presentation and share your findings with your class.

Buyer's Guide 2007:
How to Purchase a Personal Computer

(a) desktop computer

At some point, perhaps while you are taking this course, you may decide to buy a personal computer. The decision is an important one and will require an investment of both time and money. Like many buyers, you may have little computer experience and find yourself unsure of how to proceed. You can get started by talking to your friends, coworkers, and instructors about their computers. What type of computers did they buy? Why? For what purposes do they use their computers? You also should answer the following four questions to help narrow your choices to a specific computer type, before reading this Buyer's Guide.

(b) mobile computer (notebook computer or Tablet PC)

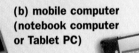

(c) personal mobile device (smart phone or PDA)

Should I buy a desktop or mobile computer or personal mobile device?

For what purposes will I use the computer?

Should the computer I buy be compatible with the computers at school or work?

Should I buy a Mac or PC?

1 **Do you want a desktop computer, mobile computer, or personal mobile device?** A desktop computer (Figure 1a) is designed as a stationary device that sits on or below a desk or table in a location such as a home, office, or dormitory room. A desktop computer must be plugged into an electrical outlet to operate. A mobile computer, such as a notebook computer or Tablet PC (Figure 1b), is smaller than a desktop computer, more portable, and has a battery that allows you to operate it for a period without an electrical outlet. A personal mobile device (Figure 1c) runs on a battery for a longer period of time than a notebook computer or Tablet PC and can fit in your pocket.

Desktop computers are a good option if you work mostly in one place and have plenty of space in your work area. Desktop computers generally give you more performance for your money.

Increasingly, more desktop computer users are buying mobile computers to take advantage of their portability to work in the library, at school, while traveling, and at home. The past disadvantages of mobile computers, such as lower processor speeds, poor-quality monitors, weight, short battery life, and significantly higher prices, have all but disappeared when compared with desktop computers.

FIGURE 1

If you are thinking of using a mobile computer to take notes in class or in business meetings, then consider a Tablet PC with handwriting and drawing capabilities. Typically, note-taking involves writing text notes and drawing charts, schematics, and other illustrations. By allowing you to write and draw directly on the screen with a digital pen, a Tablet PC eliminates the distracting sound of the notebook keyboard tapping and allows you to capture drawings. Some notebook computers can convert to Tablet PCs.

A personal mobile device, such as a smart phone or a PDA, is ideal if you require a pocket-sized computing device as you move from place to place. Personal mobile devices provide personal organizer functions, such as a calendar, appointment book, address book, and many other applications. The small size of the processor, screen, and keyboard, however, limit a personal mobile device's capabilities when compared with a desktop or notebook computer or a Tablet PC. For this reason, most people who purchase personal mobile devices also have a desktop or notebook computer to handle heavy-duty applications.

Drawbacks of mobile computers and personal mobile devices are that they tend to have a shorter useful lifetime than desktop computers and lack the high-end capabilities. Their portability makes them susceptible to vibrations, heat or cold, and accidental drops, which can cause components such as hard disks or display devices to fail. Also, because of their size and portability, they are easy to lose and are the prime targets of thieves.

 For what purposes will you use the computer?
Having a general idea of the purposes for which you want to use your computer will help you decide on the type of computer to buy. At this point in your research, it is not necessary to know the exact application software titles or version numbers you might want to use. Knowing that you plan to use the computer primarily to create word processing, spreadsheet, database, and presentation documents, however, will point you in the direction of a desktop or notebook computer. If you want the portability of a smart phone or PDA, but you need more computing power, then a Tablet PC may be the best alternative. You also must consider that some application software runs only on a Mac, while others run only on a PC with the Windows operating system. Still other software may run only on a PC running the UNIX or Linux operating system.

Should the computer be compatible with the computers at school or work? If you plan to bring work home, telecommute, or take distance education courses, then you should purchase a computer that is compatible with those at school or work.

Compatibility is primarily a software issue. If your computer runs the same operating system version, such as Microsoft Windows XP, and the same application software, such as Microsoft Office, then your computer will be able to read documents created at school or work and vice versa. Incompatible hardware can become an issue if you plan to connect directly to a school or office network using a cable or wireless technology. You usually can obtain the minimum system requirements from the Information Technology department at your school or workplace.

Should the computer be a Mac or PC? If you ask a friend, coworker, or instructor, which is better — a Mac or a PC — you may be surprised by the strong opinion expressed in the response. No other topic in the computer industry causes more heated debate. The Mac has strengths, especially in the areas of graphics, movies, photos, and music. The PC, however, has become the industry standard with 95 percent of the market share. Figure 2 compares features of the Mac and PC in several different areas. Overall, the Mac and PC have more similarities than differences, and you should consider cost, compatibility, and other factors when choosing whether to purchase a Mac or PC.

Area	Comparison
Cost and availability	A Mac is priced slightly higher than a PC. Mac peripherals also are more expensive. The PC offers more available models from a wide range of vendors. You can custom build, upgrade, and expand a PC for less money than a Mac.
Exterior design	The Mac has a more distinct and stylish appearance than most PCs.
Free software	Although free software for the Mac is available on the Internet, significantly more free software applications are available for the PC.
Market share	The PC dominates the personal computer market. While the Mac sells well in education, publishing, Web design, graphics, and music, the PC is the overwhelming favorite of businesses.
Operating system	Users claim that Mac OS X provides a better all-around user experience than Microsoft Windows XP. Both the Mac and PC supports other operating systems, such as Linux and UNIX.
Program control	Both have simple and intuitive graphical user interfaces. The Mac relies more on the mouse and less on keyboard shortcuts than the PC. The mouse on the Mac has one button, whereas the mouse on a PC has a minimum of two buttons.
Software availability	The basic application software most users require, such as Microsoft Office, is available for both the Mac and PC. More specialized software, however, often is available only for PCs. Many programs are released for PCs long before they are released for Macs.
Speed	Historically, the PC has provided faster processors than the Mac. Apple, however, has begun to ship some models of the Mac with PC-like Intel processors.
Viruses	Dramatically fewer viruses attack Macs. Mac viruses also generally are less infectious than PC viruses.

FIGURE 2 Comparison of Mac and PC features.

After evaluating the answers to these four questions, you should have a general idea of how you plan to use your computer and the type of computer you want to buy. Once you have decided on the type of computer you want, you can follow the guidelines presented in this Buyer's Guide to help you purchase a specific computer, along with software, peripherals, and other accessories.

Many of the desktop computer guidelines presented also apply to the purchase of a notebook computer, Tablet PC, and personal mobile device. Later in this Buyer's Guide, sections on purchasing a notebook computer or Tablet PC address additional considerations specific to those computer types.

This Buyer's Guide concentrates on recommendations for purchasing a desktop computer or mobile computer. For recommendations on purchasing a personal mobile device, see page 296 in the Personal Mobile Devices feature that follows Chapter 5.

Type of Computer	Web Site	Web Address
PC	CNET Shopper	shopper.cnet.com
	PC World Magazine	pcworld.com
	BYTE Magazine	byte.com
	PC Magazine	zdnet.com/reviews
	Yahoo! Computers	computers.yahoo.com
	MSN Shopping	shopping.msn.com
	Dave's Guide to Buying a Home Computer	css.msu.edu/PC-Guide
Mac	Macworld Magazine	macworld.com
	Apple	apple.com
	Switch to Mac Campaign	apple.com/switch

For an updated list of hardware and software reviews and their Web site addresses, visit scsite.com/dc2007/ch8/buyers.

FIGURE 3 Hardware and software reviews.

HOW TO PURCHASE A DESKTOP COMPUTER

Once you have decided that a desktop computer is most suited to your computing needs, the next step is to determine specific software, hardware, peripheral devices, and services to purchase, as well as where to buy the computer.

1 Determine the specific software you want to use on your computer. Before deciding to purchase software, be sure it contains the features necessary for the tasks you want to perform. Rely on the computer users in whom you have confidence to help you decide on the software to use. The minimum requirements of the software you select may determine the operating system (Microsoft Windows XP, Linux, UNIX, Mac OS X) you need. If you have decided to use a particular operating system that does not support software you want to use, you may be able to purchase similar software from other manufacturers.

Many Web sites and trade magazines, such as those listed in Figure 3, provide reviews of software products. These Web sites frequently have articles that rate computers and software on cost, performance, and support.

Your hardware requirements depend on the minimum requirements of the software you will run on your computer. Some software requires more memory and disk space than others, as well as additional input, output, and storage devices. For example, suppose you want to run software that can copy one CD's or DVD's contents directly to another CD or DVD, without first copying the data to your hard disk. To support that, you should consider a desktop computer or a high-end notebook

computer, because the computer will need two CD or DVD drives: one that reads from a CD or DVD, and one that reads from and writes on a CD or DVD. If you plan to run software that allows your computer to work as an entertainment system, then you will need a CD or DVD drive, quality speakers, and an upgraded sound card.

2 Look for bundled software. When you purchase a computer, it may come bundled with software. Some sellers even let you choose which software you want. Remember, however, that bundled software has value only if you would have purchased the software even if it had not come with the computer. At the very least, you probably will want word processing software and a browser to access the Internet. If you need additional applications, such as a spreadsheet, a database, or presentation graphics, consider purchasing Microsoft Works, Microsoft Office, OpenOffice.org, or Sun StarOffice, which include several programs at a reduced price.

3 Avoid buying the least powerful computer available. Once you know the application software you want to use, you then can consider the following important criteria about the computer's components: (1) processor speed, (2) size and types of memory (RAM) and storage, (3) types of input/output devices, (4) types of ports and adapter cards, and (5) types of communications devices. The information in Figures 4 and 5 can help you determine what system components are best for you. Figure 4 outlines considerations for specific hardware components. Figure 5 (on page 449) provides a Base Components worksheet that lists PC recommendations for each category of user discussed in this book: Home User,

Small Office/Home Office User, Mobile User, Power User, and Large Business User. In the worksheet, the Home User category is divided into two groups: Application Home User and Game Home User. The Mobile User recommendations list criteria for a notebook computer, but do not include the PDA or Tablet PC options.

Computer technology changes rapidly, meaning a computer that seems powerful enough today may not serve your computing needs in a few years. In fact, studies show that many users regret not buying a more powerful computer. To avoid this, plan to buy a computer that will last you for two to three years. You can help delay obsolescence by purchasing the fastest processor, the most memory, and the largest hard disk you can afford. If you must buy a less powerful computer, be sure you can upgrade it with additional memory, components, and peripheral devices as your computer requirements grow.

CD/DVD Drives: Most computers come with a CD-RW drive. A CD-RW drive allows you to create your own custom data CDs for data backup or data transfer purposes. It also will allow you to store and share video files, digital photos, and other large files with other people who have access to a CD-ROM drive. An even better alternative is to upgrade to a DVD±RW combination drive. It allows you to read DVDs and CDs and to write data on (burn) a DVD or CD. A DVD has a capacity of at least 4.7 GB versus the 650 MB capacity of a CD.

Card Reader/Writer: A card reader/writer is useful for transferring data directly to and from a removable flash memory card, such as the ones used in your camera or audio player. Make sure the card reader/writer can read from and write on the flash memory cards that you use.

Digital Camera: Consider an inexpensive point-and-shoot digital camera. They are small enough to carry around, usually operate automatically in terms of lighting and focus, and contain storage cards for storing photographs. A 3- to 4-megapixel camera with a 64 MB, 128 MB, or 256 MB storage card is fine for creating images for use on the Web or to send via e-mail.

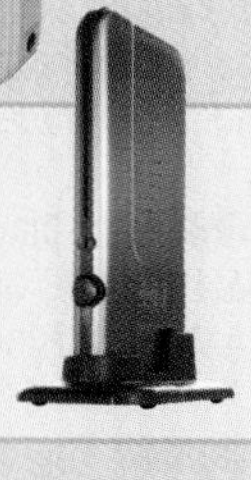

Digital Video Capture Device: A digital video capture device allows you to connect your computer to a camcorder or VCR and record, edit, manage, and then write video back on a VCR tape, a CD, or a DVD. The digital video capture device can be an external device or an adapter card. To create quality video (true 30 frames per second, full-sized TV), the digital video capture device should have a USB 2.0 or FireWire port. You will find that a standard USB port is too slow to maintain video quality. You also will need sufficient storage: an hour of data on a VCR tape takes up about 5 GB of disk storage.

Floppy Disk Drive: The floppy disk drive is useful for backing up and transferring small files, collectively less than 1.44 MB. Users prefer the faster and higher capacity USB flash drives and CD/DVD drives for backup and file transfer purposes. Consider a floppy disk drive only if your work environment requires it.

Hard Disk: It is recommended that you buy a computer with 60 to 80 GB if your primary interests are browsing the Web and using e-mail and Office suite-type applications; 80 to 100 GB if you also want to edit digital photographs; 100 to 120 GB if you plan to edit digital video or manipulate large audio files even occasionally; and 120 to 300 GB if you will edit digital video, movies, or photography often; store audio files and music; or consider yourself to be a power user.

Joystick/Wheel: If you use your computer to play games, then you will want to purchase a joystick or a wheel. These devices, especially the more expensive ones, provide for realistic game play with force feedback, programmable buttons, and specialized levers and wheels.

Keyboard: The keyboard is one of the more important devices used to communicate with the computer. For this reason, make sure the keyboard you purchase has 101 to 105 keys, is comfortable and easy to use, and has a USB connection. A wireless keyboard should be considered, especially if you have a small desk area.

Microphone: If you plan to record audio or use speech recognition to enter text and commands, then purchase a close-talk headset with gain adjustment support.

Modem: Most computers come with a modem so that you can use your telephone line to dial out and access the Internet. Some modems also have fax capabilities. Your modem should be rated at 56 Kbps.

Monitor: The monitor is where you will view documents, read e-mail messages, and view pictures. A minimum of a 17" screen is recommended, but if you are planning to use your computer for graphic design or game playing, then you may want to purchase a 19" or 21" monitor. The LCD flat panel monitor should be considered, especially if space is an issue.

FIGURE 4 Hardware guidelines.

(continued on next page)

(continued from previous page)

Mouse: As you work with your computer, you use the mouse constantly. For this reason, spend a few extra dollars, if necessary, and purchase a mouse with an optical sensor and USB connection. The optical sensor replaces the need for a mouse ball, which means you do not need a mouse pad. For a PC, make sure your mouse has a wheel, which acts as a third button in addition to the top two buttons on the left and right. An ergonomic design is also important because your hand is on the mouse most of the time when you are using your computer. A wireless mouse should be considered to eliminate the cord and allow you to work at short distances from your computer.

Network Card: Most computers come with a network card. A network card allows you to connect to a network or use broadband (cable or DSL) to connect to the Internet.

Port Hub Expander: If you plan to connect several peripheral devices to your computer at the same time, then you need to be concerned with the number of ports available on your computer. If your computer does not have enough ports, then you should purchase a port hub expander. A port hub expander plugs into a single FireWire port or USB port and gives several additional ports.

Printer: Your two basic printer choices are ink-jet and laser. Color ink-jet printers cost on average between $50 and $300. Laser printers cost from $200 to $2,000. In general, the cheaper the printer, the lower the resolution and speed, and the more often you are required to change the ink cartridge or toner. Laser printers print faster and with a higher quality than an ink-jet, and their toner on average costs less. If you want color, then go with a high-end ink-jet printer to ensure quality of print. Duty cycle (the number of pages you expect to print each month) also should be a determining factor. If your duty cycle is on the low end — hundreds of pages per month — then stay with a high-end ink-jet printer, rather than purchasing a laser printer. If you plan to print photographs taken with a digital camera, then you should purchase a photo printer. A photo printer is a dye-sublimation printer or an ink-jet printer with higher resolution and features that allow you to print quality photographs.

Processor: For a PC, a 2.8 GHz Intel or AMD processor is more than enough processor power for application home and small office/home office users. Game home, large business, and power users should upgrade to faster processors.

RAM: RAM plays a vital role in the speed of your computer. Make sure the computer you purchase has at least 512 MB of RAM. If you have extra money to invest in your computer, then consider increasing the RAM to 1 GB or more. The extra money for RAM will be well spent.

Scanner: The most popular scanner purchased with a computer today is the flatbed scanner. When evaluating a flatbed scanner, check the color depth and resolution. Do not buy anything less than a color depth of 48 bits and a resolution of 1200 x 2400 dpi. The higher the color depth, the more accurate the color. A higher resolution picks up the more subtle gradations of color.

Sound Card: Computers come with a standard sound card that supports the Sound Blaster and General MIDI standards and should be capable of recording and playing digital audio. If you plan to turn your computer into an entertainment system or are a game home user, then you will want to spend the extra money and upgrade from the standard sound card.

Speakers: Once you have a good sound card, quality speakers and a separate subwoofer that amplifies the bass frequencies of the speakers can turn your computer into a premium stereo system.

PC Video Camera: A PC video camera is a small camera used to capture and display live video (in some cases with sound), primarily on a Web page. You also can capture, edit, and share video and still photos. The camera sits on your monitor or desk. Recommended minimum specifications include 640 x 480 resolution, a video with a rate of 30 frames per second, and a USB 2.0 or FireWire port.

USB Flash Drive: If you work on different computers and need access to the same data and information, then this portable miniature mobile storage device is ideal. USB flash drive capacity varies from 16 MB to 4 GB.

Video Graphics Card: Most standard video cards satisfy the monitor display needs of application home and small office users. If you are a game home user or a graphic designer, you will want to upgrade to a higher quality video card. The higher refresh rates will further enhance the display of games, graphics, and movies.

Wireless LAN Access Point: A Wireless LAN Access Point allows you to network several computers, so they can share files and access the Internet through a single cable modem or DSL connection. Each device that you connect requires a wireless card. A Wireless LAN Access Point can offer a range of operations up to several hundred feet, so be sure the device has a high-powered antenna.

BASE COMPONENTS

	Application Home User	Game Home User	Small Office/Home Office User	Mobile User	Large Business User	Power User
HARDWARE						
Processor	Pentium⁽ᵖ⁾ 4 at 2.8 GHz	Pentium⁽ᵖ⁾ 4 at 3.0 GHz	Pentium⁽ᵖ⁾ 4 at 3.0 GHz	Pentium⁽ᵖ⁾ 4M at 2.4 GHz	Pentium⁽ᵖ⁾ 4 at 3.4 GHz	Multiple Itanium⁽ᵗᵐ⁾ at 1.6 GHz
RAM	512 MB	1 GB	512 MB	512 MB	2 GB	2 GB
Cache	256 KB L2	512 KB L2	512 KB L2	512 KB L2	512 KB L2	2 MB L3
Hard Disk	80 GB	120 GB	120 GB	60 GB	160 GB	300 GB
Monitor/LCD Flat Panel	17" or 19"	21"	19" or 21"	15.7" Wide Display	19" or 21"	23"
Video Graphics Card	256 MB	512 MB	256 MB	32 MB	128 MB	256 MB
CD/DVD Bay 1	CD-RW	CD-RW	CD-RW	CD-RW/DVD	CD-RW	CR-RW/DVD
CD/DVD Bay 2	DVD+RW	DVD+RW	DVD+RW	DVD+RW	DVD+RW	DVD+RW
Printer	Color Ink-Jet	Color Ink-Jet	18 ppm Laser	Portable Ink-Jet	50 ppm Laser	10 ppm Laser
PC Video Camera	Yes	Yes	Yes	Yes	Yes	Yes
Fax/Modem	Yes	Yes	Yes	Yes	Yes	Yes
Microphone	Close-Talk Headset With Gain Adjustment	Close-Talk Headset With Gain Adjustment	Close-Talk Headset With Gain Adjustment	Close-Talk Headset With Gain Adjustment	Close-Talk Headset With Gain Adjustment	Close-Talk Headset With Gain Adjustment
Speakers	Stereo	Full-Dolby Surround	Stereo	Stereo	Stereo	Full-Dolby Surround
Pointing Device	IntelliMouse or Optical Mouse	Laser Mouse and Joystick	IntelliMouse or Optical Mouse	Touchpad or Pointing Stick and Laser Mouse	IntelliMouse or Optical Mouse	IntelliMouse or Laser Mouse and Joystick
Keyboard	Yes	Yes	Yes	Built-In	Yes	Yes
Backup Disk/Tape Drive	250 MB Zip®	External or Removable Hard Disk	External or Removable Hard Disk	External or Removable Hard Disk	Tape Drive	External or Removable Hard Disk
USB Flash Drive	128 MB	256 MB	256 MB	256 MB	4 GB	2 GB
Sound Card	Sound Blaster Compatible	Sound Blaster Audigy 2	Sound Blaster Compatible	Built-In	Sound Blaster Compatible	Sound Blaster Audigy 2
Network Card	Yes	Yes	Yes	Yes	Yes	Yes
TV-Out Connector	Yes	Yes	Yes	Yes	Yes	Yes
USB Port	6	8	6	2	8	8
FireWire Port	2	2	2	1	2	2
SOFTWARE						
Operating System	Windows XP Home Edition with Service Pack 2	Windows XP Home Edition with Service Pack 2	Windows XP Professional with Service Pack 2	Windows XP Professional with Service Pack 2	Windows XP Professional with Service Pack 2	Windows XP Professional with Service Pack 2
Application Suite	Office 2003 Standard Edition	Office 2003 Standard Edition	Office 2003 Small Business Edition	Office 2003 Small Business Edition	Office 2003 Professional	Office 2003 Professional
Antivirus	Yes, 12-Mo. Subscription	Yes, 12-Mo. Subscription	Yes, 12-Mo. Subscription	Yes, 12-Mo. Subscription	Yes, 12-Mo. Subscription	Yes, 12-Mo. Subscription
Internet Access	Cable, DSL, or Dial-up	Cable or DSL	Cable, DSL, or Dial-up	Wireless or Dial-up	LAN/WAN (T1/T3)	Cable or DSL
OTHER						
Surge Protector	Yes	Yes	Yes	Portable	Yes	Yes
Warranty	3-Year Limited, 1-Year Next Business Day On-Site Service	3-Year Limited, 1-Year Next Business Day On-Site Service	3-year On-Site Service	3-Year Limited, 1-Year Next Business Day On-Site Service	3-year On-Site Service	3-year On-Site Service
Other		Wheel	Postage Printer	Docking Station Carrying Case Fingerprint Scanner Portable Data Projector		Graphics Tablet Plotter or Large-Format Printer

Optional Components for all Categories	
802.11g Wireless Card	Graphics Tablet
Bluetooth™ Enabled	iPod Audio Player
Biometric Input Device	IrDA Port
Card Reader/Writer	Mouse Pad/Wrist Rest
Digital Camera	Multifunction Peripheral
Digital Video Capture	Photo Printer
Digital Video Camera	Port Hub Expander
Dual-Monitor Support with Second Monitor	Portable Data Projector
Ergonomic Keyboard	Scanner
External Hard Disk	TV/FM Tuner
Floppy Disk Drive	Uninterruptible Power Supply

FIGURE 5 Base desktop and mobile computer components and optional components. A copy of the Base Components worksheet is part of the Data Files for Students. To obtain a copy of the Data Files for Students, see the inside back cover of this book for instructions.

Consider upgrades to the mouse, keyboard, monitor, printer, microphone, and speakers.

You use these peripheral devices to interact with your computer, so you should make sure they are up to your standards. Review the peripheral devices listed in Figure 4 on pages 447 and 448 and then visit both local computer dealers and large retail stores to test the computers on display. Ask the salesperson what input and output devices would be best for you and whether you should upgrade beyond what comes standard. Consider purchasing a wireless keyboard and wireless mouse to eliminate bothersome wires on your desktop. A few extra dollars spent on these components when you initially purchase a computer can extend its usefulness by years.

Determine whether you want to use telephone lines or broadband (cable or DSL) to access the Internet.

If your computer has a modem, then you can access the Internet using a standard telephone line. Ordinarily, you call a local or toll-free 800 number to connect to an ISP (see Guideline 6 on the next page). Using a dial-up Internet connection is relatively inexpensive but slow.

DSL and cable connections provide much faster Internet connections, which are ideal if you want faster file download speeds for software, digital photos, and music. As you would expect, they also are more expensive. DSL, which is available through local telephone companies, also may require that you subscribe to an ISP. Cable is available through your local cable television provider and some online service providers (OSPs). If you get cable, then you would not use a separate Internet service provider or online service provider.

6 **If you are using a dial-up or wireless connection to connect to the Internet, then select an ISP or OSP.** You can access the Internet via telephone lines in one of two ways: an ISP or an OSP. Both provide Internet access for a monthly fee that ranges from $6 to $25. Local ISPs offer Internet access to users in a limited geographic region, through local telephone numbers. National ISPs provide access for users nationwide (including mobile users), through local and toll-free telephone numbers and cable. Because of their size, national ISPs generally offer more services and have a larger technical support staff than local ISPs. OSPs furnish Internet access as well as members-only features for users nationwide. Figure 6 lists several national ISPs and OSPs. Before you choose an ISP or OSP, compare such features as the number of access hours, monthly fees, available services (e-mail, Web page hosting, chat), and reliability.

Company	Service	Web Address
America Online	OSP	aol.com
AT&T Worldnet	ISP	www.att.net
Comcast	OSP	comcast.net
CompuServe	OSP	compuserve.com
EarthLink	ISP	earthlink.net
Juno	OSP	juno.com
NetZero	OSP	netzero.com
MSN	OSP	msn.com
SBC Yahoo!	ISP/OSP	myhome.prodigy.net

For an updated list of national ISPs and OSPs and their Web site addresses, visit scsite.com/dc2007/ch8/buyers.

FIGURE 6 National ISPs and OSPs.

7 **Use a worksheet to compare computers, services, and other considerations.** You can use a separate sheet of paper to take notes on each vendor's computer and then summarize the information on a worksheet, such as the one shown in Figure 7. You can use Figure 7 to compare prices for either a PC or a Mac. Most companies advertise a price for a base computer that includes components housed in the system unit (processor, RAM, sound card, video card), disk drives (floppy disk, hard disk, CD-ROM, CD-RW, DVD-ROM, and DVD±RW), a keyboard, mouse, monitor, printer, speakers, and modem. Be aware, however, that some advertisements list prices for computers with only some of these components. Monitors and printers, for example, often are not included in a base computer's price. Depending on how you plan to use the computer, you may want to invest in additional or more powerful components. When you are comparing the prices of computers, make sure you are comparing identical or similar configurations.

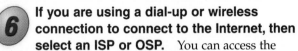

PC or MAC Cost Comparison Worksheet

Dealers list prices for computers with most of these components (instead of listing individual component costs). Some dealers do not supply a monitor. Some dealers offer significant discounts, but you must subscribe to an Internet service for a specified period to receive the discounted price. To compare computers, enter overall system price at top and enter a 0 (zero) for components <u>included in the system cost</u>. For any additional components not covered in the system price, enter the cost in the appropriate cells.

Items to Purchase	Desired System (PC)	Desired System (Mac)	Local Dealer #1	Local Dealer #2	Online Dealer #1	Online Dealer #2	Comments
OVERALL SYSTEM							
Overall System Price	< $1,500	< $1500					
HARDWARE							
Processor	Pentium(R) 4 at 2.8 GHz	Power PC G5 at 1.6 GHz					
RAM	1 GB	1 GB					
Cache	256 KB L2	256 KB L2					
Hard Disk	120 GB	120 GB					
Monitor/LCD Flat Panel	17 Inch	17 Inch					
Video Graphics Card	128 MB	128 MB					
Floppy Disk Drive	3.5 Inch	NA					
USB Flash Drive	128 MB	128 MB					
CD/DVD Bay 1	CD-RW	DVD±RW					
CD/DVD Bay 2	DVD±RW	NA					
Speakers	Stereo	Stereo					
Sound Card	Sound Blaster Compatible	Sound Blaster Compatible					
USB Ports	6	6					
FireWire Port	2	2					
Network Card	Yes	Yes					
Fax/Modem	56 Kbps	56 Kbps					
Keyboard	Standard	Apple Pro Keyboard					
Pointing Device	IntelliMouse	Intellimouse or Apple Pro Mouse					
Microphone	Close-Talk Headset with Gain Adjustment	Close-Talk Headset with Gain Adjustment					
Printer	Color Ink-Jet	Color Ink-Jet					
SOFTWARE							
Operating System	Windows XP Media Center Edition	Mac OS X					
Application Software	Office 2003 Small Business Edition	Office 2004 for Mac					
Antivirus	Yes - 12 Mo. Subscription	Yes - 12 Mo. Subscription					
OTHER							
Card Reader							
Digital Camera	4-Megapixel	4-Megapixel					
Floppy Disk Drive	3.5 Inch	NA					
Internet Connection	1-Year Subscription	1-Year Subscription					
Joystick	Yes	Yes					
PC Video Camera	With Microphone	With Microphone					
Port Hub Expander							
Scanner							
Surge Protector							
Warranty	3-Year On-Site Service	3-Year On-Site Service					
Wireless Card	Internal	Internal					
Wireless LAN Access Point	LinkSys	Apple AirPort					
Total Cost			$.	$.	$.	$.	

FIGURE 7 A worksheet is an effective tool for summarizing and comparing components and prices of different computer vendors. A copy of the Computer Cost Comparison Worksheet is part of the Data Files for Students. To obtain a copy of the Data Files for Students, see the inside back cover of this book for instructions.

8 **If you are buying a new computer, you have several purchasing options: buying from your school bookstore, a local computer dealer, a local large retail store, or ordering by mail via telephone or the Web.** Each purchasing option has certain advantages. Many college bookstores, for example, sign exclusive pricing agreements with computer manufacturers and, thus, can offer student discounts. Local dealers and local large retail stores, however, more easily can provide hands-on support. Mail-order companies that sell computers by telephone or online via the Web (Figure 8) often provide the lowest prices, but extend less personal service. Some major mail-order companies, however, have started to provide next-business-day, on-site services. A credit card usually is required to buy from a mail-order company. Figure 9 lists some of the more popular mail-order companies and their Web site addresses.

9 **If you are buying a used computer, stay with name brands such as Dell, Gateway, Hewlett-Packard, and Apple.** Although brand-name equipment can cost more, most brand-name computers have longer, more comprehensive warranties, are better supported, and have more authorized centers for repair services. As with new computers, you can purchase a used computer from local computer dealers, local large retail stores, or mail

order via the telephone or the Web. Classified ads and used computer sellers offer additional outlets for purchasing used computers. Figure 10 lists several major used computer brokers and their Web site addresses.

10 **If you have a computer and are upgrading to a new one, then consider selling or trading in the old one.** If you are a replacement buyer, your older computer still may have value. If you cannot sell the computer through the classified ads, via a Web site, or to a friend, then ask if the computer dealer will buy your old computer. An increasing number of companies are taking trade-ins, but do not expect too much money for your old computer. Other companies offer free disposal of your old PC.

11 **Be aware of hidden costs.** Before purchasing, be sure to consider any additional costs associated with buying a computer, such as an additional telephone line, a cable or DSL modem, an uninterruptible power supply (UPS), computer furniture, a USB flash drive, paper, and computer training classes you may want to take. Depending on where you buy your computer, the seller may be willing to include some or all of these in the computer purchase price.

Type of Computer	Company	Web Address
PC	CNET Shopper	shopper.cnet.com
	Hewlett-Packard	hp.com
	CompUSA	compusa.com
	TigerDirect	tigerdirect.com
	Dell	dell.com
	Gateway	gateway.com
Macintosh	Apple Computer	store.apple.com
	ClubMac	clubmac.com
	MacConnection	macconnection.com
	PC & MacExchange	macx.com

For an updated list of new mail-order computer companies and their Web site addresses, visit scsite.com/dc2007/ch8/buyers.

FIGURE 9 Computer mail-order companies.

FIGURE 8 Mail-order companies, such as Dell, sell computers online.

Company	Web Address
Amazon.com	amazon.com
TECHAGAIN	techagain.com
American Computer Exchange	americancomputerex.com
U.S. Computer Exchange	usce.org
eBay	ebay.com

For an updated list of used computer mail-order companies and their Web site addresses, visit scsite.com/dc2007/ch8/buyers.

FIGURE 10 Used computer mail-order companies.

Consider more than just price. The lowest-cost computer may not be the best long-term buy. Consider such intangibles as the vendor's time in business, the vendor's regard for quality, and the vendor's reputation for support. If you need to upgrade your computer often, you may want to consider a leasing arrangement, in which you pay monthly lease fees, but can upgrade or add on to your computer as your equipment needs change. No matter what type of buyer you are, insist on a 30-day, no-questions-asked return policy on your computer.

 Avoid restocking fees. Some companies charge a restocking fee of 10 to 20 percent as part of their money-back return policy. In some cases, no restocking fee for hardware is applied, but it is applied for software. Ask about the existence and terms of any restocking policies before you buy.

 Use a credit card to purchase your new computer. Many credit cards offer purchase protection and extended warranty benefits that cover you in case of loss of or damage to purchased goods. Paying by credit card also gives you time to install and use the computer before you have to pay for it. Finally, if you are dissatisfied with the computer and are unable to reach an agreement with the seller, paying by credit card gives you certain rights regarding withholding payment until the dispute is resolved. Check your credit card terms for specific details.

 Consider purchasing an extended warranty or service plan. If you use your computer for business or require fast resolution to major computer problems, consider purchasing an extended warranty or a service plan through a local dealer or third-party company. Most extended warranties cover the repair and replacement of computer components beyond the standard warranty. Most service plans ensure that your technical support calls receive priority response from technicians. You also can purchase an on-site service plan that states that a technician will come to your home, work, or school within 24 hours. If your computer includes a warranty and service agreement for a year or less, think about extending the service for two or three years when you buy the computer.

HOW TO PURCHASE A NOTEBOOK COMPUTER

If you need computing capability when you travel or to use in lecture or meetings, you may find a notebook computer to be an appropriate choice. The guidelines mentioned in the previous section also apply to the purchase of a notebook computer. The following are additional considerations unique to notebook computers.

1 **Purchase a notebook computer with a sufficiently large active-matrix screen.**
Active-matrix screens display high-quality color that is viewable from all angles. Less expensive, passive-matrix screens sometimes are difficult to see in low-light conditions and cannot be viewed from an angle. Notebook computers typically come with a 12.1-inch, 13.3-inch, 14.1-inch, 15.4-inch, or 17-inch display. For most users, a 14.1-inch display is satisfactory. If you intend to use your notebook computer as a desktop computer replacement, however, you may opt for a 15.7-inch or 17-inch display. Notebook computers with these larger displays weigh seven to ten pounds, however, so if you travel a lot and portability is essential, you might want a lighter computer with a smaller display. The lightest notebook computers, which weigh less than 3 pounds, are equipped with a 12.1-inch display. Regardless of size, the resolution of the display should be at least 1024 x 768 pixels. To compare the monitor size on various notebook computers, visit the company Web sites in Figure 11.

Type of Notebook	Company	Web Address
PC	Acer	global.acer.com
	Dell	dell.com
	Fujitsu	fujitsu.com
	Gateway	gateway.com
	Hewlett-Packard	hp.com
	Lenovo	lenovo.com/us/en/
	NEC	nec.com
	Sony	sony.com
	Toshiba	toshiba.com
Mac	Apple	apple.com

For an updated list of companies and their Web site addresses, visit scsite.com/dc2007/ch8/buyers.

FIGURE 11 Companies that sell notebook computers.

CENTURY COMPUTERS
Performance Guarantee
(See reverse for terms & conditions of this contract)

Invoice #: 1984409 Effective Date: 10/12/07
Invoice Date: 10/12/07 Expiration Date: 10/12/10

Customer Name: Leon, Richard System & Serial Numbers
Date: 10/12/07 IMB computer
Address: 1123 Roxbury S/N: US759290C
Sycamore, IL 60178
Day phone: (815) 555-0303
Evening Phone: (728) 555-0203

John Smith 10/12/07
Print Name of Century's Authorized Signature Date

Experiment with different keyboards and pointing devices. Notebook computer keyboards are far less standardized than those for desktop computers. Some notebook computers, for example, have wide wrist rests, while others have none. Notebook computers also use a range of pointing devices, including pointing sticks, touchpads, and trackballs. Before you purchase a notebook computer, try various types of keyboard and pointing devices to determine which is easiest for you to use. Regardless of the pointing device you select, you also may want to purchase a regular mouse to use when you are working at a desk or other large surface.

 Make sure the notebook computer you purchase has a CD and/or DVD drive. Most notebook computers come with a CD and/or a DVD drive. Although DVD drives are slightly more expensive, they allow you to play CDs and DVD movies using your notebook computer and a headset.

If necessary, upgrade the processor, memory, and disk storage at the time of purchase. As with a desktop computer, upgrading your notebook computer's memory and disk storage usually is less expensive at the time of initial purchase. Some disk storage is custom designed for notebook computer manufacturers, meaning an upgrade might not be available in the future. If you are purchasing a lightweight notebook computer, then it should include at least a 2.4 GHz processor, 512 MB RAM, and 80 GB of storage.

The availability of built-in ports and a port extender on a notebook computer is important. A notebook computer does not have a lot of room to add adapter cards. If you know the purpose for which you plan to use your notebook computer, then you can determine the ports you will need. Most notebooks come with common ports, such as a mouse port, IrDA port, serial port, parallel port, video port, a FireWire port, and multiple USB ports. If you plan to connect your notebook computer to a TV, however, then you will need a PCtoTV port. If you want to connect to networks at school or in various offices via a network cable, make sure the notebook computer you purchase has a network port. If your notebook computer does not come with a network port, then you will have to purchase an external network card that slides into an expansion slot in your notebook computer, as well as a network cable. While newer iPod audio players connect to a USB port, older ones require a FireWire port.

 If you plan to use your notebook computer for note-taking at school or in meetings, consider a notebook computer that converts to a Tablet PC. Some computer manufacturers have developed convertible notebook computers that allow the screen to rotate 180 degrees on a central hinge and then fold down to cover the keyboard and become a Tablet PC (Figure 12). You then can use a stylus to enter text or drawings into the computer by writing on the screen.

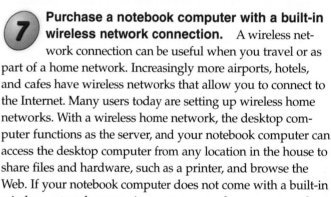

FIGURE 12
The HP Compaq tc4200 Tablet PC converts to a notebook computer.

Purchase a notebook computer with a built-in wireless network connection. A wireless network connection can be useful when you travel or as part of a home network. Increasingly more airports, hotels, and cafes have wireless networks that allow you to connect to the Internet. Many users today are setting up wireless home networks. With a wireless home network, the desktop computer functions as the server, and your notebook computer can access the desktop computer from any location in the house to share files and hardware, such as a printer, and browse the Web. If your notebook computer does not come with a built-in wireless network connection, you can purchase an external one that slides into your notebook computer. Most home wireless networks allow connections from distances of 150 to 800 feet.

If you are going to use your notebook computer for long periods without access to an electrical outlet, purchase a second battery. The trend among notebook computer users today is power and size over battery life, and notebook computer manufacturers have picked up on this. Many notebook computer users today are willing to give up longer battery life for a larger screen, faster processor, and more storage. In addition, some manufacturers typically sell the notebook with the lowest capacity battery. For this reason, you need to be careful in choosing a notebook computer if you plan to use it without access to electrical outlets for long periods, such as an airplane flight. You also might want to purchase a second battery as a backup. If you anticipate running your notebook computer on batteries frequently, choose a computer that uses lithium-ion batteries, which last longer than nickel cadmium or nickel hydride batteries.

9 **Purchase a well-padded and well-designed carrying case.** An amply padded carrying case will protect your notebook computer from the bumps it will receive while traveling. A well-designed carrying case will have room for accessories such as spare floppy disks, CDs and DVDs, a user manual, pens, and paperwork (Figure 13).

FIGURE 13
A well-designed notebook computer carrying case.

10 **If you travel overseas, obtain a set of electrical and telephone adapters.** Different countries use different outlets for electrical and telephone connections. Several manufacturers sell sets of adapters that will work in most countries.

11 **If you plan to connect your notebook computer to a video projector, make sure the notebook computer is compatible with the video projector.** You should check, for example, to be sure that your notebook computer will allow you to display an image on the computer screen and projection device at the same time (Figure 14). Also, ensure that your notebook computer has the ports required to connect to the video projector.

12 **For improved security, consider a fingerprint scanner.** More than a quarter of a million notebook computers are stolen or lost each year. If you have critical information stored on your notebook computer, then consider purchasing one with a fingerprint scanner (Figure 15) to protect the data if your computer is stolen or lost. Fingerprint security offers a level of protection that extends well beyond the standard password protection.

FIGURE 15 Fingerprint scanner technology offers greater security than passwords.

FIGURE 14
A notebook computer connected to a video projector projects the image displayed on the screen.

HOW TO PURCHASE A TABLET PC

The Tablet PC (Figure 16) combines the mobility features of a traditional notebook computer with the simplicity of pencil and paper, because you can create and save Office-type documents by writing and drawing directly on the screen with a digital pen. Tablet PCs use the Windows XP Tablet PC Edition operating system, which expands on Windows XP Professional by including digital pen and speech capabilities. A notebook computer and a Tablet PC have many similarities. For this reason, if you are considering purchasing a Tablet PC, review the guidelines for purchasing a notebook computer, as well as the guidelines below.

FIGURE 16 The lightweight Tablet PC, with its handwriting capabilities, is the latest addition to the family of mobile computers.

 Make sure the Tablet PC fits your mobile computing needs. The Tablet PC is not for every mobile user. If you find yourself in need of a computer in class or you are spending more time in meetings than in your office, then the Tablet PC may be the answer. Before you invest money in a Tablet PC, however, determine the programs you plan to use on it. You should not buy a Tablet PC simply because it is a new and interesting type of computer. For additional information on the Tablet PC, visit the Web sites listed in Figure 17. You may have to use the search capabilities on the home page of the companies listed to locate information about the Tablet PC.

Company	Web Address
Fujitsu	fujitsu.com
Hewlett-Packard	hp.com
Microsoft	microsoft.com/windowsxp/tabletpc
ViewSonic	viewsonic.com
For an updated list of companies and their Web site addresses, visit scsite.com/dc2007/ch8/buyers.	

FIGURE 17 Companies involved with Tablet PCs and their Web sites.

 Decide whether you want a convertible or pure Tablet PC. Convertible Tablet PCs have an attached keyboard and look like a notebook computer. You rotate the screen and lay it flat against the computer for note-taking. The pure Tablet PCs are slim and lightweight, weighing less than four pounds. They have the capability of easily docking at a desktop to gain access to a large monitor, keyboard, and mouse. If you spend a lot of time attending lectures or meetings, then the pure Tablet PC is ideal. Acceptable specifications for a Tablet PC are shown in Figure 18.

TABLET PC SPECIFICATIONS

Dimensions	12" × 9" × 1.2"
Weight	Less than 4 Pounds
Processor	Pentium M processor at 1 GHz
RAM	1 GB
Hard Disk	40 GB
Display	12.1" TFT
Digitizer	Electromagnetic Digitizer
Battery	4-Cell (3-Hour)
USB	2
FireWire	1
Docking Station	Grab and Go with CD-ROM, Keyboard, and Mouse
Bluetooth Port	Yes
Wireless	802.11a/b/g Card
Network Card	10/100 Ethernet
Modem	56 Kbps
Speakers	Internal
Microphone	Internal
Operating System	Windows XP Tablet PC Edition
Application Software	Office Small Business Edition
Antivirus Software	Yes – 12 Month Subscription
Warranty	1-Year Limited Warranty Parts and Labor

FIGURE 18 Tablet PC specifications.

Be sure the weight and dimensions are conducive to portability. The weight and dimensions of the Tablet PC are important because you carry it around like a notepad. The Tablet PC you buy should weigh four pounds or less. Its dimensions should be approximately 12 inches by 9 inches by 1.2 inches.

Port availability, battery life, and durability are even more important with a Tablet PC than they are with a notebook computer. Make sure the Tablet PC you purchase has the ports required for the applications you plan to run. As with any mobile computer, battery life is important especially if you plan to use your Tablet PC for long periods without access to an electrical outlet. A Tablet PC must be durable because if you use it the way it was designed to be used, then you will be handling it much like you handle a pad of paper.

 Experiment with different models of the Tablet PC to find the digital pen that works best for you. The key to making use of the Tablet PC is to be comfortable with its handwriting capabilities and on-screen keyboard. Not only is the digital pen used to write on the screen (Figure 19), you also use it to make gestures to complete tasks, in a manner similar to the way you use a mouse. Figure 20 compares the standard point-and-click of a mouse with the gestures made with a digital pen. Other gestures with the digital pen replicate some of the commonly used keys on a keyboard.

FIGURE 19 A Tablet PC lets you handwrite notes and draw on the screen using a digital pen.

Mouse	Digital Pen
Point	Point
Click	Tap
Double-click	Double-tap
Right-click	Tap and hold
Click and drag	Drag

FIGURE 20 Standard point-and-click of a mouse compared with the gestures made with a digital pen.

 Check out the comfort level of handwriting in different positions. You should be able to handwrite on a Tablet PC with your hand resting on the screen. You also should be able to handwrite holding the Tablet PC in one hand, as well as with it sitting in your lap.

 Make sure the LCD display device has a resolution high enough to take advantage of Microsoft's ClearType technologies. Tablet PCs use a digitizer under a standard 10.4-inch motion-sensitive LCD display to make the digital ink on the screen look like real ink on paper. To ensure you get the maximum benefits from the new ClearType technology, make sure the LCD display has a resolution of 800 × 600 in landscape mode and a 600 × 800 in portrait mode.

Test the built-in Tablet PC microphone and speakers. With many application software packages recognizing human speech, such as Microsoft Office, it is important that the Tablet PC's built-in microphone operates at an acceptable level. If the microphone is not to your liking, you may want to purchase a close-talk headset with your Tablet PC. Increasingly more users are sending information as audio files, rather than relying solely on text. For this reason, you also should check the speakers on the Tablet PC to make sure they meet your standards.

Consider a Tablet PC with a built-in PC video camera. A PC video camera adds streaming video and still photography capabilities to your Tablet PC, while still allowing you to take notes in lectures or meetings.

Review the docking capabilities of the Tablet PC. The Microsoft Windows XP Tablet PC Edition operating system supports a grab-and-go form of docking, so you can pick up and take a docked Tablet PC with you, just as you would pick up a notepad on your way to a meeting (Figure 21).

FIGURE 21 A Tablet PC docked to create a desktop computer with the Tablet PC as the monitor.

Wireless access to the Internet and your e-mail is essential with a Tablet PC. Make sure the Tablet PC has wireless networking, so you can access the Internet and your e-mail anytime and anywhere. Your Tablet PC also should include standard network connections, such as dial-up and Ethernet connections.

Review available accessories to purchase with your Tablet PC. Tablet PC accessories include docking stations, mouse units, keyboards, security cables, additional memory and storage, protective handgrips, screen protectors, and various types of digital pens.

NOTES

Communications and Networks

Picture Yourself Communicating Wirelessly

While driving to a small, quaint village for a weekend getaway, you realize you forgot to pay bills before leaving on the trip. All you need is an Internet connection because you pay your bills online. Along the roadside, you see a Starbucks Coffee billboard that says, "Stay connected with T-Mobile Hot Spot." After four hours of driving, a white chocolate mocha sounds real good. Not sure how to get to the Starbucks Coffee advertised on the billboard, you pull off the road and use the GPS feature of your PDA to access a city map.

At the coffee shop, you order your coffee, sit down at a table, open up your notebook computer that has Intel's built-in Centrino wireless technology, connect to the Internet, access your bank's Web site, and pay your bills.

Later that night at the bed and breakfast, you decide to check e-mail messages. Although the inn provides a central telephone line for dial-up Internet connections, you use your wireless PC modem card to connect to your wireless Internet service provider and download e-mail messages wirelessly. This way you can stay in your room and relax.

While shopping for antiques the next day, you see a clock your mom would love. Before buying it, you take a picture of it with your smart phone and use picture messaging to send the picture to your dad's e-mail address — you want to be sure she does not have it already. He sends back a text message that says, "Buy it!"

Read Chapter 9 to learn about wireless communications with a notebook computer, PDA, and smart phone and to discover other uses of communications.

COMMUNICATIONS

Computer **communications** describes a process in which two or more computers or devices transfer data, instructions, and information. Today, even the smallest computers and devices communicate directly with one another, with hundreds of computers on a company network, or with millions of other computers around the globe — often via the Internet.

Figure 9-1 shows a sample communications system. Some communications involve cables and wires; others are sent wirelessly through the air. For successful communications, you need the following:

- A **sending device** that initiates an instruction to transmit data, instructions, or information.
- A communications device that connects the sending device to a communications channel.
- A **communications channel**, or transmission media on which the data, instructions, or information travel.

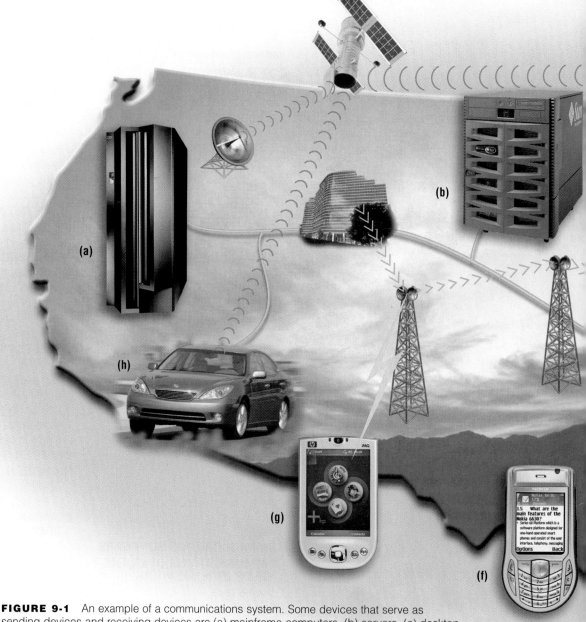

FIGURE 9-1 An example of a communications system. Some devices that serve as sending devices and receiving devices are (a) mainframe computers, (b) servers, (c) desktop computers, (d) notebook computers, (e) Tablet PCs, (f) smart phones, (g) Internet-enabled PDAs, and (h) GPS receivers. The communications channel consists of telephone lines, cable television and other underground lines, microwave stations, and satellites.

- A communications device that connects the communications channel to a receiving device.
- A **receiving device** that accepts the transmission of data, instructions, or information.

As shown in Figure 9-1, all types of computers and mobile devices serve as sending and receiving devices in a communications system. This includes mainframe computers, servers, desktop computers, notebook computers,

Tablet PCs, smart phones, PDAs, and GPS receivers. One type of communications device that connects a communications channel to a sending or receiving device such as a computer is a modem. Two examples of communications channels are cable television lines and telephone lines.

This chapter presents various uses of communications, discusses different types of networks, and then examines several types of communications devices and communications channels.

(c)

(d)

(e)

USES OF COMPUTER COMMUNICATIONS

Computer communications are everywhere. Many require that users subscribe to an Internet access provider. With other computer communications, an organization such as a business or school provides communications services to employees, students, or customers. The following pages discuss a variety of computer communications.

Internet, Web, E-Mail, Instant Messaging, Chat Rooms, Newsgroups, Internet Telephony, FTP, Web Folders, Video Conferencing, and Fax

Previous chapters discussed many uses of computer communications as they related to a particular topic. In the course of a day, it is likely you use, or use information generated by, one or more of these previously discussed communications technologies. The table in Figure 9-2 reviews the features of these modes of communications.

The following pages discuss a variety of other uses of communications that have not been discussed previously. These include wireless messaging services, wireless Internet access points, cybercafés, global positioning systems, groupware, collaboration, voice mail, and Web services.

Wireless Messaging Services

Users can send and receive wireless messages to and from smart phones, cellular telephones, or PDAs using three techniques: text messaging, wireless instant messaging, and picture messaging (Figure 9-3). The type of messaging you use depends primarily on the services offered by the wireless Internet service provider (WISP) that works with the cellular phone or PDA you select. In most cases, you can receive these messages at no cost but pay a per use or monthly fee to send messages to others. Read Ethics & Issues 9-1 for a related discussion.

PREVIOUSLY DISCUSSED USES OF COMMUNICATIONS

Internet — Worldwide collection of networks that links millions of businesses, government agencies, educational institutions, and individuals

Web — Worldwide collection of electronic documents on the Internet that users access through a Web browser

E-Mail — Transmission of messages and files via a computer network

Instant Messaging — Real-time Internet communications service that notifies you when one or more people are online and then allows you to exchange messages, pictures, files, audio, and video

Chat Rooms — Real-time typed conversation that takes place on a computer connected to a network that also may allow the exchange of messages, pictures, files, audio, and video

Newsgroups — Online areas in which users have written discussions about a particular subject

Internet Telephony — Conversation that takes place over the Internet using a telephone connected to a desktop computer, mobile computer, or mobile device

FTP — Internet standard that permits users to upload and download files to and from FTP servers on the Internet

Web Folders — Location on a Web server (also known as an HTTP server) to which users publish documents and other files

Video Conferencing — Real-time meeting between two or more geographically separated people who use a network to transmit audio and video data

Fax Machine or Computer Fax/Modem — Transmits and receives documents over telephone lines

FIGURE 9-2 Uses of communications discussed in earlier chapters.

ETHICS & ISSUES 9-1

Should Cell Phones Be Banned in Public Places?

Most people would never consider cutting in line at the bank or checking out with too many items in the 10-items-or-fewer lane at the grocery store. This courtesy seems to elude many people when it comes to cellular phone etiquette. In movie theatres, libraries, schools, restaurants, and on the sidewalk, more and more people are engaging in loud cell phone conversations. Psychologists have found that it may not be the cell phone users' speech volume that annoys us, but rather that the person is having a seemingly one-way conversation with no one, which is a much more difficult background noise for the brain to filter out. New York City recently banned the use of cell phones in places of public performance, including theatres, lectures, museums, and libraries. Some states and cities have banned the use of cell phones while driving, or required the use of hands-free devices while driving and using a cell phone. Opponents of such strict rules claim that the phones make people more productive and are convenient in an emergency. Should governments do more to discourage the use of cell phones in public places? Why or why not? Should simple rules of etiquette for cell phone use be more publicized or enforced? Why or why not? If so, by whom?

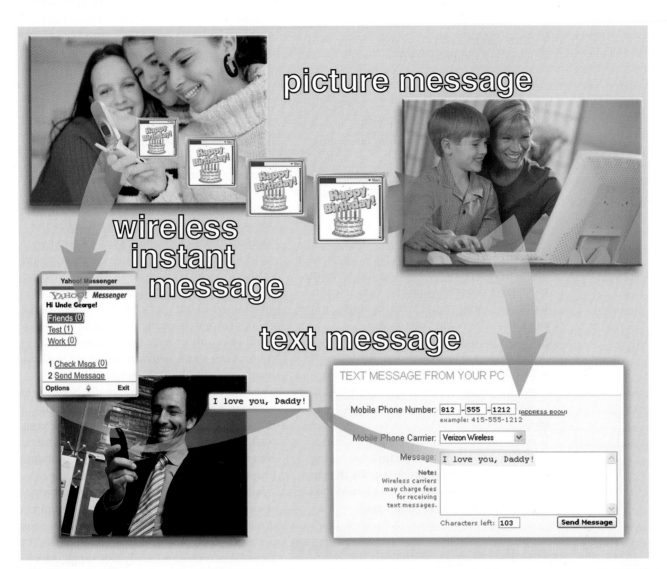

FIGURE 9-3   Users can send and receive text messages, wireless instant messages, and picture messages to and from their smart phones and other computers and devices.

TEXT MESSAGING   A mobile device with **text messaging**, also called **SMS** (*short message service*), capability allows users to send and receive short text messages on a smart phone or PDA. Most text messaging services limit messages to a specific number of characters, usually fewer than 300 characters. Text messaging services typically provide users with several options for sending and receiving messages:

- Mobile to Mobile: send the message from your mobile device to another mobile device
- Mobile to E-Mail: send the message from your mobile device to an e-mail address anywhere in the world
- Web to Mobile: send the message from a text messaging Web site to a mobile device

Most services store incoming text messages for about 72 hours. After that time, the WISP deletes any unread messages from its server.

WIRELESS INSTANT MESSAGING   Wireless instant messaging (IM) is a real-time Internet communications service that allows wireless mobile devices to exchange messages with one or more mobile devices or online users. Some WISPs partner with IM services so you can use your smart phone or PDA to send and receive wireless instant messages. Cingular Wireless service, for example, allows communications through various instant messengers such as AOL Instant Messenger and Yahoo! Messenger. With a compatible IM service, users have these IM options:

- Mobile to Mobile: use a wireless instant messenger to communicate between two mobile devices
- Mobile to Personal Computer: use a wireless instant messenger to communicate between a mobile device and a personal computer

Many services also allow users to forward wireless instant messages from a personal computer to their smart phone.

PICTURE MESSAGING   Users can send graphics, pictures, video clips, and sound files, as well as short text messages with **picture messaging**, also called *MMS* (*multimedia message service*) to another smart phone, PDA, or computer. Smart phones and PDAs with picture messaging capability typically have a digital camera built into the device. Read Ethics & Issues 9-2 for a related discussion.

Picture messaging services typically provide users these options for sending and receiving messages (some messaging services use the term, *video messaging*, to refer separately to the capability of sending video clips):

• Mobile to Mobile: send the picture from your mobile device to another mobile device
• Mobile to E-Mail: send the picture from your mobile device to an e-mail address anywhere in the world

If you send a picture message to a cellular phone that does not have picture messaging capability, the cellular phone usually displays a text message directing the user to a Web page that contains the picture message.

Wireless Internet Access Points

At home, work, school, and in many public locations, people connect wirelessly to the Internet through a **wireless Internet access point** using mobile computers or other devices. Two types of wireless Internet access points are hot spots and 3G networks.

A *hot spot* is a wireless network that provides Internet connections to mobile computers and other devices. Through the hot spot, mobile users check e-mail, browse the Web, and access any service on the Internet — as long as their computers or devices have built-in wireless capability or the appropriate wireless network card or PC Card (Figure 9-4). Two popular hot spot technologies are Wi-Fi and WiMAX. In general, Wi-Fi hot spots have an indoor range of 100 feet and an outdoor range of 300 feet. Wi-Fi hot spots provide wireless network connections to users in airports, train stations, hotels, convention centers, schools, campgrounds, marinas, shopping malls, bookstores, libraries, restaurants, and coffee shops. The coverage range for WiMAX hot spots, by contrast, can extend to more than 30 miles and cover entire cities. Sections later in this chapter discuss Wi-Fi and WiMAX in more detail.

Some hot spots provide free Internet access, some charge a per-use fee, and others require users to subscribe to a WISP, to which they pay per access fees, daily fees, or a monthly fee. Per access fees average $3, daily fees range from $5 to $20, and monthly fees range from $30 to $50 for unlimited access.

Instead of hot spots, some users access the Internet wirelessly through 3G networks. A *3G network* uses cellular radio technology to provide users with high-speed wireless Internet connections, as long as they are in the network's range. A 3G network usually includes most major cities and airports. Users access the 3G network through a cellular phone or notebook computer equipped with the appropriate PC Card. Subscription fees for unlimited monthly Internet access through a cellular phone range from $30 to $50. Fees for notebook computer access are higher, ranging from $60 to $80 per month. A section later in this chapter discusses 3G technology in more depth.

ETHICS & ISSUES 9-2

High-Tech Cheating via Wireless Messaging Services

Several schools have banned student cellular telephones claiming that they disrupt classes and sometimes are used for illegal activities, such as drug sales. Now, schools may have another reason to prohibit cellular telephones and other wireless devices among students.

Once, teachers only had to watch test-takers to make sure that no one was copying from a neighbor's paper or secretly referring to notes concealed under a desk. Recently, however, some students have been caught using their cellular phones' messaging service to send each other answers to test questions. Others have been caught using camera-enabled cellular phones to take pictures of tests and forwarding the images to other students who were scheduled to take the test at a later time. Some teachers fear that more students soon may be using wireless devices, such as gaming devices, to communicate covertly with classmates during a test, or even to receive messages from sources outside the classroom. To eliminate this high-tech method of cheating, should cellular telephones, digital cameras, notebook computers, Tablet PCs, PDAs, and other wireless devices be banned during lectures and exams? Why or why not? Short of banning these devices, what, if anything, can schools do to prevent students from using them to cheat? Is it possible for schools to seek a point of compromise so that they can both embrace the new technology and control it?

FIGURE 9-4   Mobile users in this hot spot access the Internet through their notebook computers. One computer uses a wireless network PC Card. The other has Intel's built-in wireless Centrino technology.

WEB LINK 9-1

Hot Spots
For more information, visit scsite.com/ dc2007/ch9/weblink and then click Hot Spots.

Cybercafés

When mobile users travel without their notebook computer or Internet-enabled mobile device, they can visit a cybercafé to access e-mail, the Web, and other Internet services. A **cybercafé** is a coffeehouse or restaurant that provides personal computers with Internet access to its customers (Figure 9-5). More than 5,700 cybercafés exist in cities around the world. Although some provide free Internet access, most charge a per-hour or per-minute fee. Some cybercafés also are hot spots, providing wireless Internet connections to users with mobile computers and devices.

FIGURE 9-5   People using Internet-connected computers in a cybercafé.

Global Positioning System

A **global positioning system (GPS)** is a navigation system that consists of one or more earth-based receivers that accept and analyze signals sent by satellites in order to determine the receiver's geographic location (Figure 9-6). A *GPS receiver* is a handheld, mountable, or embedded device that contains an antenna, a radio receiver, and a processor. Many include a screen display that shows an individual's location on a map.

Many mobile devices such as PDAs and smart phones have GPS capability built into the device or as an add-on feature. Some users carry a handheld GPS receiver; others mount a receiver to an object such as an automobile, boat, airplane, farm and construction equipment, or computer.

The first and most used application of GPS technology is to assist people with determining where they are located. The data obtained from a GPS, however, can be applied to a variety of other uses: creating a map, ascertaining the best route between two points, locating a lost person or stolen object, or monitoring the movement of a person or object. Many vehicles use GPSs to provide drivers with directions or other information, automatically call for help if the airbag is deployed, dispatch roadside assistance, unlock the driver's side door if keys are locked in the car, and track the vehicle if it is stolen. Hikers and remote campers may carry GPS receivers in case they need emergency help or directions.

For applications that locate or track people, the GPS receiver typically works in conjunction

FIGURE 9-6   HOW A GPS WORKS

Step 1:
GPS satellites orbit Earth. Every thousandth of a second, each satellite sends a signal that indicates its current position to the GPS receiver.

L O C A T E   M E

Step 2:
A GPS receiver (such as in a car, a watch, a smart phone, a handheld device, or a collar) determines its location on Earth by analyzing at least 3 separate satellite signals from the 24 satellites in orbit.

with a cellular wireless network. When a user presses a button on the GPS receiver or at regularly scheduled times, the GPS receiver captures data from the satellite and sends location information to a cellular wireless network. Once the cellular wireless network receives the data, its computer calculates the exact location of a person or object.

A new use of GPS places the GPS receiver on a computer chip that is worn as a wristwatch or chain or woven into fabric. The chip measures and sends a person's biological information to a cellular wireless network. If the information relayed indicates a person needs medical attention, dispatchers use data from the GPS receiver to calculate the person's location and immediately send emergency medical help. Other possible uses include locating a missing person or pet, tracking parolees, and protecting valuables.

Collaboration

Many programs provide a means to **collaborate**, or work online, with other users connected to a server. With Microsoft Office, for example, users can conduct online meetings (Figure 9-7). An *online meeting* allows users to share documents with others in real time. That is, all participants see the document at the same time. As someone changes the document, everyone in the meeting sees the changes being made. During the online meeting, participants have the ability to open a separate window and type messages to one another. Some programs refer to this window as a chat room.

Instead of interacting in a live meeting, users often collaborate via e-mail. For example, if users want others to review a document, they can attach a routing slip to the document and send it via e-mail to everyone on the routing slip. When the first person on the routing slip receives the document, he or she may add comments to the document. As changes are made to the document, both the original text and the changes are displayed. When subsequent persons on the routing slip receive the document via e-mail, they see all the previous users' changes and can make additional changes. Once everyone on the routing slip has reviewed the document, it automatically returns to the sender.

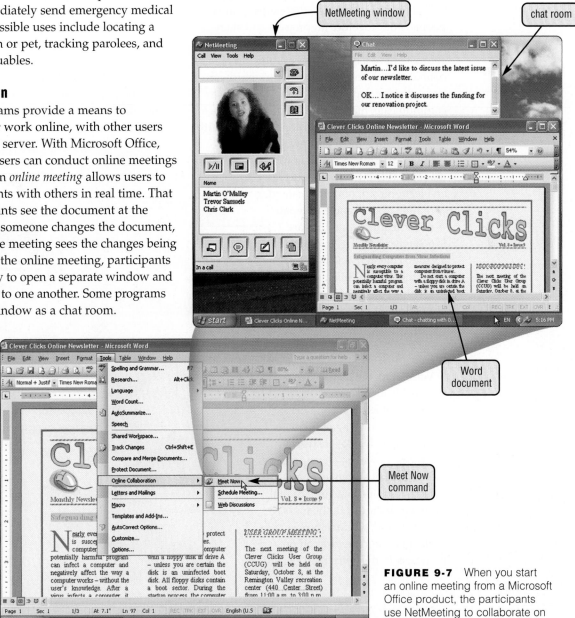

FIGURE 9-7 When you start an online meeting from a Microsoft Office product, the participants use NetMeeting to collaborate on the document.

Some companies use document management systems to make collaboration possible among employees. A *document management system* provides for storage and management of a company's documents, such as word processing documents, presentations, and spreadsheets. Users then access these documents, depending on their needs. A document management system can track all changes made to a document. It also can store additional information such as the document's creation date, the user who created the document, a summary of the document, and any keywords associated with the document.

Groupware

Groupware is software that helps groups of people work together on projects and share information over a network. Groupware is a component of a broad concept called *workgroup computing*, which includes network hardware and software that enables group members to communicate, manage projects, schedule meetings, and make group decisions. To assist with these activities, most groupware provides personal information manager (PIM) functions, such as an electronic appointment calendar, an address book, and a notepad. A major feature of groupware is group scheduling, in which a group calendar tracks the schedules of multiple users and helps coordinate appointments and meeting times.

Voice Mail

Voice mail, which functions much like an answering machine, allows someone to leave a voice message for one or more people. Unlike answering machines, however, a computer in the voice mail system converts an analog voice message into digital form. Once digitized, the message is stored in a voice mailbox. A *voice mailbox* is a storage location on a hard disk in the voice mail system.

Web Services

Web services describe standardized software that enables programmers to create applications that communicate with other remote computers over the Internet or on an internal business network (Figure 9-8). Businesses are the primary users of Web services because this technology provides a means for departments to communicate with each other, suppliers, vendors, and with clients. For example, third-party vendors can use Web services to communicate with their online retailer's Web site to manage their inventory levels.

Web services do not require a specific programming language, operating system, or Web browser. Different applications from different platforms can communicate with each other by sending properly formatted *XML* (eXtensible Markup Language) files to the Web services. A Windows application, for example, can communicate with a UNIX application. Web services do not have a user interface because the application's user interface interacts with the Web service.

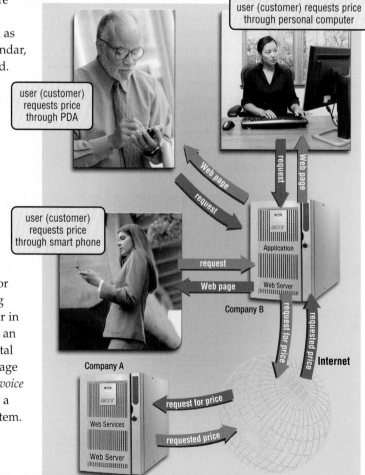

FIGURE 9-8 An example of Web services.

Test your knowledge of pages 460 through 468 in Quiz Yourself 9-1.

NETWORKS

As discussed in Chapter 1, a **network** is a collection of computers and devices connected together via communications devices and transmission media. Many businesses network their computers together to facilitate communications, share hardware, share data and information, share software, and transfer funds (Figure 9-9). The next page elaborates on how businesses use networks.

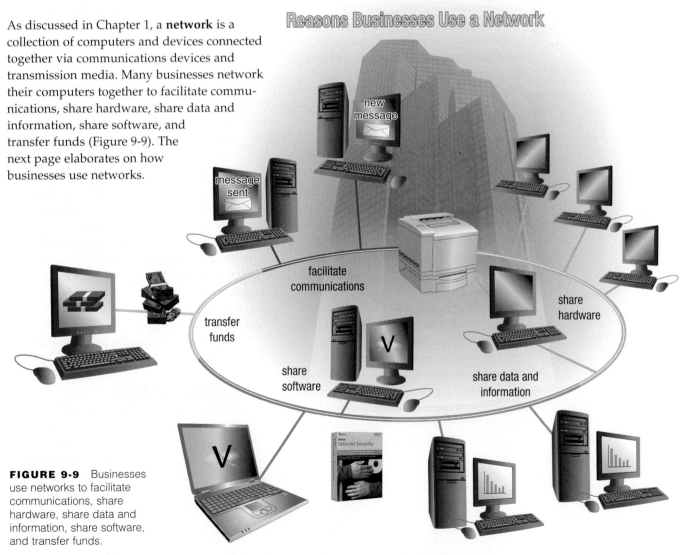

FIGURE 9-9 Businesses use networks to facilitate communications, share hardware, share data and information, share software, and transfer funds.

A network can be internal to an organization or span the world by connecting itself to the Internet. Networks facilitate communications among users and allow users to share resources, such as data, information, hardware, and software, with other users. The following paragraphs explain the advantages of using a network.

- Facilitating communications — Using a network, people communicate efficiently and easily via e-mail, instant messaging, chat rooms, blogs, video telephone calls, video conferencing, Internet telephony, wireless messaging services, and groupware. Some of these communications, such as e-mail, occur within a business's internal network. Other times, they occur globally over the Internet.

- Sharing hardware — In a networked environment, each computer on the network has access to hardware on the network. Business and home users network their hardware to save money. That is, it may be too costly to provide each user with the same piece of hardware such as a printer. If the computers and a laser printer are connected to a network, the computer users each access the laser printer on the network, as they need it.

- Sharing data and information — In a networked environment, any authorized computer user can access data and information stored on other computers on the network. A large company, for example, might have a database of customer information. Any authorized person, including a mobile user with a PDA or smart phone connected to the network, has access to the database.

  Most businesses use a standard, such as *EDI* (*electronic data interchange*), that defines how data transmits across telephone lines or other means. For example, companies use EDI to handle product catalog distribution, bids, requests for quotations, proposals, order placement, shipping notifications, invoicing, and payment processing. EDI enables businesses to operate with a minimum amount of paperwork.

- Sharing software — Users connected to a network have access to software on the network. To support multiple users' access of software, most vendors sell network versions or site licenses of their software, which usually cost less than buying individual copies of the software for each computer. A *network license* is a legal agreement that allows multiple users to access the software on a server simultaneously. The network license fee usually is based on the number of users or the number of computers attached to the network. A *site license* is a legal agreement that permits users to install the software on multiple computers — usually at a volume discount.

- Transferring funds — Called *electronic funds transfer* (*EFT*), it allows users connected to a network to transfer money from one bank account to another via transmission media. Both businesses and consumers use EFT. Consumers use an ATM to access their bank account. Businesses deposit payroll checks directly in employees' bank accounts. Consumers use credit cards to make purchases from a retail Web site. Businesses use EFT to purchase and pay for goods purchased from vendors. Both businesses and consumers pay bills online, with which they instruct a bank to use EFT to pay creditors.

Instead of using the Internet or investing in and administering an internal network, some companies hire a value-added network provider for network functions. A *value-added network* (*VAN*) is a third-party business that provides networking services such as secure data and information transfer, storage, e-mail, and management reports. Some VANs charge an annual or monthly fee; others charge by service used.

For a technical discussion about networks, read the High-Tech Talk article on page 498.

LANs, MANs, and WANs

Networks usually are classified as a local area network, metropolitan area network, or wide area network. The main differentiation among these classifications is their area of coverage, as described in the following paragraphs.

LAN   A **local area network (LAN)** is a network that connects computers and devices in a limited geographical area such as a home, school computer laboratory, office building (Figure 9-10), or closely positioned group of buildings. Each computer or device on the network, called a *node*, often shares resources such as printers, large hard disks, and programs. Often, the nodes are connected via cables.

A **wireless LAN (WLAN)** is a LAN that uses no physical wires. Computers and devices that access a wireless LAN must have built-in wireless capability or the appropriate wireless network card, PC Card, or flash card. Very often, a WLAN communicates with a wired LAN for access to its resources, such as software, hardware, and the Internet (Figure 9-11).

WEB LINK 9-3

WLANs

For more information, visit scsite.com/ dc2007/ch9/weblink and then click Wireless Local Area Networks.

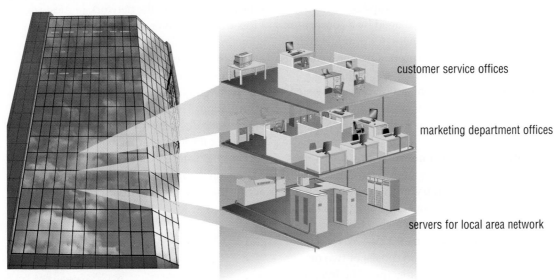

customer service offices

marketing department offices

servers for local area network

FIGURE 9-10   Computers on different floors access the same local area network (LAN) in an office building.

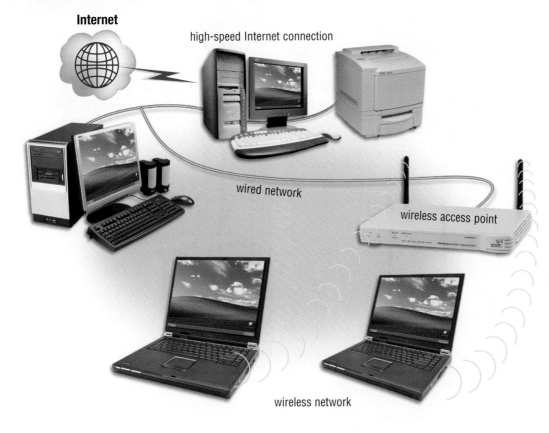

Internet

high-speed Internet connection

wired network

wireless access point

wireless network

FIGURE 9-11
Computers on a wireless LAN often communicate via an access point with a wired LAN to access its software, printer, the Internet, and other resources.

MAN   A *metropolitan area network* (*MAN*) is a high-speed network that connects local area networks in a metropolitan area such as a city or town and handles the bulk of communications activity across that region. A MAN typically includes one or more LANs, but covers a smaller geographic area than a WAN. The state of Pennsylvania, for example, has a MAN that connects state agencies and individual users in the region around the state capital.

A MAN usually is managed by a consortium of users or by a single network provider that sells the service to the users. Local and state governments, for example, regulate some MANs. Telephone companies, cable television operators, and other organizations provide users with connections to the MAN.

WAN   A **wide area network** (**WAN**) is a network that covers a large geographic area (such as a city, country, or the world) using a communications channel that combines many types of media such as telephone lines, cables, and radio waves (Figure 9-12). A WAN can be one large network or can consist of two or more LANs connected together. The Internet is the world's largest WAN.

Network Architectures

The design of computers, devices, and media in a network, sometimes called the *network architecture*, is categorized as either client/server or peer-to-peer. The following paragraphs discuss these network architectures.

CLIENT/SERVER   On a **client/server network**, one or more computers act as a server, and the other computers on the network request services from the server (Figure 9-13). A **server**, sometimes called a *host computer*, controls access to the hardware, software, and other resources on the network and provides a centralized storage area for programs, data, and information. The **clients** are other computers and mobile devices on the network that rely on the server for its resources. For example, a server might store a database of customers. Clients on the network (company employees) access the customer database on the server.

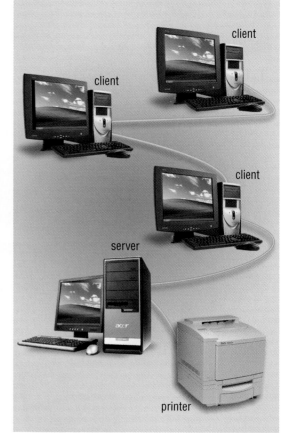

FIGURE 9-13   On a client/server network, one or more computers act as a server, and the clients access the server(s).

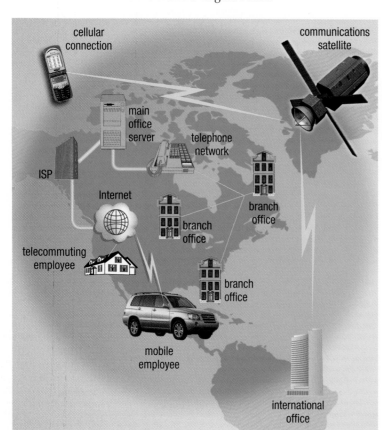

FIGURE 9-12   An example of a WAN.

Some servers, called *dedicated servers*, perform a specific task and can be placed with other dedicated servers to perform multiple tasks. For example, a *file server* stores and manages files. A *print server* manages printers and print jobs. A *database server* stores and provides access to a database. A *network server* manages network traffic (activity).

Although it can connect a smaller number of computers, a client/server network typically provides an efficient means to connect 10 or more computers. Most client/server networks require a person to serve as a network administrator because of the large size of the network.

PEER-TO-PEER One type of *peer-to-peer network* is a simple, inexpensive network that typically connects fewer than 10 computers. Each computer, called a *peer*, has equal responsibilities and capabilities, sharing hardware (such as a printer), data, or information with other computers on the peer-to-peer network (Figure 9-14). Each computer stores files on its own storage devices. Thus, each computer on the network contains both the network operating system and application software. All computers on the network share any peripheral device(s) attached

to any computer. For example, one computer may have a laser printer and a scanner, while another has an ink-jet printer and an external hard disk.

Peer-to-peer networks are ideal for very small businesses and home users. Some operating systems, such as Windows, include a peer-to-peer networking utility that allows users to set up a peer-to-peer network.

INTERNET PEER-TO-PEER Another type of peer-to-peer, called *P2P*, describes an Internet network on which users access each other's hard disks and exchange files directly over the Internet (Figure 9-15). This type of peer-to-peer network sometimes is called a *file sharing network* because users with compatible software and an Internet connection copy files from someone else's hard disk to their hard disks. As more users connect to the network, each user has access to shared files on other users' hard disks. When users log off the network, others no longer have access to their hard disks. To maintain an acceptable speed for communications, some implementations of P2P limit the number of users.

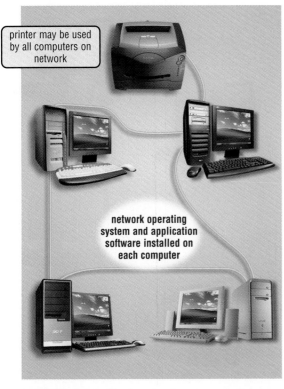

printer may be used by all computers on network

network operating system and application software installed on each computer

FIGURE 9-14 Each computer on a peer-to-peer network shares its hardware and software with other computers on the network.

hard disk

Internet

hard disk

hard disk

FIGURE 9-15 P2P describes an Internet network on which users connect to each other's hard disks and exchange files directly.

Examples of networking software that support P2P are BitTorrent, Grokster, Gnutella, and Kazaa, which allow users to swap MP3 music and other files via the Web. For example, when one user requests a song, the program searches through lists of shared files — which are stored on one or more connected computers, called supernodes. If a match is found, the MP3 file is copied from the computer on which it resides to the requesting computer. These programs initially stirred much controversy with respect to copyright infringement of music because they allowed users easily to copy MP3 music files free from one computer to another. To help reduce copyright infringement, today's music-sharing services typically are fee based, and music files often are encrypted as they travel across the Internet.

Many businesses also see an advantage to using P2P. That is, companies and employees can exchange files using P2P, freeing the company from maintaining a network server for this purpose. Business-to-business e-commerce Web sites find that P2P easily allows buyers and sellers to share company information such as product databases.

Network Topologies

A **network topology** refers to the layout of the computers and devices in a communications network. Three commonly used network topologies are bus, ring, and star. Networks usually use combinations of these topologies.

BUS NETWORK   A *bus network* consists of a single central cable, to which all computers and other devices connect (Figure 9-16). The *bus* is the physical cable that connects the computers and other devices. The bus in a bus network

transmits data, instructions, and information in both directions. When a sending device transmits data, the address of the receiving device is included with the transmission so the data is routed to the appropriate receiving device.

Bus networks are popular on LANs because they are inexpensive and easy to install. One advantage of the bus network is that computers and other devices can be attached and detached at any point on the bus without disturbing the rest of the network. Another advantage is that failure of one device usually does not affect the rest of the bus network. The greatest risk to a bus network is that the bus itself might become inoperable. If that happens, the network remains inoperative until the bus is back in working order.

RING NETWORK   On a *ring network*, a cable forms a closed loop (ring) with all computers and devices arranged along the ring (Figure 9-17). Data transmitted on a ring network travels from device to device around the entire ring, in one direction. When a computer or device sends data, the data travels to each computer on the ring until it reaches its destination.

WEB LINK 9-4

P2P

For more information, visit scsite.com/ dc2007/ch9/weblink and then click P2P.

FIGURE 9-17   On a ring network, all connected devices form a continuous loop.

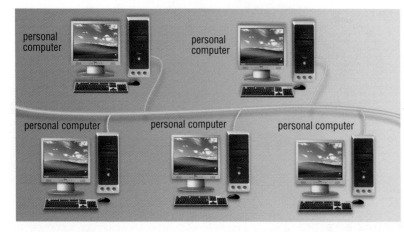

personal computer

personal computer

personal computer   personal computer   personal computer

FIGURE 9-16   Devices in a bus network share a single data path.

If a computer or device on a ring network fails, all devices before the failed device are unaffected, but those after the failed device cannot function. A ring network can span a larger distance than a bus network, but it is more difficult to install. The ring topology primarily is used for LANs, but also is used in WANs.

STAR NETWORK On a *star network*, all of the computers and devices (nodes) on the network connect to a central device, thus forming a star (Figure 9-18). The central device that provides a common connection point for nodes on the network often is called the *hub*. All data that transfers from one node to another passes through the hub.

Star networks are fairly easy to install and maintain. Nodes can be added to and removed from the network with little or no disruption to the network.

On a star network, if one node fails, only that node is affected. The other nodes continue to operate normally. If the hub fails, however, the entire network is inoperable until the hub is repaired. Most large star networks, therefore, keep backup hubs available in case the primary hub fails.

Intranets

Recognizing the efficiency and power of the Internet, many organizations apply Internet and Web technologies to their own internal networks. An *intranet* (intra means within) is an internal network that uses Internet technologies. Intranets generally make company information accessible to employees and facilitate working in groups.

Simple intranet applications include electronic publishing of organizational materials such as telephone directories, event calendars, procedure manuals, employee benefits information, and job postings. Additionally, an intranet typically includes a connection to the Internet. More sophisticated uses of intranets include groupware applications such as project management, chat rooms, newsgroups, group scheduling, and video conferencing.

An intranet essentially is a small version of the Internet that exists within an organization. It has a Web server, supports multimedia Web pages coded in HTML, and is accessible via a Web browser such as Microsoft Internet Explorer or Netscape Navigator. Users update information on the intranet by creating and posting a Web page, using a method similar to that used on the Internet.

Sometimes a company uses an *extranet*, which allows customers or suppliers to access part of its intranet. Package shipping companies, for example, allow customers to access their intranet to print air bills, schedule pickups, and even track shipped packages as the packages travel to their destinations.

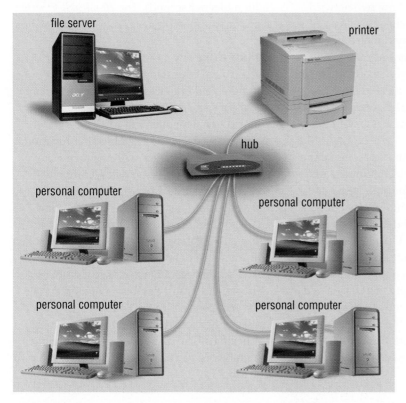

FIGURE 9-18 A star network contains a single, centralized hub through which all the devices in the network communicate.

NETWORK COMMUNICATIONS STANDARDS

Today's networks connect terminals, devices, and computers from many different manufacturers across many types of networks, such as wide area, local area, and wireless. For the different devices on various types of networks to be able to communicate, the network must use similar techniques of moving data through the network from one application to another. For example, an IBM mainframe computer cannot communicate directly with an Apple Macintosh network — some form of translation must occur for devices on these two types of networks to communicate.

To alleviate the problems of incompatibility and ensure that hardware and software components can be integrated into any network, various organizations such as ANSI and IEEE (pronounced I triple E) propose, develop, and approve network standards. A *network standard* defines guidelines that specify the way computers access the medium to which they are attached, the type(s) of medium used, the speeds used on different types of networks, and the type(s) of physical cable and/or the wireless technology used. A standard that outlines characteristics of how two network devices communicate is called a *protocol*. Specifically, a protocol may define data format, coding schemes, error handling, and sequencing techniques. Hardware and software manufacturers design their products to meet the guidelines specified in a particular standard, so their devices can communicate with the network.

The following sections discuss some of the more widely used network communications standards and protocols for both wired and wireless networks including Ethernet, token ring, TCP/IP, 802.11 (Wi-Fi), Bluetooth, IrDA, RFID, WiMAX, and WAP. Oftentimes, these network standards and protocols work together to move data through a network. Some of these standards define how a network is arranged physically; others specify how messages travel along the network, and so on. Thus, as data moves through the network from one application to another, it may use one or more of these standards.

Ethernet

Ethernet is a network standard that specifies no central computer or device on the network (nodes) should control when data can be transmitted; that is, each node attempts to transmit data when it determines the network is available to receive communications. If two computers on an Ethernet network attempt to send data at the same time, a collision will occur, and the computers must attempt to send their messages again.

Ethernet is based on a bus topology, but Ethernet networks can be wired in a star pattern. The Ethernet standard defines guidelines for the physical configuration of a network, e.g., cabling, network cards, and nodes. Today, Ethernet is the most popular network standard for LANs because it is relatively inexpensive and easy to install and maintain.

Ethernet networks often use cables to transmit data. At a 10 Mbps (million bits per second) data transfer rate, the original Ethernet standard is not very fast by today's standards. A more recent Ethernet standard, called *Fast Ethernet*, has a data transfer rate of 100 Mbps, ten times faster than the original standard. *Gigabit Ethernet* provides an even higher speed of transmission, with transfer rates of 1 Gbps (1 billion bits per second). The *10-Gigabit Ethernet* standard supports transfer rates up to 10 Gbps.

Token Ring

The **token ring** standard specifies that computers and devices on the network share or pass a special signal, called a token, in a unidirectional manner and in a preset order. A *token* is a special series of bits that function like a ticket. The device with the token can transmit data over the network. Only one token exists per network. This ensures that only one computer transmits data at a time.

Token ring is based on a ring topology (although it can use a star topology). The token ring standard defines guidelines for the physical configuration of a network, e.g., cabling, network cards, and devices. Some token ring networks connect up to 72 devices. Others use a special type of wiring that allows up to 260 connections. The data transfer rate on a token ring network can be 4 Mbps, 16 Mbps, or up to 100 Mbps.

WEB LINK 9-5

Ethernet

For more information, visit scsite.com/dc2007/ch9/weblink and then click Ethernet.

TCP/IP

Short for *Transmission Control Protocol/Internet Protocol*, **TCP/IP** is a network standard, specifically a protocol, that defines how messages (data) are routed from one end of a network to the other, ensuring the data arrives correctly. TCP/IP describes rules for dividing messages into small pieces, called *packets*; providing addresses for each packet; checking for and detecting errors; sequencing packets; and regulating the flow of messages along the network.

TCP/IP has been adopted as a network standard for Internet communications. Thus, all hosts on the Internet follow the rules defined in this standard. As shown in Figure 9-19, Internet communications also use other standards, such as the Ethernet standard, as data is routed to its destination.

When a computer sends data over the Internet, the data is divided into packets. Each packet contains the data, as well as the recipient (destination), the origin (sender), and the sequence information used to reassemble the data at the destination. Each packet travels along the fastest individual available path to the recipient's computer via communications devices called routers.

This technique of breaking a message into individual packets, sending the packets along the best route available, and then reassembling the data is called *packet switching*.

FAQ 9-1

Do HTTP, SMTP, and POP work with TCP/IP?

Yes. HTTP (Hypertext Transfer Protocol), SMTP (Simple Mail Transfer Protocol), and POP (Post Office Protocol) are standards that define the format of data as it transmits over networks that use the TCP/IP standard. HTTP works with Web browsers, and SMTP and POP work with e-mail programs. For more information, visit scsite.com/dc2007/ch9/faq and then click HTTP, SMTP, and POP.

EXAMPLE OF HOW COMMUNICATIONS STANDARDS WORK TOGETHER

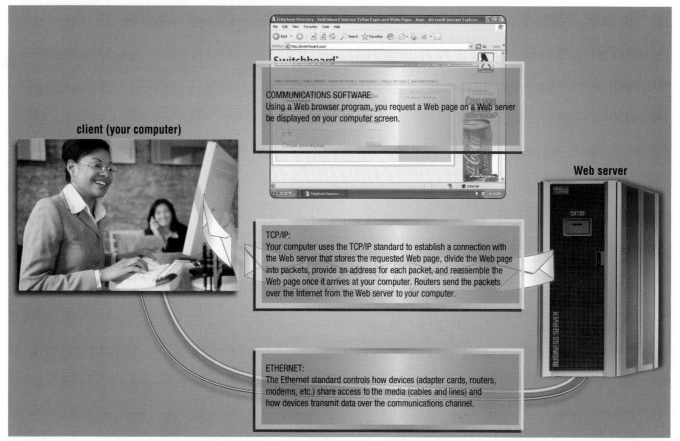

FIGURE 9-19 Network communications use a variety of standards to ensure that data travels correctly to its destination. Some standards used in Internet communications include the TCP/IP and Ethernet standards, as shown in this figure.

802.11 (Wi-Fi)

Developed by IEEE, **802.11** is a series of network standards that specifies how two wireless devices communicate over the air with each other. Using the 802.11 standard, computers or devices that have built-in wireless capability or the appropriate wireless network card or PC Card communicate via radio waves with other computers or devices. The table in Figure 9-20 outlines various 802.11 standards and their data transfer rates. As shown in the table, *802.11g* has a data transfer rate of 54 Mbps and higher. A designation of 802.11 a/b/g on a computer or device indicates it supports all three standards. The newest standard, *802.11n*, uses multiple transmitters and receivers, known as *MIMO* (multiple-input multiple-output), to reach speeds from 2 to 10 times faster than 802.11g. An *802.11i* network standard specifies enhanced security for wireless communications.

The 802.11 standard often is called the *wireless Ethernet standard* because it uses techniques similar to the Ethernet standard to specify how physically to configure a wireless network. Thus, 802.11 networks easily can be integrated with wired Ethernet networks. When an 802.11 network accesses the Internet, it works in conjunction with the TCP/IP network standard.

The term **Wi-Fi** (*wireless fidelity*) identifies any network based on the 802.11 series of standards. Wi-Fi Certified products are guaranteed to be able to communicate with each other. Windows XP and Windows Mobile include support for Wi-Fi.

One popular use of the Wi-Fi network standard is in hot spots (discussed earlier in this chapter) that offer mobile users the ability to connect to the Internet with their wireless computers and devices. Many homes and small businesses also use Wi-Fi to network computers and devices together wirelessly. In open or outdoor areas free from interference, the computers or devices should be within 300 feet of each other. In closed areas, the wireless network range is about 100 feet. To obtain communications at the maximum distances, you may need to install extra antennas.

Some entire cities are set up as a *Wi-Fi mesh network*, in which each mesh node routes its data to the next available node until the data reaches its destination — usually an Internet connection. A Wi-Fi mesh network is more flexible than a hot spot because each node in a mesh network does not have to be directly connected to the Internet.

802.11 SERIES OF STANDARDS

Standard	Transfer Rates
802.11	1 or 2 Mbps
802.11a	Up to 54 Mbps
802.11b	Up to 11 Mbps
802.11g	54 Mbps and higher
802.11n	108 Mbps and higher

FIGURE 9-20
A comparison of standards in the 802.11 series.

Bluetooth

Bluetooth is a network standard, specifically a protocol, that defines how two Bluetooth devices use short-range radio waves to transmit data. The data transfers between devices at a rate of up to 2 Mbps. To communicate with each other, Bluetooth devices often must be within about 10 meters (about 33 feet) but can be extended to 100 meters with additional equipment.

A Bluetooth device contains a small chip that allows it to communicate with other Bluetooth devices. Examples of Bluetooth-enabled devices can include desktop computers, notebook computers, handheld computers, PDAs, smart phones, headsets, microphones, digital cameras, fax machines, and printers. For computers and devices not Bluetooth-enabled, you can purchase a Bluetooth wireless port adapter that will convert an existing USB port or serial port into a Bluetooth port. Windows XP has built-in Bluetooth support that allows users easily to configure Bluetooth communications.

FAQ 9-3

Are Wi-Fi and Bluetooth competing technologies?

Not really. Bluetooth is designed for limited data transfer between two devices, one of which usually is a mobile device (e.g., a notebook computer and a printer, a digital camera and a desktop computer, two PDAs). Wi-Fi, which supports much faster data transfer rates, allows users to network many computers and devices together wirelessly. For more information, visit scsite.com/dc2007/ch9/faq and then click Wi-Fi and Bluetooth.

IrDA

As discussed in Chapter 4, some computers and devices use the **IrDA** standard to transmit data wirelessly to each other via infrared (IR) light waves. The devices transfer data at rates from 115 Kbps (thousand bits per second) to 4 Mbps between their IrDA ports.

Infrared requires a *line-of-sight transmission*; that is, the sending device and the receiving device must be in line with each other so that nothing obstructs the path of the infrared light wave. Because Bluetooth does not require line-of-sight transmission, some industry experts predict that Bluetooth will replace infrared.

FAQ 9-2

How prevalent are hot spots?

Very. In the next few years, experts predict that more than 120,000 hot spots will exist worldwide. The United States has the most hot spots, followed by the United Kingdom, France, Germany, and Japan. In the United States, New York City has the most hot spots. For more information, visit scsite.com/dc2007/ch9/faq and then click Hot Spots.

RFID

RFID (*radio frequency identification*) is a standard, specifically a protocol, that defines how a network uses radio signals to communicate with a tag placed in or attached to an object, an animal, or a person. The tag, called a transponder, consists of an antenna and a memory chip that contains the information to be transmitted via radio waves. Through an antenna, an RFID reader, also called a transceiver, reads the radio signals and transfers the information to a computer or computing device.

RFID tags are passive or active. An active RFID tag contains a battery that runs the chip's circuitry and broadcasts a signal to the RFID reader. A passive RFID tag does not contain a battery and thus cannot send a signal until the reader activates the tag's antenna by sending out electromagnetic waves. Because passive RFID tags contain no battery, these can be small enough to be embedded in skin.

Depending on the type of RFID reader, the distance between the tag and the reader ranges from 5 inches to 15 feet. Readers can be handheld or embedded in an object such as the tollbooth shown in Figure 9-21.

WiMAX

WiMAX (Worldwide Interoperability for Microwave Access), also known as **802.16**, is a newer network standard developed by IEEE that specifies how wireless devices communicate over the air in a wide area. Using the WiMAX standard, computers or devices with built-in WiMAX wireless capability or the appropriate wireless network card or PC Card communicate via radio waves with other computers or devices via a WiMAX tower. The WiMAX tower, which can cover up to a 30 mile radius, connects to the Internet or to another WiMAX tower.

The WiMAX Forum is a wireless industry association of more than 240 suppliers and service providers dedicated to developing specifications and testing equipment. Current WiMAX standards have data transfer rates from 54 Mbps to 70 Mbps.

The WiMAX standard provides wireless broadband Internet access at a reasonable cost over long distances to business and home users. Experts predict that WiMAX service eventually could surpass other broadband Internet access services such as DSL and cable because it can reach rural and remote areas easily and inexpensively. The WiMAX standard, similar to the Wi-Fi standard, connects mobile users to the Internet via hot spots. The next generation of game consoles also plans to support the WiMAX standard.

FIGURE 9-21   HOW ELECTRONIC RFID TOLL COLLECTION WORKS

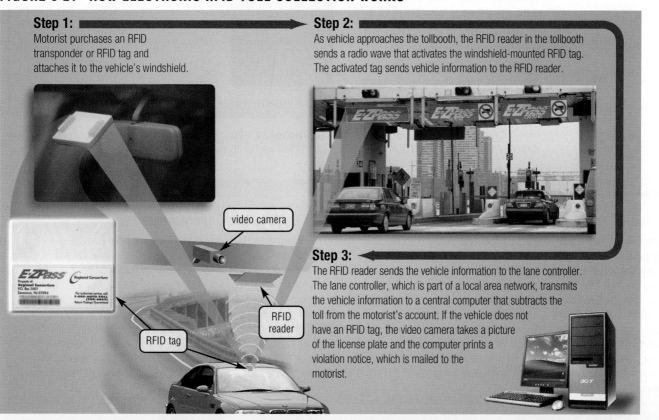

Step 1:
Motorist purchases an RFID transponder or RFID tag and attaches it to the vehicle's windshield.

Step 2:
As vehicle approaches the tollbooth, the RFID reader in the tollbooth sends a radio wave that activates the windshield-mounted RFID tag. The activated tag sends vehicle information to the RFID reader.

Step 3:
The RFID reader sends the vehicle information to the lane controller. The lane controller, which is part of a local area network, transmits the vehicle information to a central computer that subtracts the toll from the motorist's account. If the vehicle does not have an RFID tag, the video camera takes a picture of the license plate and the computer prints a violation notice, which is mailed to the motorist.

video camera

RFID reader

RFID tag

WAP

The **Wireless Application Protocol (WAP)** is a standard, specifically a protocol, that specifies how some wireless mobile devices such as smart phones and PDAs can display the content of Internet services such as the Web, e-mail, chat rooms, and newsgroups. For example, to display a Web page on a smart phone, the phone would be WAP enabled and contain a microbrowser. WAP works in conjunction with the TCP/IP network standard.

WAP uses a client/server network. The wireless device contains the client software, which connects to the Internet service provider's server. On WAP-enabled devices, data transfer rates range from 9.6 to 153 Kbps depending on the type of service.

COMMUNICATIONS SOFTWARE

Communications software consists of programs that (1) help users establish a connection to another computer or network; (2) manage the transmission of data, instructions, and information; and (3) provide an interface for users to communicate with one another. The first two are system software and the third is application software. Chapter 3 presented a variety of examples of application software for communications: e-mail, FTP, Web browser, newsgroup/message boards, chat rooms, instant messaging, video conferencing, and Internet telephony. Read Ethics & Issues 9-3 for a discussion related to Web browser communications.

Sometimes, communications devices are preprogrammed to accomplish communications tasks. Other communications devices require separate communications software to ensure proper transmission of data. Communications software works with the network standards and protocols just discussed to ensure data moves through the network or the Internet correctly. Communications software usually is bundled with the operating system or purchased network devices.

Often, a computer has various types of communications software, each serving a different purpose. One type of communications software, for example, helps users establish an Internet connection using wizards, dialog boxes, and other on-screen messages. Another allows home and small office users to configure wired and wireless networks and connect devices to an existing network (Figure 9-22).

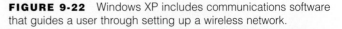

FIGURE 9-22 Windows XP includes communications software that guides a user through setting up a wireless network.

Should Libraries Be Required to Hand Over Web Browser Logs to the Government?

Most libraries offer computers that adults and children can use to connect to the Internet. In 2001, the USA PATRIOT Act that became law included a provision that libraries must hand over library patron Web browser logs when requested by law enforcement. Libraries are not allowed to disclose to anyone that they gave the information to law enforcement. The requirement directly violates the librarians' professional ethics, which hold that patrons have a right to privacy in a library. Supporters of the USA PATRIOT Act claim that the right to privacy is not absolute and that every reasonable means necessary to counteract terrorism should be employed. In addition, they claim that the records are public records. In response, many libraries have updated their privacy policies and no longer keep such records. When a patron is finished using a computer, any information related to the patron is deleted. Every effort is made to gather as little information as possible about patrons' computer habits. Should law enforcement be able secretly to gather Web browsing habits from public libraries? Why or why not? Do you think terrorists are more likely to use public libraries if they know that the library will delete all of their Web browsing records? If you knew that information about your Web browsing habits were being stored and could be gathered by law enforcement agencies, would you be less likely to use the computers in the library? Why?

COMMUNICATIONS OVER THE TELEPHONE NETWORK

The *public switched telephone network* (*PSTN*) is the worldwide telephone system that handles voice-oriented telephone calls (Figure 9-23). Nearly the entire telephone network today uses digital technology, with the exception of the final link from the local telephone company to a home, which often is analog.

The telephone network is an integral part of computer communications. Data, instructions, and information are transmitted over the telephone network using dial-up lines or dedicated lines. The following sections discuss dial-up lines and the various types of dedicated lines that use the telephone network for data communications.

Dial-Up Lines

A **dial-up line** is a temporary connection that uses one or more analog telephone lines for communications. A dial-up connection is not permanent. Using a dial-up line to transmit data is similar to using the telephone to make a call. A modem at the sending end dials the telephone number of a modem at the receiving end. When the modem at the receiving end answers the call, a connection is established and data can be transmitted. When either modem hangs up, the communications end.

Using a dial-up line to connect computers costs no more than making a regular telephone call. Computers at any two locations establish an Internet or network connection using modems and the telephone network. Mobile users, for example, can use dial-up lines in hotels to connect to their main office network to read e-mail messages, access the Internet, and upload files.

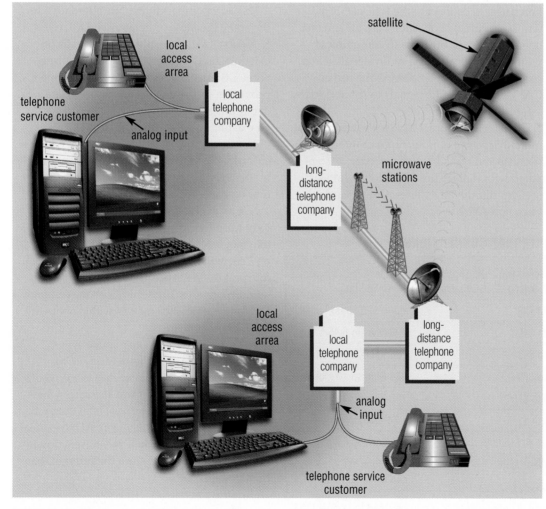

FIGURE 9-23   A sample telephone network configuration.

Dedicated Lines

A **dedicated line** is a type of always-on connection that is established between two communications devices (unlike a dial-up line where the connection is reestablished each time it is used). The quality and consistency of the connection on a dedicated line are better than a dial-up line because dedicated lines provide a constant connection.

Businesses often use dedicated lines to connect geographically distant offices. Dedicated lines can be either analog or digital. Digital lines increasingly are connecting home and business users to networks around the globe because they transmit data and information at faster rates than analog lines.

Four types of digital dedicated lines are ISDN lines, DSL, T-carrier lines, and ATM. Although cable television (CATV) lines and fixed wireless are not a type of standard telephone line, they are very popular ways for the home user to connect to the Internet. Fixed wireless Internet connections use an antenna on your house or business to communicate with a tower location via radio signals. Later sections in this chapter discuss the use of CATV lines and radio signals to connect to the Internet.

The table in Figure 9-24 lists the approximate monthly costs of various types of Internet connections and transfer rates (speeds), as compared with dial-up lines. The following sections discuss ISDN lines, DSL, T-carrier lines, and ATM.

ISDN Lines

For the small business and home user, an ISDN line provides faster transfer rates than dial-up telephone lines. Not as widely used today as in the past, *ISDN* (*Integrated Services Digital Network*) is a set of standards for digital transmission of data over standard copper telephone lines. With ISDN, the same telephone line that could carry only one computer signal now can carry three or more signals at once through the same line, using a technique called *multiplexing*.

ISDN requires that both ends of the connection have an ISDN modem. This type of modem is different from the type used in dial-up connections. The ISDN modem at your location must be within about 3.5 miles of the telephone company's ISDN modem. Thus, ISDN may not be an option for rural residents.

DSL

DSL is a popular digital line alternative for the small business or home user. **DSL** (*Digital Subscriber Line*) transmits at fast speeds on existing standard copper telephone wiring. Some DSL installations include a dial tone, providing users with both voice and data communications. Others share services with an existing telephone line.

To connect to DSL, a customer must have a special network card and a DSL modem. A DSL modem is different from the modem used for dial-up connections.

Not all areas offer DSL service because the local telephone company or the lines in the area may not be capable of supporting DSL technology. As with ISDN, DSL may not be an option for rural residents because the user's location (and DSL modem) and the telephone company's DSL modem must be located within about 3.5 miles of each other.

ADSL is one of the more popular types of DSLs. As shown in Figure 9-25, *ADSL* (*asymmetric digital subscriber line*) is a type of DSL that supports faster transfer rates when receiving data (the *downstream rate*) than when sending data (the *upstream rate*). ADSL is ideal for Internet access because most users download more information from the Internet than they upload.

SPEEDS OF VARIOUS INTERNET CONNECTIONS

Type of Line	Approximate Monthly Cost	Transfer Rates
Dial-up	Local or long-distance rates	Up to 56 Kbps
ISDN	$10 to $40	Up to 128 Kbps
DSL	$15 to $40	128 Kbps to 8.45 Mbps
Cable TV (CATV)	$20 to $45	128 Kbps to 36 Mbps
Fixed Wireless	$35 to $70	256 Kbps to 10 Mbps
Fractional T1	$200 to $700	128 Kbps to 768 Kbps
T1	$500 to $1,000	1.544 Mbps
T3	$5,000 to $15,000	44.736 Mbps
ATM	$3,000 or more	155 Mbps to 622 Mbps, can reach 10 Gbps

FIGURE 9-24   The speeds of various lines that can be used to connect to the Internet.

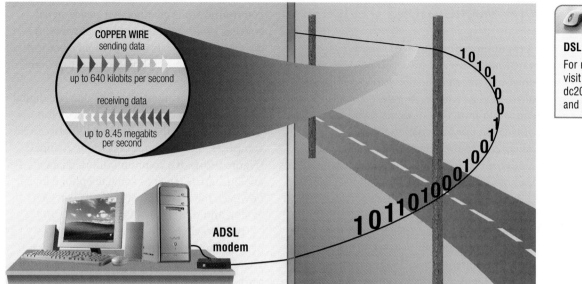

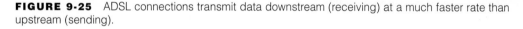

COPPER WIRE
sending data

up to 640 kilobits per second

receiving data

up to 8.45 megabits
per second

ADSL
modem

FIGURE 9-25 ADSL connections transmit data downstream (receiving) at a much faster rate than upstream (sending).

WEB LINK 9-7

DSL
For more information, visit scsite.com/dc2007/ch9/weblink and then click DSL.

T-Carrier Lines

A **T-carrier line** is any of several types of long-distance digital telephone lines that carry multiple signals over a single communications line. Whereas a standard dial-up telephone line carries only one signal, digital T-carrier lines use multiplexing so that multiple signals share the line. T-carrier lines provide very fast data transfer rates. Only medium to large companies usually can afford the investment in T-carrier lines because these lines are so expensive.

The most popular T-carrier line is the *T1 line*. Businesses often use T1 lines to connect to the Internet. Many Internet access providers use T1 lines to connect to the Internet backbone. Home and small business users purchase *fractional T1*, in which they share a connection to the T1 line with other users. Fractional T1 is slower than a dedicated T1 line, but it also is less expensive. Users who do not have other high-speed Internet access in their areas can opt for fractional T1.

A *T3 line* is equal in speed to 28 T1 lines. T3 lines are quite expensive. Main users of T3 lines include large companies, telephone companies, and Internet access providers connecting to the Internet backbone. The Internet backbone itself also uses T3 lines.

ATM

ATM (*Asynchronous Transfer Mode*) is a service that carries voice, data, video, and multimedia at very high speeds. Telephone networks, the

Internet, and other networks with large amounts of traffic use ATM. Some experts predict that ATM eventually will become the Internet standard for data transmission, replacing T3 lines.

Test your knowledge of pages 469 through 483 in Quiz Yourself 9-2.

QUIZ YOURSELF 9-2

Instructions: Find the true statement below. Then, rewrite the remaining false statements so they are true.

1. A wireless LAN is a LAN that uses physical wires.

2. An intranet is an internal network that uses video conferencing technologies.

3. Four types of digital dial-up lines are ISDN lines, DSL, T-carrier lines, and ATM.

4. In a client/server network, servers on the network access resources on the client.

5. In a networked environment, any unauthorized computer user can access data and information stored on other computers on the network.

6. P2P describes an Internet network on which users access each other's hard disks and exchange files directly over the Internet.

Quiz Yourself Online: To further check your knowledge of networks, network communications standards, communications software, and communications over the telephone network, visit scsite.com/dc2007/ch9/quiz and then click Objectives 4 – 8.

COMMUNICATIONS DEVICES

A **communications device** is any type of hardware capable of transmitting data, instructions, and information between a sending device and a receiving device. At the sending end, a communications device sends the data, instructions, or information from the sending device to a communications channel. At the receiving end, a communications device receives the signals from the communications channel.

One type of communications device that connects a communications channel to a sending or receiving device such as a computer is a modem. Computers process data as digital signals. Data, instructions, and information travel along a communications channel in either analog or digital form, depending on the communications channel. An *analog signal* consists of a continuous electrical wave. A *digital signal* consists of individual electrical pulses that represent bits grouped together into bytes.

For communications channels that use digital signals (such as cable television lines), the modem transfers the digital signals between the computer and the communications channel (Figure 9-26a). If a communications channel uses analog signals (such as some telephone lines), however, the modem first converts between analog and digital signals (Figure 9-26b).

The following pages describe these types of communications devices: dial-up modems, ISDN and DSL modems, cable modems, network cards, wireless access points, routers, and hubs.

FIGURE 9-26a   (all digital communications channel)

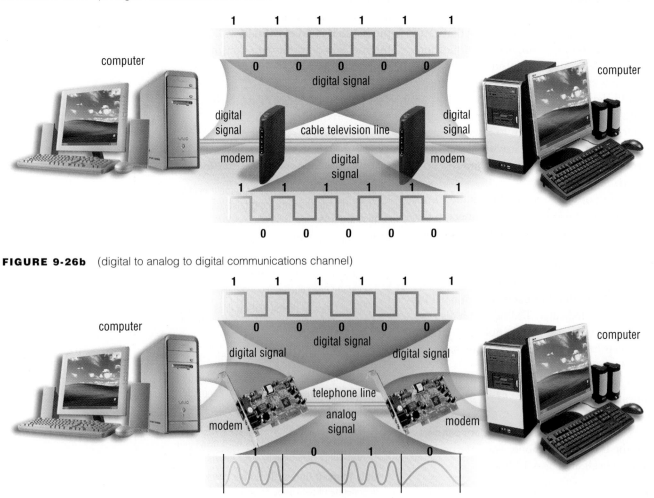

FIGURE 9-26b   (digital to analog to digital communications channel)

FIGURE 9-26   A modem connects a communications channel, such as a cable television line or a telephone line, to a sending or receiving device such as a computer. Depending on the type of communications channel, a modem may need to convert digital signals to analog signals (and vice versa) before transferring data, instructions, and information to or from a sending or receiving device.

Dial-Up Modems

As previously discussed, a computer's digital signals must be converted to analog signals before they are transmitted over standard telephone lines. The communications device that performs this conversion is a **modem**, sometimes called a *dial-up modem*. The word, modem, is derived from the combination of the words, *modulate*, to change into an analog signal, and *demodulate*, to convert an analog signal into a digital signal.

Both the sending and receiving ends of a standard telephone line (communications channel) must have a dial-up modem for data transmission to occur. For example, a dial-up modem connected to a sending computer converts the computer's digital signals into analog signals. The analog signals then can travel over a standard telephone line. At the receiving end, if necessary, another dial-up modem converts the analog signals back into digital signals that a receiving computer can process.

A dial-up modem usually is in the form of an adapter card that you insert in an expansion slot on a computer's motherboard (Figure 9-27). One end of a standard telephone cord attaches to a port on the modem card and the other end plugs into a telephone outlet. Devices other than computers also use modems. A stand-alone fax machine, for example, has a modem that converts a scanned digitized image into an analog signal that is sent to a recipient's fax machine.

If a notebook or other mobile computer does not have built-in modem capabilities, mobile users can insert a PC Card modem in a PC Card slot on the computer. The PC Card modem attaches to a telephone outlet with a standard telephone cord. Mobile users without access to a telephone outlet also can use a special cable to attach the PC Card modem to a cellular telephone, thus enabling them to transmit data over a cellular telephone.

ISDN and DSL Modems

If you access the Internet using ISDN or DSL, you need a communications device to send and receive the digital ISDN or DSL signals. A *digital modem* is a modem that sends and receives data and information to and from a digital telephone line such as ISDN or DSL. An *ISDN modem* sends digital data and information from a computer to an ISDN line and receives digital data and information from an ISDN line. A **DSL modem** sends digital data and information from a computer to a DSL line and receives digital data and information from a DSL line. ISDN and DSL modems usually are external devices, in which one end connects to the telephone line and the other end connects to a port on the system unit.

FAQ 9-4

Are digital modems really modems?

According to the definition of a modem (to convert from analog to digital signals and vice versa), the use of the term modem in this context is not correct. Although the original term for these devices was terminal adapter, the industry refers to ISDN, DSL, and cable modems as digital modems. For more information, visit scsite.com/dc2007/ch9/faq and then click Digital Modems.

Cable Modems

A **cable modem**, sometimes called a *broadband modem*, is a digital modem that sends and receives digital data over the cable television (CATV) network. With more than 100 million homes wired for cable television, cable modems provide a faster Internet access alternative to dial-up for the home user and have speeds similar to DSL. Cable modems currently can transmit data at speeds that are much faster than either a dial-up modem or ISDN (Figure 9-24 on page 482).

FIGURE 9-27 A dial-up modem for a desktop computer usually is in the form of an adapter card you install in the system unit.

As shown in Figure 9-28, CATV service enters your home through a single line. To access the Internet using the CATV service, the CATV company installs a splitter inside your house. From the splitter, one part of the cable runs to your televisions and the other part connects to the cable modem. Many CATV operators provide a cable modem as part of the installation; some offer a rental plan; and others require that you purchase one separately. A cable modem usually is an external (separate) device, in which one end of a cable connects to a CATV wall outlet and the other end plugs in a port, such as on an Ethernet card, in the system unit. An Ethernet card is a type of network card. A later section discusses network cards.

WEB LINK 9-8

Cable Modems

For more information, visit scsite.com/ dc2007/ch9/weblink and then click Cable Modems.

FAQ 9-5

Which is better, DSL or cable Internet service?

Each has its own advantages. DSL uses a line that is not shared with other users in the neighborhood. With cable Internet service, by contrast, users share the node with up to 500 other cable Internet users. Simultaneous access by many users can cause the cable Internet service to slow down. Cable Internet service, however, has widespread availability. For more information, visit scsite.com/dc2007/ch9/faq and then click DSL and Cable Internet Service.

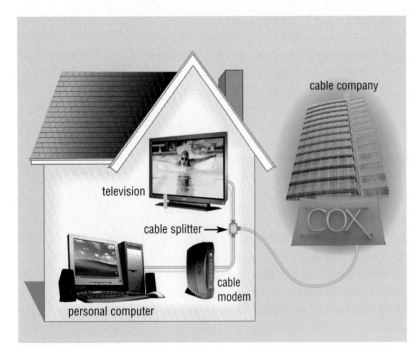

FIGURE 9-28   A typical cable modem installation.

Wireless Modems

Some mobile users have a **wireless modem** that allows access to the Web wirelessly from a notebook computer, a PDA, a smart phone, or other mobile device (Figure 9-29). Wireless modems, which have an external or built-in antenna, typically use the same waves used by cellular telephones. These modems are available as PC Cards and flash cards.

antenna on wireless PC Card modem communicates with wireless Internet service provider

wireless PC Card modem inserted in PC slot on notebook computer

FIGURE 9-29   Wireless modems, in the form of a PC Card or flash card, allow users to access the Internet wirelessly using their mobile computers and devices.

Network Cards

A **network card**, sometimes called a *network interface card* (*NIC* pronounced nick), is an adapter card, PC Card, or flash card that enables the computer or device to access a network. Although some computers and devices have networking capabilities integrated in their circuitry, most personal computers on a LAN contain a network card. The network card coordinates the transmission and receipt of data, instructions, and information to and from the computer or device containing the network card.

Network cards are available in a variety of styles (Figure 9-30). A network card for a desktop computer is an adapter card that has a port to which a cable connects. A network card for mobile computers and devices is in the form of a Type II PC Card or a flash card. Many of these network cards have more than one type of port, which enable different types of cables to attach to the card. For example, some cable modems and DSL modems require that one end of a cable plug in the modem and the other end in a network card. (If your computer does not have a network card, these modems often allow connections to a USB port also.)

Network cards that provide wireless data transmission also are available. This type of card, called a *wireless network card*, often has an antenna. Sometimes the antenna is detachable, allowing the user to position it in a location with the best signal strength. Some network cards include support for both wired and wireless networks.

A network card follows the guidelines of a particular network communications standard, such as Ethernet or token ring. An Ethernet card is the most common type of network card. Depending on the type of wiring used, the transfer rate on an Ethernet network is 10 Mbps, 100 Mbps, or 1,000 Mbps (1 Gbps). Ethernet cards typically support one or more of these speeds. For example, some are called 10/100 because they support both 10 Mbps and 100 Mbps. Some network cards also are a combination Ethernet and dial-up modem card.

FAQ 9-6

Do I need a wireless network card to access a wireless network?

No. Some computers and devices have built-in 802.11 (Wi-Fi) hardware, such as those with Intel's *Centrino technology*. For computers and devices requiring a wireless network card, some users purchase a wireless USB network adapter that connects to a USB port on the computer instead of a network card. Wireless USB network adapters are ideal for users who have no empty expansion slots in their computers or for users not comfortable working inside the system unit. For more information, visit scsite.com/dc2007/ch9/faq and then click Wireless Network Cards and Adapters.

Wireless Access Points

A *wireless access point* is a central communications device that allows computers and devices to transfer data wirelessly among themselves or to transfer data wirelessly to a wired network (Figure 9-31). Wireless access points have high-quality antennas for optimal signals. For the best signal, some manufacturers suggest positioning the wireless access point at the highest possible location.

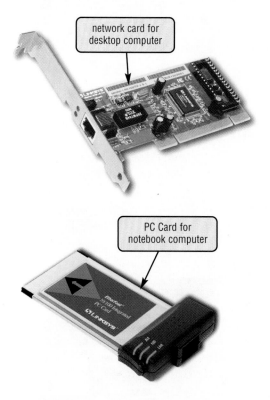

FIGURE 9-30 Network cards are available for both desktop and notebook computers.

FIGURE 9-31 Wireless access points around campus allow students to access the school network wirelessly from their classrooms, the library, dorms, and other campus locations. To access the network, the notebook computer or mobile device must have built-in wireless capability or a wireless network card.

Routers

A *router* is a communications device that connects multiple computers or other routers together and transmits data to its correct destination on the network. A router can be used on any size of network. On the largest scale, routers along the Internet backbone forward data packets to their destination using the fastest available path. For smaller business and home networks, a router allows multiple computers to share a single high-speed Internet connection such as through a cable modem or DSL modem (Figure 9-32). These routers connect from 2 to 250 computers.

To prevent unauthorized users from accessing files and computers, many routers are protected by a built-in firewall, called a *hardware firewall*. Some also have built-in antivirus protection. Routers also support wireless communications, eliminating the need for a separate wireless access point in a wireless network. If the network has a separate wireless access point, it connects to the router via a cable. Some routers also include additional functionality such as including a built-in print server.

Connecting Networks

Today, thousands of computer networks exist, ranging from small networks operated by home users to global networks operated by numerous telecommunications firms. Interconnecting these many types of networks requires various types of communications devices. For example, as shown in Figure 9-33, a *hub* is a device that provides a central point for cables in a network. Some hubs include routers. That is, the hub receives data from many directions and then forwards it to one or more destinations.

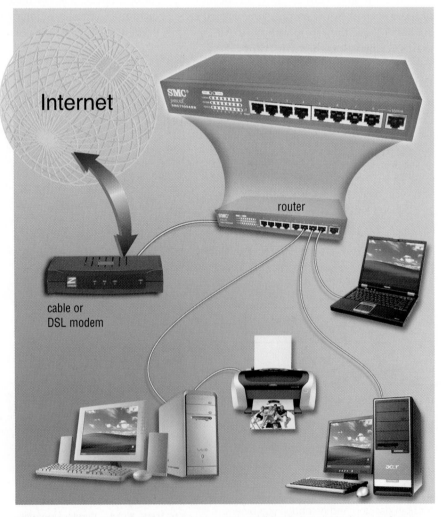

FIGURE 9-32   Through a router, home and small business networks can share access to a high-speed Internet connection such as through a cable or DSL modem.

- Share peripherals such as a printer, scanner, external hard disk, or DVD drive
- Play multiplayer games with players on other computers in the house

Many vendors offer home networking packages that include all the necessary hardware and software to network your home using wired or wireless techniques. Some of these packages also offer intelligent networking capabilities. An *intelligent home network* extends the basic home network to include features such as lighting control, thermostat adjustment, and a security system.

WEB LINK 9-10

Home Networks
For more information, visit scsite.com/dc2007/ch9/weblink and then click Home Networks.

Wired Home Networks

As with other networks, a home network can use wires, be wireless, or use a combination of wired and wireless. Three types of wired home networks are Ethernet, powerline cable, and phoneline.

ETHERNET Some home users have an Ethernet network. As discussed earlier in this chapter, traditional Ethernet networks require that each computer have built-in network capabilities or contain a network card, which connects to a central network hub or similar device with a physical cable. This may involve running cable through walls, ceilings, and floors in the house. For the average home user, the hardware and software of an Ethernet network can be difficult to configure.

POWERLINE CABLE NETWORK A home *powerline cable network* is a network that uses the same lines that bring electricity into the house. This network requires no additional wiring. One end of a cable plugs in the computer's parallel or USB port and the other end of the cable plugs in a wall outlet. The data transmits through the existing power lines in the house.

PHONELINE NETWORK A *phoneline network* is an easy-to-install and inexpensive network that uses existing telephone lines in the home. With this network, one end of a cable connects to an adapter card or PC Card in the computer and the other end plugs in a wall telephone jack. The phoneline network does not interfere with voice and data transmissions on the telephone lines. That is, you can talk on the telephone and use the same line to connect to the Internet. One slight disadvantage is that the room with the computer must have a wall telephone jack.

FIGURE 9-33 A hub is a central point that connects several devices in a network together.

HOME NETWORKS

An estimated 39 million homes have more than one computer. Thus, many home users are connecting multiple computers and devices together in a **home network**. Home networking saves the home user money and provides many conveniences. Each networked computer in the house has the following capabilities:

- Connect to the Internet at the same time
- Share a single high-speed Internet connection
- Access files and programs on the other computers in the house

Wireless Home Networks

To network computers and devices that span multiple rooms or floors in a home, it may be more convenient to use a wireless strategy. One advantage of wireless networks is that you can take a mobile computer outside, for example in the backyard, and connect to the Internet through the home network, as long as you are in the network's range. Two types of wireless home networks are HomeRF and Wi-Fi.

A *HomeRF* (*radio frequency*) *network* uses radio waves, instead of cables, to transmit data. A HomeRF network sends signals through the air over distances up to 150 feet. One end of a cable connects to a special card in the computer and the other end connects to a transmitter/receiver that has an antenna to pick up signals.

A HomeRF network usually can connect up to 10 computers.

Another home network that uses radio waves is a Wi-Fi network, which sends signals over a wider distance than the HomeRF network — up to 1,500 feet in some configurations. A Wi-Fi home network is more expensive than a HomeRF network. Despite the higher costs, increasingly more home users set up Wi-Fi networks in their homes because they are fairly easy to configure. Each computer that accesses the network needs built-in wireless networking capabilities (such as Intel's Centrino technology) or a wireless network card, which communicates either with a wireless access point or a combination router/wireless access point (Figure 9-34). Even in a wireless home network,

FIGURE 9-34   HOW TO SET UP HARDWARE FOR A WI-FI HOME NETWORK

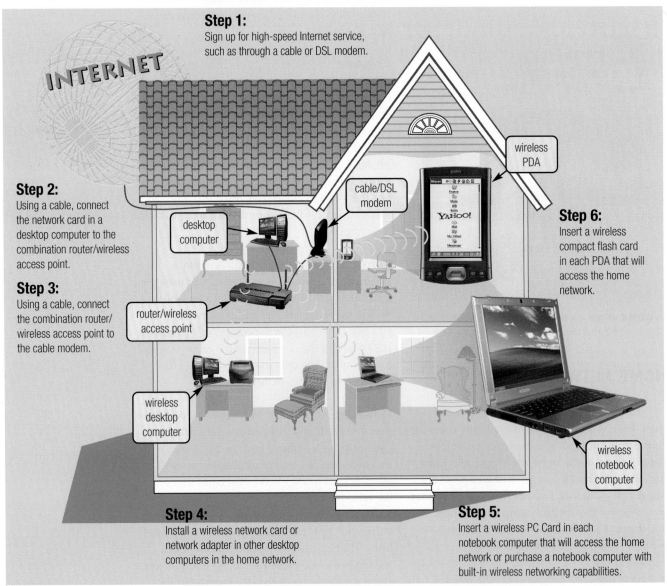

Step 1:
Sign up for high-speed Internet service, such as through a cable or DSL modem.

Step 2:
Using a cable, connect the network card in a desktop computer to the combination router/wireless access point.

Step 3:
Using a cable, connect the combination router/wireless access point to the cable modem.

Step 4:
Install a wireless network card or network adapter in other desktop computers in the home network.

Step 5:
Insert a wireless PC Card in each notebook computer that will access the home network or purchase a notebook computer with built-in wireless networking capabilities.

Step 6:
Insert a wireless compact flash card in each PDA that will access the home network.

INTERNET

cable/DSL modem

desktop computer

router/wireless access point

wireless desktop computer

wireless PDA

wireless notebook computer

one desktop computer usually connects to the router/wireless access point using a cable.

Wireless networks do have the disadvantage of interference. Walls, ceilings, and electrical devices such as cordless telephones and microwave ovens can disrupt wireless communications.

COMMUNICATIONS CHANNEL

As described at the beginning of the chapter, a communications channel is the transmission media on which data, instructions, or information travel in a communications system. The amount of data, instructions, and information that can travel over a communications channel sometimes is called the **bandwidth**. The higher the bandwidth, the more the channel transmits. For example, a cable modem has more bandwidth than a dial-up modem.

For transmission of text only, a lower bandwidth is acceptable. For transmission of music, graphics, photographs, virtual reality images, or 3-D games, however, you need a higher bandwidth. When the bandwidth is too low for the application, you will notice a considerable slow-down in system performance.

Latency is the time it takes a signal to travel from one location to another on a network. Several factors that negatively can affect latency include the distance between the two points, the type of transmission media, and the number of nodes through which the data must travel over the communications channel. For best performance, bandwidth should be high and latency low.

A communications channel consists of one or more transmission media. **Transmission media** consist of materials or substances capable of carrying one or more signals. When you send data from a computer, the signal that carries the data may travel over various transmission media. This is especially true when the transmission spans a long distance.

Figure 9-35 illustrates a typical communications channel and shows the variety of transmission media used to complete the connection. Although many media and devices are involved, the entire communications process could take less than one second.

FIGURE 9-35 AN EXAMPLE OF SENDING A REQUEST OVER THE INTERNET USING A COMMUNICATIONS CHANNEL

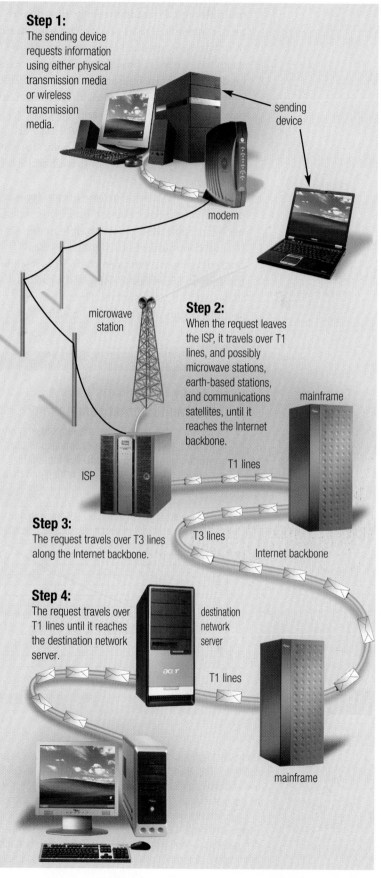

Step 1:
The sending device requests information using either physical transmission media or wireless transmission media.

sending device

modem

microwave station

Step 2:
When the request leaves the ISP, it travels over T1 lines, and possibly microwave stations, earth-based stations, and communications satellites, until it reaches the Internet backbone.

mainframe

ISP

T1 lines

Step 3:
The request travels over T3 lines along the Internet backbone.

T3 lines

Internet backbone

Step 4:
The request travels over T1 lines until it reaches the destination network server.

destination network server

T1 lines

mainframe

Baseband media transmit only one signal at a time. By contrast, **broadband** media transmit multiple signals simultaneously. Broadband media transmit signals at a much faster speed than baseband media. Home and business users today opt for broadband Internet access because of the much faster transfer rates. Two previously discussed services that offer broadband transmission are DSL and the cable television Internet service. Satellites also offer broadband transmission. Read Looking Ahead 9-1 for a look at the future of broadband over power lines (BPL).

Transmission media are one of two types: physical or wireless. *Physical transmission media* use wire, cable, and other tangible materials to send communications signals. *Wireless transmission media* send communications signals through the air or space using radio, microwave, and infrared signals. The following sections discuss these types of media.

PHYSICAL TRANSMISSION MEDIA

Physical transmission media used in communications include twisted-pair cable, coaxial cable, and fiber-optic cable. These cables typically are used within or underground between buildings. Ethernet and token ring LANs often use physical transmission media. The table in Figure 9-36 lists the transfer rates of LANs using various physical transmission media. The following sections discuss each of these types of cables.

TRANSFER RATES FOR VARIOUS TYPES OF LANS USING PHYSICAL TRANSMISSION MEDIA

Type of Cable and LAN	Maximum Transfer Rate
Twisted-Pair Cable	
• 10Base-T (Ethernet)	10 Mbps
• 100Base-T (Fast Ethernet)	100 Mbps
• 1000Base-T (Gigabit Ethernet)	1 Gbps
• Token ring	4 Mbps to 16 Mbps
Coaxial Cable	
• 10Base2 (ThinWire Ethernet)	10 Mbps
• 10Base5 (ThickWire Ethernet)	10 Mbps
Fiber-Optic Cable	
• 10Base-F (Ethernet)	10 Mbps
• 100Base-FX (Fast Ethernet)	100 Mbps
• FDDI (Fiber Distributed Data Interface) token ring	100 Mbps
• Gigabit Ethernet	1 Gbps
• 10-Gigabit Ethernet	10 Gbps

FIGURE 9-36 The speeds of various physical communications media when they are used in LANs.

FAQ 9-8

Do many home users have a broadband Internet connection?

As shown in the chart below, the number of home users with a broadband Internet connection has grown to more than 75 percent. For more information, visit scsite.com/dc2007/ch9/faq and then click Broadband Usage.

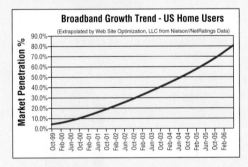

Broadband Growth Trend - US Home Users
(Extrapolated by Web Site Optimization, LLC from Nielson/NetRatings Data)

Market Penetration %

90.0%
80.0%
70.0%
60.0%
50.0%
40.0%
30.0%
20.0%
10.0%
0.0%

Oct-99, Feb-00, Jun-00, Oct-00, Feb-01, Jun-01, Feb-02, Jun-02, Oct-02, Feb-03, Jun-03, Oct-03, Feb-04, Jun-04, Oct-04, Feb-05, Jun-05, Oct-05, Feb-06

LOOKING AHEAD 9-1

Tech Firms Supporting Broadband over Power Lines (BPL)

Every electrical outlet in your house can become a high-speed gateway to the Internet if experimental technology is deployed. This always-on *broadband over power lines* (BPL) connection is predicted to compete with digital subscriber line and cable modem services by increasing coverage, decreasing prices, and bridging the digital divide. It is expected to be popular in rural communities where high-speed Internet currently is unavailable.

Engineers are working to eliminate system problems, especially unstable connections riddled with interference. Intel, Google, Motorola, Cisco, and IBM, as well as cable companies and the Federal Communications Commission are backing companies developing this technology. Data transmission speeds roughly will equal current broadband service. For more information, visit scsite.com/dc2007/ch9/looking and then click BPL.

Twisted-Pair Cable

One of the more widely used transmission media for network cabling and telephone systems is twisted-pair cable. **Twisted-pair cable** consists of one or more twisted-pair wires bundled together (Figure 9-37). Each *twisted-pair wire* consists of two separate insulated copper wires that are twisted together. The wires are twisted together to reduce noise. **Noise** is an electrical disturbance that can degrade communications.

Coaxial Cable

Coaxial cable, often referred to as *coax* (pronounced KO-ax), consists of a single copper wire surrounded by at least three layers: (1) an insulating material, (2) a woven or braided metal, and (3) a plastic outer coating (Figure 9-38).

Cable television (CATV) network wiring often uses coaxial cable because it can be cabled over longer distances than twisted-pair cable. Most of today's computer networks, however, do not use coaxial cable because other transmission media such as fiber-optic cable transmit signals at faster rates.

Fiber-Optic Cable

The core of a **fiber-optic cable** consists of dozens or hundreds of thin strands of glass or plastic that use light to transmit signals. Each strand, called an *optical fiber*, is as thin as a human hair. Inside the fiber-optic cable, an insulating glass cladding and a protective coating surround each optical fiber (Figure 9-39).

Fiber-optic cables have the following advantages over cables that use wire, such as twisted-pair and coaxial cables:

- Capability of carrying significantly more signals than wire cables
- Faster data transmission
- Less susceptible to noise (interference) from other devices such as a copy machine
- Better security for signals during transmission because they are less susceptible to noise
- Smaller size (much thinner and lighter weight)

Disadvantages of fiber-optic cable are it costs more than twisted-pair or coaxial cable and can be difficult to install and modify. Despite these limitations, many local and long-distance telephone companies are replacing existing telephone lines with fiber-optic cables. Businesses also are using fiber-optic cables in high-traffic networks or as the backbone in a network.

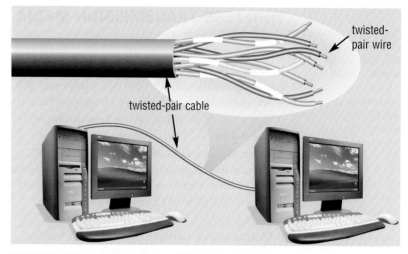

FIGURE 9-37 A twisted-pair cable consists of one or more twisted-pair wires. Each twisted-pair wire usually is color coded for identification. Telephone networks and LANs often use twisted-pair cable.

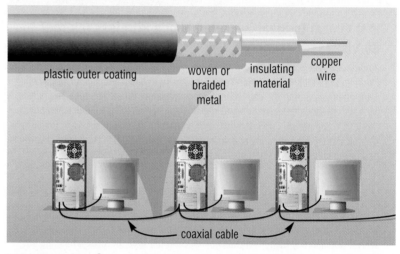

FIGURE 9-38 On a coaxial cable, data travels through a copper wire. This illustration shows computers networked together with coaxial cable.

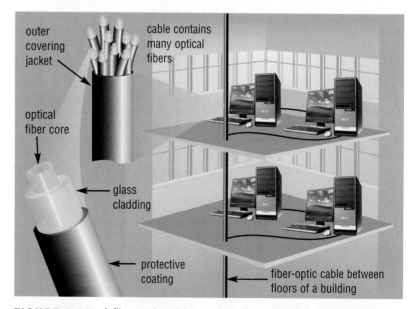

FIGURE 9-39 A fiber-optic cable consists of hair-thin strands of glass or plastic that carry data as pulses of light.

WIRELESS TRANSMISSION MEDIA

Many users opt for wireless transmission media because it is more convenient than installing cables. In addition to convenience, businesses use wireless transmission media in locations where it is impossible to install cables. Read Ethics & Issues 9-4 for a related discussion.

Types of wireless transmission media used in communications include infrared, broadcast radio, cellular radio, microwaves, and communications satellites. The table in Figure 9-40 lists transfer rates of various wireless transmission media. The following sections discuss these types of wireless transmission media.

ETHICS & ISSUES 9-4

Is It Ethical to Steal Your Neighbor's Wireless Internet Service?

If you knew that your neighbor often left her door unlocked while she went to work, you probably never would consider walking in and watching her premium cable channels during the day without her permission. But, if you turn on your wireless notebook computer only to see that you can connect to your neighbor's wireless home network and access the Internet for free, you may find yourself in an ethical quandary. Because of a lack of knowledge about how to secure a wireless home network, many people have accidentally left their networks open to use by the whole neighborhood and by people driving or walking past. One study found that 14 percent of wireless network owners have accessed their neighbor's wireless connection. In some cases, people drive around town until they find a house with an open wireless connection and then park in front of the house for hours at a time while surfing the Internet. Many are canceling their own costly service and secretly using the stolen connection full-time. In most areas, the law is unclear or nonexistent regarding such unauthorized use. Would you borrow your neighbor's wireless home network? Why or why not? What would you do if you found out that someone was using your wireless home network? How should the law handle such abuse, and how should violators be punished?

TRANSFER RATES FOR VARIOUS TYPES OF WIRELESS TRANSMISSION MEDIA

Transmission Medium	Maximum Transfer Rate
Infrared	115 Kbps to 4 Mbps
Broadcast radio	
• Bluetooth	1 Mbps to 2 Mbps
• HomeRF	1.6 Mbps to 10 Mbps
• 802.11b	11 Mbps
• 802.11g	54 Mbps
• 802.11a	54 Mbps
Cellular radio	
• 2G	9.6 Kbps to 19.2 Kbps
• 3G	144 Kbps to 2.4 Mbps
Microwave radio	150 Mbps
Communications satellite	1 Gbps

FIGURE 9-40 The transfer rates of various wireless transmission media.

Infrared

As discussed earlier in the chapter, *infrared* (*IR*) is a wireless transmission medium that sends signals using infrared light waves. Mobile computers and devices, such as a mouse, printer, and smart phone, often have an IrDA port that enables the transfer of data from one device to another using infrared light waves. If your notebook computer has an IrDA port, simply position the port in front of the IrDA port on a printer to print a document wirelessly. Many PDAs also have IrDA ports that allow users to transfer data to another PDA or a network wirelessly.

Broadcast Radio

Broadcast radio is a wireless transmission medium that distributes radio signals through the air over long distances such as between cities, regions, and countries and short distances such as within an office or home.

For radio transmissions, you need a transmitter to send the broadcast radio signal and a receiver to accept it. To receive the broadcast radio signal, the receiver has an antenna that is located in the range of the signal. Some networks use a transceiver, which both sends and receives signals from wireless devices. Broadcast radio is slower and more susceptible to noise than physical transmission media but it provides flexibility and portability.

Bluetooth, HomeRF, Wi-Fi, and WiMAX communications technologies discussed earlier in this chapter use broadcast radio signals. Bluetooth is an alternative to infrared communications, and HomeRF and Wi-Fi are competing technologies for home and small business networks. Hot spots use Wi-Fi and WiMAX networks. In a Wi-Fi business network, employees have access to the network from their notebook computers while roaming from one meeting room to another.

Cellular Radio

Cellular radio is a form of broadcast radio that is used widely for mobile communications, specifically wireless modems and cellular telephones (Figure 9-41). A cellular telephone is a telephone device that uses high-frequency radio waves to transmit voice and digital data messages. Because only a limited number of radio frequencies exist, cellular network providers reuse frequencies so they can accommodate the large number of users.

Some mobile users connect their notebook computer or other mobile computer to a cellular telephone to access the Web, send and receive e-mail, enter a chat room, or connect to an office

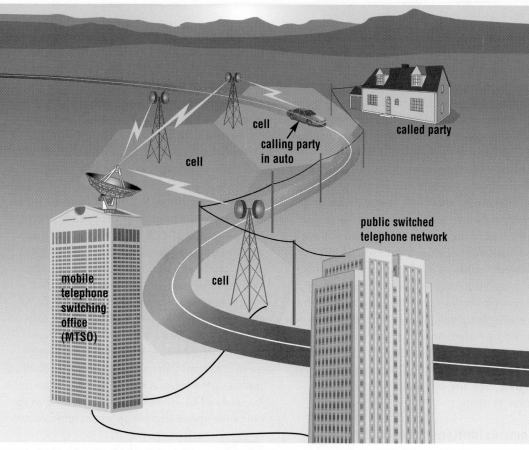

FIGURE 9-41 As a person with a cellular telephone drives from one cell to another, the radio signals transfer from the base station (microwave station) in one cell to a base station in another cell.

WEB LINK 9-11

Cellular Communications

For more information, visit scsite.com/dc2007/ch9/weblink and then click Cellular Communications.

or school network while away from a standard telephone line.

Several categories of cellular transmissions exist, defining the development of cellular networks:

- *1G* (first generation) transmitted analog data
- *2G* (second generation) transmit digital data at speeds from 9.6 Kbps to 19.2 Kbps
- *3G* (third generation) transmit digital data at speeds from 144 Kbps to 2.4 Mbps

Examples of 3G standards include *GSM* (Global System for Mobile Communications), *UMTS* (Universal Mobile Telecommunications System), *GPRS* (General Packet Radio Service), *CDMA* (Code Division Multiple Access), and *EDGE* (Enhanced Data GSM Environment). These 3G standards allow users quickly to display multimedia and graphics, browse the Web, watch television or a video, have a video conference, and transfer data on a cellular device. Providers that offer 3G service include Sprint, Verizon, Cingular, Motorola, Ericsson, and Nokia.

Personal Communications Services (PCS) is the term used by the U. S. Federal Communications Commission (FCC) to identify all wireless digital communications. Devices that use PCS include cellular telephones, PDAs, pagers, and fax machines. These devices have voice mail, call forwarding, fax capability, caller ID, and wireless modems for Internet and e-mail access.

Microwaves

Microwaves are radio waves that provide a high-speed signal transmission. Microwave transmission, often called *fixed wireless*, involves sending signals from one microwave station to another (Figure 9-42). Microwaves can transmit data at rates up to 4,500 times faster than a dial-up modem.

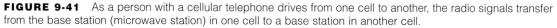

microwave stations

FIGURE 9-42 A microwave station is a ground-based reflective dish that contains the antenna, transceivers, and other equipment necessary for microwave communications.

A *microwave station* is an earth-based reflective dish that contains the antenna, transceivers, and other equipment necessary for microwave communications. As with infrared, microwaves use line-of-sight transmission. To avoid possible obstructions, such as buildings or mountains, microwave stations often sit on the tops of buildings, towers, or mountains.

Microwave transmission typically is used in environments where installing physical transmission media is difficult or impossible and where line-of-sight transmission is available. For example, microwave transmission is used in wide-open areas such as deserts or lakes; between buildings in a close geographic area; or to communicate with a satellite. Current users of microwave transmission include universities, hospitals, city governments, cable television providers, and telephone companies. Homes and small businesses that do not have other high-speed Internet connections available in their area also opt for lower-cost fixed wireless plans.

Communications Satellite

A **communications satellite** is a space station that receives microwave signals from an earth-based station, amplifies (strengthens) the signals, and broadcasts the signals back over a wide area to any number of earth-based stations (Figure 9-43).

These earth-based stations often are microwave stations. Other devices, such as PDAs and GPS receivers, also can function as earth-based stations. Transmission from an earth-based station to a satellite is an *uplink*. Transmission from a satellite to an earth-based station is a *downlink*.

Applications such as air navigation, television and radio broadcasts, weather forecasting, video conferencing, paging, global positioning systems (read Looking Ahead 9-2 for a look at the future of GPS), and Internet connections use communications satellites. With the proper satellite dish and a satellite modem card, consumers can access the Internet using satellite technology. With satellite Internet connections, however, uplink transmissions usually are slower than downlink transmissions. This difference in speeds usually is acceptable to most Internet satellite users because they download much more data than they upload. Although a satellite Internet connection is more expensive than cable Internet or DSL connections, sometimes it is the only high-speed Internet option in remote areas.

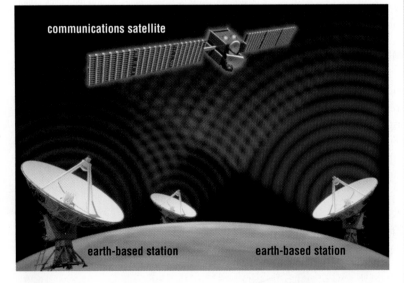

communications satellite

earth-based station   earth-based station

FIGURE 9-43 Communications satellites are placed about 22,300 miles above the Earth's equator.

LOOKING AHEAD 9-2

Europe Develops Satellite Navigation System

The European Union is developing its own satellite navigation system similar to the United States' global positioning system. Called Galileo, the multi-billion-dollar system is expected to be operational by 2008.

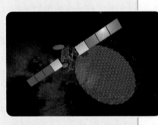

Although the U.S. GPS signals are beamed worldwide at no cost, the European countries desired to build their own system that would provide uninterrupted, independent service and would not rely on the U.S. military. Some of these countries have laws stating that navigational aids must be based within their own territorial borders and controlled by their own governments.

Galileo will be used to help civilians navigate in their vehicles and on foot, track livestock and shipments, and perform search and rescue operations. It will use 30 satellites positioned 15,000 miles above the Earth. For more information, visit scsite.com/dc2007/ch9/looking and then click Galileo.

Test your knowledge of pages 484 through 496 in Quiz Yourself 9-3.

QUIZ YOURSELF 9-3

Instructions: Find the true statement below. Then, rewrite the remaining false statements so they are true.

1. A cable modem converts a computer's digital signals to analog signals before they are transmitted over standard telephone lines.

2. A hardware firewall is a communications device that allows computers and devices to transfer data wirelessly among themselves or to transfer data wirelessly to a wired network.

3. A network card is an adapter card, PC Card, or flash card that enables the computer or device to access a network.

4. Analog signals consist of individual electrical pulses that represent bits grouped together into bytes.

5. Physical transmission media send communications signals through the air or space using radio, microwave, and infrared signals.

6. The lower the bandwidth, the more data, instructions, and information the channel transmits.

7. Two types of wireless home networks are HomeRF and powerline cable.

Quiz Yourself Online: To further check your knowledge of communications devices, home networks, and transmission media, visit scsite.com/dc2007/ch9/quiz and then click Objectives 9 – 11.

CHAPTER SUMMARY

This chapter provided an overview of communications terminology and applications. It also discussed how to join computers into a network, allowing them to communicate and share resources such as hardware, software, data, and information. It also explained various communications devices, media, and procedures as they relate to computers.

CAREER CORNER

Network Specialist

As more companies rely on networks, the demand for network specialists will continue to grow. A *network specialist* must have a working knowledge of local area networks and their application within wide area networks. A network specialist also must be familiar with the Internet, its connectivity to LANs and WANs, and Web server management. Responsibilities of a network specialist include installing, configuring, and troubleshooting network systems. Other responsibilities may include managing system and client software, Web page integration and creation, network security measures, user accounting, and monitoring network event logs for problem resolution. A network specialist must possess good problem-solving skills and the ability to work independently. They also must have the ability to concentrate on detailed projects for long periods of time. Good oral, written, and team-oriented interpersonal skills also are beneficial.

Many institutions offer two-year network specialist programs. In addition to a college degree, industry certifications are available for further career enhancement. Two of the more notable certifications are the Novell CNA (Certified Novell Administrator) and the Cisco CCNA (Certified Cisco Networking Associate). Network specialist salaries will vary depending on education, certifications, and experience. Individuals with certifications can expect an approximate starting salary between $49,500 and $65,000. For more information, visit scsite.com/dc2007/ch9/careers and then click Network Specialist.

High-Tech Talk

OSI REFERENCE MODEL: THE DRIVING FORCE BEHIND NETWORK COMMUNICATIONS

Every message sent over a network — even the simplest e-mail message — must be divided into discrete packages of data and routed via transmission media such as telephone lines. While traveling from the sending computer to the receiving computer, each data package can take a different path over the network. How do these messages get to their destination, intact and accurate?

The *Open Systems Interconnection (OSI) reference model*, a communications standard developed by the International Organization for Standardization (ISO), offers an answer. The OSI reference model describes the flow of data in a network through seven layers, from the user's application to the physical transmission media.

A simple way to understand the OSI reference model is to think of it as an elevator (Figure 9-44). On the sending end, data enters at the top floor (the application layer) and travels to the bottom floor (the physical layer). Each layer communicates with the layers immediately above and below it. When a layer receives data, it performs specific functions, adds control information to the data, and passes it to the next layer. The control information contains error-checking, routing, and other information needed to ensure proper transmission along the network.

The top layer, the *application layer*, serves as the interface between the user and the network. Using application software, such as an e-mail program, a user can type a message and specify a recipient. The application then prepares the message for delivery by converting the message data into bits and attaching a header identifying the sending and receiving computers.

The *presentation layer* translates the converted message data into a language the receiving computer can process (from ASCII to EBCDIC, for example) and also may compress or encrypt the data. Finally, the layer attaches another header specifying the language, compression, and encryption schemes.

The next layer, called the *session layer*, establishes and maintains communications sessions. A *session* is the period between establishment of a connection, transmission of the data, and termination of the connection.

The *transport layer*, also called the end-to-end layer, ensures that data arrives correctly and in proper sequence. The transport layer divides the data into segments and creates a *checksum*, a mathematical sum based on the data, and puts this information in the transport header. The checksum later is used to determine if the data was scrambled during transmission.

The *network layer* routes the message from sender to receiver. This layer splits the data segments from the transport layer into smaller groups of bits called *packets*. Next, it adds a header containing the packet sequence, the receiving computer address, and routing information. The network layer also manages network problems by rerouting packets to avoid network congestion.

The *data link layer* supervises the transmission of the message to the next network node by specifying the network technology (such as Ethernet or token ring) and grouping data accordingly. The data link layer also calculates the checksum and keeps a copy of each packet until it receives confirmation that the packet arrived undamaged at the next node.

Finally, the *physical layer* encodes the packets into a signal recognized by the medium that will carry them — such as an analog signal to be sent over a telephone line — and sends the packets along that medium to the receiving computer.

At the receiving computer, the process is reversed and the data moves back through the seven layers from the physical layer to the application layer, which identifies the recipient, converts the bits into readable data, removes some of the error-checking and control information from the data, and directs it to the appropriate application. The next time you send an e-mail message to a friend, consider the network communications processes described by the OSI reference model, which ensure that your message travels safely over many networks to your friend's computer. For more information, visit scsite.com/dc2007/ch9/tech and then click OSI Reference Model.

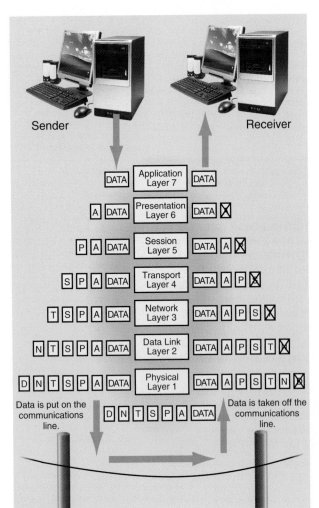

FIGURE 9-44 The seven layers of the OSI model.

Companies on the Cutting Edge

CISCO SYSTEMS
NETWORKING THE INTERNET

As the world leader in networking equipment, *Cisco Systems* strives to empower the Internet generation by connecting people and networks regardless of differences in locations, time, or types of computers. The company offers a broad line of networking equipment for transporting data within a building, across a campus, or across the globe.

A group of computer scientists from Stanford University founded Cisco in 1984. From the start, the company focused on communicating over networks. Today, Cisco's Internet Protocol-based (IP) networking equipment is the basis of the Internet and most networks.

Its key products focus on the areas of home and wireless networking, network security, and communications. The company set a Guinness world record for having the highest capacity Internet router of 92 terabits (92 trillion bits per second). For more information, visit scsite.com/dc2007/ch9/companies and then click Cisco.

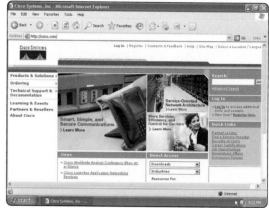

QUALCOMM
WIRELESS COMMUNICATIONS LEADER

When you speak into your cellular telephone, your voice is converted into digital information that is transmitted as a radio signal with a unique code. This wireless communications process is based on Code Division Multiple Access (CDMA), which *QUALCOMM* engineers first conceptualized in 1988.

Commercial CDMA networks were unveiled in 1995, and they provided about 10 times the capacity of analog networks. Today, QUALCOMM is the world's largest provider of 3G technology and has shipped more than 1 million chips to the 125 telecommunications equipment manufacturers using the CDMA standard.

In 2005, QUALCOMM announced powerful improvements to its wireless location services, which will increase accuracy in GPS positioning for E911 calls, child locators, and turn-by-turn navigation systems. For more information, visit scsite.com/dc2007/ch9/companies and then click QUALCOMM.

Technology Trailblazers

ROBERT METCALFE
ETHERNET INVENTOR

The Internet will be filled with video within 20 years, according to *Robert Metcalfe*. His prediction is likely to be correct based on his visionary track record. While studying for his doctorate degree at Harvard and working at Xerox's Palo Alto Research Center (PARC), he combined hardware with a high-speed network interface and envisioned that his invention would be used widely. This network technology developed into Ethernet, today's most popular LAN technology that links millions of computers worldwide.

In 1979, Metcalfe left Xerox to found 3Com Corporation and make Ethernet the standard for computer communications. After he retired from that company, he became a general partner in the venture capital firm, Polaris Ventures. In 2005, he received the National Medal of Technology for his pioneering work at PARC. For more information, visit scsite.com/dc2007/ch9/people and then click Robert Metcalfe.

PATRICIA RUSSO
LUCENT TECHNOLOGIES CHAIRMAN AND CEO

As captain of her high school cheerleading squad, *Patricia Russo* had to project a spirit of optimism, build teamwork, and solve problems. She uses these same skills in her current job as chairman and chief executive officer of Lucent Technologies, which designs and delivers communications hardware, software, and services to communications service providers worldwide.

Russo helped found Lucent in 1996 and oversaw various critical corporate functions, including global sales, strategy and business development, human resources, and public relations. She left Lucent to serve as CEO for Eastman Kodak, but nine months later Lucent asked her to return and appointed her CEO in 2002 and chairman the following year. Forbes.com listed Russo as the thirteenth most powerful woman in the world in its 2005 rankings. For more information, visit scsite.com/dc2007/ch9/people and then click Patricia Russo.

Chapter Review

The Chapter Review section summarizes the concepts presented in this chapter. To listen to the audio version of this Chapter Review, visit scsite.com/dc2007/ch9/review. To obtain help from other students regarding any subject in this chapter, visit scsite.com/dc2007/ch9/forum and post your thoughts or questions.

(1) **What Components Are Required for Successful Communications?** Computer **communications** describes a process in which two or more computers or devices transfer data, instructions, and information. Successful communications requires a **sending device** that initiates a transmission instruction, a communications device that connects the sending device to a communications channel, a **communications channel** on which the data travels, a communications device that connects the communications channel to a receiving device, and a **receiving device** that accepts the transmission.

(2) **What Are Various Sending and Receiving Devices?** All types of computers and mobile devices serve as sending and receiving devices. This includes mainframe computers, servers, desktop computers, notebook computers, Tablet PCs, smart phones, PDAs, and GPS receivers.

(3) **How Are Computer Communications Used?** Communications technologies include the Internet, Web, e-mail, instant messaging, chat rooms, newsgroups, Internet telephony, FTP, Web folders, video conferencing, and fax machine or computer fax/modem. Users can send and receive wireless messages to and from smart phones, cellular telephones, or PDAs using **text messaging**, wireless instant messaging, and **picture messaging**. A *3G network* uses cellular radio technology to provide users with high-speed wireless Internet connections. A **wireless Internet access point** lets people connect wirelessly to the Internet. A *hot spot* is a wireless network that provides Internet connections to mobile computers and devices. A **cybercafé** is a coffeehouse or restaurant that provides computers with Internet access. A **global positioning system** (**GPS**) analyzes signals sent by satellites to determine an earth-based receiver's geographic location. Many software products provide a means to **collaborate**, or work online with other users. A *document management system* provides for storage and management of a company's documents, such as word processing documents, presentations, and spreadsheets. **Groupware** is software that helps people share information over a network. **Voice mail** allows someone to leave a voice message for one or more people.

 Visit scsite.com/dc2007/ch9/quiz or click the Quiz Yourself button. Click Objectives 1 – 3.

(4) **What Are Advantages of Using a Network?** A **network** is a collection of computers and devices connected together via communications devices and transmission media. Advantages of using a network include facilitating communications, sharing hardware, sharing data and information, sharing software, and transferring funds.

(5) **How Are Client/Server, Peer-to-Peer, and P2P Networks Different?** On a **client/server network**, one or more computers acts as a **server**, which controls access to network resources and provides a centralized storage area, while the other computers on the network are **clients** that rely on the server for resources. A *peer-to-peer network* is a simple network that typically connects fewer than 10 computers, each called a *peer*, that have equal responsibilities and capabilities. *P2P* is an Internet peer-to-peer network on which users connect directly to each other's hard disks and exchange files over the Internet.

(6) **What Are Various Network Communications Standards?** A *network standard* defines guidelines that specify the way computers access a medium, the type(s) of medium, the speeds on different types of networks, and the type of physical cable or wireless technology used. Network communications standards include Ethernet, token ring, TCP/IP, 802.11 (Wi-Fi), Bluetooth, IrDA, RFID, WiMAX, and WAP. **Ethernet** allows nodes to contend for access to the network. **Token ring** requires devices to share or pass a special signal, called a *token*. **TCP/IP** divides data up into

Chapter Review

packets. **802.11** is a series of standards for wireless devices. **Bluetooth** uses short-range radio waves to transmit data. **IrDA** transmits data wirelessly via infrared light waves. **RFID** uses radio signals for communications. **WiMAX** is a newer network standard developed by IEEE that specifies how wireless devices communicate over the air in a wide area. The **Wireless Application Protocol (WAP)** allows wireless mobile devices to access the Internet.

(7) What Is the Purpose of Communications Software? **Communications software** helps users establish a connection to another computer or network, manages the transmission of data, and provides an interface for users to communicate with one another.

(8) What Are Various Types of Lines for Communications Over the Telephone Network? The telephone network uses dial-up lines or dedicated lines. A **dial-up line** is a temporary connection that uses one or more analog telephone lines for communications. A **dedicated line** is an always-on connection established between two communications devices. Dedicated lines include ISDN lines, DSL, T-carrier lines, and ATM. *ISDN* is a set of standards for digital transmission over standard copper telephone lines. **DSL** transmits at fast speeds on existing standard copper telephone wiring. A **T-carrier line** is a long-distance digital telephone line that carries multiple signals over a single communications line. **ATM** (*Asynchronous Transfer Mode*) is a service that carries voice, data, video, and multimedia at extremely high speeds.

connect Visit scsite.com/dc2007/ch9/quiz or click the Quiz Yourself button. Click Objectives 4 – 8.

(9) What Are Commonly Used Communications Devices? A **communications device** is hardware capable of transmitting data between a sending device and a receiving device. A **modem** converts a computer's digital signals to analog signals for transmission over standard telephone lines. An *ISDN modem* transmits digital data to and from an ISDN line, while a **DSL modem** transmits digital data to and from a DSL line. A **cable modem** is a digital modem that sends and receives digital data over the cable television network. A **wireless modem** allows wireless access to the Web. A **network card** is an adapter card, PC Card, or flash card that enables a computer or device to access a network. A *wireless access point* allows computers and devices to transfer data wirelessly. A *router* connects multiple computers together and transmits data to its destination on the network. A *hub* provides a central point for cables in a network.

(10) How Can a Home Network Be Set Up? A **home network** connects multiple computers and devices in a home. An Ethernet network connects each computer to a hub with a physical cable. A home *powerline cable network* uses the same lines that bring electricity into the house. A *phoneline network* uses existing telephone lines in a home. A *HomeRF (radio frequency) network* and **Wi-Fi** network use radio waves, instead of cable, to transmit data.

(11) What Are Various Physical and Wireless Transmission Media? **Transmission media** consist of materials or substances capable of carrying one or more signals. *Physical transmission media* use tangible materials to send communications signals. **Twisted-pair cable** consists of one or more twisted-pair wires bundled together. **Coaxial cable** consists of a single copper wire surrounded by at least three layers: an insulating material, a woven or braided metal, and a plastic outer coating. **Fiber-optic cable** consists of thin strands of glass or plastic that use light to transmit signals. *Wireless transmission media* send communications signals through the air or space. *Infrared (IR)* sends signals using infrared light waves. **Broadcast radio** distributes radio signals through the air over long and short distances. **Cellular radio** is a form of broadcast radio that is used widely for mobile communications. **Microwaves** are radio waves that provide a high-speed signal transmission. A **communications satellite** is a space station that receives microwave signals from an earth-based station, amplifies the signals, and broadcasts the signals back over a wide area.

connect Visit scsite.com/dc2007/ch9/quiz or click the Quiz Yourself button. Click Objectives 9 – 11.

Quizzes and Learning Games

Computer Genius
Crossword Puzzle
DC Track and Field
Practice Test
Quiz Yourself
Wheel of Terms
You're Hired!

Exercises

Case Studies
Chapter Review
Checkpoint
▸ Key Terms
Learn How To
Learn It Online
Web Research

Beyond the Book

Career Corner
Companies
FAQs
High-Tech Talk
Looking Ahead
Making Use of the Web
Trailblazers
Web Links

Features

Chapter Forum
Install Computer
Lab Exercises
Maintain Computer
Tech News
Timeline 2007

Key Terms

You should know the Primary Terms and be familiar with the Secondary Terms. Use the list below to help focus your study. To further enhance your understanding of the Key Terms in this chapter, visit scsite.com/dc2007/ch9/terms. See an example of and a definition for each term, and access current and additional information about the term from the Web.

Primary Terms

(shown in bold-black characters in the chapter)

802.11 (478)
802.16 (479)
ATM (483)
bandwidth (491)
Bluetooth (478)
broadband (492)
broadcast radio (494)
cable modem (485)
cellular radio (494)
client/server network (472)
clients (472)
coaxial cable (493)
collaborate (467)
communications (460)
communications channel (460)
communications device (484)
communications satellite (496)
communications software (480)
cybercafé (465)
dedicated line (482)
dial-up line (481)
DSL (482)
DSL modem (485)
Ethernet (476)
fiber-optic cable (493)
global positioning system (GPS) (466)
groupware (468)
home network (489)
IrDA (478)
latency (491)

local area network (LAN) (471)
microwaves (495)
modem (485)
network (469)
network card (486)
network topology (474)
noise (493)
picture messaging (464)
receiving device (461)
RFID (479)
sending device (460)
server (472)
SMS (463)
text messaging (463)
T-carrier line (483)
TCP/IP (477)
token ring (476)
transmission media (491)
twisted-pair cable (493)
voice mail (468)
wide area network (WAN) (472)
WiMAX (479)
Wi-Fi (478)
Wireless Application Protocol (WAP) (480)
wireless Internet access point (464)
wireless LAN (WLAN) (471)
wireless modem (486)

Secondary Terms

(shown in italic characters in the chapter)

3G network (464)
802.11g (478)
802.11i (478)
802.11n (478)
10-Gigabit Ethernet (476)
1G (495)
2G (495)
3G (495)
ADSL (asymmetric digital subscriber line) (482)
analog signal (484)
Asynchronous Transfer Mode (483)
baseband (492)
broadband modem (485)
bus (474)
bus network (474)
CDMA (495)
coax (493)
database server (473)
dedicated servers (473)
demodulate (485)
dial-up modem (485)
digital modem (485)
digital signal (484)
Digital Subscriber Line (482)
document management system (468)
downlink (496)
downstream rate (482)
EDGE (495)
EDI (electronic data interchange) (470)
electronic funds transfer (EFT) (470)
extranet (475)
Fast Ethernet (476)
file server (473)
file sharing network (473)
fixed wireless (495)
fractional T1 (483)
Gigabit Ethernet (476)
GPRS (495)
GPS receiver (466)
GSM (495)
hardware firewall (488)
HomeRF (radio frequency) network (490)
host computer (472)
hot spot (464)
hub (connecting networks) (488)
hub (star network) (475)
infrared (IR) (494)
intelligent home network (489)
intranet (475)
ISDN (Integrated Services Digital Network) (482)
ISDN modem (485)
line-of-sight transmission (478)

metropolitan area network (MAN) (472)
microwave station (496)
MIMO (478)
MMS (multimedia message service) (464)
modulate (485)
multiplexing (482)
network architecture (472)
network interface card (NIC) (486)
network license (470)
network server (473)
network standard (476)
node (471)
online meeting (467)
optical fiber (493)
P2P (473)
packet switching (477)
packets (477)
peer (473)
peer-to-peer network (473)
Personal Communications Services (PCS) (495)
phoneline network (489)
physical transmission media (492)
powerline cable network (489)
print server (473)
protocol (476)
public switched telephone network (PSTN) (481)
radio frequency identification (479)
ring network (474)
router (488)
short message service (463)
site license (470)
star network (475)
T1 line (483)
T3 line (483)
token (476)
Transmission Control Protocol/Internet Protocol (477)
twisted-pair wire (493)
UMTS (495)
uplink (496)
upstream rate (482)
value-added network (VAN) (470)
video messaging (464)
voice mailbox (468)
Web services (468)
Wi-Fi mesh network (478)
wireless access point (487)
wireless Ethernet standard (478)
wireless fidelity (478)
wireless network card (487)
wireless transmission media (492)
workgroup computing (468)
XML (468)

Checkpoint

Use the Checkpoint exercises to check your knowledge level of the chapter. The Beyond the Book exercises will help broaden your understanding of the concepts presented in this chapter. To complete the Checkpoint exercises interactively, visit scsite.com/dc2007/ch9/check.

Label the Figure

Identify the elements in this sample communications system.

a. Internet-enabled PDAs

b. GPS receivers

c. smart phones

d. desktop computers

e. Tablet PCs

f. notebook computers

g. mainframe computers

h. servers

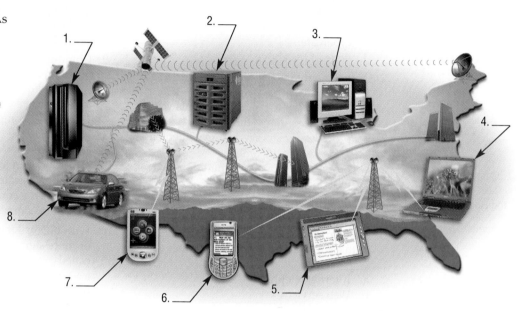

True/False

Mark T for True and F for False. (See page numbers in parentheses.)

_____ 1. A communications channel is the media on which data, instructions, or information travel. (460)

_____ 2. A 3G network uses infrared technology to provide users with high-speed wireless Internet connections. (464)

_____ 3. The first and most used application of GPS technology is to locate a lost person or stolen object. (466)

_____ 4. A network is a collection of computers and devices connected together via communications devices and transmission media. (469)

_____ 5. A local area network (LAN) is a network that covers a large geographic area using a communications channel that combines many types of media such as telephone lines, cables, and radio waves. (472)

_____ 6. An intranet is an internal network that uses Internet technologies. (475)

_____ 7. A packet is a special series of bits that function like a ticket. (476)

_____ 8. Bluetooth does not require line-of-sight transmission. (478)

_____ 9. A cable modem is a digital modem that sends and receives digital data over the cable television network. (485)

_____ 10. Latency is the time it takes a signal to travel from one location to another on a network. (491)

_____ 11. Broadcast radio is media that sends signals using infrared light waves. (494)

Checkpoint

Multiple Choice   Select the best answer. (See page numbers in parentheses.)

1. A _____ is a coffeehouse or restaurant that provides personal computers with Internet access to its customers. (465)
   a. hot spot
   b. wireless Internet access point
   c. cybercafé
   d. none of the above

2. A document management system _____. (468)
   a. allows users to share documents with other users in real time
   b. provides for storage and management of a company's documents
   c. provides personal information manager functions
   d. prints to a Web address associated with a particular printer

3. Different applications can communicate with each other by sending XML files to the _____. (468)
   a. Internet telephony
   b. Web services
   c. instant messenger
   d. global positioning system

4. Many businesses network their computers together to _____. (469)
   a. facilitate communications
   b. share hardware, software, data, and information
   c. transfer funds
   d. all of the above

5. A(n) _____ is a legal agreement that allows multiple users to access the software on a server simultaneously. (470)
   a. site license
   b. EDI
   c. value-added network
   d. network license

6. Today, _____ is the most popular network standard for LANs because it is relatively inexpensive and easy to install and maintain. (476)
   a. token ring   b. Ethernet
   c. TCP/IP   d. Bluetooth

7. When a computer uses TCP/IP to send data over the Internet, the data is divided into small pieces, or _____. (477)
   a. tokens   b. packets
   c. hubs   d. nodes

8. _____ is a newer network standard developed by IEEE that specifies how wireless devices communicate over the air in a wide area. (479)
   a. Wi-Fi   b. WiMAX
   c. 802.16   d. Both b and c

9. Communications software consists of programs that do all of the following except _____. (480)
   a. help users establish a connection to another computer or network
   b. manage the transmission of data, instructions, and information
   c. provide an interface for users to communicate with one another
   d. convert a computer's analog signals into digital signals for transmission

10. With ISDN, a telephone line can carry three or more signals at once using a technique called _____. (482)
    a. packet switching
    b. multiplexing
    c. file sharing
    d. collaborating

11. The most popular T-carrier line is the _____. (483)
    a. T3 line   b. ATM
    c. T1 line   d. DSL

12. A(n) _____ allows access to the Web wirelessly from a notebook computer, a PDA, a smart phone, or other mobile device. (486)
    a. wireless modem
    b. ISDN modem
    c. network card
    d. DSL modem

13. Two types of wireless home networks are _____. (490)
    a. Ethernet and powerline
    b. phoneline and HomeRF
    c. Ethernet and Wi-Fi
    d. HomeRF and Wi-Fi

14. _____ consists of a single copper wire surrounded by at least three layers. (493)
    a. Fiber-optic cable
    b. Coaxial cable
    c. Twisted-pair cable
    d. Infrared

Checkpoint

Matching

Match the terms with their definitions. (See page numbers in parentheses.)

_____ 1. wireless instant messaging (463)

_____ 2. picture messaging (464)

_____ 3. groupware (468)

_____ 4. Web services (468)

_____ 5. intranet (475)

_____ 6. extranet (475)

_____ 7. network standard (476)

_____ 8. ATM (483)

_____ 9. bandwidth (491)

_____ 10. latency (491)

a. online area in which users have written discussions about a subject

b. standardized software that enables programmers to create applications that communicate over the Internet or an internal network

c. guidelines that specify the way computers access a medium, type of medium, speed, and physical technology used

d. allows customers or suppliers to access part of a company's intranet

e. allows users to send graphics, pictures, video clips, and sound files, as well as short text messages to another smart phone, PDA, or computer

f. amount of data, instructions, and information that can travel over a communications channel

g. software that helps groups of people share information over a network

h. time it takes a signal to travel from one network location to another

i. service that carries voice, data, video, and multimedia at very high speeds

j. type of media that transmits only one signal at a time

k. real-time Internet communications service that allows wireless mobile devices to exchange messages with one or more mobile devices or online users

l. internal network that uses Internet technologies

Short Answer

Write a brief answer to each of the following questions.

1. What is a wireless Internet access point? _____ What is a hot spot? _____

2. How are a local area network (LAN), a metropolitan area network (MAN), and a wide area network (WAN) different? _____ What is a wireless LAN? _____

3. What is a peer-to-peer network? _____ What is a P2P network? _____

4. What is a network topology? _____ How are a bus network, a ring network, and a star network different? _____

5. What are the various 802.11 standards? _____ How do the standards differ? _____

Beyond the Book

Read the following book elements, learn more about each using the Web, and then write a brief report.

1. Ethics & Issues — Should Cell Phones Be Banned in Public Places? (462), High-Tech Cheating via Wireless Messaging Services (464), Should Libraries Be Required to Hand Over Web Browser Logs to the Government? (480), and Is It Ethical to Steal Your Neighbor's Wireless Internet Service? (494)

2. Career Corner — Network Specialist (497)

3. Companies on the Cutting Edge — Cisco Systems or QUALCOMM (499)

4. FAQs (477, 478, 485, 486, 487, 488, 492)

5. High-Tech Talk — OSI Reference Model: The Driving Force Behind Network Communications (498)

6. Looking Ahead — Tech Firms Supporting Broadband over Power Lines (BPL) (492) and Europe Develops Satellite Navigation System (496)

7. Making Use of the Web — Learning (125)

8. Picture Yourself Communicating Wirelessly (458)

9. Technology Trailblazers — Robert Metcalfe or Patricia Russo (499)

10. Web Links (465, 466, 471, 474, 476, 479, 483, 486, 488, 489, 495)

Learn It Online

Use the Learn It Online exercises to reinforce your understanding of the chapter concepts. To access the Learn It Online exercises, visit scsite.com/dc2007/ch9/learn.

① At the Movies — Bluetooth in Action

To view the Bluetooth in Action movie, click the number 1 button. Locate your video and click the corresponding High-Speed or Dial-Up link, depending on your Internet connection. Watch the movie and then complete the exercise by answering the questions that follow. When Bluetooth works, it can be a great way to optimize your personal area network (PAN). How can Bluetooth change your personal area network (PAN) into a wireless network? What are the dangers of using Bluetooth without proper security?

② At the Movies — Tracking Kids with GPS

To view the Tracking Kids With GPS movie, click the number 2 button. Locate your video and click the corresponding High-Speed or Dial-Up link, depending on your Internet connection. Watch the movie and then complete the exercise by answering the questions that follow. Inventors using a new miniaturization process have merged cellular and GPS tracking technology into a valuable instrument for parents who want an extra measure of security in protecting their children. Disguised as a simple wrist-watch, this device is able to provide parents with a way to track children who may become lost in a crowd or become a victim of kidnapping. By placing the

watch on their child and signing up for a tracking service, parents can locate lost or stolen children in a short period of time. What are the pros and cons of using technologies such as Digital Angel to track children? Under what situations might the watch become a danger to the child?

③ Student Edition Labs — Networking Basics

Click the number 3 button. A new browser window will open, displaying the Student Edition Labs. Follow the on-screen instructions to complete the Networking Basics Lab. When finished, click the Exit button. If required, submit your results to your instructor.

④ Student Edition Labs — Wireless Networking

Click the number 4 button. A new browser window will open, displaying the Student Edition Labs. Follow the on-screen instructions to complete the Wireless Networking Lab. When finished, click the Exit button. If required, submit your results to your instructor.

⑤ Practice Test

Click the number 5 button. Answer each question. When completed, enter your name and click the Grade Test button to submit the quiz for grading. Make a note of any missed questions. If required, submit your results to your instructor.

⑥ Who Wants To Be a Computer Genius²?

Click the number 6 button to find out if you are a computer genius. Directions about how to play the game will be displayed. When you are ready to play, click the Play button. Submit your score to your instructor.

Learn It Online

(7) Wheel of Terms

Click the number 7 button to reinforce important terms you learned in this chapter by playing the Shelly Cashman Series version of this popular game. Directions about how to play the game will be displayed. When you are ready to play, click the Play button. Submit your score to your instructor.

(8) DC Track and Field

Click the number 8 button to use what you have learned in this chapter to compete against other students in three track and field events. Directions about how to play the game will be displayed. When you are ready to play, click the start first event button. If required, submit your score to your instructor.

(9) You're Hired!

Click the number 9 button to use what you have learned in this chapter to embark on the path to a career in computers. Directions about how to play the game will be displayed. When you are ready to play, click the begin game button. If required, submit your score to your instructor.

(10) Crossword Puzzle Challenge

Click the number 10 button. Complete the puzzle to reinforce skills you learned in this chapter. Directions about how to play the game will be displayed. When you are ready to play, click the Submit button. Submit the completed puzzle to your instructor.

(11) Lab Exercises

Click the number 11 button. When the Lab Exercises menu appears, click the exercise assigned by your instructor. A new browser window will open. Follow the on-screen instructions to complete the exercise. When finished, click the Exit button. If required, submit your results to your instructor.

(12) In the News

Theoretically, business travelers can access e-mail, fax documents, and transmit data from anywhere in the world. In practice, however, incompatible telephone standards and mismatched telephone jacks can frustrate even experienced globetrotters. The 3Com Megahertz LAN PC Card addresses this problem. The modem and accompanying software allow travelers to use computer communications with more than 250 telephone systems worldwide simply by selecting the appropriate country from a menu and attaching a suitable adapter plug. Click the number 12 button and read a news article about a product that is changing computer communications. What is the product? What does it do? Who is likely to use this product?

(13) Chapter Discussion Forum

Select an objective from this chapter on page 459 about which you would like more information. Click the number 13 button and post a short message listing a meaningful message title accompanied by one or more questions concerning the selected objective. In two days, return to the threaded discussion by clicking the number 13 button. Submit to your instructor your original message and at least one response to your message.

(14) Online Radio

Click the number 14 button to learn how to use the Internet to find and listen to various radio stations. Follow the instructions to use Windows Media Player to find and listen to a radio station of your choice. Once you have selected a genre, use the Zip Code search text box to display a list of Internet radio stations within your area. Listen to at least three different radio stations. Write a report comparing the quality of sound of each station. Include in your report any difficulties you may have encountered as well as any features you found interesting. Print your report, and submit it to your instructor.

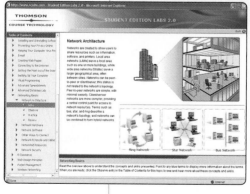

Learn How To

Use the Learn How To activities to learn fundamental skills when using a computer and accompanying technology. Complete the exercises and submit them to your instructor. To see a video of a Learn How To activity, visit scsite.com/dc2007/ch9/howto.

LEARN HOW TO 1: Set Up and Install a Wi-Fi Home Network

In this chapter you learned about home networks and their advantages (see page 489, Home Networks). Creating a Wi-Fi home network consists of four phases: 1) subscribe to a high-speed Internet connection; 2) purchase the Wi-Fi equipment; 3) connect the physical devices; and 4) create the network through the use of software.

SUBSCRIBE TO A HIGH-SPEED INTERNET CONNECTION A high-speed Internet connection is advisable to connect all computers on the home network to the Internet. The three primary ways for home users to obtain a fast connection to the Internet are DSL, cable, and satellite. DSL is provided by telephone companies, cable is provided by cable TV companies, and satellite connections are provided by satellite TV providers. Each has its advantages and disadvantages, including the minimum and maximum speed of Internet access, cost, and availability.

Determining the optimal high-speed Internet connection depends largely on where the network will be located, local costs, and service availability. The way to obtain the best high-speed Internet connection is to research the options available in your area.

Exercise

1. Assume you live near Coeur d'Alene, Idaho. You have decided that high-speed Internet access and a Wi-Fi network would be advantageous for your at-home business. Find answers to the following questions for this Idaho town or a town specified by your instructor: What methods of high-speed Internet access are available? Which provides the best service? Which is the cheapest? Based on the information you gather, write a plan for subscribing to a high-speed Internet connection service. Submit the answers to the questions and your plan to your instructor.

PURCHASE THE WI-FI EQUIPMENT As part of the service when you subscribe to fast access on the Internet, you receive a modem that is capable of connecting to the Internet. In most cases, the modem is not a wireless transmitter. So, in order to establish a wireless connection between the Internet and the home network, you will need a wireless router that establishes the wireless access point.

You can visit any retail electronics store and find a wide variety of wireless routers. A key to purchasing the correct router is to ensure it will work with your modem and Internet access service. Some Internet service providers support only certain brands of routers and, while it is true that other routers may work, you might be taking a risk if you purchase an unsupported router. With the popularity of wireless home networks, though, some Internet service providers now provide a wireless router as part of the subscription service, often for an additional fee. You should investigate closely the needs for the Wi-Fi router to ensure compatibility with your Internet access service.

In addition to the router, each computer that is to be part of the Wi-Fi network needs a wireless network adapter. This device allows the computers to communicate with one another. Most external wireless network adapters plug in either a PC Card slot or a USB connection. Many notebook computers have a built-in wireless network adapter.

Finally, in the better designed home networks, one computer is designated the Internet Connection Sharing (ICS) host. This is the computer that is connected directly to the wireless router, then to the modem and the Internet. Most of the time, this computer, which normally is a desktop and the most powerful computer in the network, is connected using an Ethernet network adapter and cable.

Once the Wi-Fi equipment is assembled, you are ready to connect your home network.

Learn How To

Exercise

1. Using your Web research skills, determine the type of IEEE 802.11 standard used by modems available from Internet service providers. What percentage use 802.11b? What percentage use 802.11g? If your modem uses 802.11b but your wireless network router is 802.11g, what happens? Based on your research, which router do you recommend? Submit your answers to your instructor.

CONNECT THE PHYSICAL DEVICES   Once you have assembled your equipment, you can connect the devices in the network. Usually, the modem will be connected to the source of the Internet transmission (DSL, cable, or satellite). Then the modem is connected to the wireless router, which in turn is connected to the Internet Connection Sharing computer.

After these connections are completed, each of the computers that will be used in the network that do not have a built-in wireless network adapter must have the adapter attached, often by using a USB connection. Once these connections are made, the network can be created.

CREATE THE NETWORK   To establish a network, operating system software must be configured based on the design of your network. To begin the process on a Windows XP computer with Service Pack 2, you should run the Wireless Network Setup Wizard by completing the following steps:

1. Click the Start button on the Windows taskbar and then click Control Panel on the Start menu.
2. In Category view, click Network and Internet Connections.
3. In the Network and Internet Connections window, click Set up a wireless network for home or small office. *The first Wireless Network Setup Wizard dialog box is displayed.*
4. Click the Next button. If the next Wireless Network Setup Wizard dialog box asks "What do you want to do?," click Set up a new wireless network and then click the Next button.
5. In the Network name (SSID) text box, type a name for the wireless network you are creating. Use a name that you will recognize as the name for the network. Make sure the Automatically assign a network key option button is selected. If your devices are so equipped, click the Use WPA encryption instead of WEP check box. This will give your network stronger security. Then, click the Next button.
6. In the next Wireless Network Setup Wizard dialog box (Figure 9-45), click Use a USB flash drive if you have a USB drive to use; otherwise, click Set up a network manually (these steps assume you have a USB drive). Click the Next button.
7. Insert your flash drive in a USB port and wait for the drive letter to appear. Click the Next button.
8. Follow the steps specified in the wizard to configure each computer in the network and then click the Next button.
9. The network has been created. Click the Finish button to close the wizard.

Next, you must run the Network Setup Wizard to configure the network by completing the following steps:

1. Open the Network and Internet Connections window in Control Panel. Click Set up or change your home or small office network. *The Network Setup Wizard is displayed (Figure 9-46).*
2. Follow the instructions in the wizard.

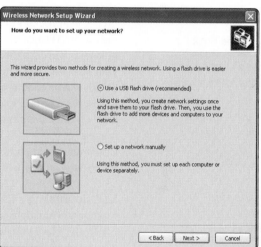

FIGURE 9-45

FIGURE 9-46

Exercise

1. Form a three-person team whose responsibility is to create a Wi-Fi network for a small business in your local area. Assign tasks to each member of the team. Write a detailed plan for creating the Wi-Fi network, including the brand and type of equipment to be purchased, costs, and a schedule for completing the work. Submit the plan to your instructor.

Web Research

Use the Internet-based Web Research exercises to broaden your understanding of the concepts presented in this chapter. Visit scsite.com/dc2007/ch9/research to obtain more information pertaining to each exercise. To discuss any of the Web Research exercises in this chapter with other students, post your thoughts or questions at scsite.com/dc2007/ch9/forum.

① Scavenger Hunt Use one of the <u>search engines</u> listed in Figure 2-10 in Chapter 2 on page 78 or your own favorite search engine to find the answers to the questions that follow. Copy and paste the Web address from the Web page where you found the answer. Some questions may have more than one answer. If required, submit your answers to your instructor. (1) How is Boeing using RFID in its aircraft? (2) What is geocaching? (3) What is the most common bridge used to connect two dissimilar networks? (4) What company developed the token ring protocol? What is the data transfer rate for token ring technology? (5) What is the purpose of the Bluetooth Special Interest Group? Where is the headquarters of this organization? (6) How many cybercafés are located in London, England? In Uganda?

② Search Sleuth <u>Subject directories</u> are used to find specialized topics, such as information about automobiles, travel, and real estate. Most subject directories are arranged by topic and then displayed in a series of menus. Yahoo! is one of the more popular directories. Visit this Web site and then use your word processing program to answer the following questions. Then, if required, submit your answers to your instructor. (1) Click the Shopping link in the Y! Services area at the top of the page, click the Computers link, and then click the Printers link. What are the top three printers displayed and their prices? (2) Click your browser's Back button or press the BACKSPACE key to return to the Yahoo! home page. Click the Search text box and type "digital camera" and "7.1 megapixels" in the box. Sort the cameras by lowest price by clicking the Lowest Price link near the top of the page. Which camera is the least expensive? (3) Click your browser's Back button or press the BACKSPACE key several times to return to the Yahoo! home page. Click the Computers link in the Yahoo! Web Directory at the bottom of the page. Click the Communications and Networking link in the Computers Additional Categories area, click one of the links in the Site Listings area, and then review the articles. Write a 50-word summary of your findings.

③ Journaling Respond to your readings in this chapter by writing at least one page about your reactions, evaluations, and reflections on computer communications. For example, have you visited a <u>cybercafé</u>? Have you used a device equipped with a global positioning system? How would you react if a classmate used a cell phone with text and picture messaging to cheat on an exam? You also can write about the new terms you learned by reading this chapter. If required, submit your journal to your instructor.

④ Expanding Your Understanding More than a million drivers are finding their commutes more enjoyable with the advent of <u>satellite radio</u>. The two major providers, XM Radio and Sirius, offer hundreds of channels of specific music, talk shows, news, and sports programming. Traditional broadcasters have complained to the Federal Communication Commission, stating that the satellite companies have violated their original licenses because they have expanded their channels to include local weather and traffic advisories and plan to introduce video channels to air on back seat video screens. View Web sites to learn more about satellite radio's popularity. What is the monthly subscription fee for both services? What programming is available in your area? Write a report summarizing your findings, focusing on the broadcasters' objections. If required, submit your report to your instructor.

⑤ Ethics in Action Products such as cell phones with global positioning system tracking capabilities certainly can be beneficial. The tracking information, however, could be used in detrimental ways if your electronic device always is turned on, according to privacy experts. If, for example, you regularly eat at fast-food establishments, your health insurance company could obtain the data regarding your whereabouts and then increase your premiums. Your automobile insurance company could drop your coverage if it learns you drive farther to work than you stated on your application. View online sites that provide arguments about trading <u>privacy</u> for information. Write a report summarizing your findings, and include a table of links to Web sites that provide additional details. If required, submit your report to your instructor.

Case Studies

Use the Case Studies to apply the concepts presented in the chapter to real-world situations. Visit scsite.com/dc2007/ch9/cases to obtain more information pertaining to each exercise. To discuss the Case Studies in this chapter with other students, visit scsite.com/dc2007/ch9/forum and post your thoughts or questions.

CASE STUDY 1 — Class Discussion   Your aunt owns a major development firm in the southeast. The company specializes in designing and constructing retirement communities throughout the United States. One of her biggest expenses is the cost of her project management team traveling to meetings with on-site personnel. She recently learned about the collaboration features of Microsoft Office. She is aware that you are studying about computers and has asked you to examine <u>online collaboration</u> as an alternative to some or all of the face-to-face meetings with on-site personnel. What are the advantages and disadvantages of collaborating online? What is a whiteboard? How are online meetings set up? What is NetMeeting? Does collaboration require additional hardware? Write a brief report and be prepared to discuss your findings in class.

CASE STUDY 2 — Class Discussion   You work as an intern in the Information Technology department for the *Star Journal*, a local newspaper. The newspaper's board of directors recently approved a budget for redesigning the interior of its century-old building as part of an inner-city rehabilitation project. Your manager has been asked to recommend the type of <u>transmission media</u> (hardwire or wireless) to use for the newspaper's local area network. He has asked you to submit a feature/benefit report that summarizes the advantages of hardwiring the building versus using wireless transmission media. Which transmission media would have a greater startup cost? Which transmission media do you think is the most secure? Do the walls in the building present a problem for a wireless network? Does a wireless network present any health hazards? Be prepared to discuss your findings in class.

CASE STUDY 3 — Research   You are employed as a communications advisor at Telemark, a telemarketing firm with over 1,500 telemarketers. The president of the company recently attended the annual Internet Telephony Conference & Expo and came away with the idea that the company can save hundreds of thousands of dollars annually on local, long distance, and international calls by using <u>Internet telephony</u>, rather than the conventional public switched telephone network (PSTN). She has asked you to look into the feasibility of making the switch. Use the Web and/or print media to research the advantages and disadvantages of Internet telephony. How does Internet telephony work? What type of hardware and software must the company purchase to make calls over the Internet? Submit your report or use PowerPoint to create a presentation and share your findings with your class.

CASE STUDY 4 — Research   You recently were hired as a network consultant by P. J. Hoff Enterprises, the only local supplier of business equipment and office supplies in Macomb County. Because of the lack of competition, the owners have not reinvested in the business. A nationally recognized competitor recently opened for business with plans to put P. J. Hoff out of business. In response, the owners have decided to reinvest substantial sums of money in the company. One of their first projects is to develop a <u>local area network</u> that will link employee computers. Before they invest money in the network, they want to know more about networks. Use the Web and/or print media material to answer the following questions put forward by the owners. What are the advantages of having a network? What are the disadvantages? What type of network is best suited for our company — a peer-to-peer network or a client/server network? What transmission media should the company use? Why? What types of problems can we expect with a network? Write a brief report or use PowerPoint to create a presentation and share your findings with your class.

CASE STUDY 5 — Team Challenge   Your school offers free student-intern assistance to the county government. The county in turn assigns a manager to each team of students, who is responsible for defining the project assigned to the student team and ensuring that dates are met. Your team has been assigned to the manager of communications in the information technology department. Next year, he plans to select an <u>ISP — DSL, cable, or wireless</u> — to handle all Internet communications in the county buildings. Form a three-member team and have each team member choose a different type of ISP. Using the Web and/or print media, have each team member determine the advantages and disadvantages of their chosen ISP. Include such features as start-up costs, e-mail disk storage, speed, online protection, and recurring costs. As a team, merge your findings into a team report and/or PowerPoint presentation and share your recommendations with your class.

CHAPTER TEN

Database Management

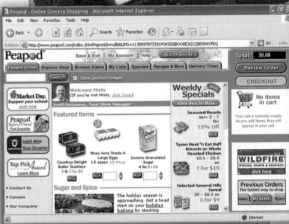

Picture Yourself Using Web Databases

During a break, you think about everything you have to do after work today. Grocery shop . . . stop by the bank . . . pick up your niece — you promised her a movie and pizza tonight. Before leaving the office at the end of the day, you check show times using the Internet Movie Database (IMDb) Web site. You notice the movie has a rating of 8.2 out of 10 — it must be pretty good. The movie starts at 7:30 p.m., which gives you plenty of time.

At home, you log on to the grocery store's Web site and begin filling your shopping cart. Each time you search for an item, the screen says "accessing our database of thousands of products." When finished shopping, you select a time for the groceries to be delivered to your house, enter credit card information, and then click the Submit Order button.

Next, you drop off the application for a personal loan at the bank. The loan officer explains that the credit check, which is done online through Equifax's credit database, will take just a few minutes. Approved! You can pick up your check in the morning. While leaving the bank, you run into a friend you have not seen since high school. He asks if you are going to the class reunion next month. You ask him for more information because you had not heard about it. He explains if you log on to classmates.com and enter the year you graduated from high school, you will have access to the reunion information — and your high school classmates in the database of more than 60 million people.

To learn about Web databases, read Chapter 10 and discover the many features and functions of databases and database software.

OBJECTIVES

After completing this chapter, you will be able to:

1. Define the term, database

2. Identify the qualities of valuable information

3. Explain why data is important to an organization

4. Discuss the terms character, field, record, and file

5. Identify file maintenance techniques

6. Differentiate between a file processing system approach and the database approach

7. Discuss the functions common to most DBMSs

8. Describe characteristics of relational, object-oriented, and multidimensional databases

9. Explain how to interact with Web databases

10. Discuss the responsibilities of database analysts and administrators

CONTENTS

DATABASES, DATA, AND INFORMATION

As presented in Chapter 3, a **database** is a collection of data organized in a manner that allows access, retrieval, and use of that data. *Data* can include text, numbers, images, audio, and video. For example, you can type text on a keyboard, talk into a computer's microphone, transfer photographs taken with a digital camera to a computer, and capture motion and sounds with a video camera and store the recordings on a computer.

Information is processed data; that is, it is organized, meaningful, and useful. In addition to documents, information can be in the form of audio, images, and video. For example, voice communications can be sent in an e-mail message for a family member, friend, or coworker to hear. You can post photographs taken with a digital camera on a Web page for others to view. With a PC video camera, others can see you in real time during a conference call.

Computers process data in a database into information. A database at a members-only discount warehouse, for example, contains data about its club members, e.g., member data, purchases data, etc. When someone wishes to become a warehouse club member, a membership services associate enters several

FIGURE 10-1   HOW A MEMBERS-ONLY DISCOUNT WAREHOUSE MIGHT PROCESS DATA INTO INFORMATION

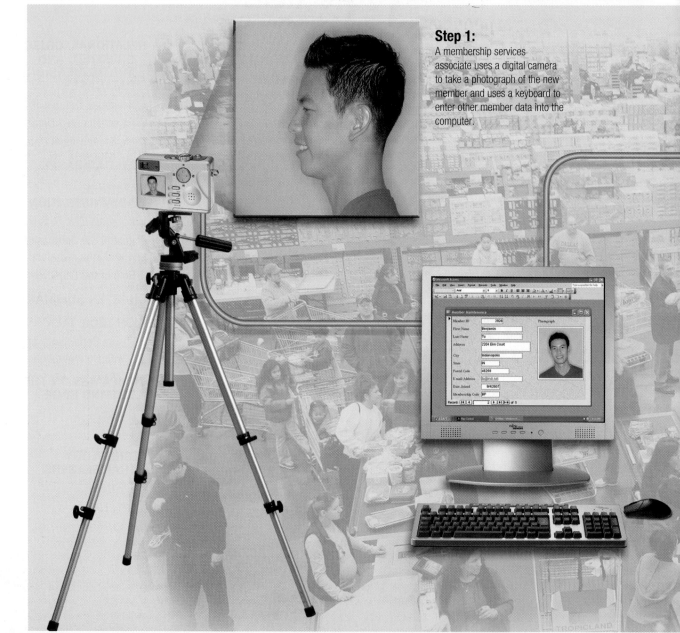

Step 1:
A membership services associate uses a digital camera to take a photograph of the new member and uses a keyboard to enter other member data into the computer.

data items into a computer. The associate also uses a digital camera to photograph the new member. This picture, along with the other entered data, is stored in a database on a server's hard disk. A computer at the discount warehouse then processes the new member data and then sends receipt information to a laser printer and member ID card information to an ID card printer (Figure 10-1).

With **database software**, often called a **database management system** (**DBMS**), users create a computerized database; add, change, and delete data in the database; sort and retrieve data from the database; and create forms and reports from the data in the database. A discount warehouse might use Microsoft Access as its database software.

Database software includes many powerful features, as you will discover later in this chapter.

Most companies realize that data is one of their more valuable assets — because data is used to generate information. Many business transactions take less time when employees have instant access to information. For example, if membership services associates at a discount warehouse have instant access to member records, they can determine when a membership is due for renewal upon member request. When employees are more productive, customers (members, in this case) usually are more satisfied. When customers are happy, typically they become loyal to that business. Loyal customers can lead to referrals and an increase in profits.

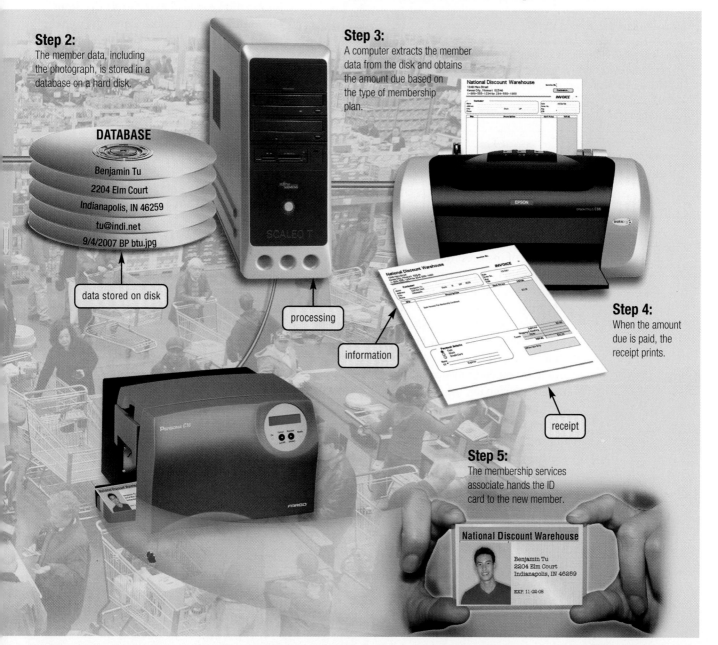

Step 2:
The member data, including the photograph, is stored in a database on a hard disk.

DATABASE

Benjamin Tu
2204 Elm Court
Indianapolis, IN 46259
tu@indi.net
9/4/2007 BP btu.jpg

data stored on disk

processing

information

Step 3:
A computer extracts the member data from the disk and obtains the amount due based on the type of membership plan.

Step 4:
When the amount due is paid, the receipt prints.

receipt

Step 5:
The membership services associate hands the ID card to the new member.

National Discount Warehouse

Benjamin Tu
2204 Elm Court
Indianapolis, IN 46259

EXP. 11-02-08

To ensure that data is accessible on demand, a company must manage and protect its data just as it would any other resource. Thus, it is vital that the data has integrity and is kept secure. Read Ethics & Issues 10-1 for a related discussion. Chapter 11 discusses data security.

ETHICS & ISSUES 10-1

Are Portable Storage Devices a Threat to Businesses?

For years, and to the dismay of many companies, workers have carted portable storage devices loaded with valuable company information. Today's miniscule USB flash drives, MP3 players, and external hard disks allow employees to pack volumes of valuable information in their pockets. Companies now must be concerned with disgruntled employees walking off with complete customer lists, employee databases, or secret product designs and strategies. Some companies have gone as far as banning some MP3 players and other portable storage devices from the company premises. Other companies have begun disabling USB and FireWire ports on employee computers, thereby preventing the devices from being used at all.

How can companies control employee use of portable storage devices to copy company information? Should companies be allowed to dictate the types of personal devices that employees bring to work? Why or why not? Is the problem solvable, just manageable, or should the company find other ways to secure its information? Why? Is it ethical for employees to take corporate information home if only for work purposes? Why or why not?

Data Integrity

For a computer to produce correct information, the data that is entered into a database must have integrity. *Data integrity* identifies the quality of the data. An erroneous member address in a member database is an example of incorrect data. When a database contains this type of error, it loses integrity. The more errors the data contains, the lower its integrity.

Garbage in, garbage out (*GIGO*) is a computing phrase that points out the accuracy of a computer's output depends on the accuracy of the input. If you enter incorrect data into a computer (garbage in), the computer will produce incorrect information (garbage out).

Data integrity is important because computers and people use information to make decisions and take actions. When you sign up for a warehouse club membership and pay with a credit card, a process begins that charges an amount to your credit card. If the membership price is not correct in the discount warehouse's database, an incorrect amount will be billed to your credit card. This type of error causes both you and the membership services associate extra time and effort to remedy.

Qualities of Valuable Information

The information that data generates also is an important asset. People make decisions daily using all types of information such as receipts, bank statements, pension plan summaries, stock analyses, and credit reports. At school, students use grade reports and degree audits to make decisions. In a business, managers make decisions based on sales trends, competitors' products and services, production processes, and even employee skills.

To assist with sound decision making, the information must have value. For it to be valuable, information should be accurate, verifiable, timely, organized, accessible, useful, and cost-effective.

- *Accurate information* is error free. Inaccurate information can lead to incorrect decisions. For example, consumers assume their credit report is accurate. If your credit report incorrectly shows past due payments, a bank may not lend you money for a car or house.
- *Verifiable information* can be proven as correct or incorrect. For example, security personnel at an airport usually request some type of photo identification to verify that you are the person named on the ticket.
- *Timely information* has an age suited to its use. A decision to build additional schools in a particular district should be based on the most recent census report — not on one that is 20 years old. Most information loses value with time. Some information, such as information about trends, gains value as time passes and more information is obtained. For example, your transcript gains value as you take more classes.
- *Organized information* is arranged to suit the needs and requirements of the decision maker. Two different people may need the same information presented in a different manner. For example, an inventory manager may want an inventory report to list out-of-stock items first. The purchasing agent, instead, wants the report alphabetized by vendor.
- *Accessible information* is available when the decision maker needs it. Having to wait for information may delay an important decision. For example, a sales manager cannot decide which sales representative deserves the award for highest annual sales if the final sales have not yet been placed in the database.

- *Useful information* has meaning to the person who receives it. Most information is important only to certain people or groups of people. Always consider the audience when collecting and reporting information. Avoid distributing useless information. For example, an announcement of an alumni association meeting is not useful to students not yet graduated.

- *Cost-effective information* should give more value than it costs to produce. A company occasionally should review the information it produces to determine if it still is cost-effective to produce. Sometimes, it is not easy to place a value on information. For this reason, some companies create information only on demand, that is, as people request it, instead of on a regular basis. Many companies make information available online. Users then can access and print online information as they need it. For example, sending a printed benefits manual to each employee in a company could be quite costly. Instead, employees can access an online benefits manual, when they need to review it.

FAQ 10-1

How can I verify the accuracy of my credit report?

The three credit reporting companies (Equifax, Experian, and TransUnion) developed a central Web site at annualcreditreport.com. Through this Web site, you can request a free copy of your credit report from each credit reporting company every 12 months. You also can request the reports by mailing a form or calling a toll-free number. For more information, visit scsite.com/dc2007/ch10/faq and then click Verifying Credit Report Accuracy.

THE HIERARCHY OF DATA

Data is organized in layers. In the computer profession, data is classified in a hierarchy. Each higher level of data consists of one or more items from the lower level. For example, a member has an address, and an address consists of letters and numbers. Depending on the application and the user, different terms describe the various levels of the hierarchy.

As shown in Figure 10-2, a database contains files, a file contains records, a record contains fields, and a field is made up of one or more characters. The Discount Warehouse database contains four files: Member, Membership Plans, Member Purchases, and Products. The Member file contains records about current members. The Membership Plans file contains records identifying a type of membership and its annual fee. The Member Purchases file contains records about members' purchases at the discount warehouse, and the Products file contains records about items for sale. Each field in a record contains many characteristics, one of which is the field size.

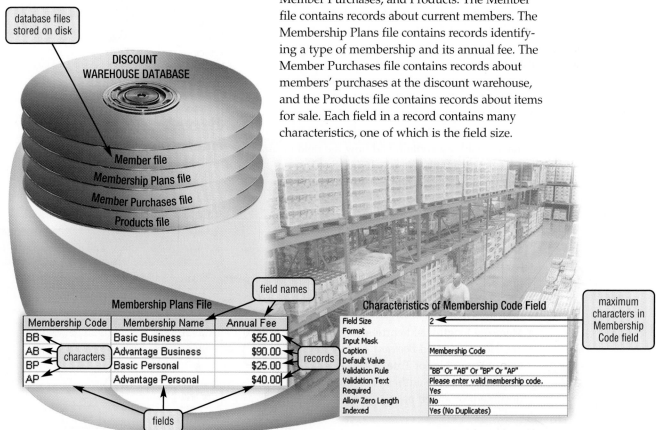

FIGURE 10-2 A sample discount warehouse database with four files: Member, Membership Plans, Member Purchases, and Products. The sample Membership Plans file contains four records. Each record contains three fields. The Membership Code field can contain a maximum of two characters (bytes).

Characters

As discussed in Chapter 4, a bit is the smallest unit of data the computer can process. Eight bits grouped together in a unit comprise a byte. In the ASCII and EBCDIC coding schemes, each byte represents a single **character**, which can be a number (4), letter (R), punctuation mark (?), or other symbol (&). The Unicode coding scheme, by contrast, uses one or two bytes to represent a character. (Read Appendix A for more information about coding schemes.)

Fields

A **field** is a combination of one or more related characters or bytes and is the smallest unit of data a user accesses. A **field name** uniquely identifies each field. When searching for data in a database, you often specify the field name. Field names for the data in the Membership Plans file are Membership Code, Membership Name, and Annual Fee.

A database uses a variety of characteristics, such as field size and data type, to define each field. The **field size** defines the maximum number of characters a field can contain. For example, the Membership Code field contains two characters. Valid entries include BB (Basic Business), AB (Advantage Business), BP (Basic Personal), and AP (Advantage Personal). Thus, as shown in Figure 10-2 on the previous page, the Membership Code field has a field size of 2.

The type of data in a field is an important consideration. Figure 10-3 identifies the data types for fields in the Membership Plans and Member files. The **data type** specifies the kind of data a field can contain and how the field is used. Common data types include:

- Text (also called *alphanumeric*) — letters, numbers, or special characters
- Numeric — numbers only
- AutoNumber — unique number automatically assigned by the DBMS to each added record
- Currency — dollar and cent amounts or numbers containing decimal values
- Date — month, day, year, and sometimes time information
- Memo — lengthy text entries
- Yes/No (also called *Boolean*) — only the values Yes or No (or True or False)
- Hyperlink — Web address that links to a document or a Web page

- Object (also called *BLOB* for binary large object) — photograph, audio, video, or a document created in other programs such as word processing or spreadsheet

In the Membership Plans file, two fields (Membership Code and Membership Name) have a text data type; the third field (Annual Fee) has a currency data type (Figure 10-3). In the Member file, the Member ID field has an AutoNumber data type. The First Name, Last Name, Address, City, State, Postal Code, and Membership Code fields have a text data type. E-mail Address field has a hyperlink data type, Date Joined a date/time data type, and Photograph an object data type.

Membership Plans file

Membership Code	Text
Membership Name	Text
Annual Fee	Currency

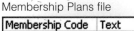

Member file

Member ID	AutoNumber
First Name	Text
Last Name	Text
Address	Text
City	Text
State	Text
Postal Code	Text
E-mail Address	Hyperlink
Date Joined	Date/Time
Membership Code	Text
Photograph	Object

FIGURE 10-3 Data types of fields in the Membership Plans and Member files.

SAMPLE MEMBER FILE

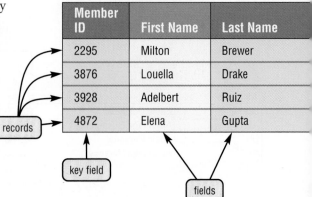

Member ID	First Name	Last Name
2295	Milton	Brewer
3876	Louella	Drake
3928	Adelbert	Ruiz
4872	Elena	Gupta

records

key field

fields

Records

A **record** is a group of related fields. For example, a member record includes a set of fields about one member. A **key field**, or **primary key**, is a field that uniquely identifies each record in a file. The data in a key field is unique to a specific record. For example, the Member ID field uniquely identifies each member because no two members can have the same Member ID.

FAQ 10-2

What are examples of primary keys?

Examples of primary key values that uniquely identify records in a file include driver's license numbers, student identification numbers, checking account numbers, credit card numbers, product codes, and order numbers. Often, the database program automatically assigns a unique primary key number to each newly added record. For more information, visit scsite.com/dc2007/ch10/faq and then click Primary Key Fields.

Files

A **data file** is a collection of related records stored on a storage medium such as a hard disk, CD, or DVD. A Member file at a discount warehouse might consist of hundreds of individual member records. Each member record in the file contains the same fields. Each field, however, contains different data. Figure 10-4 shows a small sample Member file that contains four member records, each with eleven fields. Typical fields

about people often include First Name, Last Name, Address, City, State, Postal Code, and E-mail Address.

A database includes a group of related data files. With a DBMS, users access data and set relationships among the data in data files. Read Ethics & Issues 10-2 for a discussion related to a use of databases.

ETHICS & ISSUES 10-2

Is a National Identification Card Necessary for the Security of the Nation?

Calls for a national identification card in the United States have sparked heated debate, although such cards are the norm in many parts of the world. A *national ID card* could do more than simply assert the cardholder's identity. Some card proponents have called for embedding a biometric identifier, such as a fingerprint or facial scan, in the cards as an added security measure. In the near future, the Department of Homeland Security will require nearly everyone to carry a federally approved photo identification card. Information that citizens provide to obtain a card will be stored in a national database. Law enforcement officials contend that national ID cards would provide tamper-resistant proof of identification and improve national security. Civil liberties groups fear that the cards would facilitate information sharing among government agencies, increase police power, and lead to unjustified suspicion when someone fails to produce a card. Should the United States require a national identification card? Why or why not? If a national ID card is used, should it have biometric identifiers or be tied to a national database? Why?

Address	City	State	Postal Code	E-mail Address	Date Joined	Membership Code	Photograph
54 Lucy Court	Shelbyville	IN	46176		6/10/2006	AB	mbrewer.jpg
33 Timmons Place	Cincinnati	OH	45208	lou@world.com	8/9/2006	AP	ldrake.jpg
99 Tenth Street	Carmel	IN	46033		10/8/2006	BP	aruiz.jpg
2 East Penn Drive	Pittsboro	IN	46167	eg@earth.net	11/6/2006	BB	egupta.jpg

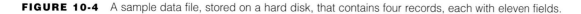

fields

FIGURE 10-4 A sample data file, stored on a hard disk, that contains four records, each with eleven fields.

MAINTAINING DATA

File maintenance refers to the procedures that keep data current. File maintenance procedures include adding records to, changing records in, and deleting records from a file.

Adding Records

Users add new records to a file when they obtain new data. If a new member wants to join the discount warehouse club, a membership services associate adds a new record to the Member file at the discount warehouse. The process required to add this record to the file might include the following steps:

1. A membership services associate uses the database management system (DBMS) to display a Member Maintenance form that gives him or her access to the Member file. The associate then clicks the New Record button, which begins the process of adding a record to the Member file.

2. The associate fills in the fields of the member record with data (except for the Member ID, which automatically is assigned by the DBMS). In this example, the data entered is kept to a minimum.

3. The associate takes a picture of the member using a digital camera. The DBMS stores this picture in the Member file and prints it on a member ID card.

4. The membership services associate verifies the data on the screen and then presses a key on the keyboard or clicks a button on the screen to add the new member record to the Member file. The system software determines where to write the record on the disk, depending on the location of enough free space on the disk. In some cases, it writes the new record at the end of the file. In other cases, such as illustrated in Figure 10-5, it writes the new record for Benjamin Tu between existing records in the file.

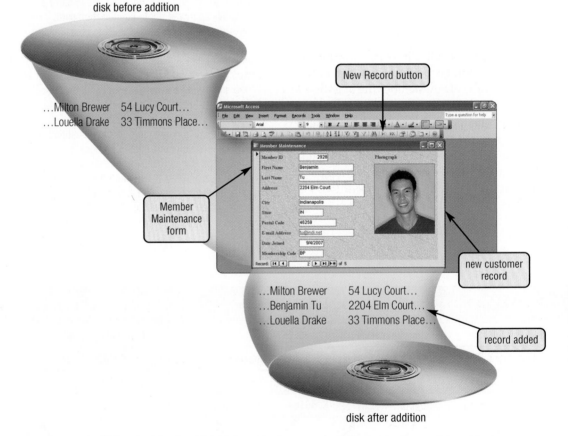

FIGURE 10-5 Using the Member Maintenance form, a membership services associate adds a new member record for Benjamin Tu. After the associate takes the photograph with the digital camera and confirms the data is correct, he or she adds the record to the database file.

Changing Records

Generally, users change a record in a file for two reasons: (1) to correct inaccurate data or (2) to update old data with new data.

As an example of the first type of change, assume that a membership services associate enters a member's e-mail address as ge@earth.net, instead of eg@earth.net. The member notices the error when she reviews her membership agreement at home. The next time she visits the discount warehouse, she requests that a membership services associate correct her e-mail address.

A more common reason to change a record is to update old data with new data. Suppose, for example, that Benjamin Tu moves from 2204 Elm Court to 76 Ash Street. The process to change the address and update Benjamin Tu's record might include the following steps:

1. The membership services associate displays the Member Maintenance form.

2. Assuming Benjamin Tu is present, the associate inserts Benjamin's member ID card in a card reader to display his member record on the screen. If Benjamin did not have his ID card or was not present, the associate could enter Benjamin's member ID — if Benjamin knew it. Otherwise, the associate could enter Tu in the Last Name field, which would retrieve all members with that same last name. The associate then would scroll through all of the retrieved records to determine which one is Benjamin's.

3. The DBMS displays data about Benjamin Tu so that the associate can confirm the correct member record is displayed.

4. The associate enters the new street address, 76 Ash Street.

5. The membership services associate verifies the data on the screen and then clicks the Save button to change the record in the Member file. The DBMS changes the record on the disk (Figure 10-6).

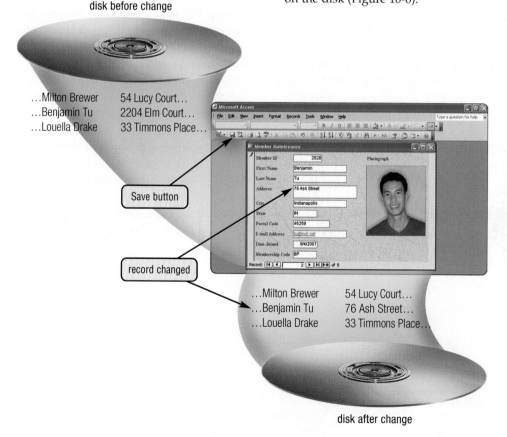

FIGURE 10-6 The membership services associate scans the membership ID card to display the member's record. After looking at the photograph on the screen to confirm that the correct member record is displayed, the associate changes the member's address.

Deleting Records

When a record no longer is needed, a user deletes it from a file. Assume a member named Elena Gupta is moving out of the country. The process required to delete a record from a file includes the following steps:

1. The membership services associate displays the Member Maintenance form.
2. The associate displays Elena Gupta's member record on the screen.
3. The associate confirms the correct member record is displayed. Then, the associate clicks the Delete Record button to delete the record from the Member file and then clicks the Save button to save the modified file.

DBMSs use a variety of techniques to manage deleted records. Sometimes, the DBMS removes the record from the file immediately. Other times, the record is flagged, or marked, so the DBMS will not process it again. In this case, the DBMS places an asterisk (*) or some other character at the beginning of the record (Figure 10-7).

DBMSs that maintain inactive data for an extended period commonly flag records. For example, a discount warehouse might flag canceled memberships. When a DBMS flags a deleted record, the record remains physically on the disk. The record, however, is deleted logically because the DBMS will not process it. DBMSs will ignore flagged records unless an instruction is issued to process them.

From time to time, users should run a utility program that removes flagged records and reorganizes current records. For example, the discount warehouse may remove from disk any accounts that have been canceled for more than one year. Deleting unneeded records reduces the size of files and frees up storage space.

Validating Data

Validation is the process of comparing data with a set of rules or values to find out if the data is correct. Many programs perform a *validity check* that analyzes entered data to help ensure that it is correct. For instance, when a membership services associate adds or changes data in a member record, the DBMS tests the entered data.

With an annual membership fee, you would expect to see numbers before and after a decimal point. For example, a valid annual membership fee is 30.00. An entry of XR.WP clearly is not correct. If the entered data fails a validity check, the computer should display an error message that instructs the user to enter the data again. Validity checks, sometimes called *validation rules*, reduce data entry errors and thus enhance the data's integrity.

Various types of validity checks include alphabetic checks, numeric checks, range checks, consistency checks, and completeness checks. Check digits also validate data accuracy. The following paragraphs describe the purpose of these validity checks. The table in Figure 10-8 illustrates several of these validity checks and shows valid data that passes the check and invalid data that fails the check.

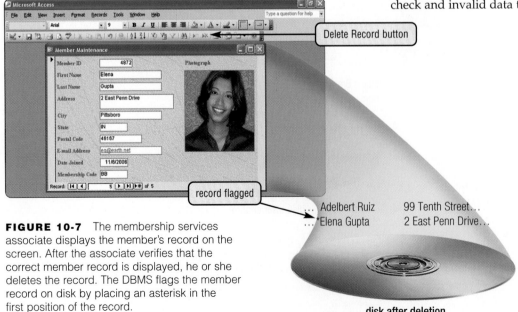

FIGURE 10-7 The membership services associate displays the member's record on the screen. After the associate verifies that the correct member record is displayed, he or she deletes the record. The DBMS flags the member record on disk by placing an asterisk in the first position of the record.

SAMPLE VALID AND INVALID DATA

Validity Check	Field Being Checked	Valid Data	Invalid Data
Alphabetic Check	First Name	Karen	Ka24n
Numeric Check	Postal Code	46322	4tr22
Range Check	Annual Fee	$30.00	$120.00
Consistency Check	Date Joined Birth Date	9/20/2006 8/27/1983	9/20/2006 8/27/2007
Completeness Check	Last Name	Tu	

FIGURE 10-8 In this table of sample valid and invalid data, the first column lists commonly used validity checks. The second column lists the name of the field that contains data being checked. The third column shows valid data that passes the validity checks. The fourth column shows invalid data that fails the validity checks.

ALPHABETIC/NUMERIC CHECK An *alphabetic check* ensures that users enter only alphabetic data into a field. A *numeric check* ensures that users enter only numeric data into a field. For example, data in a First Name field should contain only characters from the alphabet. Data in a postal code field should contain numbers (with the exception of the special characters such as a hyphen).

RANGE CHECK A *range check* determines whether a number is within a specified range. Assume the lowest annual membership fee at the discount warehouse is $25.00 and the highest is $90.00. A range check on the Annual Fee field ensures it is a value between $25.00 and $90.00.

CONSISTENCY CHECK A *consistency check* tests the data in two or more associated fields to ensure that the relationship is logical. For example, the value in a Date Joined field cannot occur earlier in time than a value in a Birth Date field.

COMPLETENESS CHECK A *completeness check* verifies that a required field contains data. For example, in many programs, you cannot leave the Last Name field blank. The completeness check ensures that data exists in the Last Name field.

CHECK DIGIT A *check digit* is a number(s) or character(s) that is appended to or inserted in a primary key value. A check digit often confirms the accuracy of a primary key value. Bank account, credit card, and other identification numbers often include one or more check digits.

A program determines the check digit by applying a formula to the numbers in the primary key value. An oversimplified illustration of a check digit formula is to add the numbers in the primary key. For example, if the primary key is 1367, this formula would add these numbers (1 + 3 + 6 + 7) for a sum of 17. Next, the formula would add the numbers in the result (1 + 7) to generate a check digit of 8. The primary key then is 13678. This example began with the original primary key value, 1367, then the check digit, 8, was appended.

When a data entry clerk enters the primary key of 13678, for example, to look up an existing record, the program determines whether the check digit is valid. The program applies the check digit formula to the first four digits of the primary key. If the calculated check digit matches the entered check digit (8, in this example), the program assumes the entered primary key is valid. If the clerk enters an incorrect primary key, such as 13778, the check digit entered (8) will not match the computed check digit (9). In this case, the program displays an error message that instructs the user to enter the primary key value again.

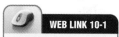

WEB LINK 10-1

Check Digits

For more information, visit scsite.com/dc2007/ch10/weblink and then click Check Digits.

Test your knowledge of pages 514 through 523 in Quiz Yourself 10-1.

QUIZ YOURSELF 10-1

Instructions: Find the true statement below. Then, rewrite the remaining false statements so they are true.

1. A coding scheme is a number(s) or character(s) that is appended to or inserted in a primary key value.
2. A database is a combination of one or more related characters or bytes and is the smallest unit of data a user accesses.
3. A record is a collection of data organized in a manner that allows access, retrieval, and use of that data.
4. Data is processed information.
5. Hierarchy of data procedures include adding records to, changing records in, and deleting records from a file.
6. To be valuable, information should be accurate, verifiable, timely, organized, accessible, useful, and cost-effective.

Quiz Yourself Online: To further check your knowledge of databases, qualities of valuable information, the hierarchy of data, and file maintenance techniques, visit scsite.com/dc2007/ch10/quiz and then click Objectives 1 – 5.

FILE PROCESSING VERSUS DATABASES

Almost all application programs use the file processing approach, the database approach, or a combination of both approaches to store and manage data. The next sections discuss these two approaches.

File Processing Systems

In the past, many organizations exclusively used file processing systems to store and manage data. In a typical **file processing system**, each department or area within an organization has its own set of files. The records in one file may not relate to the records in any other file.

Companies have used file processing systems for many years. A lot of these systems, however, have two major weaknesses: they have redundant data and they isolate data.

- Data Redundancy — Each department or area in a company has its own files in a file processing system. Thus, the same fields are stored in multiple files. If a file processing system is used at the discount warehouse, for example, the Member file and the Member Purchases file store the same members' names and addresses.

   Duplicating data in this manner wastes resources such as storage space and people's time. When new members are added or member data is changed, file maintenance tasks consume additional time because people

must update multiple files that contain the same data.

   Data redundancy also can increase the chance of errors. If a member changes his or her address, for example, the discount warehouse must update the address wherever it appears. In this example, the Address field is in the Member file and also in the Member Purchases file. If the Address field is not changed in all the files where it is stored, then discrepancies among the files exist.

- Isolated Data — Often it is difficult to access data stored in separate files in different departments. Assume that the member e-mail addresses exist in the Member files, and items on sale are in the Products files. To send an e-mail message informing members about items on sale, data is needed from both the Member file and the Products file. Sharing data from multiple, separate files to generate such a list in a file processing system often is a complicated procedure and usually requires the experience of a computer programmer.

The Database Approach

When a company uses the **database approach**, many programs and users share the data in the database. A discount warehouse's database most likely contains data about members, membership plans, member purchases, and products. As shown in Figure 10-9, various areas within the discount warehouse share and

Programs on
Membership Services
Associate's Computer

Database
Management System

Programs on
Computer for
Checkout Lanes

Member File
Membership Plans File
Member Purchases File
Products File

Discount Warehouse Database

FIGURE 10-9 In a discount warehouse that uses a database, the computer used by a membership services associate and the computer used in a checkout lane access data in a single database through the DBMS.

interact with the data in this database. The database does secure its data, however, so only authorized users can access certain data items.

While a user is working with the database, the DBMS resides in the memory of the computer. Instead of working directly with the DBMS, some users interact with a front end. A *front end* is a program that generally has a more user-friendly interface than the DBMS. For example, a membership services associate interacts with the Membership program. This front-end program interacts with the DBMS, which in turn, interacts with the database. Many programs today have a Web page as their front end. An application that supports a front-end program sometimes is called the *back end*. In this case, the DBMS is the back end.

The database approach addresses many of the weaknesses associated with file processing systems. The following paragraphs present some strengths of the database approach.

- Reduced Data Redundancy — Most data items are stored in only one file, which greatly reduces duplicate data. For example, a discount warehouse's database would record a member's name and address only once. When member data is entered or changed, one employee makes the change once. Figure 10-10 demonstrates the differences between how a database application and a file processing application might store data.

- Improved Data Integrity — When users modify data in the database, they make changes to one file instead of multiple files. Thus, the database approach increases the data's integrity by reducing the possibility of introducing inconsistencies.

- Shared Data — The data in a database environment belongs to and is shared, usually over a network, by the entire organization. This data is independent of, or separate from, the programs that access the data. Companies that use databases typically have security settings to define who can access, add, change, and delete the data in a database. Read Ethics & Issues 10-3 for a related discussion.

- Easier Access — The database approach allows nontechnical users to access and maintain data, providing they have the necessary privileges. Many computer users also can develop smaller databases themselves, without professional assistance.

- Reduced Development Time — It often is easier and faster to develop programs that use the database approach. Many DBMSs include several tools to assist in developing programs, which further reduces the development time. The next section discusses these tools and other DBMS features.

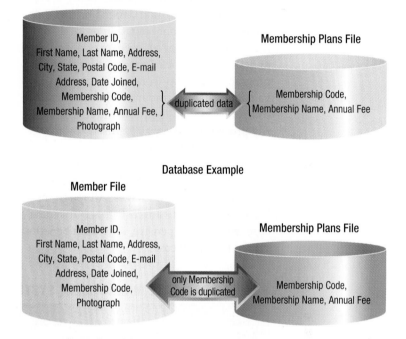

FIGURE 10-10 In the file processing environment, both files contain all three membership plans data fields. In a database environment, only the Membership Plans file contains the Membership Name and Annual Fee fields. Other files, however, such as the Member file, contain the Membership Code, which links to the Membership Plans file when membership plans data is needed.

ETHICS & ISSUES 10-3

Should States Share Criminal Databases?

California was the first state to employ a controversial database. Based on Megan's Law — the statute named for a seven year old girl who was violated and killed by a paroled felon — the database listed the names and addresses of people convicted of crimes against children. Today, all states employ similar databases and are required to share the information with a national database. Most states now allow you to use these databases to find out if these felons live near you. In some communities, when a paroled offender moves in, the police inform the local school system, which in turn sends parents a notification that includes a history, address, and picture of the wrongdoer. Some states share information with each other regarding almost all criminals, and some allow citizens to search for these offenders by name. Touted as a valuable tool in crime prevention, some feel that publishing this information makes it impossible for an offender to lead a normal life and can result in vigilantism — one paroled lawbreaker's car was firebombed only days after his name was released. Should a database of people paroled or released for crimes be made public? Why or why not? What about those who have committed other types of crimes? Who should have access to the database? Why?

Databases have many advantages as well as some disadvantages. A database can be more complex than a file processing system. People with special training usually develop larger databases and their associated applications. Databases also require more memory, storage, and processing power than file processing systems.

Data in a database is more vulnerable than data in file processing systems. A database stores most data in a single file. Many users and programs share and depend on this data. If the database is not operating properly or is damaged or destroyed, users may not be able to perform their jobs. In some cases, certain programs may stop working. To protect their valuable database resource, individuals and companies should establish and follow security procedures. Chapter 11 discusses a variety of security methods.

Despite these limitations, many business and home users work with databases because of their tremendous advantages. Although the hardware and software costs to set up a database may seem expensive, long-term benefits exceed the initial costs.

FAQ 10-3

Can a database eliminate redundant data completely?

No, a database reduces redundant data — it does not eliminate it. Key fields link data together in a database. For example, the Member ID field will exist in any database file that requires access to member data. Thus, the Member ID is duplicated (exists in many database files) in the database. For more information, visit scsite.com/dc2007/ch10/faq and then click Database Relationships.

DATABASE MANAGEMENT SYSTEMS

As previously discussed, a database management system (DBMS), or database program, is software that allows you to create, access, and manage a database. DBMSs are available for many sizes and types of computers (Figure 10-11). Whether designed for a small or large computer, most DBMSs perform common functions. The following pages discuss functions common to most DBMSs.

POPULAR DATABASE MANAGEMENT SYSTEMS

Database	Manufacturer	Computer Type
Access	Microsoft Corporation	Personal computer, server, mobile devices
Adabas	Software AG	Server, mainframe
D³	Raining Data	Personal computer, server
DB2	IBM Corporation	Personal computer, server, mainframe
Essbase	Hyperion Solutions Corporation	Personal computer, server
FastObjects	Versant Corporation	Personal computer, server
GemFire	GemStone Systems, Inc.	Server
Informix	IBM Corporation	Personal computer, server, mainframe
Ingres	Computer Associates International, Inc.	Personal computer, server, mainframe
InterBase	Borland Software Corporation	Personal computer, server
JDataStore	Borland Software Corporation	Personal computer, server
KE Texpress	KE Software, Inc.	Personal computer, server
MySQL	MySQL AB	Personal computer, server
ObjectStore	Progress Software Corporation	Personal computer, server
Oracle Database	Oracle Corporation	Personal computer, server, mainframe, mobile devices
SQL Server	Microsoft Corporation	Server, personal computer, PDA
Sybase	Sybase Inc.	Personal computer, server, mobile devices
Versant	Versant Corporation	Personal computer, server
Visual FoxPro	Microsoft Corporation	Personal computer, server

FIGURE 10-11 Many database management systems run on multiple types of computers.

WEB LINK 10-2

Database Management System

For more information, visit scsite.com/dc2007/ch10/weblink and then click Database Management System.

FAQ 10-4

Which companies have the largest database presence?

As shown in the chart below, Oracle has the largest market share, followed by IBM and Microsoft. For more information, visit scsite.com/dc2007/ch10/faq and then click Database Market Share.

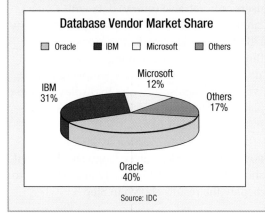

Database Vendor Market Share

☐ Oracle ■ IBM ☐ Microsoft ■ Others

Microsoft 12%

IBM 31%

Others 17%

Oracle 40%

Source: IDC

Data Dictionary

A **data dictionary**, sometimes called a *repository*, contains data about each file in the database and each field in those files. For each file, it stores details such as the file name, description, the file's relationship to other files,

and the number of records in the file. For each field, it stores details such as the field name, description, field type, field size, default value, validation rules, and the field's relationship to other fields. Figure 10-12 shows how a data dictionary might list data for a Member file.

Because the data dictionary contains details about data, some call it *metadata* (meta means more comprehensive). Sometimes, a data dictionary also contains data about programs and users. It might keep track of who accessed data and when they accessed it. The data dictionary is a crucial backbone to a DBMS. Thus, only skilled professionals should update the contents of a data dictionary.

A DBMS uses the data dictionary to perform validation checks. When users enter data, the data dictionary verifies that the entered data matches the field's data type. For example, the data dictionary allows only dates to be entered in a Date Joined field. The data dictionary also can limit the type of data that can be entered, often allowing a user to select from a list. For example, the data dictionary ensures that the State field contains a valid two-letter state code, such as IN, by presenting a list of valid state codes to the user. By validating data, the data dictionary helps to maintain the integrity of the data.

fields in Member file

Field Name	Data Type	Description
Member ID	Number	Member's ID Number
First Name	Text	Member's First Name
Last Name	Text	Member's Last Name
Address	Text	Member's Address
City	Text	City Member Lives
State	Text	State Member Lives
Postal Code	Text	Member's Postal Code
E-mail Address	Hyperlink	Member's E-mail Address
Date Joined	Date/Time	Date Member Joined Center
Membership Code	Text	Membership Code for Membership Plan
Photograph	OLE Object	Digital Photograph of Member

Field Properties

General | Lookup

Field Size	2
Format	
Input Mask	
Caption	State
Default Value	"IN"
Validation Rule	
Validation Text	
Required	Yes
Allow Zero Length	No
Indexed	No

data about State field

A field name can be up to 64 characters long, including spaces. Press F1 for help on field names.

FIGURE 10-12 A sample data dictionary entry shows the fields in the Member file and the properties of the State field.

A data dictionary allows users to specify a default value for a field. A *default value* is a value that the DBMS initially displays in a field. If most members who join the warehouse club live in Indiana, then the DBMS initially could display IN in the State field. The user does not have to type in a default value. Displaying a default value reduces the possibility of errors. A user typically can override a default value if it does not apply for a certain record. For example, you can change the value from IN to OH if the member lives in Ohio.

File Retrieval and Maintenance

A DBMS provides several tools that allow users and programs to retrieve and maintain data in the database. As discussed earlier in this chapter, file maintenance involves adding new records, changing data in existing records, and removing unwanted records from the database.

To retrieve or select data in a database, you query it. A **query** is a request for specific data from the database. Users can instruct the DBMS to display, print, or store the results of a query. The capability of querying a database is one of the more powerful database features.

To meet the needs of a wide variety of database users, from trained experts to nontechnical staff, a DBMS offers several methods to retrieve and maintain its data. The four more commonly used are query languages, query by example, forms, and report generators. The following paragraphs describe each of these methods. Read Looking Ahead 10-1 for a look at Microsoft's next generation of organizing data for retrieval.

QUERY LANGUAGE A **query language** consists of simple, English-like statements that allow users to specify the data to display, print, or store. Each query language has its own grammar and vocabulary. A person without a programming background usually can learn a query language in a short time.

Although a query language can be used to maintain (add, change, and delete) data, most users only retrieve (query) data with a query language. To simplify the query process, many DBMSs provide wizards to guide users through the steps of creating a query. Figure 10-13 shows how to use the Simple Query Wizard in Microsoft Access to display the First Name, Last Name, and E-mail Address fields from the Member file.

Instead of using the Simple Query Wizard, you could enter the query language statement shown in Figure 10-13 directly in the DBMS to display the results shown in Step 3.

QUERY BY EXAMPLE Most DBMSs include **query by example** (**QBE**), a feature that has a graphical user interface to assist users with retrieving data. Figure 10-14 shows a sample QBE screen for a query that searches for and lists members on the Basic Personal plan; that is, their Membership Code field value is equal to BP. Later in the chapter, specific query languages are presented in more depth.

WEB LINK 10-3

Query

For more information, visit scsite.com/dc2007/ch10/weblink and then click Query.

LOOKING AHEAD 10-1

WinFS Offers Improved File Organizing System

Organizing your files may become less of a chore with *Windows Future Storage* (*WinFS*), Microsoft's newest relational file system. This technology promises to improve productivity by reducing search times and using memory effectively. Ultimately, Microsoft's goal is for users to "unify, organize, explore, and innovate" in new ways.

Rather than using directories, WinFS creates multiple file indexes. Microsoft explains that the software really is both a file system and a database using rules. These rules are based on logic, such as determining whether a student attended class today or finding a computer lab equipped with a particular software upgrade. WinFS is one part of Microsoft's integrated data initiative, which is a group of technologies designed to integrate data effectively across applications. For more information, visit scsite.com/dc2007/ch10/looking and then click WinFS.

FIGURE 10-13 HOW TO USE THE SIMPLE QUERY WIZARD

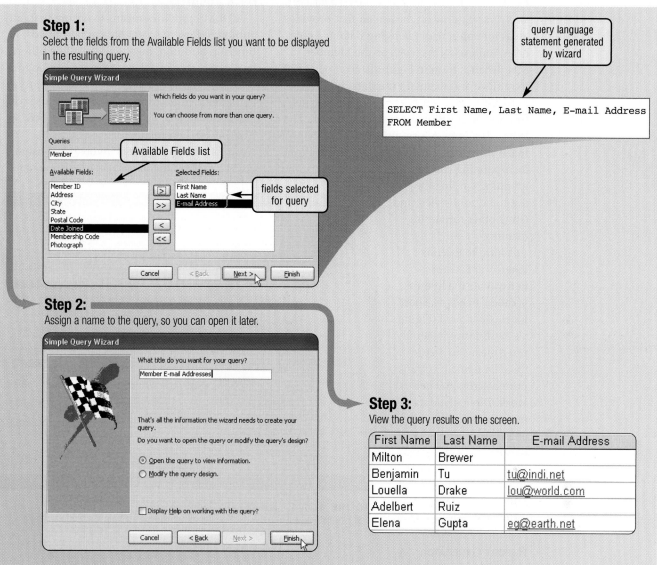

Step 1:
Select the fields from the Available Fields list you want to be displayed in the resulting query.

query language statement generated by wizard

SELECT First Name, Last Name, E-mail Address
FROM Member

Step 2:
Assign a name to the query, so you can open it later.

Step 3:
View the query results on the screen.

First Name	Last Name	E-mail Address
Milton	Brewer	
Benjamin	Tu	tu@indi.net
Louella	Drake	lou@world.com
Adelbert	Ruiz	
Elena	Gupta	eg@earth.net

FIGURE 10-14a   (query by example screen)

Member: Filter by Form

Last Name	Address	City	State	Postal Code	E-mail Address	Date Joined	Membership Code
							BP

Look for   Or

criteria

FIGURE 10-14b   (query results)

Member

		Last Name	Address	City	State	Postal Code	E-mail Address	Date Joined	Membership Code
▶	+	Tu	76 Ash Street	Indianapolis	IN	46259	tu@indi.net	9/4/2007	BP
	+	Ruiz	99 Tenth Street	Carmel	IN	46033		10/8/2006	BP

Record: 1 of 2 (Filtered)

FIGURE 10-14   Access has many QBE capabilities. One QBE technique is Filter by Form, which uses a form to show available fields. The database program retrieves records that match criteria you enter in the form fields. This example searches for members whose Membership Code is equal to BP.

FORM   A **form**, sometimes called a *data entry form*, is a window on the screen that provides areas for entering or changing data in a database. You use forms (such as the Member Maintenance form in Figure 10-5 on page 520) to retrieve and maintain the data in a database.

To reduce data entry errors, well-designed forms should validate data as it is entered. When designing a form using a DBMS, you can make the form attractive and easy to use by incorporating color, shading, lines, boxes, and graphics; varying the fonts and font styles; and using other formatting features.

A form that sends entered data across a network or the Internet is called an *e-form*, short for *electronic form* (Figure 10-15). E-forms generally use a means to secure the data while it is transported across the network. Often, the data in the e-form automatically enters in, or updates existing data in, a database on the network or the Internet. Thus, many DBMSs include the capability of creating e-forms.

REPORT GENERATOR   A **report generator**, also called a *report writer*, allows users to design a report on the screen, retrieve data into the report design, and then display or print the report (Figure 10-16). Unlike a form, you use a report generator only to retrieve data. Report generators usually allow you to format page numbers and dates; titles and column headings; subtotals and totals; and fonts, font sizes, color, and shading.

Data Security

A DBMS provides means to ensure that only authorized users access data at permitted times. In addition, most DBMSs allow different levels of access privileges to be identified for each field in the database. These access privileges define the actions that a specific user or group of users can perform. Read Ethics & Issues 10-4 for a related discussion.

Access privileges for data involve establishing who can enter new data, change existing data,

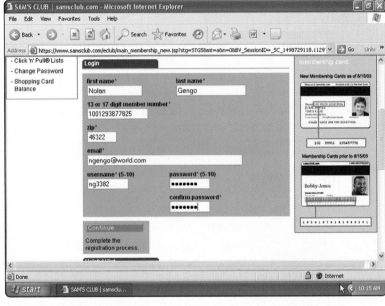

FIGURE 10-15   Through this e-form, users register in an online membership database.

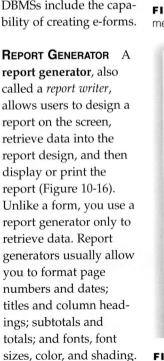

FIGURE 10-16   This report, created in Access, displays member information by the type of membership in which members are enrolled.

Who Should Be Granted Access to Student Records?

Most database management systems specify various access privileges. When a database is created, access policies are determined. Individuals may be granted no access privileges, read only privileges (data can be read but not changed), limited access privileges (only certain data can be read and/or changed), or full update privileges (all data can be read and changed). A student file, for example, contains each student's name, address, and grades, and also may contain data about ethnicity, gender, finances, family, health, activities, discipline, and so on. In a recent case, due to lax security and a simple desire to "see if it could be done," a student at a community college accessed and read all of the grades of students at the school. Being satisfied that he had done nothing wrong, the student did not alter any of the information. Using this situation as an example, what access privileges should be granted to the student, other students, faculty, administrators, financial aid officers, potential employers, and other outside groups? Explain your answers. Is it a crime to access confidential information without authorization? Why? Does it depend on the information? Does it depend on whether the information is altered? Does it depend on how the information is used? Would it be a crime for a student to access a school database of instructors' salaries? Why or why not?

delete unwanted data, and view data. In the Products file, a checkout clerk might have read-only privileges for product prices. That is, the clerk could view the prices, but cannot change them. An inventory manager, by contrast, would have full-update privileges to product data, meaning he or she can view and change the data. Finally, some users have no access privileges to the data; that is, they cannot view or change any data in the database. Chapter 11 discusses access privileges and other security techniques in more depth.

Backup and Recovery

Occasionally a database is damaged or destroyed because of hardware failure, a problem with the software, human error, or a catastrophe such as fire or flood. A DBMS provides a variety of techniques to restore the database to a usable form in case it is damaged or destroyed.

- A **backup**, or copy, of the entire database should be made on a regular basis. Some DBMSs have their own built-in backup utilities. Others require users to purchase a separate backup utility, or use one included with the operating system.

- More complex DBMSs maintain a **log**, which is a listing of activities that change the contents of the database. If a membership services associate modifies a member's address, for example, the change appears in the log. The DBMS places the following in the log: (1) a copy of the member record prior to the change, called the *before image* (Figure 10-17a); (2) the actual change of address data (Figure 10-17b); and (3) a copy of the member record after the change, called the *after image* (Figure 10-17c). The log also might store who made the change, when it was made, and from which computer it was made.

FIGURE 10-17a (before image)

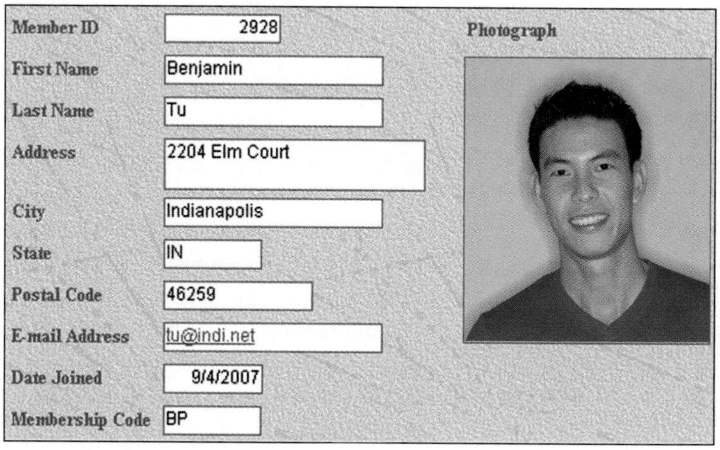

FIGURE 10-17b (change)

FIGURE 10-17c (after image)

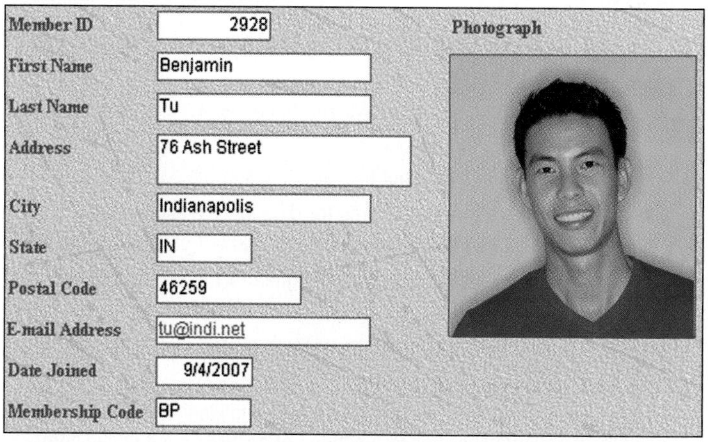

FIGURE 10-17 When the contents of a record are changed, the DBMS places three items in the log: the before image of the record, the actual change, and the after image of the record.

- A DBMS that creates a log usually provides a recovery utility. A **recovery utility** uses the logs and/or backups to restore a database when it becomes damaged or destroyed. The recovery utility restores the database using rollforward and rollback techniques. In a *rollforward*, also called *forward recovery*, the DBMS uses the log to reenter changes made to the database since the last save or backup. In a *rollback*, also called *backward recovery*, the DBMS uses the log to undo any changes made to the database during a certain period. The rollback restores the database to its condition prior to the failure. Depending on the type of failure, the DBMS determines which type of recovery technique to use. For example, if the database is destroyed by a lightning strike, the DBMS would rollforward from the last backup. Assume, however, that a power failure happens at 3:15 p.m. and shuts down all computers, but does not destroy any data. Because some users may have been in the middle of entering transactions, the DBMS would rollback the database to 3:00 p.m. and send a message to all users that they need to reenter any transactions made after that time.

- *Continuous backup* is a backup plan in which all data is backed up whenever a change is made. This backup technique is costly but is growing in popularity because of its benefits. Continuous backup provides recovery of damaged data in a matter of seconds.

WEB LINK 10-4

Continuous Backup

For more information, visit scsite.com/ dc2007/ch10/weblink and then click Continuous Backup.

Test your knowledge of pages 524 through 532 in Quiz Yourself 10-2.

QUIZ YOURSELF 10-2

Instructions: Find the true statement below. Then, rewrite the remaining false statements so they are true.

1. A DBMS is hardware that allows you to create, access, and manage an operating system.

2. A query contains data about files and fields in the database.

3. Backup and recovery procedures for data involve establishing who can enter new data, change existing data, delete unwanted data, and view data.

4. To reduce data entry errors, well-designed forms should rollback data as it is entered.

5. Two major weaknesses of file processing systems are data redundancy and isolated data.

Quiz Yourself Online: To further check your knowledge of file processing systems versus databases and functions of a DBMS, visit scsite.com/ dc2007/ch10/quiz and then click Objectives 6 – 7.

RELATIONAL, OBJECT-ORIENTED, AND MULTIDIMENSIONAL DATABASES

Every database and DBMS is based on a specific data model. A **data model** consists of rules and standards that define how the database organizes data. A data model defines how users view the organization of the data. It does not define how the operating system actually arranges the data on the disk.

Three popular data models in use today are relational, object-oriented, and multidimensional. A database typically is based on one data model. For example, when using a relational database, users work with the relational data model. Some databases are called *object-relational databases* because they combine features of the relational and object-oriented data models.

The table in Figure 10-18 lists some popular DBMSs and the data model on which they are based. The following sections discuss the features of relational, object-oriented, and multidimensional databases.

DATA MODELS FOR POPULAR DBMSs

Data Model	Popular DBMSs
Relational	Access Adabas Informix Ingres InterBase MySQL SQL Server Sybase
Object-oriented	FastObjects GemFire KE Texpress ObjectStore Versant
Object-relational	DB2 JDataStore Oracle Polyhedra PostgreSQL Visual FoxPro
Multidimensional	D^3 Essbase Oracle Express

FIGURE 10-18 Four popular data models are relational, object-oriented, object-relational, and multidimensional. Most DBMSs are based on one of these models.

DATA TERMINOLOGY

File Processing Environment	Relational Database Developer	Relational Database User
File	Relation	Table
Record	Tuple	Row
Field	Attribute	Column

FIGURE 10-19   In this data terminology table, the first column identifies the terms used in a file processing environment. The second column presents the terms used by developers of a relational database. The third column indicates terms to which the users of a relational database refer.

Relational Databases

Today, a relational database is a widely used type of database. A **relational database** is a database that stores data in tables that consist of rows and columns. Each row has a primary key and each column has a unique name.

As discussed earlier in this chapter, a file processing environment uses the terms file, record, and field to represent data. A relational database uses terms different from a file processing system. A developer of a relational database refers to a file as a *relation*, a record as a *tuple*, and a field as an *attribute*. A user of a relational database, by contrast, refers to a file as a **table**, a record as a **row**, and a field as a **column**. Figure 10-19 summarizes this varied terminology.

In addition to storing data, a relational database also stores data relationships. A **relationship** is a connection within the data. In a relational database, you can set up a relationship between tables at any time. The tables must have a common column (field). For example, you would relate the Member table and the Membership Plans table using the Membership Code column. Figure 10-20 illustrates these relational database concepts. In a relational database, the only data redundancy (duplication) exists in the common columns (fields). The database uses these common columns for relationships.

Applications best suited for relational databases are those whose data can be organized into a two-dimensional table. Many businesses use relational databases for payroll, accounts receivable, accounts payable, general ledger, inventory, order entry, invoicing, and other business-related functions.

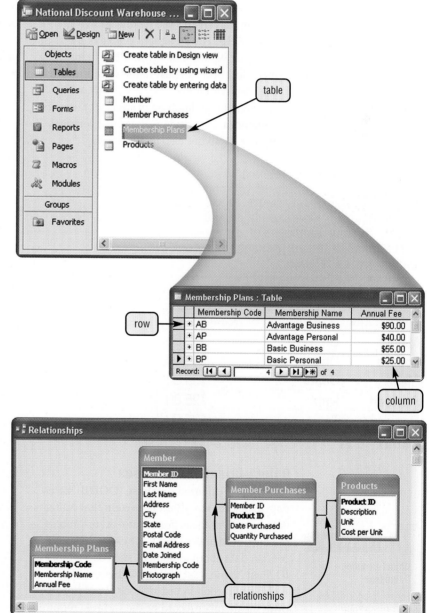

FIGURE 10-20   The Member table is linked to the Membership Plans table through the Membership Code column. The Member table is linked to the Member Purchases table through the Member ID column. The Products table is linked to the Member Purchases table through the Product ID column.

A developer of relational databases uses normalization to organize the data. *Normalization* is a process designed to ensure the data within the relations (tables) contains the least amount of duplication. For a technical discussion about normalization, read the High-Tech Talk article on page 540.

SQL   Structured Query Language (**SQL**) is a query language that allows users to manage, update, and retrieve data. SQL has special keywords and rules that users include in SQL statements. For example, the SQL statement in Figure 10-21a shows how to write the join operation that creates the results shown in Figure 10-21b. The statement displays the First Name, Last Name, and Annual Fee fields in alphabetical order by last name for all records in the Member table.

Most relational database products for servers and mainframes include SQL. Many personal computer databases also include SQL.

Object-oriented databases have several advantages compared with relational databases: they can store more types of data, access this data faster, and allow programmers to reuse objects. An object-oriented database stores unstructured data more efficiently than a relational database. Unstructured data includes photographs, video clips, audio clips, and documents. When users query an object-oriented database, the results often are displayed more quickly than the same query of a relational database. If an object already exists, programmers can reuse it instead of recreating a new object — saving on program development time.

Examples of applications appropriate for an object-oriented database include the following:

- A *multimedia database* stores images, audio clips, and/or video clips. For example, a geographic information system (GIS) database stores maps. A voice mail system database stores audio messages. A television news station database stores audio and video clips.

- A *groupware database* stores documents such as schedules, calendars, manuals, memos, and reports. Users perform queries to search the document contents. For example, you can search people's schedules for available meeting times.

- A *computer-aided design* (CAD) *database* stores data about engineering, architectural, and scientific designs. Data in the database includes a list of components of the item being designed, the relationship among the components, and previous versions of the design drafts.

- A *hypertext database* contains text links to other types of documents. A *hypermedia database* contains text, graphics, video, and sound. The Web contains a variety of hypertext and hypermedia databases. You can search these databases for items such as documents, graphics (Figure 10-22), audio and video clips, and links to Web pages.

- A *Web database* links to an e-form on a Web page. The Web browser sends and receives data between the form and the database. A later section in this chapter discusses Web databases in more depth.

FIGURE 10-21a   (SQL statement)

```
SELECT FIRST NAME, LAST NAME, ANNUAL FEE
FROM MEMBER, MEMBERSHIP PLANS
WHERE MEMBER.MEMBERSHIP CODE =
  MEMBERSHIP PLANS.MEMBERSHIP CODE
ORDER BY LAST NAME
```

FIGURE 10-21b   (SQL statement results)

First Name	Last Name	Annual Fee
Milton	Brewer	$90.00
Louella	Drake	$40.00
Elena	Gupta	$55.00
Adelbert	Ruiz	$25.00
Benjamin	Tu	$25.00

FIGURE 10-21   A sample SQL statement and its results.

Object-Oriented Databases

An **object-oriented database** (**OODB**) stores data in objects. An **object** is an item that contains data, as well as the actions that read or process the data. A Member object, for example, might contain data about a member such as Member ID, First Name, Last Name, Address, and so on. It also could contain instructions about how to print the member record or the formula required to calculate a member's balance due. A record in a relational database, by contrast, would contain only data about a member.

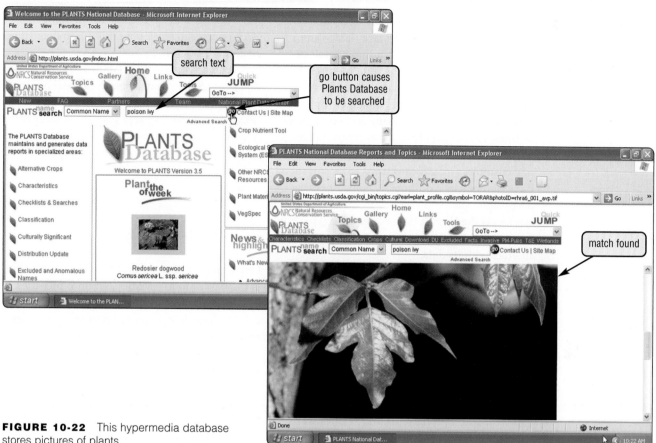

FIGURE 10-22 This hypermedia database stores pictures of plants.

OBJECT QUERY LANGUAGE   Object-oriented and object-relational databases often use a query language called *object query language* (*OQL*) to manipulate and retrieve data. OQL is similar to SQL. OQL and SQL use many of the same rules, grammar, and keywords. Because OQL is a relatively new query language, not all object databases support it.

Multidimensional Databases

A **multidimensional database** stores data in dimensions. Whereas a relational database is a two-dimensional table, a multidimensional database can store more than two dimensions of data. These multiple dimensions, sometimes known as a *hypercube*, allow users to access and analyze any view of the database data.

A Webmaster at a retailing business may want information about product sales and customer sales for each region spanning a given time. A manager at the same business may want information about product sales by department for each sales representative spanning a given time. A multidimensional database can consolidate this type of data from multiple dimensions at very high rates of speed.

The number of dimensions in a multidimensional database varies. A retail business might have four dimensions: products, customers, regions, and time. A multidimensional database for a hospital procedure could have six dimensions: time, procedure type, patient, hospital, physician, and diagnosis. A multidimensional database for an insurance policy may include five dimensions: time, policy type, agent, customer, and coverage. Nearly every multidimensional database has a dimension of time. The content of other dimensions varies depending on the subject.

The key advantage of the multidimensional database is that it can consolidate data much faster than a relational database. A relational database typically does not process and summarize large numbers of records efficiently. With a multidimensional database, users obtain summarized results very quickly. For example, a query that takes minutes or hours to execute in a relational database will take only seconds to execute in a multidimensional database.

No standard query language exists for multidimensional databases. Each database uses its own language. Most are similar to SQL.

WEB LINK 10-8

Multidimensional Databases

For more information, visit scsite.com/dc2007/ch10/weblink and then click Multidimensional Databases.

DATA WAREHOUSES One application that uses multidimensional databases is a data warehouse. A **data warehouse** is a huge database that stores and manages the data required to analyze historical and current transactions. Through a data warehouse, managers and other users access transactions and summaries of transactions quickly and efficiently. Some major credit card companies monitor and manage customers' credit card transactions using a data warehouse. Additionally, consumers can access their own transactions in the data warehouse via the Web. A data warehouse typically has a user-friendly interface, so users easily can interact with its data.

The databases in a data warehouse usually are quite large. Often, the database is distributed. The data in a *distributed database* exists in many separate locations throughout a network or the Internet. The data is accessible through a single server. The data's location is transparent to the user, who usually is unaware that the data is stored in multiple servers.

Data warehouses often use a process called *data mining* to find patterns and relationships among data. A state government could mine through data to check if the number of births

has a relationship to income level. Many e-commerce sites use data mining to determine customer preferences.

A smaller version of a data warehouse is the *data mart*. A data mart contains a database that helps a specific group or department make decisions. Marketing and sales departments may have their own separate data marts. Individual groups or departments often extract data from the data warehouse to create their data marts.

WEB DATABASES

One of the more profound features of the Web is the vast amount of information it provides. The Web offers information about jobs, travel destinations, television programming, movies and videos (Figure 10-23), local and national weather, sporting events, legislative information, and movies. You can shop for just about any product or service, buy or sell stocks, search for a job, and make airline reservations. Much of this and other information on the Web exists in databases. Read Ethics & Issues 10-5 for a related discussion.

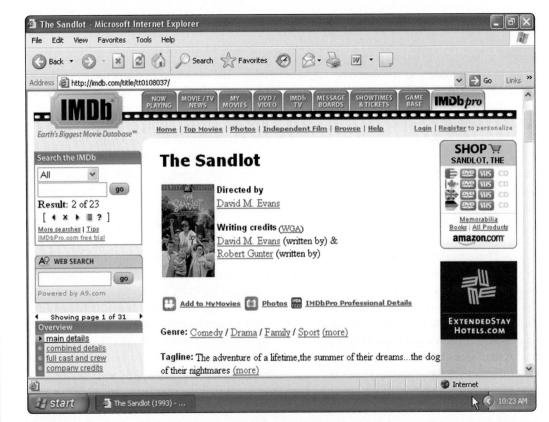

WEB LINK 10-9

Web Databases

For more information, visit scsite.com/dc2007/ch10/weblink and then click Web Databases.

FIGURE 10-23 Through the Internet Movie Database (IMDb) Web site, users can access a huge database loaded with content about current and classic movies.

Can the Government Be Trusted with Personal Data?

Despite laws, policies, and procedures to the contrary, a New York state government subcontractor posted a confidential database containing information about children involved in various government programs. The database remained on the Web until a news organization notified the state of the security breach. In another case of government mishandling data, a judge ordered all of the Web sites of the Interior Department to be shut down for 10 weeks because a database system handling billions of dollars of payments to Native Americans was found to be vulnerable to hackers. In a recent survey, concern over many well-publicized security lapses and computer crime incidents resulted in 63 percent of adults being less likely to provide personal information to the government. In addition, 81 percent worried about the government misusing the information. Because of the volumes of information kept by the government in massive databases, the lack of resources, and an increase in outsourcing work to subcontractors, information is increasingly insecure in many government agencies. Who should be held accountable for lapses in security, privacy, and ethics with regards to government data? Why? Should governments be limited in any way in the amount of information they store, types of information they store, or the duration for which they store the information? Why or why not?

To access data in a Web database, you fill in a form on a Web page. The Web page is the front end to the database. Many search engines such as Yahoo! use databases to store Web site descriptions. Thus, the search engine's home page is the front end to the database. To access the database, you enter search text into the search engine.

A Web database usually resides on a database server. A *database server* is a computer that stores and provides access to a database. One type of program that manages the sending and receiving of data between the front end and the database server is a *CGI (Common Gateway Interface)* script. CGI scripts run automatically — as soon as you click the button to send or receive information. Writing a CGI script requires computer programming skills.

In addition to accessing information, users provide information to Web databases. Many Web sites request users to enter personal information, such as name, address, telephone number, and preferences, into an e-form. The database then stores this personal information for future use. A company, for example, may send e-mail messages to certain groups of customers. If you are a frequent flyer, you may receive travel information.

For smaller databases, many personal computer database programs provide a variety of Web publishing tools. Microsoft FrontPage, for example, has a Database Results Wizard that requires no computer programming. The wizard publishes a Web page that links to your existing database such as a Microsoft Access or Oracle database.

DATABASE ADMINISTRATION

Managing a company's database requires a great deal of coordination. The role of coordinating the use of the database belongs to the database analysts and administrators. To carry out their responsibilities, these IT (information technology) professionals follow database design guidelines and need cooperation from all database users.

Database Design Guidelines

A carefully designed database makes it easier for a user to query the database, modify the data, and create reports. The guidelines shown in Figure 10-24 apply to databases of all sizes.

DATABASE DESIGN GUIDELINES

1. Determine the purpose of the database.

2. Design the tables.
   - Design tables on paper first.
   - Each table should contain data about one subject. The Member table, for example, contains data about members.

3. Design the records and fields for each table.
   - Be sure every record has a unique primary key.
   - Use separate fields for logically distinct items. For example, a name could be stored in six fields: Title (Mr., Mrs., Dr., etc.), First Name, Middle Name, Last Name, Suffix (Jr., Sr., etc.), and Nickname.
   - Do not create fields for information that can be derived from entries in other fields. For example, do not include a field for Age. Instead, store the birthdate and compute the age.
   - Allow enough space for each field.
   - Set default values for frequently entered data.

4. Determine the relationships among the tables.

FIGURE 10-24 Guidelines for developing a database.

Role of the Database Analysts and Administrators

The database analysts and administrators are responsible for managing and coordinating all database activities. The **database analyst (DA)**, or *data modeler*, focuses on the meaning and usage of data. The DA decides on the proper placement of fields, defines the relationships among data, and identifies users' access privileges. The **database administrator (DBA)** requires a more technical inside view of the data. The DBA creates and maintains the data dictionary, manages security of the database, monitors the performance of the database, and checks backup and recovery procedures.

In small companies, one person often is both the DA and DBA. In larger companies, the responsibilities of the DA and DBA are split among two or more people.

FAQ 10-6

Does DBA have two meanings?

Yes; DBA stands for either database administration or database administrator. The first, database administration, is the act of managing a database. The second, database administrator, is the person who manages the database. For more information, visit scsite.com/dc2007/ch10/faq and then click DBA.

Role of the Employee as a User

Employees should learn how to use the data in the database effectively. The amount of information available often amazes first-time database users. Instant access to this information helps employees perform their jobs more effectively. For example, assume a car backed into your parked car. You call your insurance agent to find out where to repair your car. The agent reads to you a list of authorized car repair shops in your area. Today, employees access databases from their office desktop computers, notebook computers, or even smart phones, PDAs, and other mobile devices (Figure 10-25).

Employees also must take an active role in identifying new data for the database. For example, maybe the insurance agent does not have access to the list of car repair shops on the computer. Instead, the agent looks them up in the telephone book. The agent's job would be much easier if this information was available on the computer.

The maintenance of a database is an ongoing task that companies measure constantly against their overall goals. Users can take part in designing the database that will help them achieve those goals.

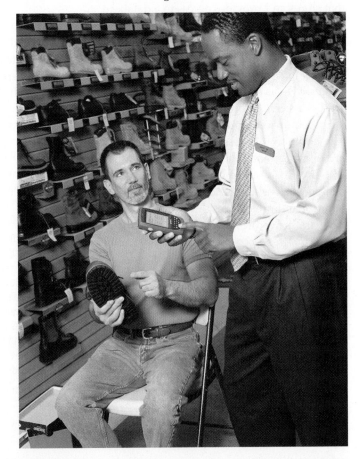

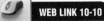
FIGURE 10-25 This sales clerk checks inventory to see if the requested shoe size is in inventory.

Test your knowledge of pages 532 through 538 in Quiz Yourself 10-3.

QUIZ YOURSELF 10-3

Instructions: Find the true statement below. Then, rewrite the remaining false statements so they are true.

1. Data warehouses often use a process called OQL to find patterns and relationships among data.

2. Object-oriented databases store data in tables.

3. One type of program that manages the sending and receiving of data between the front end and the database server is a CGI script.

4. Relational database users refer to a file as a table, a record as a column, and a field as a row.

5. SQL is a data modeling language that allows users to manage, update, and retrieve data.

6. The database analyst requires a more technical inside view of the data than does the database administrator.

Quiz Yourself Online: To further check your knowledge of relational, object-oriented, and multidimensional databases; Web databases; and database administration, visit scsite.com/dc2007/ch10/quiz and then click Objectives 8 – 10.

CHAPTER SUMMARY

This chapter discussed how data and information are valuable assets to an organization (read Looking Ahead 10-2 for a look at the next generation of preserving data and information). The chapter also presented methods for maintaining high-quality data and assessing the quality of valuable information. It then discussed the advantages of organizing data in a database and described various types of databases. It also presented the roles of the database analysts and administrators.

LOOKING AHEAD 10-2

Preserving Electronic Files for Future Generations

Historians and researchers are concerned that Web content and rare and unique electronic works may be lost forever because they exist only in digital form.

In an attempt to gather, organize, and preserve digital files, the United States Congress approved the *National Digital Information Infrastructure & Preservation Program* and commissioned The Library of Congress to supervise the project. Six digital formats have been identified: large Web sites, electronic journals, electronic books, digitally recorded sound, digital moving images, and digital television.

Library officials have partnered with industry and educational experts to discuss how to create and maintain the database. In addition, the National Science Foundation has awarded research grants to address these preservation issues. For more information, visit scsite.com/dc2007/ch10/looking and then click Preservation.

CAREER CORNER

Database Administrator

Most businesses and organizations are built around databases. Access to timely, accurate, and relevant information is a company's lifeline. A database administrator (DBA) creates, applies, supports, and administers the policies and procedures for maintaining a company's database. Database administrators construct logical and physical descriptions of the database, establish database parameters, develop data models characterizing data elements, ensure database integrity, and coordinate database security measures including developing and implementing disaster recovery and archiving procedures. They also use query languages to obtain reports of the information in the database. With the large amounts of sensitive data generated, data integrity, backup, and security have become increasingly important aspects of the administrator's responsibilities.

Administering a database requires a great deal of mental work and the ability to focus on finite details. Database administrators must be able to read and comprehend business related information, organize data in a logical manner, apply general rules to specific problems, identify business principles and practices, and communicate clearly with database users. Being proficient with a particular database such as Oracle, Informix, or SQL Server is an added advantage. The real key, however, is learning, understanding, and becoming an expert in database design.

Database administrators usually have a bachelor or associate degree and experience with computer programming, relational databases, query languages, and online analytical processing. Typical salaries for database administrators are between $71,500 and $95,000, depending on experience. For more information, visit scsite.com/dc2007/ch10/careers and then click Database Administrator.

High-Tech Talk

ENSURE CONSISTENCY OF YOUR DATA WITH NORMALIZATION

Normalization organizes a database into one of several normal forms to remove ambiguous relationships between data and minimize data redundancy. In *zero normal form* (*0NF*), the database is completely nonnormalized, and all of the data fields are included in one relation or table. Repeating groups are listed within parentheses (Figure 10-26a). The table has large rows due to the repeating groups and wastes disk space when an order has only one item.

To normalize the data from 0NF to *1NF* (*first normal form*), you remove the repeating groups (fields 3 through 7 and 8 through 12) and place them in a second table (Figure 10-26b). You then assign a primary key to the second table (Line Item), by combining the primary key of the nonrepeating group (Order #) with the primary key of the repeating group (Product #). Primary keys are underlined to distinguish them from other fields.

To further normalize the database from 1NF to *2NF* (*second normal form*), you remove partial dependencies. A *partial dependency* exists when fields in the table depend on only part of the primary key. In the Line Item table (Figure 10-26b), Product Name is dependent on Product #, which is only part of the primary key. Second normal form requires you to place the product information in a separate Product table to remove the partial dependency (Figure 10-26c).

To move from 2NF to *3NF* (*third normal form*), you move transitive dependencies. A *transitive dependency* exists when a nonprimary key field depends on another nonprimary key field. As shown in Figure 10-26c, Vendor Name is dependent on Vendor #, both of which are nonprimary key fields. If Vendor Name is left in the Order table, the database will store redundant data each time a product is ordered from the same vendor.

Third normal form requires Vendor Name to be placed in a separate Vendor table, with Vendor # as the primary key. The field that is the primary key in the new table — in this case, Vendor # — also remains in the original table as a *foreign key* and is identified by a dotted underline (Figure 10-26d). In 3NF, the database now is logically organized in four separate tables and is easier to maintain. For instance, to add, delete, or change a Vendor or Product Name, you make the change in just one table. For more information, visit scsite.com/dc2007/ch10/tech and then click Normalization.

FIGURE 10-26
The process of normalizing a database.

repeating group I   repeating group II

Order Table

Order #	Order Date	Product #	Product Name	Qty Ordered	Vendor #	Vendor Name	Product #	Product Name	Qty Ordered	Vendor #	Vendor Name
1001	6/8/2007	605	8.5" x 11" White Copy Paper	2	321	Hammermill	203	CD Jewel Cases	5	110	Fellowes
1002	6/10/2007	751	Ballpoint Pens	6	166	Pilot					
1003	6/10/2007	321	1" Ring Binder, Blue	12	450	Globe					
1004	6/11/2007	605	8.5" x 11" White Copy Paper	2	321	Hammermill	102	Interior File Folders	2	450	Globe

(a) Zero Normal Form (0NF)
(Order #, Order Date, (Product #, Product Name, Quantity Ordered, Vendor #, Vendor Name))

(b) First Normal Form (1NF)
Order (<u>Order #</u>, Order Date)
Line Item (<u>Order # + Product #</u>, Product Name, Quantity Ordered, Vendor #, Vendor Name)

(c) Second Normal Form (2NF)
Order (<u>Order #</u>, Order Date)
Line Item (<u>Order # + Product #</u>, Quantity Ordered, Vendor #, Vendor Name)
Product (<u>Product #</u>, Product Name)

(d) Third Normal Form (3NF)
Order (<u>Order #</u>, Order Date)
Line Item (<u>Order # + Product #</u>, Quantity Ordered, Vendor #)
Product (<u>Product #</u>, Product Name)
Vendor (<u>Vendor #</u>, Vendor Name)

Order

Order #	Order Date
1001	6/8/2007
1002	6/10/2007
1003	6/10/2007
1004	6/11/2007

Line Item

Order # + Product #	Qty Ordered	Vendor #
1001605	2	321
1001203	5	110
1002751	6	166
1003321	12	450
1004605	2	321
1004102	2	450

Product

Product #	Product Name
102	Interior File Folders
203	CD Jewel Cases
321	1" Ring Binder, Blue
605	8.5" x 11" White Copy Paper
751	Ballpoint Pens

Vendor

Vendor #	Vendor Name
110	Fellowes
166	Pilot
321	Hammermill
450	Globe

Companies on the Cutting Edge

ORACLE
DATABASE SOFTWARE DEVELOPER

More than half of the FORTUNE 100 companies use an *Oracle* product as their primary database, but Oracle's quest, according to CEO Larry Ellison, is to have its customers convert all their database applications to Oracle's software.

Ellison and two partners founded the company in 1977 with the intent of developing a commercially viable relational database. When their Oracle database was released, it was an immediate success and changed the way companies stored and managed information. For the first time, separate data tables could be connected by a common field.

The company is the world's second largest independent software company behind Microsoft. With the recent $10.3 billion acquisition of PeopleSoft and $5.85 billion acquisition of Siebel Systems, Oracle also will control more than 25 percent of the corporate application-software market. For more information, visit scsite.com/ dc2007/ch10/companies and then click Oracle.

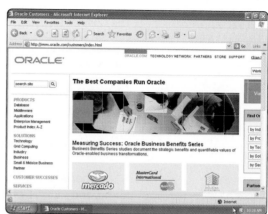

SYBASE
MANAGING DATA FOR THE UNWIRED ENTERPRISE

Researchers at the University of California, Berkeley, estimate that 95 percent of the data produced by major corporations never is used after it is stored in a database because it is disorganized and inaccessible.

Sybase helps companies unlock and use this data whenever and wherever needed through its unwired enterprise. This data access solution helps mobile database users tap into corporate networks, often wirelessly. The company focuses especially on Enterprise Portal (EP) solutions, which convert stored data into information that can be used by customers, partners, and suppliers.

For more than 20 years, Sybase has produced software that links platforms, servers, databases, applications, and mobile devices. The company aggressively is marketing its technologies abroad; it plans to showcase its wireless technologies during Beijing's 2008 Olympic Games. For more information, visit scsite.com/dc2007/ ch10/companies and then click Sybase.

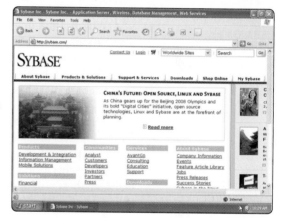

Technology Trailblazers

E. F. CODD
RELATIONAL DATABASE MODEL INVENTOR

The majority of large and small databases are structured on the relational model, which is considered one of the greatest technological inventions of the 20th Century. *E. F. Codd* single-handedly is credited with developing and promoting that model in a series of research papers beginning with his 1969 IBM Research Report, "Derivability, Redundancy, and Consistency of Relations Stored in Large Data Banks."

Edgar F. Codd began his career in 1949 when he joined IBM as a programming mathematician after graduating from Oxford University. Throughout the 1950s he helped develop several IBM computers and then turned his attention to database management. Among his achievements is earning the prestigious A. M. Turing Award, which is the Association for Computing Machinery's highest technical achievement honor given to an individual, for his relational database theory. For more information, visit scsite.com/dc2007/ch10/people and then click E. F. Codd.

LARRY ELLISON
ORACLE CEO

On a visit to Kyoto, Japan, *Larry Ellison* became intrigued with the country's culture and the citizens' combination of confidence and humility. He says he applies these philosophical principles to his work at Oracle, where he serves as CEO.

As a young man, Ellison was interested in science and mathematics. He was inspired by E. F. Codd's relational database model and founded Oracle in 1977 under the name Software Development Laboratories with a $1,200 investment.

Under Ellison's leadership, the company doubled its sales in 11 of its first 12 years. He is known for his uncanny ability to motivate his employees and business partners toward a common goal. In 2005, he was the fifth-richest American, according to *Forbes*'s annual survey. For more information, visit scsite.com/dc2007/ch10/people and then click Larry Ellison.

Quizzes and
Learning Games

Computer Genius
Crossword Puzzle
DC Track and Field
Practice Test
Quiz Yourself
Wheel of Terms
You're Hired!

Exercises

Case Studies
▶ Chapter Review
Checkpoint
Key Terms
Learn How To
Learn It Online
Web Research

Beyond the Book

Career Corner
Companies
FAQs
High-Tech Talk
Looking Ahead
Making Use of
the Web
Trailblazers
Web Links

Features

Chapter Forum
Install Computer
Lab Exercises
Maintain Computer
Tech News
Timeline 2007

Chapter Review

The Chapter Review section summarizes the concepts presented in this chapter. To listen to the audio version of this Chapter Review, visit scsite.com/dc2007/ch10/review. To obtain help from other students regarding any subject in this chapter, visit scsite.com/dc2007/ch10/forum and post your thoughts or questions.

① What Is a Database?   A **database** is a collection of data organized in a manner that allows access, retrieval, and use of that data. **Database software**, often called a **database management system (DBMS)**, allows users to create a computerized database; add, change, and delete the data; sort and retrieve the data; and create forms and reports from the data.

② What Are the Qualities of Valuable Information?   *Data* can include text, numbers, images, audio, and video. Computers process data into information. *Information* is processed data; that is, it is organized, meaningful, and useful. For information to be valuable, it should be accurate, verifiable, timely, organized, accessible, useful, and cost-effective.

③ Why Is Data Important to an Organization?   Because data is used to generate information, many companies realize that data is one of their more valuable assets. *Data integrity* identifies the quality of data. Data integrity is important because computers and people use information to make decisions and take actions. For a computer to produce correct information, the data that is entered in a database must have integrity.

④ What Is Meant by Character, Field, Record, and File?   Data is classified in a hierarchy, with each level of data consisting of one or more items from the lower level. A bit is the smallest unit of data a computer can process. Eight bits grouped together in a unit form a byte, and each byte represents a single **character**. A **field** is a combination of one or more related characters and is the smallest unit of data a user accesses. A **record** is a group of related fields. A **data file** is a collection of related records stored on a storage medium such as a hard disk, CD, or DVD.

⑤ How Are Files Maintained?   **File maintenance** refers to the procedures that keep data current. File maintenance procedures include adding records when new data is obtained, changing records to correct inaccurate data or to update old data with new data, and deleting records when they no longer are needed. **Validation** is the process of comparing data with a set of rules or values to find out if the data is correct. Many programs perform a *validity check* that analyzes entered data to help ensure that it is correct. Types of validity checks include an *alphabetic check*, a *numeric check*, a *range check*, a *consistency check*, a *completeness check*, and a *check digit*.

> Visit scsite.com/dc2007/ch10/quiz or click the Quiz Yourself button. Click Objectives 1 – 5.

⑥ How Is a File Processing System Approach Different from the Database Approach?
In a **file processing system**, each department or area within an organization has its own set of data files. Two major weaknesses of file processing systems are redundant data (duplicated data) and isolated data. With a **database approach**, many programs and users share the data in a database. The database approach reduces data redundancy, improves data integrity, shares data, permits easier access, and reduces development time. A database, however, can be more complex than a file processing system, requiring special training and more computer memory, storage, and processing power. Data in a database also is more vulnerable than data in file processing systems.

⑦ What Functions Are Common to Most DBMSs?   Most DBMSs perform common functions. A **data dictionary** contains data about each file in the database and each field within those files. A DBMS offers several methods to maintain and retrieve data, such as query languages, query by example, forms, and report generators. A **query language** consists of simple, English-like

Chapter Review

statements that allow users to specify the data to display, print, or store. **Query by example (QBE)** has a graphical user interface that assists users with retrieving data. A **form** is a window on the screen that provides areas for entering or changing data. A **report generator** allows users to design a report on the screen, retrieve data into the report design, and then display or print the report. To supply security, most DBMSs can identify different levels of *access privileges* that define the actions a specific user or group of users can perform for each field in a database. If a database is damaged or destroyed, a DBMS provides techniques to return the database to a usable form. A **backup** is a copy of the database. A **log** is a listing of activities that change the contents of the database. A **recovery utility** uses the logs and/or backups to restore the database. *Continuous backup* is a backup plan in which all data is backed up whenever a change is made.

connect

Visit scsite.com/dc2007/ch10/quiz or click the Quiz Yourself button. Click Objectives 6 – 7.

8 **What Are Characteristics of Relational, Object-Oriented, and Multidimensional Databases?**   A **data model** consists of rules and standards that define how the database organizes data. Three popular data models are relational, object-oriented, and multidimensional. A **relational database** stores data in tables that consist of rows and columns. A relational database developer refers to a file as a *relation*, a record as a *tuple*, and a field as an *attribute*. A relational database user refers to a file as a **table**, a record as a **row**, and a field as a **column**. A **relationship** is a connection within the data in a relational database. **Structured Query Language (SQL)** allows users to manage, update, and retrieve data. An **object-oriented database (OODB)** stores data in objects. An **object** is an item that contains data, as well as the actions that read or process the data. Applications appropriate for an object-oriented database include a *multimedia database*, a *groupware database*, a *computer-aided design (CAD) database*, a *hypertext database*, a *hypermedia database*, and a *Web database*. Object-oriented databases often use an *object query language (OQL)* to manipulate and retrieve data. A **multidimensional database** stores data in dimensions. These multiple dimensions, sometimes known as a *hypercube*, allow users to access and analyze any view of the database data. One application that uses multidimensional databases is a **data warehouse**, which is a huge database that stores and manages the data required to analyze historical and current transactions. No standard query language exists for multidimensional databases.

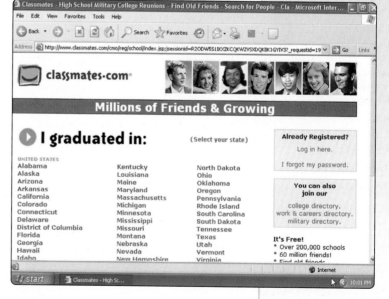

9 **How Do Web Databases Work?**   To access data in a *Web database*, you fill in a form on a Web page, which is the *front end* to the database. A Web database usually resides on a *database server*, which is a computer that stores and provides access to a database. One type of program that manages the sending and receiving of data between the front end and the database is a *CGI (Common Gateway Interface)* script.

10 **What Are the Responsibilities of Database Analysts and Administrators?**   A **database analyst (DA)**, or *data modeler*, focuses on the meaning and usage of data. The DA decides on the placement of fields, defines data relationships, and identifies access privileges. A **database administrator (DBA)** requires a more technical view of the data. The DBA creates and maintains the data dictionary, manages database security, monitors database performance, and checks backup and recovery procedures.

connect

Visit scsite.com/dc2007/ch10/quiz or click the Quiz Yourself button. Click Objectives 8 – 10.

Key Terms

You should know the Primary Terms and be familiar with the Secondary Terms. Use the list below to help focus your study. To further enhance your understanding of the Key Terms in this chapter, visit scsite.com/dc2007/ch10/terms. See an example of and a definition for each term, and access current and additional information about the term from the Web.

Primary Terms

(shown in bold-black characters in the chapter)

backup (531)
character (518)
column (533)
data dictionary (527)
data file (519)
data model (532)
data type (518)
data warehouse (536)
database (514)
database administrator (DBA) (538)
database analyst (DA) (538)
database approach (524)
database management system (DBMS) (515)
database software (515)
field (518)
field name (518)
field size (518)
file maintenance (520)
file processing system (524)
form (530)

key field (519)
log (531)
multidimensional database (535)
object (534)
object-oriented database (OODB) (534)
primary key (519)
query (528)
query by example (QBE) (528)
query language (528)
record (519)
recovery utility (532)
relational database (533)
relationship (533)
report generator (530)
row (533)
Structured Query Language (SQL) (534)
table (533)
validation (522)

Secondary Terms

(shown in italic characters in the chapter)

access privileges (530)
accessible information (516)
accurate information (516)
after image (531)
alphabetic check (523)
alphanumeric (518)
attribute (533)
back end (525)
backward recovery (532)
before image (531)
BLOB (518)
Boolean (518)
CGI (Common Gateway Interface) script (537)
check digit (523)
completeness check (523)
computer-aided design (CAD) database (534)
consistency check (523)
continuous backup (532)
cost-effective information (517)
data (514)
data entry form (530)
data integrity (516)
data mart (536)
data mining (536)
data modeler (538)
database server (537)
default value (528)
distributed database (536)
e-form (530)
electronic form (530)

forward recovery (532)
front end (525)
garbage in, garbage out (GIGO) (516)
groupware database (534)
hypercube (535)
hypermedia database (534)
hypertext database (534)
information (514)
metadata (527)
multimedia database (534)
normalization (534)
numeric check (523)
object query language (OQL) (535)
object-relational databases (532)
organized information (516)
range check (523)
relation (533)
report writer (530)
repository (527)
rollback (532)
rollforward (532)
timely information (516)
tuple (533)
useful information (517)
validation rules (522)
validity check (522)
verifiable information (516)
Web database (534)

Checkpoint

Use the Checkpoint exercises to check your knowledge level of the chapter. The Beyond the Book exercises will help broaden your understanding of the concepts presented in this chapter. To complete the Checkpoint exercises interactively, visit scsite.com/dc2007/ch10/check.

Label the Figure

Identify the database elements.

a. relationships

b. column

c. table

d. form

e. row

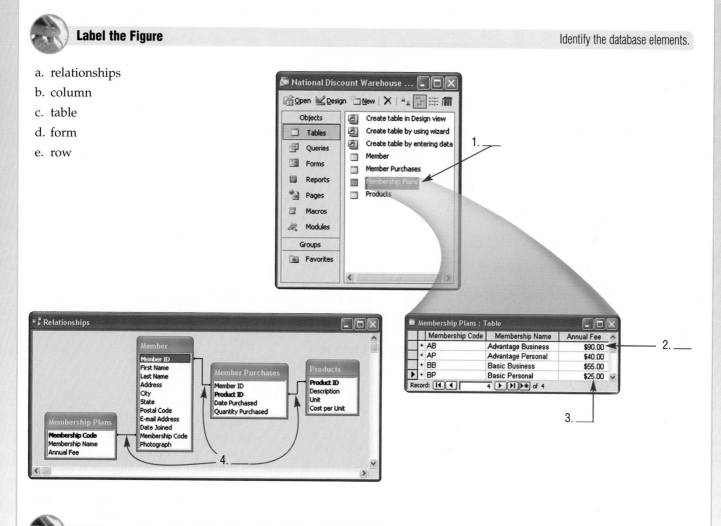

True/False

Mark T for True and F for False. (See page numbers in parentheses.)

_____ 1. Data can include text, numbers, sounds, images, audio, and video. (514)

_____ 2. Organized information has meaning to the person who receives it. (516)

_____ 3. A character is the smallest unit of data a computer can process. (518)

_____ 4. The data in a key field is the same for every record in a file. (519)

_____ 5. Validation is the process of comparing data with a set of rules or values to find out if the data is correct. (522)

_____ 6. A consistency check tests the data in two or more associated fields to ensure that the relationship is logical. (523)

_____ 7. Databases require more memory, storage, and processing power than a file processing system. (526)

_____ 8. To retrieve or select data in a database, you query it. (528)

_____ 9. Access privileges refer to the rules and standards that define how the database organizes data. (531)

_____ 10. The data in a distributed database exists in many separate locations throughout a network or the Internet. (536)

Checkpoint

Multiple Choice   Select the best answer. (See page numbers in parentheses.)

1. Data _____ identifies the quality of data. (516)
   a. integrity
   b. modeling
   c. security
   d. mining

2. _____ information has an age suited to its use. (516)
   a. Timely   b. Organized
   c. Cost-effective d. Verifiable

3. Accessible information _____. (516)
   a. is error free
   b. has an age suited to its use
   c. has meaning to the person who receives it
   d. is available when the decision maker needs it

4. The _____ data type is used for lengthy text entries. (518)
   a. memo   b. numeric
   c. hyperlink   d. data

5. A _____ is a field that uniquely identifies each record in a file. (519)
   a. data type
   b. data file
   c. primary key
   d. data character

6. _____ analyzes entered data to help ensure that it is correct. (522)
   a. Data integrity
   b. An access privilege
   c. A validity check
   d. A data model

7. A range check _____. (523)
   a. ensures that users enter only alphabetic data into a field
   b. determines whether a number is within a specified range
   c. ensures that users enter only numeric data into a field
   d. verifies that a required field contains data

8. All of the following are strengths of the database approach, except _____. (525)
   a. less complexity
   b. improved data integrity
   c. easier access
   d. reduced development time

9. Because the _____ contains details about data, some call it metadata (meta means more comprehensive). (527)
   a. data mart
   b. data warehouse
   c. data modeler
   d. data dictionary

10. _____ has a graphical user interface that assists users with retrieving data. (528)
    a. A query language
    b. Query by example (QBE)
    c. A report generator
    d. A form

11. A(n) _____ sends entered data across a network or the Internet. (530)
    a. e-form
    b. groupware database
    c. report generator
    d. log

12. _____ is a backup plan in which all data is backed up whenever a change is made. (532)
    a. Rollback
    b. Backward recovery
    c. Continuous backup
    d. Forward recovery

13. The key advantage of the multidimensional database is that _____. (535)
    a. the number of dimensions in a multidimensional database is always the same
    b. a standard query language exists for multidimensional databases
    c. it requires less disk space than a relational database
    d. it can consolidate data much faster than a relational database

14. The database analyst (DA) _____. (538)
    a. decides on the proper placement of fields
    b. creates and maintains the data dictionary
    c. monitors the performance of the database
    d. checks backup and recovery procedures

Checkpoint

Matching

Match the terms with their definitions. (See page numbers in parentheses.)

_____ 1. database (514)

_____ 2. field name (518)

_____ 3. field size (518)

_____ 4. data type (518)

_____ 5. key field (519)

_____ 6. default value (528)

_____ 7. query (528)

_____ 8. data model (532)

_____ 9. data modeler (538)

_____ 10. database administrator (538)

a. uniquely identifies each field

b. smaller version of a data warehouse

c. defines the maximum number of characters a field can contain

d. collection of data organized in a manner that allows access, retrieval, and use of that data

e. person who focuses on the meaning and usage of data

f. rules and standards that define how the database organizes data

g. value that a DBMS initially displays in a field

h. creates and maintains the data dictionary, manages security of the database, monitors the performance of the database, and checks backup and recovery procedures

i. specifies the kind of data a field can contain and how the field is used

j. uniquely identifies each record in a file

k. request for specific data from a database

Short Answer

Write a brief answer to each of the following questions.

1. How is a field different from a record? _____ What is a data file? _____

2. What is validation? _____ What are five types of validity checks? _____

3. Why is data redundancy a weakness of file processing systems? _____ How does the database approach reduce data redundancy? _____

4. In a log, how is a before image different from an after image? _____ How is rollforward different from rollback? _____

5. What are Structured Query Language (SQL) and Object Query Language (OQL)? _____ How are they similar? _____

Beyond the Book

Read the following book elements, learn more about each using the Web, and then write a brief report.

1. Ethics & Issues — Are Portable Storage Devices a Threat to Businesses? (516), Is a National Identification Card Necessary for the Security of the Nation? (519), Should States Share Criminal Databases? (525), Who Should Be Granted Access to Student Records? (531), or Can the Government Be Trusted with Personal Data? (537)

2. Career Corner — Database Administrator (539)

3. Companies on the Cutting Edge — Oracle or Sybase (541)

4. FAQs (517, 519, 526, 527, 533, 538)

5. High-Tech Talk — Ensure Consistency of Your Data with Normalization (540)

6. Looking Ahead — WinFS Offers Improved File Organizing System (528) or Preserving Electronic Files for Future Generations (539)

7. Making Use of the Web — Science (128)

8. Picture Yourself Using Web Databases (512)

9. Technology Trailblazers — E. F. Codd or Larry Ellison (541)

10. Web Links (523, 526, 528, 532, 534, 535, 536, 538)

Learn It Online

Use the Learn It Online exercises to reinforce your understanding of the chapter concepts. To access the Learn It Online exercises, visit scsite.com/dc2007/ch10/learn.

1 At the Movies — Internet Movie Database

To view the Internet Movie Database movie, click the number 1 button. Locate your video and click the corresponding High-Speed or Dial-Up link, depending on your Internet connection. Watch the movie and then complete the exercise by answering the question that follows. Using Rottentomatoes.com could help you save time and money by allowing you to view movie trailers and view customer reviews. Explain how the "tomato picker" works and how using that feature of Rottentomatoes.com could save you time and money.

2 At the Movies — National Identity Card

To view the National Identity Card movie, click the number 2 button. Locate your video and click the corresponding High-Speed or Dial-Up link, depending on your Internet connection. Watch the movie and then complete the exercise by answering the question that follows. Identity theft is a burgeoning problem. One solution is a national identity card, but other groups have proposed a national driver's license. Both of these ideas have spawned widespread controversy due to the ease with which the cards' opponents feel that the cards can be fraudulently reproduced. Explain the three security measures that AAMVA has proposed as safeguards against fraud should national driver's licenses be issued.

3 Student Edition Labs — Advanced Databases

Click the number 3 button. A new browser window will open, displaying the Student Edition Labs. Follow the on-screen instructions to complete the Advanced Databases Lab. When finished, click the Exit button. If required, submit your results to your instructor.

4 Student Edition Labs — Advanced Spreadsheets

Click the number 4 button. A new browser window will open, displaying the Student Edition Labs. Follow the on-screen instructions to complete the Advanced Spreadsheets Lab. When finished, click the Exit button. If required, submit your results to your instructor.

5 Practice Test

Click the number 5 button. Answer each question. When completed, enter your name and click the Grade Test button to submit the quiz for grading. Make a note of any missed questions. If required, submit your results to your instructor.

6 Who Wants To Be a Computer Genius²?

Click the number 6 button to find out if you are a computer genius. Directions about how to play the game will be displayed. When you are ready to play, click the Play button. Submit your score to your instructor.

Learn It Online

7 Wheel of Terms

Click the number 7 button to reinforce important terms you learned in this chapter by playing the Shelly Cashman Series version of this popular game. Directions about how to play the game will be displayed. When you are ready to play, click the Play button. Submit your score to your instructor.

8 DC Track and Field

Click the number 8 button to use what you have learned in this chapter to compete against other students in three track and field events. Directions about how to play the game will be displayed. When you are ready to play, click the start first event button. If required, submit your score to your instructor.

9 You're Hired!

Click the number 9 button to use what you have learned in this chapter to embark on the path to a career in computers. Directions about how to play the game will be displayed. When you are ready to play, click the begin game button. If required, submit your score to your instructor.

10 Crossword Puzzle Challenge

Click the number 10 button. Complete the puzzle to reinforce skills you learned in this chapter. Directions about how to play the game will be displayed. When you are ready to play, click the Submit button. Submit the completed puzzle to your instructor.

11 Lab Exercises

Click the number 11 button. When the Lab Exercises menu appears, click the exercise assigned by your instructor. A new browser window will open. Follow the on-screen instructions to complete the exercise. When finished, click the Exit button. If required, submit your results to your instructor.

12 In the News

To spare harried dispatchers, police officers used to request suspect information only when it was urgent. Now, IBM's eNetwork Law Enforcement Express lets officers directly access real-time databases of stolen cars, mug shots, and warrants. With a few taps on a notebook computer keyboard, police officers can search a database to see if a suspect in custody has a past criminal record. They also can find out if a suspect stopped for speeding is wanted for any more serious infractions. Click the number 12 button and read a news article about a database that is being used in a new way. Who is using the database? How is it being used? How will the database benefit the user?

13 Chapter Discussion Forum

Select an objective from this chapter on page 513 about which you would like more information. Click the number 13 button and post a short message listing a meaningful message title accompanied by one or more questions concerning the selected objective. In two days, return to the threaded discussion by clicking the number 13 button. Submit to your instructor your original message and at least one response to your message.

14 Financial Calculators

Click the number 14 button to learn how to use the Internet to calculate a mortgage payment, car payment, or retirement savings. Follow the instructions to use USA Today's Mortgaged calculator to determine what your monthly payment would be on a $150,000 mortgage calculated over 30 years using an interest rate of 5.5%. Use the Autos calculator to figure your monthly payment on a $20,000 auto loan calculated over 60 months using an interest rate of 7.75%. Use the Retirement calculator to determine what type of retirement savings plan will provide you with the most income. Print each calculation result and then submit it to your instructor.

Learn How To

Use the Learn How To activities to learn fundamental skills when using a computer and accompanying technology. Complete the exercises and submit them to your instructor. To see a video of a Learn How To activity, visit scsite.com/dc2007/ch10/howto.

LEARN HOW TO 1: Organize and Manage Files on a Computer

Introduction   In Learn How To 1 in Chapter 3 (page 178), you learned the procedure for saving a file. In this Learn How To activity, you will learn how to manage files using folders and how to find a file if you cannot remember where you saved it.

Folders   A folder is a virtual container where you can store a file on media. When you store any file, the file must be stored in a folder. The folder symbol, together with the folder name, identifies a folder. 📁

You can create folders in a variety of ways. To create a folder on the desktop, complete the following steps:
1. Right-click the desktop in a location that does not contain an icon or toolbar.
2. Point to New on the shortcut menu that is displayed (Figure 10-27).
3. Click Folder on the New submenu.
4. When the folder icon is displayed on the desktop, type the name you want to assign to the folder and then press the ENTER key. You should choose a name that identifies the contents of the folder.

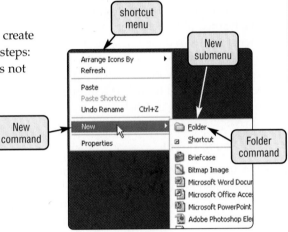

FIGURE 10-27

A folder can contain other folders. This allows you to organize your files in a hierarchical manner so that the highest-level folder contains all the folders for a given subject, and lower-level folders contain more specific files and folders. For example, your highest-level folder could be named Fall Semester. For each class, such as Computer Information Systems 110, you could define a folder within the Fall Semester folder. Within each class folder, you could define folders for each week of the class, or for each project or assignment within the class. In this manner, you would have a set of folders, each designated for a specific use. You then would save your files in the appropriate folder.

To create a folder within a folder, complete the following steps:
1. Double-click the folder name either on the desktop or in the window or dialog box in which the folder name appears.
2. Right-click a blank space in the window that is displayed.
3. Point to New on the shortcut menu that is displayed and then click Folder on the New submenu.
4. When the folder icon is displayed, type the name you want to assign to the folder, and then press the ENTER key.

To delete a folder, complete the following steps:
1. Right-click the folder.
2. On the shortcut menu that is displayed (Figure 10-28), click Delete.
3. In the Confirm Folder Delete dialog box, click the Yes button.

FIGURE 10-28

Learn How To

When you delete a folder, all the files and folders contained in the folder you are deleting, together with all files and folders on the lower hierarchical levels, are deleted. If you accidentally delete a folder, complete the following steps:
1. Double-click the Recycle Bin icon on the desktop.
2. In the Recycle Bin window, select the folder you wish to restore.
3. Click File on the menu bar and then click Restore on the File menu.

Using folders effectively will aid you in keeping track of files you create for your classes.

Exercise

1. Assume you are taking the following courses: Computer Information Systems 120, History 210, English 145, Marketing 221, and Business Law 120. Define the hierarchy of folders you would create for these classes. In which folder would you store an assignment from English 145 that was assigned in the sixth week of class? Submit your answers to your instructor.

LEARN HOW TO 2:   Search for Files and Folders

At times, you might store a file in a folder and then forget where you stored the file. The Search Companion feature of Windows XP enables you to search storage media on a computer to find the file. To use the Search Companion, complete the following steps:
1. Click the Start button on the Windows taskbar.
2. Click Search on the Start menu.
3. Click All files and folders in the What do you want to search for balloon.
4. In the All or part of the file name text box, type the name of the file for which you are searching. If you do not know the entire file name, enter as much of the file name as you can remember. If you do not know any portion of the file name, use the other options in the balloon to provide the search criteria (Figure 10-29).
5. Click the Search button in the balloon.
6. All items containing the file name or partial file name will be displayed in the Search Results window. If the file was not found, a message to that effect is displayed.
7. To open the file you found, double-click the file name in the list. The file will be opened by the appropriate program.
8. Before you close the Search Results window, make a note of the location of the file. If this is not the location where you want the file to be stored, store the file in the correct location.

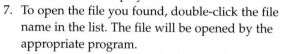

FIGURE 10-29

Exercise

1. Using the Windows XP Search Companion, locate the file named Soap Bubbles. How many file names were returned? Which folder contains the Soap Bubbles file? Submit your answers to your instructor.
2. On the computer you are using, create a hierarchy of folders for your classes. Create a WordPad file that contains the following text: `This file will be found using Search Companion.` Save the file in one of the folders using a file name of your choice. Using Search Companion, search for the file you just created. How many files were returned from your search? Delete all folders and files you created in this exercise. Write a paragraph describing the steps you will take to organize your files for the coming semester. Submit your responses to your instructor.

Web Research

Use the Internet-based Web Research exercises to broaden your understanding of the concepts presented in this chapter. Visit scsite.com/dc2007/ch10/research to obtain more information pertaining to each exercise. To discuss any of the Web Research exercises in this chapter with other students, post your thoughts or questions at scsite.com/dc2007/ch10/forum.

① Scavenger Hunt   Use one of the search engines listed in Figure 2-10 in Chapter 2 on page 78 or your own favorite search engine to find the answers to the questions that follow. Copy and paste the Web address from the Web page where you found the answer. Some questions may have more than one answer. If required, submit your answers to your instructor. (1) How does click-stream analysis examine data from Web site usage patterns? (2) What geographic information system (GIS) functions does ArcExplorer perform? (3) What company that was incorporated in 1911 developed the relational database? (4) What query language did the System R database system develop? (5) What is the purpose of the European Union (EU) directive?

② Search Sleuth   Major United States newspapers helped design Clusty the Clustering Engine (clusty.com). One of its unique features is returning search results for Web sites, news stories, images, and shopping sites in clusters, which are categories of folders, along with a list of links. Visit this Web site and then use your word processing program to answer the following questions. Then, if required, submit your answers to your instructor. (1) Click the Web+ tab, click the Request text box, and then type `relational database` in the box. Click the Cluster button. Browse the clusters on the left side of the page and then expand the Applications cluster by clicking the + icon next to the Applications link. (2) Click the Wikipedia tab. What is one definition retrieved and its source? (3) Click the News tab and then click the News Page link. What are two stories listed in the Top News category? (4) Click two links in the Business category and review the articles. Write a 50-word summary of your findings.

③ Journaling   Respond to your readings in this chapter by writing at least one page about your reactions, evaluations, and reflections on databases. For example, have you created a database to store details about your movie and music collections? Have you shopped online and accessed a merchant's database? Have you experienced problems with data integrity and tried to correct errors? Should Americans have a national identification card? You also can write about the new terms you learned by reading this chapter. If required, submit your journal to your instructor.

④ Expanding Your Understanding   Public records contain details about professional licenses, civil court filings, adoptions, foreclosures, driving records, and much other personal data. The Internet makes searching for this data quite easy, and many of the databases can be browsed for free. One of the more comprehensive free public records databases is the Search Systems Public Records Directories. View Web sites to learn more about searching public records. Which databases are free, and which require a subscription fee? What state records are available where you live? Write a report summarizing your findings, focusing on searching the public records databases. If required, submit your report to your instructor.

⑤ Ethics in Action   When you shop online, enter contests, and complete warranty registration cards, businesses automatically store data about you and your transactions in a marketing database. They often use this data to analyze sales and develop advertising campaigns. Unbeknownst to many consumers, some companies also sell this data to third parties for financial gain. Consumers can refuse to receive targeted e-mail messages and marketing materials, but they actively must search the Web sites or paper forms for check boxes to indicate these opt-out preferences. Some privacy experts, however, view this practice as unethical and urge businesses to default to not adding consumers' information to databases unless the consumer opts in to receive additional materials. View online sites that include opt-in or opt-out provisions. Write a report summarizing your findings, and include a table of links to Web sites that provide additional details about protecting consumers' data. If required, submit your report to your instructor.

Case Studies

Use the Case Studies to apply the concepts presented in the chapter to real-world situations. Visit scsite.com/dc2007/ch10/cases to obtain more information pertaining to each exercise. To discuss the Case Studies in this chapter with other students, visit scsite.com/dc2007/ch10/forum and post your thoughts or questions.

CASE STUDY 1 — Class Discussion   While attending college, you work 20 hours a week as an instructor's assistant. You earn $8.00 an hour and are paid every two weeks. You recently received a payroll check that was $160.00 less than you expected for 40 hours of work. What error do you think the data entry clerk made that resulted in the wrong check being generated? Errors such as the one illustrated here show why <u>data integrity</u> is as important to a successful information management system as the hardware and software being used. The phrase garbage in, garbage out (GIGO) has been used to explain that you cannot create correct information from incorrect data. Write a brief report that includes your suggestion regarding the error made by the data entry clerk, and summarize the various data validation techniques described in this chapter. Be prepared to discuss your findings in class.

CASE STUDY 2 — Class Discussion   Reviews of movies on a video store's new release shelf are fairly easy to find, but critiques of other movies in stock may be less accessible. To help film buffs, information on more than 100,000 movie titles is available from a database on the World Wide Web. The Internet Movie Database Ltd. can be searched using a movie's title, cast members, year produced, characters, genre, awards, or other criteria. Each movie's page offers a brief description and rating and includes links to such items as stars, summary, trivia, reviews, quotes, goofs, and recommendations. Visit the movie database and write a brief report outlining how visitors can <u>query</u> the movie database. Search for several movies. How complete was the information provided? Who would benefit most from using the movie database? Why? Be prepared to discuss your findings in class.

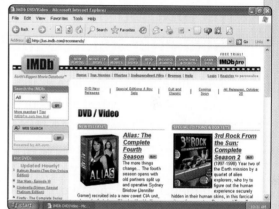

CASE STUDY 3 — Research   While taking computer classes at the local community college, you also work as a data entry clerk for a restaurant supply company. The company uses a network of personal computers and a twenty-year-old file processing system to handle its applications. Your supervisor has been told that it is time to convert the file processing system to a modern <u>database management system</u>. Because you are taking computer classes, he has asked you to submit an initial report that summarizes the features of three database management systems — Access, Visual FoxPro, and Oracle. Use the Web and/or print media to complete your evaluation. Which system is the least expensive to purchase? Which one offers the easiest conversion? Which one offers a query language, query by example, forms, a report generator, and backup and recovery procedures? Submit your report or use PowerPoint to create a presentation and share your findings with your class.

CASE STUDY 4 — Research   You recently were hired as a student intern to assist a local insurance agency in reorganizing their customer files. The agency employs a file processing system to maintain three distinct customer files — billing, claims, and promotion. The manager indicates that data entry has become unwieldy because of unclear relationships between data and data redundancy. Furthermore, customers are complaining about inconsistencies in the information they receive. The problem is beginning to affect business in a negative way. As a first step, she has asked you to prepare a report summarizing the benefits of <u>normalizing</u> the data in the three files. Use the Web and/or print media and High-Tech Talk on page 540 to gain an understanding of the normalization process. What is zero normal form? First normal form? Second normal form? Third normal form? Define and give an example of each of the following terms: data redundancy, primary key, and repeating group. Write a brief report or use PowerPoint to create a presentation and share your findings with your class.

CASE STUDY 5 – Team Challenge   When deciding on which database management system to use, companies have a choice of three <u>data models</u> — relational, object-oriented, and multidimensional. A major retail company has hired your team as database specialists to determine the data model best suited for their applications. Form a three-member team and have each team member choose a different data model. Have each member use the Web and/or print media to develop a feature/benefit report for each data model. Does the data model allow for query by example? How does the data model allow users to manage, update, and retrieve data? As a team, merge your findings into a team report and/or PowerPoint presentation and share your findings with your class.

CHAPTER ELEVEN

Computer Security, Ethics, and Privacy

Picture Yourself Aware of Computer-Related Risks

According to the old adage, things happen in threes. If that is true, your streak of bad luck is over because you plan to prevent each of these three situations from ever occurring again.

While working at your computer last week, you received an e-mail message from your credit card company (or so you thought). The message explained that your account temporarily would be unavailable until you updated some information. You clicked a link to display what appeared to be the credit card company's Web page. You entered your credit card number, name, address, and telephone number. Unfortunately, you supplied enough information to the scammer who later used the information to make purchases in your name.

During a severe storm yesterday, a lightning strike caused a loss of power in your house. Once power was restored, you discovered that your printer no longer worked. After talking with a technician, you learned the printer will need to be replaced because it was damaged by a power surge.

At the doctor's office this morning, you were diagnosed with tendonitis in your arm. She said the tendonitis was caused from improperly using the mouse while working on the computer.

Each of these unfortunate incidents taught you valuable lessons about safeguarding against identity theft, protecting computers and devices, and preventing computer-related health injuries. Read Chapter 11 to learn about these and many other computer safeguards.

OBJECTIVES

After completing this chapter, you will be able to:

1. Describe the types of computer security risks
2. Identify ways to safeguard against computer viruses, worms, Trojan horses, denial of service attacks, back doors, and spoofing
3. Discuss techniques to prevent unauthorized computer access and use
4. Identify safeguards against hardware theft and vandalism
5. Explain the ways software manufacturers protect against software piracy
6. Define encryption and explain why it is necessary
7. Discuss the types of devices available that protect computers from system failure
8. Explain the options available for backing up computer resources
9. Identify risks and safeguards associated with wireless communications
10. Recognize issues related to information accuracy, rights, and conduct
11. Discuss issues surrounding information privacy
12. Discuss ways to prevent health-related disorders and injuries due to computer use

CONTENTS

Encrypting Credit Card Data...

EUROCARD

MasterCard

COMPUTER SECURITY RISKS

Today, people rely on computers to create, store, and manage critical information. Thus, it is important that the computers and the data they store are accessible and available when needed. It also is crucial that users take measures to protect their computers and data from loss, damage, and misuse. For example, businesses must ensure that information such as credit records, employee and customer data, and purchase information is secure and confidential. Home users must ensure that their credit card number is secure when they use it to purchase goods and services from Web-based businesses.

A **computer security risk** is any event or action that could cause a loss of or damage to computer hardware, software, data, information, or processing capability. Some breaches to computer security are accidental. Others are planned intrusions. Some intruders do no damage; they merely access data, information, or programs on the computer before logging off. Other intruders indicate some evidence of their presence either by leaving a message or by deliberately altering or damaging data.

An intentional breach of computer security often involves a deliberate act that is against the law. Any illegal act involving a computer generally is referred to as a **computer crime**. The term **cybercrime** refers to online or Internet-based illegal acts. Today, cybercrime is one of the FBI's top three priorities.

Perpetrators of cybercrime and other intrusions fall into seven basic categories: hacker, cracker, script kiddie, corporate spy, unethical employee, cyberextortionist, and cyberterrorist.

- The term **hacker**, although originally a complimentary word for a computer enthusiast, now has a derogatory meaning and refers to someone who accesses a computer or network illegally. Hackers often claim the intent of their security breaches is to improve security.
- A **cracker** also is someone who accesses a computer or network illegally but has the intent of destroying data, stealing information, or other malicious action. Both hackers and crackers have advanced computer and network skills.
- A **script kiddie** has the same intent as a cracker but does not have the technical skills

and knowledge. Script kiddies often are teenagers that use prewritten hacking and cracking programs to break into computers.
- Some corporate spies have excellent computer and network skills and are hired to break into a specific computer and steal its proprietary data and information. Unscrupulous companies hire corporate spies, a practice known as corporate espionage, to gain a competitive advantage.
- Unethical employees break into their employers' computers for a variety of reasons. Some simply want to exploit a security weakness. Others seek financial gains from selling confidential information. Disgruntled employees may want revenge.

Internet and network attacks

"Attacked by Sasser"

system failure

Credit Card
Credit Card Nu
Exp. Date
Name:

STOLEN IDENTITY

information theft

- A **cyberextortionist** is someone who uses e-mail as a vehicle for extortion. These perpetrators send a company a threatening e-mail message indicating they will expose confidential information, exploit a security flaw, or launch an attack that will compromise the company's network — if they are not paid a sum of money.
- A **cyberterrorist** is someone who uses the Internet or network to destroy or damage computers for political reasons. The extensive damage might destroy the nation's air traffic control system, electricity-generating companies, or a telecommunications infrastructure.

Cyberterrorism usually requires a team of highly skilled individuals, millions of dollars, and several years of planning.

Business and home users must protect, or safeguard, their computers from breaches of security and other computer security risks. The more common computer security risks include Internet and network attacks, unauthorized access and use, hardware theft, software theft, information theft, and system failure (Figure 11-1). The following pages describe these computer security risks and also discuss safeguards users might take to minimize or prevent their consequences.

unauthorized access and use

hardware theft

STOLEN COMPUTER

software theft

ILLEGAL COPYING

FIGURE 11-1 Computers are exposed to several types of security risks.

INTERNET AND NETWORK ATTACKS

Information transmitted over networks has a higher degree of security risk than information kept on a company's premises. In a business, network administrators usually take measures to protect a network from security risks. On the Internet, where no central administrator is present, the security risk is greater.

To determine if your computer is vulnerable to an Internet or network attack, you could use an online security service. An **online security service** is a Web site that evaluates your computer to check for Internet and e-mail vulnerabilities. The service then provides recommendations of how to address the vulnerabilities.

Companies and individuals requiring assistance or information about Internet security breaches can contact or visit the Web site for the *Computer Emergency Response Team Coordination Center*, or *CERT/CC*, which is a federally funded Internet security research and development center.

Internet and network attacks that jeopardize security include computer viruses, worms, and Trojan horses; denial of service attacks; and spoofing. The following pages address these computer security risks and suggest measures businesses and individuals can take to protect their computers while on the Internet or connected to a network.

Computer Viruses, Worms, and Trojan Horses

Every unprotected computer is susceptible to the first type of computer security risk — a computer virus, worm, and/or Trojan horse.
- A computer **virus** is a potentially damaging computer program that affects, or infects, a computer negatively by altering the way the computer works without the user's knowledge or permission. Once the virus infects the computer, it can spread throughout and may damage files and system software, including the operating system.
- A **worm** is a program that copies itself repeatedly, for example in memory or on a network, using up resources and possibly shutting down the computer or network.
- A **Trojan horse** (named after the Greek myth) is a program that hides within or looks like a legitimate program. A certain condition or action usually triggers the Trojan horse. Unlike a virus or worm, a Trojan horse does not replicate itself to other computers.

Computer viruses, worms, and Trojan horses are classified as *malware* (short for *malicious software*), which are programs that act without a user's knowledge and deliberately alter the computer's operations. Other classes of malware include back doors and spyware, which are discussed later in this chapter. Although malware often falls in one of these classes (virus, worm, Trojan horse, back door, or spyware), some malware has characteristics of two or more classes. For example, MyDoom and Blaster are worms; Melissa has elements of a virus, worm, and Trojan horse.

Unscrupulous programmers write malware and then test it to ensure it can deliver its payload (read Ethics & Issues 11-1 for a related discussion). The *payload* is the destructive event or prank the program is intended to deliver. A computer infected by a virus, worm, or Trojan horse often has one or more of the following symptoms:
- Screen displays unusual message or image
- Music or unusual sound plays randomly
- Available memory is less than expected
- Existing programs and files disappear
- Files become corrupted

ETHICS & ISSUES 11-1

How Should Virus Authors Be Punished?

Recently, the author of an Internet virus that caused millions or billions of dollars in alleged damages pleaded guilty to the crime and faced 18 to 37 months in prison — about the same as that for auto theft. The author of the Sasser worm, which shut down an airline, hospitals, and government agencies, was sentenced to 21 months of probation after causing a similar amount of damage. Many experts and computer administrators claim that the punishment for the crime is out of proportion with the damages caused by the crime. Some legal experts claim that lax security on the part of Internet users is to blame, and perhaps those who help to spread the viruses via lax security should be punished as well. Others claim that some companies provide exorbitant estimates of true damages that viruses cause and that these alleged damages provoke an emotional overreaction to the crimes. The types of crimes and international extent of possible damages is relatively new territory in criminal law. Should the government create new laws specifically aimed at punishing those who spread viruses and worms? Why or why not? Should virus authors be punished in proportion to the alleged damages that they cause? Why or why not? Because the Internet is an international medium, how should countries coordinate law enforcement and punishment for virus authors?

- Programs or files do not work properly
- Unknown programs or files mysteriously appear
- System properties change

Computer viruses, worms, and Trojan horses deliver their payload on a computer in four basic ways: when a user (1) opens an infected file, (2) runs an infected program, (3) boots the computer with infected removable media inserted in a drive or plugged in a port, or (4) connects an unprotected computer to a network. Today, a common way computers become infected with viruses, worms, and Trojan horses is through users opening infected e-mail attachments. Figure 11-2 shows how a virus can spread from one computer to another through an infected e-mail attachment.

Currently, more than 81,000 known viruses, worms, and Trojan horse programs exist with an estimated 6 new programs discovered each day. Many Web sites maintain lists of all known viruses, worms, and Trojan horses. For a technical discussion about viruses, worms, and Trojan horses, read the High-Tech Talk article on page 168 in Chapter 3.

FAQ 11-1

How long is an unprotected computer safe from intruders?

One security expert maintains that 50 percent of unprotected computers are compromised by an intruder within 12 minutes. Slammer and Nimda, two devastating worms, wreaked worldwide havoc in 10 and 30 minutes, respectively. For more information, visit scsite.com/dc2007/ch11/faq and then click Viruses and Worms.

FIGURE 11-2 HOW A VIRUS CAN SPREAD THROUGH AN E-MAIL MESSAGE

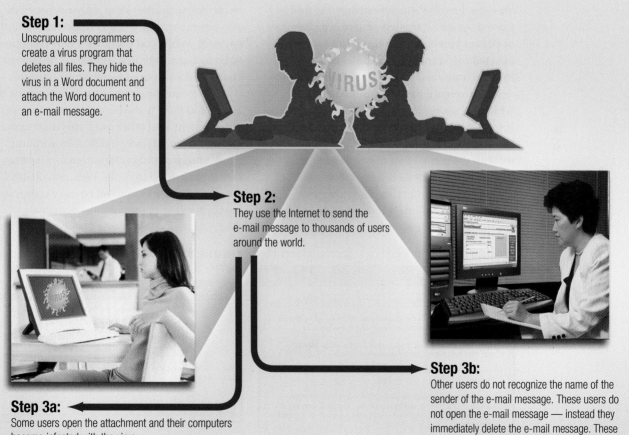

Step 1:
Unscrupulous programmers create a virus program that deletes all files. They hide the virus in a Word document and attach the Word document to an e-mail message.

Step 2:
They use the Internet to send the e-mail message to thousands of users around the world.

Step 3a:
Some users open the attachment and their computers become infected with the virus.

Step 3b:
Other users do not recognize the name of the sender of the e-mail message. These users do not open the e-mail message — instead they immediately delete the e-mail message. These users' computers are not infected with the virus.

Safeguards against Computer Viruses, Worms, and Trojan Horses

Methods that guarantee a computer or network is safe from computer viruses, worms, and Trojan horses simply do not exist. Users can take several precautions, however, to protect their home and work computers from these malicious infections. The following paragraphs discuss these precautionary measures.

Do not start a computer with removable media inserted in the drives or plugged in the ports. That is, CD and DVD drives should be empty, a USB port should not contain a USB flash drive, etc. During the startup process, a computer may attempt to execute the boot sector on media in certain drives and ports. Even if the attempt is unsuccessful, any virus on the boot sector of removable media can infect the computer's hard disk. If you must start the computer with media in a drive or port, be certain the media is uninfected.

Never open an e-mail attachment unless you are expecting the attachment *and* it is from a trusted source. A **trusted source** is a company or person you believe will not send a virus-infected file knowingly. If the e-mail message is from an unknown source or untrusted source, delete the e-mail message immediately — without opening or executing any attachments. If the e-mail message is from a trusted source, but you were not expecting an attachment, verify with the source that they intended to send you an attachment — before opening it.

Many e-mail programs allow users to preview an e-mail message before or without opening it. Some viruses and worms can deliver their payload when a user simply previews the message. Thus, you should turn off message preview in your e-mail program.

Some viruses are hidden in *macros*, which are instructions saved in an application such as a word processing or spreadsheet program. In applications that allow users to write macros, you should set the macro security level to medium (Figure 11-3a). With a medium security level, the application software warns users that a document they are attempting to open contains a macro (Figure 11-3b). From this warning, a user chooses to disable or enable the macro. If the document is from a trusted source, the user can enable the macro. Otherwise, it should be disabled.

Users should install an antivirus program and update it frequently. As discussed in Chapter 8, an **antivirus program** protects a computer against viruses by identifying and removing any computer viruses found in memory, on storage media, or on incoming files. Most antivirus programs also protect against worms, Trojan horses, and spyware. When you purchase a new computer, it often includes antivirus software. The table in Figure 11-4 lists popular antivirus programs.

An antivirus program scans for programs that attempt to modify the boot program, the operating system, and other programs that normally are read from but not modified. In addition, many antivirus programs automatically scan files downloaded from the Web, e-mail attachments, opened files, and all types of removable media inserted in the computer.

FIGURE 11-3a   (dialog box to set macro security)

FIGURE 11-3b   (warning is displayed because security is set to medium)

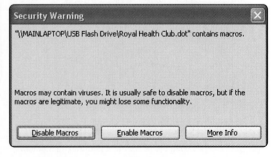

FIGURE 11-3   Many application programs, such as Microsoft Word, allow users to set security levels for macros. To display the dialog box shown in Figure 11-3a in Word, click Tools on the menu bar, point to Macro, and then click Security.

POPULAR ANTIVIRUS PROGRAMS

- AVG Anti-Virus
- eTrust EZ Antivirus
- F-Secure Anti-Virus
- Kaspersky Anti-Virus Personal
- McAfee VirusScan
- Norton AntiVirus
- Trend Micro PC-cillin
- Vexira Antivirus

FIGURE 11-4 Popular antivirus programs.

One technique that antivirus programs use to identify a virus is to look for virus signatures. A **virus signature**, also called a **virus definition**, is a known specific pattern of virus code. Computer users should update their antivirus program's signature files regularly. Updating signature files downloads any new virus definitions that have been added since the last update (Figure 11-5). This extremely important activity allows the antivirus program to protect against viruses written since the antivirus program was released. Most antivirus programs contain an automatic update feature that regularly prompts users to download the virus signature. The vendor usually provides this service to registered users at no cost for a specified time.

Another technique that antivirus programs use to detect viruses is to inoculate existing program files. To **inoculate** a program file, the antivirus program records information such as the file size and file creation date in a separate inoculation file. The antivirus program then uses this information to detect if a virus tampers with the data describing the inoculated program file.

If an antivirus program identifies an infected file, it attempts to remove its virus, worm, or Trojan horse. If the antivirus program cannot remove the infection, it often quarantines the infected file. A **quarantine** is a separate area of a hard disk that holds the infected file until the infection can be removed. This step ensures other files will not become infected. Users also can quarantine suspicious files themselves.

In extreme cases, you may need to reformat the hard disk to remove a virus. Having uninfected, or clean, backups of all files is important. A later section in this chapter covers backup and restore techniques in detail.

In addition to an antivirus program, users often install a personal firewall program to protect a computer and its data from unauthorized intrusions. A later section discusses firewalls.

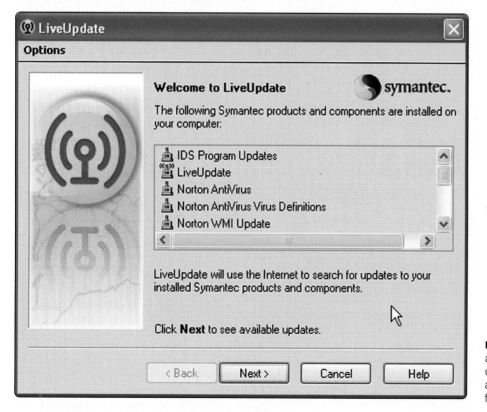

FIGURE 11-5 Many vendors of antivirus programs allow registered users to update virus signature files automatically from the Web at no cost for a specified time.

Finally, stay informed about new virus alerts and virus hoaxes. A **virus hoax** is an e-mail message that warns users of a nonexistent virus, worm, or Trojan horse. Often, these virus hoaxes are in the form of a chain letter that requests the user to send a copy of the e-mail message to as many people as possible. Instead of forwarding the message, visit a Web site that publishes a list of virus alerts and virus hoaxes.

The list in Figure 11-6 summarizes important tips for protecting your computer from virus, worm, and Trojan horse infection.

WEB LINK 11-2

Virus Hoaxes

For more information, visit scsite.com/dc2007/ch11/weblink and then click Virus Hoaxes.

FAQ 11-2

Should I inform others if my computer gets a virus, worm, or Trojan horse?

If you share data with other users, such as via e-mail attachments, instant message attachments, or removable media, then you should inform these users of your virus, worm, or Trojan horse infection. This courteous gesture allows fellow users to check their computers for the same type of infection. Be careful not to spread the virus inadvertently. For more information, visit scsite.com/dc2007/ch11/faq and then click Safeguards against Viruses, Worms, and Trojan Horses.

TIPS FOR PREVENTING VIRUS, WORM, AND TROJAN HORSE INFECTIONS

1. Never start a computer with removable media inserted in the drives or plugged in the ports, unless the media is uninfected.
2. Never open an e-mail attachment unless you are expecting it *and* it is from a trusted source. Turn off message preview.
3. Set the macro security in programs so you can enable or disable macros. Enable macros only if the document is from a trusted source and you are expecting it.
4. Install an antivirus program on all of your computers. Obtain updates to the virus signature files on a regular basis.
5. Check all downloaded programs for viruses, worms, or Trojan horses. This malware often is placed in seemingly innocent programs, so it will affect a large number of users.
6. If the antivirus program flags an e-mail attachment as infected, delete the attachment immediately.
7. Before using any removable media, use the antivirus scan program to check the media for infection. Incorporate this procedure even for shrink-wrapped software from major developers. Some commercial software has been infected and distributed to unsuspecting users this way.
8. Install a personal firewall program.

FIGURE 11-6 With the growing number of new viruses, worms, and Trojan horses, it is crucial that users take steps to protect their computers.

Denial of Service Attacks

A **denial of service attack**, or **DoS attack**, is an assault whose purpose is to disrupt computer access to an Internet service such as the Web or e-mail. Perpetrators carry out a DoS attack in a variety of ways. For example, they may use an unsuspecting computer to send an influx of confusing data messages or useless traffic to a computer network. The victim computer network eventually jams, blocking legitimate visitors from accessing the network.

A more devastating type of DoS attack is the *DDoS (distributed DoS) attack*, in which multiple unsuspecting computers are used to attack multiple computer networks. DDoS attacks have been able to stop operations temporarily at numerous Web sites, including powerhouses such as Yahoo!, Amazon.com, eBay, and CNN.com.

Some perpetrators use zombies to execute a DoS or DDoS attack. A **zombie** is a computer that is completely unaware it is being used as part of a network that attacks other systems.

FAQ 11-3

How many computers are zombies?

One study estimated that computers in United States accounted for 18 percent of zombies worldwide. For more information, visit scsite.com/dc2007/ch11/faq and then click Zombies.

Back Doors

A **back door** is a program or set of instructions in a program that allow users to bypass security controls when accessing a program, computer, or network. Once perpetrators gain access to unsecure computers, they often install a back door or modify an existing program to include a back door, which allows them to continue to access the computer remotely without the user's knowledge. Some worms leave back doors, which have been used to spread other worms or to distribute junk e-mail from the unsuspecting victim computers.

Programmers often build back doors into programs during system development. These back doors save development time because the programmer can bypass security controls while writing and testing programs. If the programmer fails to remove the back door before releasing the software, a perpetrator could use the back door to gain entry to a computer or network.

Spoofing

Spoofing is a technique intruders use to make their network or Internet transmission appear legitimate to a victim computer or network. Several types of spoofing schemes exist. One type, called IP spoofing, occurs when an intruder computer fools a network into believing its IP address is associated with a trusted source.

Perpetrators of IP spoofing trick their victims into interacting with the phony Web site. For example, the victim may provide confidential information or download files containing viruses, worms, or other malware.

Safeguards against DoS Attacks, Back Doors, and IP Spoofing

Some of the latest antivirus programs include provisions to protect a computer from DoS and DDoS attacks. To further defend against these and other Internet and network attacks, users can implement firewall solutions, install intrusion detection software, and set up honeypots.

Firewalls

A **firewall** is hardware and/or software that protects a network's resources from intrusion by users on another network such as the Internet (Figure 11-7). All networked and online computer users should implement a firewall solution.

Companies use firewalls to protect network resources from outsiders and to restrict employees' access to sensitive data such as payroll or personnel records. Businesses can implement a firewall solution themselves or outsource their needs to a company specializing in providing firewall protection.

Large companies often route all their communications through a proxy server, which typically is a component of the firewall. A *proxy server* is a server outside the company's network that controls which communications pass into the company's network. That is, the proxy server carefully screens all incoming and outgoing messages. Proxy servers use a variety of screening techniques. Some check the domain name or IP address of the message for legitimacy. Others require that the messages have digital signatures. A section later in this chapter discusses digital signatures.

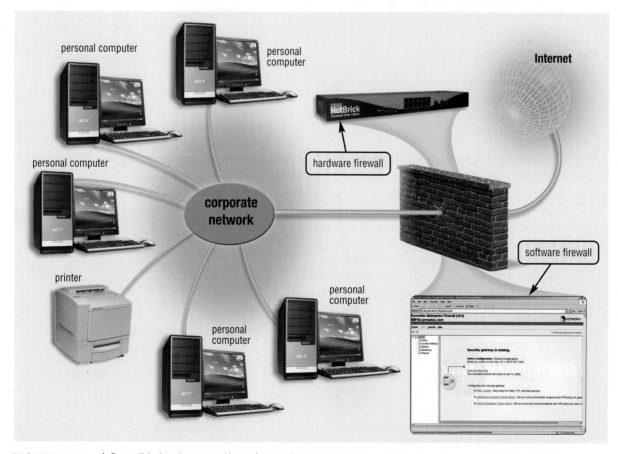

FIGURE 11-7 A firewall is hardware and/or software that protects a network's resources from intrusion by users on another network such as the Internet.

Home and small office/home office users often protect their computers with a personal firewall. As discussed in Chapter 8, a **personal firewall** is a utility that detects and protects a personal computer and its data from unauthorized intrusions. Personal firewalls constantly monitor all transmissions to and from the computer and inform you of any attempted intrusion. Some operating systems, such as Windows XP, include personal firewalls. For enhanced firewall protection, many users purchase stand-alone personal firewall software (Figure 11-8), usually for less than $50.

Some small office/home office users purchase a hardware firewall, such as a router or other device that has a built-in firewall, in addition to or instead of personal firewall software. Hardware firewalls stop intrusions before they break in your computer.

WEB LINK 11-3

Personal Firewall Software

For more information, visit scsite.com/ dc2007/ch11/weblink and then click Personal Firewall Software.

PERSONAL FIREWALL SOFTWARE
BlackICE PC Protection
McAfee Personal Firewall Plus
Norton Personal Firewall
Sygate Personal Firewall Pro
Tiny Personal Firewall
ZoneAlarm Pro

FIGURE 11-8 Popular personal firewall software.

Intrusion Detection Software

To provide extra protection against hackers and other intruders, large companies sometimes use intrusion detection software to identify possible security breaches. *Intrusion detection software* automatically analyzes all network traffic, assesses system vulnerabilities, identifies any unauthorized intrusions, and notifies network administrators of suspicious behavior patterns or system breaches.

To utilize intrusion detection software requires the expertise of a network administrator because the programs are complex and difficult to use and interpret. These programs also are quite expensive. This software, however, when combined with a firewall, provides an added layer of protection to companies with highly sensitive data such as credit card databases.

Honeypots

Some companies and organizations use honeypots so they can analyze an attack being perpetrated. A *honeypot* is a vulnerable computer that is set up to entice an intruder to break into it. These computers, which appear real to the intruder, actually are separated safely from the company or organization's network. Honeypots allow the company or organization to learn how intruders are exploiting their network and also attempt to catch perpetrators who have been doing damage elsewhere on their network. Large Web hosting companies, such as Yahoo! and AT&T, and law enforcement agencies frequently use honeypots.

UNAUTHORIZED ACCESS AND USE

Another type of computer security risk is unauthorized access and use. **Unauthorized access** is the use of a computer or network without permission. **Unauthorized use** is the use of a computer or its data for unapproved or possibly illegal activities. Unauthorized use includes a variety of activities: an employee using an organization's computer to send personal e-mail messages, an employee using the organization's word processing software to track his or her child's soccer league scores, or someone gaining access to a bank computer and performing an unauthorized transfer. For the home user, most unauthorized use occurs on computers that have always-on Internet connections, such as through Internet cable or DSL.

FAQ 11-4

Why do hackers and other intruders want to access my home computer?

Some hackers and other intruders access home computers to use the computer's resources to spread malicious code, carry out a DoS attack, or get away with other nefarious acts. Once they break into your home computer, these intruders often install a back door so they can continue to use your computer as a launching pad for their activities. For more information, visit scsite.com/dc2007/ch11/faq and then click Protecting Home Computers.

Safeguards against Unauthorized Access and Use

Companies take several measures to help prevent unauthorized access and use. At a minimum, they should have a written acceptable use policy (AUP) that outlines the computer activities for which the computer and network may and may not be used. A company's AUP should specify the acceptable use of computers by employees for personal reasons. Some companies prohibit such use entirely. Others allow personal use on the employee's own time such as a lunch hour. Whatever the policy, a company should document and explain it to employees.

To protect your personal computer from unauthorized intrusions, you should disable file and printer sharing on your Internet connection (Figure 11-9). This security measure attempts to ensure that others cannot access your files or your printer. To display the dialog box shown in Figure 11-9 in Windows XP, click the Start button on the taskbar, point to All Programs, point to Accessories, point to Communications, and then click Network Connections. Right-click the appropriate network connection in the list and then click Properties on the shortcut menu.

Other measures that safeguard against unauthorized access and use include firewalls and intrusion detection software, which were discussed in the previous section, and identifying and authenticating users.

FAQ 11-5

Are Stand-Alone Browsers More Secure?

Some users believe that a browser independent of the operating system, such as Firefox or Opera, is more secure than a browser built in an operating system, such as Internet Explorer. For more information, visit scsite.com/dc2007/ch11/faq and then click Browser Security.

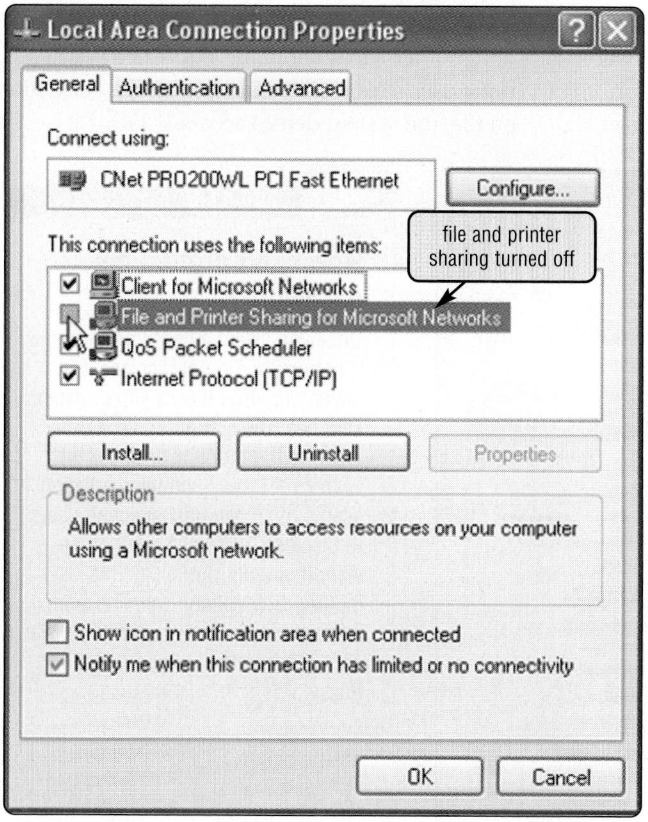

Identifying and Authenticating Users

Many companies use access controls to minimize the chance that a perpetrator intentionally may access or an employee accidentally may access confidential information on a computer. An *access control* is a security measure that defines who can access a computer, when they can access it, and what actions they can take while accessing the computer. In addition, the computer should maintain an **audit trail** that records in a file both successful and unsuccessful access attempts. An unsuccessful access attempt could result from a user mistyping his or her password, or it could result from a hacker trying thousands of passwords.

Companies should investigate unsuccessful access attempts immediately to ensure they are not intentional breaches of security. They also should review successful access for irregularities, such as use of the computer after normal working hours or from remote computers. In addition, a company regularly should review users' access privilege levels to determine whether they still are appropriate.

FIGURE 11-9 To protect files on your local hard disk from hackers and other intruders, turn off file and printer sharing on your Internet connection.

Many systems implement access controls using a two-phase process called identification and authentication. *Identification* verifies that an individual is a valid user. *Authentication* verifies that the individual is the person he or she claims to be. Three methods of identification and authentication include user names and passwords, possessed objects, and biometric devices. The technique(s) a company uses should correspond to the degree of risk associated with the unauthorized access. The following paragraphs discuss each of the identification and authentication methods.

USER NAMES AND PASSWORDS   A **user name**, or *user ID* (identification), is a unique combination of characters, such as letters of the alphabet or numbers, that identifies one specific user. A **password** is a private combination of characters associated with the user name that allows access to certain computer resources.

Most multiuser (networked) operating systems require that users correctly enter a user name and a password before they can access the data, information, and programs stored on a computer or network. Many other systems that maintain financial, personal, and other confidential information also require a user name and password as part of their logon procedure (Figure 11-10).

Some systems assign a user name or user ID to each user. For example, a school may use the student identification number as a user ID. With other systems, users select their own user name or user ID. Many users select a combination of their first and last names.

Most systems require that users select their own passwords. Users typically choose an easy-to-remember word or series of characters for passwords. If your password is too obvious, however, such as your initials or birthday, others can guess it easily. Easy passwords make it simple for hackers and other intruders to break into a system. Hackers use computer automated tools to assist them with guessing passwords. Thus, you should select a password carefully. Longer passwords provide greater security than shorter ones. Each character added to a password significantly increases the number of possible combinations and the length of time it might take for someone or for a hacker's computer to guess the password (Figure 11-11).

In addition to a user name and password, some systems ask users to enter one of several pieces of personal information. Such items can include a spouse's first name, a birth date, a place of birth, or a mother's maiden name. As with a password, if the user's response does not match information on file, the system denies access.

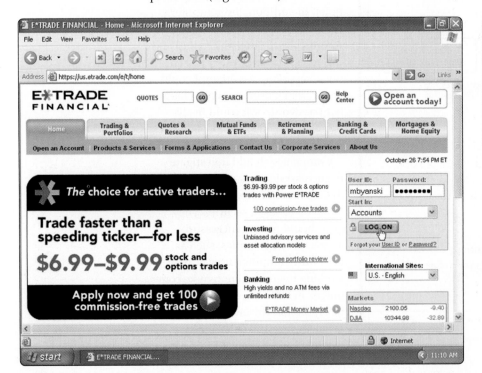

FIGURE 11-10   Many Web sites that maintain personal and confidential data require a user to enter a user name (user ID) and password.

PASSWORD PROTECTION

Number of Characters	Possible Combinations	AVERAGE TIME TO DISCOVER	
		Human	Computer
1	36	3 minutes	.000018 second
2	1,300	2 hours	.00065 second
3	47,000	3 days	.02 second
4	1,700,000	3 months	1 second
5	60,000,000	10 years	30 seconds
10	3,700,000,000,000,000	580 million years	59 years

- Possible characters include the letters A–Z and numbers 0–9
- Human discovery assumes 1 try every 10 seconds
- Computer discovery assumes 1 million tries per second
- Average time assumes the password would be discovered in approximately half the time it would take to try all possible combinations

FIGURE 11-11   This table shows the effect of increasing the length of a password that consists of letters and numbers. The longer the password, the more effort required to discover it. Long passwords, however, are more difficult for users to remember.

POSSESSED OBJECTS   A *possessed object* is any item that you must carry to gain access to a computer or computer facility. Examples of possessed objects are badges, cards, smart cards, and keys. The card you use in an automated teller machine (ATM) is a possessed object that allows access to your bank account (Figure 11-12).

FIGURE 11-12   The card you use in an automated teller machine (ATM) is a possessed object that allows access to your bank account.

Possessed objects often are used in combination with personal identification numbers. A **personal identification number (PIN)** is a numeric password, either assigned by a company or selected by a user. PINs provide an additional level of security. An ATM card typically requires a four-digit PIN. Most debit cards and some credit cards use PINs. If someone steals these cards, the thief must enter the user's PIN to access the account. PINs are passwords. Select them carefully and protect them as you do any other password.

BIOMETRIC DEVICES   As Chapter 5 discussed, a **biometric device** authenticates a person's identity by translating a personal characteristic, such as a fingerprint, into a digital code that then is compared with a digital code stored in the computer verifying a physical or behavioral characteristic. If the digital code in the computer does not match the personal characteristic code, the computer denies access to the individual.

Biometric devices grant access to programs, computers, or rooms using computer analysis of some biometric identifier. Examples of biometric devices and systems include fingerprint scanners (Figure 11-13), hand geometry systems, face recognition systems, voice verification systems, signature verification systems, iris recognition systems, and retinal scanners. Read Looking Ahead 11-1 for a look at the next generation of face recognition systems.

Biometric devices are gaining popularity as a security precaution because they are a virtually foolproof method of identification and authentication (read Ethics & Issues 11-2 for a related discussion). Users can forget their user names and passwords. Possessed objects can be lost, copied, duplicated, or stolen. Personal characteristics, by contrast, are unique and cannot be forgotten or misplaced.

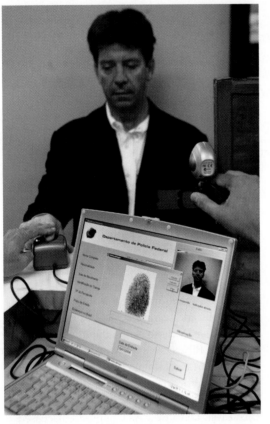

FIGURE 11-13   A fingerprint scanner verifies this traveler's identity.

ETHICS & ISSUES 11-2

Should Schools Use Biometric Devices?

Several school systems now require that students use a biometric thumbprint to pay for their school lunches. The school administrators cite the need to better track the number of free and subsidized lunches that the schools provide. In an attempt to increase security and track attendence, other school districts require thumbprint identification to enter classrooms or participate in school activities. In most cases, the schools promise to provide digital ID cards for those who oppose to the system and refuse to take part. Some experts feel that children are being trained very early to expect no privacy when they are adults. Others also are concerned that student eating habits can be tracked and then used against them in the future, or that the information could end up in the wrong hands. Should children be required to provide biometric information to engage in common public school-related activities? Why or why not? Do the school boards' reasons for the measures justify them? Why or why not? What are the privacy issues involved and should they be a concern?

LOOKING AHEAD 11-1

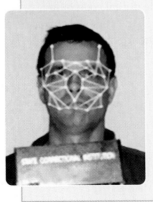

Three-Dimensional Facial Recognition Software — A Step Forward for Security

Your next passport may contain an added feature: a chip that communicates with a reader via radio frequency. The chip will contain at least one photograph of you and perhaps your fingerprints so you can be verified as the passport owner.

The facial recognition software market is expected to grow from $228 million in 2005 to $802 million in 2008 according to the International Biometric Group. Leading the way are three-dimensional systems that measure the width, height, and depth of an individual's face and then compare the dimensions to the original photographs. The software can identify an individual positively in a dark room or in a different pose than when the photographs were taken. For more information, visit scsite.com/dc2007/ch11/looking and then click Facial Recognition.

Biometric devices do have disadvantages. If you cut your finger, a fingerprint scanner might reject you as a legitimate user. Hand geometry readers can transmit germs. If you are nervous, a signature might not match the one on file. If you have a sore throat, a voice recognition system might reject you. Many people are uncomfortable with the thought of using an iris scanner.

Test your knowledge of pages 556 through 569 in Quiz Yourself 11-1.

QUIZ YOURSELF 11-1

Instructions: Find the true statement below. Then, rewrite the remaining false statements so they are true.

1. A back door attack is an assault whose purpose is to disrupt computer access to an Internet service such as the Web or e-mail.

2. All networked and online computer users should implement a firewall solution.

3. A biometric device translates a personal characteristic into an analog code that then is compared with a digital code stored in the computer.

4. Computer viruses, worms, and Trojan horses are malware that acts with a user's knowledge.

5. Perpetrators of cybercrime and other intrusions fall into seven basic categories: hacker, cracker, CERT/CC, corporate spy, unethical employee, trusted source, and cyberterrorist.

6. Shorter passwords provide greater security than longer ones.

7. Updating an antivirus program's quarantine protects a computer against viruses written since the antivirus program was released.

Quiz Yourself Online: To further check your knowledge of security risks; safeguards against viruses, worms, Trojan horses, denial of service attacks, back doors, and spoofing; and preventing unauthorized computer access and use, visit scsite.com/dc2007/ch11/quiz and then click Objectives 1 – 3.

HARDWARE THEFT AND VANDALISM

Hardware theft and vandalism are other types of computer security risks. **Hardware theft** is the act of stealing computer equipment. **Hardware vandalism** is the act of defacing or destroying computer equipment. Hardware vandalism takes many forms, from someone cutting a computer cable to individuals breaking into a business or school computer lab and aimlessly smashing computers.

Hardware theft and vandalism do not really pose a threat to the home desktop computer user. Companies and schools and other organizations that house many computers, however, are at risk to hardware theft and vandalism.

Mobile users also are susceptible to hardware theft. It is estimated that more than 600,000 notebook computers are stolen each year. The size and weight of these computers make them easy to steal. Thieves often target notebook computers of company executives, so they can use the stolen computer to access confidential company information illegally. In this case, hardware theft is combined with software and information theft.

Safeguards against Hardware Theft and Vandalism

To help reduce the chances of theft, companies and schools use a variety of security measures. Physical access controls, such as locked doors and windows, usually are adequate to protect the equipment. Many businesses, schools, and some homeowners install alarm systems for additional security. School computer labs and other areas with a large number of semifrequent users often attach additional physical security devices such as cables that lock the equipment to a desk (Figure 11-14), cabinet, or floor. Small locking devices also

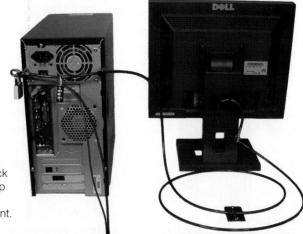

FIGURE 11-14
Using cables to lock computers can help prevent the theft of computer equipment.

exist that require a key to access a hard disk or CD/DVD drive.

Mobile computer users must take special care to protect their equipment. The best preventive measures are common sense and a constant awareness of the risk. Some users attach a physical device such as a cable to lock a mobile computer temporarily to a stationary object. For example, a hotel guest could lock a notebook computer to a desk or table in a hotel room when he or she leaves the room. Other mobile users install a mini-security system in the notebook computer. Some of these security systems shut down the computer and sound an alarm if the computer moves outside a specified distance. Notebook computer security systems and tracking software can track the location of a stolen notebook computer.

Some notebook computers use passwords, possessed objects, and biometrics as methods of security. When you boot up these computers, you must enter a password, slide a card in a card reader, or press your finger on a fingerprint scanner before the hard disk unlocks. This type of security does not prevent theft, but it renders the computer useless if it is stolen.

You also can password-protect many PDAs and smart phones. This allows only authorized users to access the device's data. You usually can instruct the password screen to display your name and telephone number, so a Good Samaritan can return it to you if lost. Several models also allow you to encrypt data in the device. A later section in this chapter discusses encryption.

SOFTWARE THEFT

Another type of computer security risk is software theft. **Software theft** occurs when someone (1) steals software media, (2) intentionally erases programs, or (3) illegally copies a program.

The first type of software theft involves a perpetrator physically stealing the media that contain the software or the hardware that contains the media, as described in the previous section. For example, an unscrupulous library patron might steal the Microsoft Encarta Encyclopedia CD-ROM.

The second type of software theft can occur when a programmer is

terminated from, or stops working for, a company. Although the programs are company property, some dishonest programmers intentionally remove the programs they have written from company computers.

The third type of software theft occurs when software is stolen from software manufacturers. This type of theft, called piracy, is by far the most common form of software theft. Software **piracy** is the unauthorized and illegal duplication of copyrighted software.

Safeguards against Software Theft

To protect software media from being stolen, owners should keep original software boxes and media in a secure location, out of sight of prying eyes. All computer users should back up their files and disks regularly, in the event of theft. When some companies terminate a programmer or if the programmer quits, they escort the employee off the premises immediately. These companies believe that allowing terminated employees to remain on the premises gives them time to sabotage files and other network procedures.

To protect themselves from software piracy, software manufacturers issue users license agreements. A **license agreement** is the right to use the software. That is, you do not own the software. The license agreement provides specific conditions for use of the software, which a user must accept before using the software (Figure 11-15). These terms usually are displayed when you install the software. Use of the software constitutes acceptance of the terms on the user's part.

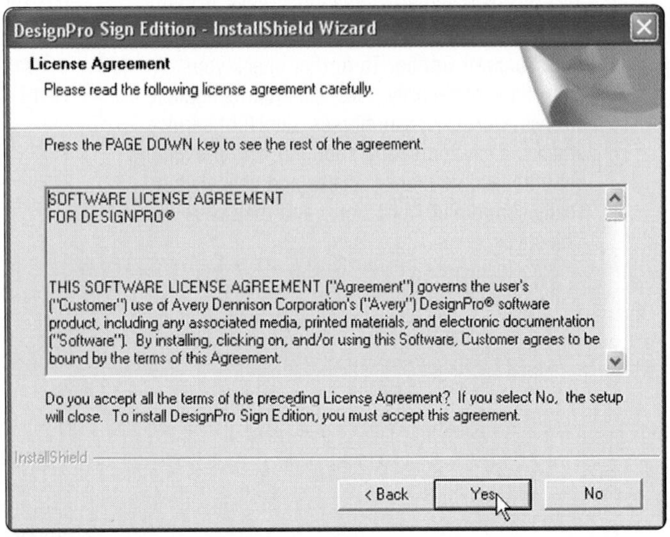

DesignPro Sign Edition - InstallShield Wizard

License Agreement
Please read the following license agreement carefully.

Press the PAGE DOWN key to see the rest of the agreement.

SOFTWARE LICENSE AGREEMENT
FOR DESIGNPRO®

THIS SOFTWARE LICENSE AGREEMENT ("Agreement") governs the user's ("Customer") use of Avery Dennison Corporation's ("Avery") DesignPro® software product, including any associated media, printed materials, and electronic documentation ("Software"). By installing, clicking on, and/or using this Software, Customer agrees to be bound by the terms of this Agreement.

Do you accept all the terms of the preceding License Agreement? If you select No, the setup will close. To install DesignPro Sign Edition, you must accept this agreement.

InstallShield

< Back   Yes   No

FIGURE 11-15 A user must accept the terms in the license agreement before using the software.

The most common type of license included with software purchased by individual users is a *single-user license agreement*, also called an *end-user license agreement* (*EULA*). A single-user license agreement typically includes many of the following conditions that specify a user's responsibility upon acceptance of the agreement.

Users are permitted to:
- Install the software on only one computer. (Some license agreements allow users to install the software on one desktop computer and one notebook computer.)
- Make one copy of the software as a backup.
- Give or sell the software to another individual, but only if the software is removed from the user's computer first.

Users are not permitted to:
- Install the software on a network, such as a school computer lab.
- Give copies to friends and colleagues, while continuing to use the software.
- Export the software.
- Rent or lease the software.

Unless otherwise specified by a license agreement, you do not have the right to copy, loan, borrow, rent, or in any way distribute software. Doing so is a violation of copyright law. It also is a federal crime. Despite this, some experts estimate for every authorized copy of software in use, at least one unauthorized copy exists.

Software piracy continues for several reasons. In some countries, legal protection for software does not exist. In other countries, laws rarely are enforced. In addition, many buyers believe they have the right to copy the software for which they pay hundreds, even thousands, of dollars. Finally, software piracy is a fairly simple crime to commit.

Software piracy, however, is a serious offense. For one, it introduces a number of risks into the software market. It increases the chance of spreading viruses, reduces your ability to receive technical support, and drives up the price of software for all users. Further, software companies take illegal copying seriously. In some cases, offenders have been prosecuted to the fullest extent of the law with penalties including fines up to $250,000 and five years in jail.

To promote a better understanding of software piracy problems and, if necessary, to take legal action, a number of major worldwide software companies formed the *Business Software Alliance* (*BSA*). The BSA operates a Web site and antipiracy hotlines in the United States and more than 60 other countries.

In an attempt to prevent software piracy, Microsoft and other manufacturers have incorporated an activation process into many of their consumer products. During the **product activation**, which is conducted either online or by telephone, users provide the software product's 25-character identification number to receive an installation identification number unique to the computer on which the software is installed. Usually, the software does not function or has limited functionality until you activate it via the Internet or telephone.

Many organizations and businesses also have strict written policies governing the installation and use of software and enforce their rules by checking networked or online computers periodically to ensure that all software is licensed properly. If you are not completely familiar with your school or employer's policies governing installation of software, check with the information technology department or your school's technology coordinator.

FAQ 11-7

How prevalent is software piracy?

A recent study showed that more than half of 86 countries polled had a piracy rate greater than 60 percent. The chart below outlines some of the piracy rates around the world. For more information, visit scsite.com/dc2007/ch11/faq and then click Software Piracy.

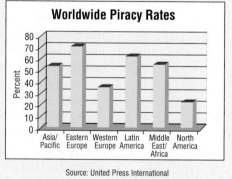

Worldwide Piracy Rates

Source: United Press International

INFORMATION THEFT

Information theft is yet another type of computer security risk. **Information theft** occurs when someone steals personal or confidential information. If stolen, the loss of information can cause as much damage as (if not more than) hardware or software theft.

Both business and home users can fall victim to information theft. An unethical company executive may steal or buy stolen information to learn about a competitor. A corrupt individual may steal credit card numbers to make fraudulent purchases. Information theft often is linked to other types of computer crime. For example, an individual first might gain unauthorized access to a computer and then steal credit card numbers stored in a firm's accounting department.

Information transmitted over networks offers a higher degree of risk because unscrupulous users can intercept it during transmission. Every computer along the path of your data can see what you send and receive.

Safeguards against Information Theft

Most companies attempt to prevent information theft by implementing the user identification and authentication controls discussed earlier in this chapter. These controls are best suited for protecting information on computers located on a company's premises.

To protect information on the Internet and networks, companies and individuals use a variety of encryption techniques to keep data secure and private.

Encryption

Encryption is a process of converting readable data into unreadable characters to prevent unauthorized access. You treat encrypted data just like any other data. That is, you can store it or send it in an e-mail message. To read the data, the recipient must **decrypt**, or decipher, it into a readable form.

In the encryption process, the unencrypted, readable data is called *plaintext*. The encrypted (scrambled) data is called *ciphertext*. To encrypt the data, the originator of the data converts the plaintext into ciphertext using an encryption key. In its simplest form, an *encryption key* is a programmed formula that the recipient of the data uses to decrypt ciphertext. For a more technical discussion about encryption keys, read the High-Tech Talk article on page 592.

Many data encryption methods exist. Figure 11-16 shows examples of some simple encryption methods. An encryption key (formula) often uses more than one of these methods, such as a combination of transposition and substitution. Most organizations use available software for encryption. Others develop their own encryption programs. Windows XP enables you easily to encrypt the contents of files and folders. To display the Windows XP dialog box shown in Figure 11-17, right-click the file or folder name in Windows Explorer, click Properties on the shortcut menu, click the General tab, and then click the Advanced button in the Properties dialog box.

When users send an e-mail message over the Internet, they never know who might intercept it, who might read it, or to whom it might be forwarded. If a message contains personal or confidential information, users can protect the message by encrypting it or signing it digitally. One of the more popular e-mail encryption programs is called *Pretty Good Privacy* (*PGP*). PGP is freeware for personal, noncommercial users. Home users can download PGP from the Web at no cost.

A **digital signature** is an encrypted code that a person, Web site, or company attaches to an electronic message to verify the identity of the message sender. The code usually consists of the user's name and a hash of all or part of the message. A *hash* is a mathematical formula that generates a code from the contents of the message.

SAMPLE ENCRYPTION METHODS

Name	Method	Plaintext	Ciphertext	Explanation
Transposition	Switch the order of characters	SOFTWARE	OSTFAWER	Adjacent characters swapped
Substitution	Replace characters with other characters	INFORMATION	WLDIMXQUWIL	Each letter replaced with another
Expansion	Insert characters between existing characters	USER	UYSYEYRY	Letter Y inserted after each character
Compaction	Remove characters and store elsewhere	ACTIVATION	ACIVTIN	Every third letter removed (T, A, O)

FIGURE 11-16 This table shows four simple methods of encryption. Most encryption programs use a combination of these four methods.

FIGURE 11-17 Through this Windows XP dialog box, you can encrypt files and folders. Only the user that encrypted the files and folders can access them.

WEB LINK 11-6

Encryption
For more information, visit scsite.com/dc2007/ch11/weblink and then click Encryption.

Thus, the hash differs for each message. Receivers of the message decrypt the digital signature. The recipient then generates a new hash of the received message and compares it with one in the digital signature to ensure they match.

Digital signatures often are used to ensure that an impostor is not participating in an Internet transaction. That is, digital signatures help to prevent e-mail forgery. A digital signature also can verify that the content of a message has not changed.

Many Web browsers also use encryption. Some browsers offer a protection level known as *40-bit encryption*. Many also offer *128-bit encryption*, which is an even higher level of protection because it has a longer encryption key. Applications requiring more security, such as banks, brokerage firms, or online retailers that use credit card or other financial information, require 128-bit encryption.

A Web site that uses encryption techniques to secure its data is known as a **secure site**. Secure sites use digital certificates along with a security protocol. Two popular security protocols are Secure Sockets Layer and Secure HTTP. The following paragraphs briefly discuss digital certificates and these security protocols.

DIGITAL CERTIFICATES A **digital certificate** is a notice that guarantees a user or a Web site is legitimate. E-commerce applications commonly use digital certificates.

A *certificate authority* (*CA*) is an authorized person or a company that issues and verifies digital certificates. Users apply for a digital certificate from a CA (Figure 11-18). A digital certificate typically contains information such as the user's name, the issuing CA's name and signature, and the serial number of the certificate. The information in a digital certificate is encrypted.

WEB LINK 11-7

Digital Certificates
For more information, visit scsite.com/dc2007/ch11/weblink and then click Digital Certificates.

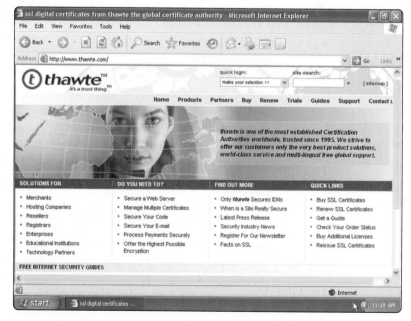

FIGURE 11-18 A company called Thawte is a certificate authority that issues and verifies digital certificates.

SECURE SOCKETS LAYER   *Secure Sockets Layer* (*SSL*) provides encryption of all data that passes between a client and an Internet server. SSL requires the client have a digital certificate. Once the server has a digital certificate, the Web browser communicates securely with the client. Web addresses of pages that use SSL typically begin with https, instead of http (Figure 11-19). SSL is available in both 40-bit and 128-bit encryption.

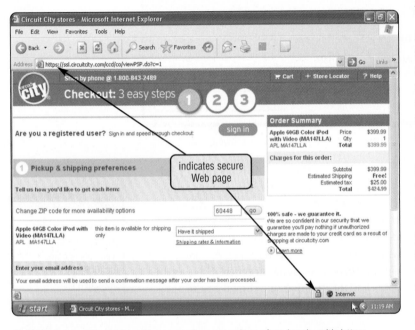

FIGURE 11-19   Web addresses of secure sites often begin with https instead of http. Secure sites also often display a lock symbol on the status bar.

SECURE HTTP   *Secure HTTP* (*S-HTTP*) allows users to choose an encryption scheme for data that passes between a client and a server. With S-HTTP, the client and server both must have digital certificates. S-HTTP is more difficult to use than SSL, but it is more secure. Applications that must verify the authenticity of a client, such as for online banking, use S-HTTP.

Mobile users today often access their company networks through a virtual private network. When a mobile user connects to a main office using a standard Internet connection, a *virtual private network* (*VPN*) provides the mobile user with a secure connection to the company network server, as if the user has a private line. VPNs help ensure that data is safe from being intercepted by unauthorized people by encrypting data as it transmits from a notebook computer, Tablet PC, PDA, or other mobile device.

SYSTEM FAILURE

System failure is yet another type of computer security risk. A *system failure* is the prolonged malfunction of a computer. System failure also can cause loss of hardware, software, data, or information. A variety of causes can lead to system failure. These include aging hardware; natural disasters such as fires, floods, or hurricanes; random events such as electrical power problems; and even errors in computer programs.

One of the more common causes of system failure is an electrical power variation. Electrical power variations can cause loss of data and loss of equipment. If the computer equipment is networked, a single power disturbance can damage multiple systems. Electrical disturbances include noise, undervoltages, and overvoltages.

Noise is any unwanted signal, usually varying quickly, that is mixed with the normal voltage entering the computer. Noise is caused by external devices such as fluorescent lighting, radios, and televisions, as well as by components within the computer itself. Noise generally is not a risk to hardware, software, or data. Computer power supplies, however, do filter out noise.

An **undervoltage** occurs when the electrical supply drops. In North America, a wall plug usually supplies electricity at approximately 120 volts. Any significant drop below 120 volts is an undervoltage. A *brownout* is a prolonged undervoltage. A *blackout* is a complete power failure. Undervoltages can cause data loss but generally do not cause equipment damage.

An **overvoltage**, or **power surge**, occurs when the incoming electrical power increases significantly above the normal 120 volts. A momentary overvoltage, called a *spike*, occurs when the increase in power lasts for less than one millisecond (one thousandth of a second). Uncontrollable disturbances such as lightning bolts cause spikes. Overvoltages can cause immediate and permanent damage to hardware.

Safeguards against System Failure

To protect against overvoltages, use a surge protector. A **surge protector**, also called a *surge suppressor*, uses special electrical components to smooth out minor noise, provide a stable current flow, and keep an overvoltage from reaching the computer and other electronic equipment (Figure 11-20). Sometimes resembling a power strip, the computer and other devices plug in the surge protector, which plugs in the power source. The surge protector absorbs small overvoltages — generally without damage to the computer and equipment. To protect the computer and other equipment from large overvoltages, such as those caused by a lightning strike, some surge protectors completely stop working when an overvoltage reaches a certain level.

No surge protectors are 100 percent effective. Large power surges can bypass the protector. Repeated small overvoltages can weaken a surge protector permanently. Some experts recommend replacing a surge protector every two to three years. Typically, the amount of protection offered by a surge protector is proportional to its cost. That is, the more expensive, the more protection the protector offers.

The surge protector you purchase should meet the safety specification for surge suppression products. This specification, which is called the *Underwriters Laboratories (UL) 1449 standard*, allows no more than 500 maximum volts to pass through the line. The response time of the surge protector should be less than one nanosecond. The surge protector also should have a Joule rating of at least 200. A *Joule* is the unit of energy a surge protection device can absorb before it can be damaged. The higher the Joule rating, the better the protection.

If your computer connects to a network or the Internet, also be sure to have protection for your modem, telephone lines, DSL lines, Internet cable lines, and network lines. Many surge protectors include plug-ins for telephone lines and other cables. If yours does not, you can purchase separate devices to protect these lines.

For additional electrical protection, some applications connect an uninterruptible power supply to the computer. An **uninterruptible power supply (UPS)** is a device that contains surge protection circuits and one or more batteries that can provide power during a temporary or permanent loss of power (Figure 11-21). A UPS connects between your computer and a power source.

Two types of UPS devices are standby and online. A *standby UPS*, sometimes called an *offline UPS*, switches to battery power when a problem occurs in the power line. The amount of time a standby UPS allows a user to continue working depends on the electrical requirements of the computer and the size of the batteries in the UPS. A UPS for a personal computer should provide from 10 to 30 minutes of use in the event of a total power loss. This should be enough time to save current work and shut down the computer properly. An *online UPS* always runs off the battery, which provides continuous protection. An online UPS is much more expensive than a standby UPS.

WEB LINK 11-8

Uninterruptible Power Supply

For more information, visit scsite.com/dc2007/ch11/weblink and then click Uninterruptible Power Supply.

FIGURE 11-20 Circuits inside a surge protector safeguard against overvoltages and undervoltages.

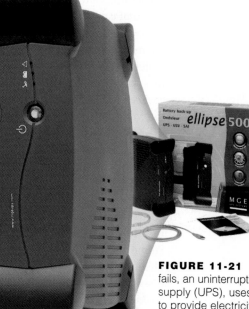

FIGURE 11-21 If power fails, an uninterruptible power supply (UPS), uses batteries to provide electricity for a limited amount of time.

Some companies use duplicate components or computers to protect against system failure. A *fault-tolerant computer* has duplicate components so it can continue to operate when one of its main components fail. Companies that must have their computers operational at all times may have two separate duplicate computers running simultaneously. Airline reservation systems, communications networks, and automated teller machines are examples of systems that duplicate components or computers to ensure that no data is lost in the event of a system failure.

FAQ 11-8

Should I use a surge protector on electronic equipment and appliances?

It is a good idea to use a surge protector on high-end, expensive electronic equipment such as entertainment systems, DVD players, fax machines, and copy machines, and also on any household appliance or device that includes a circuit board or computer such as a stove, dishwasher, and microwave. A lightning strike or other substantial power surge could damage electronics and appliances. For more information, visit scsite.com/dc2007/ch11/faq and then click Surge Protectors.

BACKING UP — THE ULTIMATE SAFEGUARD

To prevent against data loss caused by system failure or hardware/software/information theft, computer users should back up files regularly. A **backup** is a duplicate of a file, program, or disk that can be used if the original is lost, damaged, or destroyed. Thus, to **back up** a file means to make a copy of it. In the case of system failure or the discovery of corrupted files, you **restore** the files by copying the backed up files to their original location on the computer.

You can use just about any media to store backups. Be sure to use high-quality media. A good choice for a home user might be CD-RWs or DVD+RWs.

Keep backup copies in a fireproof and heatproof safe or vault, or offsite. *Offsite* means in a location separate from the computer site. Home and business users keep backup copies offsite so that a single disaster, such as a fire, does not destroy both the original and the backup copy of the data. An offsite location can be a safe deposit box at a bank or a briefcase. A growing trend is to use online storage as an offsite location. As discussed in Chapter 7, online storage is a service on the Web that provides storage to computer users.

Most backup programs for the home user provide for a full backup and a selective backup. A *full backup* copies all of the files in the computer. With a *selective backup*, users choose which folders and files to include in a backup.

Some users implement a *three-generation backup* policy to preserve three copies of important files. The *grandparent* is the oldest copy of the file. The *parent* is the second oldest copy of the file. The *child* is the most recent copy of the file.

Backup programs are available from many sources. Most operating systems include a backup program. Backup devices, such as tape and removable disk drives, also include backup programs. Numerous stand-alone backup utilities exist. Many of these can be downloaded from the Web at no cost.

Some companies choose to use an online backup service to handle their backup needs. An *online backup service* is a Web site that automatically backs up files to its online location. These sites usually charge a monthly or annual fee. If the system crashes, the online backup service typically sends the company one or more CDs that contains all of its backed up data. Users with high-speed Internet connections opt for online backup services. For slower connections, these services are not practical.

WIRELESS SECURITY

Wireless technology has made dramatic changes in the way computer users communicate worldwide. Billions of home and business users have notebook computers, PDAs, smart phones, and other devices to access the Internet, send e-mail and instant messages, chat online, or share network connections — all without wires. Home users set up wireless home networks. Mobile users access wireless networks in hot spots at airports, hotels, schools, shopping malls, bookstores, restaurants, and coffee shops. Schools have wireless networks so students can access the school network using their mobile computers and devices as they move from building to building.

Although wireless access provides many conveniences to users, it also poses additional security risks. One study showed that about 65 percent of wireless networks have no security protection. Some perpetrators connect to other's wireless networks to gain free Internet access; others may try to access a company's confidential data.

To access the network, the individual must be in range of the wireless network. Some intruders intercept and monitor communications as they transmit through the air. Others connect to a network through an unsecured wireless access point (WAP). In one technique, called *war driving*, individuals attempt to detect wireless networks via their notebook computer while driving a vehicle through areas they suspect have a wireless network. Some individuals instead use *war flying*, where they use airplanes instead of vehicles to detect unsecured wireless networks. Once located, some individuals use a GPS device to add the WAP to a war driving access point map on the Internet (Figure 11-22), making the wireless network vulnerable.

In addition to using firewalls, some safeguards that improve the security of wireless networks include reconfiguring the wireless access point and ensuring equipment uses one or more wireless security standards such as Wired Equivalent Privacy, Wi-Fi Protected Access, and 802.11i.

- A wireless access point (WAP) should be configured so it does not broadcast a network name. The WAP also should be programmed so only certain devices can access it.
- *Wired Equivalent Privacy* (WEP) is a security standard that defines how to encrypt data as it travels across wireless networks. WEP supports both 40-bit and 128-bit encryption.
- *Wi-Fi Protected Access* (WPA) is a security standard that improves on WEP by authenticating network users and providing more advanced encryption techniques.
- An *802.11i* network, the most recent network security standard, conforms to the government's security standards and uses more sophisticated encryption techniques than both WPA and WEP.

By implementing these security measures, you can help to prevent unauthorized access to wireless networks.

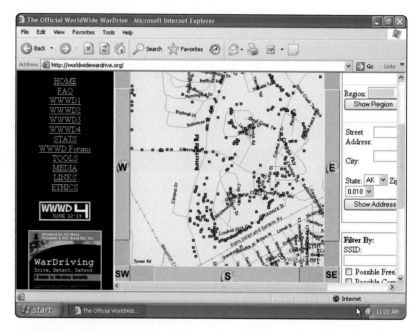

FIGURE 11-22 This Web site marks all unsecured wireless networks located during a war drive.

Test your knowledge of pages 569 through 577 in Quiz Yourself 11-2.

QUIZ YOURSELF 11-2

Instructions: Find the true statement below. Then, rewrite the remaining false statements so they are true.

1. An end-user license agreement (EULA) permits users to give copies to friends and colleagues, while continuing to use the software.

2. Encryption is a process of converting ciphertext into plaintext to prevent authorized access.

3. Mobile users are not susceptible to hardware theft.

4. Overvoltages can cause immediate and permanent damage to hardware.

5. Three backup security standards are Wired Equivalent Privacy, Wi-Fi Protected Access, and 802.11i.

6. To prevent against data loss caused by a system failure, computer users should restore files regularly.

Quiz Yourself Online: To further check your knowledge of safeguards against hardware theft and vandalism, software piracy, encryption, protection against system failure, backing up resources, and wireless security, visit scsite.com/dc2007/ch11/quiz and then click Objectives 4 – 9.

ETHICS AND SOCIETY

As with any powerful technology, computers can be used for both good and bad intentions. The standards that determine whether an action is good or bad are known as ethics.

Computer ethics are the moral guidelines that govern the use of computers and information systems. Six frequently discussed areas of computer ethics are unauthorized use of computers and networks, software theft (piracy),

information accuracy, intellectual property rights, codes of conduct, and information privacy. The questionnaire in Figure 11-23 raises issues in each of these areas.

Previous sections in this chapter discussed unauthorized use of computers and networks, and software theft (piracy). The following pages discuss issues related to information accuracy, intellectual property rights, codes of conduct, and information privacy.

	Ethical	Unethical
1. A company requires employees to wear badges that track their whereabouts while at work.	☐	☐
2. A supervisor reads an employee's e-mail.	☐	☐
3. An employee uses his computer at work to send e-mail messages to a friend.	☐	☐
4. An employee sends an e-mail message to several coworkers and blind copies his supervisor.	☐	☐
5. An employee forwards an e-mail message to a third party without permission from the sender.	☐	☐
6. An employee uses her computer at work to complete a homework assignment for school.	☐	☐
7. The vice president of your Student Government Association (SGA) downloads a photograph from the Web and uses it in a flier recruiting SGA members.	☐	☐
8. A student copies text from the Web and uses it in a research paper for his English Composition class.	☐	☐
9. An employee sends political campaign material to individuals on her employer's mailing list.	☐	☐
10. As an employee in the registration office, you have access to student grades. You look up grades for your friends, so they do not have to wait for delivery of grade reports from the postal service.	☐	☐
11. An employee makes a copy of software and installs it on her home computer. No one uses her home computer while she is at work, and she uses her home computer only to finish projects from work.	☐	☐
12. An employee who has been laid off installs a computer virus on his employer's computer.	☐	☐
13. A person designing a Web page finds one on the Web similar to his requirements, copies it, modifies it, and publishes it as his own Web page.	☐	☐
14. A student researches using only the Web to write a report.	☐	☐
15. In a society in which all transactions occur online (a cashless society), the government tracks every transaction you make and automatically deducts taxes from your bank account.	☐	☐
16. Someone copies a well-known novel to the Web and encourages others to read it.	☐	☐

FIGURE 11-23 Indicate whether you think the situation described is ethical or unethical. Discuss your answers with your instructor and other students.

Information Accuracy

Information accuracy today is a concern because many users access information maintained by other people or companies, such as on the Internet. Do not assume that because the information is on the Web that it is correct. As Chapter 2 discussed, users should evaluate the value of a Web page before relying on its content. Be aware that the company providing access to the information may not be the creator of the information.

In addition to concerns about the accuracy of computer input, some individuals and organizations raise questions about the ethics of using computers to alter output, primarily graphical output such as retouched photographs. Using graphics equipment and software, users easily can digitize photographs and then add, change, or remove images (Figure 11-24).

One group that completely opposes any manipulation of an image is the National Press Photographers Association. It believes that allowing even the slightest alteration eventually could lead to misrepresentative photographs. Others believe that digital photograph retouching is acceptable as long as the significant content or meaning of the photograph does not change. Digital retouching is an area in which legal precedents so far have not been established.

Intellectual Property Rights

Intellectual property (IP) refers to unique and original works such as ideas, inventions, art, writings, processes, company and product names, and logos. **Intellectual property rights** are the rights to which creators are entitled for their work. Certain issues arise surrounding IP today because many of these works are available digitally.

A **copyright** gives authors and artists exclusive rights to duplicate, publish, and sell their materials. A copyright protects any tangible form of expression.

A common infringement of copyright is piracy. People pirate (illegally copy) software, movies, and music. Many areas are not clear-cut with respect to the law, because copyright law gives the public fair use to copyrighted material. The issues surround the phrase, fair use, which allows use for educational and critical purposes.

FIGURE 11-24   A digitally altered photograph shows sports legend Michael Jordan (born in 1963) meeting the famous scientist Albert Einstein (who died in 1955).

This vague definition is subject to widespread interpretation and raises many questions:

- Should individuals be able to download contents of your Web site, modify it, and then put it on the Web again as their own?
- Should a faculty member have the right to print material from the Web and distribute it to all members of the class for teaching purposes only?
- Should someone be able to scan photographs or pages from a book, publish them to the Web, and allow others to download them?
- Should someone be able to put the lyrics of a song on the Web?
- Should students be able to post term papers they have written on the Web, making it tempting for other students to download and submit them as their own work?

These issues with copyright law led to the development of *digital rights management* (*DRM*), a strategy designed to prevent illegal distribution of movies, music, and other digital content. Read Ethics & Issues 11-3 for a related discussion.

ETHICS & ISSUES 11-3

Who Should Control the Content of Your CDs and DVDs?

When you purchase a CD, a DVD, or music files online, you are not purchasing the songs or movies they contain. You actually are purchasing a license to listen to or watch the digital content in a certain manner. The license limits what you can do with the CDs, DVDs, or music files. For example, you cannot play the music or movies in a public forum, or copy and distribute the digital content. Some media companies now employ electronic means of digital rights management (DRM), which automatically restricts what you can do with digital content. Media companies claim that DRM helps them to stem the tide of piracy and the sharing of content on P2P networks. Consumers argue that DRM restrictions infringe on their rights of fair use, and that oftentimes DRM makes playing the content in certain devices impossible. In some cases, DRM prevents users from making backup copies of the content or copying the content to their computers or other devices. Some people have worked around DRM restrictions, but the Digital Millennium Copyright Act (DMCA) makes any attempt to circumvent DRM an illegal activity. Because you already own a license to the content, if you scratch or lose a CD or DVD, should you be able to obtain a free or low-cost replacement for the content? Why or why not? If you already purchased a license for music by purchasing a CD, is it fair that you should pay full price again if you also would like the music in MP3 format? Why? How can the rights of media companies and consumers best be balanced?

Codes of Conduct

Recognizing that individuals need specific standards for the ethical use of computers, a number of computer-related organizations have established IT (information technology) codes of conduct (Figure 11-25). An IT **code of conduct** is a written guideline that helps determine whether a specific computer action is ethical or unethical.

IT CODE OF CONDUCT
1. Computers may not be used to harm other people.
2. Employees may not interfere with others' computer work.
3. Employees may not meddle in others' computer files.
4. Computers may not be used to steal.
5. Computers may not be used to bear false witness.
6. Employees may not copy or use software illegally.
7. Employees may not use others' computer resources without authorization.
8. Employees may not use others' intellectual property as their own.
9. Employees shall consider the social impact of programs and systems they design.
10. Employees always should use computers in a way that demonstrates consideration and respect for fellow humans.

FIGURE 11-25   Sample IT code of conduct employers may distribute to employees.

INFORMATION PRIVACY

Information privacy refers to the right of individuals and companies to deny or restrict the collection and use of information about them. In the past, information privacy was easier to maintain because information was kept in separate locations. Each retail store had its own credit files. Each government agency maintained separate records. Doctors had their own patient files.

Today, huge databases store this data online. Much of the data is personal and confidential and should be accessible only to authorized users. Many individuals and organizations, however, question whether this data really is private. That is, some companies and individuals collect and use this information without your authorization. Web sites often collect data about you, so they can customize advertisements and send you personalized e-mail messages. Some employers monitor your computer usage and e-mail messages.

Figure 11-26 lists measures you can take to make your personal data more private. The following sections address techniques companies and employers use to collect your personal data.

Electronic Profiles

When you fill out a form such as a magazine subscription, product warranty registration card, or contest entry form, the merchant that receives the form usually enters it into a database. Likewise, every time you click an advertisement on the Web or register software online, your information and preferences enter a database. Merchants then sell the contents of their databases to national marketing firms and Internet advertising firms. By combining this data with information from public sources such as driver's licenses and vehicle registrations,

HOW TO SAFEGUARD PERSONAL INFORMATION

1. Fill in only necessary information on rebate, warranty, and registration forms.

2. Do not preprint your telephone number or Social Security number on personal checks.

3. Have an unlisted or unpublished telephone number.

4. If Caller ID is available in your area, find out how to block your number from displaying on the receiver's system.

5. Do not write your telephone number on charge or credit receipts.

6. Ask merchants not to write credit card numbers, telephone numbers, Social Security numbers, and driver's license numbers on the back of your personal checks.

7. Purchase goods with cash, rather than credit or checks.

8. Avoid shopping club and buyer cards.

9. If merchants ask personal questions, find out why they want to know before releasing the information.

10. Inform merchants that you do not want them to distribute your personal information.

11. Request, in writing, to be removed from mailing lists.

12. Obtain your credit report once a year from each of the three major credit reporting agencies (Equifax, Experian, and TransUnion) and correct any errors.

13. Request a free copy of your medical records once a year from the Medical Information Bureau.

14. Limit the amount of information you provide to Web sites. Fill in only required information.

15. Install a cookie manager to filter cookies.

16. Clear your history file when you are finished browsing.

17. Set up a free e-mail account. Use this e-mail address for merchant forms.

18. Turn off file and printer sharing on your Internet connection.

19. Install a personal firewall.

20. Sign-up for e-mail filtering through your Internet service provider or use an anti-spam program such as Brightmail.

21. Do not reply to spam for any reason.

22. Surf the Web anonymously with a program such as Freedom WebSecure or through an anonymous Web site such as Anonymizer.com.

FIGURE 11-26 Techniques to keep personal data private.

these firms create an electronic profile of individuals. The information in these electronic profiles includes personal details such as your age, address, telephone number, spending habits, marital status, number of dependents, ages of dependents, and so on.

Direct marketing supporters say that using information in this way lowers overall selling costs, which lowers product prices. Critics contend that the information in an electronic profile reveals more about an individual than anyone has a right to know. They claim that companies should inform people if they plan to provide personal information to others, and people should have the right to deny such use. Many companies today allow people to specify whether they want their personal information distributed (Figure 11-27).

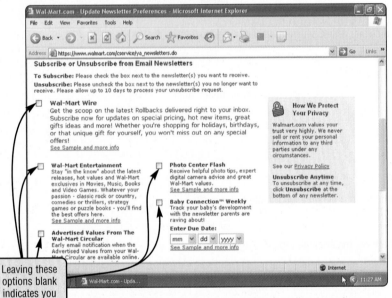

Leaving these options blank indicates you do not want to be contacted.

FIGURE 11-27 Many companies today allow people to specify whether they want their personal information distributed.

Cookies

E-commerce and other Web applications often rely on cookies to identify users and customize Web pages. A **cookie** is a small text file that a Web server stores on your computer. Cookie files typically contain data about you, such as your user name or viewing preferences.

Web sites use cookies for a variety of purposes.

• Most Web sites that allow for personalization use cookies to track user preferences. On such sites, users may be asked to fill in a form requesting personal information, such as their name, postal code, or site preferences. A news Web site, for example, might allow users to customize their viewing preferences to display certain stock quotes. The Web site stores their preferences in a cookie on the users' hard disks.

• Some Web sites use cookies to store users' passwords, so they do not need to enter it every time they log in to the Web site.

• Online shopping sites generally use a *session cookie* to keep track of items in a user's shopping cart. This way, users can start an order during one Web session and finish it on another day in another session. Session cookies usually expire after a certain time, such as a week or a month.

• Some Web sites use cookies to track how regularly users visit a site and the Web pages they visit while at the site.

• Web sites may use cookies to target advertisements. These sites store a user's interests and browsing habits in the cookie.

Many commercial Web sites send a cookie to your browser, and then your computer's hard disk stores the cookie. The next time you visit the Web site, your browser retrieves the cookie from your hard disk and sends the data in the cookie to the Web site. Figure 11-28 illustrates how Web sites work with cookies.

Some Web sites do sell or trade information stored in your cookie to advertisers — a practice many believe to be unethical. If you do not want your personal information distributed, you should limit the amount of information you provide to a Web site.

You can set your browser to accept cookies automatically, prompt you if you want to accept a cookie, or disable cookie use altogether. Keep in mind if you disable cookie use, you may not be able to use many of the e-commerce Web sites. As an alternative, you can purchase software that selectively blocks cookies.

WEB LINK 11-10

Cookies

For more information, visit scsite.com/dc2007/ch11/weblink and then click Cookies.

FAQ 11-9

Can a Web site read data in all the cookie files on my computer's hard disk?

No, a Web site can read data only from its own cookie file stored on your hard disk. It cannot access or view any other data on your hard disk — including another cookie file. For more information, visit scsite.com/dc2007/ch11/faq and then click Cookies.

FIGURE 11-28 HOW COOKIES WORK

Step 1:
When you type the Web address of a Web site in your browser window, the browser program searches your hard disk for a cookie associated with the Web site.

Step 2:
If the browser finds a cookie, it sends information in the cookie file to the Web site.

cookies

Web server for www.company.com

identification number

cookie information

Step 3:
If the Web site does not receive cookie information, and is expecting it, the site creates an identification number for you in its database and sends that number to your browser. The browser in turn creates a cookie file based on that number and stores the cookie file on your hard disk. The Web site now can update information in the cookie file whenever you access the site.

Spyware and Adware

Spyware is a program placed on a computer without the user's knowledge that secretly collects information about the user. Spyware can enter a computer as a virus or as a result of a user installing a new program. The spyware program communicates information it collects to some outside source while you are online.

Some vendors or employers use spyware to collect information about program usage or employees. Internet advertising firms often collect information about users' Web browsing habits by hiding spyware in adware. *Adware* is a program that displays an online advertisement in a banner or pop-up window on Web pages, e-mail messages, or other Internet services.

Another type of spyware, called a *Web bug*, is hidden on Web pages or in e-mail messages in the form of graphical images. Web businesses use Web bugs to monitor online habits of Web site visitors. Often, Web bugs link to a cookie stored on the hard disk. (Cookies are not considered spyware because you know they exist.)

To remove spyware, you can obtain a spyware remover that can detect and delete it. Some operating systems and Web browsers include spyware removers. Read Ethics & Issues 11-4 for a related discussion.

ETHICS & ISSUES 11-4

Should Spyware Be Legal?

Legitimate businesses and illegitimate hackers use a variety of techniques to secretly install spyware on unsecured computers. Spyware can perform a number of tasks, such as monitoring the Web sites that you visit or controlling a computer remotely. Some Web pages also have cookies that count visitors and gather basic statistical information about a visitor's location and Web browser. Online advertising agencies or Internet service providers frequently place spyware cookies as part of a promotion, sometimes without the knowledge of the Web page's sponsor. When the collected information is stored in a Web database and shared among several sites, the technology can track a visitor's travels around the Web. If a visitor completes a registration, that information also can be distributed to other advertisers. Spyware and cookies help advertisers reach their markets and refine their messages, but opponents say the technology is little more than electronic stalking. Should spyware and/or cookies be banned, or is it the right of Web page owners and advertisers to collect information about visitors? Why? Should Web page authors and/or Web page visitors be made aware of spyware and cookies? Why or why not?

Spam

Spam is an unsolicited e-mail message or newsgroup posting sent to many recipients or newsgroups at once. Spam is Internet junk mail (Figure 11-29). The content of spam ranges from selling a product or service, to promoting a business opportunity, to advertising offensive material. One study indicates the average user receives more than 1,000 spam e-mail messages each year. Instead of via e-mail, some spam is sent through an instant massaging system and, thus, is called *spim*. Another type, called *spit*, is spam sent via Internet telephony.

Users can reduce the amount of spam they receive with a number of techniques. Some e-mail programs have built-in settings that allow users to delete spam automatically. Users also can sign up for e-mail filtering from their Internet service provider. **E-mail filtering** is a service that blocks e-mail messages from designated sources. These services typically collect the spam in a central location that users can view at anytime. An alternative to e-mail filtering is to purchase an **anti-spam program** that attempts to remove spam before it reaches your inbox. The disadvantage of e-mail filters and anti-spam programs is that sometimes they remove valid e-mail messages.

Phishing

Phishing is a scam in which a perpetrator sends an official looking e-mail message that attempts to obtain your personal and financial information. Some phishing e-mail messages ask you to reply with your information; others direct you to a phony Web site, or a pop-up window that looks like a Web site, that collects the information. Read Ethics & Issues 11-5 for a related discussion.

If you receive an e-mail message that looks legitimate and requests you update credit card numbers, Social Security numbers, bank account numbers, passwords, or other private information, the FTC recommends you visit the Web site directly to determine if the request is valid.

To help deter spam and phishing scams, Microsoft and others are developing standards that require e-mail messages contain sender identification so recipients can verify the legitimacy of messages.

Pharming is a scam, similar to phishing, where a perpetrator attempts to obtain your personal and financial information, except they do so via spoofing. That is, when you type a Web address in the Web browser, you are redirected to a phony Web site that looks legitimate. The phony Web site requests you enter confidential information.

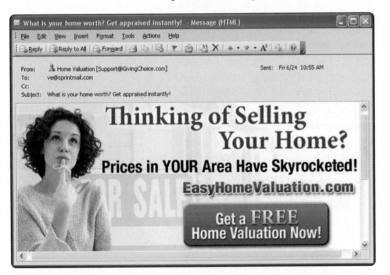

FIGURE 11-29   An example of spam.

FAQ 11-10

What do I do if I have been caught in a phishing scam?

If you have been trapped in a phishing scam, forward the phishing e-mail message to uce@ftc.gov or call the FTC help line at 1-877-FTC-HELP. For more information, visit scsite.com/dc2007/ch11/faq and then click Phishing Scams.

ETHICS & ISSUES 11-5

Who Should Protect You from Identity Theft?

If you respond to a phishing attempt, the information you submit ends up in the hands of a scammer, who then either uses the information to access your accounts and take money, or sells and trades the information with other criminals. Sadly, the result often is identity theft. Law enforcement agencies believe that many of the phishing schemes are related to organized crime. Approximately 20 percent of those targeted by phishing provide the requested information. This high level of response emboldens the scammers. Law enforcement agencies claim that these scams are difficult to stop and that people simply need to learn to ignore the requests for information. Computer users find that the scams often are impossible to distinguish from legitimate requests for information, and that the fault lies with Internet service providers or the makers of e-mail programs and Web browsers. Who should be responsible for stopping the phishing phenomenon? What can a person do to protect against phishing when e-mail messages are received from what appear to be legitimate organizations? What can be done to limit or stop the practice of phishing? Are companies and/or consumers to share in the blame for the success of phishing? Why or why not?

Privacy Laws

The concern about privacy has led to the enactment of federal and state laws regarding the storage and disclosure of personal data (Figure 11-30). Common points in some of these laws are outlined at the top of the next page.

Date	Law	Purpose
2003	**CAN-SPAM Act**	Gives law enforcement the right to impose penalties on people using the Internet to distribute spam.
2002	**Sarbanes-Oxley Act**	Requires corporate officers, auditors, and attorneys of publicly-traded companies follow strict financial reporting guidelines.
2001	**Children's Internet Protection Act (CIPA)**	Protects minors from inappropriate content when accessing the Internet in schools and libraries.
2001	**Provide Appropriate Tools Required to Intercept and Obstruct Terrorism (PATRIOT) Act**	Gives law enforcement the right to monitor people's activities, including Web and e-mail habits.
1999	**Gramm-Leach-Bliley Act (GLBA) or Financial Modernization Act**	Protects consumers from disclosure of their personal financial information and requires institutions to alert customers of information disclosure policies.
1998	**Children's Online Privacy Protection Act (COPPA)**	Requires Web sites protect personal information of children under 13 years of age.
1998	**Digital Millennium Copyright Act (DMCA)**	Makes it illegal to circumvent antipiracy schemes in commercial software; outlaws sale of devices that copy software illegally.
1997	**No Electronic Theft (NET) Act**	Closes a narrow loophole in the law that allowed people to give away copyrighted material (such as software) on the Internet without legal repercussions.
1996	**Health Insurance Portability and Accountability Act (HIPAA)**	Protects individuals against the wrongful disclosure of their health information.
1996	**National Information Infrastructure Protection Act**	Penalizes theft of information across state lines, threats against networks, and computer system trespassing.
1994	**Computer Abuse Amendments Act**	Amends 1984 act to outlaw transmission of harmful computer code such as viruses.
1992	**Cable Act**	Extends the privacy of the Cable Communications Policy Act of 1984 to include cellular and other wireless services.
1991	**Telephone Consumer Protection Act**	Restricts activities of telemarketers.
1988	**Computer Matching and Privacy Protection Act**	Regulates the use of government data to determine the eligibility of individuals for federal benefits.
1988	**Video Privacy Protection Act**	Forbids retailers from releasing or selling video-rental records without customer consent or a court order.
1986	**Electronic Communications Privacy Act (ECPA)**	Provides the same right of privacy protection for the postal delivery service and telephone companies to the new forms of electronic communications, such as voice mail, e-mail, and cellular telephones.
1984	**Cable Communications Policy Act**	Regulates disclosure of cable television subscriber records.
1984	**Computer Fraud and Abuse Act**	Outlaws unauthorized access of federal government computers.
1978	**Right to Financial Privacy Act**	Strictly outlines procedures federal agencies must follow when looking at customer records in banks.
1974	**Privacy Act**	Forbids federal agencies from allowing information to be used for a reason other than that for which it was collected.
1974	**Family Educational Rights and Privacy Act**	Gives students and parents access to school records and limits disclosure of records to unauthorized parties.
1970	**Fair Credit Reporting Act**	Prohibits credit reporting agencies from releasing credit information to unauthorized people and allows consumers to review their own credit records.

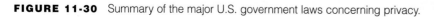

FIGURE 11-30 Summary of the major U.S. government laws concerning privacy.

1. Information collected and stored about individuals should be limited to what is necessary to carry out the function of the business or government agency collecting the data.
2. Once collected, provisions should be made to restrict access to the data to those employees within the organization who need access to it to perform their job duties.
3. Personal information should be released outside the organization collecting the data only when the person has agreed to its disclosure.
4. When information is collected about an individual, the individual should know that the data is being collected and have the opportunity to determine the accuracy of the data.

One law with an apparent legal loophole is the 1970 **Fair Credit Reporting Act**. The act limits the rights of others viewing a credit report to only those with a legitimate business need. The problem is that it does not define a legitimate business need. The result is that just about anyone can claim a legitimate business need and gain access to your credit report.

Social Engineering

As related to the use of computers, **social engineering** is defined as gaining unauthorized access or obtaining confidential information by taking advantage of the trusting human nature of some victims and the naivety of others. Some social engineers trick their victims into revealing confidential information such as user names and passwords on the telephone, in person, or on the Internet. Techniques they use include pretending to be an administrator or other authoritative figure, feigning an emergency situation, or impersonating an acquaintance. Social engineers also obtain information from users who do not destroy or conceal information properly. These perpetrators sift through company dumpsters, watch or film people dialing telephone numbers or using ATMs, and snoop around computers looking for openly displayed confidential information.

Employee Monitoring

Employee monitoring involves the use of computers to observe, record, and review an employee's use of a computer, including communications such as e-mail messages,

keyboard activity (used to measure productivity), and Web sites visited. Many programs exist that easily allow employers to monitor employees. Further, it is legal for employers to use these programs.

A frequently debated issue is whether an employer has the right to read employee e-mail messages. Actual policies vary widely. Some companies declare that they will review e-mail messages regularly, and others state that e-mail is private. In some states, if a company does not have a formal e-mail policy, it can read e-mail messages without employee notification. One survey discovered that more than 73 percent of companies search and/or read employee files, voice mail, e-mail messages, Web connections, and other networking communications. Several lawsuits have been filed against employers because many believe that such internal communications should be private.

Another controversial issue relates to the use of cameras to monitor employees, customers, and the public. Many people feel that this use of video cameras is a violation of privacy.

Content Filtering

One of the more controversial issues that surround the Internet is its widespread availability of objectionable material, such as racist literature, violence, and obscene pictures. Some believe that such materials should be banned. Others believe that the materials should be filtered, that is, restricted. **Content filtering** is the process of restricting access to certain material on the Web. Content filtering opponents argue that banning any materials violates constitutional guarantees of free speech and personal rights.

Many businesses use content filtering to limit employees' Web access. These businesses argue that employees are unproductive when visiting inappropriate or objectionable Web sites. Some schools, libraries, and parents use content filtering to restrict access to minors.

One approach to content filtering is through a rating system of the *Internet Content Rating Association* (ICRA), which is similar to those used for movies and videos. Major Web sites such as Yahoo!, AOL, and MSN use the rating system established by the ICRA. If content at the Web site goes beyond the rating limits set in the Web browser software, a user cannot access the Web site. Concerned parents can set the rating limits and prevent these limits from being changed by using a password.

Another approach to content filtering is to use filtering software. **Web filtering software** is a program that restricts access to specified Web sites. Some also filter sites that use specific words. Others allow you to filter e-mail messages, chat rooms, and programs. Many Internet security programs include a firewall, antivirus program, and filtering capabilities combined (Figure 11-31).

FIGURE 11-31 Many Internet security programs include content filtering capabilities, where users can block specified Web sites and applications.

Computer Forensics

Computer forensics, also called *digital forensics*, *network forensics*, or *cyberforensics*, is the discovery, collection, and analysis of evidence found on computers and networks. Forensic analysis involves the examination of computer media, programs, data and log files on computers, servers, and networks. Many areas use computer forensics, including law enforcement, criminal prosecutors, military intelligence, insurance agencies, and information security departments in the private sector.

A computer forensics analyst must have knowledge of the law, technical experience with many types of hardware and software products, superior communication skills, familiarity with corporate structures and policies, a willingness to learn and update skills, and a knack for problem solving. For more information about computer forensics, read the Computer Forensics Special Feature that follows this chapter. For a look at the next generation of forensics, read Looking Ahead 11-2.

LOOKING AHEAD 11-2

Computer Knowledge Assessment Using Brain Fingerprinting

A powerful forensic tool may one day replace the traditional lie detector test. Brain fingerprinting examines a subset of brain waves generated involuntarily when an individual recognizes familiar information.

To conduct the test, researchers place a strap equipped with sensors on an individual's head and then present a variety of relevant and irrelevant words, pictures, and sounds. If the stimulus is familiar, the brain generates unique brain waves 300 to 800 milliseconds after receiving the stimulus.

Computers store and then analyze the series of unique brain waves to determine if the person's brain has stored critical details of a situation, such as a fraudulent or criminal act. Researchers also have determined that brain fingerprinting could help identify the onset of Alzheimer's disease. For more information, visit scsite.com/dc2007/ch11/looking and then click Brain Fingerprinting.

WEB LINK 11-11

Computer Forensics
For more information, visit scsite.com/dc2007/ch11/weblink and then click Computer Forensics.

HEALTH CONCERNS OF COMPUTER USE

Users are a key component in any information system. Thus, protecting users is just as important as protecting hardware, software, and data.

The widespread use of computers has led to some important health concerns. Users should be proactive and minimize their chance of risk. The following sections discuss health risks and preventions, along with measures users can take to keep the environment healthy.

Computers and Health Risks

A **repetitive strain injury (RSI)** is an injury or disorder of the muscles, nerves, tendons, ligaments, and joints. Computer-related RSIs include tendonitis and carpal tunnel syndrome. RSIs are the largest job-related injury and illness problem in the United States today. For this reason, OSHA (Occupational Safety and Health Administration) has developed industry-specific and task-specific guidelines designed to prevent workplace injuries with respect to computer usage.

Tendonitis is inflammation of a tendon due to repeated motion or stress on that tendon. *Carpal tunnel syndrome* (*CTS*) is inflammation of the nerve that connects the forearm to the palm of the wrist. Repeated or forceful bending of the wrist can cause CTS or tendonitis of the wrist. Symptoms of tendonitis of the wrist include extreme pain that extends from the forearm to the hand, along with tingling in the fingers. Symptoms of CTS include burning pain when the nerve is compressed, along with numbness and tingling in the thumb and first two fingers.

Long-term computer work can lead to tendonitis or CTS. Factors that cause these disorders include prolonged typing, prolonged mouse usage, or continual shifting between the mouse and the keyboard. If untreated, these disorders can lead to permanent damage to your body.

You can take many precautions to prevent these types of injuries. Take frequent breaks during the computer session to exercise your hands and arms (Figure 11-32). To prevent injury due to typing, place a wrist rest between the keyboard and the edge of your desk. To prevent injury while using a mouse, place the mouse at least six inches from the edge of the

desk. In this position, your wrist is flat on the desk. Finally, minimize the number of times you switch between the mouse and the keyboard, and avoid using the heel of your hand as a pivot point while typing or using the mouse.

Another type of health-related condition due to computer usage is **computer vision syndrome** (*CVS*). You may have CVS if you have sore, tired, burning, itching, or dry eyes; blurred or double vision; distance blurred vision after prolonged staring at a display device; headache or sore neck; difficulty shifting focus between a display device and documents; difficulty focusing on the screen image; color fringes or after-images when you look away from the display device; and increased sensitivity to light. Eyestrain associated with CVS is not thought to have serious or long-term consequences. Figure 11-33 outlines some techniques you can follow to ease eyestrain.

People who spend their workday using the computer sometimes complain of lower back pain, muscle fatigue, and emotional fatigue. Lower back pain sometimes is caused from poor posture. Always sit properly in the chair while you work. Take a break every 30 to 60

HAND EXERCISES

- Spread fingers apart for several seconds while keeping wrists straight.
- Gently push back fingers and then thumb.
- Dangle arms loosely at sides and then shake arms and hands.

TECHNIQUES TO EASE EYESTRAIN

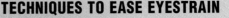

- Every 10 to 15 minutes, take an eye break.
  - Look into the distance and focus on an object for 20 to 30 seconds.
  - Roll your eyes in a complete circle.
  - Close your eyes and rest them for at least one minute.
- Blink your eyes every five seconds.
- Place your display device about an arm's length away from your eyes with the top of the screen at eye level or below.
- Use large fonts.
- If you wear glasses, ask your doctor about computer glasses.
- Adjust the lighting.

FIGURE 11-32　To reduce the chance of developing tendonitis or carpal tunnel syndrome, take frequent breaks during computer sessions to exercise your hands and arms.

FIGURE 11-33　Following these tips may help reduce eyestrain while working on a computer.

minutes — stand up, walk around, or stretch. Another way to help prevent these injuries is to be sure your workplace is designed ergonomically, which is discussed in the next section.

Ergonomics and Workplace Design

Ergonomics is an applied science devoted to incorporating comfort, efficiency, and safety into the design of items in the workplace. Ergonomic studies have shown that using the correct type and configuration of chair, keyboard, display device, and work surface helps users work comfortably and efficiently and helps protect their health. For the computer work space, experts recommend an area of at least two feet by four feet. Figure 11-34 illustrates additional guidelines for setting up the work area.

Computer Addiction

Computers can provide entertainment and enjoyment. Some computer users, however, become obsessed with the computer and the Internet. **Computer addiction** occurs when the computer consumes someone's entire social life. Computer addiction is a growing health problem.

Symptoms of a user with computer addiction include the following:
- Craves computer time
- Overjoyed when at the computer
- Unable to stop computer activity
- Irritable when not at the computer
- Neglects family and friends
- Problems at work or school

Computer addiction is a treatable illness through therapy and support groups.

viewing angle: 20° to center of screen
viewing distance: 18 to 28 inches

arms: elbows at about 90° and arms and hands approximately parallel to floor

keyboard height: 23 to 28 inches depending on height of user

adjustable height chair with 4 or 5 legs for stability

feet flat on floor

FIGURE 11-34 A well-designed work area should be flexible to allow adjustments to the height and build of different individuals. Good lighting and air quality also are important considerations.

Green Computing

Green computing involves reducing the electricity and environmental waste while using a computer. People use, and often waste, resources such as electricity and paper while using a computer. Society has become aware of this waste and is taking measures to combat it.

As discussed in Chapter 6, personal computers, display devices, and printers should comply with guidelines of the ENERGY STAR program. For example, many devices switch to standby or power save mode after a specified number of inactive minutes or hours.

Users should not store obsolete computers and devices in their basement, storage room, attic, warehouse, or any other location. Computers, monitors, and other equipment contain toxic materials and potentially dangerous elements including lead, mercury, and flame retardants. In a landfill, these materials release into the environment. Recycling and refurbishing old equipment are much safer alternatives for the environment. Manufacturers can use the millions of pounds of recycled raw materials to make products such as outdoor furniture and automotive parts.

Experts estimate that more than 500 million personal computers are obsolete. Because of the huge volumes of electronic waste, the U.S. federal government has proposed a bill that would require computer recycling across the country. Local governments are working on methods to make it easy for consumers to recycle this type of equipment. Many computer manufacturers, office supply stores, and other agencies offer free recycling to consumers and businesses.

To reduce the environmental impact of computing further, users simply can alter a few habits. Figure 11-35 lists the ways you can contribute to green computing.

FAQ 11-11

Should I turn off my computer every night?

Manufacturers claim if you use the hibernate feature of your operating system or the sleep feature on your computer, you save about the same amount of energy as when you turn off the computer. The ENERGY STAR program, however, recommends turning it off. For more information, visit scsite.com/dc2007/ch11/faq and then click ENERGY STAR.

GREEN COMPUTING SUGGESTIONS

1. Use computers and devices that comply with the ENERGY STAR program.
2. Do not leave the computer running overnight.
3. Turn off the monitor, printer, and other devices when not in use.
4. Use paperless methods to communicate.
5. Recycle paper.
6. Buy recycled paper.
7. Recycle toner cartridges.
8. Recycle old computers and printers.
9. Telecommute (saves gas).

FIGURE 11-35 A list of suggestions to make computing healthy for the environment.

Test your knowledge of pages 578 through 590 in Quiz Yourself 11-3.

QUIZ YOURSELF 11-3

Instructions: Find the true statement below. Then, rewrite the remaining false statements so they are true.

1. A code of conduct gives authors and artists exclusive rights to duplicate, publish, and sell their materials.

2. Factors that cause CVS include prolonged typing, prolonged mouse usage, or continual shifting between the mouse and the keyboard.

3. Phishing is the discovery, collection, and analysis of evidence found on computers and networks.

4. Spam is Internet junk mail.

5. Users should store obsolete computers and devices in their basement or attic.

6. Web sites use electronic profiles to track user preferences, store users' passwords, keep track of items in a user's shopping cart, and track Web site browsing habits.

7. You can assume that information on the Web is correct.

Quiz Yourself Online: To further check your knowledge of information accuracy, intellectual property rights, codes of conduct, information privacy, and computer-related health disorders and preventions, visit scsite.com/dc2007/ch11/quiz and then click Objectives 10 – 12.

CHAPTER SUMMARY

This chapter identified some potential computer risks and the safeguards that schools, businesses, and individuals can implement to minimize these risks. Wireless security risks and safeguards also were discussed.

The chapter presented ethical issues surrounding information accuracy, intellectual property rights, codes of conduct, and information privacy. The chapter ended with a discussion of computer-related health issues, their preventions, and ways to keep the environment healthy.

CAREER CORNER

Computer Forensics Specialist

Computer forensics is a rapidly growing field that involves gathering and analyzing evidence from computers and networks. It is the responsibility of the *computer forensics specialist* to take several careful steps to identify and retrieve possible evidence that may exist on a suspect's computer. These steps include protecting the suspect's computer, discovering all files, recovering deleted files, revealing hidden files, accessing protected or encrypted files, analyzing all the data, and providing expert consultation and/or testimony as required. A computer forensics specialist must have knowledge of all aspects of the computer, from the operating system to computer architecture and hardware design.

In the past, many computer forensics specialists were self-taught computer users who may have attended computer forensics seminars, or they may have been trained in the use of one or more computer forensics tools by software vendors. The computer forensics specialist of today needs extensive training, usually from several different sources. A degree in Computer Science should be supplemented with graduate courses and university level professional development certificates.

Entry level salaries for computer forensics specialists range from $50,000 to $85,000. With experience and certifications, salaries can exceed $160,000. For more information, read the Computer Forensics Special Feature that follows this chapter or visit scsite.com/dc2007/ch11/careers and then click Computer Forensics Specialist.

High-Tech Talk

THE KEY(S) TO MAKING ENCRYPTION WORK

Every day, hundreds of thousands of people carry notebook computers to and from work, even as other computer users interact electronically, via e-mail, Web sites, ATMs, and cellular telephones. The increase of electronically transmitted information has led to an increased reliance on encryption, which helps ensure that unauthorized individuals cannot obtain the contents of these electronic transmissions.

The two basic types of encryption are private key and public key. With *private key encryption*, also called *symmetric key encryption*, both the originator and the recipient use the same secret key to encrypt and decrypt the data. The most popular private key encryption system is *advanced encryption standard* (*AES*), which was adopted officially as the U.S. government standard in May 2002.

Public key encryption, also called *asymmetric key encryption*, uses two encryption keys: a public key and a private key. Public key encryption software generates both your private key and your public key. A message encrypted with your public key can be decrypted only with your private key, and vice versa.

The public key is made known to those with whom you communicate. For example, public keys are posted on a Web page or e-mailed. A central administrator can publish a list of public keys on a public key server. The private key, by contrast, should be kept confidential. To send an encrypted e-mail message with public key encryption, the sender uses the receiver's public key to encrypt the message. Then, the receiver uses his or her private key to decrypt the message (Figure 11-36). For example, if Mae wants to send Jonah an encrypted message, she would use Jonah's public key to encrypt the message. When Jonah receives the encrypted message, he would use his private key to decrypt it. Jonah's encryption software generated his public and private keys. Mae uses Jonah's public key to encrypt the message. Thus, only Jonah will be able to decrypt the message with his private key.

Windows XP includes a security feature called the *Encryption File System* (*EFS*). EFS uses a combination of public key and symmetric key encryption to ensure that files are protected from almost any method of unauthorized access. When a user encrypts a file, EFS generates a random number for the file that EFS calls the file's file encryption key (FEK) to encrypt the data. EFS then uses FEK to encrypt the file's contents with an encryption algorithm. The FEK then is encrypted with the user's public key using the RSA public-key-based encryption algorithm, and the encrypted FEK then is stored with the file. Of course, the entire encryption process happens behind the scenes for the user, who simply completes a few mouse clicks to encrypt a folder or file. That is part of the elegance of EFS: while it is simple for a user, it is very difficult for any unauthorized user without the correct keys to crack the encryption. In the end, that is the key to keeping your data safe and sound. For more information, visit scsite.com/dc2007/ch11/tech and then click Encryption.

FIGURE 11-36   AN EXAMPLE OF PUBLIC KEY ENCRYPTION

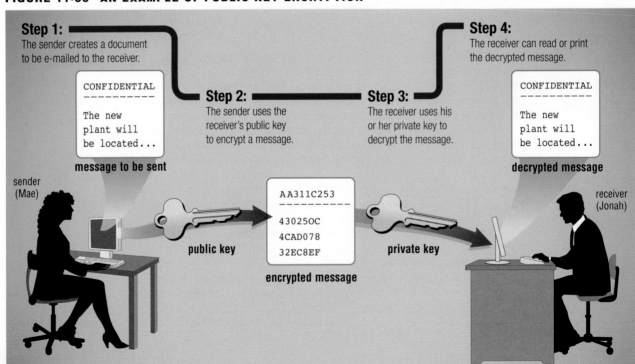

Step 1:
The sender creates a document to be e-mailed to the receiver.

CONFIDENTIAL

The new
plant will
be located...

message to be sent

Step 2:
The sender uses the receiver's public key to encrypt a message.

Step 3:
The receiver uses his or her private key to decrypt the message.

Step 4:
The receiver can read or print the decrypted message.

CONFIDENTIAL

The new
plant will
be located...

decrypted message

sender (Mae)

public key

AA311C253

43025OC
4CAD078
32EC8EF

encrypted message

private key

receiver (Jonah)

Companies on the Cutting Edge

MCAFEE
INTRUSION PREVENTION PRODUCTS DEVELOPER

Researchers in sixteen countries on five continents are hard at work at *McAfee* laboratories trying to prevent computer intrusions. The Anti-Virus Emergency Response Team (AVERT) protects desktop computers, servers, networks, and wireless devices by collecting and then disassembling malware. The researchers also monitor online bulletin board systems for suspicious messages and expect to find more than 18,000 new threats each year.

More than 70 million consumers, small- and medium-sized businesses, governmental agencies, and large corporations rely on McAfee's intrusion prevention products to shield them from viruses, worms, Trojan horses, spyware and adware, and phishing schemes. In 2005, the Santa Clara, California, company renewed its pact with Microsoft to provide online security to MSN Internet Services subscribers. For more information, visit scsite.com/dc2007/ch11/companies and then click McAfee.

SYMANTEC
COMPUTER SECURITY SOLUTIONS LEADER

Ninety percent of computer users have installed a virus protection program on their systems, but only twenty percent have a firewall to protect against malicious hackers, according to a survey conducted by Applied Marketing Research. *Symantec's* line of Norton products, including AntiVirus, Personal Firewall, and AntiSpam, can provide these users with peace of mind knowing that their systems are as secure as possible.

Gordon Eubank founded Symantec in 1982. Since then, more than 120 million users worldwide have used that company's products, helping it grow to one of the world's premier Internet security technology companies with operations in more than 35 countries. Symantec partnered with Nokia in 2005 to provide increased protection against malware threats on mobile devices. For more information, visit scsite.com/dc2007/ch11/companies and then click Symantec.

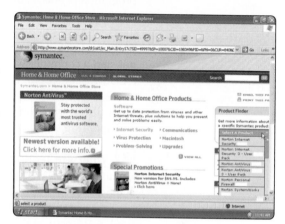

Technology Trailblazers

DONN PARKER
CYBERCRIME AUTHORITY

Computer criminals are troubled people, according to *Donn Parker*, so they violate the law in an attempt to solve their problems. In an attempt to fight cybercrime, Parker founded the International Information Integrity Institute (I-4), then interviewed hundreds of computer criminals and analyzed thousands of security crime cases during the past 30 years.

Security systems within corporations are critical, he says, but they should evolve constantly to defend against attackers. Parker says that computer criminals are unpredictable and irrational, so companies need to stay motivated to enforce their technology risk management plans.

Parker has conducted security reviews for more than 250 companies and has written 6 computer security books. For more information, visit scsite.com/dc2007/ch11/people and then click Donn Parker.

CLIFFORD STOLL
COMPUTER PHILOSOPHER

Computers have become integrated in practically every phase of our lives, but *Clifford Stoll* wants us to think about their effect on our quality of life. He questions the benefits technology and the Internet presumably provide and the role computers play in schools.

In his books, *Silicon Snake Oil — Second Thoughts on the Information Highway* and *High Tech Heretic: Why Computers Don't Belong in the Classroom*, Stoll maintains that "life in the real world is far more interesting, far more important, far richer, than anything you'll ever find on a computer screen."

He first gained fame by tracking a hacker who was part of a spy ring selling computer secrets to the Soviet Union's KGB for money and drugs. For more information, visit scsite.com/dc2007/ch11/people and then click Clifford Stoll.

Chapter Review

The Chapter Review section summarizes the concepts presented in this chapter. To listen to the audio version of this Chapter Review, visit scsite.com/dc2007/ch11/review. To obtain help from other students regarding any subject in this chapter, visit scsite.com/dc2007/ch11/forum and post your thoughts or questions.

① What Are Types of Computer Security Risks? A **computer security risk** is any event or action that could cause a loss of or damage to computer hardware, software, data, information, or processing capability. Common computer security risks include computer viruses, worms, Trojan horses, denial of service attacks, back doors, and spoofing; unauthorized access and use; hardware theft and vandalism; software theft; information theft; and system failure.

② How Can Users Safeguard against Computer Viruses, Worms, Trojan Horses, Denial of Service Attacks, Back Doors, and Spoofing? A computer **virus** is a potentially damaging program that affects, or infects, a computer negatively by altering the way the computer works. A **worm** is a program that copies itself repeatedly, using up resources and possibly shutting down the computer or network. A **Trojan horse** is a program that hides within or looks like a legitimate program. Users can take precautions to guard against this *malware*, short for *malicious software*. Do not start a computer with removable media in the drives or plugged in the ports. Never open an e-mail attachment unless it is from a **trusted source**. Disable *macros* in documents that are not from a trusted source. Install an **antivirus program** and a personal firewall. Stay informed about any new virus alert or **virus hoax**. To defend against a **denial of service attack**, improper use of a **back door**, and **spoofing**, users can install a **firewall**, install *intrusion detection software*, and set up a *honeypot*.

③ What Are Techniques to Prevent Unauthorized Computer Access and Use?
Unauthorized access is the use of a computer or network without permission. **Unauthorized use** is the use of a computer or its data for unapproved or illegal activities. A written acceptable use policy (AUP) outlines the activities for which the computer and network may and may not be used. A **firewall** consists of hardware and/or software that prevents unauthorized access to data, information, and storage media. *Intrusion detection software* analyzes network traffic, assesses vulnerability, identifies unauthorized intrusions, and notifies network administrators of suspicious behavior patterns or system breaches. An *access control* defines who can access a computer, when they can access it, and what actions they can take. Access controls include a **user name** and **password**, a *possessed object*, and a **biometric device**. An **audit trail** records in a file both successful and unsuccessful access attempts.

connect Visit scsite.com/dc2007/ch11/quiz or click the Quiz Yourself button. Click Objectives 1 – 3.

④ What Are Safeguards against Hardware Theft and Vandalism? **Hardware theft** is the act of stealing computer equipment. **Hardware vandalism** is the act of defacing or destroying computer equipment. The best preventive measures against hardware theft and vandalism are common sense and a constant awareness of the risk. Physical devices and practical security measures, passwords, possessed objects, and biometrics can reduce the risk of theft or render a computer useless if it is stolen.

⑤ How Do Software Manufacturers Protect against Software Piracy? Software **piracy** is the unauthorized and illegal duplication of copyrighted software. To protect themselves from software piracy, manufacturers issue a **license agreement** that provides specific conditions for use of the software. **Product activation** is a process during which users provide the product's identification number to receive an installation identification number unique to their computer.

⑥ What Is Encryption, and Why Is It Necessary? **Information theft** occurs when someone steals personal or confidential information. **Encryption** prevents information theft by converting readable data into unreadable characters. To read the data, a recipient must **decrypt**, or decipher, it into a readable form.

Chapter Review

(7) What Types of Devices Are Available to Protect Computers from System Failure?
A *system failure* is the prolonged malfunction of a computer. A common cause of system failure is an electrical disturbance such as **noise**, an **undervoltage**, or an **overvoltage**. A **surge protector** uses special electrical components to smooth out minor noise, provide a stable current flow, and keep an overvoltage from reaching the computer. An **uninterruptible power supply** (**UPS**) contains surge protection circuits and one or more batteries that can provide power during an undervoltage.

(8) What Are Options for Backing Up Computer Resources? A **backup** is a duplicate of a file, program, or disk that can be used to **restore** the file if the original is lost, damaged, or destroyed. Users can opt for a *full backup* or a *selective backup*. Most operating systems and backup devices include a backup program, and numerous stand-alone backup utilities exist.

(9) What Are Risks and Safeguards Associated with Wireless Communications? Wireless access poses additional security risks. Intruders connect to other wireless networks to gain free Internet access or a company's confidential data. Some individuals intercept and monitor communications as they are transmitted. Others connect to a network through an unsecured wireless access point (WAP). Some safeguards include firewalls, reconfiguring the WAP, and ensuring equipment uses a wireless security standard, such as *Wired Equivalent Privacy* (WEP), *Wi-Fi Protected Access* (WPA), and *802.11i*.

> connect
> Visit scsite.com/dc2007/ch11/quiz or click the Quiz Yourself button. Click Objectives 4 – 9.

(10) What Are Issues Related to Information Accuracy, Rights, and Conduct? **Computer ethics** govern the use of computers and information systems. Issues in computer ethics include the responsibility for information accuracy and the **intellectual property rights** to which creators are entitled for works that are available digitally. A **copyright** gives authors and artists exclusive rights to duplicate, publish, and sell their materials. An IT (information technology) **code of conduct** helps determine whether a specific computer action is ethical or unethical.

(11) What Are Issues Surrounding Information Privacy? **Information privacy** is the right of individuals and companies to deny or restrict the collection and use of information about them. Issues surrounding information privacy include electronic profiles, cookies, spyware and adware, spam, phishing, social engineering, employee monitoring, and computer forensics. An electronic profile combines data about an individual's Web use with data from public sources, which then is sold. A **cookie** is a file that a Web server stores on a computer to collect data about the user. *Spyware* is a program placed on a computer that secretly collects information about the user. *Adware* is a program that displays an online advertisement in a banner or pop-up window. **Spam** is an unsolicited e-mail message or newsgroup posting sent to many recipients. **Phishing** is a scam in which a perpetrator sends an official looking e-mail that attempts to obtain personal or financial information. **Pharming** is a scam where a perpetrator attempts to obtain your personal and financial information, except they do so via spoofing. As related to the use of computers, **social engineering** is defined as gaining unauthorized access or obtaining confidential information by taking advantage of the trusting human nature of some victims and the naivety of others. **Employee monitoring** uses computers to observe, record, and review an employee's computer use.

(12) How Can Health-Related Disorders and Injuries Due to Computer Use Be Prevented?
A **repetitive strain injury** (**RSI**) is an injury or disorder of the muscles, nerves, tendons, ligaments, and joints. Computer-related RSIs include *tendonitis* and *carpal tunnel syndrome* (CTS). Another health-related condition is eyestrain associated with **computer vision syndrome** (*CVS*). To prevent health-related disorders, take frequent breaks, use precautionary exercises and techniques, and use *ergonomics* when planning the workplace. **Computer addiction** occurs when the computer consumes someone's entire social life. Computer addiction is a treatable illness through therapy and support groups.

> connect
> Visit scsite.com/dc2007/ch11/quiz or click the Quiz Yourself button. Click Objectives 10 – 12.

Key Terms

You should know the Primary Terms and be familiar with the Secondary Terms. Use the list below to help focus your study. To further enhance your understanding of the Key Terms in this chapter, visit scsite.com/dc2007/ch11/terms. See an example of and a definition for each term, and access current and additional information about the term from the Web.

Primary Terms

(shown in bold-black characters in the chapter)

anti-spam program (584)
antivirus program (560)
audit trail (565)
back door (562)
back up (576)
backup (576)
biometric device (567)
code of conduct (580)
computer addiction (589)
computer crime (556)
computer ethics (578)
computer forensics (587)
computer security risk (556)
computer vision syndrome (588)
content filtering (586)
cookie (582)
copyright (579)
cracker (556)
cybercrime (556)
cyberextortionist (557)
cyberterrorist (557)
decrypt (572)
denial of service attack (562)
digital certificate (573)
digital signature (572)
DoS attack (562)
e-mail filtering (584)
employee monitoring (586)
encryption (572)
Fair Credit Reporting Act (586)
firewall (563)
green computing (590)
hacker (556)
hardware theft (569)
hardware vandalism (569)
information privacy (580)
information theft (571)

inoculate (561)
intellectual property rights (579)
license agreement (570)
noise (574)
online security service (558)
overvoltage (574)
password (566)
personal firewall (564)
personal identification number (PIN) (567)
pharming (584)
phishing (584)
piracy (570)
power surge (574)
product activation (571)
quarantine (561)
repetitive strain injury (RSI) (587)
restore (576)
script kiddie (556)
secure site (573)
social engineering (586)
software theft (570)
spam (584)
spoofing (563)
surge protector (574)
Trojan horse (558)
trusted source (560)
unauthorized access (564)
unauthorized use (564)
undervoltage (574)
uninterruptible power supply (UPS) (575)
user name (566)
virus (558)
virus definition (561)
virus hoax (562)
virus signature (561)
Web filtering software (587)
worm (558)
zombie (562)

Secondary Terms

(shown in italic characters in the chapter)

128-bit encryption (573)
40-bit encryption (573)
802.11i (577)
access control (565)
adware (583)
authentication (566)
blackout (574)
brownout (574)
Business Software Alliance (BSA) (571)
carpal tunnel syndrome (CTS) (588)
CERT/CC (558)
certificate authority (CA) (573)
child (576)
ciphertext (572)
Computer Emergency Response Team Coordination Center (558)
CVS (588)
cyberforensics (587)
DDoS (distributed DoS) attack (562)
digital forensics (587)
digital rights management (DRM) (580)
encryption key (572)
end-user license agreement (EULA) (571)
ergonomics (589)
fault-tolerant computer (576)
full backup (576)
grandparent (576)
hash (572)
honeypot (564)
identification (566)
intellectual property (IP) (579)
Internet Content Rating Association (ICRA) (586)
intrusion detection software (564)
Joule (575)

macros (560)
malicious software (558)
malware (558)
network forensics (587)
offline UPS (575)
offsite (576)
online backup service (576)
online UPS (575)
parent (576)
payload (558)
plaintext (572)
possessed object (567)
Pretty Good Privacy (PGP) (572)
proxy server (563)
Secure HTTP (S-HTTP) (574)
Secure Sockets Layer (SSL) (574)
selective backup (576)
session cookie (582)
single-user license agreement (571)
spike (574)
spim (584)
spit (584)
spyware (583)
standby UPS (575)
surge suppressor (574)
system failure (574)
tendonitis (588)
three-generation backup (576)
Underwriters Laboratories (UL) 1449 standard (575)
user ID (566)
virtual private network (VPN) (574)
war driving (577)
war flying (577)
Web bug (583)
Wi-Fi Protected Access (WPA) (577)
Wired Equivalent Privacy (WEP) (577)

Checkpoint

Use the Checkpoint exercises to check your knowledge level of the chapter. The Beyond the Book exercises will help broaden your understanding of the concepts presented in this chapter. To complete the Checkpoint exercises interactively, visit scsite.com/dc2007/ch11/check.

Label the Figure

Identify these common computer security risks.

a. hardware theft
b. system failure
c. information theft
d. unauthorized access and use
e. Internet and network attacks
f. software theft

1.
2.
3.
6.
5.
4.

True/False

Mark T for True and F for False. (See page numbers in parentheses.)

_____ 1. Not all breaches to computer security are planned. (556)

_____ 2. Hackers often claim the intent of their security breaches is to improve security. (556)

_____ 3. Many methods exist to guarantee completely a computer or network is safe from computer viruses, worms, and Trojan horses. (560)

_____ 4. IP spoofing occurs when an intruder computer fools a network into believing its IP address is associated with a trusted source. (563)

_____ 5. A honeypot is a computer that is set up to entice an intruder to break into it. (564)

_____ 6. Software piracy reduces the chance of spreading viruses, increases your ability to receive technical support, and drives down the price of software. (571)

_____ 7. Encrypted (scrambled) data is called ciphertext. (572)

_____ 8. A certificate authority (CA) is an authorized person or a company that issues and verifies digital certificates. (573)

_____ 9. An online UPS switches to battery power when a problem occurs in a power line. (575)

_____ 10. Digital rights management (DRM) is a strategy designed to prevent illegal distribution of computer viruses, worms, and Trojan horses. (580)

_____ 11. A cookie is a small text file that a Web server stores on your computer. (582)

_____ 12. Web filtering software is a program that restricts access to specified Web sites. (587)

Checkpoint

 **Multiple Choice**

Select the best answer. (See page numbers in parentheses.)

1. A computer infected by a virus, worm, or Trojan horse may have any of the following symptoms except _____. (558)
   a. available memory is more than expected
   b. system properties change
   c. existing programs and files disappear
   d. files become corrupted

2. Malware is a term that can be used to describe _____. (558)
   a. worms
   b. spyware
   c. back doors
   d. all of the above

3. A _____ is a computer that is completely unaware it is being used as part of a network that attacks other systems. (562)
   a. ghost
   b. zombie
   c. back door
   d. Trojan horse

4. _____ is a technique intruders use to make their network or Internet transmission appear legitimate to a victim computer or network. (563)
   a. A back door
   b. A DoS attack
   c. Spoofing
   d. A virus hoax

5. Physical access controls, such as locked doors and windows, usually are adequate to protect against _____. (569)
   a. software piracy
   b. unauthorized access
   c. hardware theft
   d. all of the above

6. Software piracy continues because _____. (571)
   a. in some countries, legal protection for software does not exist
   b. many buyers believe they have the right to copy software
   c. software piracy is a fairly simple crime to commit
   d. all of the above

7. A Web site that uses _____ to secure its data is known as a secure site. (573)
   a. hypertext
   b. decryption
   c. encryption
   d. social engineering

8. A(n) _____ is a notice that guarantees a user or a Web site is legitimate. (573)
   a. trusted source
   b. end-user license agreement
   c. surge protector
   d. digital certificate

9. A _____ is a prolonged undervoltage. (574)
   a. spike
   b. blackout
   c. joule
   d. brownout

10. To _____ a file means to make a copy of it. (576)
    a. inoculate
    b. back up
    c. quarantine
    d. encrypt

11. A _____ gives authors and artists exclusive rights to duplicate, publish, and sell their materials. (579)
    a. copyright
    b. license
    c. password
    d. firewall

12. As related to the use of computers, _____ is defined as gaining unauthorized access or obtaining confidential information by taking advantage of the trusting human nature of some victims and the naivety of others. (586)
    a. phishing
    b. social engineering
    c. a virus hoax
    d. pharming

13. Web filtering software is a program that _____. (587)
    a. uses encryption to secure a transaction on the Web
    b. backs up files to an online location
    c. restricts access to specified Web sites
    d. protects against computer viruses

14. _____ is inflammation of the nerve that connects the forearm to the palm of the wrist. (588)
    a. Carpal tunnel syndrome (CTS)
    b. Computer vision syndrome (CVS)
    c. Computer addiction
    d. Tendonitis

Checkpoint

 Matching

Match the terms with their definitions. (See page numbers in parentheses.)

____ 1. cracker (556)
____ 2. cyberterrorist (557)
____ 3. quarantine (561)
____ 4. back door (562)
____ 5. personal firewall (564)
____ 6. password (566)
____ 7. biometric device (567)
____ 8. spike (574)
____ 9. spyware (583)
____ 10. adware (583)

a. spyware hidden on Web pages or in e-mail messages in the form of a graphical image

b. private combination of characters associated with a user name

c. protects a personal computer from unauthorized intrusions

d. someone who uses the Internet or network to destroy or damage computers for political reasons

e. program that displays an online advertisement in a banner or pop-up window on Web pages, e-mail, or other Internet services

f. translates a personal characteristic into digital code

g. area of the hard disk that holds an infected file until the infection can be removed

h. someone who accesses a computer or network illegally with the intent of malicious action

i. contains an uninfected copy of key commands and startup information

j. program or set of instructions in a program that allows users to bypass security controls when accessing a program, computer, or network

k. occurs when the increase in power lasts for less than one millisecond

l. program placed on a computer without the user's knowledge that secretly collects information about the user

 Short Answer

Write a brief answer to each of the following questions.

1. How do antivirus programs detect and identify a virus? _____ What is a virus hoax? _____
2. How is identification different from authentication? _____ What are three methods of identification and authentication? _____
3. What is product activation? _____ What might be the consequences of not activating software? _____
4. What is an uninterruptible power supply (UPS)? _____ How is a standby UPS different from an online UPS? _____
5. How does phishing differ from pharming? _____ What are some social engineering techniques? _____

Beyond the Book

Read the following book elements, learn more about each using the Web, and then write a brief report.

1. Ethics & Issues — How Should Virus Authors Be Punished? (558), Should Schools Use Biometric Devices? (568), Who Should Control the Content of Your CDs and DVDs? (580), Should Spyware Be Legal? (583), or Who Should Protect You from Identity Theft? (584)
2. Career Corner — Computer Forensics Specialist (591)
3. Companies on the Cutting Edge — McAfee or Symantec (593)
4. FAQs (559, 562, 564, 565, 566, 571, 576, 582, 584, 590)

5. High-Tech Talk — The Key(s) to Making Encryption Work (592)
6. Looking Ahead — Three-Dimensional Facial Recognition Software — A Step Forward for Security (568) or Computer Knowledge Assessment Using Brain Fingerprinting (587)
7. Making Use of the Web — Environment (127)
8. Picture Yourself Aware of Computer-related Risks (554)
9. Technology Trailblazers — Donn Parker and Clifford Stoll (593)
10. Web Links (558, 562, 564, 570, 571, 573, 575, 580, 582, 587, 590)

Learn It Online

Use the Learn It Online exercises to reinforce your understanding of the chapter concepts. To access the Learn It Online exercises, visit scsite.com/dc2007/ch11/learn.

1 At the Movies — Does Biometrics Violate Employee Privacy?

To view the Does Biometrics Violate Employee Privacy? movie, click the number 1 button. Locate your video and click the corresponding High-Speed or Dial-Up link, depending on your Internet connection. Watch the movie and then complete the exercise by answering the questions that follow. Many companies are turning to high-tech methods of identifying and tracking employees. Biometric identification methods, which include fingerprinting, iris, voice, hand, and facial scans, are gaining in popularity. These methods used to be associated with high-security facilities; but due to increased risks from terrorism, they are gaining popularity in other workplaces. Biometric identification will help employers with employee fraud and security issues. Can you think of any instances where biometric identification can be used as a safety measure for employees? Are there any circumstances under which biometric technology can be abused in the workplace?

2 At the Movies — Stop Spam

To view the Stop Spam movie, click the number 2 button. Locate your video and click the corresponding High-Speed or Dial-Up link, depending on your Internet connection. Watch the movie and then complete the exercise by answering the question that follows. You have set every possible mail control and blocked every unknown e-mail address; yet each day when you open your virtual mailbox, you find unwelcome advertisements. No matter how high your security features are set, you still are bound to find some spam in your e-mail. Besides setting your e-mail controls, what are some other steps you can take to stamp out spam?

3 Student Edition Labs — Protecting Your Privacy Online

Click the number 3 button. A new browser window will open, displaying the Student Edition Labs. Follow the on-screen instructions to complete the Protecting Your Privacy Online Lab. When finished, click the Exit button. If required, submit your results to your instructor.

4 Student Edition Labs — Keeping Your Computer Virus Free

Click the number 4 button. A new browser window will open, displaying the Student Edition Labs. Follow the on-screen instructions to complete the Keeping Your Computer Virus Free Lab. When finished, click the Exit button. If required, submit your results to your instructor.

5 Practice Test

Click the number 5 button. Answer each question. When completed, enter your name and click the Grade Test button to submit the quiz for grading. Make a note of any missed questions. If required, submit your results to your instructor.

6 Who Wants To Be a Computer Genius²?

Click the number 6 button to find out if you are a computer genius. Directions about how to play the game will be displayed. When you are ready to play, click the Play button. Submit your score to your instructor.

Learn It Online

(7) Wheel of Terms

Click the number 7 button to reinforce important terms you learned in this chapter by playing the Shelly Cashman Series version of this popular game. Directions about how to play the game will be displayed. When you are ready to play, click the Play button. Submit your score to your instructor.

(8) DC Track and Field

Click the number 8 button to use what you have learned in this chapter to compete against other students in three track and field events. Directions about how to play the game will be displayed. When you are ready to play, click the start first event button. If required, submit your score to your instructor.

(9) You're Hired!

Click the number 9 button to use what you have learned in this chapter to embark on the path to a career in computers. Directions about how to play the game will be displayed. When you are ready to play, click the begin game button. If required, submit your score to your instructor.

(10) Crossword Puzzle Challenge

Click the number 10 button. Complete the puzzle to reinforce skills you learned in this chapter. Directions about how to play the game will be displayed. When you are ready to play, click the Submit button. Submit the completed puzzle to your instructor.

(11) Lab Exercises

Click the number 11 button. When the Lab Exercises menu appears, click the exercise assigned by your instructor. A new browser window will open. Follow the on-screen instructions to complete the exercise. When finished, click the Exit button. If required, submit your results to your instructor.

(12) In the News

Why own the latest video game when you can rent it from the comfort of your personal computer? IGN Entertainment has agreements with leading video-game publishers — Ripcord Games, GameSpy.com, and FilePlanet.com — that will allow broadband users to download files from the IGN Entertainment Web site to play stand-alone or multiplayer games. The IGN Web site sends users all they need to get started playing the games, and as more bytes are needed, they are sent from the server to the users. Click the number 12 button and read a news article about online games and edutainment applications. What applications have been developed? Do you think the applications will be successful? Why or why not? Do you think online games will replace the traditional, local CD-ROM game?

(13) Chapter Discussion Forum

Select an objective from this chapter on page 555 about which you would like more information. Click the number 13 button and post a short message listing a meaningful message title accompanied by one or more questions concerning the selected objective. In two days, return to the threaded discussion by clicking the number 13 button. Submit to your instructor your original message and at least one response to your message.

(14) Buying Online

Click the number 14 button to learn how to use the Internet to purchase merchandise. Follow the instructions to use Amazon.com and Barnes & Noble's Web site to compare prices and reviews of David McCullough's *1776*. How did the prices of the book compare? Which site had more favorable reviews for the book? Which site would you recommend to a friend? Write a report summarizing your findings. Print the report and then submit it to your instructor.

Learn How To

Use the Learn How To activities to learn fundamental skills when using a computer and accompanying technology. Complete the exercises and submit them to your instructor. To see a video of a Learn How To activity, visit scsite.com/dc2007/ch11/howto.

LEARN HOW TO 1: Back Up Files on an Offsite Internet Server

Note: The service described in this exercise allows 30 days of free access. After that time, you may be billed automatically for service unless you cancel your service in the given time frame.

Backing up files stored on your computer on another disk or computer located in a different geographical location is the ultimate safeguard for data on your computer. A good way to back up data is to use one of the services available on the Web. A leading service is found at www.IBackup.com. To subscribe to the IBackup service, complete the following steps:

1. Start a Web browser, type the Web address **www.IBackup.com** in the Address bar, and then press the ENTER key.
2. When the IBackup Web page is displayed, click Sign Up on the top horizontal toolbar.
3. Enter your e-mail address in the E-mail Address text box, and then click the Send Registration E-mail button.
4. In a short period, you will receive a subscription e-mail message. Because you want to subscribe to the backup service, click the backup link in the e-mail message. A form will be displayed in your browser (Figure 11-37).
5. Fill in the form. Select the plan you want in the Select a Storage Plan list. If you want to try the service for a short period of time before subscribing, select 50 MB Trial for 30 Days (Figure 11-37).
6. To continue, you must enter credit card information. If you select the 30 day trial, your credit card will not be charged, and an automatic billing at the end of 30 days will not occur. After entering the required information, click the Continue button at the bottom of the page.
7. A message is displayed that tells you the amount charged against your credit card. Also, you can click a link to go to the login page, or enter the Web address **https://www.IBackup.com**.

After establishing an account, you can use it for the time for which you subscribed. Complete the following steps to use the service:

1. Enter the Web address as noted in Step 7 above.
2. In the upper-left corner of the home page, enter your user name and password, and then click the Login button. *Your file/folder page is displayed (Figure 11-38). Initially, no files will be saved in your IBackup folder.*
3. To upload a file, click the Upload button on the IBackup toolbar, click a Browse button in the window that opened, browse your computer and locate the file you wish to upload, and then click the Upload file button. The file will be placed in the IBackup folder.

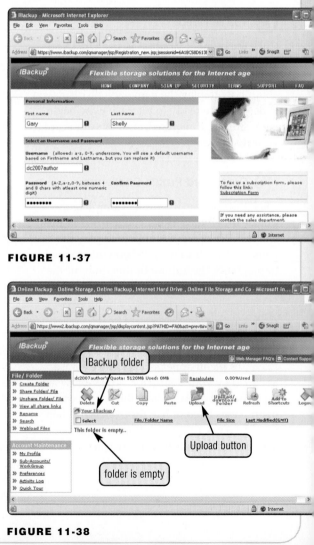

FIGURE 11-37

FIGURE 11-38

Learn How To

4. For further activities you can accomplish on this site for backing up your files, click the links in the File/Folder area and experiment.

Exercise

1. Visit the IBackup Web site. Click IBackup Tour and then follow the screen prompts to view all the services offered by IBackup. Which service is most appropriate for your home computer? Which service is most useful for the server that is used in the computer lab at your school? If you had critical data you needed to back up, would you use a service like this? Why or why not? Submit your answers to your instructor.
2. **Optional: Perform this exercise only for your own computer. Do not perform this exercise on a school computer.** Establish an account on IBackup.com. Upload two or more files from your computer. Right-click a file you uploaded on Ibackup.com and click Save Target As on the menu. What happened? Save the file on your computer. What message(s) were displayed? Download the files you uploaded back to your computer. Is this an efficient way to back up your files? Submit your answers to your instructor.

LEARN HOW TO 2: Use the Windows XP Firewall

When you use the Internet, data is sent both from your computer to the Internet and from computers on the Internet to your computer. A firewall is a barrier that checks information coming from the Internet and either turns it away or allows it to pass through to your computer, based on your firewall settings. It also checks data being sent from your computer to the Internet to ensure your computer is not sending unsolicited messages to other computers on the Internet. A firewall can be implemented using hardware or software.

Windows XP SP2 contains a software firewall that starts automatically when you boot your computer. To control the firewall usage on your computer, complete the following steps:

1. Click the Start button on the Windows taskbar, and then click Control Panel on the Start menu.
2. In the Category view of the Control Panel, click Security Center, and then click Windows Firewall in the Windows Security Center window. *The Windows Firewall dialog box is displayed (Figure 11-39).*
3. In the Windows Firewall dialog box, select On or Off to turn on or off the Windows firewall. The firewall automatically is on when you start your computer. You should NOT turn off the firewall unless you have a compelling reason to do so.
4. Click the Exceptions tab in the Windows Firewall dialog box. *The Exceptions sheet is displayed (Figure 11-40). The exceptions that are checked can communicate with the Internet without your clicking a link.*
5. You may want to allow programs that routinely communicate with the Internet, such as sports programs that display updated game scores, to have full access to your computer. To add a program to the Exceptions list, in the Exceptions sheet click the Add Program button. The Add a Program dialog box is displayed. Select a program and then click the OK button.

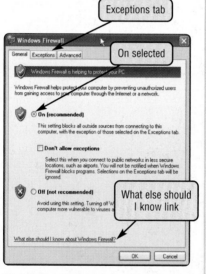

FIGURE 11-39

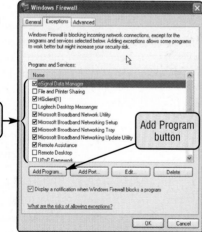

FIGURE 11-40

Exercise

1. Display the Windows Firewall dialog box. Click What else should I know about Windows Firewall in the General sheet. Read the information about Windows firewall. What did you learn that you did not know? What is a security log? How can you cause a security log to be created? Submit your answers to your instructor.

Web Research

Use the Internet-based Web Research exercises to broaden your understanding of the concepts presented in this chapter. Visit scsite.com/dc2007/ch11/research to obtain more information pertaining to each exercise. To discuss any of the Web Research exercises in this chapter with other students, post your thoughts or questions at scsite.com/dc2007/ch11/forum.

(1) Scavenger Hunt Use one of the <u>search engines</u> listed in Figure 2-10 in Chapter 2 on page 78 or your own favorite search engine to find the answers to the questions that follow. Copy and paste the Web address from the Web page where you found the answer. Some questions may have more than one answer. If required, submit your answers to your instructor. (1) What is the $800 from Microsoft hoax? (2) What term is John Scoch credited with creating at the Xerox Palo Alto Research Center in the late 1970s? (3) What is the text of the poem the Elk Cloner virus displayed? What is the significance of this virus? (4) What company developed SSL? How does SSL differ from Secure HTTP (S-HTTP)? (5) At what university is the Computer Emergency Response Team Coordination Center (CERT/CC) located? What is one of the latest advisories or incident notes reported by this organization?

(2) Search Sleuth Internet subject directories are used to find information on specialized topics. One of the oldest and more popular subject directories is the <u>WWW Virtual Library (VL)</u>. This Web site is administered by a group of volunteers who are experts in particular topics. Visit this Web site and then use your word processing program to answer the following questions. Then, if required, submit your answers to your instructor. (1) Click the Computing and Computer Science link and then click the Safety-Critical Systems link. Read two articles in the On-line Publications section and then write a 50-word summary of your findings. (2) Click the Back button twice and then click the Virtual Museum of Computing link. When did the Museum open? What are three recent additions and events? (3) Click the Back button and then type `firewall` in the Search for text box at the top of the page. How many articles were retrieved? What is the title of the most recent article posted?

(3) Journaling Respond to your readings in this chapter by writing at least one page about your reactions, evaluations, and reflections on computer security, privacy, and ethics. For example, have you suffered from a <u>repetitive strain injury</u>? Does your employer monitor your computer use? Should an employer be able to read your e-mail messages? How have you tried to decrease spam and to safeguard your personal information? You also can write about the new terms you learned by reading this chapter. If required, submit your journal to your instructor.

(4) Expanding Your Understanding Thousands of hackers are attempting to gain unauthorized access to computer systems across the world, according to computer security experts. Some of these hackers are experienced programmers, while others are <u>script kiddies</u> who are using tools developed by sophisticated programmers. All computers are vulnerable to script-kiddie assaults, especially home computers with always-on, high-speed connections. A personal firewall can help thwart these invasions. Visit a software vendor and locate a personal firewall program. What is the name of this software? Who is the manufacturer? What is the cost? What are the system requirements? How is the software installed? What tasks does the software perform? Write a report summarizing your findings. If required, submit your report to your instructor.

(5) Ethics in Action <u>Radio frequency identification (RFID) tags</u> are expected to help merchants in many ways. By placing these tags on such items as prescription drugs, computer peripherals, and clothing, retailers hope to reduce theft, track inventory, reduce labor costs, and keep their shelves stocked. Privacy experts, however, claim the tags can store information about consumers' shopping habits and whereabouts. Law enforcement officials, lawyers, marketers, and even thieves could use this electronic detailed data to track people at all times of the day. View online sites that discuss using RFID tags in stores and the privacy issues that arise from their use. Write a report summarizing your findings, and include a table of links to Web sites that provide additional details about the developing field of RFID. If required, submit your report to your instructor.

Case Studies

Use the Case Studies to apply the concepts presented in the chapter to real-world situations. Visit scsite.com/dc2007/ch11/cases to obtain more information pertaining to each exercise. To discuss the Case Studies in this chapter with other students, visit scsite.com/dc2007/ch11/forum and post your thoughts or questions.

CASE STUDY 1 — Class Discussion   As manager of the information technology department, you are responsible for maintaining the company's e-mail system. Recently, you were sent a request by a member of the senior management team to make available for her review all e-mails sent and received by non-salaried employees over the past month. Your initial reaction was that such a request is not only unethical, but possibly illegal as well. Upon contacting the human resources department, you learn that an obscure statement in the employee handbook gives senior staff the right to read anything transmitted on media owned by the company without notifying the sender or recipient. Would you immediately honor the request, or would you first try to convince senior management that internal communications between employees should be private? Why or why not? Do you think such a policy is good for employee morale? Why or why not? Write a brief report and be prepared to discuss your recommendations in class.

CASE STUDY 2 — Class Discussion   Your best friend, Matthew, spends all his free time writing computer programs that interact with the Windows operating system. He recently informed you that over fall break he had written malware that randomly erases files and displays weird messages the day before Christmas (December 24) at exactly 1:00 p.m. He plans to distribute the Trojan horse, called Merry Christmas America, via an e-mail attachment. Also included with the e-mail is a hidden program that sends the same e-mail to all the e-mail addresses in the user's address list. The e-mail with the attachment will be sent as spam the day after finals in December, so it will have plenty of time to be distributed to millions of computers worldwide before December 24. Upon learning of Matthew's plan, what would you do? You know that a hefty reward of $250,000 is offered by a large software company for turning in unscrupulous programmers. Do you think it is right to inform on a friend when no profit is involved in the crime? Why or why not? Who would you notify (i.e., Matthew's parents, the dean of students, the police, or the software company offering the reward)? Write a brief report and be prepared to discuss your recommendations in class.

CASE STUDY 3 — Research   Computer viruses have cost companies billions of dollars in lost revenue. In a recent six-month period, the number of new viruses and worms aimed at Microsoft's ubiquitous Windows operating system rose from 1,000 a year to nearly 5,000. You work as a network analyst for a large manufacturing company that uses Windows. After the most recent virus attack, your manager asked you to investigate the feasibility of switching to a different operating system, such as Linux or UNIX. Use the Web and/or print media to research the advantages and disadvantages of switching operating systems. Are alternative operating systems as susceptible to viruses as Windows? Why or why not? What is Microsoft's approach to eliminating virus attacks? Why is Windows so prone to virus attacks? What types of costs are involved in changing operating systems? Submit your report or use PowerPoint to create a presentation and share your findings with your class.

CASE STUDY 4 — Research   Internet-based companies who take advantage of consumer trust are sneaking their spyware into computers for their own purposes. Spyware secretly collects information about a user's computer activities. The owner of a chain of fast-food restaurants, Burgers & Fries, where you are employed as an application analyst wants to purge spyware from the chain's computers. Use the Web and/or print media and compare the spyware remover programs available. For each program, answer the following questions. What is the program's function? What are the system requirements? How easy is the program to use? How do you obtain updates to the program? How much does the program cost? In your opinion, is the program worth the price? Why or why not? Which one would you recommend? Why? Write a brief report or use PowerPoint to create a presentation and share your findings with your class.

CASE STUDY 5 — Team Challenge   A recent study conducted by the senior management at Consumer-Mart, a large retail company with worldwide sales, concluded that the company's computer system was at severe risk. Your team has been hired as consultants to deal with the following vulnerabilities: Internet and network attacks, unauthorized access and use, hardware theft and vandalism, software theft, information theft, system failure, and wireless security. Divide these areas of vulnerabilities between the team members. Using the Web and/or print media, have each team member summarize the issues associated with each of the areas of computer security risk assigned to them and make recommendations as to how the company can deal with them. As a team, merge your findings into a team report and/or PowerPoint presentation and share your recommendations with your class.

COMPUTER FORENSICS

Forensics is the use of science to investigate and establish facts in criminal or civil courts. Forensic scientists are able to examine a set of clues and rebuild a sequence of events. Computer forensics is the newest and fastest growing discipline in this field. As described earlier in Chapter 11, computer forensics — also called digital forensics, network forensics, or cyber-forensics — is the discovery, collection, and analysis of evidence found on computers and networks. Computer forensics techniques include analyzing log files, analyzing storage media (including deleted files), analyzing chat logs, and reviewing trace nodes (Figure 1). This field of study integrates aspects of criminal justice, computer science, and computer and network investigative techniques.

(a) Analyze Log Files

```
1)  Mar 13 03:11:55 watson ipop3d[16319]: pop3
    service init from 192.168.187.35
2)  Mar 13 03:11:55 watson ipop3d[16319]: Login
    user=kumquat host=holmes.example.net
    [192.168.187.35] nmsgs=0/0
3)  Mar 13 03:12:16 watson ipop3d[16319]: Logout
    user=kumquat host=holmes.example.net
    [192.168.187.35] nmsgs=0 ndele=0
```

(b) Analyze Deleted Files

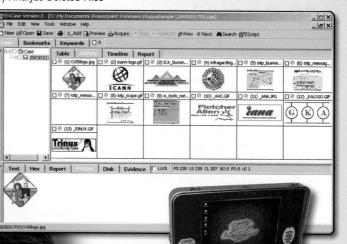

Computer Forensics Examiner

(c) Analyze Chat Logs

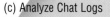

```
Session Start: Tue Mar 23 15:50:33 2007
Session Ident: #Strong&40
* Now talking in #Strong&40
* Topic is 'Welcome to the BEST little channel on the net!   www.40plus.com.html '
* Set by Bunni on Tue Mar 23 10:31:01
<BettyF> I sure beats the 20's we've been having, Cary
<BettyF> Hi, billy
<billy89> Hi
<abc_m> hi Cary:)
<abc_m> hi billy89
<`Cary> hey cd  how  be?
<billy89> Hi
<abc_m> not bad a bit cold but doing okay
<BettyF> How ya doing, billy?
<billy89> So... I'm just lookin' around irc...
<BettyF> and lo and behold you found us
<billy89> Doin' ok... also cold where I am... Minnesota... Where're you?
<BettyF> Maine here
<billy89> Yep... here I am ... :-)
<abc_m> ottawa canada here
<billy89> Sunny Ontario! :-)
<BettyF> You had some really nasty spells in January, billy
<`Cary> I gotta go again.. laters  yawl.. play safe
* `Cary has left #Strong&40
<billy89> Bitter cold in Jan. dumped on by TWO bad snow storms in December
<BettyF> I talked with my old Ottawa friend a few days ago, cdn -- but only for
about a minute ... I think he had a date. lol
<abc_m> ohhhhhhhhhhhhh
<abc_m> they have those out here?
<BettyF> I have a friend in St. Paul, billy -- she was in her house with her jacket
on in January.
```

(d) Trace Nodes

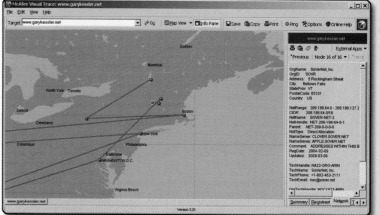

FIGURE 1   Computer forensics is the discovery, collection, and analysis of evidence found on computers and networks.

THE SCOPE OF COMPUTER FORENSICS

Computer forensics focuses on computers and networks. The forensic analysis of computers specifically involves the examination of computer media, programs, and data and log files to reconstruct the activity in which a computer was engaged, such as instant messaging conversations, Internet chats, e-mail messages, Web sites visited, documents and spreadsheets opened, and image and audio files viewed. The forensics analysis of networks focuses more on the activity of a network and includes the analysis of server contents, server and router log files, packet traffic, and information obtained from Internet service providers.

The science of computer forensics covers several overlapping areas (Figure 2). It is critical for law enforcement as an evidence gathering and criminal investigation tool. It is an increasingly important tool used for civilian and military intelligence gathering — including activities related to homeland defense. It is becoming widely employed by businesses and other private sector organizations for combating information security attacks. The core tools and skills are the same regardless of the application.

A computer forensics specialist also must have knowledge of the law regardless of whether the investigation is for law enforcement or civilian purposes. Additional complexity in this area exists because computer crime statutes and users' legitimate expectation of privacy vary widely from state to state and nation to nation. With the Internet and World Wide Web, jurisdictional boundaries are blurred, and an individual in one country can commit

crimes almost anywhere in the world without ever leaving his or her keyboard.

Although most computer forensic specialists today are engaged in law enforcement investigations, the field is not by any means limited to finding evidence of criminal guilt. Computer forensics also is a rapidly growing subspecialty for information security professionals. The traditional information security manager is responsible for proactively protecting the information technology assets within an organization. Security intrusions and other events are inevitable, however, and the computer forensics specialist often leads the incident response function to learn how an event occurred, who was behind it, and how to prevent a recurrence.

Computer forensics also is part of the toolkit of today's computer scientist. Many information security researchers purposely place a honeypot (vulnerable computer) on their networks for the specific purpose of analyzing the attacks that eventually will be perpetrated on those systems. Carefully examining the way in which a honeypot has been attacked can provide significant insight into new forms of attack, which then can be translated into new defensive tools and strategies.

THE IMPORTANCE OF COMPUTER FORENSICS

Computer forensics is a rapidly growing field for the simple reason that computers and the Internet are the fastest growing technology used for criminal activity. As computers become smaller, lighter, cheaper, and easier to use, they appear at nearly every crime scene that police investigate. Some activities, such as illegal gambling and the distribution of worms and viruses, have been given new life because of the pervasiveness of computers and the Internet.

Cybercrimes are growing rapidly in both the number of incidents as well as the cost in dollars, largely because these crimes are safer and more lucrative than crimes in the "real" world. The average bank robber, for example, nets only a few thousand dollars, and most are caught and sent to jail. Conversely, white collar computer crimes such as auction fraud, credit card theft, identity theft, and other financial scams tend to net a much larger sum of money, and the perpetrators are more difficult to catch and convict. In addition, computer criminals tend to generate more sympathy with judges, juries, and the public than violent offenders. Compounding the problem is the fact that access to corporate network resources makes insider jobs by employees easier and easier. Figure 3 shows the dollar loss reported by 269 large companies in a recent year due to telecom and financial fraud, insider abuse, unauthorized network access, theft of proprietary information, and other computer-related crimes.

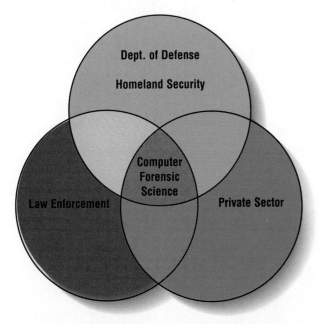

FIGURE 2 The domain of computer forensics is multidisciplinary, spanning the needs of the military and homeland security, law enforcement, and the private sector.

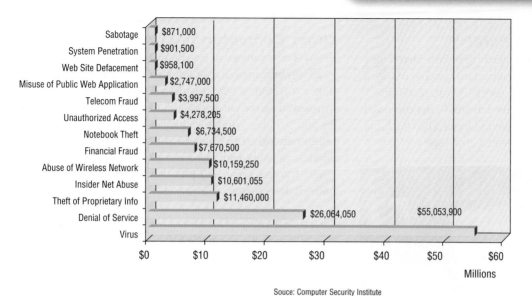

Sabotage	$871,000
System Penetration	$901,500
Web Site Defacement	$958,100
Misuse of Public Web Application	$2,747,000
Telecom Fraud	$3,997,500
Unauthorized Access	$4,278,205
Notebook Theft	$6,734,500
Financial Fraud	$7,670,500
Abuse of Wireless Network	$10,159,250
Insider Net Abuse	$10,601,055
Theft of Proprietary Info	$11,460,000
Denial of Service	$26,064,050
Virus	$55,053,900

$0 $10 $20 $30 $40 $50 $60

Millions

Souce: Computer Security Institute

FIGURE 3
Total computer security losses of $141,496,560 reported by 269 respondents in a recent year.

Computer forensics is being used not just to combat cybercrime. Terrorists around the world are known to use computers and other digital devices, so computer forensics analysis is important as an antiterrorism tool for both criminal prosecution and intelligence gathering. All organizations that employ computers, ranging from nonprofit agencies and major corporations to government agencies and utility companies, are at risk. As more information is stored digitally and more aspects of our society are under computer control, we all face increased exposure and vulnerability. Computer forensics is an important tool in understanding our digital information systems and keeping them safe, as well as tracking down the people who abuse those systems.

THE COMPUTER FORENSICS PROCESS

The computer forensics process can be simple or complex, depending upon the circumstances causing the investigation in the first place. The computer forensics specialist may be part of an investigative team, and the analysis of digital evidence may be just one part of the investigation as a whole. The specialist will look for information pertinent to the incident or event being investigated, which may be limited by a search warrant, time, and/or other circumstances.

The first step in the process is to gather the materials to analyze. This may not be quite as easy as it sounds. Law enforcement personnel will be guided by a search warrant in the seizure of materials while a corporate forensics specialist may be guided by what equipment is owned by the company. Even with clear guidelines, many items need to be considered for collection and examination as described in the following sections.

Computer Media

Computer media can be found in many places these days (Figure 4). This includes the obvious hard disk, Zip disk, floppy disk, and optical disc (CDs and DVDs). Also included are physically small, high-capacity memory devices such as USB flash drives (including the versions where the device is embedded in a watch, pen, or Swiss Army knife) and flash memory cards.

(a) hard disk

(b) Zip disk

(c) USB flash drives

(f) optical disk

(e) flash memory card

(d) floppy disk

FIGURE 4 Computer forensics experts analyze the data stored on various types of media.

Computers and Peripherals

Every part of the computer needs to be considered for examination, and it is generally important to take possession of all of the equipment. The specialist cannot assume that the spare keyboard back in the lab will fit the computer being seized. The computer shown in Figure 5 has the basic hardware one might expect to see at a crime scene.

FIGURE 5 A typical scene a computer forensics specialist encounters.

Other Computer and Network Hardware

It is imperative that other hardware devices be examined, as all might contain important log or other information (Figure 6). Homes with broadband network connections increasingly have networks and, therefore, multiple computers and a router. Wireless networks make it relatively easy to hide a networked computer; a computer using a home's wireless network could be as far as 100 yards or so from the wireless access point, and thus be situated far outside of the immediate structure.

Computer Software

Although the computer forensics specialist generally will not run software directly from the suspect drive, it may be impossible to examine files without the proper application software. In some cases, the user of a suspect computer might have installed specialized, custom, or very old software to which the specialist generally will not have access; in that case, the specialist may have to install software found at the suspect site onto a forensics lab computer. This is one reason to look around the site where the computer is found and consider seizing distribution media and manuals of any software with which the specialist is not familiar. The papers and books found near the computer also will give the specialist a clue as to the sophistication of the user and the possible types of applications to be found on the system.

FIGURE 6 Common digital hardware devices examined by a computer investigator.

In the Computer Forensics Lab

Once the materials are in the computer forensics lab, the investigation can begin. The basic steps of a computer forensics analysis are:

1. **Preserve the media** — Computer forensics analysis never should be performed on the original media except under the most extraordinary circumstances because of the potential of accidentally making a change to the original evidence. The copy also needs to be made in such a way that the original information is not altered in any way and that it can be authenticated as containing the same information as the original. This process is known as **imaging a drive**.
2. **Extract evidence** — Based upon the guidelines of the investigation, the specialist needs to determine what kind of information on the computer is pertinent to the case. Clues as to what to search for will depend upon the type of case. Spreadsheets, for example, would be highly relevant to a business fraud case, while images are important for a case of suspected child pornography, and chat and e-mail logs are of use in a case of cyberstalking. Keywords, such as pertinent phrases, slang words, names, locations, etc., must be provided to the computer forensics specialist on the case.
3. **Analyze computer media** — The actual analysis of evidence and/or the root cause of the event is the most time-consuming aspect of the process. It is important to note that the information retrieved from the computer either can be incriminating (indicating guilt) or exculpatory (indicating innocence). In addition, the specialist has to look at the entire capacity of the medium because information can be hidden anywhere. Figure 7 summarizes the common items examined during a computer forensics investigation.
4. **Document results** — The results of a computer forensics exam must be documented thoroughly, particularly if the examination is being performed for legal purposes. Everything must be written down, from the configuration of the computer and BIOS settings to each and every step taken by the computer forensic specialist and any pertinent evidence that is found. All computer equipment, media, peripherals, or other items seized must be logged, and photographs should be taken of external and internal connections, if possible. The handling of the evidence also has to be logged carefully to demonstrate that no tampering occurred. Sample computer forensics evidence worksheets are shown in Figure 8. Figure 8a is an evidence worksheet used with a computer. Figure 8b is an evidence worksheet used with a hard drive.

1. Visited Web sites
2. Downloaded files
3. Dates when files were last accessed and modified
4. Attempts to conceal, destroy, or fabricate evidence
5. Deleted or overwritten files
6. Data from RAM
7. Use of cryptography or steganography
8. File directory structure
9. Image, movie, and sound files
10. Keyword search hits
11. Contents of system files, such as the print spool and swap files
12. Installed programs
13. E-mail, chat logs, instant messaging logs
14. Registry entries
15. Contents of the Recycle Bin and unallocated space
16. Antivirus, personal firewall, and spyware detection software, as well as the presence of viruses, Trojan horses, and spyware

FIGURE 7 Common items examined during a computer forensics investigation.

(a) Computer evidence worksheet

(b) Hard drive evidence worksheet

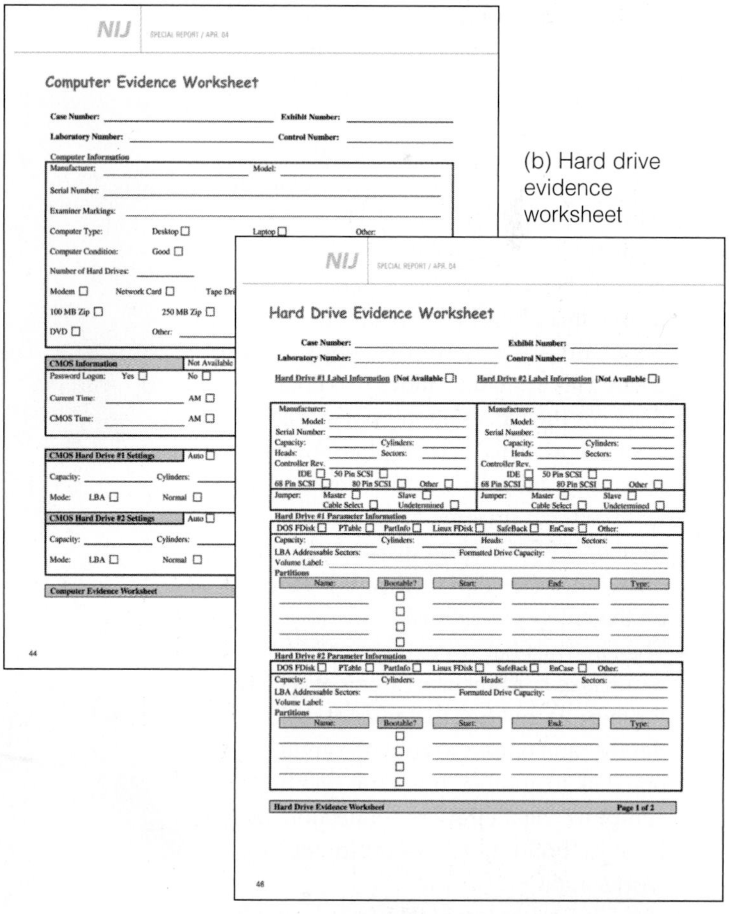
NIJ SPECIAL REPORT / APR. 04

Computer Evidence Worksheet

Case Number: Exhibit Number:
Laboratory Number: Control Number:

Computer Information
Manufacturer: Model:
Serial Number:
Examiner Markings:
Computer Type: Desktop ☐ Laptop ☐ Other:
Computer Condition: Good ☐
Number of Hard Drives:
Modem ☐ Network Card ☐
100 MB Zip ☐ 250 MB Zip ☐
DVD ☐ Other:

CMOS Information | Not Available
Password Logon: Yes ☐ No ☐
Current Time: AM ☐
CMOS Time: AM ☐

CMOS Hard Drive #1 Settings | Auto ☐
Capacity: Cylinders:
Mode: LBA ☐ Normal ☐

CMOS Hard Drive #2 Settings | Auto ☐
Capacity: Cylinders:
Mode: LBA ☐ Normal ☐

Computer Evidence Worksheet

44

NIJ SPECIAL REPORT / APR. 04

Hard Drive Evidence Worksheet

Case Number: Exhibit Number:
Laboratory Number: Control Number:

Hard Drive #1 Label Information [Not Available ☐] Hard Drive #2 Label Information [Not Available ☐]

Manufacturer: Model: Serial Number: Capacity: Cylinders: Heads: Sectors: Controller Rev. IDE ☐ 50 Pin SCSI ☐ 68 Pin SCSI ☐ 80 Pin SCSI ☐ Other ☐ Jumper: Master ☐ Slave ☐ Cable Select ☐ Undetermined ☐

Hard Drive #1 Parameter Information
DOS FDisk ☐ PTable ☐ PartInfo ☐ Linux FDisk ☐ SafeBack ☐ EnCase ☐ Other:
Capacity: Cylinders: Heads: Sectors:
LBA Addressable Sectors: Formatted Drive Capacity:
Volume Label:
Partitions
Name: Bootable? Start: End: Type:

Hard Drive #2 Parameter Information
DOS FDisk ☐ PTable ☐ PartInfo ☐ Linux FDisk ☐ SafeBack ☐ EnCase ☐ Other:
Capacity: Cylinders: Heads: Sectors:
LBA Addressable Sectors: Formatted Drive Capacity:
Volume Label:
Partitions
Name: Bootable? Start: End: Type:

Hard Drive Evidence Worksheet Page 1 of 2

46

FIGURE 8 Computer Evidence and Hard Drive Evidence Worksheets (from *Forensic Examination of Digital Evidence: A Guide for Law Enforcement*, National Institute of Justice).

612

Special Feature

In general, specialized computer forensics tools are used to perform an analysis to ensure that no information is modified on the target media and that the examination is thorough. Booting a computer changes hundreds of registry, log, and/or data files; therefore, the original hard disk never should be used to boot a computer. In addition, many operating systems, such as Linux and Windows, maintain a number of time stamps associated with every file, including the creation, last access, and last modified dates; using ordinary operating system tools to examine the contents of files usually will cause at least the last-access date to be altered. Use of specialized analysis tools maintains the integrity of the original data so that the specialist can be sure that the results of the analysis are legally and technically valid. It is important that no harm be done to the original evidence.

In some cases, specialists prefer to image hard disks in the field rather than transporting entire computers to the lab; this often is the preferable approach when the device to be imaged is a company's critical server where seizing the computer might cause undue economic hardship to the owner. Devices such as Intelligent Computer Solutions' Road MASSter-II (Figure 10) is such a device; note that it fits in a small carrying case.

Notebook computers represent a particular challenge for forensic analysis because many notebook computer hard disks have proprietary or specialty interfaces; additional hardware is available specifically for imaging drives from various models of Dell, Gateway, HP, IBM, NEC, Toshiba, and other brands of notebook computers. Other specialized hardware allows for the imaging of PDAs, smart phones, and other digital devices.

COMPUTER FORENSICS TOOLS

A wide variety of computer forensics tools are available, each with its own applications, strengths, and weaknesses. Several companies make computer forensics hardware, primarily for purposes of disk imaging. Digital Intelligence, for example, makes several forensics hardware devices, including:

- The Forensic Recovery of Digital Evidence (FRED) hardware (Figure 9a) is a stand-alone forensics workstation that can acquire data from all types of hard disk media, including IDE, ATA, SATA, and SCSI hard drives as well as floppy and Zip disks. This system includes fixed hard disks for the workstation's operating system and analysis tools plus a number of bays for other drives to be inserted and removed. For imaging applications, the contents of the suspect disk are copied to a blank disk; the analysis then is performed on the newly copied disk.
- The FireChief hardware (Figure 9b) has two removable hard disk bays, one of which is write-protected (for the original disk). This device can be used to copy the contents of one disk to another. It is connected to a computer via a FireWire connection and is ideal for building a low-cost forensics workstation.
- The FireFly hardware (Figure 9c) can plug directly into an IDE or SATA hard drive and attach to the forensics computer via a FireWire connection.

(a) Forensic Recovery of Digital Evidence (FRED) forensics workstation

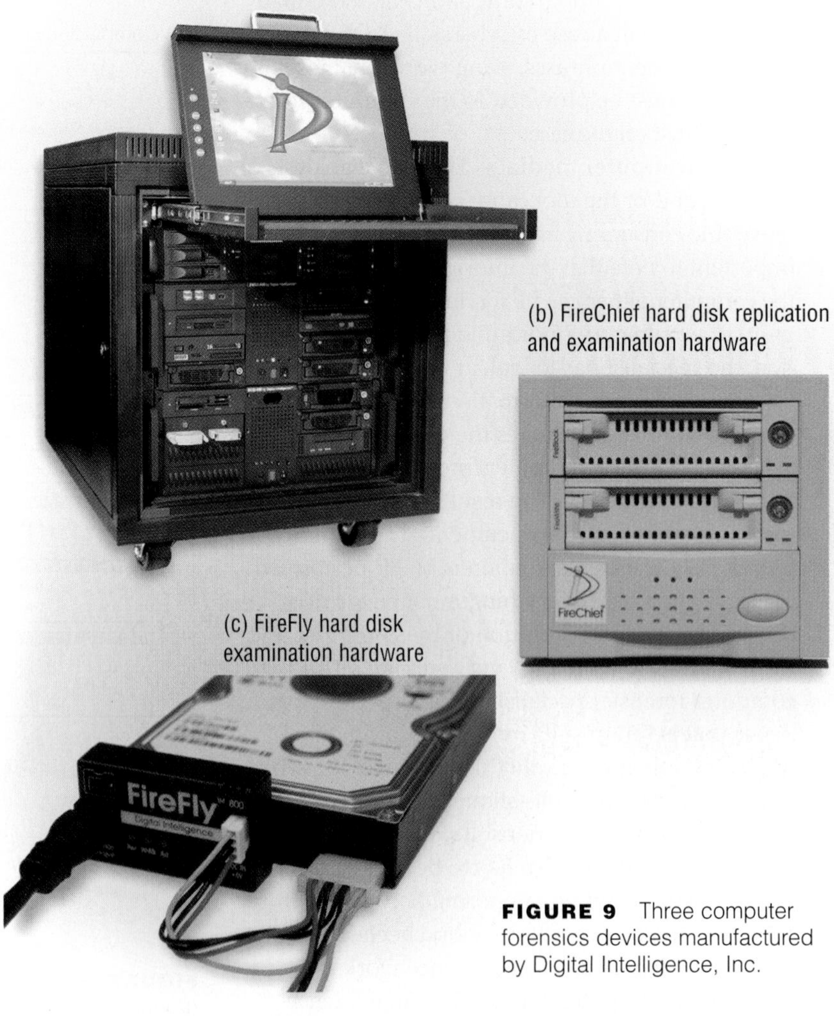

(b) FireChief hard disk replication and examination hardware

(c) FireFly hard disk examination hardware

FIGURE 9 Three computer forensics devices manufactured by Digital Intelligence, Inc.

(a) Details of the keyboard and working area of the Road MASSter

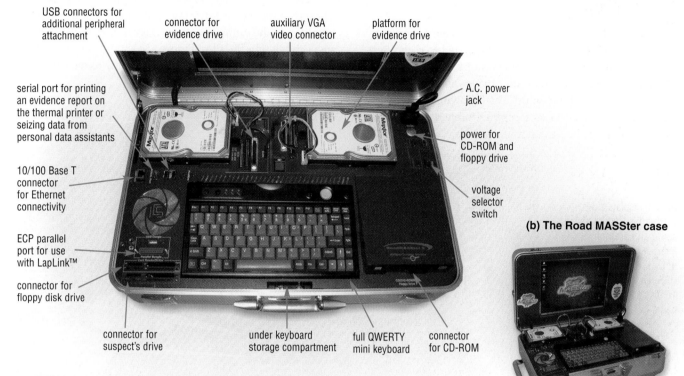

USB connectors for additional peripheral attachment

connector for evidence drive

auxiliary VGA video connector

platform for evidence drive

serial port for printing an evidence report on the thermal printer or seizing data from personal data assistants

A.C. power jack

power for CD-ROM and floppy drive

10/100 Base T connector for Ethernet connectivity

voltage selector switch

ECP parallel port for use with LapLink™

(b) The Road MASSter case

connector for floppy disk drive

connector for suspect's drive

under keyboard storage compartment

full QWERTY mini keyboard

connector for CD-ROM

FIGURE 10   The Intelligent Computer Solutions' Road MASSter-II is a portable computer forensics laboratory.

The primary computer forensics analysis tool is software. The most widely-used specialty forensics programs today are Guidance Software's EnCase and AccessData's Ultimate Toolkit (Figure 11). No single program can perform all aspects of a computer forensics analysis, although several come close. These programs provide a broad range of forensics functions (Figure 12).

(a) Guidance Software's EnCase

(b) AccessData's Ultimate Toolkit

FIGURE 11   Popular computer forensics software.

1. Create disk images
2. Recover passwords
3. Perform file access, modification, and creation time analysis
4. Create file catalogs
5. View system and application logs
6. Determine the activity of users and/or applications on a system
7. Recover "deleted" files and examine unallocated file space
8. Obtain network information such as IP addresses and host names, network routes, and Web site information
9. Track forensics activity and aid in documentation and report writing

FIGURE 12   Common tasks handled by computer forensics software.

COMPUTER FORENSICS AT WORK

A computer forensics specialist needs to have a working knowledge of a wide range of topics related to computers and networks. The most essential bit of knowledge concerns how files are stored on disk drives and the various file systems that will be found. The following sections illustrate some of the tasks computer forensic specialists use to search for clues in an investigation.

Analyzing Deleted Files

Consider the scenario shown in Figure 13. Figure 13a shows the suspect displaying the names of the files involved in the criminal activity. Figure 13b shows the suspect deleting the files. Figure 13c shows the computer forensics specialist using special programs to retrieve the deleted files.

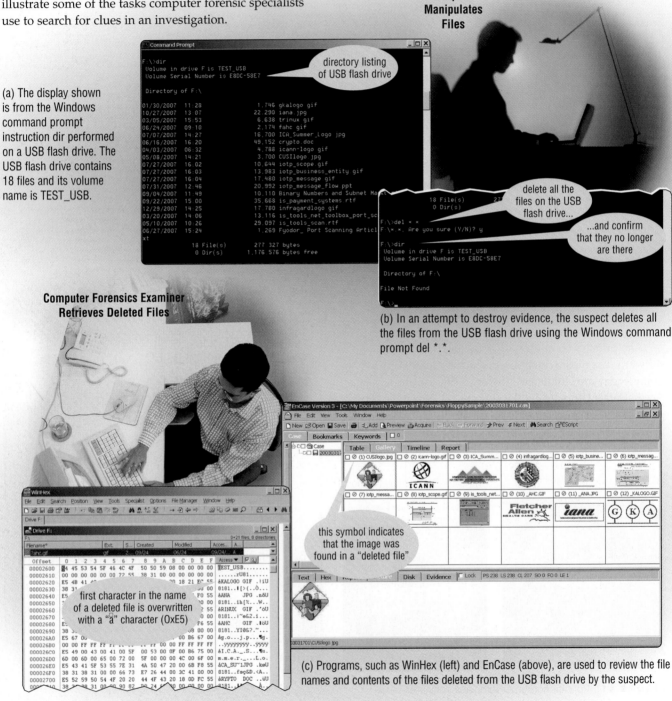

(a) The display shown is from the Windows command prompt instruction dir performed on a USB flash drive. The USB flash drive contains 18 files and its volume name is TEST_USB.

(b) In an attempt to destroy evidence, the suspect deletes all the files from the USB flash drive using the Windows command prompt del *.*.

(c) Programs, such as WinHex (left) and EnCase (above), are used to review the file names and contents of the files deleted from the USB flash drive by the suspect.

FIGURE 13 The top portion of this figure shows the suspect (a) listing the files involved in criminal activity, (b) later deleting the files in an attempt to cover-up the illegal activity, and then the lower portion of the figure shows (c) the computer forensics specialist retrieving the deleted files using special programs.

Tracing Nodes

Knowledge of the Internet is another essential skill. Figure 14a shows the output from McAfee's Visual Trace, listing the intermediate nodes between a local host computer (altamont) and a Web server (www.garykessler.net). Visual Trace is a graphical version of the tracert (DOS) and traceroute (Linux) command line utilities and lists the IP address of all hops along the path between the two computers. This display also shows the round-trip delay and can be used to show whois information about each node in the path. Visual Trace also can show a geographical map of the path (Figure 14b).

Analyzing Network Traffic

The ability to analyze network traffic also is an essential skill for a computer forensics specialist. E-mail headers are particularly important, as they provide many clues as to the origin and authenticity of e-mail messages. By now you should be familiar with the standard e-mail headers, such as To:, From:, and Subject:. But e-mail headers contain more information than what you see at the top of an e-mail; e-mail headers also can reveal the name and version of the e-mail program you use, the operating system, the name and version of your mail server, internal IP addresses, and the mail server path taken by this message.

(a) Route between two hosts, round-trip delay, and whois information.

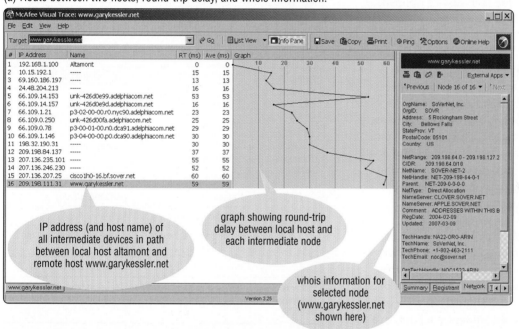

(b) Geographic map display of the route between two hosts.

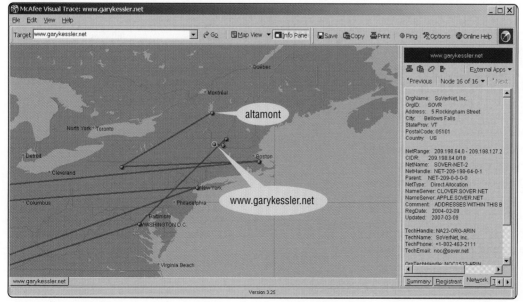

FIGURE 14 Tracing nodes between a local host computer (altamont) and a Web server using McAfee's Visual Trace.

Analyzing ISP Logs

During a computer forensics investigation, the specialist might request logs from an Internet service provider. The Internet service provider will deliver the logs, but they will be in the raw format in which they are saved.

While SMTP is used to forward e-mail across the Internet, other protocols are used to download e-mail by the client. One such protocol is the Post Office Protocol version 3 (POP3). Figure 1a on page 607 shows a set of three records from a POP3 server log showing a user logging on to check and download e-mail messages. All records show a date (March 13) and time stamp on a host named watson running the POP service (ipop3d) and access by a user on the host with IP address 192.168.187.35.

Analyzing Chat Logs

Analysis of chat logs is another important aspect of network analysis. The log shown in Figure 1c on page 607 is a conversation between BettyF, billy89, and other members of the Internet Relay Chat (IRC) Strong&40 channel. Although this conversation is relatively innocuous, analysis of logs such as these can turn up evidence of cyberstalking, criminal conspiracy, economic espionage, harassment, or other items of interest.

Analyzing a Packet Trace

Packet sniffers are an important software tool in the understanding of network traffic. A **packet sniffer** monitors all of the traffic seen on the network port of a computer and keeps a copy for later analysis. One of the most commonly used packet sniffers is tcpdump, a command line utility for UNIX/Linux; WinDump is the Windows version.

LEARNING MORE ABOUT COMPUTER FORENSICS

Every action a user takes on a computer leaves a trail. Deleting files really does not erase information. Evidence of computer activity is stored in many places on the hard disk, some obvious and some very obscure. Information about network access potentially is logged on many computers throughout the local network and global Internet. Digital tracks are everywhere.

Computer forensics specialists must possess an array of skills to uncover these tracks and recreate the activities

under investigation. They certainly must be technically knowledgeable and enjoy troubleshooting and solving puzzles. They must be aware of the legal constraints and organizational polices that guide what they can and cannot do. They must be able to communicate the process and results of their analysis in both written and oral form. Finally, they also must possess and demonstrate a high degree of honesty and ethical behavior.

Many sources for news and information about computer forensics are available online. Using the popular Web portals such as Google, Yahoo!, and others, you will find links to hundreds of computer forensics sites. Figure 15 lists sources for information about computer forensics and their Web addresses.

	WEB SITE	WEB ADDRESS
Computer Forensics Hardware Companies	Digital Intelligence, Inc.	digitalintelligence.com
	Intelligent Computer Solutions, Inc.	ics-iq.com
	WiebeTech	wiebetech.com
Computer Forensics Software	AccessData Corp. Ultimate Toolkit	accessdata.com
	Guidance Software EnCase	guidancesoftware.com
	Knoppix STD	knoppix-std.org
	SleuthKit and Autopsy	sleuthkit.org
	Technology Pathways ProDiscover	www.techpathways.com
	WinHex	winhex.com
Network Analysis Web Sites	DNSstuff.com	dnsstuff.com
	SamSpade.org	samspade.org
Network Analysis Software	McAfee Personal Firewall Plus	us.mcafee.com
	tcpdump	tcpdump.org
	WinDump	http://www.winpcap.org/windump/
Additional Information	Gary Kessler's Cybercrime and Cyberforensics-related URLs	www.garykessler.net/library/forensicsurl.html
	High Technology Crime Investigation Association (HTCIA)	htcia.org
	International Association of Computer Investigative Specialists (IACIS)	cops.org
	National White Collar Crime Center (NW3C)	nw3c.org

For an updated list, visit scsite.com/dc2007/ch11/computerforensics.

FIGURE 15 Online sources for information about computer forensics.

NOTES

Information System Development

Picture Yourself Talking with a System Development Team

During today's corporate system development planning session, the project leader reviews the current project request, some charts and diagrams, and the project's preliminary schedule. At one point, a team member asks the project leader, "When will we begin interviewing our users — you know, our cybercafé customers and employees?" The systems analyst mentions that this is a crucial step in the process — involving the users in the development of the system. The group decides that two team members will begin the interviews tomorrow.

The next morning two members of the system development team enter one of the cybercafés. While you and a friend are drinking a cup of cappuccino and browsing the Web on a café computer, one team member approaches and asks if you have a few minutes to answer some questions. How often do you visit the café? Approximately how long is each visit? What computer services do you use at the café? What food and beverages have you tried? Describe two problems you have encountered at the cybercafé. Do you have any suggestions for improving any cybercafé products or services? As a thank you for your time, he gives you a gift card for one hour of free Internet connection time at the cybercafé.

Next, you watch another member of the system development team ask the employee behind the coffee bar if he could take a few minutes to answer a few questions. As soon as he is finished making an espresso, he says he will be available.

To learn about project leaders, system development teams, and interviews, read Chapter 12 and discover other people and activities involved during system development.

After completing this chapter, you will be able to:

1. List the phases in the system development cycle
2. Identify the guidelines for system development
3. Discuss the importance of project management, feasibility assessment, documentation, and data and information gathering techniques
4. Explain the activities performed in the planning phase
5. Discuss the purpose of the activities performed in the analysis phase
6. Describe the various tools used in process modeling
7. Describe the various tools used in object modeling
8. Explain the activities performed in the design phase
9. Recognize the develop programs activity is part of the system development cycle
10. Discuss the activities performed in the implementation phase
11. Discuss the purpose of the activities performed in the operation, support, and security phase

CONTENTS

WHAT IS THE SYSTEM DEVELOPMENT CYCLE?

A **system** is a set of components that interact to achieve a common goal. You use, observe, and interact with many systems during daily activities. You drive a highway system to reach a destination. Your home maintains a comfortable temperature with its heating and cooling systems. You use the decimal number system to calculate an amount due. You see the planets in the solar system.

Businesses also use many types of systems. A billing system allows a company to send invoices and receive payments from customers. Through a payroll system, employees receive paychecks. A manufacturing system produces the goods that customers order. An inventory system keeps track of the items in a warehouse. Very often, these systems also are information systems.

An **information system** (**IS**) is a collection of hardware, software, data, people, and procedures that work together to produce quality information. An information system supports daily, short-term, and long-range activities of users. Some examples of users include store clerks, sales representatives, accountants, supervisors, managers, executives, and customers. As time passes, the type of information that users need often changes. A sales manager may want the weekly summary report grouped by district instead of by product. When information requirements change, the information system must meet the new requirements. In some cases, the members of the system development team modify the current information system. In other cases, they develop an entirely new information system.

As a computer user in a business, you someday may participate in the modification of an existing system or the development of a new system. Thus, it is important that you understand the system development cycle. The **system development cycle** is a set of activities used to build an information system.

Some activities in the system development cycle may be performed concurrently. Others are performed sequentially. Depending on the type and complexity of the information system, the length of each activity varies from one system to the next. In some cases, some activities are skipped entirely.

Phases in the System Development Cycle

System development cycles often organize activities by grouping them into larger categories called **phases**. Most system development cycles contain five phases:

1. Planning
2. Analysis
3. Design
4. Implementation
5. Operation, Support, and Security

As shown in Figure 12-1, each phase in the system development cycle consists of a series of activities, and the phases form a loop. The loop forms when the operation, support, and security phase points to the planning phase. This connection occurs when the information system requires changing. A variety of situations can lead to a change in the information system. A report might generate an incorrect total. Users may want information in a different format. A vendor may release a new version of software. Hardware might become obsolete. An unauthorized user may have gained access to the information system. When change occurs or is required, the planning

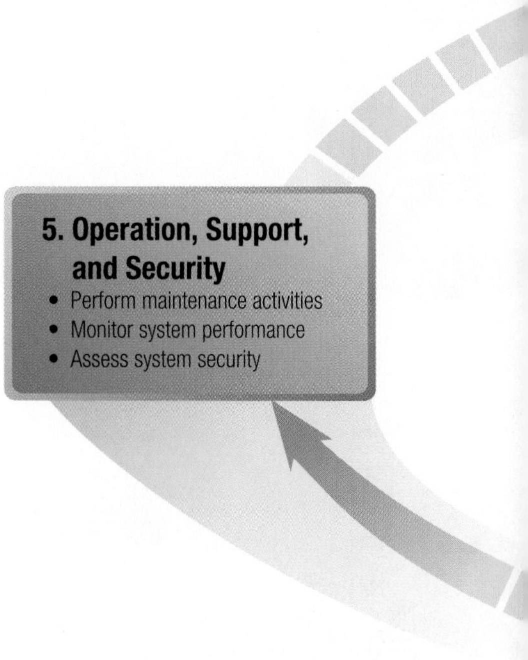

5. Operation, Support, and Security
- Perform maintenance activities
- Monitor system performance
- Assess system security

FIGURE 12-1 The system development cycle consists of five phases that form a loop. Several ongoing activities also take place throughout the entire system development cycle.

phase for a new or modified system begins and the system development cycle starts again.

In theory, the five phases in the system development cycle often appear sequentially, as shown in Figure 12-1. In reality, activities within adjacent phases often interact with one another — making the system development cycle a dynamic iterative process.

Members of the system development team follow established guidelines during the entire system development cycle. They also interact with a variety of IT professionals and others during the system development cycle. In addition, they perform several ongoing activities during all five phases of the system development cycle. The following sections discuss each of these items.

Guidelines for System Development

System development should follow three general guidelines: arrange activities into phases, involve the users, and develop standards.

1. The system development cycle should group activities or tasks into phases. Many system development cycles contain the five major phases shown in Figure 12-1. Others have more or fewer phases. Regardless, all system development cycles have similar activities. Figure 12-1 shows the Develop programs activity in the Implementation phase. Some system development cycles have another phase called Construction or Development, which includes the Develop programs activity. Other differences among system development cycles are the terminology they use, the order of their activities, and the level of detail within each phase.

2. Users must be involved throughout the entire system development cycle. **Users** include anyone for whom the system is being built. Customers, employees, students, data entry clerks, accountants, sales managers, and owners all are examples of users. You are a user of many information systems. You, as a user, might interact with an information system at your bank, library, grocery store, fitness center, work, and school. The system development team members must remember they ultimately deliver the system to the user. If the system is to be successful, the user must be included in all stages of development. Users are more apt to accept a new system if they contribute to its design.

1. Planning
- Review project requests
- Prioritize project requests
- Allocate resources
- Form project development team

Ongoing Activities
- Project management
- Feasibility assessment
- Documentation
- Data/information gathering

2. Analysis
- Conduct preliminary investigation
- Perform detailed analysis activities:
  - Study current system
  - Determine user requirements
  - Recommend solution

4. Implementation
- Develop programs, if necessary
- Install and test new system
- Train users
- Convert to new system

3. Design
- Acquire hardware and software, if necessary
- Develop details of system

3. The system development cycle should have standards clearly defined. **Standards** are sets of rules and procedures a company expects employees to accept and follow. Having standards helps people working on the same project produce consistent results. For example, one programmer might refer to a product number in a database as a product ID. Others may call it a product identification number, product code, and so on. If the system development cycle has defined standards, then everyone involved uses the same terms, such as product number. Many system development cycles implement standards by using a data dictionary.

Who Participates in the System Development Cycle?

System development should involve representatives from each department in which the proposed system will be used. This includes both nontechnical users and IT professionals. Although the roles and responsibilities of members of the system development team may change from company to company, this chapter presents general descriptions of tasks for various team members.

During the course of the system development cycle, the systems analyst meets and works with a variety of people (Figure 12-2). A **systems analyst** is responsible for designing

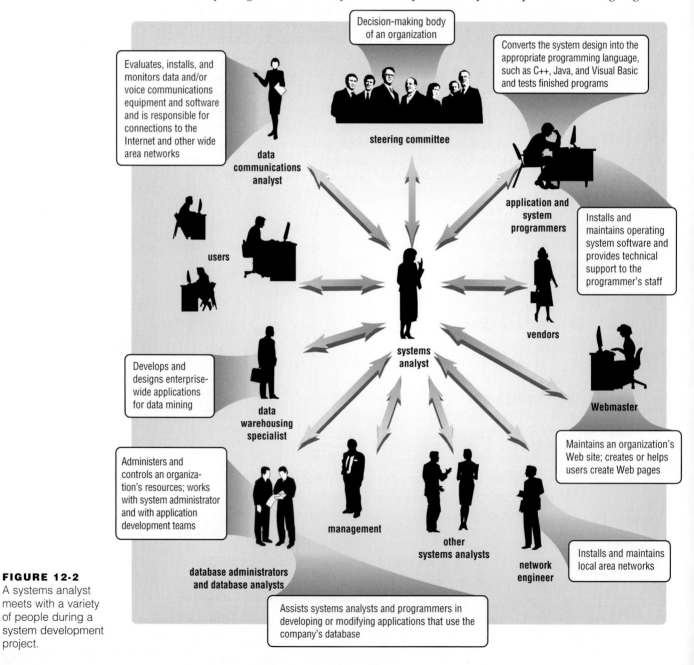

Decision-making body of an organization

Converts the system design into the appropriate programming language, such as C++, Java, and Visual Basic and tests finished programs

Evaluates, installs, and monitors data and/or voice communications equipment and software and is responsible for connections to the Internet and other wide area networks

steering committee

data communications analyst

application and system programmers

Installs and maintains operating system software and provides technical support to the programmer's staff

users

vendors

Develops and designs enterprise-wide applications for data mining

Webmaster

data warehousing specialist

Maintains an organization's Web site; creates or helps users create Web pages

Administers and controls an organization's resources; works with system administrator and with application development teams

systems analyst

management

other systems analysts

Installs and maintains local area networks

database administrators and database analysts

network engineer

Assists systems analysts and programmers in developing or modifying applications that use the company's database

FIGURE 12-2
A systems analyst meets with a variety of people during a system development project.

and developing an information system. The systems analyst is the users' primary contact person.

Depending on the size of the organization or company, the tasks performed by the systems analyst may vary. Smaller companies may have one systems analyst or even one person who assumes the roles of both systems analyst and programmer. Larger companies often have multiple systems analysts. Some companies refer to a systems analyst as a *system developer*. Read Looking Ahead 12-1 for a look at the future demand for systems analysts.

The systems analysts are the liaison between the users and the IT professionals. They convert user requests into technical specifications. Thus, systems analysts must have superior technical skills. They also must be familiar with business operations, be able to solve problems, have the ability to introduce and support change, and possess excellent communications and interpersonal skills. Systems analysts prepare many reports, drawings, and diagrams. They discuss various aspects of the development project with users, management, other analysts, database analysts, database administrators, network administrators, the Webmaster, programmers, vendors, and the steering committee. The **steering committee** is a decision-making body in a company.

For each system development project, a company usually forms a **project team** to work on the project from beginning to end. The project team consists of users, the systems analyst, and other IT professionals. One member of the team is the **project leader**, who manages and controls the budget and schedule of the project. The systems analyst may or may not be selected as the project leader of the project.

FAQ 12-1

What percentage of system development projects fall behind schedule or run over budget?

One study indicated that 84 percent of system development projects run over budget or fall behind schedule. For example, the overhaul of the Internal Revenue Service's file keeping system at one point was 40 percent over budget and more than two years behind schedule. For more information, visit scsite.com/dc2007/ch12/faq and then click IRS Modernization Plan.

LOOKING AHEAD 12-1

Computer Systems Design and the Future

The population in the United States is expected to grow by 24 million by 2012, according to the U.S. Department of Labor. This increase will trigger a demand for goods and services in a variety of fields.

The computer systems design area and related industries are some of the fields predicted to experience continued growth. The Department of Labor expects a 54.6 percent increase in this sector, which will add more than one-third of all new jobs in the professional, scientific, and technical services areas.

During a tour of universities in 2005, Microsoft Chairman Bill Gates urged students with the brightest minds to pursue a career in the computer software industry, especially because jobs are plentiful and command a high salary. Calling the field exciting and fun, Gates believes the graduates' work will be vital to the growth of the world's economy. For more information, visit scsite.com/dc2007/ch12/looking and then click Systems Design Future.

Project Management

Project management is the process of planning, scheduling, and then controlling the activities during the system development cycle. The goal of project management is to deliver an acceptable system to the user in an agreed-upon time frame, while maintaining costs.

To plan and schedule a project effectively, the project leader identifies the following elements:
- Goal, objectives, and expectations of the project, collectively called the *scope*
- Required activities
- Time estimates for each activity
- Cost estimates for each activity
- Order of activities
- Activities that can take place at the same time

When these items are identified, the project leader usually records them in a *project plan*. A popular tool used to plan and schedule the time relationships among project activities is a Gantt chart (Figure 12-3). A *Gantt chart*, developed by Henry L. Gantt, is a bar chart that uses horizontal bars to show project phases or activities. The left side, or vertical axis, displays the list of required activities. A horizontal axis across the top or bottom of the chart represents time.

ID	Task Name	Duration	Jan	Feb	Mar	Apr	May	Jun	Jul	Aug
1	**Planning**	2w	1/20	2/1						
2	**Analysis**	12w		2/8			5/10			
3	**Design**	12w			3/20			6/15		
4	**Implementation**	3w						6/16		8/9

FIGURE 12-3 A Gantt chart is an effective way to show the time relationships of a project's activities.

After a project begins, the project leader monitors and controls the project. Some activities take less time than originally planned. Others take longer. The project leader may realize that an activity is taking excessive time or that scope creep has occurred. *Scope creep* occurs when one activity has led to another that was not planned originally; thus, the scope of the project now has grown.

Project leaders should have good *change management* skills so they can recognize when a change in the project has occurred, take actions to react to the change, and plan for opportunities because of the change. For example, the project leader may recognize the team will not be able to meet the original deadline of the project due to scope creep. Thus, the project leader may extend the deadline or may reduce the scope of the system development. If the

latter occurs, the users will receive a less comprehensive system at the original deadline. In either case, the project leader revises the first project plan and presents the new plan to users for approval. It is crucial that everyone is aware of and agrees on any changes made to the project plan.

One aspect of managing projects is to ensure that everyone submits deliverables on time and according to plan. A *deliverable* is any tangible item such as a chart, diagram, report, or program file. Project leaders can use **project management software** such as Microsoft Project to assist them in planning, scheduling, and controlling development projects (Figure 12-4).

WEB LINK 12-1

Change Management

For more information, visit scsite.com/ dc2007/ch12/weblink and then click Change Management.

FAQ 12-2

What is extreme project management?

Extreme project management is a team-driven project management method in which a project manager acts more as a facilitator and participator instead of a manager during the process. Emphasis is on experimenting and rapid development. For more information, visit scsite.com/dc2007/ ch12/faq and then click Extreme Project Management.

FIGURE 12-4a (Gantt chart)

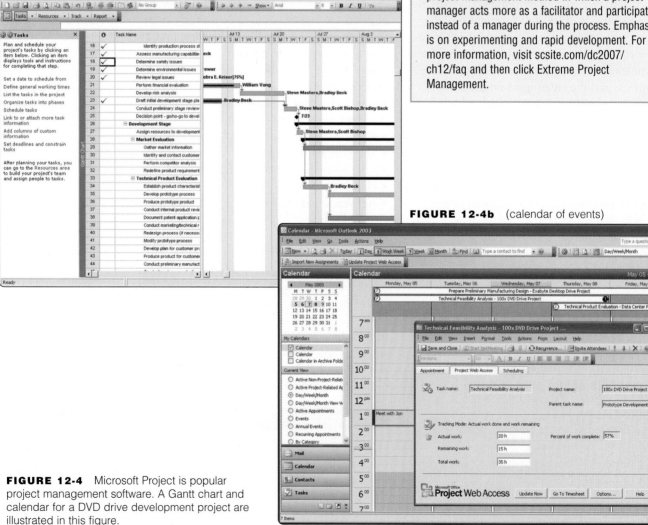

FIGURE 12-4b (calendar of events)

FIGURE 12-4 Microsoft Project is popular project management software. A Gantt chart and calendar for a DVD drive development project are illustrated in this figure.

Feasibility Assessment

Feasibility is a measure of how suitable the development of a system will be to the company. A project that is feasible at one point of the system development cycle might become infeasible at a later point. Thus, systems analysts frequently reevaluate feasibility during the system development cycle.

A systems analyst typically uses four tests to evaluate feasibility of a project: operational feasibility, schedule feasibility, technical feasibility, and economic feasibility.

- *Operational feasibility* measures how well the proposed information system will work. Will the users like the new system? Will they use it? Will it meet their requirements? Will it cause any changes in their work environment?

- *Schedule feasibility* measures whether the established deadlines for the project are reasonable. If a deadline is not reasonable, the project leader might make a new schedule. If a deadline cannot be extended, then the scope of the project might be reduced to meet the mandatory deadline.

- *Technical feasibility* measures whether the company has or can obtain the hardware, software, and people needed to deliver and then support the proposed information system. For most system projects, hardware, software, and people typically are available to support an information system. The challenge is obtaining funds to pay for these resources. Economic feasibility addresses funding.

- *Economic feasibility*, also called *cost/benefit feasibility*, measures whether the lifetime benefits of the proposed information system will be greater than its lifetime costs. A systems analyst uses many financial techniques, such as return on investment (ROI) and payback analysis, to perform the cost/benefit analysis.

FAQ 12-3

Does the systems analyst also perform the financial analysis?

Although some systems analysts perform a financial analysis, many are not familiar with financial assessment techniques. Instead, they ask a financial analyst to assist them with the financial requirements when analyzing a project's economic feasibility. For more information, visit scsite.com/dc2007/ch12/faq and then click Financial Indicators.

Documentation

During the entire system development cycle, project team members produce much documentation. **Documentation** is the collection and summarization of data and information. It includes reports, diagrams, programs, or any other deliverables generated during the system development cycle.

A *project notebook* contains all documentation for a single project. The project notebook might be a simple three-ring binder. Many companies, however, have analysis and design software that systems analysts use to create an automated project notebook.

Users and IT professionals refer to existing documentation when working with and modifying current systems. It is important that all documentation be well written, thorough, and understandable. Maintaining up-to-date documentation should be an ongoing part of the system development cycle. Too often, project team members put off documentation until the end because it is time-consuming. They mistakenly regard it as an unimportant or unproductive part of the system development cycle.

Data and Information Gathering Techniques

During the system development cycle, members of the project team gather data and information. They need accurate and timely data and information for many reasons. They must keep a project on schedule, evaluate feasibility, and be sure the system meets requirements. Systems analysts and other IT professionals use several techniques to gather data and information. They review documentation, observe, send questionnaires, interview, conduct joint-application design sessions, and do research.

- Review Documentation — By reviewing documentation such as a company's organization chart, memos, and meeting minutes, systems analysts learn about the history of a project. Documentation also provides information about the company such as its operations, weaknesses, and strengths.

- Observe — Observing people helps systems analysts understand exactly how they perform a task. Likewise, observing a machine allows you to see how it works. Read Ethics & Issues 12-1 for a related discussion.
- Questionnaire — To obtain data and information from a large number of people, systems analysts send questionnaires.
- Interview — The interview is the most important data and information gathering technique for the systems analyst. It allows the systems analyst to clarify responses and probe for face-to-face feedback.
- JAD Sessions — Instead of a single one-on-one interview, analysts often use joint-application design sessions to gather data and information. *Joint-application design (JAD)* sessions are a series of lengthy, structured, group meetings in which users and IT professionals work together to design or develop an application (Figure 12-5).

FIGURE 12-5 During a JAD session, the systems analyst is the *moderator*, or leader, of the discussion. Another member, called the *scribe*, records facts and action items assigned during the session.

- Research — Newspapers, computer magazines, reference books, trade shows, and the Web are excellent sources of information. These sources can provide the systems analyst with information such as the latest hardware and software products and explanations of new processes and procedures. In addition, systems analysts often collect Web site statistics such as the number of visitors, most visited Web pages, etc., and evaluate these statistics as part of their research.

FAQ 12-4

What types of questions are asked during an interview?

Interviewers — including systems analysts — ask two types of questions: close-ended and open-ended. Close-ended questions generally are easy to answer, such as the number of years a system has been in place. Open-ended questions, by contrast, require more explanation. For example, an open-ended question may ask the interviewee to describe three problems with the current system. For more information, visit scsite.com/dc2007/ch12/faq and then click Interviews.

WHAT INITIATES THE SYSTEM DEVELOPMENT CYCLE?

A user may request a new or modified information system for a variety of reasons. The most obvious reason is to correct a problem. The computed GPA on a grade report may be incorrect. Another reason is to improve the information system. For example, if a school wants to allow students to register for classes online, it would have to modify the existing registration system to include this new feature. Organizations may want to improve hardware, software, or other technology to enhance an information system. Allowing students to access campus labs with mobile devices, such as PDAs and smart phones, requires upgrades and changes to the information system. If an unauthorized user gains access to the information system, then changes must be made to the security of the system.

Sometimes situations outside the control of a company require a modification to an information system. Corporate management or some other governing body may mandate a change. For example, a nationwide insurance company might require all offices to use the same

ETHICS & ISSUES 12-1

Do You Work Harder When Someone Is Watching?

During the data and information gathering stage of the system development cycle, employees are involved actively in the process. They complete questionnaires, participate in interviews, and are observed while performing their jobs. Many researchers suggest that during observation, employees may not exhibit everyday behavior and may perform above and beyond their normal workday activities. They base this premise on the Hawthorne Effect, which is the result of a study performed in the 1920s in the Western Electric Company plant in Hawthorne, Illinois. The study discovered that productivity improved during observation, whether the conditions were made better or worse. Researchers concluded that productivity seemed to improve whenever the workers knew they were being observed. What is your opinion of the Hawthorne Effect? Do you agree with the research? If someone is observing you at work or if you are receiving increased attention, does this cause you to alter your behavior? Why or why not? Is such observation ethical, and can it have other psychological effects on employees? If productivity increases during observation, is observation a good data gathering technique in a system study? What precautions should be taken by the systems analyst?

calendar software. Competition also can lead to change. After one pharmacy offers online shopping, others follow for fear of losing customers. In recent years, another source of change has resulted from one company merging with or acquiring another company.

A user may request a new or modified information system verbally in a telephone conversation or written as an e-mail message (Figure 12-6a). (Read Ethics & Issues 12-2 for a discussion related to e-mail messages.) In larger companies, users write a formal request for a new or modified information system, which is called a *request for system services* or *project request* (Figure 12-6b). This document becomes the first item in the project notebook. It also triggers the first phase of the system development cycle: planning.

FIGURE 12-6a (informal project request)

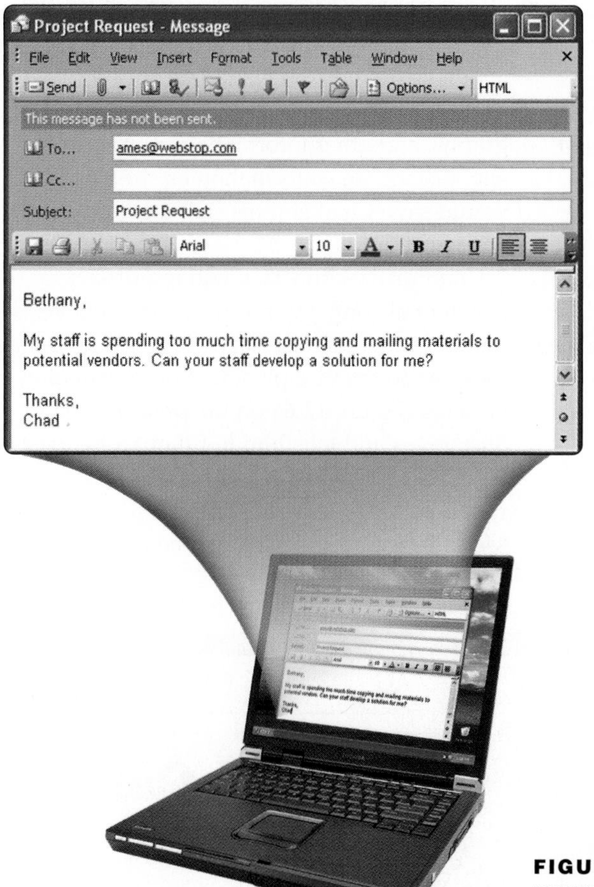

FIGURE 12-6b (formal project request)

Web Stop Café

REQUEST FOR SYSTEM SERVICES

Form IT-102A

SUBMITTED BY: Chad Goldstein

DEPARTMENT: Marketing

DATE: 12-18-2007

TYPE OF REQUEST:
New System
X Existing System Enhancement
Existing System Modification

BRIEF STATEMENT OF PROBLEM:
The staff in the marketing department is spending too much time copying and mailing materials to potential vendors.

BRIEF STATEMENT OF EXPECTED SOLUTION:
Modify our current Web site so it contains a Vendor Information Web link that displays a Vendor Information Web page. From this page, vendors could download all necessary vendor information.

ACTION (To be completed by steering committee member):
Request Approved
Request Delayed
Request Rejected
Analyst Assigned:
Start Date:
Until:
Reason:
Signature:
Date:

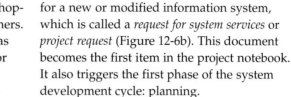

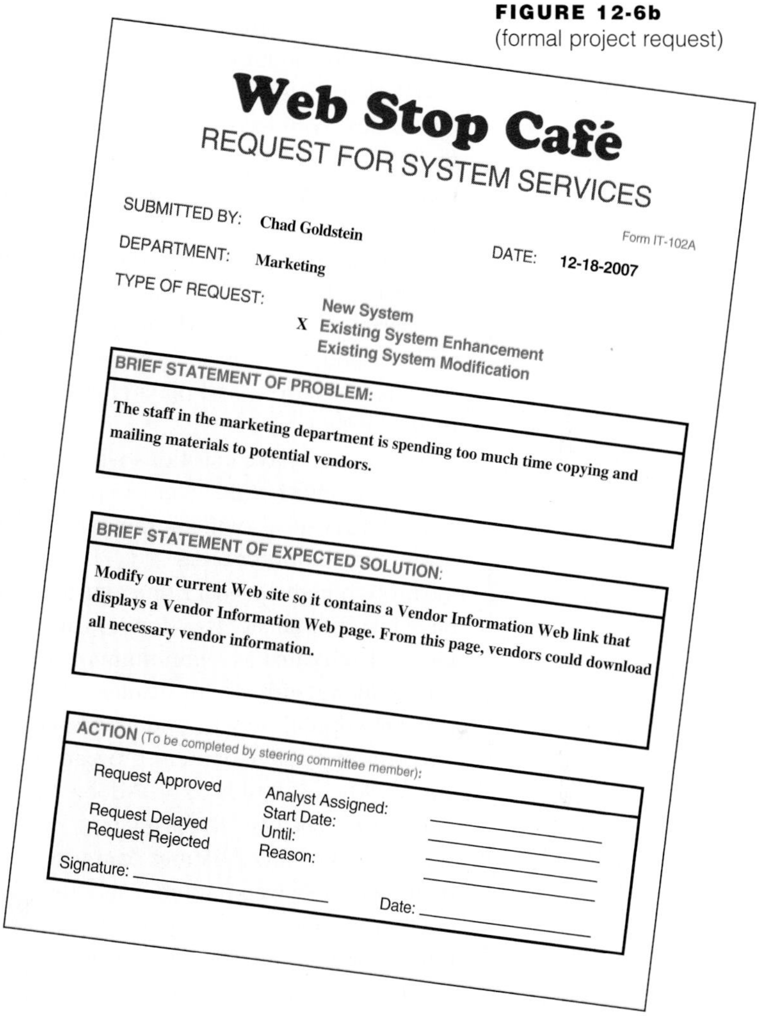

FIGURE 12-6 Sometimes users informally communicate a project request verbally or as an e-mail message. In larger companies, requests often are documented on a form such as this Request for System Services.

ETHICS & ISSUES 12-2

How Should Employers Combat Poor E-Mail Writing Skills?

E-mail may be today's most popular and influential method of communications. Millions of people around the world send and receive e-mail messages. E-mail links the geographically distanced, connects the economically separated, enables the physically challenged, and encourages the publicly timid. IT professionals are prolific e-mail writers because their job depends on a great deal of communication with users, management, vendors, and other departments. Because of e-mail, people are writing more than ever before — but is it good writing? The carefully crafted letters of an era gone by, handwritten in beautiful penmanship, have been replaced by e-mail messages stylistically equivalent to notes on the refrigerator. E-mail's immediacy often results in messages that are ill conceived, casually spelled, poorly worded, grammatically flawed, and tritely expressed (some trite phrases such as, in my humble opinion, are used so routinely they are replaced by abbreviations — IMHO). Should employers require that employees adhere to e-mail authoring policies? In general, has e-mail's impact on communications been positive or negative? Why? Should the quality of e-mail communications be a reason for concern? Why? Could someone's professional reputation be enhanced or hindered by the quality and effectiveness of his or her e-mail messages?

Web Stop Café — A Case Study

This chapter includes a case study to help you understand real-world system development applications. The case study appears shaded in green immediately after the discussion of each phase in the system development cycle. The case is based on Web Stop Café, a fictitious cybercafé. The following paragraphs present a background about Web Stop Café.

Web Stop Café is a worldwide chain of cybercafés. With locations in 45 cities around the world, Web Stop Café is one of the more technologically advanced cybercafés on the planet.

At these cafés, you can do the following: connect to the Web while drinking your favorite specialty beverage and eating a snack; chat with or send e-mail messages to coworkers, friends, and family; and play online games or read an online book.

If customers have questions while using a computer, any staff member can provide assistance. Each café also offers training courses for beginning computer users.

Through high-speed T1 lines, customers have fast Internet access. Monitors are 20 inches. Each café has a minimum of 30 computers, along with a color printer, a laser printer, a digital camera, and a scanner. All computers have popular programs such as Microsoft Office and Adobe Photoshop. The café also is a hot spot, which means customers can use their own mobile computer or mobile device to connect wirelessly to the Internet. For each beverage or snack purchased, customers receive 30 minutes of free computer and/or Web access. If they would like additional time, the fee is $5.00 per hour.

Since Web Stop Café started operations in 1997, business has been thriving. The cafés serve thousands of customers around the world. The Web site (Figure 12-7) has thousands of hits a day. Allison Popovich, chief information officer (CIO) for Web Stop Café, offers one suggestion for the company's financial success. "We do not pay for the computers and equipment in our cafés. Instead, we allow computer vendors to use our café as a storefront for their products. This provides customers with the opportunity to try out the hardware and software before making a purchase. When customers are ready to purchase computers, we direct them to the vendor's online storefront for discount pricing."

To showcase their hardware and software in the cafés, computer vendors request information from Chad Goldstein, the marketing manager. The number of these requests is rising quickly. The cost of copying and mailing this material is becoming excessive. For this reason, Chad would like this vendor information made available on the Web. Vendors could download information sheets, press releases, photographs, and other information from the Web site. Placing this information on the Web would save Chad and his staff a great deal of time and money.

Chad realizes this task will require substantial company resources. He believes a systems study is necessary. He sends an e-mail message to the vice president of information systems (Figure 12-6a on the previous page). She agrees and tells him to fill out a Request for System Services form (Figure 12-6b on the previous page) and submit it to Juanita Mendez, chair of the steering committee at Web Stop Café.

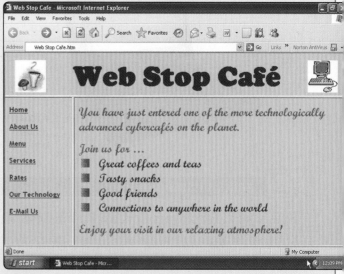

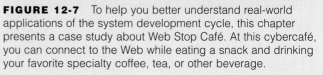

FIGURE 12-7   To help you better understand real-world applications of the system development cycle, this chapter presents a case study about Web Stop Café. At this cybercafé, you can connect to the Web while eating a snack and drinking your favorite specialty coffee, tea, or other beverage.

PLANNING PHASE

The **planning phase** for a project begins when the steering committee receives a project request. As mentioned earlier in this chapter, the steering committee is a decision-making body for a company. This committee usually consists of five to nine people. It typically includes a mix of vice presidents, managers, nonmanagement users, and IT personnel.

During the planning phase, four major activities are performed: (1) review and approve the project requests; (2) prioritize the project requests; (3) allocate resources such as money, people, and equipment to approved projects; and (4) form a project development team for each approved project.

The projects that receive the highest priority are those mandated by management or some other governing body. These requests are given immediate attention. The steering committee evaluates the remaining project requests based on their value to the company. The steering committee approves some projects and rejects others. Of the approved projects, it is likely that only a few will begin their system development cycle immediately. Others will have to wait for additional funds or resources to become available.

Planning at Web Stop Café

After receiving the project request (Figure 12-6b on page 627) from Chad, Juanita Mendez distributes it to all members of the steering committee. They will discuss the request at their next meeting. The steering committee members of Web Stop Café are Juanita Mendez, controller and chair of the steering committee; Milan Sciranka, vice president of operations; Suzy Zhao, Webmaster; Donnell Carter, training specialist; Karl Schmidt, senior systems analyst; and Bethany Ames, vice president of information systems. Juanita also invites Chad Goldstein to the next steering committee meeting. Because he originated the project request, Chad will have the knowledge to answer questions.

During the meeting, the committee decides the project request identifies an improvement to the system, instead of a problem. They feel the nature of the improvement (to make vendor information available on the Web) could lead to considerable savings for the company. It also will provide quicker service to potential vendors.

The steering committee approves the request. Juanita points out that the company has enough funds in its budget to begin the project immediately. Thus, Bethany assembles a system development project team. She assigns Karl Schmidt, senior systems analyst, as the project leader. Karl and his team immediately begin the next phase: analysis.

Test your knowledge of pages 620 through 629 in Quiz Yourself 12-1.

QUIZ YOURSELF 12-1

Instructions: Find the true statement below. Then, rewrite the remaining false statements so they are true.

1. Feasibility is the process of planning, scheduling, and then controlling the activities during the system development cycle.
2. Maintaining up-to-date documentation should be an ongoing part of the system development cycle.
3. Users should not be involved throughout the system development process.
4. The five phases in most system development cycles are programming, analysis, design, sampling, and recording.
5. The planning phase for a project begins when the steering committee receives a Gantt chart.

Quiz Yourself Online: To further check your knowledge of the names of the system development cycle phases, guidelines for system development, ongoing system development cycle activities, and the planning phase, visit scsite.com/dc2007/ch12/quiz and then click Objectives 1 – 4.

ANALYSIS PHASE

The **analysis phase** consists of two major activities: (1) conduct a preliminary investigation and (2) perform detailed analysis. The following sections discuss these activities.

The Preliminary Investigation

The main purpose of the **preliminary investigation**, sometimes called the *feasibility study*, is to determine the exact nature of the problem or improvement and decide whether it is worth pursuing. Should the company continue to assign resources to this project?

To answer this question, the systems analyst conducts a general study of the project. Then, the systems analyst presents his or her findings in a report. Figure 12-8 shows a sample feasibility report, also sometimes known as the feasibility study.

In this phase, the systems analyst defines the problem or improvement accurately. The actual problem may be different from the one suggested in the project request. For example, suppose vendors complain that the marketing department takes too long to send customer names and addresses. An investigation might reveal the marketing department is not the problem. The problem exists because some cafés wait three weeks before sending customer names and addresses to the marketing department. Thus, the preliminary investigation determines the real problem, which is the marketing department does not have instant access to the customer names and addresses.

The first activity in the preliminary investigation is to interview the user who submitted the project request. Depending on the nature

Web Stop Café
MEMORANDUM

To: Steering Committee
From: Karl Schmidt, Project Leader
Date: December 28, 2007
Subject: Feasibility Study of Vendor Web System

Following is the feasibility study in response to the request for a modification to our Web site. Your approval is necessary before the next phase of the project will begin.

The purpose of this feasibility report is to determine whether it is beneficial for Web Stop Café to continue studying the Vendor Web System. The marketing manager has indicated his staff spends a considerable amount of time duplicating and distributing materials to potential vendors. This project would affect the marketing department and customer service. Also, any person that uses the Web site would notice a change.

Background

One of the reasons for our financial success at Web Stop Café is we do not pay for the computers and equipment in our cafés. Instead, we allow computer vendors to use our cafés as a storefront for their products. This provides customers with the opportunity to try the hardware and software before making a purchase. When customers want to purchase computers, we direct them to the vendor's online storefront for discount pricing.

To showcase their hardware and software in the cafés, computer vendors request information from our marketing manager. The number of these requests is rising quickly. The cost of copying and mailing this material is becoming excessive.

Problems

The following problems have been identified with the current information system at Web Stop Café:

- Employees spend too much time copying and duplicating vendor materials

- Potential vendors do not receive material as quickly as in the past, which possibly could cause poor relations

- Resources are wasted including employee time, equipment usage, and supplies

FEASIBILITY STUDY
Page 2

Benefits of a New or Modified System

Following is a list of benefits that could be realized if the Web site at Web Stop Café were modified:

- Potential vendors would be more satisfied, leading to possible long-term relations

- Cost of supplies would be reduced by 30 percent

- Through a more efficient use of employees' time, the company could achieve a 20 percent reduction in temporary clerks in the marketing department

- Laser printers and copy machines would last 50 percent longer, due to a much lower usage rate

Feasibility of a New or Modified System

Operational

A modified system will decrease the amount of equipment use and paperwork. Vendor information will be available in an easily accessible form to any vendor. Employees will have time to complete meaningful job duties, alleviating the need to hire some temporary clerks.

Technical

Web Stop Café already has a functional Web site. To handle the increased volume of data, however, it will need to purchase a database server.

Economic

A detailed summary of the costs and benefits, including all assumptions, is available on our FTP server. The potential costs of the proposed solution could range from $15,000 to $20,000. The estimated savings in supplies and postage alone will exceed $20,000.

If you have any questions about the detailed cost/benefit summary or require further information, please contact me.

Recommendation

Based on the findings presented in this report, we recommend a continued study of the Vendor Web System.

FIGURE 12-8 A feasibility report presents the results of the preliminary investigation. The report must be prepared professionally and be well organized to be effective.

of the request, project team members may interview other users, too. In the case of the cybercafé, members of the team might interview the controller for costs of copying and mailing materials. They also might interview one or two vendors.

In addition to interviewing, members of the project team may use other data gathering techniques, such as reviewing existing documentation. The time spent on this phase of the system development cycle is quite short when compared with the remainder of the project. Often, the preliminary investigation is completed in just a few days.

Upon completion of the preliminary investigation, the systems analyst writes the feasibility report. This report presents the team's findings to the steering committee. The feasibility report contains these major sections: introduction, existing system, benefits of a new or modified system, feasibility of a new or modified system, and the recommendation.

In some cases, the project team may recommend not to continue the project. In other words, the team considers the project infeasible. If the steering committee agrees, the project ends at this point. If the project team recommends continuing and the steering committee approves this recommendation, however, then detailed analysis begins.

Detailed Analysis

Detailed analysis involves three major activities: (1) study how the current system works; (2) determine the users' wants, needs, and requirements; and (3) recommend a solution. Detailed analysis sometimes is called *logical design* because the systems analysts develop the proposed solution without regard to any specific hardware or software. That is, they make no attempt to identify the procedures that should be automated and those that should be manual.

During these activities, systems analysts use all of the data and information-gathering techniques. They review documentation, observe employees and machines, send questionnaires, interview employees, conduct JAD sessions, and do research. An important benefit from these activities is that they build valuable relationships among the systems analysts and users.

While studying the current system and identifying user requirements, the systems analyst collects a great deal of data and information. A major task for the systems analyst is to document these findings in a way that can be understood by everyone. Both users and IT professionals refer to this documentation.

Most systems analysts use either a process modeling or object modeling approach to analysis and design. The following sections discuss these approaches.

Preliminary Investigation at Web Stop Café

Karl Schmidt, senior systems analyst and project leader, meets with Chad Goldstein to discuss the project request. During the interview, Karl looks at the material that Chad's staff sends to a potential vendor. He asks Chad how many vendor requests he receives in a month. Then Karl interviews the controller, Juanita Mendez, to obtain some general cost and benefit figures for the feasibility report. He also calls a vendor. He wants to know if the material Chad's department sends is helpful.

Next, Karl prepares the feasibility report (Figure 12-8). After the project team members review it, Karl submits it to the steering committee. The report recommends proceeding to the detailed analysis phase for this project. The steering committee agrees. Karl and his team begin detailed analysis.

FAQ 12-5

Why is it necessary for the systems analyst to build relationships with users?

Systems analysts have much more credibility with users if the analysts understand user concerns. If users are involved, they are more likely to accept and use the new system — called *user buy-in*. One reason systems fail is because some systems analysts create or modify systems with little or no user participation. For more information, visit scsite.com/dc2007/ch12/faq and then click Systems Analyst.

WEB LINK 12-2

Process Modeling

For more information, visit scsite.com/dc2007/ch12/weblink and then click Process Modeling.

Process Modeling

Process modeling, sometimes called *structured analysis and design*, is an analysis and design technique that describes processes that transform inputs into outputs. Tools that a systems analyst uses for process modeling include entity-relationship diagrams, data flow diagrams, and the project dictionary. The following pages discuss these tools.

ENTITY-RELATIONSHIP DIAGRAMS An **entity-relationship diagram** (*ERD*) is a tool that graphically shows the connections among entities in a system. An *entity* is an object in the system that has data. For example, a cyber-café might have customer, order, menu item, computer, and vendor entities.

On the ERD, entity names usually are nouns written in all capital letters. Each relationship describes a connection between two entities. In the ERD shown in Figure 12-9, a vendor supplies one or more computers to the cafés. A computer is supplied by a single vendor. A customer may or may not use one of these computers during a visit to the café. A customer may or may not place an order. Some customers place multiple orders. Each order contains one or more items from the menu.

It is important that the systems analyst has an accurate understanding of the system. The systems analyst reviews the ERD with the user. After users approve the ERD, the systems analyst identifies data items associated with an entity. For example, the VENDOR entity might have these data items: Vendor Number, Vendor Name, Vendor Contact Name, Address, City, State, Postal Code, Telephone Number, and E-Mail Address.

DATA FLOW DIAGRAMS A **data flow diagram** (*DFD*) is a tool that graphically shows the flow of data in a system. The key elements of a DFD are the data flows, the processes, the data stores, and the sources (Figure 12-10). A *data flow*, indicated by a line with an arrow, shows the input or output of data or information into or out from a process. A *process*, which is drawn as a circle, transforms an input data flow into an output data flow. A *data store*, shown as a rectangle with no sides, is a holding place for data and information. Examples of data stores are filing cabinets, checkbook registers, or electronic files stored on a computer. A *source*, drawn as a square, identifies an entity outside the scope of the system. Sources send data into the system or receive information from the system.

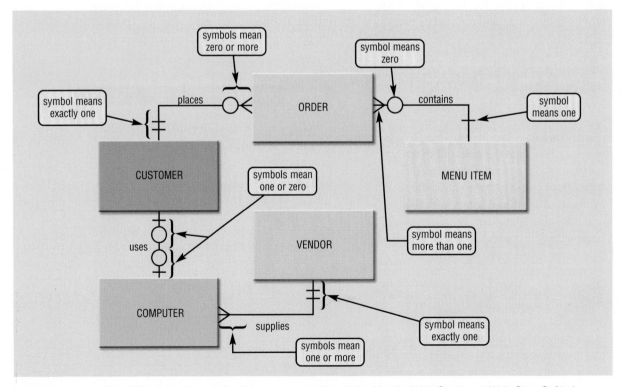

FIGURE 12-9   This ERD shows the relationships among entities in the Vendor Web System at Web Stop Café. A vendor supplies one or more computers to the cafés. A computer is supplied by a single vendor. A customer may or may not use one of these computers during a visit to the café. A customer may or may not place an order. Some customers place multiple orders. Each order contains one or more items from the menu.

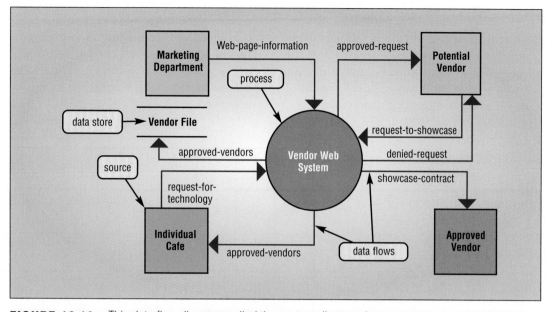

FIGURE 12-10 This data flow diagram, called the context diagram, has one process — the Vendor Web System being studied at Web Stop Café. The Vendor File is a data store. Sources both send and receive data and information to and from the system. For example, a café sends a request for technology (hardware and/or software) into the Vendor Web System, which then sends out a list of approved vendors for that technology. The list of approved vendors is stored in the Vendor File.

Like ERDs, systems analysts often use DFDs to review processes with users. Systems analysts prepare DFDs on a level-by-level basis. The top level DFD, known as a *context diagram*, identifies only the major process. Lower-level DFDs add detail and definition to the higher levels, similar to zooming in on a computer screen. The lower-level DFDs contain subprocesses. For example, Figure 12-10 shows a context diagram that contains the Vendor Web System process. This process might be split into three subprocesses: (1) gathering and organizing vendor information, (2) converting vendor information into electronic format, and (3) uploading the files to the Web page.

PROJECT DICTIONARY The **project dictionary**, sometimes called the *repository*, contains all the documentation and deliverables of a project. The project dictionary helps everyone keep track of the huge amount of details in a system. The dictionary explains every item found on DFDs and ERDs. Each process, data store, data flow, and source on every DFD has an entry in the project dictionary. Every entity on the ERD has an entry in the project dictionary. The dictionary also contains an entry for each data item associated with the entities.

The number of entries added to the dictionary at this point can be enormous. As you might imagine, this activity requires a huge amount of time.

The systems analyst uses a variety of techniques to enter these items in the project dictionary. Some of these include structured English, decision tables and decision trees, and the data dictionary.

• *Structured English* is a style of writing that describes the steps in a process. Many systems analysts use structured English to explain the details of a process. Figure 12-11 shows an example of structured English that describes the process of uploading vendor information.

UPLOADING VENDOR INFORMATION

For each item containing vendor information, perform the following steps:

      If the item is not a computer file then

            Use the scanner to convert it into a file format.

      Copy the file into the Vendor Information folder on the hard disk.

Zip all new files in the Vendor Information folder into a single file.

Save the zipped file in a Web folder.

E-mail the Webmaster with the name of the zipped file.

FIGURE 12-11 Structured English is a technique used to describe a process in the project dictionary. This structured English example describes the process of uploading vendor information to a Web page. The indented text is part of the loop.

- Sometimes, a process consists of many conditions or rules. In this case, the systems analyst may use a decision table or decision tree instead of structured English. A **decision table** is a table that lists a variety of conditions and the actions that correspond to each condition. A *decision tree* also shows conditions and actions, but it shows them graphically. Figures 12-12 and 12-13 show a decision table and decision tree for the same process: determining whether a vendor is approved.

| | | RULES | | | | | | | |
		1	2	3	4	5	6	7	8
CONDITIONS	Background check results (S = Satisfactory, U = Unsatisfactory)	S	S	S	S	U	U	U	U
	References furnished?	Y	Y	N	N	Y	Y	N	N
	Passed credit check?	Y	N	Y	N	Y	N	Y	N
ACTIONS	Vendor approved	X							
	Vendor not approved		X			X	X	X	X
	Waiting for additional information			X	X				

FIGURE 12-12 This decision table describes the policy for determining whether vendors are approved to showcase their products at Web Stop Café. Vendors are approved if they meet all conditions in Rule #1. For example, vendors are approved if their background check results are satisfactory, they have furnished all of their references, and have passed a credit check.

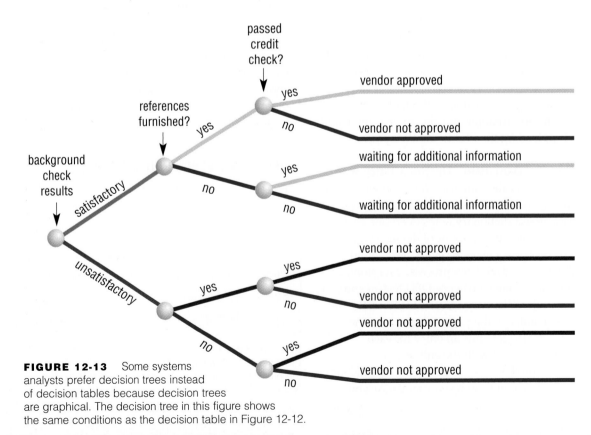

FIGURE 12-13 Some systems analysts prefer decision trees instead of decision tables because decision trees are graphical. The decision tree in this figure shows the same conditions as the decision table in Figure 12-12.

• Each data item has an entry in the data dictionary section of the project dictionary (Figure 12-14). The **data dictionary** stores the data item's name, description, and other details about each data item. The systems analyst creates the data dictionary during detailed analysis. In later phases of the system development cycle, the systems analyst refers to and updates the data dictionary.

Date: 12/29/2007 *Project:* **WEB STOP CAFE** *Page:* 11
Time: 10:36:28 AM

Detailed Listing -- Alphabetically
All Entries -- Data Flow Diagrams

Vendor ID   Data Element
Vendor File::Vendor ID
   Description:
     A unique identification number assigned to each vendor.
   Alias:
     Vendor Code
   Values & Meanings:
     Required element
     Cannot be blank
     May not be duplicated
   Data element attributes
     Storage Type: Char
     Length: 4
     Display Format: AAAA
     Null Type: NotNull
   Location:
     File -->   Vendor File
   Date Last Altered: 12/29   *Date Created:* 12/29

FIGURE 12-14 The data dictionary records details about each of the data items that make up the data flows and entities in the system. This is a dictionary entry for the Vendor ID data element.

Object Modeling

Object modeling, sometimes called *object-oriented (OO) analysis and design*, combines the data with the processes that act on that data into a single unit, called an object. An **object** is an item that can contain both data and the procedures that read or manipulate that data. For example, a Customer object might contain data about a customer (Customer ID, First Name, Last Name, Address, and so on) and instructions about how to print a customer's record or the formula required to compute a customer's amount due. Each data element is called an *attribute* or *property*. The procedure in the object, called an *operation* or *method*, contains activities that read or manipulate the data. For example, a cybercafé would create a new customer object (method) for each new customer.

Object modeling can use the same tools as those used in process modeling. Many systems analysts, however, choose to use tools defined in the UML. Although used in all types of business modeling, the **UML** (*Unified Modeling Language*) has been adopted as a standard notation for object modeling and development. The UML is a graphical tool that enables analysts to document a system. It consists of many interrelated diagrams. Each diagram conveys a view of the system.

Instead of developing their own object diagrams and steps in an object-oriented system development cycle, most companies use an existing methodology to guide them through the steps in the system development cycle. A popular methodology on the market today that uses the UML is the *Rational Unified Process* (*RUP*) by Grady Booch, Ivar Jacobsen, and James Rumbaugh.

The latest UML version includes 13 different diagrams to assist the analyst in modeling the system. Two of the more common tools are the use case diagram and class diagram. The next page describes these two diagrams.

WEB LINK 12-3

UML
For more information, visit scsite.com/dc2007/ch12/weblink and then click UML.

USE CASE DIAGRAM A use case diagram graphically shows how actors interact with the information system. An *actor* is a user or other entity such as a program. The function that the actor can perform is called the *use case*. Thus, a use case diagram shows actors and their use cases (Figure 12-15). The actor is drawn as a stick figure that connects to each use case with an arrow.

Because these diagrams are easy to understand, analysts find that the use case diagram is an ideal tool for communicating system requirements with users.

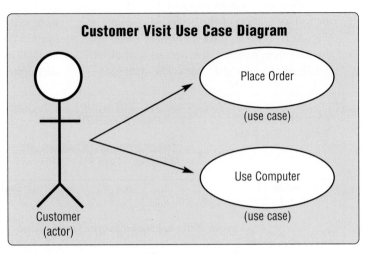

Customer Visit Use Case Diagram

FIGURE 12-15 This use case diagram shows that the customer needs the system for two use cases: place an order and use a computer.

CLASS DIAGRAM A **class diagram** graphically shows classes and subclasses in a system (Figure 12-16). On a class diagram, objects are grouped into classes. Each class can have one or more lower levels called *subclasses*. Each subclass inherits the methods and attributes of the objects in its higher-level class. Every object in a class shares methods and attributes that are part of its higher-level class. This concept of lower levels inheriting methods and attributes of higher levels is called *inheritance*. In the simplified example in Figure 12-16, Food Order and Drink Order are subclasses of the higher-level class, called Order. All orders have an Order Number and Order Date (which would be attributes in the Order object), but only drink orders have a Size attribute (with values of small, medium, or large).

The System Proposal

At this point, the systems analyst has studied the current system and determined all user requirements. The next step is to communicate possible solutions for the project in a system proposal. The purpose of the *system proposal* is to assess the feasibility of each alternative solution and then recommend the most feasible solution for the project, which often involves modifying or building on the current system. The systems analyst reevaluates feasibility at this point in the system development cycle, especially economic feasibility (often in conjunction with a financial analyst). The systems analyst presents the system proposal to the steering committee. If the steering committee approves a solution, the project enters the design phase.

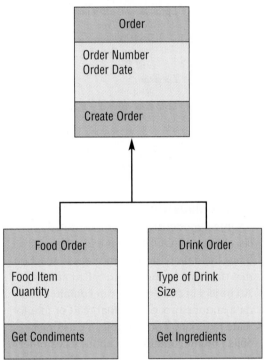

FIGURE 12-16 In this simplified class diagram, the Order class has two subclasses: Food Order and Drink Order. The subclasses inherit the attributes (Order Number and Order Date) and the method (Create Order) of the Order class and also contain some unique attributes and methods of their own.

When the steering committee discusses the system proposal and decides which alternative to pursue, it often is deciding whether to buy packaged software from an outside source, build its own custom software, or outsource some or all of its IT needs to an outside firm.

PACKAGED SOFTWARE **Packaged software** is mass-produced, copyrighted, prewritten software available for purchase. Packaged software is available for different types of computers. Chapter 3 presented many types of application software available for personal computers. These include word processing, spreadsheet, note taking, database, document management, desktop publishing, paint/image editing, Web page authoring, personal finance, legal, tax preparation, educational/reference, e-mail, and Web browser software.

Vendors offer two types of packaged software: horizontal and vertical. *Horizontal market software* meets the needs of many different types of companies. The programs discussed in Chapter 3 were horizontal. If a company has a unique way of accomplishing activities, then it also may require vertical market software. *Vertical market software* specifically is designed for a particular business or industry. Examples of companies that use vertical market software include banks, schools, hospitals, real estate offices, libraries, and insurance companies. Each of these industries has unique information processing requirements.

Horizontal market software tends to be more widely available and less expensive than vertical market software. You can search for vertical and horizontal market software on the Web. Other sources include computer magazines, trade shows, and trade publications. A *trade publication* is a magazine written for a specific business or industry. Software for these industries often is advertised in trade publications.

CUSTOM SOFTWARE Instead of buying packaged software, some companies write their own applications using programming languages such as C++, C#, Java, and Visual Basic. Application software developed by the user or at the user's request is called **custom software**.

The main advantage of custom software is that it matches the company's requirements exactly. The disadvantages usually are that it is more expensive and takes longer to design and implement than packaged software.

OUTSOURCING Companies can develop custom software in-house using their own IT personnel or *outsource* it, which means having an outside source develop it for them. Some companies outsource just the software development aspect of their IT operation. Others outsource more or all of their IT operation.

Depending on a company's needs, outside firms can handle as much of the IT requirements as desired. Some provide hardware and software. Others provide a variety of services such as Web design and development, Web hosting, sales, marketing, billing, customer service, and legal assistance. For example, an *Internet solutions provider* is a company that provides Web hosting services that include managing shopping carts, inventory, and credit card processing (Figure 12-17). A trend that has caused much controversy relates to companies that outsource to firms located outside their homeland. Read Ethics & Issues 12-3 for a discussion related to IT.

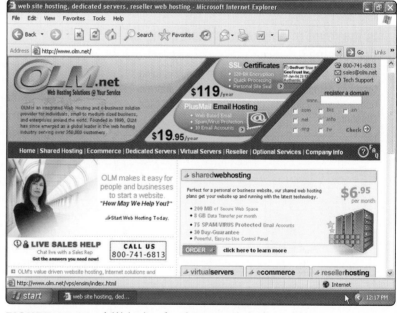

FIGURE 12-17 A Web site of an Internet solutions provider.

ETHICS & ISSUES 12-3

Does Keeping Up with Technology Provide a Strategic Advantage?

When a new technology emerges, such as the railroad or electricity, businesses that adopt the technology can gain a strategic advantage over competitors who do not. Eventually, a successful technology becomes so inexpensive and ubiquitous that the early advantage quickly disappears; the technology no longer is considered to be a competitive advantage, because all of the competition utilizes the technology. In his book *Does IT Matter*, Nicholas Carr argues that this effect already has been observed with information technology. Companies often adopt the latest information technologies with the hope of gaining an edge. Nicholas Carr, however, claims that information technology is becoming a commodity and nothing short of ordinary. Critics argue that information technology allows you to transform information and data into intelligence, which is of extreme value in an economy that greatly relies on nonmanufacturing activities, such as services, product design, and product development. Can businesses still gain an advantage over their competitors using information technology? Why or why not? Should executives rush to adopt the latest information technology in order to gain a competitive advantage? Why? If IT becomes irrelevant as a competitive advantage, what does this mean for the IT industry?

Some companies obtain software through Web services. Recall from Chapter 9 that Web services describe standardized software that enables programmers to create applications that communicate with other remote computers over the Internet or on an internal business network. Some Web services are free; others charge a fee.

WEB LINK 12-5

Outsourcing

For more information, visit scsite.com/dc2007/ch12/weblink and then click Outsourcing.

FAQ 12-6

Is the level of outsourcing increasing or decreasing?

As shown in the chart below, the level of outsourcing for many companies is on the rise. For more information, visit scsite.com/dc2007/ch12/faq and then click Outsourcing.

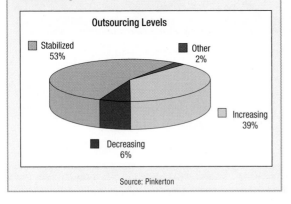

Outsourcing Levels

Stabilized 53%
Other 2%
Increasing 39%
Decreasing 6%

Source: Pinkerton

Detailed Analysis at Web Stop Café

Karl and his team begin performing the activities in the detailed analysis phase of the Vendor Web System. As part of the study and requirements activities, they use several of the data and information gathering techniques available to them. They interview employees throughout the company and meet with some vendors. They observe the marketing staff copy and mail vendor information. Because the team is using structured analysis and design techniques, they prepare many process modeling deliverables to record their findings: an entity-relationship diagram (Figure 12-9 on page 632), a data flow diagram (Figure 12-10 on page 633), a process specification using structured English (Figure 12-11 on page 633), a process specification using a decision table (Figure 12-12 on page 634), and a data dictionary entry for a Vendor ID data item (Figure 12-14 on page 635). These documents all become part of the project notebook. Members of the project team refer to these documents during the remainder of the system development cycle.

After two months of studying the existing system and obtaining user requirements, Karl discusses his findings with his supervisor, Bethany Ames. Karl recommends that a link to Vendor Information be added to their current Web site. When a vendor clicks this link, a Vendor Information page will be displayed. This Web page should contain all information that the marketing department usually sends to a vendor.

Based on Karl's findings, Bethany writes a system proposal for the steering committee to review. Suzy Zhao, Webmaster at Web Stop Café, developed the current Web site. Thus, Bethany recommends that Suzy's staff modify the Web site in-house. Bethany also recommends Web Stop Café invest in a larger database server to handle the additional vendor information.

The steering committee agrees with Bethany's proposal. Karl and his team begin the design phase of the project.

Test your knowledge of pages 630 through 638 in Quiz Yourself 12-2.

QUIZ YOURSELF 12-2

Instructions: Find the true statement below. Then, rewrite the remaining false statements so they are true.

1. Detailed analysis sometimes is called physical design because the systems analysts develop the proposed solution without regard to any specific hardware or software.

2. Entity-relationship diagrams and data flow diagrams are tools that a systems analyst uses for object modeling.

3. Horizontal market software specifically is designed for a particular business or industry.

4. The project dictionary contains all the documentation and deliverables of a project.

5. The purpose of the preliminary investigation is to assess the feasibility of each alternative solution and then recommend the most feasible solution for the project.

6. Upon completion of the preliminary investigation, the systems analyst writes the system proposal.

Quiz Yourself Online: To further check your knowledge of the analysis phase, process modeling, and object modeling, visit scsite.com/dc2007/ch12/quiz and then click Objectives 5 – 7.

DESIGN PHASE

The **design phase** consists of two major activities: (1) if necessary, acquire hardware and software and (2) develop all of the details of the new or modified information system. The systems analyst often performs these two activities at the same time instead of sequentially.

Acquiring Necessary Hardware and Software

When the steering committee approves a solution, the systems analyst begins the activity of obtaining additional hardware or software. The systems analyst may skip this activity if the approved solution does not require new hardware or software. If this activity is required, the selection of appropriate products is crucial for the success of the information system. The activity consists of four major tasks: (1) identify technical specifications, (2) solicit vendor proposals, (3) test and evaluate vendor proposals, and (4) make a decision.

Identifying Technical Specifications

The first step in acquiring the necessary hardware and software is to identify all the hardware and software requirements of the new or modified system. To do this, the systems analysts use a variety of research techniques. They talk with other systems analysts, visit vendors' stores, and search the Web. Many trade journals, newspapers, and magazines provide some or all of their printed content as e-zines. An **e-zine** (pronounced ee-zeen), or *electronic magazine*, is a publication available on the Web.

After the systems analyst defines the technical requirements, the next step is to summarize these requirements for potential vendors. The systems analyst can use three basic types of documents for this purpose: an RFQ, an RFP, or an RFI. A *request for quotation* (RFQ) identifies the required product(s). With an RFQ, the vendor quotes a price for the listed product(s). With a *request for proposal* (RFP), the vendor selects the product(s) that meets specified requirements and then quotes the price(s). Software exists that assist with the creation of a professional RFP.

Just as the depth of an information system varies, so does the length of an RFQ or RFP. Some can be as short as a couple of pages.

Others consist of more than one hundred pages. Instead of an RFQ or RFP, some companies prefer to use a request for information. A *request for information* (RFI) is a less formal method that uses a standard form to request information about a product or service.

Soliciting Vendor Proposals

Systems analysts send the RFQ, RFP, or RFI to potential hardware and software vendors. They have a variety of ways to locate vendors. Many publish their product catalogs on the Web. These online catalogs provide up-to-date information on and easy access to products, prices, technical specifications, and ordering information.

Another source for hardware and software products is a value-added reseller. A *value-added reseller* (VAR) is a company that purchases products from manufacturers and then resells these products to the public — offering additional services with the product. Examples of additional services include user support, equipment maintenance, training, installation, and warranties.

To be an authorized VAR, most manufacturers have requirements the VAR must meet. Various terms that identify a VAR's relationship with a manufacturer are strategic partner, business partner, authorized reseller, or solutions provider. Some VARs offer one product or service. Others provide complete systems, also known as a *turnkey solution* (Figure 12-18).

WEB LINK 12-6

Request for Proposals

For more information, visit scsite.com/ dc2007/ch12/weblink and then click Request for Proposals.

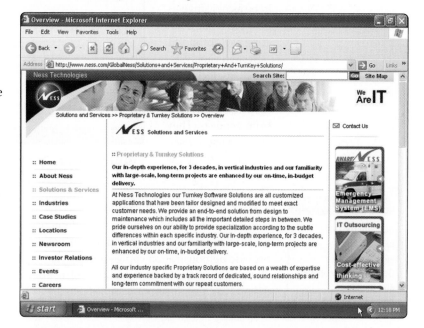

FIGURE 12-18 Many VARs advertise their services on the Web.

Instead of using vendors, some companies hire an IT consultant or a group of IT consultants; that is, they outsource this task. An *IT consultant* is a professional who is hired based on computer expertise, including service and advice. IT consultants often specialize in configuring hardware and software for businesses of all sizes.

Testing and Evaluating Vendor Proposals

After sending RFQs and RFPs to potential vendors, the systems analyst will receive completed quotations and proposals. Evaluating the proposals and then selecting the best one often is a difficult task. It is important to be as objective as possible while evaluating each proposal.

Systems analysts use many techniques to test the various software products from vendors. They obtain a list of user references from the software vendors. They also talk to current users of the software to solicit their opinions. Some vendors will give a demonstration of the product(s) specified. Other vendors provide demonstration copies or trial versions, allowing the companies to test the software themselves. Demonstration copies usually are free and have limited functionality. Trial versions

are free or have minimal fees and provide full functionality for a set time (Figure 12-19). In some cases, the demonstration copies and trial versions are available to download from the Web.

Sometimes it is important to know whether the software can process a certain volume of transactions efficiently. In this case, the systems analyst conducts a benchmark test. A *benchmark test* measures the performance of hardware or software. For example, a benchmark test could measure the time it takes a payroll program to print 50 paychecks. Comparing the time it takes various accounting programs to print the same 50 paychecks is one way of measuring each program's performance. Some computer magazines conduct benchmark tests while evaluating hardware and software and then publish these results for consumers to review. For a technical discussion about benchmark tests, read the High-Tech Talk article on page 648.

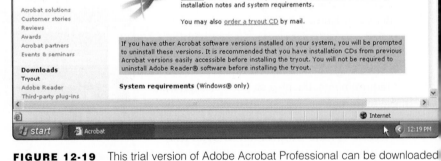

FIGURE 12-19 This trial version of Adobe Acrobat Professional can be downloaded free and expires 30 days after installation.

Making a Decision

Having rated the proposals, the systems analyst presents a recommendation to the steering committee. The recommendation could be to award a contract to a vendor or to not make any purchases at this time.

WEB LINK 12-7

Benchmark Tests

For more information, visit scsite.com/dc2007/ch12/weblink and then click Benchmark Tests.

Hardware Acquisition at Web Stop Café

Karl and his team compile a requirements list for the database server. They prepare an RFP and submit it to twelve vendors: eight through the Web and four local computer stores. Ten vendors reply within the three-week deadline.

Of the ten replies, the development team selects two to evaluate. They eliminate the other eight because these vendors did not offer adequate warranties for the database server. The project team members ask for benchmark test results for each server. In addition, they contact two current users of this database server for their opinions about its performance. After evaluating these two servers, the team selects the best one.

Karl summarizes his team's findings in a report to the steering committee. The committee gives Karl authorization to award a contract to the proposed vendor. As a courtesy and to maintain good working relationships, Karl sends a letter to all twelve vendors informing them of the committee's decision.

Detailed Design

After the systems analyst identifies the data and process requirements, the next step is to develop detailed design specifications for the components in the proposed solution. A detailed design sometimes is called a *physical design* because it specifies hardware and software — the physical components required — for automated procedures. The activities to be performed include developing designs for the databases, inputs, outputs, and programs.

The length and complexity of these activities vary depending on previous decisions. For example, the systems analyst may skip many of these activities when purchasing packaged software. If the company is developing custom software, however, these activities can be quite time-consuming.

DATABASE DESIGN   During database design, the systems analyst builds upon the data dictionary developed during the analysis phase. The systems analyst works closely with the database analysts and database administrators to identify those data elements that currently exist within the company and those that are new.

With relational database systems, the systems analyst defines the structure of each table in the system, as well as relationships among the tables. The systems analyst also addresses user access privileges. That is, the systems analyst defines which data elements each user can access, when they can access the data elements, what actions they can perform on the data elements, and under what circumstances they can access the elements. The result of database design is called a *data model*.

INPUT AND OUTPUT DESIGN   During this activity, the systems analyst carefully designs every menu, screen, and report specified in the requirements. The outputs often are designed first because they help define the requirements for the inputs. Thus, it is very important that outputs are identified correctly and that users agree to them.

The systems analyst typically develops two types of designs for each input and output: a mockup and a layout chart. A *mockup* is a sample of the input or output that contains actual data (Figure 12-20). The systems analyst shows mockups to users for their approval. Because users will work with the inputs and outputs of the system, it is crucial to involve users during input and output design. After users approve the mockup, the systems analyst develops a layout chart for the programmer. A *layout chart* is more technical and contains programming-like notations for the data items (Figure 12-21).

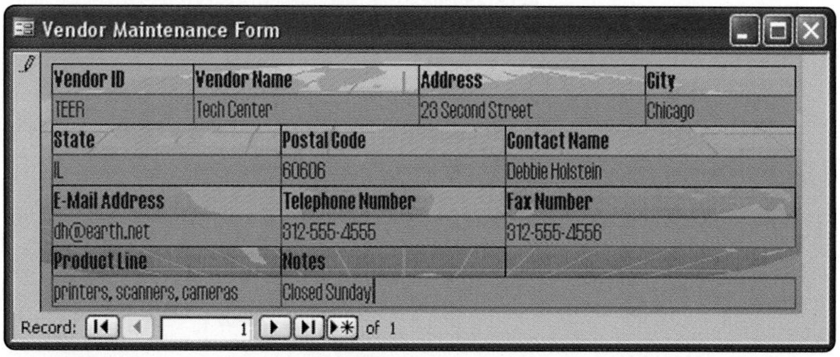

FIGURE 12-20   Users must give their approval on all inputs and outputs. This input screen is a mockup (containing actual sample data) for users to review.

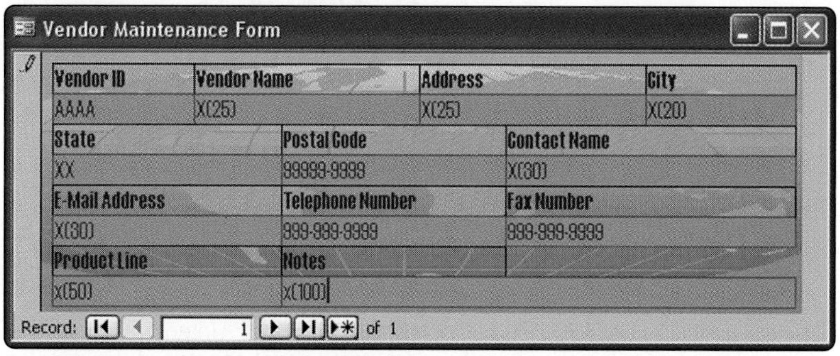

FIGURE 12-21   Once users approve a mockup, the layout chart (with technical specifications) is given to the programmer. This is the layout chart for the mockup in Figure 12-20.

Other issues that must be addressed during input and output design include the types of media to use (paper, video, audio); formats (graphical or narrative); and data entry validation techniques, which include making sure the entered data is correct (for example, a state code has to be one of the fifty valid two-letter state abbreviations).

PROGRAM DESIGN During program design, the systems analyst prepares the *program specification package*, which identifies the required programs and the relationship among each program, as well as the input, output, and database specifications.

Prototyping

Many systems analysts today use prototypes during detailed design. A **prototype** is a working model of the proposed system. The systems analyst actually builds a functional form of the solution during design. The main advantage of a prototype is users can work with the system before it is completed — to make sure it meets their needs.

The Vendor Maintenance Form shown in Figure 12-20 on the previous page could be an example of a screen in a prototype of the Vendor Web System. As soon as users approve a prototype, systems analysts can have a solution implemented more quickly than without a prototype.

Some systems analysts use prototyping during the design phase. Others begin earlier in the system development cycle — during analysis or even planning.

A common problem with prototypes is they have inadequate documentation, or worse, none at all. Another drawback is that users tend to embrace the prototype as a final system, which may not be the result of an extensive analysis. Prototyping can be an effective tool if the development team and the users discipline themselves to follow all activities within the system development cycle. Prototyping should not eliminate or replace activities; rather, it should improve the quality of these activities.

CASE Tools

Many systems analysts use computer software to assist in the system development cycle. *Computer-aided software engineering (CASE)* software tools are designed to support one or more activities of the system development cycle. CASE tools typically include diagrams to support both process and object modeling.

Some CASE tools exist separately. One program might be a dictionary and another might allow you to create drawings. The most effective tools, however, are integrated (Figure 12-22).

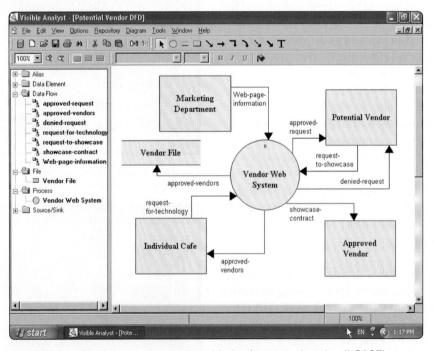

FIGURE 12-22 Integrated computer-aided software engineering (I-CASE) programs assist analysts in the development of an information system. Visible Analyst by Visible Systems Corporation enables analysts to create diagrams, as well as build the project dictionary.

Integrated case products, sometimes called *I-CASE* or a CASE workbench, include the following capabilities:

- Project Repository — Stores diagrams, specifications, descriptions, programs, and any other deliverable generated during the system development cycle.
- Graphics — Enables the drawing of diagrams, such as DFDs and ERDs.
- Prototyping — Creates models of the proposed system.
- Quality Assurance — Analyzes deliverables, such as graphs and the data dictionary, for accuracy.
- Code Generator — Creates actual computer programs from design specifications.
- Housekeeping — Establishes user accounts and provides backup and recovery functions.

Quality Review Techniques

Many people should review the detailed design specifications before they are given to the programming team. Reviewers should include users, systems analysts, managers, IT staff, and members of the system development team.

One popular review technique is an inspection. An *inspection* is a formal review of any system development cycle deliverable. A team of four to five people examines the deliverables, such as reports, diagrams, mockups, layout charts, and dictionary entries. The purpose of an inspection is to identify errors in the item being inspected. Any identified errors are summarized in a report so they can be addressed and corrected.

Once again, the systems analyst reevaluates feasibility to determine if it still is beneficial to proceed with the proposed solution. If the steering committee decides the project still is feasible, which usually is the case, the project enters the implementation phase.

FAQ 12-8

Why reassess feasibility at this late stage in system development?

It does not happen often, but companies cancel some projects at the end of the design phase because the projects become infeasible. Although much time and money may have been spent, it is less costly to cancel the project than to proceed with an inadequate or incorrect solution. For more information, visit scsite.com/dc2007/ch12/faq and then click Feasibility.

Detailed Design at Web Stop Café

As approved by the steering committee, Karl and his team begin designing the Vendor Web System. After studying current vendor information and interviewing more users and vendors, the team designs changes to the company's database, Web site, and the associated programs. They prepare several documents including a mockup (Figure 12-20 on page 641) and a layout chart (Figure 12-21 on page 641).

After completing the detailed design, Karl meets with several users and IT personnel to walk through the deliverables. They locate two errors. He corrects the errors and then presents the design to the steering committee. The committee agrees with the design solution and consents to implement it.

IMPLEMENTATION PHASE

The purpose of the **implementation phase** is to construct, or build, the new or modified system and then deliver it to the users. Members of the system development team perform four major activities in this phase: (1) develop programs, (2) install and test the new system, (3) train users, and (4) convert to the new system.

Develop Programs

If the company purchases packaged software and no modifications to the software are required, the development team may skip this activity. For custom software or packaged software that requires modification, however, programs are developed or modified either by an outside firm or in-house. Programmers write or modify programs from the program specification package created during the analysis phase. Just as the system development cycle follows an organized set of activities, so does program development. These program development activities are known as the *program development cycle*.

The program development cycle follows these six steps: (1) analyze the requirements, (2) design the solution, (3) validate the design, (4) implement the design, (5) test the solution, and (6) document the solution. Chapter 13 explains the program development cycle in depth. The important concept to understand now is that the program development cycle is a part of the implementation phase, which is part of the system development cycle.

Install and Test the New System

If the company acquires new hardware or software, someone must install and test it. The systems analysts should test individual programs. They also should be sure that all the programs work together in the system. Systems analysts do not want errors in the system after it is delivered to the users.

Systems analysts and users develop test data so they can perform various tests. The test data should include both valid (correct) and invalid (incorrect) data. When valid test data is entered, the program should produce the correct results. Invalid test data should generate an error.

Tests performed during this step include unit tests, systems tests, integration tests, and acceptance tests. A *unit test* verifies that each individual program or object works by itself. A *systems test* verifies that all programs in an application work together properly. An *integration test* verifies that an application works with other applications. An *acceptance test* is performed by end-users and checks the new system to ensure that it works with actual data. Read Looking Ahead 12-2 for a look at the next generation of software tests for Microsoft Vista.

FAQ 12-9

How much time is spent fixing errors in programs?

One study estimates that more than 34 percent of a programmer's time is devoted to fixing program bugs. For more information, visit scsite.com/dc2007/ch12/faq and then click Software Errors.

LOOKING AHEAD 12-2

Putting Vista to the Test

New security features in Microsoft Vista offer User Account Protection (UAP) against malware infection. Limited User Accounts (LUA) permit standard users to install software and change the operating system, but an administrative password is required to perform these tasks. While remembering another password may seem an inconvenience, this extra step stops changes from occurring on your computer without your knowledge.

Vista also installs device drivers and virus scanners on only the user level, not within protected areas of the system registry, as was done in previous Windows versions. This installation prevents writing to system files and modifying system-wide data. The UAP also contains antiphishing technology and promises to make the operating system less vulnerable to viruses and Trojan horses. For more information, visit scsite.com/dc2007/ch12/looking and then click Vista Validation.

Train Users

According to a recent study, poor user training is one of the top ten reasons why system development projects fail. Users must be trained properly on a system's functionality. **Training** involves showing users exactly how they will use the new hardware and software in the system. Some training takes place as one-on-one sessions or classroom-style lectures (Figure 12-23). Other companies use Web-based training, which is a self-directed, self-paced online instruction method. Whichever technique is used, it should include hands-on sessions with realistic sample data. Users should practice on the actual system during training. Users also should receive user manuals for reference. It is the systems analyst's responsibility to create user manuals, both printed and electronic.

FIGURE 12-23 Organizations must ensure that users are trained properly on the new system. One training method uses hands-on classes to learn the new system.

Convert to the New System

The final implementation activity is to change from the old system to the new system. This change can take place using one or more of the following conversion strategies: direct, parallel, phased, or pilot (Figure 12-24).

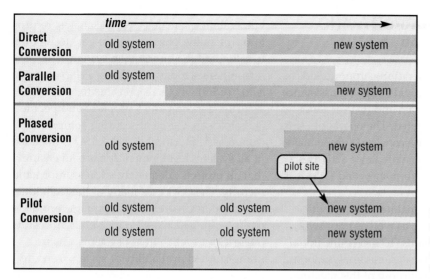

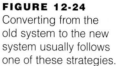

FIGURE 12-24
Converting from the old system to the new system usually follows one of these strategies.

With *direct conversion*, the user stops using the old system and begins using the new system on a certain date. The advantage of this strategy is that it requires no transition costs and is a quick implementation technique. Some systems analysts call this technique an *abrupt cutover*. The disadvantage is that it is extremely risky and can disrupt operations seriously if the new system does not work correctly the first time.

Parallel conversion consists of running the old system alongside the new system for a specified time. Results from both systems are compared. If the results are the same, the company either terminates the old system abruptly or phases it out. The advantage of this strategy is that you can fix any problems in the new system before you terminate the old system. The disadvantage is that it is costly to operate two systems at the same time.

Larger systems that have multiple sites often use a phased conversion. With a *phased conversion*, each location converts at a separate time. For example, an accounting system might convert its accounts receivable, accounts payable, general ledger, and payroll sites in separate phases. Each site can use a direct or parallel conversion.

With a *pilot conversion*, only one location in the company uses the new system — so it can be tested. After the pilot site approves the new system, other sites convert using one of the other conversion strategies. Read Ethics & Issues 12-4 for a related discussion.

At the beginning of the conversion, existing data must be made ready for the new system. Converting existing manual and computer files so the new system can use them is known as *data conversion*.

Implementation at Web Stop Café

Upon receiving the program specification package, Karl forms an implementation team of Suzy Zhao, Webmaster; Adam Rosen, programmer; and Stefan Davis, data modeler. The team works together to implement the Vendor Web System.

Karl works closely with the team to answer questions about the design and to check the progress of their work. When the team completes its work, they ask Karl to test it. He does and it works great!

Karl arranges a training class for the employees of the marketing and customer service departments. During the training session, he shows them how to use the new Vendor Information page on the company's Web site. Karl gives each attendee a printed user guide and indicates that he will e-mail them the electronic file. He wants to prepare everyone thoroughly for the new Web pages once they are posted. Karl also sends a letter to all existing vendors informing them when this new service will be available and how to use it.

ETHICS & ISSUES 12-4

What Type of System Conversion Is Best?

Any organization using an information system eventually will need to update the system. The first step most organizations take is to research and compare existing systems that can be purchased, or consider developing a new system. Once a suitable system is chosen or developed, the next step is implementation. Suppose that the educational institution you attend plans to convert to a new registration system. The administration is vacillating between direct conversion and parallel conversion. Direct conversion is less expensive, but risky. If the new system does not work correctly, student registration could be a disaster. In contrast, parallel conversion is safe, but costly and time-consuming. Student registration surely will be problem free, but the school's operating budget will suffer. If you were responsible for the decision, which method would you choose? Why? Should another alternative, such as phased conversion or pilot conversion, be considered? Why or why not? How would you prioritize budget, timeliness, and quality in any situation? Why?

OPERATION, SUPPORT, AND SECURITY PHASE

The purpose of the **operation, support, and security phase** is to provide ongoing assistance for an information system and its users after the system is implemented. The operation, support, and security phase consists of three major activities: (1) perform maintenance activities, (2) monitor system performance, and (3) assess system security.

Information system maintenance activities include fixing errors in, as well as improving on, a system's operations. To determine initial maintenance needs, the systems analyst should meet with users. The purpose of this meeting, called the *post-implementation system review*, is to discover whether the information system is performing according to the users' expectations.

Sometimes users identify errors in the system. Problems with design (logic) usually are the cause of these errors. For example, the total of a column might be incorrect. These types of errors return the analyst to the planning phase to perform *corrective maintenance*, which is the process of diagnosing and correcting errors in an information system.

Sometimes, users have enhancements or additional requirements that involve modifying or expanding an existing information system. *Adaptive maintenance* is the process of including new features or capabilities in an information system. To perform adaptive maintenance, the analyst returns to the planning phase.

During this phase, the systems analyst monitors performance of the new or modified information system. The purpose of *performance monitoring* is to determine whether the system is inefficient at any point. If it is, the systems analyst must investigate solutions to make the information system more efficient and reliable, a process called *perfective maintenance* — back to the planning phase.

Most organizations must deal with complex computer security issues. All elements of an information system — hardware, software, data, people, and procedures — must be secure from threats both inside and outside the enterprise. For example, users should be allowed access only to the data and information for which they are authorized, which typically is limited to the amount necessary to do their job. Data should be secure so intruders cannot alter, damage, or steal data. Networks need safeguards to prevent them from being compromised. If any

vulnerabilities are detected, the analyst returns to the planning phase to investigate techniques to safeguard the information system.

Companies today often have a *chief security officer* (*CSO*) who is responsible for physical security of a company's property and people and also is in charge of securing computing resources. It is critical that the CSO is included in all system development projects to ensure that all projects adequately address information security. The CSO uses many of the techniques discussed in Chapter 11 to maintain confidentiality or limited access to information, ensure integrity and reliability of systems, ensure uninterrupted availability of systems, ensure compliance with laws, and cooperate with law enforcement agencies.

Developing a Computer Security Plan

An important responsibility of the CSO is to develop a computer security plan. A **computer security plan** summarizes in writing all of the safeguards that are in place to protect a company's information assets. A computer security plan should do the following:

1. Identify all information assets of an organization, including hardware, software, documentation, procedures, people, data, facilities, and supplies.

2. Identify all security risks that may cause an information asset loss. Rank risks from most likely to least likely to occur. Place an estimated value on each risk, including lost business. For example, what is the estimated loss if customers cannot access computers for one hour, one day, or one week?

3. For each risk, identify the safeguards that exist to detect, prevent, and recover from a loss.

The CSO should evaluate the computer security plan annually or more frequently for major changes in information assets. The CSO should recognize that some degree of risk is unavoidable; further, the more secure a system is, the more difficult it is for everyone to use. The goal of a computer security plan is to match an appropriate level of safeguards against the identified risks. Fortunately, most organizations never will experience a major information system disaster.

Companies and individuals that need help with computer security plans can contact the *International Computer Security Association* (*ICSA*) *Labs* via the telephone or on the Web for assistance.

WEB LINK 12-9

Chief Security Officer

For more information, visit scsite.com/ dc2007/ch12/weblink and then click Chief Security Officer.

WEB LINK 12-10

International Computer Security Association

For more information, visit scsite.com/ dc2007/ch12/weblink and then click ICSA.

Operation, Support, and Security at Web Stop Café

During the post-implementation system review, Karl learns that the new Web page is receiving many hits. Vendors are using it and they like it. Customer service regularly receives e-mail messages from vendors that appreciate the new service. Chad says his staff is working efficiently on their primary tasks without the interruption and additional workload of making copies and sending out vendor data, now that the system has been automated. Data in the system has been accessed only by authorized users, leading him to conclude security measures work as planned.

Six months after the Vendor Web System has been in operation, Chad would like to add more information to the Vendor Information page. He sends an e-mail message to Karl requesting the change. Karl asks him to fill out a Request for System Services and puts him on the agenda of the next steering committee meeting. Back to the planning phase again!

Test your knowledge of pages 639 through 647 in Quiz Yourself 12-3.

QUIZ YOURSELF 12-3

Instructions: Find the true statement below. Then, rewrite the remaining false statements so they are true.

1. A computer training plan summarizes in writing all of the safeguards that are in place to protect a company's information assets.

2. Acceptance tests measure the performance of hardware or software.

3. Activities performed during detailed design include developing designs for the databases, inputs, outputs, and programs.

4. The program development cycle is a part of the support phase.

5. The purpose of the design phase is to provide ongoing assistance for an information system and its users after the system is implemented.

6. With a request for quotation, the vendor selects the product(s) that meets specified requirements and then quotes the price(s).

7. With parallel conversion, the user stops using the old system and begins using the new system on a certain date.

Quiz Yourself Online: To further check your knowledge of the design phase; program development; the implementation phase; and the operation, support, and security phase, visit scsite.com/dc2007/ch12/quiz and then click Objectives 8 – 11.

CHAPTER SUMMARY

This chapter discussed the phases in the system development cycle. The guidelines for system development also were presented. Activities that occur during the entire system development cycle, including project management, feasibility assessment, data and information gathering, and documentation, also were addressed. Throughout the chapter, a case study about Web Stop Café illustrated and reinforced activities performed during each phase of the system development cycle.

Systems Analyst

One of the fastest growing IT (information technology) positions in the country is that of *systems analyst*. The primary focus of this type of work is to design systems and to incorporate new technologies.

Typically, systems analysts are more involved in design issues than in day-to-day programming. The specific duties of a systems analyst vary from company to company. Systems analysts work closely with users to identify operating procedures and clarify system objectives. They must be familiar with concepts and practices within a specific field. A successful systems analyst is willing to embrace new technologies and is open to continued learning. Good communications skills are important. Systems analysts may be expected to write program documentation and operating manuals. Growing in demand are skills for the systems analyst that include e-commerce, enterprise-wide networking, and intranet technologies. Given the technology available today, telecommuting is common for computer professionals, including the systems analyst. Many analysts work as consultants.

The minimum educational requirement is a bachelor's degree, but many people opt for a master's degree. Salaries are excellent in this fast-growing occupation in the IT field. They range from $45,000 to $85,000 and up. Graduates with a master's degree can expect to earn in excess of $100,000 per year. For more information, visit scsite.com/dc2007/ch12/careers and then click Systems Analyst.

High-Tech Talk

BENCHMARKING: TESTING PERFORMANCE THROUGH CALCULATIONS

A benchmark is a surveyor's reference mark — a point of reference from which other measurements can be made. In computer technology, a benchmark is a set of conditions used to measure the performance of hardware or software. Benchmark testing involves running a set of standard tests to compare the performance of two or more systems.

Suppose you are a network administrator and need to buy new servers to support your company's e-commerce Web site. To start, you can access published benchmark results from organizations such as SPEC and TPC. Both SPEC (Standard Performance Evaluation Corporation) and TPC (Transaction Processing Performance Counsel) are nonprofit groups that define and maintain benchmarks for the computer industry. TPC, for example, tests using its TPC Benchmark W (*TPC-W*), which measures how servers perform while supporting an e-commerce Web site. Reading published benchmark test results from these groups can help you determine how one vendor's system might perform relative to another.

To understand benchmark results fully, you should understand the design and measurements (or *metrics*) used for the test. The TPC-W benchmark, for example, uses two primary metrics: WIPS and $/WIPS. *WIPS* is the number of Web Interactions Per Second that can be sustained by the *system under test*, or *SUT* (in this case, multiple servers). The *$/WIPS* is the *system cost per WIPS*, which is the total cost of the SUT divided by WIPS.

To calculate WIPS, TPC-W uses several algorithms, or formulas (Figure 12-25). One calculation is *Web Interaction Response Time* (*WIRT*), which is the time it takes to complete a Web interaction. A Web interaction might start when a user clicks a link to request a Web page and ends when the browser receives all of the data from the requested page. WIRT is calculated using the algorithm shown in Figure 12-25. Using this algorithm, if a Web interaction starts at 1:00:00 and the last byte of data is sent at 1:00:07, the WIRT is 7 seconds.

WIRT is used to calculate the number of Web interactions successfully completed during the length of the benchmark test, or *measurement interval*. During the measurement interval, the browser repeatedly cycles through requesting and then receiving a requested page, measuring the time to receive it (WIRT), and then requesting the next page. To be considered a successful Web interaction, each type of Web interaction must have a WIRT less than the TPC-specified constraint. For example, a home page Web interaction must have a WIRT of less than 3 seconds or it is not used when calculating WIPS.

The total number of successful Web interactions completed in a measurement interval is used to calculate WIPS. WIPS is calculated using the algorithm shown in Figure 12-25. Using this algorithm, if 14,009,400 Web interactions are completed successfully during a 30-minute test period, the WIPS rating for the system is 14,009,400/1,800 or 7,783 WIPs. The higher the WIPs rating, the more requests the Web server can handle per second.

The $/WIPS rating is determined by dividing the price of the SUT by the WIPS value (Figure 12-25). Using this algorithm, if a system rated as 7,783 WIPS costs $190,036, the $/WIPS rating is $190,036/7,783 or 24.42.

The TPC-W benchmark also measures the total number of connections a Web server can handle. Using the algorithm shown in Figure 12-25, if a Web site supports 35,000 browsers using 10 Web servers, each Web server is supporting 2 * (35,000/10), or 7,000 connections.

Data points such as WIPS, $/WIPS, and number of connections are the result of a benchmarking process. These data points provide the detailed information required to make informed purchasing decisions. For example, the WIPS and $/WIPS ratings in a benchmark report can help you better understand how the servers will perform in the real-world environment of your e-commerce Web site.

The TPC-W benchmark is just one of numerous industry benchmarks used to test different aspects of systems' performance. For more information, visit scsite.com/dc2007/ch12/tech and then click Benchmarking.

Web Interaction Response Time (WIRT)

Defined by the algorithm, **WIRT = T2 - T1**, where
    T1 = time when the first byte of request is sent to the Web server; and
    T2 = time after the last byte of a requested page is received by the browser

Web Interaction Per Second (WIPS)

Defined by the algorithm, **WI/(MI)**, where:
    WI = total number of Web interactions completed successfully; and
    MI = length of the measurement interval in seconds

System Cost Per WIPS ($/WIPS)

Defined by the algorithm, **System Cost/WIPS**, where:
    System Cost = entire price of the SUT, including all new hardware, software, and 3-year maintenance charges; and
    WIPS = Web interactions successfully completed

Total Number of Connections Supported by a Web Server

Defined by the algorithm, **2 * (Number of Browsers/Web Servers)**, where:
    2 represents the 2 connections per user (one nonsecure, one secure)
    Number of Browsers is the number of users browsing the Web site; and
    Web Servers is the number of Web servers supporting the Web site

FIGURE 12-25 Some benchmark algorithms.

Companies on the Cutting Edge

COMPUTER ASSOCIATES
MANAGEMENT SOFTWARE DEVELOPER

Competing in today's demanding and intricate global economy requires a variety of software to help adapt to the ever-changing needs and challenges. *Computer Associates International, Inc.* (CA) provides products to help meet these evolving business challenges.

CA's software and services range from preventing security threats to storing data intelligently. These platform-independent products help protect and optimize the operations of 95 percent of Fortune 500 companies in more than 100 countries. Charles B. Wang founded CA in 1976 with three associates, no venture capital, and one product: a sort/merge utility called CA-SORT. The company has grown to become the world's largest management software corporation. In 2005, America Online adopted CA's technology to protect subscribers from spyware and other malicious threats. For more information, visit scsite.com/dc2007/ch12/companies and then click Computer Associates.

ZEBRA TECHNOLOGIES
SPECIALTY PRINTING SOLUTIONS

The ways manufacturers move materials and retailers track inventory have changed as a result of products *Zebra Technologies* has developed.

More than 90 percent of the Fortune 500 and Global 2000 companies in such industries as automotive, health care, retail, and transportation use three million of Zebra's products. The company has sold more than four million printers, including RFID printer/encoders and wireless products. Its work in developing radio frequency identification (RFID) smart labels is helping companies save billions of dollars by expediting the flow of goods manufactured and shipped.

Wal-Mart, Best Buy, and the United States Department of Defense were among the first to require every box being shipped to have an RFID-encoded label so the correct equipment and supplies would be on hand whenever needed. For more information, visit scsite.com/dc2007/ch12/companies and then click Zebra Technologies.

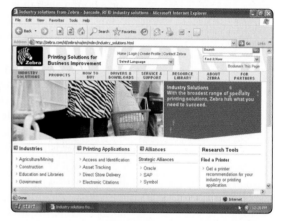

Technology Trailblazers

ED YOURDON
PROJECT MANAGEMENT CONSULTANT

Anyone contemplating working in the computer field or deciding how to advance within the business world would benefit from reading *Ed Yourdon*'s works. His latest book, *Outsource: Competing in the Global Productivity Race*, is an insider's look at the shifting of jobs from American to overseas workers.

Yourdon is considered one of the ten most influential men and women in the software field, according to *Crosstalk: The Journal of Defense Software Engineering*, and was inducted into the Computer Hall of Fame.

Yourdon began his computer career as a programmer and then founded his own consulting firm to provide advice in modern software engineering technology and project management techniques. Today, he continues his work as consultant, author, and lecturer. He was written more than 26 computer books and 550 technical articles. For more information, visit scsite.com/dc2007/ch12/people and then click Ed Yourdon.

TOM DEMARCO
SOFTWARE DEVELOPMENT EXPERT

Tom DeMarco wants to know why we all are so busy. When people and corporations focus heavily on efficiency and productivity, they cannot respond to change and embrace innovation, he claims. In his book, *Slack: Getting Past Burnout, Busywork, and the Myth of Total Efficiency*, DeMarco emphasizes the importance of giving people time to think.

He urges software developers to identify and take risks. In another of his books, *Waltzing with Bears: Managing Risk on Software Projects*, he presents the benefits of risk management and proclaims that risk brings reward, especially in the software field.

DeMarco is a principal of The Atlantic Systems Guild, Inc., which is a software think tank exploring issues facing the computer industry. For more information, visit scsite.com/dc2007/ch12/people and then click Tom DeMarco.

Chapter Review

The Chapter Review section summarizes the concepts presented in this chapter. To listen to the audio version of this Chapter Review, visit scsite.com/dc2007/ch12/review. To obtain help from other students regarding any subject in this chapter, visit scsite.com/dc2007/ch12/forum and post your thoughts or questions.

(1) What Are the System Development Cycle Phases? An **information system** (**IS**) is hardware, software, data, people, and procedures that work together to produce quality information. The **system development cycle** is a set of activities used to build an information system. Most system development cycles contain five **phases**: planning; analysis; design; implementation; and operation, support, and security.

(2) What Are Guidelines for System Development? System development should follow three general guidelines: (1) arrange activities into phases; (2) involve the **users**, which includes anyone for whom a system is being built; and (3) develop **standards**, which are sets of rules and procedures a company expects employees to accept and follow. A **systems analyst** is responsible for designing and developing an information system.

(3) Why Are Project Management, Feasibility Assessment, Documentation, and Data and Information Gathering Techniques Important? **Project management** is the process of planning, scheduling, and then controlling the activities during the system development cycle. To manage a project, the **project leader** identifies the *scope* of the project, required activities, time estimates, cost estimates, the order of activities, and activities that can take place simultaneously. The project leader records this information in a *project plan*. **Feasibility** is a measure of how suitable the development of a system will be to the company. A systems analyst typically uses four tests to evaluate feasibility of a project: *operational feasibility*, *schedule feasibility*, *technical feasibility*, and *economic feasibility*. **Documentation** is the collection and summarization of data and information. A *project notebook* contains all documentation for a single project. To gather data and information, systems analysts and other IT professionals review documentation, observe, send questionnaires, interview, participate in *joint-application design* (*JAD*) sessions, and do research.

(4) What Activities Are Performed in the Planning Phase? The **planning phase** for a project begins when the decision-making body for the company, called the **steering committee**, receives a *project request*. During the planning phase, four major activities are performed: (1) review and approve the project requests, (2) prioritize the project requests, (3) allocate resources to approved projects, and (4) form a project development team for each approved project.

> connect
> Visit scsite.com/dc2007/ch12/qui or click the Quiz Yourself button. Click Objectives 1 – 4.

(5) What Is the Purpose of Activities Performed in the Analysis Phase? The **analysis phase** consists of two major activities: (1) conduct a **preliminary investigation** to determine the exact nature of the problem or improvement and decide whether it is worth pursuing, and (2) perform detailed analysis. *Detailed analysis* involves three major activities: (1) study how the current system works; (2) determine the users' wants, needs, and requirements; and (3) recommend a solution. Most systems analysts use either a process modeling or object modeling approach to analysis and design.

(6) What Are Tools Used in Process Modeling? **Process modeling** is an analysis and design technique that describes processes that transform inputs into outputs. Tools used for process modeling include entity-relationship diagrams, data flow diagrams, and the project dictionary. An **entity-relationship diagram** (*ERD*) graphically shows the connections among entities in a system. An *entity* is an object in the system that has data. A **data flow diagram** (*DFD*) graphically shows the flow of data in a system. Key elements of a DFD are a *data flow*, which shows the input or output of data or information; a *process*, which transforms an input data flow into an output data flow;

Chapter Review

a *data store*, which is a holding place for data and information; and a *source*, which identifies an entity outside the scope of the system. The **project dictionary** contains all the documentation and deliverables of a project. Techniques used to enter items in the project dictionary include *structured English*, a **decision table** and/or a *decision tree*, and a **data dictionary**.

(7) What Are Tools Used in Object Modeling?   **Object modeling** combines the data with processes that act on the data into a single unit, called an **object**. Object modeling can use the same tools as those used in process modeling, but the **UML** (*Unified Modeling Language*) has been adopted as a standard notation for object modeling and development. Two common tools in the UML are the use case diagram and the class diagram. A **use case diagram** graphically shows how actors interact with the information system. An *actor* is a user or other entity, and the *use case* is the function that the actor can perform. A **class diagram** graphically shows classes and one or more lower levels, called *subclasses*, in a system. Lower levels (subclasses) contain attributes of higher levels (classes) in a concept called *inheritance*.

connect Visit scsite.com/dc2007/ch12/quiz or click the Quiz Yourself button. Click Objectives 5 – 7.

(8) What Activities Are Performed in the Design Phase?   The **design phase** consists of two major activities: (1) if necessary, acquire hardware and software and (2) develop all of the details of the new or modified information system. Acquiring necessary hardware and software involves identifying technical specifications, soliciting vendor proposals, testing and evaluating vendor proposals, and making a decision. Detailed design includes developing designs for the databases, inputs, outputs, and programs. During detailed design, many systems analysts use a **prototype**, which is a working model of the proposed system. *Computer-aided software engineering (CASE)* products are software tools designed to support one or more activities of the system development cycle. A popular technique used to review detailed design is an *inspection*, which is a formal review of any *deliverable*.

(9) Why Is Program Development Part of the System Development Cycle?   During the design phase, a company can purchase **packaged software**, which is mass-produced, copyrighted, prewritten software. If suitable packaged software is not available, however, a company may opt for **custom software**, which is application software developed at the user's request to match the user's requirements exactly. Programmers write custom software from the program specification package created during the analysis phase, following an organized set of activities known as the *program development cycle*.

(10) What Activities Are Performed in the Implementation Phase?   The purpose of the **implementation phase** is to construct, or build, the new or modified system and then deliver it to the users. System developers perform four major activities in this phase: (1) develop programs, (2) install and test the new system, (3) train users, and (4) convert to the new system.

(11) What Activities Are Performed In the Operations, Support, and Security Phase?

The purpose of the **operation, support, and security phase** is to provide ongoing assistance for an information system and its users after the system is implemented. The support phase consists of three major activities: (1) perform maintenance activities, (2) monitor system performance, and (3) assess system security. Companies today often have a *chief security officer (CSO)* who is responsible for physical security of a company's property and people and also is in charge of securing computing resources. The CSO develops a **computer security plan**, which summarizes in writing all current safeguards that protect the company's information assets.

connect Visit scsite.com/dc2007/ch12/quiz or click the Quiz Yourself button. Click Objectives 8 – 12.

Key Terms

You should know the Primary Terms and be familiar with the Secondary Terms. Use the list below to help focus your study. To further enhance your understanding of the Key Terms in this chapter, visit scsite.com/dc2007/ch12/terms. See an example of and a definition for each term, and access current and additional information about the term from the Web.

Primary Terms

(shown in bold-black characters in the chapter)

analysis phase (630)
class diagram (636)
computer security plan (646)
custom software (637)
data dictionary (635)
data flow diagram (632)
decision table (634)
design phase (639)
documentation (625)
entity-relationship diagram (632)
e-zine (639)
feasibility (625)
implementation phase (643)
information system (IS) (620)
object (635)
object modeling (635)
operation, support, and security phase (646)
packaged software (637)
phases (620)

planning phase (629)
preliminary investigation (630)
process modeling (632)
project dictionary (633)
project leader (623)
project management (623)
project management software (624)
project team (623)
prototype (642)
standards (622)
steering committee (623)
system (620)
system development cycle (620)
systems analyst (622)
training (644)
UML (635)
use case diagram (636)
users (621)

Secondary Terms

(shown in italic characters in the chapter)

abrupt cutover (645)
acceptance test (644)
actor (636)
adaptive maintenance (646)
attribute (635)
benchmark test (640)
change management (624)
chief security officer (CSO) (646)
computer-aided software engineering (CASE) (642)
context diagram (633)
corrective maintenance (646)
cost/benefit feasibility (625)
data conversion (645)
data flow (632)
data model (641)
data store (632)
decision tree (634)
deliverable (624)
detailed analysis (631)
DFD (632)
direct conversion (645)
economic feasibility (625)
electronic magazine (639)
entity (632)
ERD (632)
feasibility study (630)
Gantt chart (623)
horizontal market software (637)
I-CASE (643)
inheritance (636)
inspection (643)
integration test (644)
International Computer Security Association (ICSA) Labs (646)
Internet solutions provider (637)
IT consultant (640)
joint-application design (JAD) (626)
layout chart (641)
logical design (631)
method (635)
mockup (641)
object-oriented (OO) analysis and design (635)
operation (635)

operational feasibility (625)
outsource (637)
parallel conversion (645)
perfective maintenance (646)
performance monitoring (646)
phased conversion (645)
physical design (641)
pilot conversion (645)
post-implementation system review (646)
process (632)
program development cycle (643)
program specification package (642)
project notebook (625)
project plan (623)
project request (627)
property (635)
Rational Unified Process (RUP) (635)
repository (633)
request for information (RFI) (639)
request for proposal (RFP) (639)
request for quotation (RFQ) (639)
request for system services (627)
schedule feasibility (625)
scope (623)
scope creep (624)
source (632)
structured analysis and design (632)
structured English (633)
subclasses (636)
system developer (623)
system proposal (636)
systems test (644)
technical feasibility (625)
trade publication (637)
turnkey solution (639)
Unified Modeling Language (635)
unit test (644)
use case (636)
value-added reseller (VAR) (639)
vertical market software (637)

Checkpoint

Use the Checkpoint exercises to check your knowledge level of the chapter. The Beyond the Book exercises will help broaden your understanding of the concepts presented in this chapter. To complete the Checkpoint exercises interactively, visit scsite.com/dc2007/ch12/check.

Label the Figure

Identify the elements in this data flow diagram.

a. source
b. data store
c. data flows
d. process

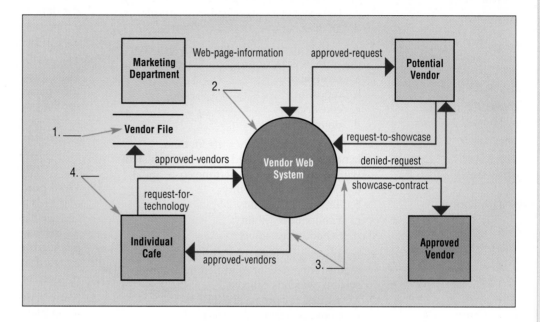

True/False

Mark T for True and F for False. (See page numbers in parentheses.)

_____ 1. An information system supports daily, short-term, and long-range activities of users. (620)

_____ 2. A systems analyst is responsible only for maintaining and troubleshooting an existing information system. (623)

_____ 3. Operational feasibility measures whether a company has the hardware, software, and people needed to support a proposed information system. (625)

_____ 4. The planning phase for a project begins when the steering committee receives a project request. (629)

_____ 5. In detailed analysis, the systems analysts develop the proposed solution with a specific hardware or software in mind. (631)

_____ 6. Structured English is a style of writing that describes the steps in a process. (633)

_____ 7. An attribute is an item that can contain both data and the procedures that read or manipulate the data. (635)

_____ 8. Horizontal market software tends to be less widely available and more expensive than vertical market software. (637)

_____ 9. A prototype is a graphical representation of the proposed system. (642)

_____ 10. With a pilot conversion, multiple locations in the company use the new system. (645)

_____ 11. Perfective maintenance involves the investigation of solutions to make an information system more efficient and reliable. (646)

Checkpoint

Multiple Choice   Select the best answer. (See page numbers in parentheses.)

1. The steering committee _____. (623)
   a. works on a project from beginning to end
   b. is a decision-making body in a company
   c. tests and evaluates vendor proposals
   d. all of the above

2. A _____ is any tangible item such as a chart, diagram, report, or program file. (624)
   a. receivable
   b. repository
   c. conservatory
   d. deliverable

3. _____ measures whether the lifetime benefits of the proposed information system will be greater than its lifetime costs. (625)
   a. Operational feasibility
   b. Technical feasibility
   c. Economic feasibility
   d. Schedule feasibility

4. In larger companies, users write a formal request for a new or modified information system, which is called a _____. (627)
   a. request for proposal (RFP)
   b. joint-application design (JAD)
   c. project request
   d. data-flow design (DFD)

5. During the planning phase, the projects that receive the highest priority are those _____. (629)
   a. mandated by management or some other governing body
   b. suggested by the greatest number of users
   c. thought to be of highest value to the company
   d. proposed by the information technology (IT) department

6. _____ is an analysis and design technique that describes processes that transform inputs into outputs. (632)
   a. Logical design
   b. Detailed analysis
   c. Process modeling
   d. Systems testing

7. The top-level DFD, known as a _____, identifies only the major process. (633)
   a. project dictionary
   b. data flow
   c. context diagram
   d. data store

8. In object modeling, the procedure in an object, called a(n) _____ or method, contains activities that read or manipulate the data. (635)
   a. property
   b. entity
   c. attribute
   d. operation

9. The purpose of the _____ is to assess the feasibility of each alternative solution and then recommend the most feasible solution for the project. (636)
   a. project plan
   b. system review
   c. project request
   d. system proposal

10. Word processing, spreadsheet, database, and Web page authoring are examples of _____ software. (637)
    a. vertical market, custom
    b. horizontal market, custom
    c. vertical market, packaged
    d. horizontal market, packaged

11. Some VARs (value-added resellers) provide a complete system, also known as a(n) _____. (639)
    a. abrupt cutover
    b. scope creep
    c. project plan
    d. turnkey solution

12. A(n) _____ test is performed by end-users and checks the new system to ensure that it works with actual data. (644)
    a. unit
    b. systems
    c. acceptance
    d. integration

13. With a parallel conversion _____. (645)
    a. the old system runs alongside the new system for a specified time
    b. only one location in the company uses the new system — so it can be tested
    c. users stop using the old system and begin using the new system on a certain date
    d. each location in the company converts at a separate time

14. _____ is the process of diagnosing and correcting errors in an information system. (646)
    a. Corrective maintenance
    b. Adaptive maintenance
    c. Performance monitoring
    d. Perfective maintenance

Checkpoint

Matching

Match the terms with their definitions. (See page numbers in parentheses.)

_____ 1. project team (623)

_____ 2. Gantt chart (623)

_____ 3. request for system services (627)

_____ 4. data dictionary (635)

_____ 5. object (635)

_____ 6. use case diagram (636)

_____ 7. value-added reseller (VAR) (639)

_____ 8. benchmark test (640)

_____ 9. mockup (641)

_____ 10. program specification package (642)

a. measures the performance of hardware or software

b. stores a name, description, and other details about each data item

c. bar chart that shows project phases or activities

d. becomes the first item in the project notebook and triggers the planning phase

e. users and IT professionals who work on a project from beginning to end

f. purchases products and then resells them along with additional services

g. an item that can contain both data and the procedures that read or manipulate that data

h. graphically shows how actors interact with the information system

i. identifies the required programs and the relationship among each program, as well as the input, output, and database specifications

j. shows how actors interact with an information system

k. sample of input or output that contains actual data

Short Answer

Write a brief answer to each of the following questions.

1. What is the difference between an entity-relationship diagram and a data flow diagram? _____ What are some examples of data stores? _____

2. What is feasibility? _____ How are operational feasibility, schedule feasibility, technical feasibility, and economic feasibility different? _____

3. What are the benefits of a project dictionary? _____ What information is contained in a project dictionary? _____

4. How is horizontal market software different from vertical market software? _____ What is an advantage and disadvantage of custom software? _____

5. How is a request for quotation (RFQ) different from a request for proposal (RFP)? _____ What is a request for information (RFI)? _____

Beyond the Book

Read the following book elements, learn more about each using the Web, and then write a brief report.

1. Ethics & Issues — Do You Work Harder When Someone Is Watching? (626), How Should Employers Combat Poor E-Mail Writing Skills? (627), Does Keeping Up with Technology Provide a Strategic Advantage? (637), or What Type of System Conversion Is Best? (645)

2. Career Corner — Systems Analyst (647)

3. Companies on the Cutting Edge — Computer Associates or Zebra Technologies (649)

4. FAQs (623, 624, 625, 626, 631, 638, 640, 643, 644)

5. High-Tech Talk — Benchmarking: Testing Performance through Calculations (648)

6. Looking Ahead — Computer Systems Design and the Future (623) or Putting Vista to the Test (644)

7. Making Use of the Web — Health (128)

8. Picture Yourself Talking with a System Development Team (618)

9. Technology Trailblazers — Ed Yourdon and Tom DeMarco (649)

10. Web Links (624, 632, 635, 637, 638, 639, 640, 642, 646)

Learn It Online

Use the Learn It Online exercises to reinforce your understanding of the chapter concepts. To access the Learn It Online exercises, visit scsite.com/dc2007/ch12/learn.

(1) At the Movies — LeapFrog

To view the LeapFrog movie, click the number 1 button. Locate your video and click the corresponding High-Speed or Dial-Up link, depending on your Internet connection. Watch the movie and then complete the exercise by answering the questions that follow. Ziff Davis Media's LeapFrog products have changed the way children across the U.S. learn their reading, writing, and arithmetic skills. The LeapPad, part toy and part teacher, uses books embedded with NearTouch technology which makes any part of a page touch-interactive. By taking the special pen and touching it to words on the book, the voice program will tell you the word. This interactive toy encourages learning and makes it fun. What do you think the pros and cons of using this technology to teach reading and math skills might be? How would using a LeapPad have changed your early education experience, if at all?

(2) At the Movies — Ed Yourdon on IT

To view the Ed Yourdon on IT movie, click the number 2 button. Locate your video and click the corresponding High-Speed or Dial-Up link, depending on your Internet connection. Watch the movie and then complete the exercise by answering the questions that follow. In his book *Time Bomb*, Ed Yourdon talked about both the worst- and best-case scenarios of Y2K, but people focused on the worst-case scenarios. Looking back, most of the Y2K incidents were minor. What do you feel helped make the Y2K transition less disruptive to daily life? Do you feel that most people worried too much about Y2K? In his book *Byte Wars*,

author Yourdon discusses how software security has changed since the 9/11 tragedy. How are software and IT security related to tragedies such as 9/11? Overall, how do you feel about the security changes? Do you think they are adequate?

(3) Student Edition Labs — Project Management

Click the number 3 button. A new browser window will open, displaying the Student Edition Labs. Follow the on-screen instructions to complete the Project Management Lab. When finished, click the Exit button. If required, submit your results to your instructor.

(4) Student Edition Labs — Web Design Principles

Click the number 4 button. A new browser window will open, displaying the Student Edition Labs. Follow the on-screen instructions to complete the Web Design Principles Lab. When finished, click the Exit button. If required, submit your results to your instructor.

(5) Practice Test

Click the number 5 button. Answer each question. When completed, enter your name and click the Grade Test button to submit the quiz for grading. Make a note of any missed questions. If required, submit your results to your instructor.

(6) Who Wants To Be a Computer Genius²?

Click the number 6 button to find out if you are a computer genius. Directions about how to play the game will be displayed. When you are ready to play, click the Play button. Submit your score to your instructor.

Learn It Online

(7) Wheel of Terms

Click the number 7 button to reinforce important terms you learned in this chapter by playing the Shelly Cashman Series version of this popular game. Directions about how to play the game will be displayed. When you are ready to play, click the Play button. Submit your score to your instructor.

(8) DC Track and Field

Click the number 8 button to use what you have learned in this chapter to compete against other students in three track and field events. Directions about how to play the game will be displayed. When you are ready to play, click the start first event button. If required, submit your score to your instructor.

(9) You're Hired!

Click the number 9 button to use what you have learned in this chapter to embark on the path to a career in computers. Directions about how to play the game will be displayed. When you are ready to play, click the begin game button. If required, submit your score to your instructor.

(10) Crossword Puzzle Challenge

Click the number 10 button. Complete the puzzle to reinforce skills you learned in this chapter. Directions about how to play the game will be displayed. When you are ready to play, click the Submit button. Submit the completed puzzle to your instructor.

(11) Lab Exercises

Click the number 11 button. When the Lab Exercises menu appears, click the exercise assigned by your instructor. A new browser window will open. Follow the on-screen instructions to complete the exercise. When finished, click the Exit button. If required, submit your results to your instructor.

(12) In the News

In the same fashion that teams from around the world gather for the World Cup Soccer Championship, more than 200 teams of researchers met at a Korean convention center for another event — the annual Robot Football World Cup. Click the number 12 button and read a news article about an innovative development or use of a computer information system. Who developed or used the system? In what way is the development or use of the system original?

(13) Chapter Discussion Forum

Select an objective from this chapter on page 619 about which you would like more information. Click the number 13 button and post a short message listing a meaningful message title accompanied by one or more questions concerning the selected objective. In two days, return to the threaded discussion by clicking the number 13 button. Submit to your instructor your original message and at least one response to your message.

(14) eMedicine

Click the number 14 button to learn how to use the Internet to obtain medical information. Follow the instructions to use eMedicine.com to research an illness or disease. What are the initial symptoms of the illness or disease you selected? What kinds of treatments are available? What preventative measures are available for the selected illness or disease? Write a report summarizing your findings. Print the report and then submit it to your instructor.

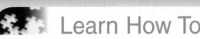
Learn How To

Use the Learn How To activities to learn fundamental skills when using a computer and accompanying technology. Complete the exercises and submit them to your instructor. Visit scsite.com/dc2007/ch12/howto to obtain more information pertaining to each activity.

LEARN HOW TO 1: Conduct an Effective Interview

As you learned in this chapter, gathering information is a critical element in the system development cycle, because without accurate facts, it is unlikely that the finished system will perform in the desired manner. An important means of gathering information is the personal interview. Interviews are used in several stages throughout the system development cycle, and they must be thorough and comprehensive.

Prior to conducting an interview, you must determine that an interview is the best means for obtaining the information you seek. You have learned a variety of ways to obtain information, and you should use each of them appropriately. Because an interview interrupts a person's work and takes time, you must be sure the information gained in the interview justifies this interruption. Once you have determined you should conduct an interview to gather information required for system development, a variety of factors become relevant.

Goal: The most important element of a successful interview is for you to determine exactly what knowledge you hope to gain as a result of the interview. If you do not have a goal, you are unlikely to emerge from the interview with much useful information.

Do Your Homework: You should complete a variety of preparatory steps that will help ensure a successful interview. These steps include the following:

1. Gather as much information as you can from the fact-gathering processes that do not require an interview. Because an interview takes a person's time and interrupts work, you must be sure the information you are seeking is not available from other sources. Additionally, if you ask someone questions to obtain information they know is available elsewhere, you will lose credibility with them during the interview process.
2. Be sure you plan to interview the best person to obtain the information you need. To do this, you must research every person you plan to interview and understand their job, their position within the department in which they work, the knowledge they should possess relative to the information you need, the culture of their work environment, how the system being developed relates to them, and an estimate of the cooperation you can expect from them. If someone is the most knowledgeable person regarding a certain subject but is unwilling to share information other than with trusted coworkers, you likely will be better served by talking to someone else.
3. Prepare the questions you want to ask prior to setting up the interview. In this way, you can have a good estimate of the time required for the interview. While other questions will occur to you as the interview proceeds, you should have a good idea of the questions you need answered to reach your goal.
4. Prior to setting an appointment for an interview, be sure the management personnel of the people you will interview have approved. Because you will be disrupting employees' work days, you must obtain management approval before even asking for an appointment.

Make an Appointment: An appointment almost always is required. By making an appointment, you ensure the person to be interviewed will be available. Normally you should request an appointment in writing, often through the use of e-mail. In this written request, you should set a time and place for the interview, inform the interviewee what you need to know, and establish an agenda with an estimated time. You must recognize that most people do not like to be interviewed, so often you will not be seen as friendly. In addition, it might be possible that the system being developed could eliminate or change the person's job, and clearly this can establish an

Learn How To

adversarial relationship. Your task when making an appointment, then, is to establish credibility with the interviewee and set the stage for a successful interview.

Conducting the Interview: When conducting an interview, remember that you are the "intruder." Therefore, you should be polite, prompt, and attentive in the interview. Always understand the perspective of the person being interviewed and understand his or her fears, doubts, and potential hostilities. Sometimes, the interviewee might feel he or she is in conflict with you, so by listening closely and being aware of the body language, you should be able to discern the amount of truth and the amount of hedging that is occurring. Some of the details of the interview of which you should be aware are as follows:

1. If possible, the interview should be conducted in a quiet environment with a minimum of interruptions.
2. The demeanor should be open and friendly, but as noted you should not expect to be welcomed with open arms.
3. Your questions should directly address the goals of the interview. Do not expect the person being interviewed to provide a tutorial. Your questions must generate answers that supply your information.
4. Your questions should be thought-provoking. Do not ask questions requiring a yes or no answer. Your questions should not lead the interviewee to an answer — rather, the questions should be open-ended and allow the person to develop the answer. As an interviewer, you never should argue with the person being interviewed, you should not suggest answers or give opinions, you should ask straight-forward questions rather than compound questions, you never should assign blame for any circumstance that might come up in the interview, and you must never interrupt while the person is talking. Finally, you, as the interviewer, should not talk much. Remember, you are conducting the interview to gain information and it is the person you are interviewing who has that information. Let him or her talk.
5. Listen carefully, with both your ears and your eyes. What you hear normally is most important, but body language and other movements often convey information as well. Concentrate on the interviewee — expect that you will make much more eye contact with the person than he or she will with you. Allow silences to linger — the normal impulse in a conversation is to fill the silence quickly; in an interview, however, if you are quiet, the person being interviewed might think of additional information.
6. As you listen, concentrate on the interviewee — when points are being made, do not take notes because that will distract from what the person is saying — stay focused. When the information has been conveyed, then jot down something so you will remember.
7. Throughout the interview, offer reinforcing comments, such as, "The way I understand what you just said is ..." Make sure when you leave the interview there are no misunderstandings between you and the person you interviewed.
8. Before you conclude the interview, be sure all your goals have been met. You likely will not have another opportunity to interview the person, so ensure you have nothing further to learn from the person.

Follow-Up: After the interview, it is recommended you send a follow-up letter or e-mail to the person you interviewed to review the information you learned. This document should invite the interviewee to correct any errors you made in summing up your findings. In addition, for all the people you interview, keep a log of the time and place of the interview. In this way, if any questions arise regarding the interview, you will have a log.

Exercise

1. Using the techniques in this activity, conduct interviews with three students on your campus. Your interview goal is to find out about both the most successful class and the least successful class the student has completed. Why was the class successful or unsuccessful? Discuss the instructor, textbook, subject matter, and other relevant items. After the interviews, write a one-page paper summarizing your findings and identify common elements found in successful classes and in unsuccessful classes. Submit this paper to your instructor.

660 **CHAPTER 12**

Discovering Computers
A Gateway to Information 2007

Select a chapter:
1 2 3 4 5 6 7 8 9 10 11 12 13 14 15

12 **Information System Development**

Web Research

Use the Internet-based Web Research exercises to broaden your understanding of the concepts presented in this chapter. Visit scsite.com/dc2007/ch12/research to obtain more information pertaining to each exercise. To discuss any of the Web Research exercises in this chapter with other students, post your thoughts or questions at scsite.com/dc2007/ch12/forum.

① **Scavenger Hunt**   Use one of the <u>search engines</u> listed in Figure 2-10 in Chapter 2 on page 78 or your own favorite search engine to find the answers to the questions that follow. Copy and paste the Web address from the Web page where you found the answer. Some questions may have more than one answer. If required, submit your answers to your instructor. (1) What resources are available for decreasing scope creep? (2) Locate a feasibility study conducted for the U.S. Department of Energy and a second study for another governmental agency. What recommendations, evaluations, or conclusions are provided? (3) What are the nine Knowledge Areas that center on management expertise for project management certification? (4) Find one company that provides outsourcing services for information technology needs. How long has the company been in business? What IT services does it offer? What aspects of the system development cycle are discussed?

② **Search Sleuth**   A meta search engine returns the results of several major search engines in one list. <u>Turbo10</u> is one meta search engine registered in the United Kingdom with computing facilities located in Texas. Its Search-o-Meter displays the number of results located, and its Turbo10 Topics feature groups results into related topic areas. Visit this Web site and then use your word processing program to answer the following questions. Then, if required, submit your answers to your instructor. (1) Type "Unified Modeling Language" UML in the search box, click the Search button, and then click the objects link in the Topic Clusters box. How many pages of results are found? (2) Click the Engines tab. What three search engines returned the most results? (3) Delete the text in the search box and then type "Gantt chart" in the search box. Click the examples topic cluster link and then review the search results. Study two examples and then write a 50-word summary of your findings.

③ **Journaling**   Respond to your readings in this chapter by writing at least one page about your reactions, evaluations, and reflections about information system development. For example, have you been a member of a <u>steering committee</u> at work or an advisory board in your community? Have you reviewed existing documentation regarding a current computer system? If so, did you find the information well written, thorough, and understandable? If not, what components of your system need documentation? You also can write about the new terms you learned by reading this chapter. If required, submit your journal to your instructor.

④ **Expanding Your Understanding**   The average home computer user may think his or her computer is safe from <u>cybercrime</u>, but a detailed survey conducted by America Online and the National Cyber Security Alliance (NCSA) reveals most people do not know what programs are on their computers. Two-thirds of the consumers surveyed did not have current antivirus software or firewall protection. Eighty percent of the computers had dozens of spyware programs, and 20 percent had at least one virus. Visit the NCSA Web site (staysafeonline.info) to read cyber security tips that can help you protect your computer. Then visit the SANS Institute Web site to learn about critical Internet security vulnerabilities. Write a report summarizing your findings. If required, submit your report to your instructor.

⑤ **Ethics in Action**   The Food and Drug Administration has approved implanting a tiny computer chip in a patient's arm for medical purposes. Millions of the <u>VeriChip</u> microchips have been implanted in pets for identification purposes, but the move to humans has alarmed security experts. The chip releases a code when a scanner is passed over it, and this code is linked to a database that retains the patient's medical information. The database can be updated each time the patient visits a health care provider. View online sites that discuss using implanted chips in humans. How can they be used to breach the confidentiality of medical records? How are they being used in nonmedical applications? Write a report summarizing your findings, and include a table of links to Web sites that provide additional details about implantable chips. If required, submit your report to your instructor.

Case Studies

Use the Case Studies to apply the concepts presented in the chapter to real-world situations. Visit scsite.com/dc2007/ch12/cases to obtain more information pertaining to each exercise. To discuss the Case Studies in this chapter with other students, visit scsite.com/dc2007/ch12/forum and post your thoughts or questions.

CASE STUDY 1 — Class Discussion Your supervisor recently has been confronted with a number of job-related procedure problems that are unrelated to computers, such as tracking sick days. She is looking for a systematic way to solve these problems. Do you think the <u>system development cycle</u> (planning, analysis, design, implementation, and support) presented in this chapter would be a good approach for her to use, even though the problems are unrelated to computers? Why or why not? If the system development cycle can be used, which steps within each phase would you change? Write a brief report and be prepared to discuss your recommendations in class.

CASE STUDY 2 — Class Discussion A recent study suggests that the United States will cumulatively lose 3.4 million jobs to offshore outsourcing by the year 2015, far fewer than are lost due to new technology, domestic competition, and consumer tastes. B&L Consulting, Inc., the company you work for as a systems analyst, has steadfastly refused to use <u>offshore outsourcing</u>, claiming it is un-American. The company's competitors, on the other hand, have been using offshore outsourcing for some time. Of particular concern is the recent outsourcing by a competitor of the entire development of an accounting system to a firm in Pakistan. Your promotion to senior system analyst gives you a voice on the B&L Consulting, Inc. senior management team. The major agenda item for next month's meeting is the outsourcing of the company's proposed accounts receivable system to a firm in India. After reading Chapter 12, do you think systems can be developed entirely overseas? Why or why not? Write a brief report that lists the major advantages and disadvantages of developing systems offshore. Is offshore outsourcing an alternative that our capitalistic economy can do without? If so, how? Be prepared to discuss your recommendations in class.

CASE STUDY 3 — Research Data sharing is critical to the success of any new IT system, especially in large organizations with employees and customers worldwide. To counteract this problem, some companies use <u>electronic data interchange</u> to facilitate the exchange of data. Use the Web and/or print media to investigate interorganizational information systems. How are these systems used? How are these systems managed? What are their benefits? What are their drawbacks? Submit your report or use PowerPoint to create a presentation and share your findings with your class.

CASE STUDY 4 — Research For many companies, information is their most valuable asset. Yet, information also can be the most difficult asset to protect. The primary problem is with employee information theft. Gaining ground quickly, however, is <u>information theft</u> by people who break into a company's computer system via the Internet. In a test of the vulnerability of various computer systems, a Web security firm was able to make unauthorized trades at a mutual fund, access employee schedules at an airline, and change information in patient files at a health care center. In an example of low-level technology, a person opened a bank account, replaced the generic deposit slips on the counter with deposit slips with his account number on them and got away with over $150,000 before the bank discovered the problem. Use the Web and/or print media to research how information can be protected from employees, customers, and other intruders. What security measures are available today? What proposals are planned for the future? Give some examples of information theft and how the company was later able to protect itself from the theft occurring again. Write a brief report or use PowerPoint to create a presentation and share your findings with your class.

CASE STUDY 5 — Team Challenge Companies convert their old systems to new systems in a variety of ways, including direct conversion, parallel conversion, phased conversion, and <u>pilot conversion</u>. Sausalito, Inc., a large manufacturing company in the Midwest, is in the process of developing a new order entry system to replace the archaic one that has been in use for the past 15 years. The company has asked your team to recommend the best way to implement the new system. Assign each team member a conversion technique. Using the Web and/or print media, have each team member summarize the advantages and disadvantages associated with the conversion techniques assigned to him or her. As a team, recommend the best way to implement a new payroll system. Merge your findings into a team report and/or PowerPoint presentation and share your recommendations with your class.

CHAPTER THIRTEEN

Programming Languages and Program Development

Microsoft® Visual Basic 2005

Microsoft® Visual J# 2005

Microsoft® Visual C++ 200

Microsoft® Visual C# 20

Picture Yourself Learning How to Program

During today's lecture on the program development cycle, you realize that computer programming involves a lot more than just entering instructions into a computer. Your instructor for your Introduction to Programming class explains, "To develop computer programs efficiently, you must follow several steps — before and after you enter the program instructions (code)." While describing the first two steps in the program development cycle, she continues, "All programs you turn in must be accompanied by a graphical representation of your program's design. For this task, you will use flowcharting software, which is on the computers in our computer lab."

Next, she mentions that everyone must form teams of three classmates to work on all programming assignments this semester. As a team, you will become familiar with a variety of programming languages and program development tools including Visual Basic 2005, Visual C# 2005 (C# is pronounced C sharp, she says), SQL, macros, VBA, HTML, XML, JavaScript, and Flash MX. You will see how programmers develop solutions for business problems, build interactive tutorials, and develop Web pages.

To learn about the program development cycle, flowcharting software, programming languages, and program development tools, read Chapter 13 and discover the details of the steps a programmer takes to build a computer program and other types of programming languages and program development tools.

After completing this chapter, you will be able to:

1. Differentiate between machine and assembly languages

2. Identify and discuss the purpose of procedural programming languages

3. Identify and discuss the characteristics of object-oriented programming languages and program development tools

4. Identify the uses of other programming languages and other program development tools

5. Describe various ways to develop Web pages, including HTML, scripting languages, DHTML, XML, WML, and Web page authoring software

6. Identify the uses of popular multimedia authoring programs

7. List the six steps in the program development cycle

8. Differentiate between structured design and object-oriented design

9. Explain the basic control structures and design tools used in designing solutions to programming problems

CONTENTS

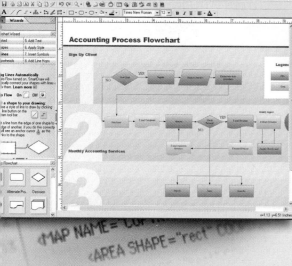

COMPUTER PROGRAMS AND PROGRAMMING LANGUAGES

Although you may never write a computer program, information you request may require a programmer to write or modify a program. Thus, you should understand how programmers develop programs to meet information requirements. A **computer program** is a series of instructions that directs a computer to perform tasks. A computer **programmer**, sometimes called a *developer*, writes and modifies computer programs.

To write a program's instructions, programmers often use a programming language. A **programming language** is a set of words, symbols, and codes that enables a programmer to communicate instructions to a computer. Just as humans speak a variety of languages (English, Spanish, French, and so on), programmers use a variety of programming languages and tools to write, or *code*, a program (Figure 13-1).

Several hundred programming languages exist today. Each language has its own rules for writing the instructions. Languages often are designed for specific purposes, such as scientific applications, business solutions, or Web page development.

Two types of languages are low-level and high-level. A *low-level language* is a programming language that is machine dependent.

FIGURE 13-1 Programmers must decide which programming languages and tools to use when they write programs.

A *machine-dependent language* runs on only one particular type of computer. These programs are not easily portable to other types of computers. Each language instruction in a low-level language usually equates to a single machine instruction. With a *high-level language*, by contrast, each language instruction typically equates to multiple machine instructions. High-level languages often are machine independent. A *machine-independent language* can run on many different types of computers and operating systems.

The following pages discuss low-level languages, as well as several types of high-level languages.

LOW-LEVEL LANGUAGES

Two types of low-level languages are machine languages and assembly languages. **Machine language**, known as the first generation of programming languages, is the only language the computer directly recognizes (Figure 13-2). Machine language instructions use a series of binary digits (1s and 0s) or a combination of numbers and letters that represents binary digits. The binary digits correspond to the on and off electrical states. As you might imagine, coding in machine language is tedious and time-consuming.

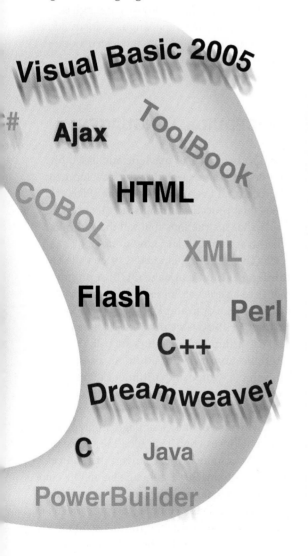

Visual Basic 2005
C#
Ajax
ToolBook
COBOL
HTML
XML
Flash
Perl
C++
Dreamweaver
C
Java
PowerBuilder

					00090
000090	50E0	30B2			010B4
000094	1B44				
000096	1B77				
000098	1B55				
00009A	F273	30D6	2C81	010D8	00C83
0000A0	4F50	30D6			010D8
0000A4	F275	30D6	2C7B	010D8	00C7D
0000AA	4F70	30D6			010D8
0000AE	5070	304A			0104C
0000B2	1C47				
0000B4	5050	304E			01050
0000B8	58E0	30B2			010B4
0000BC	07FE				
					000BE
0000BE	50E0	30B6			010B8
0000C2	95F1	2C85		00C87	
0000C6	4770	20D2		000D4	
0000CA	1B55				
0000CC	5A50	35A6			015A8
0000D0	47F0	2100		00102	
0000D4	95F2	2C85		00C87	
0000D8	4770	20E4		000E6	
0000DC	1B55				
0000DE	5A50	35AA			015AC
0000E2	47F0	2100		00102	
000102	1B77				
000104	5870	304E			01050
000108	1C47				
00010A	4E50	30D6			010D8
00010E	F075	30D6	003E	010D8	0003E
000114	4F50	30D6			010D8
000118	5050	3052			01054
00011C	58E0	30B6			010B8
000120	07FE				
					00122
000122	50E0	30BA			010BC
000126	1B55				
000128	5A50	304E			01050
00012C	5B50	3052			01054
000130	5050	305A			0105C
000134	58E0	30BA			010BC
000138	07FE				

FIGURE 13-2 A sample machine language program, coded using the hexadecimal number system. For information about hexadecimal, see Appendix A at the back of this book.

With an **assembly language**, the second generation of programming languages, a programmer writes instructions using symbolic instruction codes (Figure 13-3). *Symbolic instruction codes* are meaningful abbreviations. With an assembly language, a programmer writes abbreviations such as A for addition, C for compare, L for load, and M for multiply.

Assembly languages also use symbolic addresses. A *symbolic address* is a meaningful name that identifies a storage location. For example, a programmer can use the name RATE to refer to the storage location that contains a pay rate.

```
*             THIS MODULE CALCULATES THE REGULAR TIME PAY
CALCSTPY EQU  *
         ST   14,SAVERTPY
         SR   4,4
         SR   7,7
         SR   5,5
         PACK DOUBLE,RTHRSIN
         CVB  4,DOUBLE
         PACK DOUBLE,RATEIN
         CVB  7,DOUBLE
         ST   7,RATE
         MR   4,7
         ST   5,RTPAY
         L    14,SAVERTPY
         BR   14
*             THIS MODULE CALCULATES THE OVERTIME PAY
CALCOTPY EQU  *
         ST   14,SAVEOTPY
TEST1    CLI  CODEIN,C'O'
         BH   TEST2
         SR   5,5
         A    5,=F'0'
         ST   5,OTPAY
         B    AROUND
TEST2    SR   4,4
         SR   7,7
         SR   5,5
         PACK DOUBLE,OTHRSIN
         CVB  4,DOUBLE
         PACK DOUBLE,RATEIN
         CVB  7,RATE
         MR   4,7
         MR   4,=F'1.5'
         ST   5,OTPAY
AROUND   L    14,SAVEOTPY
         BR   14
*             THIS MODULE CALCULATES THE GROSS PAY
CALCGPAY EQU  *
         ST   14,SAVEGPAY
         SR   5,5
         A    5,RTPAY
         A    5,OTPAY
         ST   5,GRPAY
         L    14,SAVEGPAY
         BR   14
```

FIGURE 13-3 An excerpt from an assembly language payroll program. The code shows the computations for regular time pay, overtime pay, and gross pay and the decision to evaluate the overtime hours.

Despite these advantages, assembly languages can be difficult to learn. In addition, programmers must convert an assembly language program into machine language before the computer can *execute*, or run, the program. That is, the computer cannot execute the assembly source program. A **source program** is the program that contains the language instructions, or code, to be converted to machine language. To convert the assembly language source program into machine language, programmers use a program called an *assembler*.

One assembly language instruction usually equates to one machine language instruction. In some cases, however, the assembly language includes macros. An assembly language *macro* generates many machine language instructions for a single assembly language instruction. Macros save the programmer time during program development.

PROCEDURAL LANGUAGES

The disadvantages of machine and assembly (low-level) languages led to the development of procedural languages in the late 1950s and 1960s. In a **procedural language**, the programmer writes instructions that tell the computer what to accomplish and how to do it.

With a procedural language, often called a **third-generation language** (**3GL**), a programmer uses a series of English-like words to write instructions. For example, ADD stands for addition or PRINT means to print. Many 3GLs also use arithmetic operators such as * for multiplication and + for addition. These English-like words and arithmetic symbols simplify the program development process for the programmer.

As with an assembly language program, the 3GL code (instructions) is called the source program. Programmers must convert this source program into machine language before the computer can execute the program. This translation process often is very complex, because one 3GL source program instruction translates into many machine language instructions. For 3GLs, programmers typically use either a compiler or an interpreter to perform the translation.

A *compiler* is a separate program that converts the entire source program into machine language before executing it. The machine language version that results from compiling the 3GL is called the *object code* or *object program*. The compiler stores the object code on disk for execution later.

While it is compiling the source program into object code, the compiler checks the source program for errors. The compiler then produces a program listing that contains the source code and a list of any errors. This listing helps the programmer make necessary changes to the source code and correct errors in the program. Figure 13-4 shows the process of compiling a source program.

A compiler translates an entire program before executing it. An interpreter, by contrast, translates and executes one statement at a time. An *interpreter* reads a code statement, converts it to one or more machine language instructions, and then executes those machine language instructions. It does this all before moving to the next code statement in the program. Each time the source program runs, the interpreter translates and executes it, statement by statement. An interpreter does not produce an object program. Figure 13-5 shows the process of interpreting a program.

One advantage of an interpreter is that when it finds errors, it displays feedback immediately. The programmer can correct any errors before the interpreter translates the next line of code. The disadvantage is that interpreted programs do not run as fast as compiled programs. This is because an interpreter must translate the source program to machine language each time the program executes. Once a program is compiled, by contrast, users simply execute the object code to run the program.

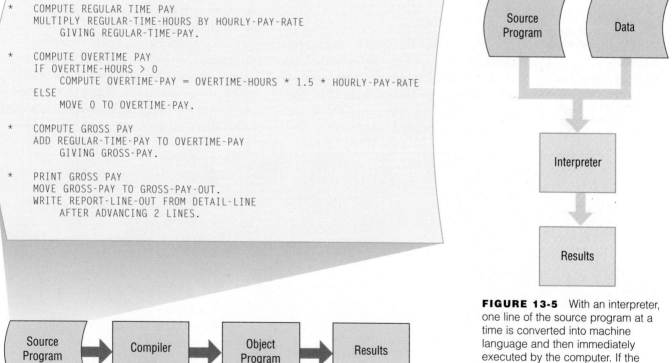

```
*    COMPUTE REGULAR TIME PAY
     MULTIPLY REGULAR-TIME-HOURS BY HOURLY-PAY-RATE
         GIVING REGULAR-TIME-PAY.

*    COMPUTE OVERTIME PAY
     IF OVERTIME-HOURS > 0
         COMPUTE OVERTIME-PAY = OVERTIME-HOURS * 1.5 * HOURLY-PAY-RATE
     ELSE
         MOVE 0 TO OVERTIME-PAY.

*    COMPUTE GROSS PAY
     ADD REGULAR-TIME-PAY TO OVERTIME-PAY
         GIVING GROSS-PAY.

*    PRINT GROSS PAY
     MOVE GROSS-PAY TO GROSS-PAY-OUT.
     WRITE REPORT-LINE-OUT FROM DETAIL-LINE
         AFTER ADVANCING 2 LINES.
```

FIGURE 13-5 With an interpreter, one line of the source program at a time is converted into machine language and then immediately executed by the computer. If the interpreter encounters an error while converting a line of code, an error message immediately is displayed on the screen and the program stops.

FIGURE 13-4 A compiler converts the entire source program into a machine language object program. If the compiler encounters any errors, it records them in the program-listing file, which the programmer may print when the entire compilation is complete. When a user wants to run the program, the object program is loaded into the memory of the computer and the program instructions begin executing.

Many programming languages include both an interpreter and a compiler. In this case, the programmer can use the interpreter during program development. When the program is complete and error free, the programmer can compile the program so it runs faster when it is placed into production for users to execute.

Hundreds of procedural languages exist. Only a few, however, are used widely enough for the industry to recognize them as standards. These include COBOL and C. To illustrate the similarities and differences among these programming languages, the following figures show program code in these languages. The code solves a simple payroll problem — computing the gross pay for an employee.

The process used to compute gross pay can vary from one system to another. The examples on the following pages use a simple *algorithm*, or set of steps, to help you easily compare one programming language with another.

COBOL

COBOL (*COmmon Business-Oriented Language*) evolved out of a joint effort between the United States government, businesses, and major universities in the early 1960s (Figure 13-6). Naval officer *Grace Hopper*, a pioneer in computer programming, was a prime developer of COBOL.

COBOL is a programming language designed for business applications. Although COBOL programs often are lengthy, their English-like statements make the code easy to read, write, and maintain. COBOL especially is useful for processing transactions, such as payroll and billing, on mainframe computers. COBOL programs also run on other types of computers. The most popular personal computer COBOL program is *Micro Focus*, which enables programmers to create and migrate COBOL programs to the Web.

C

The **C** programming language, developed in the early 1970s by Dennis Ritchie at Bell Laboratories, originally was designed for writing system software. Today, many software programs are written in C (Figure 13-7). This includes operating systems and application software such as word processing and spreadsheet programs.

C is a powerful language that requires professional programming skills. Many programmers use C for business and scientific problems. C runs on almost any type of computer with any operating system, but it is used most often with the UNIX operating system.

WEB LINK 13-1

COBOL

For more information, visit scsite.com/dc2007/ch13/weblink and then click COBOL.

```
*    COMPUTE REGULAR TIME PAY
     MULTIPLY REGULAR-TIME-HOURS BY HOURLY-PAY-RATE
         GIVING REGULAR-TIME-PAY.

*    COMPUTE OVERTIME PAY
     IF OVERTIME-HOURS > 0
         COMPUTE OVERTIME-PAY = OVERTIME-HOURS * 1.5 * HOURLY-PAY-RATE
     ELSE
         MOVE 0 TO OVERTIME-PAY.

*    COMPUTE GROSS PAY
     ADD REGULAR-TIME-PAY TO OVERTIME-PAY
         GIVING GROSS-PAY.

*    PRINT GROSS PAY
     MOVE GROSS-PAY TO GROSS-PAY-OUT.
     WRITE REPORT-LINE-OUT FROM DETAIL-LINE
         AFTER ADVANCING 2 LINES.
```

FIGURE 13-6   An excerpt from a COBOL payroll program. The code shows the computations for regular time pay, overtime pay, and gross pay; the decision to evaluate the overtime hours; and the output of the gross pay.

```
/* Compute Regular Time Pay                              */
rt_pay = rt_hrs * pay_rate;

/* Compute Overtime Pay                                  */
if (ot_hrs > 0)
    ot_pay = ot_hrs * 1.5 * pay_rate;
else
    ot_pay = 0;

/* Compute Gross Pay                                     */
gross = rt_pay + ot_pay;

/* Print Gross Pay                                       */
printf("The gross pay is %d\n", gross);
```

FIGURE 13-7   An excerpt from a C payroll program. The code shows the computations for regular time pay, overtime pay, and gross pay; the decision to evaluate the overtime hours; and the output of the gross pay.

OBJECT-ORIENTED PROGRAMMING LANGUAGES AND PROGRAM DEVELOPMENT TOOLS

Programmers use an **object-oriented programming (OOP) language** or object-oriented program development tool to implement an object-oriented design. A program that provides a user-friendly environment for building programs often is called a *program development tool*. Recall from Chapter 12 that an *object* is an item that can contain both data and the procedures that read or manipulate that data. An object represents a real person, place, event, or transaction.

A major benefit of OOP is the ability to reuse and modify existing objects. For example, once a programmer creates an Employee object, it is available for use by any other existing or future program. Thus, programmers repeatedly reuse existing objects. Programs developed using the object-oriented approach have several advantages. The objects can be reused in many systems, are designed for repeated use, and become stable over time. In addition, programmers create applications faster because they design programs using existing objects.

In addition to being able to work with objects, an OOP language is event driven. An *event* is an action to which the program responds. Examples of events include pressing a key on the keyboard, typing a value in a text box, moving the mouse, clicking a button, or speaking an instruction. An *event-driven program* checks for and responds to events. Some programming languages are event driven but are not complete OOP languages. Other programming languages, such as Java, C++, C#, and the latest versions of Visual Basic, are complete object-oriented languages.

Object-oriented programming languages and program development tools work well in a RAD environment. **RAD** (*rapid application development*) is a method of developing software, in which a programmer writes and implements a program in segments instead of waiting until the entire program is completed. Users begin working with sections of the program as they

are completed. An important concept in RAD is the use of prebuilt components. For example, programmers do not have to write code for buttons and text boxes on Windows forms because they already exist in the programming language or tools provided with the language.

The following sections discuss a variety of object-oriented programming languages and program development tools.

Java

Java is an object-oriented programming language developed by Sun Microsystems. Figure 13-8 shows a portion of a Java program and the window that the program displays.

When programmers compile a Java program, the resulting object code is called *bytecode*, which is machine independent. Java then uses a *just-in-time (JIT) compiler* to convert the bytecode into machine-dependent code that is executed immediately. Sun's Java Development Kit (JDK) includes both the Java compiler and the JIT compiler.

J2EE (Java 2 Platform, Enterprise Edition) is a set of technologies by Sun Microsystems that allows programmers to develop and deploy Web services for a company. The goal of J2EE is to simplify and reduce program development time by developing standard, reusable objects.

WEB LINK 13-2

Java

For more information, visit scsite.com/dc2007/ch13/weblink and then click Java.

```
public class BodyMassApplet extends Applet implements ActionListener
{
        //declare variables
        Image logo; //declare an Image object
        int inches, pounds;
        double meters, kilograms, index;

        //construct components
        Label companyLabel = new Label("THE SUN FITNESS CENTER BODY MASS INDEX CALCULATOR");
        Label heightLabel = new Label("Enter your height to the nearest inch  ");
            TextField heightField = new TextField(10);
        Label weightLabel = new Label ("Enter your weight to the nearest pound  ");
            TextField weightField = new TextField(10);
        Button calcButton = new Button("Calculate");
        Label outputLabel = new Label(
        "Click the Calculate button to see your Body Mass Index.");

            inches = Integer.parseInt(heightField.getText());
            pounds = Integer.parseInt(weightField.getText());
            meters = inches / 39.36;
            kilograms = pounds / 2.2;
            index = kilograms / Math.pow(meters,2);
            outputLabel.setText("YOUR BODY MASS INDEX IS " + Math.round(index) + ".");
}

public void paint(Graphics g)
{
        g.drawImage(logo,125,160,this);
}
}
```

Applet Viewer: BodyMassApplet.class
Applet
THE SUN FITNESS CENTER BODY MASS INDEX CALCULATOR
Enter your height to the nearest inch   67
Enter your weight to the nearest pound   145
Calculate
YOUR BODY MASS INDEX IS 23.
Applet started.

FIGURE 13-8 A portion of a Java program and the window the program displays.

C++

Developed in the 1980s by Bjarne Sroustrup at Bell Laboratories, **C++** (pronounced SEE-plus-plus) is an object-oriented programming language that is an extension of the C programming language. C++ includes all the elements of the C language, plus it has additional features for working with objects, classes, events, and other object-oriented concepts (Figure 13-9).

```
// portion of a C++ program that allows users to create
// a new zip code from a string or a number and expand
// zip codes, as appropriate, to a 10-digit number

ZipC::ZipC( const unsigned long zipnum )
{
   ostringstream strInt;
   strInt << zipnum;
   code = strInt.str();
}

const string ZipC::getCode()
{
   return code;
}

void ZipC::setCode(const string newCode)
{
   code = newCode;
}

void ZipC::expand( const string suffix )
{

   if(code.length() == 5 &&      // small size?
      suffix.length() == 4)      // length ok?
   {
      code += "-";
      code.append(suffix);
   }
}
```

FIGURE 13-9 Sample C++ program.

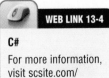

Programmers commonly use C++ to develop database and Web applications. Much application software, such as word processing and spreadsheet programs, also is written in C++. Although C++ is an outgrowth of the C programming language, a programmer does not need C programming experience to be a successful C++ programmer.

C#

C# (pronounced SEE-sharp) is an object-oriented programming language based on C++ that was developed primarily by Anders Hejlsberg, Microsoft chief architect and distinguished engineer. C# has been accepted as a standard for Web applications and XML-based Web services. Recall from Chapter 9 that Web services describe standardized software that enables programmers to create applications that communicate with other remote computers over the Internet or on an internal business network.

Like Java, C# uses a JIT compiler but its resulting code is called *Microsoft Intermediate Language* (MSIL). C# applications can be built on existing C or C++ applications, saving development time for companies migrating from C or C++. Many experts see C# as Java's main competition.

Visual Studio 2005

Visual Studio 2005 is the latest suite of program development tools from Microsoft that assists programmers in building programs for Windows, Windows Mobile, or operating systems that support Microsoft's .NET architecture. The *.NET* (pronounced dot net) architecture is a set of technologies that allows almost any type of program to run on the Internet or an internal business network, as well as stand-alone computers.

This latest version of Visual Studio includes enhanced support for building security and reliability into applications through its programming languages, RAD tools, just-in-time compilers and debuggers, and other resources that reduce development time. For example, Visual Studio 2005 includes *code snippets*, which are prewritten code and templates associated with common programming tasks. The next sections discuss the programming languages in the Visual Studio 2005 suite.

- **Visual Basic 2005** is a programming language that allows programmers easily to build complex task-oriented object-based programs. Visual Basic 2005 is based on the Visual Basic programming language, which was developed by Microsoft Corporation in the early 1990s. This language is easy to learn and use. Thus, Visual Basic 2005 is ideal for beginning programmers.

The first step in building a Visual Basic 2005 program often is to design the graphical user interface using Visual Basic 2005 objects (Steps 1 and 2 in Figure 13-10). Visual Basic 2005 objects include items such as buttons, text boxes, and labels. Next, the programmer writes instructions to define any actions that should occur in response to specific events (Step 3 in Figure 13-10). Finally, the programmer generates and tests the final program (Step 4 in Figure 13-10).

An event in Visual Basic 2005 might be the result of an action that a user initiates. For example, when a user clicks a button in a Visual Basic 2005 program, the program executes the Click event. Programmers define Visual Basic 2005 events by writing instructions (code) with its built-in programming language.

WEB LINK 13-5

Visual Studio 2005
For more information, visit scsite.com/ dc2007/ch13/weblink and then click Visual Studio 2005.

FIGURE 13-10 CREATING A VISUAL BASIC 2005 PROGRAM

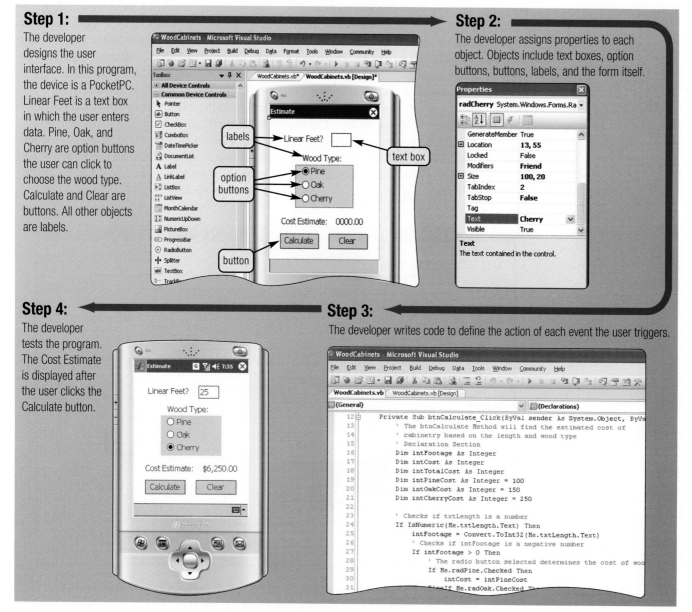

Step 1:
The developer designs the user interface. In this program, the device is a PocketPC. Linear Feet is a text box in which the user enters data. Pine, Oak, and Cherry are option buttons the user can click to choose the wood type. Calculate and Clear are buttons. All other objects are labels.

Step 2:
The developer assigns properties to each object. Objects include text boxes, option buttons, buttons, labels, and the form itself.

Step 4:
The developer tests the program. The Cost Estimate is displayed after the user clicks the Calculate button.

Step 3:
The developer writes code to define the action of each event the user triggers.

- **Visual C++ 2005** is a programming language based on C++. Not only is Visual C++ 2005 a powerful object-oriented programming language, it enables programmers to write Windows, Windows Mobile, and .NET applications quickly and efficiently. Features that make Visual C++ 2005 so powerful include reusable templates, direct access to machine level memory locations, an optimizing compiler, and advanced error reporting.

- **Visual C# 2005** is a programming language that combines programming elements of C++ with an easier, rapid development environment. The purpose of Visual C# 2005 is to take the complexity out of Visual C++ 2005 and still provide an object-oriented programming language. Programmers familiar with the C/C++ programming language family often migrate to the easier-to-use Visual C# 2005.

- **Visual J# 2005** (pronounced JAY-sharp) is a programming language that allows Java program development in the .NET environment. Programmers familiar with Java easily can migrate their skills to Visual J# 2005. Colleges today often teach a version of Visual J# in their introductory computer programming course because it is much easier to learn than the Visual C family of languages.

FAQ 13-2

What is Visual Studio 2005 Express?

Visual Studio 2005 Express is a scaled-down, easier-to-use version of the Visual Studio 2005 suite — geared for first-time programmers and less technical users. Available programs include Visual Basic 2005 Express, Visual C++ 2005 Express, Visual C# 2005 Express, and Visual J# 2005 Express. For more information, visit scsite.com/dc2007/ch13/faq and then click Visual Studio 2005 Express.

Delphi

Borland's **Delphi** is a powerful program development tool that is ideal for building large-scale enterprise and Web applications in a RAD environment (Figure 13-11). Programmers use Delphi to develop programs quickly for Windows, Linux, and .NET platforms.

Delphi also provides visual modeling tools based on the UML. Recall from Chapter 12 that the UML (Unified Modeling Language) has been adopted as a standard notation for object modeling and development. With Delphi, programmers easily link the UML designs to the working solutions.

FIGURE 13-11 The latest version of Delphi, shown in this figure, makes Windows development tasks faster, better, and easier by supporting Microsoft's .NET architecture with both Delphi and C# languages, as well as Delphi for 32-bit Windows applications, in a RAD environment.

PowerBuilder

PowerBuilder, developed by Sybase, is another powerful program development RAD tool best suited for Web-based and large-scale enterprise object-oriented applications. Programmers also use PowerBuilder to develop small- and medium-scale client/server applications. PowerBuilder includes a consistent interface, wizards, and many other features that enable programmers to develop applications quickly (Figure 13-12). In terms of complexity, PowerBuilder is comparable to Delphi.

Visual Programming Languages

A **visual programming language** is a language that uses a visual or graphical interface for creating all source code. The graphical interface, called a *visual programming environment* (*VPE*), allows programmers to drag and drop objects to develop programs. Examples of visual programming languages include Mindscript and Prograph.

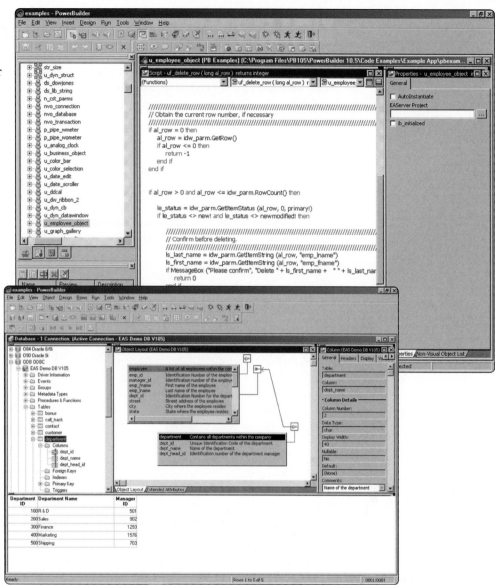

FIGURE 13-12 PowerBuilder is a program development RAD tool ideal for building large-scale and Web-based applications.

Test your knowledge of pages 664 through 673 in Quiz Yourself 13-1.

QUIZ YOURSELF 13-1

Instructions: Find the true statement below. Then, rewrite the remaining false statements so they are true.

1. An interpreter is a program that converts an entire source program into machine language before executing it.

2. COBOL and C are examples of assembly languages.

3. C# is an object-oriented programming language based on PowerBuilder.

4. Delphi is an object-oriented programming language developed by Sun Microsystems.

5. Two types of low-level languages are machine languages and source languages.

6. Visual Studio 2005 is the latest suite of program development tools from Microsoft that assists programmers in building programs for Windows, Windows Mobile, or operating systems that support Microsoft's .NET architecture.

Quiz Yourself Online: To further check your knowledge of machine languages, assembly languages, procedural languages, and object-oriented programming languages and program development tools, visit scsite.com/dc2007/ch13/quiz and then click Objectives 1 – 3.

OTHER PROGRAMMING LANGUAGES

Two programming languages also currently used that have not yet been discussed are RPG and 4GLs. The following sections discuss these programming languages.

RPG

In the early 1960s, IBM introduced **RPG** (*Report Program Generator*) to assist businesses in generating reports (Figure 13-13). Today, businesses also use RPG to access and update data in databases. Some versions of RPG are similar to procedural 3GLs, while others provide program development tools for programmers to design reports that extract data from the database. Some versions of RPG are object oriented.

Many users of RPG (and other report generators) claim it paved the way for 4GLs (discussed in the next section). RPG primarily is used for application development on IBM servers, such as the AS/400. A version is available for the personal computer.

4GLs

A **4GL** (*fourth-generation language*) is a nonprocedural language that enables users and programmers to access data in a database. With a **nonprocedural language**, the programmer writes English-like instructions or interacts with a graphical environment to retrieve data from files or a database. Nonprocedural languages typically are easier to use than procedural languages. Many object-oriented program development tools use 4GLs.

One popular 4GL is SQL. As discussed in Chapter 10, **SQL** is a query language that allows users to manage, update, and retrieve data in a relational DBMS (Figure 13-14). These powerful languages allow database administrators to define a database and its structure. They also enable users to maintain and access the data in the database.

```
C* COMPUTE REGULAR TIME PAY
C           RTHRS     MULT RATE            RTPAY     72
C*
C* COMPUTE OVERTIME PAY
C           OTHRS     IFGT 0
C           RATE      MULT 1.5             OTRATE    72
C           OTRATE    MULT OTHRS           OTPAY     72
            ELSE
C           INZ                            OTPAY     72
C
C* COMPUTE GROSS PAY
C           RTPAY     ADD  OTPAY           GRPAY     72
C
C* PRINT GROSS PAY
C                     EXCPTDETAIL
C
C*
O* OUTPUT SPECIFICATIONS
OQPRINT  E            DETAIL
O                                  23 'THE GROSS PAY IS $'
O                     GRPAY  J     34
```

FIGURE 13-13 This figure shows an excerpt from an RPG payroll program. The code shows the computations for regular time pay, overtime pay, and gross pay; the decision to evaluate the overtime hours; and the output of the gross pay.

SQL →

```
SELECT LAST_NAME, FIRST_NAME, GROSS_PAY

FROM EMPLOYEE

WHERE OVERTIME_HOURS > 0

ORDER BY LAST_NAME;
```

results →

```
LAST_NAME     FIRST_NAME     GROSS_PAY

Antiqua       Martin         780.00
Charles       Leslie         715.00
Guillan       Anita          847.50
.
.
.
```

FIGURE 13-14 SQL is a fourth-generation language that can be used to query database tables. This query produces an alphabetical list of those employees who receive overtime pay; that is, their overtime hours are greater than 0.

Classic Programming Languages

In addition to the programming languages discussed on the previous pages, programmers sometimes use other languages (Figure 13-15). Some of the languages listed in Figure 13-15, although once popular, find little use today. Read Looking Ahead 13-1 for a look at the next generation of programming languages.

FAQ 13-3

What are the more popular programming languages?

According to a recent study, Java, C, and C++ are the top programming languages, with Visual Basic, Perl, Delphi, SQL, and JavaScript not far behind. For more information, visit scsite.com/dc2007/ch13/faq and then click Popular Programming Languages.

LOOKING AHEAD 13-1

The Future of Programming Languages

The programming languages of today may not be the programming languages of tomorrow, according to some computer experts. While today's programmers follow the program development cycle, future programmers may not need to write even one line of code. Instead, they might ask their computers a question, such as "What are the top ranked NCAA football programs?" Intelligent programs then will write the correct code automatically to generate the answer.

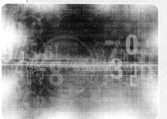

These programs will create appropriate interfaces that allow human interaction. With this self-generating code, programmers will be able to focus on planning, analyzing, and validating a design rather than spending many tedious hours implementing their design. Intelligent programs also will modify themselves as new maintenance issues arise. For more information, visit scsite.com/dc2007/ch13/looking and then click Future Programming Languages.

Ada	Derived from Pascal, developed by the U.S. Department of Defense, named after Augusta Ada Lovelace Byron, who is thought to be the first female computer programmer
ALGOL	ALGOrithmic Language, the first structured procedural language
APL	A Programming Language, a scientific language designed to manipulate tables of numbers
BASIC	Beginners All-purpose Symbolic Instruction Code, developed by John Kemeny and Thomas Kurtz as a simple, interactive problem-solving language
Forth	Similar to C, used for small computerized devices
Fortran	FORmula TRANslator, one of the first high-level programming languages used for scientific applications
HyperTalk	An object-oriented programming language developed by Apple to manipulate cards that can contain text, graphics, and sound
LISP	LISt Processing, a language used for artificial intelligence applications
Logo	An educational tool used to teach programming and problem-solving to children
Modula-2	A successor to Pascal used for developing systems software
Pascal	Developed to teach students structured programming concepts, named in honor of Blaise Pascal, a French mathematician who developed one of the earliest calculating machines
PILOT	Programmed Inquiry Learning Or Teaching, used to write computer-aided instruction programs
PL/1	Programming Language One, a business and scientific language that combines many features of Fortran and COBOL
Prolog	PROgramming LOGic, used for development of artificial intelligence applications
Smalltalk	Object-oriented programming language

FIGURE 13-15 Other programming languages.

OTHER PROGRAM DEVELOPMENT TOOLS

As mentioned earlier, program development tools are user-friendly programs designed to assist both programmers and users in creating programs. In many cases, the program automatically generates the procedural instructions necessary to communicate with the computer. The following sections discuss application generators and macros.

Application Generators

An **application generator** is a program that creates source code or machine code from a specification of the required functionality. When using an application generator, a programmer or user works with menu-driven tools and graphical user interfaces to define the desired specifications. Application generators most often are bundled with or are included as part of a DBMS.

An application generator typically consists of a report writer, form, and menu generator. As discussed in Chapter 10, a *report writer* allows you to design a report on the screen, retrieve data into the report design, and then display or print the report. A *form* is a window on the screen that provides areas for entering or changing data in a database. Figure 13-16 shows a sample form design and the resulting form it generates showing sample data a user may enter in the form. A *menu generator* enables you to create a menu for the application options. If you create three reports and two forms for an application, for example, the menu would contain at least six options: one for each report, one for each form, and one to exit, or quit, the application.

Macros

A **macro** is a series of statements that instructs an application how to complete a task. Macros allow users to automate routine, repetitive, or difficult tasks in application software such as word processing, spreadsheet, or database programs. That is, users can create simple programs within the software by writing macros. You usually create a macro in one of two ways: (1) record the macro or (2) write the macro.

If you want to automate a routine or repetitive task such as formatting or editing, you would record a macro. A *macro recorder* is similar to a movie camera because both record all actions until turned off. To record a macro,

FIGURE 13-16a   (form design)

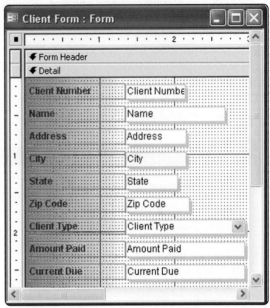

FIGURE 13-16b   (resulting filled-in form)

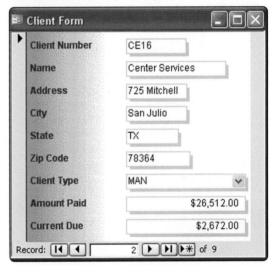

FIGURE 13-16   A form design and the resulting filled-in form created with Microsoft Access.

start the macro recorder in the software. Then, perform the steps to be part of the macro, such as clicks of the mouse or keystrokes. Once the macro is recorded, you can run it anytime you want to perform that same sequence of actions. For example, if you always print three copies of certain documents, you could record the actions required to print three copies. To print three copies, you would run the macro called PrintThreeCopies.

When you become familiar with programming techniques, you can write your own macros instead of recording them. Many programs use *Visual Basic for applications* (*VBA*), which integrates with Visual Studio 2005, or a similar language as their macro programming language. The macro in Figure 13-17a shows an Excel VBA macro that automates the data entry process to determine the contributions and future value of a retirement plan. Figure 13-17b shows the dialog box generated from the macro that prompts the user to enter the annual salary. Read Ethics & Issues 13-1 for a related discussion.

FAQ 13-4

How do I record a macro?

In the latest Microsoft Office programs, click Tools on the menu bar, point to Macro, click Record New Macro, and then click the OK button. As you click the mouse and make choices on menus and in dialog boxes, the macro recorder records every action you take. To stop recording the macro, click the Stop Recording button on the Stop Recording toolbar. For more information, visit scsite.com/dc2007/ch13/faq and then click Macros.

WEB LINK 13-6

Macros

For more information, visit scsite.com/dc2007/ch13/weblink and then click Macros.

FIGURE 13-17a (VBA Macro)

FIGURE 13-17b
(macro dialog box in Excel window)

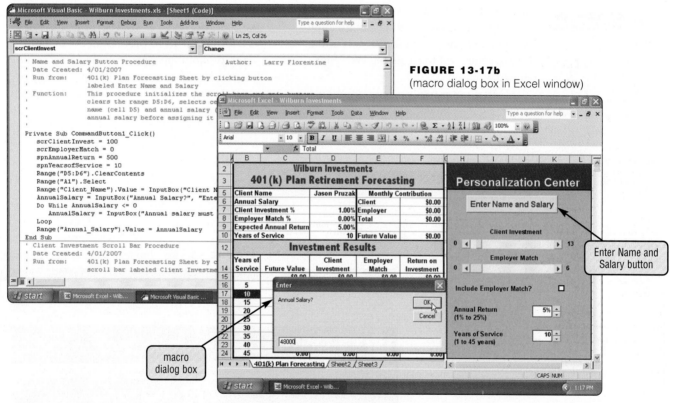

FIGURE 13-17 The left screen shows a VBA macro used to automate a retirement plan forecast. After a macro is written, the user clicks the Enter Name and Salary button to run the macro. The right screen shows the macro guiding the user through the data entry process.

ETHICS & ISSUES 13-1

Should All Students Be Required to Learn Computer Programming?

When computers first were introduced in schools, instructors taught programming routinely. As time passed, however, the emphasis turned towards learning to use application software and the Internet. Many educators feel programming still should be an integral part of computer education, and some believe that all students should learn fundamental computer programming. They point out that application software often includes a programming language, such as Visual Basic for Applications (VBA), with which users can customize the software. People who have knowledge of programming can recognize more readily the kinds of problems that computers are likely to be able to solve. Many researchers claim that programming improves logical reasoning and critical thinking skills. Yet, other instructors feel that program development is irrelevant for most students, an unnecessary impediment to achieving computer literacy, and may create negative attitudes towards computers. How important is it to learn programming? Why? Should programming in some form be a part of computer education? Why or why not? Should everyone be taught computer programming? Why? How might you react if you were required to learn computer programming?

WEB PAGE DEVELOPMENT

The designers of Web pages, known as *Web page authors*, use a variety of techniques to develop Web pages. These include some of the languages previously discussed and the languages discussed in the following sections.

HTML

HTML (*Hypertext Markup Language*) is a special formatting language that programmers use to format documents for display on the Web. You view a Web page written with HTML in a Web browser such as Internet Explorer, Netscape Navigator, Mozilla, Safari, Firefox, or Opera. Figure 13-18a shows part of the HTML code used to create the Web page shown in Figure 13-18b.

HTML is not actually a programming language. It is, however, a language that has specific rules for defining the placement and format of text, graphics, video, and audio on a Web page. HTML uses *tags*, which are codes that specify links to other documents and indicate how a Web page is displayed when viewed on the Web.

A Web page, thus, is a file that contains both text and HTML tags. Examples of tags are <B> to bold text, <P> to indicate a new paragraph, and <HR> to display a horizontal rule across the page.

You can write HTML code using any text editor such as Notepad. The HTML code also can be entered into any standard word processing program, such as Word. You must save the code, however, as an ASCII file, instead of as a formatted word processing document. Many programmers never write HTML code because HTML is generated automatically by several programming languages and program development tools.

FIGURE 13-18a   (portion of HTML program)

FIGURE 13-18b   (portion of resulting Web page)

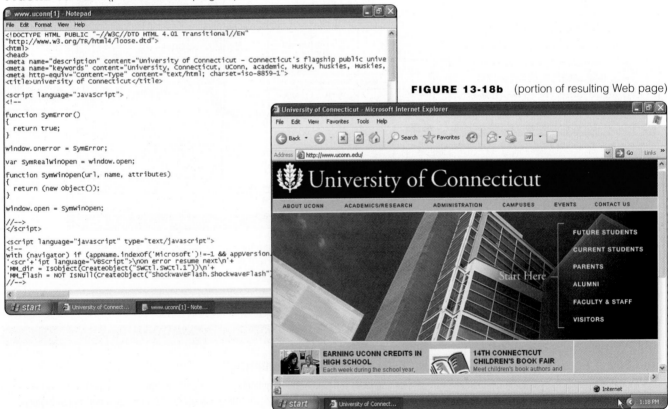

FIGURE 13-18   HTML (Hypertext Markup Language) is used to create Web pages. The portion of the HTML code in the top figure generates a portion of a Web page shown in the bottom figure.

FAQ 13-5

What is an ASCII file?

An *ASCII file* is a file that does not contain any formatting. That is, ASCII files do not contain graphics, italics, bold, underlining, styles, bullets, shading, color, or any other type of graphical format. Word processing programs typically have an option to save a file as text only, which means ASCII. For more information, visit scsite.com/dc2007/ch13/faq and then click ASCII Files.

Scripts, Applets, Servlets, and ActiveX Controls

HTML tells a browser how to display text and images, set up lists and option buttons, and establish links on a Web page. By adding dynamic content and interactive elements such as scrolling messages, animated graphics, forms, pop-up windows, and interaction, Web pages become much more interesting. To add these elements, Web page authors write small programs called scripts, applets, servlets, and ActiveX controls. These programs run inside of another program. This is different from programs discussed thus far, which are executed by the operating system. In this case, the Web browser executes these short programs.

As discussed in Chapter 9, your computer is the client computer when it is connected to the Web. A **script** is an interpreted program that runs on the client. That is, a script runs on your computer, instead of running on a Web server. An **applet** also usually runs on the client, but it is compiled. Thus, an applet usually runs faster than a script. Scripts and applets shift the computational work from the Web server to the client. A **servlet** is an applet that runs on the server.

Similar to an applet, an **ActiveX control** is a small program that runs on the client computer, instead of the server. ActiveX controls use ActiveX technology. **ActiveX** is a set of object-oriented technologies by Microsoft that allows components on a network to communicate with one another. To run an ActiveX control, the Web browser must support ActiveX technology. If it does not, you will need a plug-in program to run ActiveX controls.

One reason Web page authors use scripts, applets, servlets, and ActiveX controls is to add special multimedia effects to Web pages. Examples include animated graphics, scrolling messages, calendars, and advertisements. Another reason to use these programs is to include interactive capabilities on Web pages. Cookies, shopping carts, games, counters, image maps, and processing forms are types of scripts, applets, servlets, and ActiveX controls that allow you to transfer information to and from a Web server.

A **counter** tracks the number of visitors to a Web site. An **image map** is a graphical image that points to a Web address. Web pages use image maps in place of, or in addition to, text links. When you click a certain part of the graphical image, the Web browser sends the coordinates of the clicked location to the Web server, which in turn locates the corresponding Web address and sends the Web page to your computer.

A **processing form** collects data from visitors to a Web site, who fill in blank fields and then click a button that sends the information. When a user clicks that button on the processing form, that action executes the script or applet. It transmits the data to the server, processes it, and then, if appropriate, sends information back to your Web browser via the server.

To send and receive information between your computer and a Web server, the script, applet, or servlet uses the CGI. The *CGI* (*common gateway interface*) is the communications standard that defines how a Web server communicates with outside sources. Many times, the outside source is a database. The program that manages the sending and receiving across the CGI is a *CGI script*.

The steps in Figure 13-19 show how a CGI script works.

A CGI script can be in the form of a script, applet, servlet, or ActiveX control. You can download CGI scripts from the Web and purchase them. If one does not exist that meets your needs, you can write your own CGI script using a scripting language. The next section discusses scripting languages.

Scripting Languages

Programmers write scripts, applets, servlets, or ActiveX controls using a variety of languages. These include some of the languages previously discussed, such as Java, C++, C#, and Visual Basic 2005. Some programmers use scripting languages. A *scripting language* is an interpreted language that typically is easy to learn and use. Popular scripting languages include JavaScript, Perl, Rexx, Tcl, and VBScript.

FIGURE 13-19 HOW A CGI SCRIPT WORKS

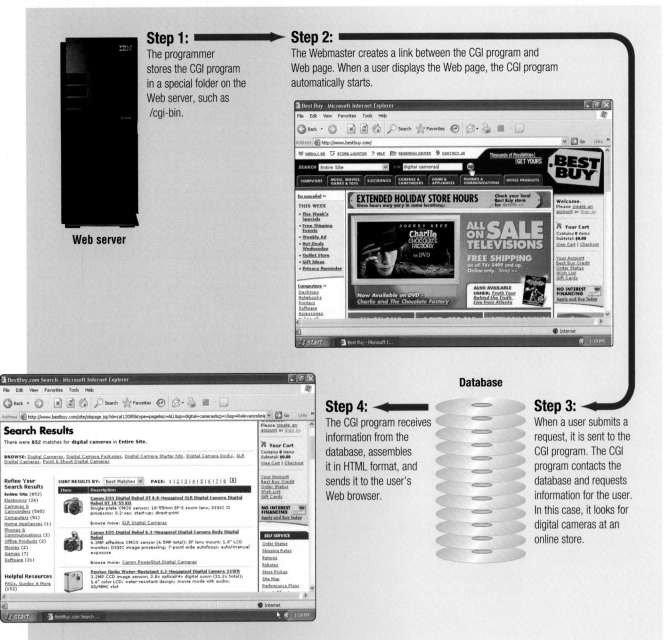

Step 1:
The programmer stores the CGI program in a special folder on the Web server, such as /cgi-bin.

Web server

Step 2:
The Webmaster creates a link between the CGI program and Web page. When a user displays the Web page, the CGI program automatically starts.

Database

Step 4:
The CGI program receives information from the database, assembles it in HTML format, and sends it to the user's Web browser.

Step 3:
When a user submits a request, it is sent to the CGI program. The CGI program contacts the database and requests information for the user. In this case, it looks for digital cameras at an online store.

- **JavaScript** is an interpreted language that allows a programmer to add dynamic content and interactive elements to a Web page (Figure 13-20). These elements include alert messages, scrolling text, animations, drop-down menus, data input forms, pop-up windows, interactive quizzes, and mouse rollovers. A *mouse rollover* or *mouseover* occurs when text, a graphic, or other object changes as the user moves the mouse pointer over the object on the screen.

  Web page authors insert JavaScript code directly in an HTML document. Although it shares many of the features of the full Java language, JavaScript is a much simpler language. JavaScript is an *open language*, which means anyone can use it without purchasing a license. JavaScript thus allows the programmer to improve the appearance of Web pages without spending a large amount of money.
- **Perl** (*Practical Extraction and Report Language*) originally was developed by Larry Wall at NASA's Jet Propulsion Laboratory as a procedural language similar to C and C++. The latest release of Perl, however, is an interpreted scripting language. Because Perl has powerful text processing capabilities, it has become a popular language for writing scripts.
- **Rexx** (*REstructured eXtended eXecutor*) was developed by Mike Cowlishaw at IBM as a procedural interpreted scripting language for both the professional programmer and the nontechnical user. In addition to all IBM operating systems, Rexx works with Windows, Mac OS X, and most UNIX operating systems.
- **Tcl** (*Tool Command Language*) is an interpreted scripting language created by Dr. John Ousterhout and maintained by Sun Microsystems Laboratories. Tcl has a companion program, called Tool Kit (Tk), that allows Web page authors to build graphical user interfaces.
- **VBScript** (*Visual Basic, Scripting Edition*) is a subset of the Visual Basic language that allows programmers to add intelligence and interactivity to Web pages. As with JavaScript, Web page authors embed VBScript code directly into an HTML document. Programmers already familiar with Visual Basic choose VBScript as their scripting language, so they do not have to learn a new scripting language. The latest version of Internet Explorer includes VBScript.

FIGURE 13-20a (pop-up window)

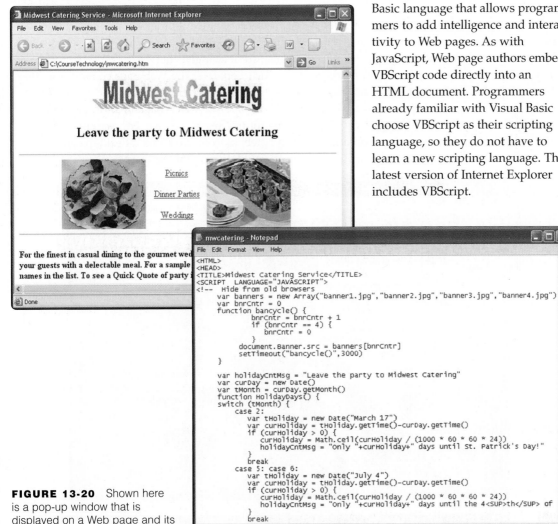

FIGURE 13-20b (JavaScript code)

```
<HTML>
<HEAD>
<TITLE>Midwest Catering Service</TITLE>
<SCRIPT  LANGUAGE="JAVASCRIPT">
<!--  Hide from old browsers
     var banners = new Array("banner1.jpg","banner2.jpg","banner3.jpg","banner4.jpg")
     var bnrCntr = 0
     function bancycle() {
             bnrCntr = bnrCntr + 1
             if (bnrCntr == 4) {
                bnrCntr = 0
             }
          document.Banner.src = banners[bnrCntr]
          setTimeout("bancycle()",3000)
     }

     var holidayCntMsg = "Leave the party to Midwest Catering"
     var curDay = new Date()
     var tMonth = curDay.getMonth()
     function HolidayDays() {
     switch (tMonth) {
         case 2:
            var tHoliday = new Date("March 17")
            var curHoliday = tHoliday.getTime()-curDay.getTime()
            if (curHoliday > 0) {
               curHoliday = Math.ceil(curHoliday / (1000 * 60 * 60 * 24))
               holidayCntMsg = "Only "+curHoliday+" days until St. Patrick's Day!"
            }
            break
         case 5: case 6:
            var tHoliday = new Date("July 4")
            var curHoliday = tHoliday.getTime()-curDay.getTime()
            if (curHoliday > 0) {
               curHoliday = Math.ceil(curHoliday / (1000 * 60 * 60 * 24))
               holidayCntMsg = "Only "+curHoliday+" days until the 4<SUP>th</SUP> of
            }
            break
```

FIGURE 13-20 Shown here is a pop-up window that is displayed on a Web page and its associated JavaScript code.

Dynamic HTML

Dynamic HTML (DHTML) is a newer type of HTML that allows Web page authors to include more graphical interest and interactivity in a Web page, without the Web page accessing the Web server. That is, the client's computer automatically updates and changes its own content. These Web pages display much faster than Web pages created with HTML.

Typically, Web pages created with DHTML are more animated and responsive to user interaction. Colors change, font sizes grow, objects appear and disappear as a user moves the mouse (Figure 13-21), and animations dance around the screen.

Dynamic HTML works by using the document object model, style sheets, and scripting languages. *The document object model (DOM)* defines every item on a Web page as an object. Fonts, graphics, headlines, tables, and every other page element are objects. With DOM, Web page authors can change properties, such as color or size, of any or all of these objects on the Web page.

A *style sheet* contains descriptions of a document's characteristics. Many word processing documents use style sheets to define formats of characters and paragraphs. *Cascading style sheets (CSS)* contain the formats for how a particular object should be displayed in a Web browser. For example, the CSS specify items such as background colors, image and link colors, fonts, and font sizes. A single HTML document can contain multiple cascading style sheets, thus, the name cascading. As a user moves the mouse or clicks an item, a new style sheet can be applied to change the appearance of the screen.

After a Web page author has defined and formatted objects on a Web page, a scripting language such as JavaScript manipulates them. A script can move, display, hide, or change the appearance of an object as the user performs actions such as a mouse rollover.

XHTML, XML, and WML

XHTML (*eXtensible HTML*) is a markup language that enables Web sites to be displayed more easily on microbrowsers in PDAs and smart phones. XHTML includes features of HTML and XML. **XML** (*eXtensible Markup Language*) is an increasingly popular format for sharing data that allows Web page authors to create customized tags, as well as use predefined tags. With XML, a server sends an entire record to the client, enabling the client to do much of the processing without going back to the server. In XML, programmers also can define a link that points to multiple Web sites instead of a single site.

XML separates the Web page content from its format, allowing the Web browser to display the contents of a Web page in a form appropriate for the display device. For example, a PDA, a notebook computer, and a desktop computer all could display the same XML page. A Web

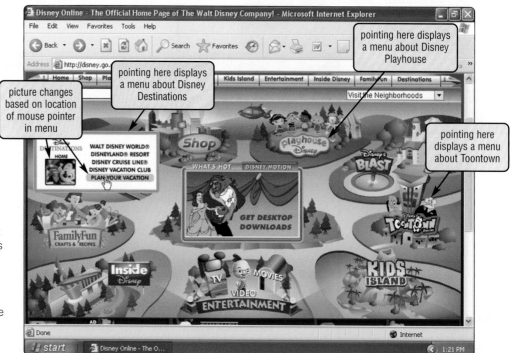

FIGURE 13-21 Web pages at Disney's Web site use DHTML. As you move the mouse around the window, a menu is displayed at the location of the mouse pointer that relates to the object to which you are pointing. As you move the mouse through menus, pictures change based on location of the mouse pointer in the menu.

page written with only HTML probably would require multiple versions to run on each of these types of computers. For a technical discussion about XML, read the High-Tech Talk article on page 698.

One application of XML is the RSS 2.0 specification. **RSS 2.0**, which stands for *Really Simple Syndication*, is a specification that content aggregators use to distribute content to subscribers. The online publisher creates an RSS document that is made available to Web sites for publication. News Web sites often use RSS to publish headlines and stories. Most Web browsers can read RSS documents.

Wireless devices use a subset of XML called WML. **WML** (*wireless markup language*) allows Web page authors to design pages specifically for microbrowsers. Many Internet-enabled PDAs and smart phones use WML as their markup language.

Ajax

Ajax, which stands for Asynchronous JavaScript and XML, is a method of creating interactive Web applications designed to provide immediate response to user requests. Instead of refreshing entire Web pages, Ajax works with the Web browser to update only changes to the Web page. This technique saves time because the Web application does not spend time repeatedly sending unchanged information across the network.

Ajax combines several programming tools: JavaScript, HTML or XHTML, XML, and cascading style sheets. Web browsers that support Ajax include Internet Explorer, Netscape Navigator, Mozilla, Safari, Firefox, and Opera. Examples of Web sites that use Ajax are Google Maps and Flickr.

Web Page Authoring Software

As Chapter 3 discussed, you do not need to learn HTML to develop a Web page. You can use **Web page authoring software** to create sophisticated Web pages that include images, video, audio, animation, and other effects.

Web page authoring software generates HTML tags from your Web page design. With the Web page authoring software, you can view or modify the HTML associated with a Web page. Sometimes, you may add an HTML tag that the Web page authoring software does not provide. Learning HTML basics will enable you to fine-tune Web page formats created with authoring software. Read Ethics & Issues 13-2 for a related discussion.

Three popular Web page authoring programs are Dreamweaver MX, Flash MX, and FrontPage.

- **Dreamweaver MX**, originally developed by Macromedia, is a Web page authoring program that allows Web site developers to create, maintain, and manage professional Web sites. Some features of Dreamweaver MX include its visual environment, use of cascading style sheets, capability of manipulating code, built-in graphics editor (called Fireworks), and XML support.
- **Flash MX**, also originally developed by Macromedia, is a Web page authoring program that enables Web site programmers to combine interactive content with text, graphics, audio, and video. For example, marketing and WBT (Web-based training) sites often use Flash MX. Features of Flash MX include its animation and interactive tools, professional video capabilities, easy deployment to mobile devices such as PDAs and smart phones, and XML support.
- **FrontPage**, developed by Microsoft, is a Web page authoring program that provides nontechnical and professional users with the ability to create and manage Web sites easily. FrontPage is part of the Microsoft Office System. Features of FrontPage include its easy-to-use graphics tools, HTML code generator, scripting tools, and XML support.

FAQ 13-6

What is the breakdown of Web page authors by age?

As shown in the chart below, the greatest number of Web page authors falls between 30 and 49 years of age. For more information, visit scsite.com/dc2007/ch13/faq and then click Web Page Authors.

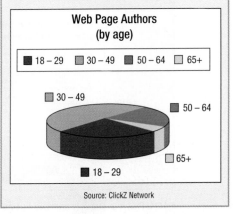

Web Page Authors (by age)

■ 18 – 29 ■ 30 – 49 ■ 50 – 64 □ 65+

Source: ClickZ Network

MULTIMEDIA PROGRAM DEVELOPMENT

Multimedia authoring software allows programmers to combine text, graphics, animation, audio, and video in an interactive presentation. Many programmers use multimedia authoring software for computer-based training (CBT) and Web-based training (WBT). Popular Web page authoring programs typically share similar features and are capable of creating similar applications. Popular programs include ToolBook, Authorware, and Director MX.

- **ToolBook**, from SumTotal Systems, has a graphical user interface and uses an object-oriented approach, so programmers can design multimedia applications using basic objects. These objects include buttons, fields, graphics, backgrounds, and pages.

  In ToolBook, programmers can convert a multimedia application into HTML, so it can be distributed over the Internet. Figure 13-22 shows a sample Web application developed in ToolBook that uses DHTML. Many businesses and colleges use ToolBook to create content for distance learning courses.

- **Authorware**, originally from Macromedia, is a multimedia authoring program that provides the tools programmers need to build interactive multimedia training and educational programs. Authorware offers a powerful authoring environment for the development of interactive multimedia magazines, catalogs, reference titles for CDs and DVDs, and applications for kiosks. Authorware also offers tools for bundling the content, student tracking, and course management components of a WBT or other distance learning course. Users view Authorware applications distributed over the Web using the Shockwave plug-in.

- **Director MX**, also originally from Macromedia, is a popular multimedia authoring program with powerful features that allow programmers to create highly interactive multimedia applications.

  Director MX includes Lingo, which is a built-in object-oriented scripting language. Director MX also supports JavaScript. Director MX's powerful features make it well suited for developing electronic presentations, CDs or DVDs for education and entertainment, simulations, and applications for kiosks and the Internet. Web-based applications can include streaming audio and video, interactivity, and multiuser functionality. As with Authorware, users view applications developed in Director MX on the Web using the Shockwave plug-in.

Test your knowledge of pages 674 through 684 in Quiz Yourself 13-2.

QUIZ YOURSELF 13-2

Instructions: Find the true statement below. Then, rewrite the remaining false statements so they are true.

1. HTML is a language that has specific rules for defining the placement and format of text, graphics, video, and audio on a Web page.

2. Interpreted HTML works by using the document object model, style sheets, and scripting languages.

3. Maps allow users to automate routine, repetitive, or difficult tasks in application software such as word processing, spreadsheet, or database programs.

4. Popular first-generation languages include JavaScript, Perl, Rexx, Tcl, and VBScript.

5. Rexx separates the Web page content from its format, allowing the Web browser to display the contents of a Web page in a form appropriate for the display device.

6. SQL is an example of a second generation language.

7. Three popular markup languages are Dreamweaver MX, Flash MX, and FrontPage.

Quiz Yourself Online: To further check your knowledge of other programming languages and program development, Web page program development, and multimedia authoring programs, visit scsite.com/dc2007/ch13/quiz and then click Objectives 4 – 6.

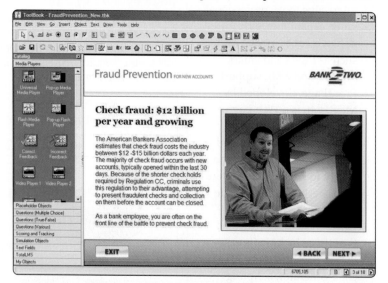

FIGURE 13-22   A sample ToolBook application.

THE PROGRAM DEVELOPMENT CYCLE

The program development cycle is a series of steps programmers use to build computer programs. As Chapter 12 discussed, the system development cycle guides information technology (IT) professionals through the development of an information system. Likewise, the program development cycle guides computer programmers through the development of a program. The program development cycle consists of six steps (Figure 13-23):

1. Analyze Requirements
2. Design Solution
3. Validate Design
4. Implement Design
5. Test Solution
6. Document Solution

As shown in Figure 13-23, the steps in the program development cycle form a loop. Program development is an ongoing process within system development. Each time someone identifies errors in or improvements to a program and requests program modifications, the Analyze Requirements step begins again. When programmers correct errors or add enhancements to an existing program, they are said to be **maintaining** the program.

What Initiates the Program Development Cycle?

As discussed in Chapter 12, the system development cycle consists of five phases: planning; analysis; design; implementation; and operation, support, and security. During the analysis phase, the development team recommends how to handle software needs. Choices include purchasing packaged software, building custom software in-house, or outsourcing some or all of the IT activities.

If the company opts for in-house development, the design and implementation phases of the system development cycle become quite extensive. In the design phase, the systems analyst creates a detailed set of requirements for the programmers. Once the programmers receive the requirements, the implementation phase begins. At this time, the programmer analyzes the requirements of the problem to be solved. The program development cycle thus begins at the start of the implementation phase in the system development cycle.

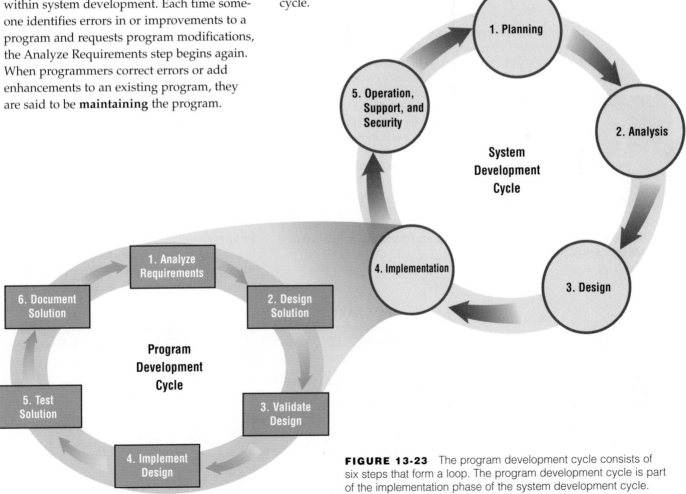

FIGURE 13-23 The program development cycle consists of six steps that form a loop. The program development cycle is part of the implementation phase of the system development cycle.

The scope of the requirements largely determines how many programmers work on the program development. If the scope is large, a **programming team** that consists of a group of programmers may develop the programs. If the specifications are simple, a single programmer might complete all the development tasks. Whether a single programmer or a programming team, all the programmers involved must interact with users and members of the development team throughout the program development cycle.

By following the steps in the program development cycle, programmers create programs that are correct (produce accurate information) and maintainable (easy to modify). The following sections address each of the steps in the program development cycle. Read Looking Ahead 13-2 for a look at the next generation of programming.

STEP 1 — ANALYZE REQUIREMENTS

The first step in the program development cycle is to analyze the requirements of the problem the program(s) should solve, so the programmer can begin to develop an appropriate solution. In most cases, the solution requires more than one program. The Analyze Requirements step consists of three major tasks: (1) review the requirements, (2) meet with the systems analyst and users, and (3) identify input, processing, output, and data components.

First, the programmer reviews the requirements. The requirements may be in the form of deliverables such as charts, diagrams, and reports. For example, screen and report layout charts show input and output requirements. Structured English, decision tables, and decision trees convey processing requirements. The data dictionary identifies the data requirements. By thoroughly reviewing these deliverables, the programmer understands the nature of the requirements.

During this step, the programmer also meets with the systems analyst and the users. This enables the programmer to understand the purpose of the requirements from the users' perspective. Recall from Chapter 12 that a guideline of system development is to involve users throughout the entire system development cycle.

After design specifications are established, the programmer defines the input, processing, output (IPO), and data requirements for each program. Many programmers use an IPO chart to show the input, processing, and output components (Figure 13-24). An *IPO chart* identifies a program's inputs, its outputs, and the processing steps required to transform the inputs into the outputs. Programmers review the contents of the IPO chart with the systems analyst and

---

LOOKING AHEAD 13-2

Robotic Vehicles Move Forward

Your morning commute will take a new turn when robotic cars, trucks, and motorcycles drive themselves without any human guidance or intervention.

This technology is emerging, in part, from the Grand Challenge contest sponsored by the Pentagon's Defense Advanced Research Projects Agency

(DARPA). The winning team receives $2 million when their vehicle travels unassisted through 132 miles of the Mojave Desert's rugged terrain in less than 10 hours without human intervention.

When the first DARPA challenge was held in 2004, no vehicle finished the race. In 2005, however, five vehicles crossed the finish line, led by Stanford University's Volkswagen Touareg that completed the course in less than seven hours. For more information, visit scsite.com/dc2007/ch13/looking and then click Robotic Vehicles.

IPO CHART

Input	Processing	Output
Regular Time Hours Worked Overtime Hours Worked Hourly Pay Rate	Read regular time hours worked, overtime hours worked, hourly pay rate. Calculate regular time pay. If employee worked overtime, calculate overtime pay. Calculate gross pay. Print gross pay.	Gross Pay

FIGURE 13-24 An IPO (Input Process Output) chart is a tool that assists the programmer in analyzing a program.

the users. This allows programmers to be sure they completely understand the purpose of the program.

STEP 2 — DESIGN SOLUTION

The next step is to design the solution that will meet the users' requirements. Designing the solution involves devising a solution algorithm to satisfy the requirements. A *solution algorithm*, also called *program logic*, is a graphical or written description of the step-by-step procedures to solve the problem. Determining the logic for a program often is a programmer's most challenging task. It requires that the programmer understand programming concepts, as well as use creativity in problem solving.

Recall from Chapter 12 that a system can be designed using process modeling (structured analysis and design) or object modeling (object-oriented analysis and design). The approach used during the system development cycle determines the techniques a programmer uses in designing a solution.

Structured Design

In **structured design**, sometimes called *top-down design*, the programmer typically begins with a general design and moves toward a more detailed design. This approach breaks down the original set of requirements into smaller, more manageable sections.

The first step in top-down design is to identify the major function of a program, sometimes called the *main routine* or *main module*. Next, the programmer decomposes (breaks down) the main routine into smaller sections, called *subroutines or modules*. Then, the programmer analyzes each subroutine to determine if it can be decomposed further.

Programmers use a **hierarchy chart**, also called a *structure chart*, to show program modules graphically (Figure 13-25). A hierarchy chart contains rectangles and lines. The rectangles are the modules. The main module is at the top of the chart. All other modules are placed below the main module. Modules connect by lines to indicate their relationships. In Figure 13-25, for example, the Initialization, Process, and Wrap-Up modules are subordinate to the MAIN module.

Programs developed using structured design benefit from their simplicity, reliability, readability, and maintainability. Structured design, however, does not provide a way to keep the data and the program (or procedure) together. Each program has to define how it will use the data. This can result in redundant programming code that must change every time the structure of the data changes. To eliminate this problem, some IT professionals use the object-oriented approach for program development.

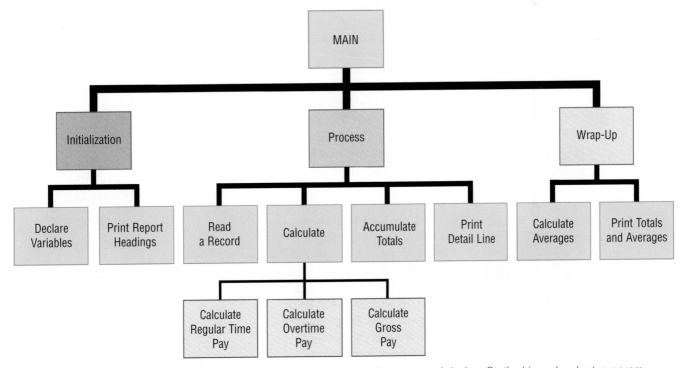

FIGURE 13-25 The hierarchy chart is a tool the programmer uses during structured design. On the hierarchy chart, program modules are drawn as rectangles. All modules are subordinate to the main module.

Object-Oriented Design

With **object-oriented (OO) design**, the programmer packages the data and the program (or procedure) into a single unit, an object. When the structure of an object changes, any program that accesses the object automatically accesses the change.

The concept of packaging data and procedures into a single object is called *encapsulation*. That is, an object encapsulates (hides) the details of the object. Think of an object as a box, and you cannot see inside the box. The box sends and receives messages. It also contains code and data. For example, when users want to print a document, they click the Print button (the object). They probably do not know how the Print button actually communicates with the hardware to print the document. Thus, the details of the print object are encapsulated (hidden) from the user. Programmers, however, need to know how the object works, so they can send messages to it and use it effectively.

As described in Chapter 12, objects are grouped into classes. To represent classes and their hierarchical relationships graphically, programmers use a class diagram. Figure 13-26 shows a high-level class diagram. In this diagram, a construction site needs many jobs performed, a job is completed by several workers, and each worker receives one paycheck for work performed. The 1 below the Construction Site class indicates that each Construction Site class must have at least one Job class associated with it. The 1..* above the Job class indicates that each Job class must be associated with at least one Construction Site class above it.

With the high-level class diagram complete, the programmer develops a detailed class diagram that provides a visual representation of each object, its attributes, and its methods. Then, the programmer translates the methods into program instructions.

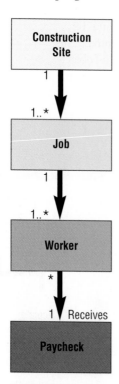

FIGURE 13-26
A class diagram is a hierarchical tool the programmer uses during object-oriented design.

Control Structures

Whether using structured design or object-oriented design, programmers typically use control structures to describe the tasks a program is to perform. A **control structure**, also known as a *construct*, depicts the logical order of program instructions. Three basic control structures are sequence, selection, and repetition.

SEQUENCE CONTROL STRUCTURE A *sequence control structure* shows one or more actions following each other in order (Figure 13-27). Actions include inputs, processes, and outputs. Examples of actions are reading a record, calculating averages or totals, and printing totals.

FIGURE 13-27 The sequence control structure shows one or more actions followed by another.

SELECTION CONTROL STRUCTURE   A *selection control structure* tells the program which action to take, based on a certain condition. Two common types of selection control structures are the if-then-else and the case.

When a program evaluates the condition in an *if-then-else control structure*, it yields one of two possibilities: true or false. Figure 13-28 shows the condition as a diamond symbol. If the result of the condition is true, then the program performs one action. If the result is false, the program performs a different (or possibly no) action. For example, the if-then-else control structure can determine if an employee should receive overtime pay. A possible condition might be the following: Is Overtime Hours greater than 0? If the response is yes (true), then the action would calculate overtime pay. If the response is no (false), then the action would set overtime pay equal to 0.

With the *case control structure*, a condition can yield one of three or more possibilities (Figure 13-29). The size of a beverage, for example, might be one of these options: small, medium, large, or extra large. A case control structure would determine the price of the beverage based on the size purchased.

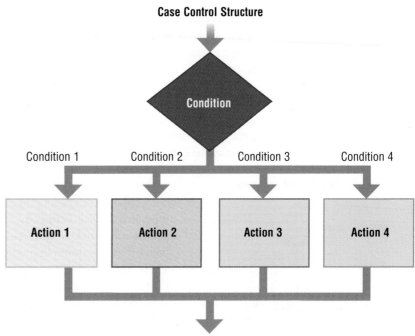

Case Control Structure

FIGURE 13-29   The case control structure allows for more than two alternatives when a condition is evaluated.

Repetition Control Structure   The *repetition control structure* enables a program to perform one or more actions repeatedly as long as a certain condition is met. Many programmers refer to this construct as a *loop*. Two forms of the repetition control structure are the do-while and do-until.

A *do-while control structure* repeats one or more times as long as a condition is true (Figure 13-30). This control structure tests a condition at the beginning of the loop. If the result of the condition is true, the program executes the action(s) inside the loop. Then, the program loops back and tests the condition again. If the result of the condition still is true, the program executes the action(s) inside the loop again. This looping process continues until the condition being tested becomes false. At that time, the program stops looping and moves to another set of actions.

The do-while control structure normally is used when occurrence of an event is not quantifiable or predictable. For example, programmers frequently use the do-while control structure to process all records in a file.

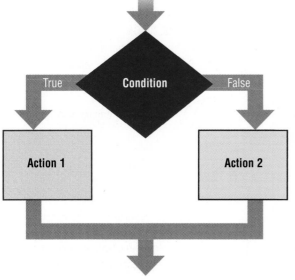

If-Then-Else Control Structure

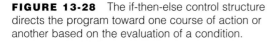

FIGURE 13-28   The if-then-else control structure directs the program toward one course of action or another based on the evaluation of a condition.

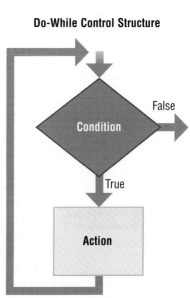

Do-While Control Structure

FIGURE 13-30   The do-while control structure tests the condition at the beginning of the loop. It exits the loop when the result of the condition is false.

A payroll program using a do-while control structure loops once for each employee. This program stops looping when it processes the last employee's record.

The *do-until control structure* is similar to the do-while but has two major differences: where it tests the condition and when it stops looping. First, the do-until control structure tests the condition at the end of the loop (Figure 13-31). The action(s) in a do-until control structure thus always will execute at least once. The loop in a do-while control structure, by contrast, might not execute at all. That is, if the condition immediately is false, the action or actions in the do-while loop never execute. Second, a do-until control structure continues looping until the condition is true — and then stops. This is different from the do-while control structure, which continues to loop while the condition is true.

Design Tools

To help document a solution algorithm, programmers use *design tools*. Two structured design tools are program flowcharts and pseudocode. A design tool for object-oriented design is the UML.

- A *program flowchart*, or simply **flowchart**, graphically shows the logic in a solution algorithm. The American National Standards Institute (ANSI) published a set of standards for program flowcharts in the early 1960s. These standards, still used today, specify symbols for various operations in a program's logic (Figure 13-32).

  Programmers connect most symbols on a program flowchart with solid lines. These lines show the direction of the program. Dotted lines on a flowchart connect comment symbols. A *comment symbol*, also called an *annotation symbol*, explains or clarifies logic in the solution algorithm. Figure 13-33 shows the program flowchart for three modules of the program shown in the hierarchy chart in Figure 13-25 on page 687.

  In the past, programmers used a template to trace the symbols for a flowchart on a piece of paper. Today, programmers use commercial **flowcharting software** to develop flowcharts. This software makes it easy to modify and update flowcharts. Two popular flowcharting programs are SmartDraw and Visio (Figure 13-34).

- *Pseudocode* uses a condensed form of English to convey program logic. Some programmers prefer to explain the logic of a solution algorithm with words (pseudocode), instead of a graphical flowcharting technique. Pseudocode also uses indentation to identify the control structures. The beginning and ending of the module start at the left margin.

Do-Until Control Structure

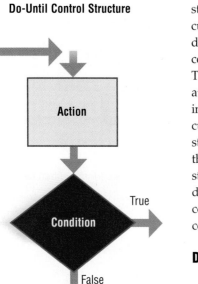

FIGURE 13-31   The do-until control structure tests the condition at the end of the loop. It exits the loop when the result of the condition is true.

WEB LINK 13-11

Flowcharting Software

For more information, visit scsite.com/dc2007/ch13/weblink and then click Flowcharting Software.

ANSI FLOWCHART SYMBOLS

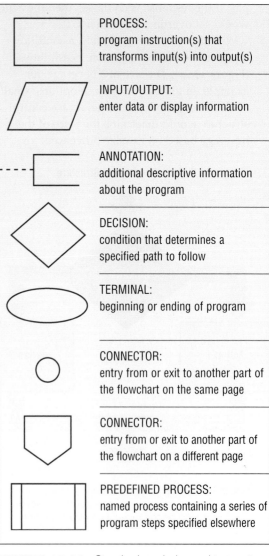

PROCESS:
program instruction(s) that transforms input(s) into output(s)

INPUT/OUTPUT:
enter data or display information

ANNOTATION:
additional descriptive information about the program

DECISION:
condition that determines a specified path to follow

TERMINAL:
beginning or ending of program

CONNECTOR:
entry from or exit to another part of the flowchart on the same page

CONNECTOR:
entry from or exit to another part of the flowchart on a different page

PREDEFINED PROCESS:
named process containing a series of program steps specified elsewhere

FIGURE 13-32   Standard symbols used to create program flowcharts.

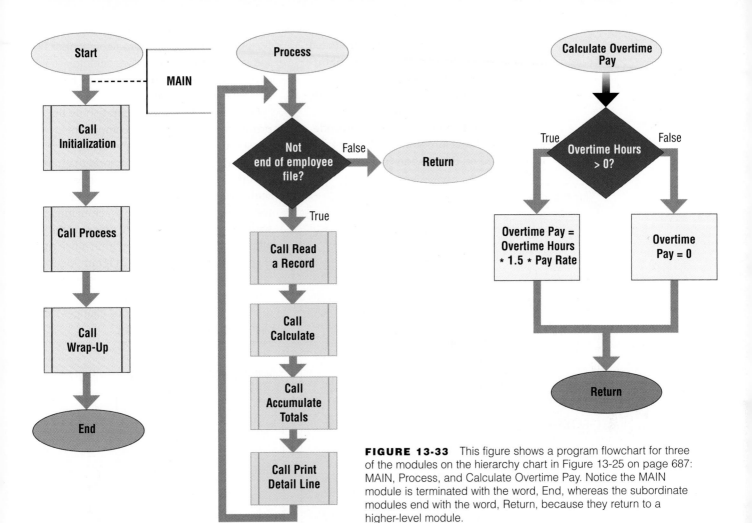

FIGURE 13-33 This figure shows a program flowchart for three of the modules on the hierarchy chart in Figure 13-25 on page 687: MAIN, Process, and Calculate Overtime Pay. Notice the MAIN module is terminated with the word, End, whereas the subordinate modules end with the word, Return, because they return to a higher-level module.

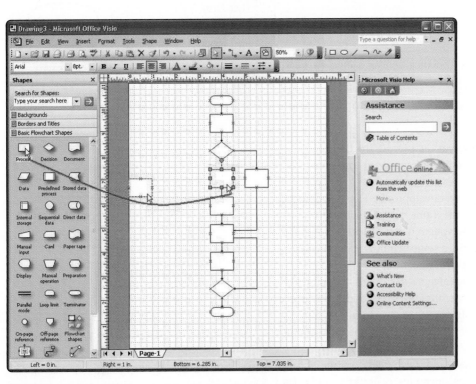

FIGURE 13-34 Visio is a popular flowcharting program.

The actions within the module are indented. The actions within a selection or repetition control structure are indented again. This allows the programmer to identify the beginning and ending of the control structure clearly. Figure 13-35 shows the pseudocode for the same three program modules as in Figure 13-33 on the previous page.

```
MAIN MODULE:

    CALL Initialization
    CALL Process
    CALL Wrap-Up

END

PROCESS MODULE:

    DO WHILE Not EOF
        CALL Read a Record
        CALL Calculate
        CALL Accumulate Totals
        CALL Print Detail Line
    ENDDO

RETURN

CALCULATE OVERTIME PAY MODULE:

    IF Overtime Hours > 0 THEN
        Overtime Pay = Overtime Hours * 1.5 * Pay Rate
    ELSE
        Overtime Pay = 0
    ENDIF

RETURN
```

FIGURE 13-35 Pseudocode is another alternative method of showing program logic. This figure shows the same three modules (MAIN, Process, and Calculate Overtime Pay) as illustrated in Figure 13-33 with program flowcharts.

- As discussed in Chapter 12, the UML (Unified Modeling Language) has been adopted as a standard notation for object modeling and development. These notations are used in diagrams that present various views of the system being developed. Figure 13-36 identifies some symbols used in each of these types of diagrams.

  Two basic categories of diagrams in the UML are structural diagrams and behavioral diagrams. Examples of structural diagrams include class diagrams, component diagrams, and deployment diagrams. A class diagram shows classes and their subclasses and relationships, attributes, operations, and roles.

A component diagram shows how the software components of a system interact. A deployment diagram illustrates how hardware components are connected.

Behavioral diagrams illustrate how the processes flow among the components, classes, users, and the system being designed. Examples of behavioral diagrams include use case diagrams, activity diagrams, sequence diagrams, and state diagrams. A use case diagram shows how actors interact with the system. An activity diagram shows all the activities that occur within a use case (Figure 13-37). A sequence diagram identifies all possible paths a message takes as it moves among the actors and objects. A state diagram identifies the various changes that occur to an object over time.

SOME SYMBOLS USED IN THE UML DIAGRAMS

Class	
Interface	
Actor	
Use Case	
Association	
Generalization	
Dependency	
Package	
Note	
State	
Activity	
Decision	

FIGURE 13-36 Symbols used to create diagrams in the UML.

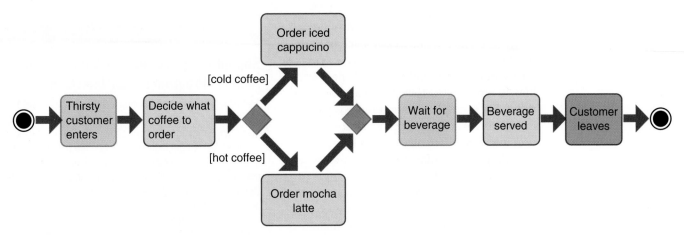

FIGURE 13-37   A UML activity diagram illustrating a Place Coffee Order use case.

STEP 3 — VALIDATE DESIGN

Once programmers develop the solution algorithm, they should *validate*, or check, the program design for accuracy. During this step, the programmer checks the logic for accuracy and attempts to uncover logic errors. A **logic error** is a flaw in the design that causes inaccurate results. Two techniques for reviewing a solution algorithm are a desk check and an inspection.

When programmers do a *desk check*, they use test data to step through its logic. **Test data** is sample data that mimics real data the program will process once it is in production. Users should assist in the development of test data. The programmer who developed the solution algorithm usually performs the desk check, but another programmer also can perform this task. Desk checking involves five steps.

1. Develop various sets of test data (inputs).
2. Determine the expected result (output) for each set of data, without using the solution algorithm.
3. Step through the solution algorithm using one set of test data and write down the actual result obtained (output) using the solution algorithm.
4. Compare the expected result from Step 2 to the actual result from Step 3.
5. Repeat Steps 3 and 4 for each set of test data.

If the expected result and actual result do not match for any set of data, the program has a logic error. When this occurs, the programmer must review the logic of the solution algorithm to determine the reason for the error and then correct it.

A more formal technique for checking the solution algorithm is an inspection. As discussed in Chapter 12, a systems analyst often uses an inspection to review deliverables during the system development cycle. Likewise, programmers use inspections to review solution algorithms during the program development cycle.

Usually, a programmer easily can correct errors or improvements identified at this point. After the programmer begins implementing the design, errors are more difficult to fix. Thus, detecting errors and making improvements early in the program development cycle reduces the overall time and cost of program development.

STEP 4 — IMPLEMENT DESIGN

Implementation of the design includes using a program development tool that assists the programmer by generating or providing some or all code, or includes writing the code that translates the design into a computer program and, if necessary, creating the user interface. **Coding** a program involves translating the solution algorithm into a programming language (usually on paper) and then typing the programming language code into the computer.

As previously mentioned, many different programming languages exist. Each of these has a particular syntax. A language's **syntax** is the set of grammar and rules that specifies how to write instructions for a solution algorithm. For example, a programmer writes an instruction to add three numbers or create a user interface differently in each language, according to its syntax. Read Ethics & Issues 13-3 for a related discussion.

As programmers enter code into a computer, they should document the code thoroughly so the programs can be maintained easily. Programs should include both global and internal documentation, called *comments* (Figure 13-38). *Global comments*, which usually are at the top of a program, explain the program's purpose and identify the program name, its author, and the date written. *Internal comments*, which appear throughout the body of the program, explain the purpose of the code statements within the program.

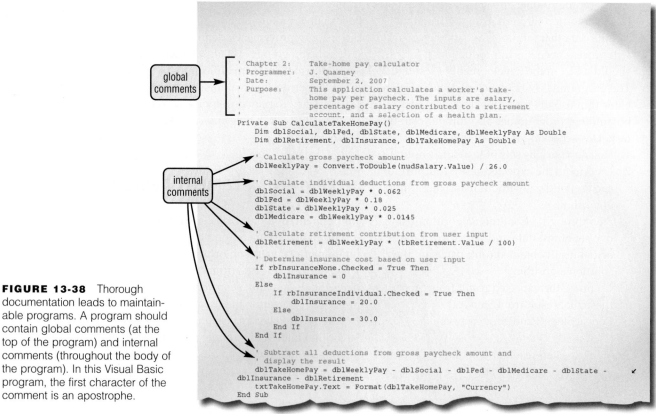

FIGURE 13-38 Thorough documentation leads to maintainable programs. A program should contain global comments (at the top of the program) and internal comments (throughout the body of the program). In this Visual Basic program, the first character of the comment is an apostrophe.

Extreme Programming

As an alternative to coding in this step of the program development cycle, some companies use extreme programming to develop programs. *Extreme programming* (*XP*) is a strategy that proposes that programmers should immediately begin coding and testing solutions as soon as requirements are defined. The code continually is tested and refined until it works. This strategy essentially eliminates the Design Solution and Validate Design steps of the traditional program development cycle. Extreme programming also suggests that programmers work in pairs, with each communicating code to the other and generating ideas for proper solutions. Proponents of extreme programming claim it reduces the time required for the program development cycle. Extreme programming most often is used in object-oriented design.

STEP 5 — TEST SOLUTION

Once a programmer codes and enters the program, the next step is to test it. Thorough testing is very important. After programmers place the program into production, many users rely on the program and its output to support their daily activities and decisions.

The goal of program testing is to ensure the program runs correctly and is error free. Errors uncovered during this step usually are one of two types: (1) syntax errors or (2) logic errors. A **syntax error** occurs when the code violates the syntax, or grammar, of the programming language. Misspelling a command, leaving out required punctuation, or typing command words out of order all will cause syntax errors. Programmers usually discover syntax errors the first time they attempt to compile or interpret the program code on the computer. When a syntax error is located, a message either is displayed on the screen immediately or is written to a log file. Either way, the programmer must review and correct all syntax errors. The procedure for testing for logic errors at this step is much like the desk checking techniques used in the Validate Design step.

Another purpose of using test data is to try to cause a **run-time error**, which is an error that occurs while the program is running. If the pay rate for employees cannot exceed $55.00 per hour, then the test data should use some valid pay rates, such as $25.00 and $10.50, as well as some invalid ones, such as $-32.00 and $72.50. When entering an invalid pay rate, the program should display an error message and allow the user to reenter the pay rate. If the program accepts an invalid pay rate, then it contains a logic error. In addition, the program should handle data exception errors such as division by zero.

The process of locating and correcting syntax and logic errors in a program is known as **debugging** the program. The program errors themselves are the **bugs**. Thus, removing the errors is de*bug*ging. The term bug originated when the failure of one of the first computers supposedly was traced to an actual bug. A moth lodged in the computer's electronic components was the cause of the failure (Figure 13-39).

WEB LINK 13-12

Extreme Programming

For more information, visit scsite.com/ dc2007/ch13/weblink and then click Extreme Programming.

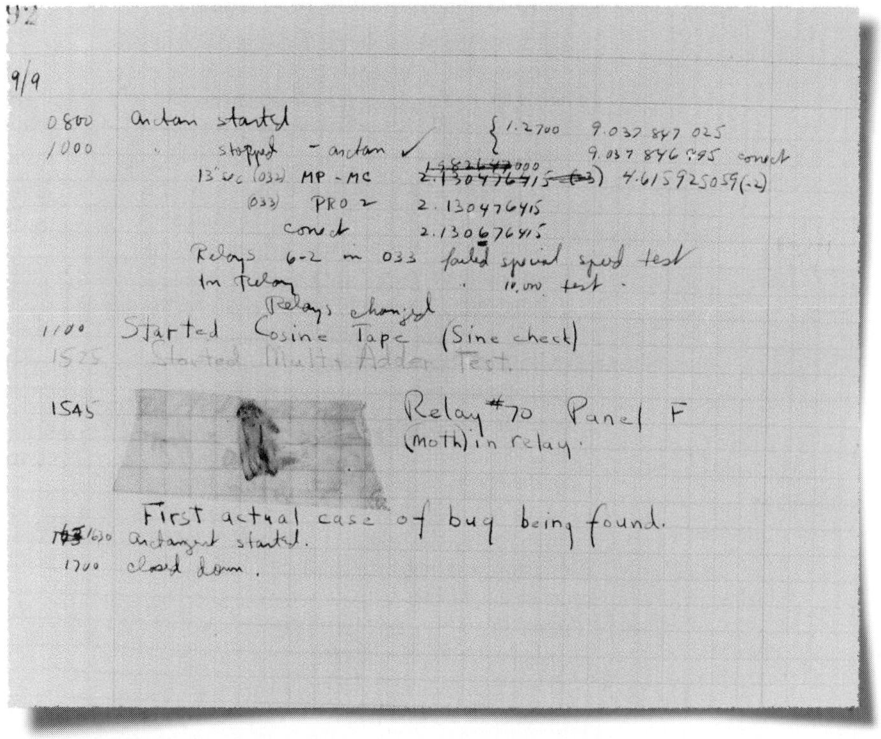

FIGURE 13-39 The temporary failure of one of the first computers was traced to a dead moth (shown taped to the log book) caught in the electrical components. Some say this event is the origin of the term bug, which means computer error.

Most programming languages include a debug utility. A *debug utility*, or *debugger*, assists programmers with identifying syntax errors and finding logic errors. With a debugger, a programmer examines program values (such as the result of a calculation) while the program runs in slow motion. Read Ethics & Issues 13-4 for a related discussion.

Some software companies distribute a beta of their software to users. A **beta** is a program that has most or all of its features and functionality implemented. Users test the beta program and send in bug reports to the software company. This enables the software manufacturer to fix any errors before the software is released to the public for sale.

If a programmer designs a program properly during the Design Solution step, then testing in this step should not require much time. As a general rule, the more time and effort programmers spend analyzing and designing the solution algorithm, the less time they spend debugging the program.

ETHICS & ISSUES 13-4

Who Is Responsible for Bugs?

The consequences of bugs, or errors, in computer programs can be staggering. An error in the code controlling a Canadian nuclear facility caused more than 3,000 gallons of radioactive water to be spilled. A bug in long-distance switching software cost AT&T more than $60 million. Users have been frustrated for years by flaws in some versions of the Windows operating system that locked up their computers and displayed the dreaded "Blue Screen of Death." Experts estimate that there are 20 to 30 bugs per 1,000 lines of code. Given that many programs contain hundreds of thousands, even millions, of code lines, bugs are not surprising. Most software licenses absolve the software creator of any responsibility for the end user getting the wrong information from a bug-riddled program. Who should be responsible for mistakes in software? Why? If users provide incomplete or inaccurate specifications, should they be held accountable for the resulting deficiencies? Why? Should those who design a system or write programs for a system be legally responsible if their product results in errors or damages? Why?

FAQ 13-8

How do I become a beta tester?

Sometimes, companies contact current users to see if they are interested in being a beta tester. Other times, you submit a beta tester application to the software company. Beta testers obtain the beta software at no cost and generally receive no compensation. For more information, visit scsite.com/dc2007/ch13/faq and then click Beta Testers.

STEP 6 — DOCUMENT SOLUTION

In documenting the solution, the programmer performs two activities: (1) review the program code and (2) review all the documentation.

First, programmers review the program for any dead code and remove it. *Dead code* is any program instructions that a program never executes. When programmers write a program, they often write a section of code at a time. Sometimes, they decide not to use the code, but leave it in the program anyway. This dead (unused) code serves no purpose and should not exist.

Next, programmers should run the program one final time to verify it still works. After reviewing the program code, the programmer gives the program and all of its documentation to the systems analyst. The documentation includes all charts, solution algorithms, test data, and program code listings that contain global and internal comments.

The programmer should be sure all documentation is complete and accurate. This becomes especially valuable if the program requires changes in the future. Proper documentation greatly reduces the amount of time a new programmer spends learning about existing programs.

Test your knowledge of pages 685 through 696 in Quiz Yourself 13-3.

QUIZ YOURSELF 13-3

Instructions: Find the true statement below. Then, rewrite the remaining false statements so they are true.

1. A language's logic is the set of grammar and rules that specifies how to write instructions for a solution algorithm.

2. An error in a program is known as a beta.

3. In structured design, the programmer typically begins with a detailed design and moves toward a more general design.

4. The concept of packaging data and procedures into a single object is called casing.

5. The program development cycle consists of these six steps: analyze requirements, design solution, validate design, implement design, test solution, and hardcode solution.

6. Three basic control structures are sequence, selection, and pseudocode.

7. Two basic categories of diagrams in the UML are structural diagrams and behavioral diagrams.

Quiz Yourself Online: To further check your knowledge of the program development cycle, structured versus object-oriented design, and basic control structures and design tools, visit scsite.com/dc2007/ch13/quiz and then click Objectives 7 – 9.

CHAPTER SUMMARY

This chapter discussed various programming languages used to write and develop computer programs. It also presented a variety of Web development and multimedia development tools. Finally, the chapter described each step in the program development cycle and presented the tools used to make this process efficient.

CAREER CORNER

Programmer

If you are the curious, creative type, enjoy solving puzzles, and gain satisfaction in making things work, you may want to consider a career in programming. A programmer designs, writes, and tests the code that tells computers what to do. Most programmers specialize in one of three fields: system programming, application programming, or Web development programming.

Some jobs may require that the programmer develop an entire program, while other jobs require program maintenance. Likewise, programmers can work for a small company in which they are responsible for the entire system development cycle, or for a larger company in which they are part of a team and individual duties are specialized. Projects can range from computer games to essential business applications. Programmers enjoy the achievements of working with computers to accomplish objectives as well as developing efficient instructions that tell computers how to perform specific tasks.

Academic credentials are essential for success in this career. A bachelor's degree in Computer Science or Information Technology usually is required. The key to success is familiarity with programming languages and a good foundation in programming logic. Surveys indicate that average salaries for entry level programmers are about $50,000 and can exceed $100,000 for senior programmers. For more information, visit scsite.com/dc2007/ch13/careers and then click Programmer.

High-Tech Talk

STRUCTURING DATA FOR THE WEB USING XML

Imagine that your marine supply company provides vendor information to clients around the world. Your clients must access the information not only from their notebook computers, but also on their wireless PDAs and smart phones. You use the same database for direct mailings to vendors.

As discussed in this chapter, XML (eXtensible Markup Language) is a format for structuring data that allows Web programmers to create one version of a Web page that then can be displayed in a form appropriate for the display device. Using HTML, a programmer must create three separate Web sites, with special coding for each device — HTML for the notebook computer, WML for the smart phone, and Web clipping (small pieces of information) for a PDA. With XML, a programmer can create just one version of the Web site and the content can be formatted to display appropriately on various devices.

How does XML differ from HTML? HTML was designed to display data and to focus on how data looks. XML, by contrast, was designed to describe data and to focus on what data is. The XML specification describes how to organize structured data into documents.

As with HTML, XML uses tags to mark various parts of a document. XML, however, uses tags to describe the structure of the data, not the display. The XML document shown in Figure 13-40, for example, uses tags to structure a list of vendors. Tags are set in pairs, with a start tag (<city>) and an end tag (</city>). A pair of tags, along with all of the text and other tags they enclose, is called an *element*. The XML document in Figure 13-40 contains eight different elements, including a <vendor> element that encloses the tags and data for each vendor and a <vendorlist> element that encloses all tags and data and constitutes the entire document.

In this example, the XML elements are nested to structure the vendor address data. Different XML documents can use different element names in different hierarchical arrangements. Although in principle every XML document can have a unique structure, XML supports the notion of a *DTD* (*document type definition*), a document that specifies a particular arrangement of elements that should be used within an XML document. For example, a DTD might specify that a vendor database consists of a vendor list element containing one or more vendor elements, and that each vendor element contains a name, address, city, state, Zip code, and Web address, in exactly that order. Using a DTD ensures that XML documents adhere to some basic guidelines for structure, to make it easier to share data with other organizations using the same DTD.

After the XML document is structured, you can apply different styles to the content so that it is usable in various formats. Remember that the XML document describes only the content, not the display or rendering of that content. By applying a different style sheet to the same document, an XML document can be rendered in different formats.

XML works with *XSL* (*Extensible Stylesheet Language*), a language for creating a style sheet that describes how to present the data described in the XML document in a Web page. For example, using XSL, you could tell a Web browser to display any data in the element <name> as left-aligned bold text.

XSLT (*Extensible Stylesheet Language Transformations*) is an extension of XSL, which is used to create stylesheets that describe how to transform XML documents into other types of documents. When a device requests a page from a Web site built with XML, a CGI script can detect what device has requested the page from the server. The server then uses the format described in the XSLT document to transform the XML into the proper format — whether a WML document for a smart phone microbrowser, a Web clipping document for a PDA, an HTML Web page for a browser on a client's notebook computer, or mailing label data for a mailing label program. For more information, visit scsite.com/dc2007/ch13/tech and then click XML.

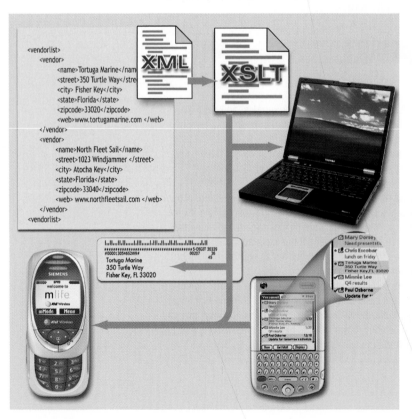

FIGURE 13-40   A sample XML document converted by an XLST document for display on various devices.

Companies on the Cutting Edge

ELECTRONIC ARTS
ENTERTAINMENT SOFTWARE DEVELOPER

Harry Potter, James Bond, John Madden, and The Sims have been found in millions of homes worldwide thanks to Electronic Arts (EA), the world's leading independent developer and publisher of interactive entertainment software. EA's yearly revenues exceed $3 billion from its games for the PlayStation, Xbox, GameCube, and Game Boy systems.

Since the company's beginnings in 1982, EA's software has had a strong market presence in video game systems, personal computers, the Internet, and cellular phones. The more popular titles are Madden NFL Football, the Need for Speed, NBA Live, and The Sims. More than 6,000 employees work at EA's studios in the United States, Canada, the United Kingdom, and Japan. In 2005, Steven Spielberg agreed to collaborate with EA to develop three original games. For more information, visit scsite.com/dc2007/ch13/companies and then click Electronic Arts.

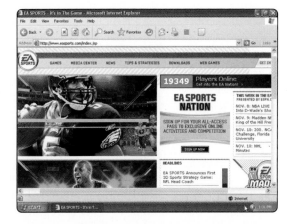

SUN MICROSYSTEMS
PRODUCTS AND SERVICES PROVIDER

More than 2.5 million programmers are hard at work developing the next generation of Java applications for *Sun Microsystems*, the creator and leading advocate of Java technology.

Since its incorporation in 1982, Sun has grown to become an industry leader of hardware, software, and services. Guided by its vision, Everyone and everything connected to the network, its major business is selling powerful networked computers. In 2005, Sun and Google entered into a multiyear agreement to develop and distribute each other's software. From controlling the Mars Rover to powering desktop productivity tools that help students stay on schedule, Java powers more than 1.75 billion devices worldwide.

Sun products are found in more than 100 countries in virtually every field, including telecommunications, retail, manufacturing, and health care. For more information, visit scsite.com/dc2007/ch13/companies and then click Sun.

Technology Trailblazers

GRACE HOPPER
COBOL DEVELOPER

Women's participation in the computer programming world was shaped by the achievements of *Grace Hopper*. She was one of the first software engineers, and in 1953 she perfected her best-known invention: the compiler.

After earning her Ph.D. degree from Yale University, she began teaching mathematics at Vassar College. She resigned that position in 1943 to join the Navy WAVES (Women Accepted for Voluntary Emergency Service). Her work developing compilers ultimately led to the creation of the COBOL programming language.

Although her achievements are the foundation of today's computers, she said during her lifetime that she was most proud of her service to her country. She was buried with full naval honors at Arlington National Cemetery. For more information, visit scsite.com/dc2007/ch13/people and then click Grace Hopper.

JAMES GOSLING
JAVA ENGINEER AND ARCHITECT

Known as the "father of Java," *James Gosling* serves as Sun Microsystems Developer Products group's chief technology officer. He is the mastermind behind Java, the network programming language running across all platforms, from servers to cellular telephones.

Gosling grew up near Calgary, Alberta, and spent much of his spare time turning spare machine parts into games. At the age of 15, he wrote software for the University of Calgary's physics department. When he was hired at Sun Microsystems, he built a multiprocessor version of UNIX, developed compilers to convert program code into machine language, engineered a window manager, and wrote a UNIX text editor.

At Sun today, he works with his research team to develop semantic modeling software that helps developers analyze an application's structure. For more information, visit scsite.com/dc2007/ch13/people and then click James Gosling.

Chapter Review

The Chapter Review section summarizes the concepts presented in this chapter. To listen to the audio version of this Chapter Review, visit scsite.com/dc2007/ch13/review. To obtain help from other students regarding any subject in this chapter, visit scsite.com/dc2007/ch13/forum and post your thoughts or questions.

(1) How Are Machine Languages Different from Assembly Languages? A **computer program** is a series of instructions that directs a computer to perform tasks. A **programming language** is a set of words, symbols, and codes that enables a **programmer** to communicate instructions to a computer. Two low-level programming languages are machine language and assembly language. A **machine language** uses a series of binary digits, or combinations of numbers and letters that represent binary digits, and is the only language a computer directly recognizes. With an **assembly language**, a programmer writes instructions using *symbolic instruction codes*, which are meaningful abbreviations.

(2) What Is the Purpose of Procedural Programming Languages? In a **procedural language**, or **third-generation language** (3GL), a programmer writes instructions that tell a computer what to accomplish and how to do it. Programmers use English-like words to write instructions, which simplifies the program development process. A *compiler* or an *interpreter* translates the 3GL **source program** into machine language *object code* that a computer can execute. Standard procedural languages include **COBOL** (a language designed for business applications) and **C** (a powerful language that requires professional programming skills).

(3) What Are the Characteristics of Object-Oriented Programming Languages and Program Development Tools? Programmers use an **object-oriented programming** (OOP) **language** or object-oriented program development tool to implement object-oriented design. A program that provides a user-friendly environment for building programs often is called a *program development tool*. An *object* is an item that can contain both data and the procedures that read or manipulate the data. A major benefit of OOP is the ability to reuse and modify existing objects, allowing programmers to create applications faster. Often used in conjunction with OOP, **RAD** (*rapid application development*) is a method of developing software, in which a programmer writes and implements a program in segments instead of waiting until the entire program is completed. OOP languages include Java, C++, and C#. **Java** uses a *just-in-time* (JIT) *compiler* to convert *bytecode* into machine-dependent code. **C++** is an object-oriented extension of the C programming language. **C#** is based on C++ and has been accepted as a standard for Web applications and XML-based Web services. Programming languages available in Microsoft's latest suite of program development tools include **Visual Basic 2005**, **Visual C++ 2005**, **Visual C# 2005**, and **Visual J# 2005**. A **visual programming language** uses a visual or graphical interface, called a *visual programming environment* (VPE), for creating all source code.

 connect

Visit scsite.com/dc2007/ch13/quiz or click the Quiz Yourself button. Click Objectives 1 – 3.

(4) What Are the Uses of Other Programming Languages and Other Program Development Tools? **RPG** (*Report Program Generator*) is a language that helps businesses generate reports. A **4GL** (*fourth-generation language*) is a **nonprocedural language** that enables users to access data in a database. A popular 4GL is **SQL**, a query language for relational databases. An **application generator** creates source code or machine code from a specification of the required functionality. A **macro** is a series of statements that instructs an application how to complete a task.

(5) What Are Web Page Program Development Techniques such as HTML, Scripting Languages, DHTML, XML, WML, and Web Page Authoring Software? *Web page authors* use a variety of techniques to design and develop Web pages. **HTML** (*Hypertext Markup Language*) is a special formatting language that programmers use to format documents for display on the Web.

Chapter Review

A *scripting language* is an easy-to-use, interpreted language that programmers use to add dynamic content and interactive elements to Web pages. **Dynamic HTML (DHTML)** is a newer type of HTML that allows developers to include more graphical interest and interactivity in a Web page. **XML** (*eXtensible Markup Language*) is a popular format for sharing data that allows Web page developers to create customized tags, as well as predefined tags. **RSS 2.0** is a specification that content aggregators use to distribute content to subscribers. **WML** is a subset of XML used to design Web pages for microbrowsers. **Ajax** is a method of creating interactive Web applications designed to provide immediate response to user requests. Developers use **Web page authoring software** to create sophisticated Web pages that include graphical images, video, audio, animation, and other special effects.

macromedia
FLASH
REMOTING MX

(6) How Are Popular Multimedia Authoring Programs Used? Multimedia authoring **software** allows developers to combine text, graphics, animation, audio, and video into an interactive presentation. Popular authoring software includes ToolBook, Authorware, and Director MX. **ToolBook** has a graphical user interface and uses an object-oriented approach. **Authorware** provides the tools developers need to build interactive multimedia training and educational programs. **Director MX** has powerful features that allow developers to create highly interactive multimedia applications.

connect
Visit scsite.com/dc2007/ch13/quiz or click the Quiz Yourself button. Click Objectives 4 – 6.

(7) What Are the Six Steps in the Program Development Cycle? The **program development cycle** is a series of steps programmers use to build computer programs. The program development cycle consists of six steps: (1) analyze requirements, (2) design solution, (3) validate design, (4) implement design, (5) test solution, and (6) document solution.

(8) How Is Structured Design Different from Object-Oriented Design? In **structured design**, a programmer typically begins with a general design and moves toward a more detailed design. A programmer starts with the program's major function, called the *main routine*, and breaks it down into smaller sections, called *subroutines*. Structured design results in programs that are reliable and easy to read and maintain, but it does not provide a way to keep the data and the program together and can result in redundant programming code. With **object-oriented (OO) design**, the programmer packages the data and the program (or procedure) into a single unit, an object. Objects are grouped into classes. A detailed class diagram represents each object, its attributes (data), and its methods (procedures). The programmer translates the methods into program instructions.

(9) What Are the Basic Control Structures and Design Tools Used in Designing Solutions to Programming Problems? A **control structure** depicts the logical order of program instructions. A *sequence control structure* shows one or more actions following each other. A *selection control structure* tells the program which action to take, based on a certain condition. Two types of selection control structures are the *if-then-else control structure*, which yields one of two possibilities (true or false), and the *case control structure*, which can yield one of three or more possibilities. The *repetition control structure* enables a program to perform one or more actions repeatedly as long as a certain condition is met. Two forms of the repetition control structure are the *do-while control structure*, which tests a condition at the beginning of the loop and continues looping as long as a condition is true, and the *do-until control structure*, which tests a condition at the end of the loop and continues looping until the condition is true. Some *design tools* include a *program flowchart*, or simply **flowchart**; *pseudocode*; and the UML.

connect
Visit scsite.com/dc2007/ch13/quiz or click the Quiz Yourself button. Click Objectives 7 – 9.

Key Terms

You should know the Primary Terms and be familiar with the Secondary Terms. Use the list below to help focus your study. To further enhance your understanding of the Key Terms in this chapter, visit scsite.com/dc2007/ch13/terms. See an example of and a definition for each term, and access current and additional information about the term from the Web.

Primary Terms

(shown in bold-black characters in the chapter)

4GL (674)
ActiveX (679)
ActiveX control (679)
Ada (675)
Ajax (683)
ALGOL (675)
APL (675)
applet (679)
application generator (676)
assembly language (666)
Authorware (684)
BASIC (675)
beta (696)
bugs (695)
C (668)
C# (670)
C++ (670)
COBOL (668)
coding (693)
computer program (664)
control structure (688)
counter (679)
debugging (695)
Delphi (672)
Director MX (684)
Dreamweaver MX (683)
dynamic HTML (DHTML) (682)
Flash MX (683)
flowchart (690)
flowcharting software (690)
Forth (675)
Fortran (675)
FrontPage (683)
hierarchy chart (687)
HTML (678)
HyperTalk (675)
image map (679)
implementation (693)
Java (669)
JavaScript (681)
LISP (675)
logic error (693)
Logo (675)
machine language (665)
macro (application program) (676)
maintaining (685)
Modula-2 (675)
multimedia authoring software (684)

nonprocedural language (674)
object-oriented (OO) design (688)
object-oriented programming (OOP) language (669)
Pascal (675)
Perl (681)
PILOT (675)
PL/1 (675))
PowerBuilder (673)
procedural language (666)
processing form (679)
program development cycle (685)
programmer (664)
programming language (664)
programming team (686)
Prolog (675)
RAD (669)
Rexx (681)
RPG (674)
RSS 2.0 (683)
run-time error (695)
script (679)
servlet (679)
Smalltalk (675)
source program (666)
SQL (674)
structured design (687)
syntax (694)
syntax error (695)
Tcl (681)
test data (693)
third-generation language (3GL) (666)
ToolBook (684)
VBScript (681)
Visual Basic 2005 (671)
Visual C++ 2005 (672)
Visual C# 2005 (672)
Visual J# 2005 (672)
visual programming language (673)
Visual Studio 2005 (670)
Web page authoring software (683)
WML (683)
XHTML (682)
XML (682)

Secondary Terms

(shown in italic characters in the chapter)

algorithm (668)
annotation symbol (690)
assembler (666)
bytecode (669)
cascading style sheets (CSS) (682)
case control structure (689)
CGI (common gateway interface) (679)
CGI script (679)
code (664)
code snippets (670)
comment symbol (690)
comments (694)
COmmon Business-Oriented Language (668)
compiler (666)
construct (688)
dead code (696)
debug utility (696)
debugger (696)
design tools (690)
desk check (693)
developer (664)
document object model (DOM) (682)
do-until control structure (690)
do-while control structure (689)
encapsulation (688)
event (669)
event-driven program (669)
execute (666)
Extensible HTML (682)
eXtensible Markup Language (682)
extreme programming (XP) (695)
form (676)
fourth-generation language (674)
global comments (694)
high-level language (665)
Hypertext Markup Language (678)
if-then-else control structure (689)
internal comments (694)
interpreter (667)
IPO chart (686)
J2EE (Java 2 Platform, Enterprise Edition) (669)
just-in-time (JIT) compiler (669)
loop (689)
low-level language (664)
machine-dependent language (665)

machine-independent language (665)
macro (assembly language) (666)
macro recorder (676)
main module (687)
main routine (687)
menu generator (676)
Micro Focus (668)
Microsoft Intermediate Language (670)
modules (687)
mouse rollover (681)
mouseover (681)
.NET (670)
object (669)
object code (667)
object program (667)
open language (681)
Practical Extraction and Report Language (681)
program development tool (669)
program flowchart (690)
program logic (687)
pseudocode (690)
rapid application development (669)
Really Simple Syndication (683)
repetition control structure (689)
Report Program Generator (674)
report writer (676)
REstructured eXtended eXecutor (681)
scripting language (680)
selection control structure (689)
sequence control structure (688)
solution algorithm (687)
structure chart (687)
style sheet (682)
subroutines (687)
symbolic address (666)
symbolic instruction codes (666)
tags (678)
Tool Command Language (681)
top-down design (687)
validate (693)
Visual Basic for Applications (VBA) (676)
Visual Basic, Scripting Edition (681)
visual programming environment (VPE) (673)
Web page authors (678)
wireless markup language (683)

Checkpoint

Use the Checkpoint exercises to check your knowledge level of the chapter. The Beyond the Book exercises will help broaden your understanding of the concepts presented in this chapter. To complete the Checkpoint exercises interactively, visit scsite.com/dc2007/ch13/check.

Label the Figure

Identify the steps in the program development cycle.

a. document solution
b. test solution
c. analyze requirements
d. implement design
e. design solution
f. validate design

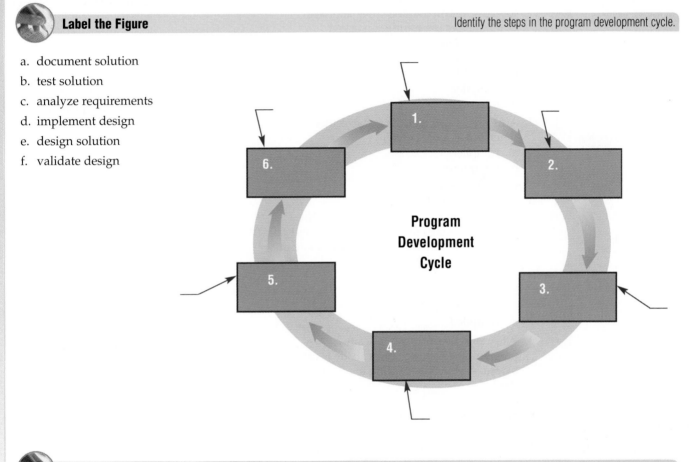

True/False

Mark T for True and F for False. (See page numbers in parentheses.)

_____ 1. Just as humans speak a variety of languages, programmers use a variety of programming languages and tools to write, or code, a program. (664)

_____ 2. Programmers must convert an assembly language program into machine language before the computer can execute, or run, the program. (666)

_____ 3. A compiler is a separate program that converts the entire source program into a high-level language before executing it. (666)

_____ 4. A disadvantage of OOP is the inability to reuse and modify existing objects. (669)

_____ 5. With RAD, users begin working with sections of programs as they are completed. (669)

_____ 6. A Web page is a file that contains both text and HTML tags. (678)

_____ 7. A script is an interpreted program that runs on your computer instead of running on a Web server. (679)

_____ 8. RSS 2.0 is a specification that content aggregators use to distribute content to subscribers. (683)

_____ 9. Programmers use a sequence control structure to show program modules graphically. (687)

_____ 10. A sequence control structure tells the program which action to take, based on a certain condition. (689)

Checkpoint

Multiple Choice Select the best answer. (See page numbers in parentheses.)

1. To convert an assembly language source program into machine language, programmers use a program called a(n) _____. (666)
   a. debugger
   b. assembler
   c. compiler
   d. interpreter

2. A(n) _____ translates and executes one statement at a time. (667)
   a. compiler
   b. interpreter
   c. source program
   d. symbolic address

3. An OOP language is _____, which means an OOP language program checks for and responds to events such as pressing a key or typing a value. (669)
   a. event based
   b. interpreted
   c. event driven
   d. compiled

4. When programmers compile a(n) _____ program, the resulting object code is called bytecode, which is machine independent. (669)
   a. C
   b. assembly language
   c. Java
   d. all of the above

5. _____ is a programming language that allows Java program development in the .NET environment. (672)
   a. Visual C# 2005
   b. Visual C++ 2005
   c. Visual J# 2005
   d. Visual Basic 2005

6. _____ is a popular fourth-generation query language that allows users to manage, update, and retrieve data in a relational DBMS. (674)
   a. RPG   b. COBOL
   c. XML   d. SQL

7. _____ is not actually a programming language, but it has specific rules for defining the placement and format of text, graphics, and video on a Web page. (678)
   a. VBA (Visual Basic for Applications)
   b. HTML (Hypertext Markup Language)
   c. RPG (Report Program Generator)
   d. C

8. Examples of _____ are <B> to bold text and <P> to indicate a new paragraph. (678)
   a. bugs
   b. macros
   c. tags
   d. objects

9. _____ is a newer type of HTML that allows Web page authors to include more graphical interest and interactivity in a Web page, without the Web page accessing the Web server. (682)
   a. XML
   b. DHTML
   c. XHTML
   d. A style sheet

10. Instead of refreshing entire Web pages, _____ works with the Web browser to update only changes to the Web page. (683)
    a. Ajax
    b. Director MX
    c. XHTML
    d. none of the above

11. Many programmers use a(n) _____ to identify a program's inputs, its outputs, and the processing steps required to transform the inputs into the outputs. (686)
    a. IPO chart
    b. case diagram
    c. program flowchart
    d. hierarchy chart

12. The concept of packaging data and procedures into a single object is called _____. (688).
    a. encapsulation
    b. object code
    c. an object program
    d. a control structure

13. A _____ control structure tells a program what action to take, based on a certain condition. (689)
    a. repetition
    b. sequence
    c. loop
    d. selection

14. When programmers review program code, they remove any _____, which is any program instructions that a program never executes. (696)
    a. dead code
    b. test code
    c. object code
    d. source code

Checkpoint

Matching

Match the terms with their definitions. (See page numbers in parentheses.)

_____ 1. C (668)

_____ 2. Java (669)

_____ 3. C++ (670)

_____ 4. C# (670)

_____ 5. PowerBuilder (673)

_____ 6. 4GL (674)

_____ 7. application generator (676)

_____ 8. image map (679)

_____ 9. Perl (681)

_____ 10. XHTML (682)

a. program that creates source code or machine code from a specification of the required functionality

b. object-oriented language that uses a just-in-time compiler

c. program development RAD tool best suited for Web-based enterprises

d. simple, interactive, problem-solving procedural language

e. programming language, developed in the early 1970s for writing system software

f. graphical image that points to a Web address

g. object-oriented language based on C++

h. once a procedural language, but the latest release is an interpreted scripting language

i. nonprocedural language that enables users and programmers to access data in a database

j. visual programming language used for object-based programs

k. markup language that enables Web sites to be displayed more easily on microbrowsers

l. object-oriented extension of the C programming language

Short Answer

Write a brief answer to each of the following questions.

1. How is a compiler different from an interpreter? _____ What is the advantage, and disadvantage, of an interpreter? _____

2. What is one major advantage of OOP? _____ In relation to OOP, what are some examples of events? _____

3. What is a script, an applet, a servlet, and an ActiveX control? _____ Why are they used? _____

4. What are program flowcharts and pseudocode? _____ How is a desk check different from an inspection? _____

5. How is a logic error different from a syntax error? _____ When is dead code dealt with and why? _____

Beyond the Book

Read the following book elements, learn more about each using the Web, and then write a brief report.

1. Ethics & Issues — Should All Students Be Required to Learn Computer Programming? (677), Should a Web Page Author Know HTML? (683), Should Programmers Be Able to Copy Another Program's User Interface? (694), or Who Is Responsible for Bugs? (696)

2. Career Corner — Programmer (697)

3. Companies on the Cutting Edge — Electronic Arts or Sun Microsystems (699)

4. FAQs (672, 675, 677, 679, 683, 688, 696)

5. High-Tech Talk — Structuring Data for the Web Using XML (698)

6. Looking Ahead — The Future of Programming Languages (675) or Robotic Vehicles Move Forward (686)

7. Making Use of the Web — Research (129)

8. Picture Yourself Learning How to Program (662)

9. Technology Trailblazers — Grace Hopper or James Gosling (699)

10. Web Links (668, 669, 670, 671, 677, 678, 682, 683, 688, 690, 695)

Learn It Online

Use the Learn It Online exercises to reinforce your understanding of the chapter concepts. To access the Learn It Online exercises, visit scsite.com/dc2007/ch13/learn.

① At the Movies — VeriChip

To view the VeriChip movie, click the number 1 button. Locate your video and click the corresponding High-Speed or Dial-Up link, depending on your Internet connection. Watch the movie and then complete the exercise by answering the question that follows. In December of 2001, Applied Digital Solutions introduced the VeriChip, which is similar to a MedicAlert bracelet. The chip is implanted under the skin instead of being worn externally. It is digitally inscribed with a number that, when read with a special scanner and entered into a database, will give doctors access to medical records. The company says the chip could be a lifesaver for people with illnesses that may inhibit their ability to communicate with doctors or life-squad personnel. It also could help locate Alzheimer's patients who have wandered away from home. Privacy rights experts say the chip could be used as a means of tracking people remotely who are unaware they have been implanted with the chip. What do you feel are the pros and cons of making this technology widely available?

② At the Movies — Inoculate Your E-mail

To view the Inoculate Your E-mail movie, click the number 2 button. Locate your video and click the corresponding High-Speed or Dial-Up link, depending on your Internet connection. Watch the movie and then complete the exercise by answering the questions that follow. It used to be enough just to ignore e-mail attachments from people you did not know. An exe attachment raised a red flag, and you knew not to open it. Now, just opening your e-mail exposes your computer to new kinds of attacks, and viruses such as BubbleBoy and KakWorm have changed the safety of e-mail forever. In addition to viruses, spammers have begun to use Web bugs hidden in the HTML that can track anyone who opens their e-mail. What is the function of a Web bug? What steps can you take to protect your computer from viruses and bugs, yet still receive HTML e-mail from people you trust?

③ Student Edition Labs — Visual Programming

Click the number 3 button. A new browser window will open, displaying the Student Edition Labs. Follow the on-screen instructions to complete the Visual Programming Lab. When finished, click the Exit button. If required, submit your results to your instructor.

④ Student Edition Labs — Creating Web Pages

Click the number 4 button. A new browser window will open, displaying the Student Edition Labs. Follow the on-screen instructions to complete the Creating Web Pages Lab. When finished, click the Exit button. If required, submit your results to your instructor.

⑤ Practice Test

Click the number 5 button. Answer each question. When completed, enter your name and click the Grade Test button to submit the quiz for grading. Make a note of any missed questions. If required, submit your results to your instructor.

⑥ Who Wants To Be a Computer Genius²?

Click the number 6 button to find out if you are a computer genius. Directions about how to play the game will be displayed. When you are

Learn It Online

ready to play, click the Play button. Submit your score to your instructor.

7 Wheel of Terms

Click the number 7 button to reinforce important terms you learned in this chapter by playing the Shelly Cashman Series version of this popular game. Directions about how to play the game will be displayed. When you are ready to play, click the Play button. Submit your score to your instructor.

8 DC Track and Field

Click the number 8 button to use what you have learned in this chapter to compete against other students in three track and field events. Directions about how to play the game will be displayed. When you are ready to play, click the start first event button. If required, submit your score to your instructor.

9 You're Hired!

Click the number 9 button to use what you have learned in this chapter to embark on the path to a career in computers. Directions about how to play the game will be displayed. When you are ready to play, click the begin game button. If required, submit your score to your instructor.

10 Crossword Puzzle Challenge

Click the number 10 button. Complete the puzzle to reinforce skills you learned in this chapter. Directions about how to play the game will be displayed. When you are ready to play, click the Submit button. Submit the completed puzzle to your instructor.

11 Lab Exercises

Click the number 11 button. When the Lab Exercises menu appears, click the exercise assigned by your instructor. A new browser window will open. Follow the on-screen instructions to complete the exercise. When finished, click the Exit button. If required, submit your results to your instructor.

12 In the News

Programming is not just for programmers anymore. "Yaroze" is a Japanese expression meaning, let us work together. Net Yaroze is a project that lets members and educational institutions work together with Sony to create their own games for Sony's PlayStation. Increasingly, entertainment and productivity applications are offering tools, such as macros, that allow users to program their own innovations. Click the number 12 button and read a news article about programming. Who is doing the programming? How is the programming different?

13 Chapter Discussion Forum

Select an objective from this chapter on page 663 about which you would like more information. Click the number 13 button and post a short message listing a meaningful message title accompanied by one or more questions concerning the selected objective. In two days, return to the threaded discussion by clicking the number 13 button. Submit to your instructor your original message and at least one response to your message.

14 Wikipedia

Click the number 14 button to learn how to use the Internet to locate and edit articles in an online encyclopedia. Follow the instructions to use Wikipedia.org to locate an article relating to a current event. Read the article and determine if there is anything you can add or edit. To edit articles, you first must create an account. Follow the instructions to create an account. Print the article that you selected and then submit it to your instructor. Be sure to identify any edits or additions you made.

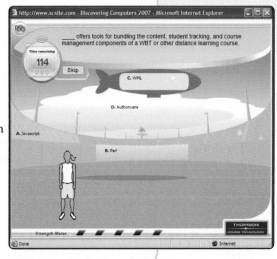

Learn How To

Use the Learn How To activities to learn fundamental skills when using a computer and accompanying technology. Complete the exercises and submit them to your instructor. Visit scsite.com/dc2007/ch13/howto to obtain more information pertaining to each activity.

LEARN HOW TO 1: Design and/or Evaluate a Graphical User Interface (GUI)

In most cases, when you interact with a program or a Web site, you are looking at and responding to a graphical user interface (GUI). Often, your ability to use the application or Web site effectively will depend on the design of the GUI. If it is easy to use and follow, your experience will be productive and enjoyable. Conversely, if you have to struggle to figure out how to enter data or which button to click, the GUI is defeating the purpose of the application.

Modern program designers spend 25 percent to 40 percent of their time creating and perfecting the user interface, sometimes called the presentation layer of a program. They do this because they realize the importance of user interaction with the application. If the user interface is not productive and easy to use, the user will not be satisfied with the application regardless of how well it does its work.

The user interface includes both the graphics and text shown on the screen, as well as the methods a user can use to interact with the software and cause operations to occur. Three primary means of interacting in a user interface are the keyboard, a pointing device such as a mouse, and voice input. The correct use of these tools significantly will increase the success of a user interface.

The ultimate goal of a user interface is to allow a user to interact with the interface and the underlying software in an intuitive and familiar way. If the user must stop and think how to use the interface, then the interface has failed. Therefore, if you are designing a user interface for a program or application, or merely evaluating software and its user interface, you should apply a variety of guidelines to a user interface to determine its usability, including the following:

1. Using the interface should feel natural and normal. This requirement means the software developer must be aware of who the user is and the manner in which the user is accustomed to working. For example, the interface for a banking application where a teller is entering account information will be different from that of a graphic arts program that allows manipulation of graphics and photographs. Both must reflect the needs of the user.

2. A graphical user interface offers a wide variety of elements (Figure 13-41), many of which can be used for similar purposes. A good user interface uses the most appropriate element for each requirement. In addition, once an element is used for a particular purpose, such as a button being used to cause a particular action, then that same element should be used for the same purpose through the application interface.

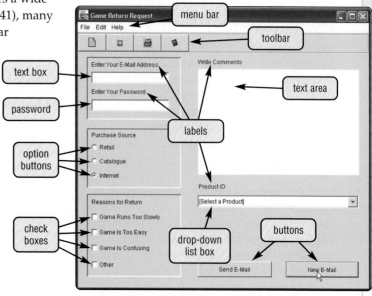

FIGURE 13-41

Learn How To

3. The elements must be arranged in the sequence in which they are used so the user is able to move from item to item on the screen in a logical, straightforward manner. This requirement once again requires the designer to understand the needs of the user. When this rule is not followed, a confusing interface can occur (Figure 13-42). If it is followed, however, the interface is clear and easy to use (Figure 13-43).

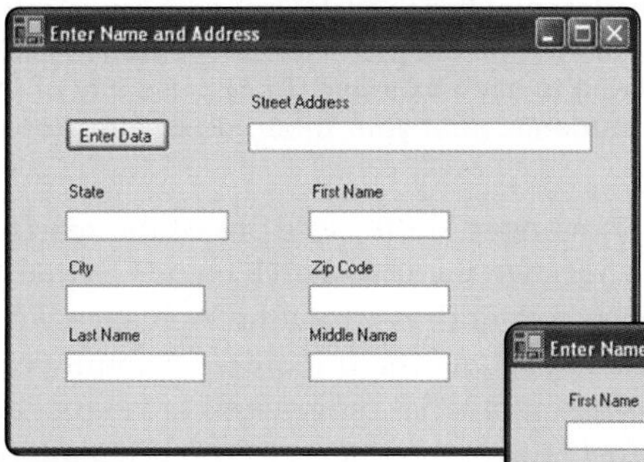

4. The interface should be kept as simple as possible, while containing all the functionality required for the application. Generally, the simpler the interface, the more effective the interface will be.

5. When implemented, the user interface should be intuitive, which means the user should be able to use it with little or no instruction. In fact, the user should feel that no other interface could have been designed because the one they are using is the most "natural."

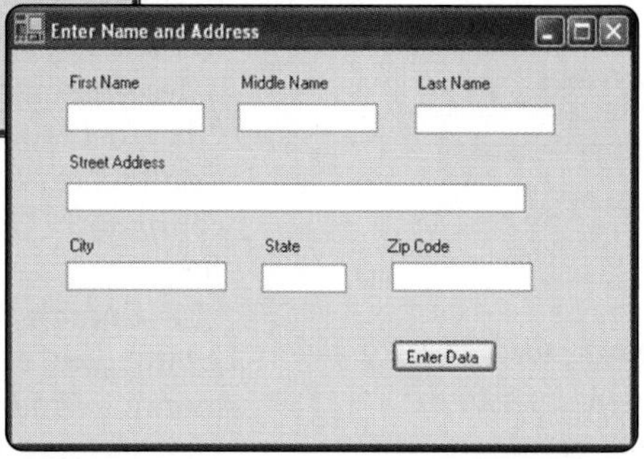

FIGURE 13-42

FIGURE 13-43

Implementing the Interface

In most cases, a graphical user interface is designed using a visual programming environment such as Visual Studio 2005. This product allows the developer to place the GUI elements on a form, which becomes the window when the program runs. Often, the developer will produce a prototype interface, in which the elements are placed in the window but few of them are functional. This prototype allows the user to see and "feel" the interface well before the application is ready for actual implementation. Then, the users can provide feedback to the developer regarding their likes and dislikes. The developer will make adjustments, or sometimes whole new designs, to meet the needs of the users. This process can occur multiple times until the users are satisfied with the GUI design.

Evaluating Application Software

One important factor when you are a user or purchaser of software is your analysis of the user interface. As you evaluate software, it is critical to remember that the user interface is as important as the functions the software performs. If you cannot use the software effectively through the user interface, then no matter how wonderful the functions of the software might be, the software cannot be useful to you.

Exercise

1. Start three different programs from three different application software developers. For example, you could start a program from Microsoft, one from Apple, and one from Adobe. What similarities do you find in the user interface for each of these programs? What differences do you observe? Does one use color more than the others? Are different fonts used? Which do you find most effective? Why? If you had to choose one interface, which one would you choose? Why? Submit your answers to your instructor.

2. Web sites also should follow the principles of good user interface design. Visit three different sites where you can make purchases, including at least one airline site where you can make an airline reservation. Without actually buying anything (unless you want to), evaluate the procedures you had to follow in order to make the reservation or purchase. Which was the easiest to use? Which was the most difficult? Why? Did the usefulness of the user interface on the Web site influence whether you would use the Web site again? Why? Submit your answers to your instructor.

3. While both the Apple Mac and Windows XP interfaces are GUIs, they differ considerably. Conduct some common operations, such as opening and closing an application, copying and pasting, and deleting on both a Windows machine and an Apple Mac. How does using each of the interfaces differ? (Remember that the mouse is part of the user interface). Also, open the same application, such as Microsoft Word or Adobe Photoshop Elements, on both a Windows machine and an Apple Mac. What differences between the application interfaces do you observe? Which interface do you prefer? Why? Submit your answers to your instructor.

Web Research

Use the Internet-based Web Research exercises to broaden your understanding of the concepts presented in this chapter. Visit scsite.com/dc2007/ch13/research to obtain more information pertaining to each exercise. To discuss any of the Web Research exercises in this chapter with other students, post your thoughts or questions at scsite.com/dc2007/ch13/forum.

①   **Scavenger Hunt**   Use one of the <u>search engines</u> listed in Figure 2-10 in Chapter 2 on page 78 or your own favorite search engine to find the answers to the questions that follow. Copy and paste the Web address from the Web page where you found the answer. Some questions may have more than one answer. If required, submit your answers to your instructor. (1) Borland's Delphi is a descendant of what programming language? (2) What programming language has been called "the duct tape of the Internet"? (3) What are some highlights from the most recent JavaOne Conference? (4) What is the name of the artificial intelligence system that ran the Deep Space 1 computer?

②   **Search Sleuth**   An international network of knowledgeable people provide the content for **About.com**, one of the top search Web sites. More than 20 million people view this resource every month to find practical advice and solutions to questions on more than 50,000 topics. Visit this Web site and then use your word processing program to answer the following questions. Then, if required, submit your answers to your instructor. (1) Click the Computing & Technology link in the Channels section. Browse the Computing & Technology Resources section. What are the latest security alerts and headlines? (2) What are the most popular topics in the What Our Readers Think section? (3) Type **"Flash MX"** in the Search box and then click the Go button. How many results were found? What are the titles of two Flash MX tutorials? (4) Delete any text in the Search box, type **C++** in the Search box, and then click the Go button. Click a link that discusses C++ programming basics and then write a 50-word summary of your findings.

③   **Journaling**   Respond to your readings in this chapter by writing at least one page about your reactions, evaluations, and reflections on programming languages and program development. For example, would you like to be a <u>beta tester</u>? How can software be tested more accurately to eliminate the 20 to 30 errors that occur in every 1,000 lines of code? Should a software manufacturer be required to compensate a corporation when buggy software causes damages? You also can write about the new terms you learned by reading this chapter. If required, submit your journal to your instructor.

④   **Expanding Your Understanding**   Corporations and individual computer users share similar concerns: their software often crashes or is riddled with errors. The source code for proprietary software, such as Microsoft Office, is not available to computer users, despite the fact that they own the product. The source code for <u>open-source software</u>, on the other hand, is available, and users are encouraged to review and improve the code. Visit the Red Hat (redhat.com) and Linspire (linspire.com) Web sites to learn the features of their software. Why do more people choose proprietary software over open-source software? What are the more popular open-source programs? What factors will encourage the development and use of more open-source software? Write a report summarizing your findings. If required, submit your report to your instructor.

⑤   **Ethics in Action**   Although hackers can be prosecuted under the <u>Computer Fraud and Abuse Act</u>, the challenge of breaking into a computer often outweighs the threat of punishment. Some hackers believe their actions should cause corporations to practice better programming and security efforts and to test their programs and systems more thoroughly. Other hackers attempt to protect free speech and human rights throughout the world. For example, visit the Hacktivismo Web site (hacktivismo.com) to read about the members' programming efforts to develop software that increases freedom of expression. Then visit Web sites that describe how the USA Patriot Act of 2001 increases the scope and penalties of the Computer Fraud and Abuse Act. Should all hackers be prosecuted, or should some be exonerated if their efforts are done with a greater purpose, such as furthering a political concern? Write a report summarizing your findings, and include a table of links to Web sites that provide additional details about hackers. If required, submit your report to your instructor.

Case Studies

Use the Case Studies to apply the concepts presented in the chapter to real-world situations. Visit scsite.com/dc2007/ch13/cases to obtain more information pertaining to each exercise. To discuss the Case Studies in this chapter with other students, visit scsite.com/dc2007/ch13/forum and post your thoughts or questions.

CASE STUDY 1 — Class Discussion   You work as a senior programmer/analyst for an aerospace company that has used the <u>C programming language</u> for all the programming projects developed over the past 10 years. Your manager has informed you that the company will be switching to the Java programming language for all new programming projects. She wants you to be proficient in the use of the new language within six months if you want to continue working for the company. What steps would you take to become proficient in the use of the Java programming language? Write a brief report and be prepared to discuss your recommendations in class.

CASE STUDY 2 — Class Discussion   You work as an administrative assistant for the president of a local marketing company. Much of your time is spent using application software, such as Word, Excel, Outlook, and Access. Your manager has asked you to consider using <u>macros</u> to automate some of the repetitive tasks in the word processing work you do. Give two examples of common repetitive tasks in word processing that are not already available via buttons or commands. What is a macro? How does a macro automate a routine? Do you have to learn how to program to create a macro? How do you invoke a macro? Write a brief report about macros and be prepared to discuss your findings in class.

CASE STUDY 3 — Research   You manage the Information Technology department at National Insurance, a worldwide insurance company that specializes in high-risk policies. There are over 1,250 system analysts and programmers in your department. For the past 40 years the company has used COBOL, a procedural language, to implement new systems, such as payroll, accounts receivable, and accounts payable. Because of heavy maintenance over the years, the programs have become sluggish and difficult to maintain. Your department is about to begin a five-year major overhaul of all the current systems. Your senior advisors in the department have recommended that the company move to an <u>object-oriented language</u> to replace the current systems. You are not sure that this is best for the company. Use the Web and/or print media to research the advantages and disadvantages of object-oriented programming. How difficult is it for procedural language programmers and system analysts to switch to an object-oriented language? Which is easier to implement, systems implemented in a procedural language or an object-oriented language? Why? Submit your report or use PowerPoint to create a presentation and share your findings with your class.

CASE STUDY 4 — Research   Just a decade ago, computer programs consisting of 5,000 lines of code were considered long. Today, programs used in automobile transmissions have almost 20,000 lines of code, word processing programs can be more than 500,000 lines, and operating systems, such as Windows XP, contain millions of lines of code. What will computer programming be like in the future? Some experts see such trends as continued movement towards <u>object-oriented languages</u>, greater participation in programming by computer users, and computers taking a more active part in programming themselves. Using the Web and/or print media, prepare a report on what programming will be like in 10 years. How will programming be different from what it is today? Who will be doing the programming? How will they be doing it? What effect might developments in computer hardware have on programming? Prepare a brief report or use PowerPoint to create a presentation and share your findings with your class.

CASE STUDY 5 — Team Challenge   Choosing a suitable programming language is one of the most important decisions an organization has to make when developing custom software. A poor choice can be a costly mistake, resulting in a program that is difficult to maintain, incompatible with other software, unproductive when used, or irreconcilable with existing <u>platforms</u>. Diamond Brokerage Services, a worldwide brokerage house, has hired your team as consultants to recommend the programming language to use for Windows-based systems developed in-house. The company currently uses COBOL and Fortran. Three popular programming languages are C++, Java, and Visual Basic. Form a three-member team and assign each team member one of these languages. Have the team members use the Web and/or print media to research their assignments. Which of the considerations that were outlined in this chapter for selecting a programming language was most important? Why? Which was least important? Why? Were any other factors considered (such as the expertise of available programmers)? Combine your findings in a table listing the advantages and disadvantages of each programming language. Share your findings with your class. Merge your findings into a team report and/or PowerPoint presentation and share your recommendations with your class.

Enterprise Computing

Picture Yourself in Need of Technical Support

As you turn on your computer to pay some bills and finish a paper for your class this evening, you gasp at the cryptic error message that is displayed. After finding the elusive computer manual, you quickly locate the technical support number and dial. You punch in your customer number after being asked by the voice prompt. A technician answers and greets you by name.

After you provide the error message, the technician tells you that you need a new memory module. She says you either can get the part for free under warranty, or pay a small fee to be able to pick up the part immediately at a local store with which the company partners. You opt to pay the fee, so she transfers you to the billing department, which says that all they need is to confirm the credit card number that they have on file for you. You finish the call, run to the store, and pick up the part, which somehow is waiting for you.

You pay your bills, receive e-mail confirmation of the payments from the companies and your bank, and then finish your paper. Before class, you navigate to your computer company's Web site and find a summary of your call to technical support. You click the Respond button, and as you type a note thanking the technician, you are shocked at how quickly all this happened. How did the technician know about you and your computer just from your customer number? How did she communicate so quickly with the billing department and the store where you shop?

As you read Chapter 14, you will learn about enterprise computing and how large organizations manage data and information.

After completing this chapter, you will be able to:

1. Discuss the special information requirements of an enterprise-sized corporation
2. Identify information systems used in the functional units of an enterprise
3. List general purpose and integrated information systems used throughout an enterprise
4. List types of technologies used throughout an enterprise
5. Describe the major types of e-commerce
6. Discuss the computer hardware needs and solutions for an enterprise
7. Determine why computer backup is important and how it is accomplished
8. Discuss the steps in a disaster recovery plan

CONTENTS

WHAT IS ENTERPRISE COMPUTING?

The term, **enterprise**, commonly describes a business or venture of any size. In this chapter, the term enterprise refers to large multinational corporations, universities, hospitals, research laboratories, and government organizations. **Enterprise computing** involves the use of computers in networks, such as LANs and WANs, or a series of interconnected networks that encompass a variety of different operating systems, protocols, and network architectures.

Enterprises produce and gather enormous volumes of information regarding customer, supplier, and employee activity. The information flows among an assortment of entities both inside and outside of the enterprise, and users consume the information during a number of activities (Figure 14-1). Customers, suppliers, and employees interact with the enterprise in a number of ways, and computers track each interaction. Each sale of a product, purchase of a piece of equipment, or paycheck generates activity involving information systems.

A typical enterprise consists of corporate headquarters, remote offices, international offices, and hundreds of individual operating entities, called *functional units*, including departments, centers, and divisions. Often,

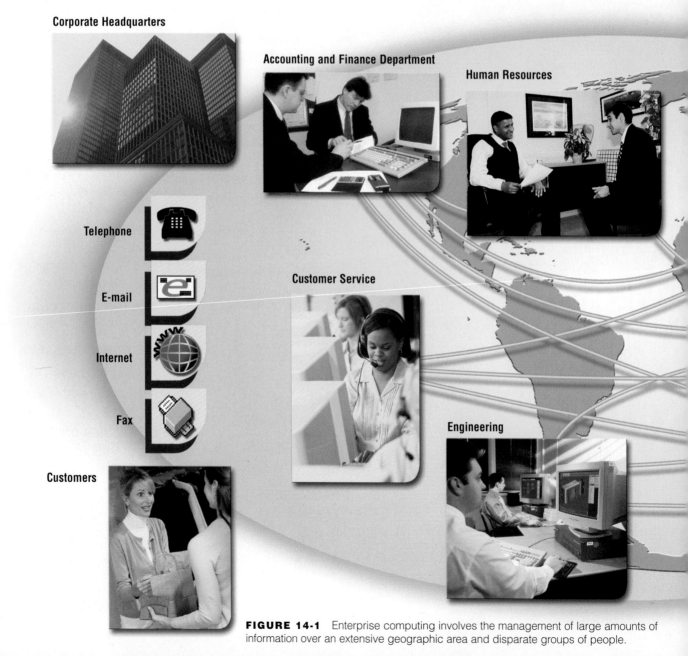

Corporate Headquarters

Accounting and Finance Department

Human Resources

Telephone

E-mail

Internet

Fax

Customer Service

Engineering

Customers

FIGURE 14-1 Enterprise computing involves the management of large amounts of information over an extensive geographic area and disparate groups of people.

organizations within the enterprise may have similar responsibilities within the divisions to which they belong. For example, a large automobile company may organize its divisions based on the model of car that the business unit produces. Each division includes a group of engineers that designs the automobiles. Each of the engineering groups may have similar or different information systems based on its needs or the culture of the company. Some companies allow for independence within their divisions, while others attempt to standardize systems across the enterprise.

Each type of functional unit has specialized requirements for their information systems.

These units can be grouped by the functions they perform. The types of functional units within a typical manufacturing enterprise are accounting and finance, human resources, engineering, manufacturing, marketing, sales, distribution, customer service, and information technology. These functional units are summarized later in this chapter.

Large computers connected by vast networks allow the enterprise to manage and distribute information quickly and efficiently. Procedures safeguard information when disaster strikes. Security policies ensure that people, computers, and networks access only the information they require.

Sales Department

Remote Office

IT Department

Marketing Department

Television

Internet

Newspaper

Distribution

Manufacturing

International Office

For example, when a customer purchases goods or services on a Web site, many activities occur behind the scenes at a company. A customer views an advertisement on a Web site created by the company's marketing department. The customer purchases a product at a Web site. The customer makes a credit card payment that is processed by a financial system connected to the company's bank. The company's accounting system records the payment and transaction. The distribution center receives a message telling it to ship the product. The marketing department notes the advertising that was successful in generating the sale to the customer and informs the sales department that this customer may be interested in purchasing complementary products.

When the customer calls to check the status of an order, a computer routes the telephone call to the proper customer service representative who checks the status of the order in a database shared with the distribution department. Finally, the activity generated by the purchase finds its way onto management reports, and managers

make decisions based on the information collected in the purchase process. For example, a manager may make a decision to order more parts for inventory because a product is selling particularly well.

As just illustrated, information is combined and analyzed by the management, and decisions are made based on the information. The divisions and departments within the enterprise use specialized hardware and software to perform their tasks. These same units may share hardware and software with each other to become more effective. Some large organizations employ enterprise-wide networks that help manage all aspects of a company and are used by many or all of the divisions and departments.

Organizational Structure of an Enterprise

Most traditional enterprises are organized in a hierarchical manner. Figure 14-2 shows an example of an organization chart of a large manufacturing company. Managers at the first two levels at the top of the chart, including the

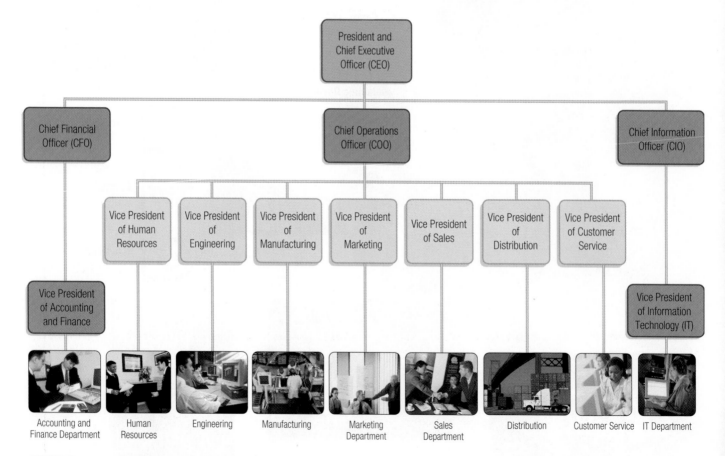

FIGURE 14-2 A typical organization chart for an enterprise illustrates the hierarchy within an enterprise.

chief executive officer (CEO), mainly concern themselves with strategic decisions and long-term planning.

The activities relating to running the business are called *supporting activities*. Supporting activities usually are separated from those activities that relate to the main mission of the company which are the *core activities*. *Operations* refer to the core activities of a business, and involve the creation, selling, and support of the products and services that the company produces. In Figure 14-2, the chief operations officer (COO) manages the core activities. The supporting activities include financial departments and information technology (IT) departments. The chief financial officer (CFO) and the chief information officer (CIO) lead these supporting roles.

Each enterprise includes its own special needs and the organizational structure of every enterprise varies. Companies may include all or some of the managers and departments shown in Figure 14-2. Companies also may include additional departments or combine some of those shown.

A *decentralized* approach to information technology exists when departments and divisions maintain their own information systems. Some companies maintain central computers, supported by a central information technology department, which is referred to as a *centralized* approach to information technology. Companies decide whether to support a centralized or decentralized approach based on a number of factors, including cost, efficiency, and the interdependence of departments. A centralized approach to information systems usually reduces costs of maintenance and increases manageability.

A decentralized approach allows for greater flexibility, allowing each functional unit or department to customize information systems to their particular needs. Both centralized and decentralized approaches focus on the sharing of information with other departments and divisions.

Levels of Users

In an enterprise, users typically fall into one of four categories: executive management, middle management, operational management, and nonmanagement employees (Figure 14-3). The types of information that users require often depend on their employee level in the company. The following paragraphs discuss the four categories of users and their information requirements.

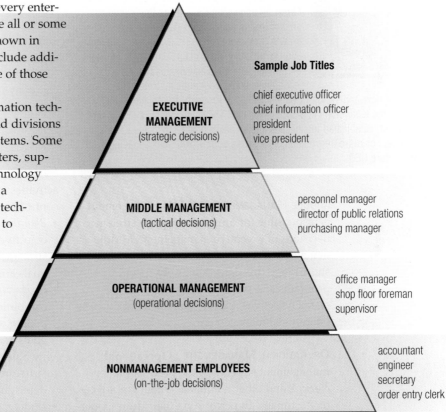

Sample Job Titles

EXECUTIVE MANAGEMENT
(strategic decisions)

chief executive officer
chief information officer
president
vice president

MIDDLE MANAGEMENT
(tactical decisions)

personnel manager
director of public relations
purchasing manager

OPERATIONAL MANAGEMENT
(operational decisions)

office manager
shop floor foreman
supervisor

NONMANAGEMENT EMPLOYEES
(on-the-job decisions)

accountant
engineer
secretary
order entry clerk

FIGURE 14-3 This pyramid illustrates the levels of users, sample job titles of each level of user, and the types of decisions these users make.

EXECUTIVE MANAGEMENT   Executive **management**, which includes the highest management positions in a company, focuses on the long-range direction of the company. These managers primarily are responsible for *strategic decisions* that center on the company's overall goals and objectives. Executive management oversees middle management. Read Looking Ahead 14-1 for a look at the changing roles of the next generation of CEOs.

MIDDLE MANAGEMENT   **Middle management** is responsible for implementing the strategic decisions of executive management. Middle managers make *tactical decisions*, which are short-range decisions that apply specific programs and plans necessary to meet the stated objectives. Middle management oversees operational management.

OPERATIONAL MANAGEMENT   Operational **management** supervises the production, clerical, and other nonmanagement employees of a company. In performing their duties, operational managers make numerous operational decisions. An *operational decision* involves day-to-day activities within the company. These decisions should be consistent with and support the tactical decisions made by middle management.

NONMANAGEMENT EMPLOYEES **Nonmanagement employees** include production, clerical, and other personnel. Nonmanagement employees frequently need information to perform their jobs. Today, these employees have more information available to them than in the past. They have access to the information necessary to make decisions that previously were made by managers — a trend called *empowering* users.

How Managers Use Information

Enterprise information is the information gathered in the ongoing operations of an enterprise-sized organization. Enterprise information begins with the day-to-day transactions that occur within a company, such as sales receipts or time cards. The company gathers and stores the information. Over time, employees collect, combine, and analyze the information. Ultimately, the role of information gathered in this way is to allow managers to make better decisions.

All employees, including managers, in a company need accurate information to perform their jobs effectively. **Managers** are responsible for coordinating and controlling an organization's resources. Resources include people, money, materials, and information. Managers coordinate these resources by performing four activities: planning, organizing, leading, and controlling.

- *Planning* involves establishing goals and objectives. It also includes deciding on the strategies and tactics needed to meet these goals and objectives.
- *Organizing* includes identifying and combining resources, such as money and people, so that the company can reach its goals and objectives. Organizing also involves determining the management structure of a company, such as the departments and reporting relationships.
- *Leading*, sometimes referred to as directing, involves communicating instructions and authorizing others to perform the necessary work.
- *Controlling* involves measuring performance and, if necessary, taking corrective action.

Figure 14-4 shows how these four management activities usually occur in an order that forms an endless cycle. During the controlling activity, managers measure actual performance against a previously established plan. Following this measurement, they may revise the plan. Revised plans may result in additional organizational and leadership activities. Managers then measure performance against the revised plan, and the cycle repeats itself. The four tasks are linked. A change in one task usually affects one or more of the other tasks.

Managers utilize a variety of tools and techniques to focus on information that is important to the decision-making process. These tools and techniques, including business intelligence, business process management, and business process automation, are described in the following sections.

• *Business intelligence* (*BI*) includes several types of applications and technologies for acquiring, storing, analyzing, and providing access to information to help users make more sound business decisions. BI applications include decision support systems, query and reporting, online analytical processing (OLAP), statistical analysis, and data mining. These activities are described later in this chapter.

• *Business process management* (*BPM*) includes a set of activities that enterprises perform to optimize their business processes, such as accounting and finance, hiring employees, and purchasing goods and services. BPM almost always is aided by specialized software designed to assist in these activities.

• *Business process automation* (*BPA*) provides easy exchange of information among business applications, reduces the need for human intervention in processes, and utilizes software to automate processes wherever possible. BPA offers greater efficiency and reduces risks by making processes more predictable.

WEB LINK 14-1

Business Intelligence
For more information, visit scsite.com/dc2007/ch14/weblink and then click Business Intelligence.

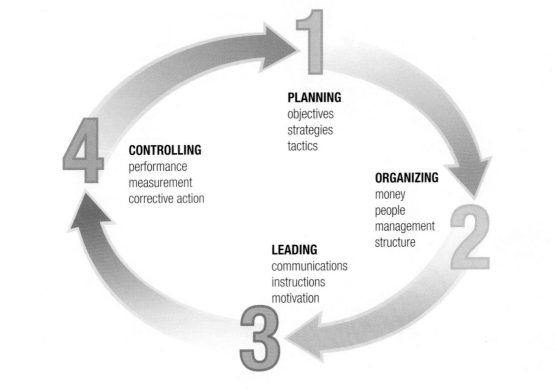

PLANNING
objectives
strategies
tactics

ORGANIZING
money
people
management
structure

LEADING
communications
instructions
motivation

CONTROLLING
performance
measurement
corrective action

FIGURE 14-4 The four management activities include planning, organizing, leading, and controlling. The activities usually are performed in a continuous sequence.

INFORMATION SYSTEMS IN THE ENTERPRISE

An **information system** is a set of hardware, software, data, people, and procedures that works together to produce information (Figure 14-5). A *procedure* is an instruction, or set of instructions, a user follows to accomplish an activity. An information system supports daily, short-term, and long-range activities of users in a company.

Some information systems are used exclusively by only one type of department, or functional unit, within the enterprise. General purpose information systems include categories of information systems that can be used by almost any department within the enterprise. Integrated information systems are used by multiple departments and facilitate information sharing and communication within the enterprise.

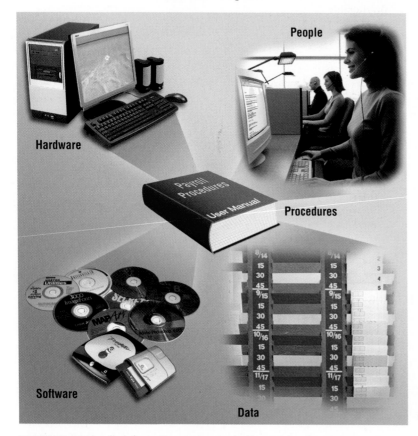

FIGURE 14-5 An information system typically contains five components: hardware, software, data, people, and procedures.

Information Systems within Functional Units

Figure 14-6 lists typical functional units and their purpose within an enterprise. The sections that follow discuss the types of information systems and software used within these units.

FUNCTIONAL UNITS WITHIN AN ENTERPRISE

Functional Unit	Description
Accounting and Finance	Responsible for managing the business' money. Accounting department tracks every financial transaction that occurs within the company. Finance department manages the business' money as efficiently as possible.
Human Resources (HR)	Responsible for recruiting and promoting employees, maintaining employee records, evaluating employees, training employees, and managing employee benefits and compensation.
Engineering or Product Development	Responsible for developing ideas into a product that can be used by customers. Ensures that the product can be manufactured effectively and designs the methods for manufacturing the product.
Manufacturing	Responsible for converting raw materials into physical products.
Marketing	Responsible for researching the market in which a business operates to determine the products and features that the business should develop. Determines the demographics to target with sales efforts and informs the target market about the company's products through advertising and education.
Sales	Responsible for selling the company's products and services.
Distribution	Responsible for delivery of products to customers.
Customer Service	Responsible for maintaining a relationship with a customer both before and after a sale has been made.
Information Technology	Responsible for designing, purchasing, implementing, testing, and maintaining information systems for the rest of the organization. Sometimes called the information services (IS) department.

FIGURE 14-6 An enterprise is composed of several functional units.

ACCOUNTING AND FINANCE

Figure 14-7 illustrates the separate functions of accounting and financial systems used by accounting and finance departments. Accounting software manages everyday transactions, such as sales and payments to suppliers. Financial software helps managers budget, forecast, and analyze. Both types of software include comprehensive and flexible reporting tools to assist managers in making decisions, provide historical documentation, and meet regulatory requirements.

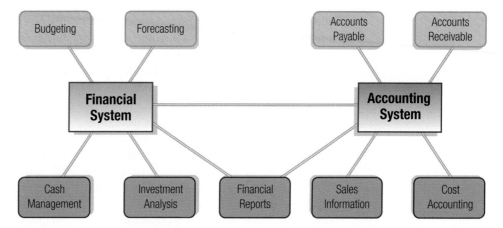

FIGURE 14-7 Accounting and financial systems perform different tasks but share information and produce financial reports that help management make decisions.

HUMAN RESOURCES

A **human resources information system** (**HRIS**) manages one or more human resources functions (Figure 14-8). A human resources information system and its associated software help a company such as Wal-Mart maintain records on its 1.3 million employees.

An *employee relationship management* (*ERM*) *system* automates and manages much of the communications between employees and the business. For example, an employee may interact with employee relationship management software to gather information regarding the employee's retirement account. Most employee relationship management software includes a Web interface for the employees and the human resources personnel, allowing both to interact with the system when they are in the office or at home.

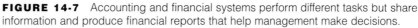

FIGURE 14-8 A human resources information system (HRIS) allows human resources personnel to manage employee information, such as benefits, personal information, performance evaluations, training, and vacation time.

WEB LINK 14-2

Employee Relationship Management

For more information, visit scsite.com/dc2007/ch14/weblink and then click Employee Relationship Management.

ENGINEERING OR PRODUCT DEVELOPMENT

Professional workers, such as engineers, require specialized software and systems to perform their tasks. **Computer-aided design (CAD)** uses a computer and special software to aid in engineering, drafting, and design (Figure 14-9). Using computer-aided design offers several advantages over traditional manual drafting methods. Computer-aided design software, for example, allows a designer to modify a design more easily than before, as well as dynamically change the size of some or all of the subject and view the design from different angles.

Computer-aided engineering (CAE) uses computers to test product designs. Using computer-aided engineering, engineers can test the design of a car or bridge before it is built. These sophisticated programs simulate the effects of wind, temperature, weight, and stress on product shapes and materials. Computer-aided engineering also allows engineers to create a computer prototype for use in testing under a variety of conditions, such as hurricanes and earthquakes. Engineers sometimes use *3-D visualization*, which allows them to interact with a product without the need to build a prototype.

MANUFACTURING Manufacturing information systems and software not only assist in the actual assembly process, but also assist in scheduling and managing the inventory of parts and products. **Computer-aided manufacturing (CAM)** is the use of computers to control production equipment. Computer-aided manufacturing production equipment includes software-controlled drilling, lathe, welding, and milling machines.

Computer-integrated manufacturing (CIM) uses computers to integrate the many different operations of the manufacturing process, using such technologies as computer-aided design, computer-aided engineering, and computer-aided manufacturing. Using computer-integrated manufacturing (Figure 14-10), for example, a factory can link individual processes so that production is balanced, efficient, driven by customer demand, and results in high-quality products.

Formal manufacturing methods help guide enterprises in their manufacturing processes.

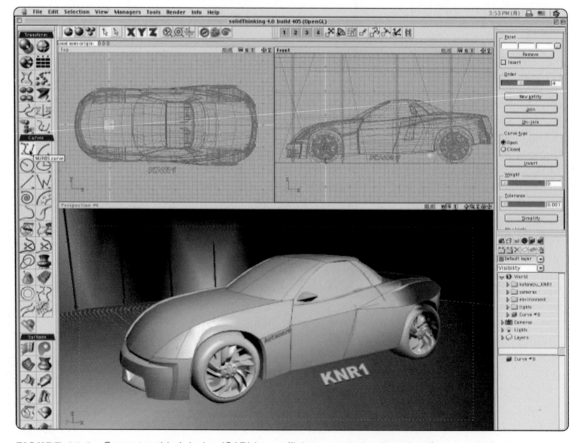

FIGURE 14-9 Computer-aided design (CAD) is an efficient way to develop plans for new products.

FIGURE 14-10 Computer-integrated manufacturing (CIM) speeds the manufacturing process and reduces product defects.

Material Requirements Planning (MRP) is an approach to information management in a manufacturing environment that uses software to help monitor and control processes related to production. Material Requirements Planning focuses on issues related to inventory of parts and forecasting future demand so that materials needed for manufacturing can be on hand when they are needed. **Manufacturing Resource Planning II (MRP II)** is an extension of MRP and also includes software that helps in scheduling, tracking production in real time, and monitoring product quality. Companies use Material Requirements Planning and Manufacturing Resource Planning II systems to facilitate an MRP or MRP II approach to their manufacturing.

MARKETING A *marketing information system* serves as a central repository for the tasks of the marketing functional unit (Figure 14-11). One type of marketing information system is a *market research system*, which stores and analyzes data gathered from demographics and surveys. Many

companies gather information via the Web and store information about individuals' Web browsing habits and interests. Market research software assists in target marketing by allowing marketing personnel to query databases based on criteria such as income, gender, previous purchases, and favorite recreational activities. The relationship between marketing and the Internet is discussed later in this chapter.

WEB LINK 14-3

MRP II

For more information, visit scsite.com/ dc2007/ch14/weblink and then click MRP II.

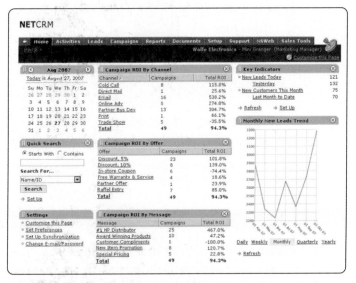

FIGURE 14-11 Marketing information systems allow marketing departments to create marketing campaigns and track their effectiveness.

SALES Sales force automation (SFA) software equips traveling salespeople with the electronic tools they need to be more productive. Sales force automation software helps salespeople manage customer contacts, schedule customer meetings, log customer interactions, manage product information, and take orders from customers.

Sales force automation software (Figure 14-12) often runs on PDAs or notebook computers. The PDA or notebook computer may connect wirelessly to the central office, allowing the salesperson to access up-to-date corporate information in real time no matter where he or she is.

Alternatively, some sales force automation programs allow the salesperson to upload information to the central office at the end of the day or end of the week. The programs also allow salespeople to download updated product and pricing information.

DISTRIBUTION *Distribution systems* provide forecasting for inventory control, manage and track shipping of products, and provide information and analysis on inventory in warehouses. Some distribution systems rely on GPS and other navigation technologies to track shipping in real time. Distribution systems strive to maximize the value of each shipment made by the company while keeping costs to a minimum.

CUSTOMER SERVICE Customer interaction management (CIM) software (Figure 14-13) manages the day-to-day interactions with customers, such as telephone calls, e-mail interactions, Web interactions, and instant messaging sessions. A customer interaction management program routes customer telephone calls to the most appropriate support person depending on the identity of the customer or responses the customer gives to prompts.

Customer interaction management software also assists support personnel in providing the best solutions for customers. The customer interaction management program may provide a customer support representative with a choice of several e-mail messages to send to a customer in response to the problem. The representative chooses the best response and requests that the CIM software sends the e-mail message. Information gathered by such a program during interactions, such as reasons for the interaction and the resolution of the interaction, may be collected and made available through other information systems throughout the company.

WEB LINK 14-4

Sales Force Automation

For more information, visit scsite.com/dc2007/ch14/weblink and then click Sales Force Automation.

FIGURE 14-12 Sales force automation (SFA) software allows the sales force to manage customer and prospective customer relationships more effectively.

FAQ 14-1

When should I supply personal information to a company?

Companies gather personal information about consumers for a variety of reasons. Unless you are sure you want the company to communicate with you in some way, few reasons exist to supply personal information to a company. Ask the company why it needs the information and use your judgment. Most companies can supply you with a privacy policy upon request. For more information, visit scsite.com/dc2007/ch14/faq and then click Sharing Personal Information.

NETCRM

Change Role | Sign Out | Help | Global Search [   ] Go

Home | Cases | Customers | Reports | Setup | Support | Knowledge Base

Home »

Wolfe Electronics [2006] - A Wolfe (Support Lead)

Reminders ⊗
- 3 Cases to respond to
- 1 Event Invitation to respond to
→ Update → Set Up

Quick Search ⊗
- Starts With ○ Contains
[   ]
Search For...
Name/ID ▾
[Search]
→ Set Up

Settings
- Add Content
- Set Preferences
- Set Up Synchronization
- Change E-mail/Password

Key Performance Indicators ⊗

Indicator	Period	Current	Previous	Change
My Open Cases	Current	6		
My New Cases	This Week vs Last Week	4	0 ↑	100.0%
My Closed Cases	This Week vs Last Week	3	0 ↑	100.0%

→ Update → Set Up

Marquee Customers ⊗

New	Edit	View	Name	Sales Rep	Phone
	Edit	View	Adley Electric Systems	Krista Barton	(858) 916-0015
	Edit	View	Amarillo Apartments Distributors	A Wolfe	(302) 334-0426
	Edit	View	Anderson Boughton Inc.	A Wolfe	206-555-1302
	Edit	View	Apfel Electric Co.	Corporate Sales Team	(563) 268-0679
	Edit	View	B-Sharp Music	Krista Barton	800-555-4681
	Edit	View	Bakkala Catering Distributors	Corporate Sales Team	(605) 781-0775
	Edit	View	Bartkus Automotive Company	Krista Barton	(802) 364-0790
	Edit	View	Bay Media Research	Sam R Cruz	800-555-0609
	Edit	View	Bayas Hardware Dynamics	Sam R Cruz	(242) 669-0561
	Edit	View	Big Bear Lake Plumbing Holding Corp.	A Wolfe	(706) 997-0248
	Edit	View	Boise Publishing Co.		(253) 417-0081
	Edit	View	Bridgham Electric Inc.		(718) 429-0726
	Edit	View	CVM Business Solutions	Mark Grogan	650-555-7709
	Edit	View	Carpinteria Leasing Services		(985) 630-0633
	Edit	View	Clayton and Bubash Telecom Services		(416) 905-0562
	Edit	View	Cosimini Software Agency		(716) 862-0213
	Edit	View	Deblasio Painting Holding Corp.		(772) 383-0172
	Edit	View	Diekema Attorneys Manufacturing		(814) 943-0419
	Edit	View	Downey and Sweezer Electric Group		(775) 229-0480
	Edit	View	Duman Windows Sales		(469) 750-0919

FIGURE 14-13 A customer interaction management (CIM) system manages and reports on daily interactions with customers, such as telephone support calls or customer support requests via e-mail.

INFORMATION TECHNOLOGY The information technology department makes technology decisions for the enterprise, such as a decision whether to build or buy new information systems or when a computer or information system has outlived its useful life. The overall technology strategy often is referred to as the *information architecture* of the company. Many companies elevate the importance of information technology by including a *chief information officer* (*CIO*) executive position that reports to the CEO.

The information technology department uses software to maintain hardware and software. For example, *Web site management programs* allow the information technology department to track Web site usage and statistics. *Security software* enables the department to limit access to sensitive information.

General Purpose Information Systems

Some information systems in an enterprise cross the boundaries of functional units and are used by one or more functional units in an enterprise. These general purpose, or *enterprise-wide systems*, become necessary in an enterprise for two reasons. First, functional units within an enterprise have a significant need to share data among the units. Second, enterprise-wide systems can collect and combine data more quickly and provide executive management access to a more up-to-date and accurate view of what is happening in the organization. Advances in computing speed, storage capacity, security, and networking have made enterprise-wide systems more attractive to companies in recent years.

FAQ 14-2

How do companies allocate their IT budgets?

One study estimates that on average, companies allocate approximately two percent of their total revenues to information technology. The chart to the right shows the results of one survey regarding how companies typically allocate their IT budgets. For more information, visit scsite.com/dc2007/ch14/faq and then click Information Technology Budgets.

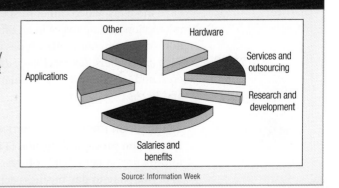

Other | Hardware | Services and outsourcing | Research and development | Salaries and benefits | Applications

Source: Information Week

General purpose information systems generally fall into one of five categories: office information systems, transaction processing systems, management information systems, decision support systems, and expert systems. The following sections present each type of these general purpose information systems.

OFFICE INFORMATION SYSTEMS   An **office information system** (**OIS**) is an information system that enables employees to perform tasks using computers and other electronic devices, instead of manually. An office information system increases employee productivity and assists with communications among employees. Some people describe an office information system as *office automation*.

Just about every type of business or organization uses some form of office information system. For example, a school might post its class schedules on the Internet. When the school updates the schedule, students receive an e-mail notification. In a manual system, the school would photocopy the schedule and mail it to each student's house.

An office information system supports many administrative activities. With this type of a system, users create and distribute graphics and documents, send messages, schedule appointments, browse the Web, and publish Web pages. All levels of users utilize and benefit from the features of an office information system.

An office information system uses many common software products to support its activities. Typical software in such a system includes word processing, spreadsheet, database, presentation graphics, e-mail, Web browser, Web page authoring, personal information management, and groupware. To send text, graphics, audio, and video to others, an office information system uses communications technology such as voice mail, fax, videoconferencing, and electronic data interchange.

In an office information system, computers have modems, video cameras, speakers, and microphones. Employees in an office information system often use other types of hardware such as scanners, fax machines, digital cameras, and Internet-enabled cellular telephones and PDAs.

TRANSACTION PROCESSING SYSTEMS   A **transaction processing system** (**TPS**) is an information system that captures and processes data from day-to-day business activities. When you make a purchase with a credit card at a store, you are interacting with a transaction processing system (Figure 14-14). A *transaction* is an individual business activity. Examples of transactions are deposits, payments, orders, and reservations. In a company, clerical staff typically uses computers and special software to perform the following activities associated with a transaction processing system:

1. Recording a transaction such as a student's registration, a customer's order, an employee's time card, or a car owner's payment.
2. Confirming an action or causing a response, such as printing a student's schedule, sending a thank-you note to a customer, printing an employee's paycheck, or issuing a receipt to a car owner.
3. Maintaining data, which involves adding new data, changing existing data, or removing unwanted data.

Transaction processing systems were among the first computerized systems that processed business data. Many people initially referred to the functions of such systems as *data processing*. The first transaction processing systems computerized an existing manual system. The intent of these systems was to process faster, reduce clerical costs, and improve customer service.

FIGURE 14-14   When you make a purchase with a credit card, you are using a transaction processing system.

Early transaction processing systems mostly used batch processing. With *batch processing*, the computer collects data over time and processes all transactions later, as a group. As computers became more powerful, system developers created online transaction processing information systems. With *online transaction processing (OLTP)*, the computer processes each transaction as it is entered.

For example, when you register for classes, your school probably uses online transaction processing. The registration clerk enters your desired schedule. The computer immediately prints your statement of classes. The invoices often print using batch processing. That is, the computer later prints the student invoices, which then are mailed out.

Today, most transaction processing systems use online transaction processing. For some routine processing tasks, they also use batch processing. Many enterprise-sized organizations use batch processing to calculate paychecks and print invoices.

MANAGEMENT INFORMATION SYSTEMS A **management information system (MIS)** is an information system that generates accurate, timely, and organized information, so managers and other users can make decisions, solve problems, supervise activities, and track progress. Management information systems evolved from transaction processing systems. Managers realized the computer and its software had more potential than just supporting a transaction processing system. Its capability of quickly computing and comparing data could produce meaningful information for managers.

Management information systems often are integrated with transaction processing systems. To process a sales order, the transaction processing system records the sale, updates the customer's account balance, and reduces the inventory count. Using this information, the related management information system produces reports that recap daily sales activities, summarize weekly and monthly sales activities, list customers with past due account balances, chart slow- or fast-selling products, and highlight inventory items that need reordering. A management information system focuses on creating information that managers and other users need to perform their jobs.

A management information system creates three basic types of reports: detailed, summary,

and exception (Figure 14-15). A *detailed report* usually lists just transactions. For example, a Detailed Order Report lists orders taken during a given period. A *summary report* consolidates data usually with totals, tables, or graphs, so managers can review it quickly and easily.

FIGURE 14-15a   (detailed report)

DETAILED ORDER REPORT for May 3, 2007

Part Number	Part Description	Customer	Quantity Purchased
93814	Dorm refrigerator	Union Bookstore University Supplies	5 2
10761	Large futon	Eddes Rentals Middleton Furnishings	3 6
88732	Hot plate	Union Bookstore Sam's Quick-Mart University Supplies	9 12 7
30021	Closet organizer	Eddes Rentals Lilac Imports	3 4

FIGURE 14-15b   (summary report)

SUMMARY REPORT for May 3, 2007

Part Number	Part Description	Total Quantity Sold	Supplier
93814	Dorm refrigerator	7	Van Electric
10761	Large futon	9	Carolina
88732	Hot plate	28	Chen Imports
30021	Closet organizer	7	Wilson Enterprises

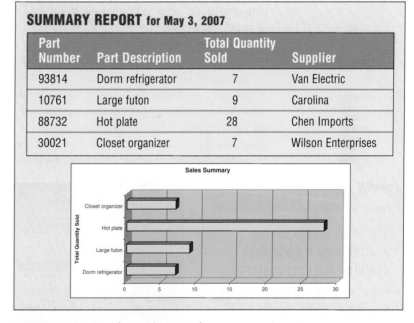

FIGURE 14-15c   (exception report)

INVENTORY EXCEPTION REPORT for May 3, 2007

Part Number	Part Description	Total Quantity on Hand	Reorder Point
93814	Dorm refrigerator	2	5
30021	Closet organizer	7	20

FIGURE 14-15 Three basic types of information generated in an MIS are detailed, summary, and exception.

An *exception report* identifies data outside of a normal condition. These out-of-the-ordinary conditions, called the *exception criteria*, define the normal activity or status range. For example, an Inventory Exception Report notifies the purchasing department of items it needs to reorder.

Exception reports save managers time. Instead of searching through a detailed report, managers simply review the exception report. These reports help managers focus on situations that require immediate decisions or actions. Most information systems support all three types of reports shown in Figure 14-15 on the previous page.

DECISION SUPPORT SYSTEMS   A **decision support system** (**DSS**) helps users analyze data and make decisions. Often, a transaction processing system or management information system does not generate the type of report a manager needs to make a decision. This is where a decision support system can help. A marketing manager might need to know how much he or she has spent on Internet advertising in the past three months, whereas an office manager might need to know how many pads of paper were used.

A variety of decision support systems exist. Some are company specific and designed solely for managers. Others are available to everyone on the Web. Programs that analyze data, such as those in a decision support system, sometimes are called *online analytical processing* (*OLAP*) programs. Because they summarize information, these programs process many records at a time.

This is different from online transaction processing programs, which process individual records at one time.

A decision support system uses data from internal and external sources. *Internal sources* of data might include sales orders, Material Requirements Planning and Manufacturing Resource Planning II results, inventory records, or financial data from accounting and financial analyses. Data from *external sources* could include interest rates, population trends, costs of new housing construction, or raw material pricing.

Some decision support systems include their own query languages, statistical analyses, spreadsheets, and graphics that help users retrieve data and analyze the results. Some also allow managers to create a model of the factors affecting a decision. A product manager might need to decide on a price for a new product. A simple model for finding the best price would include factors for the expected sales volume at various price levels. The model allows the user to ask what-if questions and view the expected results.

A special type of decision support system, called an *executive information system* (*EIS*), supports the strategic information needs of executive management (Figure 14-16). An executive information system presents information as charts and tables that show trends, ratios, and statistics. Such a system typically uses external data sources such as the Dow Jones Interactive or the Internet. These external data sources provide current information about interest rates, commodity prices, and other leading economic indicators.

FAQ 14-3

Are other alternatives available to a complete decision support system?

Instead of buying a DSS, many people use their application software to perform decision support system functions. With Microsoft Excel, for example, you can model data and create what-if scenarios. For more information, visit scsite.com/dc2007/ch14/faq and then click Decision Support Systems.

FIGURE 14-16   This executive information system (EIS) presents information to senior management in the form of graphics and reports.

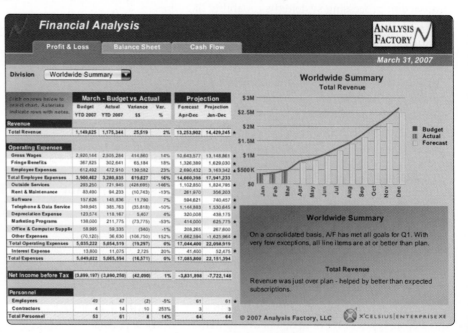

EXPERT SYSTEMS An **expert system** is an information system that captures and stores the knowledge of human experts and then imitates human reasoning and decision making. Figure 14-17 shows how one expert system assists with a medical diagnosis.

Expert systems consist of two main components: a knowledge base and inference rules. A *knowledge base* is the combined subject knowledge and experiences of the human experts. The *inference rules* are a set of logical judgments that are applied to the knowledge base each time a user describes a situation to the expert system.

Expert systems help all levels of users make decisions. Nonmanagement employees use them

FIGURE 14-17 A SAMPLE EXPERT SYSTEM

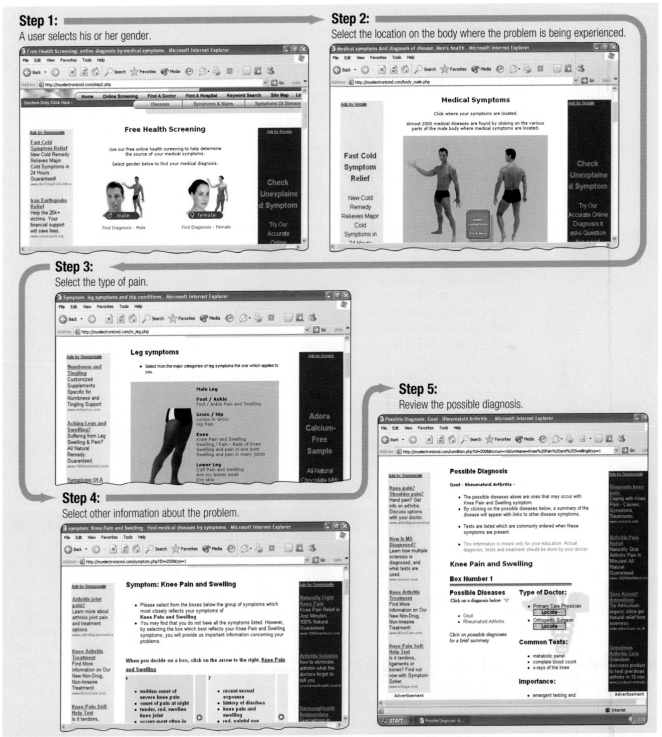

Step 1:
A user selects his or her gender.

Step 2:
Select the location on the body where the problem is being experienced.

Step 3:
Select the type of pain.

Step 4:
Select other information about the problem.

Step 5:
Review the possible diagnosis.

to help with job-related decisions. Expert systems also successfully have resolved such diverse problems as diagnosing illnesses, searching for oil, and making soup.

Expert systems are one aspect of an exciting branch of computer science called artificial intelligence. **Artificial intelligence (AI)** is the application of human intelligence to computers. Artificial intelligence technology senses a person's actions and, based on logical assumptions and prior experience, takes the appropriate action to complete the task. Artificial intelligence has a variety of capabilities, including speech recognition, logical reasoning, and creative responses. New research in the field of artificial intelligence tries to mimic the way that human memory works in order to expedite searches for information.

Enterprises employ expert systems in a variety of roles, such as answering customer questions, training new employees, and analyzing data.

The knowledge and experience of a professional worker is an important asset to any business. *Knowledge workers*, such as accountants, engineers, and other professionals, include individuals whose jobs center on the collection, processing, and application of information. *Knowledge management* (*KM*) is the process by which an enterprise collects, archives, indexes, and retrieves its knowledge, or resources. The knowledge worker performs the tasks to develop or use the knowledge. Organizations implement *knowledge management software* (*KMS*) to assist in the task of knowledge management. Knowledge management software captures the expertise of knowledge workers, so their knowledge is not lost when they leave the company. For a more technical discussion about artificial intelligence, read the High-Tech Talk article on page 750.

Integrated Information Systems

It often is difficult to classify an information system as belonging to only one of the five general types of information systems. Much of today's application software, such as enterprise resource planning and Manufacturing Resource Planning II software, supports transaction processing and creates management information system reports. Other applications provide transaction processing, management information, and decision support.

CUSTOMER RELATIONSHIP MANAGEMENT A **customer relationship management (CRM)** system manages information about customers, interactions with customers, past purchases, and interests. Customer relationship management mainly is used across sales, marketing, and customer service departments. Customer relationship management software tracks leads and inquiries from customers, stores a history of all correspondence and sales to a customer, and allows for tracking of outstanding issues with customers. Enterprise resource planning systems often serve as a basis for customer relationship management. Read Ethics & Issues 14-1 for a related discussion.

Marketing departments use customer relationship management software to learn about current customers and design new products based on customer experiences. The sales department utilizes customer relationship management software to track the sales process from initial contact through the final purchase. The customer support organization tracks ongoing correspondence with the customer, and the customer relationship management system may be linked to a customer interaction management system. All of the functional units have access to each other's information, allowing for a

---

ETHICS & ISSUES 14-1

Should Companies Share Customer Information?

Under state and federal law, it is illegal for video rental stores to inform anyone as to which movies their customers have rented. But in most industries, companies are at liberty to share customer information, such as contact information, purchasing habits, and interests. In recent years, Internet access providers have become a focus of this issue. A proposed law would make Internet access providers subject to similar constraints as video rental stores. Under the law, Internet access providers would have to notify customers whenever they disclose information about accounts, such as e-mail addresses or Web pages visited, and explain why the information is being shared. Internet access provider contracts would have to inform customers how they could prevent such information sharing. Major Internet access providers oppose the law, claiming that any state regulations would be unwieldy for companies that operate on a national, and even international, level. Supporters of the law claim that sharing customer information violates customer privacy. Some argue that the law should go further, making it illegal to disclose any customer information, even to law enforcement agencies. Should companies have to inform customers when they disclose personal information, such as the Web sites that a customer visits? Why? Should any such disclosure be illegal, or should it be restricted to law enforcement agencies? Why or why not?

more consistent, knowledgeable approach to managing interactions with the customer.

ENTERPRISE RESOURCE PLANNING **Enterprise resource planning (ERP)** provides centralized, integrated software to help manage and coordinate the ongoing activities of the enterprise, including manufacturing and distribution, accounting, finance, sales, product planning, and human resources. Figure 14-18 shows how enterprise resource planning fits into the operations of an enterprise. Companies such as SAP provide the fundamental framework for building these software-based systems.

The enterprise resource planning system installed at each company must be customized to match the business requirements of the enterprise. At a large company, such a system may take four to six years to implement and cost hundreds of millions of dollars. The company hopes

to regain the investment through the advantages offered by enterprise resource planning.

Advantages of enterprise resource planning include complete integration of information systems across departments, better project management, and better customer service. Complete integration means information is shared rapidly and management receives a more complete and timely view of the organization through the information. Better and faster reporting of the state of the enterprise leads managers to better decisions. Enterprise resource planning also helps management in a company to better manage the global nature of many enterprises. The reliance on one information system, rather than up to several hundred systems, allows the information technology department to focus on one type of technology and simplifies relationships with information technology vendors.

WEB LINK 14-5

Enterprise Resource Planning

For more information, visit scsite.com/dc2007/ch14/weblink and then click Enterprise Resource Planning.

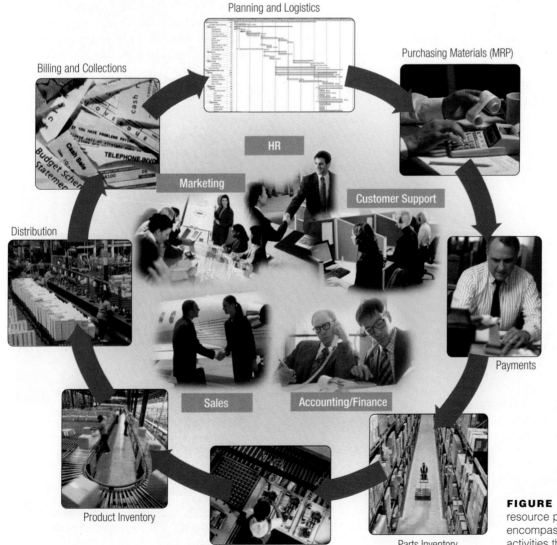

FIGURE 14-18 Enterprise resource planning (ERP) encompasses all of the major activities throughout a business.

CONTENT MANAGEMENT SYSTEMS A **content management system** (**CMS**) is an information system that is a combination of databases, software, and procedures that organizes and allows access to various forms of documents and other files, including images and multimedia content. A content management system includes information about the files and data, called *metadata*. For example, the metadata for a company's employee manual may include the author's name, revision number, a brief summary, and last revision date. The content management system also provides security controls for the content, such as who is allowed to add, view, and modify content and on which content the user is allowed to perform those operations.

Users add content to a content management system using a graphical user interface or Web page. Based on the user's actions, the content management system processes content, categorizes the content, *indexes* the content so that it can later be searched, and stores the content. Users then have access to the content stored in such a system through other applications, such as an enterprise portal (Figure 14-19).

An enterprise portal gathers information from the content management system, other information sources from within the enterprise, and information external to the enterprise, such as news services.

Publishing entities, such as news services, use content management systems to keep Web sites up-to-date. As news or information is published, it is categorized and updated on the appropriate sections of the Web site. For example, a sports writer may submit a story to the content management system and add metadata that indicates that the story is a headline story. The content management system categorizes the story so that it is displayed as the first item with a large headline on the sports section of the Web site. The content management system indexes the information in the story so that users who search the Web site based on keywords in the story will find a link to the story.

Many content management systems serve to enhance the effectiveness of groupware and collaboration software. Groupware, such as Lotus Notes from IBM, can be integrated with content management systems.

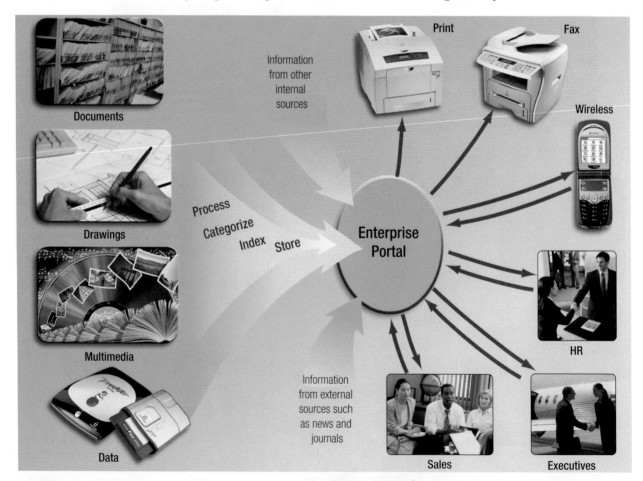

FIGURE 14-19 A content management system (CMS) helps a company classify and manage volumes of documents and media for future retrieval and use.

Test your knowledge of pages 714 through 732 in Quiz Yourself 14-1.

ENTERPRISE-WIDE TECHNOLOGIES

Several technologies adopted by enterprises allow companies flexibility and the ability to move swiftly in a business environment. By using standard and accepted technologies, the company does not need to reengineer solutions to typical problems. Commonly used technologies provide the organization with a starting point to solve problems present in many large organizations.

Some of the common technologies used in enterprises include portals, data warehouses, electronic data interchange, extranets, Web services, document management systems, workflow, and virtual private networks. The following sections discuss each of these technologies.

Portals

A **portal** is a collection of links, content, and services presented on a Web page and designed to guide users to information they likely are to find interesting for their particular job function. A service may include a portion of a Web page that allows the user to check package shipment status for an overnight delivery service or the ability to check airline flight schedules or flight status. Portals combine information from several business sources, both inside and outside the enterprise (Figure 14-20). A portal often includes searching

capabilities or a link to a search engine, such as Google. Organizations often deploy *enterprise search* technology that allows users to perform searches across many enterprise-wide information systems and databases. Users typically can customize the portal Web site to meet their needs. The customization of users' portal pages to meet their needs is called *personalization*.

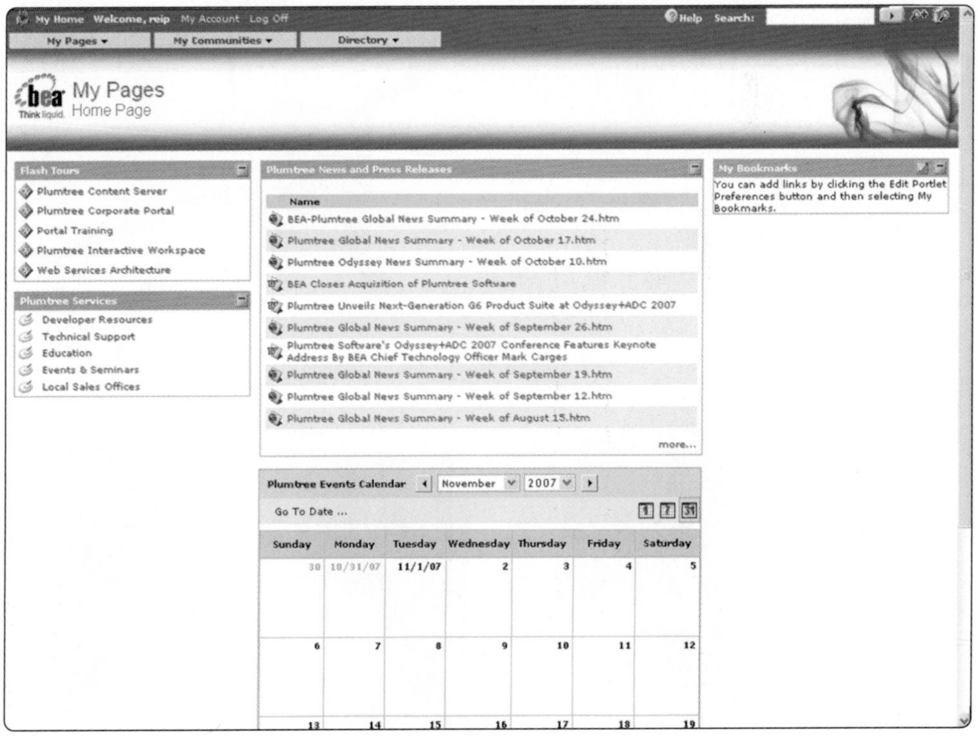

FIGURE 14-20 Portals allow users quick access to a multitude of information sources that they access on a regular basis.

Users within a department or those working together on a project often have similar views of the portal. An executive may have access to daily financial summaries on the portal Web page, while a customer service representative views updates to product problems. Information from external sources included on a portal Web page can include weather, news, reference tools, and instant messaging.

Data Warehouses

A **data warehouse** is a huge database that stores and manages the data required to analyze historical and current transactions. Software, such as enterprise resource planning and Manufacturing Resource Planning II programs, store and access data in a data warehouse.

Most data warehouses include one or more databases and one or more information systems storing data in the data warehouse. The data in the databases consists of transaction data required for decision making. This data may come from internal or external sources (Figure 14-21). Some data warehouses use Web farming for their external data. *Web farming* is the process of collecting data from the Internet as a source for the data warehouse. With Web resources, the company must convert the data to a form suitable for the data warehouse.

Another growing external source of information is a click stream. A *click stream* is a collection of every action that users make as they move through a Web site. By analyzing visitors' click streams, companies identify consumer preferences and determine which Web pages are most attractive to visitors.

The data in a data warehouse is accurate as of a moment in time. It contains snapshots of current and historical transactions. Thus, you usually do not change the content of existing data in a data warehouse. As time passes, you simply add new data. The data warehouse also contains summarizations of this data.

WEB LINK 14-7

Data Warehouse

For more information, visit scsite.com/dc2007/ch14/weblink and then click Data Warehouse.

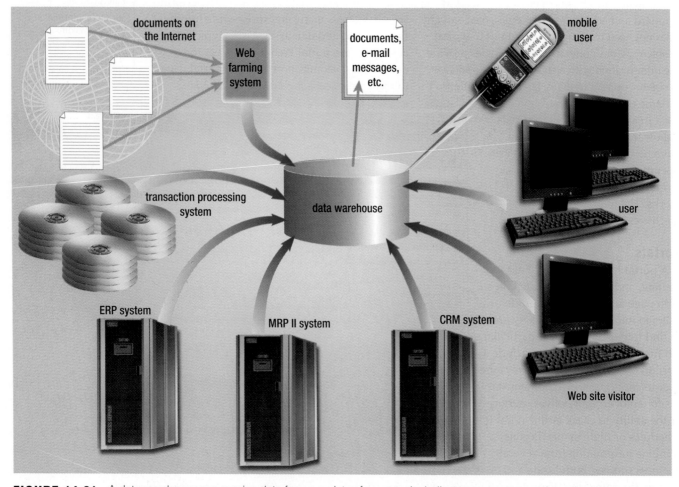

FIGURE 14-21 A data warehouse can receive data from a variety of sources, including company transactions, the Internet, and Web site visitor click streams.

EDI

EDI (**electronic data interchange**) is a set of standards that controls the transfer of business data and information among computers both within and among enterprises. One of the first steps in the development of e-commerce was electronic data interchange, which originally was created to eliminate paperwork and improve response time in business interactions. Today, businesses use these standards to communicate with industry partners over the Internet and telephone lines.

Despite the introduction of newer technologies, electronic data interchange continues to thrive in many businesses. Companies can set up their own electronic data interchange networks or subscribe to a third party electronic data interchange service provider. Errors in processing are reduced because the technology validates information that is communicated by both parties.

Extranets

An **extranet** is the portion of a company's network that allows customers or suppliers of a company to access parts of an enterprise's intranet. An extranet provides a secure, physical connection to the company's network. Customers may use the extranet to place and monitor orders electronically or to make payments. Suppliers may check inventory levels of the parts they supply to the company and receive orders and payments from the company. Extranets improve efficiency by replacing the postal service, faxes, or telephone calls as the communications medium of choice. Recently, extranets have replaced or supplemented existing electronic data interchange systems.

Web Services

Web services include a relatively new set of software technologies that allows businesses to create products and B2B (business-to-business) interactions over the Internet. Web services represent an evolutionary step when compared with electronic data interchange. They send and receive requests for information from an enterprise's Web site using XML. Recall that XML was discussed in Chapter 12. Web services are made available either internally or externally.

Web services do not include traditional user interfaces, such as a Web page. Rather, users build their own interfaces to the Web services when necessary. This means that companies provide a critical piece of business functionality to a user without worrying about providing a complete solution. Two popular platforms for building and running Web services are the Sun Microsystems J2EE platform and the Microsoft .NET platform.

For example, a company may provide inventory information as a Web service (Figure 14-22). Customers or suppliers that want to access this information need to use an Internet connection to communicate with the Web service and request the information from the Web service. A customer may ask for a quantity of an item in stock and receive back a number from the Web service. How the customer uses that information, whether displayed to an end user or stored in a database, is up to the customer. Typically, the customer, or consumer, of the Web service must write a program to use the Web service.

FAQ 14-4

Can I use someone else's Web service?

If an individual or a company has made its Web service available to the public, you can use the Web service. You may need some minimal Web programming skills or an application that can understand how to communicate with others' Web services. Some third parties, such as the Google Maps Web site, allow you to use their Web services free. For more information, visit scsite.com/dc2007/ch14/faq and then click Web Services.

FIGURE 14-22 HOW A WEB SERVICE MIGHT WORK

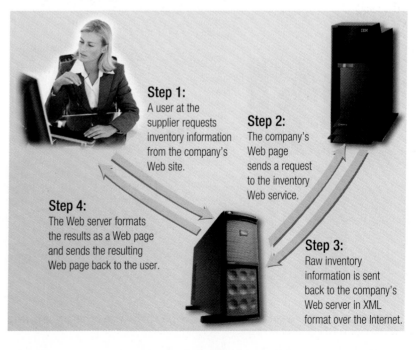

Step 1:
A user at the supplier requests inventory information from the company's Web site.

Step 2:
The company's Web page sends a request to the inventory Web service.

Step 3:
Raw inventory information is sent back to the company's Web server in XML format over the Internet.

Step 4:
The Web server formats the results as a Web page and sends the resulting Web page back to the user.

Document Management Systems

A **document management system (DMS)** allows for storage and management of a company's documents, such as word processing documents, presentations, and spreadsheets. A central library, or *repository*, stores all documents within a company or department. The system supports access control, security, version tracking of documents, search capabilities, and the ability for users to check-in and check-out documents. Users are granted access to certain parts of the repository depending on their needs. For example, one user may be responsible for creating promotional material, and therefore has the ability to create, read, and write presentations in the marketing department's repository. Salespersons only need to be able to read or copy the presentations from the repository, and therefore are granted only read privileges to the marketing department's repository.

A document management system has the benefit of tracking a document throughout its life cycle, from creation, through changes, and finally to archival. Additional information can be stored along with the document that describes the uses and history of the document. This information can include the document's creation date, the user who created the document, the project to which the document belongs, copyright information, a summary of the document, and any keywords associated with the document. This information can be used for searches within the document repository.

Workflow

A **workflow** is a defined process that identifies the specific set of steps involved in completing a particular project or business process. A workflow may be a written set of rules or a set of rules that exists in an information system. When an insurance company receives a claim from a customer, a workflow in the insurance company defines how the claim is validated, processed, and paid. Workflow rules trigger particular actions to be taken within the company. On an insurance claim, the first step may be to validate that the customer has a current policy and the claim form is filled out correctly. If not, the claim is rejected and the customer is notified.

A **workflow application** is a program that assists in the management and tracking of all the activities in a business process from start to finish. Enterprises use workflow applications to assist in defining complex workflows. Workflow applications also enforce the rules of the workflow once the workflow is defined and in place.

Virtual Private Network

Many companies today allow access to their company networks through a virtual private network. When a mobile user, remote office, vendor, or customer connects to a company's network using the Internet, a **virtual private network (VPN)** provides them with a secure connection to the company network server, as if they had a private line. Virtual private networks help to ensure that transmitted data is safe from being intercepted by unauthorized people (Figure 14-23). VPNs securely extend

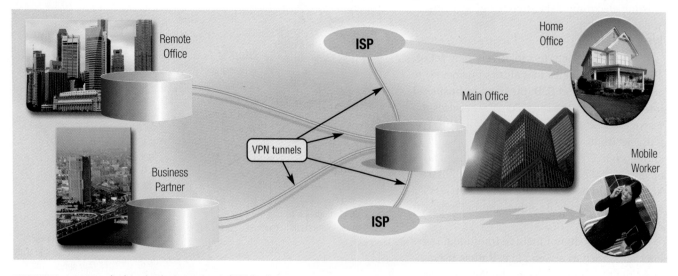

FIGURE 14-23   A virtual private network (VPN) allows a company to extend its internal network securely.

the company's internal network beyond the physical boundaries of the company. The secure connection created over the Internet between the user's computer and the company's network is called a *VPN tunnel*.

E-COMMERCE

Several market sectors have taken advantage of business opportunities on the Web. The more popular market segments include retail, finance, entertainment and media, travel, and health. The following paragraphs describe how the general public interacts with each of these types of enterprises on the Web.

E-Retailing

Retailing is one of the more visible market sectors of e-commerce. In retail, merchants sell products and services directly to a buyer. **E-retail**, also called *e-tail*, occurs when retailers use the Web to sell their products and services. Enterprises have adopted e-retail as a new way to reach customers. E-retailers constantly are challenging the old ways of conducting business as they bring new products and services to market. All e-retailers, however, operate in a similar way. Figure 14-24 shows an example of how an e-retail transaction might occur.

FIGURE 14-24 HOW A BUSINESS-TO-CONSUMER (B2C) E-COMMERCE TRANSACTION TAKES PLACE

Step 1:
The customer displays the e-retailer's electronic storefront.

Step 2:
The customer collects purchases in an electronic shopping cart.

Step 3:
The customer enters payment information in a secure Web site. The e-retailer sends financial information to a bank.

Step 4:
The bank performs security checks and sends authorization back to the e-retailer.

Step 7:
While the order travels to the customer, shipping information is posted on the Web.

Step 6:
The fulfillment center packages the order, prepares it for shipment, and then sends a report to the server where records are updated.

Step 5:
The e-retailer's Web server sends confirmation to the customer, processes the order, and then sends it to the fulfillment center.

Step 8:
The order is delivered to the customer.

For example, a customer (consumer) visits an online business at the company's electronic storefront and adds items to a shopping cart. When ready to complete the sale, the customer proceeds to the checkout. At this time, the customer enters personal and financial data through a secure Web connection. The transaction and financial data automatically are verified at a banking Web site. Several methods are available through which a company can accept payments from a customer. Companies sometimes bill customers through traditional paper invoices.

If the bank or merchant account provider approves the transaction, the customer receives a confirmation notice of the purchase. Then, the e-retailer processes the order and sends it to the fulfillment center where it is packaged and shipped. Inventory systems then are updated. The e-retailer notifies the bank of the shipment, and payment is sent via electronic channels to the e-retailer. Shipping information is posted on the Internet, so the customer can track the order. The customer typically receives the order a few days after the purchase. Read Ethics & Issues 14-2 for a related discussion.

Finance

Financial institutions include any business that manages the circulation of money, grants credit, makes investments, or meets banking needs. These include banks, mortgage companies, brokerage firms, and insurance companies. In the past, financial institutions often were strictly traditional bricks-and-mortar institutions. Today, many also conduct business on the Internet.

Online banking allows users to pay bills from their computer, that is, transfer money electronically from their account to a payee's account such as the electric company or telephone company. At anytime, online banking users also can download transactions such as cleared checks, ATM withdrawals, and deposits, which allows them to have an up-to-date bank statement.

With **online trading**, users invest in stocks, options, bonds, treasuries, certificates of deposit, money markets, annuities, mutual funds, and so on — without using a broker. Many investors prefer online stock trading because the transaction fee for each trade usually is substantially less than when trading through a broker. Many of these online businesses also provide other financial services such as life insurance and retirement plans.

ETHICS & ISSUES 14-2

Would You Buy Merchandise Online?

Customers at a bricks-and-mortar business can examine products and walk out with their purchases in hand and the knowledge that, should a problem arise, the vendor will be there tomorrow to correct the difficulty. For customers at an online storefront, however, products are pictured or described, purchases are ordered, sellers are anonymous, and the storefront itself is as short-lived as the image on a computer screen. Because Internet transactions are faceless, a business has to generate trust to turn window shoppers into buyers, especially when purchasing potentially dangerous products such as prescription medications. Reputable online merchants often display an address and telephone number and indicate membership in an Internet protection group such as Netcheck, TRUSTe, or the BBBOnLine. Many e-businesses display a security or privacy statement to encourage customer confidence. Would you be comfortable purchasing a product online? Why or why not? How would such factors as your familiarity with the vendor, notifications on the vendor's Web site, the type of product, and the cost of the product influence your decision? Why?

FAQ 14-5

How can I tell that a financial Web site is secure?

Make sure that the Web site address begins with https:// rather than http:// whenever you are viewing or transmitting personal financial information on a Web site. Financial Web sites should include both privacy and security policies for you to read. The security policy should tell you how the information is both transmitted and then stored securely once the company has the information. For more information, visit scsite.com/dc2007/ch14/faq and then click Web Site Security.

Travel

The Web provides many travel-related services. If you need directions, you simply can enter a starting point and destination, and many Web sites provide detailed directions along with a map. Users can make airline reservations and reserve a hotel or car.

Some of these Web sites are shopping bots that save users time by doing all the investigative cost-comparison work. A **shopping bot** is a Web site that searches the Internet for the best price on a product or service in which you are interested (Figure 14-25).

With airline reservations, for example, simply name the price you are willing to pay per ticket, your travel dates, and the cities between which you are traveling. The shopping bot finds an available flight arrangement that meets your budget.

FIGURE 14-25 At Priceline.com, you name the price you are willing to pay and Priceline.com finds available commodities such as flights, hotel rooms, and car rentals that meet your budget.

Entertainment and Media

The technology behind the Web has enabled entertainment and media to take many forms. Music, videos, news, sporting events, and 3-D multiplayer games are a growing part of the Web's future. Newsprint on the Web is not replacing the newspaper, but enhancing it and reaching different populations. Streaming technology currently supports live radio broadcasting, live videos, and live concerts. As discussed in Chapter 2, streaming allows users to access and use a file while it is transmitting. Users can purchase music online and download MP3 files directly to a computer hard disk, allowing them to listen to the purchased music immediately from a computer or any MP3 player. For additional types of entertainment and media, read the Digital Entertainment feature that follows Chapter 15.

Health

Many Web sites provide up-to-date medical, fitness, nutrition, or exercise information. As with any other information on the Web, users should verify the legitimacy of the Web site before relying on its information.

Some of these health-related Web sites maintain databases of doctors and dentists to help individuals find the one who suits their needs. They also may have chat rooms, so people can talk to others diagnosed with similar conditions. Read Ethics & Issues 14-3 for a related discussion.

WEB LINK 14-8

Online Travel

For more information, visit scsite.com/dc2007/ch14/weblink and then click Online Travel.

ETHICS & ISSUES 14-3

Would You Trust an Online Medical Diagnosis?

More than 2.5 million consumers have turned to a medical-practice Web site for a diagnosis, and 35 million people claim they would be willing to try such a Web site. Most physicians' Web sites structure an online doctor's visit by having patients complete a form containing a series of questions and decision trees. Based on the responses, doctors suggest probable diagnoses and even may offer an order form that can be used, along with a credit card, to order prescribed medicines. Medical-practice Web sites provide greater access to medical information and allow doctors more time to see patients with urgent problems. Some people, though, question any medical diagnosis based on a form, worry about patient privacy, and believe obtaining prescription medicines online is unsafe. Should a physician be allowed to diagnose an ailment and/or dispense prescription medicine online? Why or why not? Does the nature of the ailment make a difference? If a problem occurs, should a medical-practice Web site be open to a malpractice lawsuit? Why? Would you trust an online medical diagnosis? Why or why not?

Many bricks-and-mortar pharmacies have an online counterpart that exists on the Web, allowing customers to refill prescriptions and ask pharmacists questions using customer interaction management software. Some Web sites even allow consumers to order prescription drugs online and have them delivered directly to their door (Figure 14-26).

Other Business Services

Enterprises use the Web to provide services to consumers and other businesses. Public relations, online advertising, direct mail, recruiting, credit, sales, market research, technical support, training, software consulting, and Internet access represent a few of the areas of service.

FIGURE 14-26 At drugstore.com, you can fill prescriptions online and have them delivered directly to your door.

Test your knowledge of pages 733 through 740 in Quiz Yourself 14-2.

QUIZ YOURSELF 14-2

Instructions: Find the true statement below. Then, rewrite the remaining false statements so they are true.

1. A portal is the portion of a company's network that allows customers or suppliers of a company to access parts of an enterprise's intranet.

2. A data warehouse is a huge database that stores and manages the data required to analyze historical and current transactions.

3. A VPN is a server that is placed on a network with the sole purpose of providing storage to users and information systems attached to the network.

4. A workflow application helps an enterprise collect, archive, index, and retrieve its resources.

Quiz Yourself Online: To further check your knowledge of technologies used throughout the enterprise and e-commerce, visit scsite.com/dc2007/ch14/quiz and then click Objectives 4 – 5.

ENTERPRISE HARDWARE

Enterprise hardware allows large organizations to manage and store information and data using devices geared for heavy use, maximum availability, and maximum efficiency. To meet these needs, enterprise hardware often includes levels of *redundancy*, which means that if one piece of the hardware breaks, another part can assume its tasks. (Redundant components are discussed later in this chapter.)

One of the goals of an enterprise's hardware is to maintain a high level of availability to end users. The *availability* of hardware to users is a measure of how often it is online. Highly available hardware is accessible 24 hours a day, 365 days a year.

Enterprises use a variety of hardware types to meet their large-scale needs. The following sections discuss a variety of enterprise hardware solutions.

RAID

For applications that depend on reliable data access, users must have the data available when they attempt to access it. Some manufacturers provide a type of hard disk system that connects several smaller disks into a single unit that acts like a single large hard disk. A group of two or more integrated hard disks is called a **RAID (redundant array of independent disks)**. Although quite expensive for large computers, RAID (Figure 14-27) is more reliable than traditional hard disks. Networks and Internet servers often use RAID.

FIGURE 14-27 A group of two or more integrated hard disks, called a RAID (redundant array of independent disks), often is used with network servers. Shown here is a rack-mounted RAID chassis including the hard disks.

RAID duplicates data, instructions, and information to improve data reliability. RAID implements this duplication in different ways, depending on the storage design, or level, being used. (These levels are not hierarchical. That is, higher levels are not necessarily better than lower levels.) The simplest RAID storage design is *level 1*, called *mirroring*, which writes data on two disks at the same time to duplicate the data (Figure 14-28a). A level 1 configuration enhances storage reliability because, if a drive should fail, a duplicate of the requested item is available elsewhere within the array of disks.

Other RAID levels use a technique called *striping*, which splits data, instructions, and information across multiple disks in the array (Figure 14-28b). Striping improves disk access times, but does not offer data duplication. For this reason, some RAID levels combine both mirroring and striping.

FAQ 14-6

Can I use RAID in my personal computer?

Yes. RAID is becoming more common in personal computers. Using RAID level 1 in a personal computer is relatively inexpensive. All you need are a second hard disk and an inexpensive RAID controller to implement your own RAID storage. Using RAID at home protects your data from hard disk glitches and crashes and gives you peace of mind. For more information, visit scsite.com/dc2007/ch14/faq and then click RAID.

FIGURE 14-28a (mirroring)

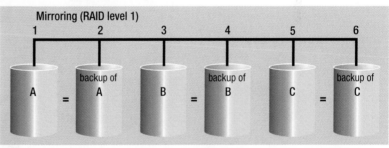

FIGURE 14-28b (striping)

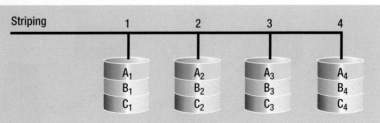

FIGURE 14-28 In RAID level 1, called mirroring, a backup disk exists for each disk. Other RAID levels use striping; that is, portions of each disk are placed on multiple disks.

Network Attached Storage and Storage Area Networks

Network attached storage (**NAS**) is a server that is placed on a network with the sole purpose of providing storage to users and information systems attached to the network (Figure 14-29a). A network attached storage server often is called a *storage appliance* because it is a piece of equipment with only one function — to provide additional storage. Administrators quickly add storage to an existing network simply by attaching a new network attached storage server to the network.

A **storage area network** (**SAN**) is a high-speed network with the sole purpose of providing storage to other servers to which it is attached (Figure 14-29b). A storage area network is a network that includes only storage devices. High-speed fiber-optic cable connects other networks and servers to the storage area network, so the networks and servers have fast access to large storage capacities. A storage area network connects to networks and other servers up to seven miles away using high-speed network connections.

Both network attached storage and storage area network solutions offer easier management of storage, fast access to storage, sharing of storage, and isolation of storage from other servers. Isolation of storage from other servers lets other servers concentrate on performing a

WEB LINK 14-9

NAS and SAN

For more information, visit scsite.com/dc2007/ch14/weblink and then click NAS and SAN.

FIGURE 14-29a   (network attached storage on a LAN)

FIGURE 14-29b   (a SAN provides centralized storage for servers and networks)

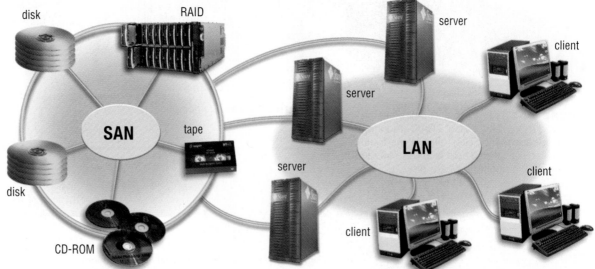

FIGURE 14-29   Network attached storage (NAS) and a storage area network (SAN) connect to existing servers and networks in different ways.

specific task, rather than consuming resources involved in the tasks related to storage. Network attached storage and storage area network systems connect to existing networks and servers in different manners as shown in Figure 14-29. Both storage solutions include disk, tape, DVD-ROM, and CD-ROM types of storage.

Enterprises sometimes choose to implement both network attached storage and storage area network solutions. A network attached storage server is better suited for adding additional storage to an existing network, such as a department's file server. A company typically implements a storage area network solution as central storage for an entire enterprise or a large information system, such as an enterprise resource planning system.

Enterprise Storage Systems

Many companies use networks. Data, information, and instructions stored on the network must be easily accessible to all authorized users. The data, information, and instructions also must be secure, so unauthorized users cannot access the network. An **enterprise storage system** is a strategy that focuses on the availability, protection, organization, and backup of storage in a company.

The goal of an enterprise storage system is to consolidate storage so operations run as efficiently as possible. Most enterprise storage systems manage extraordinary amounts of data. For example, one large retailer manages a 485-terabyte (485,000,000,000,000 bytes) storage system to store sales data. Read Ethics & Issues 14-4 for a related discussion.

To implement an enterprise storage system, a company uses a combination of techniques. As shown in Figure 14-30, an enterprise storage system may use servers, RAID, a tape library, CD-ROM and DVD-ROM jukeboxes, Internet backup, network attached storage devices, and/or a storage area network. Enterprises often use *Fibre Channel* technology to connect to storage systems at data rates up to 4 Gbps. The list on the next page explains these storage techniques.

WEB LINK 14-10

Fibre Channel
For more information, visit scsite.com/ dc2007/ch14/weblink and then click Fibre Channel.

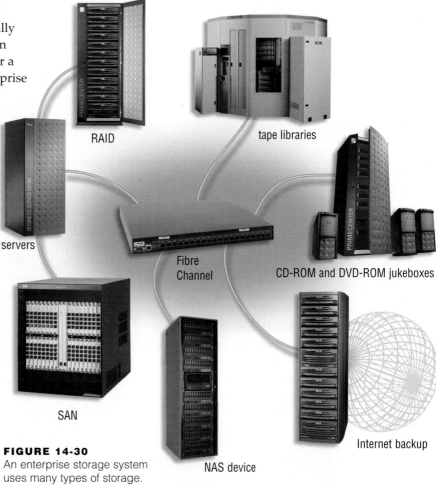

RAID

tape libraries

servers

Fibre Channel

CD-ROM and DVD-ROM jukeboxes

SAN

Internet backup

FIGURE 14-30
An enterprise storage system uses many types of storage.

NAS device

How Much Data Should Companies Be Required to Keep?

In 2002, the Sarbanes-Oxley Act was signed into law, providing a myriad of financial reporting requirements and guidelines for public companies. A main focus of the law is the retention of business records. As provisions of the law slowly have come into effect, companies have been faced with massive new data storage requirements for these records. For example, all e-mail messages within a company are considered to be business records and must be retained. Deleting stored e-mail messages constitutes a destruction of evidence infraction. Penalties include 20 years of prison for any employee who alters or destroys records or documents. IT departments are faced not only with understanding this complex law, but also with ensuring accuracy of financial data, determining policies for record retention, and building storage capacity to hold all of the data. Supporters of the law cite its need due to the recent wave of corporate scandals. Opponents say that the law is overreaching and costs too much for the added benefits. Is the Sarbanes-Oxley Act an unfair burden on companies? Why or why not? Should companies be able to engage in internal communications without the fear that those communications could be used against them later? Why or why not? How should companies go about reacting to the law? Are such laws necessary in order to protect the public? Why or why not?

- A server stores data, information, and instructions needed by users on the network.
- RAID ensures that data is not lost if one drive fails.
- A *tape library* is a high-capacity tape system that works with multiple tape cartridges for storing backups.
- A **CD-ROM server**, or **DVD-ROM server**, also called a *CD-ROM jukebox*, or *DVD-ROM jukebox*, holds hundreds of CD-ROMs or DVD-ROMs that can contain programs and data.
- Companies using *Internet backup* store data, information, and instructions on the Web.
- A network attached storage device is an easy way to add additional hard disk space to the network.
- A storage area network is a high-speed network that connects storage devices.

Some companies manage an enterprise storage system in-house. Other enterprises elect to offload all (or at least the backup) storage management to an outside organization or online Web service. This practice is known as *outsourcing*. Some vendors focus on providing enterprise storage systems to clients. A data warehouse might seek this type of outside service.

Blade Servers

Blade servers, sometimes called *ultradense servers*, pack a complete computer server, such as a Web server or network server, on a single card, or *blade*, rather than a system unit. Each blade server includes a processor, memory, hard disk, network card, and ports on the card. The individual blades insert in a *blade server chassis* that can hold many blades. Using blade servers allows an organization to fit 16 or more blades in the physical space occupied by a single server. Figure 14-31 shows a blade and a chassis that holds many blades.

Besides the savings in space offered by blade servers, blade servers require less maintenance, use less energy, generate less heat, and easily are replaced or upgraded. The hardware industry, however, disagrees on a standard for blade servers. A blade server made by one manufacturer often is incompatible with the blade server chassis of another manufacturer.

FAQ 14-7

How popular are blade servers?

One study estimates that while blade servers accounted for less than 10 percent of server sales today, they will account for at least 29 percent of server sales by 2008, worth more than $2.5 billion in sales. For more information, visit scsite.com/dc2007/ch14/faq and then click Blade Servers.

Thin Clients

Thin clients are small terminal-like computers that mostly rely on a server for data storage and processing. These computers are inexpensive compared to a personal computer. As shown in Figure 14-32, the system unit of a thin client usually consists of a monitor and optical drive. A keyboard and a mouse, or other pointing device, are attached to the system unit. A thin client typically does not contain a hard drive, and the lack of many components usually seen on a personal computer makes thin clients much easier and less expensive to maintain and repair.

FIGURE 14-32   A thin client usually consists of a monitor, optical drive, keyboard, and mouse.

FIGURE 14-31   A blade server contains several very small servers, each on its own blade within the server.

The processing for a thin client usually is done on a server to which the client is attached over a network. The server may be configured in two ways — either as a virtual server on a central server or as a personal computer blade. In the first configuration, a single server is virtually divided into several personal computers. That is, one server may run 20 to 50 virtual servers at the same time. Each thin client shares the resources of the central server, but each individual virtual server has its own place in the memory of the central server. The second type of configuration, the *personal computer blade*, works in much the same manner as blade servers. Individual PC blades in a blade server each act as a separate personal computer, containing a processor, memory, and hard disk.

High-Availability Systems

High-availability systems continue running and performing tasks for at least 99 percent of the time. Some users demand that high-availability systems be available for 99.9 percent or 99.99 percent of the time. *Uptime* is a measurement of availability. A system that has uptime of 99.99 percent is nonfunctional for less than one hour per year. That one hour, called *downtime*, includes any time that the computer crashes, needs repairs, or requires installation of replacement or upgrade parts.

Critical business systems demand high levels of availability. Telecommunications companies, such as local telephone companies, rely on high-availability systems to deliver telephone service. Emergency 911 communications centers require almost 100 percent uptime for their hardware and software applications as mandated by law. Centralized accounting or financial systems must be available to gather sales and other accounting information from locations scattered around the globe.

High-availability systems often include a feature called hot-swapping. *Hot-swapping* allows components, such as a RAID hard disk or power supplies, to be replaced while the rest of the system continues to perform its tasks. A high-availability system also may include redundant components. **Redundant components**, such as redundant power supplies, allow for a functioning component to take over automatically the tasks of a similar component that fails. When a component fails, the system administrator is notified, but the computer continues to perform its tasks because a redundant component has taken its place automatically in the system.

Scalability

As an enterprise grows, its information systems either must grow with it or must be replaced. **Scalability** is a measure of how well computer hardware, software, or an information system can grow to meet increasing performance demands. A system that is designed, built, or purchased when the company is small may be inadequate when the company doubles in size.

A company may find that its Web site is becoming overwhelmed by customers and prospective customers. If the Web site is scalable, then the Web administrator can add more Web servers to handle the additional visitors to the Web site. Similarly, an enterprise's storage needs usually grow daily, meaning that storage systems should be scalable to store the ever-growing data generated by users.

Adding additional hardware often is the easiest method to grow, or scale, an information system. Because of software constraints, however, information systems may grow to a point at which adding more hardware does not achieve the return on investment required to justify the cost of the hardware. Often, at some point, a system no longer scales and must be replaced with a new system.

Utility and Grid Computing

As the need for scalability increases, companies often find that using outside computing resources is more economical than building new computing capacity internally. Utility and grid computing are two new technologies that provide flexible and massive online computing power. *Utility computing*, or *on demand computing*, allows companies to use the processing power sitting idle in a network located somewhere else in the world. For example, an employee working during the day in California could use computing power in a Paris network system located in an office that is closed for the evening. When the company uses the computing resources, they pay a fee based on the amount of computing time and other resources that they consume, much in the way that consumers pay utility companies, such as the electric company, based on how much electricity they use.

Grid computing combines many servers and/or personal computers on a network, such as the Internet, to act as one large computer. As with utility computing, a company may pay for the use of a grid based on the amount of processing time that it needs. Grid computing often is used in research environments, such as climate research and life science problems. Read Looking Ahead 14-2 for a look at the next generation of grid computing.

LOOKING AHEAD 14-2

The Future of Grid Computing

Depression, stroke, and epilepsy may be diagnosed and treated much more quickly with advances in grid computing. This same form of technology may help interpret signals from radio telescopes and discover the genetic information housed within proteins.

Near the end of this decade, scientists and engineers foresee using grid computing to study the climate and to conduct biomedical research that will end deadly diseases. In the business world, commercial applications for grid computing are expected to rake in more than $15 billion by 2009. For more information, visit scsite.com/dc2007/ch14/looking and then click Grid Computing.

Interoperability

Enterprises typically build and buy a diverse set of information systems. An information system often must share information, or have **interoperability**, with other information systems within the enterprise. Information systems that more easily share information with other information systems are said to be *open*. Information systems that are more difficult to interoperate with other information systems are said to be *closed*, or *proprietary*. Recent open systems employ XML and Web services to allow a greater level of interoperability.

Enterprises own diverse hardware, software, and information systems for a variety of reasons. The enterprise may want to diversify its technology to reduce the risk of relying on just one type of technology. When a company relies on one type of technology, it risks that the technology may be limited in its ability to grow or change with the company, that the technology may become obsolete, and that the technology may become more expensive relative to competing technologies. Enterprises also grow through acquisitions of other companies, and the systems of the acquired companies must be integrated into the enterprise's existing systems.

BACKUP PROCEDURES

Business and home users can perform four types of backup: full, differential, incremental, or selective. A fifth type, continuous data protection, is used by large enterprises. A full backup, sometimes called an archival backup, copies all of the files in the computer. A full backup provides the best protection against data loss because it copies all program and data files. Performing a full backup can be time-consuming. Users often combine full backups with differential and incremental backups. A differential backup copies only the files that have changed since the last full backup. An incremental backup copies only the files that have changed since the last full or last incremental backup. A selective backup, sometimes called a partial backup, allows the user to choose specific files to back up, regardless of whether or not the files have changed since the last incremental backup.

The main differences between a differential backup and an incremental backup is the number of backup files and the time required for backup. With a differential backup, you always have two backups: the full backup and the differential backup that contains all changes since the last full backup.

With incremental backups, you have the full backup and one or more incremental backups. The first incremental backup contains changes since the last full backup. Each subsequent incremental backup contains changes only since the previous incremental backup. For files that contain many changes and are comprised of a large portion of the total data, incremental backup usually is fastest. If files contain only a few changes, differential backups may be appropriate. For the greatest flexibility or if backup space is limited, a selective backup allows you to choose specific files that you would like to back up. Figure 14-33 outlines the advantages and disadvantages of each type of backup.

VARIOUS BACKUP METHODS

TYPE OF BACKUP	ADVANTAGES	DISADVANTAGES
Full	Fastest recovery method. All files are saved.	Longest backup time.
Differential	Fast backup method. Requires minimal storage space to back up.	Recovery is time-consuming because the last full backup plus the differential backup are needed.
Incremental	Fastest backup method. Requires minimal storage space to back up. Only most recent changes saved.	Recovery is most time-consuming because the last full backup and all incremental backups since the last full backup are needed.
Selective	Fast backup method. Provides great flexibility.	Difficult to manage individual file backups. Least manageable of all the backup methods.
Continuous	The only real-time backup. Very fast recovery of data.	Very expensive and requires a great amount of storage.

FIGURE 14-33 The advantages and disadvantages of various backup methods.

Continuous data protection (CDP), or continuous backup, is a backup plan in which all data is backed up whenever a change is made. Because CDP is costly, few organizations have implemented continuous data protection, but its popularity is growing quickly as the cost for the technology falls. Backup procedures specify a regular plan of copying and storing important data and program files. Generally, users should perform a full backup at regular intervals, such as at the end of each week and at the end of the month. Between full backups, you can perform differential or incremental backups. Figure 14-34 illustrates a sample approach a company might follow for backing up its computer for one month. This combination of full and incremental backups provides an efficient way to protect data. Whatever backup procedures a company adopts, they should be stated clearly, documented in writing, and followed consistently.

Disaster Recovery Plan

A **disaster recovery plan** is a written plan describing the steps a company would take to restore computer operations in the event of a disaster. Every company and each department or division within an enterprise usually has its own disaster recovery plans. A disaster recovery plan contains four major components: the emergency plan, the backup plan, the recovery plan, and the test plan.

FIGURE 14-34
This calendar shows a backup method strategy for a month. End-of-month backups usually are kept for at least one year.

November 2007

MONDAY	TUESDAY	WEDNESDAY	THURSDAY	FRIDAY	SAT/SUN
29 DAILY INCREMENTAL	30 DAILY INCREMENTAL	31 END OF MONTH FULL BACKUP	1 DAILY INCREMENTAL	2 WEEKLY FULL BACKUP	3/4
5 DAILY INCREMENTAL	6 DAILY INCREMENTAL	7 DAILY INCREMENTAL	8 DAILY INCREMENTAL	9 WEEKLY FULL BACKUP	10/11
12 DAILY INCREMENTAL	13 DAILY INCREMENTAL	14 DAILY INCREMENTAL	15 DAILY INCREMENTAL	16 WEEKLY FULL BACKUP	17/18
19 DAILY INCREMENTAL	20 DAILY INCREMENTAL	21 DAILY INCREMENTAL	22 DAILY INCREMENTAL	23 WEEKLY FULL BACKUP	24/25
26 DAILY INCREMENTAL	27 DAILY INCREMENTAL	28 DAILY INCREMENTAL	29 DAILY INCREMENTAL	30 END OF MONTH FULL BACKUP	1/2

THE EMERGENCY PLAN   An *emergency plan* specifies the steps to be taken immediately after a disaster strikes. The emergency plan usually is organized by type of disaster, such as fire, flood, or earthquake. Depending on the nature and extent of the disaster, the procedures that are followed in an emergency will differ. All emergency plans should contain the following information:

1. Names and telephone numbers of people and organizations to notify (e.g., management, fire department, police department)
2. Procedures to follow with the computer equipment (e.g., equipment shutdown, power shutoff, file removal)
3. Employee evacuation procedures
4. Return procedures; that is, who can reenter the facility and what actions they are to perform

THE BACKUP PLAN   Once the procedures in the emergency plan have been executed, the next step is to follow the backup plan. The *backup plan* specifies how a company uses backup files and equipment to resume information processing. The backup plan should specify the location of an alternate computer facility in the event the company's normal location is destroyed or unusable.

When operations are so important that a company cannot afford to lose the operations to a disaster, the company often maintains a *hot site*, which is a separate facility that mirrors the systems and operations of the critical site. The hot site always operates concurrently with the main site, so that if either site becomes unavailable, the other site continues to meet the company's needs. The process of one system automatically taking the place of a failed system is called *failover*. A *cold site* is a site that mirrors the critical site, but does not become operational until the critical site becomes unavailable. When using a cold site, some time elapses between the disaster and when the cold site becomes functional.

The backup plan identifies these items:

1. The location of backup data, supplies, and equipment
2. The personnel responsible for gathering backup resources and transporting them to the alternate computer facility
3. A schedule indicating the order in which, and approximate time by which, each application should be up and running

For a backup plan to be successful, the company must back up all critical resources. Also, additional people, including possibly nonemployees, must be trained in the backup and recovery procedures because company personnel could be injured in a disaster.

The location of the alternate computer facility is important. It should be close enough to be convenient, yet not too close that a single disaster, such as an earthquake, could destroy both the main and alternate computer facilities. Some companies preinstall all the necessary hardware, software, and communications devices at the alternate computer facility. These facilities immediately are ready in the event of a disaster. In other cases, the alternate computer facility is simply an empty facility that can accommodate the necessary computer resources, if needed. One more alternative is to enter into a *reciprocal backup relationship* with another firm, where one firm provides space and sometimes equipment to the other in case of a disaster.

FAQ 14-8

Should I have a backup plan?

Yes! Even home computers need a backup plan. You probably know someone who lost valuable personal information due to a hard disk crash or other problem. Most modern operating systems include backup software. You should familiarize yourself with the software, develop a plan, and test both backing up and recovering data. For more information, visit scsite.com/dc2007/ch14/faq and then click Backup Software.

THE RECOVERY PLAN   The *recovery plan* specifies the actions to be taken to restore full information processing operations. As with the emergency plan, the recovery plan differs for each type of disaster. To prepare for disaster recovery, a company should establish planning committees, with each one responsible for different forms of recovery. For example, one committee is in charge of hardware replacement. Another is responsible for software replacement.

THE TEST PLAN   To provide assurance that the disaster plan is complete, it should be tested. A disaster recovery *test plan* contains information for simulating various levels of disasters and recording an organization's ability to recover. In a simulation, all personnel follow the steps in the disaster recovery plan. Any needed recovery actions that are not specified in the plan should be added. Although simulations can be scheduled, the best test of the plan is to simulate a disaster without advance notice.

Test your knowledge of pages 741 through 749 in Quiz Yourself 14-3.

QUIZ YOURSELF 14-3

Instructions: Find the true statement below. Then, rewrite the remaining false statements so they are true.

1. Network attached storage is a high-speed network with the sole purpose of providing storage to other servers to which it is attached.

2. Scalability refers to the ability of an information system to share information with other information systems.

3. A differential backup copies only the files that have changed since the last full or last incremental backup.

4. A full backup is the fastest backup method, requiring only minimal storage.

5. An emergency plan specifies how a company uses backup files and equipment to resume information processing.

6. The recovery plan specifies the actions to be taken to restore full information processing operations.

Quiz Yourself Online: To further check your knowledge of enterprise hardware, backup procedures, and a disaster recovery plan, visit scsite.com/dc2007/ch14/quiz and then click Objectives 6 – 8.

CHAPTER SUMMARY

This chapter reviewed the special computing requirements present in an enterprise-sized organization. Various types of users within an organization require different types of information systems. Large information systems become more valuable when they communicate with each other and offer users a great deal of flexibility in interacting with the information system and other users. The chapter discussed e-retailing and the types of businesses that use e-commerce.

Enterprises manage complex hardware, including storage area networks, RAID, and blade servers. Requirements for this enterprise hardware often include high-availability, scalability, and interoperability, which they meet with technologies such as grid and utility computing. The chapter also discussed the backup procedures present in a large organization.

CAREER CORNER

CIO

CIO (*chief information officer*) is the highest-ranking position in an information technology (IT) department. The CIO manages all of a company's information systems and computer resources. In large organizations, the CIO typically is a vice president and reports directly to the organization's CEO.

Depending on the organization, a CIO can be called an MIS (management information systems) manager, an IS (information systems) manager, or an IT (information technology) manager. Regardless of the title, the CIO determines an organization's information needs and provides the systems to meet those needs. The CIO sets an IT department's goals, policies, and procedures. In addition, the CIO evaluates technology, hires and supervises staff, oversees the network, directs user services, develops backup and disaster recovery plans, and manages the department budget. Perhaps most important, the CIO provides leadership, creating a vision for an IT department and helping the department deliver that vision.

Some CIOs work as consultants, providing corporate IT departments with short-term or long-term guidance. Most CIOs rise through the ranks of an organization's IT department. Generally, CIOs have a bachelor's degree or higher in computer science and at least ten years of experience in an IT department. Today, many CIOs also have an MBA. Pay reflects the importance of the CIO, with average salaries in excess of $200,000. For more information, visit scsite.com/dc2007/ch14/careers and then click CIO.

High-Tech Talk

NEURAL NETWORKS: LEARNING FROM EXPERIENCE

A *neural network* is a type of artificial intelligence system that attempts to emulate the way the human brain works. Neural networks are named after *neurons*, which are the billons of cells in the human brain that perform intelligent operations. Each neuron is like a small computer with basic capabilities. When billions of neurons are connected together, however, these cells are the intellectual capacity in the human brain, the most intelligent system known.

Neural networks are modeled on the human brain. A neural network uses an interconnected system of hundreds or thousands of specially designed circuits, also called *artificial neurons*. Like the brain's neurons, these circuits are connected together. Neural networks also are called *artificial neural networks* (*ANNs*) to differentiate the network of artificial neurons from the network of biological neurons in the human brain.

A neural network uses these circuits to create connections between inputs and outputs. The most common neural network model is the *multilayer perceptron* (*MLP*), which consists of at least three layers of circuits: a layer of input circuits, which is connected to one or more layers of hidden circuits, which are connected to a layer of output circuits (Figure 14-35). The knowledge of a neural network is housed in the hidden layers, which store the information that defines relationships between inputs and outputs.

Just as people do, neural networks learn from experience. Some neural networks are trained using a process called backpropagation, as shown in Figure 14-35. During *backpropagation*, the input data, which is the information used to make a decision, repeatedly is presented to the neural network via the input layer. The neural network then generates an output, which is the resulting decision, prediction, or response, based on the weighted connections between the inputs and outputs, as stored in the hidden layers.

The output of the neural network then is compared with the desired output, and the error is calculated based on historical or known data. This error then is fed back, or backpropagated, to the hidden layer to adjust the weights of the connection. During each repetition, the neural network learns to associate the weight of the relationship between certain inputs and outputs. It then adjusts the weights of the connections between the inputs and outputs accordingly. The hidden layers thus store a neural network's knowledge as weighted connections between inputs and outputs, which are known as *synaptic weights*. As training continues, the extent of the error decreases with each iteration, until the neural network reaches a fully trained state where it reliably produces the desired output. The neural network then is ready to produce outputs when the desired output is unknown.

Unlike humans, once trained fully, a neural network recognizes and classifies patterns in huge quantities of complex data, at high speeds that humans cannot duplicate. Uses of neural networks include a wide range of applications, such as sorting mail at the U.S. Postal Service, determining the number of jurors to call at county courthouses, and identifying police officers with a potential for misconduct. Scientists use neural networks to predict rainfall and forecast air quality. Manufacturers benefit from neural networks that allow them to test the quality of plastics and welding and determine which type of concrete to use on a highway. In health care, neural networks help predict heart attacks and cancer risk, while helping to improve treatment. For more information visit scsite.com/dc2007/ch14/tech and then click Neural Networks.

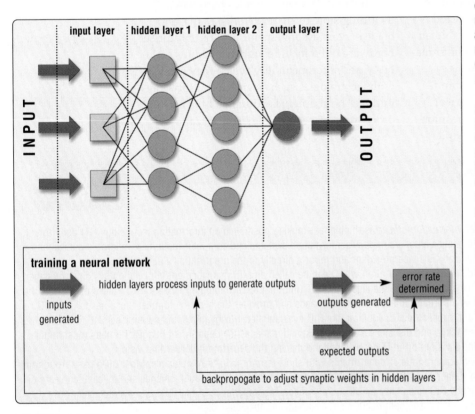

FIGURE 14-35 How a neural network works.

Companies on the Cutting Edge

SAP
INNOVATIVE ENTERPRISE SOFTWARE DEVELOPER

SAP wants to make innovation happen. Each employee is focused on turning new concepts into real economical and technological business benefits for customers.

Innovation was the foundation of the company. When IBM rejected an offer more than 30 years ago to develop a fully integrated software product that would support all facets of a company's operation, five of IBM's system engineers decided to form their own company in Germany to create such a product. In 1972 they founded SAP, an acronym for Systeme, Anwendugen, und Produkte in der Datenverarbeitung (Systems, Applications, and Products in Data Processing).

More than 12 million people worldwide use SAP's enterprise software products, which combine and link multiple applications to a central database and help business partners, employees, and customers work together. For more information, visit scsite.com/dc2007/ch14/companies and then click SAP.

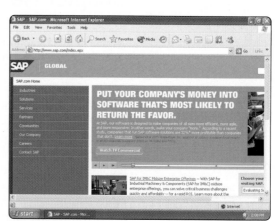

IBM
WORLD'S LARGEST INFORMATION TECHNOLOGY COMPANY

In a survey of the world's 100 most powerful computers, 55 of *IBM*'s products top the list in computing power with a total of 188 teraflops (trillions of calculations per second). But the company's products reach more than power users; IBM is the world's largest information technology corporation and works with consumers of all sizes.

IBM has a reputation for pioneering products. In 1911, three companies merged to sell a variety of business-related gadgets, including a machine that used punched cards to catalogue data. Nine years later, the company changed its name to International Business Machines (IBM). In its history of computer innovation, the company has developed the first family of computers with interchangeable software and peripherals, the personal computer with 16 KB of memory and a floppy disk drive, and the ThinkPad notebook computer. For more information, visit scsite.com/dc2007/ch14/companies and then click IBM.

Technology Trailblazers

MARK HURD
HEWLETT-PACKARD CEO AND PRESIDENT

Mark Hurd faced a difficult situation when he was hired at Hewlett-Packard in 2005: return the company to its prominence in the technology industry. After a 25-year tenure at NCR Corporation that culminated in being CEO and president, he assumed the same duties at HP. Shares of HP stock surged more than 10 percent when his appointment was announced.

Hurd, who holds a bachelor's degree in business administration from Baylor University, says a number of opportunities are afforded by HP's problems. His key to business success is focusing on the customer, and he believes this operating principle should drive every decision. He is working to gain customers' trust that HP will deliver on its commitments. For more information, visit scsite.com/dc2007/ch14/people and then click Mark Hurd.

JIM CLARK
TECHNOLOGY INNOVATOR

When *Jim Clark* has an idea, people listen. As a professor at Stanford University, he developed a computer chip that processed 3-D images in real time. The high-powered chip formed the basis of Clark's first company, Silicon Graphics, and was used to create everything from suspension bridges to scenes in Hollywood movies.

Seeking more innovation opportunities, Clark contacted Marc Andreessen, creator of the Web browser, Mosaic. Together, they launched Netscape Communications Corporation, the source of one of the world's more successful Web browsers, Netscape Navigator.

Since then, Clark has started other computer-related companies: Healtheon, which links doctors, patients, and health insurance providers; MyCFO, a Web-based financial advisory firm; and Shutterfly, an online digital photo printing service. For more information, visit scsite.com/dc2007/ch14/people and then click Jim Clark.

Chapter Review

The Chapter Review section summarizes the concepts presented in this chapter. To listen to the audio version of this Chapter Review, visit scsite.com/dc2007/ch14/review. To obtain help from other students regarding any subject in this chapter, visit scsite.com/dc2007/ch14/forum and post your thoughts or questions.

① What Are the Special Information Requirements of an Enterprise-Sized Corporation?
A large organization, or **enterprise**, requires special computing solutions because of its size and geographical extent. **Enterprise computing** uses computers in networks or series of interconnected networks to satisfy the information needs of an enterprise. The types of information employees require depend on their level in the company. **Executive management** needs information to make *strategic decisions* that center on a company's overall goals and objectives. **Middle management** needs information to make *tactical decisions* that apply specific programs and plans to meet stated objectives. **Operational management** needs information to make an *operational decision* that involves day-to-day activities. **Nonmanagement employees** also need information to perform their jobs and make on-the-job decisions. Managers utilize tools and techniques such as *business intelligence, business process management,* and *business process automation* to focus on information that is important to the decision-making process.

② What Information Systems Are Used in the Functional Units of an Enterprise? An **information system** is a set of hardware, software, data, people, and procedures that works together to produce information. In an enterprise, the individual operating entities, called *functional units*, have specialized requirements for their information systems. Accounting and financial systems manage everyday transactions and help budget. A **human resources information system** (HRIS) manages one or more human resources functions. **Computer-aided design** (CAD) assists engineers in product design, and **computer-aided engineering** (CAE) tests product designs. **Computer-aided manufacturing** (CAM) controls production equipment, and **computer-integrated manufacturing** (CIM) integrates operations in the manufacturing process. A *marketing information system* serves as a central repository for marketing tasks. **Sales force automation** (SFA) software equips salespeople with the tools they need. *Distribution systems* control inventory and manage shipping. **Customer interaction management** (CIM) software manages interactions with customers. The information technology (IT) department makes technology decisions for an enterprise and maintains hardware and software applications.

③ What Information Systems Are Used throughout an Enterprise? Some general purpose information systems, called *enterprise-wide systems*, are used throughout an enterprise. An **office information system** (OIS) enables employees to perform tasks using computers and other electronic devices. A **transaction processing system** (TPS) captures and processes data from day-to-day business activities. A **management information system** (MIS) generates accurate, timely, and organized information, so users can make decisions, solve problems, and track progress. A **decision support system** (DSS) helps users analyze data and make decisions. An **expert system** stores the knowledge of human experts and then imitates human reasoning and decision making. **Customer relationship management** (CRM) systems manage information about customers. **Enterprise resource planning** (ERP) provides software to help manage and coordinate ongoing activities. A **content management system** (CMS) organizes and allows access to various forms of documents and files.

Visit scsite.com/dc2007/ch14/quiz or click the Quiz Yourself button. Click Objectives 1 – 3.

④ What Are Types of Technologies Used throughout an Enterprise? Technologies used throughout an enterprise include portals, data warehouses, electronic data interchange, extranets, Web services, document management systems, workflow, and virtual private networks. A **portal** is a collection of links, content, and services on a Web page designed to guide users to information

Chapter Review

related to their jobs. A **data warehouse** is a huge database that stores and manages the data required to analyze transactions. **EDI (electronic data interchange)** controls the transfer of data and information among computers. An **extranet** allows customers or suppliers to access part of an enterprise's intranet. **Web services** allow businesses to create products and B2B interactions. A **workflow application** assists in the management and tracking of the activities in a business process. A **virtual private network** (**VPN**) provides users with a secure connection to a company's network server.

(5) What Are the Major Types of E-Commerce?   **E-retail** occurs when retailers use the Web to sell their products and services. **Online banking** allows users to pay bills from their computers, and **online trading** lets users invest without using a broker. Travel-related services on the Web include directions; airline, hotel, or car reservations; and a **shopping bot** that searches for the best price on a product or service. Entertainment and media on the Web include music, videos, news, sporting events, and 3-D multiplayer games. Many Web sites provide medical, fitness, nutrition, or exercise information.

connect
Visit scsite.com/dc2007/ch14/quiz or click the Quiz Yourself button. Click Objectives 4 – 5.

(6) What Are the Computer Hardware Needs and Solutions for an Enterprise?   **Enterprise hardware** allows large organizations to manage and share information and data using devices geared for maximum availability and efficiency. Enterprises use a variety of hardware types to meet their needs. A **RAID (redundant array of independent disks)** is a group of integrated disks that duplicates data and information to improve data reliability. **Network attached storage** (**NAS**) is a server that provides storage for users and information systems. A **storage area network** (**SAN**) provides storage to other servers. An **enterprise storage system** uses a combination of techniques to consolidate storage so operations run efficiently. **Blade servers** pack a complete computer server on a single card. **Thin clients** rely on a server for data storage and processing. **High-availability systems** continue running and performing tasks for at least 99 percent of the time. *Utility computing* allows companies to use the processing power sitting idle in a network at another location. **Grid computing** combines servers and personal computers on a network to act as one large computer.

(7) Why Is Computer Backup Important, and How Is It Accomplished?
A backup duplicates a file or program to protect an enterprise if the original is lost or damaged. A full backup copies all of the files in a computer. A differential backup copies only files that have changed since the last full backup. An incremental backup copies only files that have changed since the last full or incremental backup. A selective backup allows users to back up specific files. Growing in popularity is continuous data protection *(CDP)*, or continuous backup, in which data is backed up whenever a change is made. Backup procedures specify a regular plan of copying and storing data and program files.

(8) What Are the Steps in a Disaster Recovery Plan?   A **disaster recovery plan** describes the steps a company would take to restore computer operations in the event of a disaster. A disaster recovery plan contains four components. The *emergency plan* specifies the steps to be taken immediately after a disaster strikes. The *backup plan* stipulates how a company uses backup files and equipment to resume information processing. The *recovery plan* identifies the actions to be taken to restore full information processing operations. The *test plan* contains information for simulating disasters and recording an organization's ability to recover.

connect
Visit scsite.com/dc2007/ch14/quiz or click the Quiz Yourself button. Click Objectives 6 – 8.

Quizzes and
Learning Games

Computer Genius
Crossword Puzzle
DC Track and Field
Practice Test
Quiz Yourself
Wheel of Terms
You're Hired!

Exercises

Case Studies
Chapter Review
Checkpoint
Key Terms
Learn How To
Learn It Online
Web Research

Beyond the Book

Career Corner
Companies
FAQs
High-Tech Talk
Looking Ahead
Making Use of
the Web
Trailblazers
Web Links

Features

Chapter Forum
Install Computer
Lab Exercises
Maintain Computer
Tech News
Timeline 2007

Key Terms

You should know the Primary Terms and be familiar with the Secondary Terms. Use the list below to help focus your study. To further enhance your understanding of the Key Terms in this chapter, visit scsite.com/dc2007/ch14/terms. See an example of and a definition for each term, and access current and additional information about the term from the Web.

Primary Terms

(shown in bold-black characters in the chapter)

artificial intelligence (AI) (730)
blade servers (744)
CD-ROM server (744)
computer-aided design (CAD) (722)
computer-aided engineering (CAE) (722)
computer-aided manufacturing (CAM) (722)
computer-integrated manufacturing (CIM) (722)
content management system (CMS) (732)
customer interaction management (CIM) (724)
customer relationship management (CRM) (730)
data warehouse (734)
decision support system (DSS) (728)
disaster recovery plan (747)
document management systems (DMS) (736)
DVD-ROM server (744)
EDI (electronic data interchange) (735)
enterprise (714)
enterprise computing (714)
enterprise hardware (741)
enterprise information (718)
enterprise resource planning (ERP) (731)
enterprise storage system (743)
e-retail (737)
executive management (718)
expert system (729)
extranet (735)
grid computing (746)

high-availability systems (745)
human resources information system (HRIS) (721)
information system (720)
interoperability (746)
management information system (MIS) (727)
managers (718)
Manufacturing Resource Planning II (MRP II) (723)
Material Requirements Planning (MRP) (723)
middle management (718)
network attached storage (NAS) (742)
nonmanagement employees (718)
office information system (OIS) (726)
online banking (738)
online trading (738)
operational management (718)
portal (733)
RAID (redundant array of independent disks) (741)
redundant components (745)
sales force automation (SFA) (724)
scalability (745)
shopping bot (739)
storage area network (SAN) (742)
thin clients (744)
transaction processing system (TPS) (726)
virtual private network (VPN) (736)
Web services (735)
workflow (736)
workflow application (736)

Secondary Terms

(shown in italic characters in the chapter)

3-D visualization (722)
availability (741)
backup plan (748)
batch processing (727)
blade (744)
blade server chassis (744)
business intelligence (BI) (719)
business process automation (BPA) (719)
business process management (BPM) (719)
CD-ROM jukebox (744)
centralized (717)
chief information officer (CIO) (725)
click stream (734)
closed (746)
cold site (748)
controlling (718)
core activities (717)
data processing (726)
decentralized (717)
detailed report (727)
distribution systems (724)
downtime (745)
DVD-ROM jukebox (744)
emergency plan (748)
employee relationship management (ERM) system (721)
empowering (718)
enterprise search (733)
enterprise-wide systems (725)
e-tail (737)
exception criteria (728)
exception report (728)
executive information system (EIS) (728)
external sources (728)
failover (748)
Fibre Channel (743)
functional units (714)
hot site (748)
hot-swapping (745)
indexes (732)
inference rules (729)
information architecture (725)
internal sources (728)
Internet backup (744)
knowledge base (729)

knowledge management (KM) (730)
knowledge management software (KMS) (730)
knowledge workers (730)
leading (718)
level 1 (741)
market research system (723)
marketing information system (723)
metadata (732)
mirroring (741)
office automation (726)
on demand computing (745)
online analytical processing (OLAP) (728)
online transaction processing (OLTP) (727)
open (746)
operational decision (718)
operations (717)
organizing (718)
outsourcing (744)
personal computer blade (745)
personalization (733)
planning (718)
procedure (720)
proprietary (746)
reciprocal backup relationship (748)
recovery plan (748)
redundancy (741)
repository (736)
security software (725)
storage appliance (742)
strategic decisions (718)
striping (741)
summary report (727)
supporting activities (717)
tactical decisions (718)
tape library (744)
test plan (748)
transaction (726)
ultradense servers (744)
uptime (745)
utility computing (745)
VPN tunnel (737)
Web farming (734)
Web site management programs (725)

Checkpoint

Use the Checkpoint exercises to check your knowledge level of the chapter. The Beyond the Book exercises will help broaden your understanding of the concepts presented in this chapter. To complete the Checkpoint exercises interactively, visit scsite.com/dc2007/ch14/check.

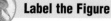

Label the Figure   Identify the components of an enterprise storage system.

a. Internet backup

b. RAID

c. tape libraries

d. CD-ROM and DVD-ROM jukeboxes

e. SAN

f. servers

g. NAS device

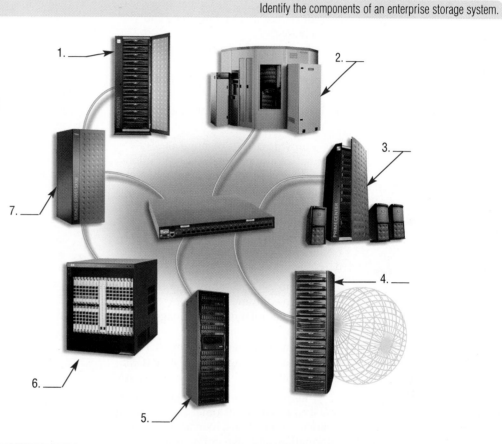

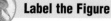

True/False   Mark T for True and F for False. (See page numbers in parentheses.)

_____ 1. Enterprises produce and gather enormous volumes of information. (714)

_____ 2. The activities relating to running the business are called supporting activities. (717)

_____ 3. Business process management rarely is aided by specialized software designed to assist in these activities. (719)

_____ 4. An information system is a set of hardware, software, data, people, and procedures that works together to produce information. (720)

_____ 5. Manufacturing Resource Planning II includes software that helps in scheduling and tracking production in real time, and monitoring product quality. (723)

_____ 6. An MIS summary report usually lists only transactions. (727)

_____ 7. Enterprise search technology allows users to perform searches across many enterprise-wide information systems and databases. (733)

_____ 8. A content management system is a program that assists in the management and tracking of all the activities in a business from start to finish. (736)

_____ 9. Blade servers pack a complete computer server on a single card rather than a system unit. (744)

_____ 10. Information systems that have interoperability and easily share information with other information systems are said to be open. (746)

Checkpoint

Quizzes and Learning Games

Computer Genius
Crossword Puzzle
DC Track and Field
Practice Test
Quiz Yourself
Wheel of Terms
You're Hired!

Exercises

Case Studies
Chapter Review
▶ Checkpoint
Key Terms
Learn How To
Learn It Online
Web Research

Beyond the Book

Career Corner
Companies
FAQs
High-Tech Talk
Looking Ahead
Making Use of the Web
Trailblazers
Web Links

Features

Chapter Forum
Install Computer
Lab Exercises
Maintain Computer
Tech News
Timeline 2007

Multiple Choice   Select the best answer. (See page numbers in parentheses.)

1. A centralized approach to information systems usually _____ manageability. (717)
   a. reduces costs of maintenance and increases
   b. reduces costs of maintenance and reduces
   c. increases costs of maintenance and increases
   d. increases costs of maintenance and reduces

2. _____ provides easy exchange of information among business applications, reduces the need for human intervention in processes, and utilizes software to automate processes wherever possible. (719)
   a. Business process automation
   b. Business intelligence
   c. Business process management
   d. None of the above

3. _____ is the use of computers to control production equipment. (722)
   a. Computer relationship management (CRM)
   b. Computer-aided engineering (CAE)
   c. Computer management system (CMS)
   d. Computer-aided manufacturing (CAM)

4. _____ helps salespeople manage customer contacts, schedule customer meetings, log customer interactions, manage product information, and take orders from customers. (724)
   a. Marketing information system
   b. Sales force automation
   c. Customer interaction management
   d. Customer relationship management

5. An advantage of ERP is _____. (731)
   a. complete integration of information systems across departments
   b. better project management
   c. better customer service
   d. all of the above

6. A _____ is a collection of every action that users make as they move through a Web site. (734)
   a. cold site   b. workflow
   c. click stream   d. hot site

7. The secure connection created between a user's computer and a company's network is called a(n) _____. (737)
   a. VPN tunnel   b. blade server
   c. EDI portal   d. data warehouse

8. _____ allows users to pay bills from their computer, that is, transfer money electronically, from their account to a payee's account such as the electric company or telephone company. (738)
   a. Online trading
   b. Online banking
   c. E-retail
   d. A shopping bot

9. The _____ of hardware to users is a measure of how often it is online. (741)
   a. redundancy
   b. scalability
   c. availability
   d. interoperability

10. Enterprises often use _____ technology to connect to storage systems at data rates up to 4 Gbps. (743)
    a. RAID
    b. NAS
    c. Fibre Channel
    d. SAN

11. A thin client _____. (744)
    a. is a small, terminal-like computer
    b. is expensive compared to a personal computer
    c. contains its own hard drive and all other components seen on a personal computer
    d. all of the above

12. A(n) _____ allows a user to choose specific files to back up, regardless of whether or not the files have changed. (746)
    a. full backup
    b. differential backup
    c. incremental backup
    d. selective backup

13. To aid in disaster planning, a company often maintains a _____, which is a separate facility that mirrors the systems and operations of the critical site. (748)
    a. hot site   b. backup facility
    c. cold site   d. test site

14. A(n) _____ contains information for simulating various levels of disaster and recording an organization's ability to recover from the simulation. (748)
    a. emergency plan   b. test plan
    c. backup plan   d. recovery plan

Checkpoint

Matching

Match the terms with their definitions. (See page numbers in parentheses.)

_____ 1. supporting activities (717)

_____ 2. core activities (717)

_____ 3. 3-D visualization (722)

_____ 4. MRP (723)

_____ 5. Web farming (734)

_____ 6. workflow (736)

_____ 7. CD-ROM server (744)

_____ 8. scalability (745)

_____ 9. interoperability (746)

_____ 10. failover (748)

a. holds hundreds of CD-ROMs that can contain programs and data

b. instructing and authorizing others to perform necessary work

c. process of one system automatically taking the place of a failed system

d. allows engineers to interact with a product without the need to build a prototype

e. process of collecting data from the Internet as a source for a data warehouse

f. monitors and controls processes related to production

g. business activities that relate to the main mission of a business

h. process that identifies the specific set of steps involved in completing a project

i. measure of how well computer hardware, software, or an information system can grow to meet increasing performance demands

j. activities relating to running a business

k. allow business to create products and B2B interactions

l. capability of an information system to share information with other information systems

Short Answer

Write a brief answer to each of the following questions.

1. What are the responsibilities of managers? _____ What four activities do managers perform to coordinate resources? _____

2. What are the advantages of using computer-aided design? _____ What are the benefits of computer-aided engineering? _____

3. What is a management information system (MIS)? _____ How are a detailed report, a summary report, and an exception report different? _____

4. What is RAID? _____ How is mirroring different from striping? _____

5. Who should have a disaster recovery plan? _____ What are a disaster recovery plan's four major components? _____

Beyond the Book

Read the following book elements, learn more about each using the Web, and then write a brief report.

1. Ethics & Issues — Should Companies Share Customer Information? (730), Would You Buy Merchandise Online? (738), Would You Trust an Online Medical Diagnosis? (739), and How Much Data Should Companies Be Required to Keep? (743)

2. Career Corner — CIO (749)

3. Companies on the Cutting Edge — SAP or IBM (751)

4. FAQs (724, 725, 728, 735, 738, 741, 744, 748)

5. High-Tech Talk — Neural Networks: Learning from Experience (750)

6. Looking Ahead — The CEO of the Future (718) and The Future of Grid Computing (746)

7. Making Use of the Web — Careers (130)

8. Picture Yourself in Need of Technical Support (712)

9. Technology Trailblazers — Mark Hurd or Jim Clark (751)

10. Web Links (719, 721, 723, 724, 731, 733, 734, 739, 742, 743)

Learn It Online

Use the Learn It Online exercises to reinforce your understanding of the chapter concepts. To access the Learn It Online exercises, visit scsite.com/dc2007/ch14/learn.

① At the Movies — Conferencing with Video Phones

To view the Conferencing with Video Phones movie, click the number 1 button. Locate your video and click the corresponding High-Speed or Dial-Up link, depending on your Internet connection. Watch the movie and then complete the exercise by answering the question that follows. Interest in videoconferencing has surged since 9/11 as companies scramble to find a way to have face-to-face meetings without the hassles of flying. Another practical use for videoconferencing is to monitor an elderly or disabled loved one. Some programs can even send health information directly to health-care providers or create small video e-mails. How could videoconferencing make communication within your family easier?

② At the Movies — Confessions of a Software Pirate

To view the Confessions of a Software Pirate movie, click the number 2 button. Locate your video and click the corresponding High-Speed or Dial-Up link, depending on your Internet connection. Watch the movie and then complete the exercise by answering the questions that follow. The bulk of pirated software can be found online via FTP and peer-to-peer file-sharing networks. How do the pirated programs find their way to these sites? Software pirate Chris Tresco had more than one and a half terabytes of illegal software (equal to 2 to the 40th power or about a thousand billion bytes) available for download on a Web site

he ran through the servers of his employer, MIT (Massachusetts Institute of Technology). How did the federal government finally catch Chris? Chris did not make money from his piracy, but his actions potentially cost software companies millions of dollars. After his arrest and conviction, what was Chris's punishment?

③ Student Edition Labs — E-Commerce

Click the number 3 button. A new browser window will open, displaying the Student Edition Labs. Follow the on-screen instructions to complete the E-Commerce Lab. When finished, click the Exit button. If required, print a copy of your results to submit to your instructor.

④ Student Edition Labs — Backing Up Your Computer

Click the number 4 button. A new browser window will open, displaying the Student Edition Labs. Follow the on-screen instructions to complete the Backing Up Your Computer Lab. When finished, click the Exit button. If required, print a copy of your results to submit to your instructor.

⑤ Practice Test

Click the number 5 button. Answer each question. When completed, enter your name and click the Grade Test button to submit the quiz for grading. Make a note of any missed questions. If required, submit your results to your instructor.

⑥ Who Wants To Be a Computer Genius²?

Click the number 6 button to find out if you are a computer genius. Directions about how to play the game will be displayed. When you are ready to play, click the Play button. Submit your score to your instructor.

⑦ Wheel of Terms

Click the number 7 button to reinforce important terms you learned in this chapter by playing the Shelly Cashman Series version

Learn It Online

of this popular game. Directions about how to play the game will be displayed. When you are ready to play, click the Play button. Submit your score to your instructor.

8 DC Track and Field

Click the number 8 button to use what you have learned in this chapter to compete against other students in three track and field events. Directions about how to play the game will be displayed. When you are ready to play, click the start first event button. If required, submit your score to your instructor.

9 You're Hired!

Click the number 9 button to use what you have learned in this chapter to embark on the path to a career in computers. Directions about how to play the game will be displayed. When you are ready to play, click the begin game button. If required, submit your score to your instructor.

10 Crossword Puzzle Challenge

Click the number 10 button. Complete the puzzle to reinforce skills you learned in this chapter. Directions about how to play the game will be displayed. When you are ready to play, click the Submit button. Submit the completed puzzle to your instructor.

11 Lab Exercises

Click the number 11 button. When the Lab Exercises menu appears, click the exercise assigned by your instructor. A new browser window will open. Follow the on-screen instructions to complete the exercise. When finished, click the Exit button. If required, submit your results to your instructor.

12 In the News

The Internet has become a driving force in both the new and used vehicle market. A survey released by the National Automobile Dealers Association indicates that over 90 percent of all new car dealers have a well-established Internet presence. As dealerships recognize the Web's power as a sales tool, online sales will continue to increase. Click the number 12 button and read a news article about a recent e-commerce success story. What is the product or company? How has it been successful? Is this success expected to continue?

13 Chapter Discussion Forum

Select an objective from this chapter on page 713 about which you would like more information. Click the number 13 button and post a short message listing a meaningful message title accompanied by one or more questions concerning the selected objective. In two days, return to the threaded discussion by clicking the number 13 button. Submit to your instructor your original message and at least one response to your message.

14 Online Automobile Shopping

Click the number 14 button to learn how to use the Internet to price an automobile online. Follow the instructions to use Ford.com to research and price an automobile. Use the Vehicle Showroom Tool to select an SUV in the $30,000 to $51,000 price range. You may choose from any of the brands listed (Ford, Lincoln, Mazda, etc.). Once you have selected your vehicle, click the More Information button to proceed with customizing your vehicle. When you have completed pricing your vehicle, print the specifications and price and then submit them to your instructor. If available, use the payment calculator to calculate your monthly payments.

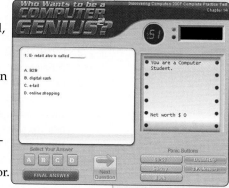

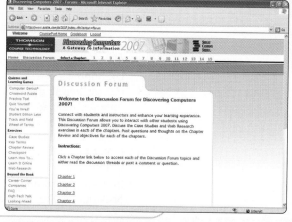

Learn How To

Use the Learn How To activities to learn fundamental skills when using a computer and accompanying technology. Complete the exercises and submit them to your instructor. To see a video of a Learn How To activity, visit scsite.com/dc2007/ch14/howto.

LEARN HOW TO 1: Use Internet Telephony — Voice over the Internet (VoIP)

Every enterprise organization depends on reliable communications. An important means of communication is voice, or telephone, communications. In most organizations today, a telephone company is the primary vendor for providing telephone communications. In the near future, however, the Internet might be the largest provider of telephone communications.

You learned in a previous chapter about Voice over Internet Protocol (VoIP), sometimes called Internet telephony, which provides for voice communications using the Internet instead of standard telephone connections. Two advantages claimed for VoIP are improved reliability and much lower costs. Both of these advantages are attractive to businesses, and VoIP is forecasted to become the standard voice communications method within the next 5-10 years.

VoIP also is available to individual users. One primary means to use VoIP is through the service offered by Skype, a company that offers free, unlimited calls through an Internet connection. The Skype software also is free. Using Skype, you can talk to another Skype user via the Internet anywhere in the world for no cost whatsoever. If the person you call is not a Skype user, you can use Skype to call their ordinary landline or mobile telephone quite inexpensively. For example, to call someone on a landline telephone in the United Kingdom from anywhere in the world, the cost is approximately 2 cents per minute.

The following quote indicates the potential future of VoIP and services like Skype:

"I knew it was over when I downloaded Skype," Michael Powell, chairman of the Federal Communications Commission, explained. "When the inventors of KaZaA are distributing for free a little program that you can use to talk to anybody else, and the quality is fantastic, and it's free — it's over. The world will change now inevitably."

Fortune Magazine, February 16, 2004

To download Skype, complete the following steps:
1. Start your Internet browser, type `www.skype.com` in the Address bar, and then press the ENTER key.
2. When the Skype home page is displayed, explore the Web site for information about using Skype. When you are ready, click the Download Skype now. It's free. button.
3. In the next window, the version of Skype required for your operating system is identified, along with the hardware requirements. Notice that in order to use Skype, you need, at a minimum, a sound card, speakers, and a microphone. A headset or a USB telephone provide better service. After reading the information on the screen, click the Download link.
4. When the File Download — Security Warning dialog box is displayed, click the Save button.
5. In the Save As dialog box, select the Desktop for the location of the saved file. Then, click the Save button. The Skype Setup file will download. This may take a few minutes, depending on the speed of your Internet connection, because of the large file size.
6. When the Download complete window is displayed, click the Close button. The SkypeSetup icon is displayed on the desktop.
7. Double-click the SkypeSetup icon on the desktop. If any warning dialog boxes appear, click the Run button.
8. In the Select Setup Language window, select the language you would like to use and then click the OK button.
9. If your firewall displays a message asking whether the application should have access to the Internet, grant access.
10. In the Setup-Skype window, click the Next button. Select the I accept the agreement option button in the License Agreement window and then click the Next button.
11. In the Select Destination Location window, you normally should use the default, so click the Next button.
12. In the Select Additional Tasks window, check the boxes that apply to your choices and then click the Next button. For this example, be sure to install the Skype icon on the desktop.

Learn How To

13. Skype will be installed on your computer. When the Completing the Skype Setup Wizard window opens, remove the check from the Launch Skype check box, and then click the Finish button.

Skype now is installed on your computer. The Skype icon should appear on your desktop. To start and use Skype, complete the following steps:

1. Double-click the Skype icon on your desktop. The first time you start Skype, the Create a new Skype account dialog box is displayed (Figure 14-36). In this dialog box, you enter your Skype name, password, and e-mail address. The Skype name is the name you will use to start Skype each time, together with the password. You can use any name and password that has not already been used on Skype. Also, be sure to check the Skype End User License Agreement check box, and then click the Next button. The Creating Account message is displayed.

2. If your Skype name and password have not been used, the Skype - User Profile dialog box is displayed (Figure 14-37). If your Skype name or password already have been used by another user, you must select another Skype name or password.

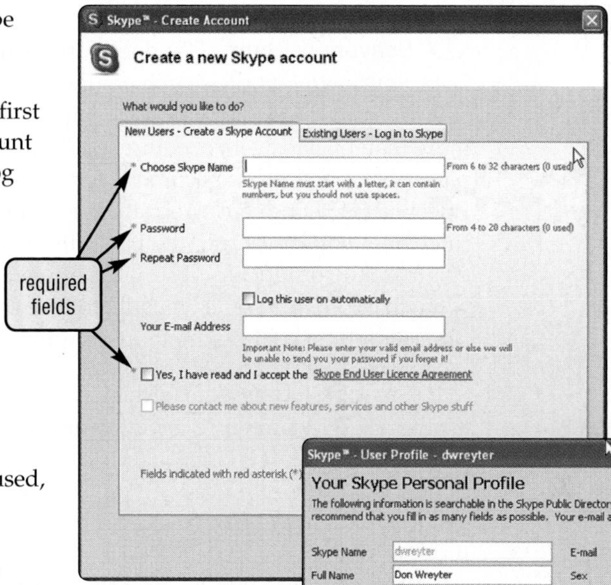

3. In the Skype - User Profile dialog box, provide as much information about yourself as you feel comfortable with, keeping in mind that this profile window will be available to other Skype users. Many users might have the same name as you, so the more details you provide, the chances are better that another Skype user will identify you as a friend or acquaintance who uses Skype. At a minimum, you should provide your full name, country, and state (if applicable) where you live. When you have entered the information, click the Update button. You can change the information in this personal profile at anytime when using the Skype program.

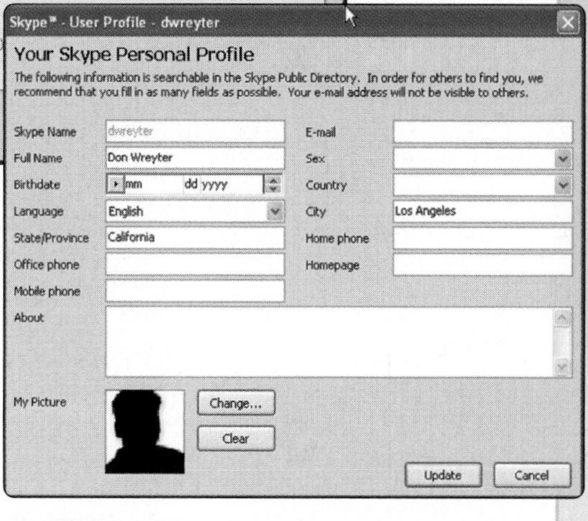

4. The Skype program starts and opens the Skype window (Figure 14-38).

5. After installing Skype, you can make calls to other Skype users anywhere in the world for no cost. If you want to dial a telephone number for a regular landline telephone, you must subscribe to SkypeOut. This service, which costs .017 euros (about two cents in U.S. currency) to call many places in the world, can be obtained by clicking the SkypeOut:Global calling at local rates link in the Skype window.

6. To learn the techniques for calling another Skype user and for using SkypeOut, click Help on the menu bar in the Skype window, click Help on the Help menu, and then select the subject about which you want to learn.

FIGURE 14-36

FIGURE 14-37

FIGURE 14-38

Exercise

1. Visit the Skype Web site. Examine the various screens and examples shown on the Web site. Do you think this type of service can be useful to you? Why? What are the advantages and disadvantages of using Skype? If you were calling a friend in Australia on a regular telephone, how much per minute would you have to pay? Submit your answers to your instructor.

2. **Optional: Perform this exercise only on your own computer. Do not perform this exercise on a school computer.** Establish an account on Skype. Call another member of your class who also has established a Skype account. What do you like about Skype? What do you not like? If you know someone in Europe or Asia who is a Skype user, call him or her. Do you like the fact the call is free anywhere in the world? As an option, subscribe to SkypeOut and then call someone somewhere else in the world on his or her regular telephone. Is the quality of the call good? What did you like or not like about the call? Submit your answers to your instructor.

Web Research

Use the Internet-based Web Research exercises to broaden your understanding of the concepts presented in this chapter. Visit scsite.com/dc2007/ch14/research to obtain more information pertaining to each exercise. To discuss any of the Web Research exercises in this chapter with other students, post your thoughts or questions at scsite.com/dc2007/ch14/forum.

(1) Scavenger Hunt   Use one of the search engines listed in Figure 2-10 in Chapter 2 on page 78 or your own favorite search engine to find the answers to the questions that follow. Copy and paste the Web address from the Web page where you found the answer. Some questions may have more than one answer. If required, submit your answers to your instructor. (1) How does a company obtain a VeriSign Secured Seal for its Web site? (2) Using both the Orbitz (orbitz.com) and Priceline (priceline.com) Web sites, search for an 8:00 a.m. one-way flight from Houston's Intercontinental airport to the Hololulu, Hawaii, airport. Which airline offers the lowest fare? (3) Compare the products and services offered by two online banks, such as Citibank and Chase. What loan programs are available to finance a college education? (4) What are three "Spam Scams" protection tips the Federal Trade Commission offers to consumers?

(2) Search Sleuth   One of the newer online academic research tools is Google Scholar (scholar.google.com). It uses newly developed algorithms to provide search results composed of books, technical reports, abstracts, peer-reviewed articles, and theses. Visit this Web site and then use your word processing program to answer the following questions. Then, if required, submit your answers to your instructor. (1) Type e-commerce in the Search box and then click the Search button. How many results were found? (2) Click one of the e-commerce links for an article published within the past three years. What is the article's title, and who is the author? What journal published the article? When? (3) Click your browser's Back button or press the BACKSPACE key to return to the Google Scholar home page. Delete the text in the Search box, type "grid computing" in the Search box, and then click the Search button. Find two articles published within the past three years that have been cited by more than 100 other works. Write a 50-word summary of these two articles.

(3) Journaling   Respond to your readings in this chapter by writing at least one page about your reactions, evaluations, and reflections on enterprise computing. For example, how often do you and your employer back up computer files? What experiences have you had using e-commerce market sectors, such as finance, entertainment and media, travel, and health? You also can write about the new terms you learned by reading this chapter. If required, submit your journal to your instructor.

(4) Expanding Your Understanding   Most e-retailers experience their highest profits of the year during the Christmas holiday season. Spammers and phishers, likewise, increase their activities as the holiday shopping season kicks into high gear; e-mail scams surged more than 1,200 percent in 2004. SurfControl (surfcontrol.com) attempts to filter e-mail and Web sites, and the National Fraud Information Center (fraud.org) tracks consumer losses through telemarketing and Internet schemes. Visit these Web sites to learn how to protect yourself from phishing. Because many employees shop online during business hours, how can companies protect themselves from Internet scams? How have online merchants attempted to fight fraud? Write a report summarizing your findings. If required, submit your report to your instructor.

(5) Ethics in Action   Using grid computing, your computer can join millions of other computers throughout the world when you are connected to the Internet and have idle processing time. While grid computing turns inactive computer time into computational power, critics believe some grid projects are immoral, may compromise intellectual property, and are undertaking work for-profit companies should perform. Visit Grid.org, the Global Grid Forum (gridforum.org), the Globus Alliance (globus.org), and other Web sites to learn about current grid computing projects. Should for-profit companies pay grid participants for their computer time? Is data security compromised? Who sets standardization guidelines? How will companies track network resources? Write a report summarizing your findings, and include a table of links to Web sites that provide additional details about grid computing. If required, submit your report to your instructor.

Case Studies

Use the Case Studies to apply the concepts presented in the chapter to real-world situations. Visit scsite.com/dc2007/ch14/cases to obtain more information pertaining to each exercise. To discuss the Case Studies in this chapter with other students, visit scsite.com/dc2007/ch14/forum and post your thoughts or questions.

Case Study 1 — Class Discussion   Half of all new e-commerce businesses fail within five years of their creation, and many do not last that long. What do you need to be part of the successful 50 percent? While experts point to several factors, two of the most important factors to consider before embarking are a good idea and financial backing. Regrettably, without the first, it often is difficult to get the second. Select a product you feel will sell well online. Then, use Google or another search engine to learn about <u>Web hosting</u>. Write a brief report about why you believe the product you selected will sell online and how Web hosting works. Be prepared to discuss your recommendations and findings in class.

Case Study 2 — Class Discussion   You are employed as senior systems analyst for a large international company created through several mergers. The company has organized the merged companies into divisions, with each having its own <u>IT department</u>. You have been asked to develop a company-wide five-year IT plan. What are the advantages and disadvantages of requiring the divisions to move towards common hardware and software? Write a brief report and share your findings in class.

Case Study 3 — Research   <u>Intelligent machines</u> have intrigued humans for centuries. Today, computers and artificial intelligence (AI) capture our imagination. Categories within this topic include expert systems, neural networks, artificial life, fuzzy logic, natural language processing, and robotics. Select one of these categories and explore it using printed material and the Web. Then, create a PowerPoint presentation to share with the class how the category of artificial intelligence is used today and might be used in the future.

Case Study 4 — Research   The CEO of eBay recently said that the popular online auction site is "enabling a kind of e-commerce that didn't exist to any extent before, and that's person-to-person e-commerce." Like garage sales, online auctions bring together buyers and sellers. Web auction sites have been described as combining extensive classified ads with the excitement of a television game show. To foster trust in brokers and bidders, some online auctions even provide chat boards where people can share tips and feedback. Web auction sites are particularly useful for buyers and sellers of unusual items. Pierre Omidyar, who founded <u>eBay</u> in 1995, started the site in an effort to add to his girlfriend's collection of Pez candy dispensers. Today, you can use Web auction sites to buy everything from Beanie Babies and baseball cards to expensive jewelry and art. Visit a Web auction site. How does the site work? What types of items are available on the site? Could you find similar items elsewhere? What, if any, guarantees are available? Are any additional services available (such as a chat board)? Some people insist that, although Web auction sites are entertaining, they are not necessarily inexpensive (after all, the selling price is the highest price offered). In general, are costs at the Web auction site low or high? Would you make a purchase at a Web auction site? Why or why not? Write a brief report or use PowerPoint to create a presentation and share your findings with your class.

Case Study 5 – Team Challenge   A major national retail chain has grown enormously over the past several years. It has hired your team as consultants to investigate the use of <u>radio frequency identification</u> (RFID) as a solution to its growing inventory and supplier problems. The company wants to require that all of its suppliers use RFID on all shipments sent to the company's warehouses. The plan will require changes to every one of the company's computer systems, as well as fundamental changes in how the company does business with its stores, suppliers, and customers. Using the Web and/or print media, have each team member investigate the costs and barriers to using RFID, and contrast those with the benefits of the technology. Should a large company force a specific technology on its suppliers? Why might the company opt to not include the RFID tags on individual items? Investigate how Wal-Mart or another major retailer used RFID to solve its inventory and supplier problems. Summarize the advantages and disadvantages of RFID. Merge your findings into a team report and/or PowerPoint presentation and share your recommendations with your class.

Enterprise Order Processing:
A Case Study

E very enterprise builds an enterprise computing infrastructure in a unique manner that reflects its own specific needs. This feature presents a case study of the enterprise computing environment for a fictional company. The case study introduces the hardware, software, data, people, and procedures necessary for a computer manufacturing company to fulfill a customer's e-commerce order for a new computer. A customer order may trigger a complex chain of activities behind the scenes at the company. Figure 1 shows a timeline for the processing of a customer order. Some of the information systems and processes required at each step also are shown. Orders must be tracked, inventory must be stocked and up-to-date, payments from customers and to vendors must be processed properly, employees must receive precise information about procedures, and management must be kept informed about the state of the company. Information systems within departments and across the company help to manage all of these activities and more.

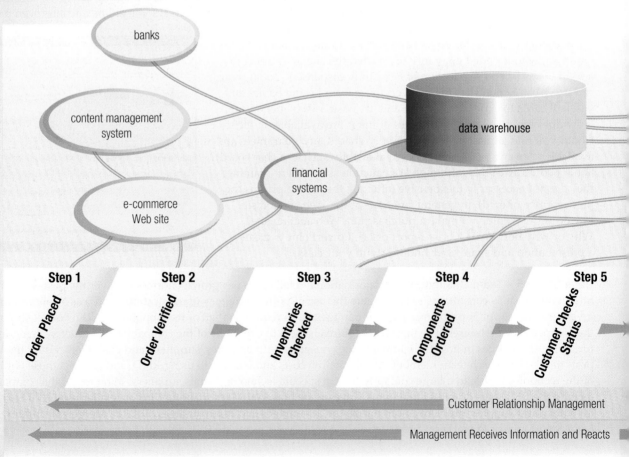

FIGURE 1

Mecha Computers is a large manufacturer of computers with 30,000 employees and 45 locations worldwide. The company accepts orders on its Web page or over the telephone. Customers select the custom components and peripherals that they would like included with their computer.

After a customer places an order, the order is verified, meaning that the customer's credit card number is validated and the customer's shipping information is deemed accurate. Mecha Computers does not keep prebuilt computers in stock. Rather, each customer's order is assembled after the order has been verified. The company also tries not to keep the components for computers in stock. As soon as a customer's order is verified, inventory is checked, the components are ordered from various suppliers, such as a hard disk supplier, a power supply vendor, and a DVD drive supplier. This reduces the company's cost of holding inventory in stock and makes certain that the company does not purchase components that become obsolete or unpopular. All components ordered from suppliers must include RFID tags (tiny computer chips attached to products for identification and read via radio

waves) so that Mecha can track the components as they move through the manufacturing process.

During the process or after the customer receives the computer, the customer may call for assistance, either to check on an order or for technical help. Once the components for a computer are received, they are put in a bin with an RFID tag and sent down an assembly line. Workers assemble the computer, and when the computer reaches the shipping dock, the payment for the computer is processed. The computer then is shipped. A customer interaction management (CIM) system helps to manage customer support requests at Mecha Computers. A customer relationship management (CRM) system is used throughout the process to track customer information and order history. Mecha's executive information system (EIS) provides up-to-the-minute reporting of the state of many processes within the company, such as the number of orders being manufactured, delays in receiving components from suppliers, and the amount of payments and orders processed that day.

The following pages describe in more detail each of the steps in the process outlined in Figure 1.

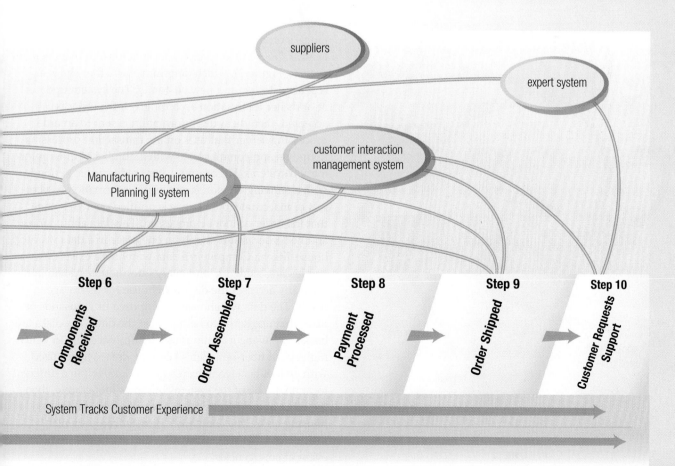

Step 1 — *Order Placed*

Janice Oberweis needs to purchase a new computer to replace her aging and underpowered computer. After investigating computer companies and possible configurations for her new computer, she navigates to the Mecha Computers e-commerce Web site to place an order (Figure 2). The Web site is maintained on a set of approximately 1,000 high-availability blade servers. While at the Web site, Janice investigates various processor types and components. The information about the components is kept up-to-date through Mecha Computers's content management system (CMS). All information systems at Mecha Computers store their data in a common data warehouse. A group in the marketing department is responsible for accurately maintaining this information in the CMS. After selecting the components and peripherals for her computer, Janice receives pricing information and chooses to check out. The checkout Web page is a secure Web page that requires customer data, such as name, e-mail address, address, and credit card information. The chief security officer at Mecha is responsible for maintaining the privacy of this information, and she sets policies regarding who can access the information. Any access to customer information is logged in a database, and the logs frequently are audited for unauthorized or unusual access.

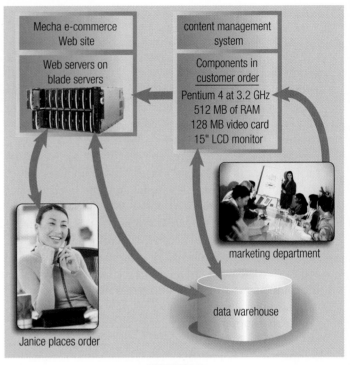

FIGURE 2

Step 2 — *Order Verified*

After submitting the required information, Janice's order and customer information is checked against the company's customer relationship management system (Figure 3), which determines whether she is a repeat customer or a new customer. The system updates or adds her information accordingly. If the order is accepted, then the order information is sent to an order processing server that uses online transaction processing to update and communicate with a number of other information systems. For example, her credit card is verified with a banking vendor. If any of the information is incorrect or inaccurate, then Janice is notified on a Web page that the order cannot be processed. The data about Janice and her order is stored only in one place in a data warehouse. Mecha Computers's data warehouse exists on a storage area network, and every information system in the company accesses the data warehouse for its storage needs. The data warehouse is composed of thousands of disks that use RAID to help protect the data. The disks are backed up using a continuous backup procedure in which high-speed fiber-optic lines keep the data synchronized with an identical storage area network (SAN) in a different location. If one of the systems becomes inoperative, then the other automatically takes over all of the data warehousing tasks. The company's disaster recovery plan includes a third backup location that is utilized in the event of emergencies.

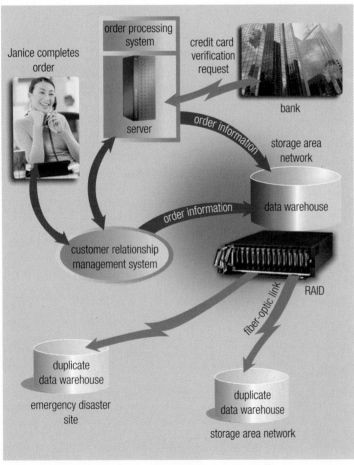

FIGURE 3

Step 3 — Inventories Checked

After an order is accepted for manufacturing, the order is broken down into a list of components required from Mecha Computers's suppliers (Figure 4). This processing is done by specialized software within the company's Manufacturing Resources Planning II (MRP II) information system. While the company does not like to keep an inventory of components in stock, some situations arise in which a component may be in inventory. For example, if a component was returned or an order cancelled, the company usually chooses to keep the component on hand. If a component is found in the database of components in the inventory on hand, then the component is flagged as being necessary for the particular order. A report is sent to the stock room containing the component to tell a worker there to set the component aside for this particular order.

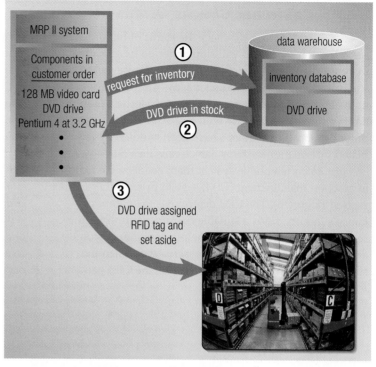

FIGURE 4

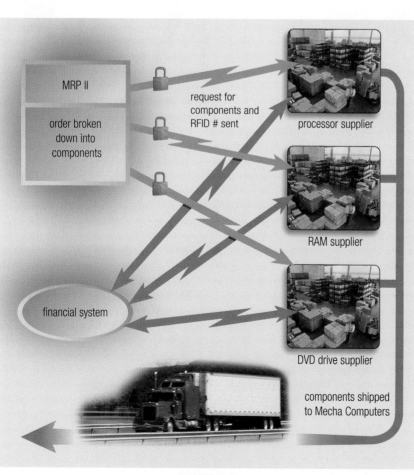

FIGURE 5

Step 4 — Components Ordered

When it is time to order components from suppliers, the MRP II system uses secure Web services on the supplier's extranet Web servers to place the orders (Figure 5). Mecha Computers demands just-in-time delivery, meaning that the supplier must get the components to Mecha exactly on the date that Mecha indicates it wants the components. Mecha also automatically provides an RFID identification number that the supplier should use on each component, and the supplier is required to affix an RFID tag to each component. Mecha Computers will use the RFID tags to track the component throughout the manufacturing process. Alternatively, the company allows its suppliers to choose an identification number for the RFID tag and notify Mecha Computers of the number. To pay its suppliers for components, Mecha Computers asks that its suppliers use an electronic data interchange (EDI) system to send invoices to the company. Invoices from suppliers then are placed into the accounting system, which, using another EDI system, requests that its bank pay the supplier at the appropriate time. Payment information is recorded and reported by the company's financial information system.

Step 5 *Customer Checks Status*

Janice wants to check the status of her order to see if the computer still will ship to her on time. Rather than use the Web site to check the order, Janice feels that she would like to talk to someone instead. Up to this point in the ordering process, no employee of Mecha Computers has been involved directly with Janice Oberweis's computer order. All of the steps have been handled by automated information systems. Janice calls the company, and an automated telephone system managed by a customer interaction management (CIM) system prompts her for her request (Figure 6). The CIM determines the nature of Janice's inquiry, finds a suitable customer support representative who is not currently helping another customer, and forwards the call to the representative. When the support representative receives the call, the CIM gathers

customer information and order information from the customer relationship management (CRM) and Manufacturing Resources Planning II (MRP II) systems to display on the representative's computer screen. The information quickly is relayed to the customer. The CIM also records the call and stores the recording and information about the call in the data warehouse. The 400 support representatives at Mecha use thin clients — small terminal-like computers that primarily rely on a server for data storage and processing for their work. The thin clients connect to servers, and each server can support 50 virtual servers at once. That is, 50 representatives can all share one server at a time. The use of inexpensive thin clients requires much less maintenance than standard personal computers.

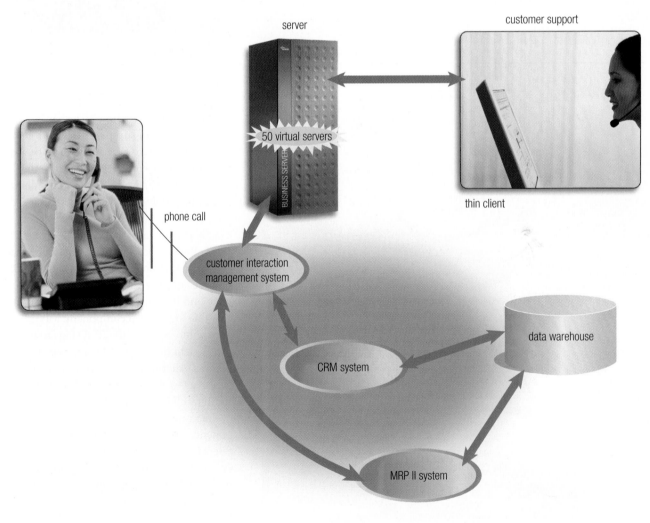

FIGURE 6

Components Received

As workers at the loading docks receive components and components are acquired from inventory stocks, the components are scanned in using the RFID tags assigned to and placed on them (Figure 7). The Manufacturing Resources Planning II (MRP II) system, therefore, is able to track automatically the requests for components from various vendors. The MRP II system informs the dock workers where to store the components for future recovery when all components have been received for an order. When all the components are received, the MRP II system generates a report and assigns an RFID tag to the entire order. The MRP II system is updated with the current status of the order. The workers, aided by the RFID tags on the components, gather the components, place them together in a bin, tag them with the new RFID tag, and place them on a conveyor belt. A computer-integrated manufacturing information system then uses the order information to determine the best path along the assembly floor for the new computer. The path determined by the computer-integrated manufacturing (CIM) system depends on the type of computer, the components to be installed, the urgency of the order, and the availability of workers. The CIM uses automation to send the bin of components along the factory floor in the predetermined path.

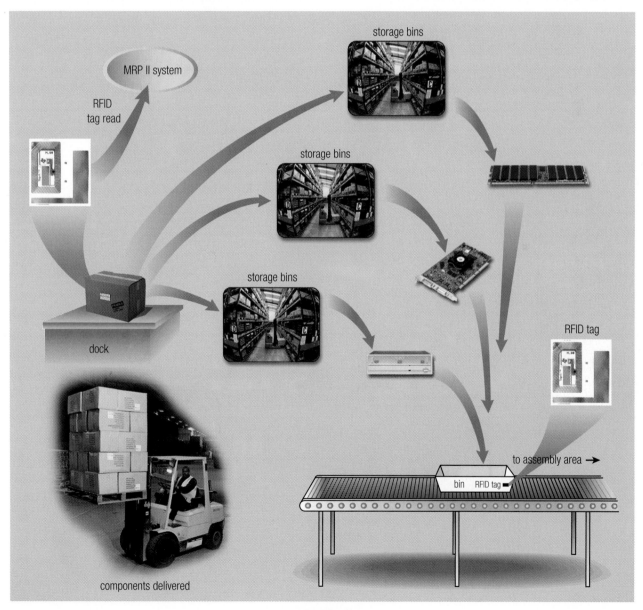

FIGURE 7

Step 7 *Order Assembled*

As the computer-integrated manufacturing system guides the bin of components along the manufacturing floor, it keeps a record of what processes have been completed. When the conveyor belt brings the worker a bin, the worker uses an RFID reader to verify that he or she has the correct bin and each individual component (Figure 8). The worker's thin client displays the work needed to be performed by that worker. For example, the instructions may be "Install processor, RAM, and video card." More detailed instructions are available upon request by the worker. The detailed instructions are maintained in a content management system. The RFID tags on each individual component are removed as they are installed in the computer. The worker can interact with the Manufacturing Resources Planning II (MRP II) system if the worker has a special request, such as informing the system that the bin contains a broken component. The MRP II system will instruct the computer-integrated manufacturing (CIM) system to send the worker a replacement component. When the worker is done with the instructed work, he or she informs the MRP II system of the work and places the bin back on the conveyor belt. The CIM system takes the bin to the next worker and proceeds with this process until the computer is assembled. The last step is to take the computer to a testing environment, where the functionality of the computer is verified.

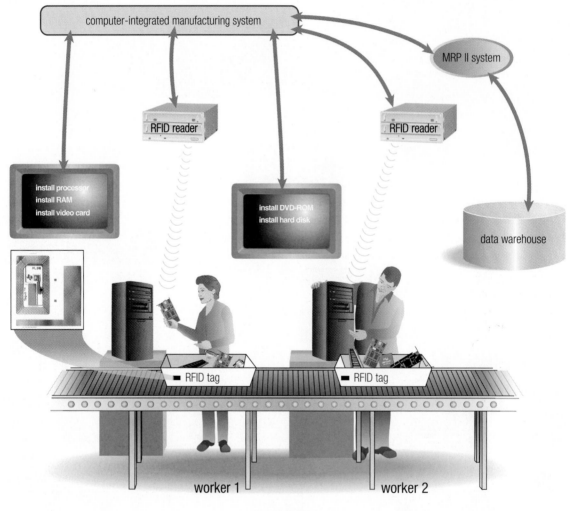

FIGURE 8

Step 8 — Payment Processed

Once Janice's computer is assembled, tested, and ready for shipment, Mecha Computers processes the customer's payment before shipping the computer to her (Figure 9). A financial system receives notification of the request to process the payment and uses a transaction processing system to apply the charge to the customer's credit card. When the transaction processing system completes the transaction, the accounting system is updated to reflect the amount and type of transaction. The entire transaction takes less than a second. On a daily basis, Mecha's bank uses electronic data interchange (EDI) to receive the money from the credit card company. Upon deposit in the bank, the bank electronically notifies Mecha Computers's accounting system to inform the company of the fund transfer.

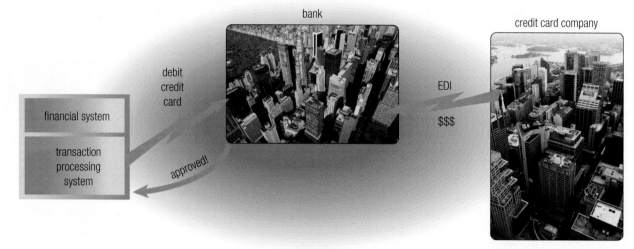

FIGURE 9

Step 9 — Order Shipped

With the payment accepted, the Manufacturing Resources Planning II (MRP II) system receives its final confirmation that the order is complete (Figure 10). The MRP II system interacts with the customer relationship management (CRM) system to inform the CRM system that it should send an e-mail to Janice to let her know that her order has been shipped. At the same time, the last step for the computer-integrated manufacturing information system is to make sure that the completed computer is sent to the shipping area. Software and hardware in the distribution system automatically read the RFID tag and determine the most cost-efficient manner in which to package the computer. A worker receives the instructions and packages the computer. The distribution system then uses artificial intelligence to determine the most cost-effective and quickest shipping method. The computer then is shipped to Janice, and the status of the order is updated. Mecha Computers uses Web services at various freight and package delivery companies to track its packages automatically. Any abnormalities in the tracking of the shipment are reported to a customer support representative who takes appropriate action to remedy the situation.

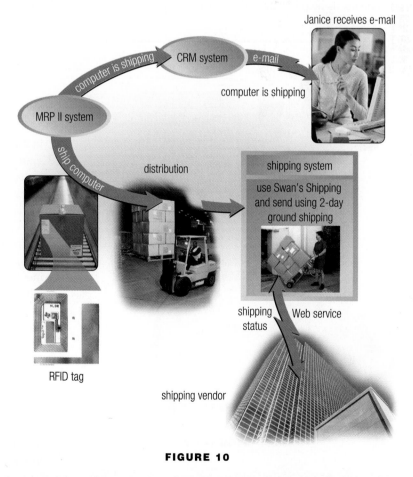

FIGURE 10

Step 10 Customer Requests Support

When her new computer arrives, Janice sets up the computer and quickly begins to move all of her files from her old computer to the new one using CD-R discs. She discovers that the DVD drive on the new computer will not read the discs as it should. She navigates to the Mecha Computers Web site and clicks the technical support link (Figure 11). An expert system, loaded with documentation and information from a content management system, guides her through the diagnosis of the problem. It seems that the drive simply needs to be replaced due to damage during shipping, and the customer interaction management system supplies her with a telephone number and support reference number. When she calls, the customer interaction management (CIM) system requests her support reference number and then routes her call and customer information to a components replacement specialist. The specialist uses the Manufacturing Resources Planning II (MRP II) system to report the problem with the drive and then orders a new drive from the supplier using the supplier's extranet. The supplier's extranet allows the specialist to ship the drive directly from the supplier to Janice. When the part arrives, the distribution system notifies the technical support personnel who call her and ask her if she needs help installing the replacement.

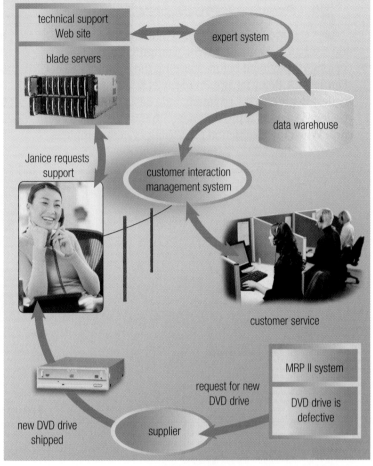

FIGURE 11

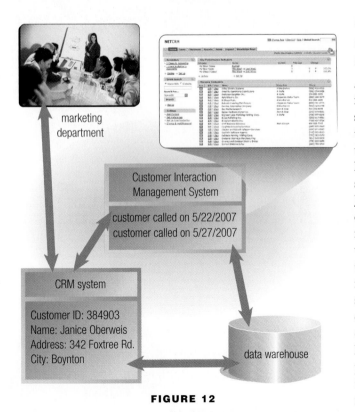

FIGURE 12

Customer Relationship Management Information System Tracks Customer Experience

All of Janice's interactions with Mecha Computers are tracked in the company's customer relationship management (CRM) system (Figure 12). The CRM system performs additional tasks such as assigning Janice a unique customer number, using the United States Postal Service update files to update her address automatically when she moves, and helps the sales team to identify when might be a good time to contact Janice again about purchasing her next new computer. The company tightly integrates the customer interaction management system with the CRM system. Anyone in the company who ever interacts with Janice in the future will have access to this history. Janice will not have to explain her past dealings with the company to the next customer support representative with whom she speaks. The CRM system stores all of its information in the data warehouse. The marketing department uses the CRM system to track customer buying habits and to target customers for future marketing campaigns based on their purchasing history. For example, a customer who purchased a system with only 256 MB of RAM may be an ideal candidate to receive a special offer regarding memory upgrades.

Management Receives Information and Reacts

The executive information system at Mecha Computers is a decision support system that allows managers and executives to obtain real-time information from any information system in the company. The executive information system (EIS) consolidates information that is important to executives and presents a summary of information such as sales, financial, manufacturing, and service information (Figure 13). If the manager needs to get more detail, they can "zoom in" on a piece of information to see what comprises it. For example, a manager may be presented with the total number of defective components reported by customers in the last month. The manager can zoom in on that number to get a comparison of the defects from week to week within that month, and then day to day in order to look for trends. In the case of Janice Oberweis's defective DVD drive, the chief operating officer notices a sharp increase in the number of defective drives from one particular supplier. The executive uses the Manufacturing Resources Planning II (MRP II) system to request that this supplier be excluded from future orders until the problem can be analyzed further. The marketing department receives the request as well and removes the component from availability on the e-commerce Web site via the content management system (CMS). When at home or traveling, managers use a virtual private network to interact securely with the EIS.

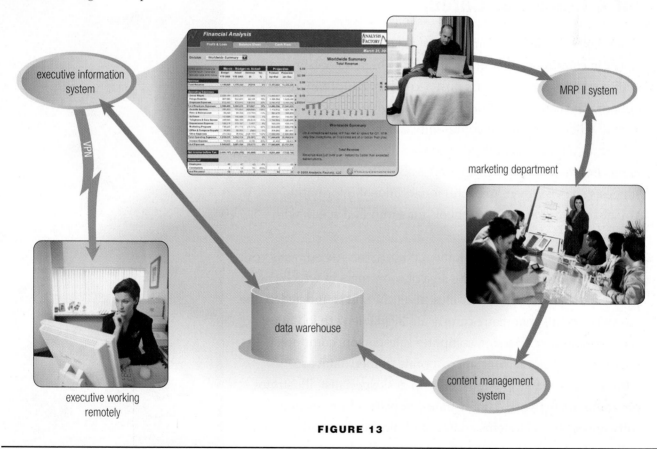

FIGURE 13

Enterprise Order Processing: *Summary*

Every interaction that you have with a large company triggers a chain of events across many information systems. This case study provides an example of how hardware, software, data, people, and procedures work together to satisfy customers and meet the objectives of an enterprise.

CHAPTER FIFTEEN

Computer Careers and Certification

Picture Yourself Planning for a Computer Career

Yesterday, your daughter informed you she wants to pursue a career in computers after graduating from high school. She meets with her counselor to discuss post-secondary education options. The counselor indicates your daughter can attend a trade school, a two-year community college or junior college, or a four-year college or university. The counselor hands her many brochures and tapes about local schools and suggests she visit their Web sites for additional information. You also can call any of the schools for a tour and speak with an advisor.

During a visit to one of the junior colleges, the advisor asks your daughter if she has decided the area of computers in which she would like to specialize. After indicating she still is undecided, the advisor explains that many careers are available with job titles such as computer operator, computer salesperson, computer scientist, computer technician, corporate trainer, database administrator, desktop publisher, help desk specialist, illustrator, programmer, network administrator, security administrator, software engineer, systems analyst, technical writer, and Web page author. She suggests your daughter browse the Web to explore careers in the computer field. After doing her research, your daughter eagerly signs up for her first college computer course and imagines herself working in the computer field.

To learn about careers in the computer industry, read Chapter 15 and also discover types of information technology certifications.

After completing this chapter, you will be able to:

1. Describe career opportunities available in various segments of the computer industry

2. Discuss functions of jobs available in an IT department

3. Distinguish between trade schools and colleges

4. Differentiate among various computer-related majors for college students

5. Identify ways to stay current with changing technology after graduation

6. List the benefits of certification for employers, employees, and vendors

7. Identify ways to prepare for certification

8. List the general areas of IT certification

9. Name some specific IT certifications in each certification area

CONTENTS

THE COMPUTER INDUSTRY

In today's technology-rich world, a demand for computer professionals continues to grow. The U.S. Department of Labor's Bureau of Labor Statistics (BLS) reports that more than 20 percent of the fastest growing occupations are in computer-related fields. These include network administrators, software engineers, database administrators, and systems analysts. Figure 15-1 identifies these and other computer-related careers available to today's college graduates.

The Information Technology Association of America (ITAA) estimates that the current IT (information technology) workforce is about 10.5 million people with an expected increase

of about 2 to 3 percent per year. More than 79 percent of IT employees work at companies whose primary business is not computer-related, such as banking, finance, food service, manufacturing, or transportation.

While the use of computers and the demand for computer professionals continue to grow, the number of students majoring in computer-related fields is declining. One primary reason is students fear homeland IT-related jobs could be outsourced (read Ethics & Issues 15-1 for a related discussion). On the other hand, administrators at colleges and universities and business executives worry that if this decline in enrollment continues, the demand for graduates majoring in computers will exceed the actual number of students graduating with

Systems analyst

Help desk specialist

Computer operator

Software engineer

Computer technician

Programmer/Developer

Technical lead

FIGURE 15-1
The computer industry offers many rewarding careers.

computer-related degrees. To reassure students that a future in IT holds promise and to dispel concerns related to outsourcing, Bill Gates, Microsoft's founder, recently gave presentations to students at several well-known schools — encouraging students to consider majoring in computers.

As presented in the Career Corner feature at the end of each chapter of this book, the computer industry offers many rewarding careers. These computer-related careers often require a unique combination of hands-on skills, creative problem solving, and an understanding of business needs. This chapter discusses a variety of careers in the computer industry, how to prepare for these types of jobs, and available certifications.

ETHICS & ISSUES 15-1

Outsourcing Computer Jobs — A Threat to American Workers?

While the cost of skilled computer professionals has risen for companies in the United States, other countries have begun producing much less expensive skilled IT workers. To remain competitive, many companies have chosen to send computer jobs overseas, a practice known as outsourcing. Proponents say that the United States has a long history of outsourcing all types of work when the economics of the situation demands it. Furthermore, with an anticipated IT worker shortage, if the government were to place restrictions on outsourcing, then American businesses could not be as competitive with their foreign counterparts. Opponents say that outsourcing results in unemployment and decreases student interest in majoring in IT-related fields. Also, sending high-paying jobs overseas harms the economy. Outsourcing of sensitive work, such as health record maintenance or military work, could place U.S. citizens at risk. Should the government limit a company's ability to outsource computer jobs to other countries? Why or why not? Should companies be criticized for outsourcing jobs? Why or why not? What are some possible alternatives to outsourcing that would help to keep a company competitive?

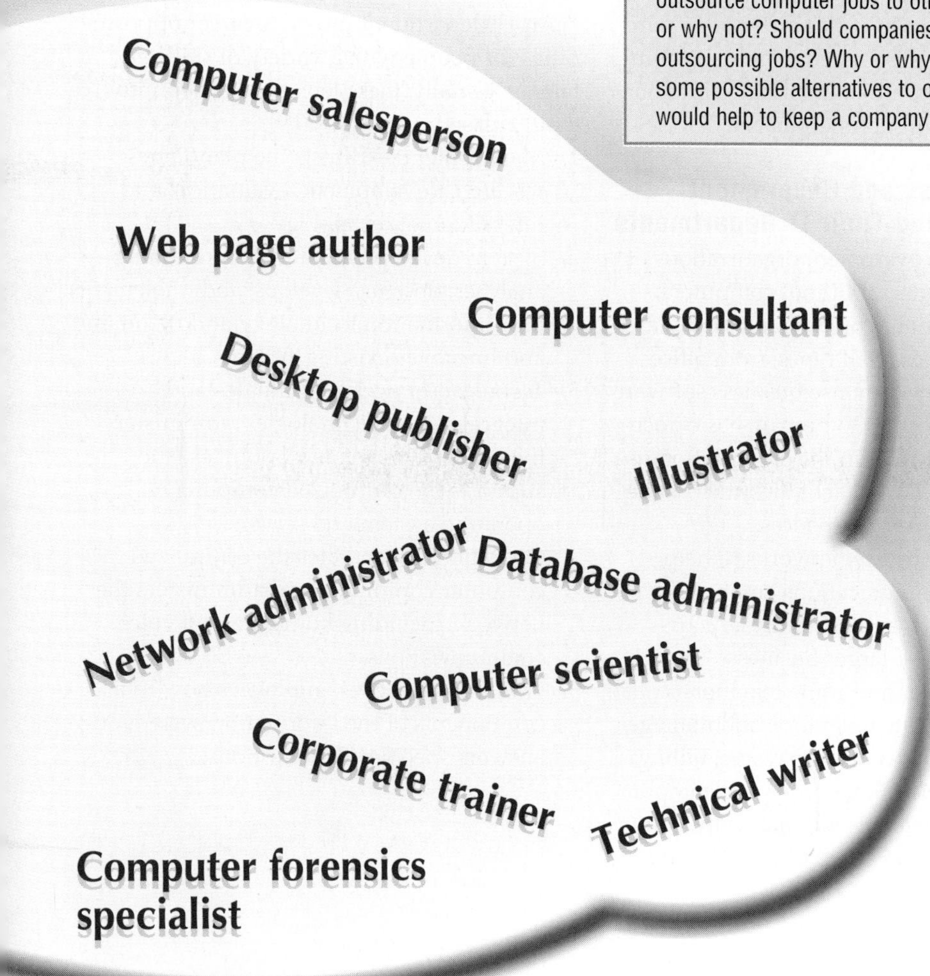

Computer salesperson

Web page author

Computer consultant

Desktop publisher

Illustrator

Network administrator Database administrator

Computer scientist

Corporate trainer Technical writer

Computer forensics specialist

CAREERS IN THE COMPUTER INDUSTRY

With billions of dollars in annual revenue, the computer industry is one of the larger worldwide industries. This industry has created thousands of high-tech jobs, even in companies whose primary business is not computer-related. Job opportunities in the computer industry generally are available in one or more of these areas:

- General business and government organizations and their IT departments
- Computer equipment field
- Computer software field
- Computer service and repair field
- Computer sales
- Computer education and training field
- IT consulting field

The following pages discuss each of these areas and the career opportunities and jobs available within the areas. In the fast-paced world of technology, job titles are not standardized. Some companies are reducing their number of job titles or combining job titles into one position such as programmer/analyst.

General Business and Government Organizations and Their IT Departments

Businesses and government organizations of all sizes use computers. Without computers, very few organizations could operate in today's economy. Employees of all types, from office workers to shop foremen, use business software such as word processing to prepare basic documents. Other employees in the organization use computers for specialized activities such as the management of company finances.

Most organizations use networks to help ensure smooth communications among employees, vendors, and customers. As discussed in Chapter 14, larger businesses use computers to answer and route telephone calls, process orders, update inventory, and manage accounts receivable, accounts payable, billing, and payroll activities. Some firms use computers to order raw materials automatically, control manufacturing, and ship finished goods.

Businesses and government offices use computers and the Web to provide the public with a means to access their facilities. For example, people in the United States use computers to file taxes, apply for permits and licenses, pay parking tickets, buy stamps, report crimes, apply for financial aid, and renew vehicle registrations and driver's licenses.

To manage their computers and operations, businesses and government organizations need employees to fill a variety of computer-related jobs. Most medium and large businesses and government organizations include an IT department that employs people in computer-related jobs (Figure 15-2). Employees in the **IT department** work together as a team to meet the information requirements of their organization and are responsible for keeping all the computer operations and networks running smoothly. They also determine when and if the company requires new hardware or software. Read Looking Ahead 15-1 for a look at the future of IT careers.

An IT department provides career opportunities for people with a variety of skills and talents. Usually, these jobs are divided into five main areas:

1. Management — directs the planning, research, development, evaluation, and integration of technology.
2. System development and programming — analyzes, designs, develops, and implements new information technology and maintains and improves existing systems.
3. Technical services — evaluates and integrates new technologies, administers the organization's data resources, and supports the centralized computer operating system and servers.
4. Operations — operates the centralized computer equipment and administers the network, including both data and voice communications.
5. Training — teaches employees how to use components of the information system or answers specific user questions.

FIGURE 15-2 In larger businesses and government organizations, the IT department includes professionals who set up and manage the computer equipment and software to ensure that it produces quality information for users.

LOOKING AHEAD 15-1

Tomorrow's Jobs in Information Technology

By 2012, the total United States workforce is expected to increase 14.8 percent to 165 million. Of the 21 million jobs that will be added, more than one-third will be in the professional, scientific, and technical services, according to the U.S. Department of Labor's Bureau of Labor Statistics (BLS).

Growth in these areas will fuel the need for expanded computer support. As a result, employment in computer systems and design and related fields is projected to increase by 54.6 percent. Of the 20 fastest growing occupations, five are in information systems.

Increased demand for employees will occur in the areas of software and Web publishing, Internet service providers, and Web search portals. While these job openings may exist, there is a shortage of qualified U.S. applicants to hire, according to Microsoft chairman Bill Gates. He expresses deep concern about the decrease in the number of students entering the computer science field and urges technology companies to cultivate positive images of the interesting and challenging jobs available. For more information, visit scsite.com/ dc2007/ch15/looking and then click Tomorrow's Jobs.

FAQ 15-1

What are the fastest growing IT jobs?

The U.S. Department of Labor predicts that by 2010, demand for software engineers and support specialists will nearly double. Demand for many other computer professionals will grow by more than 50 percent, including jobs such as computer scientists, data communications analysts, database administrators, desktop publishers, network administrators, and systems analysts. For more information, visit scsite.com/dc2007/ ch15/faq and then click Fast Growing IT Jobs.

The table in Figure 15-3 shows some of the jobs in each of the areas of a typical IT department along with job functions, usual educational requirements, and national average salary ranges.

IT DEPARTMENT JOBS

Area	Job Title	Function	Usual Education Required	Annual Salary Range
Management	Chief information officer (CIO)/Vice president of IT	Directs the company's information service and communications functions	Bachelor's degree in Management Information Technology	$159,000 to $249,000
	Chief security officer (CSO)	Responsible for physical security of a company's property and people; in charge of securing computing resources	Bachelor's degree in Computer Science or Management Information Technology	$118,000 to $163,000
	E-commerce administrator	Supervises the development and execution of Internet or e-commerce systems; works with the company's marketing and customer service divisions	Bachelor's degree in Management Information Technology	$48,000 to $165,000
	Network administrator	Installs, configures, and maintains LANs, WANs, intranets, and Internet systems; identifies and resolves connectivity issues	Bachelor's degree in Computer Information Systems or Electrical Engineering Technology	$39,000 to $92,000
	Project leader/manager	Oversees all assigned projects; allocates resources; selects teams; performs systems analysis and programming tasks; conducts performance appraisals	Bachelor's degree in Management Information Technology	$77,000 to $92,000
System development and programming	Application programmer/developer	Converts the system design into the appropriate computer language, such as Visual Basic 2005, Java, and C++	Associate's or Bachelor's degree in Computer Information Systems	$50,000 to $100,000
	Computer scientist	Researches, invents, and develops innovative solutions to complex software requirements or problems	Bachelor's or Master's degree in Computer Science or Engineering	$60,000 to $110,000
	Database analyst	Uses data modeling techniques and tools to analyze, tune, and specify data usage within an application area	Bachelor's degree in Computer Science or Computer Information Systems	$43,000 to $106,000
	Software engineer	Specifies, designs, implements, tests, and documents high-quality software in a variety of fields, including robotics, operating systems, animation, and applications	Bachelor's degree in Computer Science or Software Engineering	$45,000 to $123,000
	Systems analyst	Works closely with users to analyze their requirements, designs and develops new information systems, and incorporates new technologies	Bachelor's degree in Computer Information Systems	$45,000 to $85,000
	Systems programmer	Installs and maintains operating system software and provides technical support to the programming staff	Bachelor's degree in Computer Science or Computer Information Systems	$55,000 to $110,000
	Technical writer	Works with the analyst, programmer, and user to create system documentation and user materials	Associate's or Bachelor's degree in Computer Information Systems or in English	$36,000 to $81,000
	Technical lead	Guides design, development, and maintenance tasks; serves as interface between programmer/developer and management	Bachelor's degree in Computer Science	$77,000 to $91,000
	Web page author	Analyzes, designs, implements, and supports Web applications; works with HTML, JavaScript, and multimedia	Bachelor's degree in Computer Information Systems	$58,000 to $92,000

FIGURE 15-3 Some of the jobs available in each of the five main areas of a typical IT department.

(continued)

Area	Job Title	Function	Usual Education Required	Annual Salary Range
Technical services	Computer forensics specialist	Collects and analyzes evidence found on computers and networks	Bachelor's degree in Computer Science	$50,000 to $85,000
	Computer technician	Installs, maintains, and repairs hardware; installs, upgrades, and configures software; troubleshoots hardware problems	Associate's degree in Computer Information Systems or Electrical Engineering	$34,000 to $60,000
	Database administrator	Creates and maintains the data dictionary; manages security and monitors performance of the database	Bachelor's degree in Computer Information Systems	$72,000 to $95,000
	Desktop publisher	Produces documents such as newsletters, brochures, and books by combining text and graphics	Certificate	$24,000 to $60,000
	Graphic designer/ illustrator	Creates visual impressions of products and advertisements in the fields of graphics, theater, and fashion	Certificate	$30,000 to $80,000
	Network security specialist	Configures routers and firewalls; specifies Web protocols and enterprise technologies	Bachelor's degree in Computer Science or Computer Information Systems	$58,000 to $96,000
	Quality assurance specialist	Reviews programs and documentation to ensure they meet the organization's standards	Bachelor's degree in Computer Information Systems	$48,000 to $100,000
	Security administrator	Administers network security access; monitors and protects against unauthorized access	Bachelor's degree in Computer Science or Computer Information Systems	$56,000 to $79,000
	Web administrator	Oversees Web site performance; maintains links between company's Web server and Internet access provider	Bachelor's degree in Computer Information Systems	$51,000 to $152,000
	Web graphic designer	Develops graphical content using Photoshop, Flash, and other multimedia tools	Bachelor's degree in Computer Information Systems	$51,000 to $99,000
	Webmaster	Maintains an organization's Web site; creates or helps users create Web pages	Bachelor's degree in Computer Information Systems	$54,000 to $78,000
Operations	Computer operator	Performs equipment-related activities such as monitoring performance, running jobs, backup, and restore	Associate's degree in Computer Information Systems	$27,000 to $47,000
	Data communications analyst	Evaluates, installs, and monitors data and/or voice communications equipment and software; maintains connections to the Internet and other WANs	Bachelor's degree in Computer Information Systems or Electrical Engineering Technology	$41,000 to $75,000
Training	Corporate trainer	Teaches employees how to use software, design and develop systems, program, and perform other computer-related activities	Certificate or Bachelor's degree in Computer Information Systems	$54,000 to $125,000
	Help desk specialist	Answers hardware, software, or networking questions in person, over the telephone, and/or in a chat room	Associate's degree in Computer Information Systems	$37,000 to $60,000

Computer Equipment Field

The **computer equipment field** consists of manufacturers and distributors of computers and computer-related hardware such as disk and tape drives, monitors, printers, and communications and networking devices. In addition to the companies that make end-user equipment, thousands of companies manufacture components used inside a computer such as chips, motherboards, and power supplies.

Careers in this field are available with companies that design, manufacture, and produce computers and devices such as input, output, communications, and networking devices. Jobs include designing and fabricating computer chips, testing internal components (Figure 15-4), assembling computers and devices, and packing computers and peripherals. In addition to computer equipment related jobs, most companies of this type include an IT department, where job opportunities may be available.

Computer equipment manufacturers include such companies as AMD, Apple Computer, Cisco Systems, Dell, Gateway, Hewlett-Packard, IBM, Intel, Logitech, Lucent Technologies, Motorola, Nokia, QUALCOMM, Sun Microsystems, and 3Com. Many of these firms are huge organizations with thousands of employees worldwide. IBM, for example, is one of the larger computer companies with more than 329,000 employees and annual revenues of more than $96 billion.

The computer equipment industry also is well known for the many startup companies it spawns each year. These new companies take advantage of rapid changes in equipment technology, such as wireless communications, networking, multimedia, and fiber optics, to create new products and new job opportunities. Often these companies offer special incentives to influence college graduates to join their firms instead of the larger, more established companies. Read Ethics & Issues 15-2 for a discussion related to other IT hiring practices.

ETHICS & ISSUES 15-2

Should Work Visas Be Issued to Foreign IT Workers?

Millions of Americans are employed today in IT and communications industries. In order for companies to remain competitive, they often send work overseas to take advantage of cheaper labor. Another way to cut costs and fill positions is to bring foreign workers to the United States under the H-1B Visa program. This program is authorized by the United States Congress and grants a fixed number of work visas each year. Many argue that the expansion of the H-1B Visa program is crucial to the future development of the United States' economy. They contend that some of the world's better high-tech employees come from places other than the United States, so legislation should expand the H-1B Visa program. Additionally, the inability to bring in a greater number of foreign workers may force more companies simply to send the work overseas or leave job openings vacant. Others argue that the H-1B Visa program is a method for American companies to bring in low-cost labor and drive down salaries of American workers. Should Congress expand the H-1B Visa program to admit additional IT workers? Why or why not? Should a time limit be set on those coming into the United States? Should a minimum wage be established for IT workers?

FIGURE 15-4 Computer-related manufacturing jobs are found throughout the computer equipment industry.

Computer Software Field

The **computer software field** consists of companies that develop, manufacture, and support a wide range of software. Some software companies specialize in a particular type of software such as business software or utility programs. Other software companies, especially larger firms such as Microsoft, produce and sell many types of software.

Career opportunities in the computer software field involve designing and programming a variety of software, including operating systems and utility programs; business, graphics, multimedia, home, personal, educational, and entertainment software; network software; software development tools; and Internet and Web page authoring software.

Job titles for careers related to the development of software include project leader or project manager, programmer, developer, technical lead, software engineer, and computer scientist. Some employees develop application software such as business programs, games, simulations, Web sites, and more; others develop system software or utility programs. For a more technical discussion about programming computer games, read the High-Tech Talk article on page 802.

A project leader or project manager analyzes software requirements, designs software solutions, and oversees the software development process. A programmer writes and tests computer programs. Programmers of Internet and Web applications often use the title, developer, instead of programmer. Technical lead personnel guide the design, development, and maintenance tasks and serve as interface between programmer/developer and management. A software engineer designs and develops software. Computer scientists draw on their theoretical educational background to research, invent, and develop innovative solutions to complex software requirements or problems.

The software industry is huge, with annual sales exceeding $100 billion. Leading software companies include Adobe Systems, BMC Software, Computer Associates, IBM, Intuit, McAfee, Microsoft, Novell, Oracle, RealNetworks, Red Hat, Riverdeep, Sybase, and Symantec. The largest software company, Microsoft, has more than 57,000 employees and annual revenues of more than $36 billion.

Computer Service and Repair Field

The **computer service and repair field** provides preventive maintenance, component installation, and repair services to customers. Typical job titles for workers in this field include service technician, computer repairperson, repair technician, and computer technician — all of which perform similar responsibilities.

A computer technician installs, maintains, and repairs hardware; installs, upgrades, and configures software; and troubleshoots hardware problems (Figure 15-5). Being a computer technician is a challenging job for people who like to troubleshoot and solve problems and possess a strong background in electronics. Computer technicians often replace a malfunctioning component, such as a hard disk, at the site of the computer equipment and then take the faulty part back for repair at an office or special repair facility.

Many computer equipment manufacturers include diagnostic software with their computer equipment that assists computer technicians in identifying problems. Today's technology also allows computer technicians to diagnose and repair software problems from a remote location; that is, the technician accesses the user's hard disk from a different location.

FIGURE 15-5 A computer technician job requires a knowledge of electronics.

Computer Sales

Computer salespeople must possess a general understanding of computers and a specific knowledge of the product they are selling. Strong people skills are important, including a keen listening ability and superior oral communications skills. Computer salespeople generally determine a buyer's needs and match these needs to the correct hardware and software. Effective computer salespeople need a thorough understanding of available products. They also must be able to discuss computers without using technical jargon.

WEB LINK 15-2

Computer Salespeople

For more information, visit scsite.com/ dc2007/ch15/weblink and then click Computer Salespeople.

Some salespeople work directly for computer equipment and software manufacturers such as Apple Computer, Dell, Hewlett-Packard, IBM, and Palm. Others work for resellers, including retailers that sell personal computer products, such as Best Buy, Circuit City, CompUSA, OfficeMax, Office Depot, and Staples.

The computer salesperson in a retail store often is a suitable entry-level job for students majoring in computers (Figure 15-6). Salespeople often are paid based on the amount of product they sell. More experienced corporate salespeople can be among an organization's more highly paid employees.

FIGURE 15-6 Computer retailers need salespeople who understand the products they sell and have solid people skills.

Computer Education and Training Field

The increased sophistication and complexity of today's computer products have opened extensive opportunities in computer-related education and training. Schools, colleges, universities, and private companies all need qualified educators. In fact, the high demand has led to a shortage of qualified instructors at the college level as instructors increasingly move to careers in private industry with the promise of higher pay.

Corporate trainers teach employees how to use software, design and develop systems, write programs, and perform other computer-related activities (Figure 15-7). Many companies use their own training departments. Corporations usually require less educational

background for trainers than educational institutions require for instructors.

In a more informal setting, a help desk specialist answers hardware, software, and networking questions in person, over the telephone, or via a chat room. Educational requirements for help desk specialists are less stringent than they are for other jobs in the computer field. The help desk specialist position is an ideal entryway into the IT field.

FIGURE 15-7 Corporate trainers lead continuing education classes and introduce new software.

IT Consulting

Computer professionals sometimes decide to become IT consultants after gaining experience in one or more computer-related areas, such as programming, systems analysis and design, network configuration, or Web page development. An **IT consultant**, typically hired based on computer expertise, provides computer services to his or her clients. Many companies hire an IT consultant to fill in for an employee on an extended leave of absence. Large enterprises often hire teams of consultants to offer advice about technology-related concerns.

IT consultants must possess strong technical skills in their specialized area and must be able to communicate effectively to clients. Qualified consultants are in high demand for tasks such as computer selection, information system design, communications, hardware and software configuration, network design and installation, and Web development.

WEB LINK 15-3

Help Desk Specialist

For more information, visit scsite.com/ dc2007/ch15/weblink and then click Help Desk Specialist.

Test your knowledge of pages 776 through 784 in Quiz Yourself 15-1.

PREPARING FOR A CAREER IN THE COMPUTER INDUSTRY

To prepare for a career in the computer industry, you first must decide on the area in which you are interested and then become educated in that field. If you desire a formal education, several options are available, which include attending a trade school, a college that offers two-year degrees, or a college or university that offers four-year degrees. After obtaining your education, you must keep abreast of changes in the field. The following sections discuss various options for obtaining formal computer education and methods of remaining current after embarking on a career in the computer industry.

Attending a Trade School

A **trade school**, also called a technical school, vocational school, or career college, offers programs primarily in the areas of programming, Web design and development, graphics design, hardware maintenance, networking, personal computer support, and security. One advantage of attending a trade school is time savings. Trade schools teach specific skills instead of requiring students take a broad range of courses in the sciences and humanities. For this reason, students often complete trade school programs in a shorter time than college and university programs.

Upon completion of trade school education, students often receive a certificate. Some receive an associate's degree or higher. Many students seek full-time employment with their certificate or degree and then continue their education on a part-time basis with a two-year or four-year college. To ensure coursework will transfer, it is important that students ask their advisor if the trade school has an articulation agreement with a nearby college or university. An *articulation agreement* ensures that if you transfer to a college or university, you will receive credit for most of the courses taken at your current school.

As with any post-secondary school, when deciding on a trade school, you should compare curricula, laboratory facilities, instructors, and the types of jobs the school's graduates have obtained.

Entry-level jobs for students with a certificate or degree from a trade school include computer technician, desktop publisher, graphic designer/illustrator, help desk specialist, technical writer, and Web page author.

WEB LINK 15-4

Trade Schools
For more information, visit scsite.com/dc2007/ch15/weblink and then click Trade Schools.

FAQ 15-2

Do post-secondary schools test computer proficiency of incoming students?

Many use the ETS ICT (Educational Testing Service Information and Communication Technology) Literacy Assessment to measure incoming students' level of computer literacy. For more information, visit scsite.com/dc2007/ch15/faq and then click ETS ICT Literacy Assessment.

Attending a College or University

Some students attend a two-year school, called a community college or junior college. Others attend a four-year college or university. If attending a community college, students should ask their advisor if the school has an articulation agreement with a nearby college or university. As in most other industries, individuals with advanced degrees in specific fields have a better chance of success. To round out their education, many graduates augment their computer degree with a master's degree in business, education, or other field of study.

At colleges and universities, three broad disciplines produce the majority of entry-level employees in the computer industry: computer information systems, computer science (also referred to as software engineering), and computer engineering. The characteristics of each program are summarized in Figure 15-8 and discussed in the following paragraphs.

WEB LINK 15-5

College Computer Majors

For more information, visit scsite.com/dc2007/ch15/weblink and then click College Computer Majors.

FAQ 15-3

What programming languages should I learn so that I am marketable?

According to a recent study, the programming languages currently in high demand include C++, C#, Java, Perl, SQL, and Visual Basic. For more information, visit scsite.com/dc2007/ch15/faq and then click Computer Hiring Trends.

COMPUTER DISCIPLINE DIFFERENCES

Computer Information Systems*	Computer Science/ Software Engineering	Computer Engineering
Practical and application oriented	Theory oriented	Design oriented
Business and management oriented	Mathematics and science oriented	Mathematics and science oriented
Understand how to design and implement information systems	Understand the fundamental nature of hardware and software	Understand the fundamental nature of hardware and electronics
Certificates Degrees include A.A., A.A.S., A.S., B.A., B.S., M.S., Ph.D	Degrees include B.S., M.S., Ph.D.	Degrees include B.S., M.S., Ph.D.

*Sometimes called Information Technology or Management Information Systems

FIGURE 15-8   The major differences among the computer information systems, computer science/software engineering, and computer engineering disciplines.

MAJOR IN COMPUTER INFORMATION SYSTEMS   A **computer information systems** (**CIS**), or information technology (IT), curriculum teaches students technical knowledge and skills and focuses on how to apply these skills. Types of computer courses required in a typical CIS curriculum emphasize application programming and include courses in programming, operating systems, systems analysis and design, databases, networking, and Web development. CIS curricula typically do not require majors to have a strong mathematics or physics background. In addition to academic skills, CIS majors should possess excellent people skills, a keen understanding of business operations and organizational behavior, the ability to work in teams, and solid presentation skills.

After two years of study in a CIS curriculum, students may receive an associate's degree or certificate. Entry-level jobs for students with a two-year CIS degree include application programmer, computer operator, computer sales representative, computer technician, graphic designer, help desk specialist, and technical writer.

Students enrolled in four-year programs can receive a bachelor's degree with an emphasis in software development, systems analysis and design, or networking. Entry-level jobs for CIS students graduating with a bachelor's degree include application programmer, database analyst, graphic designer, IT consultant, network security specialist, systems analyst, Web page author, and Web programmer.

Instead of CIS, some schools refer to this curriculum as *management information systems* (*MIS*) or *management information technology*. The main difference between a CIS curriculum and an MIS curriculum is that the ratio of business courses to computer courses is greater in a MIS curriculum.

MAJOR IN COMPUTER SCIENCE   A **computer science** (**CS**), also called **software engineering**, curriculum focuses on the theory of programming and operating systems. A computer science curriculum typically emphasizes system programming instead of application programming. CS computer courses typically include subjects such as artificial intelligence, data communications, data and file structures, operating systems, application and systems programming, and systems analysis and design (read Ethics & Issues 15-3 for a discussion about another type of computer course). Students also are required to take

ETHICS & ISSUES 15-3

Should Colleges Teach Students How to Create Computer Viruses?

Taking the traditional admonition "know thy enemy" literally, a university recently began offering a course that teaches students how to write computer viruses. A high school runs an after-school program that challenges students to break into computers. Proponents of such courses and programs claim that these hacking skills enable the next generation of security experts to think like the virus authors, thereby helping to stop viruses. Critics claim that this practice will only encourage more virus authoring and hacking. Others claim that knowing how to write a virus does not make someone more capable of stopping viruses. Questions remain about who is responsible legally, financially, and morally if one of the students in the course or program releases malicious code to the Internet. Should virus writing be taught in schools? Why? Should companies hire people who are trained virus writers? Why or why not? What precautions should schools take if they plan to offer such courses? Who should be held responsible if a student in such a course or program causes a computer virus infection? Why?

higher-level mathematics, such as calculus, and physics courses in the CS curriculum.

Entry-level jobs for graduating CS students include software engineer, systems programmer, computer forensics specialist, and IT consultant.

MAJOR IN COMPUTER ENGINEERING A **computer engineering** (CE) curriculum teaches students how to design and develop the electronic components found in computers and peripheral devices. Required computer courses include application and systems programming, data and file structures, networks, and operating systems. Students also are required to take several high-level mathematics courses, at least two semesters of physics, and several electronic engineering courses in the CE curriculum.

Entry-level jobs for graduating CE students include software engineer, network security specialist, computer hardware designer, new hardware tester, and IT consultant. Computer engineers work independently or with teams of other engineers.

Searching for Computer-Related Jobs

Many companies list their job openings, internship opportunities, and career opportunities on their Web sites (Figure 15-9). They typically offer excellent career opportunities but usually require initial and continuing formal education. If you are serious about interviewing with a company, you often can obtain a wealth of information about the firm, its employment opportunities, and its educational requirements by visiting the company's Web site. Some companies even allow job seekers to submit their resumes online.

FAQ 15-4

How do computer graduates' starting salaries compare to other fields?

As shown in the chart below, computer-related majors are among the top ten highest college graduates' starting salaries. For more information, visit scsite.com/dc2007/ch15/faq and then click Computer Graduates' Starting Salaries.

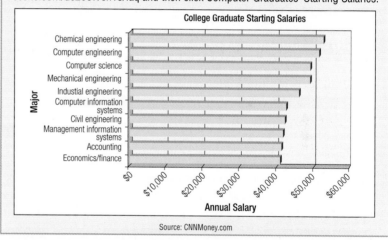

Source: CNNMoney.com

FIGURE 15-9 Many companies' Web sites provide information about their career opportunities.

Some Web sites, such as Monster, specialize in helping people find jobs (Figure 15-10). These job-search Web sites provide services free to job seekers — it is the employers who typically pay the fees. In addition to providing users with access to millions of job postings, these Web sites offer a variety of services, including resume writing tips, resume posting, interviewing advice, and current salary information.

FIGURE 15-10 HOW TO USE MONSTER TO SEARCH FOR AN ENTRY-LEVEL PROGRAMMING JOB ANYWHERE IN THE UNITED STATES

Step 1:
With your personal Monster Web page displaying on the screen, click the Find Jobs tab.

Step 2:
With the job search screen displayed, type `entry-level programmer` in the Enter Keyword(s) text box; click Select all in the Select Location list; scroll to and then click Computers, Software in the Select Job Category list; and then click the Get Results button.

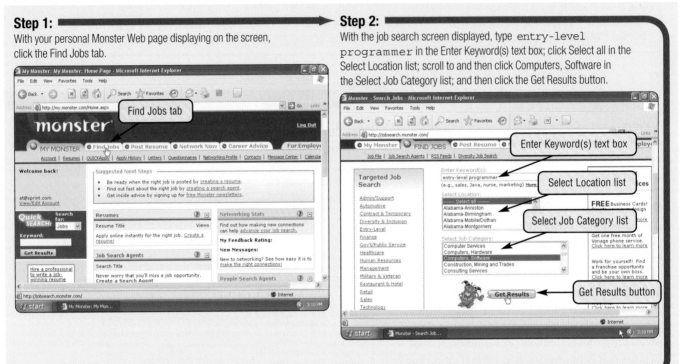

Step 4:
Read the job description. If it appeals to you, send your resume to the contact listed at the bottom of the screen.

Step 3:
When the results of the search are displayed, click the job title about which you would like more information.

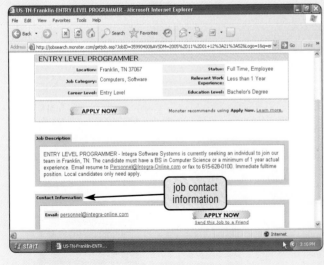

Planning for Career Development

Managers and educators emphasize that to remain competitive, workers in computer-related fields must keep their skills current. Someone who is an expert today finds that as technology changes, his or her career path also must change and grow. As a computer professional, you must seek methods to keep up to date on industry trends and technologies and to develop new skills. Four primary means of achieving these objectives are through professional organizations, professional growth and continuing education activities, computer publications and Web sites, and certification.

Professional Organizations

Computer professionals with common interests and a desire to extend their proficiency form computer-related professional organizations to share their knowledge (read Looking Ahead 15-2 for a look at how women in technology share knowledge). Two organizations that are influential in the computer industry are the Association for Computing Machinery and the Association of Information Technology Professionals.

The **Association for Computing Machinery** (**ACM**) is a scientific and educational organization dedicated to advancing knowledge and proficiency of information technology. The ACM enjoys a membership of more than 80,000 professional and student members in more than 40 countries. The focus of the ACM is computer science and computer science education. A large number of college and university computer educators are members of the ACM.

The **Association of Information Technology Professionals** (**AITP**), formerly called the *Data Processing Management Association* (*DPMA*), is a professional association with nearly 9,000 members consisting of programmers, systems analysts, and information processing managers.

Both ACM and AITP offer the following features and benefits:

- Chapters throughout the United States, for both professionals and students
- Monthly meetings
- Workshops, seminars, and conventions
- Publications, including magazines, journals, and books that help computing professionals negotiate industry and career changes
- *Special Interest Groups* (*SIGs*) that bring together members with shared interests, needs, knowledge, and experience
- Programs to help with continuing education needs

Figure 15-11 lists several professional computer organizations.

PROFESSIONAL COMPUTER ORGANIZATIONS

Association for Computing Machinery (ACM)

Association for Information Systems (AIS)

Association for Women in Computing (AWC)

Association of Information Technology Professionals (AITP) (formerly DPMA)

IEEE Computer Society

Independent Computer Consultants Association (ICCA)

Information Systems Security Association (ISSA)

Institute of Electrical and Electronics Engineers (IEEE)

National Association of Programmers (NAP)

FIGURE 15-11 Professional organizations help members remain current with trends in information technology.

Attending professional meetings as a guest or student member provides an excellent opportunity for students to learn about the IT industry and to meet and talk with professionals in the field. Often, student chapters of professional organizations exist on college campuses. The student chapters provide students with the opportunity to develop leadership skills and to become acquainted with professionals who speak at their chapter meetings.

In addition to professional organizations, many user groups exist for a wide range of computers, operating systems, application software, and more. A *user group* is a collection of people with common computer equipment or software interests that meets regularly to share information. Most metropolitan areas have one or more local computer user groups that meet monthly to discuss mutual interests about computers (Figure 15-12). For anyone employed or simply interested in the computer industry, these groups can be an effective and rewarding way to learn about and continue career development.

Professional Growth and Continuing Education

Staying aware of new products and services in the computer industry is a challenging task because technology changes so rapidly. One way to stay informed is to participate in professional growth and continuing education activities such as workshops, seminars, conferences, conventions, and trade shows. These types of events provide both general and specific information about equipment, software, services, and issues affecting the computer industry.

Workshops and seminars usually last one or two days. Many companies offer training about their products in the form of books, video-based training, computer-based training (CBT), Web-based training (WBT), and instructor-led training in a classroom.

Conferences, conventions, and trade shows often last for a week. One of the larger technology trade shows in the world is the *International Consumer Electronics Show* (*CES*), which brings together more than 2,500 exhibitors and more than 130,000 attendees (Figure 15-13). At this trade show, many exhibitors demonstrate the latest developments in personal computer hardware and related peripheral devices.

FAQ 15-6

How much does it cost to join a professional organization such as ACM or AITP?

An annual professional membership in ACM is $99. ACM has a student membership plan for high school and undergraduate students that ranges in cost from $19 to $62, depending on the membership package selected. AITP dues range from $105 to $299 per year, depending on the chapter. Students can join for $35. For more information, visit scsite.com/dc2007/ch15/faq and then click ACM and AITP.

EXAMPLES OF USER GROUPS

Apple User Groups

Association of Personal Computer User Groups (APCUG)

C/C++ Users Group (CUG)

Independent Oracle Users Group (IOUG)

Java Users Groups (JUG)

Linux Users Groups WorldWide (LUGWW)

.NET User Groups

UNIX User Groups

FIGURE 15-12   User groups provide computer users with a means of sharing ideas and information.

WEB LINK 15-6

International Consumer Electronics Show

For more information, visit scsite.com/dc2007/ch15/weblink and then click Consumer Electronics Show.

FIGURE 15-13   The International Consumer Electronics Show (CES) shown here was held in Las Vegas, Nevada. More than 2,500 exhibitors displayed their newest products and services to more than 130,000 attendees.

Computer Publications and Web Sites

Another way to keep up to date about industry trends and technologies is to read one or more computer industry publications regularly (Figure 15-14) or visit news, blogs, or technical Web sites (Figure 15-15).

Hundreds of computer industry publications are available. Some magazines, such as *Computerworld, InfoWorld, PC Magazine,* and *PC World*, are similar to newspapers and cover a wide range of topics. Other periodicals are oriented toward a particular subject such as

communications, personal computers, or a specific equipment manufacturer. Many of the more popular publications are available in public or school libraries. Most also have Web sites to visit for news about the latest developments in the computer industry.

Another source for information is Web sites that discuss or share opinions, analysis, reviews, or news about technology. Popular Web sites in this category include Slashdot, The Register, AnandTech, and Tom's Hardware Guide.

FIGURE 15-14 Numerous computer industry publications are available.

FIGURE 15-15 The Register is a popular technology Web site that provides information and viewpoints to its visitors.

Test your knowledge of pages 785 through 791 in Quiz Yourself 15-2.

QUIZ YOURSELF 15-2

Instructions: Find the true statement below. Then, rewrite the remaining false statements so they are true.

1. A transfer statement ensures that if you transfer to a college or university, you will receive credit for most of the courses taken at your current school.
2. Computer science programs focus on how to apply computing skills.
3. Job-search Web sites such as Monster provide job-search services for a fee to job seekers.
4. Students often complete trade school programs in a longer time than college and university programs.
5. Two organizations that are influential in the computer industry are the Association for Computing Machinery and the Association of Information Technology Professionals.

Quiz Yourself Online: To further check your knowledge of trade schools and colleges, computer-related majors, and methods of staying current with IT technology, visit scsite.com/dc2007/ch15/quiz and then click Objectives 3 – 5.

CERTIFICATION

Certification is the process of verifying the technical knowledge of an individual who has demonstrated competence in a particular area. Companies often require certification to ensure quality and workmanship standards and to confirm their workforce remains up to date with respect to computers and technology.

Computer certification demonstrates the mastery of a skill set and knowledge base in a specific IT area. Certifications are available in many areas, including application software, operating systems, programming, hardware, networking, computer forensics, security, the Internet, and database systems. The last section of this chapter discusses specific certifications in each of these areas.

Computing professionals typically obtain a certification by taking and passing an examination. Preparation for a certification exam requires experience or special classes, many of which are offered by trade schools, community colleges, and adult education centers. After certification requirements are met, proficiency in an area is acknowledged with a certificate.

Many vendors, such as Microsoft and Novell, offer technical certification programs for their products. These vendors, called *sponsoring organizations*, develop and administer the examinations to determine whether a person is qualified for certification. Sponsors of IT certifications include computer equipment and software vendors, independent training companies, and professional organizations.

Both IT professionals and users should be familiar with IT certifications. The following sections discuss certification benefits, choosing a certification, preparing for a certification, and certification examinations.

Certification Benefits

IT certification can enhance employees' careers, provide them with a better standing as industry professionals, and increase their salaries. The following paragraphs explain the benefits of certification for employees.

- Career: A certification is one of the first accomplishments an employer notices on a resume. It provides a benchmark, or a means, to measure a person's skills. It can set an individual apart from other potential candidates who may be vying for a similar advancement or position.

- Professional: Certification is a personal achievement that adds credibility among peers and employers. Certification also authorizes the certificate holder to use the product's official logo or symbol on personal items, such as business cards and Web pages. As an additional bonus, some certification training can be used for college credit. Although nothing guarantees job security, certification helps give the IT professional an edge over employees without certification.

- Salary: Numerous salary surveys show that certification helps influence pay increases. As depicted in Figure 15-16, a salary survey conducted by Microsoft reported that 47 percent of the respondents had a salary increase due to certification, with 23 percent of these

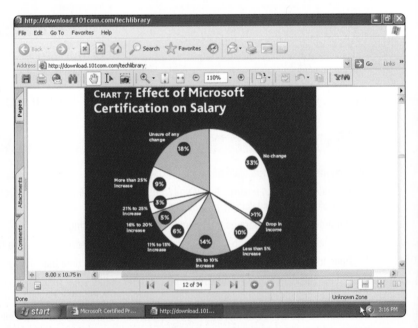

FIGURE 15-16 Microsoft's Tenth Annual Salary Survey of Microsoft Certified Professionals shows that certification can increase salary.

workers reporting significant raises of more than 10 percent. Individuals with more than one area of certification can command even higher salaries. Companies often pay a bonus as an incentive for certification.

Many job listings ask for specific skills represented by certifications, and the number of companies requiring these skills is expected to grow in the future.

Vendor-sponsored certifications offer many special benefits as incentives. As shown in Figure 15-17, vendors often provide special privileges to certified professionals, such as access to technical and product information. This may include access to secure online electronic resources, special technical support, automatic notification of updates, and access to beta products. In addition, vendors may offer advanced training opportunities to certificate holders. Free vendor magazine subscriptions and discounts on product-support publications and tools sometimes are available. Some vendors even have authorized clothing lines embellished with the certification logo.

Professional organizations that offer certifications, such as the *Institute for the Certification of Computing Professionals* (ICCP), define

standards designed to raise the competence level for the computer industry.

Certification also offers many benefits to customers, employers, and industry, as explained in the following paragraphs.

- Customer benefits of certification: Customers gain confidence in a company when IT professionals have earned a certification. Multiple certifications show that the professional can deal with many aspects of a problem, drawing from several areas of expertise. Certification implies motivation to expend extra effort, which often benefits the customer.
- Employer benefits of certification: An industry-sponsored study indicates that certified workers are more productive and knowledgeable than noncertified employees. Certified workers within the company have higher morale and job contentment, which benefits the employer.
- Industry benefits of certification: Certification is a form of industry self-regulation. It sets computer professionals' competence standards and raises the level of expertise and knowledge in the IT industry as a whole. This, in turn, enhances the reputation of the professionals in the industry.

WEB LINK 15-7

Institute for the Certification of Computing Professionals

For more information, visit scsite.com/dc2007/ch15/weblink and then click Institute for the Certification of Computing Professionals.

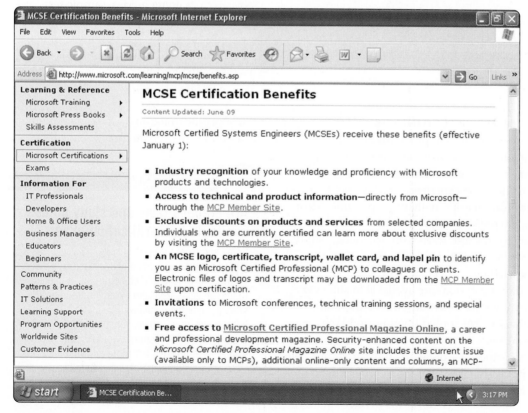

FIGURE 15-17 Certification sponsors often offer a variety of benefits to certificate holders.

Choosing a Certification

Certifications are not the same with respect to training and options. Selecting a certification is a personal process that requires careful thought and research. If you are considering obtaining a certification, reflect on your career goals and interests. Consider your career path during the long term. Then, assess your background knowledge and experience. Finally, research certifications to find those that best match your needs. Figure 15-18 describes factors to consider.

If you are new to the computer field, it is best to start with a general, entry-level certification. You may want to choose a certification that has immediate benefits for your current job. If you are more experienced, consider building on your existing experience with a certification that helps you reach career goals.

A certification represents a major commitment in time and money. Thoughtful research and planning can serve to guide your career to your chosen destination.

FACTORS TO CONSIDER IN SELECTING A CERTIFICATION

- Consider the expenses and the time involved to obtain the certification
- Examine employment projections
- Look at job listings to see what certifications are sought
- Read evaluations of certifications
- Talk to people in the industry
- Think about complementary combinations of certifications to meet your goals

---

FIGURE 15-18 Factors to consider when selecting a certification.

Preparing for Certification

Most certification programs do not require academic coursework. Test results alone determine certification. Very few professionals, however, have the experience and skill set to take a certification exam without preparation. Most people prefer to follow a study program to prepare for the test. Even with experience, study serves as a review and may help to fill gaps in knowledge.

Training options are available to suit every learning style: self-study, online training classes, instructor-led training, and Web resources.

- Self-study: Flexible self-study programs help professionals prepare for certification at their own pace and supplement other training

methods. Self-study requires high motivation and discipline but is the least expensive option. Hundreds of books, videotapes, and computer-based training programs on CD or DVD are available.

- Online training classes: Online training allows students to set their own pace in an interactive environment and combines the technological advantages of computer-based training with the connectivity of the Internet or a company's intranet. Online programs can cost about one-third the price of the traditional instructor-led programs.
- Instructor-led training: Instructor-led training is available in a variety of forms, including seminars, which typically are held for several days during a week; boot camps, which immerse students in intensive coursework for up to two weeks; and academic-style classes, which span a period of several weeks or months. Some sponsors hold their own training sessions and also authorize independent training centers.
- Web resources: The certification sponsor's Web site generally contains descriptions of the available certifications, with FAQs and links to authorized training and testing centers. Many include detailed course objectives, training guides, sample test questions, chat rooms, and discussion groups. Most sell books and other training resources. Private individuals often set up Web sites to offer their own views and tips on the testing process.

Most people prefer to use a combination of these options to prepare for a certification test.

WEB LINK 15-8

Instructor-Led Certification Classes

For more information, visit scsite.com/dc2007/ch15/weblink and then click Instructor-Led Certification Classes.

FAQ 15-7

Are practice tests and study guides available for certification exams?

Some sponsors make practice tests available. If your sponsoring company does not, try visiting a certification Web community such as CramSession. Certification Web communities often provide the public with news, resources, information, study guides, chat rooms, newsgroups, and other resources for IT certification exams — at no cost. For more information, visit scsite.com/dc2007/ch15/faq and then click Certification Web Communities.

Certification Examinations

Authorized testing companies, such as Thomson Prometric (Figure 15-19), Pearson VUE, and Brainbench, provide most certification exams. Many colleges also are authorized testing facilities. Certification sponsors often have a link to the testing company's Web site from their own Web page.

At the sponsor's Web site, you can use the test center locator to find a list of testing centers near you, including addresses and telephone numbers. Most testing centers allow you to pay for the test either online or by telephone with a credit card. Fees for each test range from $50 to more than $1,500, depending on the type of test. Typically, the more technical tests require higher fees. On the day of the test, you usually must present two forms of identification, one of which must be a type of photo identification.

At the testing centers, examinations are taken using computers, which process the results as you take a test. You will know immediately whether you pass the examination. Some tests are in a multiple-choice format; others are skill based.

Some tests use a technique known as *computerized adaptive testing* (*CAT*), where the tests analyze a person's responses while taking the test. The number and order of the test questions are modified to correspond to each individual's progress and demonstrated ability. Occasionally, a certification requires a hands-on lab test. The certification sponsor typically administers these tests. These examinations are much more expensive than the computerized tests. In addition, the number of testing facilities is limited.

If you do not pass an exam, you must pay the fee again to retake the test. In some cases, you can retake the test immediately; however, most people opt to review before trying to take the test again. Some training centers offer a guarantee for their program. They provide discounts, or even free sessions, for individuals who have completed their program, yet do not pass a test. Most sponsors allow candidates a set time, such as a year, in which to complete the test.

FAQ 15-8

Do computer certifications expire?

Most certifications expire after a set time because product-based skills remain current for only 18 months or so. Sponsors specify training or examinations to maintain the certification. In addition, if a vendor issues a product update, certificate holders must retrain almost immediately. For more information, visit scsite.com/dc2007/ch15/faq and then click Computer Certifications.

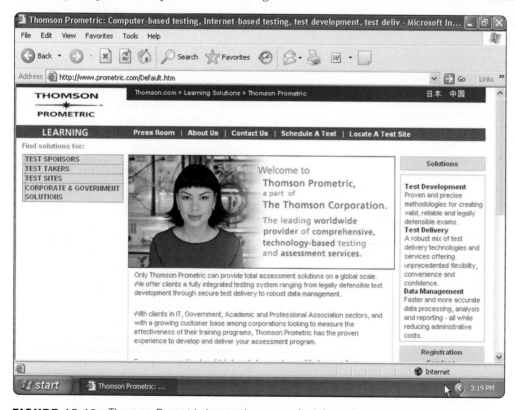

FIGURE 15-19 Thomson Prometric is a testing center for information technology certifications.

A GUIDE TO CERTIFICATION

Today, more than 200 certifications are available. Some certifications have a broad focus, and others require an in-depth knowledge of a single computing aspect. Often, a sponsor establishes a series of related certifications to show levels of expertise within a single area.

Certifications usually are classified based on the computer industry area to which they most closely relate: application software, operating systems, programming, hardware, networking, computer forensics, security, the Internet, and database systems. Some certifications are related to more than one category. For example, a certification in networking also may indicate knowledge of hardware and operating systems.

This section describes the major certifications and certification sponsors in each industry area. Some certifications have components that span multiple categories. In this case, they are placed in the area for which they are known best. Read Ethics & Issues 15-4 for a related discussion.

Application Software Certifications

Although numerous types of application software exist, several applications have achieved national recognition for use as business and graphics tools. Figure 15-20 identifies some popular application software certifications, sometimes called *end-user certifications*, and their sponsors. Most sponsors of application software certifications have a partner training program and encourage computer-training centers to be authorized training representatives.

As with most other certifications, vendor-authorized testing facilities take registrations and administer the certification test. People in the following careers may be interested in application software certification:

- Computer sales representatives
- Computer teachers
- Corporate trainers
- Desktop publishers
- Graphic designers
- Help desk specialists
- Office managers/ workers

WEB LINK 15-9

Microsoft Office Specialist

For more information, visit scsite.com/ dc2007/ch15/weblink and then click Microsoft Office Specialist.

ETHICS & ISSUES 15-4

Should Lifetime Certification Be Granted for Computer Professionals?

While some professions grant lifetime certification once a certification test or tests are passed, the vast majority do not. They require recertification after a certain period or when software or hardware changes significantly. Proponents of lifetime certification claim that many recertifications are simply a way for computer companies and industry associations to increase revenue. Also, once a skill is proved, a person's knowledge should not be discounted. Opponents say that the rapid pace of change in technology requires that those who are certified remain current. In the computer industry, where change occurs at a very rapid rate, are lifetime certifications meaningful? Why or why not? Should individuals be required to take a certification examination every year, 3 years, or 5 years to be able to indicate on their resume that they are certified in a particular area? Why or why not? Should the government regulate certification to ensure that companies are not taking advantage of workers? Why?

APPLICATION SOFTWARE CERTIFICATIONS

Certification	Description	Sponsor
Microsoft Office Specialist (Office Specialist)	Tests a user's basic (specialist) and advanced (expert) skills of Microsoft Office programs	Microsoft
Microsoft Certified Desktop Support Technician (MCDST)	Tests a user's skills solving problems associated with applications that run on Windows XP and the operating system itself	Microsoft
Adobe Certified Expert (ACE)	Tests a user's expertise on Adobe software	Adobe Systems
IBM Certified Professional for Lotus Software	Tests knowledge of Lotus programs	IBM
Macromedia Certified Professional	Tests user's expertise in a variety of Macromedia software including Flash MX and Dreamweaver MX	Macromedia

FIGURE 15-20 Application software certifications are available to anyone who works in the computer industry.

Operating System Certifications

Several options for different knowledge levels are available to those seeking operating system certifications. These certifications focus on particular skills of the user, the operator, the system administrator, and the software engineer. The table in Figure 15-21 lists a few of the certifications available in the operating systems area.

If you are interested in an occupation as an operating system administrator or software engineer, you also may benefit from certifications in networking, hardware, and the Internet. These additional certifications are linked closely to the operating system and serve to broaden expertise in that area. People in the following jobs may be interested in a certification in operating systems:

- Hardware technicians
- Help desk specialists
- Network security specialists
- IT consultants
- System administrators

OPERATING SYSTEMS CERTIFICATIONS

Certification	Description	Sponsor
Microsoft Certified Systems Administrator (MCSA)	Tests technical expertise in one of several areas including managing and troubleshooting Windows operating systems	Microsoft
Certified Linux Professional (CLP)	Tests technical expertise in installing, managing, and troubleshooting the Linux operating system	Novell
Red Hat Certified Engineer (RHCE)	Tests technical expertise of setting up and administering network services and security administration of the Linux operating system	Red Hat
Red Hat Certified Technician (RHCT)	Tests basic knowledge of setting up and managing a Linux operating system	Red Hat
Sun Certified System Administrator	Tests knowledge of administering the Solaris operating system	Sun
IBM Certified Specialist	Tests knowledge of AIX operating system and network security	IBM

FIGURE 15-21 Operating system certifications test knowledge level of a specific operating system.

FAQ 15-9

What is a Microsoft Certified Architect?

A *Microsoft Certified Architect (MCA)* is a top IT expert who has at least 10 years of IT experience with 3 years experience in developing and managing technical projects during the entire system development cycle. A Microsoft Certified Architect often holds certifications in many areas. For more information, visit scsite.com/dc2007/ch15/faq and then click Microsoft Certified Architect.

Programmer/Developer Certifications

Various certifications are available in the programmer/developer area. These certifications usually are supported with training programs that prepare applicants for the certification test.

If you are interested in writing application software, you also may benefit from certifications in networking and Web design. These certifications are tied closely to programming and may broaden employment opportunities.

The table shown in Figure 15-22 identifies a few of the certifications available in the programmer/developer area. People in the following jobs may be interested in a programmer/developer certification:

- Java programmers
- Oracle database managers
- Programming consultants
- SQL programmers
- Web page designers
- XML programmers

PROGRAMMER/DEVELOPER CERTIFICATIONS

Certification	Description	Sponsor
Certified Software Development Professional (CSDP)	Tests knowledge of software development process and tools	IEEE Computer Society
IBM Certified Solution Developer	Tests knowledge of developing XML applications with Web services	IBM
Microsoft Certified Professional Developer (MCPD)	Tests knowledge of developing Web or Windows-based applications using programs in the Visual Studio 2005 suite and the .NET framework	Microsoft
Sun Certified Enterprise Architect	Tests knowledge of creating and maintaining J2EE applications	Sun
Sun Certified Developer	Tests advanced knowledge of Java programming language	Sun
Sun Certified Programmer	Tests basic knowledge of Java programming language	Sun

FIGURE 15-22 Various certifications are available in programming.

Hardware Certifications

Hardware certifications vary in scope from a narrow focus with an emphasis on the repair of a specific device to an integrated hardware solution that addresses a company's current and future computing needs. Obtaining an advanced certification in hardware implies that you have achieved a standard of competence in assessing a company's hardware needs, and you can implement solutions to help the company achieve its computing goals.

People interested in hardware certifications also may benefit from networking and operating system software certifications, which are tied closely to advanced hardware knowledge. The table in Figure 15-23 lists a few available hardware certifications. People in the following careers may be interested in hardware certification:

- Cable installation technicians
- Computer repair technicians
- Corporate trainers
- Help desk specialists
- IT consultants
- System engineers and administrators

Networking Certifications

Network expertise is acquired through years of experience and training because so many variables exist for a total network solution. Obtaining an advanced certification in networking implies that you have achieved a standard of competence, enabling you to address the complex issues that arise when planning, installing, managing, and troubleshooting a network. Networking certification holders earn salary levels from 5 to 30 percent more than those without certification.

The table shown in Figure 15-24 identifies a few of the certifications available in the networking area. People in the following careers may be interested in network certification:

- Hardware service technicians
- Network consultants
- Network managers
- Network engineers
- System administrators

WEB LINK 15-10

A+ Certification

For more information, visit scsite.com/dc2007/ch15/weblink and then click A+ Certification.

WEB LINK 15-11

Certified Novell Administrator

For more information, visit scsite.com/dc2007/ch15/weblink and then click Certified Novell Administrator.

HARDWARE CERTIFICATIONS

Certification	Description	Sponsor
A+	Tests entry-level knowledge of personal computer setup, configuration, maintenance, troubleshooting; basic networking skills; and system software	Computing Technology Industry Association (CompTIA)
IBM eServer Certified Specialist	Tests knowledge of IBM eServer line	IBM
NACSE Network Technician (NNT)	Tests basic knowledge of personal computers, operating systems, networks, and cabling	National Association of Communication System Engineers (NACSE)

FIGURE 15-23 Hardware certifications may test general knowledge of hardware or test knowledge of a specific type of hardware.

NETWORKING CERTIFICATIONS

Certification	Description	Sponsor
Certified Novell Administrator (CNA)	Tests knowledge of Novell's networking products including NetWare, intraNetWare, and GroupWise	Novell
Certified Novell Engineer (CNE)	Tests in-depth knowledge of designing, configuring, implementing, administering, and troubleshooting the Novell network system	Novell
Cisco Certified Network Professional (CCNP)	Tests advanced knowledge of installing, configuring, and operating LANs and WANs	Cisco
Network+	Tests competency in several network areas including transmission media and topologies, protocols, and standards	Computing Technology Industry Association (CompTIA)
Sun Certified Network Administrator	Tests knowledge of administering Sun networks	Sun

FIGURE 15-24 Networking certifications usually test knowledge of a company-specific network.

Computer Forensics Certifications

As discussed in Chapter 11, computer forensics is the discovery, collection, and analysis of evidence found on computers and networks. According to the Investigative Services Bureau, the testimonies of computer forensics certificate holders are considered highly credible during computer crimes cases.

The table shown in Figure 15-25 identifies a few of the certifications available in the computer forensics area. People in the following careers may be interested in computer forensics certification:

- Information security officers and managers
- Law enforcement officials
- Military intelligence officers
- Network administrators
- Network security specialists
- Security administrators

COMPUTER FORENSICS CERTIFICATIONS

Certification	Description	Sponsor
Certified Electronic Evidence Collection Specialist (CEECS)	Tests basic knowledge of forensic ethics, imaging, examination, collection, and reporting	International Association of Computer Investigative Specialists (IACIS)
Certified Forensic Computer Examiner (CFCE)	Tests in-depth knowledge of forensic imaging, examination, collection, and reporting	International Association of Computer Investigative Specialists (IACIS)
Certified Computer Examiner (CCE)	Tests core knowledge of acquisition, marking, handling, and storage of computer evidence using a particular operating system	International Society of Forensic Computer Examiners (ISFCE)

FIGURE 15-25 Computer forensics certifications usually test knowledge of the examining, collecting, and reporting of computer evidence.

Security Certifications

Security certifications measure a candidate's ability to identify and control security risks associated with any event or action that could cause a loss of or damage to computer hardware, software, data, information, or processing capability. While some security certifications focus solely on network and Internet security, others include measures to secure operating systems, application programs, and information systems, as well as the physical facility and its people.

The table shown in Figure 15-26 identifies a few of the certifications available in the security area. People in the following careers may be interested in security certification:

- Information security officers and managers
- Network administrators
- Network security specialists
- Security administrators

SECURITY CERTIFICATIONS

Certification	Description	Sponsor
Certified Information Systems Security Professional (CISSP)	Tests in-depth knowledge of access control methods, information systems development, cryptography, operations security, physical security, and network and Internet security	International Information Systems Security Certification Consortium (ISC)²
Systems Security Certified Practitioner (SSCP)	Tests basic knowledge of access controls, cryptography, data communications, and malicious code	International Information Systems Security Certification Consortium (ISC)²
Security Certified Network Professional (SCNP)	Tests skills with firewalls and defending against network intrusions	The Security Certified Program (SCP)
Security Certified Network Architect (SCNA)	Tests network security skills related to wireless security, e-mail security, digital certificates, digital signatures, and biometrics	The Security Certified Program (SCP)

FIGURE 15-26 Some security certifications focus on network security, while others include security for the entire enterprise.

Internet Certifications

Internet certifications are demanding and require technical expertise in networking hardware and configuration before enrollment in an Internet certification-sponsored training program. These certifications include Web management, Web programming, and Web development certifications.

Internet-related occupations also benefit from certifications in hardware, networking, operating systems, and programming. The table shown in Figure 15-27 lists a few of the certifications available in the Internet area. People in the following careers may be interested in Internet certification:

- Internet and intranet managers
- Internet service provider staff
- Network administrators
- Webmasters
- Web page designers
- Web programmers

Database System Certifications

Supporting a large database management system requires a professional staff. The various tasks the staff performs form a core on which the database management certifications are based. If you are interested in working with a database management system, you also may benefit from certifications in hardware, the Internet, networking, and programming.

The table shown in Figure 15-28 outlines a few of the certifications available in the database area. People in the following careers may be interested in database certification:

- Database administrators
- Database analysts
- Database application developers
- Database designers

WEB LINK 15-12

Certified Web Professional

For more information, visit scsite.com/ dc2007/ch15/weblink and then click Certified Web Professional.

INTERNET CERTIFICATIONS

Certification	Description	Sponsor
Certified Internet Webmaster (CIW)	Tests knowledge of Web development, security, and administration	Prosoft Learning
Cisco Certified Internetwork Expert (CCIE)	Tests expert level knowledge in areas of internetwork communications, security, routing, and switching	Cisco
Certified Web Professional (CWP)	Tests advanced knowledge in areas of Web site design and development, and server administration and security	International Webmasters Association

FIGURE 15-27   Internet certifications are demanding and require technical expertise in networking hardware.

DATABASE CERTIFICATIONS

Certification	Description	Sponsor
IBM Certified Solutions Expert – DB2	Tests advanced skills of administration of the DB2 database management system	IBM
IBM Certified Solutions Expert – Informix	Tests advanced skills of administration of the Informix database management system	IBM
Microsoft Certified IT Professional (MCITP)	Tests skills required to use SQL Server 2005 to design or install, manage, and maintain a database system	Microsoft
Oracle Certified Professional (OCP)	Tests knowledge of developing and deploying large-scale Oracle database management systems	Oracle
Sybase Certified Professional	Tests skills in developing and administering Sybase database management systems	Sybase

FIGURE 15-28   Database certifications usually test knowledge of a specific database management system.

Test your knowledge of pages 792 through 800 in Quiz Yourself 15-3.

QUIZ YOURSELF 15-3

Instructions: Find the true statement below. Then, rewrite the remaining false statements so they are true.

1. Computer forensics certifications usually test knowledge of the examining, collecting, and reporting of computer evidence.

2. If you do not pass a certification exam, you do not have to pay a fee again to retake the test.

3. Industrialization is a process of verifying the technical knowledge of an individual who has demonstrated competence in a particular area.

4. Salary surveys show that certification helps influence pay decreases.

5. The Microsoft Certified Professional Developer certification tests a user's basic (specialist) and advanced (expert) skills of Microsoft Office programs.

Quiz Yourself Online: To further check your knowledge of benefits of certification, preparing for certification, areas of certification, and specific certifications, visit scsite.com/dc2007/ch15/quiz and then click Objectives 6 – 9.

CHAPTER SUMMARY

This chapter discussed the strong demand for computer and IT professionals and presented a variety of available computer-related careers. For additional discussion about 15 of the more popular careers, read the Career Corner features at the end of each chapter in this book. The table in Figure 15-29 lists the page number on which each career is presented.

This chapter also focused on computer education at trade schools, computer-related majors at colleges and universities, job searches, career development planning, professional organizations, and professional growth. Information about certification preparation, examinations, and resources also was presented. Finally, specific certifications were discussed.

CAREER CORNER FEATURES

Chapter Number	Chapter Title	Job Title	Page Number
1	Introduction to Computers	Personal Computer Salesperson	37
2	The Internet and World Wide Web	Web Developer	101
3	Application Software	Help Desk Specialist	167
4	The Components of the System Unit	Computer Engineer	217
5	Input	Data Entry Clerk	267
6	Output	Graphic Designer/Illustrator	327
7	Storage	Computer Technician	381
8	Operating Systems and Utility Programs	Systems Programmer	429
9	Communications and Networks	Network Specialist	497
10	Database Management	Database Administrator	539
11	Computer Security, Ethics, and Privacy	Computer Forensics Specialist	591
12	Information System Development	Systems Analyst	647
13	Program Languages and Program Development	Programmer	697
14	Enterprise Computing	CIO	749
15	Computer Careers and Certification	Computer Science/IT Instructor	801

FIGURE 15-29 Each chapter in this book ends with a Career Corner feature. This table lists the job title and page number for each career corner.

CAREER CORNER

Computer Science/IT Instructor

Computer science/IT instructors are in demand. In both the educational and business sectors, skilled teachers are reaping the many benefits and rewards of being in a highly sought after occupation.

Instructors in K-12 usually teach computer literacy or specific computer applications. Teaching in K-12 requires at least a bachelor's degree with some computer related courses. Instructors in higher education teach basic computer courses in addition to specialized classes such as computer engineering, Internet development, networking, programming, or systems analysis and design. Generally, these instructors have at least a master's degree with 18 graduate hours in the subject area. Teaching software and/or hardware design usually requires a master's degree and/or a Ph.D. in software engineering or electrical engineering.

Corporate trainers teach employees systems development, programming, and other computer-related skills. They also lead continuing education classes and introduce new software. Many companies have their own training departments. Qualifications for the corporate world are less stringent than those for educational institutions. Often, companies hire instructors with trainer certifications, such as the Microsoft Certified Trainer (MCT) and Cisco Certified Trainer.

Salaries range widely. In a traditional educational setting, salaries vary from about $40,000 to $90,000, depending on the area of expertise, years of experience, and location. At the professor level, salaries range from $50,000 to $130,000. In the corporate world, salaries are considerably higher, ranging up to $125,000 and beyond. For more information, visit scsite.com/dc2007/ch15/careers and then click Computer Science/IT Instructor.

High-Tech Talk

MAGNETIC MOTION CAPTURE: MAKING THE GAME

That lifelike power forward slam dunking in your favorite computer game most likely got his moves thanks to motion capture. *Motion capture technology* is where actors are tracked by computers to provide the movements for computer-generated characters. Motion capture is achieved by fitting an actor with a special suit containing several sensors. A computer uses the sensors to record every nuance of the actor's performance and apply it to a character in a computer. As computer gamers demand increasingly realistic action and animation in games, motion capture technology is allowing programmers to develop computer games populated by animated characters with natural, highly realistic human movements.

Several technologies are available for motion capture, including optical, inertial, and AC and DC magnetic. DC magnetic motion capture generally provides more accurate capture than the other technologies, because the sensors involved do not need line-of-sight transmission and are not affected greatly if other metals, such as steel or aluminum, are located near the sensors.

How does motion capture work? In a DC *magnetic motion capture system*, a transmitter is located at the center of a measured space that encloses an electromagnetic field. To start the process of motion capture, a performer must secure magnetic sensors to various points on his or her body. A simple way to attach the sensors is to require performers wear a motion capture body suit with sensor holders where sensors are mounted (Figure 15-30). Performers also can wear peripherals, such as data gloves, which are able to capture subtle movements like hand gestures and finger movements.

The sensors on the suit and peripherals use the electromagnetic field to measure their spatial relationship to the transmitter in the center of the measured space. In developing a basketball computer game, for example, you could attach up to 20 sensors to key points on several athlete-performers. As the performers complete the motion of a jump shot, the motion capture system tracks the position and orientation of each magnetic sensor more than 100 times per second to identify the location of the performers' bodies in space. This rapid tracking records every bodily motion and provides highly accurate capture of such actions as a batter's home run swing, a gymnast's handspring, or a golfer's putt.

Input from these sensors is transmitted to a recording device via cables (a *tethered system*) or via wireless connections (an *untethered system*). In an untethered or wireless system, input from the sensors travels over sensor cables within the suit to a battery-powered electronic unit mounted in a small, lightweight backpack worn by the performer. The body suit and peripherals have channeled tubes and closures that secure and guide the sensor cables into the electronic unit. A wireless system thus allows performers to complete complex motions without tangling cables.

The motion data captured by the sensors then is sent over a wireless connection to a base station for final processing. This data then can be mapped instantly to the corresponding features of a computer-generated animated character, which gives it the exact movements of the live performers. Because many motion capture systems can track up to 90 sensors, a developer can create four or five animated characters and then track and map movements to multiple characters as several performers interact with each other. This makes magnetic motion capture technology ideal for creating highly realistic multiplayer sports games.

The entertainment industry rapidly has embraced this dynamic technology. Magnetic motion capture was used to create complex, multiple-character interactions for movies such as *Polar Express* and *I, ROBOT*, to give the Pillsbury Doughboy lifelike movement, and to add life to characters in Nike commercials. Game programmers such as Sony, SEGA, and Microsoft are using magnetic motion capture to give animated characters hundreds of body motions.

That realistic motion makes characters more believable and keeps players interested in the game. Motion capture also gives games star quality. By using motion capture to capture the movements and expressions of a leading athlete, a game programmer captures both the athletic and personal qualities of these stars and then gives the game player a chance to coach these stars. Motion capture provides an excitement and realism that engages players and viewers — and that makes motion capture captivating to programmers. For more information visit scsite.com/dc2007/ch15/tech and then click Motion Capture.

FIGURE 15-30　A motion capture body suit.

Companies on the Cutting Edge

MONSTER
ONLINE CAREER OPPORTUNITIES

Helping you achieve your goals and realize your life's ambitions are part of *Monster*'s objectives. When Chief Monster Jeff Taylor founded the company in 1994, his ad agency had been operating on the premise of developing "big ideas." One of his customers requested a "monster idea," so Taylor envisioned the possibility of connecting potential employees and employers online to provide real-world career opportunities.

The world's largest and most popular job-search and career-management Web site has more than 46 million online resumes, 800,000 job postings, and 130,000 employers in more than 20 countries.

Employers state that their foremost challenge is recruiting and retaining qualified employees, and Monster believes its services will help with these employment needs. For more information, visit scsite.com/dc2007/ch15/companies and then click Monster.

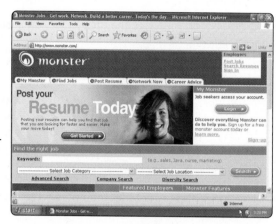

ZDNET
TECHNOLOGY AND BUSINESS WEB SITE

Looking for a good, basic notebook computer? Want to find the best antivirus tools to fight hackers? Searching for a job in the information technology field? One Web site can provide help: *ZDNet* (zdnet.com).

Winner of the Computer Press Association's Best Overall Site award for two consecutive years, ZDNet combines a variety of resources that help professionals in the computer and business fields maximize their technology investments. Content includes news updates, blogs, technical reports, downloads, product reviews, and current hardware and software pricing.

The Web site helps readers stay informed of developments in their careers by providing a site directory with links to emerging technology trends, computer-based training, and educational reports on industry issues. Its Water Cooler page offers recreational and entertainment news, including car technology and Tech Tales from the IT trenches. For more information, visit scsite.com/dc2007/ch15/companies and then click ZDNet.

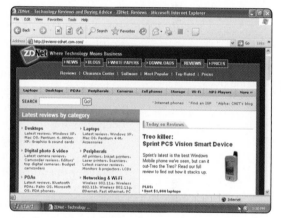

Technology Trailblazers

STEVE BALLMER
MICROSOFT CEO

As Microsoft's CEO since 2000, *Steve Ballmer* is leading the most comprehensive reinvention in the company's history by helping develop the .NET platform for desktop personal computers, servers, and the Internet.

Ballmer is known for his energy, determination, charm, sense of humor, and dedication to his company and its customers. In 1980, when Microsoft was five years old, he served as Bill Gates's first business manager; since that time, the Harvard University graduate has brought this enthusiasm and leadership to the world's leading software company.

In a speech delivered to Stanford University students in 2005, Ballmer said he believes the computer industry barely has begun to tap the potential of software and computing and that the industry's potential is "unbelievable." For more information, visit scsite.com/dc2007/ch15/people and then click Steve Ballmer.

STEVE WOZNIAK
APPLE COMPUTER COFOUNDER

Steve Wozniak's visions have helped turn Apple Computer into an industry leader. He designed the original Apple computer in 1976 with Apple's current CEO, Steve Jobs; ten years later, he cofounded Pixar, the award winning animation studio. He left Apple in 1985 to spend time with his family, work on community projects, and teach, but he still serves as an advisor to the corporation.

Wozniak was inducted into the Consumer Electronics Hall of Fame in 2004 and the National Inventors Hall of Fame in 2000. In 2005, he became an advisor to the board of VeriLAN, a Portland-based wireless company planning to offer inexpensive Internet access in cities throughout the United States. For more information, visit scsite.com/dc2007/ch15/people and then click Steve Wozniak.

Chapter Review

The Chapter Review section summarizes the concepts presented in this chapter. To listen to the audio version of this Chapter Review, visit scsite.com/dc2007/ch15/review. To obtain help from other students regarding any subject in this chapter, visit scsite.com/dc2007/ch15/forum and post your thoughts or questions.

(1) What Career Opportunities Are Available in the Computer Industry? Career opportunities in the computer industry fall into several areas. In most medium and large businesses and government offices, staff in an **IT department** is responsible for keeping all computer operations and networks running smoothly. Workers in the **computer equipment field** manufacture and distribute computers and computer-related hardware. Employees in the **computer software field** develop, manufacture, and support a wide range of software. People in the **computer service and repair field** provide preventive maintenance, component installation, and repair services to customers. **Computer salespeople** determine a buyer's needs and match them to the correct hardware and software. Computer educators and corporate trainers teach students and employees how to use software, design and develop systems, program, and perform other computer-related activities. An **IT consultant** is a professional who draws upon his or her expertise in a specialized area of computers and provides computer services to clients.

(2) What Are the Functions of Jobs in an IT Department? Jobs in an IT department fall into five main areas. Management directs the planning, research, development, evaluation, and integration of technology. System development and programming analyzes, designs, develops, and implements new information technology and maintains and improves existing systems. Technical services evaluates and integrates new technologies, administers the organization's data resources, and supports the centralized computer operating system and servers. Operations operates the centralized computer equipment and administers the network including both data and voice communications. Training teaches employees how to use components of the information system or answers specific questions.

> *connect*
> Visit scsite.com/dc2007/ch15/quiz or click the Quiz Yourself button. Click Objectives 1 – 2.

(3) How Are Trade Schools and Colleges Different? A **trade school**, also called a technical school, vocational school, or career college, offers programs primarily in the areas of programming, Web design and development, graphics design, hardware maintenance, networking, personal computer support, and security. Students learn specific skills instead of taking a broad range of science and humanities courses, often resulting in time savings for students.

(4) How Are the Various College Computer-Related Courses of Study Different? Three broad disciplines in higher education produce the majority of entry-level employees in the computer industry. **Computer information systems (CIS)**, or information technology (IT), programs teach technical knowledge and skills and focus on how to apply these skills. **Computer science (CS)**, also called **software engineering**, programs stress the theoretical side of programming and operating systems. **Computer engineering (CE)** programs teach students how to design and develop the electronic components found in computers and peripheral devices.

(5) How Can People Stay Current with Changing Technology? Four primary ways to stay current with computer technology are professional organizations, professional growth and continuing education activities, computer publications and Web sites, and certification. Professional organizations are formed by computer professionals with common interests and a desire to extend their proficiency. The **Association for Computing Machinery (ACM)** is a scientific and educational organization dedicated to advancing knowledge and proficiency of information technology. The **Association of Information Technology Professionals (AITP)** is a professional association of programmers, systems analysts, and managers. Professional growth and continuing education include events such as workshops, seminars, conferences, conventions, and trade shows. The *International Consumer Electronics Show (CES)* is one of the larger technology trade shows, bringing together

Chapter Review

thousands of vendors and more than 130,000 attendees. Computer industry publications, such as *Computerworld*, *InfoWorld*, *PC Magazine*, and *PC World* also help to keep people informed about the latest developments in the computer industry. Web sites are another source for information or to share opinions, analysis, or news about technology. **Certification** is a process of verifying the technical knowledge of an individual who has demonstrated competence in a particular area.

Visit scsite.com/dc2007/ch15/quiz or click the Quiz Yourself button. Click Objectives 3 – 5.

(6) What Are the Benefits of Certification for Employers, Employees, and Vendors?
For employers, certification ensures quality workmanship standards and can help keep their workforce up to date with respect to computers and technology. For employees, certification can enhance careers, provide better standing as industry professionals, and increase salaries. For vendors, certification is a form of industry self-regulation that sets computer professionals' competence standards and raises the level of expertise and knowledge.

(7) How Can People Prepare for Certification? Certification training options are available to suit every learning style. Self-study programs help professionals prepare for certification at their own pace and supplement other training methods. Online training classes, which are available on the Internet and on many company intranets, allow students to set their own pace in an interactive environment. Instructor-led training classes are available in a variety of forms, including seminars, boot camps, and academic-style classes. Web resources include the certification sponsor's Web site and individual Web sites. The certification sponsor's Web site can contain descriptions of certifications with FAQs and links to training and testing centers. Training guides, sample test questions, chat rooms, and discussion groups often are provided. Individuals also set up Web sites to offer their own views and tips.

(8) What Are the General Areas of IT Certification? Certifications usually are classified based on the computer industry area to which they most closely relate: application software, operating systems, programmer/developer, hardware, networking, computer forensics, security, the Internet, and database systems.

(9) What Are Some Specific IT Certifications in Each Certification Area? Application software certifications, sometimes called *end-user certifications*, include *Microsoft Office Specialist (Office Specialist)*, *Microsoft Certified Desktop Support Technician (MCDST)*, *Adobe Certified Expert (ACE)*, *IBM Certified Professional for Lotus Software*, and *Macromedia Certified Professional*. Operating system certifications include *Microsoft Certified System Administrator (MCSA)*, *Certified Linux Professional (CLP)*, *Red Hat Certified Engineer (RHCE)*, *Red Hat Certified Technician (RHCT)*, *Sun Certified System Administrator*, and *IBM Certified Specialist*. Programmer/developer certifications include *Certified Software Development Professional (CSDP)*, *IBM Certified Solution Developer*, *Microsoft Certified Professional Developer (MCPD)*, *Sun Certified Enterprise Architect*, *Sun Certified Developer*, and *Sun Certified Programmer*. Hardware certifications include *A+*, *IBM eServer Certified Specialist*, and *NACSE Network Technician (NNT)*. Networking certifications include *Certified Novell Administrator (CNA)*, *Certified Novell Engineer (CNE)*, *Cisco Certified Network Professional (CCNP)*, *Network+*, and *Sun Certified Network Administrator*. Computer forensics certifications include *Certified Electronic Evidence Collection Specialist (CEECS)*, *Certified Forensic Computer Examiner (CFCE)*, and *Certified Computer Examiner (CCE)*. Security certifications include *Certified Information Systems Security Professional (CISSP)*, *Systems Security Certified Professional (SSCP)*, *Security Certified Network Professional (SCNP)*, and *Security Certified Network Architect (SCNA)*. Internet certifications include *Certified Internet Webmaster (CIW)*, *Cisco Certified Internetwork Expert (CCIE)*, and *Certified Web Professional (CWP)*. Database certifications include *IBM Certified Solutions Expert – DB2*, *IBM Certified Solutions Expert – Informix*, *Microsoft Certified IT Professional (MCITP)*, *Oracle Certified Professional (OCP)*, and *Sybase Certified Professional*.

Visit scsite.com/dc2007/ch15/quiz or click the Quiz Yourself button. Click Objectives 6 – 9.

Quizzes and Learning Games

Computer Genius
Crossword Puzzle
DC Track and Field
Practice Test
Quiz Yourself
Wheel of Terms
You're Hired!

Exercises

Case Studies
Chapter Review
Checkpoint
Key Terms
Learn How To
Learn It Online
Web Research

Beyond the Book

Career Corner
Companies
FAQs
High-Tech Talk
Looking Ahead
Making Use of the Web
Trailblazers
Web Links

Features

Chapter Forum
Install Computer
Lab Exercises
Maintain Computer
Tech News
Timeline 2007

Key Terms

You should know the Primary Terms and be familiar with the Secondary Terms. Use the list below to help focus your study. To further enhance your understanding of the Key Terms in this chapter, visit scsite.com/dc2007/ch15/terms. See an example of and a definition for each term, and access current and additional information about the term from the Web.

Primary Terms

(shown in bold-black characters in the chapter)

application programmer/ developer (780)
Association for Computing Machinery (ACM) (789)
Association of Information Technology Professionals (AITP) (789)
certification (792)
chief information officer (CIO) (780)
chief security officer (CSO) (780)
computer engineering (CE) (787)
computer equipment field (782)
computer forensics specialist (781)
computer information systems (CIS) (786)
computer operator (781)
computer salespeople (783)
computer science (CS) (786)
computer scientist (780)
computer service and repair field (783)
computer software field (782)
computer technician (781)
corporate trainer (781)
data communications analyst (781)

database administrator (781)
database analyst (780)
desktop publisher (781)
e-commerce administrator (780)
graphic designer/illustrator (781)
Help desk specialist (781)
IT consultant (784)
IT department (778)
network administrator (780)
network security specialist (781)
project leader/manager (780)
quality assurance specialist (781)
security administrator (781)
software engineer (780)
software engineering (786)
systems analyst (780)
systems programmer (780)
technical lead (780)
technical writer (780)
trade school (785)
vice president of IT (780)
Web administrator (781)
Web graphic designer (781)
Web page author (780)
Webmaster (781)

Secondary Terms

(shown in italic characters in the chapter)

A+ (798)
Adobe Certified Expert (ACE) (796)
articulation agreement (785)
Certified Computer Examiner (CCE) (799)
Certified Electronic Evidence Collection Specialist (CEECS) (799)
Certified Forensic Computer Examiner (CFCE) (799)
Certified Information Systems Security Professional (CISSP) (799)
Certified Internet Webmaster (CIW) (800)
Certified Linux Professional (CLP) (797)
Certified Novell Administrator (CNA) (798)
Certified Novell Engineer (CNE) (798)
Certified Software Development Professional (CSDP) (797)
Certified Web Professional (CWP) (800)
Cisco Certified Internetwork Expert (CCIE) (800)
Cisco Certified Network Professional (CCNP) (798)
computerized adaptive testing (CAT) (795)
computer science/IT instructors (801)
Computerworld (791)
Data Processing Management Association (DPMA) (789)
end-user certifications (796)
IBM Certified Professional for Lotus Software (796)
IBM Certified Solution Developer (797)
IBM Certified Solutions Expert – DB2 (800)
IBM Certified Solutions Expert – Informix (800)
IBM Certified Specialist (797)
IBM eServer Certified Specialist (798)
InfoWorld (791)
Institute for the Certification of Computing Professionals (ICCP) (793)

International Consumer Electronics Show (CES) (790)
Macromedia Certified Professional (796)
management information systems (MIS) (786)
management information technology (786)
Microsoft Certified Desktop Support Technician (MCDST) (796)
Microsoft Certified IT Professional (MCITP) (800)
Microsoft Certified Professional Developer (MCPD) (797)
Microsoft Office Specialist (Office Specialist) (796)
Microsoft Certified Systems Administrator (MCSA) (797)
NACSE Network Technician (NNT) (798)
Network+ (798)
Oracle Certified Professional (OCP) (800)
PC Magazine (791)
PC World (791)
Red Hat Certified Engineer (RHCE) (797)
Red Hat Certified Technician (RHCT) (797)
Security Certified Network Architect (SCNA) (799)
Security Certified Network Professional (SCNP) (799)
Special Interest Groups (SIGs) (789)
sponsoring organizations (792)
Sun Certified Developer (797)
Sun Certified Enterprise Architect (797)
Sun Certified Network Administrator (798)
Sun Certified Programmer (797)
Sun Certified System Administrator (797)
Sybase Certified Professional (800)
Systems Security Certified Practitioner (SSCP) (799)
user group (790)

Checkpoint

Use the Checkpoint exercises to check your knowledge level of the chapter. The Beyond the Book exercises will help broaden your understanding of the concepts presented in this chapter. To complete the Checkpoint exercises interactively, visit scsite.com/dc2007/ch15/check.

Label the Figure

Identify these computer disciplines.

a. Computer Information Systems
b. Computer Engineering
c. Computer Science

1. ___   2. ___   3. ___

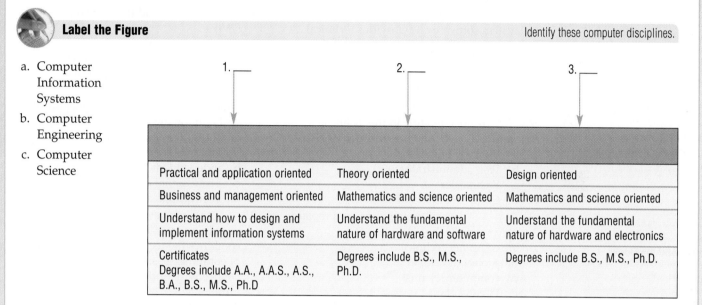

Practical and application oriented	Theory oriented	Design oriented
Business and management oriented	Mathematics and science oriented	Mathematics and science oriented
Understand how to design and implement information systems	Understand the fundamental nature of hardware and software	Understand the fundamental nature of hardware and electronics
Certificates Degrees include A.A., A.A.S., A.S., B.A., B.S., M.S., Ph.D	Degrees include B.S., M.S., Ph.D.	Degrees include B.S., M.S., Ph.D.

True/False

Mark T for True and F for False. (See page numbers in parentheses.)

_____ 1. As the use of computers and the demand for computer professionals continues to decline, the number of students majoring in computer-related fields is much more than what the industry needs. (776)

_____ 2. An IT department is responsible for keeping all the computer operations and networks running smoothly. (778)

_____ 3. Computer salesperson in a retail store is a position reserved for highly trained and experienced computer professionals. (784)

_____ 4. An IT consultant is a professional who draws upon his or her expertise in a specialized area of computers. (784)

_____ 5. After two years of study in a CIS curriculum, students may receive a master's degree or certificate. (786)

_____ 6. In general, a CS curriculum focuses on theory of programming and operating systems and typically emphasizes system programming instead of application programming. (786)

_____ 7. The Association for Computing Machinery (ACM) is a scientific and educational organization dedicated to advancing knowledge and proficiency of information technology. (789)

_____ 8. Staying aware of new products and services in the computer industry is a relatively easy task because technology changes so slowly. (790)

_____ 9. Most certification programs do not require academic coursework. (794)

_____ 10. If you are interested in writing application software, you also may benefit from certifications in networking and Web design. (797)

Checkpoint

Multiple Choice   Select the best answer. (See page numbers in parentheses.)

1. A _____ installs and maintains operating system software and provides technical support to the programming staff. (780)
   a. software engineer
   b. systems programmer
   c. systems analyst
   d. Web administrator

2. _____ is not a job title in the technical services area of an IT department. (781)
   a. Desktop publisher
   b. Web administrator
   c. Webmaster
   d. Computer operator

3. A(n) _____ installs, maintains, and repairs hardware. (781)
   a. computer technician
   b. project developer
   c. computer scientist
   d. IT consultant

4. Many companies hire a(n) _____ to fill in for an employee on an extended leave of absence. (784)
   a. computer technician
   b. IT consultant
   c. computer scientist
   d. project developer

5. A(n) _____ ensures that if a student transfers to a college or university, he or she will receive credit for most of the courses taken at the trade school level. (785)
   a. technical service
   b. articulation agreement
   c. tethered system
   d. user group

6. _____ is a business and management oriented computer discipline. (786)
   a. Computer information systems (CIS)
   b. Computer science (CS)
   c. Computer engineering (CE)
   d. All of the above

7. A _____ curriculum teaches students how to design and develop the electronic components found in computers and peripheral devices. (787)
   a. computer science (CS)
   b. computer engineering (CE)
   c. computer information systems (CIS)
   d. management information systems (MIS)

8. Both the ACM and the AITP offer _____. (789)
   a. chapters throughout the United States
   b. workshops, seminars, and conventions
   c. Special Interest Groups (SIGs)
   d. all of the above

9. Sponsors of IT certifications include all of the following except _____. (792)
   a. computer equipment and software vendors
   b. independent training companies
   c. professional organizations
   d. user groups and trade schools

10. _____ allow(s) students to set their own pace in an interactive environment and combines the technological advantages of computer-based training with the connectivity of the Internet or a company's intranet. (794)
    a. Self-study   b. Online training classes
    c. Web study   d. Instructor-led training

11. _____ is/are available in a variety of forms, including seminars, boot camps, and academic-style classes. (794)
    a. Instructor-led training
    b. Online training classes
    c. Self-study
    d. Web resources

12. Certifications usually are classified based on the _____. (796)
    a. location and availability of the certification program
    b. computer industry area to which they most closely relate
    c. amount of time and money required to obtain certification
    d. difficulty of the requirements

13. _____ certifications include Microsoft Office Specialist (Office Specialist), Adobe Certified Expert (ACE), and IBM Certified Professional for Lotus Software. (796)
    a. Programmer/developer
    b. Application software
    c. Internet
    d. Operating system

14. Database certification may be of interest to _____. (800)
    a. database administrators
    b. database analysts
    c. database designers
    d. all of the above

Checkpoint

Matching

Match the terms with their definitions. (See page numbers in parentheses.)

_____ 1. chief security officer (CSO) (780)

_____ 2. project manager (780)

_____ 3. chief information officer (CIO) (780)

_____ 4. systems analyst (780)

_____ 5. technical lead (780)

_____ 6. database administrator (781)

_____ 7. network security specialist (781)

_____ 8. quality assurance specialist (781)

_____ 9. data communications analyst (781)

_____ 10. corporate trainer (781)

a. supervises the execution of Internet or e-commerce systems

b. configures routers and firewalls and specifies Web protocols

c. guides design, development, and maintenance tasks

d. directs information service and communications functions

e. manages database security and monitors database performance

f. reviews programs and documentation to ensure they meet the organizations's standards

g. combines text and graphics to produce documents such as brochures and books

h. oversees projects, allocates resources, selects teams, and appraises performance

i. evaluates, installs, and monitors communications equipment and software

j. responsible for physical security of a company's property and people

k. teaches employees how to use software, design and develop systems, program, and perform other computer-related activities

l. analyzes user requirements and designs and develops new information systems

Short Answer

Write a brief answer to each of the following questions.

1. What is an advantage of attending a trade school? _____ What factors should you consider when selecting a trade school? _____

2. What do student chapters of professional organizations offer students? _____ What is a user group? _____

3. What is the Institute for Certification of Computing Professionals? _____ What should be considered when choosing a certification? _____

4. How are tests taken at certification testing centers? _____ What is CAT? _____

5. What is a benefit of computer forensics certification? _____ Who might be interested in computer forensics certification? _____

Beyond the Book

Read the following book elements, learn more about each using the Web, and then write a brief report.

1. Ethics & Issues — Outsourcing Computer Jobs — A Threat to American Workers? (777), Should Work Visas Be Issued to Foreign IT Workers? (782), Should Colleges Teach Students How to Create Computer Viruses? (787), or Should Lifetime Certification Be Granted for Computer Professionals? (796)

2. Career Corner — Computer Science/IT Instructor (801)

3. Companies on the Cutting Edge — Monster or ZDNet (803)

4. FAQs (779, 785, 786, 787, 789, 790, 794, 795, 797)

5. High-Tech Talk — Magnetic Motion Capture: Making the Game (802)

6. Looking Ahead — Tomorrow's Jobs in Information Technology (779) or Women Connect Professionally Online (789)

7. Making Use of the Web — Arts and Literature (131)

8. Picture Yourself Planning for a Computer Career (774)

9. Technology Trailblazers — Steve Ballmer or Steve Wozniak (803)

10. Web Links (779, 783, 784, 785, 786, 790, 793, 794, 796, 798, 800)

Learn It Online

Use the Learn It Online exercises to reinforce your understanding of the chapter concepts. To access the Learn It Online exercises, visit scsite.com/dc2007/ch15/learn.

① At the Movies — Find a Job Online

To view the Find a Job Online movie, click the number 1 button. Locate your video and click the corresponding High-Speed or Dial-Up link, depending on your Internet connection. Watch the movie and then complete the exercise by answering the questions that follow. It is easy to get discouraged while searching for employment. You cannot seem to find the right company, and the right company cannot find you. Today more companies are posting their job listings on the Internet, but less than half of all job seekers use the Internet to find work. How could you get the most out of your job hunting experience by using the Internet? What do you feel is the most effective way to let potential employers know about you?

② At the Movies — Design Your Own Video Game

To view the Design Your Own Video Game movie, click the number 2 button. Locate your video and click the corresponding High-Speed or Dial-Up link, depending on your Internet connection. Watch the movie and then complete the exercise by answering the question that follows. Maneesh Sethi studied books from the library and friends in order to learn C++, the programming language in which most professional video games are written. What other programming languages does Maneesh Sethi encourage anyone who plans on being a professional programmer to learn?

③ Interviewing for an IT Career

Being prepared for an interview is vital in making a good impression and one of the more important steps to getting a job. To begin your preparation, compose a list of common questions that you may be asked. Most employers will ask about experience, qualifications, and future plans. Next, prepare a list of questions that you can ask your potential employer. Some common questions are about benefits, types of training programs, and available career paths. Then practice, practice, practice. One way to practice in a safe environment is through a virtual interview. Click the number 3 button and complete the virtual interview. Was the interview helpful? What questions were the most difficult?

④ Microsoft Office Specialist Certification

One of the more popular software certifications is the Microsoft Office Specialist (Office Specialist) certification. The certification recognizes individuals who have achieved a certain level of mastery with Microsoft Office products and provides a framework for measuring end-user proficiency with Microsoft Office programs. Attaining Microsoft Office Specialist certification proves you have met an industry-recognized standard for measuring an individual's mastery of Office programs, demonstrates proficiency in a given Office program to employers, and provides a competitive edge in the job marketplace. Click the number 4 button for a list of frequently asked questions (FAQs) about the Office Specialist certification. Read the questions. What types of certifications are available? What kind of preparation is necessary for certification? Does your educational institution offer Office Specialist courses?

⑤ Practice Test

Click the number 5 button. Answer each question. When completed, enter your name and click the Grade Test button to submit the quiz for grading. Make a note of any missed questions. If required, submit your results to your instructor.

Learn It Online

⑥ Who Wants To Be a Computer Genius²?

Click the number 6 button to find out if you are a computer genius. Directions about how to play the game will be displayed. When you are ready to play, click the Play button. Submit your score to your instructor.

⑦ Wheel of Terms

Click the number 7 button to reinforce important terms you learned in this chapter by playing the Shelly Cashman Series version of this popular game. Directions about how to play the game will be displayed. When you are ready to play, click the Play button. Submit your score to your instructor.

⑧ DC Track and Field

Click the number 8 button to use what you have learned in this chapter to compete against other students in three track and field events. Directions about how to play the game will be displayed. When you are ready to play, click the start first event button. If required, submit your score to your instructor.

⑨ You're Hired!

Click the number 9 button to use what you have learned in this chapter to embark on the path to a career in computers. Directions about how to play the game will be displayed. When you are ready to play, click the begin game button. If required, submit your score to your instructor.

⑩ Crossword Puzzle Challenge

Click the number 10 button. Complete the puzzle to reinforce skills you learned in this chapter. Directions about how to play the game will be displayed. When you are ready to play, click the Submit button. Submit the completed puzzle to your instructor.

⑪ Lab Exercises

Click the number 11 button. When the Lab Exercises menu appears, click the exercise assigned by your instructor. A new browser window will open. Follow the on-screen instructions to complete the exercise. When finished, click the Exit button. If required, submit your results to your instructor.

⑫ In the News

As the IT professionals shortage continues, several certification sponsors have started offering certification training and testing to high school students. The students choose computers as a major and take courses in certification programs such as A+ and MCSE. Many states have magnet schools where most of the curriculum is focused on technology. Click the number 12 button and read a news article about a recent high school certification story. Could this trend cause a potential problem with students not attending college?

⑬ Chapter Discussion Forum

Select an objective from this chapter on page 775 about which you would like more information. Click the number 13 button and post a short message listing a meaningful message title accompanied by one or more questions concerning the selected objective. In two days, return to the threaded discussion by clicking the number 13 button. Submit to your instructor your original message and at least one response to your message.

⑭ Flickr.com

Click the number 14 button to learn how to use the Internet to search for photographs online. Follow the instructions to sign up for a free flickr.com account and then use flickr.com to search for photographs of a chosen topic. Click the photo search link at the bottom of the Home page. Enter a topic in the Search with one or more tags box (a current or historical event, a specific location, etc.). View some of the photographs. Select two of them, print them, and then submit them to your instructor.

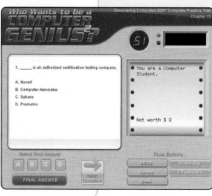

Learn How To

Use the Learn How To activities to learn fundamental skills when using a computer and accompanying technology. Complete the exercises and submit them to your instructor.
To see a video of a Learn How To activity, visit scsite.com/dc2007/ch15/howto.

LEARN HOW TO 1: Create a Video for Your Electronic Resume

Resumes are used to inform potential employers about your experience, education, qualifications, and other important information. When using job search services such as Monster.com (see Figure 15-10 on page 788), you often will submit your resume electronically.

An electronic resume can contain multimedia elements. For example, an electronic resume can contain a video of you speaking to your potential employer, explaining your interest in the job and why you think you are the best qualified candidate.

To create a video for your resume complete the following steps:

Obtain the Video Camera   The first step is to obtain a video camera with which you can record your presentation. You can purchase a PC video camera or a more sophisticated camera.

Record the Video   When you record the video, you must be aware of several important elements:
1. Prepare your script: Before you start recording, write and memorize the words you will say in the video. The video should be no longer than one minute, so write your script accordingly. Remember — you are trying to impress your potential employer.
2. Set the stage: The lighting and picture in the video are critical to making a professional-appearing video. You should use adequate light so the video is clear. Generally, you should arrange the camera for a head-and-shoulders shot.
3. Practice: You must practice your presentation in front of the camera. You can record and play back your practice recordings until you feel confident about your presentation.
4. Dress for the part: When on camera, the impression you make will be influenced by your attire and your personal grooming. You should dress as if you were doing a live interview.
5. Record the video: Your video should be no longer than one minute, but you might want to divide it into segments. For example, you could separate your statement about why you want to work for a company from your statement about your educational background. So, when you create the actual video, you may record several clips of shorter duration, and then join them together when you edit the video. To capture the video you can use the software provided with your camera, or you can use Windows Movie Maker.

To use Windows Movie Maker, complete the following steps:
1. Click the Start button on the Windows taskbar, point to All Programs on the Start menu, point to Accessories on the All Programs submenu, and then click Windows Movie Maker on the Accessories submenu.
2. Click File on the menu bar and then on the File menu click Capture Video. *The first Video Capture Wizard dialog box is displayed (Figure 15-31). This wizard identifies the video capture devices connected to your computer. You can set the microphone's audio level for recording the video.*
3. Click the Next button, give the video a name, and then identify where on your computer the video file should be stored.
4. Click the Next button and then select the quality level for the video. Generally, you will select Best quality for playback on my computer. Click the Next button. *The next wizard dialog box is displayed (Figure 15-32).*
5. Ensure the image in the window is the way you want it to appear on the video, and then click the Start Capture button. Your video is being recorded. When you are ready, begin your presentation.
6. When you have completed your presentation, click the Stop Capture button. The recording process will end. Then, click the Finish button. The video file will be stored in the location you selected, and the video will be placed in the Collection area in Windows Movie Maker.

Learn How To

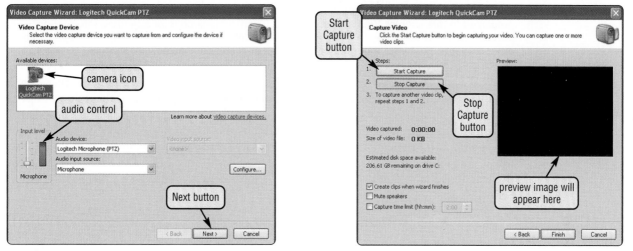

FIGURE 15-31

FIGURE 15-32

Edit the Video After recording the video, you normally should edit it and save it in a format that can be placed in your resume. To use Windows Movie Maker for this process, complete the following steps:
1. To create your movie, you first must import the video clips that will comprise the movie. If you recorded the video as specified above, the video will be in your collection window. If you have additional clips you would like to include, click File on the menu bar, click Import into Collections on the File menu, locate the video clip you want to import using the Import File dialog box, select the video clip, and then click the Import button. You should continue this process until all the video clips you will use in your resume video have been imported into the Collections window.
2. At the bottom of the screen, ensure the Storyboard area is displayed. If the Show Timeline button is displayed, then the Storyboard area is on the screen. If not, click the Show Storyboard button.
3. Drag the first clip in sequence to the leftmost window in the Storyboard. Continue this process until all clips have been placed in the Storyboard. To play the video, click the Play Storyboard button next to the Show Timeline button.
4. To learn how to further edit your resume video, review each subject in the Movie Tasks pane. If the Movie Tasks pane does not appear on the left of the window, click the Tasks button on the toolbar.
5. After you have completed your video, save the project by clicking the Save button on the toolbar.
6. To save your video for inclusion in your resume, click File on the menu bar, click Save Movie File on the File menu, and then follow the instructions in the Save Movie Wizard that is displayed.

Import the Video into Your Resume Import the video into your resume by completing the following steps:
1. Start Microsoft Word, open the resume document, and then place the insertion point at the location where you want your video to appear.
2. Click Insert on the menu bar and then click Object on the Insert menu.
3. In the Object type list in the Create New sheet in the Object dialog box, select Video Clip, and then click the OK button.
4. In the window that opens, click Insert on the menu bar, and then click Video for Windows on the menu. Identify where your video is stored, select the file, and then click the Open button.
5. To return to the normal Word window, click anywhere in the document except the video. To play the video in the Word window, double-click the video icon.

Exercise

1. Write the script you would use for your resume video. Submit the script to your instructor.
2. Using Windows Movie Maker, create a video using the Windows Movie Maker sample file (C:\Program Files\Movie Maker\SAMPLE). Add transitions to make the video more interesting. Submit the video to your instructor.
3. If you have access to a video camera, use Windows Movie Maker to create a video for your resume. Place a title on the video, edit it with transitions if appropriate, trim the clip if necessary, ensure the clip is to your liking, and then submit the video to your instructor.

Web Research

Use the Internet-based Web Research exercises to broaden your understanding of the concepts presented in this chapter. Visit scsite.com/dc2007/ch15/research to obtain more information pertaining to each exercise. To discuss any of the Web Research exercises in this chapter with other students, post your thoughts or questions at scsite.com/dc2007/ch15/forum.

1 **Scavenger Hunt**   Use one of the search engines listed in Figure 2-10 in Chapter 2 on page 78 or your own favorite search engine to find the answers to the questions that follow. Copy and paste the Web address from the Web page where you found the answer. Some questions may have more than one answer. If required, submit your answers to your instructor. (1) What are three topics posted in the Association for Computing Machinery (ACM) Education forum? (2) What are the Microsoft Office Specialist certification tracks? Where is the nearest iQcenter? (3) What are two stories featured in the Latest News section of the ZDNet.com Web site? (4) Describe three Computer Services jobs listed at the Monster.com Web site.

2 **Search Sleuth**   When people have questions about breaking news, consumer products, and popular topics, they frequently turn to the Ask Jeeves Web site (ask.com). Visit this Web site and then use your word processing program to answer the following questions. Then, if required, submit your answers to your instructor. (1) Type "`magnetic motion capture`" in the Search the Web box and then click the Search button. How many pages of results are found? (2) Click your browser's Back button or press the BACKSPACE key several times to return to the Ask Jeeves home page. Click the Bloglines icon at the bottom of the Web page. What are three hot topics and three new blogs in the Cool features section? (3) Click the links describing how to create your personal Bloglines page, read the information, and then write a 50-word summary of your findings.

3 **Journaling**   Respond to your readings in this chapter by writing at least one page about your reactions, evaluations, and reflections on computer careers and certification. For example, have you prepared an online resume? If so, did you use resume building software? Have you searched for a job using a Web site? Would you consider obtaining a certificate to demonstrate your competence in the IT industry? Do you read computer publications? You also can write about the new terms you learned by reading this chapter. If required, submit your journal to your instructor.

4 **Expanding Your Understanding**   One of the newer IT jobs is a computer security officer or consultant. People employed in this field protect the privacy of an organization's computer files, develop company privacy policies, and help prosecute people who violate these laws and policies regarding computers. The International Information Systems Security Certification Consortium, Inc., called (ISC)² for short, provides training and resources to assist information security professionals and offers two certifications: Certified Information Systems Security Professional (CISSP) and Systems Security Certified Practitioner (SSCP). Visit the (ISC)² Web site (isc2.org) to read about these certification tests, careers in the field, and publications. Then visit the National Security Institute (nsi.org) Web site to learn about its information security services and products. Write a report summarizing your findings. If required, submit your report to your instructor.

5 **Ethics in Action**   People studying for certification exams sometimes turn to braindump Web sites to obtain test questions that test takers recall and then post to the Web site after taking an exam. Major certification companies require test takers to sign a nondisclosure agreement. Some potential test takers, however, believe that buying these test questions makes studying efficient and effective. View online sites that contain braindumps, such as BrainDumps.com, and describe what questions are available. What is the cost of obtaining this information? Then view the Microsoft and Cicso Systems Web sites to read their nondisclosure policies. What information is permitted for posting? What happens to test takers caught revealing exam information? Write a report summarizing your findings, and include a table of links to Web sites that provide additional details about braindumps. If required, submit your report to your instructor.

Case Studies

Use the Case Studies to apply the concepts presented in the chapter to real-world situations. Visit scsite.com/dc2007/ch15/cases to obtain more information pertaining to each exercise. To discuss the Case Studies in this chapter with other students, visit scsite.com/dc2007/ch15/forum and post your thoughts or questions.

CASE STUDY 1 — Class Discussion   You are employed as a computer programmer for a company that writes assessment software for institutions of higher learning. Your salary is $75,000, plus $25,000 in benefits. The company you work for is very profitable. It primarily markets its software in the United States and Canada. You recently learned from your manager that the company plans to **outsource** its software development to India, where it can hire programmers for one-fifth the salary and benefits it pays you. If the company goes ahead as planned, then you will be out of a job. Your manager, who will lose her job as well, has asked you and the other members of the programming staff to come up with reasons why the company should not move its software development overseas. Write a report that includes three reasons why the company should keep its software development in the United States. Be prepared to discuss your recommendations in class.

CASE STUDY 2 — Class Discussion   Your manager has informed you that the company will be upgrading their application software within the next six months to Microsoft Office 2003. She states that you need to pass the Microsoft Word 2003 Specialist and Microsoft Excel 2003 Specialist certification examinations by the time the upgrade is completed if you want to continue in your current word processing position. For additional information about Microsoft Office Specialist Certification, visit the **Shelly Cashman Series Certification Web site**. What steps would you take to become proficient in the use of the new software so that you could pass the examination? Write a brief report and be prepared to discuss your recommendations in class.

CASE STUDY 3 — Research   Some programmers consider themselves artists, and they may be right — although perhaps not in the sense they had in mind. With the growing popularity of computer-animated movies, computer games, and virtual media, the call for graphic artists who also are computer programmers is expected to become a shout. The U.S. Department of Labor predicts that the demand for commercial artists with computer ability will climb 25 percent by 2008. What does it take to succeed in these jobs that combine artistic talent with digital skills? To learn about this challenging career, use the Web and/or print media to research companies that create art and movies with computers. In particular, research the animation technology internships and career opportunities with **DreamWorks**, the company that produced *Shrek, Shrek 2,* and *Madagascar.* From what you discover, do you think you have the interest, and the talent, to pursue this type of work? Why or why not? Submit your report or use PowerPoint to create a presentation and share your findings with your class.

CASE STUDY 4 — Research   You are the assistant manager of the Information Technology (IT) department at Century Merchandising, a large retail company. Senior management is considering using certification as a means to identify employees who deserve raises and/or promotions. You have been asked to chair a committee on **IT certification**. Use the Web and/or print media to research IT certification. Who determines certification requirements? Which IT certifications are rigorous, requiring extensive training and success on a number of tests? Which IT certifications require less training or are easier to obtain? Which IT certifications are the more respected and in higher demand? In your opinion, is certification a valid way to determine an employee's worth? Why or why not? Which IT certifications would you recommend your company recognize? Why? Write a brief report or use PowerPoint to create a presentation and share your findings with your class.

CASE STUDY 5 — Team Challenge   The computer class you are enrolled in has whet your classmates' appetite to a point where several students seriously are considering majoring in one of the three **computer disciplines** — Computer Information Systems, Computer Science, or Computer Engineering. Form a three-member team and have each team member choose a different discipline. Using the Web, school catalogs, other print media, or interviews with school counselors or advisors, have each team member determine the advantages and disadvantages of the discipline assigned to them. Which option is more application oriented? Theory oriented? Are advanced degrees in the assigned discipline awarded at your school? As a team, merge your findings into a team report and/or PowerPoint presentation and share your recommendations with your class. Make sure you include in the merged report the planning and prerequisites necessary, along with which discipline offers the greatest potential for career growth and advancement.

Digital Entertainment

The Revolution Is Underway

COMPUTING

GAMING

RECORDING

AUDIO

VIDEO

This feature looks at the components that comprise the world of digital entertainment. Ever since the world heard "Mary Had a Little Lamb" on Thomas Edison's newest invention — the phonograph — in 1877, the worlds of entertainment and technology began to converge. Next came mass media in the form of radio, movies, and television, followed by personal entertainment products, such as video games, CDs, and DVDs. Today, our homes have become electronic playgrounds, with powerful media center computers functioning as an interface to digital media and television tasks. Our digital world of computing, gaming, recording, audio, and video is evolving quickly, and the entertainment breakthroughs are bound to bring hours of excitement and fun to our lives.

Convergence

The Personal Computer and Television

The personal computer and television can serve as the focal points of the entertainment system. A mid-size flat-screen CRT television delivers excellent picture quality for far less money than a plasma, LCD, or projection unit, but a plasma display gives rich, fluid image quality from a variety of viewing angles.

FIGURE 1 Microsoft's Media Center software can use wireless networking to feed programs, movies, music, and e-mail from a media center personal computer to a television in the room or elsewhere in the house.

FIGURE 2 A desktop computer can double as an entertainment center. A wide-screen LCD monitor's large viewing area can be used for both computer applications and watching television or movies.

FIGURE 3 Media Center PCs deliver high-definition surround sound that can bring live sports action into your media room. They have multiple TV tuners, so you can watch one program while recording another. A single remote lets you select all your television shows, music, and digital photos.

Recording Audio and Video

Whether you are in the mood for an action-packed movie or some soothing new-age music, your digital entertainment products can fulfill your needs. Burn your favorite songs to a CD and play them in your car or while you work out at the gym, burn footage recorded on your camcorder to a DVD to take to Grandma's house, or record movies and television programs on your digital video recorder when you are not at home and then play them at your convenience. The video-capable iPod expanded the ability to view music videos, animated short films, and popular television programs. In 2005, Apple sold 1 million video downloads at $1.99 each during the first 20 days this content was available through its iTunes store.

FIGURE 4 Millions of audiophiles use dedicated network audio receivers and legal music download services to hear their preferred musical bands and songs. They then record these digital audio files in MP3, WMA, and other formats and burn them to CDs.

FIGURE 5 DVD burners are considered essential peripherals and can be internally mounted in your computer or externally connected using USB or FireWire cables. Dual-format, dual-layer drives allow you to copy full DVDs without recompression, which preserves the original image quality.

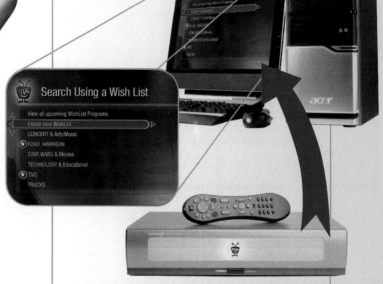

FIGURE 6 Convergence technologies have made storing and sharing video content a breeze. With digital video recorders, such as TiVo, you can record all episodes of one television show with one click, skip commercials, stream video from one unit to another, and then control recording features from a remote Web browser.

Bring Music to Your Ears

A computer now can be considered an essential component of a home entertainment system. A multimedia computer should have at least 200 GB of storage space to save thousands of CDs or digital audio files, a CD burner, a DVD drive to play multichannel audio DVDs, and several USB 2.0 ports to connect peripherals.

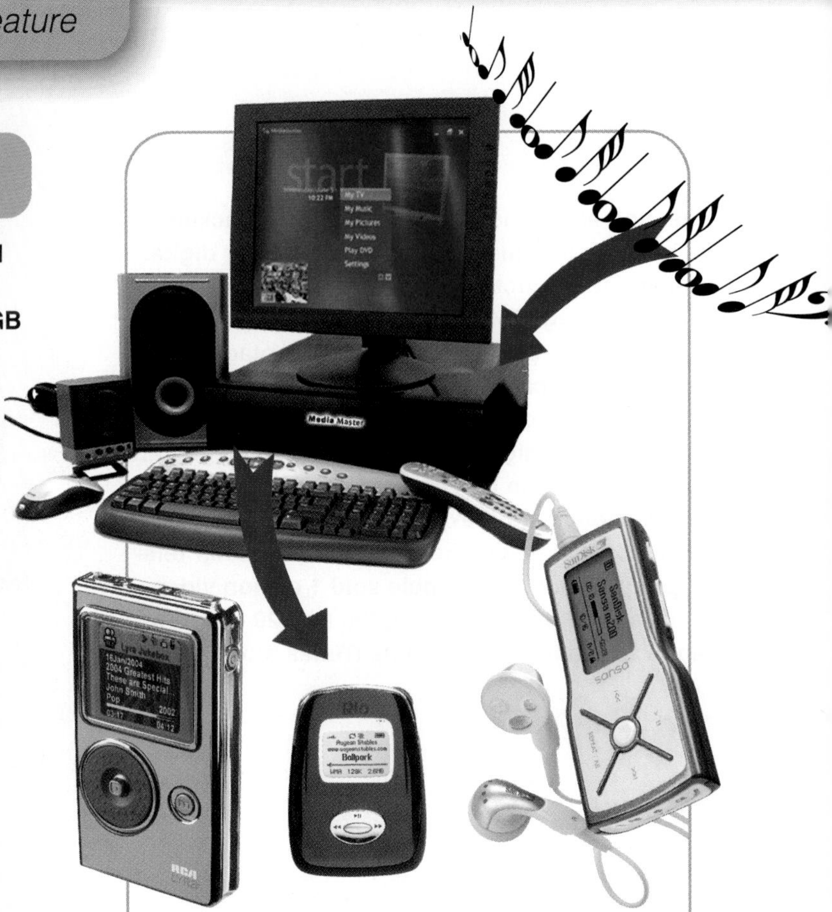

FIGURE 7 Music downloading services allow you to purchase individual tracks or entire albums, download the music to your computer, and then transfer the files to a portable player or burn them to a CD. Top downloading services are Apple iTunes Music Store and Microsoft's MSN Music.

FIGURE 8 Apple's creativity software, GarageBand, uses a Macintosh computer to transform any room of the house into a recording studio. The program includes more than 1,000 pieces of music and more than 50 virtual instruments to mix and edit.

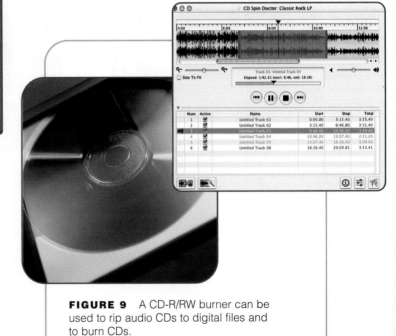

FIGURE 9 A CD-R/RW burner can be used to rip audio CDs to digital files and to burn CDs.

FIGURE 10 Manage your music with digital jukebox software, including Windows Media Player, RealPlayer, Musicmatch Jukebox, and iTunes. These programs allow you to listen to streaming audio, CDs, and downloaded files in a variety of formats. The Microsoft Windows PlaysForSure initiative assures consumers that specific devices are compatible with downloaded content.

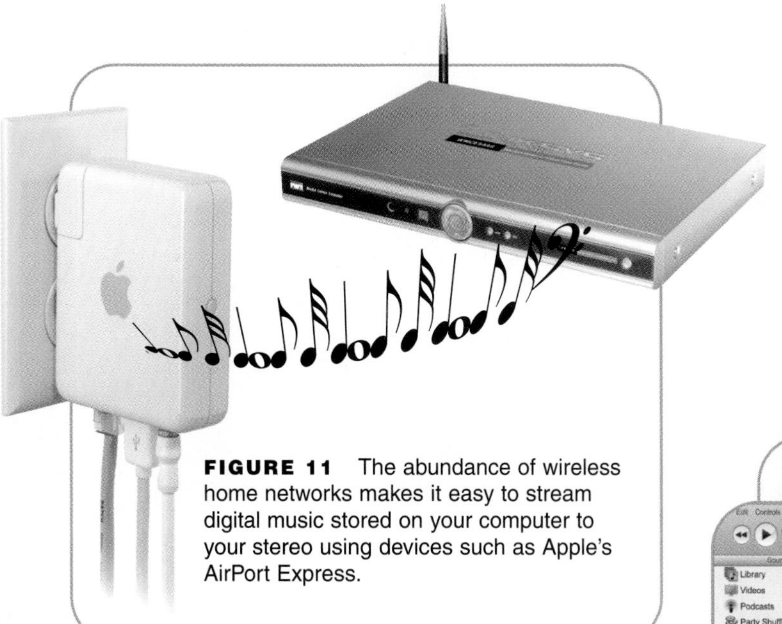

FIGURE 11 The abundance of wireless home networks makes it easy to stream digital music stored on your computer to your stereo using devices such as Apple's AirPort Express.

FIGURE 12 iTunes jukebox software allows you to play tracks downloaded from the iTunes Music Store, create playlists, and then transfer the tunes to the trendy iPod.

All the World Is a Game

With thousands of available game titles, it is easy to quench a thirst for fun. From one-player games to serious competition with fellow gamers, it is easy to find sports, strategy, and action games to suit everyone's interests. Gaming hardware can be sorted into three categories: personal computer, console, and handheld. With a broadband connection and home network, you can compete online and tie together multiple personal computer and game consoles.

FIGURE 13 Millions of gamers worldwide are competing with friends living across the street or across the globe with massively multiplayer online games (MMOGs). Ultra-fast processors, enormous amounts of memory, a high-end graphics card, large monitor, superb speakers, and case fans are necessary components.

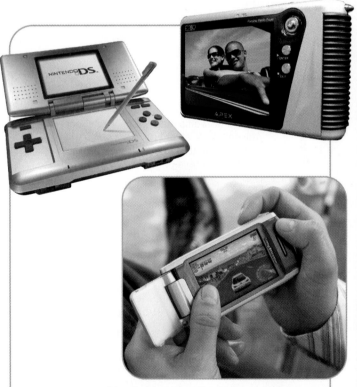

FIGURE 14 The three gaming consoles — Nintendo Revolution, Sony PlayStation 3, and Microsoft Xbox 360 — offer a variety of game titles.

FIGURE 15 Handheld multimedia devices weigh less than one pound and have large, high-resolution screens and incredible sound to play audio, video, and photos. Bluetooth technology allows networked gaming and syncing with other handheld units or a personal computer.

Convergence: Tying the Loose Ends Together

With wired and wireless home networking and broadband, all components are connected to provide entertainment in innovative ways. A central media hub, digital video recorder, and other devices can stream music and video files, Internet radio, and slide shows of photographs seamlessly throughout your house.

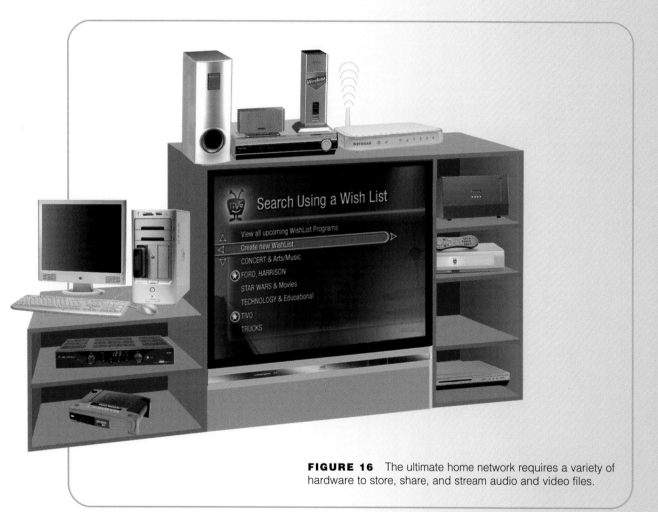

FIGURE 16 The ultimate home network requires a variety of hardware to store, share, and stream audio and video files.

The entertainment revolution has worked its way into virtually every facet of our lives. From the largest media rooms to the smallest portable media centers, we can watch our favorite television programs and movies any place at anytime. We can surf the Internet, play games with partners on the other side of the world, listen to personalized music, and have fun wherever life takes us. No matter where we are, we always can have the best seat in the house for digital entertainment.

APPENDIX A

Coding Schemes and Number Systems

CODING SCHEMES

As discussed in Chapter 4, a computer uses a coding scheme to represent characters. This section of the appendix presents the ASCII, EBCDIC, and Unicode coding schemes and discusses parity.

ASCII and EBCDIC

Two popular coding schemes that represent characters in a computer are ASCII and EBCDIC. The **American Standard Code for Information Interchange**, or ASCII (pronounced ASK-ee), coding scheme is the most widely used coding scheme to represent data. Many personal computers and midrange servers use ASCII. The **Extended Binary Coded Decimal Interchange Code**, or EBCDIC (pronounced EB-see-dik), coding scheme is used primarily on mainframe computers and high-end servers. As shown in Figure A-1, the combination of bits (0s and 1s) is unique for each character in the ASCII and EBCDIC coding schemes.

When a computer uses the ASCII or EBCDIC coding scheme, it stores each represented character in one byte of memory. Other binary formats exist, however, that the computer sometimes uses to represent numeric data. For example, a computer may store, or pack, two numeric characters in one byte of memory. The computer uses these binary formats to increase storage and processing efficiency.

Unicode

The 256 characters and symbols that are represented by ASCII and EBCDIC codes are sufficient for English and western European languages but are not large enough for Asian and other languages that use different alphabets. Further compounding the problem is that many of these languages use symbols, called **ideograms**, to represent multiple words and ideas. One solution to this situation is Unicode. **Unicode** is a 16-bit coding scheme that has the capacity of representing all the world's current languages, as well as classic and historical languages, in more than 65,000 characters and symbols.

ASCII	SYMBOL	EBCDIC
00110000	0	11110000
00110001	1	11110001
00110010	2	11110010
00110011	3	11110011
00110100	4	11110100
00110101	5	11110101
00110110	6	11110110
00110111	7	11110111
00111000	8	11111000
00111001	9	11111001
01000001	A	11000001
01000010	B	11000010
01000011	C	11000011
01000100	D	11000100
01000101	E	11000101
01000110	F	11000110
01000111	G	11000111
01001000	H	11001000
01001001	I	11001001
01001010	J	11010001
01001011	K	11010010
01001100	L	11010011
01001101	M	11010100
01001110	N	11010101
01001111	O	11010110
01010000	P	11010111
01010001	Q	11011000
01010010	R	11011001
01010011	S	11100010
01010100	T	11100011
01010101	U	11100100
01010110	V	11100101
01010111	W	11100110
01011000	X	11100111
01011001	Y	11101000
01011010	Z	11101001
00100001	!	01011010
00100010	"	01111111
00100011	#	01111011
00100100	$	01011011
00100101	%	01101100
00100110	&	01010000
00101000	(	01001101
00101001	)	01011101
00101010	*	01011100
00101011	+	01001110

FIGURE A-1

A Unicode code for a symbol, as shown in Figure A-2, is obtained by appending the symbol's corresponding digit in the left-most column to the end of the symbol's corresponding three-digit code in the column heading. For

	003	004	005	006	007
0	0 0030	@ 0040	P 0050	` 0060	p 0070
1	1 0031	A 0041	Q 0051	a 0061	q 0071
2	2 0032	B 0042	R 0052	b 0062	r 0072
3	3 0033	C 0043	S 0053	c 0063	s 0073
4	4 0034	D 0044	T 0054	d 0064	t 0074
5	5 0035	E 0045	U 0055	e 0065	u 0075
6	6 0036	F 0046	V 0056	f 0066	v 0076
7	7 0037	G 0047	W 0057	g 0067	w 0077
8	8 0038	H 0048	X 0058	h 0068	x 0078
9	9 0039	I 0049	Y 0059	i 0069	y 0079
A	: 003A	J 004A	Z 005A	j 006A	z 007A
B	; 003B	K 004B	[005B	k 006B	{ 007B
C	< 003C	L 004C	\ 005C	l 006C	| 007C
D	= 003D	M 004D	] 005D	m 006D	} 007D
E	> 003E	N 004E	^ 005E	n 006E	~ 007E
F	? 003F	O 004F	_ 005F	o 006F	DEL 007F

FIGURE A-2

example, the Unicode for the capital letter C is 0043. In Unicode, 30,000 codes are reserved for future use, such as ancient languages, and 6,000 codes are reserved for private use. Existing ASCII coded data is fully compatible with Unicode because the first 256 codes are the same. Unicode is implemented in several operating systems, including Windows XP, Mac OS X, and Linux. Unicode-enabled programming languages and software include Java, XML, Microsoft Office, and Oracle. Some experts believe that Unicode eventually will replace all other coding schemes.

Parity

Regardless of the coding scheme used to represent characters in memory, it is important that the computer store characters accurately. For each byte of memory, most computers have at least one extra bit, called a **parity bit**, that the computer uses for error checking. A parity bit can detect if one of the bits in a byte has been changed inadvertently. While such errors are extremely rare (most computers never have a parity error during their lifetime), they can occur because of voltage fluctuations, static electricity, or a memory failure.

Computers are either odd- or even-parity machines. In computers with odd-parity, the total number of on bits in the byte (including the parity bit) must be an odd number (Figure A-3). In computers with even parity, the total number of on bits must be an even number. The computer checks parity each time it uses a memory location. When the computer moves data from one location to another in memory, it compares the parity bits of both the sending and receiving locations to see if they are the same. If the computer detects a difference or if the wrong number of bits is on (e.g., an odd number in a computer with even parity), an error message is displayed. Many computers use multiple parity bits that enable them to detect and correct a single-bit error and detect multiple-bit errors.

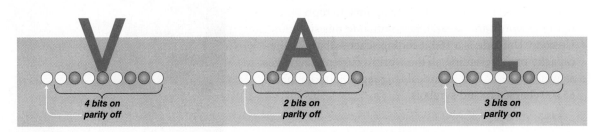

FIGURE A-3

NUMBER SYSTEMS

This section of the appendix describes the number systems used with computers. Technical computer personnel require a thorough knowledge of this subject, but most users need only a general understanding of number systems and how they relate to computers.

The binary (base 2) number system is used to represent the electronic status of the bits in memory. It also is used for other purposes such as addressing the memory locations. Another number system commonly used with computers is **hexadecimal** (base 16). The computer uses the hexadecimal number system to communicate with a programmer when a problem with a program exists, because it would be difficult for the programmer to understand the 0s and 1s of binary code. Figure A-4 shows how the decimal values 0 through 15 are represented in binary and hexadecimal number systems.

DECIMAL	BINARY	HEXADECIMAL
0	0000	0
1	0001	1
2	0010	2
3	0011	3
4	0100	4
5	0101	5
6	0110	6
7	0111	7
8	1000	8
9	1001	9
10	1010	A
11	1011	B
12	1100	C
13	1101	D
14	1110	E
15	1111	F

FIGURE A-4

The mathematical principles that apply to the binary and hexadecimal number systems are the same as those that apply to the decimal number system. To help you better understand these principles, this section starts with the familiar decimal system, then progresses to the binary and hexadecimal number systems.

The Decimal Number System

The decimal number system is a base 10 number system (deci means ten). The base of a number system indicates how many symbols it uses. The decimal number system uses 10 symbols: 0 through 9. Each of the symbols in the number system has a value associated with it. For example, 3 represents a quantity of three and 5 represents a quantity of five.

The decimal number system also is a positional number system. This means that in a number such as 143, each position in the number has a value associated with it. When you look at the decimal number 143, the 3 is in the ones, or units, position and represents three ones (3×1); the 4 is in the tens position and represents four tens (4×10); and the 1 is in the hundreds position and represents one hundred (1×100). The number 143 is the sum of the values in each position of the number ($100 + 40 + 3 = 143$). The chart in Figure A-5 shows how you can calculate the positional values (hundreds, tens, and units) for a number system. Starting on the right and working to the left, the base of the number system, in this case 10, is raised to consecutive powers (10^0, 10^1, 10^2). These calculations are a mathematical way of determining the place values in a number system.

When you use number systems other than decimal, the same principles apply. The base of the number system indicates the number of symbols that it uses, and each position in a number system has a value associated with it. By raising the base of the number system to consecutive powers beginning with zero, you can calculate the positional value.

power of 10	10^2	10^1	10^0	1	4	3	=
				(1×10^2) +	(4×10^1) +	(3×10^0)	=
positional value	100	10	1	(1×100) +	(4×10) +	(3×1)	=
number	1	4	3	100 +	40 +	3	= 143

FIGURE A-5

The Binary Number System

As previously discussed, binary is a base 2 number system (bi means two), and the symbols it uses are 0 and 1. Just as each position in a decimal number has a place value associated with it, so does each position in a binary number. In binary, the place values, moving from right to left, are successive powers of two (2^0, 2^1, 2^2, 2^3 or 1, 2, 4, 8). To construct a binary number, place ones in the positions where the corresponding values add up to the quantity you want to represent and place zeros in the other positions. For example, in a four-digit binary number, the binary place values are (from right to left) 1, 2, 4, and 8. The binary number 1001 has ones in the positions for the values 1 and 8 and zeros in the positions for 2 and 4. Therefore, as shown in Figure A-6, the quantity represented by binary 1001 is 9 (8 + 0 + 0 + 1).

The Hexadecimal Number System

The hexadecimal number system uses 16 symbols to represent values (hex means six). These include the symbols 0 through 9 and A through F (Figure A-4 on the previous page). The mathematical principles previously discussed also apply to hexadecimal (Figure A-7).

The primary reasons the hexadecimal number system is used with computers are (1) it can represent binary values in a more compact and readable form, and (2) the conversion between the binary and the hexadecimal number systems is very efficient.

An eight-digit binary number (a byte) can be represented by a two-digit hexadecimal number. For example, in the ASCII code, the character M is represented as 01001101. This value can be represented in the hexadecimal number system as 4D. One way to convert this binary number (4D) to a hexadecimal number is to divide the binary number (from right to left) into groups of four digits, calculate the value of each group, and then change any two-digit values (10 through 15) to the symbols A through F that are used in the hexadecimal number system (Figure A-8).

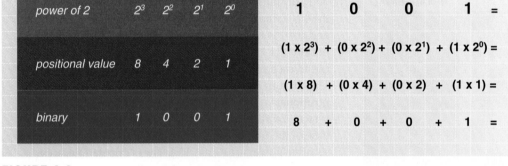

power of 2	2^3	2^2	2^1	2^0
positional value	8	4	2	1
binary	1	0	0	1

$$1 \quad 0 \quad 0 \quad 1 =$$
$$(1 \times 2^3) + (0 \times 2^2) + (0 \times 2^1) + (1 \times 2^0) =$$
$$(1 \times 8) + (0 \times 4) + (0 \times 2) + (1 \times 1) =$$
$$8 + 0 + 0 + 1 = 9$$

FIGURE A-6

power of 16	16^1	16^0
positional value	16	1
hexadecimal	A	5

$$A \quad 5 \quad =$$
$$(10 \times 16^1) + (5 \times 16^0) =$$
$$(10 \times 16) + (5 \times 1) =$$
$$160 + 5 = 165$$

FIGURE A-7

positional value	8421	8421
binary	0100	1101
decimal	4	13
hexadecimal	4	D

FIGURE A-8

APPENDIX B
Quiz Yourself Answers

Following are possible answers to the Quiz Yourself boxes throughout the book.

Quiz Yourself 1-1

1. A computer is ~~a motorized~~an electronic device that processes ~~output~~input into ~~input~~output.
2. A storage device records (~~reads~~writes) and/or retrieves (~~writes~~reads) items to and from storage media.
3. An ~~output~~input device is any hardware component that allows you to enter data and instructions into a computer.
4. True Statement
5. Computers have the ~~dis~~advantages of fast speeds, ~~high~~low failure rates, producing consistent results, storing ~~small~~enormous amounts of data, and communicating with others.
6. Three commonly used ~~input~~output devices are a printer, a monitor, and speakers.

Quiz Yourself 1-2

1. A ~~resource~~network is a collection of computers and devices connected together via communications devices and transmission media.
2. True Statement
3. Popular ~~system~~application software includes Web browsers, word processing software, spreadsheet software, database software, and presentation graphics software.
4. The ~~Internet~~Web is one of the more popular services on the ~~Web~~Internet.
5. Two types of ~~application~~system software are the operating system and utility programs.

Quiz Yourself 1-3

1. A ~~desktop computer~~notebook computer (or laptop computer) is a portable, personal computer designed to fit on your lap.
2. True Statement
3. Each ~~large business~~home user spends time on the computer for different reasons that include budgeting and personal financial management, Web access, communications, and entertainment.
4. A ~~home~~power user requires the capabilities of a workstation or other powerful computer.
5. ~~Mainframes~~Supercomputers are the fastest, most powerful computers — and the most expensive.
6. The elements of an information system are hardware, ~~e-mail~~software, data, people, and ~~the Internet~~procedures.
7. With ~~embedded computers~~online banking, users access account balances, pay bills, and copy monthly transactions from the bank's computer right into their personal computers.

Quiz Yourself 2-1

1. True Statement
2. ~~A WISP~~An IP address (or Internet Protocol address) is a number that uniquely identifies each computer or device connected to the Internet.
3. ~~An IP address~~A domain name, such as www.google.com, is the text version of ~~a domain name~~an IP address.
4. Dial-up access takes place when the modem in your computer uses ~~the cable television network~~a standard telephone line to connect to the Internet.
5. The World Wide Web Consortium (W3C) oversees research and ~~owns~~sets standards and guidelines for many areas of the Internet.

Quiz Yourself 2-2

1. True Statement
2. A ~~Web browser~~subject directory classifies Web pages in an organized set of categories, such as sports or shopping, and related subcategories.
3. Audio and video files are ~~downloaded~~compressed to reduce their file sizes.
4. Popular ~~portals~~players include iTunes, RealPlayer, and Windows Media Player.
5. The more widely used ~~search engines~~Web browsers for personal computers are Internet Explorer, Netscape, Firefox, Mozilla, Opera, and Safari.
6. To develop a Web page, you do not have to be a computer programmer.
7. To improve your Web searches, use ~~general~~specific nouns and put the ~~least~~ most important terms first in the search text.

Quiz Yourself 2-3

1. True Statement
2. An e-mail address is a combination of a user name and ~~an e-mail program~~a domain name that identifies a user so he or she can receive Internet e-mail.
3. ~~Business~~Consumer-to-consumer e-commerce occurs when one consumer sells directly to another, such as in an online auction.
4. FTP is an Internet standard that permits file ~~reading~~uploading and ~~writing~~downloading with other computers on the Internet.
5. ~~Spam~~Internet telephony uses the Internet (instead of the public switched telephone network) to connect a calling party to one or more called parties.
6. Netiquette is the code of ~~un~~acceptable behaviors while on the Internet.
7. On a newsgroup, a ~~subscription~~thread (or threaded discussion) consists of the original article and all subsequent related replies.

Quiz Yourself 3-1

1. True Statement
2. ~~Public domain~~Packaged software is mass produced, copyrighted retail software that meets the needs of a wide variety of users, not just a single user or company.
3. To use ~~system~~application software, your computer must be running ~~application~~system software.
4. When an application is started, the program's instructions load from ~~memory~~a storage medium into ~~a storage medium~~memory.

Quiz Yourself 3-2

1. ~~Audio~~Video editing software typically includes ~~video~~audio editing capabilities.
2. ~~Enterprise computing~~Image editing software provides the capabilities of paint software and also includes the ability to modify existing images.
3. Millions of people use ~~spreadsheet~~word processing software every day to develop documents such as letters, memos, reports, fax cover sheets, mailing labels, newsletters, and Web pages.
4. Professional ~~accounting~~DTP (or desktop publishing) software is ideal for the production of high-quality color documents such as textbooks, corporate newsletters, marketing literature, product catalogs, and annual reports.
5. ~~Spreadsheet~~Presentation graphics software is application software that allows users to create visual aids for presentations to communicate ideas, messages, and other information to a group.
6. Two of the more widely used ~~CAD programs~~software suites are Microsoft Office and Sun StarOffice.
7. True Statement

Quiz Yourself 3-3

1. An ~~anti-spam~~antivirus program protects a computer against viruses by identifying and removing any computer viruses found in memory, on storage media, or in incoming files.
2. ~~Computer~~Web-based training is a type of ~~Web~~computer-based training that uses Internet technology and consists of application software on the Web.
3. True Statement
4. ~~Legal~~Personal finance software is a simplified accounting program that helps home users and small office/home office users balance their checkbooks, pay bills, track investments, and evaluate financial plans.
5. ~~Personal DTP~~Photo editing software is a popular type of image editing software that allows users to edit digital photographs.

Quiz Yourself 4-1

1. True Statement
2. Four basic operations in a machine cycle are: (1) ~~comparing~~fetching, (2) decoding, (3) executing, and, if necessary, (4) ~~pipelining~~storing.
3. Processors contain a ~~motherboard~~control unit and an arithmetic logic unit (ALU).
4. The ~~central processing unit~~motherboard, sometimes called a system board, is the main circuit board of the system unit.
5. The leading processor chip manufacturers for personal computers are ~~Microsoft~~Intel, AMD, IBM, Motorola, and Transmeta.
6. The pace of the system clock, called the clock speed, is measured by the number of ticks per ~~minute~~second.
7. The system unit is a case that contains ~~mechanical~~electronic components of the computer used to process data.

Quiz Yourself 4-2

1. True Statement
2. A gigabyte (GB) equals approximately 1 ~~trillion~~billion bytes.
3. Memory cache helps speed the processes of the computer because it stores ~~seldom~~frequently used instructions and data.
4. Most computers are ~~analog~~digital, which means they recognize only two discrete states: on and off.
5. Most RAM ~~retains~~loses its contents when the power is removed from the computer.
6. Read-only memory (ROM) refers to memory chips storing ~~temporary~~permanent data and instructions.

Quiz Yourself 4-3

1. A ~~bus~~port is the point at which a peripheral attaches to or communicates with a system unit so the peripheral can send data to or receive information from the computer.
2. An ~~AC adapter~~expansion slot is a socket on the motherboard that can hold an adapter card.
3. Built into the power supply is a ~~heater~~fan that keeps components of the system unit ~~warm~~cool.
4. ~~Serial~~USB ports can connect up to 127 different peripherals together with a single connector type.
5. The higher the bus clock speed, the ~~slower~~faster the transmission of data.
6. True Statement

Quiz Yourself 5-1

1. A keyboard is an ~~output~~input device that contains keys users press to enter data in a computer.
2. A ~~light pen~~graphics tablet is a flat, rectangular, electronic plastic board.

3. A ~~trackball~~ touch pad is a small, flat, rectangular pointing device commonly found on notebook computers.
4. True Statement
5. Operations you can perform with a ~~wheel~~ mouse include point, click, right-click, double-click, triple-click, drag, right-drag, rotate wheel, press wheel button, and tilt wheel.
6. ~~PDAs~~ Tablet PCs use a pressure-sensitive digital pen, and ~~Tablet PCs~~ PDAs use a stylus.

Quiz Yourself 5-2

1. True Statement
2. DV cameras record video as ~~analog~~ digital signals.
3. ~~Instant messaging~~ Voice recognition (or speech recognition) is the computer's capability of distinguishing spoken words.
4. Many smart phones today have a built-in camera so users easily can send ~~text~~ picture messages.
5. The ~~lower~~ higher the resolution of a digital camera, the better the image quality, but the more expensive the camera.

Quiz Yourself 5-3

1. A fingerprint scanner captures curves and indentations of a ~~signature~~ fingerprint.
2. After swiping a credit card through ~~an MICR~~ a magstripe (or magnetic stripe card) reader, a POS terminal connects to a system that authenticates the purchase.
3. ATMs ask you to enter a password, called a ~~biometric identifier~~ PIN (or personal identification number), which verifies that you are the holder of the bankcard.
4. Four types of ~~source documents~~ scanners are flatbed, pen, sheet-fed, and drum.
5. Retail and grocery stores use the ~~POSTNET~~ UPC (Universal Product Code) bar code.
6. RFID is a technology that uses ~~laser~~ radio signals to communicate with a tag placed in an object, an animal, or a person.
7. True Statement

Quiz Yourself 6-1

1. A ~~lower~~ higher resolution uses a greater number of pixels and thus provides a smoother image.
2. An output device is any type of ~~software~~ hardware component that conveys information to one or more people.
3. Documents often include ~~text~~ graphics to enhance their visual appeal and convey information.
4. ~~LCD~~ CRT monitors have a larger footprint than ~~CRT~~ LCD monitors.
5. Types of ~~CRTs~~ flat-panel displays include LCD monitors, LCD screens, and plasma monitors.
6. True Statement

Quiz Yourself 6-2

1. A ~~laser~~ thermal printer generates images by pushing electrically heated pins against heat-sensitive paper.
2. A ~~photo~~ laser printer creates images using a laser beam and powdered ink, called toner.
3. An ink-jet printer is a type of impact printer that forms characters and graphics by spraying tiny drops of liquid ~~nitrogen~~ ink onto a piece of paper.
4. Printed information is called ~~soft~~ hard copy.
5. Two commonly used types of impact printers are ~~ink-jet~~ dot-matrix printers and line printers.
6. True Statement

Quiz Yourself 6-3

1. A digital light processing (DLP) projector uses tiny ~~lightbulbs~~ mirrors to reflect light.
2. True Statement
3. Many personal computer users add surround sound ~~printer systems~~ speakers to their computers to generate a higher-quality sound.
4. Multifunction peripherals require ~~more~~ less space than having a separate printer, scanner, copy machine, and fax machine.
5. Some joysticks, wheels, and gamepads include ~~real-time action~~ force feedback, which is a technology that sends resistance to the device in response to actions of the user.

Quiz Yourself 7-1

1. Miniature hard disks are a type of ~~optical disc~~ magnetic disk.
2. True Statement
3. SATA is a hard disk interface that uses ~~parallel~~ serial signals to transfer data, instructions, and information.
4. ~~Storage media~~ A storage device is the computer hardware that records and/or retrieves items to and from a ~~storage device~~ media.
5. Three types of ~~manual~~ magnetic disks are hard disks, floppy disks, and Zip disks.
6. Users can move an ~~internal~~ external Zip drive from computer to computer as needed by connecting the drive to a USB port or FireWire port on the system unit.

Quiz Yourself 7-2

1. A ~~CD-RW~~ CD-ROM is a type of optical disc on which users can read but not write (record) or erase.
2. A ~~DVD-RAM~~ Picture CD is a single-session disc that stores digital versions of a single roll of film using a jpg file format.
3. DVDs have ~~the same~~ much greater storage capacities ~~as~~ than CDs.
4. Optical discs are written and read by ~~mirrors~~ a laser.

5. ~~Single session~~Multisession means you can write on part of the disc at one time and another part at a later time.
6. True Statement

Quiz Yourself 7-3

1. A smart card stores data on a thin ~~magnetic stripe~~microprocessor embedded in the card.
2. A USB flash drive is a flash memory storage device that plugs in a ~~parallel~~USB port on a computer or mobile device.
3. Flash memory cards are a type of ~~magnetic~~solid-state media, which means they consist entirely of electronic components and contain no moving parts.
4. Microfilm and microfiche have the ~~shortest~~longest life of any storage media.
5. Tape storage requires ~~direct~~sequential access, which refers to reading or writing data consecutively.
6. True Statement

Quiz Yourself 8-1

1. A ~~buffer~~driver is a small program that tells the operating system how to communicate with a specific device.
2. A ~~cold~~warm boot is the process of using the operating system to restart a computer.
3. A password is a ~~public~~private combination of characters associated with the user name that allows access to certain computer resources.
4. Firmware that contains the computer's startup instructions is called the ~~kernel~~BIOS.
5. The program you currently are using is in the ~~background~~foreground, and the other programs running but not in use are in the ~~foreground~~background.
6. Two types of system software are operating systems and ~~application~~utility programs.
7. True Statement

Quiz Yourself 8-2

1. A ~~file manager~~firewall is a utility that detects and protects a personal computer from unauthorized intrusions.
2. ~~Fragmenting~~Defragmenting a disk is the process of reorganizing it so the files are stored in contiguous sectors.
3. ~~Linux~~Windows XP is available in five editions: Home Edition, Professional, Media Center Edition, Tablet PC Edition, and Professional x64 Edition.
4. True Statement
5. ~~Windows XP~~Linux is a UNIX-type operating system that is open source software.
6. You should ~~uninstall~~back up files and disks regularly in the event your originals are lost, damaged, or destroyed.

Quiz Yourself 8-3

1. A ~~pop-up blocker~~file compression utility shrinks the size of a file(s).
2. An ~~anti-spam~~antivirus program protects a computer against viruses by identifying and removing any computer viruses found in memory, on storage media, or on incoming files.
3. True Statement
4. Pocket PCs use ~~Palm OS~~Windows Mobile as their operating system.
5. ~~Web filtering~~CD/DVD burning software writes text, graphics, audio, and video files to a recordable or rewritable CD or DVD.

Quiz Yourself 9-1

1. A ~~cybercafé~~hot spot is a wireless network that provides Internet connections to mobile computers and other devices.
2. A ~~Web folder~~GPS (global positioning system) is a navigation system that consists of one or more earth-based receivers that accept and analyze signals sent by satellites in order to determine the receiver's geographic location.
3. True Statement
4. ~~Receiving~~Sending devices initiate an instruction to transmit data, instructions, or information.
5. Users can send graphics, pictures, video clips, and sound files, as well as short text messages with ~~text~~picture messaging.

Quiz Yourself 9-2

1. A wireless LAN is a LAN that uses no physical wires.
2. An intranet is an internal network that uses ~~video conferencing~~Internet technologies.
3. Four types of digital ~~dial-up~~dedicated lines are ISDN lines, DSL, T-carrier lines, and ATM.
4. In a client/server network, ~~servers~~clients on the network access resources on the ~~client~~server.
5. In a networked environment, any ~~un~~authorized computer user can access data and information stored on other computers on the network.
6. True Statement

Quiz Yourself 9-3

1. A ~~cable~~dial-up modem converts a computer's digital signals to analog signals before they are transmitted over standard telephone lines.
2. A ~~hardware firewall~~wireless access point is a communications device that allows computers and devices to transfer data wirelessly among themselves or to transfer data wirelessly to a wired network.
3. True Statement
4. ~~Analog~~Digital signals consist of individual electrical pulses that represent bits grouped together into bytes.

5. ~~Physical~~ Wireless transmission media send communications signals through the air or space using radio, microwave, and infrared signals.
6. The ~~lower~~ higher the bandwidth, the more data, instructions, and information the channel transmits.
7. Two types of wireless home networks are HomeRF and ~~powerline cable~~ Wi-Fi.

Quiz Yourself 10-1

1. A ~~coding scheme~~ check digit is a number(s) or character(s) that is appended to or inserted in a primary key value.
2. A ~~database~~ field is a combination of one or more related characters or bytes and is the smallest unit of data a user accesses.
3. A ~~record~~ database is a collection of data organized in a manner that allows access, retrieval, and use of that data.
4. ~~Data~~ Information is processed ~~information~~ data.
5. ~~Hierarchy of data~~ File maintenance procedures include adding records to, changing records in, and deleting records from a file.
6. True Statement

Quiz Yourself 10-2

1. A DBMS is ~~hardware~~ software that allows you to create, access, and manage ~~an operating system~~ a database.
2. A ~~query~~ data dictionary contains data about files and fields in the database.
3. ~~Backup and recovery procedures~~ Access privileges for data involve establishing who can enter new data, change existing data, delete unwanted data, and view data.
4. Strengths of the database approach include ~~increased~~ reduced data redundancy, ~~reduced~~ improved data integrity, shared data, easier access, and ~~increased~~ reduced development time.
5. To reduce data entry errors, well-designed forms should ~~rollback~~ validate data as it is entered.
6. True Statement

Quiz Yourself 10-3

1. Data warehouses often use a process called ~~OQL~~ data mining to find patterns and relationships among data.
2. ~~Object oriented~~ Relational databases store data in tables.
3. True Statement
4. Relational database users refer to a file as a table, a record as a ~~column~~ row, and a field as a ~~row~~ column.
5. SQL is a ~~data modeling~~ query language that allows users to manage, update, and retrieve data.
6. The database ~~analyst~~ administrator requires a more technical inside view of the data than does the ~~database administrator~~ data analyst.

Quiz Yourself 11-1

1. A ~~back door~~ denial of service (DoS) attack is an assault whose purpose is to disrupt computer access to an Internet service such as the Web or e-mail.
2. True Statement
3. A biometric device translates a personal characteristic into ~~an analog~~ a digital code that then is compared with a digital code stored in the computer.
4. Computer viruses, worms, and Trojan horses are malware that acts with~~out~~ a user's knowledge.
5. Perpetrators of cybercrime and other intrusions fall into seven basic categories: hacker, cracker, ~~CERT/CC~~ script kiddie, corporate spy, unethical employee, ~~trusted source~~ cyberextortionist, and cyberterrorist.
6. ~~Shorter~~ Longer passwords provide greater security than ~~longer~~ shorter ones.
7. Updating an antivirus program's ~~quarantine~~ signature file protects a computer against viruses written since the antivirus program was released.

Quiz Yourself 11-2

1. An end-user license agreement (EULA) ~~permits~~ does not permit users to give copies to friends and colleagues, while continuing to use the software.
2. Encryption is a process of converting ~~ciphertext~~ plaintext into ~~plaintext~~ ciphertext to prevent authorized access.
3. Mobile users are ~~not~~ susceptible to hardware theft.
4. True Statement
5. Three ~~backup~~ wireless security standards are Wired Equivalent Privacy, Wi-Fi Protected Access, and 802.11i.
6. To prevent against data loss caused by a system failure, computer users should ~~restore~~ back up files regularly.

Quiz Yourself 11-3

1. A ~~code of conduct~~ copyright gives authors and artists exclusive rights to duplicate, publish, and sell their materials.
2. Factors that cause ~~CVS~~ tendonitis or CTS (carpal tunnel syndrome) include prolonged typing, prolonged mouse usage, or continual shifting between the mouse and the keyboard.
3. ~~Phishing~~ Computer forensics is the discovery, collection, and analysis of evidence found on computers and networks.
4. True Statement
5. Users should not store obsolete computers and devices in their basement or attic.
6. Web sites use ~~electronic profiles~~ cookies to track user preferences, store users' passwords, keep track of items in a user's shopping cart, and track Web site browsing habits.
7. You can~~not~~ assume that information on the Web is correct.

Quiz Yourself 12-1

1. ~~Feasibility~~ Project management is the process of planning, scheduling, and then controlling the activities during the system development cycle.
2. True Statement
3. Users should ~~not~~ be involved throughout the system development process.
4. The five phases in most system development cycles are ~~programming~~planning; analysis; design; ~~sampling~~implementation; and ~~recording~~ operation, support, and security.
5. The planning phase for a project begins when the steering committee receives a ~~Gantt chart~~project request.

Quiz Yourself 12-2

1. Detailed analysis sometimes is called ~~physical~~logical design because the systems analysts develop the proposed solution without regard to any specific hardware or software.
2. Entity-relationship diagrams and data flow diagrams are tools that a systems analyst uses for ~~object~~process modeling.
3. ~~Horizontal~~Vertical market software specifically is designed for a particular business or industry.
4. True Statement
5. The purpose of the ~~preliminary investigation~~system proposal is to assess the feasibility of each alternative solution and then recommend the most feasible solution for the project.
6. Upon completion of the preliminary investigation, the systems analyst writes the ~~system proposal~~feasibility report.

Quiz Yourself 12-3

1. A computer ~~training~~security plan summarizes in writing all of the safeguards that are in place to protect a company's information assets.
2. ~~Acceptance~~Benchmark tests measure the performance of hardware or software.
3. True Statement
4. The program development cycle is a part of the ~~support~~implementation phase.
5. The purpose of the ~~design~~operation, support, and security phase is to provide ongoing assistance for an information system and its users after the system is implemented.
6. With a request for ~~quotation~~proposal, the vendor selects the product(s) that meets specified requirements and then quotes the price(s).
7. With ~~parallel~~direct conversion, the user stops using the old system and begins using the new system on a certain date.

Quiz Yourself 13-1

1. An ~~interpreter~~compiler is a program that converts an entire source program into machine language before executing it.
2. COBOL and C are examples of ~~assembly~~procedural languages.
3. C# is an object-oriented programming language based on ~~PowerBuilder~~C++.
4. ~~Delphi~~Java is an object-oriented programming language developed by Sun Microsystems.
5. Two types of low-level languages are machine languages and ~~source~~assembly languages.
6. True Statement

Quiz Yourself 13-2

1. True Statement
2. ~~Interpreted~~Dynamic HTML works by using the document object model, style sheets, and scripting languages.
3. ~~Maps~~Macros allow users to automate routine, repetitive, or difficult tasks in application software such as word processing, spreadsheet, or database programs.
4. Popular ~~first generation~~scripting languages include JavaScript, Perl, Rexx, Tcl, and VBScript.
5. ~~Rexx~~XML separates the Web page content from its format, allowing the Web browser to display the contents of a Web page in a form appropriate for the display device.
6. SQL is an example of a ~~second~~fourth generation language.
7. Three popular ~~markup languages~~Web page authoring programs are Dreamweaver MX, Flash MX, and FrontPage.

Quiz Yourself 13-3

1. A language's ~~logic~~syntax is the set of grammar and rules that specifies how to write instructions for a solution algorithm.
2. An error in a program is known as a ~~beta~~bug.
3. In structured design, the programmer typically begins with a ~~detailed~~ general design and moves toward a more ~~general~~detailed design.
4. The concept of packaging data and procedures into a single object is called ~~easing~~encapsulation.
5. The program development cycle consists of these six steps: analyze requirements, design solution, validate design, implement design, test solution, and ~~hardcode~~document solution.
6. Three basic control structures are sequence, selection, and ~~pseudocode~~repetition.
7. True Statement

Quiz Yourself 14-1

1. The main task of executive managers is to make ~~short~~long-term, ~~tactical~~strategic decisions.
2. An information system is a set of hardware, software, data, procedures, and people that works together to produce information.
3. A ~~human resources~~marketing information system serves as a central repository for the tasks of the marketing functional unit.
4. True Statement
5. Decision support systems ~~capture and store the knowledge of human experts and then imitate human reasoning and decision making~~help users analyze data and make decisions.
6. Enterprise resource planning ~~is a combination of databases, software, and procedures that organizes and allows access to various forms of documents and files~~provides centralized integrated software to help manage and coordinate the ongoing activities of the functional units of an enterprise, including manufacturing and distribution, accounting, finance, sales, product planning, and human resources.

Quiz Yourself 14-2

1. ~~A portal~~An extranet is the portion of a company's network that allows customers or suppliers of a company to access parts of an enterprise's intranet.
2. True Statement
3. A VPN ~~is a server that is placed on a network with the sole purpose of providing storage to users and information systems attached to the network~~provides mobile users, remote offices, vendors, or customers a secure connection to the company network server, as if they had a private line.
4. A workflow application ~~helps an enterprise collect, archive, index, and retrieve its resources~~is a program that assists in the management and tracking of all the activities in a business process from start to finish.

Quiz Yourself 14-3

1. ~~Network attached storage~~A storage area network is a high-speed network with the sole purpose of providing storage to other servers to which it is attached.
2. Scalability ~~refers to the ability of an information system to share information with other information systems~~is a measure of how well computer hardware, software, or an information system can grow to meet increasing performance demands.
3. A differential backup copies only the files that have changed since the last full ~~or last incremental~~ backup.
4. ~~A full~~An incremental backup is the fastest backup method, requiring only minimal storage.

5. An ~~emergency~~backup plan specifies how a company's users back up files and equipment to resume information processing.
6. True Statement

Quiz Yourself 15-1

1. A ~~corporate trainer~~computer technician installs, maintains, and repairs hardware; installs, upgrades, and configures software; and troubleshoots hardware problems.
2. A ~~Webmaster~~chief security officer is responsible for physical security of a company's property and people and in charge of securing computing resources.
3. Career opportunities in the computer ~~equipment~~software field involve designing and programming a variety of software.
4. True Statement
5. More than 79 percent of IT employees work at companies whose primary business is not computer-related.
6. ~~Network administrators~~Help desk specialists answer hardware, software, or networking questions in person, over the telephone, and/or in a chat room.

Quiz Yourself 15-2

1. ~~A transfer statement~~An articulation agreement ensures that if you transfer to a college or university, you will receive credit for most of the courses taken at your current school.
2. Computer ~~science~~information systems programs focus on how to apply computing skills.
3. Job-search Web sites such as Monster provide job-search services for ~~a fee~~free to job seekers.
4. Students often complete trade school programs in a ~~longer~~shorter time than college and university programs.
5. True Statement

Quiz Yourself 15-3

1. True Statement
2. If you do not pass a certification exam, you ~~do not~~ have to pay a fee again to retake the test.
3. ~~Industrialization~~Certification is a process of verifying the technical knowledge of an individual who has demonstrated competence in a particular area.
4. Salary surveys show that certification helps influence pay ~~decreases~~increases.
5. The Microsoft ~~Certified Professional Developer~~Office Specialist certification tests a user's basic (specialist) and advanced (expert) skills of Microsoft Office programs.

APPENDIX C
Computer Acronyms

Acronym	Description	Page
0NF	zero normal form	540
1NF	first normal form	540
2NF	second normal form	540
3GL	third-generation language	666
3NF	third normal form	540
4GL	fourth-generation language	674
AA	Audible Audio	87
AAC	Advanced Audio Coding	87
AC	alternating current	213
ACE	Adobe Certified Expert	796
ACM	Association for Computing Machinery	789, 790
ADA	Americans with Disabilities Act	266
ADC	analog-to-digital converter	38
ADSL	asymmetric digital subscriber line	482
AES	advanced encryption standard	592
AGP	Accelerated Graphics Port	212
AI	artificial intelligence	730
AIFF	Audio Interchange File Format	87
AIS	Association for Information Systems	789
AITP	Association of Information Technology Professionals	789, 790
Ajax	Asynchronous JavaScript and XML	683
ALGOL	ALGOrithmic Language	675
ALU	arithmetic logic unit	188
AMD	Advanced Micro Devices	219
ANN	artificial neural network	750
ANSI	American National Standards Institute	690
AOL	America Online	72, 82
APCUG	Association of Personal Computer Users Group	790
APL	A Programming Language	675
ARPA	Advanced Research Projects Agency	69
ARPANET	Advanced Research Projects Agency network	69
ASCII	American Standard Code for Information Interchange	195, 518
ASF	Advanced Streaming (or Systems) Format	87
ASP	application service provider	164
ATC	advanced transfer cache	201
ATM	Asynchronous Transfer Mode	482, 483
ATM	automated teller machine	262
AUP	acceptable use policy	565
AWC	Association for Women in Computing	789
B2B	business-to-business	92, 735
B2C	business-to-consumer	92
BASIC	Beginner's All-purpose Symbolic Instruction Code	675
BI	business intelligence	719
BIOS	basic input/output system	400
Bit	binary digit	195, 518
BLOB	binary large object	518
BLS	Bureau of Labor Statistics	779
BMP	bit map	85
BPA	business process automation	719
BPL	broadband over power lines	492

Acronym	Description	Page
BPM	business process management	719
BSA	Business Software Alliance	571
BTW	by the way	100
C2C	consumer-to-consumer	92
CA	certificate authority	573
CAD	computer-aided design	151, 327, 722
CAE	computer-aided engineering	722
CAI	computer-aided instruction	160
CAM	computer-aided manufacturing	36, 722
CASE	computer-aided software engineering	642-43
CAT	computerized adaptive testing	795
CATV	cable television	482
CBT	computer-based training	160, 790
CCD	charge-coupled device	251
CCE	Certified Computer Examiner	799
CCIE	Cisco Certified Internetwork Expert	800
CCNP	Cisco Certified Network Professional	798
CD	compact disc	8, 9, 17, 27, 89, 357, 819
CDMA	Code Division Multiple Access	494, 499
CDP	continuous data protection	747
CD-R	compact disc-recordable	371
CD-ROM	compact disc read-only memory	369-70
CD-RW	compact disc-rewritable	371, 576
CE	computer engineering	787
CEECS	Certified Electronic Evidence Collection Specialist	799
CEO	Chief Executive Officer	717, 718
CERT/CC	Computer Emergency Response Team Coordination Center	558
CES	Consumer Electronics Show	790
CF	CompactFlash	376
CFCE	Certified Forensic Computer Examiner	799
CFO	Chief Financial Officer	717
CGI	Common Gateway Interface	679
CIM	computer-integrated manufacturing	722, 724, 765, 768, 769, 770, 772
CIO	chief information officer	717, 725, 749, 780
CIPA	Children's Internet Protection Act	480, 585
CIS	computer information systems	786
CISSP	Certified Information Systems Security Professional	799
CIW	Certified Internet Webmaster	800
CLP	Certified Linux Professional	797
CMOS	complementary metal-oxide semiconductor	203
CMS	content management system	732, 766
CNA	Certified Novell Administrator	798
CNE	Certified Novell Engineer	798
Coax	coaxial cable	493
COBOL	COmmon Business-Oriented Language	53, 668, 699
COM port	communications port	207
COM+	Component Object Model extension	688
COO	Chief Operations Officer	717
COPPA	Children's Online Privacy Protection Act	585

Appendix C *Computer Acronyms*

Acronym	Description	Page
CORBA	Common Object Request Broker Architecture	688
CPU	central processing unit	8, 187
CRM	customer relationship management	730, 751, 765, 768
CRT	cathode-ray tube	307
CS	computer science	786-87
CSDP	Certified Software Development Professional	797
CSO	chief security officer	646
CSS	cascading style sheets	682
CST	Computer Service Technician	381
CTS	carpal tunnel syndrome	588
CUG	C/C++ Users Group	790
CVS	computer vision syndrome	588
CWP	Certified Web Professional	800
DA	database analyst	538, 780, 786
DAC	digital-to-analog converter	38
DBA	database administrator	538, 781
DBMS	database management system	515
DDoS attack	distributed denial of service attack	562
DDR SDRAM	double data rate synchronous dynamic random access memory	199
DFD	data flow diagram	632-33
DHCP	Dynamic Host Configuration Protocol	102
DHTML	Dynamic Hypertext Markup Language	682
DIMM	dual inline memory module	199
DL	distance learning	166
DLP projector	digital light processing projector	324
DMCA	Digital Millennium Copyright Act	585
DMS	Document Management System	736
DNS	domain name system	74
DOM	document object model	682
DOS	Disk Operating System	417
DoS attack	denial of service attack	562
Dpi	dots per inch	252, 313
DPMA	Data Processing Management Association	789
DRAM	dynamic random access memory	199
DSL	Digital Subscriber Line	70, 449, 482, 486
DSP	digital signal processor	38
DSS	decision support system	728
DTD	document type definition	698
DTP	desktop publishing	152
DTV	digital television	306
DV camera	digital video camera	253
DVD	digital versatile disc or digital video disc	8, 17, 59, 89, 357, 819
DVD+R	digital versatile disc or digital video disc recordable	373
DVD-R	digital versatile disc or digital video disc recordable	373
DVD+RAM	digital versatile disc or digital video disc + random access memory	373
DVD-ROM	digital versatile disc or digital video disc read-only memory	9, 372
DVD+RW	digital versatile disc or digital video disc + rewritable	373
DVD-RW	digital versatile disc or digital video disc + rewritable	373
DVI	Digital Video Interface	305

Acronym	Description	Page
EB	exabyte	356
EBCDIC	Extended Binary Coded Decimal Interchange Code	195, 518
E-book	electronic book	61, 303
E-commerce	electronic commerce	28, 30, 60, 61, 91-92
ECPA	Electronic Communications Privacy Act	585
EDGE	Enhanced Data GSM Environment	494
EDI	electronic data interchange	470, 735, 767, 771
EEPROM	electrically erasable programmable read-only memory	202
E-file	electronic filing	157
E-form	electronic form	530
EFS	Encryption File System	592
EFT	electronic funds transfer	470
EIDE	Enhanced Integrated Drive Electronics	363
EIS	executive information system	728, 765, 773
E-mail	electronic mail	12, 31, 69, 92-95, 101, 161, 462
EMR	electromagnetic radiation	308
ENIAC	Electronic Numerical Integrator and Computer	52
EP	Enterprise Portal	541
ERD	entity-relationship diagram	632
E-retail	electronic retail	737-38
ERM system	employee relationship management system	721
ERP	enterprise resource planning	731
E-tail	electronic retail	737–38
ETS ICT	Education Testing Service Information and Communication Technology	785
EULA	end-user license agreement	571
E-zine	electronic magazine	639
FAQ	frequently asked questions	6, 100
Fax	facsimile	322-23
Fortran	FORmula TRANslator	53, 675
FRED	Forensic Recovery of Digital Evidence	612
FTP	File Transfer Protocol	68, 96, 134, 161, 462
FWIW	for what it's worth	100
FYI	for your information	100
GB	gigabyte	197, 356
Gbps	giga [billion] bits per second	476
GHz	gigahertz	189
GIF	Graphics Interchange Format	85
GIGO	garbage in, garbage out	10, 516
GLBA	Graham-Leach-Bliley Act	585
GPRS	General Packet Radio Service	494
GPS	global positioning system	466, 513
GPU	graphics processing unit	305
GSM	Global System for Mobile Communications	494
GUI	graphical user interface	15, 137, 402, 420, 421
HD	high density	364
HD-DVD	high-density-DVD	372
HDTV	high-definition television	306-7
HIPAA	Health Insurance Portability and Accountability Act	381, 585
HomeRF network	home radio frequency network	490
HP	Hewlett-Packard	329
HR	Human Resources	720
HRIS	Human Resources Information Systems	721
HTML	Hypertext Markup Language	678

Acronym	Description	Page
http	Hypertext Transfer Protocol	76, 477
Hz	hertz	189
I-4	International Information Integrity Institute	593
IBM	International Business Machines	53, 54, 55, 138, 751, 783
IC	integrated circuit	186
ICANN	Internet Corporation for Assigned Names and Numbers	74
I-CASE	integrated computer-aided software engineering	643
ICCA	Independent Computer Consultants Association	789
ICCP	Institute for Certification of Computer Professionals	793
ICRA	Internet Content Rating Association	587
ICSA Labs	International Computer Security Association Labs	647
IEEE	Institute of Electrical and Electronics Engineers	789
IM	instant messaging	98
IMDb	Internet Movie Database	536
IMHO	in my humble opinion	100, 627
Interactive TV	interactive television	307
IOUG	Independent Oracle Users Group	790
IP	intellectual property	579
IP address	Internet Protocol address	73, 102
IPng	Internet Protocol Next Generation	102
IPO chart	input, processing, output chart	686
IPv6	Internet Protocol version 6	102
IR	infrared	494
IrDA	Infrared Data Association	210, 478
IRQ	interrupt request	409
IS	information system	25, 620, 720-32
ISDN	Integrated Services Digital Network	482
ISP	Internet service provider	72
ISSA	Information Systems Security Association	789
IT	information technology	25, 717, 778
ITAA	Information Technology Association of America	776
J2EE	Java 2 Platform, Enterprise Edition	669, 735, 797
JAD session	joint-application design session	626
JIT compiler	just-in-time compiler	669, 670
JPEG	Joint Photographic Experts Group	85, 345
JUG	Java Users Groups	790
K	kilobyte	197
KB	kilobyte	197
KBps	kilobytes per second	357, 369
Kbps	kilo [thousand] bits per second	478
KM	knowledge management	730
KMS	knowledge management software	730
L1 cache	Level 1 cache	201
L2 cache	Level 2 cache	201
L3 cache	Level 3 cache	201
LAN	local area network	55, 471
LCD	liquid crystal display	304, 818
LISP	LISt Processing	675
LUGWW	Linux Users Group WorldWide	790
Mac OS	Macintosh Operating System	19
Mac OS X	Macintosh Operating System X	39, 135, 195, 420
MAN	metropolitan area network	472
MB	megabyte	197, 356
MBps	megabytes per second	357, 365

Acronym	Description	Page
Mbps	megabits per second	365, 476, 492, 494
MCA	Microsoft Certified Architect	797
MCDST	Microsoft Certified Desktop Support Technician	796
MCITP	Microsoft Certified IT Professional	800
M-commerce	mobile commerce	91
MCPD	Microsoft Certified Professional Developer	797
MCSA	Microsoft Certified Systems Administrator	797
MHz	megahertz	203
MIB	Medical Information Bureau	381, 581
MICR	magnetic-ink character recognition	260
MIDI	Musical Instrument Digital Interface	209, 246
MIPS	millions of instructions per second	190
MIS	management information system	727
MLP	multilayer perception	750
MMOG	massively multiplayer online game	822
MMS	multimedia message service	464
Modem	modulate/demodulate	9, 462, 485-86
MP	million pixels	252
MP3	Moving Pictures Experts Group Audio Layer 3 (MPEG-3)	86, 87, 89, 202
MPEG	Moving Pictures Experts Group	88
MRAM	magnetoresistive random access memory	199
MRP	Material Requirements Planning	723
MRP II	Manufacturing Resource Planning II	723, 767, 768, 769, 770, 771, 772, 773
μs	microsecond	203
ms	millisecond	203
MS-DOS	Microsoft Disk Operating System	417, 430
MSIL	Microsoft Intermediate Language	670
MSN	Microsoft Network, The	72, 82
MT/ST	Magnetic Tape/Selectric Typewriter	54
MTBF	mean time between failures	361
NACSE	National Association of Communication Systems Engineers	798
NAP	National Association of Programmers	789
NAS	network attached storage	742-43
NET Act	No Electronic Theft Act	585
Netiquette	Internet etiquette	100
NIC	network interface card	486
NLQ	near letter quality	318
NNT	NASCE Network Technician	798
ns	nanosecond	203
NSF	National Science Foundation	70
OCP	Oracle Certified Professional	800
OCR	optical character recognition	257
OIS	office information system	726
OLAP	online analytical processing	728
OLE	object linking and embedding	57
OLED	organic light emitting diode	304
OLTP	online transaction processing	727
OMR	optical mark recognition	257
OO	object-oriented	635
OODB	object-oriented database	534
OOP language	object-oriented programming language	669
OQL	object query language	535
OS	operating system	15-16, 398-425
OSI reference model	Open Systems Interconnection reference model	498

Acronym	Description	Page
OSP	online service provider	72
P2P	peer-to-peer	473-74
PATRIOT Act	Provide Appropriate Tools Required to Intercept and Obstruct Terrorism Act	585
PB	petabyte	356
PC	personal computer	19-20, 445
PC-DOS	personal computer Disk Operating System	417
PCI bus	Peripheral Component Interconnect bus	212
PCL	Printer Control Language	316
PCMCIA	Personal Computer Memory Card International Association	205
PCS	Personal Communications Services	495
PC-to-TV port	personal computer-to-television port	453
PDA	personal digital assistant	22, 31, 265, 282, 325
PDF	Portable Document Format	150
PDL	page description language	316
Perl	Practical Extraction and Report Language	680, 681, 786
PGP	Pretty Good Privacy	572
PILOT	Programmed Inquiry Learning Or Teaching	675
PIM	personal information manager	148
PIN	personal identification number	262, 567
Pixel	picture element	252, 304
PL/I	Programming Language One	675
PNG format	Portable Network Graphics format	85
POP	point of presence	72
POP	Post Office Protocol	95, 477
POP3	Post Office Protocol 3	95
POS	point of sale	261
POST	power-on self test	400
ppi	pixels (picture elements) per inch	252
Prolog	PROgramming LOGic	675
PROM chip	programmable read-only memory chip	202
ps	picosecond	203
PSTN	public switched telephone network	481
QBE	query by example	528
QT	QuickTime	87
RA	RealAudio	87
RAD	rapid application development	669, 671, 672, 673
RAID	redundant array of independent disks	741
RAM	random access memory	197, 198-200
RDRAM	Rambus dynamic random access memory	199
Rexx	REstructured eXtended eXecutor	680, 681
RFI	request for information	639
RFID	radio frequency identification	259, 476, 479
RFP	request for proposal	639
RFQ	request for quotation	639
RHCE	Red Hat Certified Engineer	797
RHCT	Red Hat Certified Technician	797
RIAA	Recording Industry Association of America	63
RIMM	Rambus inline memory module	199
ROM	read-only memory	201-2
RPG	Report Program Generator	674
Rpm	revolutions per minute	360
RSI	repetitive strain injury	587
RSS 2.0	Really Simple Syndication	84, 683
RUP	Rational Unified Process	635

Acronym	Description	Page
SAN	storage area network	742-43, 766
SATA	Serial Advanced Technology Attachment	362-63
SCNA	Security Certified Network Architect	799
SCNP	Security Certified Network Professional	799
SCSI	small computer system interface	210
SD	Secure Digital	376
SDRAM	synchronous dynamic random access memory	199, 203
SFA	sales force automation	724
S-HTTP	secure hypertext transfer protocol	574
SIGs	Special Interest Groups	789
SIMM	single inline memory module	199
SMS	short message service	463
SMTP	simple mail transfer protocol	94, 477
SOHO	small office/home office	28
SQL	Structured Query Language	534, 674
SRAM	static random access memory	199
SSCP	Systems Security Certified Practitioner	799
SSL	Secure Sockets Layer	574
SUT	system under test	648
SVGA	super video graphics array	305
SXGA	Super Extended Graphics Array	305
TB	terabyte	197, 356
Tcl	Tool Command Language	680, 681
TCP/IP	Transmission Control Protocol/Internet Protocol	477
TFT display	thin-film transistor display	304
TIFF	Tagged Image File Format	85, 345
TPC-W	Transaction Processing Performance Council Workload	648
TPS	transaction processing system	726
TRACERT	traceroute	430
TTFN	ta ta for now	100
TYVM	thank you very much	100
UGA	Ultra Extended Graphics Array	305
UL 1449 standard	Underwriters Laboratories 1449 standard	575
Ultra XGA	Ultra Extended Graphics Array	305
UMD	Universal Media Disc	372
UML	Unified Modeling Language	635, 673
UMTS	Universal Mobile Telecommunications System	494
UNIVAC I	UNIVersal Automatic Computer	52
uPC	ultra personal computer	21
UPC	Universal Product Code	258
UPS	uninterruptible power supply	451, 575
URL	Uniform Resource Locator	76
USB	universal serial bus	207, 212
User ID	user identification	410, 566
VAN	value-added network	470
VAR	value-added reseller	639
VBA	Visual Basic for Applications	676-77
VBScript	Visual Basic, Scripting Edition	680, 681
VCD	video CD	351
VoiceXML	Voice eXtensible Markup Language	528
Voice over IP	voice over Internet Protocol	99
VPE	visual programming environment	673
VPN	virtual private network	574, 736-37
VR	virtual reality	88

Acronym	Description	Page
W3C	World Wide Web Consortium	70, 327, 528
WAN	wide area network	472
WAP	Wireless Application Protocol	480
WAV	Windows waveform	87
WBT	Web-based training	166, 790
WEP	Wired Equivalent Privacy	577
Wi-Fi	wireless fidelity	478
WiMAX	Worldwide Interoperability for Microwave Access	479
WinFS	Windows Future Storage	382
WIPS	Web Interactions Per Second	648
WIRT	Web Interaction Response Time	648
WISP	wireless Internet service provider	72, 463
WLAN	wireless local area network	471

Acronym	Description	Page
WMA	Windows Media Audio	87, 89, 202
WML	wireless markup language	683, 698
WPA	Wi-Fi Protected Access	577
WWW	World Wide Web	75, 103
WYSIWYG	what you see is what you get	137
XGA	Extended Graphics Array	305
XHTML	eXtensible Hypertext Markup Language	682
XML	eXtensible Markup Language	468, 682-83, 698, 735
XP	extreme programming	695
XSL	Extensible Stylesheet Language	698
XSLT	Extensible Style Language Transformations	698
YB	yottabyte	356
ZB	zettabyte	356

INDEX

Micro Focus: The most popular personal computer COBOL program, which enables programmers to create and migrate COBOL programs to the Web. **668**

Microbrowser: Special type of browser designed for the small screens and limited computing power of Internet-enabled mobile devices. **76**

Microcode: Instructions programmers use to program a PROM chip. **202**

Microfiche: A small sheet of film, usually about 4 inches by 6 inches in size, on which microscopic images of documents are stored. **379**

Microfilm: A roll of film, usually 100 to 215 feet long, on which microscopic images of documents are stored. **379**

Microphone, 7, 322
  input using, 245, 246
  purchasing desktop computer and, 447, 449
  purchasing Tablet PC and, 456
  sound card and, 204
  video conference using, 254

Microprocessor: Term used by some computer and chip manufacturers to refer to a processor chip for a personal computer. **187.** *See also* **Processor**
  development of, 55

Microsecond (μs), 203

Microsoft, 39, 55, 56, 57, 58, 59, 60, 61, 62, 63, 65, **169**
  ActiveX, 679
  application software, 148
  CEO of, 803
  certification programs, 792, 796, 797, 800
  ClearType technologies, 456
  legal issues, 60, 62
  MS-DOS, 195
  .NET architecture, 671
  operating system, 15, 135, 195. *See also* **Windows XP**
  software piracy prevention and, 571

Microsoft Certified Desktop Support Technician (MCDST): Application software certification that tests a user's skills solving problems associated with applications that run on Windows XP and the operating system itself. **796.** *See also* **MCDST**

Microsoft Certified IT Professional (MCITP): Database certification that tests skills required to use SQL Server 2005 to design or install, manage, and maintain a database system. **800**

Microsoft Certified Professional Developer (MCPD): Programmer/developer certification that tests knowledge of developing Web or Windows-based applications using programs in the Visual Studio 2005 suite and the .NET framework. **797**

Microsoft Certified Systems Administrator (MCSA): Operating systems certification that tests technical expertise in one of several areas, including managing and troubleshooting Windows operating systems. **797**

Microsoft FrontPage, 537

Microsoft Intermediate Language (MSIL): Resulting object code in C#. **670.** *See also* **MSIL**

Microsoft Internet Explorer: Web browser included with the Windows operating system, starting with Windows 98. 59, 75, **417**
  VBScript and, 681

Microsoft Network, The (MSN), 72, 82
  rating system for Web sites, 587

Microsoft Office, 60, 148
  elements of, 148
  online meetings using, 467

Microsoft Office, recording macro using, 677

Microsoft Office OneNote 2003, 138

Microsoft Office Specialist (Office Specialist): Application software certification that tests a user's basic (specialist) and advanced (expert) skills of Microsoft Office products. **796**

Microsoft Office System, 148

Microsoft Outlook, 93

Microsoft Reader, 303

Microsoft Windows operating system. *See* Windows operating system

Microsoft Word, 138, 141

Microwave station: Earth-based reflective dish that contains the antenna, transceivers, and other equipment necessary for microwave communications. **496**

Microwaves: Radio waves that provide a high-speed signal transmission. **495**

Middle management: Level of management responsible for implementing the strategic decision of executive management. **718**

MIDI: Short for Musical Instrument Digital Interface. **209, 246.** *See also* **Musical Instrument Digital Interface**

MIDI port: Special type of serial port that connects the system unit to a musical instrument, such as an electronic keyboard. **209**

Midrange server: Server that is more powerful and larger than a workstation computer, typically supporting several hundred and sometimes up to a few thousand connected computers at the same time. 19, **23**

Military intelligence officers, certification of, 799

Millisecond (ms), 203

Millions of instructions per second, 190. *See also* **MIPS**

Millipede, 360

MIMO: Multiple-input multiple-output. **478**

Miniature mobile storage media, 375–78

Mini disc, digital cameras using, 250

Mini discs: Optical disc with a size of three inches or less used by smaller computers and devices. **366**

Mini-DVD media, 373

Minutiae, 268

MIPS (millions of instructions per second): Measurement of a system clock's speed. **190**

Mirroring: RAID storage design that writes data on two disks at the same time to duplicate the data. **741.** *See also* **Level 1**

MIS, 727. *See also* **Management information system (MIS)**

MIS (management information system) manager, 749

Missing person or pet, GPS tracking and, 466–67

MITS, Inc., 55

MLP, 750. *See also* **Multilayer perceptron (MLP)**

MMOG. *See* Massively multiplayer online game

MMS (Multimedia message service): Service that allows users to send graphics, pictures, video clips, and sound files, as well as short text messages to another smart phone, PDA, or computer. **464.** *See also* **Picture messaging**

Mobile commerce. *See* **M-commerce**

Mobile computer: Personal computer that a user can carry from place to place. 19, **20**
  purchasing, 444–45, 452–56

Mobile device: Computing device small enough for a user to hold in his or her hand. 19, **20**, 21–22
  data collection using, 261
  display device, 303
  flash memory and, 202, 205
  GPS capability, 466
  input devices, 243, 244, 247–49
  Internet access, 462, 478, 480
  LCD screens, 302
  miniature hard disk, 363
  personal, 282–97
  PC Card modem, 485
  PDA. *See* **PDA (personal digital assistant)**
  printer, 317
  security risks, 570
  storage media for, 355, 375–78, 380
  system unit, 185
  theft of, 569, 570
  touch screens, 243
  viruses and, 250
  Web access and, 72, 683, 698

Mobile printer: Small, lightweight, battery-powered printer used by a mobile user to print from a notebook computer, Tablet PC, PDA, or smart phone while traveling. **317**

Mobile users: Users who work on a computer while away from a main office or school. 26, **29**, 31
  e-commerce and, 91
  input devices, 265
  Internet access by, 70–71
  mobile printers, 317
  output devices, 303, 317, 325
  processor selection, 215, 219
  sales force, 724
  storage and, 355, 375–78, 380
  system unit, 213–15
  virtual private network use, 736
  wireless security and, 576

Mockup: Sample of the input or output that contains actual data. **641**

Models, decision support system (DSS), 728

Modem: Communications device that converts a computer's digital signals to analog signals. 9, 462, **485–86.** *See also* **Dial-up modem**
  broadband, 485, 492
  bus connection, 212
  cable, 70, 485
  dial-up, 485
  digital, 482, 485
  DSL, 482, 485, 486
  fax, 322, 323
  Internet access using, 70
  ISDN, 482, 485
  PC Card, 485
  port, 207
  purchasing desktop computer and, 447
  surge protection and, 575, 576
  wireless, 485

Moderated newsgroup: A newsgroup with a moderator who decides if an article is relevant to the discussion. **97**

Moderator: Person who reviews content of a newsgroup article and then posts it, if appropriate. **97**

Moderator (JAD session), 626

Modula-2: A successor to Pascal used for developing systems software. **675**

Modulate/modulation: To change into an analog signal. 38, **485**

Module: Smaller sections into which a main routine is broken down by a programmer during structured design. **687.** *See also* **Subroutines**
  flowchart, 690
  pseudocode, 690–92

Money
  counterfeiting, 315
  transferring using network, 470

Monitor: Display device that is packaged as a separate peripheral. 8, **302–8**
  CRT. *See* **CRT monitor**
  flat-panel, 302–6
  health issues, 588
  largest, 306
  purchasing desktop computer and, 447, 449
  purchasing notebook computer and, 452

Mono, 328

Monochrome: Display device capability in which information appears in one color on a different color background. **302**

Monster, 803

Moore, Gordon, 193, 219

Moore's Law, 193, 219

Morphing, 350

Motherboard: Main circuit board of the system unit, which has some electronic components attached to it and others built into it. 8, 185, **186.** *See also* **System board**
  memory slots on, 199

Motion capture technology, 802

Motorola, 782

Motorola processor: Processor used in Apple computers that have a design different from the Intel-style processor. **190, 191, 192**

Mouse: Pointing device that fits comfortably under the palm of a user's hand. 7, **239–40**
  BIOS testing, 400
  connections, 239
  creator of, 269
  left-handed users, 240
  manufacturer, 269
  purchasing desktop computer and, 448, 449
  repetitive strain injuries and, 238, 587
  types, 239
  using, 136, 240

Mouse gestures: Capability that allows users to perform certain operations by holding a mouse button while moving the mouse in a particular pattern. **240**

Mouse pad: Rectangular rubber or foam pad that provides traction for a mechanical mouse. **239**

Mouse pointer: Small symbol displayed on a computer screen whose location and shape changes as a user moves a mouse. **239**

Mouse rollover: Event that occurs when text, a graphic, or other object changes as the user moves the mouse pointer over an object on the screen. **681.** *See also* **mouseover**

Mouseover: Event that occurs when text, a graphic, or other object changes as the user moves the mouse pointer over an object on the screen. **681.** *See also* **mouse rollover**

PHOTO CREDITS

rights reserved.; Figure 5-34b, Copyright © Colin Young-Wolff/Photo Edit — All rights reserved.; Figure 5-35, Copyright ©Susan Van Etten/Photo Edit — All rights reserved.; Figure 5-36, Courtesy of Tibbett & Britten Group; Looking Ahead 5-1, © Michael Pohuski/Getty Images; Figure 5-37, Copyright © Spencer Grant/Photo Edit — All rights reserved.; Figure 5-39, Courtesy of Symbol Technologies; Figure 5-40, Copyright ©Dennis MacDonald/Photo Edit — All rights reserved.; Figure 5-41, © Steve Dunwell/Index Stock Imagery; Figure 5-42a, © AP/WIDE WORLD PHOTOS; Figure 5-42b, Courtesy of Microsoft Corporation; Figure 5-43, Courtesy of Recognition Systems, Inc.; Figure 5-44, © BORIS ROESSLER/dpa/Landov; Figure 5-45a, Courtesy of Athena Smartcard Solutions - www.athena-scs.com; Figure 5-46a, © Comstock Images; Figure 5-46b, © Paul Barton/CORBIS; Figure 5-46c, © C. Görling/zefa/Corbis; Figure 5-46d, © Mark Harmel/Alamy; Figure 5-46e, © Dynamic Graphics Group/IT Stock Free/Alamy; Figure 5-47, Courtesy of www.keytools.com; Figure 5-49, Courtesy of NaturalPoint, Inc.; Looking Ahead 5-2, Courtesy of rosner | touch | mp3blue; Career Corner, © Romilly Lockyer/Getty Images; Technology Trailblazer 1, © 2002 Gary Reyes/San Jose Mercury News. All rights reserved; Technology Trailblazer 2, © AP/WIDE WORLD PHOTOS; **Special Feature 5 — Personal Mobile Devices:** Opener1, © PicturePress; Opener2, © Photo by China Photos/Getty Images; Opener 3, Courtesy of Research In Motion Limited (RIM); Figure 1a, © Medioimages; Figure 1b, © Thinkstock/Getty Images; Figure 1c, © Jiri Rezac/Alamy; Figure 1d, Courtesy of Research In Motion Limited (RIM); Figure 2a, Courtesy of Nokia; Figure 2b, © AP/WIDE WORLD PHOTOS; Figure 2c, Courtesy of Samsung; Figure 3a, © SUNNYphotography.com/Alamy; Figure 3b, Courtesy of palm, Inc. Palm, Treo, Tungsten, Zire, LifeDrive, VersaMail,; Blazer, Addit, Handspring, "T" stylized, "Z" stylized, stylizations and design marks associated with all the preceding, and trade dress associated with; Palm, Inc.'s products, are among the trademarks or registered trademarks owned by or licensed to Palm, Inc.; Figure 3c, Courtesy of Garmin Ltd.; Figure 3d, Courtesy of Think Outside Inc.; Figure 3e1, ©2005 Veo Intl., All Rights Reserved.; Figure 3e2, © 2005 Dell Inc. All Rights Reserved.; Figure 4a, Courtesy of Palm, Inc. Palm, Treo, Tungsten, Zire, LifeDrive, VersaMail, Blazer, Addit, Handspring, "T" stylized, "Z" stylized, stylizations and design marks associated with all the preceding, and trade dress associated with; Palm, Inc.'s products, are among the trademarks or registered trademarks owned by or licensed to Palm, Inc.; Figure 6a, © Art Vandalay/Getty Images; Figure 6g, Courtesy of Blue Nomad Software; Figure 7a, © Peter Griffith/Masterfile www.masterfile.com; Figure 7b, Courtesy of Snapperfish, Ltd.; Figure 8a, Courtesy of Symbol Technologies; Figure 8a, © CRIS BOURONCLE/AFP/Getty Images; Figure 8c2, Courtesy of ASUSTeK Computer Inc.; Figure 9a, © Dynamic Graphics Group/Creatas/Alamy; Figure 10a, Courtesy of Symbol Technologies; Figure 10a, © Orbit/Masterfile www.masterfile.com; Figure 11a, © Erik Dreyer/Getty Images; Figure 12a1, Copyright ©Michael Newman/Photo Edit — All rights reserved.; Figure 12b,c,d, Courtesy of TruSmart Technologies; Figure 12a2, © AP/WIDE WORLD PHOTOS; Figure 15, Courtesy of Motorola, Inc.; Figure 16, Courtesy of Danger, Inc.; Figure 17, Courtesy of Motorola, Inc.; **Chapter 6:** © Stewart Cohen/Getty Images; © Comstock Images/Alamy; © Comstock Images/Alamy; © 2003 Riverdeep Interactive Learning Limited, and its licensors.; Courtesy of Hewlett-Packard Company; Courtesy of Hewlett-Packard Company; Courtesy of Hewlett-Packard Company; Courtesy of Hewlett-Packard Company; Courtesy of Hewlett-Packard Company; Figure 6-1a1, Courtesy of Nokia; Figure 6-1a2, Courtesy of IBM Corporation; Figure 6-1a3, Courtesy of NEC Display Solutions of America, Inc.; Figure 6-1b1, Courtesy of Motion Computing; Figure 6-1b1, Courtesy of FranklinCovey; Figure 6-1b2, Courtesy of Epson America, Inc.; Figure 6-1b3, Courtesy of ASUSTeK Computer Inc.; Figure 6-1b3, Courtesy of Handmark Inc.; Figure 6-1c1, Courtesy of Logitech; Figure 6-1c2, Courtesy of Apple Computer, Inc.; Figure 6-1d1, Courtesy of Nokia; Figure 6-1d2, Courtesy of NEC Display Solutions of America, Inc.; Figure 6-2, Courtesy of ViewSonic® Corporation; Figure 6-3, Courtesy of ViewSonic® Corporation; Figure 6-4a, Courtesy of Acer America Corp.; Figure 6-4b, Courtesy of Acer America Corp.; Figure 6-4c, Courtesy of palm, Inc. Palm, Treo, Tungsten, Zire, LifeDrive, VersaMail,; Blazer, Addit, Handspring, "T" stylized, "Z" stylized, stylizations and design marks associated with all the preceding, and trade dress associated with; Palm, Inc.'s products, are among the trademarks or registered trademarks owned by or licensed to Palm, Inc.; Figure 6-4d, Courtesy of Sony Ericsson Mobile Communications AB. All Rights Reserved; Looking Ahead 6-1, Courtesy of Polymer Vision; Figure 6-6, "FireGL™ V5100 is[are] used under license and is [are] a registered; trademark[s] or trademark[s] of ATI Technologies Inc. in the United States and other countries."; Figure 6-7, Courtesy of BenQ; Figure 6-8, © BananaStock/Alamy; Figure 6-9, Courtesy of NEC-Mitsubishi Electronics Display of America Inc.; Figure 6-10 Step 1, Courtesy of Intel Corporation; Figure 6-13a1, © David Muir/Masterfile; Figure 6-13a2, © Royalty-Free/CORBIS; Figure 6-13a3, © Chuck Savage/CORBIS; Figure 6-13b1, Courtesy of Nokia; Figure 6-13b2, © OSHIKAZU TSUNO/AFP/Getty Images; Figure 6-13c, © Najlah Feanny/Corbis; Figure 6-13d, Courtesy of Sony Electronics Inc.; Figure 6-13e, Courtesy of Eastman Kodak Company; Figure 6-13f, Courtesy of Epson America, Inc.; Figure 6-13g, QV3000EX camera photo courtesy of Casio Inc.; Figure 6-14a, Courtesy of Xerox Corporation; Figure 6-14a2, Courtesy of Sony Electronics Inc.; Figure 6-14b1, Courtesy of Epson America, Inc.; Figure 6-14b2, Courtesy of Epson America, Inc.; Figure 6-14c, Courtesy of Epson America, Inc.; Figure 6-16, © Gary Herrington Photography; Figure 6-17a, Courtesy of Epson America, Inc.; Figure 6-17b, Courtesy of Epson America, Inc.; Figure 6-17c1, Courtesy of Canon U.S.A, Inc.; Figure 6-17c2, © Jon Feingersh/Masterfile www.masterfile.com; Figure 6-18a, Courtesy of Xerox Corporation; Figure 6-18b, Courtesy of Xerox Corporation; Figure 6-20a, Courtesy of Mitsubishi Digital Electronics America, Inc.; Figure 6-20a2, © Royalty-Free/Corbis; Figure 6-20b, Courtesy of Canon U.S.A, Inc.; Figure 6-21, Courtesy of Canon U.S.A, Inc.; Figure 6-22, Courtesy of Seiko Instruments USA Inc.; Figure 6-23, Courtesy of MacDermid ColorSpan, Inc.; Figure 6-24, Courtesy of Oki Data Amercas, Inc.; Figure 6-25, Courtesy of Printronix, Inc.; Figure 6-26, Courtesy of Mind Computer Products; Figure 6-27, ©Jeff Greenberg/PhotoEdit Inc.; Figure 6-29, © John A Rizzo/Getty Images; Figure 6-30a, ©Spencer Grant/Photo Edit Inc.; Figure 6-30b, Courtesy of U.S. Robotics Corporation; Figure 6-30c, Courtesy of MPC Computers, LLC.; Figure 6-30d, Courtesy of MPC Computers, LLC.; Figure 6-31, Courtesy of Xerox Corporation; Figure 6-32a, Courtesy of InFocus® Corporation; Figure 6-32b, Courtesy of InFocus® Corporation; Looking Ahead 6-2, © Nick Koudis/Getty Images; Figure 6-33a, © 2005 Guillemot Corporation S.A. All rights reserved. Thrustmaster® is a; registered trademark of Guillemot Corporation S.A. Ferrari® is a registered trademark of Ferrari S.p.A. All other trademarks and brand names are hereby acknowledged and are property of their respective owners. Figure 6-33b, © 2005 Guillemot Corporation S.A. All rights reserved. Thrustmaster® is a registered trademark of Guillemot Corporation S.A. Ferrari® is a registered trademark of Ferrari S.p.A. All other trademarks and brand names are hereby acknowledged and are property of their respective owners.; Figure 6-34a, © Comstock Images; Figure 6-34b, © Paul Barton/CORBIS; Figure 6-34c, © C. Görling/zefa/Corbis; Figure 6-34d, © Mark Harmel/Alamy; Figure 6-34e, © Dynamic Graphics Group/IT Stock Free/Alamy; Figure 6-36a, Courtesy of Enabling Technologies; Figure 6-36b, © Don Farrall/Getty Images; Figure 6-37, Courtesy of Intel Corporation; Career Corner, © Robert Llewellyn/Imagestate; Technology Trailblazer 1, ©Fujifotos/The Image Works; Technology Trailblazer 2, © AP/WIDE WORLD PHOTOS; **Special Feature 6 —Digital Imaging and Video Technology:** Opener, © Photo Resource Hawaii/Alamy; Opener, ©Masterfile (Royalty-Free Div.) www.masterfile.com; Opener, © Design Pics Inc./Alamy; Opener, © Brian Pieters/Masterfile www.masterfile.com; Opener, © BananaStock/Alamy; Figure 1, © David Madison/Getty Images; Figure 1a, Courtesy of Nikon USA; Figure 1b, Courtesy of Sony Electronics Inc.; Figure 1c, Courtesy of BenQ; Figure 1d, Courtesy of Sony Electronics Inc.; Figure 1e, Courtesy of Canon USA Inc.; Figure 1f, Courtesy of Sony Electronics Inc.; Figure 1g, Courtesy of JVC Company of America; Figure 2a, Courtesy of Sony Electronics Inc.; Figure 2b, Courtesy of Canon U.S.A, Inc.; Figure 2c, Courtesy of Phase One Inc.; Figure 5a, Courtesy of Pretec Electronics Corp.; Figure 5b, Courtesy of Lexar Media, Inc.; Figure 5c, Courtesy of Sony Electronics Inc.; Figure 6, Courtesy of SanDisk Corporation; Fgure 08, Courtesy of Pixel Magic Imaging™, Inc; Figure 9, Courtesy of Nero Inc.; Figure 10a, Courtesy of Sony Electronics Inc.; Figure 10b, Courtesy of Matsushita Electric Corporation of America; Figure 10c, Courtesy of Logitech; Figure 11a, Courtesy of Sony Electronics Inc.; Figure 11b, © Art Vandalay/Getty Images; Figure 12a, Courtesy of JVC Company of America; Figure 12b, Courtesy of Pinnacle Systems, Inc.; Figure 12c, Courtesy of Matsushita Electric Corporation of America; Figure 12d, © Meeke/zefa/Corbis; Figure 13, Courtesy of Adobe Systems Incorporated; Figure 16, Courtesy of Adobe Systems Incorporated; Figure 17, Courtesy of Microsoft Corporation; Figure 18, Courtesy of Microsoft Corporation; Figure 19, Courtesy of Mediachance; **Chapter 7:** © Ken Welsh/Alamy; © Leslie Garland Picture Library/Alamy; © Alex Mares-Manton/Getty Images; © Cale Merege/Bloomberg News /Landov; © John Froschauer/Bloomberg News /Landov; © Steve Allen/Alamy; © Mark Wilson/Getty Images; Courtesy of Iomega; Courtesy of SanDisk Corporation; Figure 7-1a, © Masterfile (Royalty Free Div.) www.masterfile.com; Figure 7-1b, Photo Courtesy of Iomega Corporation. Copyright © 2003 Iomega; Corporation. All Rights Reserved. Zip is a registered trademark in the United States and/or other countries. Iomega, the stylized "i" logo and product images; are property of Iomega Corporation in the United States and/or other countries.; Figure 7-1c, Courtesy of Seagate Technology; Figure 7-1d, Courtesy of Toshiba America Information Systems, Inc.; Figure 7-1e, Courtesy of Western Digital; Figure 7-1f, Courtesy of Fujitsu Siemens Computers; Figure 7-1g, Courtesy of Quantum Corporation; Figure 7-1h, Courtesy of Kingston Technology Company, Inc.; Figure 7-1i, Courtesy of Sandisk Corporation; Figure 7-1j, Courtesy of Lexar Media, Inc.; Figure 7-1k, © Aaron Flaum/Alamy; Figure 7-6a, © Gary Herrington Photography; Figure 7-6b, Courtesy of Western Digital; Figure 7-8, Courtesy of Maxtor Corporation; Figure 7-11, Courtesy of Intel Corporation; Figure 7-13a, Courtesy of Maxtor Corporation; Figure 7-13b, Photo Courtesy of Iomega Corporation. Copyright © 2005 Iomega; Corporation. All Rights Reserved. Zip is a registered trademark in the United States and/or other countries. Iomega, the stylized "i" logo and product images; are property of Iomega Corporation in the United States and/or other countries.; Figure 7-14a, Courtesy of Quantum Corp.; Figure 7-14b,c, Photo Courtesy of Iomega Corporation. Copyright © 2005 Iomega; Corporation. All Rights Reserved. Zip is a registered trademark in the United States and/or other countries. Iomega, the stylized "i" logo and product images; are property of Iomega Corporation in the United States and/or other countries; Figure 7-15a, b, Photo Courtesy of Iomega Corporation. Copyright © 2005 Iomega; Corporation. All Rights Reserved. Zip is a registered trademark in the United States and/or other countries. Iomega, the stylized "i" logo and product images; are property of Iomega Corporation in the United States and/or other countries.; Looking Ahead 7-1, Courtesy of IBM Corporation; Figure 7-17, © Gary Herrington Photography; Figure 7-21a, Courtesy of Merriam-Webster Inc.; Figure 7-21b, c, Courtesy of Memorex Products, Inc.; Figure 7-21d, Coutesy of DeLorme; Figure 7-21e, f, Courtesy of Memorex Products, Inc.; Figure 7-22a, Courtesy of Encyclopædia Britannica, Inc.; Figure 7-22b, Courtesy of Microsoft Corporation; Figure 7-22c, © Gary Herrington Photography; Figure 7-23c, Courtesy of NEC Solutions (America), Inc.; Figure 7-23d, Courtesy of Ulead Systems, Inc.; Figure 7-23e, © Steven Brahms/Bloomberg News /Landov; Figure 7-24a, © 2005 Dell Inc. All Rights Reserved.; Figure 7-24b, Courtesy of DeLorme; Figure 7-26, Courtesy of Sony DADC; Looking Ahead 7-2, Courtesy of Blu-ray Disc Association; Looking Ahead 7-2, HD DVD logo is a Trademark of DVD Format/Logo Licensing Corporation.; Figure 7-27, Courtesy of Sony Electronics Inc.; Figure 7-28a, Courtesy of Toshiba America Information Systems, Inc.; Figure 7-28b, Courtesy of Toshiba America Information Systems, Inc.; Figure 7-30a, ©Sonda Dawes/The Image Works; Figure 7-30b, Courtesy of Delkin Devices, Inc.; Figure 7-30c, Courtesy of Lexar Media, Inc.; Figure 7-31, Courtesy of Sandisk Corporation; Figure 7-32, Courtesy of Delkin Devices, Inc.; Figure 7-33, Toshiba America Information Systems, Inc.; Figure 7-34, © Jean-Yves Bruel/Masterfile; Figure 7-35a, Copyright ©Bill Aron/Photo Edit — All rights reserved.; Figure 7-35b, Copyright ©Bill Aron/Photo Edit — All rights reserved.; Figure 7-37, © Wes Thompson/CORBIS; Figure 7-38a, © Comstock Images; Figure 7-38b, © Paul Barton/CORBIS; Figure 7-38c, © C. Görling/zefa/Corbis; Figure 7-38d, © Mark Harmel/Alamy; Figure 7-38e, © Dynamic Graphics Group/IT Stock Free/Alamy; Career Corner, © Noel Hendrickson/Masterfile; Technology Trailblazer 1, Courtesy of Al Shugart International; Technology Trailblazer 2, Courtesy of IBM Research; **Chapter 8:** © Daisuke Morita/Getty Images; © Masterfile (Royalty-Free Division); Courtesy of Microsoft Corporation; Courtesy of Symantec Corporation; © Royalty-Free/Corbis; © David Young-Wolff/Alamy; © Koopman/CORBIS; Courtesy of Microsoft Corporation; Courtesy of Sony Ericsson Mobile Communications AB. All Rights Reserved.; Figure 8-1a,; Figure 8-1b, Courtesy of Kingston Technology; Figure 8-1c, Courtesy of Lexmark; Figure 8-1d, Courtesy of Acer America Corp.; Figure 8-1e, Courtesy of Hewlett-Packard Company; Figure 8-3, Step 7, Courtesy of Hewlett-Packard Company; Figure 8-5, Courtesy of Fujitsu Siemens Computers; Figure 8-7a, Courtesy of Kingston Technology; Figure 8-7b, Courtesy of Seagate Technology; Figure 8-8a, Courtesy of IBM Corporation; Figure 8-8b, Courtesy of Seagate Technology; Figure 8-8c, Courtesy of Lexmark; Figure 8-25a, © Getty Images; Figure 8-25b, Courtesy of Microsoft Corporation; Figure 8-26, Courtesy of Microsoft Corporation; Figure 8-28, Courtesy of Apple Computer, Inc.; Figure 8-29, Courtesy of K Desktop Environment, KDE.org; Figure 8-30, Courtesy of Red Hat; Looking Ahead 8-1, Courtesy of The Gimp, ewing@isc.tamu.edu; Figure 8-31, Courtesy of BERNINA® of America, Inc.; Figure 8-32a, © 2005 Dell Inc. All Rights Reserved.; Figure 8-32b, Courtesy of Audiovox; Figure 8-33a, Courtesy of palm, Inc. Palm, Treo, Tungsten, Zire, LifeDrive, VersaMail, Blazer, Addit, Handspring, "T" stylized, "Z" stylized, stylizations and design marks associated with all the preceding, and trade dress associated with; Palm, Inc.'s products, are among the trademarks or registered trademarks owned by or licensed to Palm, Inc.; Figure 8-33b, Courtesy of Kyocera; Figure 8-34, Courtesy of Sharp Electronics; Figure 8-35a, Courtesy of UIQ Technology; Figure 8-35b, Courtesy of Sony Ericsson Mobile Communications AB. All Rights Reserved.; Figure 8-37, Courtesy of Symantec Corporation; Figure 8-38, Courtesy of WinZip International L LC. WinZip is a registered trademark of; WinZip International LLC. All rights reserved. Figure 8-39, Courtesy of Nero Inc.; Figure 8-40, Courtesy of Symatec Corporation; Career Corner, © MTPA Stock/Masterfile; Technology Trailblazer 1, © AP/WIDE WORLD PHOTOS; Technology Trailblazer 2, © Kim Kulish/CORBIS; **Special Feature 8 Buyer's Guide:** Opener 1, Courtesy of Acer America, Inc.; Opener 2, Courtesy of Apple Computer; Opener 3, Courtesy of Acer America, Inc.; Figure 1a, Courtesy of Acer America, Inc.; Figure 1b1, Courtesy of Acer America, Inc.; Figure 1b2, Courtesy of ViewSonic; Figure 1b3, Courtesy of UTStarcom Personal Communications, a division of UTStarcom,; Inc.; Figure 1b4, Courtesy of palm, Inc. Palm, Treo, Tungsten, Zire, LifeDrive, VersaMail,; Blazer, Addit, Handspring, "T" stylized, "Z" stylized, stylizations and design marks associated with all the preceding, and trade dress associated with; Palm, Inc.'s products, are among the trademarks or registered trademarks owned by or licensed to Palm, Inc.; Figure 1c, © White Packert/Getty Images; Figure 4a, Courtesy of JVC; Figure 4b, Courtesy of Sandisk; Figure 4c, PRNewsFoto/SANYO Fisher Company; Figure 4d, Copyright © 2000-2005 Avid Technology, Inc. All Rights Reserved; Figure 4f, Courtesy of Seagate; Figure 4g, Courtesy of Logitech; Figure 4h, Courtesy of Microsoft; Figure 4j, Courtesy of Zoom Technologies Inc.; Figure 4k, Courtesy of ViewSonic Corporation; Figure 4l, Courtesy of Logitech; Figure 4m, Courtesy of 3Com Corporation; Figure 4n, Courtesy of EPSON America, Inc.; Figure 4o, Courtesy of Intel Corporation; Figure 4p, Courtesy of Kingston Technology; Figure 4q, Courtesy of UMAX; Figure 4s, Courtesy of Logitech; Figure 4t, Courtesy of Logitech; Figure 4u, Courtesy of Sandisk; Figure 4v, Courtesy of 3Com Corporation; Figure 4w, Courtesy of D-Link Corporation/D-Link Systems, Inc; Figure 4x, Courtesy of Iomega; Figure 12, PRNewsFoto/Mindjet LLC; Figure 13, Courtesy of Toshiba America Information Systems, Inc.; Figure 14, Courtesy of InFocus Corporation; Figure 15, Courtesy of IBM Corporation; Figure 16, Copyright ©Patrick Olear/Photo Edit — All rights reserved.; Figure 19, © 2005 by Electrovaya Inc. www.electrovaya.com; Figure 21, Courtesy of ViewSonic Corporation; **Chapter 9:** Courtesy of Sierra Wireless Inc.; Courtesy of Socket Communications; © Comstock Images/Alamy; © George Simhoni/Masterfile; © Eric Meola/Getty Images; © Brand X Pictures/Alamy; Courtesy of Intel Corporation; © James Leynse/Corbis; © Siemens AG Press Pictures; Figure 9-1b, Courtesy of Sun Microsystems, Inc.; Figure 9-1c, Courtesy of Hewlett-Packard Company; Figure 9-1d, Courtesy of Acer America Corp.; Figure 9-1e, Courtesy of Motion Computing, Inc.; Figure 9-1f, Courtesy of Nokia; Figure 9-1g1, Courtesy of Hewlett-Packard Company; Figure 9-1h, Toyota photo; Figure 9-1i, © Ingram Publishing/Alamy; Figure 9-1j, © Digital Stock; Figure 9-1k, © Digital Stock; Figure 9-1l, © Digital Stock; Figure 9-3a, © Kaz Mori/Getty Images; Figure 9-3b, © Royalty-Free/Corbis; Figure 9-3c, © Digital Vision; Figure 9-4a, © Justin Sullivan/Getty Images; Figure 9-4b, Courtesy of Intel Corporation; Figure 9-4c, Courtesy of Linksys, a Division of Cisco Systems Inc.; Figure 9-4d, © James Leynse/Corbis; Figure 9-5, © Chuck Pefley/Alamy; Figure 9-6a1, Courtesy of Garmin Ltd.; Figure 9-6a2, © George Simhoni/Masterfile; Figure 9-6b1, Courtesy of Wherify Wireless, Inc.; Figure 9-6b2, Courtesy of Wherify Wireless, Inc.; Figure 9-6c1, © Siemens AG Press Pictures; Figure 9-6c2, © Jasper James/Getty Images; Figure 9-6d1, Courtesy of Garmin Ltd.; Figure 9-6d2, © Ron Chapple/Getty Images; Figure 9-6e1, © Dante Burn-Forti/Getty Images; Figure 9-6e2, Courtesy of GPS Tracks, Inc.; Figure 9-7, © First Light/Imagestate; Figure 9-8a, © Javier Pierini/Getty Images; Figure 9-8b, © Jon Feingersh/CORBIS; Figure 9-8c, © Andersen Ross/Brand X Pictures; Figure 9-8d, Courtesy of Sun Microsystems; Figure 9-8d2, Courtesy of Sun Microsystems; Figure 9-9, Courtesy of Symantec Corporation; Figure 9-10, © Image Source/Imagestate; Figure 9-11, Courtesy of 3Com Corporation; Figure 9-11, Courtesy of Acer America Corp.; Figure 9-14, Courtesy of Acer America Corp.; Figure 9-14, Courtesy of Sony Electronics Inc.; Figure 9-18, Courtesy of SMC Networks Inc.; Figure 9-18, Courtesy of Sony Electronics Inc.; Figure 9-18, Courtesy of TallyGenicom; Figure 9-19a, © Jose Luis Pelaez, Inc./CORBIS; Figure 9-19b, Courtesy of Fujitsu Siemens Computers; Figure 9-21a1, © E-ZPass/Getty Images; Figure 9-21a2, © James Leynse/CORBIS; Figure 9-21b, © James Leynse/CORBIS; Figure 9-25, Courtesy of Zoom Technologies, Inc.; Figure 9-26a, Courtesy of Courtesy of Toshiba America Information Systems, Inc.; Figure 9-29a, Courtesy of Sony Electronics Inc.; Figure 9-29a, Courtesy of Acer America Corp.; Figure 9-26b, Courtesy of Cnet USA, Inc.; Figure 9-27, Courtesy of U.S. Robotics Corporation; Figure 9-28a, © Erik S. Lesser/Bloomberg News /Landov; Figure 9-28b, Courtesy of Motorola, Inc.; Figure 9-28c, Courtesy of Saenix Technology Inc.; Figure 9-28d, Courtesy of Panasonic; Figure 9-28e, © image100/Alamy; Figure 9-29a, Courtesy of Sierra Wireless Inc.; Figure 9-29b, Courtesy of Toshiba America Information Systems, Inc.; Figure 9-30a, Courtesy of Linksys, a Division of Cisco Systems Inc.; Figure 9-30b, Courtesy of Linksys, a Division of Cisco Systems Inc.; Figure 9-31a, Courtesy of Linksys, a Division of Cisco Systems Inc.; Figure 9-31b, © F64/Getty Images; Figure 9-31c, Copyright ©Michael Newman/Photo Edit — All rights reserved.; Figure 9-31d, Copyright ©CLEO PHOTOGRAPHY/Photo Edit — All rights reserved.; Figure 9-31e, Copyright ©Bonnie Kamin/Photo Edit — All rights reserved.; Figure 9-32a, Courtesy of Zoom Technologies, Inc.; Figure 9-32b, Courtesy of SMC Networks Inc.; Figure 9-33, Courtesy of 3Com Corporation; Figure 9-34a, © Photo by Business Wire via Getty Images; Figure 9-34b, Courtesy of Seanix Technology Inc.; Figure 9-34b, Courtesy of Toshiba America Information Systems, Inc.; Figure 9-34c, Courtesy of U.S. Robotics Corporation; FAQ 9-9, Reprinted with permission of WebSiteOptimization.com; Looking Ahead 9-1, © davies & starr/Getty Images; Figure 9-42, © Vince Streano/CORBIS; Figure 9-43, © Antonio M Rosario/Getty Images; Looking Ahead 9-2, Courtesy of